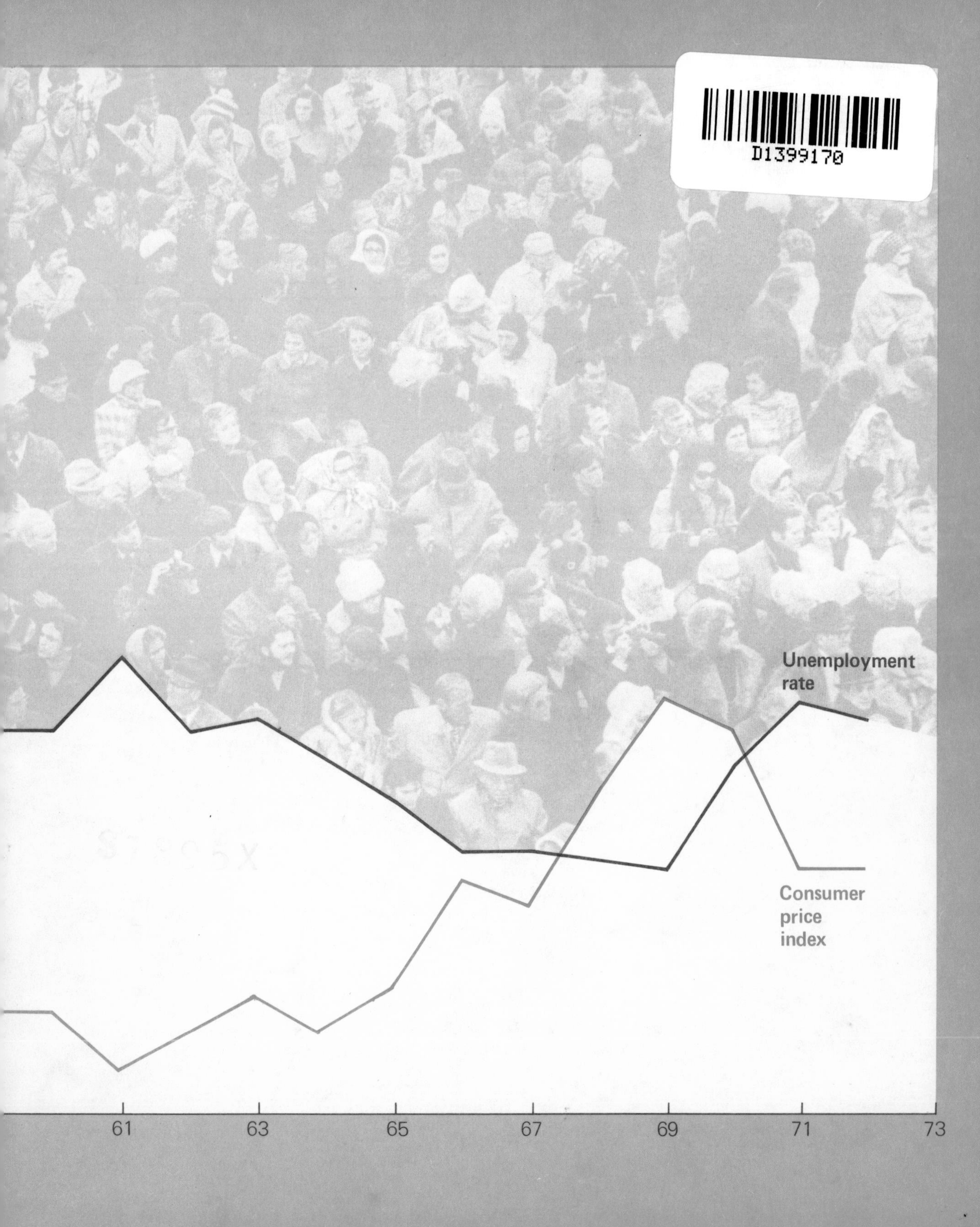
D1399170
Unemployment rate
Consumer price index
61
63
65
67
69
71
73

ECONOMICS

ECONOMICS

William P. Albrecht, Jr.
University of Iowa

PRENTICE-HALL, INC.
Englewood Cliffs, N.J.

13-227439-6

Library of Congress Catalog Card Number 73-15275

Printed in the United States of America

10 9 8 7 6 5 4 3

Designer: J. Paul Kirouac, A Good Thing, Inc.
Illustrations: Vantage Art

Prentice-Hall International, Inc., London
Prentice-Hall of Australia, Pty. Ltd., Sydney
Prentice-Hall of Canada, Ltd., Toronto
Prentice-Hall of India Private Limited, New Delhi
Prentice-Hall of Japan, Inc., Tokyo

Contents

PART 1 BASIC CONCEPTS

Preface

This book is designed for the introductory economics course at the college level. However, we might as easily say that it is designed for today's student—the student who expects to be introduced to the basic concepts of economics, but who also wants the intellectual satisfaction of applying these concepts to problems in the real world. In this text, basic concepts and models are thoroughly and graphically explained: these are the tools of the science. But tools are, of course, to be used. As early as the second chapter, the student is shown how to use economic concepts in analyzing a contemporary problem. Throughout, a pedagogical balance is maintained between basic concepts and topical application.

APPROACH

The means to this balance is the unifying theme of efficiency and equity—how to provide what society wants at the lowest cost without sacrificing economic justice. Economics emerges as a science that matters—a science to be used. Therefore, policy issues appear where appropriate—integrated into the chapter, as short commentaries, or as full chapters directly after the theory they elucidate—not as an isolated, last-minute section. Since no text can remain as current as today's headlines, each issue of contemporary interest also illustrates a point about the basic concepts of economics. The part on growth exemplifies this approach as it develops a broader definition of economic growth to include the quality of life as well as material abundance, and offers students some economic tools for evaluating proposals toward these goals.

The inclusion of questions of equity or normative issues is imperative in a time of ferment in the field of economics. The same analysis may be evaluated quite differently by a Monetarist, a Keynesian, or a radical economist. Each school has its day, so students are challenged to take an active approach to the theories, to see the underlying assumptions and the implications that different scholars draw from them. This theme also allows the introduction of material from other disciplines such as political science or sociology, to widen the traditional coverage.

COVERAGE

The book is structured into seven parts, flexible enough to allow the professor to tailor the order to suit the course syllabus. Part One offers an overview of the theory of both microeconomics and macroeconomics, including an intellectual history of the subject in Chapter 5. Part Two treats macroeconomic theory, and includes a chapter on the effects of fiscal policy on the content of federal programs. Part Three introduces money, the debate over its role in the economy and alternative stabilization policies, such as wage-price controls. Part Four treats economic growth, focusing on the problems of affluent nations. Part Five begins the microeconomic section, treating problems of efficiency and equity in the product market, such as consumerism, corporate responsibility, agricultural policy, and economic concentration. Part Six presents the theory of the factor market and general equilibrium as a prelude to questions of income distribution, concluding with a chapter on the radical critique of traditional theory. Part Seven considers equity and efficiency in the international sphere—the alternatives to the market and the forces behind international trade and exchange.

PEDAGOGY

The theme of the book provides a convenient pedagogical tool for reinforcing related concepts within these disparate parts. It provides students with a clear sense of the coherence and internal consistency of the subject.

The commentaries included throughout the book present the more controversial topics, discussing the findings and opinions of economists and other scholars. They are intended to whet the interest of the student and many may serve as a springboard to class discussions.

Special attention has been given to providing a clear, uncluttered visual format. Photographs have been introduced to suggest the real world upon which the models and theories are ultimately founded. Graph and other visual elements are indispensable in aiding comprehension, and each is carefully captioned to clarify the analysis. The student wishing to review important concepts is directed to the end-of-chapter summaries and questions, and to the glossary at the back of the book. Readings of various levels of difficulty are suggested for each chapter.

ACKNOWLEDGMENTS

Many people contributed to the development and production of this book. Foremost among them is Karen Reixach, who did a magnificent job as the project editor. Others who deserve special thanks are Lydia Castle and Stephen Slavin, who did most of the research, and Mary Schieck, who offered helpful editorial support. Despite their efforts, however, some errors may be found. They are, of course, my responsibility.

Finally, I wish to thank my wife, Alice, and our children, Ken, Alison, Jon, and Jeff, for their encouragement and willingness to grant me the time to complete this project.

William P. Albrecht, Jr.

ECONOMICS

PART

1

BASIC CONCEPTS

CHAPTER 1

ECONO-MIZING

"If the United States can get a sophisticated spacecraft to the moon, why can't it get decent train service to Milwaukee?" It's a familiar enough complaint. Although American technical know-how and wealth are unparalleled, many of the basic problems of society remain unsolved.

The paradoxes come easily to mind: With only about 10 percent of the arable land in the world, the United States produces a far larger percentage of the world's food; in fact, American farmers are such efficient producers of food that the government has had to devise ways of discouraging them lest they inundate the nation with wheat and butter. Nevertheless, 12 million Americans go to bed hungry each night. In 1973 alone, the United States turned out well over a trillion dollars' worth of goods and services. But in the process, it produced about 50 billion cans and 30 billion bottles and jars which seem to have ended up mostly on the roadside—along with 4 to 5 million tons of iron and steel scrap from derelict cars.

Suddenly aware that things are getting out of hand, many Americans on both sides of the political spectrum are asking, "What's wrong? Why can't we get things done?" Answers and explanations have come from a number of contemporary thinkers.

Edward C. Banfield, for example, has pinned the responsibility on the liberals, who have designed many of the ambitious social programs of our time. He charges that liberals have been more interested in assuaging their consciences through social action than in finding out if their solutions are feasible. Banfield doubts that they can be. He asserts, for example, that the poor are "present-oriented" and that this is the chief obstacle to the elimination of poverty: The poor are simply unable to defer gratification or organize their lives sufficiently to accumulate assets. In Banfield's opinion, welfare only worsens the situation. "Believing that any problem can be solved if only we try hard enough, we do not hesitate to attempt what we do not have the least idea of how to do and what, in some instances, reason and experience both tell us cannot be done. Not recognizing any bounds to what is feasible . . . we do not even perceive . . . the necessity, so frequently arising, of choosing the least objectionable among courses of action that are all very unsatisfactory."[1]

Opening photo by Burk Uzzle, Magnum

Inappropriate solutions to real problems is Milton Friedman's diagnosis as well. "Is it an accident that so many of the governmental reforms of recent decades have gone awry?" asks Friedman. "Is it simply because the programs are faulty in detail? I believe the answer is clearly in the negative. The central defect of these measures is that they seek through government to force people to act against their own immediate interests in order to promote a supposedly general interest."[2] Friedman believes that the answer is a free enterprise system in which each person *can* act in his own interest—in other words, a capitalist system. Government intervention, he feels, is necessary only in a limited number of circumstances. The concentration of power, even in the hands of well-intentioned people, he maintains, is the gravest danger to society and the source of many of today's problems.

To Friedman, the solution is greater reliance on capitalism; to the Marxists, however, the problem is capitalism itself. "The elimination of basic capitalist institutions is necessary, though not sufficient, to eliminate the oppressive problems of the modern world," asserts a recent book by three young Marxist academics.[3] They feel that only strong direction from government can free us from the problems created by capitalism.

To Charles Reich, Americans simply need a change in consciousness. Reich asserts that what is responsible for the present state of affairs is a consciousness shaped by technological ends and the desire for efficiency. He suggests that a change in culture can disarm the corporate state we live in without a shot being fired. Greed, pollution, and other problems bred by the economy can be replaced with harmony among men and between man and nature—all through the cultivation of an attitude Reich calls

1 Edward C. Banfield, *The Unheavenly City: The Nature and Future of Our Urban Crisis* (Boston: Little, Brown, 1970), pp. 249–250.
2 Milton Friedman, *Capitalism and Freedom* (Chicago: University of Chicago Press, 1962), p. 200.
3 Richard C. Edwards, Michael Reich, and Thomas E. Weisskopf, *The Capitalist System: A Radical Analysis of American Society* (Englewood Cliffs, N.J.: Prentice-Hall, 1972), p. 5.

Consciousness III. Because the state administers according to prevailing values, a change in values can alter the state's direction.[4]

THE INEVITABILITY OF SCARCITY

Between these problems and their solution is an economic "fact of life": People cannot have everything they want, neither in goods nor in services. The United States is an immensely rich country, but even its wealth is limited.

The concept of scarcity is difficult for Americans to accept because for so long and in so many ways we seem to have lived in the middle of plenty. In America's early years, if people wanted land, all they had to do was go west, take possession of a tract, pay a modest claim fee, improve the land—and it was theirs to keep. With the frontier still somewhere beyond them and free land always accessible, it was difficult to conceive of land as a limited resource. So it was with minerals and other scarce resources. Nonetheless, Americans have always faced scarcity: a scarcity of labor and capital in America's early periods, and a scarcity of less tangible things, like pure air or quality education, today.

In the presence of scarcity, people will always disagree about priorities. As they look for solutions to the problems of society, they will disagree about who should benefit and who might be hurt. Self-interest enters into their opinions. In fact, much of the malaise today stems from the conviction that solutions *are* possible but are being prevented by entrenched groups who fear the effect of change on their well-being. In a world where no one suffered scarcity, such groups would have little reason to cling to privilege, but in our world they do. This is the real heart of the economic problem: how to use scarce resources for competing ends.

4 Charles A. Reich, *The Greening of America* (New York: Bantam Books, 1970), pp. 322–335.

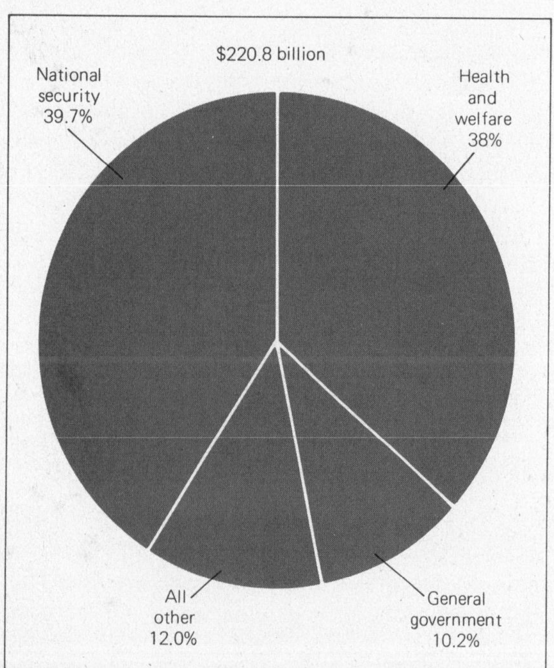

FIGURE 1-1 FEDERAL SPENDING PRIORITIES (Calendar year 1971) A most visible set of choices in the use of resources is the federal budget. This reflects national priorities at a glance. The two largest categories of federal expenditures are for national security (including space and international relations as well as defense) and for health and welfare (primarily social security and other income supports). Given the enormous size of the budget, it is easy to forget that each item implies a sacrifice: It represents all the goods and services that must be forgone to enable that expenditure.

SOURCE: Michael E. Levy et al., *The Federal Budget: Its Impact on the Economy*, fiscal 1974 ed. (New York: The Conference Board, 1973), p. 59.

Insatiable Wants

Scarcity would be less of a problem if society—once it attained a certain level of well-being—were satisfied with what it had. But human needs and wants are insatiable.

It may seem odd to talk of insatiable wants in a society where it takes a great deal of business ingenuity to "make a sale." After all, advertisers must spend over $20 billion annually persuading people to buy all the gadgets and gizmos industry dreams up. A single advertising campaign such as Avis's "We Try Harder" cost $4 million in 1972 alone. Where are insatiable wants, when it takes that much money to promote a product?

Editorial cartoon by Pat Oliphant. © *The Denver Post.* Reprinted with permission of *Los Angeles Times Syndicate.*

Advertising to make people buy more proves only that people's desires for a given product may be limited. What advertising does is to educate people to need and want products and services that did not exist or were unknown before. And advertising works only because people are predisposed to want things. Insatiable wants, then, means simply that when one want or need is fulfilled, another pops up in its place. Once we have something, we seldom want to do without it. And no matter what we have, we want more of it or of something else.

Needs and wants are not simply biological: They extend well beyond our basic physical needs. When King Lear's daughters tried to cut expenses by trimming his retinue, he raged, "Reason not the need." When dignity and authority are at stake, as in King Lear's case, biological survival—even comfort—is not enough.

Nor are tangible consumer goods enough. If they were, we might appear like the character in *The Yellow Submarine,* the one with the vacuum-cleaner mouth that pulled in everything on the screen; when he had nothing else to consume, he proceeded to inhale himself, leaving a blank screen. Unlike this fellow, we desire services as well as products. A student may live quite ascetically, without steaks, stereos, or new clothes, yet may demand interesting professors, a well-run library, and perhaps even a championship football team. The desire for a good education, like the desire for consumer goods, comes from various needs.

In the unlikely event that everyone reacted against what he saw as a surfeit of goods in the United States, might it not be possible to eliminate scarcity? Might we not simply curb our desires? Probably not, for desires are virtually unlimited in the aggregate. There will always be competing uses for given resources.

Since our wants and needs are unlimited and our resources are limited, we are inevitably confronted by the basic condition of economic life—scarcity.

Resources, Products, and Income

The satisfaction of people's needs and wants begins with unprocessed resources, such as our no-longer pure water and air. Less directly, a population needs certain natural resources which, though limited in quantity, are indispensable to the highly complex, highly vulnerable network of exchanges that constitute our economy.

Soil is needed for what it, with the help of the farmer and the weather, can produce: tomatoes, wheat, corn, potatoes, strawberries, and all the other foods man wants. Americans do not always want these products in the form of fresh produce, but prefer the tomatoes peeled, canned, and delivered to the supermarket shelf; the wheat milled and baked into bread and packaged; the corn fed to steers and sheep that are slaughtered, processed, and sold at meat counters; and the strawberries made into jam and sold in jars at a variety of stores. Similarly, consumers are not interested in having a ton of iron ore parked in the driveway, but would be delighted to have it in processed form as a Vega or a Mustang.

Very few of our needs and wants are satisfied by resources directly, but rather by products that have come from production processes, often very complicated ones. Products, then, are derived from resources, and because resources are limited in quantity, it follows that the products that can be produced from them will also be limited.

Factors of Production The resources that go into making products are called **factors of production.** These resources are generally grouped into four categories: land, capital, labor, and entrepreneurship. It may seem odd to use the term *resource* in so broad a manner, for by resource we usually mean a natural resource, something that has existed apart from man. In economic terms, however, a resource may refer to man himself as well as to man-made goods.

LAND To the economist, the term *land* means more than real estate. Land refers to every natural resource: water, air, sunshine, vegetation, wild animals, and also deposits of minerals under the land and sea.

CAPITAL The term *capital,* too, has a different meaning to the economist than to the layman, for whom it sometimes means simply money. To an economist, capital refers to man-made resources that are not consumed, but are used to make other products. Some examples of capital resources are factories with their presses, stamping machines, and assembly lines; railroads, trucks, and highways. Money is called capital when it is used to buy these productive resources.

The difference between capital goods and consumer goods is important in economic terms. Toasters and TV sets are consumer products, but the machines and transportation that went into making those products are capital resources. Toasters and TV sets are only good for toasting and viewing, but the machines and systems that produced them are capable of making more toasters and TV sets. The basic difference between capital goods and consumer goods, then, is that consumer goods are consumed and capital goods remain, turning out more and more products.

LABOR Labor is, quite simply, people working. It includes people who farm the land to produce foodstuffs, people who mine the earth so that its resources can be used in the production process, people who make finished products in factories, and people who perform the innumerable services that are needed by the population as a whole. Of course, labor also includes people who sit at desks and keep track of the work other people are doing. All expend energy in return for money.

ENTREPRENEURSHIP Before products can arise from resources, someone needs to discover the resources, invent a production process, or create a business firm. The functions of organizing, directing, and managing the factors of production are performed by the entrepreneur. An entrepreneur may be an individual acting on his own behalf in search of a profit. He may be a corporate executive acting on behalf of the stockholders and other absentee owners of the firm. Or he may be a bureaucrat planning goals for a state-run enterprise. But regardless of who performs them, the entrepreneurial functions are essential if the factors of production are to be organized in a process that turns out goods and services.

Entrepreneurship, like the other factors of production, is in scarce supply. It is not a common talent, and not everyone who has it chooses to use it. Limited resources and limited entrepreneurship mean a limitation on products. Given unlimited needs and wants, there will never be enough goods and services to satisfy everyone.

Income from Factors of Production Entrepreneurs garner profits (or their equivalent in a state-run enterprise), labor receives compensation, land furnishes rent to its owner, and capital earns interest. Each resource or productive factor provides its own type of income. Because some people control more resources—or scarcer, more costly resources—than other people, income is not evenly distributed. And because resources are scarce, the income from these resources is necessarily limited—as are the goods and services that it buys.

THE NECESSITY OF CHOICE

Faced with the dilemma of limited products, limited income, and unlimited wants and needs, society must make choices. The inevitability of scarcity leads directly to the necessity of choice. How are the resources to be used? What products should be made with the limited resources and in what quantity? Who should get them? These questions and the choices they call forth form the basis of the economic organization of a society.

Technological Efficiency

Technological efficiency is the answer to our first basic question of economics: How should the scarce resources of a society be used to produce products that satisfy the needs and wants of consumers? With needs and wants for products unlimited, and resources limited, it would be self-defeating to waste resources by producing goods in any but the most efficient way.

Many economists liken the technological efficiency of the economy to the efficiency of an engine. If 100 units of raw energy placed in an engine turn out 100 units of refined energy, the engine is said to be 100 percent efficient.

An economy is operating at 100 percent technological efficiency when no change can be made in the use of resources that would lead to an increase in the output of one product without necessitating a decrease in the output of another product.

Every resource is then being used to its utmost capacity. At this point, the only way to get more of a particular product is to make less of another product.

Technological efficiency is not synonymous with complete utilization of all resources. Indeed, it would hardly be efficient to use up limited resources all at once. Built into the concept of efficiency is the notion that some of each resource will be saved for later production. Thus, the consumption of oil and coal and gold and clean air is scheduled in such a way that some is left for later use.

And the same is true for labor. We might try working around the clock 24 hours, but sooner or later we would all drop from exhaustion and be unable to work at all. Built into the concept of full employment, then, is the assumption that people will work only as much as they want, not every hour of every day. They will have some time off to sleep and refresh themselves, the better to tackle tomorrow's work and be more efficient at it.

Allocative Efficiency

Technological efficiency is not enough, however. The most productive machinery in the world is essentially useless if it produces something no one wants. The economy must also produce the combina-

SCARCITY OR SURFEIT?

Back in the 1950s some social thinkers began to predict a society of unprecedented abundance. Scarcity would be hardly possible in wealthy post-industrial America. David Riesman, for example, envisioned a "leisure society," in which the major problem of most of us would be to occupy the free time that technology had thrown our way.

Today this vision of a world without scarcity seems even closer—at least superficially. Americans today have a per capita income of over $4000 and their income is projected to rise to $6000 by 1985. In 1972 alone they spent $4 billion on pets and $17.7 billion on liquor. Such a world seems far removed from one in which scarcity reigns.

But many people today see the United States running up against the limits of its resources. Their vision is of a post-industrial society, too, but one in which industry has created an ecological disaster.

In *The Coming of Post-Industrial Society*, sociologist Daniel Bell* suggests that neither vision is realistic. He reminds the prophets of environmental doom that resources should be measured in economic rather than physical terms. In an economic sense, our resources may in fact be expanding:

* Daniel Bell, *The Coming of Post-Industrial Society* (New York: Basic Books, 1973).

United Press International

Swamplands have been turned to dry farmland, and obscure minerals, like taconite, have been found to yield iron ore. But Bell objects equally to the vision of a world without scarcity. He reminds us that scarcity, too, is an economic rather than a physical term. Even if everyone could have all the material goods he wanted, he would still be confronted by scarcity—for example, a scarcity of time in which to enjoy them, and, no less, to clean, polish, and repair them. For post-industrial society brings with its technological bounty a whole new set of scarcities, all measurable in terms of rising costs.

Information is one such scarcity. As the economy expands, as political and social institutions become ever more complicated—as history becomes longer and science more difficult—the cost of gathering and interpreting information rises. We can never absorb all the information we need in order to make the best decisions. And as more and more information becomes available, we become relatively less informed. The rising costs are evident in longer schooling, more specialized journals, and a generally expanded communications industry.

Another scarce resource in the post-industrial society will be *coordination*. The cost of regulation, planning, and other forms of coordination is high in a society in which billions of telephone calls are exchanged, millions of votes are cast in every national election, and a number of companies employ over 100,000 persons. Simply getting and spending our increased incomes will require a multitude of transactions, each with its own cost.

A third resource that is invariably limited is *time*—the one economic resource that cannot be accumulated. When productivity is high, as in the post-industrial society, time is relatively expensive. As Bell notes, the very pleasures of consumption take time. So does the maintenance of our many goods—and for this reason we are likely to buy from others such services as dry cleaning and gardening. Ironically, the post-industrial man has little "free time" despite his many leisure options. Indeed he may need to work longer hours to make sure that he can afford the kinds of goods and services that give him a high yield on his leisure hours.

Bell concludes that the post-industrial society, with its heavy emphasis on social interaction, leads to increased collective regulation. And since nobody likes to follow regulations that he has had no hand in forming, everyone will have to bear increased costs: the cost of being informed, the cost of interacting in an organized way with his fellows, and the cost of the time-saving goods and services that will enable him to spend his energies well. Scarcity will continue to be a reality.

tion of goods and services that most satisfies society. If it does this, it has achieved what is known as allocative efficiency.

When no change in resource allocation can be made without making someone worse off, then the economy is operating at allocative efficiency.

The decision-making process depends in part on the political organization of the society. In a socialist society, deciding what products will be made with the available scarce resources is primarily the function of political administrators who base their decisions on what they think will be good for the people or for the future of the society.

In a market economy, the question of what products will be made is usually decided by consumer demand, and the force that maintains demand is the consumers' satisfaction with the product. Consumers demand those products that best satisfy their needs and wants, and the economic system responds to supply them. If the demand for mink-lined umbrellas is sufficient for an entrepreneur to make a profit by supplying them, then mink-lined umbrellas will be supplied. In a market system consumer demand is king; it dictates that those products will be produced that satisfy the needs and wants of consumers.

Together, technological and allocative efficiency form a central objective of economic endeavor. Everybody tries to get the most at the least cost. Such goals seem relatively noncontroversial since failure to meet them would make someone worse off, either in the amount or selection of output. Economic analysis can show under what conditions such goals are met and can predict the effects of changes in economic conditions on these goals. For these reasons, the study of efficiency has absorbed much of the energy of economists.

The Problem of Equity

The concept of equity deals with the question of whose needs and wants are to be provided for and depends not on objective, scientific criteria but on values and judgments. The degree of equity is determined by the political context. In a centralized society, decisions on priorities are made primarily by the state. In the more decentralized system of capitalism, where consumer demand reigns supreme, it is the distribution of income that decides this question. The focus of this book is upon capitalism, where the working out of equity occurs less by design than by the accumulation of individual decisions based on self-interest.

Many books liken the capitalist process to that of voting. But the consumer is not really like a voter. Although the consumer takes his dollar and buys a product, in effect "voting" for that product, the analogy has a significant flaw. In the political arena, every voter has one vote, but in the economic arena, some consumers have many more dollars than others. Not all consumers are equal because not all consumers control the same amount of resources and have the same income. The question of who is to receive satisfaction is decided on the basis of economic power—who has the income? The answer to this question tells who will be the recipient of satisfaction.

People with large incomes receive satisfaction for many of their material needs and wants (never all, because no matter how many products or services they have, they will always want more). People with moderate incomes receive some satisfaction of their material needs and wants. Poor people receive relatively little satisfaction of most of their material needs and wants.

This is the way our economic system works. The distribution of goods and services follows the distribution of income. The more income, the more goods and services. The less income, the fewer goods and services.

This raises the problem of justice or equity. Is income a fair basis on which to distribute the material wealth of a society? Is there a more equitable means of distributing income than the one existing in America?

One alternative is the equal distribution of income among all citizens, regardless of the amount of resources they control. But this would be no guarantee of fairness, for under this kind of income distribution those people who contributed greater resources or worked harder would receive no more than those who made no contribution.

At the other extreme is the idea that income should flow only to those people who provide goods and services that meet consumer demand. Anyone who did not contribute to meeting consumer demand would receive no income. Obviously, this would not be fair to people who, through no fault of their own, found themselves outside the main productive stream, with no marketable resources or with labor skills no longer needed by society. And what about people who have no chance to acquire profitable skills or resources because they are neglected by society? Should they be penalized in the interest of rewarding those lucky enough to find themselves profitably productive? Such a system, too, violates our desire for equity.

An equitable system probably lies somewhere between these two extremes. But it would derive from an extra-economic decision, essentially beyond the realm of purely economic analysis. The scientific approach that works in dealing with matters of efficiency fails to cope with normative issues of equity. This is not to say that economists cannot participate in such decisions, for indeed they can greatly help in clarifying the issues involved. An economist might point out, for example, that when incomes are all on the same level, the incentive to produce may also be leveled. Nowhere in economic history can we find examples of producers who were consistently willing to produce without profit to themselves. The economist might also point out that if income distribution becomes too inequitable, the system will not work, for a large part of society will have insufficient income to create demand for products. Politically, such a system is extremely volatile. Beyond this, the decision becomes a question not of fact but of preference or power.

Equitable distribution of income, as a prerequisite for the equitable distribution of the scarce products of society, is a difficult and complex issue, central to any study of economics, but it is one that involves controversy and conclusions of less certainty than those about efficiency. The problem becomes even more complex if we broaden the definition of equity to include not only the fulfillment of material needs represented by equitable income distribution but also other, less tangible needs such as justice and freedom. Equity in its broadest use encompasses far more slippery concepts than income distribution. We shall use the term *equity* in both senses as we develop the theories and applications of economics.

THE NATURE OF ECONOMICS

At the heart of economics is the idea of economizing, of allocating the limited material resources of a society for the efficient production of inevitably scarce goods and services to satisfy best the needs and wants of society. Economics can be defined in various ways, but this definition serves the purposes of this book, emphasizing its dominant concerns:

> The process of exchange and allocation; the effect of individual and collective decisions on that process; satisfaction-seeking as the basis for these decisions; and the necessity of choice that results from the inevitability of scarcity.

Underlying this definition of economics is the potential tension between efficiency and equity. The most efficient way to use resources may not be equitable, and the most equitable way may not be efficient. The tension between these two valid goals, and how society deals with it, is the central focus of this book. To arrive at answers to the policy questions of the day, economists must determine ways of reconciling the often conflicting aims of efficiency and equity. In doing so, it is not their job to dictate policy decisions—which is a political function—but rather to point out the cost of options so that decisions can be made on a more rational, a more "economical" basis.

Economics, Science, and Society

The tension between efficiency and equity in society is reflected within the discipline of economics. Some economists favor a value-oriented, humanistic approach; others, a scientific one. Economists who emphasize questions of justice at all stages of economic study are adherents of normative economics; those who approach economics as a science and treat matters of value as separate issues are adherents of positive economics. The adherents of positive economics do not exclude questions of value and justice entirely, but claim to deal with them after scientific analysis has been made. Today the traditional approach is identified with the positive school.

Economics as a Social Science Traditional economics favors the positivist position and has developed powerful mathematical tools to deal with questions of resource allocation and technological efficiency. Critics of the traditionalists say that they have concentrated on the use of tools and ignored the underlying nature of the problems.

To radical economist Paul M. Sweezy this situation occurs because traditional economics uses a paradigm (or view of the world) that is both exhausted and obsolete. Each discipline shapes the questions that can be asked and the investigations undertaken. In the hard sciences when the questions are exhausted, a new conception of the world must be sought. Today traditional economics is asking more and more esoteric questions because the power of its paradigm is spent. Moreover, according to Sweezy, economics also faces a problem different from that in the hard sciences. In truly scientific disciplines the underlying reality does not change, but in economics the world itself changes as new institutions evolve and others pass away. Thus, explanations for conditions that prevailed a century ago may no longer apply to today's conditions. Galbraith points out, for example, that in a poor society, economic questions are foremost, but once that nation becomes rich, it is bothered by questions that are not strictly economic, such as "how much beauty should be sacrificed for increased output . . . how much discipline should be enforced on men to insure greater output . . . how completely should the individual subordinate his personality to the organization which was created to supply his wants?"[5]

Members of the radical school of economic thought contend that the greatest flaw of traditional economics has been its tendency to accept the social system as fixed and to concentrate on questions of efficiency at the expense of equity. Charles Schultze, who belongs to the traditional branch of economics, has summarized the charges of the radical school:

> Because economics ignores the substantial economic power now concentrated in large firms and unions, and because on a larger scale it accepts the fundamental status quo of current power relationships in society and ignores the relationship between the distribution of power and the distribution of income, it either has no policy prescriptions for pressing social problems or offers ameliorative remedies that only scratch the surface.[6]

Economics as a Science Although science rests on facts and logic, scientists are concerned not simply with accumulating boxcars of data; they also wish to make meaningful statements about the world. Simon Kuznets of Harvard won the Nobel Prize for economics, not because he had made a vast contribution to the store of facts about economic conditions in various nations at different times, but because of the powerful tools he developed to measure national income and his use of facts to gain insights into the process of economic development.

In attacking a problem, the scientific economist follows a general procedure. First he decides what he wishes to test and formulates a statement or hypothesis that can be tested—for example, a statement to the effect that productivity in a zipper factory is adversely affected by bad weather. He then defines his terms and assumptions. For example, he would need to state more definitely what his measure of productivity is (total number of zippers or zippers per worker?) and what he means by bad weather (rain or heat?). The economist must be especially careful to ensure that the hypothesis can be tested by steps that are clearly defined rather than by a

5 John Kenneth Galbraith, *The New Industrial State* (Boston: Houghton Mifflin, 1967), p. 407.

6 Charles Schultze, "Is Economics Obsolete? No, Underemployed," *Saturday Review*, January 22, 1972, p. 43.

generalized observation about reality; and he must know what kinds of evidence prove or disprove his hypothesis. For example, if an economist set out to prove that competition is the best means for reducing racial prejudice, his study would be virtually meaningless unless there were some way to compare competitive and noncompetitive systems and to measure the degrees of racial prejudice in each. Once tested and verified, the hypothesis becomes useful in explaining past and present instances and in predicting events. If the hypothesis explains a number of related phenomena, it may be accepted as a theory.

Although economics is investigated in this scientific way, economic issues—especially controversial ones—are often subjected to illogical arguments. Everyone is familiar with the rebuttal, "What can you expect from a ______?" (fill in radical, conservative, professor, politician, or other convenient epithet). Appeals to popular acceptance or to authority are of the same ilk ("Everyone knows that . . ."). Leaving out one side of the case is also a convenient tactic.

A theory may be attacked on sounder grounds, however. Two logical fallacies that may creep into economic discussions are the false-cause and composition/division fallacies. The false-cause fallacy assumes that because two events occur together, one must be a cause of the other. If gamblers have a high rate of emphysema, can we say that gambling is bad for the lungs as well as for the pocketbook? The fallacy of composition/division argues that what is true of the parts must be true of the whole or what is true of the whole must be true of the parts. For example, if a company raises its prices, it may make a higher profit; but if all prices go up in the economy at the same rate, this is inflation, and the company is no better off. This is an example of the fallacy of composition, since one cannot reason from part to whole.

Economists may also attack the assumptions of the theory. Or they may accept the assumptions but draw different implications, or no implications at all. This is often possible when the theorist has deliberately oversimplified a problem to illustrate the effect of one variable on an economic factor by holding all other variables constant; this technique is called by the Latin *ceteris paribus* ("other things being equal"). Economists may accept a theory but regard it as trivial, or powerless in dealing with central questions in economics. Other objections may be made, not to the values behind the theory but to the facts or the logic of the case.

If economics were a pure science, it probably would have little direct concern for values and policy questions, but would deal instead with mathematical relationships between economic variables and careful theory building. But as most economists admit, economics is an applied science and a handmaiden of policy. Its tools can help decision-makers determine how to allocate public and private resources. They can identify incompatible objectives, for example, or suggest kinds of incentives to achieve politically determined ends, such as clean water or lower welfare costs. The final section of this chapter shows how some goals of a society may be defined through the use of one scientific tool, a simple model of economizing.

MODEL BUILDING

One important technique in scientific analysis is the use of models. A model is a simplified version of reality. In it, the small inconsistencies are averaged out; the tangential points are eliminated. A model allows us to focus attention on the relationship between two or three basic factors without being distracted by numerous factors of the complex reality. A model is also a convenient, clear way to demonstrate and explain basic principles.

Model building is at the heart of the scientific method. First, the real situation must be examined, and the facts that relate to it are gathered and studied. What these facts mean, and how they relate to other facts, are considered, as well as the implications that can be drawn from them. A model is then constructed to express the economist's understanding of how reality works. From that model he can then draw hypotheses about other aspects of the reality on which the model is based, and from those hypotheses develop questions and research objectives for ideas that he wishes to test. When he does, either the new data he gathers confirm his hypothesis—and he has additional evidence that his model is accurate—or the new data contradict his model. When this happens he has to adjust the model to incorporate the new data and to retest the accuracy. Only through this time-consuming and careful process has the body of economic facts been slowly built up, tested and retested, and finally accepted as knowledge.

The Production-Possibilities Frontier

From the ideas presented in this chapter we can build an important economic model—a model of economizing. We will want the model to show the scarcity of resources, the necessity of choice, the goal of efficiency, and the problem of equity. And we will want it to serve as the source for other ideas derived from these concepts.

To build the model, let us assume that the entire productive capacity of the country is directed toward turning out only two products. Since World War II, Adolf Hitler's exhortation about choosing between guns and butter has generally been used to illustrate this model. We might update this example by assuming that all the economic resources of the United States are to be directed toward producing either F-15 Tomcat fighter airplanes or low-income urban housing projects.

Assume that the United States has a total national economic output of exactly $1 trillion. Since the F-15 Tomcats cost about $13 million each, the United States can have a total of 76,923 Tomcat airplanes, if it is willing to have nothing else. Given the usual cost overruns, the airplanes probably will cost more than $13 million each, so we might lower the figure to a round 75,000. The economy does not have the resources to make 75,001, and if it came up with only 74,999, this would mean that production was not technologically efficient.

Let us assume that instead, we take the option of building only low-income urban housing developments. We shall envision these as well-designed, well-constructed, roomy, pleasant but not plush apartment houses with attendant parks, garages, shopping areas, and the cultural and community centers that make urban living enjoyable. We can assume that each such project would cost $20 million. And again, having a total productive output of $1 trillion, the United States could construct a total of 50,000 such housing developments.

What we have done, in effect, is to pose a choice between a military good and a civilian good. While in our model we list only one military good (Tomcat fighter aircraft) and only one civilian good (urban housing developments), we can imagine that the Tomcats stand for all military goods and the urban housing developments, for all civilian goods. Stating the problem in terms of two specific products simply helps to make the model clearer.

Next, let us draw up a hypothetical list of alternative choices between these two products:

Choice	Housing projects	Tomcats
A	0	75,000
B	10,000	70,000
C	20,000	60,000
D	30,000	45,000
E	40,000	25,000
F	50,000	0

We can plot these points on a graph and draw a curve that connects them. We will then have a model of the production-possibilities frontier.

Opportunity Costs The frontier limits the mix of products available. Suppose that 70,000 Tomcats are scheduled for production instead of 40,000 housing projects. Then only 10,000 housing projects can be built. In this case some well-meaning observers might comment: "O.K., let them have their Tomcats, but why should they stop us from building more housing?" The answer, of course, is that there are no more resources because the economy is operating on its production-possibilities frontier. To obtain resources to build more housing, society has to give

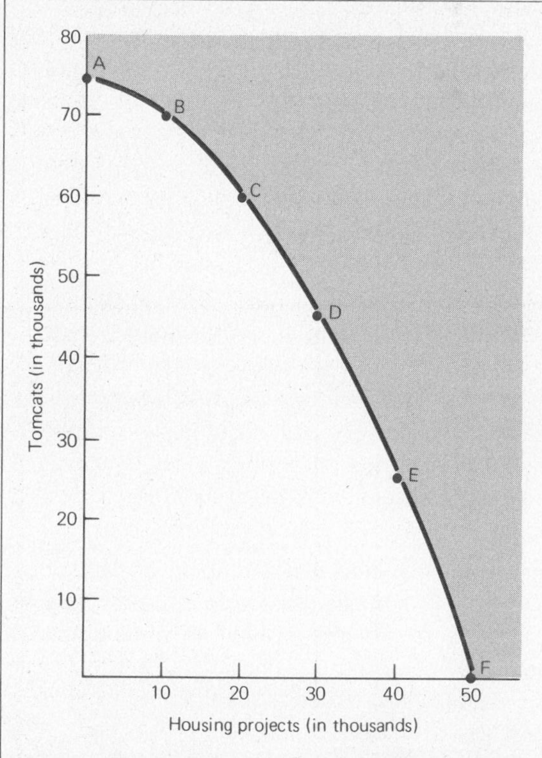

FIGURE 1-2 THE PRODUCTION-POSSIBILITIES FRONTIER The line ABCDEF represents the maximum combination of Tomcats and housing projects that our economy can produce, given our resources and technology. Any point on this frontier represents technological efficiency. If the economy produces that combination of Tomcats and housing projects demanded by society (represented by a single point on the frontier), then it has achieved allocative efficiency as well.

up some Tomcats. It is faced with the fact that it cannot have more housing if it wants more fighter planes—not, at least, in the simplified model of reality we are dealing with. If, for example, it should be decided that the point of production should be at point C, with 60,000 Tomcats and 20,000 housing developments, society will have given up the opportunity to have 30,000 housing developments in order to have 60,000 Tomcats. It cannot have 60,000 Tomcats (point C) and 30,000 housing developments (point D) at the same time.

If society decides to have 30,000 housing developments instead of 20,000, it can achieve this goal only by accepting 45,000 Tomcats. The cost of having 10,000 more housing developments (from 20,000 to 30,000) is to give up 15,000 Tomcats (from 60,000 to 45,000). The number of aircraft given up represents what it costs to get the additional number of housing projects.

What must be given up in order to get something else is called an opportunity cost.

It results from a choice of options, such as someone might make by giving up an opportunity to go to Paris, instead of Peoria, because it is impossible for him to be in both places at the same time.

Increasing Costs Another factor that enters into choosing the mix of output is the cost of converting from one product to the other. This cost increases as we approach a society of all Tomcats or all housing developments; in other words, it increases as we move toward the upper and lower points on the curve. In moving from point B to point C, society gives up 10,000 aircraft in order to get 10,000 more housing projects. In moving from point C to point D, society has to give up 15,000 aircraft to get 10,000 more housing projects. There is not a constant trade-off between Tomcats and housing developments because the cost of converting from one good to the other increases as we approach a one-product economy.

One explanation for this is that resources are not always equally suited for different uses. Some resources may not be at all suited for production of fighter planes; but if we decide to make fighter planes anyway, the cost of the additional planes would be quite high—forcing us to sacrifice a lot of housing projects. In addition, the production system may be better geared for one product than another. Since in the past there was more demand to build fighter aircraft than urban housing developments, the economy has developed a better ability to build aircraft.

If society decided to build even more housing, say 40,000 developments, the cost in lost airplanes would be even greater. To move from 30,000 to 40,000 housing projects, it would have to give up 20,000 Tomcats. And to move altogether into housing and out of aircraft, point F, would cost 25,000 airplanes for only 10,000 additional housing projects.

Every choice is made at the cost of things that were not chosen. Thus, the more we want the more we may have to give up. The term to express this concept is **increasing cost of convertibility**.

Efficiency and Equity Any point on this curve represents the greatest possible output given the resources of the society and the existing distribution of income. It represents technological efficiency. In our model, there simply are not more resources available to produce anything beyond the frontier. And if production is set within the frontier, some resources are not being used fully and society is losing potential output.

Whatever combination of Tomcats and housing projects society chooses determines its place on the production-possibilities frontier. If for some reason the mix of output differs from the desired combination, the society is experiencing allocative inefficiency.

Efficiency depends upon the distribution of income. There is one point on the frontier that represents allocative efficiency for a given income distribution. If the distribution of income is changed to one considered more equitable, the point of allocative efficiency will probably change also, since redistributed income will mean that different people, with different wants and needs, will be having a larger say in the mix of products. Since the production-possibilities model usually accepts the given income distribution, some people consider it appropriate to say that efficiency ignores rather than conflicts with equity. Others point out that the policy decisions designed to achieve equity may cause some inefficiency, and vice versa. The most cynical say that economists' obsession with efficiency leads them to ignore the question of equity and that it is little more than a matter of semantics as to whether *ignores* or *conflicts with* is the appropriate term.

ECONOMIC GOALS

A choice between guns and butter, housing and fighter aircraft, represents not simply a choice between two very different goods. It may also represent a choice between competing interests; at the very least it involves a recognition of society's shared goals—goals that are broader, more general than a choice between any two goods, or kinds of goods, would suggest.

We have said that in the highest sense our economic goals are efficiency and equity. Yet these are not the terms that dominate public discussion of economic issues. The headliners are *inflation, unemployment,* and *welfare*. And our editorials assure us that we want in their places price stability, full employment, and a decent standard of living for every member of society.

One reason that *efficiency* and *equity* do not appear so frequently in public discussion is that they are not operational terms—that is, they cannot be practically defined, measured, or demonstrated in a real situation. A policy-maker can argue that the economy is operating at maximum efficiency, but he cannot prove this without referring to the unemployment rate and the Gross National Product (GNP), both of which *can* be measured. Similarly, a politician can declare that his administration has achieved greater economic stability or more equality of opportunity than ever before, but we need to see the price indices and income distribution tables before accepting these claims. On a conceptual level our economic goals may be efficiency and equity, but on an operational level they become full employment, price stability, and other clearly defined goals.

Full Employment

As a goal, full employment is very directly related to the concept of efficiency: Unless all resources are fully and wisely employed, technical inefficiencies will result. In such cases we will get fewer Tomcats and housing projects. We will not be on the frontier, but somewhere inside it.

Failure to achieve the goal of full employment is most apparent when the resource that is unemployed

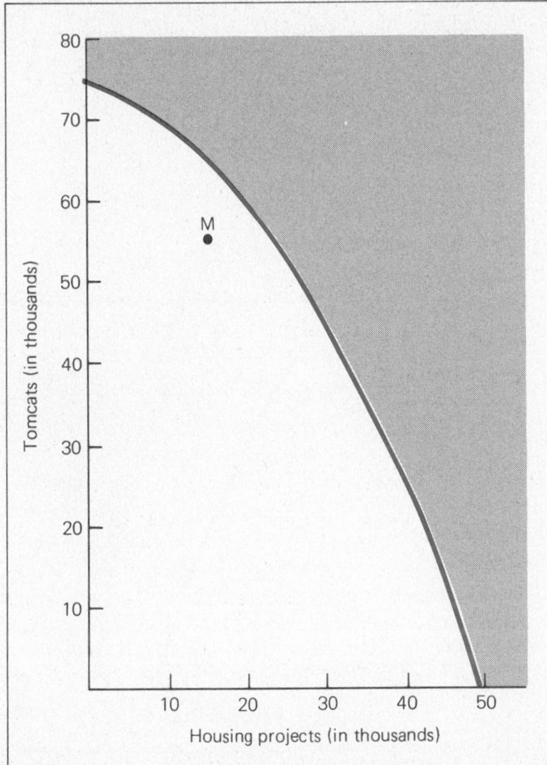

FIGURE 1-3 PRODUCTION AT LESS THAN FULL EFFICIENCY **Seldom does an economy produce on its production-possibilities frontier. To do so would mean full employment of all resources as well as utilization of its most advanced technology. Point M, which lies within the production-possibilities frontier, represents a more probable combination of goods produced, in which some resources are still either unemployed or underemployed.**

is labor—men and women without jobs. Less obvious is the unemployment of land and capital resources. A waterway may be undeveloped, a factory lie idle; these things will not affect us nearly so strongly as the man in the breadline, even though the loss in production may be far greater. Human unemployment, in addition to being inefficient, touches upon our conception of equity: We tend to believe that everyone has a right to be gainfully employed because unemployment cuts income. The level of employment affects income distribution and personal well-being.

A related goal is to ensure that every worker is employed to the fullest of his capabilities. An economy really cannot be efficient if a man who wants full-time work must take a part-time job, or if a specialized engineer has no opportunity to work in his field. Such underemployment of resources results in a serious loss of production. So, too, does the underemployment of land and capital resources.

Price Stability

Another goal that relates to efficiency and equity is price stability. As the economy moves toward the production-possibilities frontier—that is, toward maximum efficiency—all available resources become scarcer. People are willing to pay more and more for the resources and products that remain. In our economy, as prices go up, wage demands become correspondingly higher. To the employer this means that the cost of his labor, as well as the costs of resources, will increase and he will have to raise his prices. The cost of a high level of employment, then, may be rising prices.

Not only does inflation complicate the elimination of unemployment; it may also encourage inefficient use of money resources, especially in periods of extreme or hyperinflation. Instead of investing in production (which has become more expensive), the entrepreneur may invest in vacation lands, Steinway pianos, or porcelain sculptures in the hope that he can sell these items for much more than he paid for them. This kind of speculation ties up money without really contributing to the production of new goods in society.

Inflation also affects income distribution, thus raising problems of equity. When prices rise, some people are in the position of having less real income, in the sense that their money can no longer buy what it did just a short time ago. Those who depend solely on pensions, savings, disability payments, and other kinds of fixed income will be relatively worse off. This group usually includes the elderly and others who can ill afford the reduction. The affluent, on the other hand, have the resources with which to take advantage of inflation, through early purchase of costly goods, through speculation, and so on. This is not to imply that inflation causes a simple redistribution of income from poor to rich. Actually the effect is uneven. For example, a blue-collar worker who belongs to a union and whose contract assures him "cost of living increases" will be hurt less than a manager who is not protected against an increase in the cost of living. Borrowers in all walks of life will benefit, for the money they ultimately pay back will be worth less in purchasing power than the money they originally borrowed. Lenders are adversely affected, as are those who put most of their money in savings.

Growth

If the economy stayed at the same level of output very long, this would be cause for worry. We think of economic growth in positive terms, and we expect the capacity of the economy to expand over time. In time and with better technology, we expect to be able to have more Tomcats *and* more housing projects.

In our production-possibilities model, an overall expansion of the economy is represented by a shifting of the entire frontier to the right. Suppose, for example, that a newly developed aluminum substitute makes it possible for us to produce 75,000 Tomcats and 30,000 housing projects. This position is represented by point G. To show the other choice combinations that are now possible, we need to draw a completely new frontier to the right of the old one. The frontier need not be equidistant from the earlier frontier at all points, since growth may not occur in all sectors. The aluminum substitute may be more suitable to aircraft use and enable us to build many more Tomcats. The frontier shown reflects this fact.

The goal of economic growth is complicated by the necessity of choosing between consumer and capital goods. When policy-makers choose to divert resources from consumer items, such as wheat or radios, to capital goods, such as mines or factories, it is with the expectation that consumption will, in the long run, be increased. But such cutbacks can have drastic immediate effects. In countries where most of the productive capacity is devoted to food, any cutback in consumption to increase capital may result

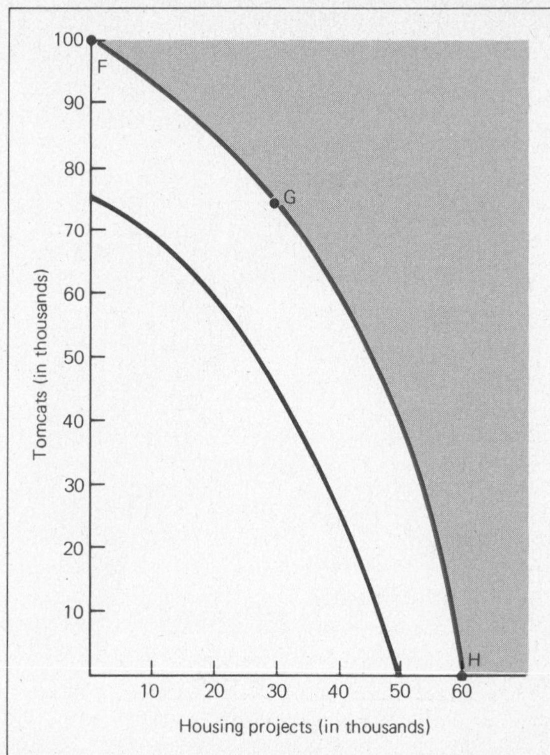

FIGURE 1-4 A SHIFT IN THE PRODUCTION-POSSIBILITIES FRONTIER Economic growth shifts the production-possibilities frontier upward and to the right. The growth in the capacity of the economy enables it to produce more Tomcats *and* more housing projects. For example, point G indicates that it can produce 75,000 Tomcats, but now can have 30,000 housing projects (instead of none as before). Note that the growth of the economy, represented by the overall shift in the curve, is not symmetrical; with the added capacity devoted entirely to Tomcats (F), we may have 25,000 more planes, but if we used the capacity solely for housing (H), we could get only 10,000 more, not the full 25,000 that would make growth symmetrical.

in widespread starvation. The different combinations of capital and consumer goods that are available to a given country can be shown using the production-possibilities model. It is, metaphorically, a choice between butter now and dairy processing plants for the future.

In our society, we do not hear much about the need for increasing capital goods at the expense of consumer goods. This is because the United States, like other highly industrialized countries, has a large store of capital goods. What we do sometimes hear is an appeal to turn our production from private consumer needs to public goods, or to public goods of a certain kind. Thus, some critics call for less colored toilet paper and more drug-treatment centers, while others, looking at the public budget, want to use the money marked for fighter planes for housing and drug treatment instead. Choices such as these involve issues of equity, since growth in some areas, such as public housing, effects a redistribution of income and advantage. Clearly, economic growth is a goal that is not easy to pursue to everybody's satisfaction.

Balance of Payments

The production-possibilities model assumes that our economy is a closed system, that we do not purchase resources and products from other countries, and that we do not sell to them. In fact, we enter into all kinds of international transactions, and one of our goals is to maintain a balance between income and expenditures. We do not wish to spend more of our money abroad than foreigners are willing to spend here, as has been the case. Ideally, we want to achieve a balance of payments, receiving as much currency from foreign nations as they receive from us.

We have, moreover, certain other purposes in international trade. We want to avoid becoming dependent on any one country for the production of a vital material. We need to be sure that we do not import so much of a product that American industry suffers and American workers are laid off. But neither do we want to prevent Americans from buying those foreign products that the United States cannot produce efficiently, economically, or in sufficient quantity. Thus, we might encourage importation of foreign meat, for example, as a means of increasing the quantity of meat available, and thereby prevent a rise in meat prices. One of our economic goals, then, is to manage our international trade in a manner that is consistent with other goals, such as full employment and price stability.

Elimination of Poverty

The production-possibilities model ignores the issues of equity in accepting as given whatever income distribution already exists. To some policymakers, a more equitable distribution of income is one of the by-products of an efficient economy. To others, it is an end in itself—so much so that they are even willing to accept a certain amount of inflation in the economy as a whole if this is the only way of providing lower-income groups with sufficient means. Of course, the definition of what is sufficient varies; but once this is determined, it is relatively easy to measure the extent to which a society has succeeded in eliminating whatever it defines as poverty.

How to have efficiency with equity is the central theme of this text. This problem is examined in specific relationship to health care in the next chapter. Later, in Parts Two and Three, the question of efficiency (with equity) on the aggregate level will be studied. Part Four is a more detailed study of the concept and goal of growth. Parts Five and Six deal with small economic units—individuals and firms—in their struggle with efficiency and equity. And Part Seven covers international trade, where the concepts of efficiency and equity deal with economic activity among nations.

SUMMARY

1 Although the United States is the richest nation in the world, even *its* wealth is limited. The use of finite resources for competing ends is the central economic problem in all societies.

2 Scarcity occurs because resources are limited but wants and needs are insatiable.

These needs are not simply for biological survival or for consumer goods. Even if everyone lived ascetically, there would probably be competing uses for different resources, and therefore, there would be scarcity.

3 Limited resources are the basis of limited products and limited income. Very few wants are satisfied directly by resources. Production processes turn resources into the goods and services that fulfill the wants of society. These resources are called factors of production and are grouped into four categories: land, capital, labor, and entrepreneurship. Each of these factors receives its own type of income. Land furnishes rent; capital, interest; labor, compensation; and entrepreneurship, profit. The control of resources is the basis of income.

4 Faced with limited products, limited incomes, and unlimited wants, society must make choices. The central choices involve how products are to be made, what those products will be, and who is to get them. Technological efficiency, which refers to how products are made, occurs when no change can be made in the use of resources that would increase the output of one product without necessitating a decrease in the output of another product. Every resource is being used to its utmost. The economy must also produce the combination of goods and services that most satisfies society. If it does this, it has achieved what is known as allocative efficiency. The study of efficiency has been central to economics, but there is also the question of whose needs and wants are to be satisfied, or the equity of the economic system. The strict definition of equity refers to income distribution; at one pole is total equality of income despite differing individual contributions to the economy and at the other pole is income distribution based solely on the control of factors. The broader definition of equity refers to how well the economy promotes such intangibles as justice and freedom.

5 At the heart of economics is the idea of economizing, of allocating the limited material resources of a society for the efficient production of inevitably scarce goods and services to satisfy best the needs and wants of society. Underlying this definition is the potential tension between efficiency and equity. Positive economists, who have developed powerful mathematical tools, separate scientific analysis about questions of efficiency from value judgments about the direction of society. Adherents of normative economics insist that such a view of the discipline uses a narrow and obsolete approach that accepts the social system as relatively fixed and concentrates on efficiency at the expense of equity.

6 The scientific approach involves a general procedure of formulating a hypothesis that can be tested, defining terms and assumptions in an operational way, and testing the hypothesis through observation and use of logic. One important technique is the use of models, or simplified versions of reality that enable the scientist to focus attention on the relationship between two or three variables, holding all others constant.

7 One important economic model is the production-possibilities frontier, which shows the different combinations of goods possible given the limited resources of society. If the economy is operating at technological efficiency, it will be at some point on the frontier. If it is operating at allocative efficiency, it will be producing that combination of goods most desired by the society. If a society wants

one more of one good, it will have to give up some of another good. What it gives up is known as the opportunity cost. As resources are converted from one use to another, the opportunity cost increases. This is known as the increasing cost of convertibility.

8 The central goals of a society are efficiency and equity, but these concepts may be made operational. It is easier to measure how we are meeting these goals using levels of unemployment, price stability, rate of growth, balance of payments, and progress in eradicating poverty.

SUGGESTED READINGS

Dorfman, Robert. *Prices and Markets.* Chap. 1. Englewood Cliffs, N.J.: Prentice-Hall, 1967.

Lipsey, Richard G., and **Peter O. Steiner.** *Economics.* 3rd ed. Chaps. 1–3. New York: Harper & Row, 1972.

Mansfield, Edwin. *Microeconomics: Theory and Applications.* Chap. 1. New York: W. W. Norton, 1970.

Rivlin, Alice M. "Why Can't We Get Things Done?" *The Brookings Bulletin* 9, no. 2 (Spring 1972): 5–9.

QUESTIONS

1 Review
   a. the roles of scarcity and wants in the "economic" problem,
   b. efficiency and equity,
   c. positive and normative economics,
   d. the formulation, testing, and refutation or support of a hypothesis,
   e. the chacteristics and use of a model,
   f. the uses of the production-possibilities frontier.

2 Gold conducts electricity better than other metals. However, gold is rarely used for this purpose. Why? Why is even copper not used for heavy, long-distance cables?

3 Most traditional economic models assume that sellers and buyers of goods compete with each other basically in terms of price. Baran and Sweezy have argued that big oligopolies do not compete in terms of price but in terms of the "sales effort."* If Baran and Sweezy are correct, on what basis are they criticizing traditional models? What effects might this have on prices?

4 A fellow student of yours tells you that he is going to try to break the curve on the next economics exam by memorizing everything in the book. He is therefore confident, he says, of getting an A. Would you adopt his approach? Give your reasons.

5 What is the significance of the bowed shape of the production-possibilities curve shown below? Assume that the economy is producing 80,000 units of wheat and 20,000 tractors. What is the opportunity cost of 10,000 additional units of wheat?

* Paul Baran and Paul Sweezy, "The Tendency of Surplus to Rise," in David Mermelstein, ed., *Economics: Mainstream Readings and Radical Critiques,* 1st ed. (New York: Random House, 1970).

Where on the diagram would the economy be producing if factors are unemployed or underemployed?

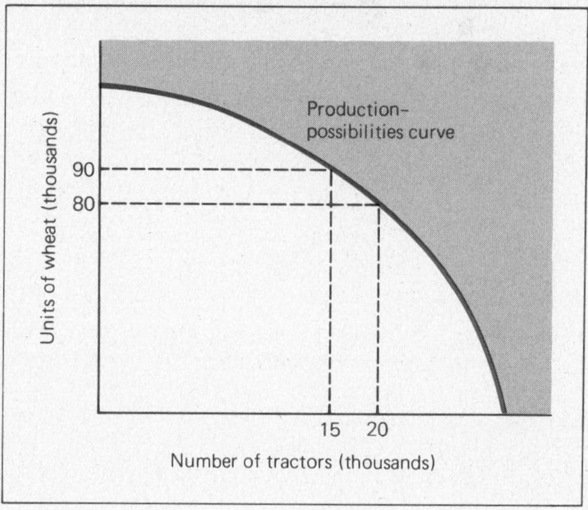

6 Suppose that an economy has resources that can be used equally well for the production of wheat or rye. How might the shape of the production-possibilities curve differ from that shown above? Suppose that an economy produces wine and cars. At some point on the production-possibilities curve, there is no way to use wine-producing resources to make additional cars. What would be the shape of the curve over this range?

7 Suppose that you advance the hypothesis that as unemployment rises, enrollment in educational institutions increases. On what grounds might this hypothesis be attacked?

8 In the interest of equity, some economists have argued for a guaranteed minimum income for all households in the United States. Herbert Gans, however, argues that the middle and upper classes face a dilemma: They believe that all should live at a minimum standard, but suspect that at least some people may decide not to work if that standard is provided by the government. The people who are likely to make that choice, says Gans, are those who are underpaid and those who do society's "dirty work."† Why would people be tempted to take the guaranteed income? How might the production processes be affected? What might happen to the wages for "dirty work"? How does this example illustrate the general conflict between efficiency and equity?

† Herbert J. Gans, "Income Grants and 'Dirty Work,'" in David Mermelstein, ed., *Economics: Mainstream Readings and Radical Critiques*, 1st ed. (New York: Random House, 1970).

Opening photo by J. Paul Kirouac

CHAPTER 2
CHOICES

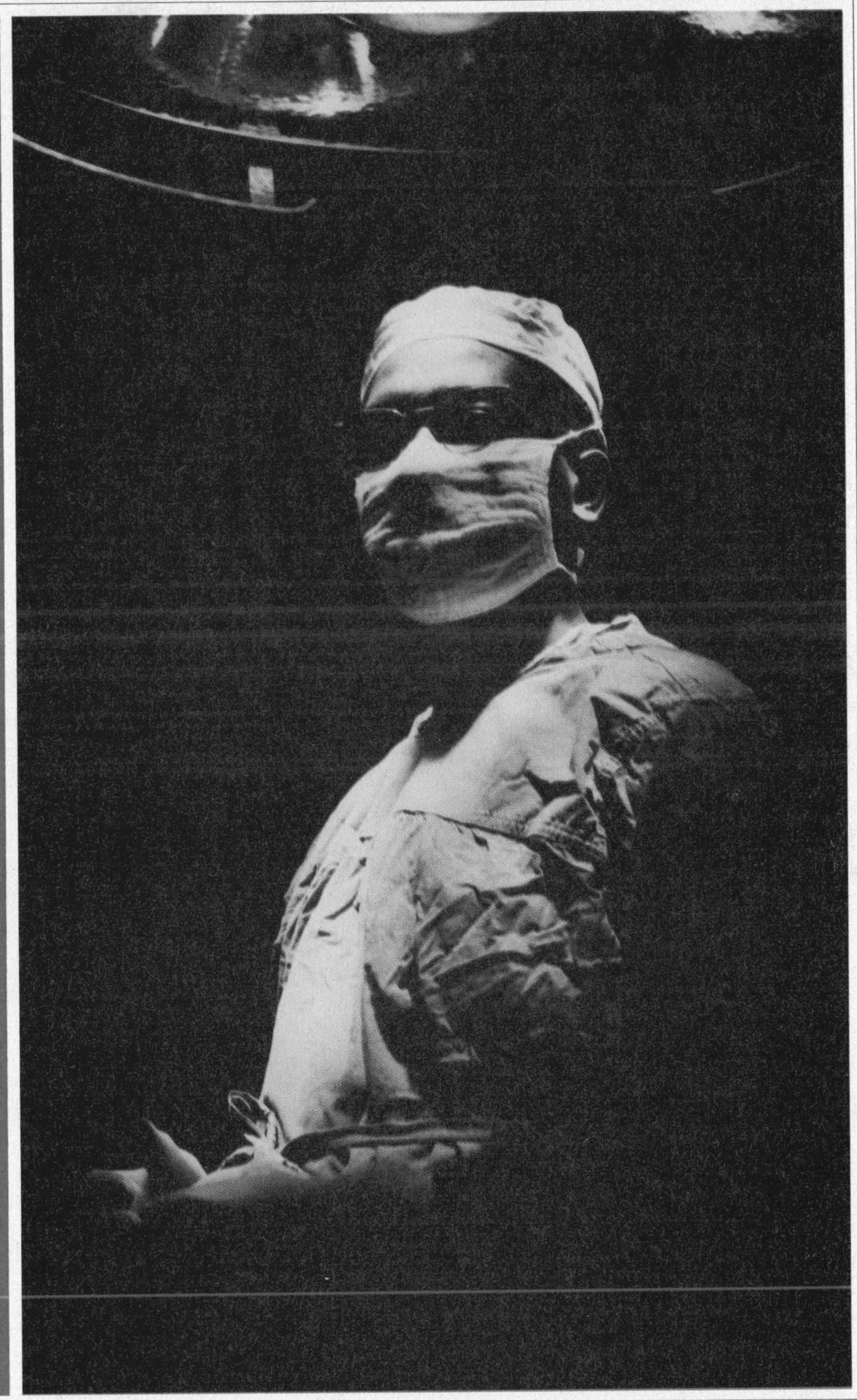

In testimony before the Senate Health Subcommittee, when that panel was investigating the national health care system, a young college man related how an injury resulting from a football game had left him paralyzed from the neck down. His father estimated for the committee that, in the period immediately following the accident, the young man's medical bills had been about $40,000. He also estimated that his son would probably have medical expenses of between $75,000 and $100,000 every year from then on.[1]

Of course, most individuals' medical expenses are not in this catastrophic range. But even for noncatastrophic injury or illness, the cost is expensive and becoming more so. In the decade between 1960 and 1970, hospital costs increased by 170 percent and doctor's fees by 60 percent, and the upward trend continues.

The average sum that each American spent on health care in 1970 was roughly $300, the highest per capita amount in the world. Overall in that year, Americans spent about $60 billion on personal health care and related services. That means that about 7 percent of the Gross National Product—all the money spent on all the goods and services in the country—went for health care.

That is a lot of money—7 cents out of every dollar—and should buy the American people good health care. Whether it does is difficult to tell because it is almost impossible to design a meaningful, workable way to measure what constitutes good health, much less good health care. But the following statistics are illuminating, particularly as they compare with those of other countries.

—In 1971, the life expectancy of each baby born in the United States was 70.8 years. In Europe alone, 10 countries have a longer life expectancy for newborn infants.

—In 1970, the infant mortality rate in the United States was 19.8; that is, nearly 20 out of every 1000 babies born in the United States died before reaching the age of one. Ten European nations have a lower mortality rate.

These statistics for the United States are for the entire population of the country. The figures for different income groups within the United States tell another story. Among people with high incomes ($10,000 a year and above) the infant mortality rate in 1964 was 19.9 deaths per 1000 live births. In contrast, among low-income people (under $3000 per year), the infant mortality rate was 32.1, with the black infant mortality rate even higher at 42.5 deaths per 1000 live births. A white born in 1955 can expect to live nearly seven years longer than a black person born in the same year.

Our society, then, has allocated a large amount of its available resources—7 percent—to health care, but there is at least some question, judging from the com-

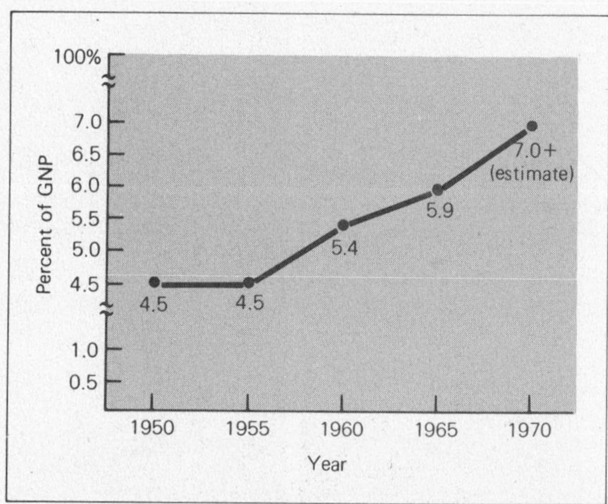

FIGURE 2-1 NATIONAL HEALTH EXPENDITURES AS A PERCENTAGE OF GNP, 1950–70 **Since 1950, national health expenditures have risen, as a percent of GNP, from 4.5 percent to over 7 percent. This startling rise is explained largely by the rapidly rising cost of medical care relative to other prices. Furthermore, as GNP rises, one would expect an increasing percent to be spent on medical care, because only the relatively well-to-do can afford to spend as much as they would like on medical care. As GNP rises, then, an increasing percentage of the population is able to spend on medical care what would have otherwise (had they been poorer) gone to more pressing needs such as food and essential clothing. Source: Howard R. Bowen and James R. Jeffers, *The Economics of Health Services* (New York: General Learning, 1972), p. 5.**

1 Edward M. Kennedy, *In Critical Condition: The Crisis in America's Health Care* (New York: Simon and Schuster, 1972), pp. 27–35.

parisons with other countries, that these resources are being used with technological efficiency, and there is evidence that these health care resources, or more precisely, the output of these resources, is not being distributed with equity. This chapter develops these ideas—allocative efficiency, technological efficiency, and equity—as they apply to the way health care resources are used in the United States.

HEALTH CARE: A RIGHT OR A PRIVILEGE?

A Question of Equity

In a free-market economy, income rationing of the available goods and services is a fact of life. Part of the market's function is to provide a means of allocating the scarce goods and services among people's unlimited needs and wants, and that allocation almost invariably follows the distribution of income. People who have high incomes usually have better housing, better food, better clothing, better transportation, and better leisure activities than low-income people.

The traditional view of health care is that it too is a service, available to those who want or need it at the going price. Health care is a privilege afforded to those who have the money to buy it. To the extent that poor people receive health care at all, it is charity, for which the poor are expected to be grateful and not to complain.

But recently society's view about health care has begun to change. There is a new social attitude coming into being that sees health care as a basic right of all people, regardless of their income. This new viewpoint holds that, while income rationing may be an acceptable way to distribute cars and TV sets and vacations, it is an unacceptable way to distribute health care. Since the presence (or absence) of proper health care can make the difference between a productive person and a nonproductive one, and between life and death, the people who are promoting this newer attitude believe that there is a fundamental difference between health care and other, more materialistic goods and services. Their conclusion: Quality health care should be available as a right to all who need it.

A Question of Efficiency

But if this current opinion is to become public policy, several important questions are going to have to be answered first: Where is the extra health care capability going to come from? And who is going to pay for it?

It is a basic economic fact of life that nothing is free. If health care at the current level of quality is going to be made available to people who cannot now afford it, that extra capacity is going to have to come from somewhere. Either people who are now receiving adequate care will have to accept less (while still paying the same amount of money); or more health care services will have to be squeezed from the current-sized health care industry through greater efficiency; or society will have to allocate more of its resources to health care.

Some redistribution of available health care services is possible. And measures to make the health care industry more productive are also possible. But to provide the quality of health care that is now available to those who can afford it to everybody who needs it, more resources will be necessary.

Allocative Efficiency If society is going to devote appreciably more resources to health care, these resources are going to have to come at the expense of other things, be it going to the moon or buying more peanut butter. Since 7 percent of the GNP is already devoted to health care, a 50 percent increase in the amount of health care supplied would require that the country invest more than 10 percent of its resources in health (assuming that the same levels of productivity and quality were maintained); doubling the amount of health care available would take 14 percent of all the nation's resources. However, this still might not meet the increase in the amount of health care demanded, as those people who are currently rationed out of adequate care would take advantage of its new availability. At some point, society is going to have to decide how much health care is

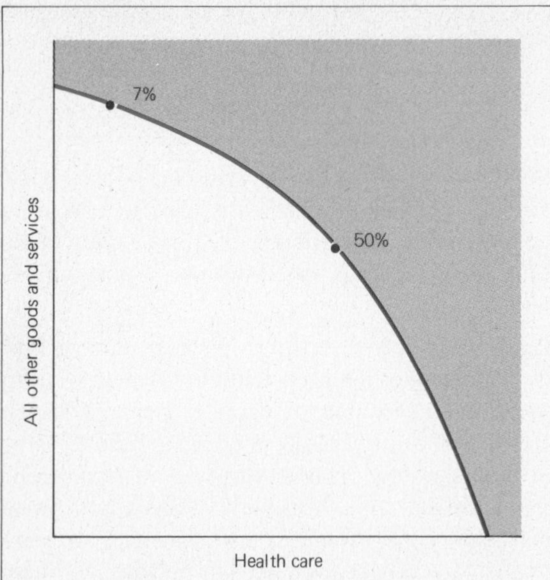

FIGURE 2-2 PRODUCTION-POSSIBILITIES CURVE FOR HEALTH CARE (Hypothetical) **If the U.S. health care system were technologically efficient and absorbing the same amount of GNP as in 1970, this would be represented by the point labeled 7 percent. Perhaps that is not enough to ensure quality health care on an equitable basis. But using 50 percent of all resources would clearly be too much. In that case, one-half of the population would be in the health care business taking care of itself and the other half of the population at the expense of many other vital goods and services.**

enough. To rephrase the issue in terms of the production-possibilities curve that was discussed in Chapter 1, society is going to have to choose how many other goods to sacrifice in order to obtain health care.

Exactly how much health care is sufficient may be determined by increasing expenditures until the benefits obtained from better health exactly offset the costs of obtaining that level of health. As a practical matter, no exact measure can be found, and the problem becomes a philosophical and political question having to do with how highly good health and life are valued by society. But it is the job of the economist to point out that, whatever level of health care the society finally decides on, it will have to pay a price, in increased taxation or in the lost opportunity to have other goods and services. Or if the level of health care remains the same or decreases, society will have to accept a certain amount of illness and death which could, given more resources, be prevented. Economists may also point out that some ways of achieving health involve needless sacrifice, because they waste precious resources through technological inefficiency.

Technological Efficiency It stands to reason that the more productively the resources devoted to health care can be used, the fewer additional resources will have to be moved into health care in order to meet the demand. If more resources are applied to a particular patient than are required to make that patient well, those extra health resources are, in effect, wasted. Overcare is as inefficient as not enough care.

But technological efficiency is needed in the health care industry, not only to make the limited resources yield as much service as possible, but also to provide as high quality care as possible. Since the consequences of poor, inefficient health care can be death itself, there is an extra urgency that health care be of a high quality, as well as that no resources be wasted. To borrow a term from the military-industrial complex, health care should be of high quality, but not "gold plated."

Goals in Health Care

From these discussions it is possible to begin to draw some conclusions about the nature of an ideal health care system. Or put another way, it is possible to write a tentative list of goals against which to measure the performance of the current health care system, as well as all the various plans that have been put forth for modifying it. Such a list of goals for an ideal health care system might look like this:

—That the cost to society would be warranted by the benefits from improved health. There is no advantage in having a health care system that is so expensive to society that other, equally important services have to be neglected.

—That whatever the resources available, they would be used economically. The objective would be to have the highest possible amount of health care, with high quality but without needless frills, and at the lowest production cost possible.

—That everybody would have equitable access to health care, regardless of where he or she lived or his or her ability to pay.

As soon as these goals are stated, two problems present themselves. First, it may well be that these goals are not mutually compatible. It may not be possible to meet all of them at the same time. To have a system with truly equitable access may preclude having one without some waste. Or to have a system with high quality and equitable access may require an unreasonable sacrifice of other goods and services.

And second, these qualities are exceedingly difficult to define. What are the measurable benefits of better health? What is high quality, efficient medical care? Exactly what is equitable access? Without precise definitions there can be no precise, objective measurements, and therefore a certain amount of fuzziness is, unfortunately, inevitable.

But using these goals, as imprecise as they must necessarily be, this chapter reviews the performance of the current health care system and weighs how well (or poorly) it measures up. Then using the same criteria, we analyze the various alternatives that have been put forth to change the current system. The objective for all this will be to show how economic analysis, particularly in terms of the tension between equity and efficiency, can be useful in evaluating various policy alternatives.

THE HEALTH CARE SYSTEM

Buying health care is not like buying most other goods or services. Usually consumers are in a position to control how much of any good or service they want to buy and how much money they will have to pay. And usually consumers have at least some knowledge about what it is they intend to buy, from advertising or word-of-mouth. For major purchases, most consumers investigate further—by looking at several different houses, or test-driving several different makes of automobiles. Consumers usually have enough information and enough of a choice that, if they want and are willing to make the effort, they can comparison shop for the best value. In most buying situations, it is the consumer who makes the decisions and pays the bills.

But in buying health care, most of these conventions are absent. The consumer makes almost no comparisons and few decisions, because most lay people have very little knowledge about health care. The health care suppliers generally decide what kind of and how much treatment the consumer will receive, and how much the services will cost. And a third party—either government or an insurance company—frequently pays the bills.

Such a system falls short of the goals we have just outlined. Probably the most obvious shortcoming is the unequal access of different groups of people to health care. Contrary to what may be the new developing social ethic, health care today is not a right that is enjoyed by everybody on an equal basis.

Equity

What in effect has developed in this country is a three-tier health care system based on income. The wealthy can afford excellent preventive medicine from their specialist doctors. If more serious problems develop, they can afford the best treatment available, and they can receive it in the finest hospitals in relative comfort. Their insurance tends to be comprehensive and covers almost all their medical expenses. And access to good health care is usually easier for upper-income persons, since doctors tend to practice in wealthier areas. For example, in Beverly Hills, California, there is one doctor for every 80 people, while in Venice, a lower-income area just 15 miles away, there is only one doctor for every 1600 people.

For the middle class, the important question is what their health insurance covers. For the elderly there is Medicare; for the rest of the middle class there are private insurance plans. To the extent that any medical problems that arise are covered by insurance, the middle class enjoys good health services provided by its family doctors and any other specialists that may be required. The middle class also tends to go to its family doctors for preventive and optional care. But since middle-class people must pay for these services directly, they tend to use less of them than the wealthy. When catastrophic or chronic illnesses or injuries exhaust the insurance coverage, the middle-class person faces financial bankruptcy, and then receives the same kind of medical care as that available to the poor.

The poor receive medical care depending on how lucky they are. If they live in one of the more than 130 rural counties that have no private doctor, they may get no care whatsoever. If they live in a state in which they can qualify for Medicaid, they may have much better access to basic health care. But it is no more than basic. Preventive care is dispensed in crowded out-patient clinics. Bed care is provided in the wards of public hospitals; and although the quality of care may be excellent in these wards—particularly if the public hospital is also a research hospital and associated with a medical school—the patients tend to be treated as either charity cases or medical specimens. The poor who cannot qualify for Medicaid and who do not live in an area served by a tax-supported public hospital that, by law, cannot refuse to treat anyone ill or injured are, simply, out of luck.

Efficiency

Almost as obvious as the unequal access to the services of the current health care industry is its inefficiency. One sign of this has been the exploding costs of health care. Between 1946 and 1971, all consumer prices rose by 71 percent, but doctors' fees went up by 109 percent. Between 1946 and 1967 hospital charges climbed 442 percent, or about six times faster than consumer prices in general. Part of this jump came from labor costs. Between 1950 and 1967, the number of hospital workers needed per 100 inpatients rose from 178 to 265, an increase of almost 50 percent. Also during this time, hospital workers began to demand and receive rapid increases in wages. Traditionally, hospital workers have been among the lowest-paid individuals in the labor force. But in 1967, two years after Medicaid and Medicare were passed, hospital workers were put under the minimum wage laws. At the same time, hospital workers began to unionize extensively. The result has been an increase not only in the amount of labor needed to run a hospital, but also in the cost of that labor. Not all of the increases in medical costs are this inevitable, however. The health care system is not organized to make maximum use of the time of physicians or the available medical facilities.

Physicians Physicians have no incentives to cut costs, since their prime interest is in healing people and since third parties or captive consumers pay the bills. Competition is strictly limited by fee schedules and by artificially created shortages because of limitations on the number of doctors educated and licensed. (The number of physicians per 100,000 population has actually declined since 1950.) Although the American Medical Association justifies the limitations on the number of physicians as a way of ensuring high quality, another result has been that doctors have the highest incomes of any professional group. The shortage is intensified by specialization (78 percent of the physicians in private practice in 1970 were specialists). In part because specialization requires a large population base to allow a full practice, doctors tend to cluster in metropolitan areas, while rural areas and inner cities suffer from a lack of physicians. Because competition is limited, doctors have few incentives to cut expenses and can maintain costly solo practices rather than group practices that might provide economies from sharing equipment and staff.

Hospitals Hospitals and other medical facilities tend to be controlled by doctors, and operate in a similar, independent manner, each intent on having for itself the latest (and most expensive) techniques and equipment, without any regard for regional planning. The result is that in the same community many medical facilities are duplicated, available in each hospital if they are needed for an emergency, but not used frequently enough to justify their duplication.

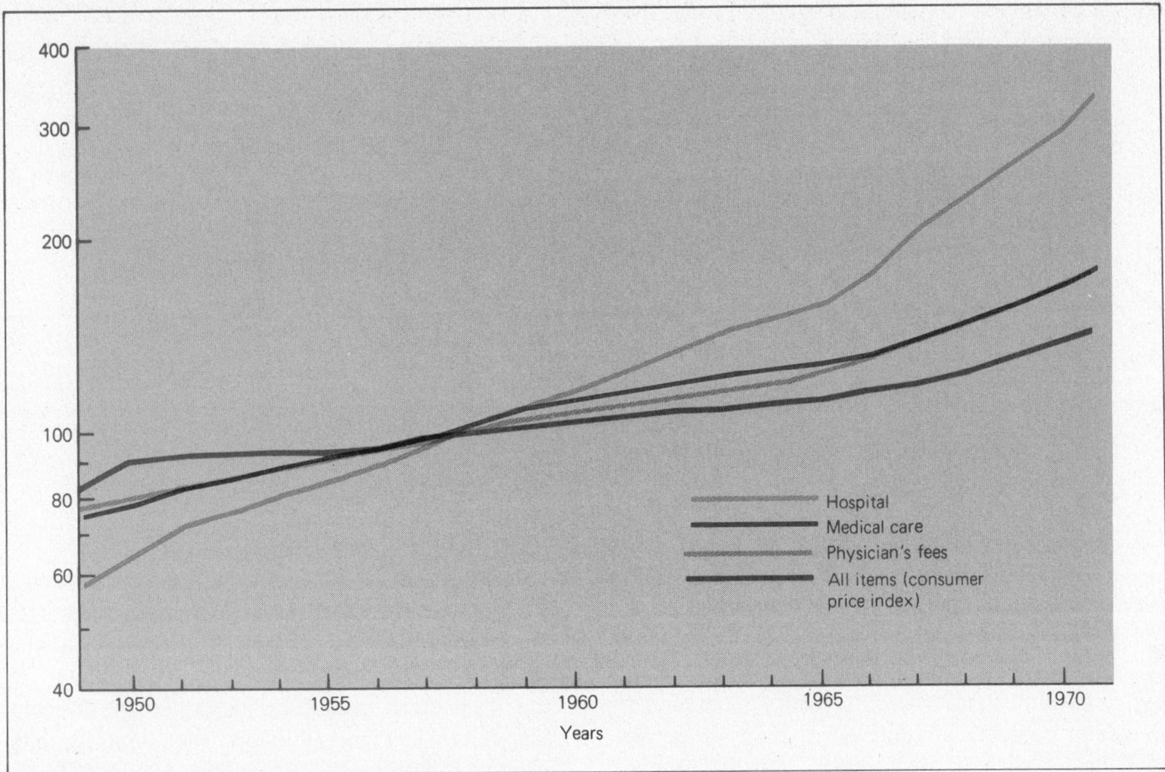

FIGURE 2-3 THE COST OF GETTING SICK, 1950–71 (1957–59 = 100) Medical costs, particularly those of hospital care, have risen much more rapidly than the Consumer Price Index, which is saying a lot in these inflationary times. Medical costs have doubled since 1950, while the cost of hospital care has increased more than fourfold. Source: Howard R. Bowen and James R. Jeffers, *The Economics of Health Services*, p. 17, © 1971 General Learning Corporation. Used by permission.

There are about 7000 hospitals and 20,000 nursing homes in the United States. Many of these units are underemployed, with utilization rates running, on an average, below 80 percent. In any ordinary economic situation, such a condition would call for reducing hospital prices to consumers, not raising them as hospitals continue to do. But like doctors, hospitals have a monopoly on a necessary service.

These and many other such factors add to the inefficiency of the health care system. But a more pervasive cause of inefficiency is the decision-making process that determines which forms of treatment and how much treatment each patient will receive. As this process has evolved in the current health care system, at almost no point are there any strong incentives for economy—that is, to control the amount of health care resources used by patients and to choose methods of treatment that are the most cost-effective. On the contrary, for most medical situations and most parts of the system, the incentives are to use as many resources as possible and to disregard economy. For hospitals this is intensified by the cost-pass-through system, in which hospitals simply pass on costs in the form of higher prices. This is acceptable because of the prevalence and structure of health insurance plans.

Health Insurance Increasingly, health care is being paid for by someone other than the consumer. Consumers indirectly contribute to these payments, by

TABLE 2-1 Paying for Health Care, 1950–71 (Percentage distribution by source)

		Consumer expenditures							
Fiscal year	Total personal health care expenditures (billions of dollars)	Private insurance benefit payments	Direct payments	Industrial in-plant services	Public expenditures: Medicare	Public expenditures: Medicaid	Public expenditures: Other	Total	Private insurance benefit payments as percentage of consumer personal health expenditures
1950	10.4	8.5	68.3	3.0	0.0	0.0	20.2	100.0	11.0
1960	22.7	20.7	55.3	2.3	0.0	2.1	19.6	100.0	27.2
1965	33.5	24.7	52.5	2.0	0.0	4.2	16.6	100.0	32.0
1968	46.3	22.5	40.8	1.7	12.9	7.6	14.5	100.0	35.6
1971	65.1	25.5	37.2	1.5	12.1	10.0	13.7	100.0	40.6

Since 1950, total personal health care expenditures have risen from $10.4 billion to $65.1 billion, an increase of over 500 percent. Private insurance and public expenditures have played an increasingly important role in financing the expense of health care, rising from 28.7 percent of these expenditures in 1950 to 61.3 percent in 1971.

SOURCE: Charles Schultze et al., *Setting National Priorities: The 1973 Budget.* P. 216. Copyright © 1972 by the Brookings Institution, Washington, D.C.

paying insurance premiums and government taxes, but they do not directly settle the bill themselves. In the 21-year period from 1950 to 1971, the figures for direct payment of health care bills and third-party payments almost reversed. In 1950, 68 percent of all health care expenditures were paid for by the consumer directly to the supplier. That left 32 percent paid indirectly through third parties. By 1971, direct payments had fallen to 37 percent, while payments through third parties had risen to 63 percent.

The trend continues toward third-party payments and away from direct payments. There seem to be two reasons for this. To protect themselves against the intermittent, unexpected, and very large costs of major illness and injury, people who can afford it are increasingly turning to the risk-sharing principle of an insurance pool. And government is paying an increasing amount of money for the health care of those people who cannot afford to pay for their own medical attention or to buy their own health insurance. Again using the years from 1950 to 1971, the percentage of health care expenditures paid for by private insurance almost tripled, from 9 percent to 26 percent. And government and other public expenditures grew from 20 percent to 36 percent. Thus, the demand for health care is to a great extent shaped indirectly, not by wants and needs, but by actuarial tables and political bargaining.

Third-party payments tend to cover hospitalization and doctors' services provided in a hospital, but not the cost of optional preventive medical care. In 1971, private insurance paid 73 percent of total outlays for hospital care but only 48 percent of doctor bills. As a result, people tend to seek health care for only those problems for which they are covered and to ignore those problems that are not covered. One example of this is surgery. Almost all health insurance covers surgery. And almost 40 percent of all the practicing physicians in the country are either general surgeons or in one or another of the surgical specialties. Further, many experts in the field believe that there is too much surgery performed in this country as compared to other countries. This is of course not evidence that excess surgery is performed because it is covered by insurances and third-party payments, but it does suggest a possible explanation.

The irony of this situation is that it takes far fewer resources to perceive a potential medical problem early and to take steps to prevent its becoming major, than it does to correct a problem once it has become debilitating and requires hospitalization. Of course, some medical conditions, no matter how early they are detected, still end up using many health care resources. But in the long run, preventive care is more efficient and a more productive way to use health care resources than later, corrective care. Yet the strongest incentive for economy in the system is directed toward limiting the amount of preventive care that is consumed, by requiring consumers to pay for this care entirely by themselves.

Since it is the third parties—the insurance carriers and the government—that pay for most health care, particularly in hospitals, it would seem to be in their interests to try to control medical and hospital costs and to push for economy. But under the current system this is not so.

Profit-making insurance carriers have no overriding incentives to attempt to control health care costs. Their strongest motivation is to show a profit, and there are two ways to do that: control costs, or just pay the claims and raise the premiums to cover the increase in outlay and still earn a profit. Often it is easier and less expensive for insurance carriers simply to raise their premium rates and write more restrictive insurance, than it is to try to control health care costs. By simply passing the higher costs along to their policy holders in the form of higher premiums, they can still show a profit, which is their only real incentive.

Private, nonprofit insurance carriers have the same choice, and often it is easier for them, too, just to raise the rates to cover the increased costs. But the nonprofit carriers, particularly the Blue Cross—Blue Shield system, face another problem in attempting to control health care costs; local physicians and hospital administrators have a strong influence on their operations. In a sense it is like the regulated regulating themselves. In some cases where a vigorous local Blue Cross–Blue Shield organization has rejected health care bills as being too high and has refused to pay them, the local health care professionals in the area have collected proxies and voted the hardline administration out and installed a more cooperative one. Ultimately it is in the insurance companies' self-interest to keep the doctors and hospitals happy. If doctors and hospitals began to refuse services to consumers with a certain kind of insurance, that insurance company would be out of business in that area.

The administrators of the Medicaid and Medicare programs ostensibly have a strong incentive to hold down the costs of health care, but they are prevented from doing so by the way the original legislation setting up these programs was written. In order to secure the acquiescence of the organized medical profession, these programs incorporated the idea that doctors and hospitals should be paid for each specific service they rendered patients and be paid the prevailing rate in the community where the services were given. The fee-for-service concept was written into the law, and it effectively stops the administrators of these programs from working for economy in the use of health care resources.

Thus, despite the help that insurance programs have provided in extending care to more Americans, these institutions have contributed to excessive cost and misallocation of resources in the health care system.

Conclusion The foregoing survey of the health care system leads to the general conclusion that despite the enormous expenditures on health care, the current health care system in the United States wastes health care resources, and in the process not only delivers services of questionable quality but delivers it better to some groups than others. The present health care system is not successful in achieving allocative efficiency, technological efficiency or equity.

SOME ALTERNATIVE PLANS

The problem, then, is to find a system that better meets the goals set out in the early part of the chapter: To achieve high-quality care distributed equitably without incurring prohibitive costs. Simply going on an economy binge is hardly the answer to rising health care costs, if lower costs are achieved by rationing more people out of the system or lowering the quality of the care. Here, then, is a real problem of economizing, and many answers are now in the air, each of which may be scrutinized according to the incentives for meeting our goals. Let us look at a few of these.

Medical Manpower

One possible long-range solution to some of the problems of the current system is to increase the number of health care professionals, particularly doctors. The assumption behind this proposal is that if there are more doctors practicing medicine, the competition among them will act as a brake on the rapidly rising costs of physicians' services and will make more physicians' services available to more people.

The Comprehensive Health Manpower Training Act of 1971 is directed toward increasing the number of physicians in two ways: by providing financial aid to medical schools so that they can increase their enrollments and improve the quality of their instruction, and by providing scholarships and loans to medical students and other students in the health care professions. The Act also attempts to correct the unequal distribution of doctors in the country through medical school and hospital construction subsidies and scholarship incentives.

The amount of federal aid for medical manpower training and education was about $1.5 billion in 1973. That provided more than half of the budgets of the medical schools in the country. And in the 1972–73 academic year, almost 76,000 would-be health care professionals received loans or scholarships from the Department of Health, Education, and Welfare. But it is still too early to know if these programs will actually result in an increase in the number of doctors and an increase in the number of doctors practicing in under-served areas.

Even if these measures work, unless some way is found to change the informal but effective way that doctors establish and maintain their fee-for-service payment schedules, or to subsidize the cost of physician care for the poor, increasing the supply of doctors will not automatically guarantee that doctors will use their time and the other health care resources more economically.

Group Practice and HMO Plans

Other ideas for reform are aimed at changing the structure of the health care delivery system, particularly the way doctor services are organized. The objective of these proposals is to give the doctors more time to practice and more incentive to provide preventive and economical care.

If doctors practiced in groups, rather than as individuals, the patient volume of the group would make it practical to have secretaries and other supporting staff members do the adminstrative, nonmedical work. Surveys have shown that doctors in partnerships or groups, with support staffs, can average about 25 percent more patients a week than their colleagues in solo practice. A group practice can also share the overhead of more extensive facilities and more expensive equipment.

Most partnerships or groups that already exist are limited to doctors of the same specialty. But if doctors of different specialties became affiliated in a group practice, consumers would have a place to go for one-stop, comprehensive, coordinated medical attention, with all the attending advantages and economies that such an arrangement would offer. Some group practices, like the Mayo Clinic in Minnesota and the Lahey Clinic in Boston, have become so extensive that they not only represent all the medical specialties; they also have their own hospital complexes.

Health Maintenance Organizations Comprehensive group medical practice combined with the prepayment of a fixed annual fee for all health care is the organizational principle of Health Maintenance Organizations (HMOs). Consumers in a particular community join an HMO by paying a flat, yearly fee that then covers all the medical services they may need for that entire year. In accepting the fees, the HMOs agree to provide whatever health care services members may need. They do not charge their members on a fee-for-service basis.

The principle behind HMOs is similar to that of insurance. It is risk sharing. If the HMO has a large enough membership, a moderate fee collected from all the members will pay for the extraordinary services required by a few members. HMOs count on the statistical probability that not all of their members will need as much medical attention as they actually paid for and that enough money will be left from this group to pay the overhead, as well as for the services that some of the members who do become seriously ill or injured need.

One of the largest HMOs currently in operation is the Kaiser Foundation Medical Care Program, which has more than a million and a half members in the Pacific Coast states. A federal survey found that on an average a Kaiser subscriber received high-quality medical attention at from 20 to 30 percent less than that available to nonsubscribers. There is also a substantial flow of members into the plan, which indicates consumer satisfaction with it.

The main promise that HMOs seem to hold is that they will deliver health care services more efficiently than the current system, because they will have strong incentives built into their design and operation to do so. HMOs receive only a set amount of money regardless of their patients' health, so profits are higher if their members stay healthy and avoid expensive hospitalizations. Therefore, the HMOs have a strong incentive to practice preventive medicine and to treat any medical problems in their early stages. And when treating illnesses, the HMOs also have a strong incentive to conserve and use as few medical resources as possible. But at the same time, an HMO has incentives to give its members good medical care, because if the members become dissatisfied and leave the program, the HMO will go bankrupt.

HMOs do seem to offer the possibility of greater efficiency in delivering health care services, but no one has had enough experience with the concept yet to know for sure. However, it does seem apparent that unless some way is found to subsidize the memberships of poor people in HMOs, the existence of HMOs by itself will do nothing to solve the problems of unequal access to health care services that exist in this country.

Establishing health maintenance organizations constituted a large part of the Nixon administration's proposals for reforming the health care system, and legislation was proposed to Congress that would provide financial and technical assistance to beginning HMOs in their critical starting-up period. But administration support for the reforms faltered and was later withdrawn.

Insurance Programs

The third major area toward which reforms are being directed is health insurance. Many ideas have been put forth, aimed at making health insurance more equitable and more available, on the assumption that a broader access to medical care would automatically follow the broader availability of health insurance coverage. Yet, to conserve medical resources, most of these plans also envision some limitations in coverage that would require at least some direct payment from consumers covered under the plans. While many of these proposals have been introduced in Congress, none that apply to the entire population have yet been enacted.

Mandatory Employer and Family Health Insurances The Nixon adminstration's proposal for restructuring health insurance coverage has two parts: a package of health insurance benefits that all employers in the country would be required to make available to their employees, and a family insurance plan that would be available to families without a working adult, which would therefore not be eligible for the mandatory package. Taken together, these plans would level out some of the difference among the coverage offered by various employers, and the difference among coverages afforded poor people because of the varying eligibility requirements for Medicaid from state to state. The two plans together would cost about $2.6 billion per year more than the current expenditures for Medicaid.

If enacted, this two-part program would alleviate some of the inequality in the current system. Under the mandatory plan, working people would at least have the option of receiving minimum, standardized coverage. But under this plan, people might have to pay up to $1500 a year in direct medical payments themselves. This amount could represent a substantial sum for working people with low wages—perhaps even a prohibitive amount, which would prevent their getting the medical help they really needed. That sum would not, however, be such a burden for working people with higher wages. The family plan would equalize some of the current inequality brought about because of the widely varying requirements for Medicaid.

But the programs do set up a difference in benefits between working and nonworking families. Nonworking families receive better coverage of initial medical expenses, but no coverage for catastrophic expenses. Working families receive coverage for catastrophic expenses, but have to pay a sizable portion of their noncatastrophic expenses themselves. Nowhere in the plans are poor, unemployed, childless couples or single people covered.

Comprehensive National Insurance This plan, called the Health Security Act, has been introduced in Congress by Senator Edward Kennedy of Massachusetts, Chairman of the Senate Subcommittee on Health, and Representative Martha Griffiths of Michigan, a senior member of the House Ways and Means Committee. It proposes a national health plan, covering the entire population, that would provide free medical care for everyone. The plan would be financed one-half by an additional federal payroll tax, paid by the country's employers, and one-half from general taxation. Unlike the Nixon plan, it attempts to build in incentives for efficiency and economy in providing health care services not simply by making the consumer pay part of the bill, but by budgeting.

Each year the plan would decide on a national health care budget, to be distributed among 1000 subareas of the country. In each subarea, an administrative agency would allocate the budget between the practitioners, the doctors and dentists, and the hospitals. Each hospital in the country would operate on a fixed, yearly budget provided by administrators at the subarea level. To assure that the hospitals were operating efficiently, a committee of consumers and professionals would monitor the use of medical resources in each hospital.

Each practitioner could choose to be paid by one of three methods: a fixed, annual salary; the standard fee-for-services-rendered basis; or a capitation basis—an amount of money that practitioners of different specialties would receive for agreeing to take care of the medical needs of one patient for one year. HMOs that were set up to provide all the health care services on a per capita basis would receive preferential treatment. And practitioners would be discouraged from choosing the fee-for-service payment basis. The practitioners would actually be paid by the subarea administration.

This plan would eliminate completely the income rationing of health services. Wealthy and poor people would have the exact same, total, financial access to health care. But the plan, at least initially, might favor the middle class and wealthy more than the poor, because at present most of the medical facilities are located in middle class and wealthy areas. To assure true equal access, some program of providing medical facilities for rural and poor areas would also have to be initiated.

To conserve medical resources and use them efficiently, the plan relies on administrative use committees in hospitals and on economic incentives similar to those of HMOs to the extent that doctors can be induced to accept the prepayment system.

Estimates of what such a comprehensive system would cost vary, depending on who is making the estimates. The Department of Health, Education, and Welfare estimates that the program would have a net cost to the government of about $60 billion annually. And according to HEW estimates, the half of the program financed by payroll taxes would require a 6.3 percent tax on wages and salaries below $15,000. Clearly, this is an expensive plan.

CONCLUSION

The policy-makers confronted with the problem of improving the health care system would do well to follow the counsel of the vizier to a medieval sultan. When asked to teach the sultan about economy in one easy lesson, the vizier replied, "TANSTAAFL," which means "There ain't no such thing as a free lunch."[2] The TANSTAAFL principle means that there is no costless way to better health care delivery—or to more of any other economic good. Such costs dictate that there is no perfect health care system. But the impossibility of perfection is not an excuse

2 For the full story, see Edwin Dolan, *TANSTAAFL: The Economic Strategy for Environmental Crisis* (New York: Holt, Rinehart and Winston, 1969).

that allows policymakers to throw up their hands and select at random. If lunch—or health care—is not free, it can be obtained at higher or lower costs. Economic analysis can point out what the costs are and who pays them in order to permit a more informed health care policy.

SUMMARY

1 An ideal health care system would be accessible to all who need care, would not absorb resources better spent on other social wants or needs, and would provide high-quality care at the lowest possible cost. In short, it would meet the goals of equity and efficiency. However, these goals are difficult to measure and may be incompatible.

2 The U.S. health care system is shaped by the facts that the producers determine how much care an individual receives and a third party often pays the bill. This results in inequities for those not covered by a third party, so that what has developed is a three-tier system based on income. The system also results in inefficiencies marked by rapidly rising costs. Some of this rise has been unavoidable; but the health care system is not organized to induce doctors or hospitals to reduce costs.

3 Because health insurance programs allow cost-pass-through, the price system does not force efficiency either. Further waste is created because insurance covers hospitalization rather than preventive medicine. Insurance does help extend health care to more Americans, but at the cost of wasted resources.

4 Although the United States has the highest per capita expenditure on health care in the world, it is neither equitable nor efficient. The problem is finding an alternative. Increasing the supply of doctors is one approach, but this does not ensure efficient use of their time. Group practices, including HMOs, offer incentives to treat patients using the fewest resources, but do little to correct inequitable access to health care. Various national insurance programs to extend access are before Congress. These involve additional expense—as much as $60 billion annually—and may produce problems of overcare and other inefficiencies. There is probably no ideal system, but there are ways of providing health care that incur fewer costs than there are now.

SUGGESTED READINGS

Bowen, Howard R., and **James R. Jeffers.** *The Economics of Health Services.* New York: General Learning, 1972.

Miller, Roger L. "Medical Care for All." In *Economics Today.* San Francisco: Canfield Press, 1973.

Schultze, Charles L., Edward R. Fried, Alice M. Rivlin, Nancy H. Teeters, and **Karen Davis.** "Health Insurance." In *Setting National Priorities.* Washington, D.C.: Brookings Institution, 1972.

Somers, Herbert M. "Economic Issues in Health Services." In *Contemporary Economic Issues.* Edited by Neil W. Chamberlain. Homewood, Ill.: Irwin, 1969.

QUESTIONS

1 Review
   a. the differences between purchases of medical care and purchases of most other types of goods and services,
   b. problems in the allocation of health care geographically and among various income groups,
   c. major efforts by government to provide for a more equitable distribution of health care,
   d. the incentives or lack of incentives for increased productivity in health care,
   e. major reform efforts.

2 Assume that the U.S. government adopts a system of national health insurance in which payments are deducted from paychecks and health care is provided when needed. What effects would you predict for resource allocation? For equity?

3 The TANSTAAFL principle may be applied to more than just the health care system. Should the economy be required to provide perfectly clean water and air, for example? Why or why not?

4 In 1910, the Flexner Report condemned the quality of medical education. The solution was to restrict the number of medical schools, thereby limiting the supply of doctors. Since Ralph Nader's book *Unsafe at Any Speed,* people have been concerned about the quality of automobiles. Would the same solution to quality apply here? What are the consequences of restricting supply in order to ensure quality? Would you rather run the risk of getting a lemon than be unable to afford a car at all? Could the same reasoning be applied to health care?

5 In the case of health care, it may be relatively easy to determine costs but difficult to determine benefits. Why would this be the case? Give some possible examples of ways in which good health care might benefit the community as a whole, as well as the individual patients.

6 When you go into a department store to buy clothes, you have a choice of price and quality. You have no such choice in the case of medical treatment. What are the differences in philosophy that produce this situation? How does this lack of choice tend to affect the supply and distribution of medical treatment?

7 It is often charged that hospitals are reluctant to increase productivity through innovations in management practices or organizational systems. Why might there be little incentive for them to do so?

8 In some cultures the "doctor" is paid only if there is a cure. How would resource allocation for health care in these cultures tend to differ from that of the United States?

9 Health insurance is one way of providing for a minimum standard of medical care. Income maintenance would also provide families with money to pay for care. What might be the differences in economic impact in the two approaches?

Opening photo by Charles Harbutt, Magnum

CHAPTER 3 MARKET & GOVERNMENT

A fundamental question confronting any society is how to organize all its scarce resources to try to fulfill its limitless wants with efficiency and equity. A system has to be devised that will determine what is to be produced, how it will be produced, and for whom it will be produced. Some relatively simple societies may be able to rely upon tradition as a means of making these decisions, but other, more complex economies must use a market system or a command system, or some combination of the two.

Socialist countries, such as China and the Soviet Union, are generally considered command systems, since decision making is in the hands of a central governmental authority, which controls economic activity and plans its objectives. The United States and most Western European nations, on the other hand, are considered capitalistic systems, for decisions are largely left up to the workings of the marketplace. In the real world, the distinction between command economies and capitalistic economies is never clear-cut, for all economies contain elements of both. Nevertheless, the two types of economies are based on different economic models. We begin our discussion with an examination of the model underlying a capitalistic system—the pure market system. At first we will exclude government. Later we will expand the discussion by considering the economic role of government.

While abstract, this chapter relates directly to current issues of how best to solve the problems of society. Should the market be left alone to achieve equity and efficiency? If the market fails, should the government intervene? What ensures that the government will work efficiently and equitably? This chapter begins a search for answers that will continue throughout this book.

WHAT IS A MARKET?

A market system represents one way in which a society may organize its economy. It can be said to have evolved naturally through the history of man's quest to satisfy his needs. In the simplest terms, a market is the interaction of supply and demand, the buying and selling of goods and services by individuals and businesses in an attempt to satisfy their own economic wants. A market, then, involves decision making not by one central authority but by many individuals, each of whom is guided not by the quest for the common good but by his own good. Consumers decide what to buy and at what price. Firms decide what goods to produce or what services to render in order to satisfy that demand. Individuals decide whether to offer their skills in the job market—and at what level of remuneration. And they decide what skills to acquire in the first place, through training and education.

It is true that in making these choices, there are certain constraints, such as personal abilities, material resources, concern for or dependence on other people. Nevertheless, in a market system there is no superior authority that plans our actions or charts our desires. It is up to the individual to choose either a station wagon or a sports car, a hamburger or a steak, a hairstyling or a home haircut. He may choose to eat hamburger in order to be able to afford to have his hair styled, or eat steak and go shaggy. But the choice is up to him.

Similarly, a firm may decide to manufacture a certain product if demand for it is strong enough to assure a profit, or it may opt to produce something else, in anticipation of an even greater profit. In either case, consumer tastes and the producer's desire for a profit are manifestations of the human self-interest that underlies all economic activity in a market system. Unless other forces interfere, each consumer will seek to maximize his own satisfaction in buying products and services, and each producer to maximize its own profits in offering them. That is the premise of a free-market economy.

Supply and Demand

In the face of all these individual decisions, we might ask how an economic system can maintain itself. How do we know that there will be ready buyers for the fresh asparagus that appears each spring? Who guarantees that there will be sufficient pharmacists to man all drugstores? And how does it happen that the numerous firms that produce soaps, cosmetics, linens, and so on, will supply the right mix of products for numerous individual consumers, each with his own shopping list? It is the price mechanism that assures that each of these needs will be met, or nearly met. If not all the asparagus is sold, the price will be lowered so that new shoppers will be attracted to the vegetable stand and regular customers will add to their usual purchase. If pharmacists are scarce, drugstore proprietors will offer a higher wage (price of labor) and this will eventually attract new members to the profession. These are reactions that we understand intuitively, but they may be explained more fully in terms of the free-market model. Basic to the free-market model is the interaction of supply and demand. In general, consumers will demand more of a good or service at a low price than at a high price: This is the reason, for example, that "sale" prices bring eager new buyers. On the other hand, firms that supply goods would prefer to see them purchased at higher prices; understandably, they supply more of a good at a high price than at a low one. Consumers are after bargains, and suppliers after profits that high prices bring. Essentially the two keep one another in line.

We can see how this mechanism works by using a demand schedule and a supply schedule for a hypothetical product (which here shall remain nameless) in Tables 3-1 and 3-2. The demand schedule shows how much of a good individuals are able and willing to buy at various prices during a given period of time. We can see that as the price goes down, the number of ounces demanded goes up, from 10 ounces at $64 each, to 50 ounces at $8 each.

TABLE 3–1 Demand Schedule for the Nameless Commodity

Price per ounce	Ounces demanded
$64	10
44	20
28	30
16	40
8	50

The nameless commodity, which is customarily retailed by the ounce, ranges in price from $8 to $64. As the price goes up, the number of ounces demanded declines. Note that this schedule represents the number of ounces people would be willing to purchase at various prices and not how much *is* sold or how much would be sold at any given price.

TABLE 3–2 Supply Schedule for the Nameless Commodity

Price per ounce	Ounces supplied
$ 4	10
16	20
28	30
40	40
52	50

The supply schedule shows the number of ounces dealers would be willing to offer at various prices. As the price increases, the number of ounces supplied also grows.

The supply schedule shows the other side of the picture—how much of a product the suppliers are willing and able to supply at every possible price during a given period of time. As the price goes down, the number of units supplied also goes down, from 50 ounces at $52 to only 10 ounces at $4. Quantity demanded and quantity supplied are dependent on price—at least when all other factors are held constant, as they are in this model.

Figures 3-1 and 3-2 plot the demand and supply curves based on these schedules. From these figures we can see the operation of the laws of supply and demand.

The law of demand states that the quantity demanded varies inversely with the price of the product.

In other words, as the price goes down, the quantity demanded goes up. The demand curve in Figure 3-1 is downward-sloping, showing the inverse relationship between price and quantity demanded.

The law of supply states that the quantity supplied varies directly with price.

In other words, as the price goes up, the quantity supplied goes up as well. The supply curve in Figure 3-2 slopes upward, denoting this direct relationship.

Equilibrium We have said that consumers will want to buy more if prices are low, and that suppliers will produce more if prices are high. Thus, at most prices

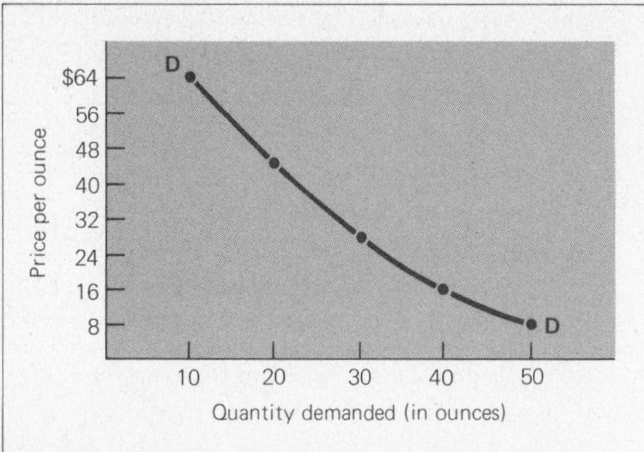

FIGURE 3–1 THE DEMAND CURVE FOR THE NAMELESS COMMODITY The demand schedule given in Table 3–1 is drawn here as curve DD. Under most circumstances the demand curve slopes downward to the right, since people are generally willing to purchase more of a commodity as its price declines. Note that price is always plotted on the vertical axis, and quantity on the horizontal.

on our schedules the desires of the two groups are not perfectly matched. At $40, for example, consumers are willing to buy only 22 ounces, but suppliers will offer 40 ounces for sale. Suppliers will glut the market, and much of the product will remain on the shelf. For the price mechanism to operate to mutual advantage, it must settle on a price at which the quantity consumers are willing to buy is exactly equal to the quantity suppliers are willing to supply.

The point of equilibrium can be obtained by superimposing the demand and supply curves on the same graph (Figure 3-3). At the point at which the two curves intersect, a dealer is willing to supply 30 ounces—as much of the product as consumers are willing to buy. The quantity demanded and the quantity supplied are equal as a result of the interaction in the marketplace.

SURPLUSES The interaction of demand and supply ensures that prices will move toward the equilibrium price. According to the model, when the price of a good is above the equilibrium price, more consumers will pass it up. The higher price will induce suppliers to produce more than consumers are demanding and will create a surplus. This in turn results in downward pressure on the price and the quantity supplied. For example, when asparagus is so expensive that most shoppers pass it up, the price will be lowered, and more will be bought. When suppliers offer more goods than consumers are willing to buy at a given price, the price is lowered until it reaches equilibrium: At that point the quantity that consumers are willing to buy equals the quantity supplied. (This interaction of supply and demand is illustrated in Figure 3-4.)

Shortages When the price of a product is lower than the equilibrium price, the quantity demanded will exceed the quantity supplied and a shortage will result. The price mechanism also acts to correct shortages. As the good becomes scarcer, prices will be driven up. As the price becomes high, suppliers will increase their output and new suppliers will open shop in the hopes of sharing greater profits. This upward pressure on price and quantity supplied will persist until the point of equilibrium is reached. (This interaction of supply and demand is illustrated in Figure 3-4.) In the market system, then, shortages and surpluses correct themselves by means of price changes.

FIGURE 3-2 THE SUPPLY CURVE FOR THE NAMELESS COMMODITY The supply schedule given in Table 3-2 is drawn here as curve SS. Under most circumstances the supply curve slopes upward to the right, since sellers are generally willing to part with more of a commodity as its price rises.

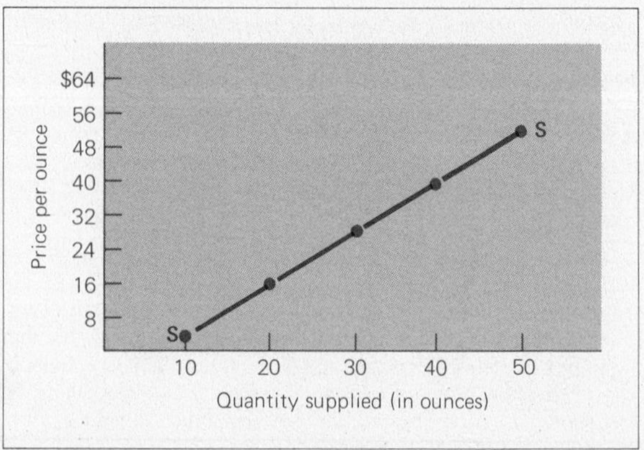

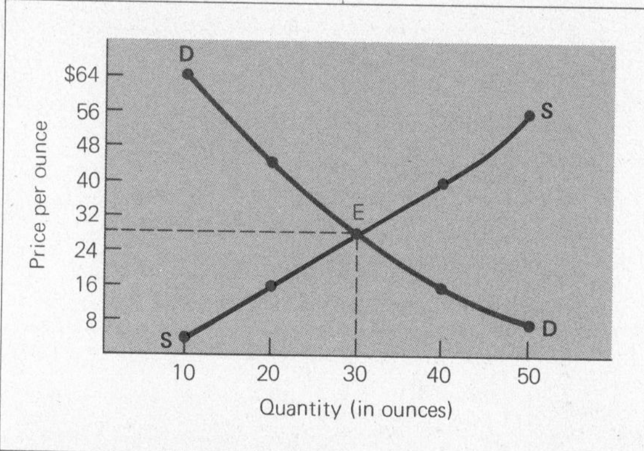

FIGURE 3-3 DEMAND, SUPPLY, AND EQUILIBRIUM The demand schedule has been reproduced from Figure 3-1, and the supply schedule from Figure 3-2. Since the demand curve slopes downward to the right and the supply curve slopes upward to the right, it is inevitable that they will cross at some point, provided they fall within the same range.

Where the two curves cross is the equilibrium point. At the market price of $28, all the buyers who are willing to buy and all the dealers who are willing to sell can do so. As will be indicated in Figure 3-4, at any other price, there will be either a shortage or a surplus of the commodity.

Changes in Supply and Demand

Changes in the quantity of goods supplied or demanded are a direct result of price changes—and price changes alone. We have assumed that all other factors have remained equal, just as in discussing the production-possibilities model we first assumed that there were no changes in total resources. But in the case of the production-possibilities model, we saw that total factors *can* increase or be put to better use and that this results in a shift of the entire curve. So, too, changes in the overall nature of demand and supply can require the drawing of new curves to the right or left of the old ones.

A simple example shows why this is so. If we suppose that the climate in the United States becomes extraordinarily rainy, this would result in a change in the demand for galoshes. But this change would have nothing to do with the price of galoshes or the number of galoshes that firms are willing to supply at any price. For this reason the change cannot be shown by simply moving from one point to another on the demand curve. At *every* price consumers will demand more galoshes. The *entire* demand curve has shifted.

Changes in the Equilibrium Price The result of a shift in a curve is a change in equilibrium price. The demand curve for galoshes shifts upward and intersects with the supply curve at a higher point. The new price of galoshes is high enough to induce suppliers to increase their output to meet the increased demand.

This example shows the difference between shifts in curves and movements along a curve. Foul weather changes the demand for galoshes; at every price more galoshes are wanted and a new curve is drawn.

FIGURE 3-4 SHORTAGES AND SURPLUSES A shortage of a commodity, such as at point Q_1, means that at a given price, fewer units of that commodity are supplied than demanded. In other words, the quantity demanded exceeds the quantity supplied. This is remedied by the competitive pricing mechanism. Since people want more than the market supplies, they will begin bidding up the commodity's price. As the price rises, the seller casts about for more of the commodity to offer for sale. This process goes on until the equilibrium price is reached.

A surplus of a commodity, shown at point Q_2, means that at a given price, fewer units of that commodity are demanded than supplied. Obviously, then, the price is too high. Some sellers will be willing to lower their price, and as they do so, they are able to sell more. Thus, the price gets bid down until it reaches $28. At that price, all sellers who are willing to sell will be able to do so.

To summarize: A shortage means that the market price is below the equilibrium price and quantity demanded exceeds the quantity supplied. A surplus means that the market price is above the equilibrium price and the quantity supplied exceeds the quantity demanded.

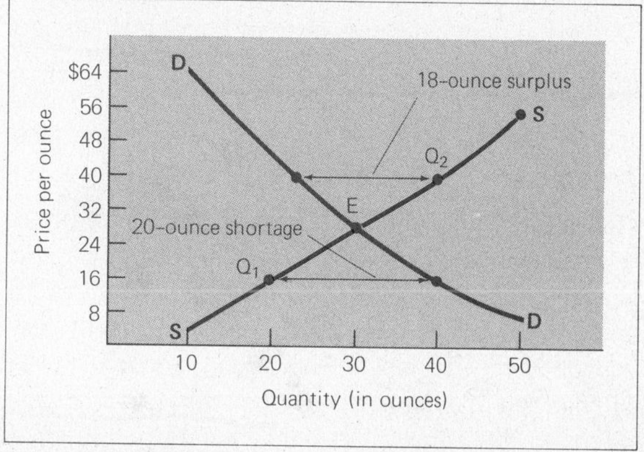

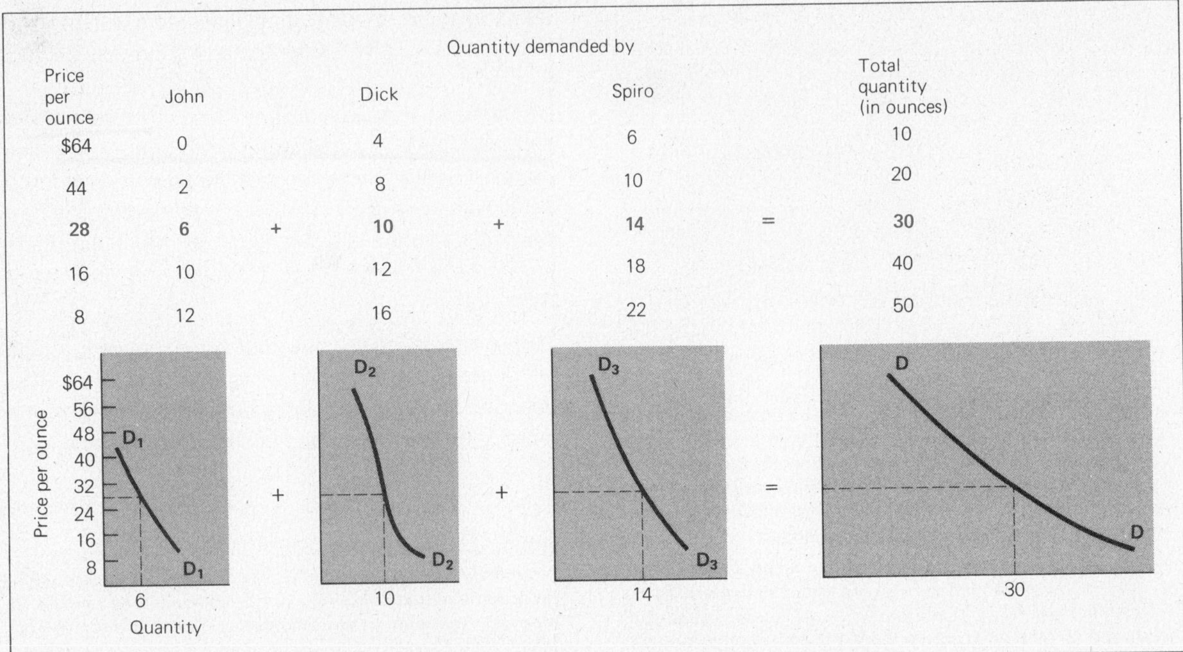

Price per ounce	Quantity demanded by John		Dick		Spiro		Total quantity (in ounces)
$64	0		4		6		10
44	2		8		10		20
28	**6**	+	**10**	+	**14**	=	**30**
16	10		12		18		40
8	12		16		22		50

FIGURE 3-5 MARKET AND INDIVIDUAL CURVES So far the curves used have been market curves, showing what groups of people will demand or supply at any price. The market demand curve DD reflects the combined quantities demanded by individuals. At a high price some individuals, such as John, will skip the product altogether. As the price is lowered, John will enter the market, while Dick and Spiro will want even more than they did before. Summing the quantity at a given price will give the total quantity demanded in this market. On the supply side the process is the same. The market supply curve expresses the sum of the quantity supplied by individual suppliers.

On the supply side there has been movement along a curve. The higher equilibrium price created by the change in demand means only that the *quantity supplied* has increased. Demand changed because of something other than price and is depicted by a shift in the demand curve; quantity supplied changed in response to a change in price. For the actual supply to change in the short run, something other than price would have to change and shift the supply curve.

Remember, changes in supply or demand occur because of changes in factors other than price and mean a shift in a curve that sets a new equilibrium price. Changes in quantity supplied or quantity demanded refer to movements along a curve in response to a change in price. When *demand* changes, affecting the equilibrium price, we do not say that *supply* changes in response; only *quantity supplied* will be affected.

Why the Demand Curve Shifts The demand curve shifts to the right to show an increase in quantity demanded at all price levels, and to the left to show a decrease in quantity demanded at all price levels. Those determinants of demand that cause a shifting of the demand curve include changes in tastes, income, and the prices of other goods.

TASTES What people want in the first place determines demand, and if their wants change, demand is affected. These preferences are different for each one of us, depending upon the utility we feel we gain from a particular item. The accumulated preferences make up the total demand, and any changes in market demand result when many different people change their minds about a product. When cholesterol is linked to heart disease, fewer eggs will be demanded, at every price, and the demand curve for eggs will shift to the left. When Army jackets are in fashion more of them will be sold at all prices, and the demand curve will shift to the right. To represent a change in demand due to a change in taste, we must draw a new demand curve.

LEVEL OF PERSONAL INCOME The level of personal income in a society is also an important determinant of demand. As personal income falls, fewer goods are demanded at *every* price. But as income increases, the demand for most products increases. More cosmetics and linens will be bought, more homes built, and so on. This occurs for two reasons: First, individuals who previously could not afford certain products will begin demanding them, and second, old buyers will want more than they were accustomed to purchasing. Not only will there be a greater willingness to purchase goods in general, but there will be a disproportionate increase in the demand for luxury goods, such as cabin cruisers and theater tickets. At the same time, there may be a decrease in the demand for certain products associated with hard times, the so-called inferior goods. For example, fewer noodles and potatoes may be sold, as families with increased incomes begin to switch to hamburger and pot roast. A change in income results in a shifting of the demand curve.

The same thing happens when people merely expect that incomes will rise. Expectations—realistic or not—affect the willingness of consumers to spend, and so affect demand. Thus, consumers will express demand for certain goods based on their expectations of salary increase. They will tend to spend heavily in periods of inflation, in an attempt to beat the high prices they expect in the future, and they will refrain from spending when economic depression is predicted. All of these decisions affect demand, and result in a shifting of the demand curve.

PRICE OF OTHER GOODS The quantity of a good demanded changes as the price is raised or lowered: This can be shown by movements along the demand curve. But the demand for a good may change as the

FIGURE 3-6 CHANGES IN DEMAND, SUPPLY, AND EQUILIBRIUM PRICES A new market demand curve is drawn every time a determinant of demand changes. Let us suppose that Nelson just got a hefty raise and is adding to what the market demands. Curve DD shifts to become curve D′D′. This raises the equilibrium price to E_2 ($40) and increases the quantity supplied from 30 to 40 ounces. If a new dealer rather than a consumer arrived on the scene, the supply curve would shift from SS to S′S′. More ounces would be available, but in order to sell them, the equilibrium price will have to go down to E_2 ($16). The effect of an increase in demand upon price and equilibrium quantity is direct (higher price, more ounces). The effect of a change in supply upon equilibrium quantity is direct but is inverse upon price (more ounces but lower price). Now trace the effects of a decrease in demand and supply.

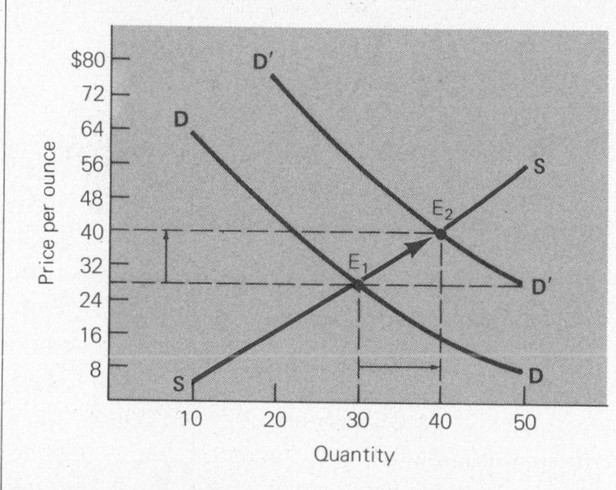

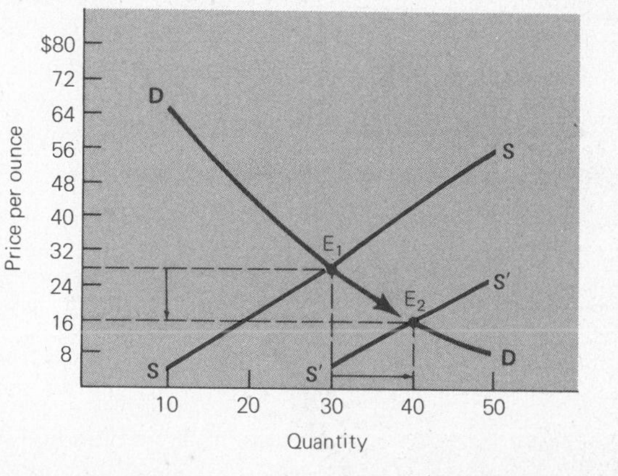

result of a change in the price of another product. This is most evident in the case of substitutes. For example, the demand for butter may change if a substitute such as margarine has become available or been newly reduced in price. As consumers substitute margarine for butter, people buy less butter, and the demand curve for butter shifts to the left.

The overall demand for a good is also influenced by the price of goods that are used with it—complementary goods. If more portable radios are sold (due to a reduction in price, for example), the demand for batteries will increase apace. This change is shown by a shift of the demand curve for batteries.

Even changes in the price of unrelated goods may affect demand for a particular item. Suppose that the price of cars goes down. This leaves consumers with a bit more income to spend on steaks, so the steak curve will shift to the right, as the demand for steaks increases.

Why the Supply Curve Shifts Like the demand curve, the supply curve shows the quantity supplied at various price levels, holding all other factors constant. But, as in the case of demand, the determinants are not always constant, and a change can mean that more or less is supplied at *all* price levels. Such changes are shown as a shifting of the supply curve, to the right when supply is increased and to the left when it is decreased.

COST OF PRODUCTION The basic determinant of supply is the cost of production. The supplier will produce goods only when the cost of producing an additional unit is covered by the price consumers are willing to pay. The supplier's costs are in turn determined by the cost of resources (iron ore, central heating, secretaries, and other factors used in the production process), and by the level of technology available to him. If any of the costs of production go up, suppliers will offer fewer goods at every price level. If the costs go down, then suppliers will be able to offer more goods at every price. Changes in the cost of production shift the supply curve.

Changes in costs are affected by the number of buyers in the market for economic resources. Suppose that a new process lowers the cost of making galoshes. In the short run, suppliers will step up production, and new suppliers will start building galoshes factories. As a result, the supply curve will shift to the right. However, as these suppliers start bidding against one another for factors of production, they will drive up the price of the factors and raise costs, so that in the long run the shift in the curve does not appear as far to the right as was expected initially.

HOW THE MODEL WORKS

We have seen that self-interest shapes the forces that determine supply and demand in a market economy. But one might ask, how does such a system, in which self-interest guides decision making, work toward achieving collective satisfaction?

The market system can work properly only under certain conditions, the most important of these being competition. In a competitive market system, no one consumer or producer can enforce his will on the other members of the economy. Each consumer is free to spend his money as he sees fit. Each producer is free to enter or leave an industry and to decide how resources are to be used. And the owners of resources may sell them freely. Competition implies large numbers of independent agents operating in the market for products and resources, preventing any one agent from affecting the prices. In a market economy, competition is the key to the efficient use of scarce resources to meet human wants.

Efficiency

Competition promotes efficiency because it relates the multitude of individual decisions made in a decentralized economy. As consumers seek to maximize utility, they look for the lowest price for any product. This forces suppliers to furnish the goods as cheaply as possible, using the lowest cost method of production. In the supplier's search for the lowest cost, factors of production are selected on the basis of their productivity, and incomes are furnished according to factor productivity. Competition ensures that those businesses which do not operate this way will eventually be eliminated.

In a truly competitive market, then, the consumer is king. Efficiency in producing and marketing is promoted by consumers, who in their decision making seek the greatest satisfaction at the lowest cost. As producers compete to satisfy consumer demand, they will strive to reduce costs to increase their profits. Their goal is to maximize profits under competitive circumstances, and the result is **technological efficiency** in the production process. Competition forces firms to seek the low-cost method of production, and those firms that cannot keep in step will be driven out of the market. The incentive for producers to furnish only those goods for which there is a demand on the market and in such quantities as will satisfy that demand creates **allocative efficiency.** Again, the profit motive is the driving force toward this type of efficiency. If a good is undersupplied, consumers will bid up its price and producers will see the profit opportunity and increase the supply of the good. If a product is oversupplied, its price will fall, reducing the profit to the producer, who will then curtail its output.

The competitive process works in the market for resources as well. Resources are allocated to the production of those goods that consumers demand. If consumers demand more shoes, due to a hiking fad, for example, some leather will be shifted from the production of belts or wallets to the production of shoes. Leather will then be distributed between shoes and other uses in a way that best meets consumer demand—an example of allocative efficiency. Suppliers will use those resources that offer the greatest productivity at the lowest cost, thus ensuring technological efficiency as well. For example, if leather can be replaced by lower-cost vinyl in shoe soles, hikers will be carried on soles of vinyl. In a competitive market, a producer who refuses to substitute the lower-cost resource or is otherwise inefficient in his technology will be ignored by consumers, who are searching for the product at the lowest price.

Here is a system that is based on two forces that would seem to divide society: self-interest and competition. Yet the system allocates its resources to the products that society most desires and furnishes them at the lowest cost, almost as if an "invisible hand" were at work reconciling the individual self-interest and competition to the collective good. It is as if a ship had left its captain ashore, yet sailed surely along, simply because the whims and interests of the individual crew members somehow worked in concert to keep her on course. Like this remarkable ship, the market system works efficiently, not as a result of centralized planning, but because individual decisions are expressed in a self-regulating price mechanism.

Government's Role in the Model

In a system such as we have described, government seems as superfluous as the captain of our metaphorical ship. Yet even in a pure market system, government is still necessary, if only to provide for the protection of private property. The terms of ownership and inheritance, the means of transfer, the enforcement of contracts—all are established and regulated by government. Even the most hidebound advocates of free enterprise approve of this kind of government intervention. The government is also involved in setting standards, such as weights, measures, and, most important, monetary standards. Without stable legal tender, a complex economy like ours could not operate. Government, then, is implicit in the idea of a market system.

HOW THE MODEL DOES NOT WORK

It would be pleasant to end the chapter at this point with the market whirring away efficiently and the government operating discreetly in the background. But this smoothly running system has within it some untidy problems. First, there are problems of equity in an economy of unregulated free enterprise. Second, there may be other difficulties, such as providing public goods like defense or education. Third, if we apply the free-market model to the real world, we see that it is often beset by imperfections which cause serious inefficiencies. In reality, it seems that the unregulated market cannot promote national welfare without some kind of government assistance. The question is no longer whether or not government should intervene, but how and to what extent it should do so. In part, our answer depends on how we view the several problems.

Equity

A competitive market system is by definition efficient —but is it equitable? Competition systematically eliminates those firms producing at high costs or offering too much of a product. This is efficient, but the cost in human terms may be high. The shoe industry in the Northeast has been virtually run out of business by cheaper, more stylish imports from Italy and Japan. To society at large this means getting shoes that better meet its wants, but to many towns in New England this has meant extreme hardship. The costs of changes caused by competition tend not to fall equally on all of society, but rather cause disproportionate hardships to certain groups.

Perhaps more significant is the fact that the market system produces only for people who can effectively demand—that is, those who can pay. Goods are allocated to consumers on the basis of their income, and the market system itself does little to ensure that income will be equitably distributed among all members of society. For example, in a market system, one's income depends on the factors of production that he controls—in most cases on labor alone. But efficiency dictates that firms pay for labor according to its productivity. As there are wide differences in the productivity of various types of labor, there are corresponding differences of income among workers. Moreover, some people control factors other than labor—a few people controlling substantial amounts of these. If the resulting distribution of income does not meet your standards of equity, neither will a market economy that allocates goods solely according to the ability to pay.

The methods for correcting these kinds of inequities lie outside the market system. For example, the system provides no incentives for raising the income of the unskilled worker when this in turn means raising the price of a good and losing buyers. Without some kind of intervention by government, many of the social inequities in income distribution would remain.

Other Inherent Problems

Externalities Another problem with the pure market system is that the prices it sets do not always reflect all of the costs incurred in producing or using a product. The result is that resources are allocated to goods that would not be demanded in such large quantities were the true costs reflected in the price. For example, we might not demand quite so many automobiles if we each had to put down an amount of money to cover the cost to society of air pollution and junked cars. Similarly, a manufacturer might not pour smoke freely into the air if he had to pay the costs of environmental clean-up, and the dry-cleaning or house-painting bills of nearby residents.

When a cost or benefit is incurred by somebody other than the producer or buyer, we say that it occurs outside of the market transaction, and is thus an **externality**. The hidden costs in our examples are called **external diseconomies**. Left to itself, the market would not correct them. After all, the profit-seeking

FIGURE 3-7 EXTERNALITIES AND RESOURCE ALLOCATION Without any externalities (as in A) the market will produce exactly the quantity that is most efficient. When not all costs are included (as in B), society will still produce at point P, which is far *more* than would be produced if the supply curve reflected the full costs as in S′S′. Resources are overallocated in this instance. When not all benefits are included (as in C), society will still produce at point P, which is far *less* than would be produced if the demand curve reflected the true desires of society as in D′D′. Resources are underallocated in this instance. Government is one means of redressing this imbalance by imposing the true costs of supplying the additional amount justified by external benefits.

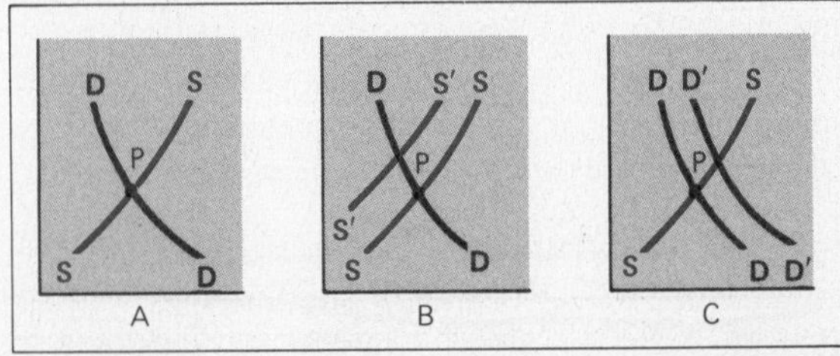

manufacturer has no incentive to expend funds on smoke "scrubbers" if he can dump wastes in the air for free.

An **external economy** is a spillover benefit derived from somebody else without the first party having to pay for it. Industrial research is a common example; what one company spends money to discover, others may apply. Unless the first firm is compensated for its discoveries, it will tend to underspend on research. This problem of underproduction is chronic for goods with external benefits.

Public Goods Another problem inherent in a pure market system is that of providing for public goods, those goods for which there is no way to charge people individually. If the members of a neighborhood want to go in together to buy a defense system, there is no way that an individual can be forced to pay his share. In such circumstances everyone will choose to hang back and let someone else buy a Minuteman missile that can also protect him. No firm would produce defense because there would be no individual or firm motivated to buy it. A product such as defense, which if provided for one person benefits all, is best furnished by a government. Furthermore, such goods are usually beyond the means of individuals and firms. Therefore, government steps in, levies taxes, and buys public goods. It reallocates resources that would have been spent on TV sets, or on new drill presses, in order to finance armaments, roads, education, and so on.

The Model and the World

Stability and Growth Any viable economic system must have the flexibility to deal with change that keeps an economy stable and the ability to produce innovations that allow an economy to grow. The model of the market economy presumes that enough income will be generated to ensure that all output will be sold. When unemployment occurs, it is thought to be a temporary phenomenon, as the market adjusts to shifts in demand and supply. When demand slackens, for example, prices should drop and output should be cleared from the market at lower prices. Theoretically, a market economy maintains a dynamic equilibrium around the level of full employment.

The capacity of the economy grows because part of the income finds its way into investment in capital goods to replace worn-out equipment and to buy new systems for production. The entrepreneur devotes current income to searching for future profits and innovates new systems for even greater gain. Resources are thus continuously diverted from less efficient to more efficient uses automatically through market forces.

In actuality, stability and growth are far harder to come by. High levels of unemployment can be chronic, as during the Depression of the 1930s when one-quarter of the work force was idled. The economy can also be troubled by persistent inflation, as recent years have shown. Nor are investment in capital goods and continued innovation by any means assured. Left to its own devices, the market cannot guarantee either full employment and price stability or growth.

Imperfect Competition The reality of the U.S. economy contrasts with the theory of the market system markedly, due to the presence of obstacles to competition. Entry into highly capitalized and technical industries is virtually closed to the small entrepreneurial firm of pure theory; firms with great market power may have incentives for growth rather than profit, may restrict the kinds of goods available, and may use advertising to induce artificial demand. The market system seems to have evolved into something quite different from the theoretical model, yet economic theory can help explain why this has occurred.

One important reason for this deviation is the growth in technological complexity. New technology can cut costs and open new fields for economic growth; at the same time it can work against the perpetuation of the competitive market system. It can bring concentration—of capital to buy the intricate new systems, of management to coordinate the application of technology, and of resource markets to ensure stable and reliable sources of raw materials. The reduced competition, while virtually inevitable, still weakens the market system. To avoid head-on com-

SHOULD THE ARTS BE SUBSIDIZED?

The performing arts in the United States are going bankrupt. Real costs have been rising faster than the price of tickets. Even the Metropolitan Opera, for which seats are virtually inherited, suffered from revenues that are about 20 percent lower than expenditures; the 25 leading orchestras in the United States have had income-expenditure gaps of 46 percent.*

One solution to bridging this gap is to raise the price of tickets to cover the deficit; another is to provide subsidies to the arts. Most European nations have long subsidized their ballet companies, theaters, opera, and symphonies. In the United States the subsidies are from private donations, with increasing amounts of government funding. Apart from arguments based on freedom from censorship and the idea that suffering produces great art, the refusal to provide large government grants in the United States is based on an economic argument. "If the arts can't pass the market test, then why tax all the people to satisfy the tastes of aesthetes?" goes the litany. The people who want art should pay the full costs of "production." Allocative efficiency would be better served this way according to this attitude.

This argument is only half true. First of all, raising the price would limit the arts to a rich elite. To deny a person the chance to hear Leontyne Price on the basis of income offends our sense of equity. In addition, the arts are a "quasi-public" commodity with features of a private and a public good. The individual does benefit directly and should pay for this, but society as a whole benefits as well. Besides conferring prestige on a nation, the arts preserve and enhance its cultural heritage for future generations. They speak to fundamental human themes and "educate" in the broadest sense. To those who insist on seeing everything in dollars and cents, the arts stimulate business in their vicinity and serve as a tourist attraction. Since there is no way of charging for exalting the human spirit (or attracting business), the use of subsidies may be justified on the grounds that not to do so actually thwarts public wants and results in allocative inefficiency.

* William J. Baumol and William G. Bowen, *Performing Arts—The Economic Dilemma* (New York: The Twentieth Century Fund, 1966), p. 387. Figures are for 1963–64 seasons.

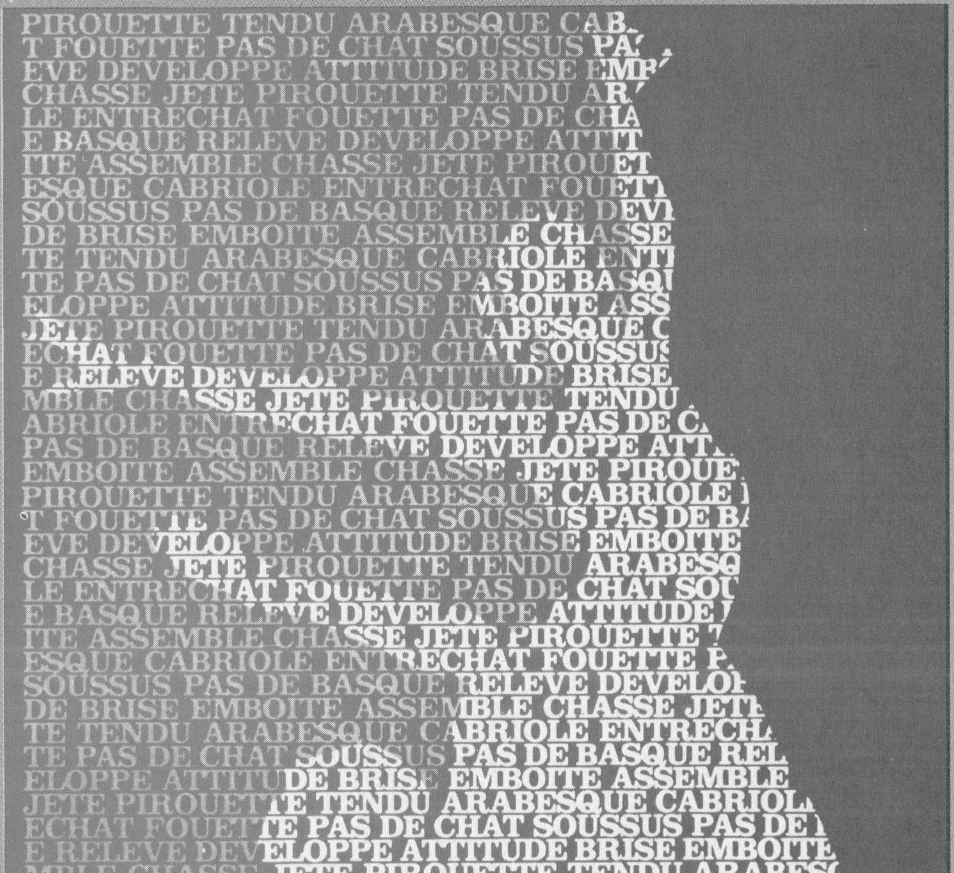

PIROUETTE TENDU ARABESQUE CAB
T FOUETTE PAS DE CHAT SOUSSUS PA
EVE DEVELOPPE ATTITUDE BRISE EMB
CHASSE JETE PIROUETTE TENDU AR
LE ENTRECHAT FOUETTE PAS DE CHA
E BASQUE RELEVE DEVELOPPE ATTIT
ITE ASSEMBLE CHASSE JETE PIROUET
ESQUE CABRIOLE ENTRECHAT FOUETT
SOUSSUS PAS DE BASQUE RELEVE DEVE
DE BRISE EMBOITE ASSEMBLE CHASSE
TE TENDU ARABESQUE CABRIOLE ENTR
TE PAS DE CHAT SOUSSUS PAS DE BASQU
ELOPPE ATTITUDE BRISE EMBOITE ASS
JETE PIROUETTE TENDU ARABESQUE C
ECHAT FOUETTE PAS DE CHAT SOUSSUS
E RELEVE DEVELOPPE ATTITUDE BRISE
MBLE CHASSE JETE PIROUETTE TENDU
ABRIOLE ENTRECHAT FOUETTE PAS DE C
PAS DE BASQUE RELEVE DEVELOPPE ATT
EMBOITE ASSEMBLE CHASSE JETE PIROUET
PIROUETTE TENDU ARABESQUE CABRIOLE
T FOUETTE PAS DE CHAT SOUSSUS PAS DE B
EVE DEVELOPPE ATTITUDE BRISE EMBOITE
CHASSE JETE PIROUETTE TENDU ARABESQ
LE ENTRECHAT FOUETTE PAS DE CHAT SOU
E BASQUE RELEVE DEVELOPPE ATTITUDE
ITE ASSEMBLE CHASSE JETE PIROUETTE T
ESQUE CABRIOLE ENTRECHAT FOUETTE P
SOUSSUS PAS DE BASQUE RELEVE DEVELOP
DE BRISE EMBOITE ASSEMBLE CHASSE JETE
TE TENDU ARABESQUE CABRIOLE ENTRECHA
TE PAS DE CHAT SOUSSUS PAS DE BASQUE REL
ELOPPE ATTITUDE BRISE EMBOITE ASSEMBLE
JETE PIROUETTE TENDU ARABESQUE CABRIOL
ECHAT FOUETTE PAS DE CHAT SOUSSUS PAS DE
E RELEVE DEVELOPPE ATTITUDE BRISE EMBOITE
MBLE CHASSE JETE PIROUETTE TENDU ARABES
ABRIOLE ENTRECHAT FOUETTE PAS DE CHAT SOUS
PAS DE BASQUE RELEVE DEVELOPPE ATTITUDE BRISE
EMBOITE ASSEMBLE CHASSE JETE PIROUETTE TENDU
PIROUETTE TENDU ARABESQUE CABRIOLE ENTREC
T FOUETTE PAS DE CHAT SOUSSUS PAS DE
EVE DEVELOPPE ATTITUDE BRISE EMBO
CHASSE JETE PIROUETTE TENDU
LE ENTRECHAT FOUETTE PAS DE
E BASQUE RELEVE DEVELOPPE
ITE ASSEMBLE CHASSE JETE PI
ESQUE CABRIOLE ENTRECHAT
SOUSSUS PAS DE BASQUE RELE
DE BRISE EMBOITE ASSEMBLE
TE TENDU ARABESQUE CABRI
TE PAS DE CHAT SOUSSUS PAS
ELOPPE ATTITUDE BRISE EMB
JETE PIROUETTE TENDU ARAB
ECHAT FOUETTE PAS DE CHAT
E RELEVE DEVELOPPE ATTITU
MBLE CHASSE JETE PIROUETT
ABRIOLE ENTRECHAT FOUETT
PAS DE BASQUE RELEVE DEV
EMBOITE ASSEMBLE CHASSE

new york city Ballet

Courtesy of the New York City Ballet

petition, firms also begin to compete in different ways, distinguishing their products on the basis of factors other than price. This practice, called product differentiation, can be readily observed in advertising. A TV commercial attempts to distinguish one toothpaste from the others on the basis of its "sex appeal." We are offered "a whole 'nother smoke," or even an "uncola"—virtually anything special and different. Firms change their images rather than their prices to attract new buyers.

Monopolistic competition—in which small firms rely on product differentiation—is only one form of imperfect competition. The extreme opposite of competition is monopoly, a situation in which a good or service is supplied by only one supplier. Without competition, the forces of supply and demand cannot be relied upon to ensure efficient resource allocation.

In the United States the few monopolies that are legally allowed to operate—mostly utility companies such as Bell Telephone—are regulated by government. There are, however, several industries in which one firm has the overwhelming share of the market. Xerox, for example, makes 81 percent of all office copying machines in the United States, and IBM has 75 percent of the computer market. There are also oligopolies, in which a very few firms are responsible for supplying nearly all of a certain product. General Motors, Ford, and Chrysler sell 97 percent of all domestic cars; and Kellogg, General Mills, and General Foods produce 82 percent of all breakfast cereals.

Oligopolies may be as capable of controlling the market as monopolies, if they decide among themselves not to compete. There are strict laws in the United States against such collusion and price-fixing, but collusion is often impossible to prove. Every year U.S. auto companies raise the prices of their models by $100 or more, citing increased costs as the reason. Their announcements of the price hikes come within a few days of each other and vary by only a few dollars. Technically, perhaps, they do not act in concert, but the end effect on the consumer is the same.

Ignorance The model assumes that the consumer exercises his choices in buying a product on the basis of complete knowledge of all products offered. In reality, no person can have such complete knowledge. The greater the number of competing products, the more fragmented will be the consumer's information on them. Advertising can go a long way to overcome the consumer's ignorance, but it may also mislead. Even the most straightforward advertising will always represent a relatively incomplete amount of information. What about the relative disadvantages of a product? What about products which are not advertised at all?

The diversity of a modern market economy is such that none of us have the time to be completely informed in all our economic decisions, and this alone amounts to an imperfection of the system. In a limited way government can address itself to this problem—requiring clear labeling, inspecting foods and drugs, and so on—but it cannot create a situation in which each of us is perfectly informed.

GOVERNMENT

Even in a relatively pure and competitive market system, the presence of government seems necessary. To what extent government should be involved, however, is a different question. Over the years, government action has been seen as the means to counteract the imperfections in the market system. Fiscal policy, pollution control laws, antitrust laws, welfare payments, and so on, are some of the corrective policies that have been tried. Many economists argue that as a result of such interventions, market failures have been or can be remedied. Others feel that we have gone too far in attempting to make the market system work better and that many of these efforts have been counterproductive.

Still others reject the market system altogether, viewing it as inherently inequitable and its premise of self-interest counterproductive to common social goals. Social thinkers who have rejected the market system have usually replaced it with some form of command system. In such a system, government is expected to plan and oversee production in order to assure an equitable distribution of goods. Instead of competing for profits by responding to consumer demand, producers are expected to cooperate in meeting the economic goals of the state. We shall analyze command systems in detail in Chapter 37, but contrast them here with what we know about the market system.

Command Systems

The dominant features of a command system are government ownership of the means of production and centralized government authority over economic goals. The problems that this system must solve are the same as those confronting a market system. But instead of supply and demand guiding the production and distribution of goods through the price mechanism, the government determines which goods will be produced and in what quantities, how to produce them, and for whom.

Technological efficiency and allocative efficiency are possible in command economies, but they are achieved in different ways from a market system. Government planners attempt to achieve technological efficiency by determining the lowest-cost methods of production and assuring that such methods are used. Allocative efficiency is achieved by comparing society's wants with its capacity to produce and determining what should be produced and in what quantities. Government then implements the policies needed to ensure that the goods and services are produced in the appropriate amounts. Allocative efficiency, of course, may have a somewhat different meaning in a command system, because production decisions reflect more than purely economic considerations.

A command system, like a market system, is never pure; in reality, a command system always contains some elements of a market economy. In the Soviet Union, for example, there are markets for labor and consumer goods, although prices and wages are not set entirely by market forces. Individuals are free to work at any job for which they are qualified and to spend their income on any of the goods produced by the state. Wages vary considerably, as the government tries to attract workers to industries it deems important. Some decisions, then, are made through the actions of supply and demand. The production process, however, is centrally planned. The result is a highly planned economy, but not a pure command system.

The command economy, like the market system, has its own problems. Most American economists argue that a command system has greater difficulty in being fully efficient, and that there are two main sources of inefficiency in the command system. First, the profit motive, and the search for low-cost production processes it inspires, has no real counterpart in command systems. This hampers full technological efficiency. Second, the mix of goods and services is not determined primarily by consumer demand. This prevents allocative efficiency.

Technological Efficiency In a command economy resource prices may not reflect productivity. Therefore, it is not clear how producers can find the lowest-cost methods of production. For example, until recently the Soviet economy put no price tag at all on land and capital. The result was a misuse of resources, for there was no incentive to put these resources to their most efficient use. A steam shovel might just as well be used to dig backyard flower beds if no costs were involved in its use. The problem of allocating land and capital has been remedied somewhat, but even today, there are differential charges for capital, depending on the industry, and the price charged does not necessarily reflect productivity.

Some defenders of command economies say that achieving technological efficiency in such a system is easier than in a free-market system because people are more highly motivated—that workers in Red China will want to be more efficient than the disgruntled assembly line workers in Detroit. But whether Chairman Mao's *Little Red Book* or educational exhortations produce efficient auto plants is a moot question, since economic goals are usually translated into concrete five- and seven-year plans with detailed quotas and resource allocations. The problem of obtaining technological efficiency depends in great part on how quotas and incentives are established. Because of quotas set in output tonnage, for example, Soviet farm machinery has been much heavier than its American counterparts, an evident waste of resources.

Allocative Efficiency When consumer preferences have little influence on the output of consumer goods, is there any reason to believe that such a system will provide what society wants? This depends to some extent on the political context. If a command system is a democracy, it can be argued that government officials are elected by the people and therefore reflect the popular will. But even if a command system is not democratic, some argue that it will do better in meeting society's wants than most market systems because property interests and concentrated economic power do not distort the distribution of goods and services. Nevertheless, most American economists would rate a command system inferior to a market system with respect to the goal of allocative efficiency.

Equity A command system may make income distribution more equitable by severing the link between private ownership of resources and income that exists in a market economy. In a planned economy, a person is likely to receive more public goods, such as subsidized housing and free health care. Therefore, although differences in wages based on labor productivity may exist, a decent standard of living is more likely for all—as long as GNP is high enough.

But the concept of equity is not limited to income distribution alone, as we have seen in Chapter 1. Liberty and freedom may depend upon how many people are involved in making the numerous choices entailed by the process of economizing. It is in meeting this second meaning of the term *equity* that a command system may fall short. Although the distribution of income may be more equitable in a command system, the centralized decision making may involve arbitrary limitations on personal choice.

Assessing Government Options

We have discussed command economies at some length because they represent the extreme of government intervention to correct the failures of a market economy. In the United States, the economic role of government is much more limited in scope, but when the market fails, the remedy is often government intervention of some sort. Not all government approaches will be equally successful, however. For example, if the government wished to obtain better housing for the poor, it might insist that slumlords meet city housing codes. But if the rents on substandard housing are extremely low and landlords cannot pay the maintenance costs on these old and sometimes vandalized buildings, then the landlords may abandon them, and slum dwellers will be worse off than before. Good intentions, then, do not prevent waste or harmful results. Today, the battle over the war-on-poverty programs is being conducted around just such issues, and the search is on for more effective methods of government intervention in all areas of the economy.

Cost of Control and Costs of Inefficiency There are two complaints frequently heard about government. One is that it costs too much—in particular, the costs of simply running the government are too high. In the federal budget the costs of operations have grown from a little over $8 billion in 1954 to $30 billion in 1973. Nearly 4 percent of the GNP goes for this outlay, and this does seem alarming.[1] The second complaint is that government is inefficient, that paying taxes is like throwing money down a hole. Thereupon, we hear examples of malfeasance, incompetence, and general waste, which are so easy to pluck out of the newspapers. In either case, the proposed solution is to take a whack out of the budget.

If the cuts are taken out of the administrative expenditures in a program, the result may be further inefficiency. Employees may spend more time at the water cooler, mistakes may go uncorrected, and a little graft may creep in. Control expenditures may actu-

1 Michael E. Levy et al., *The Federal Budget: Its Impact on the Economy*, fiscal 1974 ed. (New York: The Conference Board, 1973), p. 61.

ally need to be *increased* to ensure that the program is truly efficient. Of course, this increase can go only so far; it may be possible to make a program 100 percent efficient, but only at enormous cost. There is a trade-off, then, between the cost of control and the costs of inefficiency. A better choice can be made if we can measure the relative effectiveness of programs.

COST-BENEFIT ANALYSIS A central problem facing society, then, seems to be that of evaluating the effectiveness of government performance. A tool often used is cost-benefit analysis: The cost of a program (including the expenditures on control) is compared with the benefit derived from it. The more the benefit exceeds the cost, the more favorably we evaluate the program.

The problem with this approach, however, is that it is never possible to measure these factors accurately. Calculating the costs and benefits of a particular program may not be as easy as it seems. The cost of a highway is not simply the tax money required to buy land and lay concrete. It also includes the cost of displacing people, of the additional pollution that may be caused as a result of increased traffic, of the destruction of wildlife or recreational areas, and of many other effects. Some of these costs are easy to attach a dollar figure to; others are not. How, for example, does one calculate the emotional costs to families forced to give up their homes because of new highways? On the benefit side, it is equally difficult to identify and price some of the advantages of public investment. The determination of costs and benefits is further complicated because costs are often incurred immediately whereas benefits appear later, or vice versa.

Calculation of total benefits and costs is only the first step in evaluating the merits of a project. One must also consider the groups on which these costs and benefits fall. An urban freeway will probably not be built without a furor. Low-income slum dwellers in the path of the highway will protest losing already scarce housing in order for suburban motorists to get to work faster in the morning. Even if the total benefits exceed the total costs, the road may not be worth the burden it places on this particular group.

Among the many other shortcomings of cost-benefit analysis is that it does not assure that all possible solutions to a problem have been explored. Consider federal subsidy of flood control projects. The costs of a flood plain in terms of the destruction of property can be objectively assessed. If the flood can be contained by building a reservoir and if the cost of the reservoir is lower than the flood damage, then construction of the reservoir can be advocated on the basis of cost-benefit analysis. If dredging portions of the river would control floods and if dredging costs less than the reservoir, then it will be even more efficient to dredge. But perhaps both projects are wasteful compared with a totally different approach. For instance, government could discourage settling in flood plains by making flood insurance mandatory. If the added cost of insurance outweighs the geographical advantage of settling in the plain, then business and individuals alike would probably not want to move there. Floods would occur, but the damage would be reduced and government would bear only the cost of enforcing the law. Furthermore, it would not have to tax all of society to aid only people who live in potential flood areas.

Choice This last example indicates that when evaluating solutions to economic problems, we may not be measuring simply the pros and cons of different government programs, but we may also be weighing whether command elements or market elements are preferable. Economic analysis and observation of actual behavior should enable us to arrive at some calculations regarding the conditions under which market control or government control works better. In Chapter 2, for example, we saw the kinds of incentives that thwart the success of a program and we examined alternatives for correcting the deficiencies. How best to structure the solutions to social problems is a central theme in contemporary economic thought and forms a major theme of this book.

Many people consider this issue of secondary importance, saying that the real issue is whether a command system or a market system is more conducive to human freedom and dignity. Such questions are beyond the realm of conventional economic analysis, but should be kept in mind as we engage in this analysis.

SUMMARY

1 To fulfill the economic wants of a society, some system must be devised to determine what is to be produced, how it is to be produced, and for whom it will be produced. The market system relies on free competition to meet economic goals, and the command system relies on the government. Most societies use a combination of the two.

2 The market system is based on individual decision making. Consumers decide what to buy at what price and firms decide what goods to produce in order to satisfy that demand. Individuals decide whether to offer their skills in the job market, and at what level of remuneration.

3 Basic to the pure market model is the interaction of supply and demand. In general, consumers will demand more of a good at a low price than at a high price, which is represented graphically by a curve sloping downward to the right. On the other hand, firms that supply goods would prefer to see them purchased at higher prices, which is represented graphically by a curve sloping upward to the right When the quantity offered for sale is equal to the quantity demanded by buyers at that price, the market is in equilibrium, which is represented by the intersection of the curves. If the price is above equilibrium, there will be surpluses; if below, there will be shortages.

4 Changes in the quantity of goods demanded or supplied are a direct result of price changes and are shown by a movement along a curve. When things other than price change, the entire curve shifts—to the right for increases, and to the left for decreases. As the curve shifts, a new equilibrium price is set. The demand curve shifts as a result of changes in tastes and income and in the prices of other goods. The supply curve shifts because of changes in costs.

5 If the market is competitive, it automatically achieves allocative and technological efficiency. Government need only protect private property rights and set standards, particularly for money. However, the free-market system is inherently unable to ensure equitable income distribution, to include externalities, or to supply public goods. In reality, it also is troubled by instability and stagnation, imperfect competition, and consumer ignorance—which all impede its proper functioning.

6 Because of the failures of the market system, government intervention may be an alternative. In a command system, the government owns the means of production and sets the economic goals. There is much debate about how well such systems achieve the goals of equity and efficiency. Most societies contain some elements of government control. Assessing government options involves problems of tradeoffs between costs of control and costs of inefficiency; cost-benefit analysis is one helpful, though limited, tool in making choices about how to achieve economic goals.

SUGGESTED READINGS

Dorfman, Robert. *Prices and Markets.* Chaps. 1–5. Englewood Cliffs, N.J.: Prentice-Hall, 1967.

Downs, Anthony. "Evaluating Efficiency and Equity in Federal Urban Programs." In *The Political Economy of Federal Policy,* edited by Robert Haveman and Robert Hamrin. New York: Harper & Row, 1973.

Haveman, Robert, and Julius Margolis. "Introduction." In *Public Expenditures and Policy Analysis.* Chicago: Markham Publishing, 1970.

Hunt, E. K., and Howard J. Sherman. *Economics: An Introduction to Traditional and Radical Views.* Chaps. 36, 37, 38. New York: Harper & Row, 1972.

Lancaster, Kelvin. *Modern Economics: Principles and Policy.* Chap. 12. Chicago: Rand McNally, 1973.

Leftwich, Richard H. *The Price System and Resource Allocation.* 4th ed. Chaps. 2,3,15. New York: Holt, Rinehart and Winston, 1970.

Reynolds, Lloyd G. *Economics: A General Introduction.* 4th ed. Chaps 2,3,4,5,27,28. Homewood, Ill.: Irwin, 1973.

QUESTIONS

1 Review
   a. the characteristics of a free market,
   b. equilibrium of demand and supply, and the elimination of surpluses and shortages in the marketplace,
   c. how competition in the marketplace promotes both allocative and technological efficiency,
   d. how a command system strives for allocative and technological efficiency,
   e. problems in judging the efficiency of government activities.

2 Some surpluses and shortages in the economy may be maintained by design. Consider applications and tuition for some colleges. Where are the shortages and surpluses? How might they be eliminated if colleges were primarily motivated by profit? Why might colleges be disinclined to do so?

3 What causes might you be able to suggest for the increase in demand for energy in the United States? Many of the suppliers of energy in the United States are large power companies, each with a monopoly in a given area, and regulated by government. The regulation has been instituted primarily to ensure the supply of power to consumers at a moderate price and to eliminate monopoly profits. If shortages in energy develop, what would normally happen to the price? If the price is kept artificially low through regulation, what response would you expect on the part of producers and potential new producers? How would the price affect the possibility of future shortages?

4 For many years the American consumer enjoyed the benefits of overproduction in the agricultural sector. While the government was buying up surpluses, consumers nevertheless paid relatively low prices. Those surpluses are fast disappearing. Assume that the supply of agricultural products has been relatively stable and show how shifts in the demand curve have eliminated surpluses and resulted in increased prices. The foreign market has also increased for American agricultural goods. How would this be reflected in the demand curve? In terms of price?

5 The law of demand states that as the price of a good decreases, there will be an increase in the quantity demanded. The demand for some goods does not seem to follow this rule. For example, sometimes an increase in the price of medicine will actually increase its sales. What would the demand for this product look like? Do people think that they are buying the same product?

6 One way to hold the line on inflation may be a freeze on all payments, including profits. How might a freeze on profits interfere with allocative and technological efficiency as determined in a free-market situation?

7 There is much discussion concerning the effect of patents on innovation and growth of the economy. A private inventor may have to pay anywhere from $500 to $1000 for a patent, but may make millions when his patent is sold to a manufacturer. He may also make nothing. However, the holder of the patent can be assured of at least 17 years of protection against competitors. How might the existence of the patent system promote technological advance and economic growth? Discourage economic growth? What kinds of questions might be raised concerning the equity of the patent system?

8 The control function of government becomes extremely difficult when large profits are involved in an illegal activity. In what way might the difficulty be illustrated by Prohibition and the ban on heroin? How do the two cases differ?

9 Some local governments have hired private firms to teach selected subjects in their educational programs. The firms are on a so-called performance contract, which means that they will be paid in direct proportion to the gains in the students' scores on standardized tests. What are some of the difficulties that you see in such contracts? What are some of the improvements over the traditional form of organization? How might resources tend to be allocated among goals easily measured and those not so easily measured?

10 Arthur Hailey in his novel *Airport* describes a relatively common situation. Developers had constructed communities near the airport and had neglected to warn potential buyers that there would be noise from air traffic. Irate residents finally marched on the airport. At least one state has tried to handle this externality by reducing the amount of air traffic. In what other ways might the government have stepped in? Could it have arranged to internalize the externality? How?

Opening photo by J. Paul Kirouac

4
CHAPTER
CIRCULAR
FLOW

When a person works for a business and receives pay for that work, and when he spends portions of that pay for groceries, mortgage payments, bus fare, a movie, a savings bond, taxes, or postage stamps, it seems to him that he is merely performing certain functions of life, doing things that everybody else in society does. Were he to examine how his actions function in a market system, he might wonder how income and resources and output are exchanged so freely that he could take the process for granted. At a distance he might see himself as part of a vast pattern of economic forces. This pattern is referred to as the **circular flow.**

Economic exchange of any kind creates flows. Households sell their labor–and other resources they may possess—to businesses in return for income. They then use this income to buy products turned out by these businesses. In this simplified world–without banks, stock markets, or even a government–the different elements of the economy are linked functionally together in an eternal circle of exchanges whose directions are fixed but whose speed, volume, and composition vary considerably.

How an economy meets its goals is determined by these flows. Efficiency is determined by the forces of supply and demand that match households' wants with what businesses supply. This has been amply covered in Chapter 3. Stability is determined by the volume of flows between spending, output, resources, and income. The distribution of income and the prosperity of individual economic units is determined by where the flows are directed. In the first half of the chapter, the circular flow will be seen as it influences the aggregate level of economic activity; in the second half, it will be seen as it affects its components.

CIRCULAR FLOW AND STABILITY

Households and Businesses

The simplest model of circular flow involves only households and businesses. These terms are familiar enough, but in economics they have specific meanings.

Households Households are not just families, but may be single people and communal groups as well. What is important about them is not their cohesion or membership, but rather their economic functions. Households are, first of all, consumers. Their ultimate goal is to satisfy the needs and wants of the members. They have limited budgets and seek the most satisfaction within the constraints of their budgets. Households are, secondly, the controllers of the factors of production–land, labor, capital, and entrepreneurial talent. Labor is their main resource. Labor may be used to grow the food, make the bread, weave the cloth, and build the house that furnish the satisfaction of the household's wants. More often nowadays exchange is involved. Specialization has meant that it is more economical for households to forgo self-sufficiency and to obtain goods and services from outside sources. Even most housewives, whose labor directly satisfies household needs, no longer bake bread, can vegetables, or make soap.

Businesses The use of resources to make products or provide services is the province of the business firm. Just as the household consumes to satisfy its needs and wants, the business firm produces to make profit. What this actually means in practice is the subject of some debate. In gigantic companies a freedom from antitrust prosecution, bureaucratic power for managers, labor peace, or innovative technology may be the avowed goal, perhaps in the belief that this will increase profits. How else could we explain the approximately $125 million spent in changing the names of Standard Oil companies to Exxon, which ate into the short-run profits of that giant firm? The creation of product identity, the capture of larger market shares, the increase of earnings per share and other targets found in annual reports are secondary, short-term goals, while profit maximization may be the primary, long-term goal. For the moment, profits can be left to mean the earning potential or value of the firm.

Although every firm maximizes profit, the forms of organization differ. There are three major types in the market system of the United States: the sole proprietorship, the partnership, and the corporation.

SOLE PROPRIETORSHIP In visiting the doctor, the butcher, or the local newsstand, you are probably patronizing a sole proprietorship. This is the simplest and most prevalent form of business organization. It is also the most ephemeral; fewer than 40 percent of these small businesses survive to celebrate their fifth anniversary. Despite the difficulties in obtaining capital because business credit for these firms is really personal credit, the unlimited financial liability in case of failure, and the limitations on specialization presented by this form of business organization, close to 90 percent of all new businesses are registered in this form. The red tape in starting and conducting business is relatively uncomplicated. Income is not doubly taxed, as we shall see it is with a corporation. And the feeling of being your own boss is worth the risks to the more than 9 million sole proprietors in the United States today.

PARTNERSHIP When two or more people own the business, this is a partnership. The combined financial and managerial resources of the partners give it the main advantage over the sole proprietorship, but the potential for discord now enters as a liability along with all the others of the sole proprietorship. Only about 1 million of these businesses exist in the United States.

CORPORATION The only means of limiting financial liability, raising large sums of money, and achieving a perpetual form of organization independent of the organizer is to form a corporation. "A corporation is an artificial being, invisible, intangible, and existing only in the contemplation of law."[1] The ownership of the corporation is represented by shares of stock; profits are distributed as dividends on the stock (or retained by the corporation for future use). Liabilities are incurred by the corporation, not by its individual owners. In return for the potential for raising large sums of capital without great personal risk, the founders of a corporation must relinquish some autonomy. In most large corporations, ownership is quite distinct from management, with consequences we shall discuss later. Another disadvantage is that a corporation's profits are subject to double taxation—once on the corporation as a legal person and again on the dividends of stockholders.

Today the law "contemplates" over 1.5 million corporations in the United States. Not all are gigantic businesses; over half of these have assets of less than $100,000. Even so, corporations account for about two-thirds of all profits. Only in agriculture and the service industries does this form not predominate. The implications of this trend are detailed in Chapters 27 through 29.

1 *Dartmouth* v. *Woodward,* 4 Wheaton, 518 (1819).

Real Flows and Money Flows

As seen from the discussion of the individual proprietorship, a person may be simultaneously a business and a household. We think of households as contributing all economic resources (land, labor, capital, and entrepreneurial ability), and businesses as contributing finished goods and services. Businesses take economic resources from households, and, in return, provide the households with goods and services. These basic exchanges are known as **real flows** and are diagramed in Figure 4-1.

Real flows alone imply the existence of a barter system. Barter in a complex economy such as in the United States would be most inconvenient. To facilitate matters, we have a medium of exchange: money. **Money flows** travel in the opposite direction of real flows, as can be seen in Figure 4-1. Businesses now give money in return for economic resources, and receive money in return for goods and services supplied. From the point of view of businesses, the money that they pay out for economic resources, in the form of wages, rents, interest, and profit, is considered as costs. The money that they take in, in return for goods and services, is considered as revenue. Money has no value in itself. It has no utility. You cannot eat it or live in it. It may have some aesthetic value, but certainly not in proportion to the things we can exchange it for. Money acquires value because households and businesses agree to accept it in place of other economic goods. Households accept it in return for economic resources only because they know it will be accepted by business in return

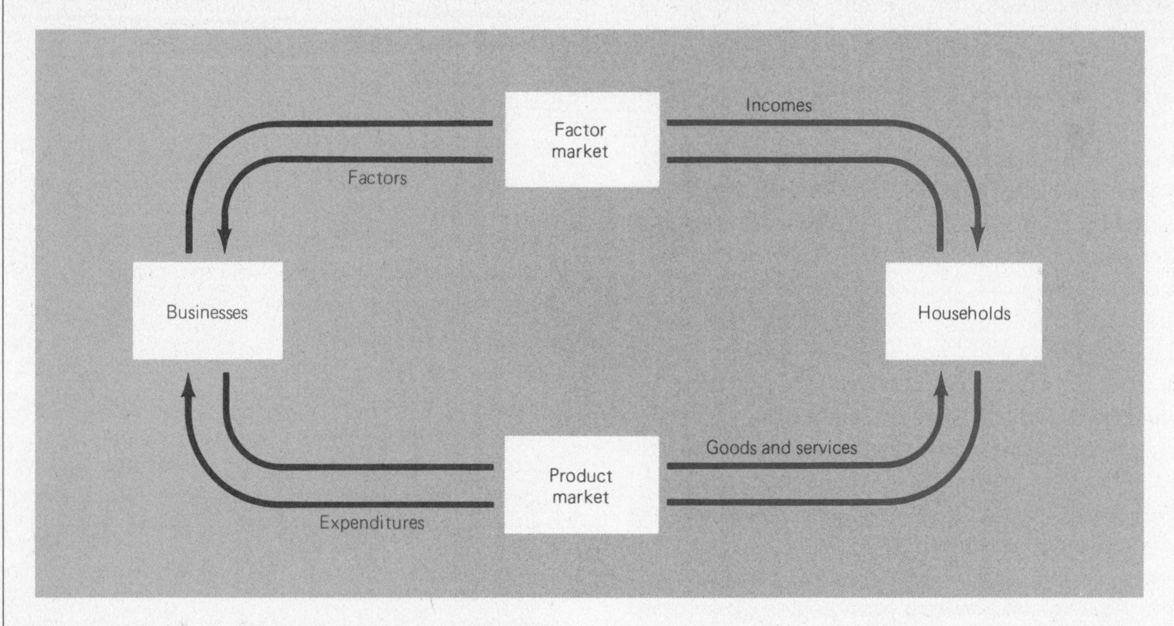

FIGURE 4-1 REAL AND MONEY FLOWS THROUGH MARKETS Businesses and households are the principals in the circular flow of real items and money which takes place in factor and product markets. In factor markets, land, labor, capital, and entrepreneurial ability are sold by households to businesses. They receive, in return, a money flow of rent, wages, interest, and profits. In product markets, real flows of goods and services are purchased from businesses with money flows of expenditures from households.

for goods and services. Money always stands for something else. This is why its flow is not "real."

Markets

But even after adding money flows to our model, we see that it is still basically dissimilar to the way things actually work. In general, businesses do not buy all economic resources directly from households, nor do households buy goods and services directly from manufacturers. Both transactions are carried out through markets. It is in the markets that prices are set through the action of the forces of supply and demand. As shown in Figure 4-1, there are two types of market: resource (or factor) market and product market. In the resource market, households supply economic resources to satisfy the demand of businesses. In the product market, businesses supply goods and services to satisfy the demand of households. Note that both real flows and money flows circulate through the markets. The size of these flows depends upon the amount demanded and supplied by businesses and households, and on the prices. The flows, however, are finite. There is only a certain amount of labor, land, and capital that households can supply. Because of this ever-present scarcity affecting the resource market, there are similar limitations on the product market. Given limited resources, business can supply only a limited amount of products. Also because of limited economic resources, households, in their role as consumers, must operate under a continuous budget constraint. Thus, we see that circular flow is affected throughout by scarcity. Scarcity makes the process of exchange necessary. Thus, we have all become accustomed to sacrificing economic resources only when we are proportionately remunerated for them.

The Roles of Saving and Investment: Stability and Growth

Up to now, we have been assuming, tacitly, that consumers are spending all of their income on the goods and services supplied by business. This, of course, is not generally the case. Consumers may save part of their income, and businesses part of their revenues. If there were no outlet for these funds, the size of the circular flow would diminish. Products supplied by business would go unsold, profits would decline, and businesses would be forced to cut production and employment. In terms of the real world, the result would be a depression. But an outlet for these funds does exist. This outlet is investment. Savings can be tapped by businesses to replace equipment, build factories, and build up inventories, for example.

Money Markets Access to savings is through borrowing in money markets. Banks are among the institutions in the money market where the forces of supply and demand establish the price of money, that is, its rate of interest. Both businesses and households save and borrow money. And there is a whole range of financial intermediaries to fulfill the various needs of each group: commercial banks, savings banks, savings and loan associations, insurance companies, credit unions. The stock market works as a money market when new issues of stock are made to raise capital for a firm. Otherwise its flows are "paper"—neither money nor real, but simply the transfer of existing assets. Although stocks are part of what is popularly known as investments, in its singular form this term does not mean the same thing to economists, who include only money spent to replace or expand the supply of capital goods as investment.

Each of these institutions allows some form of both saving and borrowing. In Figure 4-2 we see these included in the circular flow model.

Stability and Growth If the outlet of savings into investment proceeds smoothly, fluctuations in the economy are less likely and economic growth is promoted by the accumulation of capital goods. If there is insufficient investment, money deposited with savings institutions does not find its way back into the spending flow, and the level of aggregate demand declines. A certain portion of the goods and services produced by businesses goes unsold. Reduced sales means reduced profits for businesses, which must then compensate by laying off workers and by reducing their consumption of other economic resources. As a result of this reduction, households fare worse in the resource markets and, consequently, have less money to spend on consumer goods. The same reductive cycle can result from excessive saving, either by households or by businesses. Either way, it represents a leakage from the flow of spending, which serves to decrease aggregate demand.

If employment and output are to be kept at a high level, then business investments must be maintained at a proportionately high level as well. This is because when employment and output are high, savings are also high. Without large expenditures on business investments to balance these large savings, aggregate demand would begin to diminish. Money would be leaking out of the flow of spending with nothing to replace it. One function of business investment is to serve as a means of putting saved money back into the flow of spending.

Investment does, in fact, fill this function and fill it well—so well that it gives business an ever greater *capacity* to produce. The new factories and equipment, as well as more efficient processes developed with money borrowed from banks, increase the economy's total output. Investment, in other words, contributes to growth.

But if capacity rises, aggregate demand must rise too, or else the new factories and equipment would go unused. Spending must increase with capacity. But if spending increases, saving will increase as well. Investment will then have to increase still more to counterbalance these higher saving levels.

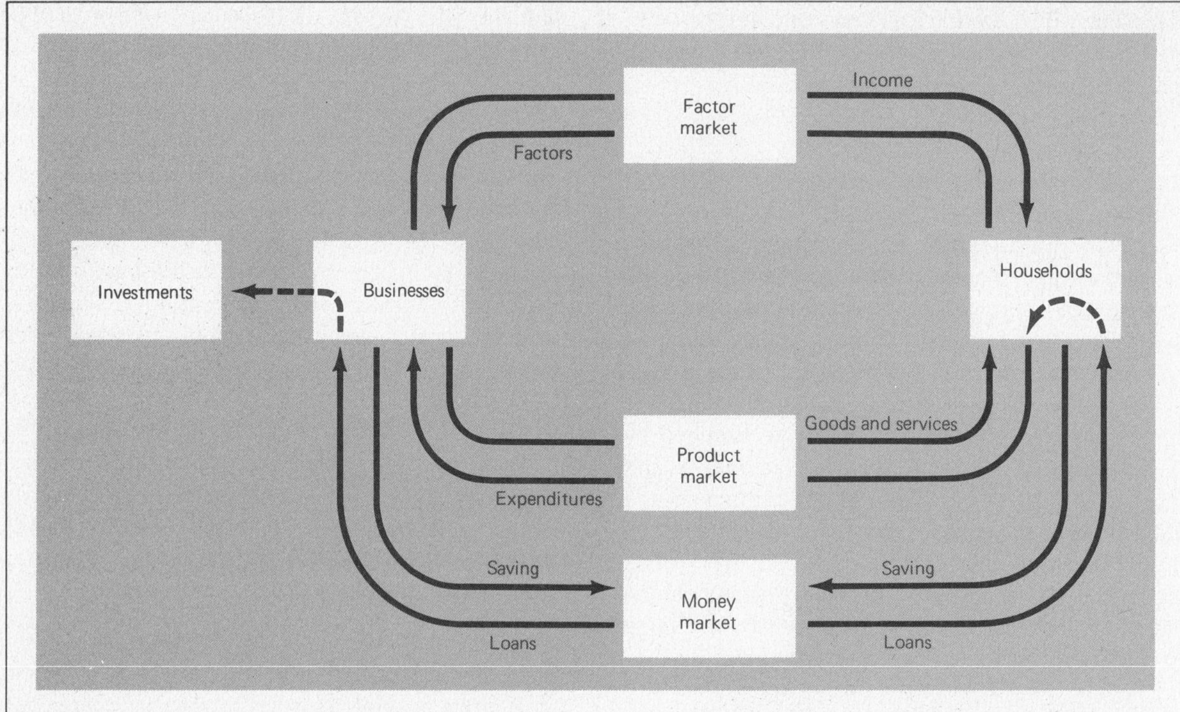

FIGURE 4-2 FACTOR, MONEY, AND PRODUCT MARKETS Without an outlet, saving would create a bottleneck in the economy. Generally, members of households as well as some businesses will put their savings into banks, life insurance, credit unions, or other financial institutions. The intermediaries form the money market and lend funds to businesses as well as to other households. There is a flow of money, then, from some businesses and households to financial intermediaries (saving) and a flow from there to other businesses and households (loans). Funds lent to businesses are generally used for investment in inventory, plant, and equipment.

To make this process clearer, let us take a hypothetical example. Let us say that the circular flow amounts to $1000 billion. Now to simplify matters, let us suppose that there is full employment and that 80 percent of total income is spent on consumption. (We will also omit the role of government.)

Circular flow	$1000 billion
Consumption	800 billion
Saving	200 billion
Investment	200 billion

The investment of $200 billion will make possible an expansion of business capacity that will, in turn, raise the potential GNP for the following year. Let us say that the new GNP figure will equal $1100 billion. Eighty percent of that will still be spent on consumption and 20 percent will be saved, which means that saving will grow to $220 billion. If the flow of spending is to be maintained, investment will have to rise to $220 billion also.

Circular flow	$1100 billion
Consumption	880 billion
Saving	220 billion
Investment	220 billion

The new investment of $220 billion will contribute to a greater rise in GNP the next year, which will mean greater consumption, greater saving, greater investment, and so on. If investment failed to meet this higher level, then GNP would falter, and surplus production capacity would soon become apparent. This would discourage further expansion and investment. The economy would take a downturn. The circular flow, then, may change in magnitude, depending on the balance of saving and investment.

Government: Stability and Growth

The government is neither household nor business, market nor bank, although it bears resemblances to all of them. We must put it in a category of its own, with its own flow of spending. Government takes money in the form of taxes collected from individuals and business alike, and dispenses public goods and services, such as law enforcement, defense, social security, education, transportation facilities, and, in some cases, power and water supplies.

Taxes, like savings, represent a leakage from the flow of spending, and just as the leakage of savings was compensated for by loans and investment, taxes

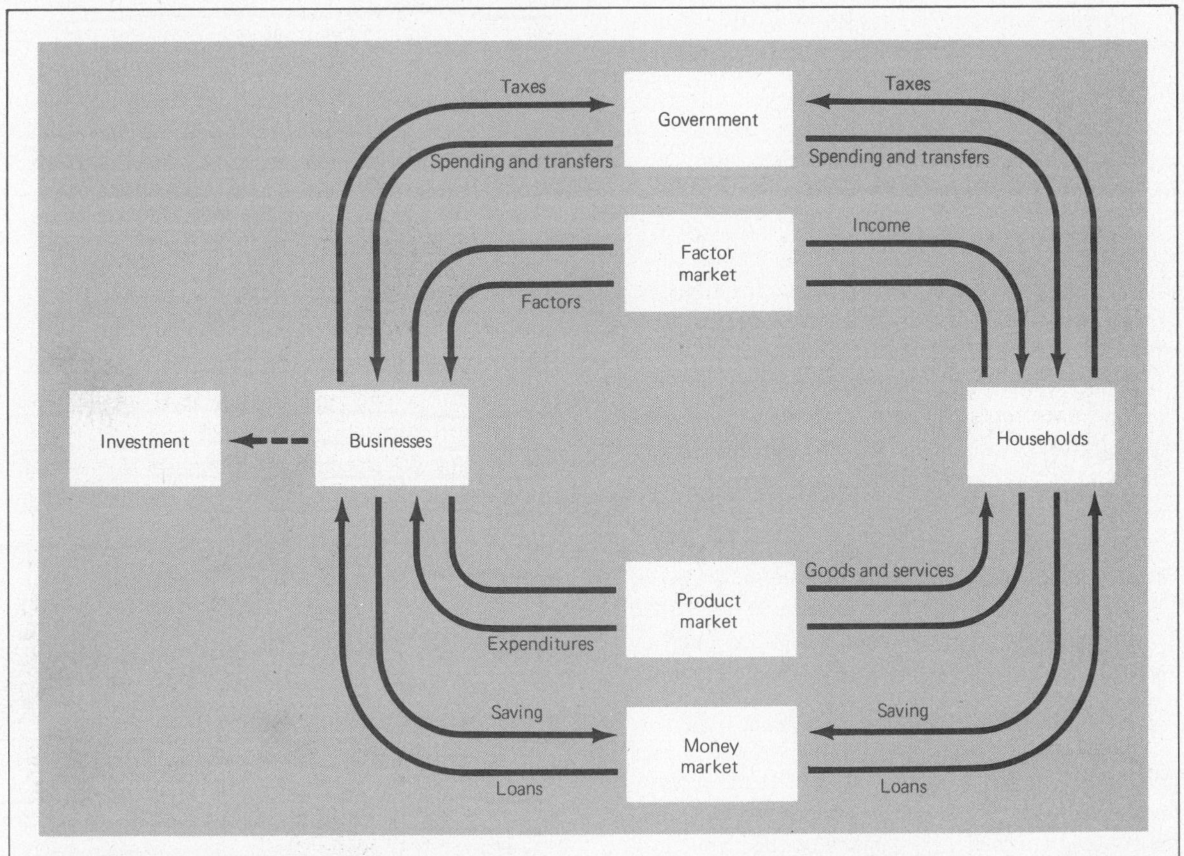

FIGURE 4-3 THE ROLE OF THE GOVERNMENT **The government collects taxes from both households and businesses, but returns this money in the form of purchase and transfer payments. By injecting and withdrawing funds, the government can stabilize the economy, affect resource allocation, and redistribute income. Our analysis of circular flows is now complete. Try to envisage a continuous flow of goods and services, resources, and money through all sectors of the economy. Since these sectors are all connected, by marking a dollar bill, one could trace its path through the various markets and its temporary stays in various households, businesses, and government agencies.**

are returned to the flow in the form of government spending. Some spending goes directly to households and businesses in the form of subsidies and transfer payments for which the government gets no product in return. But more important to the spending flows is the government's impact on the resource and product markets. The federal government is the nation's largest single employer. Thus, it constitutes a very considerable factor in the labor market. The government may also buy the output of a private industry (for instance, products of defense plants) or build plants of its own, thus giving it tremendous power in the product market. In addition, it is a buyer of land and natural resources, and a bank (through its monetary arm, the Federal Reserve). By virtue of this spending, government has great influence on the level of economic activity.

Because government has direct control over its substantial incomes and outflows, it is able to act as a regulator for the economy. Government is able to do this by adjusting the gap between taxes and government spending. There is nothing to say that one must equal the other. Just like households and businesses, government has the option of either underspending or overspending. Overspending means either increasing spending on public projects and on transfer payment programs, such as unemployment insurance, or tax cuts while maintaining government spending at the same level. These actions will have the effect of increasing spending and aggregate demand, thus increasing total income and employment. Such an undertaking on the part of government would be appropriate in a period of depression. Increased government spending has been a weapon used by all presidents since Franklin Roosevelt to stimulate the economy.

Note that when government expenditures exceed tax revenues, a deficit is created. How does the government make up this deficit? In the same way that households and businesses make up their deficits—by borrowing. Government carries out its borrowing operations through the sale of government bonds, which are actually the government's I.O.U.'s. Thus, the leakage of saving is counterbalanced in a way other than loans and investments.

Under other economic conditions, the government could decrease its spending so that a tax surplus is created. In other words, more money is collected in taxes than is spent by the government. Such a withdrawal from spending flows will have a great impact on the flow of spending. Aggregate demand will decline and, with it, income. The government will be likely to pursue such a course of action to correct an inflationary condition in the economy.

These attempts on the part of government to use its powers of taxation balanced against its purchasing power to bring stability to the economy are known as **fiscal policy.** The government also seeks stability through **monetary policy,** or the direct application of controls to the money markets. Both are powerful economic tools, and between them, ought to be capable of keeping the economy from the twin perils of inflation and depression. But the government is handicapped by its inability to procure full and accurate information on the functioning of the economy, so that its monetary and fiscal policies are rarely more than partially successful.

CIRCULAR FLOW AND INCOME DISTRIBUTION

The injections into and the withdrawals from the circular flow affect not only stability and growth but also **income distribution.** This term can be defined in two ways: first, where households get their money (or **functional distribution**) and second, who gets how much (or **personal distribution**). The relative sizes of these components can tell something about the society. A society in which rent forms a large portion of the income may be a feudal society in which the control of land is the source of power. If land ownership is highly concentrated, we can conclude that personal distribution will be quite unequal. This is the case in Kuwait, where a substantial amount of land is arid desert populated by nomadic herdsmen and where great quantities of oil under the desert are controlled by the Kuwait princes, who rent the rights to its exploitation to foreign oil companies. In the next section, we turn closer to home to examine in a preliminary way income distribution in the United States.

TABLE 4-1 Functional Distribution of National Income (Billions of dollars and percent of national income)

Item	1950		1960		1972	
National income	$241	100%	$415	100%	$935.6	100%
Compensation of employees	155	64	294	71	705.3	76
Proprietors' income	38	16	46	11	75.2	8
Rental income of persons	9	4	16	4	25.6	3
Corporate profits and inventory valuation and adjustment	38	16	50	12	88.2	9
Net interest	2	1	8	2	41.3	4

One way of looking at income distribution is to see its sources in the factors of production. Labor is by far the most important source.

SOURCES: U.S. Department of Commerce, *Statistical Abstracts of the United States*, 1972, and *Survey of Current Business*, April 1973.

Functional Distribution

As we have seen earlier, income in a market economy depends upon the factors of production. The suppliers of labor, land, and capital receive compensation, rent, and interest. To this we have added proprietors' income and corporate profits. Proprietors' income falls somewhere between wages and profits, since it accrues to the owners of small businesses. Corporate profits belong to the owners of corporations—the stockholders—and are partly paid out to them in dividends and partly reinvested.

This breakdown of the recipients of national income is called functional income distribution. Table 4-1 shows the trend of this distribution since 1950. Wages and salaries have not only always accounted for the major share of national income, but have actually increased their share at the expense of all the other categories, except interest payments. Rents, proprietors' income, and corporate profits have all declined in proportion.

The trends in functional income distribution reflect changes in production methods. Compensation and net interest payments have gone up through the years because human labor and capital accumulation have played an increasingly large role in the production of national output. An increasing population and ever higher compensation account for the rise in labor income; the large amounts of capital investment required by increasing automation in part explain the rise in interest payments.

But there are also nonmarket forces—laws, union contracts, and social changes—that affect the distribution of income to the owners of resources. Through monetary and fiscal policies government can manipulate supply and demand forces in factor markets. Population shifts from rural to urban areas have affected rental income and wages. Changes in social organization, such as increasing unionism, have affected both labor income and corporate profits.

In a way, functional income distribution reflects both the complexity and the maturity of an economy. An urban, industrial society will obviously have a different functional income distribution from an agrarian society.

Personal Distribution

In addition to functional income distribution, we also distinguish personal income distribution. The level of personal income shows whether we are a relatively rich or poor nation. The **distribution** shows what percentages of the population receive various levels of incomes, or what portion of national income goes to certain segments of the population. In a socially diverse country like the United States, personal income distribution can be related to ethnic minorities, and age and sex groups, and thus it becomes a vital tool for formulating political and social programs, as well as for providing important economic indicators.

TABLE 4-2 Personal Distribution of Income (Percent of actual income)

Color of head and year	Under $1000	$1000–1999	$2000–2999	$3000–3999	$4000–4999	$5000–5999	$6000–6999	$7000–9999	$10,000–14,999	$15,000 and over	Median income
All families											
1947	10.8	16.6	22.0	19.7	11.6	7.7	8.9		2.7		$ 3031
1950	11.5	13.2	17.8	20.7	13.6	9.0	5.2	5.8	3.3		3319
1960	5.0	8.0	8.7	9.8	10.5	12.9	10.8	20.0	10.6	3.7	5620
1970	1.6	3.0	4.3	5.1	5.3	5.8	6.0	19.9	26.8	22.3	9867
1972	1.3	2.2	3.7	4.5	4.9	5.0	5.2	16.8	26.1	30.3	11,116
White families											
1947	9.0	14.9	22.3	20.8	12.4	8.1	9.5		3.0		3157
1950	10.0	12.2	17.3	21.3	14.4	9.6	5.5	6.1	3.5		3445
1960	4.1	6.9	8.1	9.4	10.5	13.3	11.2	21.3	11.2	4.1	5835
1970	1.0	2.1	3.5	4.5	4.8	5.6	5.9	19.9	28.2	23.7	9912
1972	1.1	1.7	3.1	4.1	4.5	4.7	5.0	16.7	27.0	32.2	11,549
Nonwhite families											
1947	28.8	33.5	18.8	8.4	4.4	3.1	3.0		0.1		1614
1950	28.1	25.3	23.5	13.5	4.3	1.9	1.5	1.7	0.3		1869
1960	13.4	18.3	14.8	14.0	10.4	8.7	6.7	8.7	4.3	0.6	3233
1970	3.5	7.0	9.2	10.5	9.8	8.0	7.0	20.0	16.0	8.0	6510
1972	2.8	6.7	9.3	9.4	8.7	7.6	6.5	17.4	17.5	14.3	6864

An alternative way of looking at income distribution is to see how much goes to each income level. Further breakdowns can be made by other socioeconomic groups, in this instance race. By itself this provides strong evidence of continuing discrimination despite nonwhite gains in the post–World War II period.

SOURCE: U.S. Department of Commerce, *Current Population Reports*, Series P-60, No. 87.

Table 4-2 gives us the percentage distribution of families in the United States by income level. It also compares income trends for white and nonwhite families since 1947. Looking at the data for all families, we note immediately that income levels have shifted dramatically since 1947. That year, almost 70 percent of all families had money incomes of less than $4000. In 1970, over 70 percent earned more than $7000. The absolute shift is more pronounced for white families than for nonwhites, however.

A convenient indicator of income trends is the median income. It is not an average, but rather divides all families into two halves—50 percent receiving incomes above it. The median income in the United States rose from $3031 in 1947 to $11,116 in 1972,[2] more than tripled for white families, and more than quadrupled for nonwhite families during that period. Thus, while white families still receive substantially higher incomes than nonwhite families, the rate of increase has actually been faster for nonwhite incomes. Whether the nonwhite incomes will continue to gain on the incomes of white families is obviously a subject of social and political concern.

The fact that there are income inequalities along racial or other social lines seems to be a feature of market and nonmarket economies alike. No society has ever been able to accomplish a perfectly equal income distribution. The degree of deviation from perfect equality can be charted graphically by the so-called Lorenz curve (Figure 4-4). A curve of absolute equality would be a straight diagonal line across the graph. On that line, every percentage of the population receives a corresponding percentage

2 This trend is somewhat deceptive, since part of this increase is due to inflation. For example, the median income for all families seemed $400 higher in 1971 than in 1970, but actually remained about constant when measured without inflation.

of national income: 20 percent of the people receive 20 percent of national income, 80 percent receive 80 percent, 43 percent receive 43 percent, and so on.

Common sense, however, tells us that this is hardly so—not in the United States or elsewhere. The table in Figure 4-4 ranks 20-percent segments of the population according to aggregate income received; in addition, it gives the income received by the top 5 percent of the population. The discrepancies are obvious. The lowest 20 percent of the population receives a mere 6 percent of national income, while the highest fifth receives 40 percent. The top 5 percent, in fact, receives three times the percentage of income that they would receive under absolutely equal income distribution. The Lorenz curve simply charts these discrepancies. The vertical distance from any point on the curve to the diagonal line is the degree of deviation from absolutely equal income distribution. The greater the distance, the greater the deviation. The curvature of the Lorenz curve, then, is a simple illustration of the inequality of income distribution in an economy. The stronger the curvature, the greater the inequality. Absolute inequality is represented by the vertical and horizontal axes of the graph. Thus, at a point near the lower right end of the scale, 99 percent of the people would receive no income at all, and the remaining 1 percent would receive all of it.

Income rank of families	1950	1960	1971
Lowest fifth	4	5	6
Second fifth	12	12	12
Middle fifth	17	18	18
Fourth fifth	24	23	24
Highest fifth	43	42	40
Top 5 percent	17	17	15

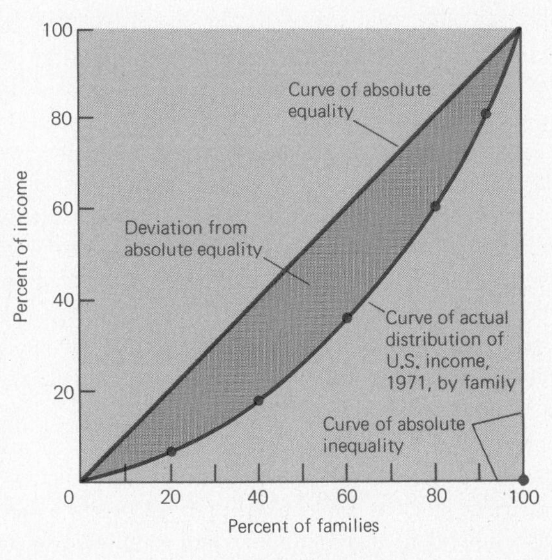

FIGURE 4-4 HOW EQUAL IS U.S. INCOME DISTRIBUTION? Equal income distribution means that any given percentage of income is received by the same percentage of families. The table shows that this was hardly the case in the United States in 1971. On the Lorenz curve, absolute equality appears as the diagonal line, and the deviation of the United States from absolute equality appears as the curve below it.

SOURCE: U.S. Department of Commerce, *Statistical Abstracts of the United States*, 1972.

The Lorenz curve may be used to compare the personal distribution of income in different nations, in different groups in a nation, or at different times in a nation's history. In the United States, for example, the distribution of income became more equal between the onset of the depression of the 1930s and the end of World War II. Since then, income shares have remained about the same.

Some Implications What difference does this inequality make? What impact does distribution of income among households have on the functioning of the economy? The answer is that the way national income is distributed among consumers affects both the quantity and the composition of national output. In extreme cases, it may lead to political instability.

Income distribution affects the quantity of goods produced because, first of all, it affects the rates of consumption and saving in an economy. The higher the income, the more people are likely to save. When a tiny minority receives most of the income, a large percentage will go into saving. This may lead to unemployment and lower income. When the same income is distributed relatively equally, there will probably be a higher rate of consumption and a better chance of full employment. Thus, when income is relatively equal and consumption forms a relatively higher proportion of income, production and employment are likely to be stimulated.

Gross inequality also affects the productivity of workers. Starving workers are poor workers. In addition, a nation may lose many bright, creative individuals to crime or to jobs below their potential because they have been unable to afford an education.

Personal distribution of income also affects the composition of output by determining the pattern of consumer spending. A highly unequal distribution will result in the production of more luxury goods than will a more equal distribution. With equal distribution of income, consumption—and therefore production—would be concentrated mostly on basic goods everybody needs and can afford. Since the size and composition of output in turn affect the use of resource factors, the cycle is complete: Output, which has determined income, is in turn determined by it.

Explanations for Income Inequality

Since perfectly equal distribution of income has never been achieved in any economy, we must ask ourselves the reasons that disparities exist. Why do some people make more money than others? In a capitalist economy, where income depends upon factor productivity, there are four major reasons.

Differences in Wealth Wealth is not income, but rather the ownership of assets that produce income, such as stocks, bonds, land, or already accumulated money. In the United States, it has been estimated that more than 70 percent of such income-producing assets are held by only one-fifth of the population. These are the recipients of interest payments, rents, and dividends. If an heiress has enough income-producing assets to assure herself a comfortable income, then she will never have to work. But if she does decide to work, then the combined income from wages, dividends, and so on will exceed the income of the average person who depends on work alone for income. In addition, unless it is grossly mismanaged, wealth tends to perpetuate itself. A worker who has only his labor from which to derive income will lose that source when he retires or dies. But property, stock, and bank accounts can be inherited by the descendants of the wealthy. The son of a working man will probably start his career from scratch—working. The heirs of the rich can devote their energies to increasing the wealth of their parents. The mere fact, therefore, that wealth is distributed unevenly contributes to an unequal distribution of income.

Differences in Ability and Opportunity This is not to say that a person cannot have a high income without being wealthy. We are all too familiar with the movie star, the professional athlete, the network newscaster, and the nationally known criminal lawyer whose incomes are way above the average. How do some people reach positions of high income while most of us plod along trying to make ends meet? The answer is, through a combination of ability and opportunity.

We were all born with different talents and aptitudes, some of which are in higher demand than others. Not everyone can be a concert pianist or a professional hockey star. But suppose that somebody has the talent but cannot afford to obtain the proper training to develop it. Then he has missed out on a high-paying career through lack of opportunity. The obstacles to equal ability are mostly biological; we do or we do not inherit certain talents. However, most of what we think of as ability is actually opportunity. The obstacles to equal opportunity are mostly social; through prejudice, neglect, or lack of motivation, some people do not have the opportunity to reach that level of income which is potentially theirs. These obstacles reinforce an unequal distribution of income. (See Figure 4-5.)

Resource Mobility If a family has money in the bank or owns stock, it can quickly shift its assets around to respond to changing demand conditions in the market. If one bank pays higher interest than another, then a family could transfer its funds. If their stock declines in value, a family can sell it and buy shares that are rising. This flexibility comes in handy when they seek to increase their income. But suppose the same family owns land for which they receive rent. Land is about as immobile as you can get. A family cannot move its plot to downtown Chicago, where

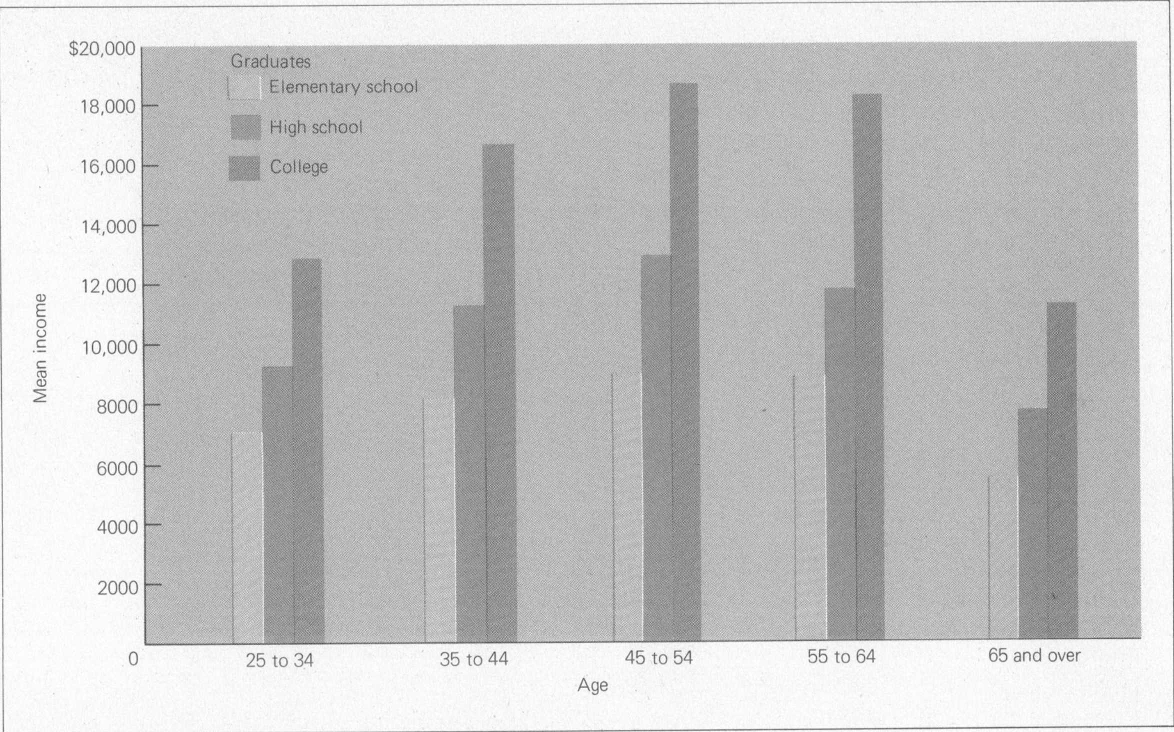

FIGURE 4-5 OPPORTUNITY FOR EDUCATION AND THE LEVEL OF INCOME The more highly educated a person is, the higher his earning potential. In every age group, college graduates earn more than high school graduates, who, in turn, earn more than elementary school graduates. These differentials apparently increase with age, until about the age of 60, when retirement starts leveling the earning power of the individual.

SOURCE: U.S. Bureau of the Census, *Current Population Reports*, Series P-60, No. 80.

rents are much higher, and furthermore, selling the plot to buy in downtown Chicago takes more time than simply shifting funds from bank to bank.

Or suppose that a family's only resource is its labor. If both parents work, they will want to stay in the same town, perhaps near other relatives, rather than move to another area where one spouse could receive higher wages. Or suppose that neither parent knows that salaries are higher outside the area they live in. Then the opportunity to earn a better income might well exist, but because of inertia or ignorance this family will not be able to cash in on it. The relative mobility of resources affects the income these resources will receive.

Regional Differences There are indeed regional differences in income distribution in the United States. Personal incomes vary by region, partly because of differences in the mix of industries and the resources that they use. Wage levels tend to be higher in urban areas than in small towns and rural areas. Banking and commerce are concentrated in big cities; real estate has higher value there, and markets are more easily accessible because they are close.

A look at Figure 4-6 indicates that the level of per capita income in the United States is higher in the industrial areas of the Northeast, Midwest, and along the Pacific Coast. Since World War II, however, the rate of increase in personal income has been highest in the Southeast and Southwest, in addition to the Far West. The Southern regions are finally making the transition from low-wage agriculture to nonfarm sectors where job and income growth rates are higher. Continuing migration to the Far West is sustaining

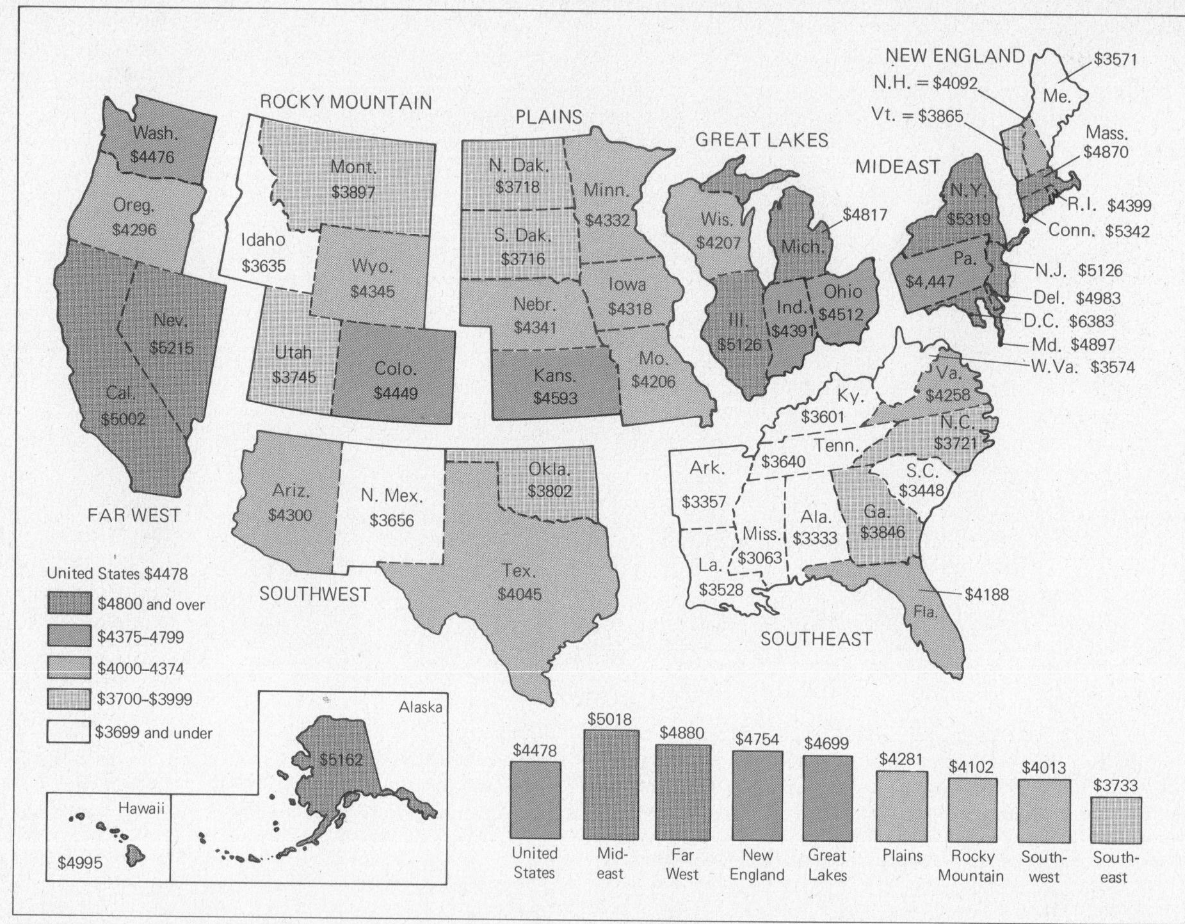

FIGURE 4-6 PER CAPITA PERSONAL INCOME IN THE UNITED STATES, 1972 Although even the poorest regions of the United States have higher per capita incomes than most other countries, there are large regional differences in per capita income. The differences from state to state are marked. They range from Connecticut's $5342 to Mississippi's $3063. The District of Columbia, with its concentration of government employees, has a per capita income of $6383, more than double Mississippi's. Most of the South is relatively poor, whereas the large industrial states are among the more well-to-do.

SOURCE: U.S. Department of Commerce, *Survey of Current Business*, April 1973.

the traditionally high rate of economic expansion there. Government spending, particularly in defense, has also shifted from the Mideast and Great Lakes to the Southern and Western regions. But despite these changes, regional differences in income distribution persist.

The Role of Government

In discussing the distribution of national income, we have so far ignored an important factor, the influence that government wields. The government can allocate resources through its spending and taxation policies. We have already seen its effects on the stability of the economy; its effects on income distribution are of equal importance. Taxes take away from income available for saving and consumption, while transfer payments such as welfare add to available income. Theoretically, then, income can be redistributed from the rich to the poor by the government. In fact, this seems to be true, as data for the United States indicate.

Increasing Size of Taxes In the past few decades, government—local, state, and federal—has assumed an increasing role in the economy of the United States. Since 1940, government expenditures have increased well over 10 times. Since government expenditures are financed overwhelmingly through the taxes it collects, it follows that tax receipts also must have gone up. While part of this increase is a result of normal economic expansion which has boosted national income, the tax rates themselves have also gone up. The rise in defense spending is one key reason. Financing World War II and the cold war has proved expensive.

Another reason for the overall rise in government outlays has been the increased demand for public goods and services we all have come to expect and depend on. This is mostly a natural consequence of the expansion and increasing complexity of economic activity, and it has particularly increased the burdens on local and state governments. Population increases and changing attitudes have called for improved sanitation, police, health, and educational services.

While all these measures entail some benefit for the entire population, their costs have risen more rapidly than other sectors for at least two reasons. First, inflation has affected government services, as it has all other economic activity. Second, productivity in government cannot be raised as easily as in some private industries. Productivity in health, education, and public safety has not increased nearly as fast as the wages of public employees in these fields. It is no wonder, then, that as the cost of government programs has risen through the years, so have the taxes required to meet these expenses.

Who Pays That the burden of taxation has increased is unquestionable. Who bears that burden affects the distribution of income. The burden of taxation is known as its **incidence**. Different taxes fall harder on different groups, and economists are often called upon to calculate the incidence of a particular tax and the consequences of adopting one form of a tax rather than another. Some taxes, for example, are borne by those who benefit from the good or service taxed; others are borne by those better able to pay.

The differential effects of taxes on income, taxes on wealth, and taxes on activities form a complex area of economic study. Table 4-3 summarizes the incidence of some common kinds of taxes.

Looking at the individual taxes is less important than viewing their overall effects. Whether corporate taxes are paid by the firm (corporate income tax) or the shareholder (taxes on dividends and capital gains) or the consumer (in the form of higher prices) makes less difference from the equity standpoint than whether poor people pay proportionately more taxes than rich people. A few millionaires slipping through loopholes may be deplorable but not alarming; the favored treatment of the entire upper class would be much more disturbing.

Table 4-4 shows the tax burdens of different income groups. From these figures, we can see:

1 The poor and the very rich bear the heaviest tax burden (in that they pay the highest percentage

TABLE 4-3 Who Pays Different Taxes

Type of tax	Probable incidence
Progressive personal income tax	Higher rates on individuals with higher incomes.
Corporate income tax	Debatable. Firms, stockholders, and consumers may all pay part.
Social security tax	Lower rates on individuals with income over $10,800. Young pay; old benefit.
Sales tax	Consumers. Falls hardest on lower-income groups.
Property tax	Owners only if land is owner-occupied; tenants if rental property; consumers if business property.
Negative tax (transfer payments)	Payments to those at lowest income levels.

The incidence of taxes is not always clear-cut, as this table indicates. Taxes on businesses are often passed on in the form of higher prices. The actual incidence depends upon the exact provisions of the law and the loopholes available.

IS CIRCULAR FLOW UNIVERSAL?

The circular flow of a market system seems so familiar to us that it is easy to mistake it for *the* pattern of economic exchange. But in some societies, the distribution of goods is based to a large extent on gift-giving or even on thievery.

The circular flow presented in this chapter has little to say about the Melanesian pig feast, for example. These elaborate slaughters are not just ostentatious displays of economic inefficiency. Pigs in Melanesia are a way of banking nutrition. When perishable vegetable crops are abundant, more pigs are raised as biological banks for bumper crops. When the pig population begins to outrun the crops, a pig feast is held to reduce the supply of pigs. This "wasteful" practice actually reduces inequalities in food consumption and sustains the delicate balance between people, crops, and pigs.

Surplus foods may be "stored" in inanimate objects, even those given away. An Indian of the northwest coast customarily would give some surpluses to relatives who needed food, in return for wealth. As wealth accumulated, the Indian would throw a gigantic feast at which large amounts of food were consumed and gifts were bestowed. Those attending were obliged to reciprocate in time with gifts of even greater value. These feasts, or potlatches, served to dispose of surpluses by turning them into prestige and into "investments" of gifts whose value had to be returned with "interest."

However quaint pig feasts and potlatches may seem to those of us accustomed to a market economy, such customs should remind us of the infinite cultural variety of man and of the danger of mistaking our own customs for the total economic reality.

Kal Muller, Woodfin Camp & Associates

TABLE 4-4 The Tax Burden at Different Income Levels, 1968 (Percentages)

	Total			Federal taxes				State and local taxes		
Adjusted money income levels	Taxes	Gov't transfer payments	Taxes minus transfer payments	Total	Income tax	Corp. profit tax	Social security tax	Total	Property tax	Sales tax
Tax and transfer rates—total	31.6	6.9	24.6	21.7	9.5	4.7	5.1	9.9	3.7	2.8
Under $2000	50.0	106.5	−56.5	22.7	1.2	6.0	7.6	27.2	16.2	6.6
$ 2000–$ 4000	34.6	48.5	−13.9	18.7	3.5	4.3	6.5	15.7	7.5	4.9
$ 4000–$ 6000	31.0	19.6	11.4	19.0	5.3	3.6	6.7	12.1	4.8	4.1
$ 6000–$ 8000	30.1	8.6	21.5	19.4	6.5	3.2	6.8	10.7	3.8	3.6
$ 8000–$10,000	29.2	5.5	23.7	19.1	7.4	2.9	6.2	10.1	3.6	3.3
$10,000–$15,000	29.8	3.9	25.9	19.9	8.7	2.9	5.8	9.9	3.6	2.9
$15,000–$25,000	30.0	3.0	27.0	20.7	9.9	3.9	4.6	9.4	3.6	2.4
$25,000–$50,000	32.8	2.1	30.7	25.0	12.9	7.5	2.5	7.8	2.7	1.8
$50,000 +	45.0	0.4	44.7	38.4	19.8	15.4	1.0	6.7	2.0	1.1

The first three columns of this table provide a summary of the effect of taxation and transfer payments on actual income. The seven columns to the right provide a more detailed breakdown of the types of taxation and the proportions of income various income groups pay. As one would expect, the personal income tax is progressive; that is, the higher one's income, the larger the percentage of one's income that goes to the government.

One should note the regressive nature of the social security tax. Since there is an income ceiling of $10,800 on which this tax must be paid, it follows that those earning less than that figure must pay a constant rate, while those earning more than $10,800 pay a declining rate.

SOURCE: Roger A. Herriott and Herman P. Miller, "The Taxes We Pay," *The Conference Board Record* (May 1971), Table 7.

of their income in taxes). In the middle brackets, everyone pays about one-third of total income to the government.

2 State and local taxes are regressive; that is, the tax burden lightens as income rises.

3 Transfer payments help offset the tax burden of the poor. In the lowest brackets, people get more in transfers than they pay through taxes. At the top level, transfers have virtually no effect.

The effect of the government upon income distribution can be depicted by the Lorenz curve. Figure 4-7 shows how the original income distribution has moved closer to absolute equality through government intervention. There are still large inequalities of income in the United States and large inequities in the tax burden, but the general effect of the tax system is to redistribute income more equally.

MEASURING CIRCULAR FLOW

The flow of income and expenditures entailed by the production and consumption of goods and services in an economy can be measured on three levels. At the national level, we can compute the total value of all productive activity and income from this activity. These form the national accounts discussed in Chapter 6. At the household level, income is derived from the sale of productive resources and then spent on the purchase of goods and services. A household budget reflects the participation of the individual in the circular flow. At the business level, participation involves outlays for productive resources (costs) and receipts from productive activity (revenues). There are a variety of accounting procedures used to measure this flow, the most important of which are the income statement and the balance sheet.

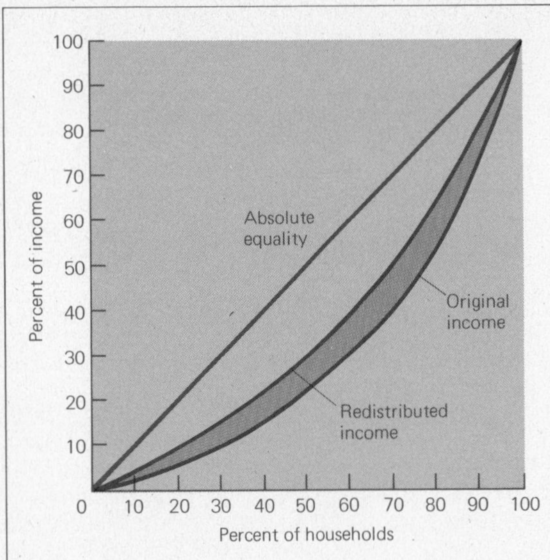

FIGURE 4-7 THE IMPACT OF GOVERNMENT ON INCOME DISTRIBUTION, 1960 Government taxation and spending programs act as an important income redistributor, as can be seen here. Obviously the direction of this redistribution has been from the wealthy to the poor. Although the middle class is generally viewed as the victim of heavy taxation, it is also the recipient of a large share of government services, which tend to return to the middle class tax payer his proportionate share of government services. Two examples are gasoline and property taxes and their corresponding governmental payoffs, highway construction and schools.

SOURCE: U.S. Bureau of the Census, Current Population Reports, Series P-60, No. 89; W. Irwin Gillespie, "Effect of Public Expenditures on the Distribution of Income," in *Essays in Fiscal Federalism,* ed. Richard A. Musgrave. P. 162. Copyright © 1965 by the Brookings Institution, Washington, D.C.

The balance sheet represents the financial position of a firm at a particular time.

It compares a firm's assets with its liabilities and points up its net worth. Assets are the things of value a firm owns, such as cash, property, inventories, and the debts it is owed. Liabilities are the monetary debts it owes in turn, such as loans, unpaid expenses, and taxes. If a firm is solvent, assets will exceed liabilities, and the difference will be its net worth. Table 4-5 presents a balance sheet for General Motors. Most of the items in it are self-explanatory. The balance sheet indicates the sheer size of a company and also its economic health. Its net worth represents the value of its stock and the amount of earnings that have not been paid out as dividends or been reinvested.

The income statement is an accounting statement that denotes a firm's flow of receipts and expenditures over a given period of time, usually the fiscal year.

It shows its income from the sale of goods and

TABLE 4-5 General Motors Corporation Balance Sheet (December 31, 1972)

Current Assets	
Cash	$ 379,618,630
Government securities and time deposits	2,567,322,841
Accounts and notes receivable	2,806,202,114
Prepaid expenses	585,214,833
Inventories	4,200,163,355
Total Current Assets	$10,538,521,773
Fixed Assets	
Real estate, plants, equipment, and special tools	$6,198,524,579
Equity in subsidiaries, other investments, and miscellaneous assets	1,234,792,852
Deferred income taxes and other	127,592,755
Total Fixed Assets	$7,560,910,186
Common Stock Held for Incentive Program	$129,540,350
Intangible Assets	
Goodwill—less amortization	$44,409,726
Total Assets	$18,273,382,035
Current Liabilities	
Accounts, drafts, and loans payable	$2,469,823,840
Income taxes payable	760,322,253
Other taxes, payrolls, and sundry accrued items	1,743,600,748
Total Current Liabilities	$4,973,746,841
Long-Term Liabilities	
Debt: Long-term and other	$1,171,242,134
Deferred credits and reserves	445,514,037
Total Long-term Liabilities	$1,616,756,171
Net Worth: Stockholders' Equity	
Capital stock:	
Preferred stock	$ 283,564,400
Common stock	479,360,875
Surplus and retained income	10,919,953,748
Total Net Worth	$11,682,879,023
Total Liabilities, Reserves, and Stockholders' Equity	$18,273,382,035

TABLE 4-6 General Motors and Consolidated Subsidiaries Statement of Consolidated Income for the Year Ending December 31, 1972

Item	Allocations	Receipts
Net sales		$30,610,010,749
Costs and expenses		
Wages and salaries	$ 8,668,223,736	
Selling, general, and administrative expenses	1,162,537,363	
Cost of sales and other operating charges	15,644,210,374	
Depreciation and obsolescence of real estate, plants, and equipment	912,432,511	26,387,403,984
Operating profit		4,222,606,765
Taxes	2,059,800,000	
Net profit after taxes		$2,162,806,765
Dividends		
Preferred stock	$12,928,270	
Common stock	$2,149,878,495	

services and the various costs it has incurred through production. The statement always balances because it includes the profit or loss the firm realized during the year. Table 4-6 presents a somewhat simplified income statement for General Motors. The left column, headed allocations, shows how receipts are apportioned between costs and profits. Again, most of the items are self-explanatory. Depreciation is an accounting device used to write off the cost of capital equipment over a succession of fiscal years. Since the cost of such equipment would distort a firm's income statement for any single year, it is spread out over the lifetime of the equipment. The table also indicates the importance of taxes as operating costs. Payroll taxes are the firm's contribution to the social security program; indirect business taxes are the sales and excise taxes it has passed on to the consumers of its products; and corporate income taxes are levied on the taxable profit of the firm. The remaining profits are distributed to stockholders as dividends or are retained as undistributed profits.

Individual firms' income statements can be combined to provide a picture of an industry or the entire business sector of the economy. Table 4-7 is an approximation of such a statement for the U.S. economy for 1972. It is assumed that there is no change in the level of inventories, so that the volume of production and sales balances for the year. We have also omitted materials from the allocations side because, if the statement is to be accurate, it cannot include transactions between businesses whose value would be duplicated by the final sale of the product. On the other hand, we have added proprietors' income because the business sector as a whole includes incorporated and nonincorporated income.

This consolidated statement serves to show the relationship between the business sector and the household and governmental sectors of the economy. All the allocations listed in the left-hand column flow either to households as income payments or to

Table 4-7 Income Statement: The Business Sector (Billions of dollars)

Allocations		Receipts	
Wages and salaries	$637	Sales of output	$1152
Interest	73	(a) To consumers	721
Rents	26	(b) To other businesses	176
Depreciation	104		
Taxes	190	(c) To government	255
(a) Payroll	39		
(b) Indirect business	110		
(c) Corporate income taxes	41		
Corporate profits (after taxes)	47		
(a) Dividends	26		
(b) Undistributed profits	21		
Proprietors' income	75		

We may view the entire business sector as a giant business, with its own income statement. Using the same format, then, as we did in Table 4-6, let us start with sales of $1152 billion. If we subtract all the costs of doing business—wages and salaries, interests, rents, depreciation, and taxes—we are left with corporate profits (after taxes) and proprietors' income. Note that wages and salaries constitute the lion's share of business costs. To obtain an even more accurate profit picture, we should subtract personal income tax paid by proprietors (owners of proprietorships and partners in partnerships) as well as those paid by the recipients of dividends.

government as taxes, or remain as undistributed receipts. Taxes and individual income, in turn, form the bases for the demand for the products that firms produce. The circular flow of production and income, as seen from the business side of the economy, is thus complete.

SUMMARY

1 There is a circular flow of goods and services, resources and money through markets to and from businesses, households, and government. Households act as consumers of goods and services from businesses and as the controllers of the factors of production—land, labor, capital, and entrepreneurial talent. Businesses use these resources to produce goods and services. Households buy these with the income received in supplying the factors of production.

2 There are three types of businesses: the sole proprietorship, the partnership, and the corporation. The proprietorship is the simplest and most prevalent form of business organization; it has only one owner. Next most numerous is the partnership, which has the advantage of combining the financial and managerial resources of its two or more owners. Limited financial liability, the ability to raise large sums of money, and perpetual life of the organization are the main advantages of the corporate form of business. Although least numerous of the three forms of American businesses, the corporations, which are legal entities, do most of the business, in terms of sales and output.

3 The balance sheet represents the financial position of a firm at a particular time: It compares a firm's assets with its liabilities to determine net worth. The flow of receipts and expenditures over a period of time, usually a year, is denoted by the income statement. By subtracting expenditures from receipts, one obtains profits, which are distributed as dividends or retained. Saving by households and businesses withdraw money from the circular flow.

4 Saving finds an outlet in the money market, where funds are loaned primarily for investment in new productive goods. An imbalance between saving and investment creates instability.

5 Government may try to stabilize the economy through withdrawals and injections into the circular flow in the form of taxation and government spending. These also affect income distribution. (The distribution of income may be represented by a Lorenz curve.) Overall, taxation in the United States does equalize income distribution to some extent, almost exclusively at the extreme ends of the income range. However, the incidence of particular taxes may not always work this way. The social security tax takes a larger percentage of income among low-income groups than among those with incomes over $10,800, for example.

SUGGESTED READINGS

Caves, Richard. *American Industry: Structure, Conduct, Performance*. 3rd ed. Englewood Cliffs, N.J.: Prentice-Hall, 1972.

Due, John F. *Government Finance*. 4th ed. Homewood, Ill.: Irwin, 1968.

Eckstein, Otto. *Public Finance*. 2nd ed. Englewood Cliffs, N.J.: Prentice-Hall, 1967.

Fusfeld, Daniel R. *Economics*. Chap. 4. Boston: D. C. Heath, 1972.

Phelps, Edmund S. *Private Wants and Public Needs.* Rev. ed. New York: W. W. Norton, 1965.
Sheppard, Harold, ed. *Poverty and Wealth in America.* Chicago: Quadrangle Books, 1970.
U.S. Department of Commerce. *Survey of Current Business.* Monthly journal of articles and data including income statistics.

QUESTIONS

1 Review
   a. the functions of households and businesses in the circular flow,
   b. the three basic forms of business enterprise,
   c. the types and directions of payments in the circular flow and the function of markets,
   d. major withdrawals and injections in the circular flow,
   e. functional and personal distribution of income,
   f. tax incidence,
   g. the balance sheet and the income statement.

2 How does the circular flow help overcome the problem of scarcity? Explain how money facilitates the exchange? How does saving complicate this flow?

3 Wealth tends to be more concentrated than annual incomes would indicate. Sketch the difference using Lorenz curves.

4 Explain whether externalities and public goods are part of the circular flow.

5 The mayor of a small town along the Mississippi River publicly states that the destruction resulting from the recent floods is actually a blessing in disguise because the process of rebuilding will stimulate the economy. How would you support or refute his argument?

6 In most developing nations, there is a conflict between equalizing income distribution and promoting a high rate of growth of the economy. Why might there be a conflict?

7 The corporation has been under attack for its concentration of decision-making power in the hands of a technocratic elite and for its lack of social responsibility. One solution to the first issue is to democratize the corporation by giving shareholders a greater say. How might this contribute to the social responsibility of the firm? How might it conflict? Consider the idea of a cooperative, as well as the traditional corporate form, in your answer.

8 Kenneth Boulding, a former president of the American Economic Association, talks about the differences between exchange economics and grants economics. The family, he points out, is based on grants economics, because the parents sustain their children with no tangible return. Name some other grant relationships. Relate this concept to that of the circular flow.

9 Given the tax structure in the United States, how could turning more power back to the states affect the distribution of income? How might revenue sharing help correct the burden state and local taxes place on lower-income groups?

10 As the owner of the Leopard Dry Cleaning chain, you have invented an all-purpose spot remover and added this to your business. The cost of the spot remover mixer is $10,000 and you anticipate it to last 10 years. Your net sales for the year

are $1 million and other costs are $749,000. Construct an income statement showing net operating profit. Taxes are $138,000. What is the net profit? As the sole proprietor, you decide to retain $72,000 for the business and distribute the remainder as profits. How much is your income? What effect would there be in the disposition of profits if you were only the chief stockholder with 60 percent of the stock?

Opening photo of engraving of Adam Smith from The New York Public Library

5
CHAPTER
ECONOMIC
THOUGHT

Up to now we have discussed the dominant concerns and various approaches of economics. We have seen the interplay of economic and social issues. We have explored the market and its life-forces. We have traced in some detail the circular flow of spending. But how did this body of knowledge arise? Or rather, how did it develop in relation to the economic settings within which everyday people have lived?

The body of knowledge we call economics has been painstakingly built block upon block. The scientists of economics are a relatively small group of thinkers who lived between the late eighteenth century and the present. They are keen observers of the economic activity around them, for the world is their laboratory. To an important extent, each has reflected the conditions of his own day, whether as defender or critic of the status quo.

The concern of economic thought has largely been with capitalism. Indeed, the growth of economics as a separate field of study coincides with the development of capitalism. Capitalism made economics necessary, because for the first time commercial forces began to dominate society. Prior to this, during the Middle Ages some trade flourished, but the conditions of life and the highly critical and limiting attitude of the official philosophy served to keep commerce in check. Under the influence of Christian teachings, the opinion leaders of medieval society branded usury (the charging of interest for loans) a sin, and condemned the merchant's struggle for profit. St. Thomas Aquinas wrote: To sell a thing for more than it is worth, or to buy it for less than it is worth, is in itself unjust and unlawful. Medieval manufacturers did not try to outdo each other in the market; the guild system made sure that products met a single standard of quality and sold at a single price. Medieval man did not have the same ideas as we do about business. It was not assumed that the businessman would strive to maximize profits, nor was the consumer expected to try to maximize pleasures, unless, of course, they were the pleasures of heaven.

This all changed. The change was slow, taking place over centuries and as the result of many forces. The discovery of the New World, the opening up of new trade routes, and the institution of enclosure in England (whereby the rural population was deprived of its communal grazing land, which encouraged migration into towns) all contributed to the development of a strong, influential business class that could afford to ignore the proscriptions of tradition and the church. By the eighteenth century, capitalism was in its early stages. The guild system no longer predominated. In this new, unaccustomed surge of economic activity, there arose an urgent need for effective rules of procedure in dealing with the bewildering vagaries of the market economy. Thus, the study of economics was born. Two of the earliest schools of economic thought were the Mercantilists and the Physiocrats.

THE FOUNDATIONS

Mercantilism

Mercantilism represented one of the first attempts at organized thinking about the behavior of business firms and the market. The Mercantilists were an array of European merchants, government officials, and pamphleteers who were active during the seventeenth century. Mercantilism was more a generalized movement than a school of thought. Since it boasted no single spokesman, many of its basic tenets remained objects of dispute. The one thing that bound its advocates together was their commitment to economic activity as it was, rather than as it ought to be. Unlike the medieval theologians, the Mercantilists were not idealists. They were men who were very much involved with the economy. They wished to decipher its mysteries, as a means of gaining control over it. They also wished to apply a standardized language to economic activity, so that those involved in the market might understand each other better. In short, they were not interested in metaphysics but in technique.

There were certain points that most of the Mercantilists agreed upon. Faced with growing chaos in the economic sphere, they demanded that government use its powers as a mediator to alleviate or regulate certain conflicts of interest between various sectors of the economy. In taking this "law and order" position, the Mercantilists were simply being pragmatic. They saw that there were situations in which people with different interests were bound to have conflicts; they felt that it was the place of the state to act as a final authority in such cases.

In other areas, however, this pragmatic attitude led the Mercantilists into error. Confusing money with wealth and confusing wealth with income, they said that the quantity of money (in the form of precious metals) a nation possessed was the factor that determined that nation's relative well-being. Although this confusion between stocks and flows is now held to be invalid, at the time the Mercantilists wrote, it may have been truer than it is today. Gold was important in maintaining a nation's armed forces or in waging war.

Nevertheless, as a consequence of the importance they attached to precious metals, the Mercantilists deduced that the best economic policy was to encourage a "favorable balance of trade." This consisted of a country's exporting more than it imported, so that the balance would be made up in gold and silver. This inflow of precious metals was assumed to be the only possible sign of gain in international trade. Later economists were to take sharp issue with this position.

The Physiocrats

Later in time and more unified as an economic philosophy than Mercantilism, the work of the Physiocrats found its most complete expression in the *Tableau Economique* of François Quesnay (1694–1774). The Frenchman Quesnay and his followers were the first to deal with the idea of economic flows. They were also the first to suggest the interdependence of the various elements of the economy, a sophisticated concept at that time. But because the Physiocrats wrote before the Industrial Revolution began to make itself felt, they assigned the dominant role in the economy to agriculture and a secondary role to industry.

The most significant aspect of the teachings of the Physiocrats was their assertion that there was a natural order that governed the economy, just as philosophers of the time believed there was a natural order that governed man and society. *Physiocracy* means "rule of nature," and it was the self-imposed task of the Physiocrats to recognize and adjust the natural rules which governed their sphere of activity. Once this reform was made, the economy would attain a state of harmony which would be beneficial to all. The Physiocrats' conception of economic harmony may seem a trifle naive, but it was to be of great significance in the development of economic thought. Almost every notable economist since the Physiocrats, from Adam Smith to the present, has made the assumption in some form or other that there are natural rules governing the economy and that it is theoretically possible to achieve (or at least approach) some sort of economic harmony by discovering and obeying these rules.

ADAM SMITH AND THE "INVISIBLE HAND"

In 1776, Adam Smith (1723–1790), a well-known scholar and philosopher at the University of Glasgow, published a book called *The Wealth of Nations*. The American colonies had declared war on the mother country that same year. In England society seemed to be in economic as well as political and social turmoil. While in London a privileged few gathered to exchange witticisms over elegant dinner tables, elsewhere the beginnings of the proletariat labored like beasts in mines and factories under conditions of unbelievable cruelty. And while prosperous merchants rode the crest of an unprecedented business boom, dispossessed peasants roamed the land looking for work and often starving.

What was so very odd about *The Wealth of Nations* was Smith's argument that, while limited government intervention was desirable, for the most part this surging, audacious world could be counted upon to regulate itself, to the benefit of all concerned. Moreover, Smith was no Doctor Pangloss, Voltaire's preposterous optimist, who believed that this was the "best of all possible worlds." Smith was not blind to the evil and folly of society, and he was distrustful of businessmen. "People of the same trade," he wrote, "seldom meet together, even for merri-

SMITH'S WEALTH OF NATIONS

. . . the annual revenue of every society is always precisely equal to the exchangeable value of the whole annual produce of its industry, or rather is precisely the same thing with that exchangeable value. As every individual, therefore, endeavours as much as he can both to employ his capital in the support of domestic industry and so to direct that industry that its produce may be of the greatest value; every individual necessarily labours to render the annual revenue of the society as great as he can. He generally, indeed, neither intends to promote the public interest, nor knows how much he is promoting it. By preferring the support of domestic to that of foreign industry, he intends only his own security; and by directing that industry in such a manner as its produce

AN

INQUIRY

INTO THE

Nature and Caufes

OF THE

WEALTH OF NATIONS.

By ADAM SMITH, LL. D. and F. R. S.

Formerly Profeffor of Moral Philofophy in the Univerfity of GLASGOW.

IN TWO VOLUMES.

VOL. I.

LONDON:

PRINTED FOR W. STRAHAN; AND T. CADELL, IN THE STRAND.

MDCCLXXVI.

may be of the greatest value, he intends only his own gain, and is in this, as in many other cases, led by an invisible hand to promote an end which was no part of his intention. Nor is it always the worse for the society that it was no part of it. By pursuing his own interest he frequently promotes that of the society more effectually than when he really intends to promote it. I have never known much good done by those who affected to trade for the public good. It is an affectation, indeed, not very common among merchants, and very few words need be employed in dissuading them from it. (From Adam Smith, *The Wealth of Nations*, Vol. 1, Book 4, Chap. 2. Edited by Edward Cannon. London: Methuen & Co., Ltd., 1961, pp. 477–478.)

CONTENTS.

CONTENTS.

ment and diversion, but the conversation ends in a conspiracy against the public, or in some contrivance to raise prices." Smith nevertheless believed that these very people, despite themselves, served to stabilize and harmonize the business realm. He proposed that an "invisible hand" guided the affairs of the economy. But Smith was no mystic, and his "invisible hand" was only a metaphor. The major portion of his book is devoted to an explanation of just how the "hand" operates, in terms of the hard, unmystical facts of a market economy.

How did Adam Smith justify his position? First of all, he was firmly convinced that businessmen, with their intimate knowledge of those things that touched on their daily sphere, were far more qualified to make business decisions than any government official. The government, he felt, was too far removed from the problems and concerns of the market to act as an effective regulator of such things as wages and prices. In Smith's view, the government should confine itself to providing defense, administering justice, and supplying certain public services (such as education for the poor) which would be in the interests of society as a whole, but which were not likely to be provided by private entrepreneurs.

Implicit in the Mercantilists' advocacy of government intervention was the belief that the purpose of international trade should be the acquisition of precious metals. Adam Smith demolished one more link in the argument for the state regulation of trade when he pointed out that gold and silver were inherently no more valuable than any other commodity. True, they make up a portion of the nation's wealth, but by no means the most important part. As Smith noted, the usefulness of money is limited: "Goods can serve many other purposes besides purchasing money, but money can serve no other purpose besides purchasing goods." This policy of confining government to a limited economic role is known as *laissez-faire* ("leave alone"). It has come to be one of the most earnestly defended points in traditional capitalist doctrine, both by businessmen whom it apparently favors, and by some economists. With equal ardor, it has been attacked, as we shall see, by the critics and detractors of capitalism.

But given laissez-faire and given a promise on the part of government that it would refrain from attempting to manipulate the mechanism of the market, who was to provide the control? Would not the mass of businessmen, out purely for individual gain, eventually tear society apart, much as a herd of rampaging beasts would tear down the pen that confined them? Adam Smith said no. There was nothing to fear. In fact, he said, not only would the competing businessmen leave the fabric of society intact, but they would contribute to the advancement of economic and social well-being.

Smith saw the struggling businessmen not as a stampeding herd but as a group which, by its very nature, serves to keep its members in check. There are two ways in which this competitive equilibrium is maintained. (1) Producers must satisfy consumer demands. They must supply what the consumer desires and at a price that he is willing to pay. (2) As a result, producers must strive to keep their costs low, pricing their products no higher than the actual "worth" of the item: "what it really costs the person who brings it to market." The consumer is king of the market.

Suppose that there were a rise in the demand for snuff. With more people buying snuff, its producers would soon find that they could raise their prices. The rise in profit would mean that snuff sales were now bringing in more than the "natural price" of snuff, that price which covers total costs. Taking advantage of the unflagging demand for snuff, producers would then use their extra profits to expand production. At this point, the consumers would have what they originally wanted—more snuff; and they would have it not because of the compassion or understanding of the producers, but because of the producers' entirely selfish desire to make money.

Competition between the different snuff producers would now have the effect of forcing them to sell their product at the lowest possible price, since each would be interested in attracting consumer patronage. Thus, the price would drop back to its "natural level," and the consumer's wishes would be doubly answered: He would get more snuff and at lower prices.

Many economists since Adam Smith have questioned whether the principle of competitive equilibrium really works as well as Smith claimed. Monopolies, for example, can arise, restricting output and inflating prices. Smith himself did not disregard the possibility of monopolies, but he did discount their probable influence, since he saw competition as a leveling force in the marketplace. Competition, then, was both self-regulating and self-perpetuating.

Economic Growth Adam Smith believed that once started, the free-market economy would steadily expand, stimulated by the processes of its own growth. First, as production would increase, employment would also increase. To attract workers, employers would pay higher wages. Better conditions for the workers would result in a growth in population, which would in turn serve to expand the number of consumers. Second, as production expanded, manufacturers would rely more heavily on division of labor. More goods could be made when the production process was broken down into its component tasks. Third, as production grew, capital would accumulate. Capital refers to both goods and property that are not held as ends in themselves, but are utilized to generate further goods or services. These greater accumulations of capital would broaden the scope of the productive process and allow it to expand still further.

Smith did not see this process as continuing forever. Eventually, the growth of the economy would stop. Population would increase to such an extent that a labor surplus would result, and wages would stabilize at a low point. At the same time, competition in the vastly expanded market would eventually eliminate all but the slimmest of profits. The only one to profit would be the landlord, who would be kept busy collecting the rents of the burgeoning population. Smith did not see this dismal prospect as coming until the distant future, however. Until then, there was plenty of self-regulating economic bustle and expansion to look forward to.

EARLY NINETEENTH CENTURY: THE HAND FALTERS

Say's Law of Markets

For several decades economic thinkers shared Smith's sanguine view of the market economy. Their optimism was buttressed by several comforting theories and assumptions, whose flaws were not to be evident until much later. One such set of theories was that of the French economist Jean-Baptiste Say (1767–1832).

Say contended that the money paid out by employers in the form of income must be sufficient to buy back the total output of production. The result would be a smooth, unbroken flow between the resource and the product markets. Supply would create its own demand, said Say's Law. Nothing could go wrong with such a system. If perchance consumers would decide not to spend all their money but to save it instead, the result, according to Say and his followers, would ultimately be about the same. If savings accumulated, the result would be a fall in the rate of interest. This would encourage people to take advantage of the lowered price of money by increasing their investments. At the same time, the low rates would make saving itself less attractive. Thus, the system would right itself unaided, and full employment would be maintained.

Many economists felt uncomfortable with Say's Law. It did not seem to correspond to reality. But the question of the effect of savings on the level of spending was not to be cleared up satisfactorily until John Maynard Keynes took up the problem in the twentieth century.

Thomas Robert Malthus

An Englishman, Thomas Robert Malthus (1766–1834), was the first professional economist (he was professor of political economy in the East India Company's college at Haileybury). He is best known for his pessimistic pronouncements on population growth. In reply to the utopian dreamer William Godwin, whose book *Political Justice* was much discussed at the time, Malthus showed that any scheme of evolutionary meliorism is bound to be imperiled by mankind's urge to reproduce. Malthus believed that while population tends to increase *geometrically* (2, 4, 8, 16, and so on), food supply increases only *arithmetically* (1, 2, 3, 4, and so on). Clearly, man would eventually breed himself into starvation.

Malthus foresaw three possible checks to the growth of population. These were "moral restraint, vice, and misery." Malthus was realistic enough not to put too much faith in moral restraint. And as a moral and religious man, he was forced to group all birth control methods under the category of vice. This left misery, which included plague, famine, and war, to carry off the surplus population periodically. Thus, any plan to better man's lot was futile and would only hasten the advent of one of the checks on population.

Malthus's thesis aroused much controversy. Numerous writers who could not accept its implications contributed refutations laced with impassioned rhetoric and scorn. It was not they, however, but history that provided the final critique of Malthus's theory. Malthus did not foresee the development of advanced agricultural methods that were to increase the yield of the land manyfold, allowing a more rapid increase in food supply. Neither did he anticipate the leveling off of population growth that has occurred in advanced nations. However, for much of the underdeveloped world, Malthus's predictions are still agonizingly relevant.

Although Malthus's essay on population became his most famous work, it was by no means his only contribution to economic thought. In his later work he raised the problem of depressions, or, as Malthus called them, "general gluts"—periods of high unemployment when more was produced than the public could consume.

In contrast with the notoriety he achieved with his work on the population question, Malthus had trouble even making people see this second problem. People generally see what they have been conditioned to see. In order to preserve the theories that they accept, they tend to ignore facts that contradict those theories. At the time Malthus wrote, Say's Law of Markets was unquestioned. As Say believed, supply creates its own demand. The economy could not produce more goods than the public could buy, because in producing the goods, manufacturers pay out exactly enough money to buy them. Sometimes general gluts did *seem* to occur, but these were only the exception that proved the rule. Such effects were due to accidental causes: a bank failure, the collapse of a large investment company, a war. They had nothing to do with the real flow of the economy.

Malthus suggested that general gluts might be the result of too much saving. If money was taken out of circulation it might detract from the public's capacity to spend. This idea was to be analyzed later by Keynes and made the cornerstone of what has now become the generally accepted explanation for the ups and downs of the economy. But in Malthus's time the idea met only with raised eyebrows. Saving was clearly irrelevant. No one saved except to eventually spend. Thus, saving was only a sort of delayed spending. Malthus was never able to reply successfully to these assertions.

David Ricardo

David Ricardo (1772–1823) and Malthus are often thought of as a pair. They were, in fact, close lifelong friends, although in economic matters they disagreed constantly in both conversation and print. Ricardo, a British businessman who made a fortune buying and selling stock, retired in middle age to devote himself to the study of economics. It is ironic that Ricardo, the amateur economist, was far more systematic and precise in method than Malthus, the professional. Ricardo is one of the great system builders of economic thought.

Like Malthus, Ricardo was a pessimist. He too prognosticated doom for mankind. Although Ricardo agreed with Malthus on the subject of population, his vision of the future was less melodramatic than his friend's. Ricardo took Malthus's population theory and combined it with his own theory of rents. As population expands, he said, more and more land will be forced into cultivation. Since the amount of good land is limited, any additions to the farmland will be of progressively inferior quality. It will cost more to make this land produce the same amount of food as the good land. Food produced on the inferior land, however, must sell in the market for the same price as food produced on the good land. Therefore, profits made on the inferior land will be lower. In order to compensate for reduced profits, producers of food will have to raise prices. And employers will also have to raise wages so that employees will be able to afford food at the higher prices.

Thus, in Ricardo's view, the expansion of the economy would work to the detriment of the capitalist. He would have to pay higher and higher wages just to maintain his workers at a subsistence level. The landlord, however, would benefit from the process. As more land was cultivated, competition for the best land would increase and the landlord would be able to charge higher rents. The idle landlord would become richer and richer while the hard-working capitalist would see his profits steadily diminish.

But Ricardo's prediction did not come to pass because (1) population began to level off, (2) laws were eventually passed in England that allowed the importation of cheaper grain from abroad, and (3) productivity increased enormously. Given conditions in Ricardo's day, however, his prediction was entirely plausible.

THE INDICTMENT OF CAPITALISM

The Utopian Socialists

Adam Smith is the founder of what is called classical economics. Although Malthus and Ricardo accepted many of Smith's ideas and assumptions, even they were pessimistic about the future of capitalism. Still they could see no viable alternative to the status quo, and so continued to advocate a hands-off policy on the part of government. But by no means were all nineteenth-century economists convinced of the tenets of classical economics. Some who were not so convinced are grouped together as the Utopian Socialists.

The Utopian Socialists include such figures as Robert Owen, a self-made industrialist. Owen invested his fortune in an ill-fated scheme to build a perfect community in Posey County, Indiana. It included a factory called New Lanark, which was a model of cleanliness, efficiency, and humanity.

Despite the mild lunacy of many of the Utopian Socialists' ideas, many thoughtful people in both Europe and America gave them serious consideration. The Utopian Socialists gained the hearing they did largely because conditions under laissez-faire capitalism were highly unsatisfactory. The impractical schemes of the Utopian Socialists were perhaps the straws that desperation forced them to grasp at. However, the very fragility of these schemes could only intensify the desire for something more solidly founded in logic and reality. At last those who could not accept the economic system as it was, were offered something more substantial in the work of Karl Marx.

Karl Marx

Karl Marx (1818–1883) was the son of a liberal Jewish lawyer in Trier, Germany. The young Marx attended the universities of Bonn and Berlin, where he was deeply influenced by the philosophy of Hegel. Hegel believed in a realm of ideas whose ceaseless development and change affected human history. The way the change occurs is that one idea immediately breeds its opposite, out of the union of which springs a third, and so on. Hegel described this process as "dialectical." Marx was eventually to adapt this theory to his own ideas on power and economics. In Marx's view, history was not created by disembodied ideas, but by economic circumstances. A society's philosophy, its religion, its codes of law, and its art are all manifestations of its particular economic adjustment. There is, in any society, a continual struggle among the different economic classes, and it is the progress of this struggle that is behind history. Because it followed Hegel, but discarded the realm of ideas for a materialist basis, Marx called his approach **dialectical materialism.**

After leaving the university, Marx supported himself through journalism, but his career is a story of lost posts, failed publications, brushes with the authorities, and frequent, often dismal, poverty. He was often helped by Friedrich Engels, Marx's lifelong friend and collaborator.

In 1848, Marx and Engels published the *Communist Manifesto*. Marx did not invent communism. It was an idea current at the time, a part of the eruption of utopianism. Marx and Engels contributed a new theory explaining why the communist state *must* come about, as a dialectical inevitability. Capitalism contains the seeds of its own destruction, they proclaimed. Such a statement in no way contradicts the basic attitudes of classical philosophers like Smith, Malthus, and Ricardo. They all saw the capitalist system as running down eventually. Yet they accepted the existing system as, if not the best of all possible worlds, then at least the only possible world. Marx, however, held very different goals as an economist. Early in his career, he decided that it was not enough merely to describe and analyze the world, as others before him had done. The object, rather, was to *change* the world. This conviction motivated Marx to blame capitalism for its built-in weaknesses, rather than merely express a detached concern for them.

Marx and Engels looked at the society of mid-nineteenth-century Europe, a society staggering under the effects of a booming industrial revolution, and drew certain conclusions about the course that society would take under capitalism. On the one hand, they saw the bourgeoisie—the owners of the means of production, their families and assistants. These early factory owners (bear in mind that a hundred years before this no one even knew what a factory was) were a rather grasping, predatory lot. By and large, they had no pity for one another, let alone for the people they employed, and, in many cases, very little regard for the public they served. These "captains of industry," said Marx and Engels, were very poorly suited to running the system they had created. The modern market economy was highly complex and could not possibly survive if it was to be continually the plaything of a gang of amoral ruffians. In this point too Marx departs from classical economics. Instead of defending a laissez-faire state as the only possible one, Marx believed that a state without central economic control is merely a state of chaos. Marx did not believe that the outcome of allowing businessmen to act purely from self-interest could be eventual harmony. There is no invisible hand, according to Marx, or, if there is, it is engaged in knocking the capitalists off their perches rather than keeping them revolving in perfect balance.

Then Marx and Engels considered the proletariat. From a craven band of landless peasants migrating into the cities, they had emerged into a distinct, established urban group, with (Marx hoped) a growing class consciousness. This class could not long remain ignorant of the wrongs that were being done to it. With the help of intellectuals like Marx himself, the proletariat would learn to understand the causes of its suffering. When this happened, class unity would intensify. The proletariat would organize against its enemy, the bourgeoisie, and using violent means if necessary, bring about its destruction.

Although Marx wrote a great deal, relatively little of his work is devoted to describing the state of society that would result after capitalism's downfall. It was in backward Russia that the seeds of Marx's thought finally germinated. There an intellectual revolutionary named V. I. Lenin worked with dogged determination to bring Marx's insights to the Russian working class. Using both the pamphlet and the speaker's platform, he evolved an interpretation of Marx suited to the needs of turn-of-the-century Russia. It was Lenin who fleshed out Marx's embryonic ideas about what was to happen after the revolution had been achieved. There would be a *dictatorship of the proletariat* that would last until true communism could be instituted. Lenin spearheaded the Bolshevik Revolution of 1917, achieving great power after its success.

Thus, the USSR became the first world power to

MARX'S CRITIQUE OF CONDITIONS UNDER CAPITALISM

In the last week of June 1863, all the London daily papers published a paragraph with the "sensational" heading, "Death from simple over-work." It dealt with the death of the milliner, Mary Anne Walkley, 20 years of age, employed in a highly-respectable dressmaking establishment, exploited by a lady with the pleasant name of Elise. The old, often-told story, was once more recounted. This girl worked, on an average, 16½ hours, during the season often 30 hours, without a break, whilst her failing labour-power was revived by occasional supplies of sherry, port, or coffee. It was just now the height of the season. It was necessary to conjure up in the twinkling of an eye the gorgeous dresses for the noble ladies bidden to the ball in honour of the newly-imported Princess of Wales. Mary Anne Walkley had worked without intermission for 26½ hours, with 60 other girls, 30 in one room, that only afforded 1/3 of the cubic feet of air required for them. At night, they slept in pairs in one of the stifling holes into which the bedroom was divided by partitions of board. And this was one of the best millinery establishments in London. Mary Anne Walkley fell ill on the Friday, died on Sunday, without, to the astonishment of Madame Elise, having previously completed the work in hand. The doctor, Mr. Keys, called too late to the death-bed, duly bore witness before the coroner's jury that "Mary Anne Walkley had died from long hours of work in an over-crowded workroom, and a too small and badly-ventilated bedroom." In order to give the doctor a lesson in good manners, the coroner's jury thereupon brought in a verdict that "the deceased had died of apoplexy, but there was reason to fear that her death had been accelerated by over-work in an over-crowded workroom, &c." "Our white slaves," cried the *Morning Star*, the organ of the Freetraders, Cobden and Bright, "our white slaves, who are toiled into the grave, for the most part silently pine and die."

"It is not in dressmakers' rooms that working to death is the order of the day, but in a thousand other places; in every place I had almost said, where 'a thriving business' has to be done . . ." (From Karl Marx, *Das Kapital*, Vol. 1: *A Critical Analysis of Capitalist Production*. Edited by Friedrich Engels. Translated from the third German edition by Samuel Moore and Edward Aveling. New York: International Publishers, 1967, pp. 254–255.)

Culver Pictures

govern itself in accordance with principles derived from Marx.

But why didn't the Marxist prediction come true in other nations? In a way, it has come true. The capitalism of the nineteenth century did break down. The harshness of early European and American capitalism spawned a leftist movement of considerable ferocity. But certain other factors exerted a counterpressure which offset the revolutionary trend. In both America and Europe the growing labor movement tended to act as a safety valve for the revolutionary ferment. The labor movement used the tactic of negotiation, and negotiation does not win victories, but compromises. The labor movement would never bring about the utopia that Marx had described and Lenin preached, but it would serve as a force for slow, relatively peaceful change. By the mid-twentieth century, few workers were forced to bear the burdens which, according to Marx, would compel them to revolt. The labor movement had undoubtedly improved conditions for the worker. And without the impetus of poverty, Marx's analysis of capitalism's failure began to sound a bit academic.

A gradual movement away from traditional laissez-faire practices also offset revolutionary pressure. In both the United States and Europe, government has found it necessary to take a larger and larger part in that realm which had been traditionally the exclusive territory of business. Labor laws, antitrust laws, income tax, and vastly increased government spending programs have given so-called capitalist governments almost as large a role in the economy as communist governments. This involvement is a far cry from the free-market economy advocated by Adam Smith. So in a sense, Marx was right. Capitalism in its pure form has broken down. But not all of its destroyers have used Marx as a textbook.

THE NINETEENTH-CENTURY MAINSTREAM: PRICE THEORY

Marx subjected economic conditions of his time to rigorous analysis in order to substantiate what was essentially a moral conviction about the wrongs of capitalism. Other economists were meanwhile engaged in equally rigorous economic analysis that extended Adam Smith's sanguine vision of the workings of capitalism. These were largely professional economists, members of the academic world, like Alfred Marshall of Cambridge University, who is probably the most important of the group.

These economists concerned themselves chiefly with one problem. Adam Smith had spoken of an "invisible hand" that maintains the equilibrium of a free-market economy. Since this hand was invisible, not much could be discovered about how it operated. The academic economists of the late nineteenth century set themselves the task of slipping onto the hand a gauntlet of hard theory, so that its movements would be visible. They began by asking themselves the question, How is value determined?

Economists since Adam Smith had been troubled by the **paradox of value**. Why does water, which is essential to life, have little or no value, while diamonds, which are mainly used as a decoration, have a very high value? Like Marx after him, Adam Smith believed that value depended on the amount of labor that went into the production of an item. Diamonds entail a great deal of labor to mine, transport, and cut; water has only to be brought from a well or a stream. This was the dominant explanation throughout the first half of the nineteenth century, and though some economists expressed dissatisfaction with the theory and offered alternatives, the labor-value assumption was accepted by the majority of economists from Smith through Marx.

Marginal Utility Theory

But the labor-value theory had flaws. There were many exceptions to the rule—too many. Certain economists applied themselves to the task of reexamining the assumptions involved and developing a more satisfactory explanation. The answer that finally emerged was based on the concept of utility. Several economists contributed to the development of utility theory. Heinrich Gossen (1810–1858) was an early, and largely ignored, forerunner. Carl Menger (1840–1921), William Stanley Jevons (1835–1882), and Alfred Marshall (1842–1924) are some important later developers of the idea. Marshall's book, *Principles of Economics,* is often considered to be the most finished and complete version of marginal utility theory.

The utility of anything is entirely subjective and may vary from person to person. It is a measure of how much we want something. Beginning with the concept of utility, Marshall and others developed a theory of **marginal utility.** Marginal utility refers to that addition to total utility which is derived from the acquisition of one additional unit of a commodity. For example, if you had nine pounds of ice cubes and were to purchase a tenth pound, the value you placed on that tenth pound would be its marginal utility.

The marginal utility theorists then offered two propositions concerning the concept of marginal utility. First, they asserted that as more of a commodity is consumed, the marginal utility of additional units eventually diminishes. In other words, the more pounds of ice cubes you have to begin with, the less you value an additional pound. The second proposition made the assumption that a person strives to maximize total utility. He does this by carefully considering the price and marginal utility of each item he buys. He maximizes utility when the marginal utility gained by the last dollar spent on one item is equal to the marginal utility of the last dollar spent on every other item he purchases. This hypothetical person who always gets exactly what he wants is an abstraction and cannot be found in reality. But the utility theorists felt that he corresponded well enough to the typical consumer to justify their leap into abstraction.

Using the theory of marginal utility, economists were able to finally explain the paradox of value in what seemed to be a satisfactory manner. Water is cheap because its marginal utility is very low. Its total utility is immense (without it life is impossible), but total utility does not determine price. We need water, but there is so much of it that people have no reason to accumulate it. It will be there when needed. Therefore, its marginal utility—and its price—is very low. In the case of diamonds, however, the marginal utility is quite high. Since marginal utility determines price, diamonds are thus very expensive.

The theory of marginal utility not only cleared up the paradox of value but had many ramifications in the study of economics in general. With some qualifications, it is still accepted today. It is the greatest contribution of the nineteenth-century academic economists.

Marginal Productivity Theory

John Bates Clark (1847–1938) was the first American economist to achieve international recognition. He carried marginal analysis to its fullest development. Like many other economists of the time, Clark was concerned with the theory of value. The marginal utility theorists focused on the consumer demand side of the marginal analysis. Clark, however, concentrated on the cost and supply side. **Marginal productivity theory** states that each input to the productive process is paid for according to what it creates. Thus, the income earned by each economic resource is the value of the additional goods and services it can produce. This theory of value differs from Marx's labor theory. The Marxian view recognizes only labor as creating value, whereas marginal productivity theory embraces all inputs that contribute to production.

Partial and General Equilibrium Theories

Given the theories of marginal utility and marginal productivity, it is still very difficult to analyze the numerous processes through which price and output decisions for all goods and services are made. There are so many variables at work.

It was Alfred Marshall who first offered the famous scissors analogy of how supply and demand work together to achieve market equilibrium. One blade of the scissors is supply, the other is demand; and it is impossible—and unnecessary—to say which of the blades does the cutting. They simply work together; neither could do the job alone.

The scissors analogy is the springboard for Marshall's **partial equilibrium analysis.** This useful tool analyzes the determinants of price in one market while keeping all other factors constant. The technique is still used today. Chapter 3 used partial equilibrium analysis to explain supply and demand.

The nineteenth century produced its greatest builder of abstract economic systems in the person of Leon Walras (1834–1910), a Frenchman who held a Swiss professorship. Walras was the first important economist to extensively employ advanced mathematical techniques in his work.

Walras addressed himself to the further working out of the principles governing Adam Smith's "invisible hand." Smith had said that market prices always tend toward their equilibrium levels. While this assumption may seem reasonable for individual markets, it is much less certain for the economy as a whole. What is it that stops prices from diverging further and further from their "natural" levels, never to return?

In order to solve this problem, Walras constructed an abstract model of the economy which is composed of two great markets: a product market in which businesses sell finished products to households, and a factor market in which households sell economic resources (labor, land, raw materials, and so forth) to businesses. We encountered this model in Chapter 4 on economic flows.

In Walras's model, both buyers and sellers are motivated by the desire to maximize utility. The result of their interaction is a state of equilibrium for the economy as a whole. This state of **general equilibrium** is defined by two conditions: (1) Each person's consumption of commodities is in perfect balance, so that it is impossible to increase utility any further, and (2) the quantity of commodities and services supplied in the economy as a whole is exactly equal to the quantity demanded.

Walras maintained that a student of economics who did not learn mathematics was at a disadvantage, since he was unprepared to grapple with the formal problems of "pure" economics. He assumed pure economics to be the foundation upon which the whole structure of economic life is built. But not all economists worked from this assumption.

By the 1920s and early 1930s theorists began to examine market imperfections such as monopoly and oligopoly. Piero Sraffa, Edward Chamberlin, and Joan Robinson were among those who applied marginal analysis to firms that did not have all the characteristics of those in Smith's model.

JOHN MAYNARD KEYNES

John Maynard Keynes (1883–1946) was a brilliant and versatile Englishman. As well as being the foremost economist of his time, he also served as a high government official, an adviser of presidents, a remarkably adept financial speculator, and bursar of King's College, Cambridge. He was also a pioneer collector of modern art, an editor, a publisher, and a member of London's Bloomsbury group, the talented and emancipated set of writers and artists that included Virginia Woolf, E. M. Forster, Lytton Strachey, and Roger Fry. All things seemed to come easily to Keynes. He was jack of all trades and master of all, but none more so than the trade of economist.

The book that contains Keynes's greatest contribution to economic thought is *The General Theory of Employment, Interest and Money*, published in 1936. The year is important, for 1936 marked the midpoint of the Great Depression which, beginning with the stock market crash of 1929, had decimated the economies of both the United States and Europe. Keynes's book attempted to deal with that problem in terms of economic theory. Such an effort was very much needed, because according to prevailing economic thought, severe depressions were not possible.

Remember Say's Law, which stated that supply creates its own demand and that markets automatically generate enough purchasing power for the consumer to buy all the goods and services produced. Malthus, you will remember, had misgivings about this principle, and suggested that, through an excess of saving, a general glut might occur, with more commodities being produced than there was ready money to buy them. Keynes provided the analysis for this idea.

In order to study the phenomenon of a depression, it is first necessary to establish an indicator for how well the economy as a whole is operating. The Mercantilists had used gold as this criterion. Keynes selected the concept of national income. When national income is high, the nation is enjoying a

KEYNES ON LAISSEZ-FAIRE

United Press International

The celebrated *optimism* of traditional economic theory, which has led to economists being looked upon as Candides, who, having left this world for the cultivation of their gardens, teach that all is for the best in the best of all possible worlds provided we will let well alone, is also to be traced, I think, to their having neglected to take account of the drag on prosperity which can be exercised by an insufficiency of effective demand. For there would obviously be a natural tendency towards the optimum employment of resources in a Society which was functioning after the manner of the classical postulates. It may well be that the classical theory represents the way in which we should like our Economy to behave. But to assume that it actually does so is to assume our difficulties away....

If the Treasury were to fill old bottles with banknotes, bury them at suitable depths in disused coal mines which are then filled up to the surface with town rubbish, and leave it to private enterprise on well-tried principles of *laissez-faire* to dig the notes up again (the right to do so being obtained, of course, by tendering for leases of the note-bearing territory), there need be no more unemployment and, with the help of the repercussions, the real income of the community, and its capital wealth also, would probably become a good deal greater than it actually is. It would, indeed, be more sensible to build houses and the like; but if there are political and practical difficulties in the way of this, the above would be better than nothing. ("The General Theory of Employment, Interest and Money" by John Maynard Keynes from *The Collected Writings of John Maynard Keynes*. Pp. 33, 129. Copyright 1958. Harcourt Brace Jovanovich, Inc. Reprinted by permission. Also by permission of the Royal Economic Society and Macmillan, London and Basingstoke.)

period of prosperity. When national income falls drastically, there is a depression. The concept of national income is part of the general approach to the study of **macroeconomics**, an approach which Keynes did not invent, but which he helped to develop and gave a place of foremost importance in modern economic theory.

Income is a flow. Money is paid out in the form of wages, then spent for goods and services. Or money may be saved in banks, in which case it again finds its way back into the spending flow in the form of loans. In trying to understand how national income falls, Keynes looked at the area of saving. He realized that although, in theory, money is saved only to be spent (by businesses or individuals who take out loans), there is no guarantee that this is so. If, for some reason, the economic climate of the country does not encourage spending and investments, saved money will remain locked in the vaults of banks. This will detract from national income, resulting in depression. This is precisely what happened during the Great Depression of the 1930s.

As a result of this analysis, Keynes concluded that the only way out of a depression was for government to do the spending and investing instead of individuals and private industry. It is this facet of his thought—the advocacy of government spending—that has come to be most often associated with Keynesian economics, but behind this program lay a large body of technical economic reasoning.

Keynes was also responsible for demonstrating that a capitalist economy is under the obligation to grow if it is to survive. As spending increases, saving also increases. This situation is all very well as long as investment remains at a sufficiently high level for savings to find their way back into the flow of spending. But if investment declines, the economy is left with a surplus of savings which, if allowed to continue, will soon begin to drag down aggregate demand.

RECENT APPROACHES

This chapter has been concerned with the evolution of systematic economic thought since its beginnings in the eighteenth century. In the early stages of development, theory was expressed in purely literary statements. Even though these early theories rested on mathematical relationships, it was not necessary to state the relationship explicitly.

In time, however, the need for more precise statement of economic variables led to the use of plane geometry as an aid to expression—the charts and graphs for which economists are so famous. Useful as they are, these tools are limited to no more than two or three variables. So plane geometry is clearly inadequate for stating complex relationships between the many variables in the economy.

By substituting mathematical symbols for economic variables, the language of mathematics enables the economic theorist to simulate relationships between variables. This was the major accomplishment of Nobel laureate Paul A. Samuelson, who tested traditional economic analysis for its consistency with mathematical tools.

An economic model is simply two or more of these relationships grouped together. Such a model can encompass an entire national economy, a business organization, or a single market. Models can be checked against statistical evidence. Some large-scale models are maintained by universities and involve whole staffs of economists, whose jobs include keeping the model up to date as well as working with it to make predictions and answer policy questions. The analysis of data for the purpose of discovering empirical relationships is referred to as **econometrics**.

Another way in which mathematics is applied to economic analysis is **game theory**. Game theory was developed largely by the mathematician John Von Neumann (1903–1957) and the economist Oskar Morgenstern (born 1902), coauthors of *Theory of Games and Economic Behavior*. Game theory uses mathematical methods to determine what each firm within a market will do when faced with a certain number of competitors.

One present-day economist who does not make much use of mathematics is John Kenneth Galbraith, a Harvard professor, adviser to presidents and a bona fide member of the liberal establishment. In most of his works he combines economic analysis with social criticism, and in this respect he resembles the nineteenth century iconoclast Thorstein Veblen. But Galbraith is more personally involved with the problems of the society than Veblen was. A friend of John F. Kennedy and a former ambassador to India, Galbraith is concerned with finding answers to the problems that face contemporary American society. In his book *The Affluent Society,* Galbraith says that we have failed to realize that our major economic problem is no longer one of scarcity but of abundance. Galbraith claims that we overemphasize private spending, to the detriment of public spending; the entrepreneur who makes a fortune selling a useless product is considered something of a hero, while government programs to provide much needed services are viewed with suspicion. Galbraith feels that we should adjust to the demands of an affluent society by reversing these priorities.

Another Galbraith work, *The New Industrial State,* scrutinizes the effects of large-scale industrial organization. Galbraith asserts that the industrial system (the large corporations) is quite literally capable of shaping society. This, he says, makes traditional theory about markets obsolete: It is the needs of the industrial system, not the needs of society, that take precedence.

Another contemporary school of economics, the Monetarists, would disagree. Led by University of Chicago economist Milton Friedman, the Monetarists take as their starting point the laissez-faire theory of Adam Smith. They put far greater faith in the inherent stability of the capitalist system than do social welfare advocates like Galbraith. Friedman and his followers believe that most attempts to control the economy from the outside actually do more to set it off its established course. Far from being mere worshippers of the past, the Monetarists support their assertions with vast quantities of statistical evidence and argue their case with great persuasiveness.

Finally, the economists of the New Left, very much like the political scientists of the New Left, deplore the dehumanization which they feel the capitalist system has produced. In rejecting the ideal of efficiency and the goal of ever more consumer goods, the New Left resembles Galbraith. But the New Left tends to be more extreme in its condemnation of the modern growth economy. It is critical both of economic conditions under capitalism and of economic research and traditional theories which share the assumptions of capitalism. The capitalists, says the New Left, have created such problems as inequitable incomes, alienation, discrimination, and imperialism, and the theorists, particularly the mathematical economists, offer few insights into correcting these conditions.

Different as each of the strains of contemporary economic thought may seem, we can see how they eventually trace back to the Scottish professor Adam Smith. We have just celebrated the 250th anniversary of his birth and are about to celebrate the 200th of the publication of *The Wealth of Nations.* Smith combined a grasp of the particulars of the economic conditions of the day with a capacity for seeing theoretical relationships that give the particulars significance. A pin factory became the symbol of specialization, a driving force in economic advance. The concern for theory and the concern for conditions are inseparable. In the remaining chapters we deal with the different traditions derived from the economic thought of Adam Smith and with the particulars of the economy that are contemporary equivalents of Smith's revealing pin factories.

SUMMARY

1 England was the first nation to industrialize, so it is not surprising that much economic thought should have originated in that country. The Industrial Revolution is said to have begun around 1750, and Adam Smith, an extremely keen observer, published his *Wealth of Nations* in 1776. Although regarded by many as the father

of economics, Smith drew heavily on the writings of the Mercantilists and the Physiocrats, two continental schools of economic thought. Smith believed that a competitive economy has self-regulating mechanisms that ensure full employment and growth. Government intervention can only distort the workings of the economy.

2 Two of Smith's immediate followers gained notoriety: Malthus for his theory of population, and Ricardo for his theory of rent and wages. Both were pessimists who did much to give economics the nickname "the dismal science." Their pessimism was based on the belief that England had reached the stage in which the limited supply of productive land placed limits on population and prosperity. Malthus paradoxically was also our first anti-Malthusian as well. In times of lagging aggregate demand (he also was the first to worry about aggregate demand, let alone *lagging* aggregate demand), a little population increase might be just the thing. John Maynard Keynes drew on this analysis for his own remedies for the secular stagnation of the 1930s.

3 As the Industrial Revolution progressed and increasing numbers of people were drawn into the factories of England, Karl Marx, drawing heavily on Ricardo and to a lesser degree on Malthus (with whom he claimed to disagree), predicted "the death knell" of capitalism. He vividly described the working conditions of his time and was sure that the proletariat would soon rise up in rebellion. They did not, largely because working conditions and pay were drastically improved during the century after *Das Kapital* was written.

4 Although several important theoretical advances were made during the last 30 years of the nineteenth century and the first 30 of the twentieth century—mainly in the area of marginal analysis and partial equilibrium analysis—it was not until the worldwide depression of the 1930s that economics again came to the fore. John Maynard Keynes addressed himself to the question, How can we raise the level of aggregate demand? Neglected since the time of Malthus, aggregate demand became the focal point of the New Economics, which refers to the body of policy prescription that grew out of Keynesian analysis.

5 The New Economists look toward government fiscal policy—the manipulation of spending and taxation to attain the proper level of aggregate demand–as the means to attain economic stability and growth. A rival group of economists, the Monetarists, or "New New Economists," led by Milton Friedman, has advocated monetary policy—control of the rate of growth of the money supply—to properly guide the economy, which, they have indicated, with varying amounts of conviction, should be left free to follow its own course. Both these heirs of Adam Smith rely on sophisticated mathematical analyses, a trend criticized by the New Left. Their radical critique attacks both capitalist theory and economic conditions under capitalism.

SUGGESTED READINGS

Fellner, William J. *Modern Economic Analysis*. New York: McGraw-Hill, 1960.

Gill, Richard J. *Evolution of Modern Economics*. Englewood Cliffs, N.J.: Prentice-Hall, 1967.

Heilbroner, Robert L. *The Worldly Philosophers*. 4th ed. New York: Simon & Schuster, 1972.

Roll, Erich. *History of Economic Thought*. 3rd ed. Englewood Cliffs, N.J.: Prentice-Hall, 1956.

QUESTIONS

1 Review
   a. the basic beliefs of the Mercantilists and the Physiocrats,
   b. the important contributions of Adam Smith,
   c. the pessimistic ideas of Malthus and Ricardo,
   d. Marxian theory,
   e. the theories of the marginalists,
   f. major contributions made by Keynes,
   g. the role of mathematics in modern schools of economic thought.

2 Thurman Arnold has argued that Americans judge private industrial organizations by their successes and government by its failures.* There is a belief that government by its very nature is wasteful and inefficient. What are the origins in economic thought that might have contributed to this belief? What might be some of the consequences for the allocation of functions between the private and public sectors?

3 Adam Smith believed that economic growth results largely from the division of labor in which small tasks can be performed repetitively by a single worker. Smith may have laid some of the groundwork for Marx when he suggested that this type of organization would render the worker stupid and ignorant. The problems of repetitive work are still with us. In what ways does our present social system recognize and try to deal with the problems of dull work? How do these changes conflict with the predictions made by Marx?

4 Though the predictions of Malthus were not borne out for most of the developed nations of the world, population growth continues to be a critical problem for the developing nations. What factors that Malthus either did or did not recognize might account for these differences?

5 How would Alfred Marshall and the marginalists explain the willingness of people to buy an energy source such as gasoline at a higher price as it becomes more scarce? Anticipating the increased scarcity of energy, some new homes are now equipped with solar energy cells that capture and store heat. Engineers say that the only cost of operating such a heating system is for a little electricity to run a small fan. Other homes are now wired to generators operated by a windmill. How might energy sources and prices illustrate the paradox of value?

6 The Victorian economist Thorstein Veblen argued that the economic man is not as reasonable or rational as suggested by the price theorists. As an example, examine the motivations for your own educational decisions: the decision to go to school, the decision as to what courses of study you would take. What kinds of social pressures influenced you, if any? Were the considerations related only to the maximization of your own benefits?

7 Galbraith argues that as a wealthy nation, we now have the problems of rethinking priorities and of more equitably distributing our wealth among our various goals. How does he argue that present priorities are inappropriate? What is the role of scarcity in Galbraith's America? What kinds of things are becoming scarce?

* Thurman Arnold, *The Folklore of Capitalism* (New Haven, Conn.: Yale University Press, 1937), Chapter 12.

8 Suppose that you have a farm in Oklahoma and have leased the oil rights to a large company. Increasingly severe shortages push up the price of gasoline and encourage the oil company to drill and operate less efficient wells than yours. Assuming that "land" includes minerals, timber, and oil, what would Ricardo have to say about the prospect for your income? Why?

PART 2

NATIONAL INCOME

CHAPTER 6 NATIONAL ACCOUNTS

As far back as the 1600s, national crises have intensified the search for some measure of national economic power. In 1665, shortly after the restoration of the Stuart monarchy in England, Sir William Petty, a physician and part-time economist, tried to determine what economic resources remained after 25 years of civil and foreign war by totaling up the individual incomes of all English persons and families. Over a century later, in 1791, the chemist Antoine Lavoisier was asked by members of the French revolutionary government to prepare a calculation of French national income in order to estimate the resources available to handle domestic problems and ward off foreign invaders.[1]

In the United States, the first efforts at measuring national income and output grew out of the mobilization for World War I. In organizing American industry to supply the materiel needed to fight the war, the War Production Board head, Bernard Baruch, recognized that "information was needed promptly on national income, inventories, prices, the labor supply, industrial capacity and other basic factors in the economy." But at the time, "the nation was poorly equipped with even the simplest economic data."[2] With the end of the war, the government suspended its efforts to collect national output and income data, but economists at various universities continued working on this problem during the twenties and thirties.

Official government efforts resumed in 1934, during the period of recovery from the Great Depression, and have continued since that time. At first the Department of Commerce began to compile statistics on how much of the nation's income was derived from wages, dividends, rents, and profits. Today, prodigious quantities of statistical material on the components of national income and output are developed each year. They are a valuable tool for appraising the current status of the economy, its rate of growth, and its potential, or for comparing its performance with that of a competing nation. The release of the latest figures on national income and product may affect the level of the stock market, the plans of entire industries, or the political fortunes of policy-makers.

1 Sam Rosen, *National Income* (New York: Holt, Rinehart and Winston, 1963), pp. 4–6.

2 From a letter by Arthur Burns to Marshall Robinson of the Ford Foundation. H. Erich Heinemann, *New York Times*, Financial Section, December 24, 1972.

Opening photo from United Press International

NATIONAL OUTPUT AND INCOME ACCOUNTS

The methods used in compiling national accounts involve not only sophisticated statistical techniques but difficult conceptual choices as to what is to be included. The indicators should provide some estimate of how well off a nation is—the value of its goods and services produced by the private and public sectors, the value of what the environment provides, the value of its home-produced goods and of its leisure. But some of these are very hard to estimate. It is easy to know how many cars are produced in a year; it is less easy to estimate the value of the roads the cars drive on, much less the value of the clean air polluted by exhaust fumes. Currently, roads—and other government goods—are measured by cost, which is not a real measure of their value. The big debate is over pollution and how to include environmental deterioration and pollution abatement in the accounts. A whole new indicator, known appropriately enough as NEW or net economic welfare, is proposed to complement the traditional measures.

The national accounts discussed in this chapter are technical indicators, involving sometimes arbitrary choices of what value means and what is to be included. The figures do explicitly define what they are going to look at and then systematically measure only what they have set out to measure. And they provide a starting point for taking the pulse of the economy.

In their calculations Lavoisier and Petty focused on one side of the account. They considered income as national wealth, or *stocks* of possessions. During World War I, the stock of productive resources of the nation was used as an indicator. Both of these accounts failed to see economic activity as a *flow* in which goods and income were aspects of the same thing.

National economic activity can be described as a circular flow of goods and services and of income measured in dollars during a given period. Business firms pay out dollars to cover the cost of producing goods or services. Such dollars are the income used by recipients to buy those goods and services. Thus, the level of national output can be measured either by the amount of income generated in the production of goods and services or by the sum of expenditures made to purchase that output.

The expenditures approach to measuring national economic activity adds up the sums that are spent by households, businesses, government, and foreign transactions. The income approach adds payments made in the form of wages and salaries, rent, interest, and profits. To arrive at a total that equals that of the expenditures side, certain nonincome items are included in the income account. Since both total expenditures (or Gross National Product) and total income (or Gross National Income) are equal indicators of the nation's economic output, economists may focus on one or the other, depending on their purposes. Although the term GNP is often used to refer to either the incomes or expenditures account, we use it in this chapter only for the expenditures side and refer to GNI when talking about incomes.

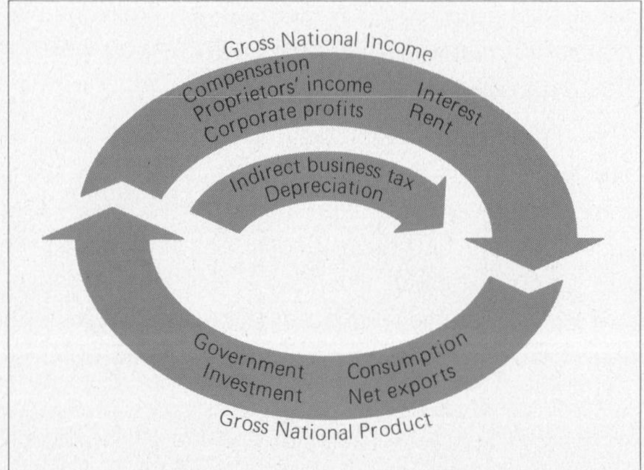

FIGURE 6-1 THE EQUALITY OF GNP AND GNI National output may be seen from two sides—either as a set of expenditures or as a set of incomes. The expenditures—consumption, investment, government, and net exports—are known as Gross National Product. The income side—compensation to labor, proprietors' income, corporate profits, interest payments, and rents plus certain balancing items—is known as Gross National Income. These flows of GNP and GNI are simply two ways of measuring the same thing.

Because these two measures are aggregates, they are not always the most sensitive barometers of economic conditions. Just as an executive inspecting the finances of his corporation does not just stop with the gross revenues but determines how the figures were derived, so economists derive the national accounts of output and income from their components. Since different components may react to different factors, their behavior provides more precise information on economic conditions.

GROSS NATIONAL PRODUCT: THE EXPENDITURES SIDE

In calculating national output, economists could simply sum up all the goods and services and leave it at that. However, trying to express national output as the sum of all products poses a major problem: finding a way of equating all the different types of units—cars, bushels of wheat, doctor visits, and haircuts, for example. The solution is to find a standard unit for measuring these products. That unit is the dollar. Attaching prices to the number of units sold in the market gives the size of national output in terms of its dollar value. In the case of government goods where no price is attached, costs are used as an estimate of value.

Gross National Product estimates the current dollar value of the goods and services produced in a nation during a year.

In 1972, the GNP of the United States equalled $1152 billion (compared with $78.9 billion in 1919 when the accounting first began).

Problems with Determining GNP

Avoiding Double Counting The chemist and part-time economist Lavoisier was the first to call attention to one statistical trap which national income statisticians must avoid—that of double counting. We have said that GNP may be calculated by multiply-

TABLE 6-1 Sales Prices and Value Added in the Production of Cake Mix

Stage of Production	Sales Price	Value Added
Farmer		
Produces and sells raw food	$ .20	$ .20
Food Processor		
Processes foods and sells ingredients to packager	.35	.15
Packager		
Combines ingredients, packages mix, and sells to supermarket	.50	.15
Supermarket		
Sells to consumer	.59	.09
Total	$1.64	$0.59

A finished product such as a box of cake mix has to pass through several stages of production. Were every intermediate payment included, the final figure would reflect double-counting items such as the ingredients which are sold and resold in different forms four times in this process. At each stage of the process some value is added to these ingredients, which is reflected in the final sales price. Using value added is another method of arriving at a total for GNP.

ing the number of units produced by the price per unit. Consider, however, the case of a box of cake mix purchased for 59 cents. Surely this 59 cents is part of GNP. But before the cake mix reached the final consumer, the supermarket bought it from the manufacturer for 50 cents. Earlier, the manufacturer had to buy 35 cents worth of refined flour, dried eggs, and milk from food processors, who in turn paid farmers 20 cents for the raw food involved. If we were to count each of these sales as a separate unit of output, the production of this one box of cake mix, valued at 59 cents, would contribute $1.64 to GNP ($.59 + $.50 + $.35 + $.20). This kind of double counting would be deceptive. The Department of Commerce prevents double counting by excluding from GNP all intermediate goods and services—that is, those goods and services bought for further processing or resale. This is accomplished by counting only final goods or, alternatively, through the use of the **value-added** method, whereby only the value added at each new step of the production process is included in the GNP.

Adjusting for Price-Level Change Expressing GNP in terms of current market prices complicates any comparisons of year-to-year price changes. If the price of a can of tuna fish is raised from 40 cents to 44 cents, and 100 million cans of tuna are sold in a year, then the tuna fish component of GNP will increase from $40 million to $44 million, with no corresponding increase in actual output. In an economy where price inflation is occurring regularly, the raw, unadjusted GNP figures would be an inaccurate reflection of actual economic activity—especially if such figures were used to compare economic performance over several years. Consequently, GNP figures are often adjusted for changes in price in in order to reflect actual changes in output. This process is referred to as "deflating" GNP. For example, if we knew that the price of tuna fish had increased by 10 percent from 1973 to 1974, we could simply reduce the 1974 tuna fish dollar component of GNP by 10 percent so as to express 1974 tuna fish production in terms of 1973 dollars. In this way we would obtain one valid basis for comparing 1974 with 1973 tuna output.

This is essentially what the Department of Commerce does in preparing its "constant dollar" or "adjusted" GNP figures. It chooses a base year and then adjusts all earlier and later GNP's accordingly. The department now prepares GNP figures with 1958 prices as the base year although it is about to revise its figures based on the 1967 economic census. Using this base, the department estimates that in 1950, prices averaged only 80.2 percent of the 1958 level. This means that 1950's actual dollar GNP of $284.8 billion would be restated as $355.3 billion in any series showing GNP in terms of constant 1958 dollars. Similarly, real GNP for 1970 rose to 135.3 percent of the 1958 level. Therefore, the 1970 actual dollar GNP of $974 billion would be stated as only $720 billion in constant 1958 dollars.

Although economists (as well as politicians and journalists) will usually use *unadjusted* GNP figures in statements describing the current performance of the economy, comparisons of adjusted dollar amounts are more meaningful. Using either current

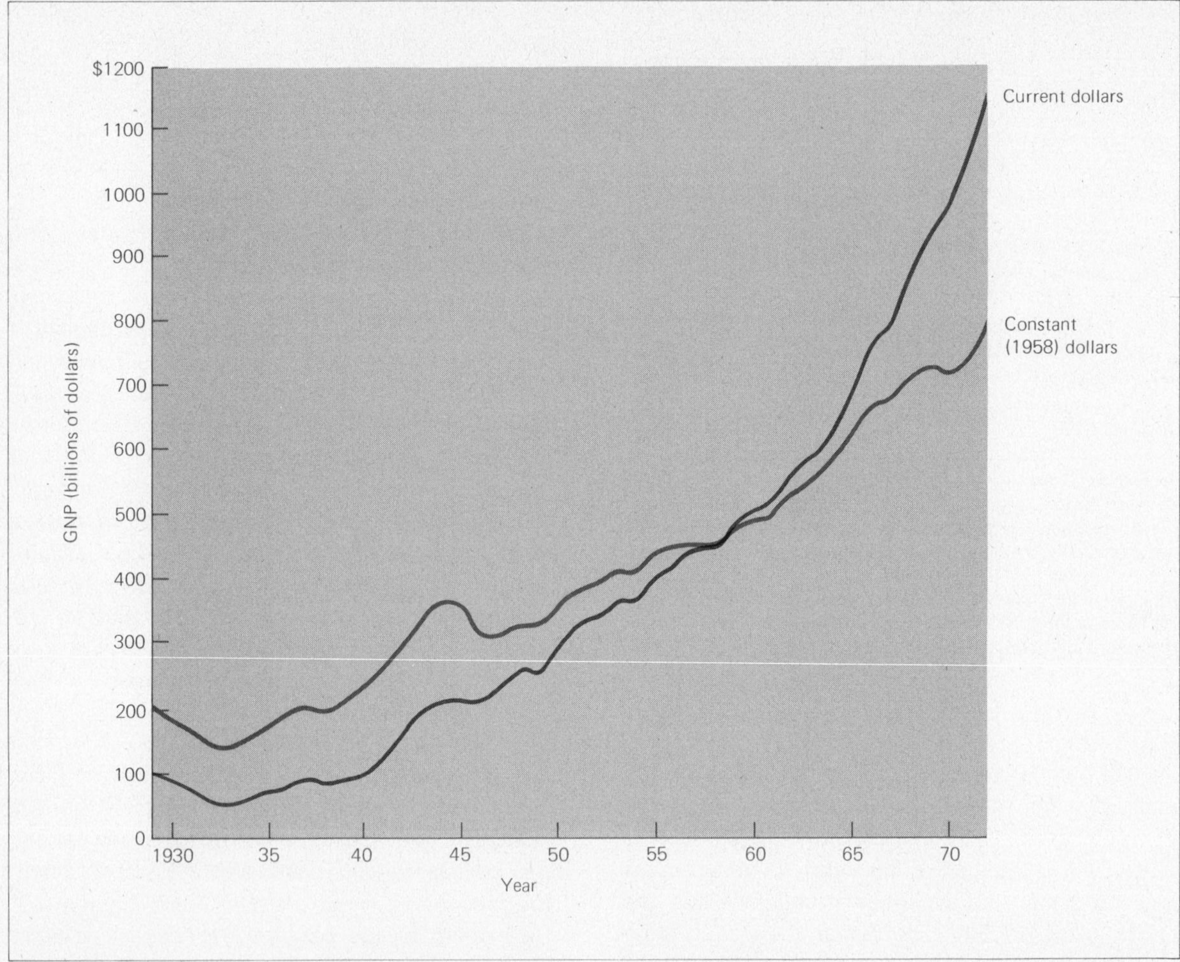

FIGURE 6-2 GNP IN CURRENT AND CONSTANT (1958) DOLLARS GNP measures the dollar level of annual production. Thus, a rise in GNP may reflect an increase in production, an increase in prices, or some combination of the two. For example, in the first quarter of 1973, GNP rose at an annual rate of 15.2 percent, but only 8.6 percent of this increase was due to rising production because 6.6 percent was due to rising prices. To find the actual rate of production increase, constant (1958) dollars may be used. These figures show what GNP would have been if the price level had been absolutely stable between 1929 and 1972. As can be seen, production rose by nearly 300 percent over this period. Had unadjusted GNP figures been used, however, the increase would appear as over 1000 percent, 650 percent of which would have been due to rising prices.

SOURCE: *Economic Report of the President,* January 1973.

or adjusted figures, actual economic output in the United States grew substantially between 1950 and 1970; but the constant dollar figures show that GNP only doubled during that period (from $355 to $720 billion), rather than tripling, as suggested by the current dollar figures.

Changes in Composition Other factors besides price change over time. Some price increases actually may reflect an improvement in the quality of the goods. For example, in looking at the prices of washing machines today compared with those in a 1950 Sears catalogue, you might still find the current model preferable because of its perma-press cycle, bleach dispenser, and other improvements. Similarly, the types of products purchased change over time. For example, we now buy more frozen convenience foods than in 1950.

Such changes create complications in the calculation of constant dollars. The constant dollar GNP figures are estimated by dividing current dollar GNP each year by an index number of prices. This index depends on the market basket of goods and services in the base year. To obtain comparability, the market basket is held constant and only the price changes are measured.

This creates problems. Comparing two years, using the earlier year as the base with its market basket, results in a different index than if the later year is used as the base with its market basket. For this reason, comparisons of GNP over the short run are more valid than those over the long run, since changes in the market basket are less dramatic.

Changes in the Proportion between Excluded and Unexcluded Items Moreover, if the proportion between excluded and included items changes, comparisons over time become difficult. The recent trend for women to go back to work, hire a housekeeper, and put their children in day-care centers is going to overinflate GNP, since their previous activities as housewives went unrecompensed and uncounted in GNP. The deceptive increase could be corrected if all housewife contributions were figured over time and included in GNP, but this is almost impossible. To change the method of calculating GNP midstream might correct the problem for future years, but frequent changes in the method of calculating GNP also create difficulties. The rules for calculating GNP may appear somewhat arbitrary and deceptive, but consistent application of these rules gives us an essential continuity.

Net National Product

One additional nonproductive expenditure that must be accounted for in compiling national output figures is the cost of replacing productive resources that have been consumed as part of the productive process. A metal-working company that manufactures garbage cans may turn out $100,000 worth of containers a year, but at the end of the year, it will find that its stock of capital goods such as drill presses and welding tools has worn out to some extent in the course of making these cans. This process of capital consumption is called **depreciation.**

Applying this concept to the economy as a whole, we can see that when describing a nation that produces $500 million of goods and services a year but uses up $50 million of capital goods in the process, it may be more realistic to quote a net figure of $450 million rather than the gross output figure. For this reason, economists often prefer to use **net national product** rather than Gross National Product in discussing output. To calculate NNP, we subtract the amount of depreciation, called the **capital consumption allowance,** from GNP. The resulting figure, net national product, represents the nation's output of goods and services, less the depreciation of its capital goods.

NNP = GNP minus depreciation

NNP is considered a more reliable indicator of economic performance than raw GNP numbers. Two nations might have nearly equal GNP levels, but one might be replacing its capital goods faster than the other. Only NNP figures would reveal this significant economic difference.

The Components of GNP

Since spending by various segments of the economy is affected by different factors, a breakdown is useful if we are to understand the reasons behind the periodic changes in total production and if we are to attempt to regulate or direct such fluctuations. Total expenditures have four component parts: Government (G), Personal Consumption (C), Investment (I), and Net Exports (X).

$$GNP = C + I + G + X$$

The distribution of total GNP among these four com-

EXCLUDING NONMARKET AND NON-PRODUCTIVE ITEMS

Since GNP focuses on measuring the dollar level of current productive activity, transactions that bypass the market, that do not involve buying and selling, or that involve only the transfer of assets are customarily excluded from GNP. But excluded transactions may have an impact on subsequent GNP. The wages of the salesman and any commissions on the sale of excluded items such as stock or a used car represent a productive service that is counted in GNP. In addition, at least some of the dollars from the sale of a stock or a secondhand car will probably be spent subsequently on an item to be counted in GNP.

Illegal Activities

Forty billion dollars in expenditures on activities such as gambling, prostitution, loan sharking, and narcotics trading are not included in GNP because they are conducted in illegal markets. This may lead to certain statistical peculiarities. During Prohibition, the value of illegally produced alcoholic beverages did not appear in GNP; once Prohibition was repealed, however, GNP immediately increased by the value of the now-legal alcoholic production.

United Press International

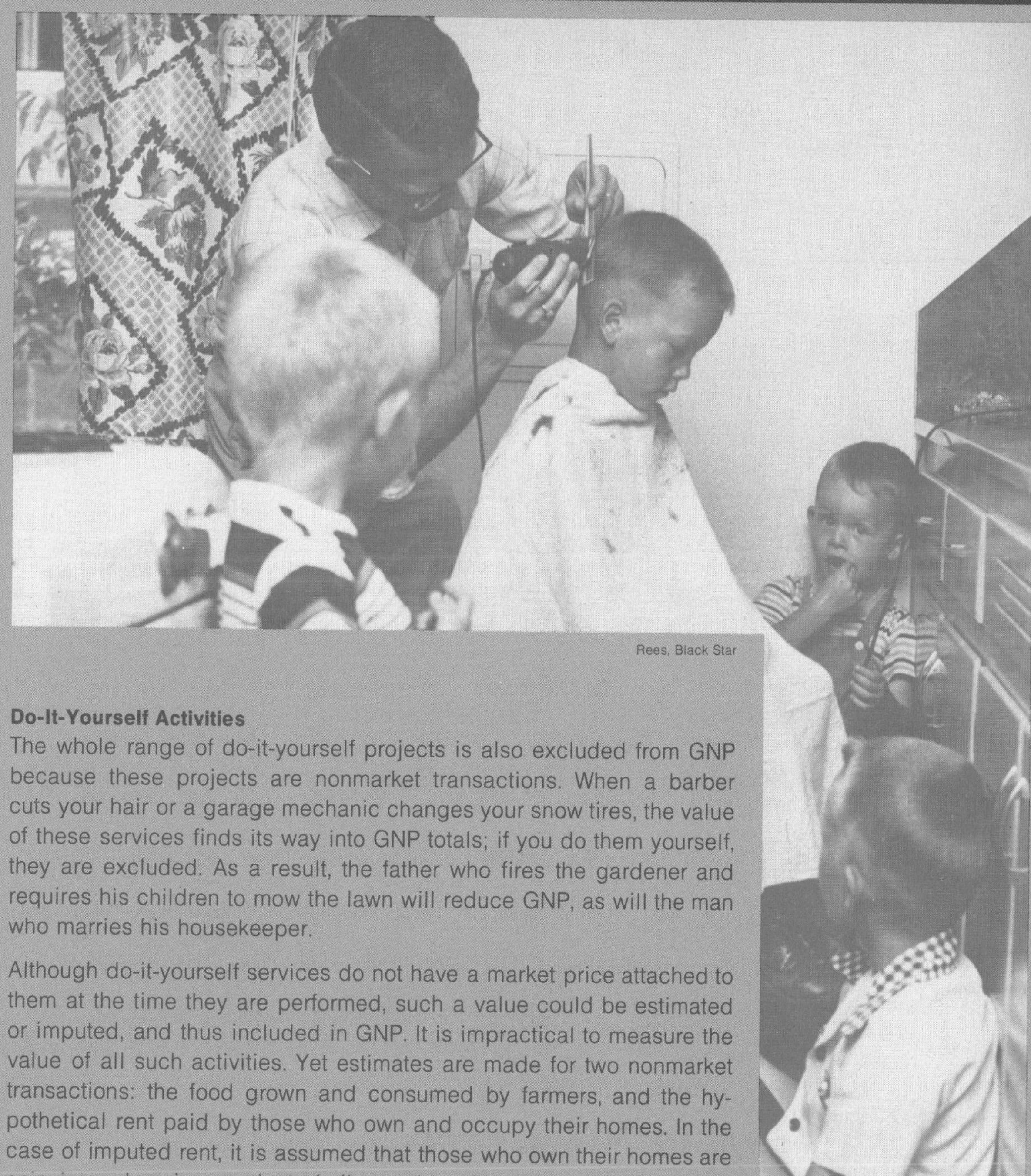

Rees, Black Star

Do-It-Yourself Activities

The whole range of do-it-yourself projects is also excluded from GNP because these projects are nonmarket transactions. When a barber cuts your hair or a garage mechanic changes your snow tires, the value of these services finds its way into GNP totals; if you do them yourself, they are excluded. As a result, the father who fires the gardener and requires his children to mow the lawn will reduce GNP, as will the man who marries his housekeeper.

Although do-it-yourself services do not have a market price attached to them at the time they are performed, such a value could be estimated or imputed, and thus included in GNP. It is impractical to measure the value of all such activities. Yet estimates are made for two nonmarket transactions: the food grown and consumed by farmers, and the hypothetical rent paid by those who own and occupy their homes. In the case of imputed rent, it is assumed that those who own their homes are enjoying a housing product similar to that of renters, even though no dollar rent is reported or paid. Therefore, government statisticians add to GNP an amount equal to the rent that home owners would have received if they had rented their houses out to others.

Securities Trades and Capital Gains

Certain financial transactions are excluded from GNP on the grounds that they do not represent productive activity, but are rather a reshuffling of output counted elsewhere. Among these are securities trades—the buying and selling of stocks and bonds among investors. When Mrs. Dow buys Mr. Jones's 100 shares of Amalgamated String Beans, it is classified as a nonproductive transaction, for nothing new has been added to total output. And the capital gains (if any) from the sale are eliminated from the accounts as well.

United Press International

United Press International

Transfer Payments

Public transfer payments—monies distributed by the government in the form of welfare, social security, and veterans' pensions—are also omitted from GNP. Because a retired person performs no current productive activity in order to receive a monthly social security check, this payment is merely a transfer of funds from the government to a private individual. In contrast, a salary check paid by the government to a postman is compensation made for a productive service—mail delivery—which increases national output.

Secondhand Goods

Secondhand goods are not counted in GNP in the year they are resold. The price you get for your used skis is not included as part of GNP the year you sell them, secondhand, to a friend. This is done to avoid another kind of double counting, for the skis had been counted previously, when first produced, as part of that earlier year's output.

Photo by Ellen Kirouac

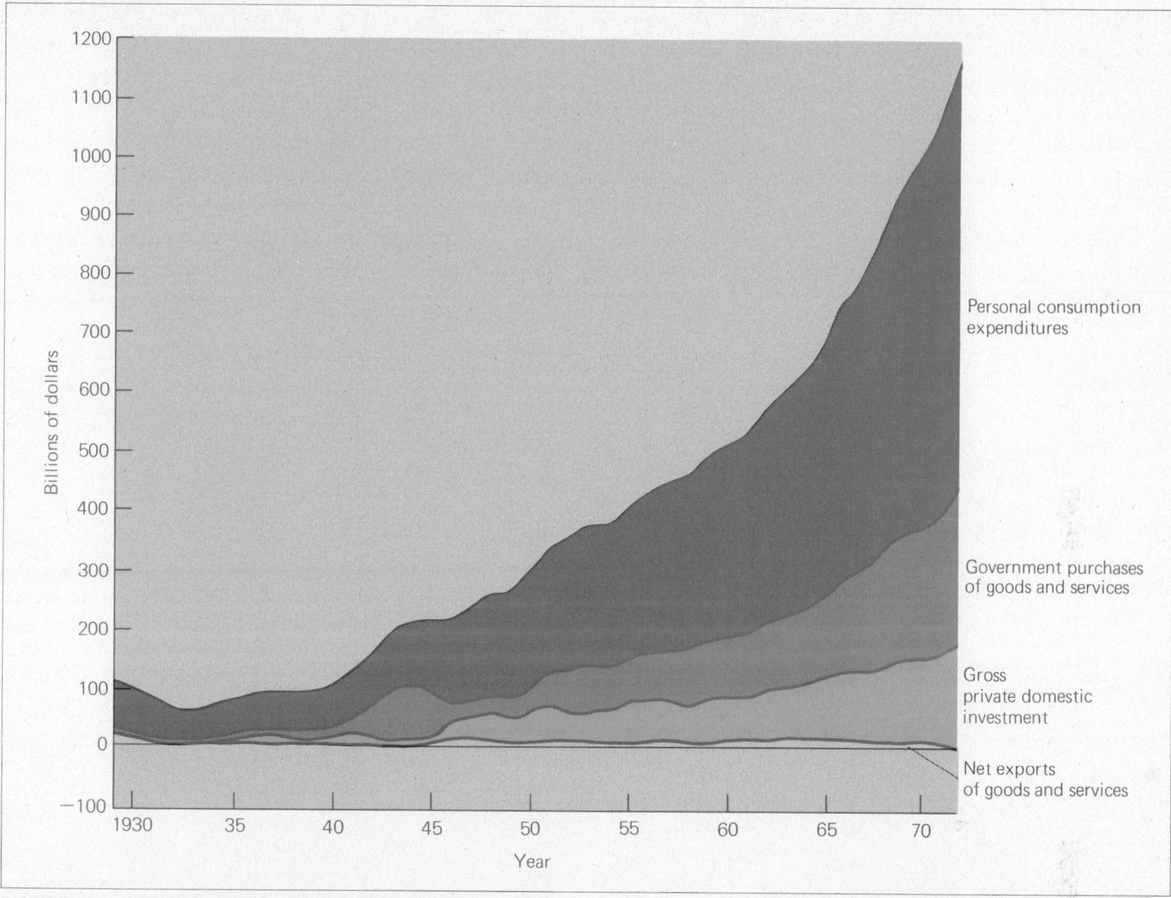

FIGURE 6-3 COMPONENTS OF GNP, 1929–72 Personal consumption expenditures have always been by far the largest component of GNP. Gross private domestic investment expenditures are the most volatile, falling precipitately during business downturns and rising rapidly during periods of prosperity. Government—federal and state and local—has played an increasing role in the U.S. economy since the Great Depression.

SOURCE: *Economic Report of the President,* January 1973.

ponents is shown in Figure 6-3 for the period 1929 to 1972. The major trend since the year 1929 has been a decline in the personal consumption sector as a percent of the total, and an increase in the government sector. This reflects changes in the way our society has decided to use its resources, with relatively more going to public expenditures for both national defense and general well-being. Because of the magnitude of government outlays, policymakers and legislators view such expenditures as a tool to help achieve and/or maintain economic stability. A prospective fall-off in business investment and personal consumption expenditures, for example, with obvious implications for the direction of GNP, might stimulate more government spending as a compensatory measure.

Personal Consumption Expenditures Personal consumption expenditures, the largest segment of GNP, include spending by households on **consumer durable goods** (cars, furniture, appliances), **consumer soft goods** (food, clothing), and **consumer**

services (accountants, dentists, roofers). The performance of the consumer durable sector has been particularly interesting in recent years. As the U.S. economy has become more affluent and more sophisticated, consumer durable spending has increased in comparison with spending on soft goods. This reflects the fact that beyond a certain point spending for food and clothing does not increase proportionately as a family's income rises. Instead, spending for another car, central air conditioning, self-cleaning ovens, or additional TV sets takes a larger percentage of any increase in income.

But the greatest increase in demand is that demonstrated for services. By 1985, the continuing shift to a service-oriented economy is expected to result in a 3:2 ratio of service to manufacturing employees. Since productivity in service industries is

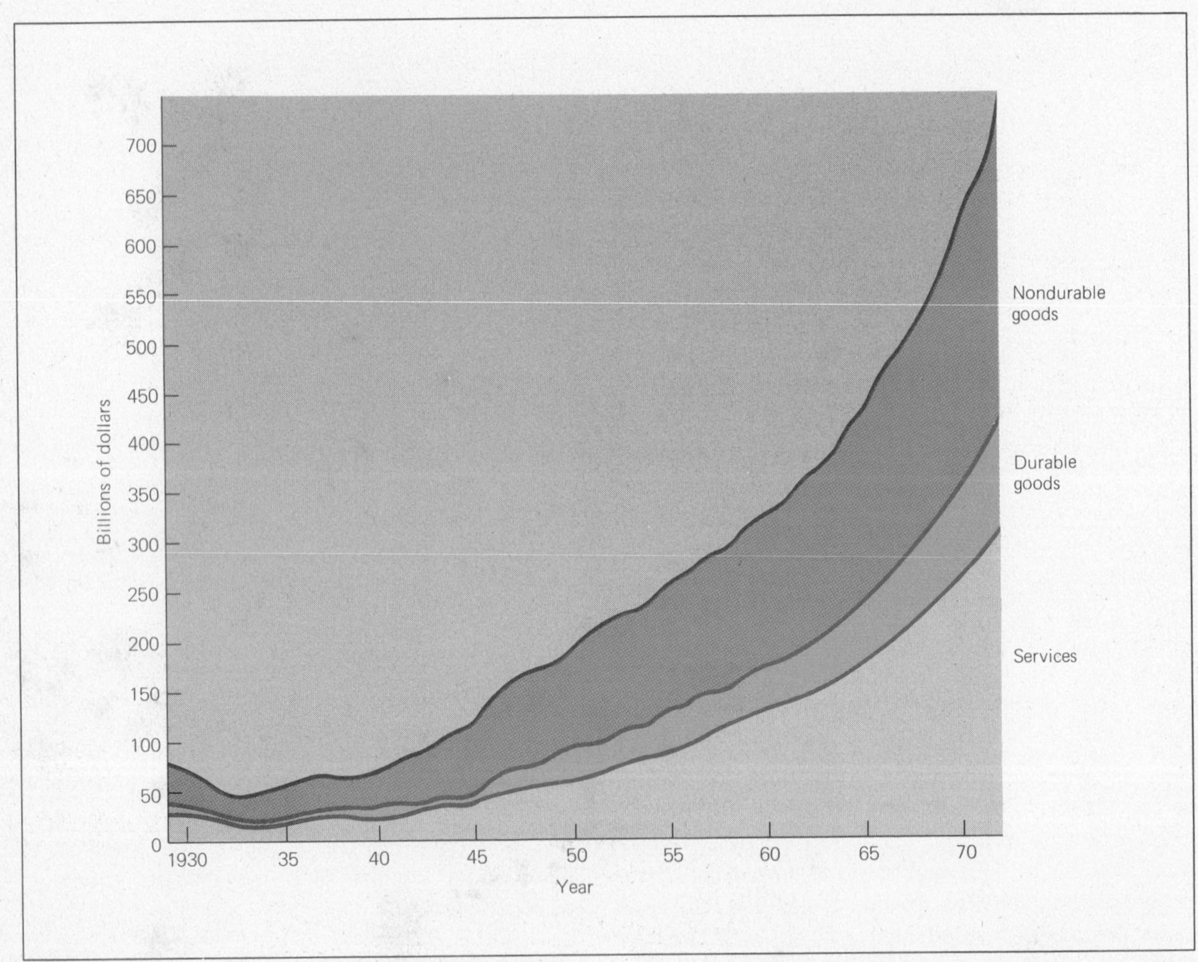

FIGURE 6-4 COMPONENTS OF PERSONAL CONSUMPTION, 1929–72 The three major components of consumption are services, durable goods, and nondurable goods. Services, the largest in magnitude, generally become the most important of the three about 50 years after a nation has attained a stage of mass consumption. Nondurable goods have declined in relative importance over the last 20 years. The consumption of durable goods has more than kept up with the rate of population increase, which means that people are consuming a slowly increasing amount per capita.

SOURCE: *Economic Report of the President*, January 1973.

primarily dependent on people, the chances for expanding productivity, and hence real economic growth, may be minimal while the inflationary potential, in terms of rising prices, is substantial.

Although the overall economic vigor of the last 45 years has resulted in a larger durable goods component today as compared with 1929, this growth has not occurred in a straight line. Durables have proven to be much more vulnerable to economic downturns than soft goods. Households increase their consumption of durables as they earn more money, but when hard times come, as in the Great Depression of the 1930s or during the much milder recession of 1970–71, a family finds it much easier to postpone the purchase of a new car than to cut spending on children's underwear or sandwich bread. As a result, spending for durables tends to be much more volatile than for soft goods. A prime example is the 1932 Depression, when spending on soft goods dropped 13 percent, but spending for durables declined by 48 percent.

Since that time government has been concerned with the development of ways to spur the private consumption sector when the economy shows signs of weakness and problems such as unemployment arise. Subsequent chapters in this book discuss the tools of fiscal policy through which government may stimulate private consumption.

Investment The investment component of GNP consists of spending by private business firms and individuals on output that increases or replaces real productive assets. It does not refer to what is commonly called purely financial "investments" such as stocks and bonds. These are not output, whereas a new house or tractor really is a tangible output.

While expenditures on electric shavers are counted in the consumption component, new factories or stamping machines or riveting guns that will be used to make shavers are included in investment. Only through a net increase in investment expenditures can a nation build up the stock of capital goods required to produce additional goods in the future.

In any year, investment expenditures may both increase and replace the existing stock of capital goods; that is, a certain number of the drill presses produced may increase our total stock, while others will merely replace older drill presses that have worn out.

In adding up the investment component, economists distinguish between the gross investment (the total new capital stock) and the net investment, which subtracts depreciation of old and obsolete equipment from the total investment component.

In our earlier comparison of Gross National Product and net national product, we explained how a capital consumption allowance is subtracted from GNP in order to calculate NNP, which measures output after depreciation. We can now phrase this same idea in a slightly different way:

GNP differs from NNP in that the investment component of GNP is gross investment, while the investment component of NNP is net investment.

Net investment is a key concept because it provides us with a measure of whether an economy is growing. When gross investment exceeds depreciation, net investment is positive and the nation's stock of capital goods expands, giving it additional productive capacity for the future. When depreciation equals gross investment, net investment is zero and productive capacity is unchanged; the economy is static. Finally, in those situations where depreciation exceeds gross investment and net investment is negative, the stock of capital is actually decreasing, and with it the economy's capacity to produce. This upsets the stability of the economy.

COMPONENTS OF INVESTMENT Investment can take various forms. **Business fixed investment** consists of buildings constructed for business purposes (offices, stores, factories) plus the equipment and machinery needed to produce goods. **Residential construction investment** includes one-family and multi-family homes, both those built for renting purposes and those constructed for occupancy by owners. Since rental housing is an income-producing asset, it is counted as an investment. Similarly, since the purchase of such a home represents the con-

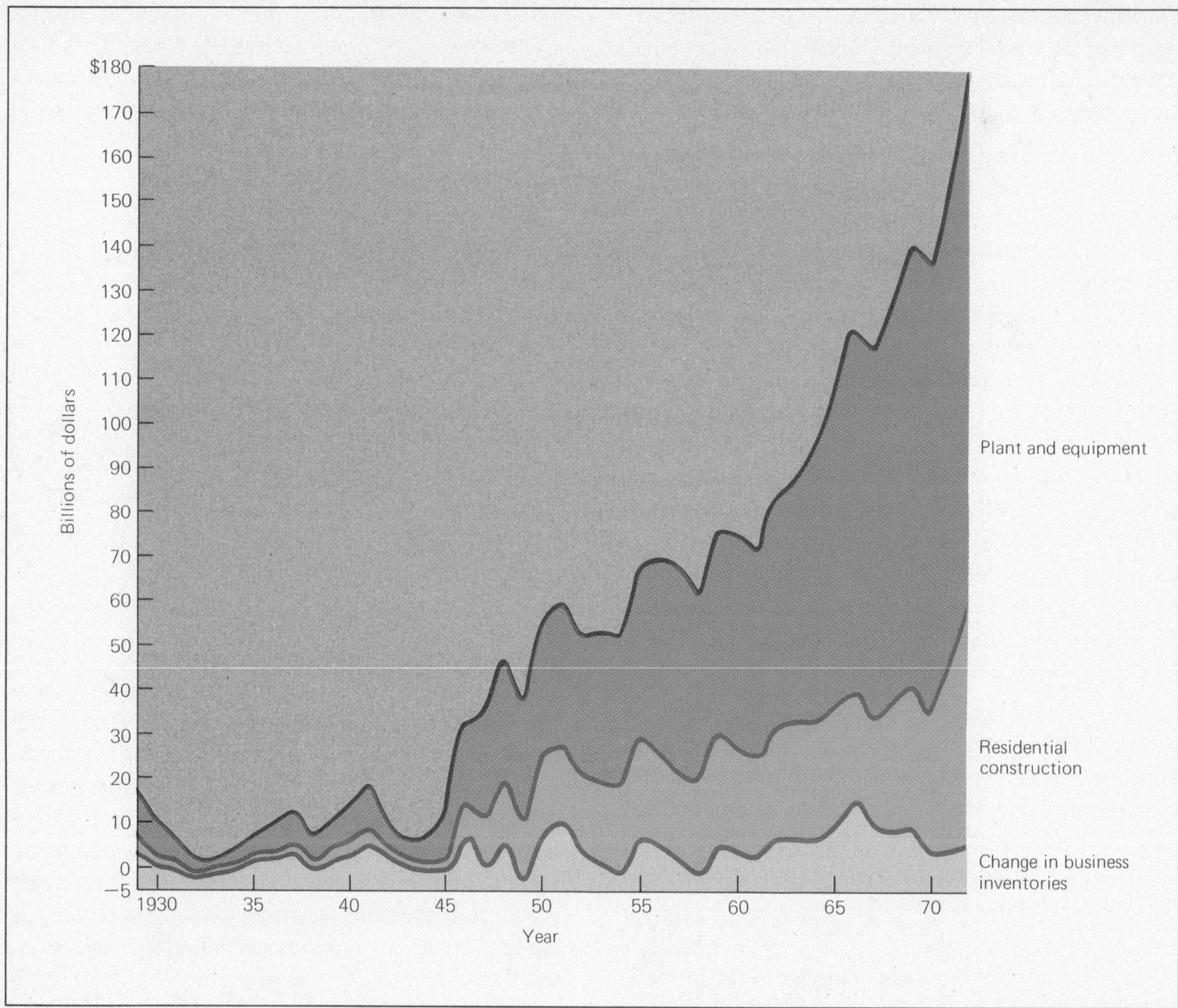

FIGURE 6-5 COMPONENTS OF GROSS PRIVATE DOMESTIC INVESTMENT, 1929–72 The most important part of investment, in terms of size, is plant and equipment. During recessions, this sector often falls precipitately, dragging the entire economy along with it. Changes in business inventories, the other part of business investment, while fluctuating even more than plant and equipment, usually have less of an impact on the economy because of their much smaller size. Finally residential construction, which is considered a part of investment, although done by people who would otherwise be considered consumers, apparently varies more with interest rates than with the business cycle, since a 1 percent rise in the interest rate might mean the difference between affording mortgage payments or not.
SOURCE: *Economic Report of the President*, January 1973.

struction of a major asset that will generate a housing product for the family over many years, the acquisition of owner-occupied, single-family homes is included under residential construction investment even though the value of that product cannot be measured by an actual cash payment.

But the concept of investment is broader than stationary capital such as structures and productive machinery. Goods on hand also will be used to generate sales and income in future periods. Consequently, **inventory accumulation** is another part of the investment segment of GNP. Assume, for example, that U.S. sales of cockroach spray totaled $10 million in a given year, but that inventories in supermarkets, which stood at $1 million at the beginning of the year, increase to $1.5 million at the year's end. Total roachicide production, then, equals the $10 million of sales, plus the $500,000 increase in inventories, or $10.5 million in all. Since this $500,000 increase in inventories cannot be included in the consumption component, it is considered an addition to business investment.

Inventory investment includes not only increased stocks of finished goods on the shelves of retail stores but also any additional supplies of chemicals in the hands of the roach spray manufacturer or of aerosol spray cans in a stockroom of his supplier. In other words, changes in inventory involve finished goods, goods in process, and raw materials.

Changes in inventory may be either planned or unplanned. Often business conditions affect inventory levels in a way different from that the business manager intended. When business is booming, inventories may fall despite the best efforts of the manager to increase stocks, as people buy goods faster than they can be produced. When business grows sluggish, inventories may pile up even though the manager is reducing production.

IMPORTANCE OF THE INVESTMENT COMPONENT The entire investment component of GNP merits emphasis because of its volatility. It reacts much more sharply than either the consumption or the government components to changes in economic conditions or expectations. When sales of blue jeans drop 10 percent, a nervous executive does not merely cut back his blue-jean factory-expansion program 10 percent. Instead, he tears it up completely. For similar reasons, the inventory accumulation phase of a boom can quickly become a period of retrenchment. An optimistic retailer may increase his inventory of jeans during a period of expanding sales; but once sales begin to decline even modestly, he not only eliminates his program of inventory accumulation, but may stop all new purchases until inventories fall to a much lower level.

This volatility has special implications. Any small downturn in economic activity can snowball into a major recession if investment spending drops precipitately. On the other hand, during optimistic periods, inflationary pressure may be compounded because of booming investment spending. In later chapters we analyze the investment component more closely and study some of the means of regulating its volatility.

Government Expenditures Government spending includes all government purchases of goods and services. Services can be those provided by state and local governments (garbage collection, traffic enforcement, education) or those supplied by the federal government (defense, weather forecasting, national park maintenance). Government purchases of goods cover the entire spectrum from space launching pads in Florida to first-grade textbooks in Chicago, from Army jeeps to carbon paper and ball-point pens. As indicated earlier, they do not include transfer payments.

Some economists have questioned the practice of including public investment (buildings, laboratories, computers, and so on) as part of the government component of GNP, believing that such expenditures belong more properly in the investment category. For example, a research facility or a school or a water purification plant built by a branch of the government is a new productive asset in much the same way as a new factory or a private college building or a computer purchased by private industry. Since most foreign national income accounts do include public investment expenditures as part of the investment component, U.S. investment figures are somewhat understated in comparison.

The fastest growing component of GNP has been government spending, which increased from $8.5 billion in 1929, or 8.2 percent of GNP, to $254.6 billion in 1972, or 22.1 percent. Growth of the government component of GNP has occurred on both the federal and the state and local level. From 1929 through World War II, expansion was primarily in federal expenditures, as the federal government mobilized first to meet the problems of the Great Depression, and then to fight the war. During this period, federal spending increased almost fivefold, whereas state and local spending were almost unchanged. After the war, however, local spending on education, road building, and welfare accelerated, growing about as rapidly as the federal component. The most recent figures suggest that state and local spending is now growing even more quickly.

Net Exports The net effect of America's foreign trade—its exports and imports—appears as the export component of GNP. In 1970, $62.9 billion of goods and services were exported, representing actual physical products like wheat and airplanes, and the value of services supplied to foreigners, such as cargo space sold to them for shipping purposes. In that same year, the United States imported $59.3 billion of goods and services from abroad, enabling Americans to enjoy $59.3 billion worth of output (vacations in France, TV sets from Japan, vodka from Russia) that were not produced with American resources.

Subtracting imports from exports provides a net figure which is called the net export component of GNP.

In 1970, net exports amounted to +$3.6 billion. Since exports exceeded imports in 1970, the net export component showed a positive balance, as has been the situation for the United States during most of the twentieth century. Since 1971, however, the United States has been importing more from abroad than it has been exporting; net exports for 1972 showed a minus or deficit balance of about $6.3 billion, and this component is therefore subtracted from the other GNP components in arriving at the final GNP figure. The importance of this change for many facets of our domestic and international economic policies is discussed later in this book.

Although the development of a net export deficit has disturbed those Americans directly concerned with foreign transactions, the overall involvement of the American economy in foreign trade has always been relatively small. In 1969, for example, U.S. exports amounted to less than 6 percent of total GNP, whereas in Great Britain, exports comprised 22 percent of GNP, in Japan 11 percent, and in Bolivia 19 percent.

GROSS NATIONAL INCOME: THE INCOME SIDE

Gross National Product—the value of the goods and services produced—is one way of measuring economic activity. Another approach to calculating this value is to total the incomes generated by the production of these goods and services. For example, we can discuss General Motors' contribution to GNP by saying that it turns out $30 billion worth of cars each year. But we can also say that the production of this $30 billion worth of cars represents nearly $30 billion worth of payments by General Motors for the use of productive resources. These payments are received as income—in the form of wages, profits, interests, and rents. To balance the ledger, GM adds certain nonincome business costs—indirect taxes and depreciation. Applying the circular flow analogy, overall national economic activity can be discussed either in terms of expenditures or in terms of incomes, understanding that, by definition, total output, or Gross National Product, must equal total incomes and costs, or Gross National Income (GNI).

Gross National Income, then, is a measure of how much is earned due to the productive process, with certain nonincome items added to balance the national accounts.

The Components of GNI

By analyzing GNI in terms of its components, we can see how national income is divided among the various groups in our society at the present time and observe changes in relative shares that have taken place over the years. For example, in the 21 years between 1950 and 1971, wages and salaries increased their share of GNI by an amount approximately equal to the decline exhibited by the corporate profit component.

National Income As we have indicated earlier, GNI consists of two kinds of items: income components and nonincome, or business cost, components. Both categories represent costs of production to the business firm. The income components—those amounts that are received by the nation's households and businesses as income—together comprise aggregate national income (NI). These components measure the actual contribution of the factors of production: labor, land, capital, and entrepreneurial talent. Labor receives compensation, land provides rent, capital earns interest, and entrepreneurial talent is rewarded by profits.

NI = the sum of all income components (compensation + rent + interest + proprietors' income + profits)

Or, to phrase it differently,

NI = GNI less nonincome components (capital consumption allowance + indirect business taxes)

National income is by far the larger part of GNI and attracts the attention of those analyzing the changes in income and the future course of the economy.

COMPENSATION In 1972, Americans received $705.3 billion in wages and salaries, part of which was in the form of various fringe benefits such as health and welfare insurance. Compensation is the largest single source of income for American households, and since 1929 it has been gradually increasing as a percentage of GNI from 59 to 75 percent in 1972. This increase may be partially an action of accounting. Proprietors' income includes an implicit salary; when a proprietor's firm is acquired by a larger company, this salary shows up as compensation rather than profit.

RENT Rents paid to those who lease out their land or facilities or equipment to those who produce goods and services comprise a second income component. Total rent amounted to $25.6 billion in 1972; it is currently the smallest of all the income categories.

INTEREST At some time, most businesses find it necessary to borrow, either from the banks or from other businesses or individuals, in the form of long-term bonds. The interest paid to these lenders is a third income component of GNI. Total interest has been growing rapidly since the post–World War II business expansion created the need for huge amounts of credit. Interest income increased eightfold from 1950 to 1972, from $5.5 billion to $41.3 billion. Interest, formerly the smallest of the income components, now surpasses rent by a comfortable margin.

PROPRIETORS' INCOME For purposes of national income accounting, government statisticians group together profits earned by unincorporated businesses, usually the smaller, owner-operated business enterprises, plus the professional practices of doctors, accountants, lawyers, and so forth. As American business has become more complex in recent years, the corporate form of organization has come to dominate the business scene. In contrast, the role of small business has been declining, as has the proprietors' share of income. For example, in 1950, corporate and proprietors' income were about equal ($37.7 billion and $37.5 billion, respectively). By 1972, however, corporate profits had grown to $93.3 billion while proprietors' income had increased to only $75.2 billion.

CORPORATE PROFITS Unlike proprietors' income, which is generally distributed in full to the owners of unincorporated businesses, corporate profits play several roles in addition to that of income to the owners. The federal government levies a special tax on the profits of corporations, and this part of profits (about 45 percent) flows immediately to the government as **corporate income tax.** In addition, the typical corporation, and especially the growing company, will retain a sizable amount of its earnings, to be used for expansion and other corporate activities. These **undistributed profits** amounted to about 27 percent of all corporate profits in 1972. The balance of corporate profits is distributed to shareholders as **dividends**; dividends are the only part of corporate profits that is actually received as income by households.

Nonincome Components of GNI Although the nonincome components of GNI are not received by households as income, they do represent costs of production to business firms and are therefore reflected in the selling price of goods and services. Thus, if GNI is equal to GNP, we must add these costs to national income to get GNI.

INDIRECT BUSINESS TAXES A customer who buys a lipstick in Phoenix, Arizona, may pay the salesclerk $2.03. Of this amount, however, only $2.00 is allocated as wages, profits, rent, and interest to those who actually produced the lipstick. The remaining 3 cents represents a state sales tax; it is handed over to the state government despite the fact that the state was not directly involved in the productive process. Local sales taxes are one of the largest of the indirect business taxes; others include excise taxes on fuel or diesel oil, business property taxes, and license fees. These taxes, although included in the prices received for goods and services, are differentiated from the income earned by the factors of production. In 1972, these taxes reached $113.5 billion.

CAPITAL CONSUMPTION ALLOWANCES Another nonincome item that every business executive must consider in pricing his merchandise—even though it does not require any immediate outlay of cash and produces no immediate income for anyone—is depreciation. Depreciation is the annual "wearing out" or "using up" of the equipment employed in the productive process.

Depreciation is often described as a "bookkeeping entry," a cost of doing business that is noted in the bookkeeping records of a company, but that, unlike wages or rent, requires no current cash outlay. This is a reflection of the fact that most of the equipment used in production (such as an electric type-

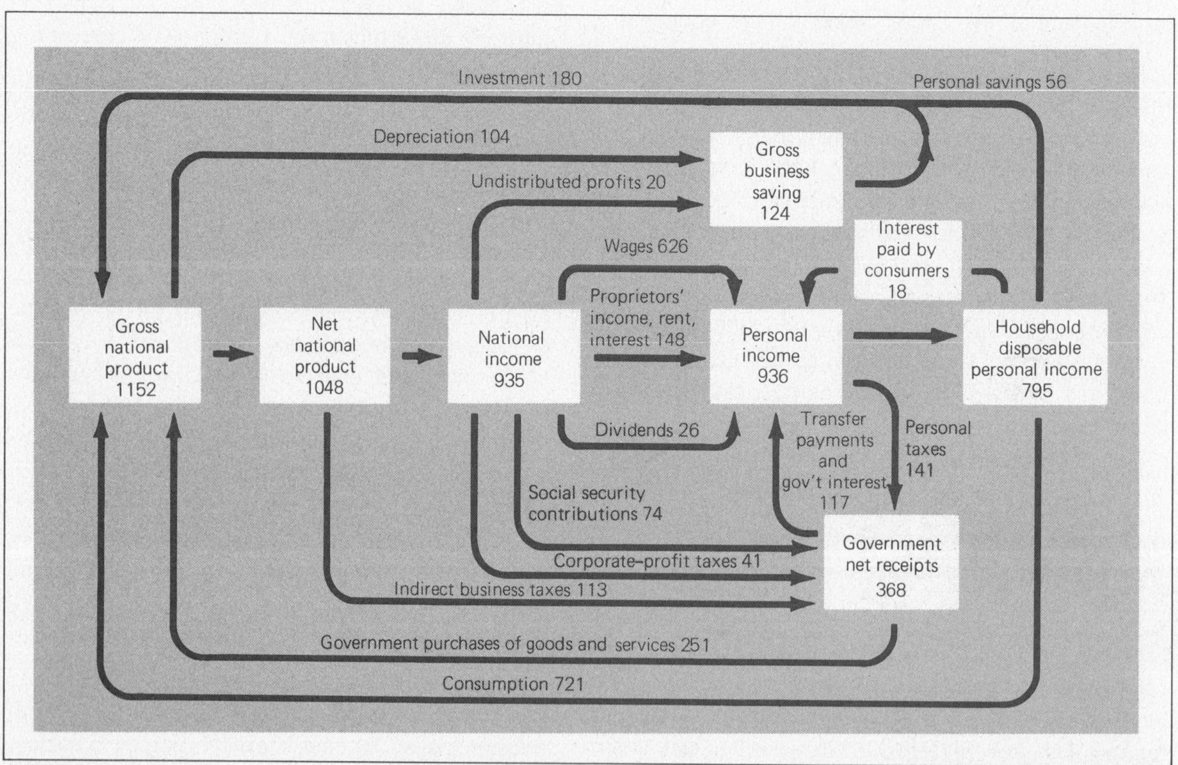

FIGURE 6-6 NATIONAL ACCOUNTS AND THE CIRCULAR FLOW The circular flow provides a means of showing the relationship of the different elements of the national accounts. Money is injected and withdrawn from different accounts, as it circulates from businesses to households and governments.

SOURCE: *Economic Report of the President*, January 1973, and U.S. Department of Commerce, *Survey of Current Business*, April 1973.

writer, an electrocardiograph machine, a fork lift) lasts for a number of years. Thus, when a gasoline station owner buys a $5000 tow truck with an estimated life of five years, presumably he will not have to buy a new truck to replace it for the next five years. Nevertheless, it would be inaccurate for the station's owner to deduct the *entire* $5000 cost of the truck from his profits in that first year when he actually bought the truck. A more realistic approach is to assume that the truck is wearing out gradually and to deduct from profits a part of the cost in each of the five years. The general policy is to allocate the cost of the truck somewhat equally over its estimated life and to include this depreciation charge each year as a cost of production. Consequently, the prices charged by the station owner will cover not only the cash payments made each year as wages to his employees or profits to himself, but also this nonincome depreciation charge. Depreciation, then, must be included as one of the components of GNI. In national income accounts, the annual depreciation charges for all businesses are called the **capital consumption allowance.**

Personal Income

When nonincome components are removed from GNI, the resulting figure is national income, which measures the income earned by families or households. NI is not the same as income **received**, however. We have noted that only one part of corporate profits, dividends, is actually received as current income by the owners of the corporation. In addition, a portion of the compensation—wage earners' contributions for Social Security—does not flow directly, as current income, to households. On the other hand, transfer payments, such as welfare or social security benefits, which are omitted from GNI because they are not currently **earned**, are currently **received**, and serve as income to those who receive them. **Personal income** (PI) measures the dollars actually received by households. PI starts with the NI total, but subtracts profits retained by corporations, corporate taxes, individuals' social security contributions, and adds transfer payments.

PI = NI minus **corporate taxes, retained earnings, social security contributions plus transfer payments and interest paid by government and consumers**

Disposable Income

Personal income measures income **received** by households. But if we are to measure the income actually available for consumption or saving, it is necessary to subtract the personal taxes on income, inheritance, and personal property paid to the government by households. Further, personal income figures alone can often be deceptive. For example, rising PI figures would normally suggest an increasing volume of sales, but if such figures are accompanied by higher personal taxes, the net effect might well be an unchanged, or an even smaller number of dollars in the pockets of potential customers. So the formula

DI = PI **minus personal taxes**

indicates **disposable income,** which is a better guide to business planners setting sales quotas or production schedules.

Government planners are equally concerned with the central role of DI. When faced with a recession and the possibility of a decline in PI, policy-makers may cut taxes to maintain DI and thus keep economic activity from plunging into further decline. This was the situation in 1971, when a personal income-tax cut was one of the tools used by the Nixon administration to increase DI in the face of growing unemployment. The same kind of logic works when applied to an economy beset by inflationary pressures. In 1968, confronted by a booming economy and rising prices, the administration advocated a tax increase to limit the growth of DI. The tax rise was enacted, and as a result, 1968 DI increased by only $45 billion, while PI showed an advance of $59 billion.

Households can do two things with their disposable income: They can spend it, or they can save it. Over the years, American households have tended to save between 5 and 7 percent of their disposable income

In 1970 the United Auto Workers struck General Motors' plants from coast to coast. The walkout, which began September 15 and ended November 20, contributed to a drop of over $1 billion in GM's net working capital for 1970 and a drop in net sales of $5.5 billion, but General Motors was not the only one to be affected.

The auto industry is a bulwark of the U.S. economy. Nearly a million people are employed in manufacturing automobiles and auto parts. In 1972 alone, $13 billion in automotive parts were supplied by the chemical, plastics, metal, glass, and other allied industries. Roughly 4 percent of total GNP is contributed by auto manufacture, sales, and servicing. General Motors accounts for about half of this, and its strike reverberated throughout the economy.

In Michigan 180,000 strikers were idled, dropping their incomes by at least two-thirds and the state's taxes by $5 million a week. During October, personal income in that state declined 5.8 percent from the October of the previous year. Some Detroit banks began redeeming food stamps for money. Estimates of the daily cost included $4 million in lost wages, $90 million in lost sales, $40 million in payment to suppliers, and $20 million in taxes excluding income taxes.

GM suppliers also were hit. On the average day in 1970 GM used 600 tons of zinc, 685 tons of aluminum, 340 tons of copper, and 175 tons of lead. About 10 percent of the steel output in the United States at that time was absorbed by GM. Although it is difficult to calculate the exact effects on allied industries directly attributable to the strike, steel production fell off 4.7 percent and shipments by 20 percent between the time the strike began and early November. Weekly losses to steel producers finally ran at an estimated $67 million.

Such effects diminish GNP. But estimating the exact extent is complicated by the other factors in the economy whose independent opera-

tion may mask or intensify strike effects. Solomon Fabricant of the National Bureau of Economic Research viewed the strike as prolonging a contraction already in progress but hesitated to go beyond that observation.*

One way of getting at the interactions of the economy that result in a final figure for aggregate economic activity is to use an econometric model. Such models can simulate the operation of the economy under varying conditions and predict levels of GNP. Early in the strike the University of Pennsylvania Wharton School model was used to simulate the impact of different durations of the strike.

A six-week strike eliminated any fourth-quarter gain in GNP; a 10-week strike caused a decline; and a 14-week strike put the economy back at the level of the second quarter of 1970.† In actuality GNP in the final quarter of 1970 was up only $3.4 billion from the third quarter, in contrast to a jump of $8.2 billion in that quarter of 1969 and $15 billion in 1968. Only the foolhardy can say that this entire amount reflected the effects of the GM strike; we can simply say that when the auto industry catches cold, GNP sneezes.

* "Recent Economic Changes and the Agenda of Business Cycle Research," *National Bureau Report Supplement 8* (New York: National Bureau of Economic Research, May 1971), p. 11.
† "Auto Strikers Take the GNP for a Ride," *Business Week*, October 3, 1970, p. 18.

in peacetime. In times of special emergency, however, unusual saving and consumption patterns have emerged. In 1932 and 1933, Americans borrowed or withdrew from their savings accounts more than the amount of net savings. Consequently, there was a net dissaving, or to put it another way, the saving rate was negative (1932, minus 1.3 percent; 1933, minus 2.0 percent). During World War II, when Americans were faced with shortages of consumer goods, rationing, and patriotic appeals to save, the saving rate reached as high as 25 percent. Variations in the rate of saving can have major implications for economic policy: for example, attempts to forestall an impending downturn by increasing disposable income may be thwarted if citizens tuck the extra income away in savings banks. Even minor changes in the saving rate can be important. In the U.S. economy, a 1 percent increase in the saving rate means a transfer of between $8 billion and $9 billion from consumption to saving.

TABLE 6-2 Components of GNP and GNI and How They Relate, 1972 (Billions of dollars)

Gross National Product (GNP)	1152.1
Capital consumption allowance	−103.7
Net national product (NNP)	1048.4
Indirect business taxes	−113.5
National income (NI)	934.9
Social security contributions	−73.9
Corporate income taxes	−41.3
Undistributed corporate profits	−19.5
Interest paid by government and consumers	+36.5
Transfer payments	+99.1
Personal income (PI)	935.8
Personal taxes	−140.7
Disposable income (DI)	795.1
Personal consumption (C)	−721.1
Interest paid by consumers	−18.2
Personal saving	55.8

The major economic accounts include GNP and GNI, from which can be derived NNP, or the value of output adjusted for the consumption of capital goods; NI, or the value of all income; PI, or the value of payments received by households; and DI, or the amount of PI available for consumption and saving.

SOURCE: *Economic Report of the President*, January 1973, and U.S. Department of Commerce, *Survey of Current Business*, April 1973.

COMPARING THE WELFARE OF NATIONS

National income accounts have long been considered one of the most useful tools for comparing national economic achievement. The tendency is to assume that a nation with a high GNP, and especially one with a high per capita GNP, is more "advanced" and that its citizens are enjoying a higher standard of living. Generally, a high GNP is taken to indicate that a society is prosperous; low figures are assumed to indicate underdevelopment. In particular, a high rate of GNP growth is considered a good measure of successful economic performance. Such assumptions often figure in attempts to demonstrate the superiority of the U.S. economy over socialist or communist states and in American efforts to aid developing nations. But GNP figures do not tell the whole story.

Cultural Differences

Despite the wide acceptance that comparative GNP figures have received, economists have long recognized that cultural differences between nations may make such comparisons less than accurate. The goods and services counted in U.S. GNP are culturally determined. In other cultures these same goods and services may be provided outside the normal "productive" channels and may therefore never appear in GNP figures. In India, for example, the extended family provides the security that Americans obtain through insurance, day-care centers, and old-age homes. In many cases, the Indians are enjoying services equivalent to those purchased by Americans, but these services will never show up in India's GNP.

To some extent, this kind of cultural undercounting also persists in the United States. The traditional American way of life prescribes that the wife engage primarily in home and community activities; in doing so, she is providing goods and services that are not included in GNP. A recent estimate of the value of such "unpaid output" for the average American family was approximately $4000 annually, consisting primarily of housework, but also including volunteer work, educational services, and other productive services.

The Uses of Leisure Time GNP counts activities in which money changes hands. Increases in leisure time reduce GNP but have a positive effect on the quality of life. Some societies may build leisure into work by choosing to talk or rest between productive efforts, even if this means turning out goods at a slower pace. In Mediterranean countries, for example, the midday siesta incorporates large slices of leisure time into the official workday. And in many less industrialized societies, people devote free time or holidays to family or community activities, which are performed in a nonmarket setting and do not contribute to GNP.

In America, leisure is an industry that counts toward GNP. The American work week has dropped from 51 hours a week in 1909 to 40 and even 35 hours in many industries today. But American leisure-time activities tend to be production-oriented in much the same way as our work: To enjoy their free time, Americans hire and train and equip professional athletes, buy sailboats or outboard motors, send their children to camp, or travel halfway across the country to take ski vacations. As a result, even though free time has increased substantially in the United States during the twentieth century because of the shorter work week and longer vacations, the growth of leisure has not had an entirely negative effect on GNP. Estimates of spending on spare-time activities run as high as $100 billion a year.

Negative Output: The Costs of GNP

Earlier in this chapter, we introduced the concept of net national product, explaining that a more accurate way of counting national output was to subtract from the gross figure an amount—the capital consumption allowance—which represented the "wearing out" or depreciation of the capital goods used in the productive process. Kenneth Boulding, a former president of the American Economic Association, sees virtually all economic activity as "depreciation."

> We have breakfast, and breakfast depreciates; so we must have lunch.... Consumption is decay—your automobile is wearing out, your clothes becoming threadbare.... Consumption is a bad, not a good thing; production is what we must undergo because of consumption.[3]

This extreme—and playful—view of GNP does question whether the accounts include outputs which are really costs. Some social scientists believe that we should develop ways of showing other costs involved in producing GNP. For example, as GNP is determined today, no provision is made for any damage to the environment created as a by-product of the manufacturing process: GNP includes the value of the copper produced by a smelting mill, but it does not allow for the costs involved in cleaning up the rivers or the air polluted by the smelter. Once we begin to consider the social and environmental costs of production that are not reflected in GNP today, it becomes increasingly clear that a high GNP may not necessarily be a sign of the best society.

Social inequities and the costs of undoing the damage caused by them may also inflate GNP in certain ways, although these inequities do adversely affect productivity and have hidden effects retarding GNP. What appears on the account, however, is not the lost output but expenditures on social workers, compensatory education, and drug prevention programs in our inner cities. These add to GNP, but might not a society without the problems and the GNP created to solve them be superior? Similar questions are now being raised in other nations too. The USSR, for example, in an attempt to encourage consumer-goods production during the 1960s, increased its vodka output sharply. This soon was followed by an increase in expenditures for medical treatment for alcoholism. In the Union of South Africa, public policy requires the building and maintenance of separate facilities for black and white citizens; this practice inflates GNP, but such an increase in GNP hardly reflects an improvement in the well-being of the society or its citizens.

3 "Fun and Games with the Gross National Product—The Role of Misleading Indicators in Social Policy," in *The Environmental Crisis: Man's Struggle to Live with Himself*, ed. Harold W. Helfrich, Jr. (New Haven: Yale University Press, 1970), pp. 161–162.

OTHER INDICES OF NATIONAL WELL-BEING

If national output data are not the most accurate measurement of national welfare and a $1.5 trillion GNP signifies neither general happiness nor effective use of resources, what are the alternatives? Is there a better system for measuring economic performance? One concept that builds upon GNP is that of Net Economic Welfare.[4] NEW, as it is called, focuses on consumption rather than production as the best measure of economic welfare.

> Conceptually it is a comprehensive measure of the annual real consumption of households. Consumption is intended to include all goods and services, marketed or not, valued at market prices or at their equivalent opportunity costs to consumers. Collective public consumption is to be included whether provided by government or otherwise; and allowance is to be made for negative externalities such as those due to environmental damage and to the disamenities and congestion of urbanization and industrialization.[5]

NEW calculations remove capital consumption expenditures and defense spending at the outset and then impute values for leisure, for nonmarket activities such as housewives' services, for services of public and private capital, and for the negative of disamenities such as the deterioration of "environmental capital." Tobin and Nordhaus find that NEW is growing slower than GNP. The quality of life is not progressing as fast as the quantity of goods and services. Chapter 21 considers how to trade some GNP for more NEW.

Such attempts to modify GNP have met with criticism from Arthur M. Okun, a former chairman of the President's Council of Economic Advisers, who warns against trying to convert GNP into a purported measure of social welfare because "producing a summary measure of social welfare is a job for a philosopher king."[6] He argues that many social goods are difficult to price and that while dollar income is a major yardstick by which to measure family welfare, this does not stop us from recognizing the importance of nonmaterial factors such as health, personal relations, and environmental pressures which, of course, affect our social welfare. By promising to do more than GNP realistically can accomplish, a reformulation of our national accounts might in fact "impede urgently needed progress toward better measurement and evaluation" of desirable changes in our social and physical environment, contends Okun.

Various other indices have been introduced as possible vehicles for measuring the satisfaction, rather than merely the quantity of goods, produced by a nation. Through periodic surveys, the National Industrial Conference Board tries to monitor how our citizens evaluate the economy. People are asked if they think business conditions are good or if jobs are hard to find. The University of Michigan Survey Research Center conducts research projects in which households are asked to estimate their intentions to buy such things as cars, appliances, or vacations, as an indication of their confidence in U.S. economic performance.

Comparisons of other kinds of statistics—life expectancy or infant mortality rates—could provide a different indication of well-being in various societies. Life expectancy in the United States for those born in 1920 was 54.1 years, while for those born in 1970, it was 70.8 years. These numbers suggest a definite advance in this regard during the intervening 50 years. On the other hand, a comparison of these same statistics with those of other nations raises provocative questions about the actual significance of our burgeoning GNP figures in ensuring proper health care.

Even among those who would prefer to limit their discussion of economic progress to the more conventional economic statistics, GNP is only one of many indicators used to assess economic conditions. Four important indicators are levels of employment and prices, rate of growth, and balance of trade. Government officials are often more concerned with the level of employment and the degree of price stability than with the size of GNP. Consequently, the

4 William Nordhaus and James Tobin, "Is Growth Obsolete?" in *Economic Growth, Fiftieth Anniversary Colloquium V* (New York: National Bureau of Economic Research, Columbia University Press, 1972). Tobin and Nordhaus use the term *Measure of Economic Welfare* or MEW in their monograph. Paul Samuelson amends this to NEW in his latest edition (9th) of *Economics* (New York: McGraw-Hill, 1973).

5 Nordhaus and Tobin, p. 24.

6 Arthur M. Okun, "Should GNP Measure Social Welfare?" *Brookings Bulletin* 8 (Summer 1971): 4–7.

unemployment and inflation rates are often headlined as the most relevant of the indices of well-being. Our intention in later chapters in this part is not merely to explain and describe the various national income accounts, but to show the relationship between employment and inflation and these accounts—to explain how the interaction of consumption spending, investment, and government spending results in economic activities that employ people and create forces that drive prices up or down.

SUMMARY

1 National economic activity can be described as a circular flow of goods and services and of income measured in dollars during a given period. It can be calculated by focusing on the expenditures side or on the income side. The expenditures approach to measuring national economic activity adds up the sums that are spent on designated goods and services by households, businesses, government, and foreign parties. This total forms Gross National Product. The income approach totals the incomes generated by production in the form of compensation, profits (including proprietors' income), interest, and rent, plus certain nonincome items to balance the account with the GNP total. This is known as Gross National Income.

2 The calculation of national output poses a problem: finding a way of equating all the different types of goods and services. The solution is to use the dollar as the standard unit; multiplying the quantity sold by the price produces the current dollar value of any item. Gross National Product estimates the current dollar level of the goods and services produced in a nation during a year.

3 In order to avoid double counting, all intermediate output is excluded, and only final goods are counted. Another way of solving this problem is by using the value-added approach, in which only the value added at each step of production and distribution is counted.

4 When comparing several years, several complications occur if GNP is expressed in current dollars. Since the price levels change, a better measure is constant dollars, using a base year and correcting for price changes. This provides a measure of what is called real GNP. Changes in quality and composition of the market basket also create difficulties.

5 GNP has four components: personal consumption (C), investment (I), government expenditures (G), and net exports (X). The consumption component, which is the largest segment of GNP, includes spending by households on consumer durable goods, consumer soft goods, and consumer services. The investment component consists of spending by private business firms and individuals on output that increases or replaces real productive assets, such as plant and equipment, residences, and inventories. Government spending excludes all transfer payments, since these do not represent real output. The export component reflects the net effect of America's foreign trade—its exports and imports. Subtracting imports from exports provides this net figure.

6 The sum that represents the wearing out of equipment used to manufacture other goods is known as depreciation, or the capital consumption allowance. Subtracting this sum from GNP gives net national product.

7 Subtracting indirect business taxes from NNP gives national income. This is the sum of compensation, proprietors' income, profits, interest, and rent. To examine what households receive, personal income is used. This equals national income plus transfer payments that add to the money a household receives but minus corporate taxes, retained earnings, and social security contributions—all of which are not income to households. The income actually available for consumption and spending, known as disposable income, may be calculated by subtracting personal taxes from PI.

8 National accounts are limited in their ability to measure national well-being. Some economists have suggested an indicator called Net Economic Welfare, which includes leisure and the value of nonmarket goods and services and those from the environment, but excludes disamenities.

SUGGESTED READINGS

Economic Report of the President. Washington, D.C.: Government Printing Office, annual. Provides summaries, predictions, and analysis of economic trends and policies for the preceding and upcoming fiscal years.

Rosen, Sam. *National Income.* New York: Holt, Rinehart and Winston, 1963.

Ruggles, Richard, and **Nancy D. Ruggles.** *National Income Accounts and Income Analysis.* 2nd ed. New York: McGraw-Hill, 1956.

Schultze, Charles L. *National Income Analysis.* 3rd ed. Englewood Cliffs, N.J.: Prentice-Hall, 1971.

Shapiro, Edward. *Macroeconomic Analysis.* 2nd ed. New York: Harcourt Brace Jovanovich, 1970.

Tobin, James, and **William Nordhaus.** "Is Growth Obsolete?" In *Economic Growth: Fiftieth Anniversary Colloquium V.* New York: National Bureau of Economic Research, Columbia University Press, 1972.

U.S. Department of Commerce. *Survey of Current Business.* July issue each year updates national accounts.

QUESTIONS

1 "It was ... the Physiocrats or 'Economists' who made the great breach, through which lay all further progress in the field of analysis, by the discovery and intellectual formulation of the circular flow of economic life."* How does this concept of the circular flow idea clarify national income accounting?

2 Although the "deflated dollar" is used as a standard unit for measuring and comparing GNP figures over time, the market basket affects its reliability. Explain.

3 Classify the following expenditures in the appropriate component of GNP:

a visit to your guru
construction of a new GM plant
launching of Apollo XVII

* Joseph A. Schumpeter, *Economic Doctrine and Method,* translated by J. C. Mohr (New York: Oxford University Press, 1967), p. 43.

President Nixon's trip to Peking
a new hat for Mrs. Nixon
a trip to Paris on Air France
a trip home on Pan American

4 What adjustments must be made in Gross National Income in order to derive a figure for net national product? A figure for national income?

5 From the information given below, compute the following: GNI, NI, PI, NNP, GNP.

personal taxes	$120	proprietors' income	$70
corporate taxes	35	corporate profit	80
retained earnings	20	capital consumption allowance	10
social security contributions	5	indirect business taxes	40
transfer payments	5		
compensation	650		
rent	25		
interest	35		

6 You sell $1000 worth of ambergris to the Comely Cosmetic Company, which uses it to produce and sell $5000 worth of Man-Trap perfume. Using the expenditures approach, calculate the increase in national income. Your value added to the ambergris is $1000. What is Comely's value-added figure? Explain how value added is used in national accounting.

7 If, because of environmental or climatic considerations, you supposed that capital equipment was much less durable in Korea than in Argentina, would you rely on GNP figures alone to compare the performance of these two economies? What other aggregate economic indicators might be more appropriate in this situation? Why?

8 There are pitfalls in relying on GNP figures alone to measure the "worth" of a society. What social and economic "costs" are never counted in GNP? What alternative indicators might be used?

9 Under what circumstances would the activities listed below be excluded from GNP? Under what circumstances would they be included?

housework
sale of an automobile
a government disbursement
betting on horse races

10 "The danger of measures is that they become ideals."† Discuss the pitfalls of relying on growth of GNP as the sole indicator of national economic progress.

†Kenneth E. Boulding, "Fun and Games with the Gross National Product—The Role of Misleading Indicators in Social Policy," in *The Environmental Crisis*, ed. Harold W. Helfrich, Jr. (New Haven: Yale University Press, 1970), p. 158.

CHAPTER 7
INSTABILITY

In an attempt to identify the major issues that would confront the United States during the next few years, the *New York Times* recently asked a group of American business leaders what they thought was the most important problem facing the country. A large number mentioned unemployment and inflation. These conditions are not only painful and undesirable in themselves, but also create many other problems. Unemployment imposes the hardships of reduced income and self-esteem, striking hardest at minorities and the poor. Inflation, defined as a general price-level increase, erodes the value of the dollar and thus penalizes the consumer and exacerbates the financial problems of the aged and the poor.

The problems of unemployment and inflation are not easy to alleviate, for a troublesome interrelation exists between the two. When measures are adopted to promote high employment, the by-product is often inflation; when primary efforts are directed at ensuring price stability, the result may be increasing unemployment. As one economist phrased it, "We know how to maintain a full-employment economy; we do not know how to do this without a significant amount of inflation. We can eliminate inflation, but the effect on unemployment is devastating."[1] And even during those periods when the economy does manage to strike a happy balance between unemployment and inflation, such a balance is likely to be precarious. It may be easily tipped by events such as droughts, floods, or wars, or by forces within the economy.

Shifts in the balance of unemployment and inflation actually indicate changes in the level of business activity. If unemployment drops, business is expanding, and if inflation subsides, business activity is slowing down. The capitalistic economy has always been subject to great swings in economic conditions. One hundred years ago these swings provided fuel for Marx's criticisms of capitalism. Today, much effort is devoted to understanding and mitigating their most serious effects.

1 *New York Times* (January 7, 1973), sec. 3, p. 37.

Opening photo by J. Paul Kirouac

A FIRST LOOK AT THE BUSINESS CYCLE

If you examine a chart of economic activity in the United States over the last few centuries, your first impression is one of enormous growth. In the twentieth century alone, actual output increased almost sixfold from 1900 to 1950, and it has more than doubled again since then. This growth trend, however, tends to obscure another equally important characteristic: The country's economic activity has risen and fallen repeatedly throughout our history. This fluctuation is clearly visible in Figure 7-1, where the long-term trend line serves as the horizontal axis, and deviations from this trend are shown above and below this line. These recurring variations in economic activity are known as business cycles.

The Business Cycle: A Description

Wesley Mitchell, the father of modern business cycle theory, defined business cycles as fluctuations in aggregate economic activity, but this description is somewhat misleading. As the term *business cycle* is used today, it does *not* refer to regular seasonal fluctuations such as the bulge in retail sales that occurs every year at Christmas and Easter. Nor should business cycles be confused with long-term trends: The 40-year pattern of annual increases in electric consumption is a unidirectional economic development, not a phase of a cycle; and the same is true for the 25-year steady decline in the number of passenger trains in operation in the United States.

Business cycles can be defined more precisely as the recurrent but irregular fluctuations of economic activity that occur over a period of several years.

These fluctuations are characterized by changes in output, employment, and price levels, and occur in a typical sequence of events.

A period of prosperity, in which output and employment are near capacity levels, characterizes the peak of a cycle. Because the public is confident, both consumption and investment spending are high. With demand high and the economy operating at near capacity, prices show a tendency to rise. Even-

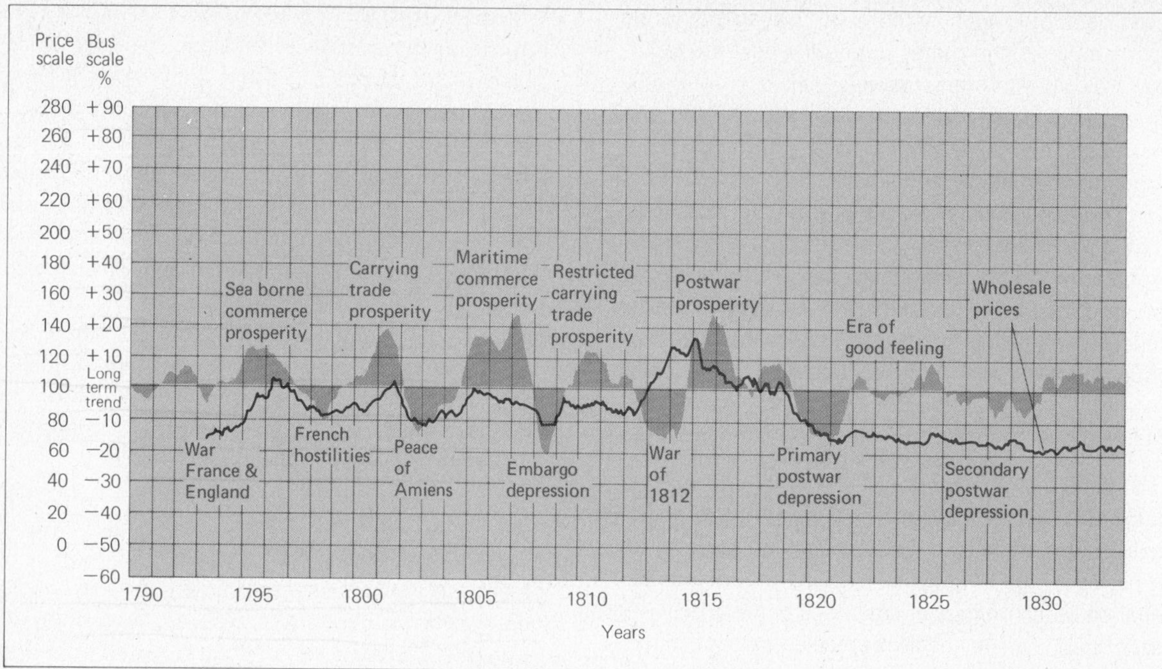

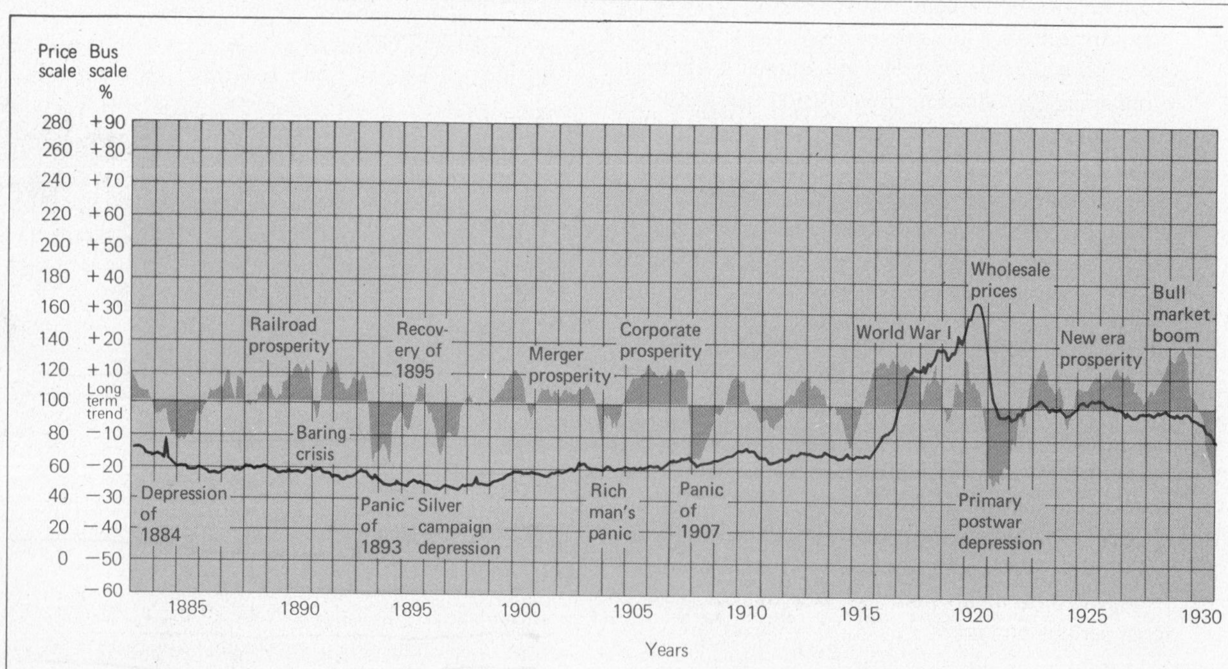

FIGURE 7-1 FLUCTUATIONS IN U.S. BUSINESS CONDITIONS, 1790–1972 Although the long-term growth of the U.S. economy has proceeded at about 3.5 percent per year, there have been large swings in business conditions around this trend. The Great Depression of the 1930s was, of course, far worse than any other downswing before or since, while every war in the last 125 years has been accompanied by prosperity. The labels for the peaks and troughs identify important features

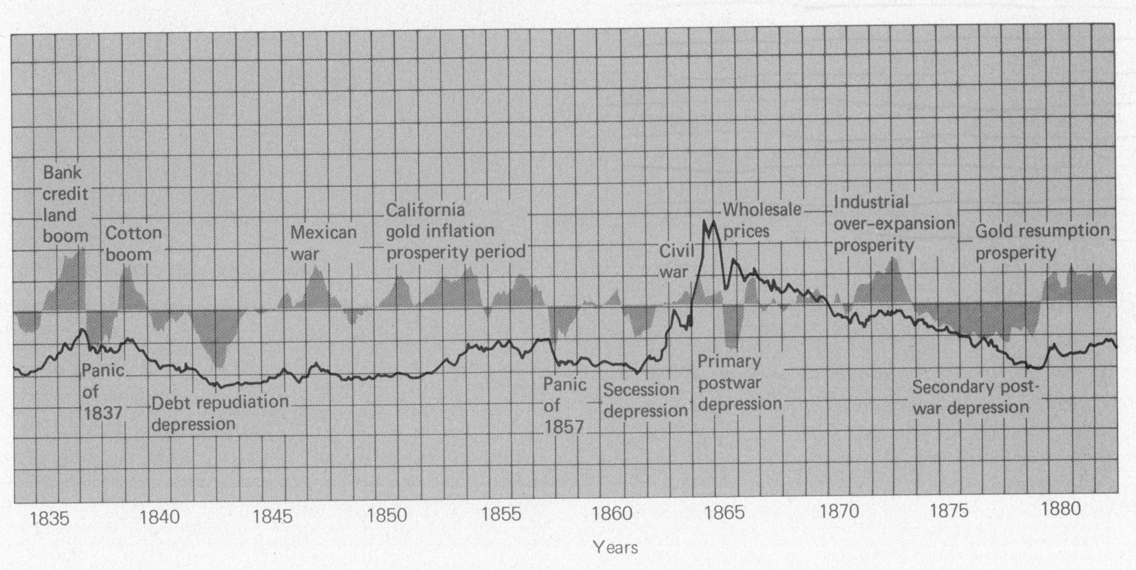

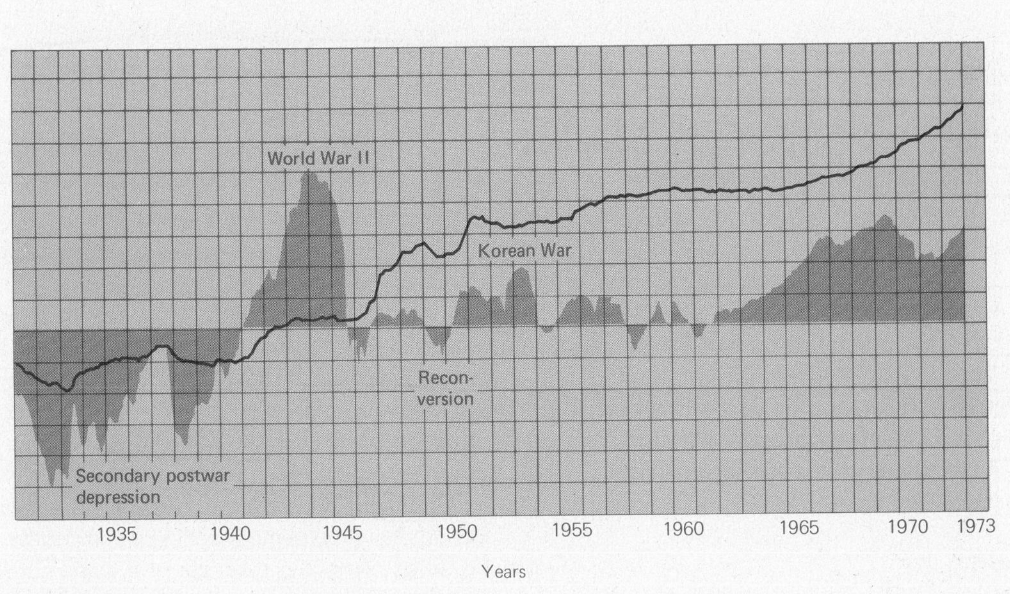

of the times that may have contributed to the prevailing economic conditions.

SOURCE: The Cleveland Trust Company. Cleveland, Ohio. Copyright 1954. Reprinted by permission.

tually, a period of downturn or contraction develops. Output and employment drop, with declines appearing in consumption and investment. Prices may also decline, as the recession or more severe depression worsens. The third stage is the trough or bottom of the recession or depression, and is characterized by low output and high unemployment. Low levels of consumption and investment spending reflect both the actual decline in demand and the fact that public confidence is at a low ebb. At some point, however, a recovery takes hold. Consumption spending increases, followed by a rise in investment spending, and soon output and employment begin to pick up as well. As the recovery develops steam, prices may start to rise. A graphic representation of a series of idealized business cycles would therefore be represented by the curves in Figure 7-2; in real life a business cycle would never be as regular as the curves shown here.

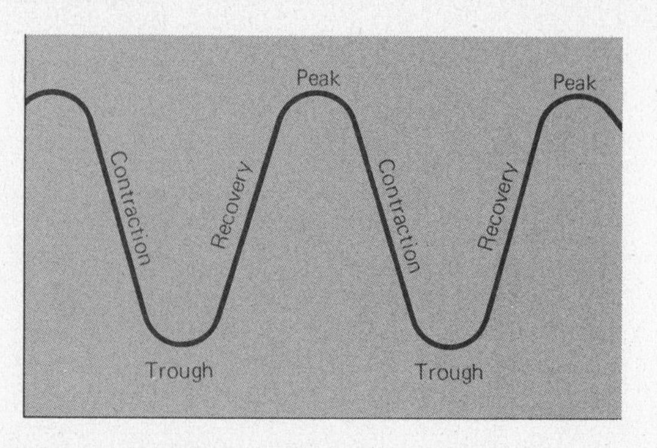

FIGURE 7-2 GENERALIZED BUSINESS CYCLE These wavelike patterns depict the three-phase business cycle. The prosperity phase is usually characterized by rising prices, high employment, full-capacity utilization, and high production. After the peak is reached, employment, production, and capacity utilization fall, and the rate of price increases declines or actually becomes negative. This is known as the contraction. At the trough the contraction ends, and the recovery phase begins. It continues until the previous real GNP is attained, when the new prosperity phase is inaugurated. The phases of real cycles may not be of identical duration, so this pattern is very generalized.

The Causes of Business Cycles

Referring again to Figure 7-1, each of the fluctuations is identified with a major social, political, or financial event of the period. We can note, for example, that there has been a period of prosperity during every major war, and a period of recession after the war's end. Classical economists assigned the primary responsibility for triggering business cycles to external, or exogenous, events. Current thought, however, emphasizes the importance of internal or endogenous factors. Our economy is not merely a yo-yo controlled by historical events; rather, there are forces inherent within the economy itself that make fluctuations an inevitable part of the system. Today, even those who believe that an external event, such as a war, may be the original impetus for a business cycle, recognize the primary role of internal factors in propelling and perpetuating the cycle once it has started, and in intensifying its effect.

Endogenous Forces within the Business Cycle

What are the structural peculiarities of our economy that shape business cycles? Three areas deserve special attention: the performance of the durable-goods sector, the behavior of investment spending, and the tendency of any trend, either up or down, to be cumulative in its effects.

Nondurable Goods versus Durable Goods During the course of a business cycle, the activity in different segments of the economy is not alike. In prosperity and recession alike, the production of nondurable goods remains fairly stable because the demand for these items is relatively constant. In bad times most families cannot postpone or reduce their purchases of food and clothing, nor do they rush out and buy greatly increased quantities of Jell-O or T-shirts during a business boom. The demand for nondurables is further stabilized by the pricing policies within the industries. Generally speaking, the sector is composed of a large number of highly competitive, relatively small firms. The manager of a small company in a competitive industry cuts his prices in bad times in order to capture or retain whatever business is available and raises them in good times to make what profit he can. Therefore, during recessions, nondurable-goods production stays relatively constant for two reasons: Sales are not likely to fall off, because consumers cannot postpone their purchases, and competitive pricing tends to stimulate sales.

The behavior of the durable-goods industries is quite different. The demand for durables fluctuates widely, reflecting the fact that these goods are long-lived and new purchases can be postponed. When hard times come, an old car can be persuaded to last another year and a family will be resigned to living a bit longer with its temperamental TV set. As a result, during a recession, purchases of durables drop sharply, while during recovery sales accelerate rapidly, a surge reflecting the normal demand plus purchases postponed in the previous period.

The pricing practices in the durables sector have tended to accentuate these fluctuations in demand. In the United States, production of automobiles, rubber, and steel is dominated by a few large corporations. Because they have sufficient assets to withstand bad times and there is relatively little competition among them, they have been able to maintain price levels even when demand declines. During a recession, instead of lowering prices to stimulate sales, the durables sector cuts back on production, laying off workers and creating unemployment. The reverse occurs during recovery periods. Thus, the activity of the durables sector varies tremendously during different phases of a business cycle.

The Behavior of Investment Spending Durable goods are to the consumer what investments in capital goods are to the entrepreneur. Both entail large–and postponable–outlays. Not surprisingly, then, investment spending is the most volatile component of GNP, on both the up side and the down side of a business cycle. As such, it is probably most directly responsible for the severity of the fluctuations during a cycle. Historical data reveal how investment spending, or the lack of it, has been a major factor in each of the cyclical swings that our economy has endured in the last 50 years. The prolonged investment spending in the prosperous 1920s, the curtailed investment in the depression of the 1930s, and the resurgence of spending in the post-World War II boom dramatize the close correlation between investment spending and business swings.

The Cumulative Effect The third characteristic of economic fluctuations involves their tendency to be cumulative in nature–that is, once a trend starts, it is likely to pick up momentum as it progresses. As a result, unless strong countermeasures are taken (by a government, for example), economic activity tends to move in extremes, with a small initial downturn snowballing into a major depression, and a minor boom developing into a production and buying binge. For example, during a recession, a small decline in overall spending can lead to a substantial decline in durable-goods industries and to drastic cutbacks in investment spending. Soon the declines in consumer-durable-goods and capital-goods industries cause growing unemployment, which results in a reduction in consumption spending. This sequence of reduced output, employment, and spending repeats itself again and again. In an expansionary period, the pattern reverses itself: A small increase in total spending can result in substantial increases in durable-goods and investment spending, each of which in turn provides more employment, more income, more spending, and an upward spiral of business.

INFLATION AND UNEMPLOYMENT

Business cycles are determined by spending levels. If spending is high, there will be a period of prosperity, and conversely, if spending drops, a business downturn will develop. Spending also has a direct bearing on prices and employment, and thus the relative health or malaise of the business sector is reflected in price trends and unemployment figures. In the following section we discuss inflation and unemployment, focusing on their relation to spending and their respective causes and effects.

Spending, Employment, and Price Levels

The relation between spending, employment, and prices is complex, varying during the phases of the business cycle. At the bottom of a recession, when total spending is low, increases in spending have little effect on prices. When demand is low, factories tend to operate at less than full capacity. If demand increases somewhat, a manufacturer will be under no pressure to raise prices because a small increase in production will not bid up the prices of the factors of production. Moreover, he will avoid increasing his prices for fear of losing sales to competitors. Instead, the manufacturer will respond to demand by utilizing unused capacity and beefing up production. Thus, when the economy is operating at low levels, increases in spending tend to be reflected in higher levels of output and employment.

As a recovery progresses and spending increases, changes in the economy will occur. Even though the entire economy is still operating below capacity, shortages of certain resources will arise. It may be difficult to obtain certain raw materials or special equipment such as giant cranes or labor with particular skills such as tool and die makers. Firms will be forced to compete for these scarce resources by offering higher prices for them. As a result, production costs will increase, putting pressure on corporate managers to raise product prices. As the recovery progresses, cost increases will spread, as certain plants operate on overtime, or pay premium prices for hard-to-find raw materials, or grant wage increases to hold or attract essential labor.

Because of these cost pressures, increases in spending during the recovery stage of a business cycle will often lead to some increases in prices. However, because *all* sectors of the economy and all resources are still not utilized at full capacity, price increases will be selective. For the economy as a whole, the average price level will rise only moderately. At this stage of the cycle, increases in spending are still reflected largely in increases in employment, with only a secondary effect on prices.

By the time the economy is operating at peak levels, the picture changes. Most of the nation's economic resources are fully utilized, and businesses cannot meet increases in demand without bidding up the cost of productive resources. Increases in output result in competition among producers for scarce resources; eventually the costs of resources rise. These higher production costs are then passed on to consumers in the form of higher product prices. In other words, at high spending levels and a full-capacity economy, further increases in spending do not result in more employment; the effect is felt primarily in higher prices.

The relation between changes in output and employment on the one hand, and prices on the other, is shown in Figure 7-3. When the economy is operating at depressed levels (Point A)—that is, when output and employment are low—*initial* increases in spending will result in higher employment, with little change in prices. During the later phase of a recovery (Point B), further spending will lead to more jobs, but it will also result in some price increases. Finally, once the economy is operating at a full-capacity–full-employment level (Point C), further increases in demand will be reflected only in higher prices.

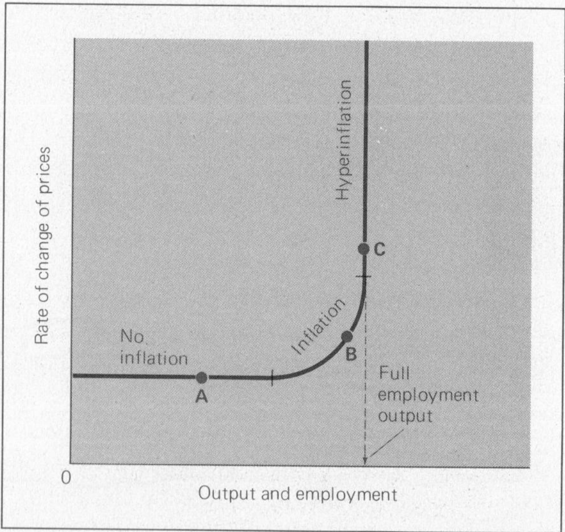

FIGURE 7-3 INFLATION AND EMPLOYMENT The relation between spending, employment, and price levels is not constant. When the level of employment and prices is low, increased spending can stimulate more jobs. As full employment is approached, further spending results in more jobs and higher prices. At full employment, increases in spending can only fuel high prices.

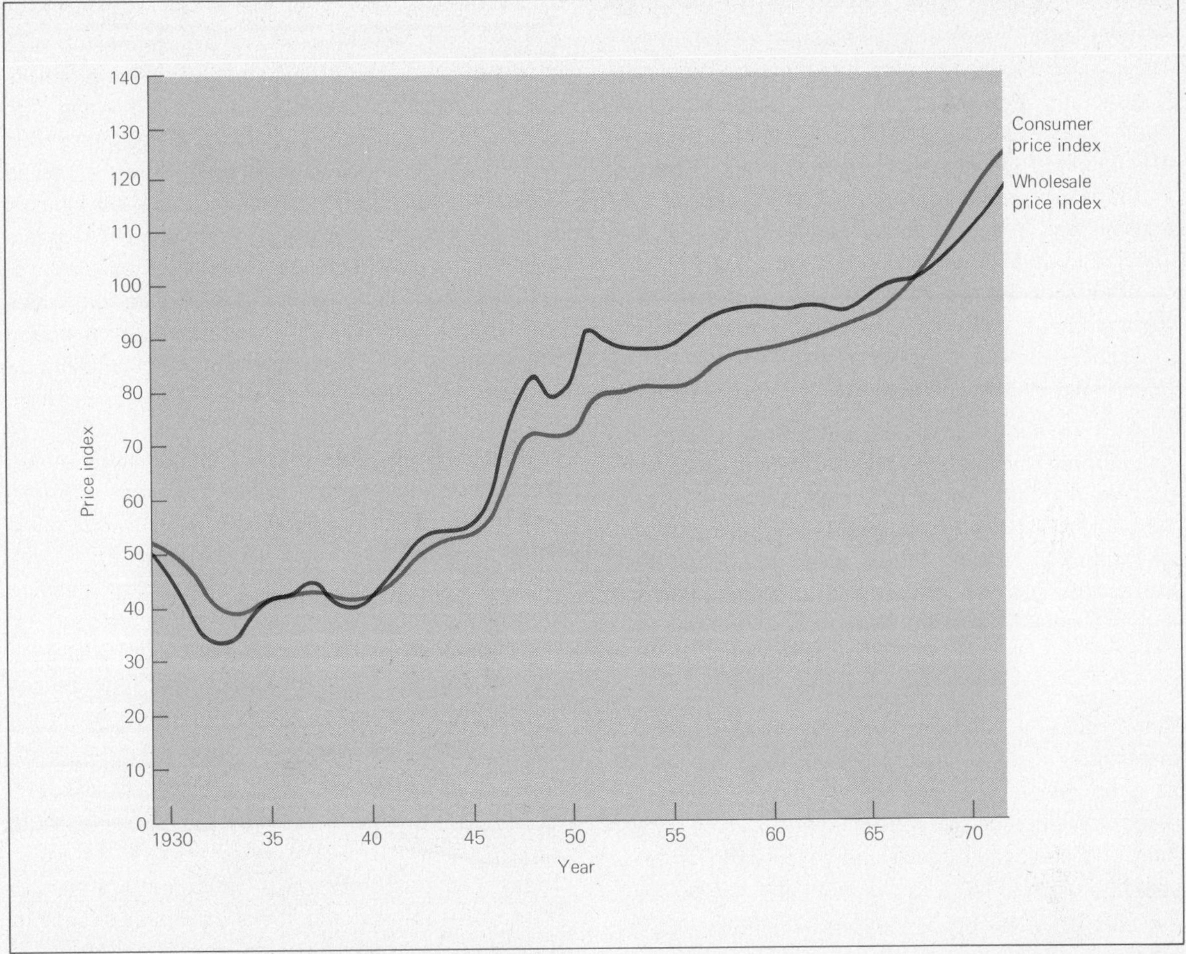

FIGURE 7-4 WHOLESALE AND CONSUMER PRICE LEVELS, 1929–1972 (1967 = 100) The wholesale price is a composite of prices paid by manufacturers to the suppliers of raw materials, while the consumer price index is based on prices paid by consumers to retailers for a specific market basket of products. Since 1933, both the consumer and wholesale price indices have been rising. However, the increases have not been uniform. During war periods these rates have generally accelerated, particularly rates of the consumer price index. During the late fifties and early sixties, the rate of inflation was apparently arrested. Unfortunately, the Vietnam War brought an end to that stability, and prices have been rising since 1964.

SOURCE: *Economic Report of the President*, January 1973.

What Is Inflation?

Inflation, defined as a generally rising level of prices, has been characteristic of our economy since the late 1930s. Strictly speaking, no American under 35 has ever lived for very long under anything but inflationary conditions. With the exception of two short breathing spells in the late forties and late fifties to early sixties, prices have risen consistently from year to year, with 1973 price levels averaging more than three times those of 1940.

Our experience of constantly rising prices tends to obscure the long-term trends. As Figure 7-4 illustrates, during other periods in our history, price behavior has been quite different. Americans have enjoyed long periods of price stability, as during the 1920s, and they have also experienced deflation (a general downward movement of prices), as in the depression years of 1930-33. Even during periods of inflation, price increases have not been steady. In 1951, for example, during the first full year of the Korean War, prices rose by almost 8 percent; in 1952, following the imposition of wage-price controls by President Truman, the increase was only 2.2 percent. From 1959 to 1964, the average annual price increase was a shade over 1 percent; in 1970, prices rose by almost 6 percent.

Finally, we should note that even when prices in general are moving up, prices are not changing uniformly in all segments of the economy. From 1960 to 1972, for example, consumer prices rose an average of 40 percent; but prices of household durable goods, such as refrigerators and dishwashers, climbed only 27 percent, while food increased 40 percent and medical costs soared by 68 percent.

The Causes of Inflation Since the 1930s, government has tried to control inflation to maximize its good effects and minimize its bad. Economists recognize a number of types of inflation, which differ from one another in cause and severity. An understanding of these types is crucial to effective policy-making because each requires different control measures.

DEMAND-PULL INFLATION Perhaps the simplest kind of inflation to understand is demand-pull inflation. It occurs when the demand for goods exceeds the supply and there is a situation of "too much money chasing too few goods."

In conditions where supply is extremely limited and demand is particularly high, inflation rockets upward. For example, in the movie *Casablanca* Humphrey Bogart has the only two exit permits in town. Paul Henreid wants to leave and is willing to offer higher and higher prices for them.

Point C of Figure 7-3 illustrates demand-pull inflation: The resources of the economy are fully utilized; in the short run, since additional demand cannot bring new resources into production, it must result in higher prices. Cost increases in the first quarter of 1973 included a number of instances of demand-pull inflation. Lumber prices went up as a continuing high demand for American lumber from forest-poor Japan bid up prices and created shortages in the United States. Increasing prices in the machine-tool industry reflected the fact that during February 1973, orders for machine tools exceeded shipments by a ratio of 2:1. Finally, plastics, too, inched higher as companies received increasing numbers of orders, even though the industry as a whole was already working at capacity.

COST-PUSH INFLATION In 1970–71, prices in the United States were advancing at a rate in excess of 5 percent a year, but since American industry was operating at only 75 percent of capacity, Americans found it hard to attribute this inflationary pressure to excess demand. Instead, attention focused on the impact of rising production costs. Cost-push inflation occurs when producers, for one reason or another, are required to pay higher prices for the factors of production. These higher resource costs, which are not offset by higher productivity, are then passed on to the consumer in the form of higher product prices.

Today, cost-push inflation is attributed to a number of causes—political and social as well as economic. Shortages, expansive monetary policies, hot and cold war, and the increasing involvement of government in human-welfare projects all contribute to cost-push inflation, but the primary causes revolve around the ability of powerful labor unions and corporations to avoid the normal consequences of reduced demand.

Labor organizations have been increasingly successful in negotiating wage and benefit increases, regardless of economic conditions; these labor costs have been passed on to the customer in higher prices. Unions have been able to land better contracts even when the supply of labor was plentiful and wages might be expected to go down. In 1971, for example, when the unemployment rate was at an eight-year high of 6.1 percent, many new wage contracts provided for annual increases as high as 10 to 20 percent or more. Under such upward pressure, cost-push inflation becomes a vicious spiral, as wage increases to offset price increases generate still higher prices, which generate still higher wage increases, and so on.

The predominance of large corporations in certain sectors has tended to exacerbate the cost-push inflation problem. Prices in these sectors are "administered" rather than set by market supply and demand; consequently, prices are rarely lowered, even in recessionary periods. In fact in 1970, when both economic activity and automobile production declined, the price of cars increased as management protected its profit margin by passing on increased labor costs to the public.

Cost-push inflation presents new policy problems. The traditional weapons against demand-pull inflation—the reduction of government spending and the raising of income taxes and interest rates—are seemingly ineffective against cost-push inflation because they operate outside the laws of supply and demand. The Nixon wage-price controls of 1971–73 were one method of attempting to rein in this potent form of inflation by directly limiting costs.

The cost-push explanation of rising prices is not accepted by all economists. There are those who argue that all inflation is fundamentally demand-pull. According to this explanation, the inflation with high unemployment of 1970–71 was started by the excess demand in the previous years that had not yet run its course. The inflation was then kept alive by continued federal deficits and too rapid expansion of the money supply.

STRUCTURAL INFLATION Structural inflation refers to the economy-wide inflation that sometimes results when price increases are initiated for one reason or another in certain basic industries, despite the fact that the economy as a whole is not experiencing an excess of demand. Such price increases can be based on either demand or cost factors, but in either case, if the industry is important enough, increases in its prices can often initiate a round of inflationary pressure throughout the economy. For example,

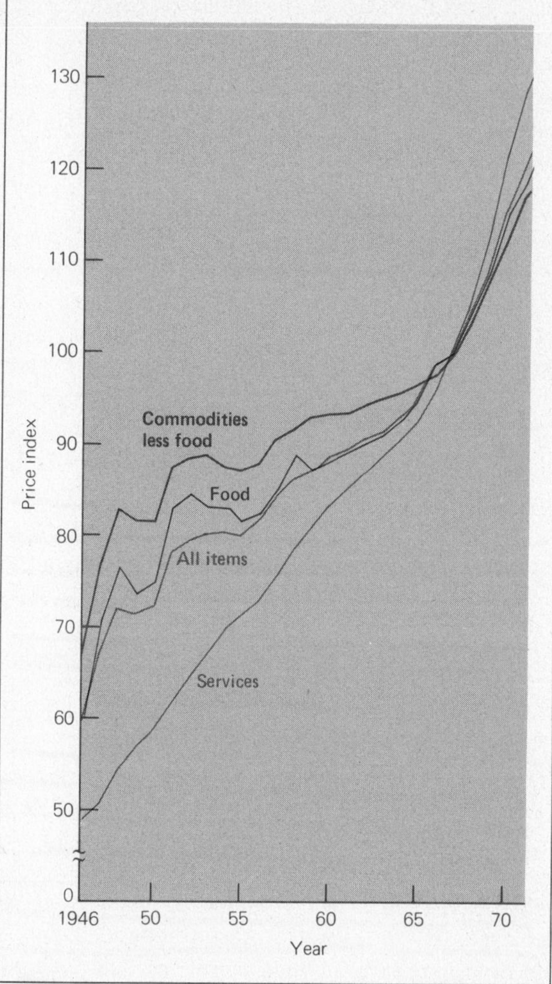

FIGURE 7-5 COMPONENTS OF THE CONSUMER PRICE INDEX (1967 = 100) The consumer price index averages three main classes of items—services, food, and commodities less food. Although food prices have been in the spotlight recently and have clearly contributed most heavily to the recent spiral in the consumer price index, since 1946 the service sector has clearly been the villain of the piece. While food prices have less than doubled since 1946, the price of services has risen by more than 180 percent!

SOURCE: *Economic Report of the President,* January 1973.

the meat price increases of 1972–73 began because a feed-grain shortage bid up the price of livestock feed. The increased cost of raising cattle was reflected in higher prices for livestock at the stockyard and higher meat prices at the butcher shop and supermarket. Food price increases in turn eroded the real value of wages and stimulated a new round of higher wage demands. Higher wages in turn were passed along in the form of higher product prices. Thus, higher prices in one key sector created pressures for higher prices throughout the economy.

HYPERINFLATION A 1973 press dispatch from Buenos Aires described the southernmost part of South America as "an economic disaster area, sick with inflation." In the preceding year, the cost-of-living index in Argentina had risen by 64 percent, in Uruguay by 94 percent, and in Chile by 163 percent. To many observers, it looked as if those nations were moving uncomfortably close to that nightmare of economists—hyperinflation. Hyperinflation occurs when prices increase, or "run away," by huge amounts. The classic case of hyperinflation occurred in Germany after World War I, when from 1919 to 1923 prices doubled every few weeks, coffee sold for 6 million marks a cup, and workmen literally needed wheelbarrows to cart home their weekly pay.

Hyperinflation occurs when a government chooses to pay its bills by printing more and more money. There results an enormous increase in the supply of money, with no corresponding increase in the supply of goods and services. In postwar Germany, the government printed so much new money that the number of marks in circulation increased from 50 billion in 1919 to almost 500 trillion billion in 1923, creating the ultimate in demand-pull inflation. Hyperinflation is generally associated with a society in trauma during war or revolution, and thus it differs from the usual demand-pull or cost-push inflation, which occurs as part of the normal operation of a healthy economy in a reasonably stable society.

How Bad Is Inflation? Inflation has generally had a "bad press" in the United States. The conventional wisdom has been that inflation is unfair to most people, injurious to the economic system, and in the long run, dangerous to the very existence of the nation. It is questionable whether such evaluations are accurate, except in the case of hyperinflation. Hyperinflation wipes out the buying power of the thrifty who have put their savings in banks, bonds, or mortgages; hyperinflation makes it impossible for those on fixed incomes to support themselves; it leads to wasteful business practices by forcing management to make decisions about the purchase of resources on the basis of inflation predictions rather than production requirements.

However, hyperinflation has never occurred in the United States, where since 1940, prices have increased at only about a 3.5 percent compounded rate. The term *creeping inflation* is often used to refer to such slow, steady increases in prices over a long period. Economists differ in their evaluation of the effects of creeping inflation. Some are disturbed by the human suffering that is caused by such an inflation, while others are convinced that "a slowly rising price level is actually preferable to a stable price level."[2]

Employment: Its Determinants

Since the level of spending in an economy influences the level of output, which, in turn, determines the level of employment, there is a direct link between employment and spending. When spending in private or government sectors is extremely high, businesses find a ready market for all the goods they can produce, and as a result, all productive resources, including labor, are fully utilized. Conversely, when spending declines, the production of goods and services also falls, and these cutbacks result almost immediately in higher unemployment rates.

Definitions of Employment Although the term *employment* is commonly used to describe the utilization of *labor* resources, to the economist it refers to the utilization of all factors of production: land and capital as well as labor. Thus, one may speak of unemployed acres as well as unemployed engineers. Nevertheless, primary attention is focused on the unemployment of labor resources for three reasons: It causes visible human suffering, it can be measured

2 Sumner Slichter, "How Bad is Inflation?" *Harper's Magazine*, August 1952, p. 53.

fairly accurately, and it is a reasonably good indicator of the degree to which the other economic resources are being utilized.

Much discussion in government and business circles centers around ways to achieve full employment. Some of the disagreement expressed in these debates may be generated by the term *full employment*, which means different things to different people. Surprisingly, the term rarely means 100 percent employment. Since very high levels of employment lead to inflation, some economists regard full employment as the highest level of employment consistent with an acceptable rate of price increase. Another definition of the term is the condition that prevails when the number of vacancies equals the number of people unemployed. English economist Lord William Beveridge would modify this to require the number of vacancies to exceed the number unemployed. These two definitions really focus on one aspect of unemployment: frictional unemployment.

FRICTIONAL AND STRUCTURAL UNEMPLOYMENT In a complex society such as ours, there will always be a certain amount of unemployment. People often leave jobs voluntarily. In addition, many people are employed in industries characterized by periodic layoffs because of weather (construction) or because of seasonal factors (farming, income-tax preparation), and they, too, will be unemployed from time to time. This temporary unemployment, called **frictional unemployment**, is believed to run between 1 and 2 percent of the total working force.

Another form of unemployment apparently inherent in our system is **structural unemployment**. Structural unemployment is caused not by an overall shortage of jobs, but by a mismatch between the jobs that are available and the skills of those who are looking for work. It reflects the changing nature of job opportunities in the United States, where technological change continuously makes the skills of many workers obsolete, while creating jobs requiring new skills in other areas. Structural unemployment hits particularly the poorly educated, unskilled worker, who is replaced in his job as a result of automation or new technology. The United States has developed many tools to deal with the special problem of structural unemployment: Workers can be taught new skills; they can be directed to communities where jobs exist; and through favorable tax treatment or government grants, business firms can be encouraged to set up plants in areas with labor surpluses or to retrain employees whose jobs have become obsolete. Hopefully, such measures will permit the eventual reentry into the job market of any particular individual affected by structural unemployment; nevertheless, because our economy changes and evolves, about 1 to 2 percent of the total labor force is believed to be structurally unemployed at any one time.

It appears, then, that a certain amount of unemployment—somewhere between 3 and 4 percent—may be inherent in our free-market economy. This is said to be the price we must pay for permitting free choice of jobs and for maintaining an acceptable level of technological change and price stability. Under these assumptions, 100 percent employment becomes an unrealistic goal, and full employment is generally defined as the highest level possible, given the inevitable occurrence of frictional and structural unemployment. In recent years, this level has been about 95 to 97 percent of the total civilian labor force.

Not all economists accept this view, however. Structural unemployment may be simply a result of there being not enough jobs to go around. Various studies of structural unemployment in the United States have found that in a period of labor surplus, employers may establish unnecessarily high qualifications for employment.[3] Utility companies, for example, may require a college degree for linemen or elaborate vocabulary tests for those hired to do telephone repair work. Prerequisites for employment irrelevant to effective job performance tend to discriminate against minorities or those whose habits of speech and dress do not conform to the norm. And the longer they remain unemployed, the more the skills they do have deteriorate, reducing further the chances of

3 U.S. Department of Commerce, *Structural Unemployment in the U.S.*, by Barbara R. Bergmann and David E. Kaun (Washington, D.C.: Government Printing Office, 1966); and Eleanor Gottesfocht Gilpatrick, *Structural Unemployment and Aggregate Demand* (Baltimore: Johns Hopkins Press, 1966).

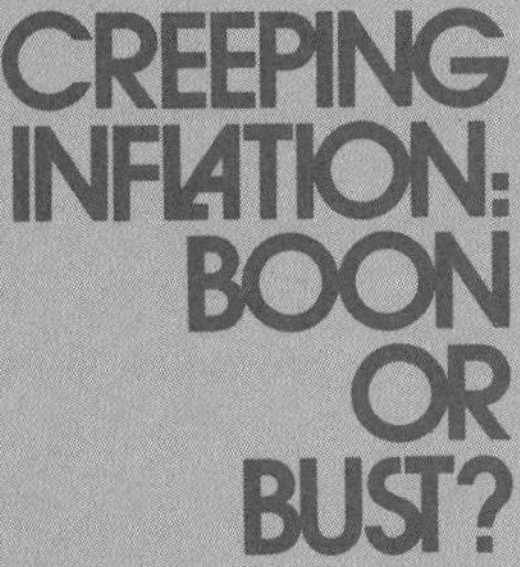

One of the hottest economic debates in the United States in recent years centers around the question of whether creeping inflation is healthy for the economy and the country. Both the economic and political communities have been polarized over the issue.

The major argument against creeping inflation is that it falls hardest on those who can least afford it: the old, the disabled, and the poor. The erosion of the real value of money eats up the resources of persons living on savings or on fixed pension or welfare payments. Even at a tame inflation rate of 3.5 percent per year, money loses half its value every 20 years, and thus a man who purchases a $20,000 endowment insurance policy at age 25 will have only $5000 of buying power when he collects at 65. In addition, inflation falls heavily on the working poor. Generally unskilled and nonunionized, they have little bargaining power to acquire wage increases that keep pace with rising prices.

The other major objection to creeping inflation is that it will become galloping inflation. Economist Milton Friedman characterized inflation as being "like drink. The first few months or years of inflation, like the first few drinks, seem just fine. . . . The hangover comes when prices start to catch up."

Friedman and others would argue that inflationary trends may get out of control. Labor, anticipating continuing inflation, may press for still higher wages, and consumers, faced with sharply rising prices, may rush to buy before prices rise any further. If such cost-push and demand-pull pressures continued, businesses might hoard raw materials and finished goods, hoping to make greater profits by selling at a later date. Ultimately shortages, excessive wages, and exorbitant prices might bring production to a grinding halt.

Current economic thought in the United States tends more and more to the view that creeping inflation is both inevitable and desirable. Those who defend it recognize its inequities but argue that its advantages outweigh its disadvantages.

Pro-inflationists argue that while inflation imposes injustices on fixed-income groups, the maintenance of price stability would create even greater hardships. To achieve price stability, the United States would have to experience periods of recession—if not depression—because only under conditions of reduced spending would there be a rollback of the price increases that inevitably occur during prosperous times. A depression and a resulting increase in unemployment would produce tremendous economic and personal hardship.

Further, the supporters of an inflationary economy hold that creeping inflation will not necessarily start to gallop uncontrollably and that its injustices can be eliminated. Accelerating inflation can be reined in by stringent government control of credit, while the erosion of fixed incomes can be countered effectively by the upward adjustment of savings-account interest rates and social security and welfare payments in accordance with the rate of inflation. Thus, the champions of creeping inflation believe that the country can enjoy the benefits of an expanding economy without the poor and aged having to pick up the tab.

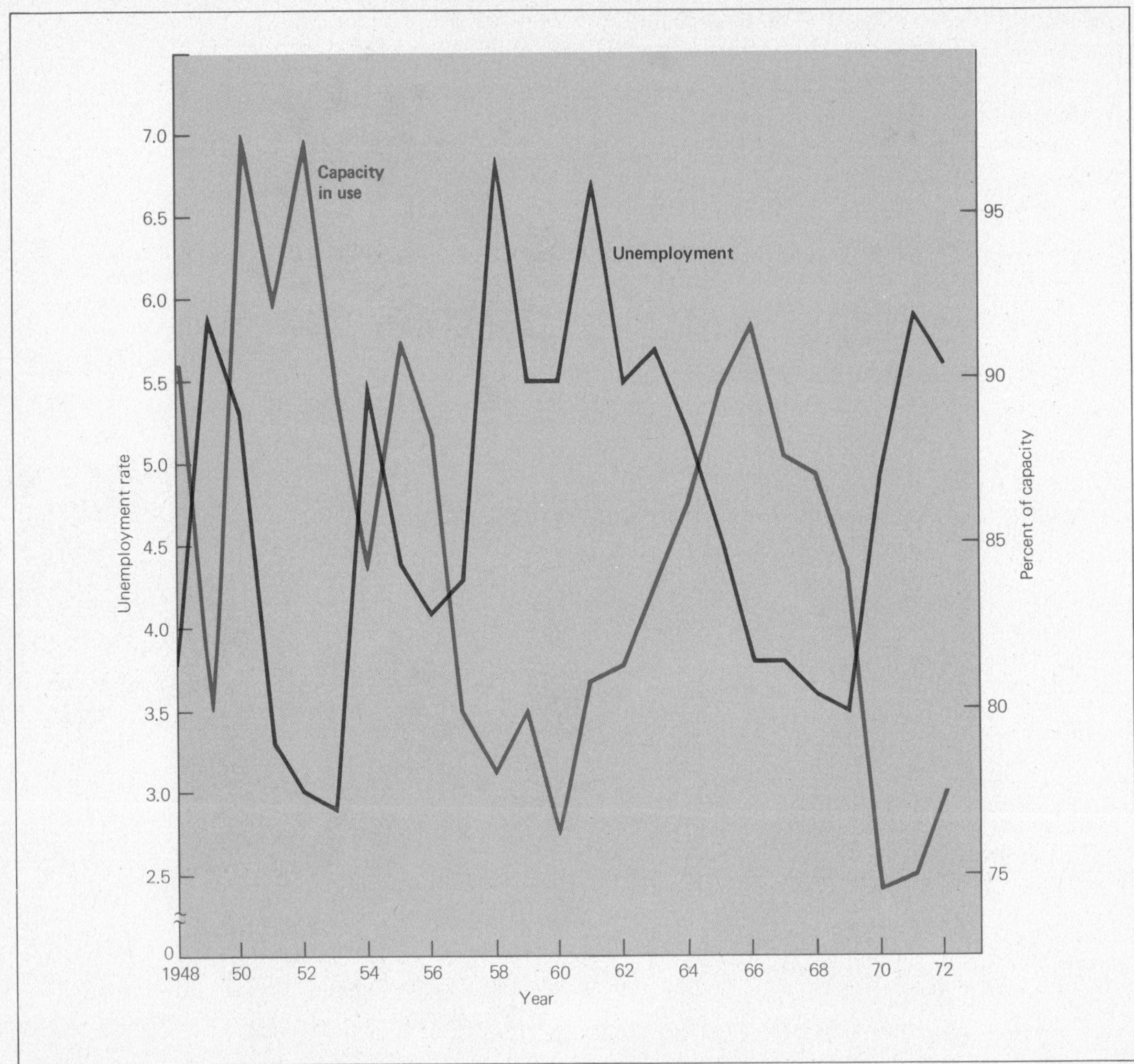

FIGURE 7-6 UNEMPLOYMENT OF LABOR AND EMPLOYMENT OF CAPITAL GOODS Employment means more than employment of labor. When factories are booming, fewer people will be unemployed. Thus, the unemployment rate of the labor force varies inversely with the rate at which manufacturing capacity is used.

SOURCE: *Economic Report of the President,* January 1973.

job success. In periods of economic expansion, employers relax their qualifications for hiring, and many of those formerly considered unemployable are hired and perform well. Apparently, much so-called structural unemployment is a function of labor surplus rather than workers' lack of skills. It is really a form of cyclical unemployment.

CYCLICAL UNEMPLOYMENT When employment drops below the full-employment level, the economy enters a period of cyclical unemployment. This is the most highly publicized form of unemployment. It is characterized by an economy-wide shortage of jobs, and occurs during those phases of the business cycle when demand declines and the economy's output is reduced. Broadly speaking, it can best be attacked through measures aimed at increasing total spending.

CONCEALED UNEMPLOYMENT The rate of unemployment in the United States is calculated by the U.S. Bureau of Labor Statistics, but these figures are somewhat deceiving. According to their definition, the unemployed are those currently not working nor "actively seeking work." The bureau does not count as unemployed those persons working part-time who want to work full-time but are unable to find jobs, nor does it include those discouraged job seekers who would like to work, but have surveyed the job market, found prospects dim, and decided not to actively seek work. Thus, the bureau consistently underestimates unemployment, particularly during periods of economic decline. At the height of the 1970–71

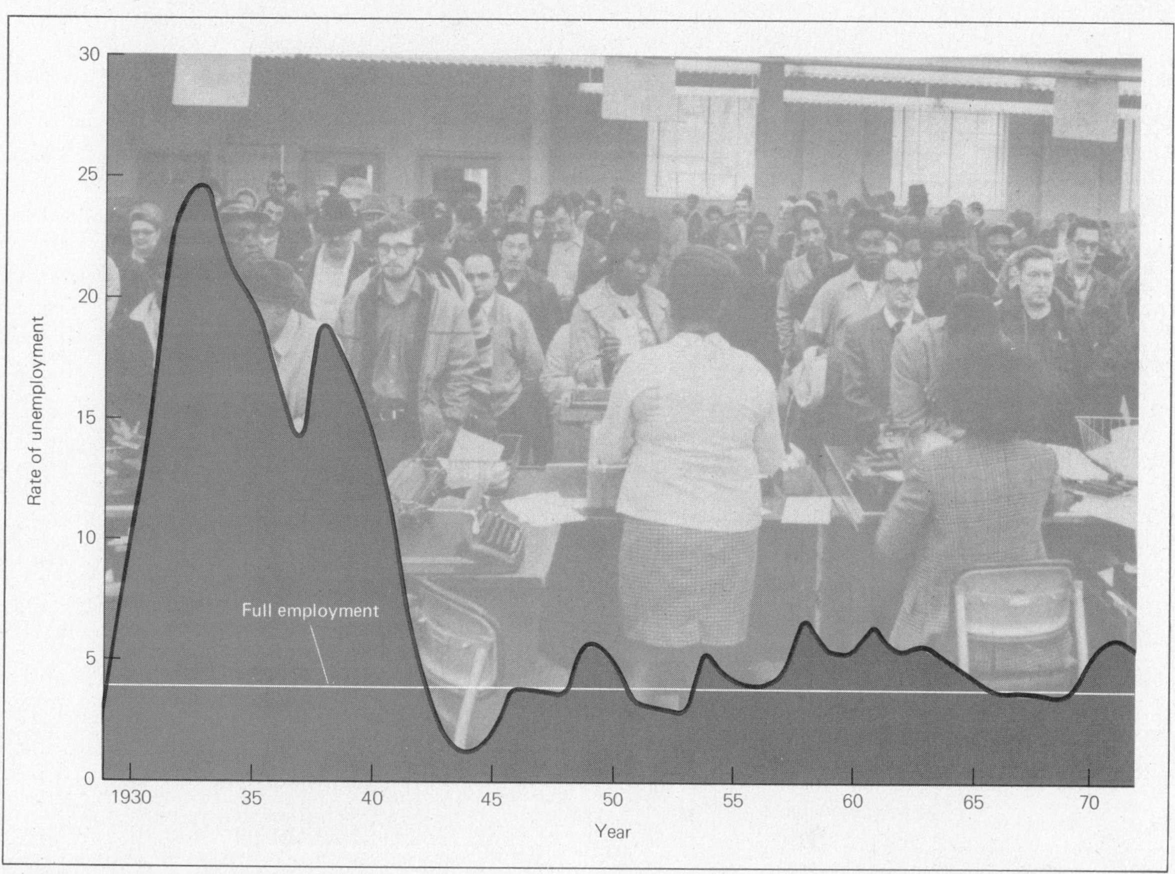

FIGURE 7-7 RATE OF UNEMPLOYMENT, 1929–1972 Full employment is generally considered to be at the 4 percent unemployment rate, since there will normally be some people between jobs, others unable to work because they are illiterate or poorly trained, and still others who either live in inconvenient locations or who cannot conform to the norms prevalent in most work situations. The rate of unemployment since 1941 has fluctuated between 4 and 7 percent. During periods of recession it has risen to close to 8 percent, while it has actually fallen below 4 percent during the wartime prosperities of the forties, fifties, and sixties. Tony Spina, *Detroit Free Press*

SOURCE: U.S. Department of Labor, Bureau of Labor Statistics, *Employment and Earnings*, Vol. 12, April 1973.

recession, for example, the stated unemployment rate was 6.1 percent, or about 5.5 million people, but some authorities estimate that the actual unemployment rate may have approached 9 percent.

The underestimation of unemployment among blacks may be particularly high. Black unemployment is already about twice that of whites, and the black labor force generally has lower education levels. Dismal employment prospects and lack of skills probably force many blacks into part-time work or discourage them from job hunting altogether, and thus they are not included in the Labor Department statistics.

The Costs of Unemployment Unemployment exacts a number of prices from the country as a whole.

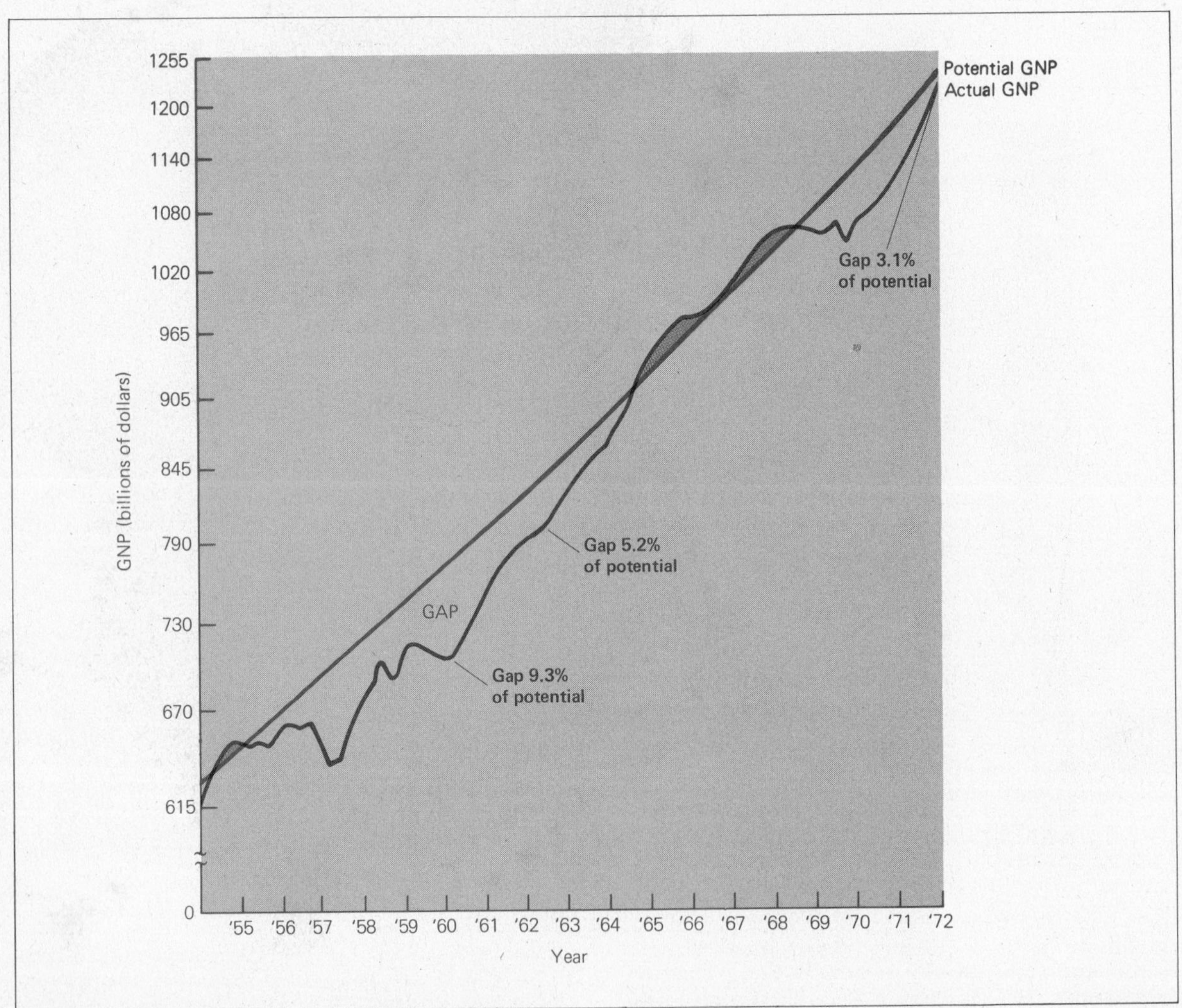

FIGURE 7-8 GNP GAP, 1955–1972 Potential GNP is what GNP would be at full employment (an unemployment rate of 4 percent). Potential GNP has generally exceeded actual GNP, the gap being greatest during periods of recession. However, during the Korean War and again during the Vietnam War, actual GNP exceeded potential GNP, since we experienced an unemployment rate of less than 4 percent during these periods.

SOURCE: Joint Economic Committee, 93rd Cong., 1st Sess. *The 1973 Joint Economic Report: Report on the January 1973 Economic Report of the President.*

The economic costs of unemployment are the goods and services that we do without because they are never produced. In 1971, for example, there were about 1.7 million unemployed in excess of the 96 percent full-employment rate. The economic cost of these unemployed workers was the production foregone because they were not working. The concept of *GNP gap* expresses this lost production. The GNP gap is the difference between actual GNP and the potential GNP that could have been achieved assuming a 4 percent unemployment level and a normal rate of GNP growth. Figure 7-8 shows the GNP gap since 1955. In the years 1970 to 1972 alone, the GNP gap totaled about $140 billion, or nearly twice as much as the federal government spent in those years on health, housing, and education.

But the economic costs do not tell the whole story; unemployment also carries a very expensive price tag in terms of social costs. Studs Terkel, in his book *Hard Times,* records the recollections of Americans about the personal disintegration and family trouble that accompanied the prolonged unemployment of the 1930s. In addition to creating personal misery, prolonged periods of high unemployment may threaten a society's political and social systems. Both Mussolini and Hitler came to power in the wake of huge unemployment rolls, overthrowing their legitimately constituted governments in the process.

THE THEORY OF INCOME AND EMPLOYMENT

The instabilities of behavior in the economy are of both practical and theoretical interest. A business that anticipates a downturn in economic conditions can hedge against this change. A government that anticipates the downturn may actually be able to avert it or cushion its impact. The reactions, however, depend to some extent on whether the business or government believes that the economy is self-regulating or not. This issue is one central to economic theory and economic policy.

The Classical Economists

Until the 1930s, economists assumed that periods of unemployment and deflation were temporary, resulting from unusual circumstances such as wars or plagues or speculative crises. Under normal conditions, economists argued, the self-regulating forces of the capitalistic system would push the economy toward full employment and price stability.

Say's Law: Supply Creates Its Own Demand The explanation of how these self-regulating forces worked is called the classical theory of income and employment, and it was developed during the early 1800s. The French economist J. B. Say first proposed the premise that forms the basis of classical theory: He thought that the demand for goods and services produced by an economy would always be equal to the supply. Say's Law, as this concept is called, is based on the reasoning that people will work only if they require income; once they obtain this income, they will spend it, and in so doing, they will create a demand for the goods and services that they have produced. In other words, when goods are produced, income is created, and this income will be used to purchase all output. To take a simplified example, an economy producing $1 million of output would simultaneously create $1 million of income (compensation, interest, rent, profits), and the recipients of this $1 million in income would use it to buy all output.

The Role of Saving Say's Law assumes that once households receive income for their work, they will spend *all* this income to purchase the output they have created. One possible loophole, of course, could be savings: What happens if a particular family decides not to spend its entire income, but to save part of it? In terms of our earlier example, what would happen if those who had received the $1 million in income decided to spend only $900,000, and to save the other $100,000? At first glance, it appears that with the demand declining to only $900,000, producers would be unable to sell their $1 million of output; consequently, cutbacks in production and employment would surely follow.

The classical economists, however, had an answer to this dilemma. It is true that if saving consisted of tucking dollar bills under a mattress, any income saved would surely be lost to the system. However, in real life, most savings do not lie idle under mat-

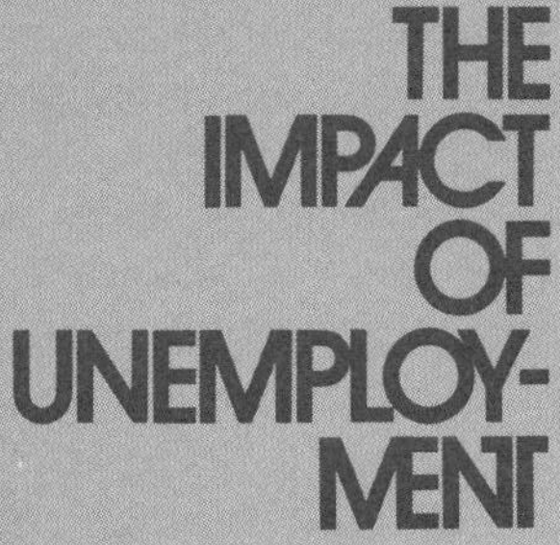

The usual defense for permitting unemployment to escalate is that such unemployment is the price we must pay to restrain inflation. The Nixon administration during its first years in office hoped to stop inflation without raising the level of unemployment, which then stood at about 3.6 percent; by 1973, the government was talking about an "acceptable" unemployment rate of 4 to 5 percent. In a country as big as the United States, with a working force of over 90 million, a 1 percent increase in the unemployment rate means 900,000 fewer jobs.

Unemployment does not affect all groups equally. From 1963 to 1973, the overall unemployment rate in the United States ranged between 3.5 and 6 percent. Yet the unemployment rate for managers and administrators never exceeded 2 percent, whereas the rate for blue-collar laborers ran as high as 12 percent and never fell below 6 percent. During the entire period, the unemployment rate for women averaged about one and one-half times that of men; for blacks twice that of whites; and for teen-aged males more than four times that of men over 20; the unemployment rate of black teen-agers ran two to three times that of their white counterparts, and occasionally rose to 10 times that of white males 20 to 64. The burdens of unemployment, then, are not shared equally among all citizens; the traditional minorities—the blacks, the young, and women—suffer more from unemployment than the average white male.

This differential burden is not always viewed as a complete misfortune. According to Herbert Stein of the Council of Economic Advisers, unemployment among older workers is more serious than that among younger workers, since the young are less likely to be supporting dependents and since some of their unemployment is frictional, as the young start hunting for first jobs. Such an argument based on differential "misery components" fails to deal with other minorities.

The concern with who bears the burdens of unemployment is important, since unemployment may be a by-product of national economic policy. As we shall see in later chapters, one of the more effective ways of containing the excess demand that encourages higher prices is to curtail economic growth and induce a recession: to cut consumption spending through higher taxes, to discourage investment spending through higher interest rates, and to reduce government spending by slashing the budget. The problem is that "these episodes of financial Puritanism" disproportionately afflict the weak.* It is primarily the blacks, the Spanish-speaking workers, women, teen-agers, the uneducated, and the

*Robert Lekachman, "The Economy: To Tame the Monster," *New York Times Magazine*, February 18, 1973, p. 73.

Photo by Herb Goro

unskilled who are called upon to accept the resulting unemployment so that the rest of the nation can enjoy price stability. The inequity is compounded by the fact that these groups are almost unrepresented in the circles of those who make the decisions to combat inflation through reduced demand, which engenders unemployment. If asked, the unemployed might very much prefer a nationwide dose of inflation, rather than the concentrated epidemic of unemployment *they* have been asked to accept.

One policy to moderate such inequities in employment is to stimulate the economy in the hopes of creating more jobs. This argument ignores the threats posed by inflation resulting from high levels of employment. Who bears the burden of price instability? How would you make a case for the importance of controlling inflation, even at the cost of some unemployment?

tresses; instead, they reenter the economic system through another door—investment. In our hypothetical case, the $100,000 in savings might be deposited in banks; the banks, in turn, would lend the money to firms, which would use it to build new plants and hire new employees. In this way, the $1 million of income resulting from the original productive process would create $1 million in demand: $900,000 would be spent on private consumption, and $100,000 on investment purchases. In other words, Say's Law would prevail: Supply and demand would be equal, and the economy would continue at full capacity and full employment.

But how can we be sure that all savings will be invested? Isn't there a possibility that firms will refuse to borrow the savings that have been set aside? Once again, the classical economists saw the capitalist system as having an inherent mechanism through which the investment of all savings was guaranteed. This mechanism was the interest rate, the price that savers received when they provided investment funds to businesses. In a market economy, the interest rate fluctuates freely in response to changes in the supply and demand for savings. These fluctuations in the interest rate would guarantee that the level of saving would be maintained at precisely that amount that investors were willing to borrow; an excess of saving would never develop. For example, if investment demand did not equal saving when interest rates were 6 percent, competition among lenders would drive the interest rate down to 3 or 4 percent. As a result, new groups of investors would now be willing to borrow, because a factory built with borrowed money costing 3 percent in interest is more likely to be profitable than a factory built with money costing 6 percent. And at the new, lower interest rate, consumers would also be less willing to save: A household might have been eager to forgo the pleasures of current consumption in order to earn 6 percent on its savings, but it would be somewhat less eager at 3 percent. Thus, a drop in the interest rate would always bring saving and investment into equilibrium. The classical economists saw no risk of an extended period during which reduced investment and absence of business growth might threaten full employment.

The Role of Flexible Prices and Flexible Wages In addition to the interest-rate mechanism, the classical economists believed that a capitalist system provided one further tool that would inevitably ensure a rapid return to full employment on those occasions when investment demand failed to materialize. This tool was flexible prices. Assume, for example, that for one reason or another business managers refused to borrow and invest the funds that households had saved. In theory, if nothing further happened, demand would no longer equal supply. Returning to our earlier example, the economy would have produced $1 million of output, but there would be only $900,000 of demand; businesses would be forced to lay off workers.

The classical economists had an answer to this difficulty. Under a competitive system, they claimed, any decline in demand would lead to price-cutting among producers, as each tried to obtain as much business as he could. A shoe manufacturer, for example, might cut the price of his shoes from $10 to $9 a pair. If similar 10-percent price cuts occurred throughout the economy, the net result would be that the reduced $900,000 demand would buy as much as the former $1 million. In other words, the total demand as expressed in *dollars* would be less than that originally considered necessary to maintain full employment, but since the $900,000 would buy the same physical volume of output, demand would continue to equal supply.

The classical economists believed that the capitalist system involved free competition not only among producers, but also among workers. Any decline in demand would lead not only to price competition among producers for the reduced amount of business available, but also to wage competition among workers for the reduced number of jobs available. The willingness of workers to accept lower wages would mean a reduction in the costs of production, and consequently business managers would be even more willing to cut prices in order to stimulate demand.

Price Stability under the Classical Theory Although price flexibility provided a second line of defense for the classical economists, they essentially focused on the interest rate as the primary mechanism for ensuring that demand would always equal supply and full employment would prevail. Occasionally, it is true, a touch of deflation might be required to return an economy to equilibrium, but this was considered a temporary condition. Inflation, if it occurred, was an aberration, probably caused by artificial increases in demand due to war or a crop failure. Inflation would quickly disappear once "normal" conditions were restored.

It is clear that classical economists saw the relation between inflation and full employment very differently than we do today. They believed that a dose of wage- and price-cutting was an effective cure for unemployment. As we have seen in our previous discussion of creeping inflation, current economic thought is that a modest amount of inflation may be necessary to achieve full employment.

In addition, classical economists believed that any government interference in the operations of the economy would upset its built-in regulating mechanisms and delay the return to full employment. This faith in the ability of the capitalist system to regulate itself was called into question by the work of John Maynard Keynes.

The Keynesian Uncoupling

To the classical economists, a capitalist economy moved continuously toward a state of full employment. They recognized the periodic bouts of unemployment encountered every few years, but explained them as temporary imbalances, brought about by forces external to the economy. With the Great Depression of the 1930s, however, it became obvious that the internal mechanisms that were supposed to work swiftly and automatically to return the economy to full employment were not doing their job. Some classical economists still hoped that in the long run the economy would rebound by itself, but as the British economist John Maynard Keynes pessimistically responded, "In the long run, we are all dead." Clearly, new theories were required to explain this apparently inexplicable depression.

Keynes's *General Theory of Employment, Interest and Money,* published in 1936, in the midst of the Depression, modified classical economic explanations of how employment levels are determined in a capitalist economy. Today, the economic policies of every major capitalist nation are based on Keynes's "new economics." During the post–World War II recessions, the limitation of the U.S. unemployment rate to 7 percent or lower is an achievement attributable to Keynes's analysis of the causes and cures of unemployment.

Saving and Investment in the Keynesian Model

Keynesian theory questioned the basic premise of the classical economists. Saving and investment are not necessarily equal, Keynes argued, because in actuality the interest rate is not the overriding consideration when saving and investment decisions are made. Keynes denied that the level of household saving is tied primarily to the interest rate. Today much of our saving is institutionalized or contractual: We commit ourselves to make regular monthly payments on insurance policies or mortgages or Christmas Clubs, and saving continues unchanged regardless of interest rates. Moreover, the real motivation for saving is the prospect of future purchases. A family saves because it wants to buy a new TV, a vacation, a college education, an income for retirement. If this is the motivation, then the amount saved will not be responsive to changes in the interest rate. In fact, occasionally changes in interest rates will have an effect exactly opposite to that predicted by classical economists. For example, a family that requires a yearly retirement income of $6000 from savings will find it necessary to save $100,000 if interest rates are 6 percent and $200,000 if interest rates are 3 percent.

Instead of viewing saving as a function of interest rates, Keynesians relate the level of savings to changes in income and expectations. Very broadly speaking, saving will increase as incomes increase, and decline as incomes decline. When incomes drop to very low levels, households will need all their funds for current expenses, and saving will cease.

Keynes not only discredited the role of interest rates in determining the level of saving, but also argued that interest rates were relatively unimportant to investment decisions. While it is true that very high interest rates may discourage investment in a few extreme cases, most business executives make investment decisions on the basis of total profit expectations. If a business executive believes that there is enough demand for output from a projected plant to make that investment profitable, he will build the plant. Conversely, if he feels pessimistic about the chances of selling a new product, he will not make additional investments, no matter how low interest rates may fall. Thus, during a depression, when demand drops, investment dries up, and even the lowest interest rates prove an ineffective stimulus to a worried executive confronted with declining markets and unused capacity. In 1934, for example, banks were willing to lend money to the biggest American corporations at 1.5 percent, a bargain rate compared to the 6 percent prevailing in 1929 and 1930. Nevertheless, gross private investment sank to about one-fifth of the earlier level.

To summarize, the New Economics emphasizes that savings decisions are based on personal motives and the level of income and that investment decisions are determined primarily by profit considerations. Since savers and investors are motivated by unrelated factors, there is no logical reason why saving should necessarily equal investment at any particular point. In fact, it is very likely that from time to time saving will exceed investment. As a result of this gap, the equality of demand and supply postulated in Say's Law will not occur, and capitalist economies can routinely expect to be confronted by periods of declining demand, output, and employment.

Wages and Prices in the Keynesian Model The classical economists claimed that even if saving and investment were not in balance, the downward flexibility of wages and prices would spur the economy to increase output and create full employment. Once again, however, Keynes was dubious, for his own observations of business indicated that wages and prices were not flexible downward.

Going even further, Keynes questioned whether price and wage cuts would restore full employment, even if they could be introduced during a period of falling demand. It is true that cutting the wages and prices of any *one* firm may lead to an expansion of demand for that firm's output and to an increased number of workers on its payroll. But the same does not hold true for the economy as a whole. If every employer reduces wages, then total money income declines, and as a result, aggregate demand for the output of the economy falls. This is an example of what logicians call the fallacy of composition—what is true about a part of the whole may not be true about the whole.

Modern Employment Theory Modern employment theory today has developed and extended the concepts originally introduced by Keynes. It assumes that full employment is not the normal condition of capitalist economies; unfortunately, there are no automatic mechanisms that drive the economy toward the level of demand that will provide full employment. Instead of the optimistic view presented by the classical economists, we now accept the fact that it is only too possible for the economy to stabilize at less than full employment. The employment level at any particular time depends on the demand for goods and services, and this demand, in turn, is dependent on total spending.

Economists are no longer sanguine enough to believe that total spending will necessarily support full employment if left to its own devices. As a result, much of current economic thought is devoted to an analysis of the components of total spending in the hope of maintaining spending at the full-employment level. Moreover, modern employment theory has accepted Keynes's view of the important role of government in an economy, a role that includes government efforts to regulate private consumption and investment, as well as direct government spending.

SUMMARY

1. Recurrent but irregular fluctuations of economic activity that occur over a period of several years are known as business cycles. The four stages in the cycles of spending, output, employment, and prices are the peak, contraction, trough, and recovery. Causes of these changes may be exogenous or endogenous. The performance of the durable-goods sector, the behavior of investment spending, and the tendency of trends to be cumulative are three destabilizing features of the economy.
2. Changes in the levels of spending affect prices and unemployment. When the economy is at low levels of employment, initial increases in spending will result in higher employment, with little change in prices. During the later phase of a recovery, further spending will lead to more jobs, but will also result in some price increases. Once the economy is operating at capacity, further spending will result only in higher prices.
3. A generally rising level of prices is defined as inflation. The situation in which too much money chases too few goods causes demand-pull inflation. When producers are required to pay higher prices for factors of production, cost-push inflation occurs. When economy-wide inflation is triggered by price increases in certain basic industries, structural inflation is the problem. When a society chooses to pay its bills by printing enormous amounts of money, run away inflation called hyperinflation results.
4. Employment refers to the utilization of all factors of production, but labor in particular. Full employment rarely means 100 percent utilization. Frictional unemployment, in which people are temporarily unemployed between jobs or between seasonal work, and structural unemployment, in which there is a mismatch between jobs available and the skills of job-seekers, are thought to be inherent. Moreover, large numbers of unemployed go unreported in the statistics. The greatest concern is for cyclical unemployment, in which there is an economy-wide shortage of jobs.
5. The costs of unemployment are reflected by the GNP gap, which measures the difference between potential GNP at full capacity and actual GNP.
6. The classical theory of income and employment, known as Say's Law, assumes that under normal conditions, supply creates its own demand, the interest rate will ensure that saving equals investment, flexible wages and prices will bring demand into line with supply, and the self-regulating mechanisms of the economy work best with minimum governmental intervention.
7. The followers of Keynes emphasize that since saving decisions are based on level of income and investment on profit considerations, the two need not necessarily be equal. As a result, the equality of demand and supply will not occur and periods of declining demand, output, and employment are inherent in an economy. Moreover, the cutting of wages and prices may simply intensify the problems of the economy. The deliberate intervention of government is necessary to ensure high levels of employment.

SUGGESTED READINGS

Dernburg, Thomas F., and **D. M. McDougall.** *Macroeconomics.* 4th ed. Chaps. 11 and 16. New York: McGraw-Hill, 1972.

Gilpatrick, Eleanor G. *Structural Unemployment and Aggregate Demand.* Baltimore: Johns Hopkins, 1966.

Keynes, John Maynard. *The General Theory of Employment, Interest and Money.* New York: Harcourt Brace Jovanovich, 1936.

Okun, Arthur, ed. *The Battle Against Unemployment.* New York: W. W. Norton, 1965.

Rowan, D. C., and **Thomas Mayer.** *Intermediate Macroeconomics.* Chaps. 15, 17, and 20. New York: W. W. Norton, 1972.

Shapiro, Edward. *Macroeconomic Analysis.* 2nd ed. New York: Harcourt Brace Jovanovich, 1970.

Sherman, Howard J. *Elementary Aggregate Economics.* Chaps. 1–4. New York: Appleton-Century-Crofts, 1966.

QUESTIONS

1 Review
   a. the typical phases of the business cycle,
   b. the major types of inflation,
   c. the types of unemployment,
   d. the relation between the interest rate, saving, and investment.

2 Immediately after World War II, there was a relatively rapid rise in the price level. There had been controls on purchasing during the war, and householders had generally postponed replacing durables. In addition, they had not had the opportunity to purchase many durables. Most had accumulated savings by the end of the war. What was probably the type of inflation occurring during this period? Why?

3 In parts of the country, weather precludes certain types of activities, such as construction for much of the winter season. In other areas, a dominant agricultural industry requires workers mainly for planting or harvest. How might a goal of full employment in these areas differ from such a goal in an area with a mild climate or diversified employment opportunities?

4 Since World War II there has been increasing concentration in many industries; that is, increasing domination by a few large firms. Would this trend tend to increase or decrease the potential for structural inflation? Why?

5 How does total spending typically change during the cycle of recovery, boom, decline, and recession? What effect does an increase in spending have on prices and employment as the economy nears full employment? As the economy reaches full employment?

6 Employers sometimes create the impression that there are vacancies when they may really have no intention of hiring. How is this done? What type of unemployment is really occurring?

7 Assume that there is a 6 percent unemployment rate in an economy presently employing 100 million. One senator argues that unemployment can be reduced to 4 percent by the creation of 2 million new jobs. Another argues that there will have to be considerably more than 2 million new jobs to get 4 percent unemployment. Why the disagreement? Which is probably right if the unemployed are defined as those actively seeking employment?

8 Keynes did not have much confidence in the ability of the interest rate to regulate saving and investment. Why? In the opinion of Keynes, when could demand remain below supply? How does this view differ from Say's Law?

9 If a classical economist happened to be the chairman of the President's Council of Economic Advisers, what course of action would he or she probably suggest to the President to combat unemployment? Would he or she be likely to worry about the dangers of inflation?

10 Who are generally the losers in the case of unemployment? Inflation? Why is there an argument concerning the amount of inflation an economy can tolerate? Shouldn't an economy have zero inflation?

11 Suppose that you have invented a special hinge that you expect to be used in cabinets for new homes. You will be paid a 6 percent royalty on each hinge sold by the manufacturer. Would you expect the income from your invention to be fairly stable or unstable over the course of the business cycle? Why?

12 Economist Milton Friedman once stated that the main problem facing the Nixon administration was an inflation psychology—the expectation of inflation. What effects would the expectation of price increases have on the purchasing decisions of householders? The wage demands of unions? The inventory policies and the stockpiling of raw materials by businesses? The "momentum" of a recovery or boom period of the business cycle?

CHAPTER 8 EQUILIBRIUM

In the early days of the Great Depression, President Hoover's laissez-faire philosophy restrained him from taking any bold, imaginative steps. He was convinced that "nature would cure all, whilst government intervention might ruin all."[1] Hoover's policy was to allow the slump to "liquidate" itself: In his own words, he was willing to "liquidate labor, liquidate stocks, liquidate the farmer, liquidate real estate"[2] in the firm belief that once this spate of liquidation was completed, the economy would return to its normal condition of full employment.

Forty-five years later, despite the growing complexity of the economy, there are still people who not only believe that free enterprise can cure its own ills, but regard government intervention as dangerous and obstructive. This view clashes with modern economic theory derived from Keynes, which questions the ability of a free-market system to maintain full employment automatically. The Keynesians say that an economy left to its own devices is as likely to have underemployment as it is to achieve full employment. From the previous chapter we know the basic reasons for this conclusion. In this chapter we explore in greater detail how levels of output and employment are determined.

AGGREGATE DEMAND

In dealing with the factors at work in the creation of full employment, we begin by taking a closer look at **aggregate demand**—the amount of money that all sectors of an economy are willing and able to spend for goods and services. Aggregate demand is the key factor in determining the level of economic output, and consequently the level of employment. A rise in the level of aggregate demand—or total spending—prompts businesses to increase their level of output, and employment climbs. Conversely, if aggregate demand is not sufficient to purchase all the goods and services produced, businesses will cut back on output, and employment will drop. Thus, a first step in analyzing overall, or macroeconomic, performance is to take a look at aggregate demand and see what determines the total amount that is spent in an economy.

As we discussed in Chapter 6, total spending (GNP) may be divided into four components: consumption spending (C), investment spending (I), government spending (G), and net exports (X). In order to simplify the discussion in this chapter, we shall temporarily ignore government spending. This means that there will be no taxation in our hypothetical private economy, and consequently, NNP, NI, and DI will be identical. To simplify even further, we shall also ignore net exports (which in the United States constitute only a very small fraction of GNP). We are then left with C and I as the components of aggregate demand.

Consumption

The United States has often been called a consumption-oriented economy. The average American household buys thousands of dollars' worth of goods and services each year—from basic necessities, such as food and clothing, to luxury goods, such as stereo equipment and vacations in Florida. What determines how much a family decides to spend in a given year and how much it decides to save for future needs?

Determinants of Consumption Economists have isolated a number of factors that influence the level of consumption spending. Of these, the amount of disposable income a family receives is unquestionably the most important variable. All other things equal, a family with an income of $14,000 will spend more than a family with an income of $10,000. But in fact, all other things are not usually equal. This is why one family with an income of $14,000 spends $12,000 and saves $2000, while another family with the same income spends all of it.

DEMOGRAPHIC FACTORS Demographic factors, such as the size of the family and the age of its members, are of considerable importance in determining how much money a given family spends. Larger families

1 Samuel Eliot Morison, *Oxford History of the American People* (New York: Oxford University Press, 1965), p. 945.

2 *Ibid.*

Opening photo by J. Paul Kirouac

spend more of their income than smaller ones. Both young and old households spend a higher percentage of their incomes than do middle-aged households. This is partially explained by the fact that family income typically peaks during the middle years, making increased saving possible, but there are other reasons. Old families, for example, no longer are saving for children's education or for retirement.

Changing demographic patterns in the United States will undoubtedly affect patterns of consumption over the next decade, although the net effect is uncertain. The declining birth rate will mean smaller families and an accompanying drop in the rate of spending, but a change in the average age of households may tend to increase the percent of income used for consumption. The Bureau of the Census estimates that by 1985 our population will show an increase in the number of young and old people relative to the total population—an increase of those groups that typically spend most of their income—and a drop in the percentage of middle-aged people—those who are likely to save a relatively large share of earnings. Thus, the long-run trends toward smaller families whose ability to save is greater may be offset by a growing proportion of the population in age brackets where saving is more difficult.

STOCK OF DURABLE GOODS The stock of durable goods on hand also influences the level of private consumption. When a family has acquired a substantial stock of durable goods, it may not want to buy additional items. A family that already owns two cars, several TV sets, and a wide assortment of washers, electric carving knives, and battery-operated toothbrushes may find it relatively easy to save a larger proportion of total income. In contrast, a family that lacks a stock of durable goods may prefer to acquire them rather than save. Such was the case for the entire economy during the early post–World War II years. Consumption expenditures soared as a consequence of the record-breaking low in the stock of consumer durable goods brought on by 16 years of depression and war.

AMOUNT OF LIQUID ASSETS AND LEVEL OF DEBT Households accumulate liquid assets, and to some degree, the amount of such assets affects consumption. The more cash, stocks, bonds, and so forth owned by a family, the more likely the family is to feel that it has saved enough; as a result, income will be used for spending, not additional saving.

The level of indebtedness also influences consumption. Up to a point, borrowing allows people to spend freely. However, high levels of debt may place restraints on household spending. When installment debt climbs and consumers find themselves committed to substantial monthly outlays to pay for previous purchases, they may cut their buying and use the income to reduce their debts. Credit availability may affect the overall level of debt, and hence the level of consumption. During the Korean War, for example, government policies that discouraged long-term, low-downpayment car loans depressed automobile sales. Interest rates in general may also influence spending, with lower interest rates stimulating consumers to borrow and buy.

PSYCHOLOGICAL FACTORS Certain psychological factors, such as confidence in the economy or expectations, may also encourage or discourage spending. If households expect a rise in prices or if they are worried about shortages, they may stock up on consumer goods. The surge in spending in 1950—at the outset of the Korean War—for example, arose partly out of public fear of impending inflation and shortages similar to those that occurred during World War II. Confidence in the economy, or lack of it, is also a very important factor. During the worst of the recession of 1970–71, consumption spending fell not merely because growing unemployment reduced incomes, but also because the savings rate increased sharply, reflecting a general fear of further layoffs.

CULTURAL FACTORS Cultural forces also influence consumption behavior. In some societies, saving confers high status. The so-called Protestant ethic makes thrift a virtue, thus encouraging saving at the expense of consumption. But overall, our culture has tended to encourage spending rather than saving. As early as 1899, the American economist Thorstein Veblen, writing in *The Theory of the Leisure Class,* described Americans as having an urge for "conspicuous consumption" that motivated such purchases as expensive cars, large wardrobes of clothing, and exotic vacations.

In societies where different cultural forces prevail, different patterns of consumption emerge. Some anthropologists believe that in societies where each person has a fixed status and rank, there may be less incentive to spend because consumption cannot acquire social position. Others have noted that the position of the older person in society affects saving for the future. In the United States, for example, the head of a family may feel compelled to limit current consumption in order to save for old age. In contrast, a study of a Philippine farming community revealed that a substantial percentage of those interviewed felt that it was not necessary to save for old age; many said that their children would provide, and others replied, "Bahala na"—God will take care.[3]

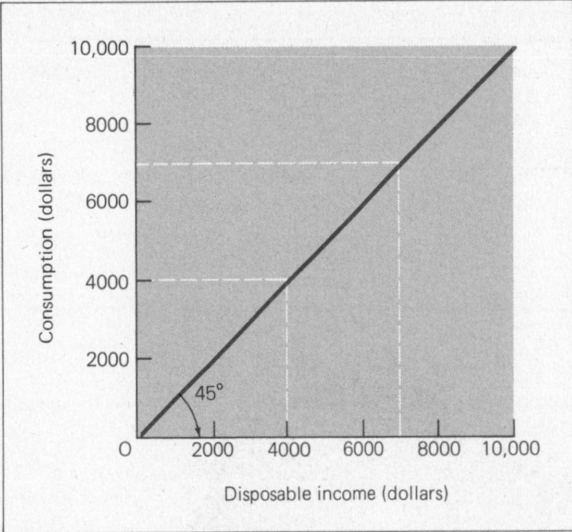

FIGURE 8-1 A HOUSEHOLD THAT CONSUMES ALL ITS DISPOSABLE INCOME (HYPOTHETICAL) The 45° line indicates that consumption and disposable income are equal at every level.

Consumption Schedules Despite the many variables that may affect consumption, the single most important factor in establishing a family's level of spending is the size of its disposable income (DI).

To analyze spending behavior, then, economists view the level of consumption as a function of the level of disposable income and assume that all the other factors affecting consumption remain constant.

The relationship between consumption and disposable income can be shown graphically. Suppose that a family always spends its entire disposable income. In other words, the family's level of consumption always equals its disposable income, regardless of the level of DI. This relationship is illustrated in Figure 8-1 by a line drawn at a 45° angle on a graph that plots DI on the horizontal axis and C on the vertical axis. The 45° line tells us that a family with a disposable income of $4000 would spend the entire $4000, that the same family with a DI of $7000 would spend the entire $7000, and so forth. Because the 45° line is equidistant from both axes, any point lying on it represents a situation in which DI and C are equal. If we were to examine the actual spending behavior of a typical American household at any one time, however, we would see that although there is a close positive correlation between C and DI, consumption and disposable income are seldom equal. Although the total amount spent increases as income increases, the amount of C does not increase as much as DI. Conversely, as a family's income falls, its consumption spending falls too, but not by as much as the decline in income.

We can illustrate this pattern by looking at a consumption and saving schedule for a typical family (Table 8-1). In its first three columns, this table shows that consumption and saving vary at different income levels. At very low levels of income, consumption exceeds DI, as a family dips into its savings or borrows. At $5000, consumption equals disposable income, but as income increases past this point, a declining percentage of total income is spent and an increasing percentage is saved. For example, a family that earns $6000 will spend $5750, or 95.8

3 G. Tagumpay-Castillo, "Sociological Factors in Saving Capital Accumulation: Some Research Findings," *Philippine Economic Journal* 3 (1964): 192.

TABLE 8-1 Consumption and Saving Schedules for an American Household (Hypothetical)

(1) Disposable income (DI)	(2) Consumption (C)	(3) Saving (S) DI–C	(4) Average propensity to consume (APC) $\frac{C}{DI}$	(5) Average propensity to save (APS) $\frac{S}{DI}$	(6) Marginal propensity to consume (MPC) $\frac{\text{change in C}}{\text{change in DI}}$	(7) Marginal propensity to save (MPS) $\frac{\text{change in S}}{\text{change in DI}}$
$ 2000	$ 2750	$–750	1.375	–.375	.75	.25
3000	3500	–500	1.167	–.167	.75	.25
4000	4250	–250	1.060	–.060	.75	.25
5000	5000	0	1.000	0	.75	.25
6000	5750	250	.958	.042	.75	.25
7000	6500	500	.929	.071	.75	.25
8000	7250	750	.906	.094	.75	.25
9000	8000	1000	.889	.111	.75	.25
10,000	8750	1250	.875	.125	.75	.25
11,000	9500	1500	.863	.137	.75	.25
12,000	10,250	1750	.854	.146	.75	.25
13,000	11,000	2000	.846	.154	.75	.25
14,000	11,750	2250	.839	,161	.75	.25

At any level of income below $5000, dissaving occurs—that is, consumption exceeds income. $5000 is the one level of income at which consumption is equal to income and saving is zero. At all incomes above $5000, there is some saving, since income exceeds consumption. Although these figures are hypothetical, it is evident that the poor have a very hard time making ends meet and are constantly in debt, while the more well-to-do are usually able to save some of their income.

percent of DI, while a family that earns $10,000 will spend $8750, or only 87.5 percent.

A table illustrating this relationship between DI and C is called a consumption schedule, or a propensity to consume schedule.

Figure 8-2 illustrates the basic characteristics of the propensity to consume by plotting the income and spending data from Table 8-1 on a graph with a 45° line. Note that although the consumption line (C) slopes upward and to the right, it does not slope as steeply as the 45° line. This is because consumption does not increase as much as DI.

AVERAGE PROPENSITY TO CONSUME Table 8-1 indicates that a family with $10,000 of income will spend $8750, or 87.5 percent.

This figure—the percentage of total income consumed—is called the average propensity to consume, or APC. The average propensity to consume for any level of income can be calculated by using the following formula:

$$APC = \frac{C}{DI} = \frac{\$\ 8750}{\$10,000} = .875$$

We have observed that the proportion of total income consumed declines as income increases. This is another way of saying that the average propensity to consume declines as income increases.

MARGINAL PROPENSITY TO CONSUME APC figures state the percentage of *total income* devoted to consumption; they do not, however, reveal how much of any *increase* in income will be consumed. For example, we know from column 4 of Table 8-1 that the APC for a family with $10,000 in disposable income is .875, or that the family spends $8750. But APC does not

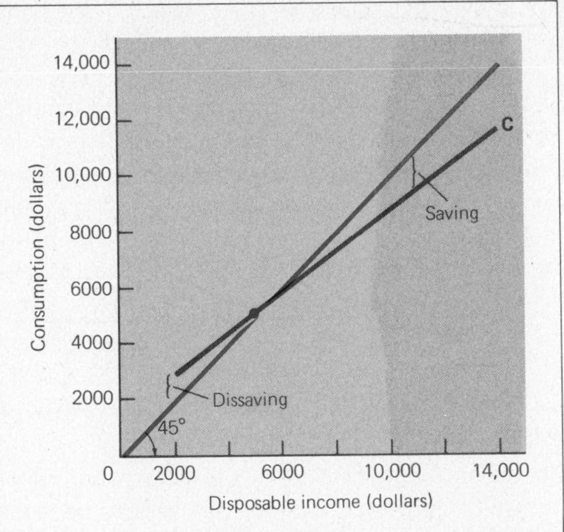

FIGURE 8-2 SAVING AND CONSUMPTION FOR AN AMERICAN HOUSEHOLD (HYPOTHETICAL) At $5000 disposable income, consumption is also $5000. Since all of disposable income is consumed, saving is 0. When disposable income is below $5000, consumption exceeds disposable income, and saving is negative. For example, when disposable income is $3000, consumption is $3500, which means that there is dissaving of $500. When disposable income exceeds $5000, saving occurs. At $10,000 disposable income, consumption is $8750 and saving, $1250.

tell us what proportion of any increment in income that family will spend.

The percentage of any additional income that is used for consumption is called the marginal propensity to consume.

Referring to Table 8-1, it is clear that a $1000 increase in income (from $10,000 to $11,000) results in a $750 increase in consumption; the marginal propensity to consume is therefore .75. The marginal propensity to consume can be calculated using the following formula:

$$\text{MPC} = \frac{\text{Change in consumption}}{\text{Change in income}} = \frac{\$\,750}{\$1000} = .75$$

Saving Schedule The portion of disposable income that is not used for consumption is saved. In other words, disposable income equals consumption plus saving (DI = C + S). Note that *saving* is not the same as *savings,* since saving is the *flow* of income into the *stock* of savings. Column 3 of Table 8-1 lists the amount a family saves at various levels of disposable income. We can see that saving plus consumption always equals DI. For example, with a DI of $10,000, a family consumes $8750 and saves $1250 ($8750 + $1250 = $10,000).

People save for reasons that are the reverse of the reasons they consume. Smaller families tend to save more, as do households headed by people in their middle years. Families are more likely to save when they fear declining economic conditions, or do not have access to credit, or are discouraged from borrowing because of high interest rates. The primary factor influencing saving, however, is the size of disposable income.

The relationship between disposable income and saving is shown graphically in Figure 8-2. Line C is the consumption function; it tells how much is consumed at each level of income. Since the 45° line represents the points at which consumption and income are equal, the distance between this line and the consumption function must represent saving or dissaving (the amount spent in excess of what one receives in income). Saving, of course, occurs when the consumption function is below the 45° line; dissaving, when it is above it.

Propensity to Save Saving behavior can also be described by the propensity to save.

The term average propensity to save (APS) refers to the proportion of total income saved at a given income level: $\text{APS} = \frac{S}{DI}$.

For example, a family that saves $1250 of its $10,000 of disposable income would have an APS of .125. Since the dollars consumed plus the dollars saved always equals total DI, then APC plus APS (the respective portions of income consumed and saved) must equal 1.00.

C + S = DI or $8750 + $1250 = $10,000

APC + APS = 0.875 + 0.125 = 1.00

Moreover, if APC declines as income increases, then by definition, APS increases as income increases.

Since marginal propensity to consume (MPC) is the percentage of any increase in income that will be spent, marginal propensity to save (MPS) is the percentage of any addition to income that will be saved.

For example, in Table 8-1, if DI increases from $9000 to $10,000, $250 of that $1000 increase in income will be saved; that is, the marginal propensity to save is .25.

$$\text{MPS} = \frac{\text{Change in saving}}{\text{Change in DI}} = \frac{\$\ 250}{\$1000} = .25$$

We know that given the same $1000 increase in DI, $750 will be consumed, or MPC=.75. Thus, MPS+MPC adds up to 1.

$$\text{MPC} + \text{MPS} \quad \text{or} \quad .75 + .25 = 1.00$$

Because this relationship between MPS and MPC is always the same, another way of finding the MPC is to subtract the MPS from 1.

$$1 - \text{MPS} = \text{MPC}$$

The National Consumption Schedule

Until now, we have been discussing consumption and saving in terms of individual households. On a national scale, a similar relationship exists between consumption and national income or net national product. A hypothetical consumption function for the entire economy would look much the same as the individual consumption schedule shown in Figure 8-2. The major difference is that we are now dealing with billions, rather than thousands, of dollars. Line C_{SR} in Figure 8-3 is a hypothetical national consumption function. This aggregate graph indicates how much every family in the economy would spend at different levels of national income.

Short-run and Long-run Aggregate Consumption

The aggregate consumption function C_{SR} in Figure 8-3 shows the relationship between consumption and income *at a given time*. It should not be misconstrued as a historical graph. If it were, one would draw the mistaken conclusion that as national income increases over time, the percentage of income consumed steadily declines, with a larger and larger proportion being held in savings. If this were the case, the implications for the economy could be disastrous. A steadily declining APC would make it more and more difficult to maintain levels of full employment. The economy would have an ever growing problem of finding ways to ensure that income saved returned to the spending stream by way of investment.

But this is not the case. A look at national consumption and income data over the past several decades reveals that the percentage of income used for consumption—APC—has remained virtually constant (except during World War II). Yet it was stated earlier in our discussion of the average propensity to consume that the APC declines as income rises. How, then, can this apparent discrepancy be explained? The answer lies in the distinction between short-run and long-run consumption functions. The long-run behavior of consumption spending can be illustrated graphically by continual upward shifts in the short-run consumption function over time. (See the right-hand graph in Figure 8-3.) Points a, b, and c represent the average level of consumption spending at each new point in time. By connecting these points, we can derive the long-run or historical consumption function—line C_{LR}.

This hypothetical long-run consumption function looks much the same as the actual long-run consumption function for the United States, shown in Figure 8-4. This figure plots aggregate spending and disposable income data for the United States since 1929. Each point represents a single year. A historical trend line has been fitted to most of the points.[4] Note that the trend line (the historical consumption function) passes almost through the point of origin.

4 You will note that the dots for 1942–45 are rather far to the right of the primary trend line, signifying that for those years, consumption grew much more slowly than income. This reflects the fact that during World War II, consumption expenditures did not expand at their normal pace because of shortages, rationing, and patriotic saving campaigns.

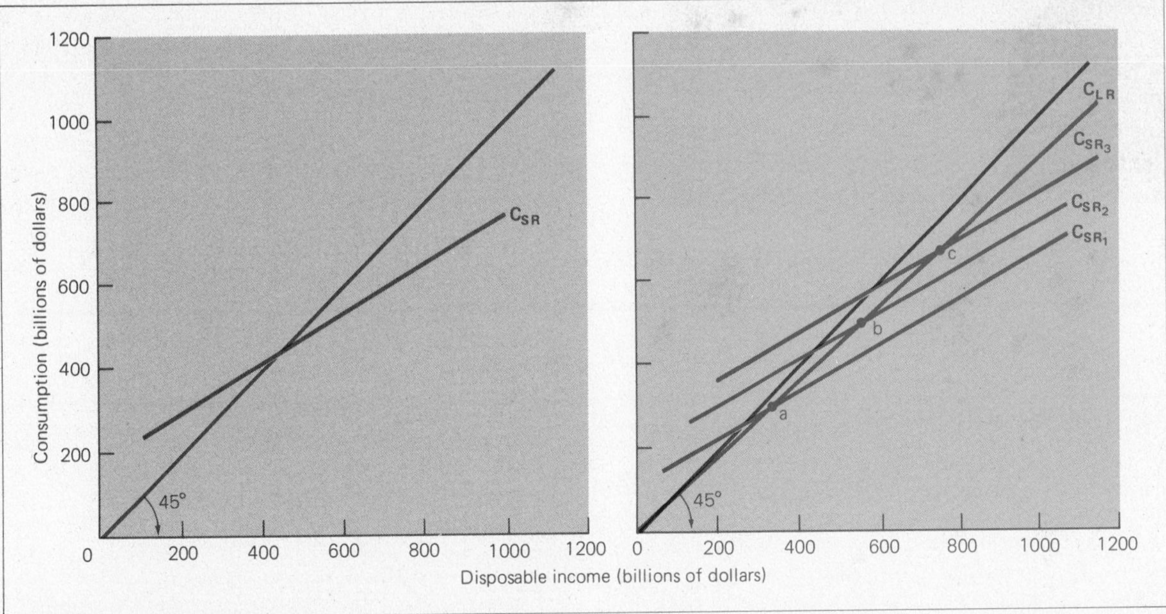

FIGURE 8-3 AGGREGATE SHORT-RUN AND LONG-RUN CONSUMPTION FUNCTIONS (HYPOTHETICAL) At any one time the aggregate consumption function resembles the individual consumption function, as C_{SR} shows. The average propensity to consume declines as income rises. However, this is not the case in the long run, as shown by C_{LR}. The average propensity to consume is relatively constant. The long-run consumption function is determined by the upward shift of the short-run curves over time.

This means that the long-run APC is virtually constant. Mathematically, it also means that APC equals MPC.

Several theories have been advanced to account for this upward shift of the consumption function over time. One is the **relative income theory** developed by James Duesenberry. This theory is based on the assumption that how much a family spends depends not merely on the total (or absolute) income it earns, but on how its income compares with that of other households. It would explain the fact that APC has remained constant during the post–World War II period by pointing out that while the absolute income of most families grew, their relative income did not change substantially. In other words, although families earned more, so did their neighbors. Therefore, consumption of additional income was forced to remain at a constant level if households were to keep up the appearance of general prosperity, or, to use the terminology of economics, their relative consumption position.

Milton Friedman has offered another theory to explain the same phenomenon. He suggests that a distinction should be made between *current income*—the income a family actually receives in a given year—and *permanent income*—the average annual income it can expect to receive over a lifetime. According to Friedman, a family makes saving and consumption decisions based on the estimated size of permanent income, not current income. Friedman argues that in a year when current income is unusually high—because of an unusual bonus or an unexpected inheritance, for example—a household will tend to save a large proportion of this temporary or transitory addition to income. However, when households feel certain that their income increments are permanent, they do not increase the percentage saved. Rather, they maintain a constant rate of consumption, even at higher income levels. This analysis would explain the fact that APC has not declined, even though incomes have increased greatly over the last several decades; most people have viewed these higher income levels as permanent.

Investment

The classical economists and the post-Keynesians recognized that, if an economy was to generate enough demand to purchase the goods and services produced, investment had to equal saving. The post-Keynesians pointed out, however, that in most cases saving decisions and investment decisions are made

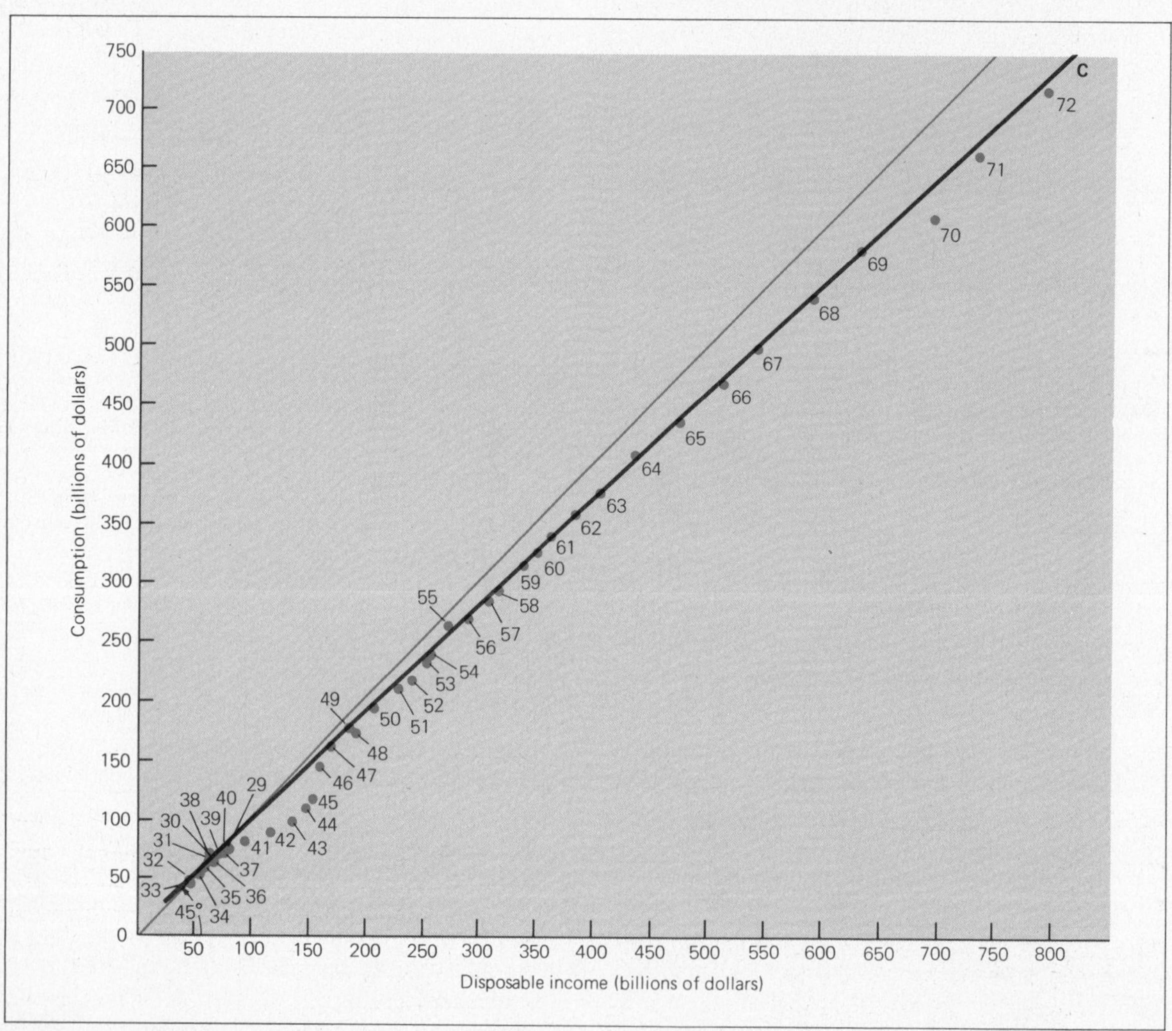

FIGURE 8-4 CONSUMPTION AND DISPOSABLE INCOME IN THE UNITED STATES, 1929–72 The consumption function for a nation is unlike that of an individual household because the percentage consumed remains relatively constant rather than declining as income rises. Compare this with Figure 8-2 to see the difference. This is actually a difference not simply between individual and aggregate curves but between a curve plotted for a single year (Figure 8-2) and a curve plotted for a number of years.

SOURCES: U.S. Bureau of the Census, *Business Conditions Digest,* August 1971; *Federal Reserve Bulletin,* March 1973.

by different people. Moreover, the forces that underlie decisions to save are quite unrelated to those that underlie decisions to invest. Thus, there is no logical reason to assume that an economy that is generating a given amount of saving will necessarily generate the same amount of investment spending.

Determinants of Investment As explained earlier, the amount of saving by households is closely tied to the amount of disposable income received. The amount of investment, however, is influenced primarily by profitability. The Board of Directors of General Motors, for example, may be eager to spend $100 million for a plant to construct a new line of minicars if they believe that the investment will yield a net profit of $10 million a year; they will be somewhat less willing if the net profit is foreseen to be only $5 million; and the investment will not be made at all if no profit is anticipated.[5]

But profitability, by itself, is not the only factor determining investment decisions. An investment may yield some profit and still not be desirable because the expected rate of return on the investment is less than the rate of interest that could be earned in the money market. If a company can put its cash into bonds and get an assured return of 5 percent, it has no incentive to invest those same funds in equipment that will offer only a 4.5 percent return. Moreover, if a company has to borrow to finance its investment, the interest it pays is part of the cost of the venture, and those costs must be covered before profits accrue. Therefore, the higher the interest rate, the less the incentive to commit funds for investment. As the rate of interest drops, more ventures become profitable and the amount of investment increases. There is an inverse relationship, then, between the rate of interest and the amount businesses are willing to invest. The rate of interest is a key determinant of the level of investment.

5 Accountants refer to such a measure of profitability as the rate of return on investment (R.O.I. = profit ÷ investment). If GM plans to earn $10 million on an investment of $100 million, the projected rate of return is 10 percent; a 5 percent rate of return on a similar $100 million investment would be $5 million.

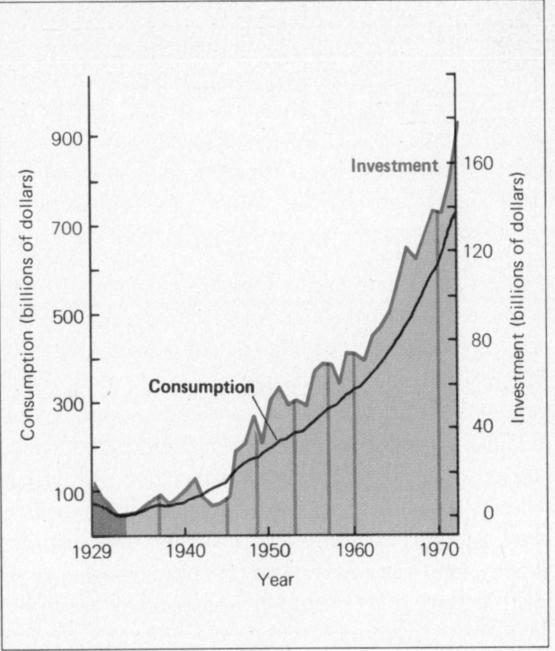

FIGURE 8-5 CONSUMPTION AND INVESTMENT, 1929–72 The volatile nature of investment and the relative stability of consumption are shown here in their historical perspective. Notice how consumption has increased steadily since World War II, while investment has fallen during each recession (signified by the colored bars).

SOURCES: *Economic Report of the President,* 1973; U.S. Department of Commerce, *Business Conditions Digest,* March 1973; U.S. Department of Commerce, *Survey of Current Business,* July 1959 and July 1960.

Volatility The investment component of aggregate demand is much more changeable, or volatile, than consumption spending (see Figure 8-5). This volatility is closely related to the durable nature of capital goods. When a business executive is unsure of or pessimistic about future profits, he can postpone buying expensive new equipment or a new plant. Actual and projected population growth, interest costs, wage rates, and taxes will influence a business executive's estimation of the future demand for and cost of producing his product. If he does not feel confident that a proposed investment will be currently profitable, he can put off his plans, awaiting more favorable conditions in the future.

Another factor that contributes to the volatility of investment is the irregular appearance of new inventions and processes that prompt waves of investment spending. The invention of the automobile, for example, induced a wave of investment spending. So did the invention of plastics and the computer. This kind of spending ends once the capital goods needed to supply the demand have been produced.

Profit expectations, and therefore investment, may also be affected by attitudes, such as a widespread feeling that government has grown more sympathetic to business—or less, as the case may be—or that unions are about to take a hard line in negotiations. Business executives may feel encouraged to spend money on new capital stock when they see indications that international tensions have eased, or they may be discouraged from investing because the stock market is shaky. Such modifications in profit expectations may result in appreciable swings in investment spending from one year to the next. In 1948, for example, buoyed by a wave of optimism following the initial post–World War II consumption boom, investment spending increased by 35 percent. The very next year, however, business executives, disturbed by the deterioration of East–West relations, the possibility of a postwar recession, and the election of a Democratic President, cut their investment spending by 22 percent.

Such volatility ir. investment spending is hardly surprising, since so little about economic conditions is under a business's direct control and so much is at stake for the firm. Perhaps the real surprise is that the swings are not even greater. But volatility is moderated because investment is a long-range activity. New factories do not appear overnight, and once the commitment to build is made, construction continues despite business downturns. A company looking for long-range profits may be willing to continue investments during hard times, hoping that it will get a jump on its competitors in the future. And during downturns, interest rates are often lower, which provides an incentive to invest, even while business conditions are not favorable.

Investment Schedule Consumption and saving are influenced primarily by disposable income, but investment is relatively independent of income. For simplicity's sake, we shall assume for the time being that investment remains constant regardless of the level of income. In Table 8-2, although income varies from $900 billion to $1500 billion, investment remains the same, at $100 billion. In reality, however, investment may increase somewhat as income rises.

Aggregate Demand Schedule

By combining the consumption and investment schedules for our hypothetical private economy, we can view the behavior of total spending. Table 8-2 is called a **schedule of aggregate demand.** Columns 2 and 3 list consumption and investment at various levels of income; column 4 is the sum of C+I, or total private aggregate demand. Although investment remains constant as income changes, consumption varies with income, and as a result, aggregate demand (C+I) must vary with income too.

This aggregate demand schedule is illustrated graphically in Figure 8-6. The C+I line is parallel to the consumption line because investment spending is exactly the same at every income level. (The

TABLE 8-2 Aggregate Demand Schedule (Hypothetical, billions of dollars)

(1) DI or NNP	(2) Consumption spending (C)	(3) Investment spending (I)	(4) Aggregate demand (C + I)
$ 900	$ 950	$100	$1050
1000	1000	100	1100
1100	1050	100	1150
1200	1100	100	1200
1300	1150	100	1250
1400	1200	100	1300
1500	1250	100	1350

Aggregate demand is the sum of consumption and investment spending. Equilibrium occurs when aggregate demand (C + I) is equal to income. This occurs at a level of $1200 billion.

equal distance between C and C + I as income rises represents the constant level of investment spending.) The fact that C + I slopes upward and to the right indicates that aggregate demand varies directly with income; this, of course, reflects the fact that consumption spending is one of its components.

Table 8-2 and Figure 8-6 illustrate how aggregate demand (C + I) varies with DI. But in a private economy where government plays no role, DI would be equal to NNP. (Review the definitions of DI and NNP in Chapter 6 to see why this is so.) Therefore, we can also say that aggregate demand changes directly with changes in the level of total output, or NNP.

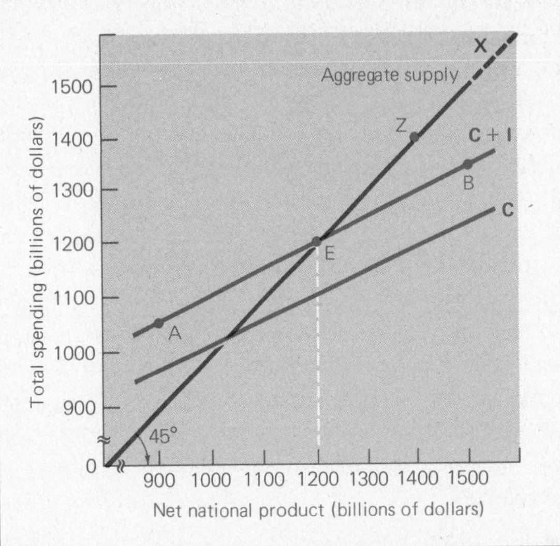

FIGURE 8-6 CONSUMPTION, INVESTMENT, AND NET NATIONAL PRODUCT (HYPOTHETICAL) The sum of consumption and investment shows the total spending, or aggregate demand, in an economy. Line OX represents aggregate supply, where spending calls forth an equal value of output. The intersection of C + I with aggregate supply forms the equilibrium point. Such an equilibrium point occurs at E. If total spending is above the aggregate supply schedule (say, at point A), there will be a tendency for spending to rise toward E. Similarly, if spending is below aggregate supply (point B), there will be a tendency for it to decline toward E.

AGGREGATE SUPPLY

Keynesian theory explains aggregate supply very neatly. Aggregate demand, said Keynes, calls forth its own supply, for businesses will try to supply as many goods as customers are willing to purchase. If total spending is $1200 billion, then businesses will supply $1200 billion worth of goods and services; if spending increases to $1300 billion, businesses will supply $1300 billion worth. To put it another way, Keynes saw aggregate supply as equal to aggregate demand at every level of NNP up to the full capacity of the economy.

In Figure 8-6, the aggregate supply curve is depicted as a straight line drawn at a 45° angle from the point of origin. Every point on this line represents an equal amount of spending and output, because the line is equidistant from both axes of the graph. Point E, for example, represents aggregate supply of $1200 billion and a $1200 billion spending level; point Z represents output of $1400 billion and spending of $1400 billion. At some point, however, the capacity of the economy is fully employed. The dotted portion of the curve represents this area.

THE SEARCH FOR EQUILIBRIUM

The ideal match between aggregate demand and aggregate supply, like an ideal marriage, is more common in theory than in practice. In either case, there is a search for equilibrium, or what is called "settling."

Aggregate Demand/Aggregate Supply Approach

One way of locating the level of output at which the economy will settle is to compare aggregate demand and aggregate supply figures.

The point at which supply and demand are equal represents market equilibrium, or the level of NNP at which the economy will tend to settle.

Table 8-3 is an aggregate supply/aggregate demand schedule for a hypothetical economy. Row (a) describes an economy producing $900 billion of output. Consumption spending at this level equals $950 billion, exceeding DI by $50 billion, so that $50 billion of dissaving occurs. Investment spending of $100 billion is projected for this economy, giving us aggregate demand, or total spending, of $1050 billion ($950 billion of consumption spending plus $100 billion of investment). In row (a), then, total desired spending of $1050 billion exceeds total output of $950 billion. Under such circumstances, demand exceeds supply, and businesses find eager customers depleting their inventories. Consequently, they step up production, not only to meet the increased demand, but also to rebuild inventories. When this happens, the economy as a whole—output, income, and employment—enjoys a period of expansion.

At the $1400 billion NNP level, row (f), we see precisely the reverse situation. Notice that here aggregate demand (C + I) of $1300 billion is less than aggregate supply; the economy is producing $1400 billion of output, but total spending equals only $1300 billion. Under these conditions, businesses are finding it impossible to sell their entire output. Inventories are accumulating, cutbacks will doubtless be made, and an economic decline will follow.

In Table 8-3, there is only one point at which aggregate supply equals aggregate demand. At a $1200 billion level of NNP, total spending (C + I) is sufficient to purchase all the output produced, and no more. At this level, businesses find a market for all the goods and services they supply. Because total spending is exactly equal to total output, there is no excess demand to deplete inventories and stimulate higher production levels. Because demand is adequate to purchase all of present output, there is no buildup of unsold inventories to lead to a decline in the level of production. Thus, an economy achieves equilibrium at that level of NNP where aggregate demand equals aggregate supply, and it will settle at a level of employment consistent with that equilibrium point.

Figure 8-6 expresses this same concept graphically. At level A, where NNP equals $900 billion, we see that the aggregate demand curve is above the aggregate supply curve, suggesting that more will be supplied in order to meet the excess demand. The

TABLE 8-3 Expanding, Declining, and Equilibrium States of the Economy (Hypothetical, billions of dollars)

(1) Aggregate supply or income (DI) or output (NNP)	(2) Consumption spending	(3) Saving	(4) Investment spending	(5) Aggregate demand (C + I)	(6) Employment level (in millions)	(7) State of the economy
(a) $ 900	$ 950	$–50	$100	$1050	75	Expanding
(b) 1000	1000	0	100	1100	80	Expanding
(c) 1100	1050	50	100	1150	85	Expanding
(d) 1200	1100	100	100	1200	90	At equilibrium
(e) 1300	1150	150	100	1250	95	Declining
(f) 1400	1200	200	100	1300	100	Declining
(g) 1500	1250	250	100	1350	105	Declining

When aggregate demand exceeds aggregate supply, the economy will tend to expand toward the equilibrium point. Similarly, when aggregate demand is smaller than aggregate supply, contraction will take place, until equilibrium is attained. At an equilibrium level of $1200 billion, aggregate demand equals aggregate supply and 90 million people are employed.

opposite is true at level B. Only at level E, where NNP equals $1200 billion, are supply and demand equal. Point E, then, is the equilibrium level for the economy.

It is important to recognize that an economy at equilibrium is not necessarily operating at full employment. In the hypothetical economy described in Table 8-3, the $1200 billion equilibrium NNP supports employment of 90 million. This figure may not, in fact, represent full employment. For example, in order to supply employment for everyone who actually wished to work, 95 million jobs may be required. Thus, it is only a coincidence if the equilibrium NNP and the full-employment NNP are the same. Unfortunately, the likelihood is that, left to its own devices, a capitalist economy may settle at equilibrium either below the full-employment level (in which case there is unemployment) or above it (in which case inflationary pressures will develop).

The Saving/Investment Approach

A somewhat different way to find the equilibrium level of NNP focuses on saving and investment. If we inspect the saving and investment columns of Table 8-3 (columns 3 and 4), we find that at the equilibrium level, $1200 billion, these two amounts are equal. At every other level of NNP, saving and investment differ, and the economy is unstable: When investment spending exceeds saving, the economy will expand; when investment spending is less than saving, the economy will contract.

To explain this, let us see what happens when investment is greater than saving. At a NNP of $1100 billion, for example, consumers may be spending $1050 billion and saving $50 billion, while businesses are committed to investment spending of $100 billion. Total spending thus equals $1150 billion, exceeding total output by $50 billion. The result is instability. This instability results directly from the fact that the amount spent for business investment is larger than saving; if business investment spending had been equal to the $50 billion of household saving, the figure for total spending would have equaled that for total output and the economy would have been in equilibrium. [Consumption spending ($1050 billion) + Investment spending ($50 billion) = NNP ($1100 billion).] Disequilibrium was created because $S \neq I$.

A similar pattern of instability is found at levels of NNP where investment is less than saving. For example, at a NNP of $1500 billion, saving exceeds investment by $150 billion. Total spending would therefore be only $1350 billion. Inadequate investment spending may result in insufficient demand, causing an accumulation of inventories, a reduction in production, and a recession.

Equilibrium, then, can be described as that level of NNP where saving and investment are equal. At levels where investment exceeds saving, aggregate demand exceeds aggregate supply, and NNP will expand. At levels where saving is greater than investment, aggregate demand is less than aggregate supply, and NNP will decline.

This kind of analysis, with its emphasis on the role of saving and investment, is useful because it highlights the importance of investment spending as a force in expanding or contracting the economy.

Figure 8-7 shows how equilibrium NNP can be found graphically using saving and investment figures. The saving and investment lines intersect at point E (NNP = $1200 billion), where saving and investment are each $100 billion; this point indicates the level of NNP at which the economy will be in equilibrium. At NNP levels to the left of E, where the investment line is above the saving line, the economy will expand in response to the excess demand created by investment spending that is greater than saving. At NNP levels to the right of E, the economy will contract, as total spending falls because households are saving more than businesses are investing.

Planned versus Unplanned Saving and Investment

It has so far been emphasized that investment and saving are rarely equal. However, in the last analysis, saving must indeed equal investment at every NNP

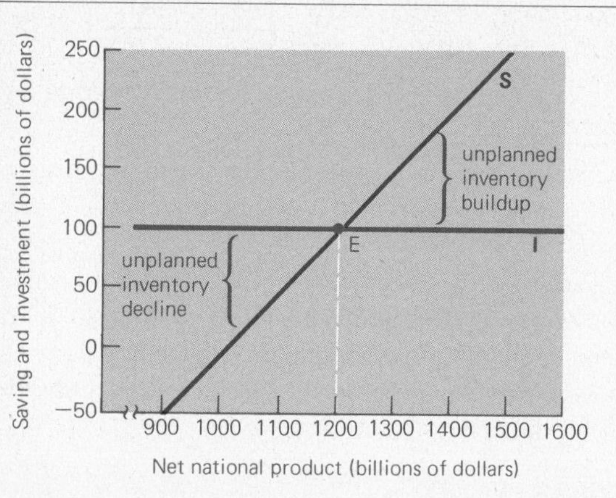

FIGURE 8-7 THE EQUILIBRIUM OF SAVING AND INVESTMENT (HYPOTHETICAL) Because investment has been assumed to equal $100 billion at all levels of net national product, it appears as a straight line. Where the saving line intersects is the equilibrium point. Above this, saving will not find an outlet in investment, and the economy will contract. Below E, the demand for investment funds will outstrip saving, and the economy will expand. These lines represent planned saving and planned investment; all levels of actual saving and actual investment are equal because inventories make up the difference.

level. This apparent contradiction can be explained by differentiating between **planned** and **actual** saving and investment.

Business investments are of two kinds: investment in plant and equipment and investment in inventories. Inventory change is as much a part of investment as the purchase of new factories and new machines. If a bicycle manufacturer, for example, buys $10,000 worth of new machinery and also increases his inventory of finished bicycles from $4000 to $5000, he has invested a total of $11,000 during the period. If, instead, his year-end inventory declines from $4000 to $3000, his total investment spending would be only $9000. In either case, the year-end totals are the firm's **actual annual investment.**

The amount that businesses intend to invest during the current year is called **planned investment.** Table 8-3 lists planned investment of $100 billion, regardless of the level of NNP. But this figure does not take into account changes in inventory that may be forced on a business because of changing economic conditions. Essentially, unplanned changes in inventory work as a kind of balancing mechanism which equates *actual* investment and *actual* saving regardless of the level of NNP. Some examples will help explain the way this mechanism works.

Suppose that our hypothetical economy is at an $1100 billion level of NNP—a level below the equilibrium point. Businesses are producing $1100 billion of output, but total spending (C+I) amounts to $1150 billion. Aggregate demand, then, is greater than total output. An additional $50 billion of output is needed to supply this excess demand, and its most likely source is from inventories. At the end of this period, businesses will find that their inventories have fallen by $50 billion—a reduction that is unplanned. As a result, actual business investment will turn out to be not the planned $100 billion listed in the schedule, but only $50 billion ($100 billion *planned* I minus $50 billion unplanned reduction in inventory equals $50 billion *actual* I). This new actual investment figure of $50 billion is exactly equal to actual saving.

The unintended reduction in inventory that occurs when aggregate demand exceeds aggregate supply will prompt businesses to step up production for the following year. These increases in output will, in turn, create increases in employment and income. As households find themselves with more money in their pockets, they will be able to save more than they had previously. Eventually, a new, higher level of intended saving will be reached which will exactly equal the amount that businesses intend to invest. At this point, equilibrium for the economy will be achieved.

The same pattern appears when insufficient demand leads to an increase in inventory. Suppose that output equals $1400 billion, but demand is only $1300 billion. As a result, businesses are unable to sell their entire output, and at the end of the period, their inventories have increased by $100 billion—the difference between output and sales. Thus, actual investment consists not only of the $100 billion initially planned, but also of the additional $100 billion of involuntary inventory increases, or unplanned investment. The new total of actual investment—$200 billion—is exactly equal to actual saving.

When businesses see that their inventories are growing, they will respond by cutting back production. As total output drops, employment and income will also drop, and households will save less. Eventually a new, lower level of intended saving will be reached, which will exactly equal intended investment. The economy is again in equilibrium.

Thus, even when the economy is not in equilibrium, actual saving will equal actual investment because of the balancing effects of unplanned changes in inventory. But these same unplanned changes in inventory will also induce changes in output, which in turn will affect the levels of income and saving. Eventually, a level of NNP will be reached at which intended saving equals intended investment. This is the equilibrium level.

CHANGES IN EQUILIBRIUM NNP

A look at actual economic performance in the United States reveals a picture far different from the idealized state of economic equilibrium. Instead of showing a relatively stable set of output and employment figures, our economy has been characterized by broad upward sweeps, broken by sharp, periodic fluctuations. In other words, our economy displays constant changes in the equilibrium point. And as the level of NNP shifts back and forth in an attempt to achieve stability, adjustments in income and employment result.

Why does the equilibrium level of NNP change? Essentially, changes in equilibrium NNP occur as a result of shifts in the consumption or investment functions. Investment, of course, is a far more volatile component of aggregate demand than is consumption. Consequently, we can assume that changes in investment are the primary cause of shifts in the equilibrium level of NNP. If investment spending increases, equilibrium NNP will rise; if investment spending decreases, equilibrium NNP will fall.

The Multiplier

That changes in investment spending lead to changes in equilibrium NNP is hardly surprising. What is surprising, however, is that any change in investment spending will cause a far greater change in the level of NNP. A few examples will illustrate this reaction.

A change in investment spending may be induced by a change in the interest rate, technological innovations, government taxing policy, foreign or domestic political developments, or any one of many other factors. The immediate effect of a change in investment is a shift in aggregate demand. If I increases by $20 billion, then C+I will be $20 billion higher at every level of NNP. This is shown graphically in Figure 8-8, where line (C+I+20) represents this new, higher level of aggregate demand. The point of intersection of this line and the aggregate supply line indicates that equilibrium NNP has shifted from $1200 billion to $1260 billion. To summarize, because of the infusion of an additional $20 billion of investment spending, a new equilibrium level of NNP is established, which is $60 billion higher than the former equilibrium level.

A decline in investment spending of $20 billion will have exactly the opposite effect. This lower aggregate demand line (C+I−20) intersects the aggregate supply line at an equilibrium NNP of $1140 billion. This indicates that given a $20 billion cut in investment spending, NNP will stabilize at a level $60 billion below the former equilibrium level.

Why do changes in investment spending cause substantially greater changes in equilibrium NNP? The answer lies in the workings of the **multiplier effect**, a term used by economists to describe the reaction of an economy to any infusion of additional spending.

The multiplier effect means that any change in aggregate demand has not one effect, but a whole series of effects on total spending.

For example, in our hypothetical economy, a $20 billion increase in investment produces an increase of $20 billion in the incomes of those hired to design and construct the new factories and equipment, house the additional inventory, operate the new machines, and so forth. What happens to this extra $20 billion in income? Assuming the marginal propensity to consume to be ⅔, those who earn the $20 billion will spend $13.3 billion on goods and services

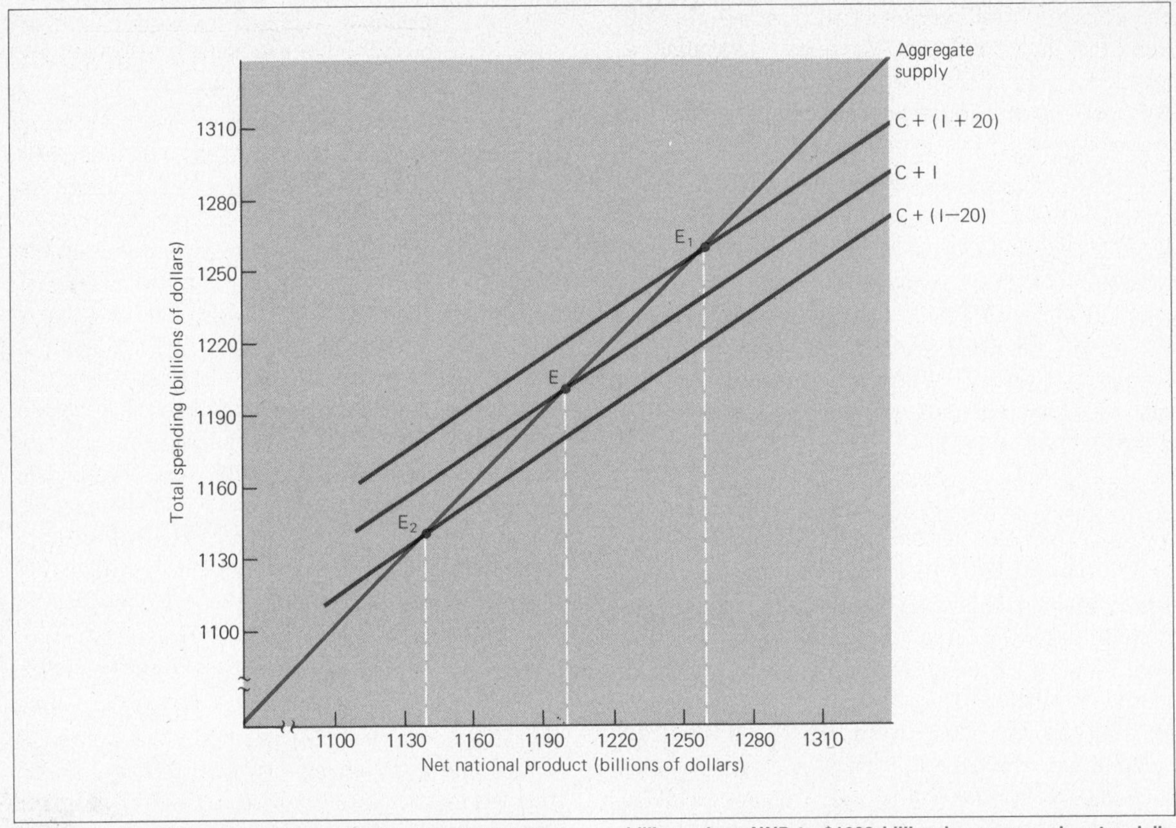

FIGURE 8-8 THE MULTIPLIER AT WORK (HYPOTHETICAL) A $20 billion change in investment spending results in more than a $20 billion change in net national product. Equilibrium is at a NNP of $1200 billion. An increase in investment of $20 billion raises NNP to $1260 billion because each extra dollar of investment is respent. The multiplier, which is based on the propensity to consume, permits a calculation of this exact amount.

and save the remaining $6.7 billion. The expended $13.3 billion will, in turn, be received as income by another group, who will spend ⅔ and save ⅓. This pattern will repeat itself again and again, until the initial $20 billion of investment spending leads to a total increment in national income of considerably more than $20 billion.

The exact size of the total increase in NI depends, of course, on the marginal propensity to consume (MPC). Once we know how much of each incremental dollar of income will be spent on consumption (the MPC), we can determine the total increase in national income that will occur as the original investment dollars spread through the economy.

The formula for the multiplier is $\frac{1}{1-\text{MPC}}$; and since we know that $1-\text{MPS}=\text{MPC}$, the formula can also be rewritten as

$$\text{Multiplier}=\frac{1}{\text{MPS}}.$$

This last equation merely says that the multiplier is the reciprocal of the MPS.

In our hypothetical example, the MPS is ⅓; therefore, the multiplier is 3. This is why the $20 billion of additional investment leads eventually to an increase in NNP that is three times its size, or $60 billion.

The Importance of the Multiplier The multiplier plays a central role in any theory about changes in national income and product. We have described its effects only in connection with changes in investment spending, but its impact on changes in consumption is identical. If we move from a purely private economy to one in which government and foreign transactions play a part, then the multiplier will also have an effect on changes in G or X. Thus, any change in one of the components of aggregate demand will be subject to the multiplier.

The multiplier is more than a simple recognition of the fact that changes in aggregate demand have a multiplied effect on changes in national income and product. The multiplier provides a means of measuring that effect. Looked at in another way, the multiplier helps determine how much of a change in spending will be required to achieve a stated change in output. With a multiplier of 3, a $90 billion increase in NNP can be induced by a $30 billion increase in spending.

Induced Investment So far, our discussion has underestimated the full importance of the multiplier somewhat because it has ignored the effects of **induced investment.** In the long run, the effects of an increase in spending would not stop with the multiple expansion of income described above, for this higher income level would, in turn, have implications for other parts of the economy. For example, in the economy illustrated in Figure 8-8, we saw how an additional investment of $20 billion would result in a new equilibrium NNP of $1260 billion. However, as incomes reached this level, businesses might very well decide to proceed with another round of increased investment spending in order to supply the output required by a higher-income economy. This is the process of induced investment.

The Acceleration Principle

The implications of induced investment become even more apparent when we investigate what is called the **acceleration principle.**

The acceleration principle refers to the relationship between increases in total output and the addition-

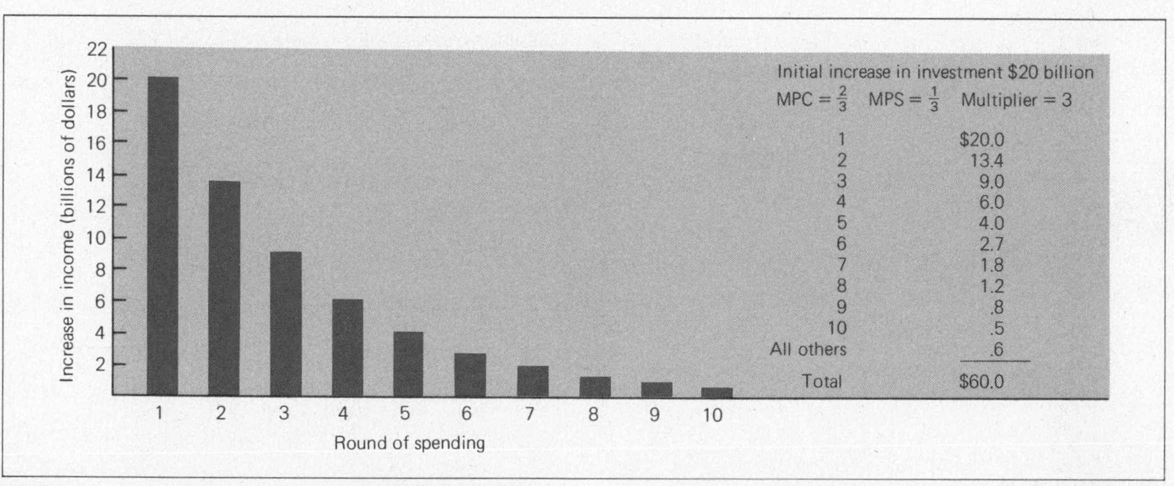

FIGURE 8-9 THE ROUND-BY-ROUND INCREASE IN INCOME CAUSED BY AN INITIAL INCREASE IN INVESTMENT OF $20 BILLION (HYPOTHETICAL) The initial increase in investment of $20 billion depicted in Figure 8-8 will lead to a $60 billion increase in income. Since two-thirds of the $20 billion is spent on consumption during the second round and two-thirds of the resultant $13.3 billion is spent on consumption during the third round, we can carry out this process through an infinite number of rounds, adding the result of each round, to reach the final $60 billion.

THE PARADOX OF THRIFT

When business conditions look bad, people start putting away a little extra for the "rainy days" ahead. And the more they save, the worse things get. This, in a nutshell, is the paradox of thrift. Although it may make good sense for an individual to save some of his current income in the expectation of having more to spend in the future, when all households attempt to save larger portions of current income, the end result will actually be a reduction in the level of national income and in the amount that people are able to save. What seems rational for an individual, then, may be a national threat in the aggregate.

Behind this paradox is the multiplier. Just as increased spending boosts national income by a greater amount, so decreased spending due to extra saving (or anything else) slams the brakes on the economy. Graphically, the increase in saving moves the saving curve upward, which leads to a drop in the equilibrium level of national income. At this new lower level of income, households find that their efforts to increase saving are thwarted. Graph A shows that when the investment curve is horizontal the initial shift in the saving curve eventually increases the level of saving not a jot!

When the investment curve slopes upward (as in B) rather than being flat (as in A), the effects are even worse. As the saving curve jumps upward, the level of income drops even more sharply than before, and savings actually declines. A "supermultiplier" is at work here.

The paradox shows that conventional wisdom is not always the best guide for national policy. Because economic health is measured in flows, not stocks, the best approach in an economic slump is to get spending moving again so that the multiplier is pushing the economy upward, not downward.

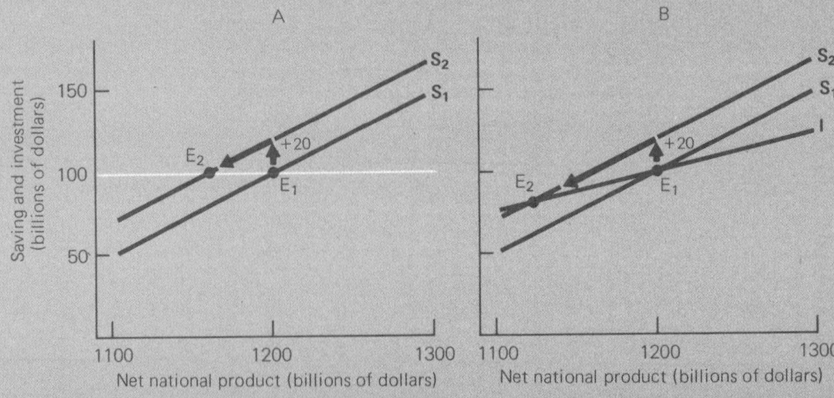

TABLE 8-4 The Acceleration Principle (Hypothetical for the Snazzy Sneaker Corporation)

				Machines purchased			
Year	Sales	Sales increase	Total machines required	New machines needed	Replacement demand	Total	Investment spending
1971	$300,000		10	–	1	1	$10,000
		30,000					
1972	330,000		11	1	1	2	20,000
		60,000					
1973	390,000		13	2	1	3	30,000
		60,000					
1974	450,000		15	2	1	3	30,000
		30,000					
1975	480,000		16	1	1	2	20,000
		0					
1976	480,000		16	–	1	1	10,000
		–30,000					
1977	450,000		15	–	–	–	0

Any change in sales (which corresponds to aggregate demand) results in larger changes in investment spending. This depends on the rate of increase in total demand. When the rate is increasing, investment spending will also increase; when the rate is constant, investment will remain at the same level; when the rate is declining, investment will be cut back.

al investment spending that such increases encourage.

In brief, it explains why an increase in NNP will often result in a proportionately larger increase in investment spending and why the amount of investment spending depends not on the absolute level of business activity, but on whether that level is increasing or decreasing. An example will help explain how the acceleration principle works.

Assume that the Snazzy Sneaker Corporation needs one stitching machine for each $30,000 worth of sneakers produced. In 1971, the company had sales of $300,000. Because it owned 10 machines, Snazzy's capacity was sufficient to meet that demand. But every year one of the firm's stitching machines wears out and must be replaced. Thus, in 1971, Snazzy's total investment spending amounted to $10,000 for one new replacement stitcher.

In 1972, the sales of Snazzy sneakers increased to $330,000. To fill the new orders, Snazzy had to buy one new stitcher plus one replacement machine; this required a total of $20,000 in investment spending. Thus, although output had increased by only 10 percent, investment spending had doubled.

The previous year's growth in sales accelerated in 1973, and the company found itself with sales of $390,000—or $60,000 more than the previous year. Investment spending of $30,000 was required: $10,000 for a replacement machine and $20,000 for two new machines to meet the additional $60,000 of demand. Note that the *rate of increase* in output was higher in 1973 than in 1972.

In 1974, sales increased again by $60,000, once more requiring the company to purchase three machines, for a total investment of $30,000. While Snazzy's output increased, the rate of increase was the same as the previous year; investment spending, although continuing at a high level, did not increase. This illustrates a fundamental point about the accelerator: Investment spending increases only if the rate of increase in output is increasing. When the rate of increase in output is constant, investment spending stabilizes.

Let us take the Snazzy story further. The year 1975 is still a very good year for Snazzy, although sales increase by only $30,000, as compared with the $60,000 advances shown during the two previous years. This $30,000 increase in sales means that Snazzy need order only two machines, and its investment spending falls from $30,000 to $20,000. In 1976, Snazzy's output is unchanged from the previous year, and investment spending falls further, dropping in half from $20,000 to $10,000. Finally, in 1977, although Snazzy suffers only a small decline in sales and output (from $480,000 to $450,000), investment spending dries up completely, for the company now has 16 machines on hand and needs only 15 to meet its production requirements.

This company's experience illustrates the operation of the acceleration principle.

This principle is based on the assumption that investment spending depends on the rate of increase in total demand: If the rate of increase is growing, investment spending will increase; if the rate of increase is stable, investment will be constant; if the rate of increase declines, investment will fall.

The acceleration principle also emphasizes the extreme volatility of investment as compared with other components of aggregate demand. At its height, investment spending for Snazzy Sneakers increased at a far greater rate than sales. But as a result of only a minor decline in total output in 1977, the company brought its investment spending to a halt. Thus, the acceleration principle suggests that any percentage change in aggregate demand may result in much larger percentage changes in investment spending.

Interaction of the Multiplier and the Accelerator

Economic instability may often be explained by the interaction of the multiplier and the accelerator. Increases or decreases in aggregate demand, from whatever source, flow through the economy, producing a multiple expansion or contraction of NNP, which is then reflected in a change in investment spending. The induced change in investment, as a result of the accelerator principle, is often sizable, and it, in turn, has a multiplied effect on NNP. The net result is that any trend in the economy, either up or down, tends to snowball. Earlier, for example, we showed how an increase of $20 billion in spending could lead to an increase of $60 billion in NNP. Applying the accelerator principle, we now see how this growth in NNP would result in a further increase in investment, which, once the multiplier effect took hold, would produce another larger increase in output, and so on.

Similarly, any decrease in total spending would cause not only an even larger decrease in NNP, but also additional declines in investment spending throughout the economy. In later chapters we explore in greater detail the sharp declines that have periodically characterized our economy which can be attributed directly to the operation of the multiplier and the accelerator.

RECAPITULATION

We began this chapter with an inquiry into the relationships between national income, aggregate spending, and full employment. First, we saw that total spending is the key to national income, or more specifically, that aggregate demand is the dynamic force that determines the level of income or output in an economy. Second, we explained how economic activity moves toward an equilibrium point; equilibrium will occur at that level of NNP where aggregate demand equals aggregate supply, or where planned saving equals planned investment. Finally, we emphasized that this equilibrium point does not invariably represent that level of output adequate to provide full employment. *There is no necessary relationship between the level of national income or output and full employment.* Operating on its own, the private sector may settle at an equilibrium level at which output is inadequate to offer jobs to all those who wish to work, or where job opportunities are so plentiful that prices are driven up in an inflationary spiral. Moreover, the equilibrium level is constantly changing. As a result, even if full-employment equilibrium were, by coincidence, achieved, it is unlikely that the economy would remain at this happy level for very long. We must therefore conclude that the private economy we have hypothesized would be unable to ensure a full-employment equilibrium without the intervention of government. In the next chapter, we investigate the resources that government may contribute to offset the inadequacies and instabilities of the private sector.

SUMMARY

1 Aggregate demand is the key factor in determining the level of economic output, and consequently the level of employment. The four components of aggregate demand are (1) consumption, (2) investment, (3) government spending, and (4) net exports. In this chapter the focus is on the first two.

2 Consumption is a function of disposable income. Population trends, stock of durable goods in the hands of consumers, amount of liquid assets and level of consumer debt, confidence in the economy, other expectations, and attitudes toward saving and consuming also have an impact on the level of consumption. These are held constant in the analysis, however.

3 A consumption schedule shows the proportion of disposable income that goes toward consumption. As income rises, consumption will rise by a smaller amount. The average propensity to consume is calculated by dividing total consumption by disposable income. The marginal propensity to consume reveals how much of any increase in income will be consumed. It is calculated by dividing the change in consumption by the change in income.

4 The amount of investment is determined primarily by profit expectations rather than by level of income. Interest rates are a gauge of the opportunity cost of any investment. The higher the rate of interest, the less the incentive to commit funds to investment. The investment component of aggregate demand is much more volatile than consumption spending.

5 Aggregate demand, said Keynes, calls forth its own supply, for businesses will try to supply as many goods as customers are willing to purchase. However, when aggregate supply is equal to aggregate demand, the economy is at equilibrium. Just because the economy is at equilibrium, it is not necessarily at full employment. It is only a coincidence that equilibrium will be at that point. Unfortunately, the likelihood is that a capitalist economy will settle at equilibrium either below the full-employment level (in which case there is unemployment) or above it (in which case inflationary pressures will develop).

6 Planned saving and planned investment are also equal at the equilibrium level: At all other levels, only actual saving and investment are equal. The difference is made up by inventory. However, this sets in motion forces to restore equilibrium. Where more has been sold than businesses had planned, national income increases and, with it, saving. If saving is greater than planned investment, the business firm will be left with unsold inventory. This will prompt a cutback in output; national income will fall and households will have less to save, thereby restoring equilibrium.

7 Economic growth dictates that the full-employment equilibrium level of GNP will rise continuously. However, the path it follows, although generally upward, is rather erratic. One destabilizing factor is the multiplier. A change in the level of aggregate demand (usually investment, since it is most volatile) will have a multiplied effect on national income. The formula for the multiplier is $\frac{1}{1 - MPC}$. Another destabilizing factor is the accelerator, which explains why an increase in national income will often result in a proportionately larger increase in investment, and why an increase in investment depends not on the absolute level of aggregate demand, but on whether that level is changing at an increasing or decreasing rate.

SUGGESTED READINGS

Dernburg, Thomas F., and **D. M. McDougall.** *Macroeconomics.* 4th ed. Chap. 5. New York: McGraw-Hill, 1972.

Reynolds, Lloyd. *Economics: A General Introduction.* 4th ed. Chap. 7. Homewood, Ill.: Irwin, 1973.

Rowan, D. C., and **Thomas Mayer.** *Intermediate Macroeconomics.* Chaps. 9 and 11. New York: W. W. Norton, 1972.

Sherman, Howard J. *Elementary Aggregate Economics.* Chap. 3. New York: Appleton-Century-Crofts, 1966.

QUESTIONS

1 Review
   a. the components of aggregate demand,
   b. the determinants of consumption,
   c. the average and marginal propensities to consume and to save,
   d. long- and short-run consumption schedules,
   e. determinants of investment spending,
   f. the determination of equilibrium income,
   g. the operation of the multiplier and acceleration principles.

2 How might the temporary freeze on food prices in the summer of 1973 have affected the consumption schedule for an American household? Sketch a graph showing the consumption function before and during the freeze.

3 Suppose that antimaterialism becomes a stronger value in the American culture. What would be the consequences for the consumption function? Saving? Investment?

4 Assume that, for some reason, the average propensity to consume begins to drop over a period of time. Government, anxious to maintain levels of full employment, would increase its expenditures. Why? The President's chief economic adviser appears on TV and argues that government's expenditures should be used to pay for consumption-type rather than investment-type expenditures, despite the opposition from Congress. Why might he advance such an argument? What would be the long-term consequences if the government pursued only those programs designed to subsidize business investment? Subsidize college educations? Build roads and other transportation facilities?

5 Calculate
   a. APC and APS when consumption is $6000 and disposable income is $8000,
   b. APS and APC if saving is $1000 and DI is $10,000,
   c. APC and APS if a household spends all of its income,
   d. MPC and the value of the multiplier if a $1000 increase in income produces an additional $800 in consumption spending,
   e. MPS and the value of the multiplier if households spend $900 of a $1000 increase in income.

6 Assume that two families presently earn the same income. However, in one family, both husband and wife are journalists and intend to pursue careers. In the other family, both husband and wife are bank tellers, but the wife intends to quit work at least for a few years when they have children. According to Friedman's permanent income hypothesis, how does the permanent income of the two families differ and how might these expectations affect the spending patterns and the APC of the two families now and in the future? Explain how their behavior might also reflect the relative income theory.

7 Since investment is a component of aggregate demand, the government seeks to influence the level of investment from time to time by affecting the interest rate. In what direction would the government seek to change the interest rate in the case of an inflationary gap? Why?

8 For the economy with the consumption and investment schedules shown below, determine the equilibrium level of income.

NNP	C	I
	(billions of dollars)	
$ 30	$200	$30
230	300	30
430	400	30
630	500	30

What is the MPC? If investment is $80 billion at each level of income, where would the economy equilibrate? What is the value of the multiplier?

9 Assume that you are a producer of miniature solar energy cells used to produce heat for private homes. As people become increasingly concerned about the shortage of fuel oil, the demand for your product rises at an increasing rate. With a small business loan, you opened shop with four machines to turn out the solar cells. Each machine cost $2000 and each is capable of producing 10,000 cells per year. You must replace one machine every three months. In the first quarter, demand is 40,000; in the second, 50,000; in the third it is 70,000; in the fourth, 100,000. In the first quarter of the next year, demand is 130,000; in the second, it remains 130,000; in the third, it drops to 120,000. Show how the changes in demand for the solar cells affect your demand for machines and your investment expenditures.

Opening photo by Rhoda Galyn

FISCAL POLICY

In Chapter 8, we saw that an economy without a government sector is essentially unstable and that this instability is compounded by built-in forces (the accelerator and the multiplier) which tend to intensify normal fluctuations. As a result, a private economy seldom rests at equilibrium; instead, it is constantly moving toward an ever changing equilibrium point.

Economic instability can have many unpleasant personal consequences. For example, workers in capital goods industries, such as machine tools, may find their employment opportunities (and their life styles) severely limited by the "boom and bust" pattern characterizing any business dependent on investment spending for its orders. Similarly, a person starting his own business may find himself at the mercy of forces beyond his control if economy-wide inventory contractions resulting from an overall decline in demand cut sharply into his projected sales during the crucial first few months of operations.

INFLATIONARY AND DEFLATIONARY GAPS

But these instabilities are only some of the problems inherent in a purely private economy. In addition, the equilibrium level in a private economy is *independent* of full employment, so that the private sector left to its own devices may settle at an output level that is below or above full capacity.

Figure 9-1 illustrates this point. Point E_1 represents an economy operating at an equilibrium NNP of $1200 billion; however, full employment (95 million) can be achieved only if output equals $1300 billion. The only way for this economy to reach full employment would be for the demand curve to shift upward by $50 billion. This new demand curve $(C+1)_2$ would intersect NNP at $1300 billion ($E_2$), thus providing full employment. In other words, the economy operating at equilibrium E_1, NNP $1200 billion, is suffering from an insufficiency of demand, or a deflationary gap of $50 billion. The effect of this gap, when subject to a multiplier of 2, is a deficiency of $100 billion in output—that is, the economy fails by $100 billion to meet its full-employment needs.

It is also possible for an economy to have an equilibrium point above the full-employment level. In Figure 9-1, the aggregate demand curve $(C+1)_3$ intersects the aggregate supply curve at a NNP of $1400 billion ($E_3$), a quantity of output that can only be produced with employment of 100 million. This economy, however, reaches full employment at 95 million, so it is obvious that there are not enough workers available to increase actual physical output to $1400 billion. As a result, the effect of this increase in demand will be expressed through prices: The economy will be turning out the same physical quantity of goods and services, but this output will be sold for $1400 billion rather than $1300 billion. This excess of demand that pushes NNP beyond its full-employment level is called an inflationary gap. In this example, the inflationary gap is $50 billion. Applying a multiplier of 2, the result is a NNP that is $100 billion higher than that which this economy can produce under full employment.

A deflationary gap represents actual physical output lost because the economy is operating below its full-employment level. An inflationary gap, on the other hand, does not represent additional physical output—merely higher prices for the same full-employment NNP.

It is precisely the occurrence of inflationary and deflationary gaps that has prompted the acceptance of an important role for government in economic matters. Since the private sector has proven unable to protect us from unemployment and inflation, we have been forced to look to the public sector for solutions.

It is generally accepted that the government has tools to influence the level of employment, prices, and growth. But this does not mean that all economists and all politicians agree about the specific policy measures that the government should undertake. And even when economists are united on their choice of methods, problems often arise if the economic stabilization objectives of government conflict with *other* government functions. Administration leaders must often make difficult choices. In

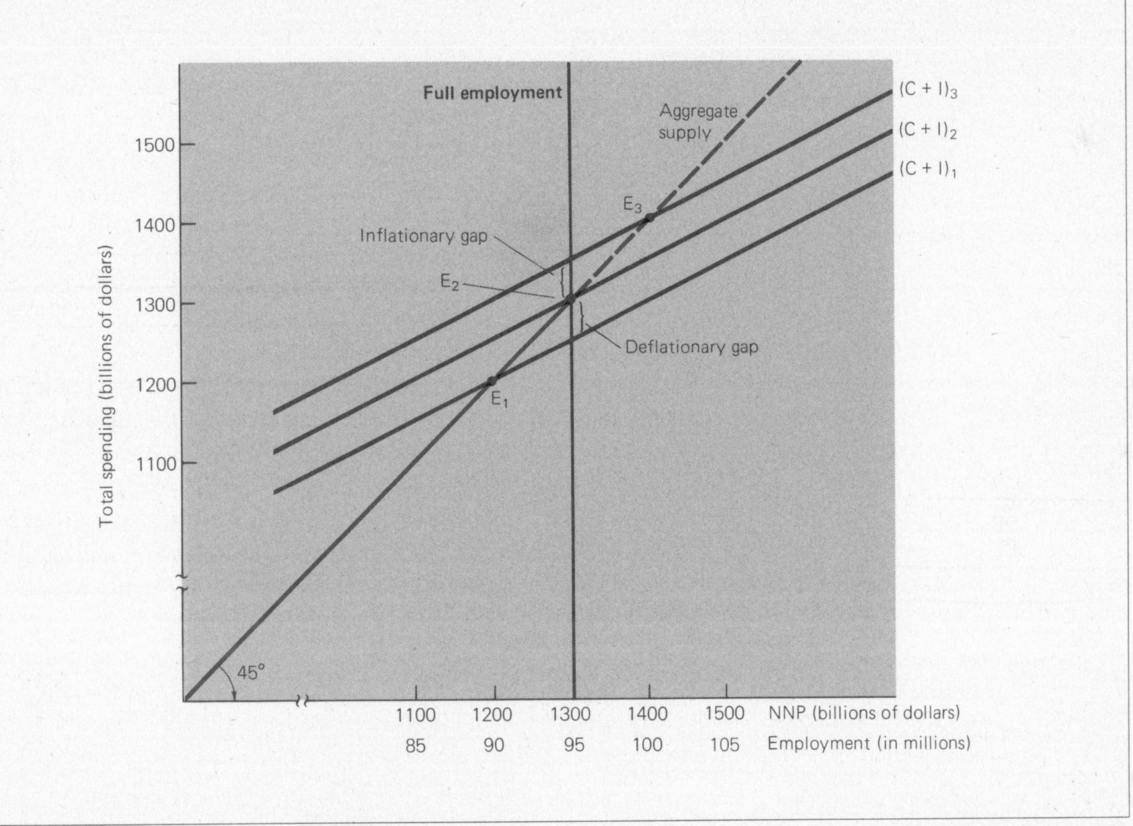

FIGURE 9-1 INFLATIONARY AND DEFLATIONARY GAPS At full-employment equilibrium (E_2), spending is equal to output, and all the resources of the economy are fully employed. However, it is possible for spending to equal output at either more than or less than full employment. Point E_1 is an equilibrium point when there is less than full employment, while E_3 indicates more than full employment. At a less than full-employment equilibrium, there is a deflationary gap—in this case $50 billion. This gap can be eliminated by an upward shift of aggregate demand from $(C+I)_1$ to $(C+I)_2$. In the case of an inflationary gap (E_3), a decrease in aggregate demand from $(C+I)_3$ to $(C+I)_2$ would result in a full-employment equilibrium at E_2.

the fall of 1965, for example, President Johnson's decision to expand spending on the Vietnam War limited the effectiveness of other government policies aimed at restraining the inflation that was developing at home. More recently, in 1973, President Nixon met with tremendous resistance from Congress in his attempts to cut government expenditures as an anti-inflationary measure; although everybody was against inflation, there was strong disagreement over which government programs should be cut.

THE ROLE OF GOVERNMENT IN DETERMINATION OF NATIONAL INCOME AND EMPLOYMENT

Government as a Component of Aggregate Demand

Since demand or spending can originate not only with households and businesses, but also with government, a third component of aggregate demand is government spending (G). The formula for aggregate demand, then, is $Y = C + I + G$.

Increments of government spending added to or

subtracted from aggregate demand in this analysis will affect NNP in exactly the same way as increments of C or I—that is, the eventual effect on output and incomes is no different when the government buys a typewriter from IBM than when a local business executive does. As a result, government spending provides a very powerful tool when changes in aggregate demand are required to bring an economy closer to its full-employment level.

However, once we admit government into the economy, we must recognize that it affects not only the spending or demand equation, but also the national income formula. In a private economy, national income is divided between consumption (C) and saving (S), but once government assumes a role, those who receive income must also allocate part of it for taxes (T). Thus, the national income formula is no longer the simple $NI = C + S$; instead, it becomes $NI = C + S + T$. With the introduction of government, we also will have to drop the assumption that disposable income, personal income, national income, and net national product are equal. Taxes and transfer payments make each of these figures different.

Reaching Equilibrium

The introduction of government spending (G) into the aggregate demand and national income equations provides an economy with interesting alternatives in the search for a satisfactory equilibrium level. In a private economy, equilibrium was defined as that level of output where aggregate demand (C + I) equaled national income (C + S).

Equilibrium: $C + I = C + S$

Or, subtracting C from both sides of the equation,

$S = I$

Now, however, we are working with equations with three rather than two variables on each side. Once again, aggregate demand must equal national income at the equilibrium level, but the formula now reads

Equilibrium: $\underset{\text{(Demand)}}{C + I + G} = \underset{\text{(National income)}}{C + S + T}$

Subtracting C from both sides, we arrive at the equation

$I + G = S + T$

which tells us that the economy will settle at that equilibrium level where the total of investment spending and government spending equals the sum of saving and taxes.

An example will clarify this new equilibrium level formula in which government spending and taxing plays such an important role. In a private economy where saving of \$150 billion exceeds investment of \$100 billion, involuntary increases in inventory will occur, and aggregate demand, output, and income will fall, until S and I are equal. However, in an economy where government is also included, we can reach equilibrium by adjusting government spending and taxes. Suppose, for example, that both T and G equal \$200 billion. Because adjustments in T and G are possible, savers can continue to save \$150 billion, and investors can continue to invest only \$100 billion. By cutting taxes and/or increasing government spending, the economy can continue at its current NNP level.

Equilibrium: $S + T = I + G$
$\$150 + \$175 = \$100 + \$225$

A Unique Aspect of the Public Sector Although in one sense changes in government spending and taxation may have effects on national income similar to changes in private spending and saving, in another sense government activities in the economic area are quite different from those initiated by private sources. In the private sector, consumption, saving, and investment decisions are based on personal choice. There are millions of households and businesses in the United States, each deciding how much to save or spend or invest in accordance with its own needs and desires and fears. As a result, although it is often possible to influence the private sector to some extent through public action (for example, through manipulating interest rates or the availability of credit), economic decisions in the private sector are not necessarily attuned to the overall requirements of the economy. In a market economy, the "right" decisions cannot be imposed on households and businesses.

In contrast, the receipts and expenditures of government are subject to deliberate control—control exercised in the public good, at least in theory. A business executive will not step up his investment spending because economists tell him that aggregate demand must rise in order to provide a full-employment economy, nor will private households obediently reduce their saving plans when similarly instructed. But in playing its role as the representative of all the people, government can deliberately design spending and taxing policies to promote stabilization goals. Of course, these may conflict with political realities or other economic objectives. Nevertheless, the government is in a unique position to deliberately regulate economic activity.

But the effective power is at the federal level since state and local governmental spending and taxation tend to move *with,* rather than *against,* fluctuations in the private sector of the economy. Thus, state and local governments are likely to cut expenditures when business conditions are depressed and to reduce taxes in periods of inflation—courses of action that reflect their comparatively limited credit standing and policy biases in favor of balanced budgets. Consequently, we must rely primarily on the national government to provide effective pressure to achieve desired overall economic results.

FISCAL TOOLS

The government can use various methods of spending and taxing to provide balance in the economy. The particular mix of such activities at any given time is referred to as the nation's **fiscal policy,** a term appropriately based on the Latin word *fiscus,* meaning a state or royal treasury. In fact, fiscal policy encompasses the entire realm of public finance, or governmental policies relating to expenditures and raising of funds by taxation and borrowing.

Government Spending

Government spending is one basic fiscal tool because of the immediate and sizable effect it produces on aggregate demand. Since government spending is a component of aggregate demand, any change in G will result in a change in the total demand schedule. Moreover, because increases or reductions in G are subject to the multiplier, their final effect on NNP (and on employment or price levels) is significantly higher than the original dollars spent.

Closing a Deflationary Gap A deflationary gap exists when demand (represented by consumer and business expenditures, new investment, and government spending) is below the aggregate dollar level required to maintain full employment in the economy. Sluggish consumer confidence as reflected in spending for soft and hard goods and new housing may be the cause; profit and growth expectations that do not encourage aggressive purchasing of inventories and supplies or net expansion of plant and equipment by business may contribute to the gap or be the prime cause. Gaps result from many factors.

Government spending can be used to close a deflationary gap by raising spending to the full-employment level. Figure 9-2 illustrates an economy operating at an equilibrium NNP of $1380 billion. At this level of output employment is 90 million, 5 million under full employment. Full-employment equilibrium can be achieved only if the aggregate demand curve, C + I + G, shifts upward by $40 billion. One way of accomplishing this is to increase government spending by $40 billion. The new demand curve, C + I + (G + 40), illustrates how such an infusion of $40 billion of government spending would eliminate the deflationary gap and move the economy to a new full-employment equilibrium NNP. Note that

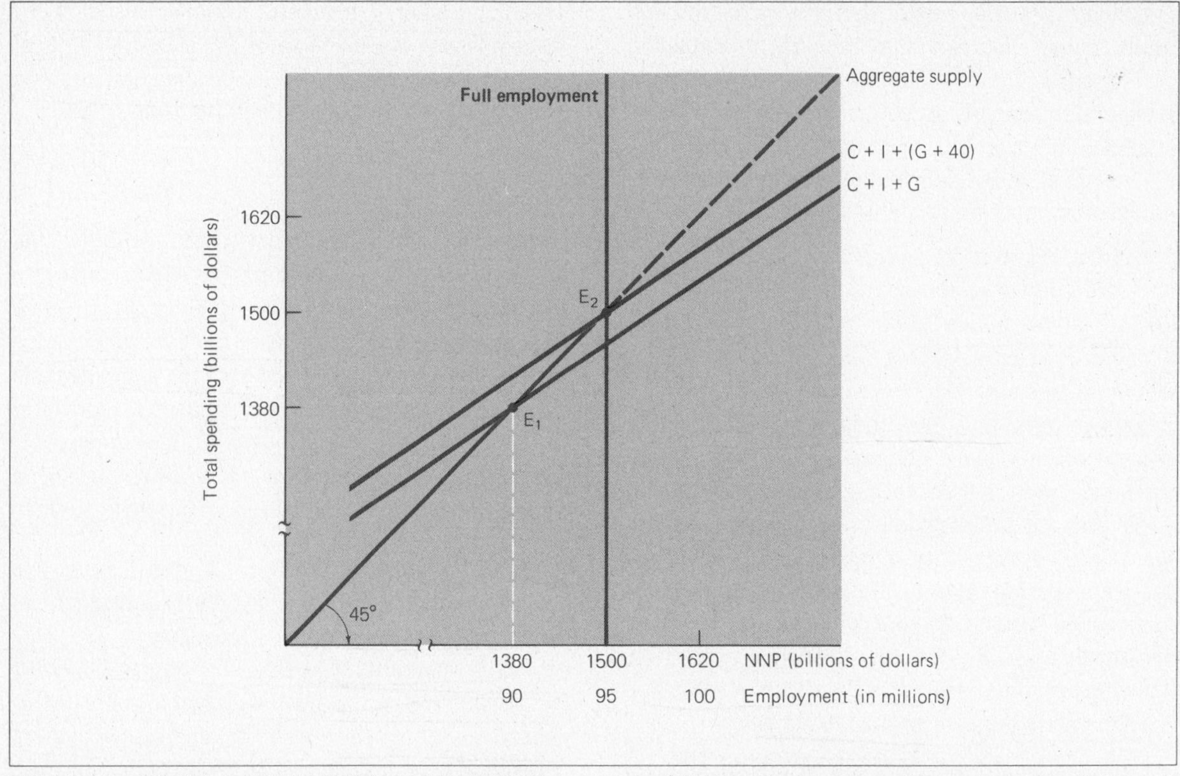

FIGURE 9-2 CLOSING A DEFLATIONARY GAP BY INCREASING GOVERNMENT SPENDING BY $40 BILLION **A deflationary gap can be eliminated by an increase in aggregate demand. The economy will move from point E_1 to point E_2 by means of a $40 billion increase in government spending. If the multiplier is 3, then net national product will be increased by $120 billion (3 × $40 billion) and full-employment equilibrium E_2 will be attained.**

although an increase of $120 billion in NNP (from $1380 to $1500 billion) was required to provide a full-employment economy, this was accomplished by adding only $40 billion in government spending. This is due to the operation of the multiplier: Since the multiplier in this economy is 3, a $40 billion infusion of spending will increase NNP by $120 billion.

The effect of the multiplier must always be considered in establishing the size of the increment of government spending that is needed to bring NNP to a desired level. Thus, if a $120 billion rise in NNP is needed to provide full employment and if the multiplier is 3, we merely divide $120 billion by 3 to arrive at the required spending of $40 billion.

$$\frac{\text{Full employment NNP} - \text{Current NNP}}{\text{Multiplier}} = \text{Required change in government spending}$$

$$\frac{\$1500 - \$1380}{3} = \$40$$

Closing an Inflationary Gap Government spending may also be an effective tool in dealing with an inflationary gap. In 1973, for example, President Nixon vetoed various appropriations bills, warning that "the big spenders" in Congress were advocating measures that would increase expenditures by as much as $50 billion and that such spending would have serious inflationary consequences. In other words, the President was advocating a reduction of government spending to eliminate a projected inflationary gap.

Figure 9-3 illustrates how such a reduction of government spending might offset inflationary pressures. In this example, total demand, C + I + G, is at such a high level that the equilibrium point (E_1) is $120 billion *above* the full-employment level of $1500 billion. Since the economy cannot physically produce a NNP higher than the full-employment NNP, the excess demand can be reflected only in higher prices.

Clearly, a reduction in aggregate demand is required. This can be accomplished by reducing the government component of aggregate demand—that is, by cutting government spending. The new aggregate demand curve, C + I + (G − 40), illustrates the effect of such a reduction in government spending. NNP now settles at a new equilibrium point (E_2) where the economy is operating at full employment and the previous inflationary pressures have been eliminated.

Once again note the effect of the multiplier. A decline in NNP of $120 billion was required, but because the multiplier is 3, this was accomplished through a $40 billion cut in spending.

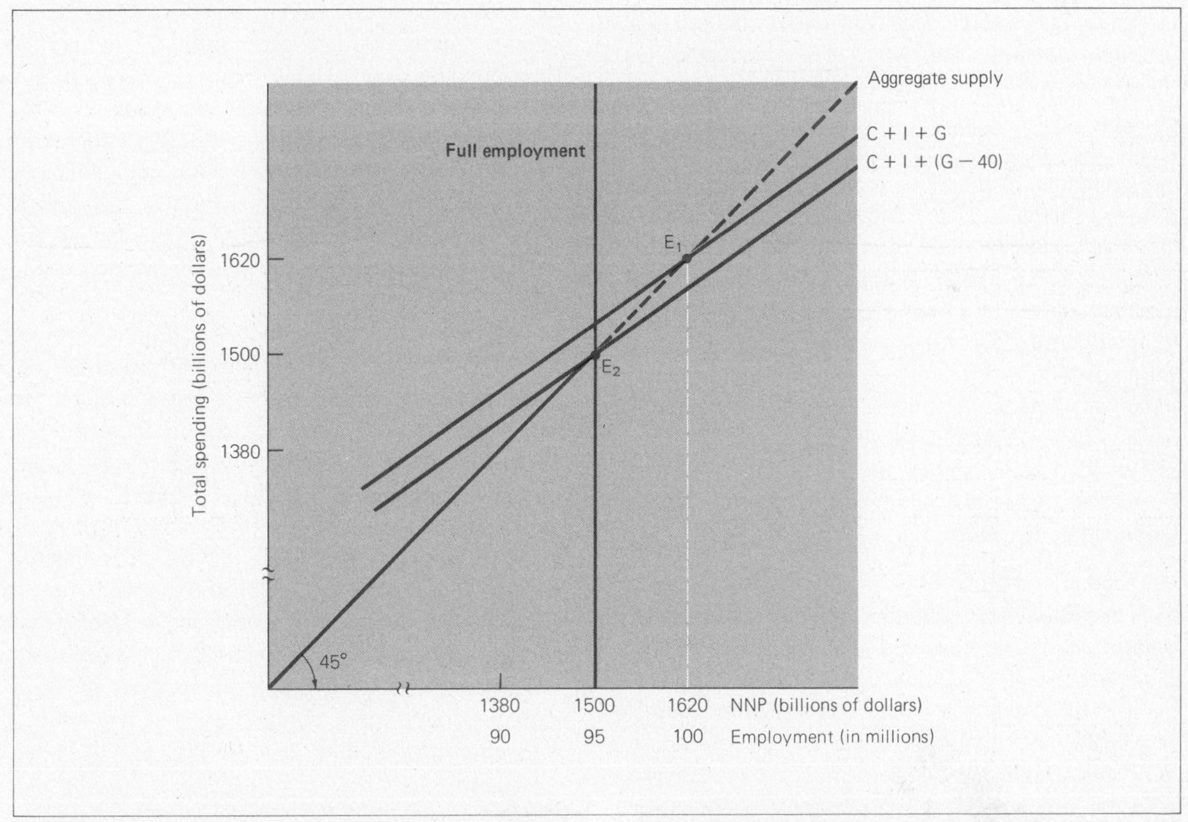

FIGURE 9-3 CLOSING AN INFLATIONARY GAP BY DECREASING GOVERNMENT SPENDING BY $40 BILLION An inflationary gap can be eliminated by a decrease in aggregate demand. The economy will move from point E_1 to point E_2 by means of a $40 billion decrease in government spending. If the multiplier is 3, then net national product will be decreased by $120 billion (3 × −$40 billion) and full-employment equilibrium E_2 will be attained.

Evaluating the Use of Government Spending as a Fiscal Tool Advocates of government spending as the primary fiscal tool to reduce unemployment base their case on unmatched efficiency. Since the actual multiplier in our economy (which is more complex than we have presented) is generally believed to run somewhere between 2 and 3, a dollar's worth of additional government spending during a recession has the effect of raising incomes and output by two to three times that amount. A secondary argument, offered by John Kenneth Galbraith[1] and others, points to the by-products of government spending: It permits our society to allocate a larger part of its resources to certain socially useful projects (pollution control, education, better health care, or helping the hard-core unemployed) that might never attract private-sector spending.

In theory, government spending could also prove a valuable tool when the nation is threatened by an inflationary excess of demand. A relatively small cut in such spending, when subject to the multiplier, could cut incomes and reduce the pressure for higher prices. In practice, however, such cuts have proven difficult to implement; every administration that has suggested budget cutting as the cure for inflation has met strong resistance. President Nixon's experience in 1973 was typical. Although he attempted to rally public support for budget cutting by warnings that any "increases in my budget . . . would mean an increase in prices for every American,"[2] many special-interest groups (ranging from the disabled aged to the cotton farmers to the health research institutes) still attempted to maintain or increase their own federal government funding.

Objections to the use of government spending as a way of increasing aggregate demand often center around the costs involved. Such spending must generally be financed through additional government debt whose costs may become burdensome. The following chapter presents this debate. More serious, perhaps, are questions raised by those who object to any increases in government spending on philosophical grounds. Economist Milton Friedman, for example, claims that "government has reached a size at which it threatens to become our master rather than our servant."[3] Friedman would distrust any fiscal policy that involved increasing the government's role in the economy.

Taxes

Traditionally, taxes have been viewed as a necessary evil, designed to meet the costs of those services a society wishes its government to provide. According to this view, taxes should be kept at the lowest possible levels consistent with the services desired. In the earliest years of our nation (1789–91), total taxes averaged about \$1.5 million annually. These were collected almost exclusively in the form of customs receipts and were used primarily to pay the interest on the public debt assumed during the Revolutionary War.[4] Today, however, taxes play a much larger role in the entire economy. In 1973, total per capita taxes were over \$2000, as compared to \$1.89 in 1800.[5] Today, taxes take on a significance that transcends the financial needs of the government. Taxes are collected not only to pay the government's bills but also to influence economic activity.

Taxes as a Tool to Influence Aggregate Demand Taxes can be used to increase or decrease aggregate demand. In this analysis, let us assume that only households pay taxes. A tax cut increases the disposable income available for households to use on consumption expenditures (C), and as a result, aggregate demand, C + I + G, increases. Conversely, an increase in taxes reduces disposable income, so that C and aggregate demand decline. This is illustrated in Figure 9-4, where the economy has settled at an equilibrium point \$120 billion above the full-employment level. Some action must be taken to reduce aggregate demand so that it intersects with aggregate supply at a NNP of \$1500 billion.

1 John Kenneth Galbraith, *The Affluent Society*, 2nd ed. (Boston: Houghton Mifflin, 1969).
2 *New York Times*, March 20, 1973, p. 16.
3 *Newsweek*, August 7, 1967, p. 68.
4 Haig Babian, "Can Taxes Do More Than Raise Revenue?" *Saturday Review*, March 22, 1969.
5 Federal taxes were \$10 million in 1800. U.S. Bureau of the Census, *Historical Statistics of U.S., Colonial Times to 1957* (Washington, D.C.: Government Printing Office, 1960).

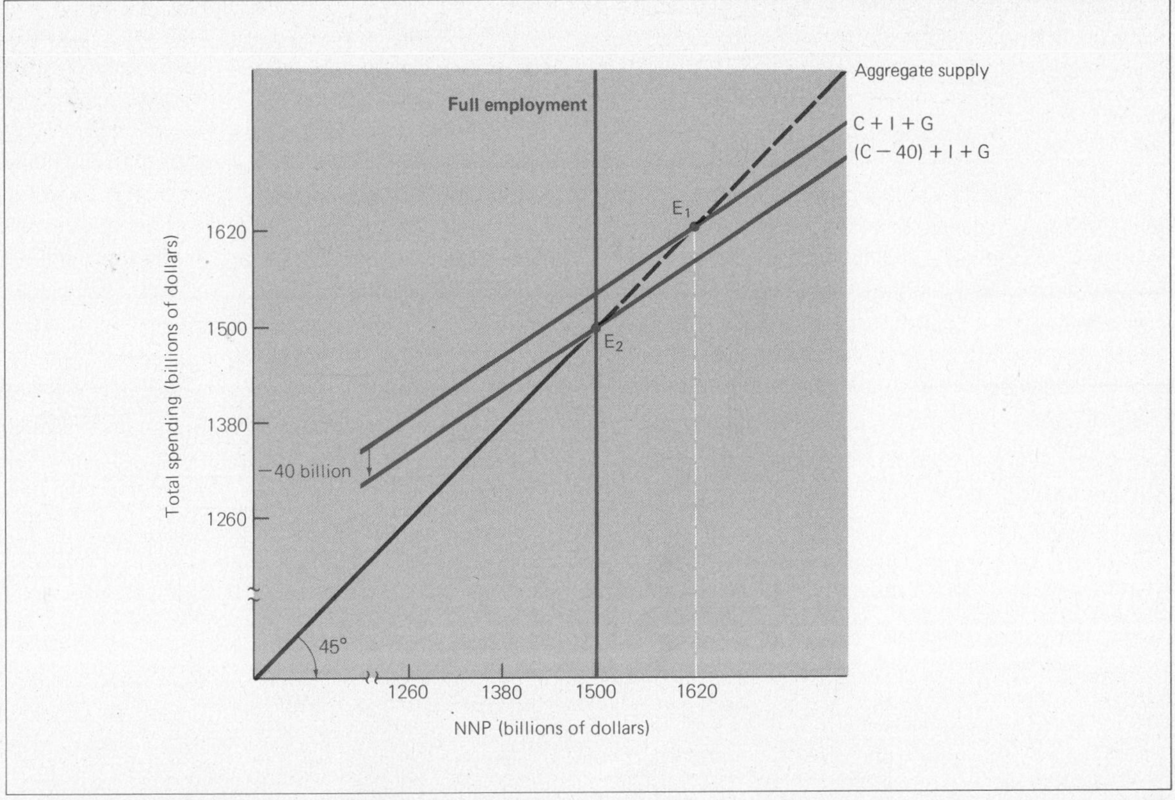

FIGURE 9-4 CLOSING AN INFLATIONARY GAP THROUGH A TAX INCREASE OF $60 BILLION **If the economy is operating beyond capacity, the government can lower net national product from $1620 billion to $1500 billion by means of a $60 billion tax increase. Given an MPC of ⅔ (and a multiplier of 3), we know that of the $60 billion no longer available to the public, some $40 billion would have been spent (that is, ⅔ of $60 billion). Thus, consumption is initially reduced by $40 billion. However, the process does not stop here, since ⅔ of the $40 billion would have been re-spent and ⅔ of that re-spent money would have been re-spent once again, and so forth. This process is summarized by the multiplier, which, in this case, is 3. Therefore, an initial decline of $40 billion in consumption causes net national product to fall by $120 billion (3 × −$40 billion).**

One way of accomplishing this would be to reduce consumption by increasing taxes, for any increase in taxes would leave less for households to devote to consumption spending. How much of a tax increase would be needed to reduce NNP by the required $120 billion? It is essential to recognize that initially consumption spending will *not* fall by the entire amount of any tax increase, for households have two choices when confronted by higher taxes: They can cut consumption spending, or they can cut down on saving and try to maintain consumption.

The immediate response when taxes are raised is a combination of both alternatives, with the exact amounts depending on the marginal propensities to consume and save. Because the economy illustrated in Figure 9-4 has an MPC of ⅔ and an MPS of ⅓, it will pay for higher taxes by cutting consumption by ⅔ of the tax increase and saving by ⅓. As a result, a tax boost of $60 billion in this economy will cut consumption spending by only $40 billion; the remainder of the tax will be paid by reductions in household saving. In other words, to determine the effect of a tax increase on C, multiply the projected tax change by the MPC; the result is the change in consumption.

MPC × Change in taxes = Change in consumption
⅔ × $60 = $40

Once the change in consumption resulting from a given change in taxes has been determined, it is necessary to apply the multiplier in order to establish the effect of this change on NNP. In an economy with a multiplier of 3, the result of a $60 billion increase in taxes will be an initial decline of $40 billion in consumption and ultimately a decline of $120 billion in NNP.

Tax cuts have a similar two-step effect on raising NNP and employment. The initial effect of a cut in taxes is an increase in consumption spending. This increase, however, will be *less* than the amount of the tax cut, the precise increase in C depending on the MPC. The increase in C is then compounded by the multiplier and the end result is an even greater increase in NNP. Figure 9-5 illustrates an economy with an MPC of ⅔ and a multiplier of 3. A tax cut of $60 billion, then, would lead to an initial increase in consumption of $40 billion and finally an increase in NNP of $120 billion.

The key point to remember is that tax changes do not affect NNP *directly;* instead, a two-step process is involved. In the first step, a change in taxes results in a change in consumption that is smaller than the original change in T. In the second step, the

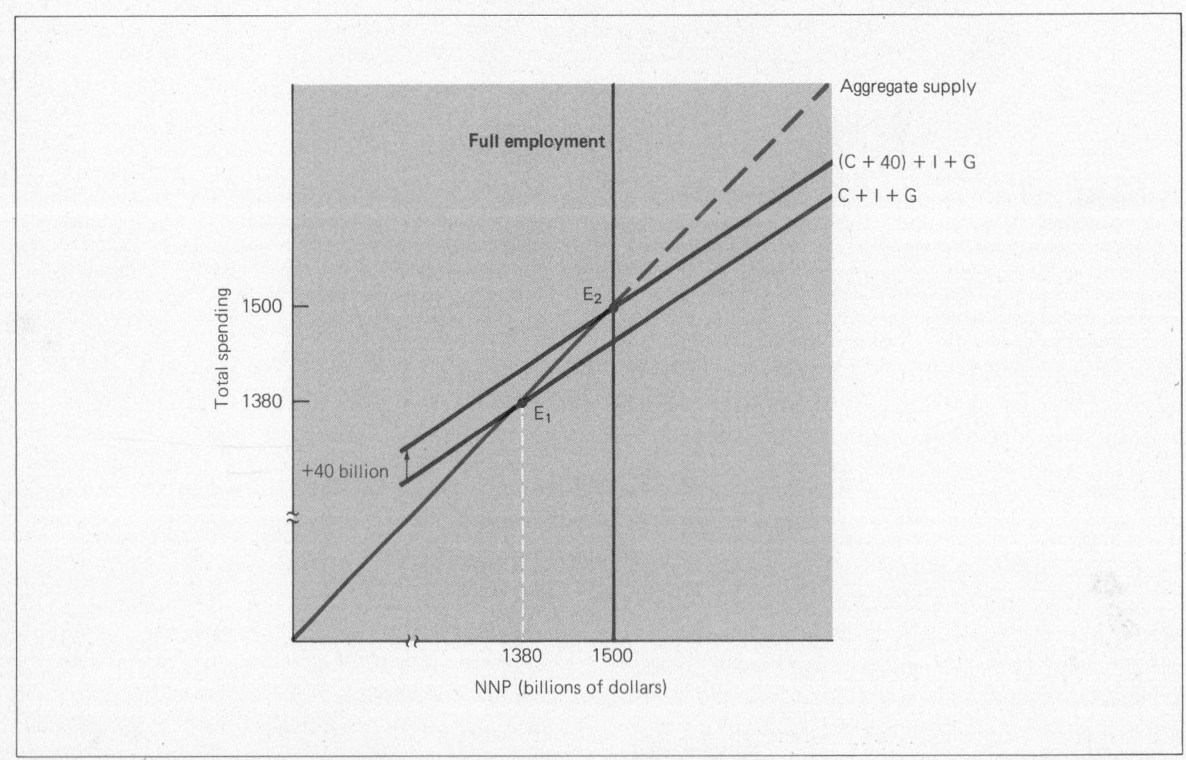

FIGURE 9-5 CLOSING A DEFLATIONARY GAP THROUGH A TAX CUT OF $60 BILLION **A tax cut will have exactly the opposite effect on NNP as a tax increase. If it is unclear how to get from E_1 to E_2 in this graph, go back to the caption of Figure 9-4 for an explanation.**

change in C is subject to the multiplier, which will determine the new equilibrium level of NNP.

How Effective Are Taxes as a Fiscal Tool? Since the 1960s there have been several significant examples of the successful use of taxes as a fiscal tool. The Revenue Act of 1964, proposed first by President Kennedy, cut personal income taxes by more than 20 percent in an ambitious attempt to reduce unemployment. Four years later, confronted by an inflationary boom, President Johnson persuaded Congress to raise taxes by a 10 percent income-tax surcharge; and in 1970, when the economy again appeared headed for serious recession, President Nixon permitted the surcharge to expire and cut taxes further in 1971 in order to promote private spending. These federal measures affected the levels of consumption and aggregate demand, providing some degree of control over the course of the economy. In addition, many authorities emphasize that using taxes as a fiscal tool does not necessarily extend the government's role in the economy. While government spending increases aggregate demand by increasing government control over the allocation of resources, tax cuts increase demand through the private sector.

One disadvantage of tax cuts concerns the relatively high cost involved in using tax reductions to stimulate the economy. For example, suppose that a $120 billion increase in NNP is needed to bring the economy to a full-employment level. In an economy with a multiplier of 3, this can be accomplished by an increase in government spending of $40 billion. However, if we attempt to achieve the same $120 billion increase in NNP through tax reductions, cuts of $60 billion in taxes will be required in order to provide that same $40 billion of additional consumption spending. In other words, if we assume that the budget was originally in balance and ignore any feedback of changes on government revenues, solving the unemployment problem through government spending will result in a deficit (and an increase in the national debt) of $40 billion; solving the same problem through tax cuts means a deficit of $60 billion.

The Balanced Budget Multiplier

We have seen that additional government spending leads to growth in NNP, while tax increases result in reductions in NNP. At first glance, then, it would appear that equal changes in government spending and tax collections would have no overall effect on the equilibrium level of NNP— that the effects of spending and taxation would tend to cancel one another. This, however, is not the case. Increments of government spending affect demand directly and are subject to the multiplier in their full amount. Increments of taxes, in contrast, affect demand indirectly; it is only that part of the tax change allocated by households to consumption that is subject to the multiplier. Consider, for example, an economy with a multiplier of 3, where additional government spending of $50 billion is projected along with an increase in taxes of $50 billion. The budget increase of $50 billion would lead to an increase in NNP of $150 billion, while the tax increase, subject as it is to an MPC of ⅔, would reduce consumption spending by only $33.3 billion and NNP by only $100 billion ($\frac{2}{3} \times \$50 = \$33.3 \times 3 = \$100$). Thus, the net result of the balanced budget would be expansionary; NNP would show a net increase of $50 billion.

This effect is called the **balanced budget multiplier**, and it explains why equal increases in spending and taxes normally result in a higher NNP. In the above example, an equal increase in government spending and taxing of $50 billion produced an increase in NNP of $50 billion; that is, the net increase in NNP was equal to the original increments of spending and taxing. In theory, this pattern will hold true regardless of the MPC or the amount of the budget change; equal increases in T and G are expansionary, and they will increase NNP by the amount of the change.

Because equal increases in government spending and taxes provide a way of increasing NNP without producing any additional budget deficit or an increase in the national debt, they are sometimes considered the most politically desirable alternative available to an administration seeking to expand economic activity. On the other hand, such an approach requires more government spending—and therefore more government involvement in the economy—than any other alternative. For example, a balanced budget with increases of $50 billion in spending and taxing will produce a net increase of $50 billion in NNP. To reach this same end through an increase in spending alone would require additional spending of only $16.6 billion (the multiplier is 3), or it could be achieved without any additional spending through a tax cut of $25 billion.

($\$25 \times 2/3 = \$16.6 \times 3 = \$50$)

While the extra government spending is undesirable to some, to others it is preferable, since they believe that the society should devote more resources to public goods. The balanced budget multiplier for them is a way of stimulating the economy and providing more money for education or health care without incurring more public debt.

ELEMENTS OF FISCAL POLICY

Discretionary Tools

So far, we have been discussing courses of action that government may *choose* to take to counteract the destabilizing effects of fluctuations in the private sector, and to move the economy toward the full-employment level of NNP. These are primarily changes in taxes and government spending, deliberate alterations which are called **discretionary fiscal tools.** Discretionary tools include such activities as the tax cuts of 1970 and 1971, and the increases in government spending and budget deficits of 1970 and 1971 which were used to stimulate a declining economy; the tax increase of 1968 and the budget surpluses of fiscal 1969 introduced in an attempt to restrain inflation are also examples of discretionary fiscal measures.

Recently, President Nixon applied the same principle to government-owned stockpiles of aluminum and other raw materials, which were originally created to assure adequate supplies of strategic materials in case of a national defense emergency. But in 1973, the President determined that they were no longer essential for this purpose. Instead, he felt that they could be a useful anti-inflationary tool, and so ordered them sold on the open market to try to restrain the sharp increases that were occurring.

The Effectiveness of Discretionary Tools The actual effects of changes in spending and taxation may depend on *how* government spends and raises funds. Expenditures on actual projects such as construction of highways and other public facilities generally are considered to have a higher multiplier effect than equal amounts of transfer payments made directly to individuals. Transfers, such as unemployment compensation and social security payments, of course, do not directly stimulate production, whereas direct spending usually does. The multiplier applies to the full amount of direct spending, but only to the amount consumed of the transfer payments.

But government outlays for projects can be counterproductive if they simply replace private investment with government spending. The drop in the private sector will offset the increased governmental outlays, and there will be little stimulus to the economy.

Similarly, increases in regressive levies such as sales and excise taxes are considered to have a more depressing effect on private spending than identical rate changes in the more progressive personal and corporate income taxes. Again, there is a counterbalancing argument that heavy additional burdens on corporate income may discourage production and investment more than can result from changes in sales and excise levies.

So in the long run the use of fiscal tools may involve consequences, both economic and social, other than immediate changes in aggregate demand. Changes in tax rates, for example, may eventually have effects on the budget quite the reverse of those originally created. In 1963, when President Kennedy asked Congress for an $11 billion tax cut without any corresponding decrease in spending, the initial reaction of many was outrage at the size of the budget deficit such a program implied. Defending his plan, however, the President claimed that his program was designed to bring about a budget *surplus,* for the "soundest way to raise revenues in the long run is to cut tax rates now."[6] The President reasoned that a tax cut would increase NNP and that an economy operating at a higher level of output would produce the higher taxes needed to eliminate the original budget deficit, and indeed move the budget to a surplus GNP increased by over 7 percent in 1964 and 8 percent in 1965, and the federal budget, which showed a deficit of nearly $6 billion in fiscal year 1964, was running a deficit of only $1.6 billion in fiscal year 1965.

But such success may be the exception rather than the rule. Economic forecasting, despite notable advances in model-building and other aids to projection, is still an inexact discipline. The result often is that policy change comes after rather than before the event it is aimed at averting. And even if the forecasts are accurate, the political process of persuading the various branches of government that must initiate and carry out shifts in economic policy and the public, which must live with the result, is time-consuming. Consequently, by the time a change in policy is set in motion, an entirely new set of conditions may exist. Furthermore, the long planning periods that are required for public works often make such measures inappropriate for coping with short periods of economic maladjustment.

Automatic Stabilizers

In contrast to discretionary fiscal policy, which must be deliberately selected and timed as circumstances require, fiscal tools also include certain "built-in" stabilizers, which work automatically as countercyclical forces. Broadly speaking, the automatic stabilizers operate to reduce income in periods when an excess of demand threatens to push the economy into inflation, and to maintain or increase income when demand drops below the full-employment level. An important advantage of these nondiscretionary tools is that they operate without the problems of timing, judgment, and political pressure which continuously beset discretionary tools. Nondiscretionary fiscal tools are activated automatically in response to business cycle pressures.

Transfer Payments and Subsidies Transfer payments and subsidies which provide income to households rise during periods of recession. Such payments automatically increase as income falls and decline as income rises. The unemployment insurance program, for example, works to stabilize the economy in this way. During a period of high employment, more unemployment taxes are collected than are paid out in benefits; during a period of recession, the reverse is true. From 1965 to 1970, unemployment insurance receipts exceeded benefits by well over $1 billion annually. Conversely, during the 1971–72 period of high unemployment, payments exceeded receipts by more than $1½ billion a year.

Welfare payments stabilize the economy. Those people in specific categories (the aged, the disabled, the blind, dependent children) who meet stated standards of need are given prescribed payments by federal, state, and local governments. Although funds distributed to certain groups (the blind, disabled, and aged) do not change very much with economic conditions, the number of recipients in other categories (dependent children, the poor) varies to some extent with the business cycle. Overall, total payments increase when incomes fall, and thus, the welfare program acts as a countercyclical device to maintain national income.

The Tax System We have seen how discretionary changes in the total amount of taxes collected can serve as a fiscal tool. In addition to this, however, the structure of the tax system itself can have extremely important implications in terms of fiscal policy. In the United States, the largest part of the federal tax burden is collected through a progressive income tax, and this structure serves as perhaps the most effective automatic stabilizer of all. Offsetting this somewhat are highly regressive state and local taxes in which people with incomes under $2000 pay 25 percent of their income to these gov-

6 *Congressional Record*, January 15, 1963.

The conflict of interest that often develops in a democracy between economic goals and other objectives is neatly demonstrated by the prolonged struggle that preceded the imposition of higher taxes in 1968. The roots of the problem can be traced back to July 1965, when President Johnson first requested more funds for Vietnam, thus adding to spending in an economy already operating at close to full capacity. Almost at once, defense spending accelerated, increasing by $3.3 billion in the third quarter of 1965 alone, and by the end of the year there were clear signs of overheating: Fourth-quarter GNP was up by an unprecedented 8.5 percent, and a Department of Commerce–Securities and Exchange Commission survey indicated that a capital spending boom was imminent. To many economists, a tax increase appeared necessary to head off these growing inflationary pressures.

In presenting his budget to Congress in January 1966, however, President Johnson did not ask for higher taxes. Reviewing his decision some years later, he explained that he did not feel he could get such legislation through Congress. Moreover, mid-term elections were scheduled for later in the year, and the President, uncertain about congressional and public support for his Vietnam policy, was apparently unwilling to provide the opposition with another gut issue—higher taxes.

Instead, the administration relied primarily on monetary policy—higher interest rates and tighter availability of credit—to control demand, and by late 1966, it looked as if these policies had met some success. By 1967, however, it appeared that inflationary pressures were once again developing. In particular, spending on Vietnam was accelerating; actual expenditures in fiscal 1967 were $10 billion higher than originally budgeted in 1966. As a result, in January 1967, Johnson asked Congress to impose a 6 percent tax surcharge on personal and corporate taxes, but Congress did not do much more than hold hearings. By midyear, home-building had rebounded, retail sales were sharply higher, and defense expenditures were continuing to increase, and the President went back to Congress again, this time requesting a 10 percent surcharge.

For the next 10 months, Congress refused to act. Initially, resistance was based on congressional skepticism toward economists' projections that serious inflation was in store: The economists were basing their warning on their readings of somewhat esoteric economic forecasts, and congressmen were reluctant to vote for an unpopular measure like a tax increase on the basis of mere forecasts. At the same time, there were those who preferred to fight any impending inflation in a different way, by cutting spending rather than raising taxes. Others worried about the social consequences of a tax rise: James Tobin, a liberal economist, claimed that higher taxes would mean more unemployment, which would hit certain groups—blacks, the young—with special severity. Others spoke of the "three million unemployed" still present in the economy despite the under 4 percent unemployment rate, and wondered whether what the country needed, in view of their plight, was *more*, rather than less, inflation. Finally, the fundamental cause of the inflation, the war, was unpopular, so that support for higher taxes could not be secured by an appeal to patriotism.

In all, it was not until June 1968, when painful evidence of real inflationary troubles could no longer be ignored (a 4 percent inflation rate, a quarterly increase of $19 billion in GNP, a deterioration of our balance of payments) that Congress finally acted, and the 10 percent surcharge was passed. And its effects did not take hold until even later.

The protracted struggle to obtain administration and congressional approval for this tax increase illustrates the institutional context in which fiscal decisions are often made. Initially, there were uncertainties about the need for restraint, and this is typical of the recognition lag that characterizes economic planning: Recommendations must be made on the basis of forecasts, and the state of the art is such that forecasts are often tentative, and are subject to controversy. The problem was complicated by the variables introduced by military considerations: When you are fighting a war, it is difficult to tell in advance how much spending it will entail, and in the 1965–68 period, the President's advisers consistently underestimated Vietnam requirements. In addition, there was the problem of trade-offs among various economic goals: Inflation was obviously undesirable, but what of the unemployment that would result from a tax increase? And finally, as one authority has phrased it, the need for a tax increase ran afoul of "the treacherous shoals of political feasibility," for it is very likely that the 1966 midyear elections made the President reluctant to ask for tax boosts early enough to secure passage in time. In summary, the history of the maneuvering that preceded the 1968 tax boosts clearly illustrates the difficulty of separating political and economic considerations in a democracy, and suggests that although the theoretical motivation behind government economic policy may be the public good, in practice, other objectives often force economic considerations to take a back seat.

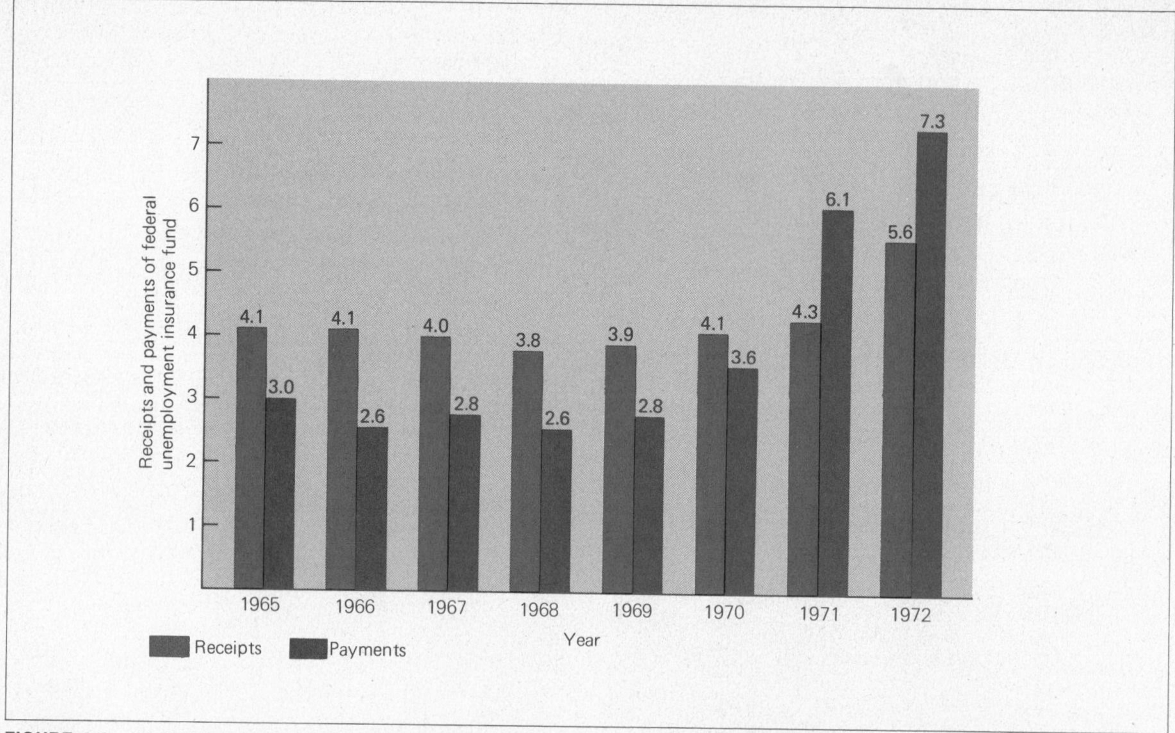

FIGURE 9-6 AUTOMATIC STABILIZATION THROUGH UNEMPLOYMENT INSURANCE, 1965–72 (Billions of dollars) Unemployment insurance tax receipts and payments work as an automatic stabilizer, curbing aggregate demand during times of inflation, but adding to aggregate demand during recessions. During the period 1965–69, the U.S. economy experienced considerable inflation, which was somewhat dampened by the surplus of unemployment insurance tax receipts over payments. 1970–72 were years of relatively high unemployment, as one might surmise from the chart. During the last two years, payments exceeded receipts, thus resulting in a net addition to aggregate demand. The net effect of these payments may not have been stabilizing, since with higher levels of unemployment the economy was also experiencing rapid price increases during the latter period.

ernments, while those with incomes of $15,000 and over pay only 7 percent.[7]

PROGRESSIVE TAX STRUCTURE The test of whether a tax is progressive, proportional, or regressive is the percentage of income paid at different income levels.

A progressive tax structure is one in which the percentage of income collected on taxes is greater for higher incomes than for lower ones.

In 1973, for example, a married taxpayer would pay only 14 percent of his first $1000 of taxable income in federal taxes, but the rate would climb quickly as his income rose. He would pay 15 percent on taxable income between $1000 and $1500, 19 percent on income between $6000 and $8000, 32 percent on income between $22,000 and $24,000, and so on up to 70 percent on income above $110,000.

One effect of this system is to reduce inflationary pressure when incomes are rising, because an ever increasing percentage of the higher incomes is collected by the government, and thus does not add to demand. In terms of the individual, a progressive tax structure means that income increments will be taxed at an increasingly higher rate. In terms of the economy as a whole, progressive taxes mean

7 Joseph A. Pechman, "The Rich, the Poor, and the Taxes They Pay," *The Public Interest* 17 (Fall 1969).

that government receipts automatically increase rapidly, and at a greater rate than increases in GNP, during an expansion, thus serving as an effective anti-inflationary force (see Table 9-1).

The progressive tax system works equally well during a recession by cushioning the effect of any decline in income. When national income drops, taxes drop at a higher rate, because taxpayers move from the higher brackets, where the government has been collecting a given percentage of their incomes, to lower brackets, where the tax bite is proportionately less. As a result, the disposable income available for household spending is maintained to some extent, despite the fall in national income.

PROPORTIONAL TAX Although the largest part of the tax burden in the United States is collected by the progressive federal income tax, other tax structures are also in use by the federal and state and local governments.

Proportional taxes are those where the percentage of income collected or rate of taxation remains the same at all levels of income.

A proportional income tax in the United States would involve the imposition of an equal percentage tax on all households; that is, every taxpayer might be asked to pay 15 percent of his earnings in taxes. Under such a tax system, what would happen to disposable income if personal income dropped by 10 percent? How would such a tax structure compare with a progressive tax structure as a stabilization device?

TABLE 9-1 How the Progressive Tax System Helps Restrain Growth in Disposable Income as the Economy Expands (Billions of dollars)

Year	Personal income	Disposable income
1966	$587.2	$511
1967	629.13	546
Percentage change	+ 7.16	+ 6.84

When the economy is growing, as in the boom years of 1966–67, taxes rise faster than personal income. As a result, disposable income rises at a slower rate. When inflation threatens, this fiscal drag from increased tax revenues helps curb private spending. When the government is trying to stimulate a sluggish economy, fiscal drag may need to be offset by increased government outlays.

TABLE 9-2 How Progressive Income Taxes as an Automatic Stabilizer Help Maintain Disposable Income for a Household during a Recession

	Personal income	Federal income tax	Disposable income
	$10,000	$901	$8099
	8000	573	7427
Percent change	–20%		–8.30%

This illustrates how the drop in personal income for an individual household during a recession is softened somewhat by the decrease in the tax bite. Although both personal income and disposable income decrease, the drop in disposable income is less, because a smaller percentage is deducted for taxes as income declines. This means that somewhat more money is available for consumption (and saving). *Note:* Figures are for married couples with two children taking standard deduction. No allowance is made for social security tax. Calculations are based on the 1972 tax tables.

REGRESSIVE TAX In absolute amounts, a rich man may pay more than a poor person under a regressive tax, but this tax takes its name from the rate structure.

A regressive tax is one where the percentage paid in taxes actually decreases as income rises.

A flat $100 head tax, for example, is 10 percent of a $1000 income and only 5 percent of a $2000 income. Strictly speaking, this type of regressive tax is not used in the United States. However, two of our most widely used taxes have regressive effects. Sales taxes, although imposed at a fixed rate, represent a larger proportion of the incomes of the poor than of the rich. Social security taxes work in a similar manner. Although they are fixed at a flat 5.85 percent rate, they are imposed against only the first $10,800 of income. Thus, a wage-earner with $10,800 of income pays the maximum of $631.80, or 5.85 percent; an employee earning $20,000, in contrast, pays the same $631.80, but this represents only 3.16 percent of his income.

IS THE U.S. FEDERAL INCOME TAX THAT BAD?

The average taxpayer spends 23 days a year working for Uncle Sam to pay his federal income tax. After every struggle with Form 1040, he tells himself there must be a better way. But is the U.S. system that bad? How does it rate in terms of its ability to raise revenue, to help stabilize the economy, and to spread the cost burden equitably?

The U.S. tax system rates high in efficiency and size. In 1973, the federal government raised about $225 billion in taxes, about $100 billion of which came from individual income taxes and $35 billion from corporate income taxes. These amounts vastly surpass the taxes collected by any other government in the world. The system itself is remarkably efficient, with actual administration costs amounting to less than 1 percent of the amount collected. Since most of the money is siphoned into the government's coffers through the withholding system, it is relatively difficult for most Americans to evade much of their responsibility, and one expert has claimed that only about 6 percent of the income that under the law should be reported, does not show up on tax returns.* In brief, from both a cost and a compliance viewpoint, the U.S. record is vastly superior to that of most foreign countries, regardless of the tax system used. Nor does our tax system compare unfavorably with those of other nations in terms of total tax burden. Americans may feel that they are overtaxed, but in 1973, total taxes amounted to only 27.9 percent of GNP in the United States—significantly less than in every other highly industrialized nation in the world except Switzerland and Japan. The German tax burden is 34 percent, the French 36.6 percent, and the Swedish a whopping 43 percent.

If our federal tax system raises huge sums of money, is efficient, and involves a relatively modest burden as compared with that of other nations, why do so many Americans find fault with it? Most complaints center around the equity of the individual income tax. Although theoretically imposed progressively, with rates varying between 14 percent and 70 percent, this tax does not, in practice, work this way at all. Because of deductions, exemptions, and qualifications, substantial amounts of income escape all taxation, and much of this income belongs to the highest-bracket taxpayers. "The income tax soaks those who live primarily on wages and salaries. . . ."† Because payroll taxes are col-

* Joseph A. Pechman, "Tax System Good, but Needs Key Reforms," *Washington Post*, April 10, 1966.
† Melville J. Ulmer, "How Unfair Are Our Taxes?" *New Republic*, November 7, 1972.

lected largely through withholding, opportunity for tax evasion is minimal. But business, agricultural, or natural resource income is subject to many deductions—such as business entertainment, depreciation, and depletion. Moreover, the chances to understate income are numerous in such fields. Further, many of the provisions of the tax code, such as charitable contributions, interest deductions, special capital gains treatment, and dividend exclusions, are often of great importance to top-bracket taxpayers and irrelevant to those in low brackets. In addition, those in the top brackets receive nontaxable forms of income. As a result, experts estimate that despite the theoretical maximum 70 percent on some kinds of income, the effective tax rate for taxpayers with incomes in excess of $200,000 per year probably averages about 30 percent.‡ Even with the institution of a minimum tax under the Revenue Act of 1969 to garner revenue from those in high brackets who paid no taxes at all on preference income such as interest from tax-exempt bonds, the fact is that 111 Americans with an adjusted gross income of over $200,000 paid no tax in 1970.§

Moreover, the distribution of the tax burden indicates a regressive shift to those on payrolls. Individual income taxes, for example, dropped from 46 percent of the total tax burden in fiscal 1969 to an estimated 44 percent in fiscal 1974; at the same time, corporate income taxes dropped from 20 percent (they were 23 percent in 1960) to 15 percent, and social insurance taxes rose from 21 percent to an estimated 31 percent of total federal receipts.

Despite the problems we have outlined, the progressive income taxes are here to stay as the prime source of government revenues. Certain improvements, such as the elimination of the more flagrant loopholes, deductions, and exemptions, would make the taxes more equitable, and might bring in enough additional revenue to permit reduction of tax rates on earned income. Overall, however, the concept of progressive income-tax structure seems particularly well suited not only to meet the growing revenue needs of a modern industrial nation, but also to help ensure full employment and price stability.

‡ Joint Economic Committee, 93rd Cong., 1st sess., *The 1973 Joint Economic Report* (Washington, D.C.: Government Printing Office, 1973), p. 51.

§ *Ibid.*, p. 53.

Under a regressive structure, tax payments increase as percentage of income when incomes fall, thus compounding the destabilizing effects of any drop in income. When incomes rise, a greater percentage is available for spending, thereby increasing inflationary pressure. Regressive taxes are doubly objectionable, since from the standpoint of equity they place a greater burden on the poor than on the rich.

NEGATIVE INCOME TAX Perhaps the most provocative new tax idea in recent years is the negative income tax.

The negative income tax guarantees all citizens that the government will pay them a certain minimum income if they are unable to earn it on their own.

Proposed originally as an alternative to welfare grants now used to fight poverty, this tax also has intriguing implications in terms of economic stabilization. A negative income tax would preserve national income and demand during those periods when the private sector was unable to provide jobs (and incomes) to some, and would therefore limit the destabilizing effects of any downturn in economic activity. Such a system was proposed under the rubric Family Assistance Plan (FAP) during the first Nixon administration, but died aborning.

TABLE 9-3 How Negative Income Tax Helps Maintain Disposable Income for a Household

Actual income	Negative income tax	Disposable income
$ 0	$2500	$2500
1000	2000	3000
2000	1500	3500
3000	1000	4000
4000	500	4500
5000	0	5000
	Income tax	
$6000	$ 200	$5800
7000	420	6580
8000	660	7340
9000	930	8070
10,000	1240	8760
15,000	2990	12,010
20,000	3500	16,500

Up to an income of $5000, the individual (say, the head of a family of four) pays no taxes. He or she is guaranteed an income of $2500, but loses one dollar of negative income tax for every two dollars earned. Thus, upon attaining an income of $5000, he or she receives no negative income tax. Individuals earning more than $5000 pay income tax. This tax acts as an extension of the progressive income tax and stabilizes income in the same manner.

Evaluation of Automatic Stabilizers Economists generally agree that "the automatic stabilizers are clearly a powerful tool for dealing with cyclical fluctuations,"[8] and that, in their absence, the economy would be subject to much greater fluctuations, especially during economic declines. The introduction of these automatic fiscal tools into the economic system simplifies the entire stabilization process by eliminating the time lags, the political pressures, and the questions of judgment that so often restrict the successful use of discretionary tools. It took the Kennedy and Johnson administrations more than a year to get their tax reduction packages through Congress, and President Johnson needed almost two years to pass his tax-increase bill. The unemployment insurance program and the progressive tax system, on the other hand, take effect immediately and automatically to increase or reduce demand when cyclical fluctuations occur. Moreover, unlike the government spending tool, the automatic stabilizers work by regulating the flow of disposable income to households, leaving the actual spending decisions—and the allocation of resources—in the hands of the private sector.

But automatic stabilizers are of limited effectiveness. When the economy is growing and operating at high levels of employment, it automatically generates rapid increases in revenues. The result is government surpluses that cut aggregate demand and may consequently slow the growth of the economy. This condition of **fiscal drag** can be offset if the government takes positive measures, such as reducing taxes, increasing federal outlays, or making grants

8 Peter Eilbott, "The Effectiveness of Automatic Stabilizers," *American Economic Review* 56 (June 1966): 463.

to state and local governmental units to be used for public expenditures.

Many suggestions about improving our economic stabilization efforts center around increasing the role of the automatic fiscal tools. Larger and more extended unemployment insurance programs have been recommended. For example, unemployment benefits are usually paid for only six months, but in 1972 Congress extended the program so that payment could run for as long as nine months where unemployment exceeded a certain rate for a certain period of time. Another possibility for improvement involves the use of automatic stabilizers that can respond flexibly to changing economic conditions.

Formula Flexibility Because of the relatively moderate effects of built-in stabilizers and the political inertia that blocks the rapid use of discretionary tools, both methods have tended to lack the timeliness and breadth necessary to cope effectively with economic downturns and low employment of productive resources during the past two decades. One possible answer is the establishment of a system of what has been called formula flexibility to trigger automatically the proper change in taxes when there is a pronounced gap between actual GNP and full-employment GNP. The object, of course, is to change disposable income and, in turn, demand.

However, because such automatic but flexible changes would have to be keyed to economic indicators, there is a technical problem of constructing a foolproof system that could cope not only with downturns and upturns but with conditions of **stagflation**, in which relatively high unemployment and rapid price increases occur simultaneously. Even were this miraculous indicator to exist, Congress might be loath to give up any more of its powers over taxes and spending.

Perhaps giving the President latitude to make changes in tax rates or government spending within a certain range could reduce the time it takes to bring discretionary changes into play. Or reforming the way in which Congress deals with economic matters could improve the responsiveness of fiscal policy to economic conditions.

SUMMARY

1 Fiscal policy, which revolves around the government's taxation and spending programs, is used to influence the level of employment, prices, and growth, and to eliminate any inherent instabilities in our economy, which, in the past, have led to a series of booms and busts. The former have been caused largely by inflationary gaps, and the latter, by deflationary gaps.

2 An excess of demand that pushes NNP beyond its full-employment level is called an inflationary gap. It does not represent additional physical output—merely higher prices for the same full-employment NNP. A deflationary gap represents actual physical output lost because the economy is operating below its full-employment level.

3 The purpose of fiscal policy is to eliminate either of these gaps. Government spending and taxation are the basic fiscal tools because of their immediate and sizable effect on aggregate demand. Reducing government spending or increasing taxes may close an inflationary gap. Increasing spending or cutting taxes may close a deflationary gap.

4 The effects of these two tools are not equal. Government spending directly affects spending and the multiplier is applied to the full amount of the change. Taxation

works in a two-step process: The part of the tax change that is affected is predicted by the MPC. The multiplier is then applied to this amount.

5 For this reason, an equal increase in taxes and spending is actually expansionary. In theory, the effect is equal to the amount of the increase. This is called the balanced budget multiplier.

6 The manipulation of spending and taxation is a discretionary tool, since it is *chosen* by the government. In contrast to discretionary fiscal policy, which must be deliberately selected and timed as circumstances require, fiscal tools also include certain built-in stabilizers, which work automatically as countercyclical forces.

7 Many transfer payments are automatic stabilizers. The two most important of those are unemployment insurance and welfare payments. The tax system itself acts as an automatic stabilizer, especially the progressive structure of the individual income tax. During periods of inflation, tax payments rise faster than income; during recessions, tax payments fall more rapidly than income.

8 It should be understood that the fiscal policy tools we have just discussed are effective in moving the economy in the right direction, but they are not sufficient to do the job alone.

SUGGESTED READINGS

Dernburg, Thomas F., and **D. M. McDougall.** *Macroeconomics.* 4th ed. Chaps. 6 and 19. New York: McGraw-Hill, 1972.

Heilbroner, Robert L., and **Peter L. Bernstein.** *Primer on Government Spending.* 2nd ed. New York: Random House, 1970.

Shapiro, Edward. *Macroeconomic Analysis.* 2nd ed. Chaps. 14 and 24. New York: Harcourt Brace Jovanovich, 1970.

Wagner, Lewis, and **Frank W. Gery.** *A Primer of Economics: Income, Employment, and Prices.* Iowa City: Bureau of Business and Economic Research, The University of Iowa, 1972.

QUESTIONS

1 Review
  a. the role of government spending and taxation in determining NNP,
  b. the equilibrium condition when government is introduced into the economy,
  c. the ways government spending and taxation affect national income,
  d. the balanced budget multiplier,
  e. discretionary and automatic stabilizers.

2 Explain what would happen in an economy in which investment was $50 billion, government spending was $100 billion, saving was $80 billion, and taxes were $60 billion.

Now assume that an economy is at equilibrium and that investment is $100 billion, saving is $75 billion, and taxes are $70 billion. What must be the value of government expenditures?

3 Assume that the multiplier is 2.5 and that the economy has an inflationary gap of $100 billion. By how much and in what direction should the government change:
   a. spending, if spending is the only action taken,
   b. taxation, if taxation is the only action taken,
   c. spending, if taxes automatically go up by $100 billion.

4 Assume that government expenditures in an economy account for 25 percent of NNP. The multiplier in this economy is 4. Now suppose that the government must raise NNP by $40 billion to eliminate a deflationary gap. Parliament, in this economy, however, will allow only a balanced budget. By how much should the budget be increased? How might the Prime Minister answer criticism that the government is becoming too large?

5 Among the many suggestions for changes in the tax structure is one designed to provide an automatic check against inflation. The proposal advocates a "... contingency tax [which] would consist of an individual and corporate income tax surcharge which would not take effect unless triggered automatically by an abnormal increase in the rate of inflation."* What specific advantages would this arrangement have over the present system? How would the tax operate to reduce or eliminate an inflationary gap? How might impounding federal appropriations have the same effect? What are the drawbacks of the two alternatives?

6 Very little is said by economic advisers about the problem of fiscal drag during periods of inflation. Why?

7 As productive capacity increases in a growing economy, what happens to the full-employment line on the graph of income and spending for the economy? How would this affect an inflationary gap? A deflationary gap?

8 The regressive nature of many state and local taxes can be attacked, not only on the grounds of equity, but also on fiscal grounds. How? How do these taxes affect the stabilization efficiency of federal taxes?

9 Many people resent welfare payments and other types of transfer payments. Especially as the economy enters a slump, people begin to feel that they can no longer afford to pay the taxes to support others. Furthermore, they argue, anyone could find a job if he were simply willing to swallow his pride and take the jobs that exist. Evaluate this position.

10 Consider the three diagrams below. Explain the differences you would find in these economies, especially in the behavior of inventories. How might G or T be used to create stability?

*A. W. Clausen, "Do We Need an Anti-Inflation Tax?" *Wall Street Journal*, April 23, 1973, p. 18.

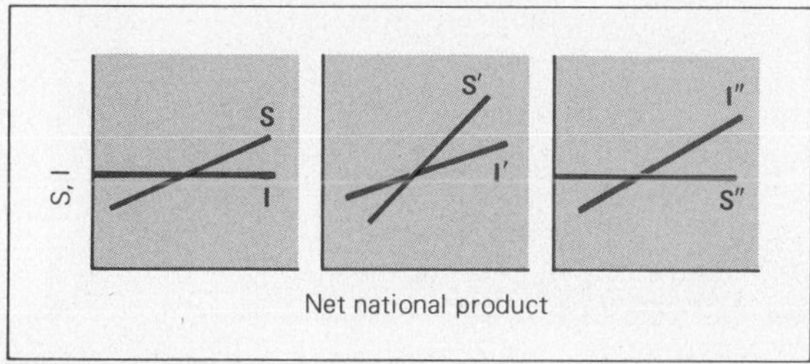

CHAPTER 10

FISCAL ISSUES

The use of fiscal policy for the purpose of stabilizing the economy is a relatively recent development. It was not until Congress enacted the Employment Act of 1946 that the responsibility for maintaining high employment and price stability was placed in the hands of the federal government. The Act states that

> ... it is the continuing policy and responsibility of the Federal Government to use all practical means ... for the purpose of creating ... conditions under which there will be afforded useful employment opportunities ... for those able, willing and seeking to work and to promote maximum employment, production and purchasing power ...

Since 1946, the federal government has struggled with this mandate. Managing the economy to provide full employment and price stability has become a primary concern of government.

The previous chapter presented the contents of the "Keynesian toolbox" and the complications in the selection of tools. But the conscious management of the economy involves problems that go beyond the choice of tools. First of all, public debt is a probable consequence of synchronizing spending and taxation with levels of economic activity. If public debt has injurious effects that outweigh the beneficial contributions of fiscal policy, the manner in which fiscal tools can be used is further limited. Second, the choice of tools is determined by the institutional and political environments. Since the control of fiscal decisions is decentralized in the United States, with some authority exercised by Congress, the President, and the Federal Reserve, the direction of fiscal policy is more a process than a decision. Third, the tools of fiscal policy are not neutral. Stabilization activities interact with spending and taxation aimed at the realization of other goals. In setting fiscal policy, questions of resource allocation and equity become inextricably involved, as was demonstrated by the battle over the level and content of spending in the 1974 budget. Finally, the manipulation of fiscal policy may be to no avail if the tools are powerless or are attacking the wrong problems. The monetarists see fiscal policy as less powerful than monetary policy. The radicals, on the other hand, see fiscal policy as unable to correct the inherent deficiencies of the capitalist system. In this chapter we shall look at these complications in the effective use of fiscal policy.

Opening photo from EPA-Tower Newsphoto

FISCAL POLICY AND THE PUBLIC DEBT

Every child born in the United States in 1973 inherited over $2000 worth of public debt. The total national debt in this country in mid-1973 was over $450 billion, and Congress was being asked to raise the "temporary" debt limit again – this time to $475 billion. Each of us pays about $100 a year in taxes simply to meet the annual interest charges. Table 10-1 shows that the national debt has increased more than twenty-five-fold since 1929; deficits in the federal budgets in 26 of the last 35 years are the cause of this increase. Whether this trend is cause for alarm depends on whether this growing debt places too heavy a burden on the economy.

The Balanced Budget Mystique

Before the 1930s, economists and politicians alike generally accepted the goal of a balanced budget. They reasoned that if businesses and families cannot accumulate ever increasing debt without disastrous consequences, the same must be true of nations. The federal government, it was argued, could not continue to increase the public debt indefinitely; at some point, future generations would have to pay.

Analogies between public and private debt, however, are misleading. Private debt is owed by one individual to another individual or to an institution. When the borrower eventually repays the debt, he will necessarily suffer a loss of assets. Public debt, on the other hand, is largely internal. In the United States, for example, the $450 billion federal debt is owed primarily to the American households, banks, and insurance companies, who have purchased government bonds. Since the United States owes the national debt to itself, repayment of the debt would not involve a loss of assets to the nation.

TABLE 10-1 U.S. Public Debt, 1929–72

Year	(1) Public debt (in billions)	(2) GNP (in billions)	(3) Interest payments (in billions)	(4) Public debt (as percent of GNP)	(5) Interest payment (as percent of GNP)	(6) Interest payment (as percent of federal budget)	(7) Per capita public debt
1929	$ 16.3	$ 103.1	$ 0.7	16%	0.7%	22.4%	$ 134
1940	50.9	99.7	1.1	51	1.1	11.5	382
1950	256.7	284.8	4.5	90	1.6	10.4	1689
1960	290.4	503.7	7.1	58	1.4	7.7	1604
1970	389.2	976.4	18.3	40	1.9	9.0	1900
1972	449.3	1151.8	20.6	39	1.8	8.8	2151

U.S. public debt has increased enormously since 1929, due to the Great Depression and the three wars fought since then. Although large in absolute terms, the burden of this debt has actually lessened. The public debt as a percentage of GNP declined from 90 percent in 1950 to only 39 percent in 1972. Because GNP measures our ultimate capability to pay back the debt, the decrease is significant. Since 1950, interest payments have increased nearly fourfold. Although this is a drain on the federal budget, interest payments, as a percentage of the budget, have actually declined.

SOURCES: *Federal Reserve Bulletin,* April 1973; U.S. Department of Commerce, *Survey of Current Business,* April 1973.

These analogies are also misleading because, unlike humans and many businesses, the lifespan of a nation has no foreseeable end. Therefore, the government can continuously renew the debt; as securities come due, the government merely sells new securities to pay off the holders of mature ones. If a nation does disappear, conditions are usually so adverse that public debt is the least of the problem.

Although it is theoretically possible to pay off the national debt, the federal debt is so large that rapid repayment would have a disastrous effect on economic stability. Taxes would have to be increased substantially in order to provide the necessary funds for debt repayments, or government funds would have to be diverted from other programs to pay off the debt. As the bonds were redeemed by the government, their former owners would be anxious to find new investments for the funds. This massive transfer of funds would disrupt the normal workings of the economy.

Is the Public Debt Too Big?

The national debt figures in column 1 of Table 10-1 reveal a substantial increase in total debt during the last 35 years. Large rises in public debt are closely tied to America's wars, with by far the biggest rise (almost $200 billion) occurring during World War II, and substantial amounts added by the Korean and Vietnam conflicts. This means that most of our debt has been caused by deficit financing during wartime rather than by budget deficits incurred to stimulate a declining economy.

Whatever its source, the United States is today faced with an enormous national debt. Most experts, however, believe that it is unrealistic to discuss the debt in absolute terms, for obviously a debt of $450 billion is much more troublesome to a poor nation than to a rich one. Therefore, it is generally more meaningful to look at national debt in relative terms. Columns 4 and 5 of Table 10-1 show total U.S. public debt and the annual interest requirements on this debt as a percent of GNP. Since the end of World War II (1946), GNP has grown fivefold, while the national debt has not even doubled. In other words, although the absolute size of the debt has increased each year, its size relative to GNP has actually declined. The same is true of interest payments. Although interest payments have grown more quickly than the debt itself (because interest *rates* have been so high in recent years), interest as a percentage of GNP is nevertheless below the 1946 level, and has remained reasonably constant during the post–World War II period. Interest as a percentage of total federal budget has stayed at about the same levels since 1960, indicating that interest charges, although higher in absolute terms, are not claiming an ever increasing share of total government expenditures.

A growing debt, then, is not necessarily dangerous. It can be argued that the $50 billion debt at the outset of World War II, when GNP was barely $100 billion, was a more serious burden than the $450 billion debt the United States carried in 1973, because by then GNP was well over $1200 billion. Thus, when an economy is growing, a rising debt may present no problem, for every year the country has more national income from which to meet the interest cost. The private sector of the economy similarly has been willing to acquire additional debt during periods of growth; while public debt has grown by about 80 percent since the end of World War II, the private borrowings of corporations and individuals have more than tripled.

The Burden of the Public Debt

An Unfair Tax Burden? Although some of the traditional arguments against a rising public debt may be unsound, there are actually certain problems connected with a sizable debt. The annual interest cost, now running over $22 billion in the United States, is a burden on taxpayers. Many feel that it is an unfair burden, contributing to greater inequality of income distribution. While taxes are paid by almost all households, the greater part of the interest on the debt is collected by upper- and middle-income families, who hold most of the government bonds. To some extent, however, this inequity is minimized by the progressive tax structure: Because upper-income households pay taxes at higher rates, they contribute a larger share of the interest charges. Thus, although a large public debt does involve some redistribution of income in favor of the wealthy, the net effect is probably negligible.

The Costs of the External Debt Although most of the U.S. debt is held internally, the 5 percent that is held by foreigners does involve a current and a future cost to Americans. Every year the U.S. government pays interest to German banks and Arabian oil sheiks who own U.S. bonds; this interest represents a transfer of money from the United States to foreigners, and as such, is a continuing cost to Americans.

Conflicts Between Refinancing and Stabilization Needs One of the major recurring problems posed by a $450 billion public debt involves the question of how this debt should be financed. Although every month billions of dollars' worth of government bonds mature and are redeemed, the Treasury sells new bonds to pay off those that have matured. This periodic refinancing of the debt may have consequences that directly conflict with the stabilization needs of the nation.

Such conflicts arise because the Treasury's primary objective in refinancing the debt is to save the taxpayers money by keeping the interest rates it pays as low as possible. Thus, during a recession, when other branches of government are trying to force interest rates down to encourage private investment, the Treasury often takes advantage of these low interest rates by selling large amounts of its own long-term bonds. Such a policy, however, tends to drive interest rates up, and draws money away from private investments. In other words, Treasury refinancing during recessions may negate the effectiveness of government monetary policy.

Somewhat similar conflicts can occur during inflationary periods. In 1950, for example, the Treasury, faced with the continuing need to refinance the public debt, wanted to keep interest rates artificially low. Inflationary pressures due to the Korean War, however, seemed to call for high interest rates to restrain demand.

Inflation and the Public Debt A final objection to a large public debt is the inflationary pressure it may cause. Government securities are very liquid assets. Consequently, the millions of Americans who own these securities tend to devote more of their current income to consumption spending than if their savings were tied up in relatively nonliquid real estate or private business investments, for example. Such an increase in consumption spending, it may be argued, can have an inflationary pull when the economy is already at its full-employment level.

A second explanation of the inflationary risk associated with the public debt is also tied to the liquidity of government bonds. Since bonds can be cashed in for money on demand, the huge supply of bonds in the hands of households represents a tremendous backlog of buying power that may be converted at inconvenient times. In 1946–47, for example, Americans cashed in many of the bonds purchased during World War II, and used the funds to finance an inflationary buying spree. In this case, though, demand had been restrained for several years—a situation that is not likely to occur frequently.

Adding to the debt is what creates the fuel for inflation. A small change in the debt may be more significant than the existing level of debt. Further, deficit spending is inflationary if it is used at the wrong time—such as during a period of full employment. But in a recession, such spending is desirable, since it tends to increase employment and output.

Solutions to Budget Imbalance

Although much of the public debt has been incurred by war, the controversy over the public debt focuses primarily on its stabilization functions. Budget surpluses and deficits affect the level of economic activity, and are used intentionally to promote full employment or to curb inflation.

> When the budget is in surplus, the federal government withdraws more from the nation's income stream through taxes than it returns through spending. With a budget deficit, the reverse occurs; more is returned to the income stream than is taken from it.... budget deficits tend to stimulate economic activity, and surpluses to restrain it.[1]

Whether to incur deficits and surpluses at all is only part of the issue. There are several different budget philosophies that accept surpluses and deficits but in different ways.

The Annually Balanced Budget At one extreme are those who favor the annually balanced budget. This was the accepted approach in the pre-Keynesian period, and its supporters are still vocal today. In 1973, for example, a special Senate-House committee investigating the congressional budget process recommended that whenever a budget deficit appears, "a surcharge... be imposed to bring in sufficient revenues in the next calendar year to eliminate that deficit."[2] This represents a clear attempt to mandate balanced budgets as part of any spending-taxing package voted by Congress.

Although it is true that an annually balanced budget would involve no additions to the public debt, consider the effect of a balanced budget on economic stability during a recession. As employment and national income declined, federal tax collections would also drop. If a balanced budget were mandatory, Congress would have only two alternatives: It could raise the tax rates, or it could cut spending. Obviously, either alternative would merely intensify the decline in aggregate spending, and depress the economy even further.

A balanced budget requirement could be equally undesirable when business conditions are very good and the economy is approaching its full-employment ceiling. As employment and incomes rose, tax collections would increase. If the budget is to be balanced, rising revenues would require an increase in government spending or a tax cut, despite the fact that either of these measures would tend to increase aggregate demand, and thus, the risk of inflation—especially if demand then rose above full-employment NNP.

An annually balanced budget, then, would compound the upward and downward swings in economic activity. Such a budget would not provide the countercyclical effects we now expect from government spending and taxing programs; instead, it would intensify economic fluctuations.

The Cyclically Balanced Budget The cyclically balanced budget represents an attempt to have the

1 Charles Schultze et al., *Setting National Priorities: The 1973 Budget* (Washington, D.C.: Brookings Institution, 1972), p. 2.

2 "Special Congressional Study Panel Drafts Major Reforms to Curb Spending," *New York Times*, May 10, 1973, p. 72.

best of all possible worlds—a budget that is a stabilization device and yet does not increase the public debt. A cyclically balanced budget would be balanced over the *entire business cycle,* rather than each year. It would run deficits in recession years, as taxes were cut and government expenditures increased, but it would show a surplus at the top of the cycle, when tax receipts were high and government spending was restrained. The difficulty with a cyclically balanced budget lies in the fact that the peaks and troughs of business cycles are not necessarily of equal duration or dimension; many recessions are longer and deeper than the periods of prosperity that follow them. Consequently, the surpluses achieved are not necessarily equal to the deficits incurred. Moreover, even full employment may require a deficit. The problems of prediction and timing are equally troublesome, since business cycles are easier to discern after they are past than when they are occurring.

Functional Finance In the functional finance approach to budget-making, the entire question of balancing the budget is irrelevant. Proponents of this approach see expenditures and revenue in terms of their function as stabilization tools, ignoring the question of whether or not the two aggregates happen to be equal. It is the government's job to provide a stable, full-employment economy, and the budget is one of the vehicles through which this can be accomplished. Any deficits or surpluses that occur in the process are minor inconveniences, considering the importance of the primary objective. Yet most proponents of the functional finance approach do not necessarily expect deficits to proliferate endlessly. *If* fiscal tools are used wisely, a deficit incurred to stimulate business activity during a recession may produce budget surpluses when recovery sets in.

Such surpluses are created because the government collects more taxes as incomes rise; if the tax system is progressive, the tax receipts grow at a faster rate than the rate at which income is rising. This creates a complication known as **fiscal drag**. If government expenditures are not increased to eliminate the surpluses, the economy is slowed before it has fully recovered. Increasing expenditures to offset fiscal drag sustains the stimulus that keeps the economy expanding.

Critics of functional financing, however, see other difficulties. They claim that once the value of balancing the budget is removed, wasteful spending is likely to occur. Politicians are more apt to evaluate projected expenditures carefully when any new spending must be balanced by an increase in taxes.

Full-Employment Budget One problem with functional finance is that the changes in economic activity can bring about changes in surpluses and deficits, just as surpluses and deficits can affect economic activity. Separating these two effects is important if fiscal policy is to achieve its intended results. The full-employment budget attempts to distinguish between policy and income effects by comparing estimated expenditures with estimated tax receipts if full employment were realized. This shows how expansionary or contractionary the budget is, regardless of the existing level of employment. The actual budget deficits reflect a mixture of the business conditions and the budget policy; the full-employment budget focuses only on the budgetary factors. For example, the original fiscal 1974 budget called for outlays of about $269 billion and receipts of about $250 billion, or an actual deficit of $19 billion. President Nixon, however, described it as a "full-employment *surplus* budget." He reasoned that if the economy were at the full-employment level of 4 percent unemployment, federal revenues would exceed the $269 billion in expenditures by $300 million. This budget, the President argued, would help fight inflation because the country would be moving away from the full-employment deficits of 1972 and 1973, toward a full-employment surplus.

As a guide to policy, the full-employment balanced budget concept retains much of the stabilization power of the functional finance budget. When unemployment rises, the budget can be adjusted to run an actual deficit to close the deflationary gap, although were the economy at full employment, the budget would be balanced. Conversely, a deflation-

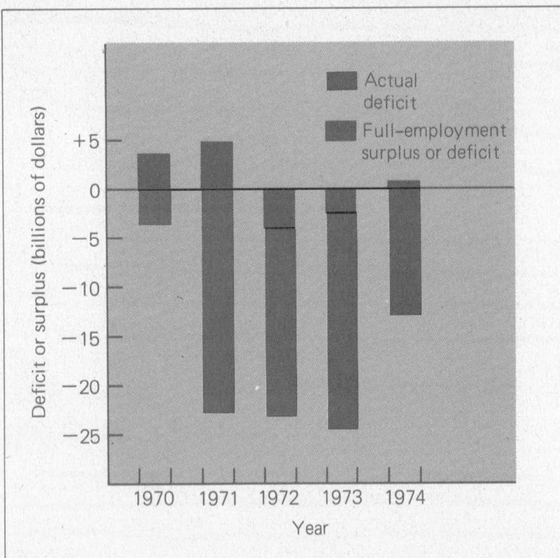

FIGURE 10-1 THE FEDERAL BUDGET: FULL-EMPLOYMENT AND ACTUAL DEFICITS AND SURPLUSES, 1970–74 (Fiscal years) **An actual budget deficit occurs when expenditures are greater than revenue. Often, although expenditures are greater than revenue, there is a full-employment surplus because if there were full employment (based on an unemployment rate of 4 percent), the present tax structure would yield enough revenue to overcome the present deficit and create a surplus. This was the case in 1970 and 1971, and will possibly be the case again in 1974.**

ary surplus may occur when inflation threatens, although again, in full-employment terms, the budget is balanced. At the same time, such a budgeting formula provides built-in controls that could help prevent some of the excessive and wasteful spending which critics say contributes to inflationary pressures.

CONTROVERSY OVER CONTROL

Although it is true that the Employment Act of 1946 gave the federal government the responsibility of providing a stable, full-employment economy, the Act is somewhat unclear when it comes to answering the question of precisely where this responsibility lies. The Act created a three-person Council of Economic Advisers (CEA) to analyze economic data and recommend stabilization policy to the President. It also established a Joint Economic Committee of Congress to assist and advise the President on economic matters. In addition, there is the Office of Management and Budget in the Executive Office of the President, the Treasury Department, and the Federal Reserve Board—all of which have strong, and not necessarily identical, feelings about the state of the economy and the most appropriate economic policies to pursue. Complicating the situation even further are conflicting interests within Congress and the political pressures to which almost all government officials—from the President to congressmen to bureaucrats—are subject. The result is a constant controversy over who will determine federal economic stabilization policy, a controversy that may at times limit the effectiveness of these efforts, but that nevertheless is an integral part of our decentralized system of government.

Controversy within the Executive Branch

Looking over the impressive list of agencies, councils, departments, and boards within the executive branch of government, it would appear that the President is liberally supplied with both economic advice and a bureaucracy to implement economic policies. A major step in this direction was the reorganization in 1970 of the old Bureau of the Budget into the Office of Management and Budget (OMB). Formerly, each government agency could submit requests for funds directly to Congress; today, however, all requests for appropriations must be channeled through OMB, giving the President close control over the size of the annual spending package.

But the final budget sent to Congress each year does not reveal the intricate process of making economic policy. Conflicts between the President's various advisers persist. The Council of Economic Advisers may call for a tax increase or for cuts in spending, but the President's political strategists may find these suggestions unacceptable in an election year. The President himself may request a limit on expenditures, as Richard Nixon did in 1973, but OMB may be subject to tremendous pressures for increased funding from specific government agencies and their clients. Thus, each group within the executive branch sees the question of priorities in terms of its own interest, and the budget that often emerges from the White House after these bitter battles has been aptly described as a "thing of patches and compromises."[3]

Controversy within Congress

Congressional control of spending and taxing is established by the Constitution. James Madison described this power of the purse as "the most complete and effectual weapon with which any constitution can arm the immediate representative of the people." But Congress is hampered in this task because its decisions are made on the merits of individual spending and taxation programs, rather than on a coherent economic program which it cannot produce. In the words of Senator Charles Mathias of Maryland, Congress "cannot perform its most basic task: to make the major decisions regarding the raising and spending of federal tax dollars."[4]

The problem is that Congress has no central authority that can evaluate the budget as a whole—as does OMB in the executive branch. Instead, authority is fragmented among dozens of individual committees and subcommittees. Except for the Joint Economic Committee, none has the staff, the interest, or the responsibility for assessing individual programs in terms of overall economic policy. And the JEC has no real authority over spending or taxing.

Of the two branches of Congress, the House of Representatives traditionally has had major responsibility for financial matters, because the Constitution requires that all revenue bills originate there. Yet the House of Representatives lacks a means of coordinating revenue collection and expenditures, because these decisions are delegated to different committees. In the House, taxes are the responsibility of the Ways and Means Committee, and expenditures are the ultimate responsibility of the Appropriations Committee. In the words of Representative Donald Riegle of Michigan, an ex-IBM finance officer, the Appropriations and Ways and Means committees "might as well be on separate planets as far as any effort is made to link expenditures and revenues." Representative Riegle found that the House fails to establish a spending-taxing goal at the outset; as a result, "everything that follows is haphazard."[5]

Moreover, spending decisions in the House have few controls. Appropriations are determined through an elaborate two-pronged system. First, a legislative committee (such as the Agriculture or the Armed Services Committee) drafts a bill and sets a fund ceiling for the program. Next, this legislation is sent to the Appropriations Committee, where specific funding is voted. In theory, the full Appropriations Committee could coordinate spending bills and establish priorities before presenting a funding proposal to the House. In practice, however, the Appropriations Committee assigns each bill to one of its 13 subcommittees for consideration, and the full committee seldom challenges the recommendations of its individual subcommittees. The same lack of coordination exists in the Senate.

Once expenditure measures go before the floor of the House or Senate, there is always pressure on a congressman or senator to vote for particular bills, more on the merits of the proposal than on the basis of stabilization needs or relative priorities. In addition, the congressional practice of "logrolling," or reciprocity, works to secure votes for many spending measures. A congressman from Chicago, for example, will support water control projects in Idaho in exchange for votes for center-city day-care facilities in his own district.

Controversy between Congress and the President

Tension between the branches of government in setting economic goals has always existed. In 1973, the debate over who should control government

3 Juan Cameron, "Those Frayed Congressional Purse Strings," *Fortune*, February 1973, p. 99.

4 *Ibid.*, p. 98.

5 *Ibid.*, p. 100.

spending and taxing policies developed into open conflict. The President, embarking on a strenuous program of budget cutting in order to hold down inflation, maintained tight control over funding requests in the fiscal 1974 budget. Congress, however, was not sympathetic. It authorized new programs requiring an additional $20 to $30 billion,[6] thus raising the spectre of a $40 to $50 billion federal deficit—by far the largest peacetime deficit in our history, and an insuperable threat to the President's anti-inflation plans.

Almost at once, there was widespread criticism of the lack of congressional control, which had permitted passage of these bills, with much of the criticism coming from Congress itself.[7] A special Senate-House committee on budget control was established to reform the congressional budget process. It recommended that Congress set an annual spending limit, create new budget committees with dual responsibility for both revenues and expenditures, and establish a congressional budget office, comparable to the White House OMB, to provide the expertise needed to allocate individual appropriations within the overall spending limit.[8]

These recommendations appeared very close to the specific suggestions made by the President in January 1973.[9] But in the meantime, the President had been faced with the immediate problem of funds already committed by Congress, funds that he believed were excessive and inflationary. The President vetoed a number of bills, including measures for rural waste and water disposal grants, low-cost loans to rural co-ops, and federal aid for hospital construction and manpower training. Moreover, he stated unequivocally that even if Congress overrode his vetoes, he would impound the funds—that is, he would refuse to spend them.

The President's position was clear. He claimed that Congress's reluctance to establish meaningful budget ceilings, if unchallenged, could destroy the effectiveness of any stabilization efforts introduced by the administration; therefore, he was forced to take control. Congressional opponents, on the other hand, felt impoundment violated the separation of powers required by the Constitution. When Congress appropriates funds, they argued, a President *must* spend them.

This episode raises fundamental questions about the responsibility for maintaining a stable economy. Assuming that an overall spending limit is required, should this limit be set by the President or by Congress? And what constitutional options are open to a President if Congress refuses to operate within the stabilization guidelines he believes necessary?

6 Cameron, p. 102.

7 "Congress Regards Cuts as Threat to Its Power," *New York Times*, January 22, 1973, p. 22.

8 "A Serious Challenge on the Hill," *New York Times*, April 15, 1973, News of the Week, p. 2.

9 *Economic Report of the President* (Washington, D.C.: Government Printing Office, January 1973), p. 75.

CONTROVERSY OVER CONTENT

The battle over the level of government funding was really a skirmish in another continuing battle: that of resource allocation. Stabilization policies would be easier to establish if spending and taxation could be varied without reference to the content of programs. But money must be spent on something and money must be raised from someone. A dollar spent on day care is very much like one spent on bombers from the point of view of economic stabilization, but cutting from one is rather different from cutting from the other in its effects on resource allocation. Moreover, once money is committed, eliminating programs becomes difficult.

The Problem of Prior Commitments Actually, the President's power to vary the level of the budget or to change allocations within it is greatly limited. Experts have estimated that a major slice of any budget consists of items over which the President can exercise no discretion at all. Of the $269-billion 1974 budget submitted by President Nixon, as much as $110 billion represents committed civilian expenditures—social security, Medicare, veterans' pensions, revenue sharing, the interest on the federal debt—mandated under legislation passed by Congress in previous years. In addition, of the $79 billion requested for military spending, a substantial amount also involved prior commitments for research, materials already ordered, and salaries. In many cases, the President was not only unable to cut spending in these categories, but was also faced with "uncontrollable" spending increases; for example, increases of $4.5 billion in federal salaries, $6 billion in social security payments, $3.5 billion in Medicare and Medicaid, and $1 to $2 billion in interest charges on the federal debt were built into the 1974 budget. This means that in 1974 "discretionary spending" probably totaled only $65 to $75 billion.

Shifting Priorities Within these limits, however, the President still has control over the allocation of a substantial sum of money. How that money is spent will, of course, be governed by the President's own priorities and those of his administration. The 1974 budget reflected two goals: to eliminate waste and inefficiency, particularly in social welfare programs, and to increase the role of state and local governments in determining and controlling expenditures for local projects. With these objectives in mind, the budget established somewhat new priorities for the allocation of funds. Approximately one hundred different programs, mostly social services, were eliminated, and certain social welfare projects—Community Action Programs, Model Cities, urban renewal, the Job Corps—were drastically cut back. These cutbacks, in turn, were offset by increases in other areas: pollution control, energy research, drug abuse control, law enforcement, cancer and heart disease research, national defense. But critics of the Nixon administration claim that the budget does not represent a basic desire for efficiency as much as a wish to use the rationale of efficiency and stabilization to eliminate programs that are philosophically repugnant to the administration.

The point is that federal stabilization policy cannot be viewed in isolation. Changes in government spending require a decision about which programs are to be expanded and which cut back. Stabilization goals, then, are not independent of other social and political goals.

TABLE 10-2 Proposed Cuts in the 1974 Budget

Program	Budget authority (millions of dollars)		
	FY 1972	FY 1973	FY 1974
Urban renewal	$1250	$1450	$138
Emergency public service employment	1000	1249	0
Office of Economic Opportunity	724	790	0
Rural electrification 2 percent loans	669	633	0
Extended unemployment compensation	600	194	0
Impacted area education aid	423	204	61
Hill-Burton hospital construction funds	358	8	0
College student loans	317	293	5
Rural environmental assistance	196	226	0
Library aid	176	138	0
Model Cities	150	500	0
Special school milk program	104	97	25

A budget reflects not only national stabilization goals but social priorities. To avoid adding extra spending that would intensify the already chronic inflation, the federal budget for fiscal year 1974 was pared by nearly $12 billion from the level it might have reached through unconstrained spending. Defense expenditures were tightened somewhat, but the lethal cuts came out of programs begun in the days of the Great Society, which the administration now deemed ineffective. The increase in revenue-sharing funds shifted power from federal to state and local social programs, completing a coherent change of priorities by the administration.

SOURCE: *Business Week*, February 3, 1973, p. 60.

Tax Changes and Income Distribution

Tax Subsidies Indeed, the federal income-tax structure confirms the influence of social value judgments in determining fiscal policy. Perhaps the clearest instance is in the choice of what not to tax.

One former Treasury Department official has asserted that all tax subsidies—including deductions, special credits, shelters, deferrals, exclusions, and preferences—are, apart from the varied terminology, species of direct government outlays that he calls "tax expenditures,"[10] akin to the expenditures that provide

10 Stanley S. Surrey, "Tax Expenditures and Tax Reform," excerpted from a statement in *The Federal Subsidy System*, Hearings of the Joint Economic Committee, U.S. Congress, January 1972, pp. 82.

THE MORATORIUM ON HOUSING SUBSIDIES

In 1973, shortly after his inauguration, President Nixon suspended new commitments for almost all federally subsidized housing for low-income groups, citing the need to keep spending within bounds and questioning the efficacy of federal low-income housing subsidies. Although over 1 million units had been built since 1968 under the suspended programs, the costs and exposés of mismanagement and corruption brought the programs under attack. One program alone had a foreclosure rate 10 times that of regular FHA loans. And St. Louis actually dynamited part of the Pruitt-Igoe public housing complex because conditions there had grown so bad. The President estimated that over the next 40 years the programs could cost between $68 and $95 billion. So an 18-month moratorium on certain housing subsidy programs was called.

Within weeks of the suspension, the Joint Economic Committee of Congress issued a rejoinder, saying that errors in management were at fault and better administration would "correct the deficiencies in these programs without killing them." What the JEC failed to examine were the actual incentives and effects of the program. Henry Aaron of the Brookings Institution has pointed out that the federal housing programs are piecemeal at best and that many involve added costs and perverse incentives.* They are concerned with building units instead of consid-

* *Shelter and Subsidies: Who Benefits from Federal Housing Policies?* (Washington, D.C.: Brookings Institution, 1972). For a brief account see the *Brookings Bulletin* 9(3):3–5.

United Press International

ering the wider needs for residential *services*. More important, they cover only a fraction of those who need help in securing proper housing.

Untouched by all the wrangling is the largest subsidy of all, the deductions of real estate tax and interest on home loans. According to Aaron, in 1970 alone, these amounted to nearly $10 billion, and Nixon's subsequent housing message in September 1973 expanded the amount of money available for mortgages. The Nixon message offered experimental support for housing allowances for the poor with hints of more to come if the initial programs succeeded. The new approach hardly matched the benefits to the middle class, but did represent a step toward a more efficient system of housing subsidies. Such subsidies, directed basically at upper- and middle-income people, result in what Aaron has called "filtering." By government's making it easier to buy new homes, older housing vacated by the unpoor filters down to the poor. Besides the expense and the inequity of subsidizing the richer segments of society, this program fails to offer incentives for what is really needed: a larger stock of decent, low-income housing.

This battle over housing subsidies is representative of many contemporary economic problems. The scarcity of resources dictates careful program design with proper incentives in mind; in reality, many other issues of social policy and power become mixed in.

an army or a national gallery of art. By not collecting more taxes because of tax subsidy privileges, the government is effectively making payments to those who receive tax-exempt interest income on municipal bonds, to those who deduct the interest paid on mortgages to buy homes, and to corporations that delay bringing overseas earnings back to the United States and thus postpone domestic tax bills.

In the 1971 Tax Act, the Nixon administration introduced a number of tax subsidies designed to counteract recession by providing encouragement to business. These included restoration of the 7 percent investment credit, more rapid depreciation of fixed assets, preferential treatment for income generated from exporting, and five-year amortization for the construction of facilities for employer on-the-job training programs and child-care facilities. Such changes are not neutral in their effects. A 1969 tax incentive for the rehabilitation of low-income housing cut amortization of capital outlays to a brief five-year period from an otherwise much longer span. This provided an effective 19 percent investment credit (assuming an expenditure with a 20-year life) for a taxpayer in the 70 percent bracket, compared with a 5 percent credit for a person in the 20 percent bracket. Clearly, such preferential tax arrangements bear directly on the distribution of income. In this case, taxpayers are being paid higher subsidies at high levels of income.

Tax Reform Such inequalities of the present tax structure in the United States were hotly debated in the 1972 Presidential election. Senator McGovern would have abolished mineral depletion allowances and ended farm-loss and real estate shelters. In addition, he would have offered generous tax subsidies to the poor. The furor over these reforms revealed the tension between the many functions of taxes: raising revenue, stabilizing the economy, promoting more efficient resource allocation, and furthering more equitable distribution of income.

The reforms offered by President Nixon following the election were hardly as far-reaching as those of Senator McGovern, but they revealed the tensions as well. One reform aimed at closing a loophole benefiting high-income people offered subsidy incentives to local and state governments issuing taxable bonds instead of relying on tax-exempt ones. Other reforms provided property tax relief for the elderly through credits for homeowners and renters and tax credits for parents sending children to private schools. It is estimated that first-year revenue loss from the enactment of all of the President's proposals will amount to $900 million. The President's proposals were advanced at a time when inflationary conditions in the economy would argue for a net increase in taxes for stabilization purposes. However, the proposal merely confirmed that the content of programs and the urgency of certain policy interests tend to take priority over stabilization needs that could be satisfied, at least in large part, by somewhat different changes in tax policies.

OBJECTIONS TO STABILIZATION POLICIES

Over the last four and a half chapters the economics of employment, income, and government stabilization policy have been outlined. Based on Keynesian analysis, the New Economics, which relies heavily on fiscal tools to regulate the economy, plays an important role in shaping economic policy in the United States. But its power is not universally accepted. So far in this chapter, some of the problems of fiscal policy have been discussed: complications of public debt, control of policy, and effects on resource allocation and income distribution. But objections go deeper than this: Radicals reject the underlying system and monetarists reject the efficacy of fiscal policy to make an essentially sound system work.

Radical Critique of Fiscal Policy

The intertwining of social, political, and economic aspects of society is particularly emphasized by the radical critics of fiscal policies based on Keynesian theory. Although the radicals acknowledge that increased government spending does reduce unemployment, they contend that in the United States such spending has been channeled into unproductive activities. The New Left argues that the content of stabilization policy is shaped by distortions of

THE TRICKLE DOWN THEORY

In 1971, when President Nixon attempted to use the fiscal tool of cutting taxes to stimulate the economy, his action was widely assailed by many labor union leaders and Democrats because it was based on what has been called the trickle-down theory. By cutting business taxes rather than individual taxes, the administration was handing business a windfall, critics charged, and benefits to individuals would only gradually trickle down in the form of lower prices, better products, higher wages, and more jobs. And there was some truth in these observations. From 1971 to 1972, after-tax corporate profits rose 14.6 percent, while per capita disposable income rose only 6.0 percent. By December 1972, unemployment was 5.1 percent, which meant that there were still 4,487,000 people out of work. The trickle seemed to be flowing into business pockets, as critics had said.

What such critics failed to realize is that in any recovery of the economy, profits increase more rapidly at first than do wages. But the benefits of the economic boom do, in fact, trickle down in time. Since most people in a primarily market economy work for profit-making institutions, rising profits are a necessary condition for a high level of employment and rising income.

Even raising incomes or employment directly boosts profits. After the great tax cut of 1964, which primarily reduced personal income taxes, the same effect occurred. After-tax profits in 1965 were up 21.1 percent over 1964, while per capita disposable income went up by 6.7 percent. As disposable income increased, consumption went up, profits rose, more jobs were created, then there was more income, in turn more profits, and so on. The same would be true if the fiscal tool of providing public service jobs were used to reduce unemployment. The money spent by the newly employed would "trickle up" to increase profits, which would in turn create more jobs, and so forth.

The implication of all this is not that we should concentrate entirely on increasing profits as a way of making everybody better off. Clearly, the equity aspects of a tax cut or increase in spending should be high among the factors considered in determining the appropriate policy. Nevertheless, in a market economy, when the economy needs a stimulus, it is not a matter of increasing wages *or* dividends, jobs *or* profits; both jobs and profits must increase, or there will be no stimulus.

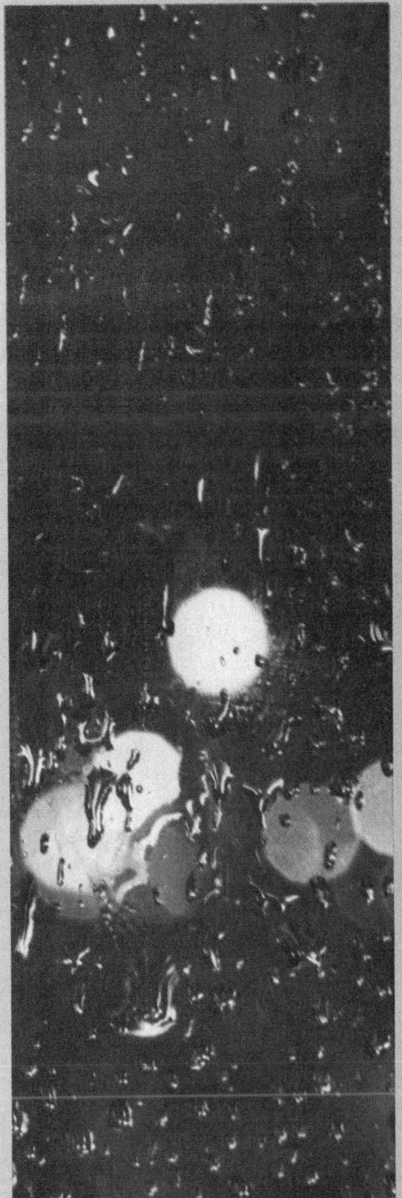

J. Paul Kirouac

monopoly capitalism and reveals its bankruptcy. During the last 30 years, the efforts to prevent a major depression by means of fiscal policies have exacted a heavy price: the consolidation of a quasi-military state, imperialist expansion, wasteful private consumption, and continuing inequality of income distribution. Furthermore, the attacks on unemployment are not aimed at eliminating this problem altogether, since fiscal policies regard a certain amount of unemployment as inevitable and "normal."

Wasteful Defense Spending The growth of the military-industrial complex under capitalism is not accidental. According to economist Paul A. Baran, once a society accepts that unregulated market forces are incapable of providing full employment, the alternatives are severely limited.[11] Although the government could disburse funds to poor people to underwrite increased consumption, capitalist ideology sees this as weakening work incentives and social discipline. Promoting collective consumption through public works goes only so far in eliminating unemployment, since entrenched interests oppose many projects. The government is barred from investing in factories and other productive facilities by capitalist interests. The only avenue left is "exhaustive government expenditures neither on objects of individual or collective consumption nor on productive purposes. . . ."[12]

The greatest spending waste is in defense expenditures. In the United States, national defense expenditures account for about 7 to 8 percent of GNP.[13] Including military-related expenditures not directly included in the budget, some experts have estimated that as much as 15 percent of GNP is tied to military spending—an amount that approximates the total GNP of the United Kingdom.[14] In every year since World War II, the United States has spent more on national defense than any other nation. The per capita outlay for defense in 1970, for example, totaled $373, as compared with $222 for the USSR, $118 for France, $116 for West Germany, $107 for the United Kingdom, and $16 for Japan.[15] Critics suggest that this military spending performs the same function in our society that pyramid building did in ancient Egypt: Although it provides opportunities for employment, it does not satisfy any of society's more urgent needs.

Some critics argue that the success of stabilization policy in the United States is closely tied to a growing defense industry. The importance of defense expenditures to the health of the economy becomes clear when one examines the consequences of cutbacks. When defense contracts to Boeing were reduced, closing aircraft plants in Seattle, the impact on employment, home mortgage foreclosures, and retail sales in that area was severe. Yet these cutbacks represented only a minor reduction in a defense budget totaling close to $80 billion. Any major decrease in defense spending, then, would be disastrous.

Imperialist Expansion Critics also charge that extensive defense expenditures have resulted in a powerful alliance between the Defense Department, the armed services, and the major corporations that supply them with arms. Paul Baran emphasized the close connection between this military-industrial complex and American foreign policy, particularly in developing nations. Baran claimed that because big business seeks to maintain these countries as sources of low-cost labor and raw materials, indigenous movements toward industrialization are thwarted. Local governments, frequently comprised largely of land-owning groups, who also have an interest in maintaining the status quo, are supported by American big business and its ally, the U.S. government. In 1973, for example, Senate hearings revealed that ITT allegedly offered the CIA $1 million to help defeat Salvador Allende when he was a leftist candidate for president in Chile. To many, this typifies the cooperation between big business

11 Paul A. Baran, *The Political Economy of Growth,* 2nd ed. (New York: Prometheus, 1960), p. 101.

12 *Ibid.*, pp. 108–109.

13 U.S. Department of Commerce, *Statistical Abstracts* (Washington, D.C.: Government Printing Office, 1972), Table 397.

14 Daniel R. Fusfeld, *Fascist Democracy in the United States.* Reprinted from Conference Papers of the Union for Radical Political Economics, December 1968, p. 11. In his estimates, Fusfeld included not only the Department of Defense and the Veterans Administration, but also the Atomic Energy Commission, the National Security Council, Civil Defense Mobilization, CIA, NASA, Selective Service, defense materials of the General Services Administration, the Department of State, and interest on the public debt.

15 However, there were several nations, including the USSR, where military spending as a percentage of GNP did exceed that of the United States, although because of reporting differences, figures may not be truly comparable. Moreover, the low figures of European countries and Japan to some extent reflect that U.S. military expenses are allowing other nations to spend less.

and the U.S. government that is an outgrowth of the powerful military-industrial complex spawned to provide full employment.

Wasteful Consumption Spending It is not government spending alone that has come under fire from critics of American capitalism. These critics are concerned about wasteful consumption spending which they believe has been encouraged as another way to provide full employment. If advertising can convince the consumer that he needs not a comb but an electric hair styler, not a sponge but an electric dishwasher, the economy will prosper.

But because of our overriding concern with the need to increase aggregate consumption, we have paid little attention to the quality of life provided by both consumer goods and the productive process that creates them. The possibilities for a shorter work week, more leisure, an improved environment, a more meaningful job are forgotten in the rush for an ever increasing quantity of goods and services.

The Problem of Income Distribution The emphasis on aggregate economic performance obscures important features of American society. An overall 4 percent unemployment rate, for example, is viewed as "acceptable," but at that aggregate level the rate of unemployment for blacks runs approximately 8 percent and the rate for teenagers about 15 percent. Thus, government spending and taxing policies may maintain unemployment at a manageable level, but critics charge that the results are not necessarily fair or equitable. By focusing on the level of unemployment or the size of GNP, policies have failed to touch on problems of discrimination and poverty. Radicals point to the inequities of the tax system and the inadequacies of spending programs in redistributing income.

The Monetarists

The conservative attack on Keynesian economics has been formulated by the monetarists. This school of thought believes that many dangers are involved in the routine use of fiscal tools to manipulate the economy. Questioning the ability of even the most knowledgeable economists to foresee the direction of the economy and prescribe the exact quantities of spending and taxing that will keep it on course, they believe that attempts at "fine tuning" the economy can be self-defeating. For example, measures taken to stimulate the economy may not begin to work until business has recovered on its own, at which time they accelerate inflationary pressures. Conservatives also criticize the New Economics on the grounds that it leads to a centralization of power over the allocation of resources in the hands of a relatively small number of government planners. The conservatives would prefer to leave such decisions to the impersonal forces of the marketplace. Nevertheless, many conservatives do accept the principle that government has a responsibility for stabilizing economic activity. They suggest, however, that this role can best be achieved through the use of monetary policy. It is by controlling the supply of money, they argue, that government can meet its responsibilities for stabilization in the most efficient and equitable manner.

The explanation of monetary policy and its theoretical basis will consume most of the next part of this book. Here again we shall encounter problems of institutional conflict and controversy over content that complicate all efforts to stabilize the economy. But more important, we shall see how the fiscal and monetary analyses fit together, how business cycles occur, and finally how economic developments in recent years pose a crisis for stabilization policy—and perhaps for economic theory.

SUMMARY

1 The use of fiscal policy for the purpose of stabilizing the economy was mandated by the Employment Act of 1946. The conscious management of the economy involves problems besides the choice of fiscal tools, however.

2 Budget deficits stimulate the economy, whereas budget surpluses restrain it.

The use of deficits as a fiscal tool has been opposed because of the burden it creates. The debt and its interest payments have been declining as a percentage of GNP, and most of the debt has been incurred by war, not by stabilizing the economy. Nonetheless, the public debt does redistribute income to holders of government securities, the externally held portions constitute an export of capital, the refinancing may interfere with stabilization needs, and an improperly timed increase in the deficit may fuel inflation.

3 The way in which deficits and surpluses are regarded depends on the budget philosophy. At one extreme is the annually balanced budget, which demands that revenues equal expenditures every fiscal year. Its more flexible relative, the cyclically balanced budget, attempts to balance things out over the course of the business cycle. Functional finance ignores the need for balancing and recommends whatever spending and taxation levels will stabilize the economy. The full-employment budget provides a tool for separating policy and income effects and is based on the level of tax receipts, were the economy at full employment.

4 Because the control over economic policy is divided among several institutions, obtaining a coherent program is difficult. Setting a spending limit and the impoundment of funds are two subjects of recent controversy.

5 Stabilization policy also affects resource allocation and income distribution. Leeway for spending cuts is limited by the magnitude of prior commitments and by the priorities of the Congress, the President, and the public. Tax subsidies provide an example of the use of taxes to promote different sectors of the economy; many of the tax reform proposals aim at changing these subsidies.

6 Objections to the use of fiscal policy may be more far-reaching. The monetarists view monetary policy as the better means to regulate the economy. The radicals assert that concern with macroeconomic policy has created a militarist society, imperialism, wasteful private consumption, and unnecessary poverty. Only through the abolition of private property can the economy be truly stabilized, they say.

SUGGESTED READINGS

Eckstein, Otto. *Public Finance.* 2nd ed. Englewood Cliffs, N.J.: Prentice-Hall, 1967.

Economic Report of the President. Washington, D.C.: Government Printing Office, annual. Contains summary and projection of economic conditions with explanations of policies.

Hamovitch, William, ed. *Federal Deficit: Fiscal Imprudence or Policy Weapon?* Lexington, Mass.: D. C. Heath, 1965.

Okun, Arthur M. *The Political Economy of Prosperity.* New York: W. W. Norton, 1970.

Pechman, Joseph A. *Federal Tax Policy.* Rev. ed. New York: W. W. Norton, 1971.

Schultze, Charles L., Edward R. Fried, Alice M. Rivlin, and **Nancy H. Teeters.** *Setting National Priorities: The 1973 Budget* and *The 1974 Budget.* Washington, D.C.: Brookings Institution, 1972, 1973.

U.S. Congress, Joint Economic Committee. *The Joint Economic Report.* Washington, D.C.: Government Printing Office, annual. Congressional evaluation of *Economic Report of the President.*

QUESTIONS

1 Review
   a. possible burdens of the national debt,
   b. potential conflicts between refinancing of the public debt and stabilization,
   c. different budget policies,
   d. problems of control and content of fiscal policy,
   e. the attacks on fiscal policy as an economic tool.

2 Walter Heller, Chairman of the Council of Economic Advisers during the Kennedy administration, criticized the Nixon budget in early 1973 by saying, "Relentless, even ruthless, in its pursuit of evil among social programs, the Nixon budget shows no comparable ruthlessness in paring military fat or challenging tax privilege."* What reasons might you offer for the tendency to ignore the military?

3 Under the present federal tax laws, charitable donations are tax deductible. With a progressive tax rate, what groups or sectors would tend to be subsidized? What rationale can be made for such deductions?

4 According to many who argue in favor of a cyclically balanced budget, the budget would be balanced over the cycle because there would be deficits during the recession and surpluses during the boom. How might you defend the idea that such a budget is actually a depressant over a long period of time?

5 There is no reason to believe that a particular surplus or deficit or a balanced budget at full employment is desirable, unless some more information is available. For example, suppose that the economy is at a full-employment equilibrium and the budget is balanced. Then, for allocative reasons Congress decides to increase spending by $50 billion. If this is offset by a tax increase of $50 billion and the multiplier in the economy is 2, what would happen to the economy? Would it help instead to cut spending by $50 billion and cut taxes by $50 billion?

6 Private debt has been growing at a rapid pace, just as public debt has. Substantial portions of private debt are used to finance investment, which ensures economic growth. Can the same be said of public debt?

7 Under present tax laws, capital gains are taxed at approximately half the rate of salaried forms of income. What might be the economic consequences of a provision to eliminate the special rate on capital gains? Could a case be made that taxpayers have subsidized business investment? Land prices? Why or why not?

8 Previously, a tax increase had been a politically dangerous way of coping with inflation. Why might a tax increase become more palatable if inflation continues? Describe the economic effects. Would fiscal drag be a problem?

9 The distribution of power cannot be ignored in the study of economics. Reject or defend this thesis as it pertains to macroeconomics.

* Walter Heller, "The Side Effects of Nixon's Budget," *Wall Street Journal*, February 22, 1973, p. 16.

PART

3

INTEGRATING MONEY

CHAPTER 11
MONEY

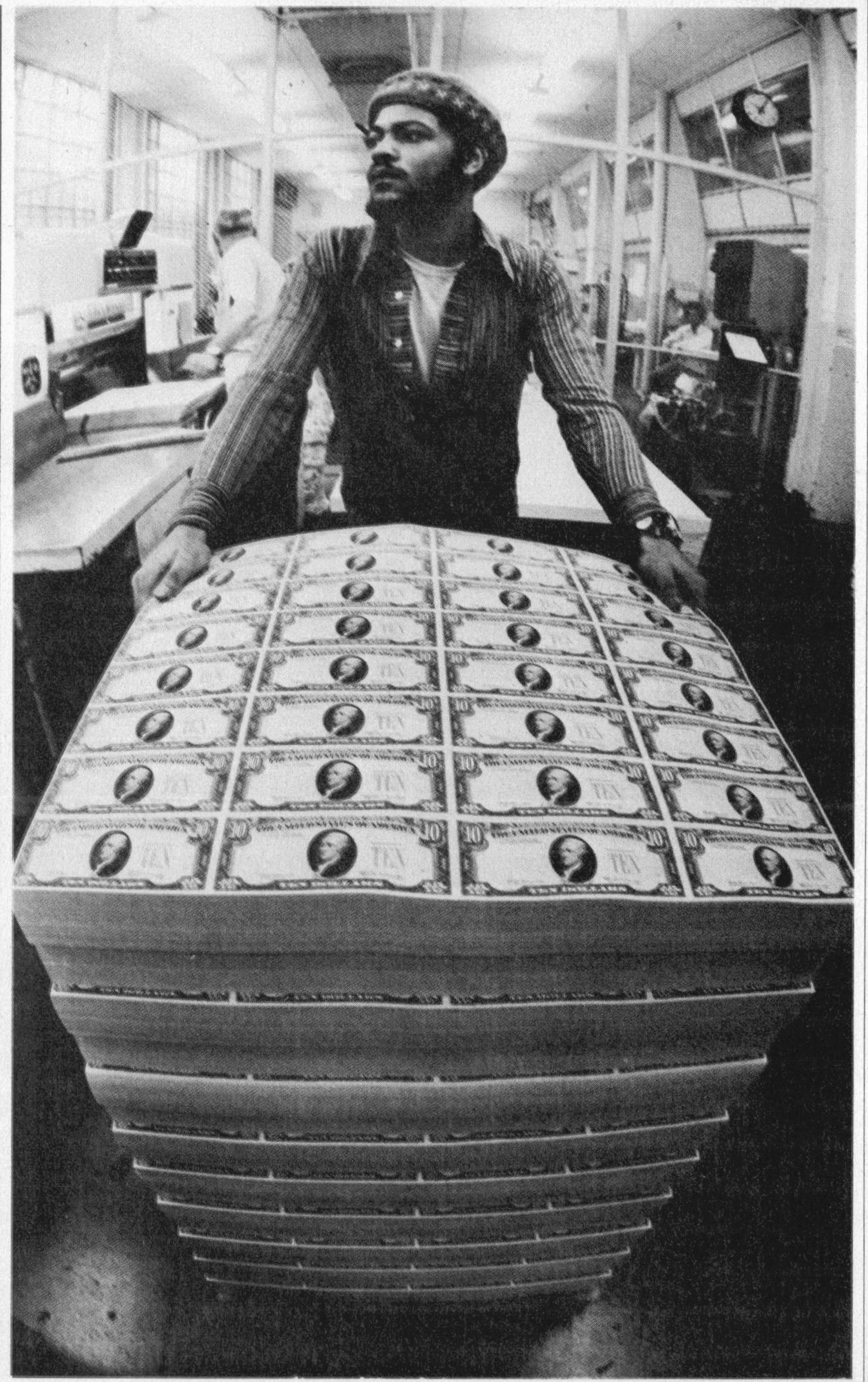

What makes a person wealthy? Why, money, of course. Then why do people spend time slaving at such jobs as digging ditches and writing economics textbooks? Why couldn't everyone become rich simply by having the government print enough money to go around? Then everyone could quit sweating over a shovel or a typewriter, sit back at ease, and let the printing presses do the work.

But in the unlikely circumstance that everyone had access to all the money he wanted and that no one found it necessary to work for a living any longer, everyone would soon find himself facing a serious problem: Money would cease to be worth anything. With no one working to produce goods and services, there would be nothing to buy and money would become just so many strips of paper. As we are about to learn, the value of money is paradoxical. The more money there is, the more careful we must be to keep its value from disappearing. Why is this so? What makes money valuable? What functions does money serve in an economy? Before demanding an unlimited supply of greenbacks, it would help to know the answers to these questions.

WHAT IS MONEY?

Generally speaking, money is whatever is accepted within an economy as a medium of exchange. Money makes the exchange of goods and services quicker and easier. If money did not exist, we would be compelled to spend much of our day in search of people who had things that we wanted in exchange for things that we had to offer. Such a barter system might be satisfactory in a relatively simple society where everyone wore much the same kind of clothes, ate the same kind of food, and engaged in similar activities. But in a society such as ours, where people have far more complex needs and wants, bartering would make life extremely difficult. If we wanted a steak for dinner, for example, we would have to offer the butcher something he desired. And if none of our possessions interested him, we would have to try the fish store or other food dealers until we found one willing to swap or else go hungry.

Opening photo by J. P. Laffont—Sygma

Not all commodities are wanted by everyone, but money is something that everybody wants. It is universally desirable because it can be exchanged for any good produced. With money, we need not concern ourselves about anything else that might be desired by the people who supply our own needs. We need only be concerned with having enough money. And since having enough money is such a major preoccupation, we can be thankful that money has simplified life for us in other ways.

The supply of money has an important effect on general economic conditions. An increase in the money supply tends to increase aggregate demand; a decrease inhibits it. This makes itself evident in the levels of economic activity, in such indices as industrial production, home building, employment, and prices.

How Money Serves Us

But the most obvious way money serves us is in helping us satisfy our day-to-day human needs. This is only one of the four basic functions of money as a medium of exchange. Money functions as (1) a means of payment, (2) a unit of value, (3) a standard of deferred payments, and (4) a store of value.

A Means of Payment In most exchange situations, money is the accepted medium through which the buyer discharges his obligation to the seller. However, barter—exchange without the use of money—still takes place between individuals and, in some cases, in major business deals, such as the trading of players by baseball teams.

But in most situations, money is the most convenient method of facilitating exchange, for it vastly increases freedom of choice. You can buy practically anything if you have the money to pay for it. People are reluctant to receive payment in a commodity other than money because if they cannot use it themselves, they will be faced with a further exchange in order to secure something that they want. Money eliminates this problem by reducing to one the number of exchanges necessary to achieve the desired commodity or service.

The absence of money renders one helpless, economically speaking. People must therefore maintain reserves of money in order to assure that they will always be prepared to meet any needs that may arise. Keeping a supply of pocket money is one way of maintaining such a reserve. Another method, widely relied on by individuals as well as by organizations, is maintaining a checking account (or demand deposit, in economics terminology).

A Unit of Value Anyone who has ever tried bartering knows that the exchange process is much simpler and quicker if each item has a designated price affixed to it. Without money, it is difficult to decide how many eggs are worth a single blanket. A complex economy could not exist if it did not have the convenience of money as a unit of value. Money, for example, gives a common unit by which to measure the various kinds of assets of a business. By assigning a monetary value to such assets as property, production machinery, and inventory, we can obtain a relatively accurate idea of the net worth of a firm. This would not be possible if people did not generally agree on how much things "cost."

In order to serve as a unit of value, however, the purchasing power of money must remain fairly stable. If we cannot agree on how much a dollar is worth, its usefulness as a unit of value diminishes. In actuality, of course, money is never perfectly stable. Its value depends on what it can buy, and since prices of goods are subject to fluctuation, the value of money is, too. Changes in the value of money reflect the average price changes of a wide range of items, some of which are rising much more rapidly, others of which are relatively stable. Nonetheless, it is this average fluctuation that is watched with a wary eye by anyone concerned about the economy.

A Standard of Deferred Payments Money not only translates the current worth of an item but allows present values to be projected into the future. Contracts that specify future payment, loan contracts, leases on property, salary contracts, the sale of rights to natural resources—each involves setting prices in the present that will apply in the future. Whenever such an arrangement is made, there is always the risk of a gain or a loss to each of the parties because of the way money fluctuates in value.

With an increase in prices, money diminishes in value. This works to the advantage of the person who has agreed to make deferred payment. A man who must pay back a loan of $1000 in ten years' time, for example, actually pays back less in value if prices have steadily risen during that time. If prices fall, the opposite is true: borrowers lose and lenders gain. But we live in an era of steadily rising prices, and thus deferred payments are consistently worth less when they fall due than when they are established. To compensate for losses incurred by inflated money, banks, whose business is making loans, raise their interest rates. Having a vested interest in the stability of the dollar, they are leading advocates of a stable money policy.

A Store of Value In economics terminology, money is a store of value. This means that it is a way to store wealth. As such, money has an advantage over other assets, as well as some disadvantages. It has more liquidity than any other form of asset. **Liquidity** means the ability of an asset to be exchanged for something else of value. Thus, money is a very convenient way to store wealth for use whenever needed, having a particular advantage in transactions that demand immediate payment.

On the debit side, aside from the fact that loose cash attracts thieves, money has a major disadvantage when it is stored as cash or demand deposits: It does not earn interest. So holding wealth in the form of money means sacrificing the income that could be made if money were held in some other form. Assets such as savings accounts and bonds are less liquid than money—we cannot spend them without first converting them into money—but they do earn us interest. This interest is actually the compensation we receive for sacrificing the liquidity of money when we convert it into other kinds of assets.

Money and Near-Money

It is not easy to say exactly what is and what is not money. Economists agree that certain types of assets qualify as money in the strictest sense, but disagree about other types. Thus, most economists, in discussing money, speak of two categories: **money** and **near-money**.

Coins, currency, and demand deposits are considered money in the strictest sense because they indisputably fulfill all the functions of money. Of these, the most important is that they are accepted as a means of payment. That is to say, they are easily transferable. This category of money is known as M_1. Certain other types of assets are not so transferable but may be included in the broader definitions of money.

FIGURE 11-1 A GROWING ECONOMY AND A GROWING MONEY SUPPLY Since 1945 the U.S. economy has doubled in size in terms of constant dollars. In that same time the money supply has more than tripled. Its major components—coins, paper currency, and demand deposits—hold about the same share they did in 1945, however. United Press International Photo

SOURCE: *Economic Report of the President*, January 1973.

Coins and Currency To children, coins are the most important form of money. When they grow older and have to pay their own bills, the coin becomes little more than a convenience. Actually, coins constitute only about 1 percent of the total money supply. At one time, U.S. coins were made of precious metals equal to the coin's face value. However, people were inclined to clip the edges off their coins and melt the the parings down, or, if the price of gold or silver rose, to melt down the entire coin and sell the metal at a profit. Coins today are token money; their face value is far more than their metallic value. They are accepted as money only because they are, by government decree, legal tender.

While coins are worth a fraction of their face value, paper money has no value other than that bestowed on it by the federal government. Nonetheless, paper money constitutes about one-fifth of the total money in the United States.

Many people have the idea that paper money is backed, dollar for dollar, by a federal store of gold. This is not true. Until 1933, holders of paper money **could** cash in their bills for gold. But generally speaking, gold no longer figures in financial transactions, and the amount of gold owned by the Treasury is enough to back only about one-fifth of the paper currency outstanding.

Demand Deposits Monies held in checking accounts in commercial banks are known as **demand deposits**. Over three-quarters of the money supply in the United States is in the form of demand deposits. They are the most important form of money in the economy. This may seem odd, since they are the most intangible. But money in a checking account is almost as liquid as cash, for its owner is able to fulfill his needs by writing checks that are, as a rule, freely accepted in place of currency. This form of payment represents the bank's promise to pay to the bearer of a check legitimately drawn on a demand deposit an amount of money equal to that specified on the check. And such is the public's faith in the banking system that this promise is usually accepted.

Time Deposits and Other Near-Monies The term **time deposits** refers to money deposited in banks and other institutions and held there to draw interest. Some economists argue that time deposits should be counted as part of the total money supply because, although such assets are not transferable, they can be converted into liquid assets rather easily. Savings banks are legally permitted to require advance notice of withdrawal, but in actuality, one can almost always withdraw savings account money in cash merely by walking up to the teller's window with a passbook. Economists group all savings accounts, whether in commercial banks, mutual savings banks, savings and loan associations, or credit unions, under the category M_2. M_2 also subsumes all M_1. In 1972, the time deposit component of M_2 was nearly $268 billion, plus $246 billion of M_1, for a total of $514 billion. It has been found that people tend to spend more freely from income when they have savings accounts—a fact of significance in inflationary periods, which are discussed later in this chapter.

The M_3 category comprises all other types of near-money—U.S. government bonds owned by individuals or businesses, and cash values of insurance policies—as well as M_2. Like savings accounts, these near-monies are not transferable, but they can be converted fairly easily into liquid assets. In 1972, near-monies in the M_3 category amounted to almost $296 billion, for a total of $810 billion in money, time deposits, and other near-monies.

Excluded from the definitions of money are the currency and demand deposits held by the government and by the Federal Reserve and commercial banks. This is partly to avoid a form of double counting and partly because it is the money in the hands of businesses and households that is most important to the level of spending.

The reasons for worrying about what constitutes the money supply are two. To find the exact relationship between money and economic activity requires that the definition of money be unchanging or we will end up comparing apples and oranges. Furthermore, if two types of money are behaving differently, policy-makers need to know which is better to attend to.

Credit Cards The use of credit cards has become extremely widespread in recent years. Credit cards serve only to establish the credit of their bearer, on the strength of which a seller grants him a loan for the amount of his purchase. They simply allow a person to "buy now, pay later"; they do not fall into the category of money or near-money. They are, rather, a device for managing money. While credit card "credit" does not, strictly speaking, add to the money supply, it has the same effect as increasing the money supply, and has grown into a factor of increasing importance in its effect upon aggregate demand, employment, and prices.

WHAT MAKES MONEY VALUABLE?

Monetary Standards

Throughout the world, people transact business in coins and paper bills that are in themselves of little intrinsic value. To define the value of its currency and whatever conditions the currency may be subject to, each nation has laws that constitute a **monetary standard.** Until recent times, silver and gold, especially gold, have served as a basis for the monetary standards of most nations. Gold was selected because it was durable, relatively scarce, widely accepted, and easily divided into exact units. Theoretically, a monetary standard can be based upon anything: ostrich plumes, lard, acorns, mercury. One reason few countries go on the lard standard is that lard fails to meet the requirements that gold fills so admirably. Over the centuries, two other standards besides gold have been employed.

Bimetallic Standard The first monetary standard in the United States was bimetallic. Under the **bimetallic standard,** the unit of currency is defined according to a fixed weight of two metals. For example, in an economy based on gold and silver, one dollar might be worth one grain of gold or fifteen grains of silver. The bimetallic standard has an inherent flaw, however, which was first noted by Sir Thomas Gresham, a sixteenth century financier and master of the mint under Elizabeth I. His observation is known as **Gresham's Law** and states: "Cheap

IS MONEY OBSOLETE?

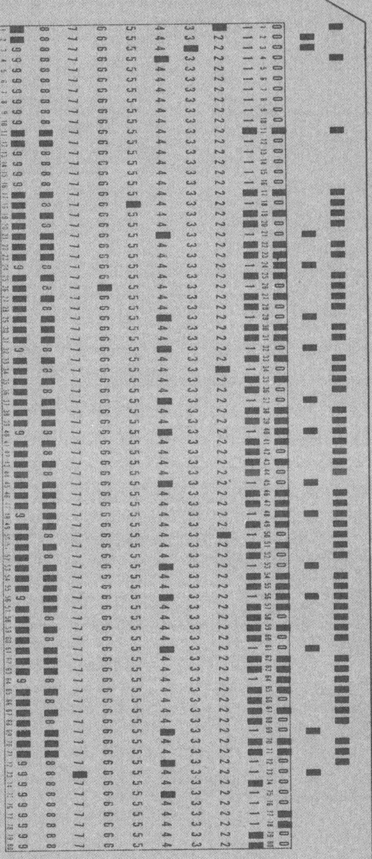

Edward Bellamy, in his late nineteenth-century novel of the future, *Looking Backward,* forecast an economy in which money, as we know it, had no place. Each citizen received credit for the amount, expressed in dollars and cents, that he had personally contributed to GNP. He could then purchase whatever he desired from the public storehouse and the purchase would be recorded on his account. While ordinary citizens were expected to budget their credit allowances on an annual basis, chronic spendthrifts might be limited to credit by the month or week. As we move ahead into the period of time envisioned by Bellamy, his predictions seem not far wrong. There are strong indications that currency, while it may not become obsolete, is almost sure to become less widely used.

A contemporary of Bellamy's might have objected that the substitution of credit for money would be impossible because of the overwhelming amount of bookkeeping entailed. But what was impossible in Bellamy's day, the computer has rendered possible in ours. There are strong indications that someday soon an employer's computer may instruct a bank's computer to make a deposit in an employee's account. Then, through additional computer-to-computer communication, charges for gas, electricity, telephone, rent, and other regular services will be deducted from the employee's "paycheck." The employee will merely get a periodic statement verifying that such operations were carried out. Such a system will not eliminate cash and personal checks entirely, but it will drastically limit their use.

A survey of consumer opinion in Atlanta, Georgia, indicates much disapproval of the proposed "electronic money." Many people reported that it gave them personal satisfaction to handle their own finances.

These rugged individualists may be forced to swallow their pride, however. The Federal Reserve System has already endorsed the concept of electronic money and put forward a preliminary plan for its implementation. In addition, California banks have begun an experiment in electronic money called SCOPE (Special Committee on Paperless Entries), under which employees' personal finances are being handled by computer.

Banking experts hailed electronic banking, pointing out that the banking system is in danger of collapsing under the sheer weight of paper it must process in checking transactions. While they anticipate that the changeover will be costly and trying, they believe that it is inevitable. As one banker remarked, the present check system is "fully satisfactory only to the bad-check artist."*

* "Approach of Electronic-Money Age Spurs Sharp Debate Among Bankers," *New York Times*, January 7, 1973, p. 67.

money drives out good." Under a bimetallic system, money is stable only if the mint value of the metals used remains equal to their market value. If the market value of one metal rises above the mint value, owners of coins made of that metal will melt them down and sell them on the market until eventually the metal will disappear from circulation. The United States was on a bimetallic standard during the nineteenth century. Between 1792 and 1834 gold disappeared from circulation; between 1834 and 1873 silver disappeared; after 1873 the western silver-producing states influenced Congress to raise the mint value of silver, and as a result, gold vanished from circulation once again.

Inconvertible Paper Standard Under an **inconvertible paper standard,** gold does not circulate and paper currency cannot be converted into gold. The unit of currency may be expressed in terms of a fixed weight of gold, but it need not be. An inconvertible paper standard allows a country the greatest flexibility in managing its economic affairs. For this reason it has been resorted to during wars and economic emergencies. The United States went on an inconvertible paper standard during the 1930s and has remained on it to this day (although there are signs in Congress of allowing private citizens to buy gold again). It is the standard used for all transactions within the domestic economy.

Currency in the United States is **fiat money.** The term comes from the fact that it has been made legal tender by fiat, or decree of the government. The currency is valuable because the government says it is. However, it is the people's confidence in the government that allows it to make this decree. Paper money is actually the circulating I.O.U.'s of the federal government. People honor these I.O.U.'s because they give the government a good credit rating. Without this rating, the government would lose its ability to create fiat money. Although you cannot now get federal gold for your paper money, you can get just about anything else for it. Currency is acceptable in virtually all financial situations. It is the government that has designated currency as "legal tender for all debts, public and private," but it is the public that maintains the status of currency as legal tender by continuing to accept it in return for goods and services. Thus, money has value because of what it will buy, because people accept it as a means of payment. If people stopped accepting it, it would, literally, not be worth the paper it was printed on. However, as long as the government remains secure and the economy is functioning, there is no reason to expect this to happen.

Variations in Value: Inflation

Under an inconvertible money standard, currency receives value from the confidence of the people; yet the holders of money cannot redeem it for gold from the treasury that issued it. Nobody seems to care very much, as long as the money still allows people to buy things and pay for services. What in fact gives money its value as a medium of exchange is that everyone feels confident that his dollars will be accepted without question by the supermarket for groceries and the Internal Revenue Service for taxes. But the amount of goods or services that a given sum of money can buy varies, so that it is said that money undergoes a change in purchasing power. It is the decline of this power that makes consumers realize, for example, that they are getting fewer groceries than they used to for the money they have budgeted for food.

We have all heard talk of a dollar's being worth less than it used to be. This simply means that it can purchase fewer goods and services than it could at an earlier time. As the sellers of goods demand more and more money, it becomes worth less and less.

The value of money fluctuates inversely to general price levels, so that the amount a dollar can buy is calculated as the reciprocal, or inverse, of the consumer price index (CPI).

When prices are low, the dollar buys more and is therefore worth more. When prices are high, the dollar buys less and is therefore worth less. When the purchasing power of money goes steadily downward and the CPI goes steadily upward, we say we are in a period of inflation.

Inflations can be creeping or they can be galloping,

with wages in pursuit of runaway prices. The galloping kind, called hyperinflation, has usually been related to wartime conditions, serving as a contributing factor to postwar disorder. It is characterized by massive doses of freshly printed money to the ailing economy, an effort to cure that all but kills the patient. In such periods money has had so little value that shoppers have had to carry buckets full of currency. In World War II, Hungarians found themselves paying 1.4 nonillion pengoes (1 nonillion = 1,000,000,000,000,000,000,000,000,000,000) for an item that had cost 1 pengo a few years earlier. In our own history, a dramatic hyperinflation took place during the Civil War, when the Confederate price index rose at an average rate of 10 percent per month for 31 consecutive months and stood at 92 times its prewar level at the time of surrender. Wealthy Southerners belatedly rushed to turn their remaining cash reserves into durable goods and Union greenbacks as the printing presses of the Confederacy poured out worthless treasury notes.

The phenomenon of inflation illustrates the influence of the money supply on a nation's economy. The quantity of money is related to prices, for example. The greater the amount of money available, the more sellers can charge for goods and services. But what about other economic factors, such as the quantity of goods produced and the rate at which money is used? Are they, too, related to the quantity of money? This question is one that has persistently engaged the attention of economists. One way of explaining the relationships between these factors is through what is known as the quantity theory of money.

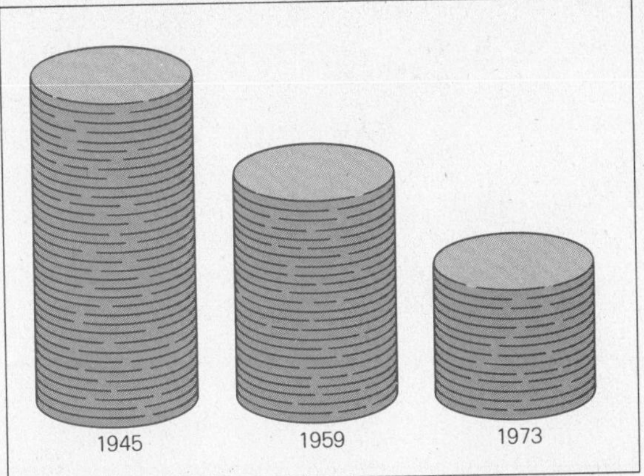

FIGURE 11-2 THE SHRINKING U.S. DOLLAR In terms of purchasing power, what you could buy for a dollar today would have cost you only 42 cents in 1945. The prices of some goods and services rose more than others since that year. Depending on where you lived in 1945, you could have purchased the following goods and services for a dollar: 10 to 20 bus rides, about two tickets for adults to a neighborhood movie (on a Saturday night), 10 to 15 ice cream cones, one-tenth of a credit at most private colleges, or three to four pounds of ground chuck. A more precise indicator of its shrinking purchasing power is the consumer price index, whose increase from 53.9 in 1945 to 125.3 in 1973 shows how price increases have been eroding the value of the dollar.

SOURCE: U.S. Department of Commerce, *Business Conditions Digest* (June 1971): 107, and (June 1973): 118.

THE QUANTITY THEORY OF MONEY

Since money is used to buy goods and services, it follows that there must be some relationship between the money supply and the level of economic activity. Net national product is one way of indicating economic activity. This total is actually the product of multiplying the goods and services in the economy by the prices paid for them, and can be expressed by PQ; these two elements correspond to the price level (P) and the level of output of the economy (Q).

Does the money supply (M), then, equal NNP (or PQ)? This is highly unlikely, since it would mean that each dollar was spent only once a year to buy newly produced goods and services. A look at the figures on NNP and the money supply shows that the NNP is by far the larger of the two. In 1970, for example, NNP was about $1 trillion. That same year the money supply was somewhat over $200 billion. To purchase the amount of goods and services represented by NNP, the money supply had to be spent several times over. This turnover rate is called **velocity** (V) in technical terminology. By multiplying it by the money supply, we find the level of economic activity, or the amount spent on all the goods and services during a year.

This relationship is expressed mathematically as $MV = PQ$, and is the form in which the **quantity theory of money** is usually expressed. This identity is also known as the **equation of exchange.** It is another way

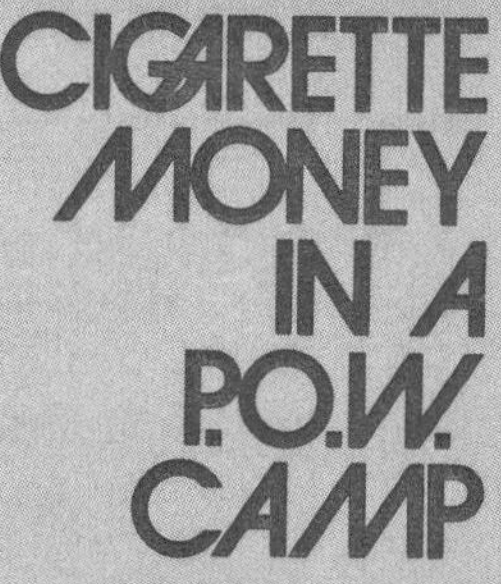

The various types of gold standards, the bimetallic standard, and the inconvertible paper standard may be the most common monetary standards in advanced countries with complex economies, but they are by no means the only ones possible. Societies have successfully used such things as sea shells, stones, sharks' teeth, and livestock as media of exchange.

In a prisoner-of-war camp during World War II, captured Allied soldiers evolved an economy based on a cigarette standard.* The prison-camp economy differed from that of the outside world in at least one important aspect: There was no production to speak of. Most of the economic activity consisted of the exchange of items issued by the prison authorities, donated by the Red Cross, or received by the prisoners in the form of personal gifts.

At first only barter was practiced. The prisoners began to develop rough standards of what things were worth relative to other things. A tin of jam, for example, was worth slightly more than one-half pound of margarine. An issue of cigarettes had several times the value of an issue of chocolate. After a time, however, cigarettes became the camp's "money." Prices of items in cigarettes were posted on notice boards and soon became standard throughout the camp.

Like our money, cigarettes served as a means of payment, a unit of value, a standard of deferred payments, and a store of value. In addition, they could be used individually for small purchases or in packs for large ones, and, like gold and silver coins, they could be clipped or, in this case, "sweated": rolled between the fingers to remove some of the tobacco. Since various brands were used, the currency soon became subject to Gresham's Law. The least desirable brands were used for trading and soon drove out the "good money," which was used for smoking.

Use of the currency for nonmonetary purposes posed one of the economy's greatest problems. As long as the regular weekly Red Cross shipments, containing 25 to 50 cigarettes per man, came through, the economy was able to operate. But when shipments were held up, the prisoners' reserves literally went up in smoke, and eventually the economy returned to a barter system. Conversely, when one of the large quarterly shipments came in and the money supply became greatly enlarged, a period of inflation set in; prices rose astronomically, only to fall gradually as reserves were consumed.

*R. A. Radford, "The Economic Organization of a P.O.W. Camp," *Economica* 12 (1945): 189–201.

During one particularly prosperous period, the men decided to open a restaurant and a shop. To avoid the effects of the periodic deflation and inflation, they decided to issue paper. These notes, called "Bully Marks" (BMk's), were issued by the shop to pay for food for the restaurant. The BMk's were then accepted, along with cigarettes, as payment in the restaurant and shop. Thus, the BMk's were backed 100 percent by food.

Eventually, food shortages and Allied bombing raids closed the restaurant.The experience of the prisoners proved, however, that economic activity is basic to human social life, and that it can, if necessary, be carried out with only the most makeshift of supplies.

American Red Cross

of expressing the identity of output and income that we discussed in Chapter 6 on national accounts. The amount spent equals the supply of money (M) times its rate of turnover (V). Since this is spent on the goods produced during a year, it must equal the quantity of output (Q) times the average price (P).

The equation expresses equality and balance among four economic factors: price, quantity of goods and services, the size of the money supply, and velocity. If any one of the factors is changed, there must be an effect on one or more of the other three factors. Thus, any change in the supply of money, or in the velocity, may be accompanied by changes in the price of goods and services, the quantities of those goods and services purchased, or both. For example, if the money supply is doubled, it might provide more purchasing power to stimulate output to double: $2MV=(2Q)P$. Or it might just raise prices twice as high: $2MV=(2P)Q$. Or if velocity fell to compensate, there would be no effect on prices: $2M(\frac{1}{2}V)=PQ$. From the equation we cannot predict which other elements will change. By holding some factors constant, however, we begin to see precise effects.

How Much Money Should There Be?

Now we can see how crucial the money supply is to the economy. Our equation makes it clear that the amount of money in the economy can directly affect prices or output. But we must also know how much money is necessary to keep prices and production at satisfactory levels. The amount of money the economy needs is enough to enable us to buy all the goods and services the economy produces. In noninflationary times, if we have less money than this and the velocity remains unchanged, items will go unsold, production will drop, and unemployment will set in. If we have more money and full employment, then goods and services will sell for higher prices, resulting in inflation. Economists have generally agreed that changes in the money supply can cause changes in price. This is consistent with the quantity theory. However, the role of the other two factors, V and Q, has long been subject to debate.

The Classical View Classical economists such as Adam Smith, David Ricardo, and Alfred Marshall were committed to the theory of *laissez faire* capitalism. According to this theory, an economy operating under a system of free competition will tend to produce at maximum capacity. These theorists assumed that labor and other resources of production would be fully utilized. Unemployment was considered a temporary and abnormal situation. In addition, they believed that velocity could not change. Thus, only two things were left subject to change, M and P. This, then, was the relationship on which the classical economists concentrated. If the money supply was doubled, they reasoned, the only possible result would be a doubling of prices. With production already at full capacity, more goods could not be produced. Thus, the people had no choice but to pay double for the goods they were already buying. Because they were convinced of this causal link, classical economists dreaded any attempt to increase the money supply unless the capacity of the economy increased, since they believed that such an increase would inevitably cause inflation. For proof they pointed to the example of Spain, which had indeed suffered inflation, ostensibly as the direct result of the introduction of new money into the economy in the form of gold from the New World.

The Keynesian View Scientific theories are generally accepted only until it becomes clear that they can no longer explain the facts. Then a new theory must be developed. This is what happened with the classical interpretation of the quantity theory of money. Between the 1920s and 1930s, unemployment in England was on the rise and showed no signs of disappearing in response to adjustments in the price of resources, as it was supposed to do according to the classical view. Economists began to ask: How can Q be a constant when the economy refuses to operate at full capacity? They reasoned that if Q is not a constant, an increase in M might create a corresponding increase in Q. In other words, it might be possible to increase production and thus alleviate the unemployment problem simply by increasing the money supply.

Such experiments were tried, but their results did not seem to bear out the expectations of the advocates of easy money. Q did not seem to be responding to M as the amended theory suggested. Clearly, some unknown factor was at work which the economists had not taken into account. John Maynard Keynes, who originally had advocated an increase in the money supply as a remedy for the unemployment problem, began to consider the problem anew. If an increase in M did not result in any corresponding increase in P or Q, then the only explanation must be a decrease in V. Keynes began to study the forces acting on V, eventually evolving the model with which his name has become associated.

According to the classical view, the only thing that people did with their money was to spend or invest it. The reason they held money was to spend it on day-to-day purchases. Any remaining money would be used to buy interest-bearing assets rather than being held in liquid form. The demand for money, then, would be limited to immediate needs and would increase as income rose because more purchases would be made. Keynes called this the **transaction demand.** But he recognized a more complicated demand for money. People hold money not only for transactions, but also if they think that interest rates are going to rise, allowing them better terms on their assets. Especially during a depression, there is an increase in the **speculative demand** for money. The extremely low interest rates resulting from depression cause people to hoard money. They reason that the low interest rates reduce the cost of holding money in a liquid form and since interest rates will eventually rise, they prefer to have money ready when the rates do go up. Keynes termed an extreme version of this condition the **liquidity trap.**

Thus, according to the Keynesian model, increases in M failed to affect Q because people were keeping the extra money in the form of nonearning reserves, rather than reinjecting it into the economy by spending and investing. Increases in M could never end the unemployment problem, but would only bring about a lower and lower velocity.

Keynes's answer to the problem was an interesting one that ultimately had widespread influence: If the people would not spend money, then the government had to do so. Keynes advocated a program of government-sponsored work projects, increases in social security and unemployment benefits, direct welfare payments, and similar measures. Keynes's ideas were an important force in the making of the New Deal under the Roosevelt administration.

Quantity Theory and the Monetarists The Keynesian view of the quantity theory of money gained wide acceptance through the post–World War II period, coming to be known as the "new" economics. In the 1950s and 1960s, however, some economists began to suggest revisions of Keynes's ideas. This school, known as the monetarists, was led by Milton Friedman of the University of Chicago. His writings came to be known as the "new" new economics, but this name is somewhat misleading, because, in certain ways Friedman's work hearkens back to the views of the classical economists.

Friedman and his followers place less emphasis on the importance of V than do the Keynesians. Research indicated to them that velocity is subject only to fairly small and predictable fluctuations. From this fact, they concluded that in a less than full-employment situation, an increase in M must result in an increase in spending. Higher spending will stimulate production, and, as production goes up, employment must increase. Monetarists concluded that the money supply should grow at a constant rate keyed to the rate of growth of the economy.

This brief account of theories about money supply has not included the institutions that affect the money supply and thereby the level of economic activity. The next two chapters deal with the banking system. Under the control of the Federal Reserve, banks can create money as well as destroy it.

SUMMARY

1 The use of money—a universally acceptable medium of exchange—is essential to all but the simplest economies. In our complex economy, money functions as a

medium of payment, a unit of value, a standard for deferred payments, and a store of value.

2 Exactly what constitutes money is a subject of debate. Coins and paper currency clearly meet the definition of money, but constitute only about one-fifth of the money supply; the rest is in the form of demand deposits. Time deposits, government bonds, and other nearly liquid assets are grouped together as near-money. The difference between these two definitions of money is important because it affects the interpretation of the effects of money upon economic activity.

3 The value of money has been pegged at different periods to fixed amounts of precious metal. At different times different standards—gold, bimetallic, and inconvertible paper—have all been tried. When two metals—usually gold and silver—are used, this is known as a bimetallic standard. Unless the mint value remains the same as the market value, one metal will disappear from the money supply, or as Gresham's Law states, "cheap money drives out good." The United States, in common with most of the rest of the world, now uses the inconvertible paper standard, under which the government issues fiat money. This takes its value from the public's faith in the solvency of the government that issues it.

4 The purchasing power of a given unit of money is indicated by the consumer price index; as prices rise, the value of the dollar declines.

5 The quantity theory of money explores the relationship between money in circulation and the level of economic activity. The relationship depends, among other things, on the rate of turnover of money, or velocity. The basic relationship is expressed mathematically as $MV = PQ$, and verbally as the supply of money times velocity is identical to the quantity of goods and services times the average price. The formula, known as the equation of exchange, suggests a vital balance among the four variables which are essential to managing the economy.

6 In the classical interpretation of quantity theory, any attempt to increase the money supply could only result in inflation, because output was usually at the full employment level and velocity was constant.

7 Keynesian economics focuses on the variable of velocity because money is not only used for transactions but also held for speculative purposes. When conditions are poor and interest rates low, people will not buy bonds, in the hope that interest rates will rise. Thus, during times of depression increasing the money supply will not stimulate economic activity as effectively as increasing government spending.

8 The monetarists' view of velocity is close to that of the classical theory. An increase in the money supply stimulates expansion only if the economy is not at full employment and the supply of money is not expanded faster than the economy can grow.

SUGGESTED READINGS

Chandler, Lester V. *The Economics of Money and Banking*. 5th ed. Chaps. 1–4. New York: Harper & Row, 1969.

Dean, Edwin, ed. *The Controversy over the Quantity Theory of Money*. Lexington, Mass.: D. C. Heath, 1965.

Duesenberry, James S. *Money and Credit: Impact and Control*. 2nd ed. Englewood Cliffs, N.J.: Prentice-Hall, 1967.

Friedman, Milton. *Studies in the Quantity Theory of Money*. Chicago: University of Chicago Press, 1956.

Ritter, Lawrence S., and **William L. Silber.** *Money*. 2nd ed. Chaps 1, 3–5, and 18. New York: Basic Books, 1973.

QUESTIONS

1 Review
   a. the four major functions of money,
   b. M_1, M_2, and M_3,
   c. the three major types of monetary standards,
   d. the relationship between the value of money and the CPI.

2 In 1973, the tiny state of Bearden had a GNP of 250 billion quibbles. Unfortunately, by 1974, the value of the quibble seemed in jeopardy both at home and abroad. It dropped in value by almost 25 percent. The GNP in 1974 was 300 billion quibbles. Had there been an increase in production? The minister of the Treasury believed that the quibble could be saved if backed by something of value. He therefore sought to rectify the situation by pledging the full value of the crown jewels against the quibble. Everyone in the cabinet sighed with relief. Should they?

3 Suppose that by social agreement people begin to exchange personal I.O.U.'s for goods and services. Should the government move to affect the supply of money? Under what circumstances?

4 What are the four major functions of money? How is its use as a store of value and a standard of deferred payment affected by inflation? Deflation?

5 What is another name for demand deposits? What do economists generally consider to be money? At present, what is the largest portion of the money supply? What are near-monies?

6 At least one culture has used large stones as a medium of exchange. In what ways is a precious metal an improvement over large stones?

7 How does Gresham's Law operate to reduce the coinage in circulation?

8 What standard does the United States have now for its currency? What gives the currency its value? How is its value related to the consumer price index? If the CPI triples during a given period of time, what has happened to the value of currency?

9 The quantity theory of money is stated as $MV = PQ$. If the quantity of money in circulation is \$200 billion and the GNP is \$600 billion, what is the number of times that a dollar exchanges hands during a year? What is this value called in the quantity theory?

10 According to classical economists, certain elements in the quantity theory equation are assumed to be constant. What are they? Why are they assumed to be constant? What would happen if the money supply increased? Decreased?

11 Why did Keynes believe an increase in the money supply to be ineffective in

raising production and employment during a depression? What is the speculative demand for money? How is it related to the interest rate? Why would people be indifferent to holding liquid or nonliquid assets?

12 Milton Friedman has argued that the money supply should grow in proportion to the increase in GNP. Why would he argue that the money supply should grow? What might happen if the money supply did not increase?

13 Some economists believe that the money supply should be reduced during a period of inflation. What effect would they be expecting? Suppose that consumers and business executives believe that prices will continue to rise, and therefore buy goods immediately rather than later at a higher price? What would be the effect on velocity? In this case, would a decrease in the money supply necessarily have the desired effect on prices? Why or why not?

14 Bank-issued credit cards are a relatively recent development in the American economy. Though economists do not consider credit cards to be part of the money supply, what effect might the widespread use of the cards have on the velocity of money? Inflation?

15 In 1965–66 there was a rapid increase in spending by the federal government. William McC. Martin, Chairman of the Federal Reserve Board, argued that the government should follow policies designed to reduce M or at least V. Why might this be an appropriate policy?

Opening photo by J. Paul Kirouac

BANKING

Without the banking system, conducting transactions involving large sums of money would be unwieldy. Instead of writing a check, people would have to cart around lots of cash. But the most important economic function of the commercial banking system lies in its power to create and destroy money. Banks make loans or buy bonds, thereby injecting new money into the economy. Over three-fourths of the money in the United States today is in the form of demand deposits, which means that the potential influence of banks on economic conditions is enormous.

THE MODERN BANKING SYSTEM

The commercial banking system in the United States consists of nearly 14,000 individual institutions. Banks have two basic functions. Through the checking process, they hold demand deposits and honor checks drawn upon them. But it is through making loans, both to individuals and corporations, and purchasing and selling government bonds and other assets, that banks create and destroy money.

The economy of the United States originally evolved as a far-flung collection of individual banks, each of them extending and contracting credit as it pleased and thereby affecting the money supply. With population and business growth, the economy became more complex and the unregulated money-creating activities of the banks began to threaten the economic stability of the nation. Some centralized authority was needed to control the banks' functions, to decide on policy, and to assure that changes in money supply would be consistent with the major shifts in economic activity. Finally, in answer to this need, the Federal Reserve System was created.

The Federal Reserve System

The Federal Reserve System came into being in 1913, in response to an epidemic of bank failures that convulsed the nation during the panic of 1907. Under the Federal Reserve System, the country is divided into 12 Federal Reserve Districts. There is a Federal Reserve Bank located in the major city of each district (New York, Chicago, San Francisco, Philadelphia, Boston, Cleveland, St. Louis, Kansas City, Atlanta, Richmond, Dallas, and Minneapolis) and a Board of Governors that sets overall policy. These are bankers' banks and have no direct dealing with the general public. All the national banks and most of the larger state banks are members of the Federal Reserve System. The smaller, nonmember banks handle only about one-sixth of the total volume of deposits, so most of the money in the American economy is under the regulation of the Federal Reserve System.

The chief purpose of the Federal Reserve (or the "Fed," as it is popularly called) is to act as a central control mechanism over the member banks and, ultimately, over the supply of money that affects the whole economy. Let us consider the nature of the activity that the Fed regulates.

Banking as a Business

Whether it is a member of the Federal Reserve System or not, every bank is a separate business institution and must contend with the same problems that any other business faces. Banks are organized to make money; that is, to earn profits for their stockholders. The main difference between banks and other enterprises is that a great portion of the holdings of banks is in the form of demand deposits, which are subject to immediate withdrawal.

Banking, in fact, began as a purely demand-deposit business. The first bankers were the goldsmiths of the Middle Ages. Along with their function as artisans, the goldsmiths began to offer to hold the gold for safekeeping, a service for which they charged a fee. In order to facilitate the return of the gold to its rightful owners, notes or certificates of ownership were issued. Eventually, people began to develop faith in the reliability of these notes and began to regard them as equal in value to the gold itself. Since the banks kept 100 percent of the gold on hand, the holder of a note could be assured of converting it into gold at any time. Moreover, the owner of a note could sign it over to another. Thus, the notes were both liquid and transferable, and soon came to be used as a medium of exchange, marking the birth of the modern system of checking.

The great change in banking came when the goldsmiths realized that if they were able to use the gold held for safekeeping to finance investments of their own, they would be able to make far more money than the small amount they received as a deposit fee. The depositors might object to the goldsmith's profiting from his use of their wealth, but in the end they had to admit the logic of his view. Since it was highly improbable that all depositors would withdraw all their money at one time, the goldsmith needed to keep only a fraction of the reserves on hand to act as a safeguard against irregularities in the daily ebb and flow of withdrawals and deposits. Depositors could still be reasonably certain of getting their gold back when they wanted it. Moreover, with the tremendous reserves at his disposal, the goldsmith could be fairly sure of a return on his investments. The failure of one venture would be more than compensated for by the success of other commitments. In fact, the goldsmith's profits might even prove advantageous to the depositors, by allowing him to lower the fee he charged for safekeeping, or even granting his depositors a dividend.

Modern Fractional Reserve Banking

When the goldsmiths began to keep only a fraction of their total deposits on hand as reserves, they had already become, in essence, modern commercial bankers.

The system of banking that they created is known as fractional reserve banking because some portion of assets is held as reserves.

Without substantially endangering their customers' deposits, banks could use nearly all their deposits for their own profit-making activities: granting loans and buying government securities. But the Fed prevents member banks from using 100 percent of deposits for investment purposes by requiring them to keep a portion of those deposits in the form of nonearning reserves with a Federal Reserve District Bank.

This legal reserve deposit is governed by the reserve ratio, which is the proportion of demand deposits that must be backed with money kept in the Federal Reserve Bank. This can be expressed by a formula:

$$\text{Reserve ratio} = \frac{\text{Required reserves}}{\text{Demand deposits}}$$

Suppose that the reserve ratio were 7 percent and a bank had $5 million of demand deposits. Using the formula above, its reserves would be .07 = required reserves/$5 million, or $350,000. The ratio may vary with the condition of the economy, from 10 to 22 percent of demand deposits for large city banks and from 7 to 14 percent for all other banks depending upon the size of total deposits. The upper and lower limits are set by Congress, but the Federal Reserve can change the ratio at its discretion, within these limits. If the ratio were changed to 10 percent, the bank's required reserves would rise from $350,000 to $5 million times 10 percent, or $500,000, so that the bank would have to keep $150,000 more on reserve in its account at the Fed.

The reserve ratio specified by the Fed is substantially greater than the funds required to cover daily cash transactions. Today, the actual amount of cash on hand in banks may be very small, usually 2 to 5 percent of the total. Such a situation is possible because in modern banking cash enters into the picture in a very subsidiary way. Most transactions involve the transfer of bank-created money represented by demand deposits rather than by cash. In fact, under favorable economic conditions, commercial banks would be able to operate quite satisfactorily with almost no cash on hand at all. Moreover, the required reserves cannot be drawn upon to meet unexpected withdrawals.

But there is a rationale for the Fed's setting a reserve requirement that is much higher than that needed to cover daily cash transactions. The granting of loans and the buying of securities are money-creating operations. Therefore, if banks were allowed to use all their assets to make loans and buy securities, an uncontrolled mushrooming of the money supply could result, eventually causing inflation. The reserve ratio, then, enables the Federal Reserve authorities to control the creation of money by the banks and consequently, to avoid, or at least moderate, inflation. When recession occurs, lowering the reserve ratio acts not to stave off the panic of a run on the bank, but rather as a control, to encourage banks not to *underextend* credit. The Board of Governors, by decreasing commercial bank reserve requirements, can influence bank credit volume to provide more money to the economy and thereby stimulate business and consumer activity.

A CLOSER LOOK AT THE BANKING PROCESS

A look behind the scenes at the way a bank conducts its everyday business will reveal what occurs when a depositor writes a check, a bank grants a loan, or other transactions occur. In order to portray these operations clearly, we will make use of a balance sheet.

A balance sheet is a device for showing the assets of a business along with the claims against these assets, at a specific time.

It is called a *balance sheet* because the total amount of assets and the total amount of claims will always be the same.

In the case of a bank, the left-hand, or **assets**, side of the balance sheet shows the bank's holdings—either on hand or owing to the bank. This will be in the form of cash or cash equivalents, money owed to the bank (loans), government securities the bank has purchased, and other investments of the bank and the property the bank owns. The right-hand side shows liabilities and net worth. In this case these are demand deposits and capital stock. This is the money that the bank owes to others. Demand deposits are referred to as **liabilities**, and capital stock—the money put up by the owners of the bank—is referred to as **net worth.** Below is a simplified version of the balance sheet of an established bank. Note that when the two sides are added up, the totals are identical.

Balance Sheet 1: Legume National Bank (Assets must equal liabilities and net worth)

Assets		Liabilities and Net Worth	
Cash and cash equivalents	$ 21,000	Demand deposits	$ 80,000
Loans	50,000	Capital stock	20,000
Government bonds	20,000		
Property	9,000		
	$100,000		$100,000

Setting Up a New Bank

Suppose that you woke up one morning with the notion of starting your own commercial bank. The first thing you would need is a lot of money. You could supply this yourself if you happened to be fabulously wealthy or if you could get a number of other people to contribute and make them owners too. This money would be your capital stock. Part of it must be used to buy or rent a building, hire a staff, and purchase the considerable amount of office equipment that is necessary in a modern bank. The money left over is cash. Assuming that you managed to start with a mere $10,000 capital stock, here is a balance sheet representing the state of your bank at this point.

Balance Sheet 2: The Dicotyledon Bank of Soy City, South Dakota (When the bank is organized and office equipment purchased)

Assets		Liabilities and Net Worth	
Cash	$ 1,000	Capital stock	$10,000
Property	9,000		

The Checking Process

The bank opens for business, and the first customer, a local farmer named Webster Hudgins, opens a checking account with an initial deposit of $1000. Now this means, of course, that the bank has $1000 more in assets. But the bank does not own this money. It must be paid back to Mr. Hudgins on demand. Therefore, the balance sheet will show a $1000 increase in both assets (cash) and liabilities (demand deposits).

Balance Sheet 3: The Dicotyledon Bank of Soy City, South Dakota (When a deposit is made)

Assets		Liabilities and Net Worth	
Cash	$ **2,000**	Demand deposits	$ **1,000**
Property	9,000	Capital stock	10,000

Excess Reserves

Assuming that The Dicotyledon Bank is a member of the Federal Reserve System, there is at this point something very important to consider. The Fed insists that a certain ratio of each member bank's deposits (let us assume 20 percent) be entrusted to the local Federal Reserve Bank or be kept on hand in cash. Since Dicotyledon now has demand deposits amounting to $1000, it sends $200 to the Federal Reserve Bank as reserves.

This leaves $800, or 80 percent, of the bank's deposits in the form of cash. Few bankers would be happy with cash rattling around in their vaults. They would prefer to see the money used to grant loans, because loans would give them the highest return on their investment. As a second choice, they would put the money in the slightly less lucrative form of government bonds. In the meantime, most bankers would send this money (save 2 or 3 percent till money) to the Federal Reserve Bank to deposit in their reserve account. This $800 forms **excess reserves,** over and above the $200 required reserves. Although excess reserves do not earn any interest, we shall see that they form the pool of funds for making loans or buying bonds.

Assume, for example, that Dicotyledon decides to send all of its cash to the Federal Reserve Bank, retaining no till money at all. Then the balance sheet would record this change as follows:

Balance Sheet 4: The Dicotyledon Bank of Soy City, South Dakota (When all cash is sent to the Federal Reserve Bank as reserves)

Assets		Liabilities and Net Worth	
Cash	$ –	Demand deposits	$ 1,000
Property	9,000	Capital stock	10,000
Reserves	**2,000**		

Clearing a Check

Since demand deposits earn no interest, people are not likely to leave their money in checking accounts for long periods of time. They *are* likely to use it, to pay for goods and services as the need arises. Let us suppose that Webster Hudgins now decides to write a check for $500 to buy a tractor.

Webster writes a check, drawn on The Dicotyledon Bank, making it out to the Gunk Machinery Company. In order to complete the transaction, Gunk Machinery must deposit Webster's check in its own account. Let us suppose that the Gunk Machinery Company's bank is not Dicotyledon, but another bank that is also a member of the Federal Reserve, the First National Bank of Storm Cellar, Iowa. First National accepts Webster's check and credits it to the account of Gunk Machinery. Gunk Machinery's demand deposit has now increased by $500.

First National's next step is to send Webster's check to the Federal Reserve Bank for collection. The Federal Reserve Bank, which serves as a clearing house for checks, responds by increasing First National's reserve assets by $500 and decreasing Dicotyledon's reserve assets by $500. The Federal Reserve Bank then returns the collected, or "cleared," check to Dicotyledon. The Dicotyledon Bank deducts $500 from Webster Hudgins' demand deposit. Dicotyledon now loses $500 in assets (the reserve money that now is deposited in First National), but it also has its demand deposit liabilities lessened by $500 (Mr. Hudgins' collected check). First National now has a $500 asset (the reserve money from Dicotyledon) and a $500 liability (the increased demand

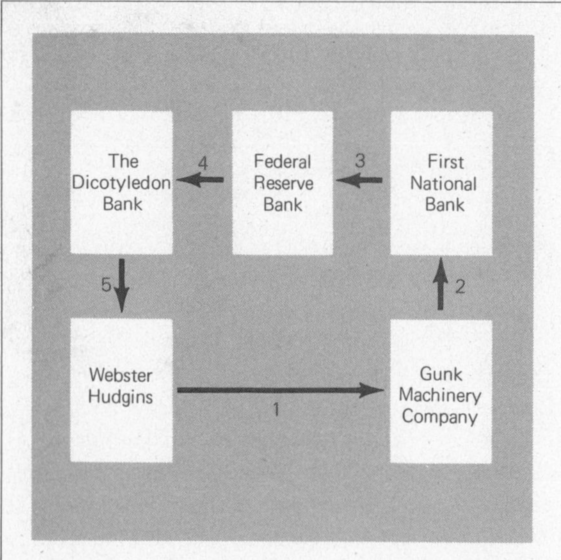

FIGURE 12-1 CLEARING A CHECK Check clearing is a vital function of the Federal Reserve System. Webster Hudgins has written a check on The Dicotyledon Bank and paid the Gunk Machinery Company for services rendered. The latter deposits that check in its account at First National Bank. That bank sends Hudgins' check to the Federal Reserve Bank, where First National's reserves are increased by the amount of the check and Dicotyledon's are decreased by the same amount. The Federal Reserve Bank returns the check to The Dicotyledon Bank, which sends it to Webster Hudgins at the end of the month. In the process, money is simply transferred from bank to bank. No money is created or destroyed.

deposit of Gunk Machinery). The transaction is now complete, and everyone's balance sheet still balances.

Balance Sheet 5: The Dicotyledon Bank of Soy City, South Dakota (When a check is drawn on a demand deposit)

Assets		Liabilities and Net Worth	
Cash	$ –	Demand deposits	$ **500**
Property	9,000	Capital stock	10,000
Reserves	**1,500**		

In such a transaction, money has neither been lost nor created. What one bank has lost in assets and liabilities, another bank has gained. The total amount of money in the banking system remains constant. To show this, we can use a T-account, which reveals only the *changes* in a balance sheet.

T–account 1: First National Bank of Storm Cellar, Iowa (When the check drawn on the other bank is deposited here)

Assets		Liabilities and Net Worth	
Reserves	+$ **500**	Demand deposits	+$ **500**

Money-Creating Transactions of Commercial Banks

Commercial banks perform other functions besides handling demand deposits. Banks may not use depositors' money to make commitments on their own behalf in the stock market. But they may function as investment counselors and in such a role properly advise their depositors to buy nongovernment stocks or bonds. Banks may also grant loans and buy and sell government bonds. It is by issuing loans and buying government bonds that banks create money.

Suppose that Latisimus Dorsey, the owner of a profitable chain of figure salons, decides to open a new establishment in a neighboring city. For this enterprise, he calculates that he will need $1400. He comes to The Dicotyledon Bank and requests a loan for that amount. The bank, satisfied with his business record and potential, grants him the loan from its excess reserves. This loan has the advantage of bearing interest.

Mr. Dorsey will, of course, not want his loan in the form of cash. He will soon have to pay contracting fees, and checks are far more convenient for such purposes than bulky wads of currency. The bank, understanding Mr. Dorsey's needs, makes his money available to him in the form of a $1400 demand deposit, which he can draw upon at any time. This demand deposit represents a new liability for the bank. But the bank also has a new asset: Mr. Dorsey's I.O.U., which represents $1400 owed *to* the bank.

Balance Sheet 6: The Dicotyledon Bank of Soy City, South Dakota (When a loan is made)

Assets		Liabilities and Net Worth	
Cash	$ –	Demand deposits	$ **1,900**
Loans	**1,400**	Capital stock	10,000
Property	9,000		
Reserves	1,500		

It is this balance sheet that shows how banks create money. Both assets and liabilities have increased by $1400, the amount of Mr. Dorsey's loan. This $1400, which previously did not exist, has now entered the economy. What has actually happened is that the bank has taken Mr. Dorsey's I.O.U., which represents his willingness and ability to pay back the amount of his loan (plus interest) in the future, and turned it into money, which he can use now. Or, to put it in financial terms, the loan has been **monetized.** By the extension of credit the bank has created money. It has accepted something that is not money (Mr. Dorsey's I.O.U.) and in return has given Mr. Dorsey a check for $1400, which certainly is money.

Shortly after receiving his loan, Mr. Dorsey writes a $1400 check to the Ozymandias Construction Company, paying it in advance for the building of the new salon. The Ozymandias Construction Company then deposits the check in its own bank, Adonais National, which sends it on to the Federal Reserve Bank for collection. The Federal Reserve Bank adds $1400 to Adonais National's reserves, subtracts $1400 from Dicotyledon's reserves, and sends the cleared check to Dicotyledon. Dicotyledon deducts $1400 from Mr. Dorsey's demand deposit.

Balance Sheet 7: The Dicotyledon Bank of Soy City, South Dakota (When a check drawn on a loan is deposited in another bank)

Assets		Liabilities and Net Worth	
Loans	$1,400	Demand deposits	$ **500**
Property	9,000	Capital stock	10,000
Reserves	**100**		

Notice that the bank no longer has any excess reserves. The process of clearing Mr. Dorsey's check has eliminated all but the required reserves of $100 (20 percent of the $500 in demand deposits). This illustrates an important principle of banking: It is extremely unwise for a bank to lend more than the amount it has in excess reserves. When money is created through loans, it is almost always used by the borrower very quickly. After all, why would a person borrow money unless he wanted to spend it? Soon after the loan money changes hands, it is sent to the Federal Reserve Bank, which reduces the lending bank's reserves proportionately. If a bank lends more than its excess reserves, a proportionate sum will soon be deducted from its reserve account, putting the bank in violation of federal law.

This is not inevitable, however, since some checks drawn on the loan deposit may be redeposited in the same bank. Indeed, if 20 percent of their loan checks normally are redeposited, the bank might feel safe in expanding its loan portfolio up to 20 percent above excess reserves.

Multiple Expansion of Deposits

So far, $1400 has been created, in the form of demand deposits lent to Mr. Dorsey. But if we follow this $1400 and see what happens to it, we shall find that the original $1400 expands due to the loan-making activities of other banks into $7000!

The $1400 originally lent to Mr. Dorsey is now in the form of a demand deposit at Adonais National. Twenty percent, or $280, must be used to meet the reserve requirement. The remaining $1120 is excess reserves, which means that $1120 more can be lent.

Adonais National decides to lend this $1120 to the No Exit Management Corporation, which plans to demolish some condemned apartment buildings it owns. Now $1120 plus $1400, or $2520, has been created. No Exit writes a check for $1120 to the Visigoth Wrecking Company in payment for the work. The Visigoth Wrecking Company deposits the check in its bank, the Dragon's Hoard Trust Company. Dragon's Hoard deducts 20 percent of the new deposit, or $224, and earmarks it as required reserves. This leaves $896 in excess reserves, which means $896 in new loans. We now have $1400 plus $1120 plus $896, or $3416, created by the banking system as a result of The Dicotyledon Bank's original loan of $1400 to Latisimus Dorsey.

This process will continue through many more similar steps. Each time a deposit is made, excess reserves of the bank in which it is deposited increase by 80 percent of the deposit. The increase in excess reserves means an identical increase in potential loans, and as these loans are made, money is created. Finally, when the process has run its course, $7000 will have been created out of the original loan of $1400 in excess reserves. A single bank can lend money up to the limit of that bank's excess reserves, but the reserves lost by one bank are not lost to the entire banking system. Thus, the three banks, Adonais National, Dragon's Hoard Trust, and Dicotyledon, all meet their reserve requirements, and at the same time the banking system as a whole creates more money. The reserves lost by one bank are gained by another, and the banking *system*, unlike a single bank, can lend by a multiple of its excess reserves because the system cannot lose reserves.

The Deposit Expansion Multiplier The deposit expansion multiplier is the formula by which we can determine, given the ratio of required reserves, how much money the banking system can create out of excess reserves. Very simply, it is the reciprocal of the reserve ratio. If the reserve ratio is 20 percent, or one-fifth, the expansion multiplier will be five. If the reserve ratio drops to 10 percent, the expansion multiplier increases to 10. Thus, the lower the reserve ratio, the more money the banking system will be able to create.

The expansion capability of the banking system as a whole from any given amount of excess reserves may be determined by applying the following formula to a given set of figures:

$$E \times M = D$$

E = excess reserves
M = expansion multiplier
D = maximum amount of money that can be created in this situation

M is calculated by dividing 1 by the reserve ratio, expressed as (1/R).

To calculate the maximum impact of the loan, the multiplier is applied to the original amount of the loan, provided, of course, that it was made from excess reserves.

TABLE 12-1 Multiple Expansion of Money

Banks	New deposits	Legal reserves	New loans (excess reserves)	Cumulative deposits
Dicotyledon	$1400	$ 280	$1120	$1400
Adonais	1120	224	896	2520
Dragon's Hoard	896	180	716	3416
All others	3584	716	2868	7000
Totals	$7000	$1400	$5600	

Given an initial loan of $1400 and a 20 percent reserve requirement, the entire banking system can create $7000. Of the initial $1400 put on deposit at Dicotyledon, $280 must be held as a legal reserve, leaving an excess reserve of $1120, which may be lent out. If all this $1120 is lent out and redeposited in another bank (or even in the same one), $224 would have to be kept on reserve, leaving $896 that could be lent out. This process continues until all $1400 is being held on reserve and cumulative deposits total $7000. That sum can also be calculated by using the formula: New deposits = Initial deposit × $\frac{1}{\text{Reserve ratio}} = \$1400 \times \frac{1}{.2} = \$1400 \times 5 = \$7000.$

Applying the numbers resulting from the Latisimus Dorsey loan, the formula would read as follows:

$$1400 \times (1/.20) = D$$
$$1400 \times 5 = D$$
$$1400 \times 5 = \$7000$$

The Destruction of Money

Just as granting a loan creates money in the form of a demand deposit, repayment of the debt shrinks the money supply. When the bank accepts repayment of a loan, it surrenders the borrower's I.O.U. The bank's demand deposits shrink by the amount of the loan, and so do the bank's loans. The I.O.U. has been destroyed as an asset; it has been **demonetized.**

The money supply also shrinks when a depositor withdraws cash from his account to buy a bond, to repay a loan, or to transact other business. If the bank has no excess reserves, this cash must come out of its required reserves, causing a multiple contraction of the money supply as the bank calls in loans or sells bonds to get its reserves up or its demand deposits down to the proper level. This multiple contraction can be calculated using the deposit multiplier formula.

Buying Government Bonds

To assure that banks concentrate on their principal task of supplying funds for productive economic uses, regulatory policy generally restricts their portfolio investments to government securities. Such holdings—especially short-term Treasury Bills and near-maturing Tax Anticipation Bills—act as **secondary reserves** because they can be quite easily converted to cash to meet liquidity demands on the banks.

The buying of government bonds by banks from individuals creates money in exactly the same way as does the granting of loans. We can see that the process is really the same if we think of government bonds as merely the government's I.O.U.'s. In return for these I.O.U.'s, the bank pays with money it has created.

Suppose that The Dicotyledon Bank decided to purchase $1400 worth of government bonds from Vergis and Dogberry, Inc., a brokerage firm specializing in government securities. Dicotyledon pays Vergis and Dogberry by opening a checking account in its name with demand deposits totaling $1400. This transaction creates both a new liability in the form of Vergis and Dogberry's demand deposit and a new asset in the form of the government bond.

Balance Sheet 8: The Dicotyledon Bank of Soy City, South Dakota (When a bank pays for government bonds with a demand deposit)

Assets		Liabilities and Net Worth	
U.S. government securities	**$1,400**	Demand deposits	**$ 1,900**
Property	9,000	Capital stock	10,000
Reserves	1,500		

In a short while, Vergis and Dogberry will probably write checks that will exhaust its demand deposit of $1400. These checks will be cleared at the Fed, resulting in Dicotyledon's reserves being decreased by $1400. As was the case when Dicotyledon lent $1400 to Latisimus Dorsey, clearing of the check has resulted in the bank's just meeting the required reserve ratio. Here is how the situation will look on the balance sheet:

Balance Sheet 9: The Dicotyledon Bank of Soy City, South Dakota (When a loan deposit is drawn upon)

Assets		Liabilities and Net Worth	
U.S. government securities	$1,400	Demand deposits	$ **500**
Property	9,000	Capital stock	10,000
Reserves	**100**		

Although The Dicotyledon Bank no longer has the $1400 that it created to pay for its government bond, the money is not lost to the banking system as a whole. In fact, when this money finds its way into another bank, it will give that bank $1120 in excess reserves. The bank may use this money to make

WHO GETS THE MONEY CREATED BY BANKS?

By making car loans, banks are indirectly responsible for the pollution that hovers over U.S. cities. By making loans to firms that do business in African countries ruled by white minorities, banks contribute to apartheid. By refusing loans to ghetto businesses, banks cut off funds that might help build up devastated lives. These issues raised by banking critics are really part of a single question: how banks are to use their power to create money.

Certainly loan policy is not neutral, as anyone who tries to buy a car or a house soon learns. Banks do not overtly discriminate against women or blacks, but they do avoid lending to those they feel are poor credit risks. They lend eagerly to people who already have vast assets or to thriving businesses, but turn away those most in need of money—the poor and the struggling.

Banks have their reasons. They do not own money; they only manage it. Profits, not philanthropy or social philosophy, are a bank's business. When a bank makes a loan, its prime concerns are safety and profit: What are its chances of getting the money back again with interest? Lending to a ghetto business *is* riskier.

Nonetheless, the banking industry has begun to acknowledge its responsibilities; its journals contain articles exhorting the banker to move with "energy" and "boldness of vision" in tackling the vital problems of the day. But these same articles are short on answers to the perennial questions: How does a bank reconcile boldness of vision with minimizing risk? How does a banker make a substantial commitment to the poor without running afoul of bank auditors and federal regulators whose commitment is decidedly less than his own?

A few firms have begun to try some solutions. Chase Manhattan Capital Corporation, for example, has instituted a program called Workshop in Business Opportunity, which not only directs loans to small businesses—some run by minorities—but also puts their owners through a sixteen-week course in small business management. Perhaps indicative of another trend, First Western Bank and Trust Company of Los Angeles has sold one of its ghetto area banks to the Bank of Finance, a black-owned bank. In addition, the U.S. government, along with large companies such as Chrysler and Olin Corporation, has begun making large deposits in black-owned banks in order to build up ghetto capital resources. And in 1970, the American Bankers Association instituted a program to provide a billion dollars in new financing to minority-owned firms by 1975.

The decision to institute these programs is still in the hands of the banking community. Increasingly, there have been proposals for government to regulate the uses to which credit is put. In 1971, David Eastburn, then President of the Federal Reserve Bank of Philadelphia, raised the possibility that the Federal Reserve might be empowered to step out of its traditional role of managing the quantity and overall flow of money to direct its uses as well. Federal Reserve Board member Arthur Brimmer has proposed giving an incentive for banks to lend funds for certain purposes through a supplemental reserve ratio that would vary with the use of the credit.

In an economics text we can hardly hope to solve the questions of redirecting credit. But we have gone beyond the traditional outline of money creation to show that this process has consequences for the society and is shaped by its institutional arrangements. This insight applies not only to banking but to much of the theory encountered throughout the text.

J. Paul Kirouac

loans or to buy government securities. In either case, the same multiple expansion of deposits can take place. Excess reserves, whether used to make loans, or to buy government bonds from private sources, or both, may eventually increase the money supply by the reciprocal of the reserve ratio. Selling a government bond works in the same way as receiving payment on a loan, in that the same end result—a reduction in the supply of money—is achieved. The sale of the bonds, if paid for by check, would reduce the amount of the bank's demand deposits. If paid in cash, circulated currency would be reduced. Both instances reduce the supply of money.

Limits to Expansion

Although the multiple expansion of deposits works in theory, there are certain modifications we must take into account to understand how the banking system actually operates. In reality, deposits never do expand to the full extent indicated by the expansion multiplier. They always fall short of it to some degree. This can be attributed to two factors.

Cash Leakages First, there is always a certain amount of leakage of cash into circulation. People taking out loans may require some of their money in the form of cash. A man who borrows money for a trip, for example, may draw most of it when he writes a check to the airline for his plane ticket, but he may convert a smaller amount into cash to pay for meals, tips, and entertainment. Some of this money will soon find its way back into the banking system. For instance, a waiter may deposit his tips in the bank at the end of the week. But if, among those tips, he finds a Kennedy half-dollar that he gives to his nephew for his collection, that 50 cents will be permanently out of circulation. Ultimately, cash leakages will result in a measurable decrease in the expansion of deposits.

Reluctance to Lend and Borrow The second factor limiting the expansion of deposits is the fact that banks do not always lend out all of their excess reserves. A bank may want to accumulate reserves in anticipation of some seasonal rush on loans, such as at Christmas time. On the other hand, it may voluntarily contract the amount of its loans because of pessimism about the state of the economy. During periods of depression and recession, banks generally keep larger reserves. Business is slack and few firms want to borrow money for expansion. And of those who do want to borrow, a greater percentage are judged poor credit risks. When the interest rate is low, banks are not as much concerned about letting cash sit idle as they would be in a more encouraging environment.

We see, then, that the expansion of money cannot be predicted by simple arithmetic. We can determine the upper limit to which deposits *can* expand, but the amount to which they actually *will* expand is dependent on the economic climate of the time.

THE ROLE OF DEBT

When an individual or an institution borrows money from a bank or when the government sells a bond, debt is created. Since a vast amount of economic activity is generated by these two processes, the importance of debt in our economic system is far greater than our folk myths about thrift would have us believe.

For many, "debt" is a word with unpleasant connotations. It conjures up images of remorseless bill collectors, financial disaster, the poorhouse. Although it may be unpleasant to owe large amounts of money, especially if one is unable to pay, it is nonetheless true that debt plays an indispensable role in our economy.

Assuming that each person in the economy has an income of some kind—large or small—three situations are possible. A person may spend the total amount of his income, and no more, on goods and services. He may spend less than his income. Or he may spend more than his income. If everyone spent exactly what he made, then the economy would be perfectly balanced for the present. But such a situation is not possible in real life. Circumstances arise which necessitate either overspending or underspending. A flourishing business may need to

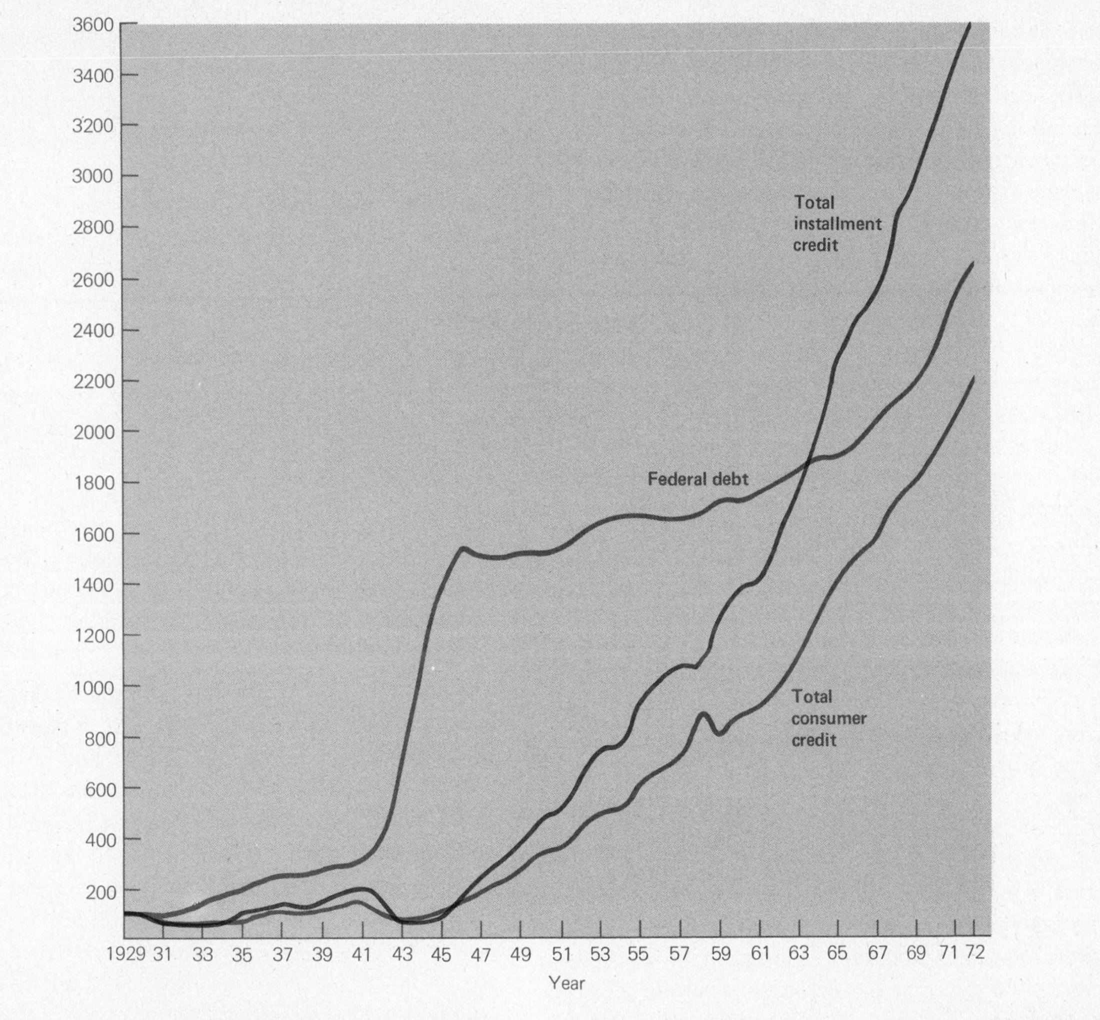

FIGURE 12-2 INDICES OF FEDERAL DEBT, TOTAL CONSUMER CREDIT, AND TOTAL INSTALLMENT CREDIT, 1929–72 (1929 = 100) Those who are alarmed over the increasing federal debt would do well to examine the rate at which U.S. private debt is rising. Most of the increase in the federal debt came during World War II, while total consumer credit, especially installment credit, has been expanding at an unparalleled pace since the late 1940s. Between 1945 and 1972, the federal debt did not quite double, while over the same period, the total consumer debt increased 21-fold and total consumer installment debt increased 35-fold. This debt contributed to consumer demand and thereby to an increasing GNP.

SOURCE: *Economic Report of the President,* January 1973.

borrow large sums of money in order to finance expansions. Couples who anticipate the need for greater amounts of money in the future—to pay for the building of a home or to send children to college—may put away portions of their income before these needs arise.

Since perfectly balanced spending is not possible, it follows that we need both underspending *and* overspending if the economy is to remain healthy. If people were allowed to save and not to borrow, the result would be a swift contraction of the economy. As money was taken out of circulation, an increasing portion of the goods produced would remain unsold. The producers of these goods would be forced to reduce their output, which would necessitate laying off employees. The country would enter a depression from which it could not extricate itself until credit was again revitalized and the volume of debt brought up to a satisfactory level. It is clear, then, that debt is not simply to be avoided, but rather to be managed and controlled according to the economic conditions of the time.

Banks: Ballast of the System, or Top-heavy Baggage?

The commercial banking system is a most important factor in the creation and control of debt through its power to create and destroy demand deposits, which constitute most of the working money supply for the economy. Because of the influence of debt on economic activity, banks can contribute to stimulating or contracting the economy through their control of both availability of funds and the terms on which such money can be borrowed. *Tight money conditions*—when funds are hard to get and borrowing costs are high—tend to moderate or even reverse the pace of business activity, if conditions are inflationary. In contrast, *easy money conditions*—when funds are readily available at low interest rates—can encourage borrowing and, in turn, stimulate employment and production, if the economy is in a recession. Certainly the banking system carries considerable weight, but in many ways, rather than serve to stabilize the system, the banks act as loose bulk, whose sliding to and fro only accentuates the pitching of the vessel. In prosperous times, when production is up, employment is rising, and businesses are expanding, banks add to the general surge by making loans readily available. The economy swells, but only to a point. Eventually, a time may be reached when excess reserves are exhausted, and the banks must restrict their loans. Thus, the banks help bring on the end of the prosperity that they themselves helped to create.

The banks may also play an influential role in prolonging recessions and depressions. As production and sales diminish, the volume of business that the economy can support falls off. Businesses are less eager to borrow money, as survival, rather than expansion, becomes their dominant concern. Other businesses lose money or fail. The banks' reaction to this situation is to protect their assets by reducing their volume of loans. This tactic, although it makes good sense as a reflex of self-preservation, serves to darken the economic skies even further. Unless loans are available, spending falls off even more, and unless spending can be encouraged, the prospects of reversing the downward economic trend are considerably reduced.

Adding to the disruptive effects of the banking system on our economy is the fact that in our country, banks are notably less centralized and controlled than in most advanced foreign nations. Our system grew up as a widely dispersed network of individual entrepreneurs. Eventually, as the economy became larger and more complex, unlimited free enterprise was found to be incompatible with the nature of banking. Thomas Jefferson's early observation, "Banks are more dangerous than standing armies" seemed indeed prescient.

Some control was needed, but it had to be control that was applied with prudence. Chapter 13 discusses how this need for control of financial conditions led, in 1913, to the creation of the Federal Reserve System.

SUMMARY

1 Banks play an important role in our economy. They can create and destroy money, determine who will get a loan and who will not, add fuel to an inflation or help curb it by no longer expanding loans. Furthermore, by making it possible to do business by check, the banking system facilitates the evolution of the national economy.

2 The Federal Reserve System has enabled the banks to carry out these roles. Prior to its creation, in 1913, the United States had periodic financial crises, often caused by overissuance of money by the banks and characterized by widespread bank failures. By requiring all member banks to keep a certain fraction of their assets on reserve, the Fed controls the volume of bank lending, and, indirectly, the nation's money supply.

3 Banks, like all other businesses, are in business for profit. Their interests may clash with the needs of the economy, and the reserve requirement is one way of controlling their expansion or contraction of the money supply.

4 Banks create (and destroy) money by exchanging a demand deposit for a borrower's promissory note (loan). On the bank's balance sheet, both demand deposits and loans will increase by the same amount. Similarly, when the loan is repaid, presumably by a check written on the borrower's account, both loans and deposits decline by the same amount.

5 Given any particular reserve requirement, any one bank can lend only up to the limit of its excess reserves. But the banking system as a whole can create a multiple amount of money from the original loan because the money is redeposited and lent again in succession. The full amount is determined by the deposit expansion multiplier, which is the reciprocal of the reserve requirement.

6 Money creation is debt creation. The loan advanced by the bank is the borrower's debt, whereas the demand deposit created for the borrower is the bank's debt. In fact, our entire money supply represents debts owned by banks (demand deposits), by the Fed (Federal Reserve Notes), and to a much smaller degree, by the Treasury (coins, silver dollars, and any Treasury notes and silver certificates still in circulation).

7 Since banks can create or destroy money, it is within their power to bring about either easy money or tight money conditions. Unfortunately, banks tend to exacerbate rather than lean against the current economic thrust. Banks will generally be expanding loans during prosperous times and contracting them during times of credit stringency. This can be particularly harmful when businesses need credit to survive, although from the banker's viewpoint, his own action is understandable, since he is merely protecting his own interests by refusing to make high-risk loans. In the next chapter we examine the role of the Federal Reserve System in making our banks more responsive to the needs of business.

SUGGESTED READINGS

Chandler, Lester V. *The Economics of Money and Banking*. 5th ed. Chaps. 5–8. New York: Harper & Row, 1969.

Duesenberry, James S. *Money and Credit: Impact and Control*. 2nd ed. Englewood Cliffs, N.J.: Prentice-Hall, 1967.

Hutchinson, Harry D. *Money, Banking and the United States Economy*. 2nd ed. Chaps. 1, 2, 4, and 5. New York: Appleton-Century-Crofts, 1971.

Ritter, Lawrence S., and **William L. Silber.** *Money*. 2nd ed. Chap. 2. New York: Basic Books, 1973.

Smith, Harlan M. *Elementary Monetary Theory*. New York: Random House, 1968.

QUESTIONS

1 Review
   a. how withdrawals and deposits in a checking account affect a bank's balance statement,
   b. how the banking system as a whole can create and destroy money,
   c. the reserve ratio and the deposit expansion multiplier,
   d. how the sale or purchase of a bond by the bank appears in the balance sheet and can affect the amount of money created or destroyed by the system.

2 What does it mean to say that we have a fractional reserve banking system? Does the Fed have unlimited power to set reserve requirements? Where does the final power rest? In what form or forms can a bank keep its required reserves?

3 Assume that you are going to establish The People's Bank of America. You have issued stock to your investors for the sum of $100,000. Construct a balance sheet to show the status of the bank. Now suppose that you have purchased space and equipment for $25,000. Change the balance sheet accordingly.

4 Mr. Nero makes a deposit in The People's Bank of $500. Enter this change in the balance sheet. If the reserve requirement is 25 percent, how much in excess reserves has been created by his deposit? Mr. Nero now writes a check for $100. Show the result in the balance sheet when his check clears. How much in excess reserves now remains from his account? What happens if the check he writes is merely deposited in another account at The People's Bank?

5 What is the value of the deposit expansion multiplier if the reserve ratio is 10 percent? 20 percent? 25 percent? 50 percent? What happens to the banking system's ability to create and destroy money as the reserve requirement ratio rises?

6 Assume that the reserve requirement ratio is 25 percent. If a little old man brings cash from the sock under his mattress into The People's Bank in the amount of $1000, how much money can be created by the banking system?

7 Why is it unlikely that the banking system will create the full amount of the money figured from the deposit expansion multiplier? If the wife of the little old man walks into The People's Bank and withdraws the $1000 and once again puts it into a sock under the bed, how would the change be reflected in the balance sheet? How much money could eventually be destroyed by the banking system? (The reserve ratio is still 25 percent.)

8 Suppose that The People's Bank has $1000 in excess reserves and decides to buy a government bond for $1000 from Garcia and Sons. How would this transaction appear in the balance sheet? Now assume that Garcia and Sons makes a deposit in The People's Bank with the $1000 they received from the sale of the bond. Show this change in the balance sheet. How much in excess reserves does the bank now have if the reserve requirement is 25 percent? How much money can eventually be created from the purchase of the bond?

9 What does it mean to say that we are in a period of tight money? Easy money? Is the banking system likely to reach its money-creation potential during a period of tight money? Why or why not? In what way are banks likely to contribute to swings in economic activity?

10 In an article some years ago in the *American Economic Review* (June 1948), Milton Friedman suggested that banks be required to keep reserves that represent 100 percent of their demand deposits. What would be the value of the deposit expansion multiplier? What is the only money the bank can create? Suppose that some quasi-governmental institution takes over granting loans. How much money could be created in the system by a loan of $5000? How much could have been created by the same loan if the required reserve ratio were 20 percent?

11 If Friedman's suggestion were put into practice and a special institution created for the purpose of granting loans, how might the policy of granting loans differ from that of banks necessarily searching for safety and high profits?

CHAPTER 13

FEDERAL RESERVE

If you look at the front of a dollar bill, at the very top, above the portrait, you will find the words *Federal Reserve Note.* Issuing paper currency is one of the functions of the Federal Reserve System—perhaps its best-known one. But the Federal Reserve has other, more specialized functions of which few people outside the financial community are aware. These functions have far-reaching consequences that affect us all. They may determine whether you can get a student loan, how much credit you can obtain when buying stocks, or whether you will pay more for a new stereo. Directly or indirectly, the influence of the Federal Reserve reaches into all areas of the economy. The Federal Reserve does not create economic conditions; they are created by the cumulative behavior of millions of economic decision-making units. But the Fed is located at the apex of the nation's financial structure, and its actions exert a profound influence on events within that structure.

FUNCTIONS OF THE FEDERAL RESERVE SYSTEM

The basic role of the Federal Reserve is to formulate and put into effect monetary policy. So that it can carry out this role, the Federal Reserve has certain special regulatory powers. In addition to its regulatory functions, the Fed also performs certain services for the convenience of the banking system.

Nonregulatory Functions

As we saw in the previous chapter, each of the 12 Federal Reserve Banks acts as a central clearinghouse for checks drawn on banks in its district. This clearing operation, which is carried out at no charge to member banks and to nonmember banks who request the service, is of immense help in simplifying and speeding up the checking process. Without the check-clearing function of the Federal Reserve Banks, our financial system, with its present level of demand deposit activity, simply could not operate .

The Federal Reserve also has several functions as a financial agent for the federal government. It acts as the nation's supplier of paper currency, or Federal Reserve Notes. Before 1968, it was permitted to issue paper money amounting to no more than four times the value of the gold reserve in Fort Knox. Now, however, collateral for Federal Reserve Notes also may include other assets such as U.S. government securities, although most Federal Reserve Banks continue to pledge a portion of their gold certificates originally issued to them by the Treasury in return for demand deposits. The Federal Reserve Banks simply print as much money as the member banks request, and deduct that much from the banks' reserve accounts. In addition to printing money, the Federal Reserve Banks provide banking services for the U.S. Treasury. Tax money collected by the Internal Revenue Service is deposited with the Federal Reserve Banks (recently the government has deposited some of it in commercial banks), and checks for tax refunds, social security payments, and other government spending are then drawn on these deposits. Finally, the Federal Reserve acts as an agent in the sale of bonds issued by the U.S. Treasury.

Regulatory Functions

The Federal Reserve's most important functions have to do with controlling the performance of the economy by means of money and credit management. When the economy is suffering from recession, marked by decreased production and by unemployment, the Board of Governors and the Federal Reserve Banks can use certain techniques—to be described in detail later in this chapter—that expand excess reserves and, hence, the lending power of commercial banks. This enables the banks to increase the supply of loanable funds to meet demand. This relative growth in available funds tends to lower the level of interest rates in the capital markets—particularly in the short-term, or money market sector—which, according to Keynesian economic theory, will

Opening photo by Raymond Juschkus, The Chase Manhattan Bank

usually stimulate borrowing for production and consumption and thus achieve the desired policy objective of reinvigorating the economy. Stimulating demand when the economy is near full employment produces rising prices. When the economy seems to be expanding too rapidly, producing an inflationary condition, the Fed will use its powers to shrink commercial banks' lending ability, thus making credit more difficult and costly to obtain. The rise in interest rates discourages borrowing and, in turn, tends to dampen or neutralize the rate of expansion of economic activity.

In recent years, policy decisions also have tended to incorporate and implement, in varying degrees, the monetarist view as to how to influence the course of the economy. This position generally holds that shifts in the size of the money supply—and not in the level of interest rates—are the main elements that historically result in change in overall economic activity and prices. Thus, expansion of the money supply will tend to raise spending, and thus the general level of business activity and prices, while shrinkage of the money supply will tend to have directly contrary effects. Hence, the monetarist position calls for monitoring and regulation of the size of the money supply itself and of reserves available to support private demand deposits through federal actions as the primary road to business and price stability.

In making these adjustments, the Fed acts in a compensatory capacity, much as the helmsman of a ship compensates for wind and current as he steers along a straight path. The long-term tendency of the economy must be expansionary. A gradual increase in credit and the supply of money is necessary if the economy is to grow and remain healthy. In order to facilitate this long-term goal, the Fed must work to reduce the magnitude of short-term fluctuations. How much such swings can or should be smoothed out is often a matter of policy dispute between those with different views on what is the best way to achieve Fed objectives without conflicting with national policy on such matters as inflation, growth, and the balance of payments.

But whatever it does, or attempts to do, the Federal Reserve can work only indirectly. Although some policy actions may influence market trends, the Federal Reserve generally cannot set specific interest rates; nor can it force banks to lend or businesses to borrow. But it can create situations which, hopefully, encourage banks and businesses to act in ways that the Federal Reserve deems favorable to the public interest.

STRUCTURE OF THE FEDERAL RESERVE SYSTEM

The United States was one of the last industrialized nations to set up a central bank. It did so at a time when the need for some effective regulatory authority over the banking business had become quite acute. Before the Civil War, banks were allowed to issue paper money against their own reserves. Although the notes of some banks were sound, the almost total lack of regulation encouraged disastrous overissues and downright fraud. Several attempts were made to set up central banks chartered by the federal government, but these proved inadequate. During the Civil War, the federal government began to issue its own paper money. This helped the situation somewhat, but the needs of the economy soon began to demand new solutions. With the growth of industry and business, checks became a popular means of payment, but there was as yet no standardized mechanism for regulating the checking process. In addition, the government had evolved no method of varying the money supply to meet changing business conditions. Occasionally, banks would be besieged by withdrawals and would have insufficient funds to handle them. Banks failed, and sometimes large-scale panics would set in, leading to severe depressions. After a series of such disasters, culminating in the panic of 1907, it was decided that a system should be established that would bring stability to the banking industry.

The Federal Reserve System was set up in 1914, after President Wilson signed the Federal Reserve Act into law in 1913. Because of regional distrust of a strong, centralized authority, 12 Federal Reserve

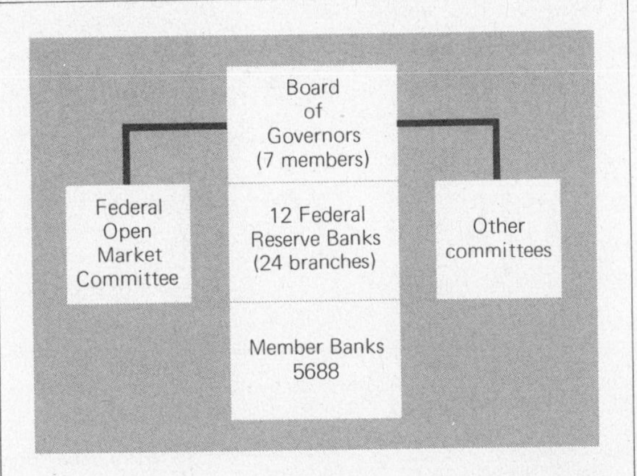

FIGURE 13-1 HOW THE FEDERAL RESERVE IS ORGANIZED **The Board of Governors exercises its broad powers, such as deciding when to expand and contract credit, as well as deciding in which areas to apply pressure. The Open Market Committee is responsible for directing the purchases and sales of federal open-market operations, while matters of regional and local concern are left to the 12 Federal Reserve Banks and their branches.**

Districts, each with its own central bank, were created. All nationally chartered banks are required to join the System. State chartered banks may join if they wish. Nominally, the Federal Reserve Banks are private corporations, owned by the member banks who have put up money for capital stock. However, although many decisions are left up to the officers of the individual banks, the System is chiefly controlled by the national Board of Governors, whose seven members are appointed for 14-year terms by the President. The terms of the Governors are staggered at two-year intervals, so that the composition of the Board at any one time reflects a broad spectrum of appointments. Acting under the direction of the Board of Governors is a group known as the Federal Open Market Committee. It is made up of the seven members of the Board of Governors plus five of the presidents of the district Federal Reserve Banks. The job of the Open Market Committee is to implement the policy decisions of the Board of Governors through the purchase or sale of government bonds. Finally, there is a 12-member group called the Federal Advisory Council. It is made up of representatives from the board of directors of each of the 12 Federal Reserve Banks. Its function is to advise the Board of Governors, but it has no power to enforce its opinions.

The Federal Reserve System, then, is privately owned, but governed by executive appointees. It is independent of the President but indirectly responsible to Congress. But although the President cannot exert direct control over its policies, the Fed is under an unofficial obligation to reach agreement on policy matters with the other federal agencies that deal with the economy, such as the Treasury, the Office of Management and Budget, and the President's Council of Economic Advisers. The close relationship to the Executive is indicated by the dual activities of Federal Reserve Board Chairman Arthur F. Burns, who also served as Chairman of the Committee on Interest and Dividends under the Economic Stabilization Program of President Nixon. Moreover, although the Fed is not directly responsible to Congress, Congress can modify the System's organization and powers. In the event of a prolonged dispute, a powerful President might, for example, put pressure on Congress to change the Federal Reserve law, bringing the Board of Governors under presidential control. Faced with this ultimate threat, the Fed usually elects to retain its independence by exercising it circumspectly.

HOW MONETARY POLICY WORKS

The goals of monetary policy are the same as those of fiscal policy: To maintain a growing economy with full employment and stable prices. The most significant way in which the Fed works to accomplish these objectives is through the use of techniques to increase or decrease the amount of excess reserves held by commercial banks. As we discovered in the preceding chapter, the amount of excess reserves a bank holds directly controls the amount of money it is able to lend. And since money lent is expanded by the banking system by the inverse of the reserve ratio, any change in the amount of money available for loans will have an enormous potential

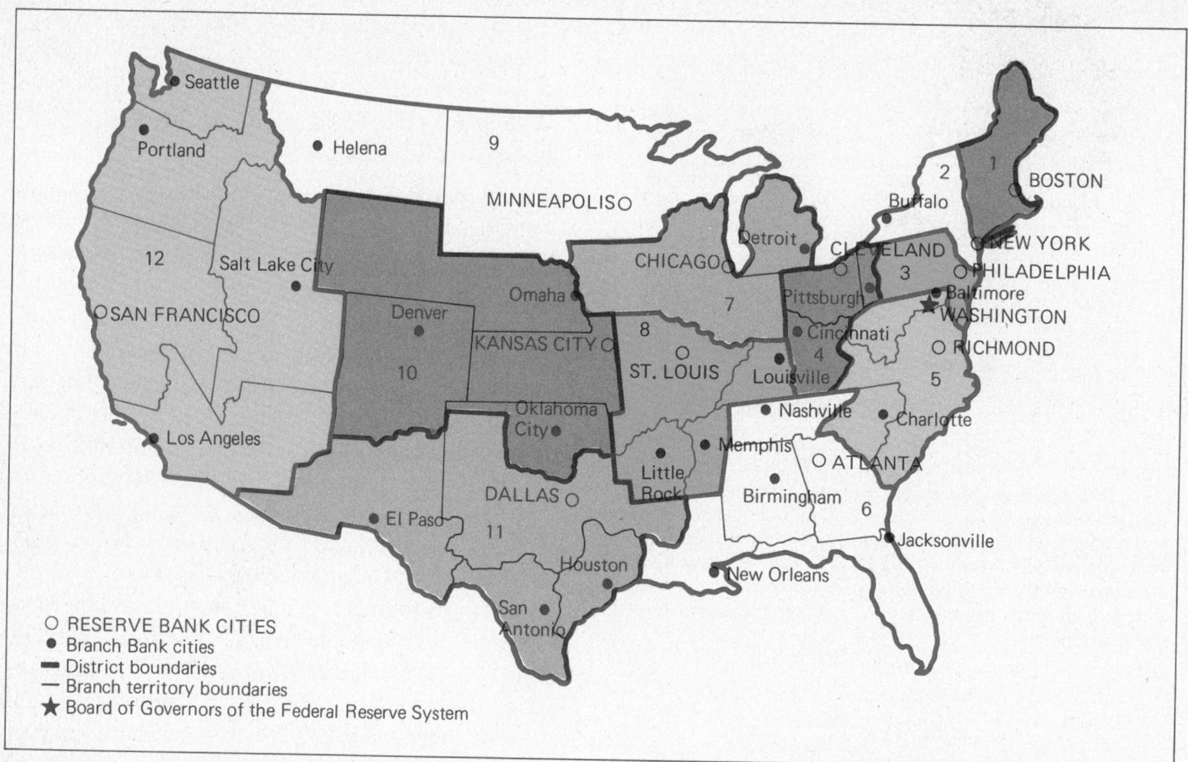

FIGURE 13-2 THE 12 FEDERAL RESERVE DISTRICTS The Federal Reserve system is divided into 12 districts to provide services and to regulate banking on a regional basis. There is a disproportionate number of districts in the Northeast because that area is heavily populated and includes several important financial and industrial centers.

effect on the supply of money in the economy. Moreover, Federal Reserve methods used to expand bank reserves often have the additional impact of directly influencing interest rate trends. Thus, open-market purchases of U.S. government securities by the Fed tend to raise their prices and, hence, lower the interest rates on those instruments. This, in turn, affects rates of return on all fixed-income investments in the same way. Similarly, when Federal Reserve Banks lower the interest or discount rate charged to System members, other interest rates will reflect the shift.

Money is subject to the law of supply and demand. The less there is, the more it will cost—that is, the higher the interest rate. Conversely, the greater the amount of money that is available, the less it will cost, or the lower will be the interest rate. While money is scarce and expensive, individuals and businesses will spend and invest less freely. When money becomes abundant and cheap, spending and investment in capital equipment will tend to rise because expectations of profit from the use of such equipment compare favorably with returns available from bonds. On the other hand, a rise in interest rates will tend to make investment in bonds more attractive. Because spending and capital investment directly influence the levels of output, employment, income, and prices, money and credit management is an effective device for regulating fluctuations in economic activity.

THE AUTONOMY OF THE FED

Under the Constitution, Congress has the power "to coin money and regulate the value thereof." Since 1913, this power has been delegated to the Federal Reserve System. The Fed is thus the creation of Congress, but at the same time it is privately owned by the System member banks, and governed by a Board of Governors appointed by the President. The Fed is responsible to the people, but it must report its policy decisions to Congress, and it must coordinate its policies with the Treasury, which is under executive jurisdiction. These multiple relationships have led to a great deal of controversy as to who really controls the Fed.

First, there are those who say that the Fed ought to be solely in the hands of the executive branch of government. In this way, monetary policy could be more easily coordinated with fiscal policy; the long-standing friction between the two could be eliminated. Moreover, such a change would take responsibility for monetary policy away from a small group of politically invisible specialists, and give it to an elected representative of the people—the President.

Others, however, would like to see the Fed remain independent of the President. These observers point out that monetary authority should be kept out of the hands of the President because of the natural executive propensity to solve economic problems by inflationary means. They fear that the President will use the Fed's power to ease money markets for the purpose of filling the government's revenue needs. Instead of raising taxes or reducing government spending—measures involving considerable political risk—the President will choose the subtler, less noticeable method of running up the federal debt at excessively low rates of interest.

These same critics also point out that although the Fed is run by specialists, they are still obligated to report annually to Congress and to work closely with the President, the Secretary of the Treasury, and the Chairman of the President's Council of Economic Advisers.

Another group of critics, those led by economist Milton Friedman, would like to see the Fed controlled, not by Congress and not by the President, but, in a sense, by the economy itself. The monetarists believe that the most important aspect of monetary policy is the size of the money supply itself. The free-market economy, they feel, is inherently stable. In their view, the Fed's "fine tuning" devices and policy of "leaning against the wind" only serve to upset this stability. The monetarists would strip the Fed of its "discretionary" powers, and limit it to acting on certain "rules." This would entail stabilizing the growth of the money supply at a steady rate—4 or 5 percent a year—and letting interest rates, price levels, and employment take care of themselves.

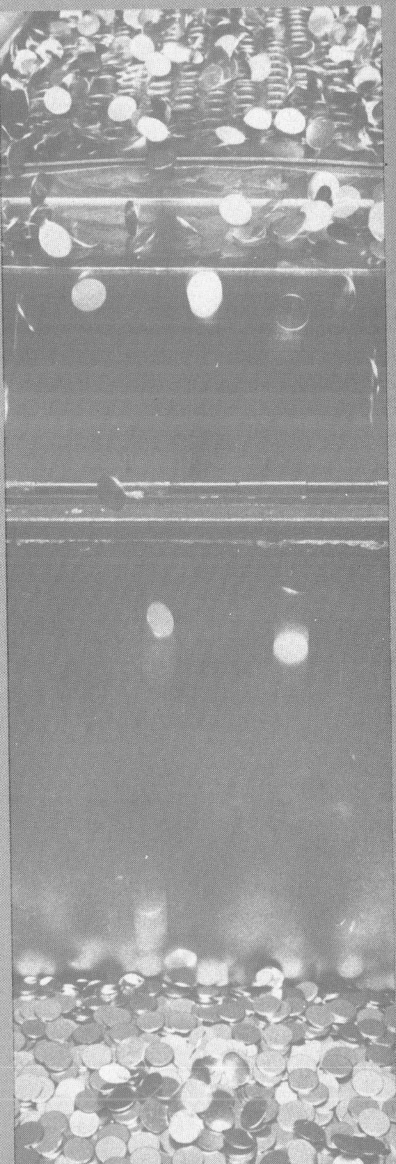

United Press International

General Controls

There are several tools that the Fed may employ to adjust the reserve positions of commercial banks. The use of any one of them will tend to result in a corresponding change in both the availability of loans and interest rates. These changes will, in turn, affect output, employment, income, and prices.

Changing the Reserve Requirement

The Board of Governors may change the reserve requirement of member banks within certain limits set by Congress. In setting these requirements, a distinction was traditionally made between "city banks" and "country banks." City banks were larger member banks located in major commercial centers. Country banks were not necessarily located in strictly rural areas, but they were outside the major commercial centers. Since the fall of 1972, the differences in reserve requirements have been based on the amount of deposits. The city banks hold well over half of all the deposits in member banks.

TABLE 13-1 Reserve Requirements, as of July 1973 (Percent of demand deposits)

	Reserve requirement
Reserve City Banks (over $400 million)	
Legal limits	10 to 22
Present requirements	18
Other banks	
Legal limits	7 to 14
Present requirements	
Up to $2 million	8
Over $2 million to $10 million	10½
Over $10 million to $100 million	12½
Over $100 million to $400 million	13½

The Federal Reserve has the authority to raise or lower reserve requirements within legal limits set by Congress. These limits distinguish between the large city banks and the remaining banks. There is no single reserve requirement, but rather a sliding scale based on the net demand deposits held by a bank. In July 1973, the Fed used the reserve requirement to curb inflation by raising the actual reserve requirements for all banks except the very smallest by ½ percent to the levels shown here.

SOURCE: *Federal Reserve Monthly Review*, July 1972; Federal Reserve Bank of New York, "Changes in Discount Rates and Reserve Requirements," Circular No. 7173 (June 29, 1973).

Because of the multiple expansion of deposits, a relatively small change in the reserve ratio can produce a large change in the money supply. For example, in 1973, in order to curb an inflationary trend, reserve requirements were raised one-half of one percent and only on that portion of an individual bank's demand deposits that exceeded $2 million. For the banking system as a whole, the effect was to transform $800 million to required reserves. Given an expansion multiplier of 5, that $800 million—if they were all excess reserves—could have supported demand deposit expansion of $4 billion. But that potential expansion was neutralized by the shift of $800 million to required reserves backing current demand deposits. This shift was used to brake the economy's expansion.

Usually the Fed refrains from using the reserve ratio adjustment method to get banks to limit their loans. As a rule, the Fed raises the reserve requirement only when there is a great deal of excess reserves in the banking system as a whole. Reserve positions of individual banks will, of course, vary because of a number of factors. At any given time, some banks will have substantial excess reserves, while others may have to borrow funds at a district Federal Reserve Bank. But Fed actions are designed to affect the level of excess reserves of the entire banking system. In 1967, for example, the Fed raised the reserve requirement only after ascertaining that there was about $345 million in excess reserves and about $62.5 billion in government securities, which the banks could liquidate to meet emergency needs. Thus, changing the reserve ratio is best used as a means of burning off excess reserves prior to making finer adjustments with a more sensitive tool of monetary policy. This more sensitive tool—one that the Fed uses far more frequently than changing the reserve requirement—is known as open-market operations.

Open-Market Operations

Once the Board of Governors of the Federal Reserve decides that a monetary policy will be executed in open-market opera-

TABLE 13-2 How Open-Market Operations Expand the Money Supply

T-Account 1. Federal Reserve (after the Fed has bought government securities from member banks)				T-Account 2. Member banks (after selling government securities to the Fed)			
Assets		Liabilities		Assets		Liabilities	
Government securities	+$100	Member bank reserves	+$100	Reserves	+$100	Demand deposits	+$500
				Loans and investments	+$400		

When the Federal Reserve buys $100 million of government securities in the open market, it pays for this by crediting $100 million to the reserve accounts of the banks from which it purchased the securities. This added reserve enables the banking system as a whole to expand the total amount of demand deposits by $500 million, if the reserve ratio is 20 percent. If you do not see the link between the added reserves and the expanded money supply, review Chapter 12.

tions, it is up to the Federal Open Market Committee (FOMC) to purchase or sell the government securities. The manager of the open-market account, who is one of the vice presidents of the Federal Reserve Bank of New York, has charge of actual purchases and sales. He deals with about 18 of the largest government security brokers, and is thus able to buy and sell quickly, as policy dictates.

When the Fed buys government securities, the effect is to expand the money supply. The manager of the open-market account buys government securities from a broker and pays him with a check drawn on the Federal Reserve Bank. The broker then turns over this check to the seller of the securities. The seller may be a commercial bank, a business, or an individual. If the seller is a commercial bank, then the bank's excess reserves increase by the amount of the check. These reserves can support an equal amount in new loans, which are then expanded by the banking system. When the seller of the securities is a business or individual, the result is again expansionary, although somewhat less so. This is because the Federal Reserve Bank's check enters the commercial banking system in the form of a demand deposit, rather than simply as reserves. A portion of these new deposits must be retained by the Federal Reserve Bank as required reserves. Thus, if the Fed buys $1000 worth of government securities from a commercial bank, that bank gains $1000 in excess reserves and can issue $1000 more in loans. But if the Fed buys $1000 in securities from an individual, the individual will deposit the check in his checking account. If the reserve ratio is 20 percent, his bank will be obligated to hold $200 in required reserves and will be left with only $800 for loans.

Even so, the power of banks to create money would support a multiple expansion of that $800 to a total of $4000 of new demand deposits in the banking system.

When the Fed sells government securities, the effect is a contraction in the money supply. If the buyer is a commercial bank, payment for the securities is deducted from the bank's excess reserves. If an individual buys, payment must be in the form of a check drawn on a commercial bank; this reduces the individual's demand deposit and the bank's reserves.

The Fed prefers to use open-market operations as a means of controlling the money supply because they are flexible, gradual, reversible, and continuously under direct control. The effects of open-market operations are not as dramatic or immediate as those of reserve ratio changes. It takes some time for the effects of government bond sales in New York to spread throughout the system. Yet it is this very absence of catastrophic, possibly unforeseen consequences that gives open-market operations their appeal.

OPEN-MARKET OPERATIONS AND INTEREST RATES One question remains. How can the Fed be so sure that commercial banks and the public will cooperate in open-market operations, that they will purchase bonds when they are offered, and that they will sell them when the Fed expresses a desire to buy? The answer lies in the mechanism of the interest rate. When the Fed wishes to buy bonds, for example, it simply offers a higher price for them, so that holders of bonds are willing to sell. Similarly, when the Fed decides to contract the money supply by selling bonds, it assures itself of finding buyers by pricing the bonds competitively.

The competitive pricing of government bonds directly affects the rate of interest paid. A 5 percent bond, for example, selling for $1000, yields $50 per year. However, if the Fed, in an effort to make bonds attractive to prospective buyers, lowers the price to $800, this change will affect the interest rate of the bond. The bond will still be earning $50 per year, but this yield will no longer represent an interest rate of 5 percent (50/1000), but of 6.25 percent (50/800). And if the government, in trying to attract sellers, raises the price of the bond from $1000 to $1200, the interest rate will fall to 4.17 percent (50/1200).

These changes in the interest rates of government securities have their own effect on the economy. For example, when the Fed is buying bonds to stimulate the economy, it bids up prices, forcing the interest rates down. As a result of lowered interest rates, government bonds suffer a decline in popularity. People would rather put their money in other things. In other words, the opportunity cost of using money to purchase bonds increases.

Because they offer top security due to the Treasury's guarantee of payment of interest and principal and play a large role in capital markets, U.S. government securities occupy a bellwether position. Consequently, interest rates on government bonds tend to be lower than on other fixed-income securities, and changes in the yields of government bonds are eventually reflected in shifts in the rate of return on other bonds. So a drop in yield on government bonds would lower the cost of borrowing money. And with borrowing costs down, people—individuals and businesses—may be stimulated to undertake projects such as home building, factory expansion, and inventory buildup. Such forms of investment tend to further stimulate the economy.

When the government sells bonds, it produces the reverse effect. The cost of bonds goes down and interest rates go up, raising interest rates throughout the economy. This has the effect of discouraging expansionary activity.

Open-market operations, then, affect the economy in two ways. First, the sale or purchase of government securities by the Fed directly affects the amount of excess reserves held by commercial banks, thus diminishing or expanding the amount of money in the economy. Second, by lowering or raising the price of government bonds, the Fed changes the interest rates of the bonds, which ultimately causes changes in interest rates throughout the economy.

OPEN-MARKET OPERATIONS AND FEDERAL DEBT Sometimes the fluctuations in interest rates caused by open-market operations have an adverse effect on the Treasury. This is because increases in interest rates on government securities raise the cost of carrying the federal debt. When the Fed raises interest rates by lowering the price of government bonds, the effect is to force the Treasury to pay higher rates when it next borrows money. During World War II, the Fed made an agreement with the Treasury to keep prices of government bonds above a certain level. Under this agreement, interest rates remained low and the cost of carrying the federal debt was kept within limits. By 1951, however, it had grown obvious that if the Fed was going to control the inflation brought on by the Korean War, it would need greater freedom in selling government securities. The Treasury agreed to let the Fed out of the original agreement, and open-market operations were carried on without regard to their effects on the federal debt. Only when the Treasury is engaged in bringing out large, new issues of securities does the Fed make a special effort to cooperate. At such a time the Fed may alter its policies in order to help stabilize government bond prices. But such actions never last more than a few days.

Changing the Discount Rate A commercial bank can borrow money from the Federal Reserve Bank in its district in just the same way that a business or individual can borrow money from a commercial bank. The percentage that the Federal Reserve Bank charges in interest is known as **the discount rate.**

Commercial banks borrow from the Federal Reserve Bank in order to increase their reserves, usually in the event of some emergency. In granting the loan, the Federal Reserve Bank simply increases the borrowing bank's reserves by the amount of the loan—first subtracting, or "discounting," the amount of interest charged over the term of the loan. An increase in bank reserves as the result of a loan, like an increase by any other means, enhances the bank's ability to make loans to the public and, thus, leads to an increase in the money supply. By lowering the discount rate, the Fed encourages borrowing; by raising the discount rate, it discourages it. The discount rate is thus another of the Fed's tools for affecting the economy through changes in the money supply. But it is a secondary tool. As a lender of last resort, the Fed must play a passive role. Like the fire axe hanging in its glass case, it must wait until circumstances compel its use. Lowering the discount rate will do little to promote borrowing, since the banks will still be reluctant to incur a debt. Raising the rates will not necessarily stop borrowing, because a bank may be going to the Fed as a last resort and must borrow, whatever the rate.

A change in the discount rate is often dictated by a change in the interest rate on short-term government securities. If the discount rate is not adjusted, the result is to undermine the Fed's open-market operations. If the discount rate for a 90-day loan from the Fed is less than the interest rate on a 90-day Treasury bill, then bankers will borrow from the Fed before they will sell their Treasury bills. Conversely, if the discount rate exceeds the interest rate on short-term securities, banks will sell their government bonds before applying for Federal Reserve loans. Because these actions may conflict with the Fed's current monetary policy, the discount rate must be adjusted to coincide closely with the interest rate on short-term government securities.

Curiously, however, this limitation actually increases the importance of the discount rate in the overall scheme of monetary policy. Because it is so closely tied to the interest rate on short-term securities, the discount rate has come to be an indicator of conditions in the money markets. When the discount rate goes up, it is taken to mean that money has become tighter. When it goes down, it is assumed that conditions have eased. These signs have the effect of encouraging further contraction or expansion. Thus, the discount rate, while relatively ineffective for directly implementing monetary policy, becomes a potent psychological device.

Relative Effectiveness of General Controls The most effective single control at the Fed's disposal is open-market operations. The other tools have drawbacks that limit their use.

The somewhat violent effects of reserve ratio changes are used primarily to burn off excess reserves. The discount rate has the disadvantages that it must be closely tied to the interest rates on short-term securities and its changes cannot compel banks to borrow or not borrow.

Open-market operations, on the other hand, have none of the disadvantages of these other methods. Moreover, they have the very significant advantage of almost unlimited resources. The Federal Reserve System now has holdings of government securities whose value is more than double the reserves of all member banks. This gives the Fed a great deal to work with, enough to expand or contract the money supply to practically any degree it wishes.

It is important to recognize, however, that all monetary tools, including open-market operations, may be more effective in contracting economic activity than in expanding it. This has been likened to the difference in effectiveness between pulling and pushing on a string. During an inflationary period, a decrease in the amount of excess reserves limits the amount of money that banks may lend. Like pulling a string taut, this will tend to contract the amount of business investment and spending and thus restrain economic activity. When, faced with the threat of recession, the Board of Governors decides to increase excess reserves in order to expand credit, it can only hope that its action will have the desired effect. But pushing on a string does not work quite as well as pulling. Banks may decide not to make their new excess reserves available for loans at all, or, if they do, customers may be unwilling to borrow. Such a situation illustrates that the Fed can only guide and direct the economy—and often the economy refuses to be directed.

Specific Controls

The reserve ratio, open-market operations, and the discount rate are monetary tools that affect the economy as a whole. They are used to contract or expand the money supply throughout the system. In this, they resemble the volume control on a stereo set; its function is to make the music loud or soft, no more. But just as a listener might want to use the treble and bass knobs to make adjustments in the quality of the sound, depending on the volume or the type of music being played, so the Fed often finds itself facing a situation in which it must affect specific aspects of the economy. For this purpose it has at its disposal a number of tools called specific controls, or selective credit controls.

Stock Market Credit Sometimes the stock market becomes sluggish or overactive while the rest of the economy continues on an even keel. In order to make adjustments that will specifically affect stock market conditions, the Fed has been empowered to set the *margin requirement* on stock purchases. The margin requirement is the percentage of the price of a stock purchase that must be paid as a down payment. For instance, a margin requirement of 50 percent means that one-half the purchase price of any stock must be paid in cash, while the rest may be borrowed from the stock broker. If the market is sluggish, the Fed may lower the margin requirement in order to stimulate stock purchases. If the market shows signs of overactivity, the margin may be raised. It was the stock market crash of 1929 that prompted Congress to grant the Fed power to set the margin requirement. Prior to the crash, the wholesale price index was fairly stable while stock prices soared. The Fed was reluctant to dampen the stock market by means of open-market activities or by raising the discount rate, as this might have brought on a general recession. If the Fed *had* been able to control the stock market specifically, the crash might have been less severe.

Consumer and Real Estate Credit During World War II, briefly between 1948 and 1949, and during the Korean War, Congress gave the Fed power to control the down payments, interest charges, and length of loans for consumer installment purchases. This control was known as "Regulation W," and was effective in limiting inflation brought on by wartime spending and in conserving resources needed for the war effort. During the 1950s, however, the enabling legislation was allowed to lapse, and Regulation W has not been invoked since. Another control enacted for similar reasons was "Regulation X," which was designed to limit the flow of money into housing construction.

Interest Rate Ceilings on Time Deposits The Fed has the power to set a ceiling on the amount of interest that member banks may pay on time deposits in the bank. This is known as "Regulation Q." The purpose of this control is to protect the competitors of commercial banks—savings banks and savings and loan associations. Both these institutions *and* commercial banks accept time deposits, but only commercial banks are subject to regulation of interest rates on such deposits. When the interest rates that member banks pay on time deposits are set below the market rates offered by savings institutions, the public will transfer their time deposits from the banks to the savings institutions. Since the deposits of savings institutions, unlike those of the commercial banks, are used chiefly for mortgage loans, increasing the reserves of savings institutions is tantamount to encouraging the housing industry. The housing industry is extremely sensitive to high interest rates. If the Fed wants to contract the money supply without creating a disproportionately large contraction in housing construction, it may keep existing ceilings on bank deposits. When the market rate on time deposits at savings institutions goes above the ceiling and funds shift to take advantage of this, the availability of money for mortgages increases, buffering the construction industry from the full effects of tight money.

Moral Suasion

Moral suasion, or, as it is sometimes irreverently called, "open-mouth policy," or "jaw boning," means the attempt by the Fed to influence bank policy by using the power of words alone, without any kind of control device to back up the request. Although moral suasion alone is the weakest monetary tool in the Fed's arsenal, it is more effective than one might expect. For one thing, it is not unknown for banks to accept pronouncements of the Fed as sound economic advice, and to follow them willingly. This is by no means always the case, but since it is the Fed's business to keep an eye on the economy and to predict future conditions, banks tend to have a certain respect for the Fed's opinions. Secondly, banks may heed moral suasion because they expect it, if not heeded, to be followed by stronger measures, especially if the chairman of the Fed is also head of the Committee on Interest and Dividends. Since the Fed's more potent tools will force banks to comply in the future, they see no point in putting up an initial, and fruitless, resistance. Finally, there is always the possible threat of direct action by the Fed against specific banks that refuse to follow the Fed's suggestions. A recalcitrant bank, for example, might find it more difficult to borrow from the Fed in the future. Whether such tactics are actually used would be difficult to say, but even the possibility might act as a deterrent.

DOES MONETARY POLICY WORK?

The various control mechanisms at the disposal of the Fed would seem to form as adequate an arsenal as any central bank could want. Surely with all those general and specific controls, meeting the goals of the economy could not be very difficult. But unfortunately, the reality is not quite as simple as the textbook model. There are numerous difficulties,

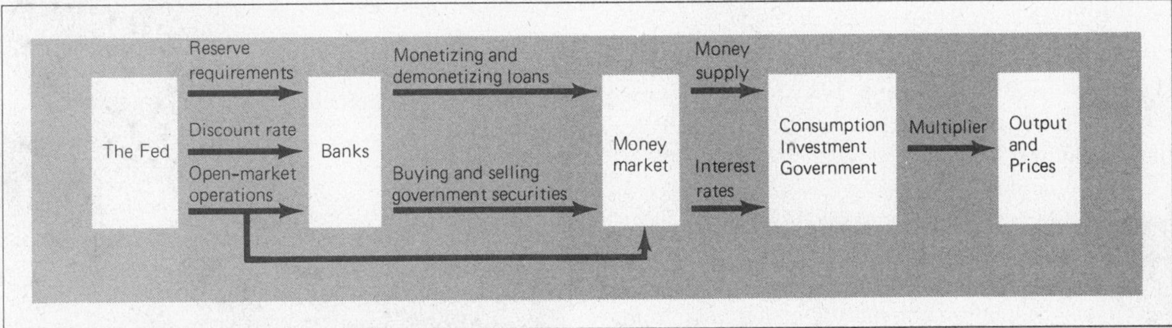

FIGURE 13-3 HOW MONETARY POLICY WORKS **When the Fed follows a policy of easy money, the flow of money from the banks tends to increase, providing consumers, businesses, and, to a lesser degree, the government with the funds to purchase goods and services. If the economy is at full employment, the result will be higher prices; below the full-employment level, the economy will respond with an increase in both production and prices (depending on how much slack exists). A policy of tight money results in an opposite sequence of events: As the flow of money to the consumers, businesses, and the government decreases, both production and prices tend to fall. However, during periods of tight money, we have experienced slowdowns in the *rate* of price increase, but no price decreases since the 1930s. Economists explain this by referring to structural changes in our economy, such as the growth of labor unions and administered (sticky) prices imposed by corporations. Furthermore, in the game of economic chicken, the monetary authorities back off well before a price decrease can take hold, for fear that tight money will cause a recession.**

numerous unforeseen events, which often conspire to make the well-equipped Fed seem very inadequate indeed. In fact, so problematic is the situation that there are critics who say that the Fed does the economy more harm than good and that there ought to be major changes in its structure.

Multiple Tools, Multiple Goals

Although the Fed possesses a number of powerful tools, their effectiveness in helping to achieve the basic objectives of full employment, reasonable price stability, and economic growth is limited by a number of conflicting factors.

First, the Fed must deal with conflict between economic objectives. In the spring of 1973, Arthur F. Burns was coping with a dilemma posed by his roles as Chairman of the Federal Reserve Board and of the Economic Stabilization Program's Committee on Interest and Dividends. In his latter role he was concerned that higher bank lending rates might add inflationary impetus to the rapidly rising cost of doing business. But as Chairman of the Federal Reserve Board, he knew that rising interest rates could help dampen inflationary pressures—shown most dramatically in rises in wholesale and consumer prices—then plaguing the economy. Furthermore, rising rates could help the nation's balance-of-payments position and bolster confidence in the dollar by attracting funds back to the United States.

At times, the Fed may have to make a choice between full employment and price stability. Historically, when economic expansion moves unemployment down to the 4 to 5 percent level, capacity utilization starts to move up to full-employment levels, prices begin to rise rapidly, and demand takes on a decidedly inflationary hue. The Fed must sense what trade-offs the public is willing to make. In short, how much unemployment will the nation tolerate in the interest of maintaining price stability? Of course, the same hard questions face other governmental decision-makers when they are considering shifts in tax and spending policies which can also affect levels of employment, investment, and income.

Moreover, the effects of monetary policy actions may be so uneven as to be somewhat self-defeating. Prices set by joint bargaining between giant corporations and labor unions seldom respond to monetary policy action. Because of substantial generation of funds from retained earnings, many large corporations may be additionally resistant to the normal consequences of a tight money policy by the Fed.

It must be remembered that the Fed is not the only arm of government seeking to fulfill those goals. Absence of action by other governmental authority can put an undue responsibility upon the shoulders of monetary policy. Thus, the failure of fiscal policy to dampen inflationary pressure generated by government financing of Vietnam War expansion in 1965 spurred the Fed to use monetary weapons to cool the economy. This, in turn, contributed heavily to the unpopular credit crunch of 1966.

On the other hand, in the interest of accommodation, the Fed may feel compelled to act inconsistently. The Treasury's job is to finance the federal debt. It does this by floating government securities, which are the Treasury's I.O.U.'s. Since it is obligated to pay interest on them, the Treasury is eager to keep interest rates low. However, when the Fed is fighting inflation with open-market operations, it must lower the price of federal securities in order to induce sales. This price reduction results in higher interest rates, so the Treasury loses money. The Fed must often temper its tight money policies in order to appease the Treasury. These compromises harmonize their relationships, but, unfortunately, tend also to pull the teeth out of the Fed's policies.

In attempting to achieve its multiple goals, then, the Fed has a difficult task indeed. One Fed official has complained: "It is like using a loose steering wheel with a sticky place in the middle. You keep overshooting."

Cyclical Asymmetry The Fed's easy money/tight money policies seem at first glance to constitute a perfectly straightforward, two-way control device, something like a water tap with knobs for hot and cold. But if the analogy is to hold, the tap must be connected to an extremely temperamental hot water heater, for while tight money controls are almost sure to have some effect, controls for bringing about an easy money condition always involve a gamble. As we noted earlier, there is no way of forcing banks to lend, once excess reserves have been made available to them, or of forcing the public to borrow. The Fed can only set the stage for deposit expansion. After that, it must sit back and wait for the actors to respond to their cues.

Private Offsets The Fed's efforts to reduce bank reserves through open-market operations may be temporarily frustrated if banks decide to sell their government securities in order to accommodate customers wanting loans. Banks may often want to shift their earning assets in this way since loans yield higher profits than securities. Besides, it is better for business to satisfy customers than to refuse them credit. If many banks respond in this same way, the velocity of money will increase and frustrate the efforts of the Fed.

Eventually, the Fed's competitive pricing of government securities will make it increasingly unprofitable for the banks to continue selling them. To compensate, the banks will have to raise interest rates on loans, which will discourage customers. Finally, there will no longer be any rationale for the banks to continue liquidating "secondary reserves." The money markets will tighten up and loans will become scarce, but this may not occur until several months after the Fed puts its tight-money policies into effect.

Velocity and Financial Intermediaries As John Maynard Keynes pointed out, increasing the money supply to revive an ailing economy may not produce the desired result, since a decrease in velocity may nullify the effect of an increase in M. The opposite may occur too. A decrease in the money supply may lead to an increase in V, thus temporarily frustrating the Fed's tight money measures.

Financial intermediaries (lending institutions outside the commercial bank system) tend to augment increases in V. These institutions do not create money as commercial banks do, but they do help to transfer savings into the hands of spenders. This activity tends to raise V and to decrease the effectiveness of tight-money policies. Many commentators believe that financial intermediaries ought to be under more direct control in order to prevent such situations.

Time Lags and Forecasting Problems Between the time the Fed changes monetary policy and the time the changes take effect throughout the economy, there is a response delay estimated at between six months and three years. That is the amount of time that economists (excluding those who wisely will not venture to guess) estimate it takes for the Fed's policies to have a decisive effect on economic activity. This delay becomes extremely serious in the event that tight-money policies finally take effect just when the economy takes a downturn of its own accord, or when easy-money policies reach their fruition in time for an unexpected inflation.

The time-lag problem is aggravated by the fact that the science of economic forecasting does not remotely approach 100 percent accuracy. With all the information at its disposal, the Fed still has only a very fragmentary picture of the economic situation at a given time. And it is not even a picture of the present, but of the past. In order to predict future conditions, this information must be compared and interpreted. Guesswork cannot be avoided. This, of course, makes the economists' predictions more liable to error. Thus, the Board of Governors faces the disquieting task of shooting at a target that may take months or years to hit. Moreover, the target is located in an area about which there can be only a speculative knowledge.

Uneven Impact of Monetary Policy When the Fed implements tight-money policies, there is no way, under the present system, that it can avoid hurting small businesses more than large ones. Small businesses rely on loans for expansion, while large businesses are more likely to have enough capital of their own to free them from dependence on the banks. Thus, when money markets contract, small businesses are soon forced to curtail expansion, whereas large businesses can continue to grow. One frequent victim of this inequity is the housing industry. Most construction companies are small

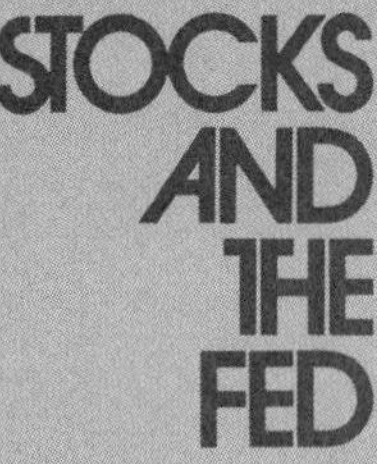

Great amounts of time and energy are spent in anticipating the course of the stock market. In the long run stock prices tend to rise. Today, the value of all stock in the United States is estimated at $900 billion, compared with about $150 billion 20 years ago.

It is the short-term fluctuations in stock prices which mystify. Is it possible that a clever investor might capitalize on some correlation between the vagaries of the stock market and the policies of the Federal Reserve System?

Perhaps the money supply is the key. After all, an increase in the money supply, by raising aggregate demand, may create a greater desire for stocks. Since this demand usually cannot be met by creating more stocks, the price of existing stocks must rise. On the other hand, contractions in the money supply reduce the demand for stocks, thus causing equity prices to fall. According to some market analysts, money market prices should rise within two months after buildup of the money supply, but fall about a year after shrinkage of available funds.

But it does not always work that way. During the stock market boom preceding the Great Crash of 1929, the money supply increased by less than 2 percent, while stock prices doubled. After 1929, the money supply shrank only 5 percent per year, but the value of stocks dropped to almost nothing.

Even a closer correlation would not necessarily mean a cause-and-effect relationship. In fact, one commentator has pointed out that between 1960 and 1966 fluctuations in stock prices and an index of the strike-out record of the Washington Senators baseball team were more closely correlated than stock prices and the money supply!*

The Fed's overall monetary policy does seem to have had a more decisive effect on stock prices during the last few years. This is due in part to the greater autonomy the Fed has assumed in economic affairs, compared with its subservience to the Treasury during and immediately after World War II. During the "credit crunch" of 1966, for example, stock prices dropped sharply, apparently as a result of the effect of the Fed's tight money policy, which raised interest rates and lowered bond prices sharply. Under such conditions investors tend to look at comparative returns on bonds and stocks and conclude that the higher returns available from bonds lower the present value of future earnings and dividend expectations from common stocks. The result is lower demand and, consequently, lower prices for stocks. In 1967 and 1968,

* Lawrence S. Ritter and William L. Silber, *Money* (New York: Basic Books, 1970), p. 134.

when an easy money policy was put into effect, the stock market went into an upswing. Lower interest rates stimulate business borrowing and reduce business operating costs; both factors improve earnings potential and, hence, increase the attractiveness of stocks. Such correlations appear to indicate that, recently at least, monetary policy may provide a fairly reliable indicator of shifts in stock market trends. But these are only marginally useful in deciding whether to dump your 10 shares of Mythical Valley in favor of three shares of gilt-edged Fauvist Mauve Records, Inc.

Arthur Lavine, The Chase Manhattan Bank

and must borrow frequently in order to stay in operation. Moreover, mortgage loans are usually quickly affected by tight money policies. Thus, contracting money markets soon leave construction firms with nothing to build with and no one to build for.

The Usefulness of Monetary Policy

Despite the deficiencies of monetary policy, a strong case can be made for its usefulness. It helped control recessions in 1949 and 1958, and during the fifties and sixties it helped keep inflation within bounds. In certain ways, it is admirably adapted as an economic tool.

Flexibility The chief device for implementing monetary policy is open-market operations. Ultimately, these operations are in the hands of the manager of the open-market account in the Federal Reserve Bank in New York. He may buy and sell bonds on a daily basis, with no more restraint than any other broker. This sort of flexibility is a far cry from the slow political processes involved in enacting fiscal policy, dominated as it is by congressional deliberations.

Political Invisibility Changes in monetary policy do not generally occasion so much political comment or opposition as do changes in fiscal policy. Fiscal matters—taxes and government spending—often make front-page news and, in addition, turn up as bones of contention in political campaigns. Monetary policy rarely enjoys such notoriety. It is quieter, more subtle, and, therefore, hopefully, more efficient.

The Debate about Monetary Policy

Still, monetary policy is a very delicate and complex instrument. As we have seen, it is greatly subject to error and misjudgment. The particular weakness of monetary policy is that it sometimes adds momentum to the very "boom and bust" swings that it is supposed to counteract. This weakness has caused many to level criticisms against overreliance on changing money and credit conditions to control the economy.

It is clear that monetary policy alone cannot regulate fluctuations in economic activity. The vital interconnection of monetary and fiscal policy demands their coordination. But then we shall have to consider what concept of money and income would be appropriate to guide such coordinated policy actions. The Keynesian approach, which has dominated U.S. monetary and fiscal policy since the 1930s, places great emphasis on relationships between interest rates and investment demand. A positive desire to invest could be stimulated into real economic activity if capital were available at reasonable interest rates and the expected return from investment would exceed the cost of borrowing funds. This is in line with traditional Fed emphasis on cost and availability of credit as being prime causes of shifts in lending capacity, interest rates, and borrowing which can result in changes in the levels of employment, investment, and national income.

But the main thrust of the Keynesian position is the necessity for active fiscal policy. Government spending and taxation policies may have to be used to stimulate investment to generate employment and income if expectations are so low that the response to shifts in cost and availability of credit is negligible. Similarly, higher taxation might be warranted to soak up inflationary purchasing power that would otherwise push demand beyond full employment of the productive capability of the economy.

The monetary view holds that changes in the money supply have been closely and rather steadily related to shifts in money income, economic activity, and prices. The monetarists, therefore, place greater emphasis on regulating the money supply and criticize the effectiveness of fiscal policy. Many suspect the usefulness of discretionary policy at all—either fiscal or monetary. The theoretical groundwork for this debate is explored in Chapter 14.

SUMMARY

1 The Federal Reserve does two types of work. It provides monetary and banking services that can be done only by a central bank and it uses its regulatory powers to carry out monetary policy. Issuing paper currency and clearing checks ensure a smooth flow of currency and checks through the economy, while the regulatory functions attempt to maintain a growing economy with full employment and stable prices.

2 The regulatory powers of the Federal Reserve include both general and selective controls. The general methods include changing the reserve ratio, changing the discount rate, and performing open-market operations. By raising the reserve ratio, raising the discount rate, or selling U.S. government securities on the open market, the Fed restricts credit. By reversing the process—lowering the reserve ratio, lowering the discount rate, or buying U.S. government securities on the open market—the Fed allows for the expansion of credit.

3 The most effective general control is that of open-market operations, since it not only changes the reserve position of banks but also affects the interest rates on government securities. The discount rate, which is the interest charged on loans to member banks, is closely tied to the rates on government securities and is therefore a less flexible tool. The reserve ratio affects all member banks, so its change combined with the deposit expansion multiplier makes it a drastic tool to use.

4 The selective controls of the Fed are not nearly as important as the general ones in terms of their overall impact, but they are used to affect particular sectors of the economy rather than total credit. Selective controls include powers of setting stock market margin requirements and Regulation Q, which limits the interest that member banks may pay on time deposits.

5 Hampered by multiple tools and multiple goals, monetary policy is apparently much more effective in curbing a credit expansion than in ameliorating a contraction. It has proven much easier to make a loan too costly or money too scarce than it has to ensure borrowing. Private offsets and the ability of financial intermediaries to increase the velocity of money create problems, as do forecasting problems and time lags in policy effects. The differential effects of monetary policy create inequities. Nonetheless, monetary policy is flexible, and implemented with fewer political complications.

SUGGESTED READINGS

Chandler, Lester V. *The Economics of Money and Banking*. 5th ed. Chaps. 9–12. New York: Harper & Row, 1968.

Dean, Edwin, ed. *The Controversy over the Quantity Theory of Money*. Lexington, Mass.: D. C. Heath, 1965.

Federal Reserve System. Board of Governors. *Federal Reserve Bulletin*. Monthly articles and data on money supply and policy issues.

Hamovitch, William, ed. *Monetary Policy: The Argument from Keynes' Treatise to Friedman.* Lexington, Mass.: D. C. Heath, 1966.

Hutchinson, Harry D. *Money, Banking, and the United States Economy*. 2nd ed. Chaps. 3, 6, 7, and 15. New York: Appleton-Century-Crofts, 1971.

Mayer, Thomas. *Elements of Monetary Policy*. Chaps. 2–3. New York: Random House, 1968.

Ritter, Lawrence S., and **William L. Silber.** *Money*. 2nd ed. Chaps. 6–8 and 15–17. New York: Basic Books, 1973.

QUESTIONS

1 Review
   a. the nonregulatory and the regulatory functions of the Fed,
   b. the structure of the Federal Reserve System,
   c. the major tools available to the Fed for affecting the money supply,
   d. tools available to the Fed for affecting specific sectors of the economy.

2 Among the functions the Fed performs for its member banks is the printing and distribution of as much cash as the member banks request. Why would the Fed be willing to undertake such a policy with respect to cash?

3 How is the Federal Reserve System organized? What was the appeal of district banks as opposed to one central bank? Describe the Board of Governors, the Federal Open Market Committee, the Federal Advisory Council. Which of the Federal Reserve Banks carries out open-market operations?

4 Assume that the Federal Open Market Committee decides to sell Treasury bonds in the amount of $1 billion. Assume that these bonds are purchased by individuals who pay for the bonds by writing checks. If the reserve requirement is 20 percent, what is the potential effect on the money supply?

5 What are the three types of general controls available to the Fed? What effects do these controls have on the money supply during periods of tight money policy? During periods of easy money policy? How may the effectiveness of these controls differ in the case of contraction and expansion?

6 Under what conditions would the Fed be most likely to change the reserve requirement of member banks? Why is the Fed at present unlikely to raise the reserve requirement by a large amount? Assume that the Fed notes that the banking system has a large quantity of excess reserves and raises the reserve requirement from 20 to 25 percent. If the original required reserves were $200 million and the excess reserves were $50 million, how much money expansion potential did the Fed eliminate?

7 Suppose that the Federal Reserve Board believes for some reason that there has been overspeculation in the stock market. What policy might the Fed follow? Suppose that the construction industry has experienced a rapid decline in activity during a period of tight money. The Federal Reserve Board wishes to provide some relief to the industry. How can it do so?

8 Why does the Fed tend to favor open-market operations as a tool of monetary policy? Trace the transactions throughout the banking system from a purchase of a $1000 bond from a member bank. Does the first transaction create money?

Why or why not? What happens if the Fed buys a bond from an individual and the individual puts the cash in his home safe?

9 What is the interest rate on a bond selling for $1000 that has a $40 per year yield? Suppose that in order to sell more of these bonds, the Fed lowers the price to $800. What is the new interest rate? How does this new rate change the opportunity costs of investing in bonds? What might be the effect on investment? How does the change in interest rates affect the cost of the public debt?

10 What is the discount rate? Why must it be closely related to the rates on short-term securities? Why is it considered to be a weather vane of Fed policy?

11 How do the multiple goals of the Fed contribute to the difficulty in managing the money supply? In the case of full employment and price stability? In the 1930s, the Fed faced a special problem because it needed to follow an expansionary domestic policy but was also facing the problem of large amounts of dollars being converted into gold, both by foreigners and Americans. How might these policies conflict?

12 Some economists believe that it is difficult not only to encourage expansion but also to discourage expansion once well underway. They point out that the key factor is the expectations of business executives and bankers. If, because of a rapid rise in optimism brought on by a boom, business executives and bankers expect a rosy future with high investment returns, what effect would there be on their willingness to pay high prices for money? Is there anything that the Fed can do about expectations? What if it uses the discount rate? Moral suasion?

CHAPTER 14
SYNTHESIS

The preceding chapters have presented two different approaches to regulating the level of economic activity. Chapters 8, 9, and 10 discussed national income analysis, explaining how changes in aggregate demand affect the level of NNP. Government, it was shown, can affect NNP—directly through changes in its expenditures, or indirectly, through its taxation policies. Then, in Chapters 11, 12, and 13, we explored monetary policy, showing how the Federal Reserve, through changes in the money supply, can also influence the level of economic activity. Now we shall attempt to integrate these two approaches. More specifically, we shall construct a single model enabling us to locate the conditions under which all the macroeconomic variables we have talked about so far will be in equilibrium. This model is admittedly a complex one; but if essentially understood, it offers an extremely valuable tool for analyzing the effectiveness of various monetary and fiscal measures.

A FIRST LOOK AT THE SYNTHESIS

A good starting point is to consider the question: How do changes in the money supply interact with changes in aggregate demand to determine the level of national income and employment? Our analysis in Chapter 13 indicated a close cause-and-effect relationship between these two variables. This relationship can be summarized by tracing the chain of events following a change in the money supply. Assume, for example, that the Federal Reserve decides to increase M. The initial effect will be a decline in interest rates (i), which will encourage businesses and households to borrow more for investment spending (I). A higher level of investment will then lead to an expanded level of aggregate demand (C+G+I), and this, in turn, will result in a multiplied increase in the equilibrium level of national income and product. Schematically, the sequence can be shown as follows:

$$\text{Increase in M} \rightarrow \text{decline in i} \rightarrow \text{increase in I} \rightarrow$$
$$\text{increase in } (C+G+I) \xrightarrow[\text{multiplier}]{} \text{increase in NI or NNP}$$

Opening photo from The Museum of Modern Art/Film Stills Archive

The reverse will occur if the Fed decides to contract the supply of money. A decrease in M will generally lead to an increase in interest rates, a decline in investment spending and aggregate demand, and through the action of the multiplier, to an even larger decline in national income and product.

$$\text{Decline in M} \rightarrow \text{increase in i} \rightarrow \text{decline in I} \rightarrow$$
$$\text{decline in } (C+G+I) \xrightarrow[\text{multiplier}]{} \text{decline in NI or NNP}$$

This is the overall framework within which our synthesis of monetary analysis and income analysis will be developed. It is composed of three steps in a chain of events:

1 Changes in the money supply tend to result in changes in interest rates.
2 Changes in interest rates tend to result in changes in investment spending.
3 Changes in investment spending tend to result in changes in aggregate demand and, through the impact of the multiplier, in even greater changes in national income.

The three-step chain can also take account of changes in consumption or government spending as a refinement of step 3 or feedback from national income to investment through the accelerator, but for the moment, let us briefly review the basic reasoning behind each of these three steps.

The Relationship Between the Money Supply and Interest Rates

Step 1 states that changes in the money supply generally lead to changes in interest rates. More specifically, we know that there is an inverse relationship between changes in M and changes in i: If the money supply is increased, interest rates will be forced downward; if the money supply is cut back, interest rates will rise. In Chapter 13, we saw how changes in the money supply are introduced. To increase excess reserves, the Federal Reserve may lower reserve requirements, reduce the discount rate, or, more commonly, increase its purchases of government bonds in the open market. Once the banking system finds itself with excess reserves, it will attempt to increase loans by offering better terms to prospective borrowers, including lower interest rates. The reverse will occur when the Fed acts to contract the money supply by reducing member bank reserves. Finding themselves with lower, or possibly even deficit reserves, commercial banks will be forced to cut back the rate at which loans are made and this, in turn, will drive interest rates up.

A Further Refinement: The Demands for Money

There are, however, certain limits on the extent to which interest rates will respond to changes in the money supply. The key to understanding these limits lies in the distinction between the various demands for money.

THE TRANSACTIONS DEMAND FOR MONEY People desire to hold money for different purposes. One of these purposes is the need for transactions balances. Both individuals and businesses need to have some money on hand, in cash or as balances in checking accounts, to meet their day-to-day expenses—paying the rent, the telephone bill, weekly salaries. It is not surprising that the amount of money required to satisfy this transactions demand is closely related to the level of national income. When national income is high, businesses and families make more purchases and therefore need more money on hand to cover their daily expenses. This is another way of saying that the transactions demand for money increases as NNP rises.

THE SPECULATIVE DEMAND FOR MONEY There is another purpose for holding money, however, that is not linked to the level of national income at all. This is the speculative demand for money—the amount of money that is held in cash balances awaiting more favorable conditions in the securities market. The speculative demand for money, then, is tied to expectations about the level of interest rates—the rate of return a money holder can expect from the purchase of bonds. When securities prices are high (which means that interest rates are low), households and businesses will be likely to hold money in cash balances waiting for bond prices to fall. Conversely, when security prices are low (interest rates are high), buyers will be eager to switch their holdings from cash balances to securities. Under normal circumstances, then, the speculative demand for money varies inversely with interest rates: At a 3 percent rate of interest a family might be willing to keep $1000 in the form of noninterest-earning cash, while at 6 percent, it might decide to put some of this money into securities instead.

Thus, there are really two purposes for which people demand money: transactions and speculative purposes. Only one of these demands for money—the speculative demand—is linked to the level of interest rates; the other demand for money—the transactions demand—is instead linked to the level of national income. Consequently, the full effect of any increase in M will not be reflected exclusively in a decline in interest rates. Instead, part of an increase in M will be absorbed into the higher transaction balances that will accompany the increase in national income resulting from the initial increase in M.

The Limits of Monetary Policy: The Liquidity Trap

Like most generalizations, the statement that increases in the supply of money will cause interest rates to fall does not hold true all of the time. When interest rates are already extremely low, increases in the money supply may be unable to budge them further. The reason is that at very low rates of interest, the prospect of buying bonds is extremely unattractive to speculators. Consequently, no matter how large an increase in the money supply is introduced, all of that increase will be held in cash balances rather than being used to purchase securities. And if the public persists in holding all of its money as idle cash, further injections of money will simply have no effect on interest rates.

The preference for cash balances over securities at very low rates of interest is encouraged by the general air of fear and pessimism that prevails during a severe depression. People with money are simply not interested in lending it, and even if they were, willing borrowers would be difficult to find.

The unresponsiveness of i to changes in M at very

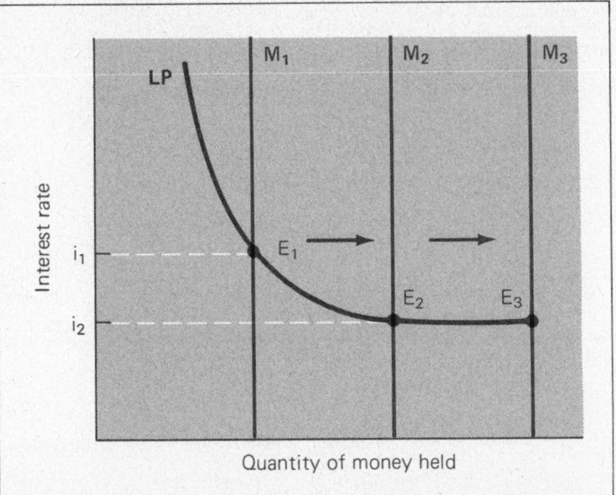

FIGURE 14-1 THE LIQUIDITY PREFERENCE CURVE The liquidity preference curve shows that at lower interest rates, people have a growing preference for liquidity. Rather than accept low interest rates for their funds, they would rather hold money, or, in technical terms, retain their liquidity. The equilibrium level of interest is set by the intersection of the LP and money supply curves. Generally, as the money supply is increased (from M_1 to M_2 to M_3), the interest rate will decline (from i_1 to i_2). However, when the interest rate i_2 is reached, people will forgo interest in exchange for liquidity. At that point (the intersection of i_2 and M_2), the economy has entered the liquidity trap; the LP line is perfectly horizontal.

low rates of interest is illustrated in the accompanying graph (Figure 14-1). The downward-sloping curve is called a **liquidity preference curve** because it shows the speculative demand for money, or liquidity, at various interest rates. The vertical line M represents the supply of money, a quantity set by the Federal Reserve. The point of intersection of the two lines locates the market rate of interest.

Now suppose that the money supply is increased, shifting the money supply line from M_1 to M_2. Such a shift will be accompanied by a decline in interest rates from i_1 to i_2. This is because the increase in M leaves the public with more money than it is willing to hold at the current interest rate of i_1. Therefore, speculators purchase securities, driving the price of bonds up and the interest rate down.

The important point to note, however, is that below a certain very low rate of interest, the liquidity preference curve becomes perfectly flat. This flat portion of the curve is known as the **liquidity trap.** At this rate of interest any increases in the money supply (from M_2 to M_3, for example) will merely be accumulated in larger and larger cash balances, and will therefore have no effect on interest rates. The policy significance of the liquidity trap is that it represents a limit to the effectiveness of monetary policy during a depression. Once the liquidity trap area of interest rates is reached, an expansionary monetary policy can have no further effect on interest rates or on investment spending.

The Relationships Between Interest Rates and Investment

To understand step 2, the link between interest rates and investment spending, it is essential to remember that we are looking at investment from the point of view of the borrower—that is, we are talking about *capital* investment rather than *financial* investment. Financial investment is investment from the point of view of the lender of financial capital. It occurs when a household or business purchases a bond or deposits money in a savings bank. Obviously, financial investments are encouraged by high interest rates; the higher the interest rate, the higher the return, and therefore the more attractive the investment will appear.

Capital investment, on the other hand, involves a decision by a business (or a prospective homeowner) to borrow funds in order to purchase a new machine, build a new factory, or buy a new house. Unlike financial investment, business investment is encouraged by lower interest rates. To a prospective borrower contemplating a business investment, interest is a cost. As we learned in Chapter 8, if a business must pay 7 percent a year on a loan of $10,000 to buy a new drill press, its interest cost in one year will be $700; if it can borrow at 5 percent, its interest cost in the first year will be only $500. Suppose that the new drill press wears out after a single year, but the business has earned net revenue of $650 as a result of its investment. By dividing this figure by the cost of

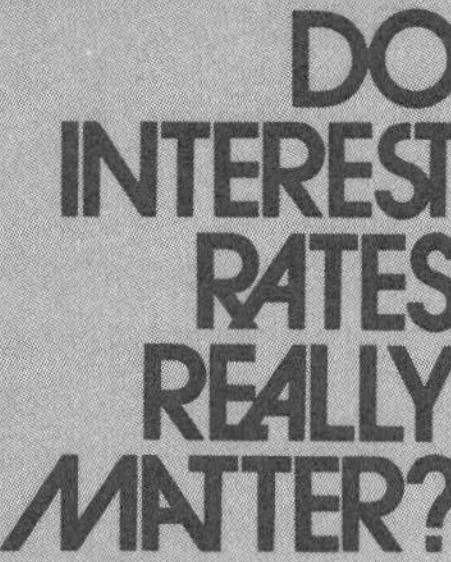

Few people would argue that the level of interest rates has no effect on the level of investment spending. But there is much debate among economists over how responsive investment spending really is to changes in i.

Clearly, the proportion of investment funds that comes from accumulated profits rather than borrowing will affect the sensitivity of investment spending to the level of interest rates. And investment from past earnings often accounts for a sizable percentage of investment spending. In 1955, 1956, and 1957, for example, internal financing accounted for 93, 81, and 88 percent, respectively, of total plant and equipment outlays. It appears that the size of a business firm influences its ability to internally finance investment spending. Large corporations, which produce most of the output in our economy, are in a better position to finance investments with accumulated profits. For example, for over 100 years, the Great Atlantic and Pacific Tea Company managed to meet most of its investment needs with retained earnings rather than from outside borrowing. In such cases, investment spending may be highly unresponsive to changes in interest rates. A company with enough accumulated earning to finance new expansion programs will not modify its investment spending plans much as interest rates rise or fall.

Some authorities also believe that even investment financed through borrowing is often relatively unresponsive to changes in interest rates. Under conditions of great optimism, when business executives believe that profit opportunities are great, investment projects will often be pursued, despite a 1 or 2 or 3 percent increase in interest rates. This was the general experience in 1969, for example. It is also possible that other considerations—such as the fear of losing a competitive advantage or a conviction that substantial inflation is imminent—may also encourage businesses to proceed with investment spending regardless of rising interest rates.

On the other hand, there are some circumstances under which investment spending may be very responsive to changes in the interest rate. This is the case in the housing industry, for example. In 1966, when interest rates rose sharply, new housing starts dropped by over 20 percent. In 1967, when interest rates began to decline, the housing industry picked up rapidly.

the investment ($10,000), we can calculate its expected rate of return to be 6.5 percent. At a 5 percent interest rate, the net revenue the firm will earn from the new drill press ($650) exceeds the one-year interest cost ($500); the investment, therefore, will be profitable. If, however, the interest rate were 7 percent, interest charges ($700) would exceed net revenue ($650), and the investment would be unprofitable.

From this we can generalize to say that whenever the expected rate of return on an investment is higher than the market rate of interest, businesses will be encouraged to make the investment. Conversely, whenever the expected rate of return is less than the interest rate, businesses will be discouraged from undertaking that particular investment project. This holds true regardless of whether the business is borrowing to invest, or investing money accumulated from past profits. This is because the interest rate is the opportunity cost of investment spending—the amount of money the firm is forgoing by not making a *financial* investment with its available funds. Consequently, even if a firm uses its own funds for investment, it must calculate the market rate of interest as an implicit cost of the investment project.

To some extent, then, investment will be responsive to changes in the interest rate. Because lower interest rates mean that an increasing number of possible investment projects will be evaluated as profitable, they will encourage borrowing and investment spending. Conversely, higher interest rates mean that the interest cost will exceed the expected rate of return on many proposed investments; therefore, borrowing and investment spending will decline.

The relationship between interest rates and investment spending can be illustrated graphically. Figure 14-2 shows the amount of investment that businesses will undertake at various interest rates. Total investment will equal $160 billion if the market rate of interest is 5 percent; as interest rates decline, additional projects become profitable and additional borrowing and investment spending occur. At a 4 percent rate of interest, for example, total investment spending will equal $180 billion.

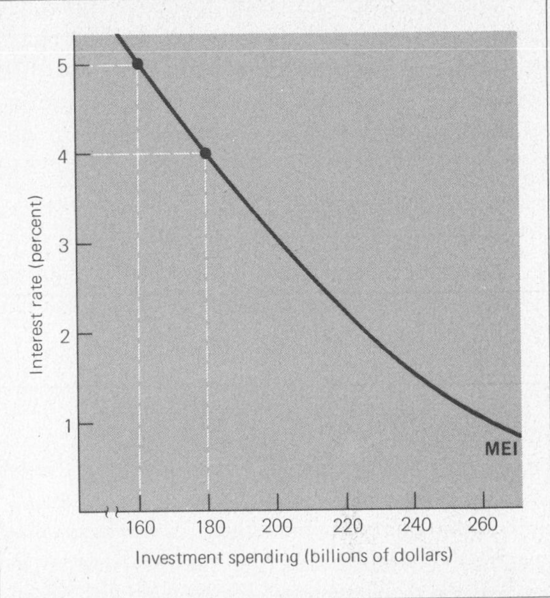

FIGURE 14-2 THE MARGINAL EFFICIENCY OF INVESTMENT **The MEI, or expected profit rate, like the LP curve, slopes downward to the right. At declining interest rates, business executives are increasingly eager to invest borrowed funds or their own retained earnings. That is so because the cost of those funds, measured by the interest, is declining. As can be seen here, at an interest rate of 5 percent, investment is only $160 billion, but at 4 percent, $180 billion is invested.**

Figure 14-2 is called an **investment demand schedule** because it shows the changes in investment demand (or investment spending) that occur with changes in interest rates. It is also called a **marginal efficiency of investment curve,** since for every level of investment it shows the expected rate of return on the last dollar spent.

The Relationship Between Investment and NNP

Now that we have explored the links between the money supply and interest rates, and interest rates and investment spending, the final step in our analysis is quite familiar. The relationship between investment spending and national income was fully discussed in Chapter 8. Because investment spending is a component of aggregate demand, a change in I will cause a corresponding change in aggregate demand, and ultimately, because of the effect of the multiplier, an even greater change in NI or NNP. Increases in investment, of course, will lead to increases in NNP; decreases in investment, to decreases in NNP.

The relationship between changes in I and changes in NNP can be shown graphically, as in Figure 14-3. As investment rises, a higher level of NNP is required to call forth the increased level of saving needed to meet the equilibrium condition S=I.

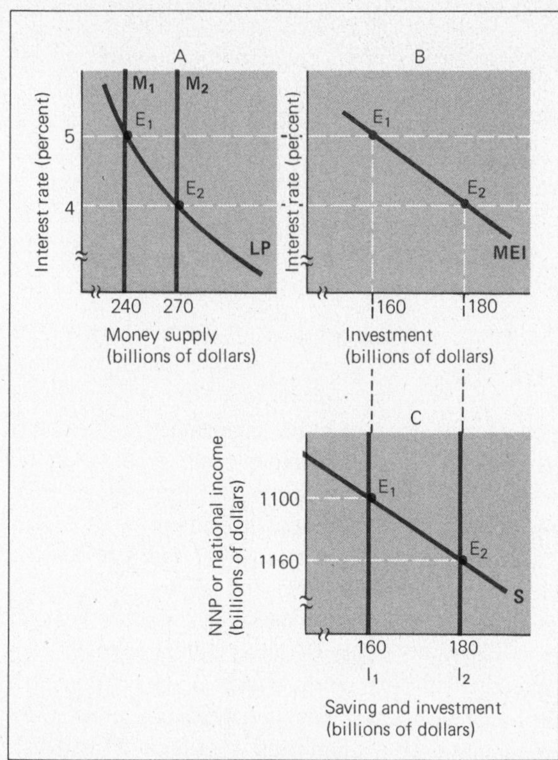

FIGURE 14-4 TRACING THE EFFECT OF MONEY ON THE ECONOMY A change in the money supply, pictured in A, has the effect of lowering the interest rate from 5 percent to 4 percent. This decline stimulates investment spending by $20 billion, as shown in B. The addition to aggregate demand raises the level of NNP, not just by $20 billion, but by $60 billion, as can be seen in C. Trace the effects of a tight-money policy on the economy using this series of graphs.

Recapitulation

Having outlined the three steps in the link between changes in the money supply and changes in national income and output, we can briefly review these steps graphically. Assume that the Federal Reserve increases the money supply by $30 billion—from $240 billion to $270 billion. The first result, as seen in Figure 14-4A, is a decline in the interest rate from 5 percent to 4 percent. This drop in the interest rate in turn affects the amount of investment spending, as shown in Figure 14-4B; investment spending, which stood at $160 billion when the interest rate was 5 percent, rises to $180 billion at a 4 percent rate. Finally, the result of this increase in investment spending is illustrated in Figure 14-4C, where an increase of $20 billion in investment spending, subject to a multiplier of 3, raises net national product by $60 billion—from $1100 billion to $1160 billion.

Figure 14-4 summarizes the impact of an increase in the money supply on national income and product. A decrease in the money supply, of course, would have exactly the reverse effect.

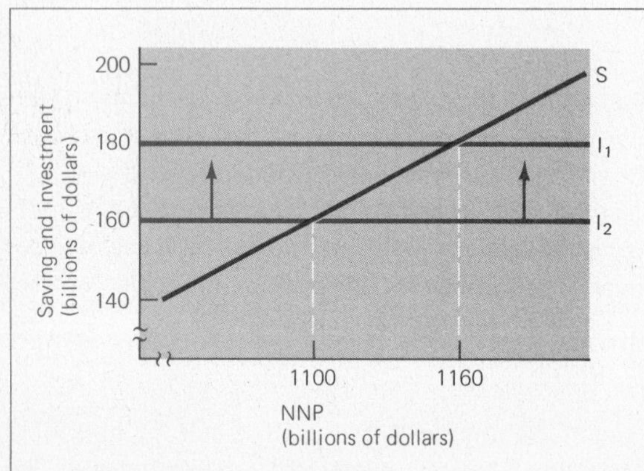

FIGURE 14-3 SAVING, INVESTMENT, AND NNP A higher investment schedule (I_2) will yield a higher NNP than will a lower one (I_1). The difference in the level also depends upon the saving schedule, shown here as S. Obviously, a steeper S schedule would result in a smaller increase in NNP. Note that if investment rose from I_1 to I_2, saving and investment would remain equal with an increase in NNP to produce an increase in the amount saved.

A FURTHER LOOK AT THE SYNTHESIS

In the preceding section we used three steps with three separate graphs to trace the relationship between changes in the money supply and changes in national income. Now we shall integrate the variables —saving and investment, demand for money and supply of money—even further by constructing a model that links changes in interest rates directly to changes in national income in a single graph of two curves.

The IS Curve

The Shape of the IS Curve In the discussion of income analysis in Chapter 8, the equilibrium level of national output was defined as that level where aggregate demand equals aggregate supply, or where intended saving equals intended investment (S = I). In that model we assumed that saving varied with the level of national income but that investment did not. In assuming a fixed level of investment, we were implicitly assuming that the interest rate remained constant. Since that earlier analysis, however, we have become more sophisticated. We now know that interest rates do indeed vary and that the level of investment spending varies inversely with the rate of interest. Therefore, in order to find the equilibrium level S = I, we must deal with two sets of variables: a saving total that varies with the level of national income and an investment total that varies with the level of interest rates. No longer can we take I as constant and merely search for that level of NI that provides saving equal to investment; instead, we must recognize that the equilibrium level of national income (where saving equals investment) will differ for different interest rates.

A few examples will clarify this point. Assume that the interest rate is 5 percent and that investment spending equals $160 billion for a given MEI. Equilibrium in this economy will exist at the level of national income where S equals $160 billion, which, let us assume, is $1100 billion. Should the interest rate drop to 4 percent, however, investment spending would increase to $180 billion, and a new equilibrium point would be established at a higher level of national income, $1160 billion, where saving would equal the required $180 billion. To generalize, we can say that at any level of interest rates (i), there will be only one level of income where I = S. Therefore, the equilibrium level of national income will change with changes in the interest rate.

This relationship between changes in the interest rate and changes in the equilibrium level of national income is shown graphically in Figure 14-5. This curve is called an IS (investment/saving) curve. Each point on the IS curve represents the equilibrium level of national income at a given interest rate. Point A shows that national income would settle at $1100 billion at an interest rate of 5 percent; point B shows that national income would settle at $1160 billion with the interest rate at 4 percent; and so on. Note that declines in the interest rate lead to increases in national income. The chain of causation is clear: At lower

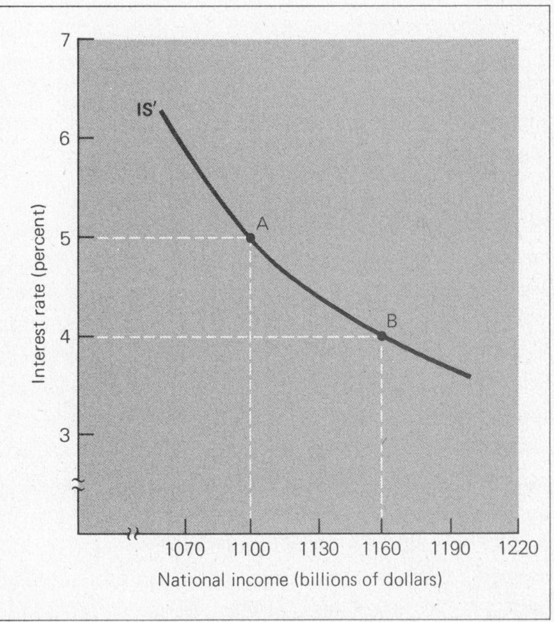

FIGURE 14-5 THE IS CURVE For any given rate of interest, there is only one level of national income at which saving equals investment. The IS curve plots this relationship. Implicit in this graph is a given relationship between i and I, reflected in the MEI curve. If this changes, then a new curve must be drawn. The IS curve shows that lowering the interest rate increases the level of national income.

interest rates, investment spending increases. As a result, a larger amount of saving is necessary in order to keep S equal to I, and it is only under conditions of higher national income that sufficient saving will be generated to meet this requirement. Conversely, higher interest rates will depress investment spending, and lower levels of national income and saving will be required to achieve the I=S equilibrium point.

The IS curve generally slopes downward and to the right, signifying that national income increases as interest rates decline. The steepness of the curve, however, will vary depending upon the extent to which investment is responsive to changes in the interest rate. If investment is relatively unaffected by changes in the interest rate, the IS curve will be very steep—almost vertical. If investment is very responsive to changes in i, the IS curve will be quite flat. Although the responsiveness of investment spending to changes in the interest rate is a much debated topic, we can assume that there is some interrelationship between the two variables. The IS curve, then, is a graphic representation of equilibrium in the product market: It indicates all the levels of national income and interest rates at which investment and saving will be equal.

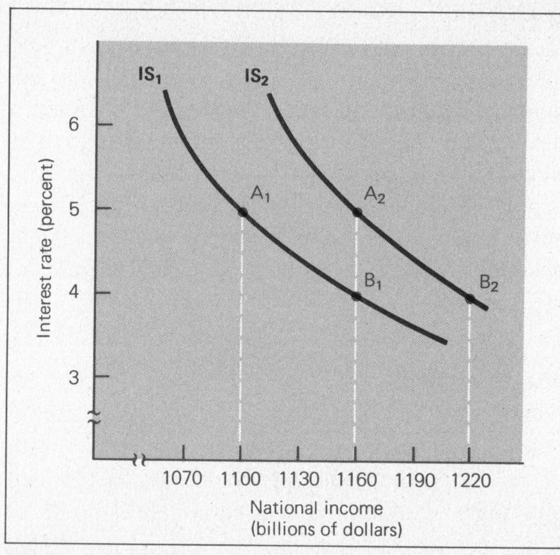

FIGURE 14-6 EFFECT OF CHANGES IN NONINVESTMENT COMPONENT OF AGGREGATE DEMAND ON THE IS CURVE **Although investment is the most volatile sector of aggregate demand, the other two sectors, consumption and government spending, may also change. Such changes can occur independently of changes in the rate of interest. Therefore, any changes in national income that result from changes in C or G may not necessarily be ascribed to a change in interest, and a new IS curve must be drawn. The effect of a $20 billion rise in G is a shift of the IS schedule from IS_1 to IS_2. This $20 billion increase in G would result in a $60 billion rise in national income.**

Shifting the IS Curve The IS curve shows how national income responds to changes in the investment component of aggregate demand initiated through changes in interest rates. This corresponds to a given responsiveness of investment to the interest rate. If this relationship changes, then the curve will also shift. But it is also possible that the other components of aggregate demand may change: Consumption spending may increase as a result of a wave of consumer optimism or a tax cut; government spending may rise or fall as a result of conscious changes in government fiscal policy. Because these increases or decreases in C or G can occur independently of any changes in interest rates, the resulting changes in NI cannot necessarily be ascribed to a change in interest rates.

Assume, for example, an IS curve where an interest rate of 5 percent produces an equilibrium NI of $1100 billion and an interest rate of 4 percent leads to an equilibrium NI of $1160 billion (see points A_1 and B_1 in Figure 14-6). If we introduce an additional $20 billion of G into this economy, the result (assuming a multiplier of 3) will be an increase of $60 billion in NI at every interest rate level. In other words, if the interest rate is at 5 percent, NI will settle at $1160 billion (point A_2) rather than $1100 billion, and if the interest rate is at 4 percent, NI will move to $1220 billion (point B_2) rather than $1160 billion. This means that any change in the noninvestment components of aggregate demand will shift the entire IS curve upward or downward. Increases in C or G will shift the IS curve higher, so that NI will be reached at higher levels for every interest rate; decreases in C or G will have the reverse effect.

The Importance of Fiscal Policy The ability of the noninvestment components of aggregate demand (which operate independently of changes in interest rates) to affect the IS curve has interesting implications for the use of fiscal policy. Looking at any single IS curve, one might conclude that monetary measures taken to increase or decrease interest rates are the obvious vehicles through which changes in national income can be effected. But when we recognize the possibility of shifting the entire IS curve through changes in C or G, the advantages of fiscal policy become more evident. Figure 14-6 shows that there are two alternative methods of increasing national income from $1100 to $1160: Either pursuing an expansionary monetary policy that will cut the interest rate from 5 percent to 4 percent (which means a movement *along* the IS curve), or cutting taxes or raising government spending so that C or G increases by $20 billion (which shifts the curve). The final result—an increase of $60 billion in national income—will be the same by either route; Figure 14-6 merely reminds us that we have a choice of tools.

The LM Curve

The Shape of the LM Curve The IS curve indicates the levels of national income at which the economy will settle at different interest rates. To the degree that interest rates are affected by the supply of money, the IS curve shows the relationship between changes in M and changes in NI.

There is, however, another way of exploring how the quantity of money, interest rates, and national income interact. We have seen how the speculative demand for M (that is, the amounts of money people are willing to hold in cash balances rather than putting it in interest-earning assets) is inversely related to interest rates: Higher interest rates mean a lower speculative demand for money, whereas lower rates encourage people to hold their money in cash balances. For example, a family earning $15,000 a year may have a demand for money of $500 if interest rates are at 6 percent, and a demand of $1000 if interest rates are 3 percent. At the same time, however, we pointed out that interest rates are not the only determinant of the total demand for money; there is also a transaction demand for money which changes with national income. Consequently, should a family's income increase from $15,000 to $20,000, its demand for money may increase from $500 to $1000, even if interest rates remain constant.

This example illustrates how the demand for money in a single household fluctuates not only with interest rates, but also with income. The same relationship also applies to the economy as a whole. Given a fixed supply of money, there is a variety of combinations of interest rates and national income where the demand for money will equal the supply of money. Figure 14-7, for example, shows that at a national

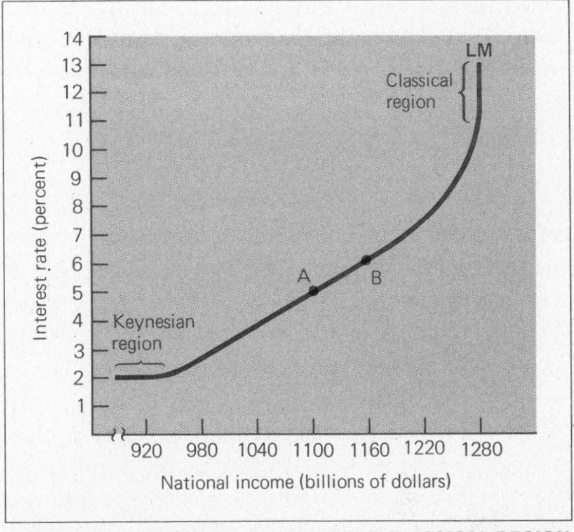

FIGURE 14-7 LM CURVE, SHOWING THE CLASSICAL REGION AND LIQUIDITY TRAP **If there is a fixed money supply established by the Fed, there is only one level of national income for every level of interest where the demand for money (L) equals the supply of money (M). The various combinations of national income and interest where this monetary equilibrium is achieved is shown by the LM curve. The LM curve slopes upward and to the right, reflecting the fact that at higher levels of national income, there is a growing demand for money which results in higher rates of interest. The classical region of the LM curve at the extreme upper right indicates that national income will remain fixed when the economy has reached the point of full employment. Any attempt to raise national income will only result in higher interest rates. In the Keynesian region, attempts to raise national income are thwarted by the low interest rates that induce people to hang onto their funds.**

income level of $1100 billion and an interest rate of 5 percent, a money supply of $200 billion will be sufficient to meet the economy's demand for money. However, if national income should increase to $1160 billion, the quantity of money demanded for transaction purposes would increase, so that a rise in interest rates to 6 percent would be required to reduce speculative balances to such a level that the existing $200 billion money supply would be adequate. In other words, assuming a fixed money supply established by the Federal Reserve, there is only one level of national income for every level of i where the demand for money (L) equals the supply of money (M). The LM curve represents the various combinations of NI and i where this monetary equilibrium is achieved.

Figure 14-7 illustrates a typical LM curve. Note that in the middle range interest rates rise as income rises, indicating that higher incomes create a higher transaction demand for money, a demand that can only be met by lowering speculative money balances by an increase in interest rates.

THE KEYNESIAN LIQUIDITY TRAP REGION But the shape of the entire LM curve is more complex than this basic analysis would suggest. The Keynesians call our attention to the special behavior of the LM curve at very low interest rates. In general, given a fixed money supply, any decline in income is accompanied by a decline in interest rates. If you cannot recall why this is so, refer to the discussion of the liquidity preference curve on p. 276. During a severe depression, when interest rates reach 1 or 2 percent, people will prefer to hold their money in idle cash balances rather than to invest in securities. As a result, when the LM curve hits the low interest rate range, it becomes a straight horizontal line, indicating that interest rates cannot be driven any lower. (See Figure 14-7.) Over this range of the curve, declines in national income are no longer accompanied by declines in interest rates. This flat area of the LM curve represents the liquidity trap.

THE CLASSICAL REGION The LM curve also has an unusual shape at its right-hand extreme. At the full-employment level of national income, further increases in output are impossible. Consequently, the LM curve becomes vertical, indicating that NI will remain fixed. Any attempt to increase NI will only drive interest rates higher. This vertical area of the LM curve is called the classical region because the classical economists believed that equilibrium usually occurs at full employment and that increasing the supply of money only results in inflation, unless the capacity of the economy has grown.

Equilibrium

The IS curve shows the possible levels of NI and i that may meet the equilibrium requirement in the product market: Saving (S) equals investment (I). The LM curve shows the possible levels in NI and i that will meet the equilibrium requirement in the money market: The supply of money (M) equals the demand for money (L). If we plot both curves on the same graph, we can now locate the single level of NI and i where both sets of requirements are fulfilled—that is, where the supply and demand for NNP as well as the supply and demand for money are in equilibrium. Figure 14-8 illustrates this condition. The IS and LM curves intersect at an interest rate of 5 percent and a national income level of $1100 billion; at this point, the economy will be in complete equilibrium.

By combining these two curves on a single graph, what we have, in effect, is a simplified model of an economy. All the multitude of changes we have been studying since Chapter 8 are here before us in a relatively simple form. What we also see is that the many variables affect one another, that the analysis in Chapters 8, 9, and 10—embodied in the IS curve—is incomplete without the analysis in Chapters 11, 12, and 13, embodied in the LM curve. The two curves are ways of sorting out a number of changes that occur simultaneously. A shift in the IS curve causes a movement along the LM curve; the resulting changes in interest rates and national income are an outgrowth of interacting events in the product market *and* the money market.

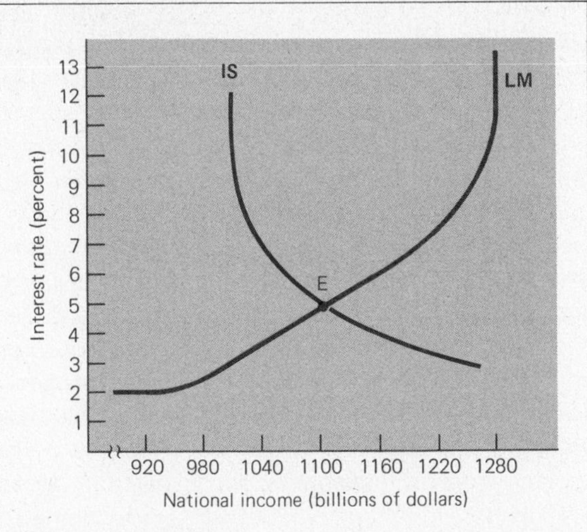

FIGURE 14-8 EQUILIBRIUM Together the IS and LM curves provide a simplified model of an economy. The IS curve shows the possible levels of NI and i that will meet the equilibrium requirement in the product market; the LM curve shows the possible levels of NI and i that will meet the equilibrium requirement in the money market. In the product market, saving equals investment; in the money market, the supply of money equals the demand for money. The intersection of the two curves indicates the single level of NI and i where both sets of equilibrium requirements are fulfilled. IS and LM intersect at 5 percent interest and $1100 billion national income.

POLICIES AT WORK: GETTING AN ECONOMY MOVING

Having established the model of the IS and LM curves and having identified the general equilibrium point at which an economy will settle, how can we use this approach to develop full-employment policies? In this section, we shall explore the use of monetary policy to shift the LM curve and fiscal policy to shift the IS curve as two methods of stimulating a declining economy.

Monetary Policy

Monetary Policy during a Recession Increasing the money supply is often suggested as an effective way of increasing economic activity during a recession. Such an increase will result in a shift in the entire LM curve. This shift is illustrated in Figure 14-9. Curve LM_1 represents the possible levels of i and NI with a money supply of $200 billion; curve LM_2 shows the possible levels of i and NI with a money supply of $240 billion. The important point to note is that LM_2 intersects the IS curve at a new equilibrium point; as a result of the increase in M, this economy will now operate at a higher level of national income ($1160 billion rather than $1100 billion) and with lower interest rates (4 percent rather than 5 percent).

The impact of an increase in the money supply, then, is a drop in interest rates, which stimulates a higher level of investment spending and ultimately a rise in the level of national income, since a higher NI is now necessary to provide saving for new investment. This chain of events indicates that monetary policy

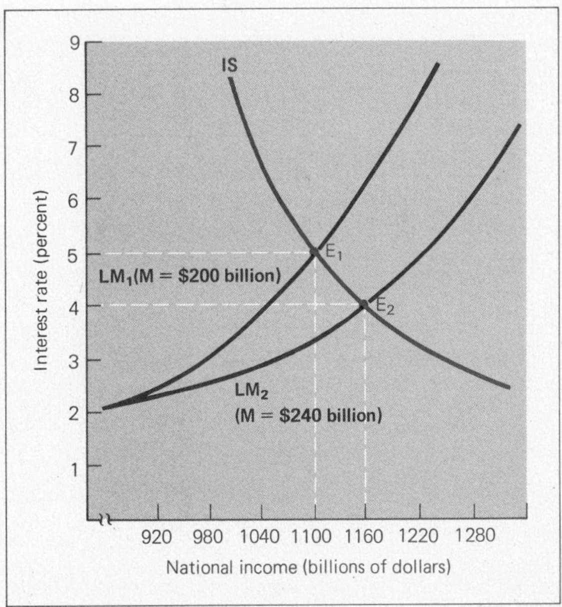

FIGURE 14-9 USING MONETARY POLICY Curve LM_1 represents the possible levels of i and NI with an M of $200 billion; curve LM_2 shows the possible levels of i and NI with an M of $240 billion. As the Fed increases the money supply, there is a shift from LM_1 to LM_2. What will result from an increase in the money supply is a lower interest rate (5 percent down to 4 percent) and a consequent rise in investment and national income.

can be effective in stimulating a stagnant economy, and this is exactly what the Federal Reserve attempts to do during a recession. Early in 1971, for example, following a year of falling industrial production and rising unemployment, the Fed boldly increased the supply of money at an almost unprecedented 11.4 percent annual rate. It is perhaps inaccurate to attribute the entire recovery that ensued to this monetary stimulation, since expansionary fiscal measures were also at work. Nevertheless, the pickup in such economic indicators as production, employment, retail sales, and personal income that occurred later in 1971 and in 1972 does appear to be related, at least in part, to this rapid and sizable increase in the money supply.

Monetary Policy during a Severe Depression Yet despite successes with the use of monetary policy, there are circumstances under which shifts in the LM curve stimulated by an increase in the money supply will be ineffective in raising national income. This is the case during a severe depression. Under depressed economic conditions the IS curve will intersect the LM curve within the area of the liquidity trap. When interest rates have dropped this low, an increase in M will have no effect on the level of the the LM curve. Consequently, there will be no change in the point at which the IS and LM curves intersect. (See Figure 14-10A.) This is because interest rates during a depression are so low that increases in the money supply will simply be accumulated in larger

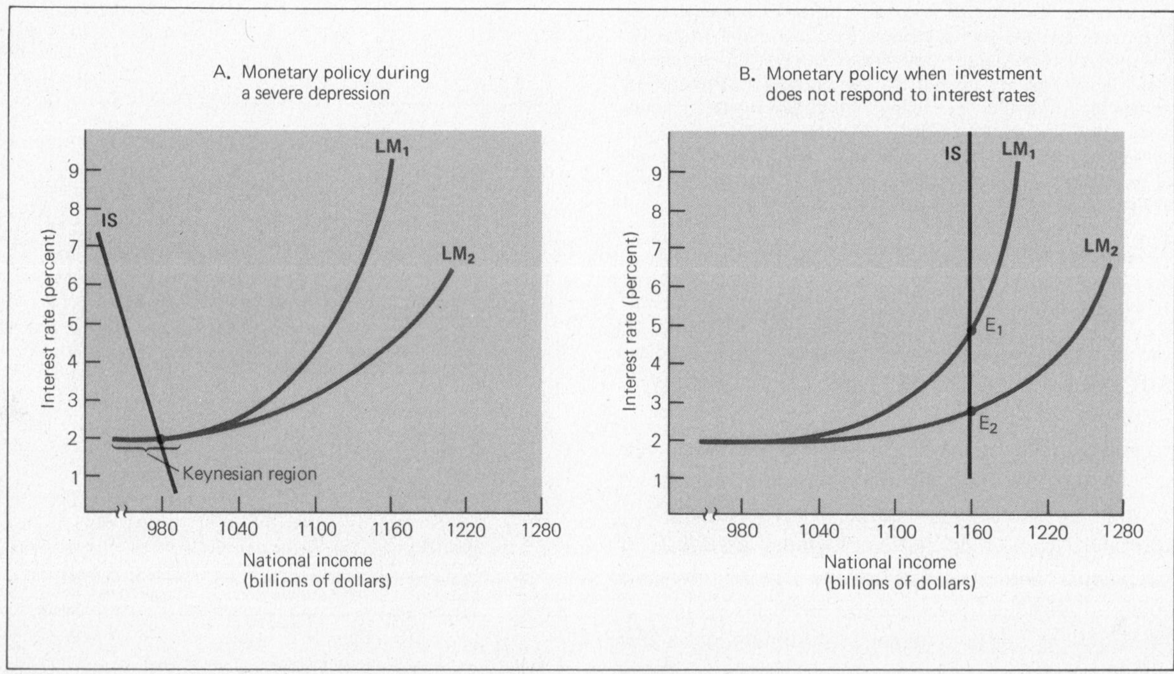

FIGURE 14-10 CONDITIONS WHEN MONETARY POLICY MAY NOT WORK An increase in the money supply is the policy prescription to cure a depression. If that depression is severe, this policy may have little effect, for when an economy is caught in the liquidity trap (as in A), people would rather hold their money than lend it out at very low interest rates, and a rise in the money supply would have little effect on interest rates, investment, and national income. This can be seen here. A change in M has no effect on the level of the LM curve, so that the LM and IS curves continue to intersect at the same equilibrium level of NI. Monetary policy will prove equally ineffective when the level of investment does not change in response to a change in the rate of interest, as in B. If business executives continue to be pessimistic about profit prospects, for example, they will not increase the level of investment, even if interest rates decline substantially. This condition is represented by a vertical IS curve, as in B.

and larger cash balances. The result is a stationary interest rate and stagnant levels of investment and income. The phenomenon of the liquidity trap was observed by Keynes during the Great Depression of the 1930s. From 1933 to 1936, the money supply in the United States increased by almost 50 percent. At first, there was some decline in interest rates, but following this initial decline, despite continued substantial increases in the money supply, it did not drop any lower.

Monetary Policy When Investment Does Not Respond to Interest Rates Another situation in which monetary policy will prove ineffective in raising the level of national income occurs when investment spending is unresponsive to changes in interest rates. Such a situation would be depicted by a vertical IS curve. (See Figure 14-10B.) Under these circumstances, a rightward shift of the LM curve, stimulated by an expansion of the money supply, will have no effect on the equilibrium level of national income. This is because investment spending remains unchanged despite lower interest rates.

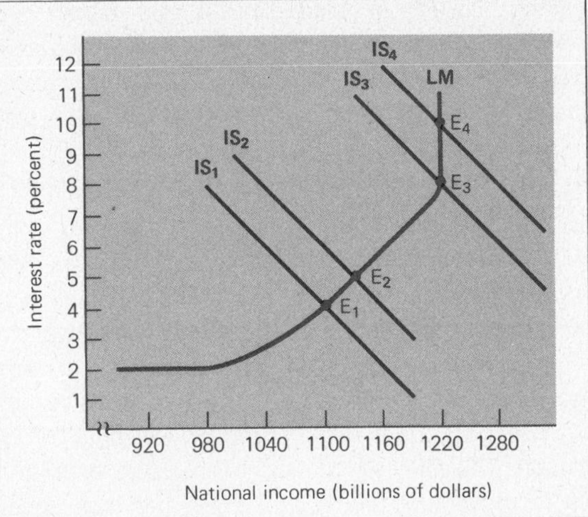

FIGURE 14-11 USING FISCAL POLICY The effect of an increase in government spending (or a cut in taxes) is to shift the IS curve upward. If the economy is operating at less than full employment (E_1), the added aggregate demand acts as a stimulant, raising national income by $60 billion in this case. Accompanying the increase, however, is a rise in interest rates that dampens the full effect of the increase. If the economy is already at full employment, then the shift in the IS curve results only in inflation.

Fiscal Policy

Fiscal Policy during a Recession The IS curve can be a helpful device for showing how fiscal policy can cause increases in aggregate spending and thus stimulate economic activity. Such increases can be introduced either through direct government outlays or through tax cuts that stimulate the private sector. The result in either case is a rightward shift of the entire IS curve—that is, increases in government spending or consumption give rise to higher levels of national income at every interest rate. However, such increases in spending have a secondary effect: The higher levels of national income they permit create a greater transactions demand for money. Since the money supply is fixed, this greater transactions demand must be met by reducing speculative money balances through an increase in the interest rate. Figure 14-11 illustrates this situation. The IS curve shifts from IS_1 to IS_2, increasing national income by over $30 billion. Had interest rates remained at 4 percent, NI would have increased by $60 billion; but interest rates also rise from 4 percent to 5 percent. The consequence of this increase is to reduce the level of investment spending somewhat, so that the full effect of the multiplier is not realized. In other words, the increase in interest rates that will result from the use of fiscal policy alone means that such measures are somewhat less expansionary than might otherwise be expected.

Expansionary Fiscal Policy at Full Employment The shift from IS_1 to IS_2 in Figure 14-11 shows a typical situation in which an increase in C or G shifts the IS curve to the right so that it intersects the LM curve at a higher level of both national income and interest rates. However, if such an increase in spending were to shift the IS curve so that it intersected the LM curve in its classical region, the effect would be very different—and much less desirable. The classical region is the portion of the LM curve where, because the economy has reached its full-employment ceiling, no further increases in real output are possible. In such a situation, illustrated by the shift from IS_3 to IS_4, further increases in spending cannot increase real income, but only interest rates and eventually prices. The implication is that expansionary fiscal policy at full employment can only be inflationary.

Our experience in the United States during the late 1960s illustrates this point. From 1965 on, escalating government expenditures to finance the war in Vietnam were introduced into an economy already operating at full employment. The immediate results were huge budget deficits and a new round of inflation. The CPI, which had been rising at from 1 to 2 percent annually during the previous seven years, shot up to a 6 percent annual rate of increase by late 1969. Interest rates rose, too, during this period. The prime rate reached 8.5 percent, for example.

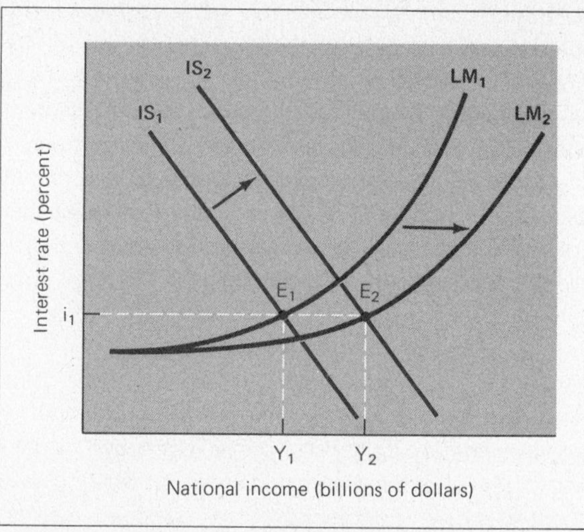

FIGURE 14-12 USING EXPANSIONARY POLICY TOOLS TOGETHER To pull an economy out of a recession, expansionary monetary and fiscal policies may be used simultaneously. Expansionary fiscal policy alone raises interest rates, thereby acting as a drag on investment spending and on national income. The increase in the money supply brought about by the expansionary monetary policy moderates the rise in interest rates. In this case, the interest rate remains at the lower level, whereas the level of national income increases to Y_2.

USING POLICIES TOGETHER

We have seen that the level of economic activity can be affected either by fiscal policy, which induces a shift in the IS curve, or by monetary policy, which stimulates a shift in the LM curve. But either method, used by itself, may have drawbacks. For example, a rightward shift of the IS curve increases national income, but it may also raise interest rates, which would have a depressing effect on investment spending, especially in areas such as housing. Similarly, there are situations in which monetary policy may be of limited value, as when the economy is stuck in the liquidity trap area or when investment does not respond to changes in interest rates. Recognizing these limitations, economic planners emphasize the importance of using fiscal policy and monetary policy together, in order to produce the most effective combination of changes in both the IS and LM curves.

Stimulating the Economy by Increasing Both the Money Supply and Aggregate Spending

The most effective way to pull an economy out of a recession is to adopt fiscal policies that will increase aggregate demand, while at the same time taking measures to expand the money supply. Figure 14-12 illustrates how expansive fiscal policy and monetary policy, used together, can be very effective. The increase in the money supply moderates the rise in interest rates that would otherwise accompany the higher level of national income; the increase in aggregate spending enables changes in the money supply to have a meaningful effect on interest rates and investment spending. The equilibrium level at which the economy settles as a result of the shifts in both the IS and LM curves is significantly higher than the equilibrium levels achieved through individual shifts in either curve.

From a practical point of view, Figure 14-12 illustrates the importance of using both monetary and fiscal measures when it is necessary to stimulate the economy. During the 1970-71 recession, for example, an expansionary budget deficit of over $23 billion was adopted for 1971; at the same time, the money supply was increased substantially.

Contracting the Economy by Reducing Spending and Pursuing Tight Money Policies

The use of only one set of tools is similarly limiting when an economy is approaching its full-employment ceiling and inflation threatens. Contractionary fiscal measures, used alone, will result in a lower level of aggregate demand, but they can also produce lower interest rates, which may have the undesirable effect of increasing investment spending. (This is illustrated in Figure 14-13, where a shift in the IS curve from IS_1 to IS_2 results in an equilibrium point on LM_1 with interest rates lower than those originally prevailing.) Nor can we be confident about the effectiveness of a contractionary monetary policy, used alone, for this will depend on the shape of the IS curve. If the IS curve is relatively flat, monetary policy might be quite effective. If the curve is almost vertical (that is, if investment is not particularly responsive to changes in interest rates), then tight money and higher interest rates may produce almost no reduction in investment spending and national income. (Figure 14-13, for example, shows that a shift in the LM curve from LM_1 to LM_2 has only a minor effect on the national income level at which the new curve intersects IS_1.)

However, if contractionary monetary and fiscal policies are introduced together, they can have substantial deflationary consequences. Tight-money policies partially counteract the lower interest rates resulting from the decline in aggregate demand; and the reduction in total spending reinforces the depressing effects of higher interest rates on new investment spending. This can be seen in Figure 14-13, where the new equilibrium level Y_2, resulting from the contractionary shifts in both the LM and IS curves, is lower than the equilibrium levels resulting from a shift in either curve by itself.

In the late 1960s and early 1970s, government relied heavily on monetary policy, unaccompanied by any really significant fiscal contraction, to fight inflation. In 1969, for example, the growth of the money stock was kept at a very restrained 2.9 percent, whereas interest rates reached heights not seen since the Civil War (the prime rate hit 8.5 percent and in subsequent years it climbed even higher). At the same time, however, the economy was still being stimulated by the huge deficit incurred in 1968. This heavy dependence on the exclusive use of monetary policy does not appear to have been satisfactory, and many authorities now believe that experience illustrates the need for joint use of fiscal and monetary measures in inflationary periods as well as in recessions.

Mitigating Dislocations

Balance of Payments Under some circumstances, policy-makers may be forced to consider factors other than full-employment objectives in determining

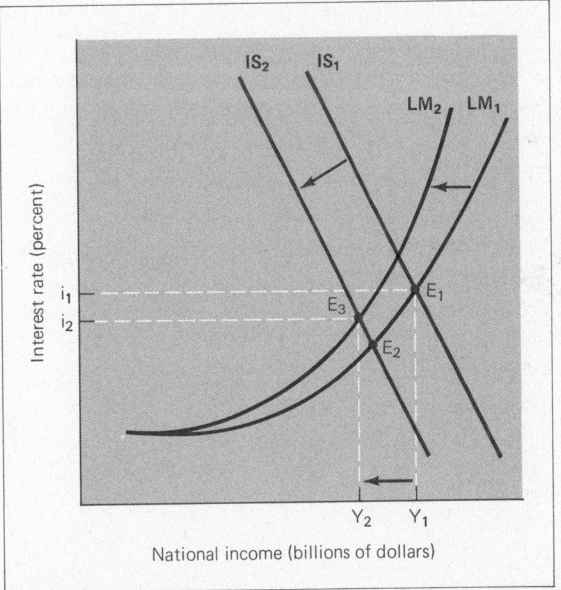

FIGURE 14-13 USING CONTRACTIONARY TOOLS TOGETHER An economy threatened by inflation may be controlled by a combination of contractionary monetary and fiscal policies. Contractionary fiscal policy alone shifts the IS curve downward from IS_1 to IS_2, and the equilibrium point changes from E_1 to E_2. This produces a drop in income but also a drop in interest rates that may stimulate the economy. By using monetary policy, the LM curve shifts from LM_1 to LM_2, and the equilibrium point from E_2 to E_3. Interest rates can be maintained at a higher level, producing an even greater contraction in the economy. Usually, the two are not used sequentially, but rather simultaneously to achieve their effects.

fiscal and monetary policy. In 1971, for example, the nation was painfully emerging from a recession, and the unemployment rate stood at over 6 percent. At the same time, however, we were experiencing severe balance of payments difficulties. Because Americans had been spending and investing more abroad than foreigners had been spending and investing in the United States, there was an excess of U.S. dollars depressing the value of the dollar in international currency markets. One possible way of solving the problem would have been for the United States to encourage short-term foreign investment in the United States by setting high interest rates. But high interest rates were undesirable from another point of view: They would have discouraged the investment spending needed to pull the economy out of the domestic recession. At the time, government officials decided not to permit the international weakness in the dollar to interfere with attempts to stimulate the economy at home, and interest rates were maintained at low levels. The result of this decision was apparent within the year: The economy recovered, but the dollar weakness accelerated into the serious international monetary crisis discussed in Chapter 39.

From a theoretical point of view, it is conceivable that a compromise could have been reached permitting both the higher interest rates needed to help the balance of payments problem and the stimulation needed to solve domestic unemployment. This solution would have consisted of a combination of a tight money supply (that is, a shift to the left in the LM curve) plus a very aggressive increase in aggregate spending (that is, a sharp upward move in the IS curve).

Offsetting Differential Effects Effective economic policy calls for tight money across the board during an inflationary period. Experience has shown, however, that certain sectors—small business and housing, in particular—are usually hit harder than others by tight money, and often, these are the very groups that for reasons of social policy we would prefer not to hurt.

Over the years, the government has explored various ways of protecting the housing industry and small business from the most severe consequences of tight money. Through the Small Business Investment Act, special tax advantages have been offered to those who lend or invest in small businesses. And the government itself stands as a low-cost lender of last resort through a small business loan corporation. Government and private funds are channeled into home building through the Federal Home Loan Bank, the Federal National Mortgage Association, and the Federal Government Mortgage Association, which in various ways, provide government guarantees for private housing loans. More subtly, the government has encouraged saving at those institutions most likely to make home loans, by permitting savings banks and savings and loan associations to pay higher interest rates than commercial banks, thereby ensuring a pool of funds for mortgages.

Despite these arrangements, every imposition of tight money as an anti-inflationary move is met by complaints, often for good reason. Representative Wright Patman of Texas, Chairman of the House Banking and Currency Committee, for example, routinely objects on the grounds that large borrowers can and do manage to obtain funds even in the tightest money markets, while the small business executive and the prospective homeowner must do without or pay very high rates.

Growth Policy: Increased Taxes with Easy Money

We have seen how monetary and fiscal policy can be used to counteract the worst consequences of the cyclical swings intrinsic to a free-market economy. Can we also use these tools to encourage long-term growth? In order to ensure long-term growth, it is necessary to provide conditions that will foster investment. Both a sufficient pool of savings and low interest rates are generally required.

One way of ensuring the availability of private savings is to restrain government's role as a borrower—that is, to run a budget surplus. Such a surplus could be created by increasing taxes rather than by cutting government spending. The government surplus, however, would serve an additional purpose, over and above its initial importance as a way of keeping the government out of the capital market. It could be used to retire the debt through government purchases of outstanding federal bonds. Such purchases of government bonds by the Federal Reserve have two immediate consequences: They increase member bank reserves and thus pave the way for an expansion of the money supply, and they lower interest rates. In this way, the initially deflationary consequences of a budget surplus would be partially counterbalanced by the expansionary effects of the increased money supply that followed closely on its heels.

In all, the sequence of higher taxes, a budget surplus, an expansion of the money supply, and lower interest rates would create conditions favoring the higher investment spending necessary for long-term growth. It is true that the contraction in spending resulting from the deflationary budget surplus would have some depressing effects on output. But if the money supply could be increased significantly enough, the overall effect would still be expansionary.

Why Policy Recommendations Differ

Laymen are often confused by the wide array of policy recommendations made by different economists to remedy the same problem. These differences are somewhat easier to understand, however, when we recognize that economics is not an exact science; we do not as yet have all the information required to provide precise descriptions of how the economy responds to monetary and fiscal measures under all conditions.

Economists differ in their basic assumptions about how the economy behaves—that is, about the shape and the location of the IS and LM curves. Those who believe that investment spending is highly responsive to interest rates will see the IS curve as fairly horizontal; those who believe that the demand for money depends almost exclusively on the level of national income rather than on interest rates will view the LM curve as almost vertical. In addition, debate exists over the level of interest rates at which the liquidity trap begins, and this, too, affects the shape of the LM curve. Such controversies obviously affect policy recommendations, for an economist who sees the IS curve as almost flat will be more willing to advocate monetary measures than those who see it as somewhat vertical. Similarly, someone who feels the economy is already in the liquidity trap area will be very dubious about the possible expansionary effects of an increase in the money supply, while those who feel the economy has not yet reached the area of the liquidity trap will hold a different opinion. In later chapters we explore these controversies in more detail, but we have now provided the background needed to understand the conflicting views that make economics such an interesting, if not exactly precise, field of study.

SUMMARY

1 Changes in both aggregate demand and the money supply affect the level of national income. The relationship of the two has been examined in two ways: The chain of causation from money to investment to national income and the IS-LM model, which depicts equilibrium in the product and money markets.

2 The effect of monetary policy may be traced through this chain of events: Changes in the money supply produce changes in interest rates· changes in interest rates produce changes in investment spending; changes in investment spending produce changes in aggregate demand and, through the impact of the multiplier, even greater changes in national income.

3 The liquidity preference curve depicts quantity of money held at different interest rates. The equilibrium level of interest rates occurs when the supply of money

equals the cash balances people wish to hold for transactional and speculative purposes. Changes in the money supply create a new equilibrium level of interest, except at low interest and national income levels, when the added funds swell the speculative balances held in hopes of higher rates.

4 The marginal efficiency of investment curve depicts the investment forthcoming at a given level of interest. It shows the cost of investment if borrowed funds finance the undertaking and the opportunity cost if retained earnings are used instead of being employed for financial investment. At high levels of interest, costs are high and the amount of investment is low.

5 The equilibrium level of saving and investment indicates the resulting level of NNP. Tracing the chain, an increase in M lowers interest rates, which increases investment, which raises aggregate demand and multiplies the increase in national income.

6 The IS-LM analysis shows the same relationships in a more concise form. At any interest rate, there will be one level of national income where saving equals investment. The IS curve plots these points to reveal how national income responds to changes in investment caused by changes in interest rates. At any interest rate there will also be one level of national income at which the demand for money equals its supply. The LM curve plots how national income responds to changes in the demand for money caused by changes in interest rates. At the intersection of the IS and LM curves, the economy will be at equilibrium, though not necessarily at full employment.

7 The level of economic activity can be affected either by fiscal policy, which induces a shift in the IS curve, or by monetary policy, which causes a shift in the LM curve.

8 During a recession, an increase in the money supply is often suggested as an effective way of increasing investment and, hence, aggregate demand. However, during a severe depression, this policy will be ineffective, because the IS curve will intersect the LM curve within the area of the liquidity trap. Another situation in which monetary policy will prove ineffective in raising the level of national income occurs when investment spending is unresponsive to changes in interest rates, reflected by a vertical IS curve.

9 Using the tools together can prove an effective way to pull an economy out of a recession. Fiscal policies will increase aggregate demand, while at the same time monetary measures will expand the money supply and keep interest rates lower than they otherwise would have been. Similarly, to fight inflation effectively, fiscal and monetary policies may both be used. The tools may also be used to avert balance of payments problems or to promote growth.

10 The choice of policy tools, however, depends on the basic assumptions about how the economy behaves, reflected in the shape of the curves.

SUGGESTED READINGS

Chandler, Lester V. *The Economics of Money and Banking*. 5th ed. Chaps. 13, 16, and 26. New York: Harper & Row, 1968.

Dernburg, Thomas F., and **D. M. McDougall.** *Macroeconomics.* 4th ed. Chaps. 7–10. New York: McGraw-Hill, 1972.

Friedman, Milton, and **Walter W. Heller.** *Monetary vs. Fiscal Policy.* New York: W. W. Norton, 1969.

Hutchinson, Harry D. *Money, Banking and the United States Economy.* 2nd ed. Chaps. 11, 13, 14, 16–18. New York: Appleton-Century-Crofts, 1971.

Mayer, Thomas. *Elements of Monetary Policy.* Chaps. 4–5. New York: Random House, 1968.

QUESTIONS

1 Review
   a. the LP and MEI curves,
   b. the chain of effects from changes in the money supply to changes in NNP and national income,
   c. the IS curve and factors that would shift the curve or change its slope,
   d. the LM curve and the slope of the LM curve in the liquidity trap and classical regions.
   e. the effectiveness of monetary or fiscal policy used alone,
   f. the use of monetary and fiscal policy together for expansion, contraction, or promotion of growth.

2 Some economists argue that an increase in the interest rate simply benefits the rich without having much effect on inflation. What must be the assumptions behind such an argument? Consider the relationship between the interest rate and investment, as well as the shape of the LM curve.

3 In the 1966–68 period, there were rapid, unplanned governmental expenditures on the Vietnam War. The expenditures were financed largely through deficits, and the economy entered a period of inflation. Use the IS and LM curves to show these changes. Recall that there may have been some reduction in the money supply and some increase in interest rates as a result of the sale of more government bonds.

4 Assume that an economy is experiencing a relatively long period of inflation, as the United States did during the late 1960s and early 1970s. People come to expect prices to rise and therefore buy as many goods as they can to hedge against future increases. Business executives also have a tendency to stockpile raw materials in preference to holding cash. How would you show the effects on the LM curve? With all other things equal, what would be the effect on NNP? What would happen if people generally expected a price decrease?

5 Though business executives throughout the country do not necessarily act in concert, they do typically read the same materials and listen to many of the same opinion leaders. Assume that business managers decide that they are in a period of uncertainty and that they decide to adopt a "wait and see" policy with respect to new investment. Show this change using the IS and LM curves. How likely is it that monetary policy will have much effect on the economy? Why?

6 In December of 1972 the Federal Reserve allowed the money supply to grow by 13.3 percent. It is not unusual for the Fed to allow the money supply to increase during December because of the increased volume of activity near Christmas and year-end trading. Why would this be the case? In 1973, however, the Fed viewed

its previous policy with some alarm and moved in January to keep the growth of the money stock to almost zero. Monetarists have frequently argued for a gradual and steady increase in the money supply instead of such sharp fluctuations. What advantages might this policy have?

7 Long-term growth policies may call for increases in taxes and low interest rates. How might these long-term policies compete with short-term political or economic interest?

8 After a relatively unsuccessful effort to control inflation through monetary and fiscal policy, the Nixon administration moved in the summer of 1973 to freeze prices for 60 days. Assume that all prices and wages were frozen. What effect, if any, would you expect upon the IS curve during the 60 days? Recall that long-term, ongoing investment projects as well as changes in inventories are also included.

9 Illustrate the paradox of thrift using the C + I + G approach from Chapter 8 and the IS–LM curves from this chapter.

10 The chain of causation M→i→I→aggregate demand→NNP does not include feedback effects. Include the accelerator in this simplified model.

Opening photo by Terrence Trimble, Design Photographers International

CHAPTER 15

BUSINESS CYCLES

In the last several chapters, we have seen how fiscal and monetary tools have been developed in an attempt to control the sieges of unemployment and inflation that periodically affect our economy. These alternate swings between prosperity and recession are called **business cycles**, and the study of their causes has intrigued economists for years. Our earlier investigation of the behavior of investment and consumption spending has explained in part the cyclical nature of the modern free-market economy. In this chapter we develop a more sophisticated business cycle theory.

Business cycles are the irregular fluctuations in economic activity between expansion and contraction that recur periodically in capitalistic economies. They can be measured in terms of a variety of economic indicators, including many different employment, production, sales, and profit figures. The cyclical fluctuations reflected in these indicators should not be confused with seasonal fluctuations. Automobile sales, for example, fluctuate with the general level of economic activity, and as such are a useful cyclical measure. But auto sales also fluctuate seasonally, with peaks appearing every year in the spring as well as in the fall, when the new models are introduced. Therefore, a sharp increase in auto sales in October as compared with August or September is not necessarily an indication that the entire economy is on the upswing; a look at October sales in previous years would be required before any meaningful conclusions could be drawn. It is also necessary to separate cyclical variations from long-term trends. In the United States, almost all indicators of economic activity show a long-term upward trend—industrial production, for example, is now almost three times the 1949 level. It is not the long-term trend, but the periodic fluctuations within this trend, that concern us here.

THEORIES OF THE BUSINESS CYCLE

The term *business cycle* implies a regularly recurring pattern of events, and earlier economists devoted considerable effort to determining if there was a definite time period within which business cycles recurred. Alvin Hansen, for example, reviewed U.S. economic performance from 1795 to 1937 and concluded that there had been 17 cycles with an average duration of 8.35 years. The performance of the U.S. economy during the first third of the twentieth century appeared to confirm Hansen's thesis: Depressions occurred with surprising regularity, in 1907, 1914, 1921, the early 1930s, and 1937.

The record during the post–World War II period, however, is less conclusive. The economy experienced declines in 1945, 1948, 1953, 1957, 1960, and 1969. Many experts now believe that the duration of the traditional business cycle has been substantially distorted because of the increasing economic role of government. Not only can government modify the level of economic activity through the use of fiscal and monetary tools, it can also determine, to some extent, the timing of cyclical fluctuations. Expansionary fiscal policy during 1968, for example, prolonged the business boom then underway, while the deliberately restrictive monetary measures adopted during 1969 and early 1970 were, in the opinion of some, directly responsible for the recession that occurred. Because of the major and apparently growing role of government in managing economic activity, traditional business cycle analysis, with its emphasis on the causes and duration of cycles, is somewhat less pertinent today. Nevertheless, we shall consider some of the more widely accepted views on why and when business cycles occur.

External Factors and the Business Cycle

To the eighteenth and nineteenth century classical economists, the peaks and troughs of business cycles were temporary aberrations. These economists accepted Say's Law, which states that supply creates its own demand. Under such ground rules, a recession caused by an insufficiency of demand or an inflationary boom caused by an excess of demand is theoretically impossible. The only way to explain their occurrence was to look to external factors that created temporary conditions of imbalance. Pre-

1930 business cycle theory, therefore, is largely devoted to a study of a wide range of external conditions that might have caused economic fluctuations. And even today some of these conditions still have validity as explanations of changes in business activity.

Weather The earliest business cycle theories emphasized the role of weather. Unusually large or small harvests were attributed to atypical weather conditions. These, in turn, affected farm income, which would soon be reflected in changes in aggregate demand throughout the economy. More elaborate theories were based on the behavior of sunspots or on the phases of the planet Venus, under the assumption that such variations determined weather conditions. Such theories were perhaps more relevant in the 1700s and 1800s, when agriculture was a significant component of total economic activity; in recent years, however, farm income as a percent of GNP and the number of those employed in agriculture have declined sharply, and changes in weather conditions and agricultural incomes must be severe to have an appreciable effect on overall economic conditions. Nevertheless, even a highly technological society cannot always escape the consequences of natural events. The purchase of enormous amounts of wheat by the Soviet Union from the United States in 1972 was the result of a severe Russian crop failure.

Technological Change Other theories attempt to tie the business cycle to technological change, suggesting that waves of expansion are induced by new inventions such as the cotton gin, the automobile, and the transistor, while recessions occur when the stimulus supplied by these inventions wanes. Alvin Hansen, writing during the 1930s, used this approach to explain the American experience. The United States, he claimed, had been able to recover from depressions through the exploitation of successive "frontiers." The lands to the west were the original "frontier"; in later years, new inventions served the same purpose. But Hansen feared that we had finally reached the end of available frontiers, for he could see no possibility of further major technological breakthroughs. As a result, he was very pessimistic about the chances of the United States recovering from the Great Depression, and he forecast a long period of stagnation at the bottom of the business cycle.

Hansen's fellow professor at Harvard Joseph Schumpeter also analyzed the role of technological change in business cycles. Schumpeter, however, called attention to the difference between invention (the actual discovery of a new product or method) and innovation (the process through which the invention is employed commercially). He emphasized the importance of the innovator—both the original innovator, who first decides to exploit the discovery, as well as others, who recognize that they too must incorporate the latest advances in order to remain competitive. The investment spending required to build the factories and machinery to produce the new product triggers an economic expansion. According to Schumpeter, expansion continues until the necessary capital goods have been acquired; then investment spending declines and a recession begins.

Random Events or Shocks Business cycles have also been ascribed to a wide variety of unexpected shocks that confront a society periodically. A strike in a major industry, such as the automobile industry, may have repercussions throughout the economy, leading to cutbacks in steel production, railroad carloadings, retail sales, home building, and so on. In late 1970, a prolonged strike at General Motors resulted in significant declines throughout the economy, intensifying the recession then underway and delaying recovery for several months.

Other shocks may come from political or military sources. Many believe, for example, that the United States never fully recovered from the Great Depression of the 1930s until the economy was stimulated by World War II; and the recessions of 1920–21 and 1947 were clearly related to the end of hostilities following World War I and World War II, respectively. Similarly, the excessive 1968–69 boom and the subsequent 1969–70 recession were closely tied to the war in Vietnam.

Psychological Theories Some observers view business cycles as an outgrowth of the waves of pessimism and optimism that periodically affect a society. The nineteenth century economist Alfred Marshall, for example, said that depressions were caused by "a want of confidence"; and the almost unprecedented 12 percent increase in retail sales in May of 1973 was ascribed by some happy department store executives to "a surge of consumer confidence we cannot explain." It is true that overall optimism will be reflected in higher consumption and investment spending and more easily available credit, whereas pessimism will result in lower spending and more restrictive loan policies. But such a psychological explanation of the business cycle merely avoids the basic issue of why these periodic changes in business and household morale occur.

Monetary Theories

Some theorists believe that monetary factors and the policies of financial institutions play the central role in creating business cycles. They claim that economic expansions are the result of a plentiful supply of money at low interest rates, whereas contractions are the result of tight money policies. Some confirmation for this approach can be found in the recent performance of the U.S. economy, with the 1967 and 1970 downturns closely associated with earlier restrictive monetary measures, and the 1971 recovery related to the introduction of easy money.

The monetarist assigns primary responsibility for such changes in monetary policy to the monetary authorities: the Federal Reserve Board and the Treasury Department. Others, including the nineteenth century British economist R. C. Hawtrey and Representative Wright Patman, Chairman of the House Banking and Currency Committee, have assigned the blame to the banking system. In their view, expansions are based on the wide availability of credit supplied by optimistic bankers in a prosperous economy. Booms finally end when bankers become reluctant to continue the expansion of credit necessary to finance further growth. The resulting slowdown is magnified by excessively restrictive credit policies typically adopted by nervous bankers during a contraction. In this way, the operations of the banking system reinforce and magnify the normal swings in business activity.

Internal Factors and the Business Cycle

One of the first efforts to explain the business cycle as an intrinsic rather than accidental characteristic of a free-market economy was made by Wesley C. Mitchell. Writing as early as 1913, Mitchell claimed that cyclical behavior is the norm in our economy and that each phase of the cycle is a necessary consequence of the previous one. Recessions, wrote Mitchell, occur because of conditions that inevitably develop during a period of prosperity; and recoveries come about as a direct result of circumstances that develop during a depression. It was not until the Great Depression, however, that internal theories about the causes and the nature of business cycles were seriously explored. Keynes laid the groundwork for later efforts through his studies of how consumption and investment spending behave in a modern economy. His view of the relationship between changes in national income and the marginal propensity to consume is the basis of modern **underconsumption** theories of the business cycle, whereas his analysis of the relationship between investment and saving provides the building blocks for contemporary **overinvestment** theories.

The Basic Multiplier/Accelerator Theory The simplest internal business cycle theory has already been suggested in our discussion of the multiplier and the accelerator in Chapter 8. According to these principles, changes in consumption and investment interact to cause changes in national income. An initial increase in consumption, for example, produces a multiple increase in national income as the spending increase moves through the economy. A further stimulus during an expansion is provided by investment spending, which, in accordance with the acceleration principle, tends to increase sharply in response to relatively minor changes in consumption. Thus, the cumulative interaction of successive injections of consumption and investment spending provides a reasonable explanation of the expansion phase of the business cycle; operating in reverse, it also explains the downturn or recession phase.

According to this theory, changes in consumption and investment are responsible not only for the periods of expansion and contraction, but also for the turning points that occur at the conclusion of each expansion or contraction phase. In a period of prosperity, for example, national income increases and the marginal propensity to consume falls, because households have a tendency to save a larger percentage of their larger incomes. This increase in saving means that although consumption is still growing in absolute terms, it is growing at a declining rate. The result is a drop in investment spending (due to the effects of the accelerator). Such a decline in investment spending is directly responsible for the shift from prosperity to contraction. A cutback in investment leads to a cutback in consumption spending on the part of those formerly employed in capital goods industries, and once the effects of the multiplier are applied to these decreasing amounts of consumption spending, a full-fledged recession is underway.

In a similar fashion, changes in the marginal propensity to consume are responsible for the turnaround that occurs at the trough of the business

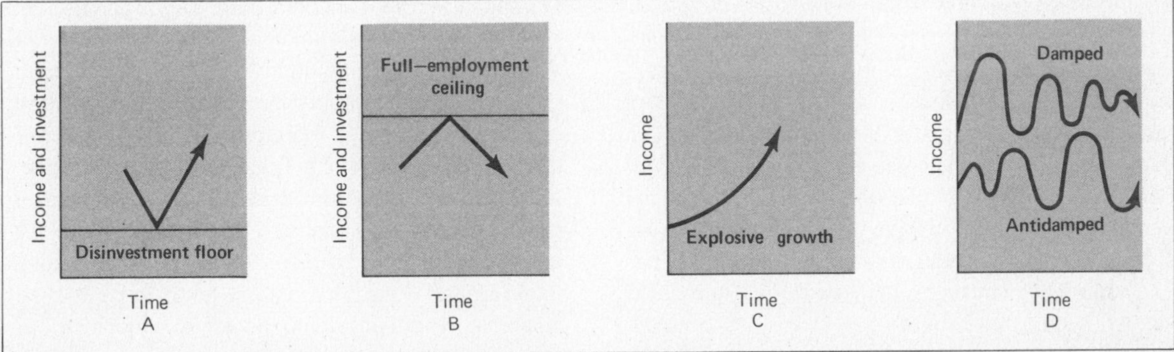

FIGURE 15-1 ACCELERATOR AND MULTIPLIER AT WORK (A) Recovery from Disinvestment Floor: In a recession, businesses disinvest because they no longer need their full productive capacity. Income and investment fall. But once the existing excess capacity has been worked off (as it depreciates or wears out and is not replaced), there is no need for further negative net investment. Net investment rises from the negative level where it has been, income is pulled up with it, and the cumulative process goes into reverse. (B) Full-Employment Ceiling and Cumulative Decline: Let us say that the interaction of the multiplier and the accelerator pushes production up to the full-employment level. Further growth of output becomes physically impossible. The acceleration principle prevents a full-employment equilibrium because income can remain high only as long as investment remains high; but investment can be high only if income is *rising*. Once the full-employment ceiling has halted the rise in income, it ceases to be necessary to add to the stock of capital, and net investment falls to zero. The fall in investment pulls down income through the multiplier, inducing a reduction of the stock of plant and equipment, bringing about a cumulative contraction. (C) Explosive Growth: At a time of high unemployment, the interaction of the multiplier and the accelerator may temporarily project the economy into a phase of explosive growth. As investment rises—say, because of increased profits or because excess capacity is worked off—income rises (by a multiplied amount), justifying an increase in the stock of plant and equipment (the accelerator), thus raising investment and income by even larger increments, and so forth. Of course, the full-employment level must eventually be reached, and furthermore, the increasing *rate* of growth cannot be maintained even short of full employment since various bottlenecks develop—shipping delays, time lags in the installation of equipment and in the building of factories, and so on. This type of growth, however, is quite possible in the short run and takes place after most recessions. (D) Damped and Antidamped Cycles: A particular shock or disturbance sets the economy temporarily off its equilibrium course. If the economy is inherently stable, it will adjust in the manner depicted by the top curve. However, if the economy is inherently unstable, a random shock will cause an ever widening tendency away from the equilibrium course, as shown in the lower curve.

cycle. As national income falls, saving rates fall even faster—that is, the marginal propensity to consume increases. This means that although both consumption and national income continue to decline, the decline in consumption is slower than the decline in income. Finally, consumption stabilizes, and the stage is set for a recovery. Eventually, there will be a pickup in investment spending, if only to replace the capital equipment that has been used up in the production of consumer goods. Such an increase in investment spending will increase national income, consumption spending will pick up, the multiplier will come into play, and the economy will begin a new round of expansion.

The Underconsumption Theory The underconsumption theory of business cycles builds on the original Keynesian thesis that the propensity to consume varies inversely with income. The term *underconsumption,* then, refers to the insufficiency of consumption spending that occurs at high levels of national income. The roots of the underconsumption theory can be traced to the early socialist view of capitalism. Socialists believed that in capitalistic economies, workers' wages would always be restricted to the subsistence level. As production became more efficient and output per worker increased, workers would not receive pay raises. As a result, wages would not be high enough to purchase all the goods and services produced, and a depression would occur. Such an interpretation is oversimplified, but it does point to the central role of wage income as a determinant of aggregate consumption—a factor of great significance in present-day underconsumption theories.

Like their predecessors, modern underconsumption theorists recognize the importance of incomes and spending as the key determinants of economic activity. Unlike their predecessors, however, they see all income as divided into two distinct categories, wages and profits, and believe that patterns of consumption spending concerning wages are different from those concerning profits. They suggest that income received as wages tends to be consumed almost entirely—that is, that the marginal propensity to consume out of wage income is close to 1. On the other hand, the marginal propensity to consume out of profit income is seen as much lower, substantial amounts of this income being devoted to saving. Several surveys appear to confirm that the MPC is higher for wage income than for nonwage income. A study of the Dutch economy from 1947 to 1954[1] revealed that the marginal propensity to consume was .85 for disposable wage income and .40 for nonwage income; an analysis[2] of the U.S. economy from 1939 to 1952 arrived at similar findings.

In addition to differentiating between the MPC for wage income and profit income, underconsumption theorists also emphasize that wage income and profit income do not fluctuate to the same extent in response to changes in national income. Increases in national income lead to proportionately greater increases in profit income than wage income, and profit income also drops much more severely during a recession. This difference is caused by a number of factors. The fixed operating costs of most modern businesses are high. Therefore, any increase in production levels once the breakeven point has been reached will result in a substantial increase in profits; conversely, relatively minor percentage cutbacks in output may wipe out earnings. Wage income in the United States, in contrast, tends to be relatively stable. The bargaining power of unions is particularly effective in preventing wage cuts during a recession, and the excess supply of labor available as an economy emerges from a depression tends to keep wages from increasing during the early stages of an expansion. Figure 15-2 shows the behavior of wages and corporate profits during two of the most recent business cycles. Note the very sharp drops in corporate profits during the recession phases, and the even sharper increases during the recovery phases; compare this with the performance of the wage sector. What is the significance of the contrasting performance of wages and profits as they respond to changes in national income?

1 Lawrence R. Klein, *An Introduction to Econometrics* (Englewood Cliffs, N.J.: Prentice-Hall, 1962). p. 228.

2 L. R. Klein and A. S. Goldberger, *An Econometric Model of the United States 1939–52* (Amsterdam: North Holland Publishing Co., 1955).

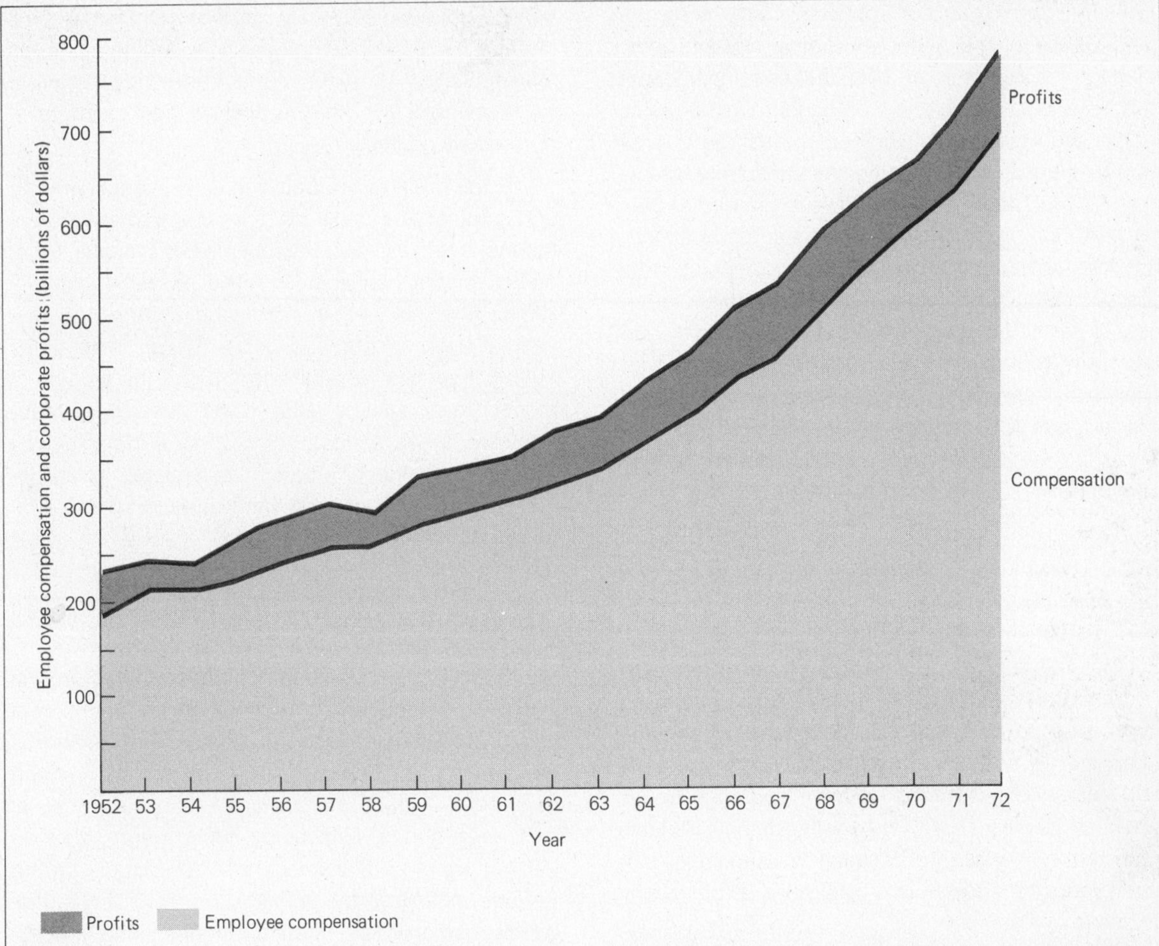

FIGURE 15-2 WAGES AND PROFITS OVER THE BUSINESS CYCLE Over the last two decades both wages and profits (before taxes) have shown some responsiveness to the business cycle. Recessions have occurred in 1953–54, 1957–58, 1960–61, and 1969–70. During each recession, profits fell, but wages remained sticky. In 1953–54 wages fell slightly, but during each of the other recessions, they rose slightly. Thus, although administered prices evidently do well in protecting margins during recessions, labor unions have an even better record of protecting wages. Few workers have been forced to take wage cuts during any of the post–World War II recessions.

SOURCES: U.S. Department of Commerce, *Business Conditions Digest*, October 1972; *Economic Report of the President*, January 1973.

Profits take an increasingly larger share of total national income during a period of prosperity. However, because the MPC for profits is lower than the MPC for wage income, such a shift in income distribution means that consumption spending will be rising at a slower rate than national income. If we accept the acceleration principle, which tells us that consumption spending must increase at a constant rate in order to maintain investment spending, the implication of this shift to profit income becomes clear. The relative decline in consumption spending will lead to a slowdown in investment spending, national income will decline, and the entire economy will slide into a recession.

The same logic can be applied to explaining the performance of the economy during a depression. Although national income falls, the wage component falls less than the profit component. As a result, wages soon represent a higher percentage of total income than they did during the prosperity phase. The MPC for wage income, however, is higher than the MPC for profit income, so consumption spending does not fall as much as national income. This relative stability of consumption spending operates to limit the decline in national income, and eventually replacement demand creates a need for investment spending. This investment spending in turn leads to increased wage and profit income, higher aggregate demand, and an economy-wide recovery.

The Overinvestment Theory In underconsumption theories of the business cycle, changes in consumption spending patterns provide the primary impetus for fluctuations in economic activity; in overinvestment theories, sharp swings in investment spending hold center stage. As early as the nineteenth century, both Ricardo and Marx wrote of the depressing effect that an excess of investment spending could have on profits. Today's overinvestment theories analyze the relationship between investment spending, production costs, and profits to explain why business cycles occur.

The key point in overinvestment theories is that investment spending is closely related to profits and that changes in the profitability of business inevitably result in changes in investment spending. When profits are high and rising, businesses increase their investment spending; when profits fall, investment is cut. The reasons for this behavior are twofold. First, a high level of current profits suggests that additional commitments will also be profitable and as such, encourages additional investment spending. Conversely, a low level of profits breeds a pessimistic climate in which businesses are reluctant to expand. The second reason for the close tie between profits and investment spending involves the importance of profits as a source of investment funds. Although it is true that money to finance investment spending can be obtained externally through borrowing, most large U.S. corporations rely heavily on internal funds for expansion. Thus, the amount of money available for investment spending is closely tied to the level of retained profits.

Given the relationship between investment spending and profits, the next step in the overinvestment theory is to explore the sources of profits. What makes profits rise and fall? The answer is simple. Profits depend on the interaction of three factors: selling price, output, and costs. Selling price times output produces revenues. Profits are the amount of money that remains after costs have been subtracted from revenues. Profits, then, depend on the interaction of these factors: If selling prices are increasing faster than costs (and quantity sold is constant or increases), profits will increase; if costs are rising more quickly than the price increases businesses can obtain in the marketplace, profits will fall.

Various studies have been conducted to explore the behavior of different groups of prices at different levels of national economic activity. They show that the prices of capital goods (plants and equipment) rise and fall much more sharply than the prices of consumer goods. One study, for example, showed that prices of capital goods rose 21 percent during periods of prosperity, whereas prices of consumer goods rose only 12 percent during the same periods. The same study showed that during recessions, capital goods prices fell by 25 percent, whereas consumer goods prices fell by only 18 percent.[3] This behavior of capital goods prices can be understood by referring to the acceleration principle. In good times, the increase in the demand for capital goods is much larger, in percentage terms, than the increase in the demand for consumer goods. Therefore, shortages develop and prices rise. On the other hand, in bad times, a relatively small decline in consumer goods leads to a major decline in the demand for capital equipment, and prices decline in response to the drop in demand.

3 F. C. Mills, *Price-Quantity Interactions in Business Cycles* (New York: National Bureau of Economic Research, 1946), pp. 132–133.

The significance of the sharply different price performances of the consumer goods sector and the capital goods sector during different phases of the business cycle lies at the heart of the overinvestment theory. During prosperity, the prices of capital goods, which represent an important cost to producers of consumer goods, rise more quickly than the prices of the finished merchandise the consumer goods manufacturer produces. As a result, the manufacturer is caught in a profit squeeze between his costs and his selling prices. His profits fall, and since profits are the main determinant of investment, investment spending declines too. Such a cut in investment spending leads to declines in employment and income and, soon, to a contraction throughout the economy. The decline will continue until the prices of capital goods have fallen to such a low level that the profit margins of consumer goods producers begin to improve. At this point, businesses will begin to experience an increase in profits because, although their prices have declined, their costs (the costs of capital goods) have declined even more. This higher level of profits will inspire a round of investment spending, and a new cycle of expansion will begin.

The overinvestment theory, like the simple multiplier/accelerator theory and the underconsumption theory, emphasizes the intrinsic nature of business cycles. In all three, each phase of the cycle is a logical and inevitable outgrowth of the preceding phase; there is no need to introduce an outside causative agent to explain changes in the level of business activity.

Synthesis Although each theory of the business cycle has some validity, perhaps the most realistic approach involves a synthesis of several theories. This synthesis could include the accelerator and multiplier principles to explain the cumulative nature of changes in economic activity. It could accept the underconsumption view that the propensity to consume is higher for wage income than for profit income and that profit income varies more widely than wage income. And it could include the overinvestment view of how investment spending behaves, with its emphasis on changes in capital goods prices and producers' profit margins as the determinants of investment spending. Combining all these elements, let us examine a general theory of business cycles.

During an expansionary period, both investment spending and consumption spending increase, and the expansion builds up steam due to the interaction of the accelerator and the multiplier. As national income increases, however, certain inevitable changes occur. The profit component of national income begins to grow faster than the wage component, and the costs of producing capital goods begin to increase faster than the prices of consumer goods. Consequently, at the peak of the cycle, both consumption spending and investment spending start to decline. Consumption spending falls because the marginal propensity to consume out of profits is less than the marginal propensity to consume out of wages; investment spending declines because profits are squeezed. This decrease in aggregate spending leads to an initial decline in national income, which is compounded through the operation of the accelerator and the multiplier, and the economy suffers a period of contraction. During this contraction, wages are more stable than profits, and the prices of consumer goods decline less than the prices of capital goods. Ultimately, these two factors lead to an increase in demand: Because wage income declines less than profit income, consumption demand eventually stabilizes and then increases; because capital goods prices are particularly low, profits and investment spending eventually pick up. These increases in consumption and investment spending lead to increases in national income, and a new cycle of expansion begins.

Although this synthesis is essentially an internal one, placing primary emphasis on forces within the economy, it could also consider the role of external forces in modifying or intensifying the trends already underway. The shock to the economy provided by the Vietnam War, for example, exaggerated the expansionary forces at work during the prosperity of 1968–69. Perhaps the major external force is caused by changes in government spending or taxing programs; these have a tremendous potential to change the aggregate spending totals that might otherwise result from the normal operation of a purely private sector economy.

FORECASTING BUSINESS CYCLES: CAN IT BE DONE?

Businesses, consumers, investors, and speculators have a real interest in trying to forecast business cycles. Department stores, for example, order Christmas merchandise in June, and need to know whether consumption buying will expand or contract six months later. Similarly, consumers often plan major purchases in advance; a home buyer who delayed purchase of a home from the peak of the 1969–70 boom until the bottom of the 1970–71 decline could have saved 1 percent or more in interest on his mortgage.[4] In the same way, buyers of stocks or bonds can also maximize yields or capital gains by timely purchases. For such reasons, attempts to forecast business cycle behavior have always been popular, and many approaches have been tried with varying success.

Methods of Forecasting

The simplest method of forecasting business cycles involves extrapolation of current trends. This method can be useful in forecasting the behavior of some of the more stable components of national economic activity. Food consumption, for example, appears to increase every year in fairly regular amounts, and a reasonable estimate for next year could probably be obtained by extending the historical trend line. For the more cyclical components, however, projections of past trend lines are almost meaningless. Given the previous years' auto production figures, for example, it would have been virtually impossible to accurately predict automobile output in 1966, 1970, or 1973.

Opinion polling is often suggested as an alternative method of forecasting business activity. The Survey Research Center of the University of Michigan makes quarterly surveys of consumer intentions to buy, and the Department of Commerce polls businesses on projected capital goods expenditures. In some cases, these surveys have served as useful indicators that the economy was either slowing down or accelerating. At other times, however, they have fallen wide of the mark.

A widely followed forecasting tool is the Bureau of the Census *Index of Leading Indicators*. This is an average of 12 economic series, including inventories, new orders of durables, stock market performance, and average work week, which in the past have started to increase or decrease several months before the economy as a whole. New orders, for example, traditionally began to drop while production (which is based on orders received earlier) is still rising. The problem with the *Index*, however, is that it will reverse direction due to freakish conditions or a statistical aberration. For this reason, most businesses prefer to wait for several months before responding to a change of direction in the leading indicators. Unfortunately, by this late date, the decline or upturn forecast by the indicators may have already occurred.

The newest approach to forecasting involves the use of sophisticated computer-based econometric models. Mathematical data about hundreds of different components of the economy—tire production, shoe production, airline travel, hospital charges—are fed into a computer, which is programmed to project changes in each component in response to changes in overall factors such as taxes, government spending, or household saving. In theory, once assumptions were made about the overall conditions that will prevail, such a model could be used to forecast both total economic performance and the performance of the individual segments. In practice, however, our society is so complex that it appears impossible to determine or accurately measure all the relevant components that should be included in such a model. Moreover, time lags in gathering the necessary data often occur. As a result, the econometric approach to forecasting, which was greeted

4 Over its lifetime, interest charges on a 20-year $20,000 7.5 percent mortgage will amount to approximately $2500 less than interest charges on a similar 8.5 percent mortgage.

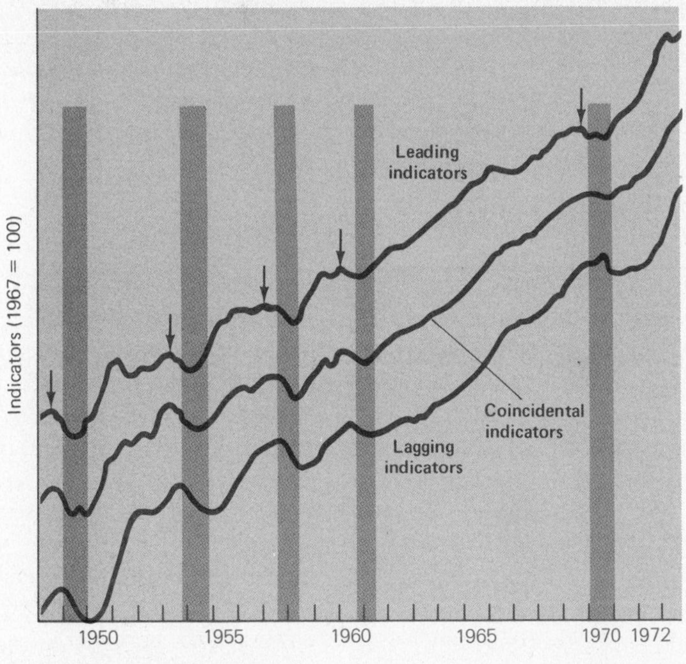

FIGURE 15-3 ECONOMIC INDICATORS Economists follow the performance of the leading economic indicators, such as the indices of net business formation, new orders, durables, new building permits, to predict turning points in business cycles. If the leading indicators are turning down (both on an individual basis and on the basis of an index), then the chances of a recession are fairly good. A substantial (more than 3 percent) and sustained (over two consecutive months) downturn indicates a very high probability of recession within the next few months. Similarly, the upturn of the leading indicators heralds the beginnings of the recovery phase. The coincident and lagging indicators obviously lack the predictive capabilities of the leading indicators. Their analytical value lies mainly in the confirmation of the cyclical turning points. For example, when a decline is predicted by the leading indicators, economic forecasters will watch the coincident indicators, such as the indices of industrial production and nonagricultural employment, for confirmation of the downturn. The economic indicators are published monthly in *Business Conditions Digest.* From it, you can fill in the chart since 1973 and perhaps predict the course of the economy for the rest of the semester.

SOURCES: U.S. Department of Commerce, *Business Conditions Digest,* 1948–73 (monthly).

with great enthusiasm when its use first became widespread in the early 1960s, has exhibited many of the same inadequacies of the older forecasting methods.

Management of Business Cycles

Proper forecasting enables the cushioning of business cycles. Although forecasting cycles is a tricky business, and then even the most painstaking work may be invalidated because of random events, the development of increasingly sophisticated monetary and fiscal tools presents government with the opportunity to manage the economy and to limit some of the most serious consequences of economic fluctuations. The growing list of automatic stabilizers—Social Security, unemployment insurance, welfare payments—provides a built-in cushion against severe downswings in aggregate demand. In all, because our society now can protect itself with reasonable effectiveness from the risk of a deep, self-perpetuating depression like that of the 1930s, the business cycle no longer has the importance it did in earlier days. On the other hand, we have been significantly less successful in handling the upper peaks of the cycle. Particularly disturbing is the fact that inflation, formerly associated only with these peaks, is now a problem during periods of both prosperity and recession, a situation for which there is no explanation in conventional business cycle theory. In the next chapter we will discuss the problem of inflation in greater detail, with emphasis on the tools that have been developed in an attempt to curb it.

SUMMARY

1 Business cycles are alternate swings between prosperity and recession. These irregular fluctuations can be measured in terms of a variety of economic indicators, including employment, production, sales, and profit figures.

2 To the eighteenth and nineteenth century economists, the peaks and troughs of business cycles were temporary aberrations, caused by exogenous factors. The earliest business cycle theories emphasized the role of weather, since farm production—and indirectly aggregate demand—was dependent upon these natural conditions.

3 Another exogenous theory attempts to tie the business cycle to technological change, suggesting that waves of expansion are induced by new inventions such as the cotton gin, the automobile, and the transistor, while recessions occur when the stimulus supplied by these inventions wanes. Business cycles have also been ascribed to a wide variety of unexpected shocks such as auto strikes or wars. Some observers view business cycles as an outgrowth of the waves of pessimism and optimism that periodically affect a society.

4 Monetary theories relate business cycles to the expansion and contraction of the money supply.

5 Wesley C. Mitchell broke new ground by claiming that cyclical behavior is endogenous to an economy, that each phase of the cycle is a necessary consequence of the previous one. The simplest endogenous business cycle theory is the multiplier/accelerator theory. According to this theory, the interaction of changes in consumption and changes in investment is responsible not only for the periods of expansion and contraction, but also for the turning points that occur at the conclusion of each expansion or contraction phase.

6 The underconsumption theory builds on the original Keynesian thesis that the propensity to consume varies inversely with income. All income is seen as divided into two distinct categories: wages and profits. The MPC out of wage income is considered to be close to 1, whereas that out of profits is much lower. Since profits take an increasingly larger share of total national income during a period of prosperity, this means that consumption spending will be rising at a slower rate than national income. This will lead to a slowdown first in investment and then in national income, as the economy slides into a recession.

7 The overinvestment theory hinges on the interdependence of investments and profits. Profits encourage investment, but investment constitutes a cost to the firm. Because in a time of prosperity the price of capital goods (which represents

the cost of investment) rises faster than the prices of finished goods (which furnish revenue to the firm), profits decline. Investment is then cut back until the price of capital goods declines rapidly enough to permit higher rates of profit.

8 Combining the simple model with the overinvestment and underconsumption models yields a general theory of the business cycle.

9 There are various methods of business cycle forecasting—extrapolation of current trends, opinion polling, and econometric models. All of these methods are used today, not only to forecast business cycles, but to manage them as well.

SUGGESTED READINGS

Dernburg, Thomas F., and **D. M. McDougall.** *Macroeconomics.* 4th ed. Chap. 17. New York: McGraw-Hill, 1972.

Estey, J. A. *Business Cycles.* 3rd ed. Englewood Cliffs, N.J.: Prentice-Hall, 1956.

Hansen, A. H. *Business Cycles and National Income.* 2nd ed. New York: W. W. Norton, 1964.

Hunt, E. K., and **Howard J. Sherman.** *Economics: An Introduction to Traditional and Radical Views.* Chap. 28. New York: Harper & Row, 1972.

U.S. Department of Commerce, Bureau of the Census. *Business Conditions Digest.* Washington, D.C.: Government Printing Office, monthly. Contains economic indicators and other data on the condition of the economy.

QUESTIONS

1 Review
   a. external causes of business cycles,
   b. the simple multiplier/accelerator theory,
   c. the overinvestment theory,
   d. the underconsumption theory,
   e. the synthesis of internal theories of the business cycle,
   f. forecasting methods.

2 During the early 1960s the American economy experienced a long period of growth with relative price stability. As growth continued, some economists began to express concern that there was a downturn looming in the near future. Why might they have expressed such concern? How might the classical economists have answered?

3 The early months of 1973 in the United States saw particularly unusual weather conditions throughout most of the country. In some sections of the country cattlemen lost up to 70 percent of their young stock, and in the Ohio and Mississippi River basins, more than 10 million acres were flooded. According to the weather theory of business cycles, what would be the prediction for business activity in general?

4 The increasing concern for energy sources in the United States has prompted large firms as well as small investors to seek increasingly efficient sources of energy. Assume that there is a major breakthrough in the technology of energy during the next few years. What might be the effects for the business cycle?

Assume, in addition, that the economy is still experiencing inflationary pressures.

5 Early in 1973, an already falling stock market experienced another blow from the disclosures of fraud and stock manipulations by a major conglomerate. What might be the psychological effects of such a stock market slump? What effects might there be on investments? And what effects in turn might there be for the business cycle?

6 Monetarists have frequently suggested that the government be prevented from attempting to correct or counterbalance short-run changes in business activity. They charge that in many instances the government's record has not been particularly good. Why do they advance such an argument? Do you think the stabilization policies of government can eliminate cycles? Why or why not?

7 During the post–World War II years, Germany experienced the strongest expansion of any of the countries of Western Europe, particularly from 1957 to 1965. In 1966, there was a decline in capital investment and in addition, financial authorities acted to restrict credit. The result was a recession. How would you explain the mechanisms that led to the decline in the German growth rate? What factors peculiar to Germany after World War II might have contributed to the high level of capital investment and the subsequent leveling off?

8 Though most small savers have a tendency to place funds in domestic banks and savings institutions, some feel encouraged to place their funds abroad when interest rates are higher abroad than they are at home. What problems might you predict concerning the availability of funds for investment if the government subscribes to a policy of long-term growth?

9 Business cycle analysis cannot explain the problems of high unemployment and accelerating inflation that have plagued the economy in the 1970s. Reject or defend, identifying the theories you are using in your answer.

10 Explain why the rates of increase and decrease of investment spending and capital goods prices are as important to know as their absolute levels.

Opening photo from United Press International

CHAPTER 16 STABILIZATION

Although it may be premature to say that business cycles are now a thing of the past, recent American experience suggests that we are now presented with problems of a different order. It appears that the economy no longer fluctuates between periods of high unemployment with stable prices and periods of full employment with inflation. Instead, the United States appears to be facing a new pattern that combines an uncomfortably high rate of unemployment with continuing inflation. **Stagflation** is the name coined to describe this new phenomenon, which seems to defy the traditional trade-off between unemployment and inflation. Because the causes of stagflation are not clear, it poses a particularly difficult problem for economic policy-makers.

Attempts to use traditional fiscal and monetary measures to handle stagflation have been unsuccessful. Expansionary monetary or fiscal policy merely exacerbates the inflation without cutting unemployment significantly, whereas contractionary monetary and fiscal measures seem to increase unemployment with little effect on inflation. Confronted with this persistent problem, policy-makers have looked to stronger tools. In August of 1971, President Nixon imposed wage-price controls, but many Americans, including the President, were doubtful about their long-term success. In January 1973, most of these controls were removed, and the immediate result was a tremendous surge in the rate of inflation: The consumer price index rose at an annual rate of 7.5 percent during February and March of 1973. Clearly, a means of controlling stagflation had not been found. Reluctantly, price controls were reinstated in June of that year.

The experience with stagflation raises many provocative questions. Is the traditional trade-off between inflation and unemployment really a thing of the past or is stagflation merely a temporary phase? What does stagflation imply in terms of economic tools? Will fiscal and monetary measures continue to be useful or must we develop new tools (such as wage-price controls) to meet the new problem? And finally, what is the relationship between our current domestic economic problems and international trade and monetary problems? Clearly, during the 1970s, we have found that attempts to cure either domestic unemployment or inflation may have extremely unpleasant consequences in these other areas.

THE PHILLIPS CURVE

Even the simplest business cycle analysis suggests that there is some relationship between the degree of inflation and the degree of unemployment in an economy, especially at the peak and trough of the cycle. It was not until 1958, however, that this relationship was analyzed in depth. In that year, A. W. Phillips, an English economist, undertook a comprehensive study of unemployment and wage increases in Great Britain from 1861 to 1957. Phillips concluded that

> . . . when the demand for labor is high and there are very few unemployed . . . employers bid wage rates up . . . each firm and each industry being continually tempted to offer a little above the prevailing rates to attract the most suitable labor from other firms and industries.[1]

As wage costs increase, producers are pressured to increase their selling prices. Consequently, higher rates of inflation are generally associated with lower rates of unemployment. The reverse occurs when unemployment is high. Because labor is unable to win substantial wage increases, the costs of production do not rise significantly, and product prices, too, remain relatively stable. Phillips presented his findings in the form of a curve showing the relationship between unemployment and wage increases during various periods. Such graphs are now known as **Phillips curves.** Since wage increases are directly linked to increases in prices, Phillips curves are commonly drawn to show the relationship between the level of unemployment and the level of inflation. Figure 16-1 is a hypothetical Phillips curve.

1 A. W. Phillips, "The Relation Between Unemployment and the Rate of Change of Money Wage Rates in the United Kingdom 1861–1957," *Economica* 25, no. 100 (November 1958):283.

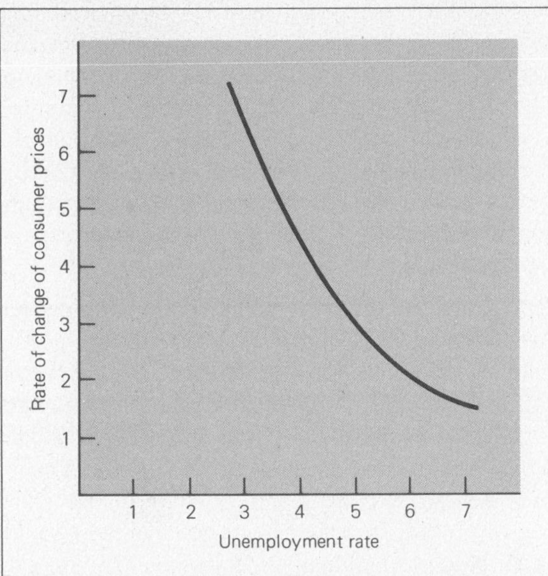

FIGURE 16-1 PHILLIPS CURVE (Hypothetical) The curve drawn here shows the trade-off between the level of unemployment and the level of inflation for a given economy. As the economy moves toward full employment, the price level will rise. Such a trade-off poses a dilemma for policymakers, since an economy cannot have low prices and high employment simultaneously.

The Phillips curve concept was generally accepted during the 1960s. Figure 16-2 shows the unemployment rates and changes in the consumer price index in the United States from 1961 to 1969. Note that inflation increased during the last half of the decade as unemployment declined. The shape of this curve is quite similar to that of the hypothetical Phillips curve in Figure 16-1.

Under the assumptions of a direct trade-off between unemployment and inflation, policy-makers enacted the contractionary fiscal and monetary measures of 1969–70. By late 1969, inflation had reached what was generally believed to be a dangerously high level—over 6 percent. Consequently, government officials decided to accept an increase in unemployment from the current 3.5 percent level to 5 or 5.5 percent, in the belief that such an increase would be accompanied by a substantial decline in the rate of inflation. The results, however, were completely unsatisfactory. By early 1971, the unemployment rate exceeded 6 percent, but there had been little apparent slowdown in rising consumer prices.

Are Traditional Tools Working?

By 1973, faced with a lack of success in combating both inflation and unemployment, some economists were asking if the standard tools were too blunted. Were the soaring inflation rate, 8 percent rise in the cost of living during the first half of 1973, and the persistent 5 percent plus unemployment rate merely the result of temporary aberrations coupled with a spell of bad luck and poor timing on the part of the Nixon administration? Or was the United States facing a new era that would require new tools to fight a new kind of inflation and unemployment?

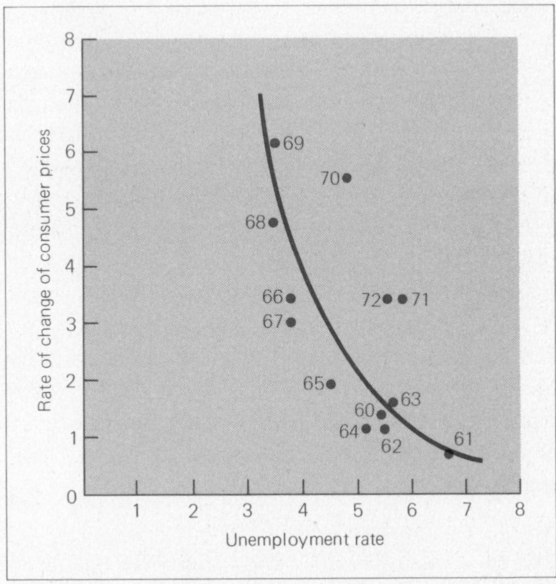

FIGURE 16-2 PHILLIPS CURVE, 1961–69 This curve is drawn from actual data, and its shape is similar to that of Figure 16-1. Note how the unemployment rate rises as the rate of price increase declines. At the upper (left-hand) end of the curve, a small increase in unemployment may be traded off against a relatively large fall in the rate of inflation. Even at high levels of unemployment, some inflation occurs because of structural elements in the economy. The years 1970–72 are included for comparison to show the changing trade-off.

Critics of the New Economics emphasize three factors that play an important role in the economic life of the 1970s, but that are to a large extent bypassed by the traditional fiscal and monetary policy approach to stabilization.

Monopolistic Power: Big Business and Big Unions The premises on which our present-day fiscal and monetary policies are based assume a fundamentally competitive system. Unemployment is believed to function as an effective counterforce to inflation because workers competing for jobs will bid wages down. Adherents of the New Economics recognize that wages and prices are not as flexible as assumed in classical economic theory, but believe that excess demand is still the fundamental cause of inflation. There are, however, other factors that create inflationary pressures. One is economic concentration. Monopolistic power in a number of key industries can raise prices without excess demand. For example, from August 1954, when the economy was in a recession, to July 1957, when the boom of that cycle peaked, prices in the seven most concentrated industries rose almost four times as fast as those in the nine least concentrated industries. Strong unions can win wage increases, even in the face of substantial national unemployment. Consequently, periodic declines in the level of aggregate demand no longer function as an effective restraint on price increases. From a policy point of view, this means that contractionary monetary and fiscal measures have little influence on price levels, for important segments of the economy apparently have the power to ignore the consequences of these contractionary measures in setting their wages and prices.

International Trade Problems Both the effectiveness of monetary and fiscal measures and the willingness of government to employ them have been enormously influenced by growing U.S. international trade problems in the 1960s and 1970s. Thus far in the 1970s the United States has experienced a balance of payments deficit—a situation in which the money value of all the goods and services bought from foreigners (plus money transferred from abroad) has exceeded the value of those items sold (or transferred) to foreigners. This continuing payments deficit poses many serious problems (see discussions of gold outflow, devaluation, and floating exchange rates in Chapters 39 and 40), and the government is under considerable foreign and domestic pressure to improve the balance of payments position.

Very often, however, a conflict occurs between these balance of payments objectives and domestic stabilization goals. For example, the U.S. payments deficit is increased when interest rates in the United States are relatively low, and businesses (either foreign or American) borrow dollars here and send them abroad to build plants or make investments. One way of discouraging such a dollar outflow would be to raise interest rates at home. Indeed, if interest rates were raised enough, they might actually encourage foreigners to transfer their funds from abroad to the United States. Moreover, tight money policies might dampen domestic inflation and thus make the prices of U.S. goods more attractive to foreign buyers. But policy-makers must also consider the domestic consequences of contractionary monetary measures. Should the Federal Reserve tighten the money supply during a recession merely to reduce a balance of payments deficit? In 1971, for example, when domestic unemployment hit 6.1 percent, the government continued its expansionary monetary policy despite an accelerating balance of payments deficit. From a domestic point of view, this seemed like the best course of action, but the price paid—a series of official and de facto dollar devaluations—was very high.

The balance of payments problem, then, seems to restrict, at least theoretically, the fiscal and monetary options available to policy-makers, particularly during recessions. This can be clearly seen in terms of policies that would lead to lower domestic interest rates, but there are also restrictions concerning fiscal measures. Can a government, worried about declining foreign markets for American goods, safely embark on an expansionary spending or tax-cutting program at home, when it knows that such policies are bound to lead to even more inflation, and thus higher prices for the goods we are trying to sell abroad? The answers to such questions are complex, for domestic stabilization policies almost always have an impact in the international sphere. When domestic and international economic goals conflict, the problems for policy-makers are great. (Some possible solutions to these problems are discussed in Chapter 40.)

The Changing Composition of the American Labor Force Another explanation for the recent failure of monetary and fiscal policy to make much of a dent in the stagflation problem involves a change in both the composition of the American labor force and the nature of the demand for labor. Since World War II, the demand for more highly skilled and well-educated workers has been increasing. At the same time, however, new entries into the labor force have consisted of a growing percentage of unskilled and poorly educated teen-agers and women, plus a large number of those whose job skills have become obsolescent through technological advances. The highly skilled and well educated maintain high employment levels, even in time of recession. They are generally unaffected by contractionary measures aimed at controlling inflation by restraining wage increases. The unskilled and poorly educated, on the other hand, often find it difficult to obtain employment, even in prosperous times, because of a declining demand for their labor. As a result, in a recession, attempts to reduce the overall unemployment rate by expanding aggregate demand tend to be unsuccessful: The skilled workers are already enjoying high employment levels despite the nationwide unemployment problem, and increases in aggregate demand do not necessarily create the kinds of jobs for which the unskilled are suited.

This analysis suggests, in the words of one economist, that "so long as we remain tied to the Keynesian approach, meek prisoners to the Phillips curve,"[2] we will be unable to emerge from the stagflation trap.

2 Melville J. Ulmer, "The Collapse of Keynesianism," *The New Republic*, May 5, 1973, p. 19.

Is There a Phillips Curve?

Confronted with the U.S. experience since 1969, some authorities have questioned whether there still is a Phillips curve—that is, whether a trade-off between inflation and unemployment continues to exist. Two hypotheses have been offered to explain the recent performance of the economy.

The Shifting Curve Some economists contend that changes in the structure of the economy mean that the Phillips curve has shifted. This explanation, offered by George Perry of the Brookings Institution, claims that the concept of an inverse relationship between inflation and unemployment is still valid, but that because of the changes in the work force, the Phillips curve has shifted upward to create a higher level of unemployment for a given level of inflation. Fifteen or twenty years ago, an unemployment rate of 4 percent was high enough to keep wage increases from exceeding increases in productivity; consequently, price increases remained at a minimum. Today, however, the changes in the composition of the labor force—proportionately more teen-agers and women—mean that a 4 percent unemployment rate is no longer sufficient to hold down wage increases.

Perry believes that it is unemployment among prime-age male workers, rather than overall unemployment rates, that is the key factor in keeping wage increases and hence inflation under control. These prime-age male workers put in more hours per week at higher wages. Therefore, their wage increases primarily determine costs and price increases. In 1955, when the overall unemployment rate was 4 percent, the unemployment rate for prime-age males was about 3 percent; 15 years later, when the unemployment rate was again 4 percent, their rate was estimated at less than 2 percent. Thus, an unemployment rate of 4 percent today has a different effect on price stabilization than it did in 1955. Perry estimated that a 4 percent unemployment rate would have resulted in a 2.75 percent rate of inflation in 1955, but a 4.5 percent rate in 1969. Consequently, a higher overall unemployment rate is required today to maintain the same degree

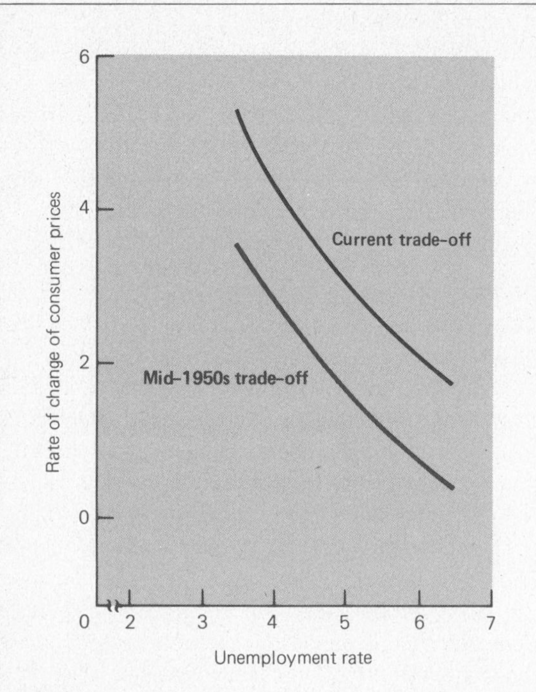

FIGURE 16-3 SHIFT IN PHILLIPS CURVE **Between 1955 and 1970, the Phillips curve has probably shifted upward. These trade-off curves are different because of a tightening of the labor market. Since prime-age males on the average work longer hours at higher wages than do other groups, their unemployment rate has greater impact on prices. Between 1955 and 1969, the proportion of teen-agers and women in the labor force rose from 35 percent to 42.6 percent. Also, the unemployment rates of the latter two groups have risen relative to that of prime-age males. Since prices are much more responsive to changes in the unemployment rate of prime-age males, whose share of total unemployment has declined considerably, it follows that it will take substantially larger increases in the unemployment rate to bring given decreases in the rate of inflation.**

SOURCE: "Changing Labor Markets and Inflation," from *Brookings Papers on Economic Activity 3: 1970*, edited by Arthur M. Okun and George L. Perry. P. 432. Copyright © 1971 by The Brookings Institution, Washington, D.C. Reprinted by permission.

of price stability that a 4 percent rate produced 15 years ago. This change can be shown graphically as a shift in the Phillips curve. (See Figure 16-3.) The shape of the curve is still the same, but higher inflation rates result from the same amount of unemployment.

The Vertical Curve Those who support the shifting Phillips curve hypothesis suggest that the curve has merely moved up a notch. The monetarists, on the other hand, have advanced the thesis that, for many economies, the Phillips curve is vertical. They claim that when an economy experiences a steady rate of inflation for a given number of years, workers will eventually recognize that their wage increases are being eroded. Soon, they will begin to expect future inflation and bargain for wage increases with this in mind. Instead of requesting wage increases that will compensate them only for current productivity gains and past inflations, workers will ask to be compensated for the price in-

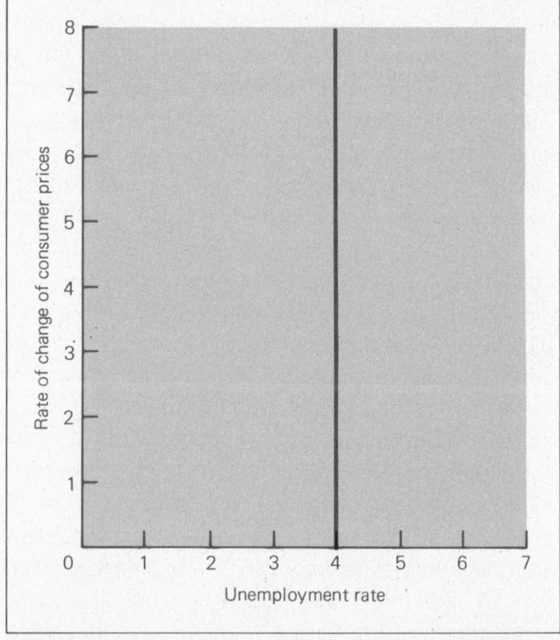

FIGURE 16-4 THE MONETARISTS' PHILLIPS CURVE: NO TRADE-OFF **During periods of inflation, unionized workers may at first accept wage increases that merely raise their money wages, while allowing their real wages to decline. This is the Keynesian "money illusion." When labor becomes aware that it is actually losing ground to inflation, it will seek to make up for lost ground as well as to obtain an allowance for anticipated inflation over the life of the contract. Thus, price increases will begin to accelerate. This acceleration will be due to expectations of future inflation, rather than to an increasingly tight employment situation. Therefore, there is no longer a trade-off between unemployment and inflation, and the Phillips curve will be a vertical line, shown here at 4 percent unemployment. This is considered a full-employment situation.**

creases they expect tomorrow. As a result, prices will begin to rise at an even faster rate. This accelerating rate of inflation is not due to an increasingly tight employment situation, but rather to expectations of future inflation. Therefore, there is no longer a trade-off between inflation and employment, and the Phillips curve, under such circumstances, will be a vertical line. (See Figure 16-4.)

This line can be thought of as the natural rate of unemployment, the point of "full employment," given the structure of the economy. If the structure changes, then the curve will shift, setting a higher or lower natural rate of unemployment.

A compromise between the original Phillips curve theory and the argument of the monetarists has been offered by James Tobin. Tobin agrees that there is an unemployment-inflation trade-off within limits, but he sees the trade-off as one "that becomes ever more fragile and vanishes once unemployment reaches a certain level."[3] Other economists have projected a "danger zone" somewhere between 4 and 5 percent unemployment. Up to this point, increases in the level of employment will produce more inflation, and the Phillips curve will have its traditional shape. However, once the level of employment reaches the danger zone, the curve rapidly becomes vertical, and further increases in inflation will bring no corresponding decreases in unemployment.

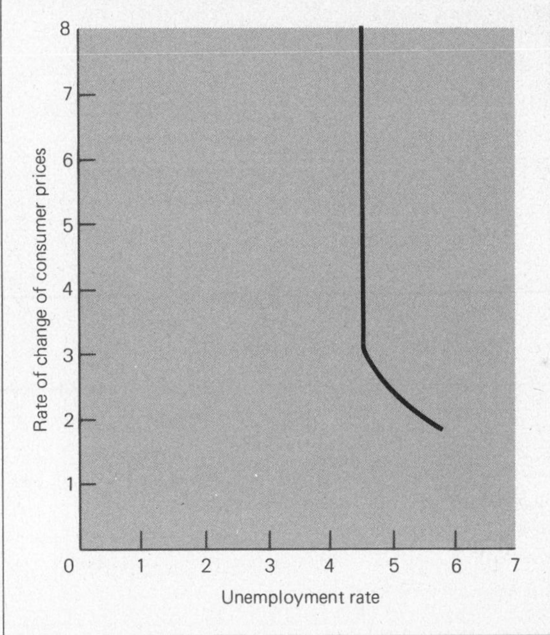

FIGURE 16-5 PHILLIPS CURVE: A COMPROMISE James Tobin has envisaged a trade-off at high levels of unemployment and slowly rising prices, but this trade-off vanishes when the unemployment rate falls to a low enough level. We have shown that level here at 4.5 percent unemployment: At that point the Phillips curve becomes completely vertical. This level may actually be a broader zone rather than a line.

STABILIZATION TOOLS FOR THE SEVENTIES

During the 1970s, there has been growing disillusionment with the manipulation of aggregate demand through monetary and fiscal policy as the preferred method of achieving full employment and price stability. Both interpretations of the Phillips curve point to the importance of structural features not responsive to macroeconomic tools. The search is now underway for new stabilization devices, with special attention being given to various forms of incomes policies as a way of fighting inflation and to the use of micro, rather than macro, tools as a method of solving our unemployment problem. To date, many of these efforts have been experimental and tentative, but it is probable that we are moving toward a stabilization approach that will include many more options than the monetary-fiscal package of the 1960s.

Incomes Policies

The term *incomes policy* is a broad one, referring to any method, voluntary or compulsory, that attempts to restrain inflation by direct limitations on increases in wages or prices. European governments have been experimenting with various forms of peacetime incomes policies since the end of World War II. In the United States, wage-price controls were imposed during World War I, World War II, and the

3 *Business Week*, April 28, 1973, p. 88.

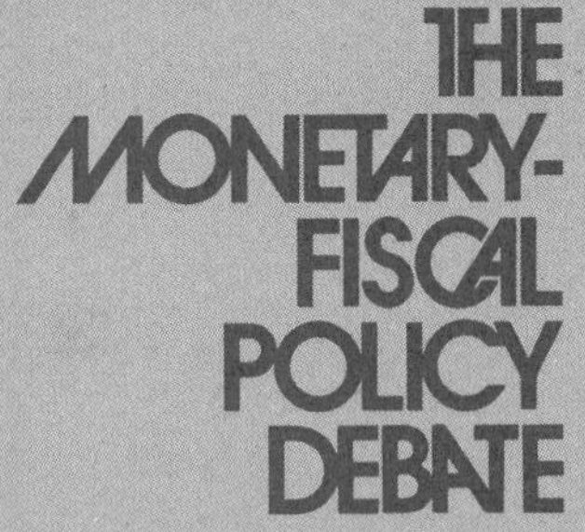

Since either monetary or fiscal policy, or some combination of the two, can be used to regulate economic activity, policy-makers are faced with a choice of methods. There is widespread disagreement, however, concerning the effectiveness of the various stabilization tools. During the 1960s, economic opinion was polarized into two distinct camps. The monetarists claimed that changing the quantity of money was the most useful tool for controlling prices and employment. The New Economists, or neo-Keynesians, opted for primary reliance on fiscal policy; that is, taxing and government spending. To a certain extent, the controversy was intensified by the close association between the monetarists and the political right, and the New Economists and the political left. Walter Heller, John Kenneth Galbraith, and Paul Samuelson, leading exponents of the New Economics, were closely associated with the Kennedy administration, while Milton Friedman, the foremost monetarist, served as Barry Goldwater's chief economic adviser.

The monetarists and New Economists hold radically different views of how the economy should be "operated on." The monetarists, according to one observer, are "neoclassical economists, who at bottom feel the patient is inherently stable; the best course ... they argue, is to let him alone as much as possible." The New Economists, in contrast, "feel that the patient is inherently unstable and must be constantly ... heated up and cooled down ... by a whole battery of government-operated devices."* Although this description may be somewhat overstated, it nevertheless points out an important philosophical difference between the monetarists and the fiscalists. The monetarists contend that their basic tool—the expansion of loans by banks—works primarily through the private sector, and therefore has the advantage of requiring fairly limited government action. The New Economists argue that decisions about the types of economic activity to be encouraged or discouraged should be regulated by government officials acting in the public interest. But the essentially philosophical question of who should make economic policy is not the only one on which the monetarists and the New Economists disagree. There are also several more concrete issues.

To the New Economists, aggregate demand is the central focus of our economy. They believe that changes in aggregate demand introduced through government spending and taxing policies are the key to maintaining full employment and price stability. In theory, their avowed aims include both of these objectives. As a practical matter, how-

* Gilbert Burck, "Must Full Employment Mean Inflation?" *Fortune*, October 1966, p. 121.

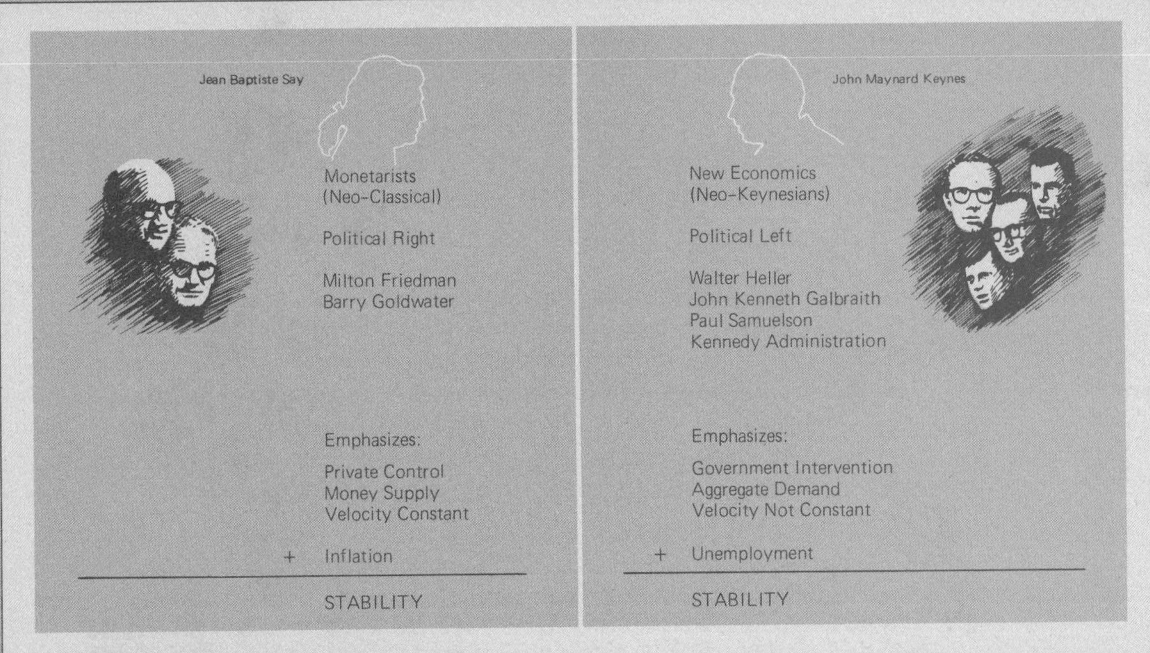

ever, their primary emphasis has always been on avoiding unemployment. The New Economists distrust the ability of monetary tools to maintain full employment. They note, for example, that despite extended use of monetary policy during the Great Depression, the unemployment rate never fell below 14 percent;† and more recently, the tight money policies used to curb inflation have led to sharp increases in unemployment. In brief, to the New Economists, expansionary monetary policy during a recession appears unable to eliminate unemployment, whereas monetary policy in a period of prosperity seems to lead inevitably to high unemployment.

From a theoretical point of view, the New Economists also question the entire premise on which monetary policy is based. They see changes in the quantity of money as only one of the determinants of aggregate demand. In fact changes in M are sometimes a result of changes in aggregate demand rather than a cause. The Fed, they say, can create conditions under which bank reserves expand or contract; however, actual changes in loans outstanding (and thus in demand deposits or M) respond to changes in general business conditions rather than to the

† This point is debatable. A monetarist might ascribe the extended length of the Great Depression to the failure of the fiscal measures employed, rather then to the ineffectiveness of the monetary measures.

wishes of the Fed. Moreover, velocity is not constant, as the monetarists insist, but may vary, upsetting the effects of monetary policy.

The concern of the New Economists with unemployment probably reflects their Keynesian roots in the Great Depression. The monetarists, on the other hand, trace their roots back to the classical economists, who believed the economy always tends toward full employment. As a result, the monetarists emphasize inflation, rather than unemployment, as the major problem with which economists deal. They also differ from the New Economists in their evaluation of the role of money. First they believe that the supply of money is the key factor behind changes in prices, income, and the level of economic activity. Second, they claim that the amount of money in the economy can be established by outside forces—that is, by the Federal Reserve Board. Given these two assumptions, it follows that once the Fed decides to increase the supply of money, this increase will be reflected in an increase in demand throughout the economy. Similarly, once the Fed cuts the supply of money, the demand for goods and services will necessarily contract.

But the monetarists do not stop here. Not only do they attempt to refute the criticisms of monetary policy offered by the New Economists, but they also take the offensive by introducing some very significant objections of their own to fiscal policy. A government spending program, they claim, will not necessarily increase aggregate demand. If such a program is financed by budget deficits, the government borrowing that supports such deficits will merely drive up interest rates and "crowd out" private spending. Government spending, then, may merely replace private spending, with little change in aggregate demand. Similarly, budget surpluses may not be deflationary, as the New Economists claim. The government may actually use a surplus to repay outstanding debt. If this is the case, the result would be a decline in interest rates, which could stimulate private sector borrowing, and thus negate the theoretically deflationary consequences of the original budget surplus. Furthermore, since the problems of lags are greater using fiscal policy, money has a more direct and powerful effect on the economy.

Korean War, but peacetime incomes policies date back only to the Kennedy administration.

Voluntary Incomes Policies In 1962, the Council of Economic Advisers (CEA), claiming that the public had a legitimate interest in the wage and price increases that resulted from collective bargaining, issued a set of voluntary guidelines for noninflationary wage and price settlements. Very broadly, the CEA suggested that wage increases be limited to the rate at which U.S. productivity was increasing—3.2 percent annually. The theory was that employers could meet such wage increases out of productivity gains, and therefore prices would remain stable. In general, the guidelines were not particularly successful. With no coercive powers, the government was unable to persuade either unions or businesses to forgo the wage or price increases they were able to obtain in the marketplace. One important exception, however, occurred in April of 1962, when President Kennedy, infuriated by a price increase announced by U.S. Steel and followed by most other steel producers, called Roger Blough, President of U.S. Steel, to the White House. The President rallied public support behind the CEA guidelines, and the steel industry soon rescinded the price rise. In several other key settlements, such "moral suasion" or "jawboning" was used by Presidents Kennedy and Johnson with various degrees of success. But by 1968, the guidelines had been largely ignored or forgotten.

When President Nixon took office in 1969, he announced that he was opposed to "jawboning" or to any other attempt by government to interfere in the collective-bargaining or price-setting process. By 1970, however, following a series of highly inflationary wage settlements or price increases in major industries, he introduced a system of "inflation alerts" through which the government would "spotlight," for public information, any wage or price settlements it believed to be inflationary. Very shortly thereafter, the construction industry negotiated a three-year, 30 percent wage increase package, and the aluminum industry announced a 6 percent price increase. Inflation alerts were issued in both cases, but in neither case were the wage or price increases withdrawn. The incidents seem to confirm the earlier American experience that voluntary incomes policies are generally ineffective.

Compulsory Incomes Policies: Nixon's "New Economic Policy" In August 1971, President Nixon announced the first peacetime compulsory incomes policy for the United States. Although most Americans were distressed by the accelerating inflation rate, and many recognized that traditional contractionary monetary and fiscal measures would be undesirable because unemployment was hovering near 6 percent, the President's bold imposition of a 90-day freeze on all wages and most prices still came as a surprise. But Phase I, as the move was called, was greeted with considerable enthusiasm and cooperation. On the next day of trading, the stock market rallied more than 30 points; auto manufacturers immediately withdrew a previously announced price rise; and there was relatively little protest from organized labor forced to forgo scheduled wage increases.

The President acted under authority previously given him by Congress in the Economic Stabilization Act of 1970. His order called for a 90-day freeze on wages, prices, and rents, and prohibited sellers from charging more for their goods than the highest price charged during the preceding 90 days. Raw agricultural foods were exempted from the freeze under the assumption that, being subject to strong competitive forces, these were impossible to regulate fairly and effectively. A cabinet-level Cost of Living Council (COLC) administered the program, with help from the Office of Emergency Preparedness, the staffs of local Internal Revenue offices, and the Justice Department. Although injunctions, prosecution by the Justice Department, and fines up to $5000 could be imposed on violators, enforcement staffs were small, and the high level of compliance was largely the result of voluntary cooperation throughout the business community.

Although compliance with Phase I was excellent, critics did point out certain inequities or dangers. Paul Samuelson, a spokesman for many liberals, claimed that the freeze was "flawed by its pro-business lopsidedness,"[4] for any productivity gains achieved during the period of the freeze would go entirely to business rather than to labor or consumers. Others seriously questioned whether the freeze would work in the long run, or whether wage-price increases would merely be postponed, to reappear in even larger amounts once the freeze was lifted. Milton Friedman referred to the freeze as "cosmetic, not therapeutic." Quoting Edmund Burke, he warned that it might turn out to be one of those "very plausible schemes with very pleasing commencements that have often shameful and lamentable conclusions."[5]

PHASE II In combating inflation, it appeared that Phase I was very successful. Although it is difficult to assign sole responsibility to the freeze, the consumer price index increased at an annual rate of only 1.9 percent—the best record in more than 10 years—and the wholesale price index actually ended the period a shade lower. Phase II, announced in October of 1971, was designed as a longer-term program, with built-in mechanisms to handle the inequities that are bound to develop during an absolute freeze. As part of the Cost of Living Council, two separate agencies were created, the Pay Board and the Price Commission. The Pay Board proceeded to establish wage guidelines of 5.5 percent within which contract settlements might be negotiated, but with some provisions for special "catch-up" exemptions for industries (like steel) caught in the middle of wage negotiations at the time Phase I was introduced. The Price Commission set guidelines for permissible price increases, which were determined by a complicated set of formulas involving costs, productivity gains, and so on. In general, these guidelines provided that prices could not be raised if such an increase would result in profit margins higher than the average experienced by the company during two of the last three years. Filing and prior approval requirements for wage and price increases were fairly rigorous, and prosecution and fines were provided for violators.

Phase II continued for more than a year, and it too was apparently successful. By the last quarter of 1972, inflation was running at a 3.2 percent rate, down from the pre-freeze rate of 4.8 in the second quarter of 1971, and not too far away from the President's stated 2.5 to 3 percent objective. At this point the administration decided to remove almost all controls. According to government forecasts, the economy was headed for a mid-year slowdown, and it was believed that inflationary pressures should subside even if controls were eliminated. With this game-plan in mind, Phase III was introduced in mid-January of 1973.

PHASE III Under Phase III, the teeth of the incomes policy were removed. To a large extent, compliance was made voluntary rather than compulsory, and the actual guidelines themselves were so watered down as to be almost meaningless. Prior approval for wage or price increases was no longer required for almost all industries; only the health, food, and construction industries had to continue with the old Phase II procedures. It is true that the very largest companies were required to file notice of wage or price changes with the COLC, and in theory, wage guidelines based roughly on the Phase II 5.5 percent standard and price guidelines based on the old profit margin limitations were continued, but all penalties for excessive wage or price increases were removed. One of the few sanctions that remained was a vague threat that the COLC could ask for a price rollback for an industry or company whose actions were "unreasonably inconsistent" with Phase III objectives.

The lack of confidence that greeted the announcement of Phase III was perhaps best illustrated by the 20-point drop in the Dow Jones stock market index the following day; and within weeks, the bad news on the inflation front confirmed this initial pessimism. In the first six months of 1973, the cost of living increased at an 8 percent annual rate; and in the month of May, the wholesale price index rose by an astounding 2.1 percent, or at an annual rate of over 25 percent. Since wholesale prices usually

4 Paul A. Samuelson, "Two Cheers for the New Nixon Program," in *Economics: Mainstream Readings and Radical Critiques*, 2nd ed., edited by David Mermelstein (New York: Random House, 1973), p. 147.

5 Milton Friedman, "Why the Freeze Is a Mistake," in Mermelstein, p. 146.

move in advance of retail prices, the outlook was grim indeed.

Pressure for remedial action by the administration increased. Congress threatened to act on its own. Nervous foreigners, frightened that U.S. inflation was reaching a runaway stage, unloaded dollars abroad, and the price of the dollar in terms of European currencies sagged. Finally, in June of 1973, President Nixon introduced Phase III½, which reimposed a price freeze (but not a wage freeze), and promised to establish a new package of controls, Phase IV, within 60 days. Most consumers and businesses doubted that the projected Phase IV would be successful, and there was extensive concern about new problems (shortages, black market, rationing) that might occur as a result.

Why did Phase III fail? Why was public enthusiasm and confidence concerning the proposed Phase IV so much less than it had been for Phases I and II? Answers to these questions will help us understand the problems underlying any incomes policy and the limitations inherent in any stabilization program tied primarily to an incomes approach.

It would appear that the failure of Phase III was due to the administration's misreading of the economic signals: Instead of slackening off, the boom accelerated. In early 1973, consumer spending soared: The saving rate declined from 8 percent in the second quarter of 1972 to 6.7 percent in the first quarter of 1973; consumer borrowing increased by $2.2 billion in the month of May alone, and retail sales showed a remarkable 12.4 percent improvement over the previous year. Throughout the nation, from meat counters to automobile salesrooms, from appliance stores to supermarkets, demand increased.

Looking back, the increase in demand should not have been totally unexpected. The considerable fiscal and monetary stimulation of the preceding year was finally having an impact. The budget had shown a $23.2 billion deficit in 1972, after a $23 billion deficit the year before; the Federal Reserve had increased the money supply by more than 8 percent during 1972. Although the fiscal 1974 budget showed a relatively small deficit and although the money supply was down to a 3.2 percent growth rate during the first four months of 1973, there is always a time lag when expansionary fiscal and monetary policies are used. Therefore, it was not until Phase III that the U.S. economy felt the full impact of the expansionary actions taken earlier.

But the demand side of the picture does not tell the whole story. Just at the time when demand was accelerating, a combination of factors was acting to restrain supply. The corn blight of 1970 was showing up in reduced meat supplies in 1973, and bad weather in the United States in the preceding fall and winter resulted in sharply reduced produce crops in many areas. In addition, the failure of snow cover for two successive years ruined two Russian wheat crops, and a drought in Asia and Australia reduced food supplies in those parts of the world. These events, in turn, triggered huge foreign purchases of the U.S. feed grains, wiping out our surpluses. Finally, worldwide prosperity, plus the devaluation of the U.S. dollar, led to increased foreign purchases of U.S. commodities such as hides, textiles, and scrap iron, reducing the supplies of these goods available to American consumers.

What was developing in the United States, then, was a classic demand-pull inflation. When supplies are inadequate to meet an expanding demand, the response is an increase in prices, and this is exactly what happened once the tough controls of Phase II were removed.

PHASE IV The introduction of Phase IV in August 1973 was accompanied by widespread skepticism. Even George Shultz, Secretary of the Treasury, and the man responsible for much of the Nixon administration stabilization game-plan, refused to make any optimistic forecasts. "It is desirable to be a little humble," said Mr. Shultz. After two years of controls, inflation, which had been running at a 4.2 percent annual rate in pre-Phase I August 1971, had accelerated to an 8 percent rate by June 1973.

Phase IV was more complicated than its predecessors and, in some ways, tougher. It continued the 6.2 percent wage guidelines of the earlier stabilization plans, restricting wage increases to 5.5 percent plus an additional .7 percent for fringe benefits. Businesses were permitted to raise prices only to pass on any higher costs they incurred, but unlike the earlier phases, they could increase their prices only by the actual amount of the higher costs, with no allowance for profit adjustment on these higher costs. In addition, price increases were subject to profit-margin constraints similar to the earlier periods: Even if specific costs increased, a company could not increase its prices if such increases would result in a higher profit margin than the average of the best of its last two out of five fiscal years. Within this framework, smaller companies (those with annual sales of less than $100 million) could increase their prices at once.

There were several important industry exceptions written into Phase IV, illustrating both the administration's desire to eliminate controls as soon as possible, and its recognition that rigid controls could have negative supply consequences in some sectors of the economy. In the oil industry, "old" crude oil (production from existing wells) was made subject to price ceilings, but "new" oil was exempted, in the hope that such an exemption would encourage the development of new domestic oil supplies. In the food sector, special rules provided that prices could be increased *without limit* to reflect changes in raw agricultural costs: The retail prices of all foodstuffs would depend on unregulated and uncontrolled free market prices at the cattle stockyards, grain pits, and produce exchanges. There was one temporary exception to this rule. Beef remained under the rigid controls of Phase III½ until September 12, in order to spread the price bulge in the supermarkets over several months. The result was to further restrict supplies and place greater pressure on the prices of other meats. This point is nicely illustrated by comparing the price and supply performance of chicken and beef during Phase III½, when chicken prices were decontrolled but beef prices remained frozen. In one typical northeastern city the price of chicken advanced from 62 cents a pound to 92 cents, but supplies were plentiful. Beef, on the other hand, when available openly in stores, did sell at the pre-freeze level, but many supermarket beef counters were empty, and part of beef supplies reached the consumer through black market or under-the-counter transactions. Moreover, trade sources suggested that the sharp increase in chicken prices was perhaps at least partially related to the beef situation: If beef had been decontrolled and permitted to sell at its free-market price, perhaps the demand for chicken and its price would not have escalated quite as much.

WILL PHASE IV WORK? In evaluating the chances for Phase IV to work, or for future incomes policies to prove successful, we must remember that the underlying economic realities were very different in mid-1973 from what they were when Phases I and II were introduced. In August of 1971, the unemployment rate exceeded 6 percent, and American industry was operating at about 75 percent of capacity. Thus, it was cost-push rather than demand-pull inflation that Phase I and Phase II controls appeared to handle so effectively. In mid-1973, in contrast, the economy was operating close to full capacity, the unemployment rate was under 5 percent, and inflation was essentially demand-pull rather than cost-push. Consequently, many believe that if Phase IV is successful, it will be due, at least in part, to the other measures taken coincidentally with the wage-price controls: In 1973, restrictions were placed on exports of important grains (such as soybeans) and raw materials (such as scrap steel); farm subsidy payments were cut back and land was removed from the soil bank in an effort to increase production of foodstuffs; President Nixon continued to press for spending cuts in the budget; the Federal Reserve proceeded to tighten money in 1973 by raising the discount rate to 7½ percent, matching the highest levels in 52 years; and there was even some talk about a possible tax increase. Thus, although it was the incomes policy that was receiving the headlines, the President's package also included many of the fiscal and monetary measures traditionally used during inflationary periods.

It appears, then, that the recent American experience with an incomes policy has taught us many useful lessons. Controls are most effective in handling cost-push inflation in a period of high unemployment. They may prove less effective, however, when used to curb demand-pull inflation; and if used overextensively during such a period, they could divert supplies to black markets and lead to shortages and rationing. Moreover, they can bottle up necessary price increases, creating a surge of inflation when controls are removed. Therefore, it appears that monetary and fiscal tools are still very useful when demand-pull inflation occurs. But because of the prevalence of cost-push inflation in the United States during periods of recession, it is likely that some form of incomes policy will be a permanent addition to our arsenal of stabilization tools during the 1970s.

Use of Micro Tools

Fighting Unemployment As we discussed earlier, it may be that structural changes in the labor force have created a situation in which even substantial increases in aggregate demand and substantial amounts of inflation have only a minor effect on reducing unemployment. Consequently, some experts have suggested that what is needed to solve the unemployment problem is not a large, general increase in aggregate demand, but rather training, education, relocation, or public works programs directed at specific groups of unemployed. Efforts could also be made to eliminate the job discrimination and limited access to union membership that still affect blacks, Puerto Ricans, Mexican Americans, and women. Some attempts in these directions were an important part of the Kennedy-Johnson Great Society program, but the cutbacks in funding for OEO and manpower training introduced as an anti-inflationary measure in the fiscal 1974 budget eliminated many of them.

Such cutbacks point up a vulnerability of microeconomic approaches. Changing the structure of an economy does not occur rapidly; it takes time to educate or retrain people in order to shift the Phillips curve to the left. During the training, large outlays for the programs may fuel inflation and make continuation of the programs politically difficult to justify.

Increasing Competition Other policy suggestions include attempts to increase competition in business and labor in order to restrain wage and price increases, at least during periods of recession. But the Nixon administration, like others before it, has shown relatively little interest in restraining the monopolistic power of big unions and big business. Although the Justice Department has taken a few widely publicized steps to force the largest conglomerates (such as ITT) to divest themselves of some recent acquisitions, the trend toward increased aggregate business concentration does not appear to have abated. In addition, the close and dearly bought alliances between President Nixon and both George Meany, President of AFL-CIO, and James Hoffa, ex-President of the Teamsters Union, suggest that no serious attempts will be made to restrain the bargaining power of the biggest unions. In practice, then, increasing competition to restrain inflationary pressures does not appear to be a politically viable scheme.

One other method for increasing competition is to remove barriers to foreign trade, both here and abroad. This could provide competition for even highly concentrated U.S. industries. Adjustment assistance for those dislocated by foreign competition could soften the impact.

Revolution

The radical economists have taken the position that the current period of stagflation is merely one step closer to the creation of a new economic system in which private property will be eliminated. They believe that the capitalist economies are now demonstrating their fundamental inadequacies and that they will continue to be unable to provide either full employment or stable prices. The introduction of an incomes policy merely verifies this conclusion, they claim, because it illustrates the inability of the free-market economy to solve its own problems without government control and planning. In other words, the radicals suggest that we are already experiencing a planned economy, but one in which the planning is done by, and for the benefit of, a big government and big business alliance. Surely, they argue, we would be better off in a socialist society, in which the "planning take[s] place under the aegis of the many rather than of the corporate few."[6]

6 David Mermelstein, "Microeconomics in Transition," *Economics: Mainstream Readings and Radical Critiques* (New York: Random House, 1973), p. 126.

SUMMARY

1 There is an inverse relationship between the unemployment rate and the rate of inflation. The Phillips curve is an attempt to define this relationship in terms of a trade-off: If we want stable prices, we must accept a certain amount of unemployment and *vice versa.* It is admittedly difficult to attain full employment (4 percent unemployment) *and* relative price stability (2 to 3 percent annual increase in the CPI). In recent years, the United States has been plagued by stagflation—high unemployment (in excess of 5 percent) and inflation (CPI rising at 4 to 9 percent annually).

2 This situation reflects structural features of the U.S. economy. Monopolistic power in a number of key industries can raise prices without excess demand; and strong unions can win wage increases, even in the face of substantial national unemployment. Consequently, periodic declines in the level of aggregate demand no longer function to effectively restrain price increases.

3 Furthermore, U.S. policy-makers have been under considerable pressure to improve our balance of payments position. One way of discouraging a dollar outflow would be to raise interest rates in the United States. To promote full employment, however, low interest rates are desirable, as well as an expansionary fiscal policy. Can we pursue such a course when we know that low interest rates would lead to a flight of dollars abroad and that an expansionary fiscal policy would lead to more inflation, and thus to higher prices for the goods we are trying to sell abroad?

4 Another factor has been the change in the composition of the labor force to include growing numbers of unskilled and poorly educated teen-agers and women. The highly skilled and well educated maintain high employment levels and are able to secure wage increases, even during recessions. The unskilled and poorly educated, however, often find it difficult to obtain employment, even in good times, because of a declining demand for their labor.

5 Confronted by persistent stagflation, economists have offered several explanations. A shifting Phillips curve, reflecting the changes in the labor market or other market structures, is one explanation for higher rates of inflation and unemployment. A vertical Phillips curve, reflecting a natural rate of unemployment combined with expectations of inflation which create further inflationary pressures, is the monetarist account.

6 The tools to cope with this problem may include more than the macroeconomic ones of monetary and fiscal policy. Incomes policy acts directly upon prices and wages, but creates dislocations in the economy. It seems more effective against

cost-push inflation than against demand-pull inflation. Microeconomic tools include training or direct public works programs, but these may add to spending and thereby to inflation before they can help shift the Phillips curve leftward. Changes in the structure of the economy, either to make it more competitive—for example, through the removal of trade barriers—or to eliminate capitalism altogether, are other options, but these seem unlikely to occur, and are of unknown efficacy.

SUGGESTED READINGS

Committee for Economic Development. *Further Weapons against Inflation: Measures to Supplement General Fiscal and Monetary Policies.* New York: CED, 1970.

Dernberg, Thomas F., and **D. M. McDougall.** *Macroeconomics.* 4th ed. Chap. 16. New York: McGraw-Hill, 1972.

Economic Report of the President. Washington, D.C.: Government Printing Office, annual. Reviews previous policies and outlines goals and tools for subsequent years.

Hunt, E. K., and **Howard J. Sherman.** *Economics: An Introduction to Traditional and Radical Views.* Chap. 30. New York: Harper & Row, 1972.

Pigott, William, and **Robert Haney Scott.** "The Monetarist Controversy in the United States." *The Banker,* October 1972, pp. 1259–1266.

Schultze, Charles L., Edward R. Fried, Alice M. Rivlin, and **Nancy H. Teeters.** *Setting National Priorities.* Washington, D.C.: Brookings Institution. Provides an annual critique of the budget with alternative approaches.

Shapiro, Edward. *Macroeconomic Analysis.* 2nd ed. Chap. 23. New York: Harcourt Brace Jovanovich, 1970.

Wallich, Henry C., and **Mable I. Wallich.** "What Have We Learned About Inflation?" *Challenge,* March–April, 1973, pp. 5–12.

QUESTIONS

1 Review
   a. the problem of stagflation,
   b. hypotheses concerning the reasons for stagflation, including the radical analysis,
   c. the debate between the monetarists and New Economists concerning the best tools to be used for stabilization,
   d. incomes policies and their use during the early 1970s,
   e. microeconomic tools.

2 By the summer of 1973, the Federal Trade Commission released a report suggesting that the gasoline shortage was largely a result of efforts by large gasoline companies to protect their profit margins. At about the same time, the state of Florida brought suit against over a dozen of the largest gasoline companies under similar charges. What are the consequences of such behavior by big business for the problem of stagflation?

3 Assume that the government provides tax allowances or subsidies for those companies that provide training for teen-agers, blacks, and women, whom they then

subsequently hire. What might be the consequences for the problem of stagflation? How might the Phillips curve be affected?

4 The debate between fiscal and monetary advocates has been covered over the last five chapters. Discuss the differences in emphasis and assumptions about three of the following:
   a. the velocity of money,
   b. the equilibrium level of the economy,
   c. the role of expectations in a severe depression,
   d. the role of expectations during inflation,
   e. the effect of the money supply upon aggregate demand,
   f. policy lags,
   g. differential effects on sectors of the economy.

5 The vertical Phillips curve extends the analysis of conditions reflected by the classical region of the LM curve. Explain or refute.

6 Wage-price controls affect the Phillips curve. Show and explain how.

7 Even rapid inflation is worth the price of reducing unemployment. Show why this prescription is impossible according to monetarist theories.

8 In June of 1973, after evidence that Phase III was not working, the Nixon administration announced a price freeze but stated that there would be no wage freeze. The administration believed that wages were not responsible for the current inflation. What reasoning was behind such a belief? What might Milton Friedman predict for future price increases and wage settlements during the freeze?

9 Select a current aspect of fiscal or monetary policy and write a short column of analysis such as might appear in *Time* or *Newsweek*. For source material, check the most recent *Economic Report of the President*, *The Report* of the Joint Economic Committee of Congress, the *New York Times* Sunday "Week in Review" and "Financial" sections, the *Wall Street Journal*, and *Business Week*.

PART 4

GROWTH

CHAPTER 17

GROWTH THEORY

The rate at which an economy grows may mean the difference between an illiterate, hungry population and one that enjoys an increasingly comfortable standard of living. For an economy must expand to provide additional jobs, goods, and income just to keep pace with population increases.

An economy that is stagnating does not maintain a constant living standard. It actually provides fewer goods and less income to each of its members. Or, as the Red Queen remarked to Alice in *Through the Looking Glass:* "It takes all the running *you* can do to keep in the same place. If you want to get somewhere, you must run twice as fast."[1]

When an economy begins to "run twice as fast," it can make real progress. The burden of scarcity is lessened, and it can undertake new projects without sacrificing old ones. It can have more guns and more butter at the same time.

DEFINING GROWTH

The basis of growth is increased output and income. But expansion of output and growth are not the same. Expansion may occur when a nation with slack in its economy starts utilizing more of its productive capacity. There is still room for increased output within the limits of present capacity. As more and more goods are produced, that capacity may eventually be met. The economy is then said to be operating at a point on its production-possibilities frontier. At this stage, unless the frontier moves outward, the economy can expand no more: It can only trade one product for another, producing more guns only at the expense of butter.

The production frontier can move outward only through economic growth. Whereas expansion is really a short-term event, closely related to business cycles, economic growth occurs over a longer period and involves increases in the actual capacity of the economy. In reality, of course, it is often difficult to tell expansion and growth apart, and the existing level of economic activity will affect the ability of a nation to push its frontier outward. But economic growth generally concerns long-term trends in the economy.

Traditionally, economic growth has been measured by the changes in Gross National Product (GNP), or the market value of all goods and services, usually adjusted for price changes. The rate of growth is based on the percentage change of GNP between two dates. These dates are usually selected with the pattern of business cycles in mind, since comparing a peak with a trough will distort the rate of growth.

A fast rate of GNP growth, however, is a deceptive signal of economic success. Statistically, the goal could be met simply by a huge migration into an area. Indeed, in a regional study for the Committee on Economic Development, Edward F. Denison noted just such a development for the period between 1929 and 1957 in the United States. By far the greatest contributor to GNP during this period was the Far West, with a growth rate of 4.4 percent, compared with a national average of 2.9 percent. It seemed an impressive comparison. But a per capita breakdown of this growth told quite another story. The rate in the Far West, Denison found, actually trailed the national figure, 1.3 to 1.7 percent, respectively. The real growth occurred in what seemed to be the sluggish parts of the country.

> The highest (per capita) rates were achieved in the Southeast and Southwest, regions that in 1929 were among the least industrialized and in which technique was least advanced, where the labor force was least educated and skilled, and where, in addition, there was substantial underutilization of labor in agriculture. In short, these are regions which shared the possibilities for rapid growth that are characteristic of nations less developed than the United States, though to a lesser degree than most.[2]

Economic growth, then, is more appropriately defined as the rate of increase of per capita income, which is reflected in an improved standard of living.

An improved standard of living involves more than growing per capita GNP, however. As we saw in

1 Lewis Carroll, *Through the Looking Glass* (New York: Random House, 1946), p. 32.

Opening photo by Sabine Weiss, Rapho Guillumette Pictures

2 Edward F. Denison, *The Sources of Economic Growth in the United States and the Alternatives Before Us* (New York: Committee on Economic Development, 1962), p. 9.

TABLE 17-1 Measuring Growth of National Income (1960–70)

	Annual rate of growth %		Total (millions of dollars)		Per capita (dollars)	
	Total	Per capita	1960	1970	1960	1970
United States	4.6	3.2	509,028	969,574	2817	4743
West Germany	4.6	3.6	72,036	186,743	1300	3034
Japan[a]	10.6	9.4	43,098	197,623	462	1911
United Kingdom	2.8	2.1	71,020	118,535	1357	2128

There are a number of ways to measure the growth of a nation. In absolute terms, the United States has had the greatest amount of growth in national income, but in terms of growth rate, Japan has been surging ahead much more rapidly. Were this to continue, Japan's absolute size would eventually surpass that of the United States. Neither of these figures tells how growth affects the standard of living. This is reflected by per capita income, which takes into account the effect of population growth.

[a] 1960–67.

SOURCE: United Nations, *Statistical Yearbook*, 1971 (New York: United Nations, 1973). Based on Gross Domestic Product, the U.N. counterpart to GNP.

Chapter 6, GNP poorly reflects pleasures like leisure time and home-baked bread and costs like foul air and traffic jams. Any measurement of growth should include not only the value of market-traded goods and services, but also the value (not costs) of goods and services provided by governments, goods and services from the environment—such as clean air and water and other environmental amenities—home-produced goods and services, and leisure time in which to enjoy the income that results from such growth. Right now such an indicator barely exists, but these elements should be kept in mind as we discuss growth in Part Four.

The Arithmetic of Growth

Although the percentage figures of growth rates are usually small, the amount of money they represent may be substantial. A gain or loss of even one percentage point in an economy with a $1 trillion GNP involves $10 billion.

In the early 1960s, Denison calculated the per capita impact of such a change between 1960 and 1980. The population of the United States, he estimated, would increase from 179.8 million to 260.0 million; that is an average annual rate of 1.9 percent. A 3 percent GNP growth rate would thus mean a 1.1 percent growth rate in per capita national product. On the other hand, a 4 percent growth rate in total product would mean a 2.1 percent growth rate in per capita national product.

Since 2.1 is 182 percent of 1.1, to achieve a 4 percent growth rate in total product over the next 20 years would require us to increase per capita national product at a rate 82 percent larger than would be necessary to achieve a 3 percent per annum rate.[3]

Over a period of time, even a relatively low, sustained rate of growth adds up. A 1.64 percent annual increase in family income, for example, would raise average U.S. family income from $10,500 in 1970 to $50,000 in 2070.

These figures show the startling effects of **compounding**, since each successive year's percentage increase is based on a figure larger than the last. Over long periods, therefore, minuscule changes in the growth rate may have immense cumulative effects. At a 3 percent rate of growth, the economy would take almost a quarter of a century to double in size, while at a 4 percent growth rate, doubling would occur in just under 18 years.[4] At 3 percent, a GNP of

3 Denison, p. 6.

4 A quick rule of thumb in figuring doubling times is the rule of 72. Divide the rate of growth into 72 to get the doubling time. If the doubling time is known, the rate of growth can be calculated by dividing 72 by the doubling time.

$1 trillion in 1970 would rise to more than $2.4 trillion in the year 2000. Should the United States grow at a steady rate of 4 percent in real terms, the nation's GNP would rise to $3.243 trillion in constant dollars. That 1 percent difference in the rate of growth would, as a result of compounding, mean a difference in GNP of nearly $1 trillion after only 30 years.

Such seemingly small differences in the arithmetic of growth turn out to be quite significant over the long term.

Why Grow?

This mesmerizing procession of doubling and tripling numbers means that the economy has more things to distribute. Theoretically at least, the market will distribute the increase to all members of the economy. Or the government can take its growth dividend and give part of it to the needy without lowering the standard of living among other sectors of the population. As its income rises, the poorer family does not buy just more food or clothes; its members can afford doctors' visits and higher education. The productivity of the once-needy is enhanced, and further growth may be expected for the entire economy.

So much for theory. True, the concept of growth has become an accepted part of national policy. Post-Keynesian economists have developed policies and tools to sustain the growth rates. But the growth dividend is not always used to such advantage, and, traditionally, too little attention is paid to the costs of growth itself. In our look at growth we need to ask such questions as: Is the lot of the poor actually improving, or are they being left behind because of policies that emphasize the rate of growth but neglect the distribution of the growth dividend? Is it worth having enough income to buy a high performance sports car if you can only drive it through heavy traffic to dirty and crowded beaches? Is prosperity unduly fueled by arms spending or wasteful private consumption?

All these issues call into question social policies that emphasize gross indicators, such as growth in GNP and employment levels, and point to a new concern with economic systems and institutions. Economic growth is a key issue. Understanding it is necessary to discussing its value.

SOURCES OF GROWTH

The political determination of targets for growth may seem to be the major factor in making a nation grow. Others, however, are far more fundamental: supply factors, demand factors, allocative factors, and other noneconomic factors. Theories of growth cluster around one or another of these categories. While Malthus, for example, emphasized the supply side of the system (the importance of the relationship of human resources to natural resources), Keynes paid close attention to capital formation and the demand factors. Yet these basic factors interact continuously, so that it is difficult to isolate any one of them, and proper balanced functioning of *all* of them is necessary for economic growth.

Supply Factors

Limiting the capacity of any economic system are the factors of supply. If the amounts of natural resources, human resources, or capital should increase, the capacity of the system may expand. Should their productivity improve—particularly through the application of new technology—the output per unit may grow. Increasing productivity may also ensue from mass production, which allows for economies of scale. The process of growth is an interplay between expansion in size and search for better ways to employ existing resources.

Natural Resources Such basic necessities as soil and water, minerals and timber are of primary importance to an economy. They must be present in sufficient quantity, and be of sufficient quality, if production is to move ahead. More than that, they must be available. (The oil on the north slope of Alaska is presently an untapped resource. Until the requisite pipeline is approved and built, the resource remains unavailable and, as such, useless for production.)

Although, strictly speaking, a nation's natural resources are limited, new discoveries and new processing techniques can create the appearance of expanding supplies. In fact, some economists contend that since untapped resources are useless until developed by human skills, they should be considered merely "neutral." Only adequate capital and labor, as well as a high enough level of demand, will turn them into positive supply factors.

Human Resources No amount of natural resources can push growth forward without human resources to shape them into products. The quantity of labor (both in size of the labor force and in hours worked) and its quality (both intrinsically and in the amount of capital goods per worker) are major determinants of a nation's productive capacity.

Population growth is the key to an expanding labor force. Yet, as important as its quantity, is the quality of a work force. Japan's economy utilizes its expanding population efficiently. Other nations, such as India, have rapidly burgeoning populations and very small rates of growth. To be effective in a growing economy, workers must be well educated and trained, healthy, and motivated; they must be able and willing to move to wherever there are job openings and to change jobs if the need arises. The average length of their work week and the quantity and quality of their capital equipment (tools and factories) are also important.

One particular and special human resource needed for economic growth is innovation. The American economist Joseph Schumpeter believed that capitalism decayed as the pioneering, risk-taking, inventive spirit of its entrepreneurs was replaced by a security-seeking bureaucracy of managers. (One example of this pioneering spirit is Edwin Land, inventor of Polaroid cameras and developer of the large company that manufactures them.)

Capital The accumulation of capital is a more complex supply factor. Natural resources cannot be tapped and human resources cannot be trained, employed, and paid without a supply of tools, equipment, and physical plants. Transportation facilities are necessary to distribute and market finished products; dams, generators, and refineries are necessary to provide power. All these can be called capital.

Where does the money for capital development come from? Basically, its source is income diverted from immediate consumption.

Both private individuals (acting through such mechanisms as securities exchanges, banks, and other financial intermediaries) and the government (federal, state, or local) can channel funds into investment. If money is to be available for investment, a society must be able and willing to give up some part of its current income for the possibility of greater return in the long run. A society with low levels of income will be hampered in its growth, because hungry people usually do not save money that they could spend on food.

If investment is possible, growth comes through changes in either the quantity or the productivity of the capital used. Building more factories or installing more equipment similar to that already available adds to the capacity of the economy. When the amount of capital increases relative to other factors, this may mean that new, more productive technology has been introduced.

Technology Technology is more than just automated production lines; it includes techniques of management and marketing. Broadly defined, it is any process or level of knowledge used in production. Improvements in technology squeeze more productivity from other inputs, even if supplies are limited.

In accounting for growth, however, the following question arises: Is technical change independent of the quantity of capital or is it actually embodied in new capital? The latter idea is closely associated with the name of Robert Solow, the economist who in the early 1960s put forth a new view of investment that suggested a much more important role for capital in the process of economic growth. He argued that capital contributes more to the growth of output than previously realized, because of the added benefits of advancing technology embodied in new capital. Since it is clear that some but not all technological change is embodied in investment, subsequent investigation has attempted to find some middle ground between those who believe change in technology is independent of capital accumulation and those who believe the two are inseparable.

Economies of Scale Increases in productivity may also ensue as the growth in a nation's economy permits more and more economies of scale. Mass production, specialization of labor, and streamlining of processes cannot be afforded by every economy. But, once the structure of production changes, economies of scale encourage further growth in size.

Demand Factors

Increases in the supply factors alone are not sufficient to maintain economic growth. Aggregate demand must keep pace to absorb the goods produced. Population growth may increase the consumption component; foreign trade may expand markets; government policies may stimulate demand in a lagging economy.

But, as the economy grows and incomes increase, a greater volume of savings is generated. Unless investments can keep pace with this constantly expanding volume of savings, then growth will lag. Even if the growth rate is constant, investments will have to expand—since investment boosts GNP, which boosts savings, which calls forth the need for more investment. No wonder officials look nervously at such investment components as inventory level or housing starts to see how well the economy is doing!

Allocative Factors

In time, the changes that inevitably occur in both supply and demand factors force changes in allocation of a country's economic resources. If these reallocations do not occur with adequate speed and completeness, the economy's growth potential will not be fully realized.

Shifts in demand are readily apparent, even over the short term. Consider what consumers were purchasing 5 or 10 years ago. Who in the sixties had heard of Boone's Farm Apple Wine or Mazda sedans? Businesses and government, too, are spending for different things. Such shifts call for the reallocation of resources.

On the supply side, scarcities may develop or new resources may be discovered. At any point, the productive capacities of some industries are expanding rapidly, while those of others grow slowly or contract. In a growing economy, changes in resource allocation are inevitable.

Advances in petroleum technology and transport, for example, have had severe effects on the coal industry. Synthetic fibers have captured a large share of the total fiber output. Obviously, labor must be shifted to the more productive areas if these sectors are to realize full growth potential.

But can miners handle oil rigs? Can cotton researchers understand synthetics? Even if they are willing to be retrained, will workers be willing to uproot their families from, say, Appalachia to the Texas desert? Population growth can supply some new workers. But a sizable outlay of capital may be needed to train and move others. When such shifts or breakthroughs occur on the supply side of growth, some mechanism to channel labor, capital, and technology may be needed in order to keep growth surging.

Noneconomic Factors

People's attitudes toward work and wealth determine just how much time and effort they will put into economic pursuits. If the dominant religion, for example, directs a people to meditate for long hours daily and to deprive themselves of abundant, rich food and posh living quarters, they will be driven neither to produce nor to consume "luxuries." Some economists have argued that Protestantism generated an ethic that led to the development of a culture of achievement and thrift—both of which are attitudes that have been vital to economic progress in the United States. Others declare that entrepreneurial spirit was the crucial ingredient in this country's economic development. Still others assert that our materialism is the value system on which an expanding market economy thrives; status seekers, spurred by hidden and forthright persuaders, are said to keep up the growth rate.

GROWTH AND ITS LIMITS

Population Growth: More Is Less

One constantly expanding factor of growth is population, which forms a larger and larger labor supply. Unless other factors also expand, per capita income is bound to drop.

As we have observed, economic growth can be graphed as an outward, or rightward, movement of the production-possibilities curve. The outward movement of such a curve depends greatly on the proportional expansion of inputs, including labor. If the labor supply doubles, then other factors of supply must expand to keep pace.

However, not all inputs can expand at the same rate. If increases in inputs are not proportionate, the production frontier may still shift to the right, although its shifts may become smaller and smaller. When the labor force continues to increase, while the rest of the inputs remain constant, production increases will be smaller than before. Such is the law of diminishing returns.

The problem, therefore, is to determine whether this limiting factor will hinder growth or if other factors will offset the limitation. Changes in the labor supply —and their effects on economic growth and well-being—occupied much of the thinking of the earliest economists.

Smith's Escape Hatches Adam Smith's concept of growth was basically optimistic. His theory of markets actually implied development. Thus, in his world, the onset of diminishing returns would call forth necessary factors through processes inherent in the market.

Smith saw that society advanced through increased productivity. This was achieved by division of labor, since a worker could master a simple task rapidly and gain speed through repetition. As machines began to contribute significantly to this process, more capital goods were needed. Capital came from the accumulation enabled by increased productivity.

So far so good. But accumulation could continue only if population expanded to supply labor for the increasing number of machines and to absorb the output as it increased. If there were not enough labor to man the machines, the scarcity would drive wages up. As wages rose, more people would survive and the population would start to increase. Population growth, then, would rescue everything since demand would increase, labor would be less scarce, and wages would drop. Accumulation would grow as wages declined, permitting the purchase of more machinery to absorb excess labor. The economy thus would spiral upward through the escape hatches of capital accumulation and population growth until the day natural resources gave out. For Smith, that day was far off.

Malthus and Misery Twenty-two years later (1798), Thomas Malthus observed the abject poverty of English workers and declared that that day had arrived. From his work on the problem of too many workers for a given land area came Malthus's law of diminishing returns:

As successive equal increments of one resource are added to a fixed resource, the consequent increases in output will, beyond a certain point, decline. If carried far enough, such increases can result in a decrease in total output.

The law of diminishing returns applies to individual businesses and economies alike. It is especially relevant to the supply factors of growth.

To expand all the resources of an economy in the same proportion may prove very difficult. Land is clearly a fixed resource—unless a nation wages war and captures or colonizes new territory. Mineral deposits and arable soil exist in limited quantities. (New coal is not being formed under the earth's surface as quickly as miners deplete rich veins.) Assume, for the moment, that technology is also fixed.

What happens, then, as the population increases? When the increase in labor supply is dispropor-

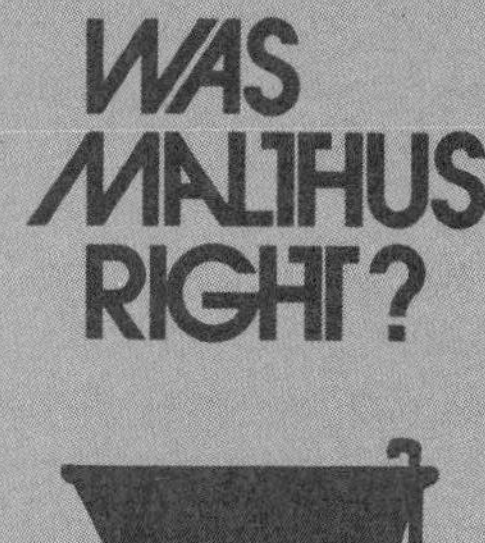

Will an increase in the standard of living always bring excess population in its wake? Evidence indicates that an improved standard of living may actually help reduce the rate of population growth after a certain point. The problem is reaching that point while having to pass through the Malthusian area of the "population trap." Over a certain range, population increases do outstrip increases in national income. Once beyond that point, population grows more slowly than the economy (Exhibit 1), and the standard of living goes up.

Exhibit 1

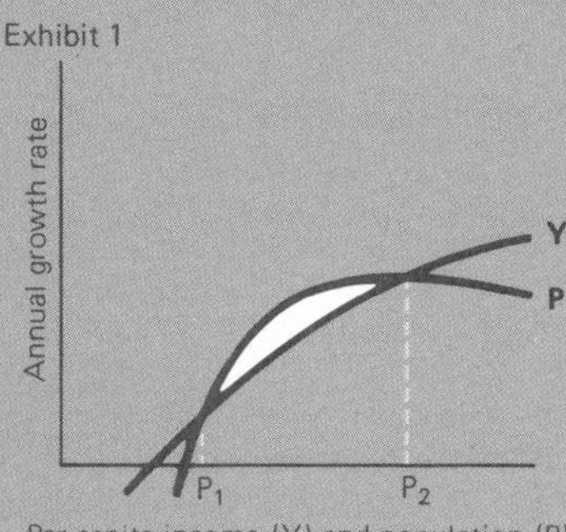

One idea about how an economy can arrive at such a population is called the "hot baths hypothesis," shown in Exhibit 2. If population growth depends on living standards, once a nation's people generally reach a certain level of living with minimal comforts (hot baths, comfortable shoes, 50 to 70 grams of protein daily), these people will want more of the same, and better. Their aspiration level will rise, and as it does, their birth rate will fall toward a level at which there are the optimal number of people to produce and enjoy the maximum national product.

Exhibit 2

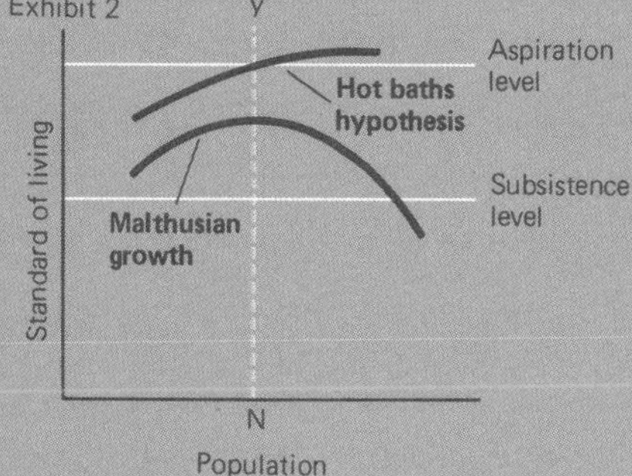

tionately high, relative to other factors, and continues over a period of time, the law of diminishing returns takes effect. The marginal product of labor (MP)—the amount of increase in total output that results from each unit of increase in labor—begins to decline. In the wake of that decline comes a diminution, too, in output per capita or average product of labor (AP), which is itself a fair measure of the standard of living within the economy.

In early stages of growth, the law of diminishing returns will seem not to apply. For example, a very small work force may underutilize a given piece of farm land. Increases in the number of laborers will, at first, bring about a rise in production. Picture a commune that has 10 people to work 100 acres of good land. A single person cannot possibly get the most out of 10 acres, but when good-hearted friends join in, and four or five can work per acre, marginal product will rise considerably, raising the standard of living. Particularly if there is underutilization of capital, added increments of labor will cause MP and output per capita to rise.

Eventually, however, as the number of workers increases, each worker will have smaller and smaller portions of the fixed capital and land to work with. If there were only enough plows for fifty, and fifty more eager young agriculturists joined in, each worker could only use a plow half as long each day. As more and more willing workers came to the land, say, 100 per acre, there would be certain hassles just to find a place to stand, much less to plant, hoe, and harvest. The standard of living would drop off, and MP would not only decrease, but would eventually reach zero. Ultimately, as the desire to farm ran high and land ran low, fighting might take the place of farming in the commune, total output would begin to decline, and MP would be negative.

Figure 17-1 and Table 17-2 illustrate that the rate of growth of the total product (TP) does, after a time, reach a maximum when a variable resource (labor) is added to fixed amounts of other resources (land and capital). Beyond that maximum, TP grows by ever smaller increments and, then, stops increasing.

A rising TP, when outstripped by rising numbers of people, results in less income per person. Growth of real GNP may continue long after growth of real GNP per capita has ceased. The AP, or output per capita, also conforms to the law of diminishing returns and reflects the same "rising-maximum-diminishing" relationship between labor and output. The highest standard of living occurs long before the downturn of total product. This point, which

TABLE 17-2 The Law of Diminishing Returns (Hypothetical)

Workers	Total product	Marginal product	Average product
1	100		100
		300	
2	400		200
		500	
3	900		300
		600	
4	1500		375
		900	
5	2400		480
		1100	
6	3500		585
		1000	
7	4500		645
		600	
8	5100		645
		300	
9	5400		600
		100	
10	5500		550
		−200	
11	5300		480
		−300	
12	5000		415

The law of diminishing returns states that if successive units of input of a given resource are added to a fixed combination of other resources, output will eventually increase by diminishing amounts until it finally decreases. It is important to distinguish between diminishing returns (declining marginal product) and negative returns (negative marginal product). In this example, the point of diminishing returns is reached after 6 units of input. After the sixth unit of input, marginal output declines from 1100 to 1000. Negative returns are reached after 10 units of input. When the eleventh unit is added, marginal output is −200. It is also important to note that average product, which represents the standard of living, is still rising after marginal product has begun to decline. Here average product reaches its peak between the seventh and eighth units of input, whereas diminishing returns sets in between the sixth and seventh.

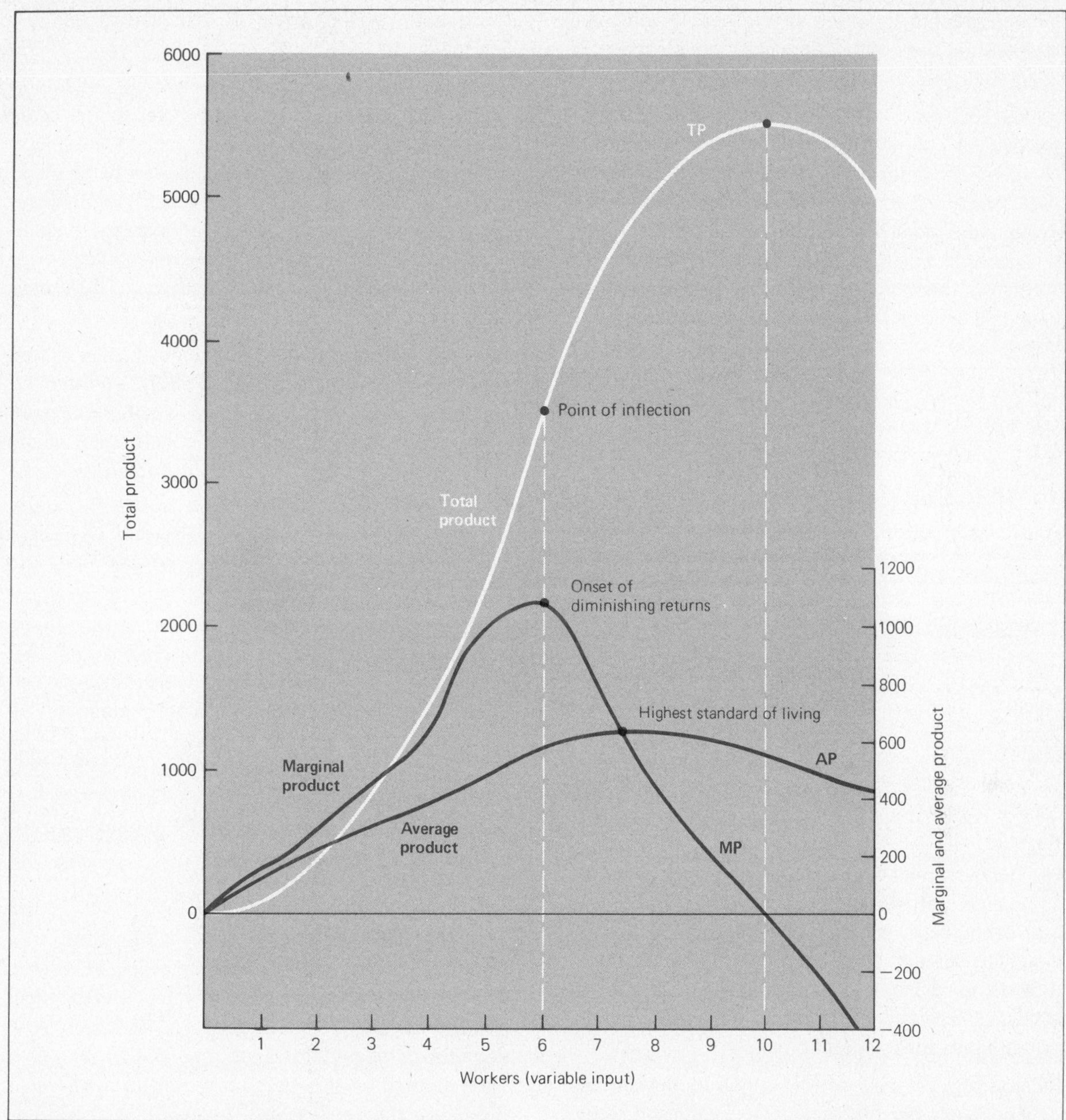

FIGURE 17-1 THE LAW OF DIMINISHING RETURNS (Hypothetical) This graph illustrates Table 17-2. The same points of diminishing returns and negative returns occur. The highest point on the MP curve marks the point of diminishing returns; the highest point on the TP curve marks the point of negative returns. Diminishing returns begins on the TP curve at the point of inflection; negative returns, on the MP curve where it crosses zero. The highest point on the AP curve indicates the point at which the standard of living is highest (meaning the greatest output per worker).

is found graphically where MP crosses AP indicates the level of population at which the standard of living is highest.

Malthus believed that the optimum level could be reached for only short periods, that the standard of living tended inexorably toward the subsistence level. Any increase would mean more children surviving, more mouths to feed, and a subsequent drop in standards again as the population overtook the economy's capacity to produce food and fiber. Malthus saw such "misery" as the equilibrium point in an economy:

> I think I may fairly make two postulata.
>
> First, that food is necessary to the existence of man.
>
> Secondly, that the passion between the sexes is necessary, and will remain nearly in its present state.
>
> Assuming, then, my postulata as granted, I say, that the power of population is indefinitely greater than the power in the earth to produce subsistence for man.
>
> Population, when unchecked, increases in a geometrical ratio. Subsistence increases only in an arithmetical ratio. A slight acquaintance with numbers will shew the immensity of the first power as compared with the second.
>
> By that law of our nature which makes food necessary to the life of man, the effects of these two unequal powers must be kept equal.
>
> This implies a strong and constantly operating check on population from the difficulty of subsistence. . . .[5]

Ricardo: The Iron Law of Wages and Profits Adam Smith saw capital accumulation as a way out of the population trap. Malthus, on the other hand, was less sanguine in his view of misery as the accommodating feature of economic equilibrium. David Ricardo, a close friend and intellectual rival of Malthus, added to this Malthusian spectre the inevitable disappearance of profits.

Ricardo argued that, if profit occurred, the capitalist would expand his enterprise. Expansion would cause competition for labor, forcing wages to rise. However, as population grew, this direct wage pressure would be relieved. (To this point, Ricardo thinks like Smith.) But to feed increased population, more land would be needed. And differences in the quality of land would be reflected in rent differentials.

As poorer land came into use, rent on the better land would rise. This, in turn, would drive up the costs of producing food. As a result, the price of food would go up, wages would keep pace with the rising cost of subsistence, and profits would therefore decline. Landlords would receive an increasing share of national income; workers, however, would remain at the subsistence level, and profits would disappear altogether.

With zero profits, the accumulation of capital necessary for economic growth would cease, and capitalists would stop investing. At the equilibrium point of zero population growth *and* subsistence wages *and* a stationary stock of capital, the economy would be characterized by stagnation.

Ricardo's arguments, while couched in somewhat abstract language, were not just an academic exercise. England was, at that time, experiencing just such a squeeze because of its Corn Laws. These laws prevented the importation of cheap grain that would tend to lower wages and enable growth to continue. "The value of corn," Ricardo claimed, "is regulated by the quantity of labour bestowed on its production on that quality of land, or with that portion of capital, which pays no rent. Corn is not high because a rent is paid, but a rent is paid because corn is high."[6]

The Doom of Capitalism

One of those who carefully read the works of Ricardo was the nineteenth century economist and political philosopher Karl Marx. (Indeed, in the course of a decade diligently spent at the British Museum, Marx studied all the major economists of his time.) But unlike Ricardo—or even Malthus—Marx was not pessimistic about the long-run effects of economic affairs on society. He believed that change was inevitable in the course of history; however, as the principles of production and of the exchange of products changed, so too would the entire social

5 *An Essay on the Principle of Population as It Affects the Future Improvement of Society*, reprinted ed. (New York: Macmillan, 1966), p. 11.

6 "Principles of Political Economy and Taxation," in *Works of David Ricardo*, edited by Piero Sraffa (London: Cambridge University Press, 1951).

order. The principle of production most evident at the time was capitalism. This, he was confident, would eventually and inevitably destroy itself as the base of production and exchange itself changed.

Fundamental to Marx's model is the labor theory of value: that everything produced has a certain value and that value embodies the amount of labor that went into producing it.

What does a worker receive in return for selling his labor to a capitalist? According to Marx's model, labor costs the capitalist exactly as much money as it takes to keep the worker alive at a subsistence level. In other words, the wage paid to a worker is what it costs to keep him working. And if a number of workers need jobs, the competition among them may lead to the worker being willing to work even longer hours for the same wage. That creates "surplus value." The value of what the laborer is producing is greater than the amount equivalent to his wage. This surplus value, then, becomes the capitalist's profits.

However, competition exists not only among workers to obtain available jobs but also among capitalists to dominate available markets. In order to produce more, a capitalist needs more workers; and he will bid the price of labor up, thereby diminishing his profits. Then, in an attempt to push profits higher, he will introduce machinery into his factory. This cuts back on the need for labor and is expected to lower costs and increase profits. However, since the man-hours that went into production of the machinery make it exceedingly expensive, the capitalist soon finds that he is not really able to generate the additional profits he had counted on. Moreover, as the workers lose their jobs, they are less and less able to afford the capitalist's product—which means that, in cutting back on his labor force, the capitalist has also reduced the size of his potential consumer market.

Does the capitalist, then, forgo machinery for labor? Of course not, says Marx. On the contrary, he may even redouble his cost-cutting efforts with the introduction of still more machinery. Soon he is producing in record quantities. But so is every other capitalist. The net result is a mad scramble to put goods on the market at whatever price is low enough to make them available to an ever smaller consumer public. The economic condition at this point is called a depression.

The capitalist system can recover to a certain extent from the first few depressions. Workers will take subvalue wages; larger and stronger companies may purchase the equipment that smaller or weaker companies have had to dump during bankruptcy. And, for a while, surplus value (profits) will reappear.

Marx saw, however, that the capitalist system was destined to repeat these boom/bust cycles, "each time more threateningly." The more frantic the competition for profits, the greater the ensuing collapse would be, until only a few immense industries would remain. In time, these, too, would fall. For they exist within the framework of an economic system that separates the technical base of industrial production from the superstructure of private property. The actual manufacturing of goods is an integrated, interdependent, highly organized process, requiring a great deal of planning and coordination that creates a working class, unified and disciplined. On the other hand, the private property that finances it is the most ruggedly individualistic of social systems, creating a class of ruthless magnates competing with one another—and against the unified working class—for survival. Capitalism thus "bears within it the seeds of its own destruction."

Outrunning Diminishing Returns

From the vantage point of a twentieth century American, it looks as though the predictions of Marx, Malthus, and Ricardo were wrong. The average laborer has a TV set and a car. Interest rates and profits fluctuate with the business cycle rather than trending to rock bottom. The U.S. economy has been growing at an average of 3.6 percent annually since 1870. The United States seems to have repealed the law of diminishing returns.

In the underdeveloped countries, of course, the enormous rates of population growth do retard economic growth. But in the industrialized nations, new developments have come to the rescue. Malthus

Growth now seems dependent upon technology. If the United States wants to keep improving productivity, it must continue to exploit technology.

But technology brings more than growth. Chemical sprays have brought about not only the "green revolution" but the "silent spring." Computers may bring better management systems, but they also throw people out of work. The problem, then, is to balance the continuing need for technological innovation with other goals and to anticipate the effects of technology.

In 1972, Congress acknowledged the importance of anticipating the impact in the Technology Assessment Act. Yet, while the search for a humane technology seems fine in the abstract, not everyone hails it in practice. One argument against the Act is that it will impede technological innovation by imposing long delays while assessment is conducted. Another is that long, costly analysis may confer false legitimacy on the results. Further, the questions involved may be so technical that policymakers will defer to the experts and lose control of decisions. Whether government or private industry should conduct this assessment is also at issue.

The ultimate critique is Norbert Weiner's: that, while we are assessing, the machines will have already taken over. "By the time we are able to react to information conveyed by our senses and stop the car we are driving, it may already have run head on into a wall."*

*"The Cost of Progress," in *The Business System*, vol. 3, ed. Clarence Walton and Richard Eells (New York: Columbia University Press, 1966), p. 2052.

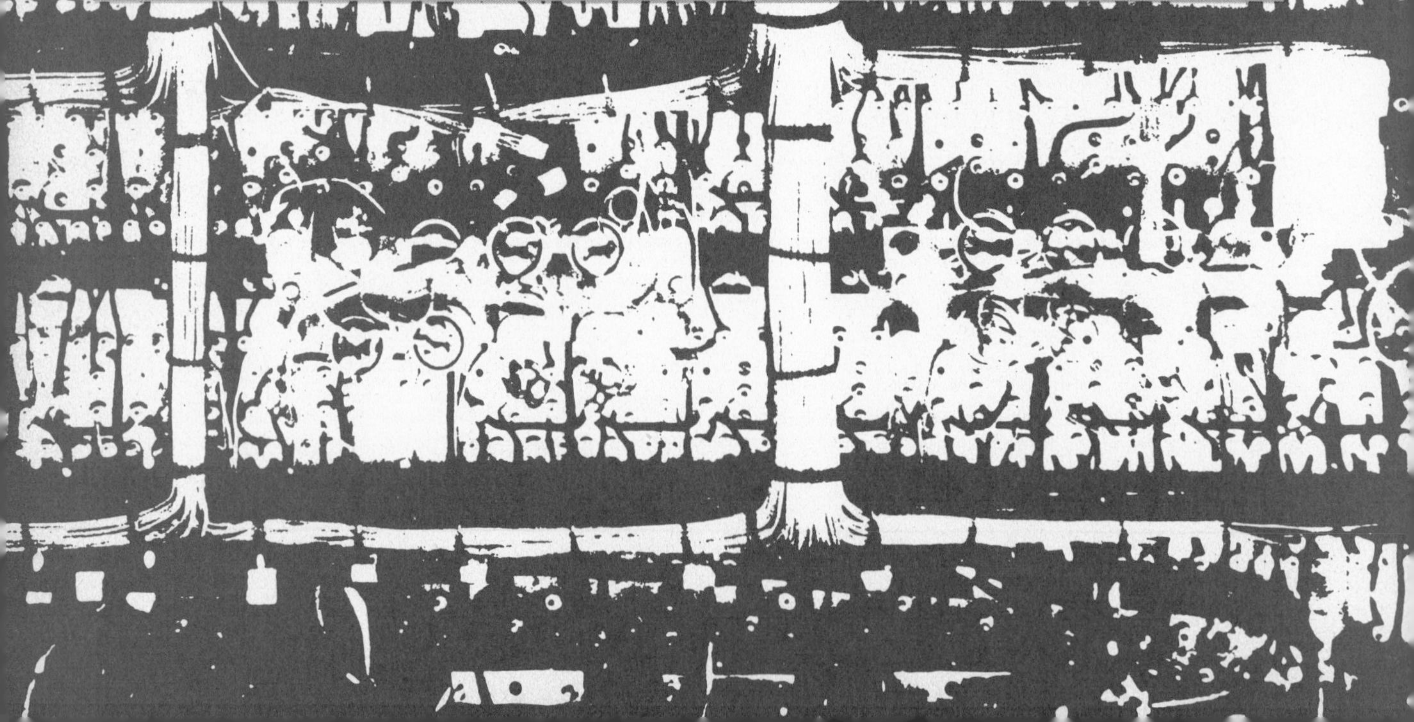

and Marx could hardly have anticipated the two centuries of technological progress that have been offsetting the forces they analyzed. Negative factors in the economy may thus be masked by positive ones, allowing for the continuity of growth.

The Neoclassicists: Harmonious Growth The neoclassical economists, coming as they did after Marx and Malthus, took a more optimistic view. They assumed that population would grow and that technological innovations would come along unbidden. They focused, therefore, on the inherent forces in economic activity that would promote growth.

The key to growth was the role of the interest rate, which matched saving to investment. Growing saving and growing investment fueled each other. Savings provided the necessary pool of funds for capital accumulation. But, in order for entrepreneurs to have access to these funds, they had to go through the capital market.

The demand and supply for investment funds were brought into line by the interest rate. When the rate charged to a business in the capital market was lower than its rate of return, the business manager would borrow to invest. Investment in capital stock raised labor productivity; increased labor productivity raised incomes, which then provided more savings available for investment. Without an increase in the productivity of capital, however, such a situation would not last, as diminishing returns set in. Technological advance provided the necessary boost to productivity. There was a continuing upward spiral as technology opened up new investment opportunities. When the opportunities for investment at a high rate of interest diminished, the demand for investment funds declined. The interest rate dropped, and less profitable investments became feasible, keeping the economy moving. Furthermore, expansion in one industry could spread to allied industries, setting off a harmonious chain reaction.

The process would depend, though, on continual technological progress to open up new and profitable investment opportunities. Otherwise, opportunities to invest would dry up, the interest rate would fall lower and lower until people would stop saving, and the economy would be at a standstill. This seemed a distant prospect.

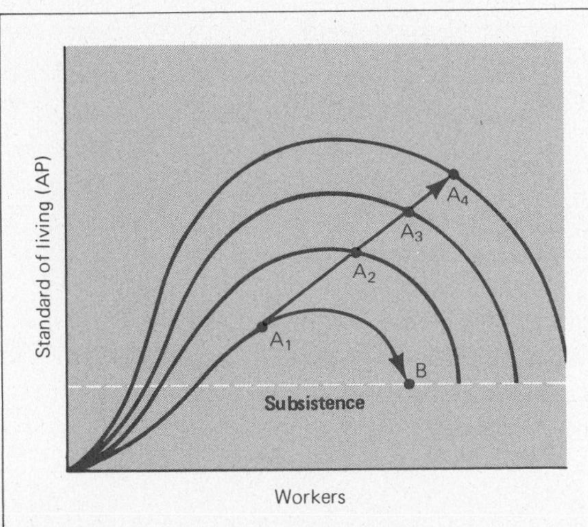

FIGURE 17-2 OUTRUNNING DIMINISHING RETURNS (Hypothetical) A growing population results in a diminished standard of living unless productivity rises. This growth path, predicted by economists from Adam Smith on, occurs from A_1 to B. As productivity grows, however, the average product curve rises. With a larger labor force and higher output per worker, the growth path is from A_1 to A_4.

Keynes and the Stagnationists

The earlier theorists seem not to have worried about demand. Their greatest concern was with the struggle to keep productivity rising by expanding the factors of supply. If the production-possibilities frontier moved outward, demand would generally keep pace with expanding capacity. Any insufficiencies of demand were temporary.

As we have seen in Part Two, Keynes asserted that an economy might operate well within its production-possibilities frontier over the long run. The equilibrium level of the economy might, therefore, remain below the full-employment level. To keep an economy moving, saving must find an outlet in investment. Moreover, in a growing economy, investment spending must constantly expand. Suppose, for example, that an economy must invest $20 billion to achieve a full-employment GNP of $1 trillion. The economy is growing at 3 percent, so the full-employment GNP for the following year will increase to $1030 billion. Part of the additional $30 billion will be saved; and, if saving accounts for one-tenth of this sum, then the economy will have to invest $3 billion on top of the basic $20 billion—which means a growth in investment of over 10 percent. Only an ever increasing volume of investment spending can keep up that kind of growth rate.

The stagnationists questioned whether investment opportunities would keep opening up. They believed that technological innovation had peaked, that there were few regions unexplored, and that even the larger markets provided by population growth, which could stimulate investment demand, were dropping off. With such limited growth prospects, chronic mass unemployment was a distinct possibility.

Keynes's solution, as we have seen, was to expand government spending. This, he argued, would keep aggregate demand up, employment levels high, and the economy growing.

Balanced Growth

Of course, investment cuts two ways. It increases aggregate demand, and it increases the productive capacity of the economy. Hence, we might have visions of demand constantly chasing an ever expanding capacity; or we might foresee a capacity always outrun by demand. Is long-run unemployment, therefore, inevitable? Or long-run inflation? Or is it possible that there might be a rate at which the two are in balance?

The Harrod–Domar model provides one way of calculating a warranted rate of growth. This model is predicated on the assumption that the problem of steady growth hinges on one major factor: investment. The investment process not only generates income; it also enhances productive capacity—which, in turn, can mean either greater output or greater unemployment. In order to bring these forces into equilibrium, conditions must be set forth to assure long-term growth sufficient to absorb savings and maintain full employment.

As the national income grows, the marginal propensity to save (MPS) predicts the increase in the amount of investment spending that is needed to absorb added saving. (Since the MPS is presumed to be constant, APS, or average propensity to save, may be substituted.) If national income increases by $30 billion and the APS is .10, the added investment must be $3 billion

This investment also adds to the capital stock and, therefore, increases the potential for producing a larger output. The amount of capacity created by an increase in investment is predicted by the capital/output ratio (K/O). This ratio demonstrates the rela-

TABLE 17-3 The Importance of Investment in Growth (Hypothetical data)

Year	Full employment output/input	Additional investment in capital stock (APS = 10)	Increase in output from additional capital (K/O = 3/1)
1	1800.00	180.00	60.00
2	1860.00	186.00	62.00
3	1922.00	192.20	64.06
4	1986.06	198.61	66.20
5	2052.26	205.23	68.41

Investment adds to both aggregate demand and capacity. The growth of national income leads to increased saving, which finds its outlet in investment in capital stock. This is predicted by the APS. The increase in output from the additional capital stock is predicted by the capital/output ratio. This raises the level of full-employment output, and requires an even higher level of investment to keep the economy on an even keel.

tionship between additional capital invested in the economy and the output that results from that investment. For example, the United States has had, for quite some time now, a capital/output ratio of about 3:1. For every $3 invested, $1 in capacity is produced. In the hypothetical economy shown in Table 17-3, this results in a $60 billion rise in output the following year. Table 17-3 also charts the course of subsequent increases.

Although the marginal increases in output continue to increase, the warranted rate of growth is constant. This growth rate balances on the razor's edge between overcapacity and insufficient investment. It is calculated by dividing the APS by the capital/output ratio:

$$\text{Warranted rate of growth} = \frac{\text{APS}}{\text{K/O}}$$

Since in our hypothetical economy, APS equals .10 and K/O equals 3/1, the warranted growth rate equals 3.3 percent; that is, 10 percent/3 = 3.3 percent.

This extremely simplistic model is subject to many qualifications, but it does teach an important lesson about stable economic growth. If national income is to grow, investment must keep growing. Too little investment leads paradoxically to overcapacity, since total spending will not rise by as much as the added capacity. Likewise, too much investment leads to the paradox of capital scarcity, since total spending will outstrip added capacity. Deviations from the path of growth, then, lead to explosive pressures upward or downward on the economy, without self-correcting mechanisms to dampen the pressures. The model does exaggerate the swings because of its assumptions, but in the short run, similar volatile behavior can be observed.

SUMMARY

1 The basis of growth is increased output, due not simply to full utilization of existing resources but to the growth in the capacity of the economy over time. The rate of growth may be measured by the percentage change in real GNP over time.

2 This definition of growth is deceptive, however. Economic growth is best defined as the rate of increase of per capita income, which is reflected in an improved standard of living. A full definition of growth would add to this nonmarket goods and services, the value of those supplied by the environment, leisure time, and other changes in amenities and disamenities.

3 Small changes in the growth rate have great consequences due to compounding.

4 The justification for growth is the improved standard of living it may afford. But growth must be more broadly defined than it has been in the past for growth policies to figure in all the factors that make living more comfortable.

5 There are four basic sources of growth: (a) supply factors, (b) demand factors, (c) allocative factors, and (d) noneconomic factors. The first of these involves an interplay between the quantitative growth and the qualitative improvement in such assets as natural and human resources, as well as the capital and technology to develop these resources adequately and economically. Economies of scale allow for the further efficiencies of mass production to keep pace with the gains in aggregate demand necessary for economic growth. Both supply and demand factors are subject to the reallocation of resources—as new resources are discovered or developed and as the population's wants shift to account for new trends in personal and public expenditures—and to such noneconomic forces as changing work attitudes and consumer awareness.

6 Unless the growth of GNP is at least proportionate to the growth in the number

of people who must be supported by output, the net result will be a *decrease* in per capita income and growth. This is precisely the condition predicted by such early economists as Malthus and Ricardo. Marx, in fact, doomed capitalism to destruction on the basis of its inherent inability to avoid the boom/bust cycles created by desperate attempts on the part of capitalists to exploit the labor force and yet maintain a strong consumer public—in effect, the same people!

7 What these early economists could not take into account was the massive technological progress that has largely succeeded in offsetting the negative forces they analyzed and in permitting a continuity of growth.

8 As Keynes observed, so long as investment spending—even deficit spending—is steadily increased, an economy may find an equilibrium level of steady growth. Since Keynes, economists have proposed a number of mathematical models by which to determine the exact rate of investment required for this steady, or "warranted," growth which steers between creating too much or too little capacity. One simplified version, the Harrod–Domar model, calculates this warranted rate of growth as $\frac{\text{APS}}{\text{K/O}}$.

SUGGESTED READINGS

Baldwin, Robert E. *Economic Development and Growth.* New York: John Wiley & Sons, 1966.

Dernburg, Thomas F., and **D. M. McDougall.** *Macroeconomics.* 4th ed. Chap. 15. New York: McGraw-Hill, 1972.

Gill, Richard T. *Economic Development: Past and Present.* 2nd ed. Englewood Cliffs, N.J.: Prentice-Hall, 1967.

Heilbroner, Robert. *The Worldly Philosophers.* 4th ed. New York: Simon and Schuster, 1972.

Schumpeter, Joseph A. *Capitalism, Socialism and Democracy.* 3rd ed. New York: Harper & Row, 1950.

QUESTIONS

1 Review
   a. definitions of economic growth and the distinction between expansion and growth,
   b. supply factors that contribute to growth,
   c. demand and allocative factors that contribute to growth,
   d. noneconomic factors such as cultural values that would aid or impede growth,
   e. Smith, Malthus, Ricardo, and Marx on the prospects for growth,
   f. the neoclassical and stagnationist views of the role of technology,
   g. the warranted rate of growth.

2 GNP rose rapidly as the United States entered World War II. Should this increase be considered economic growth? In what ways would it be growth and in what ways not?

3 In describing the circumstances of the peasants in feudal Japan in the nine-

teenth century, Angus Maddison states: "They were tied to the land and could not move around the country or change jobs. In theory, the land could not be sold and the cropping pattern was often restricted."* How would these institutional arrangements affect the chances for economic growth in Japan?

4 The introduction of modern medical techniques in many developing areas had dramatic consequences. Further, some cultures that previously practiced infanticide no longer do so. What are some of the positive and negative effects on economic growth?

5 Smith was relatively optimistic about the consequences of population growth while Malthus was not. Use Malthus's point of view to describe the difference in effects between population growth in most developing nations and that in the United States during its early history.

6 Suppose that you have inherited a fair sum of money and are deciding where to put it. If you were a strong believer in the predictions of Ricardo, where would you invest your money and why?

7 Suppose that an economy has a capital/output ratio of 4 and an average propensity to consume of .8. According to the Harrod-Domar model, what would be the warranted rate of growth?

8 What is the effect of technological advance upon the capital/output ratio, if any? How would the change affect the warranted rate of growth for an economy?

9 Assume that a new and more efficient source of energy is found. What would the stagnationists say about the prospects for both short-term and long-term growth? Why?

* Angus Maddison, *Economic Growth in Japan and the USSR* (New York: W. W. Norton, 1969), p. 5.

CHAPTER 18
DEVELOPMENT

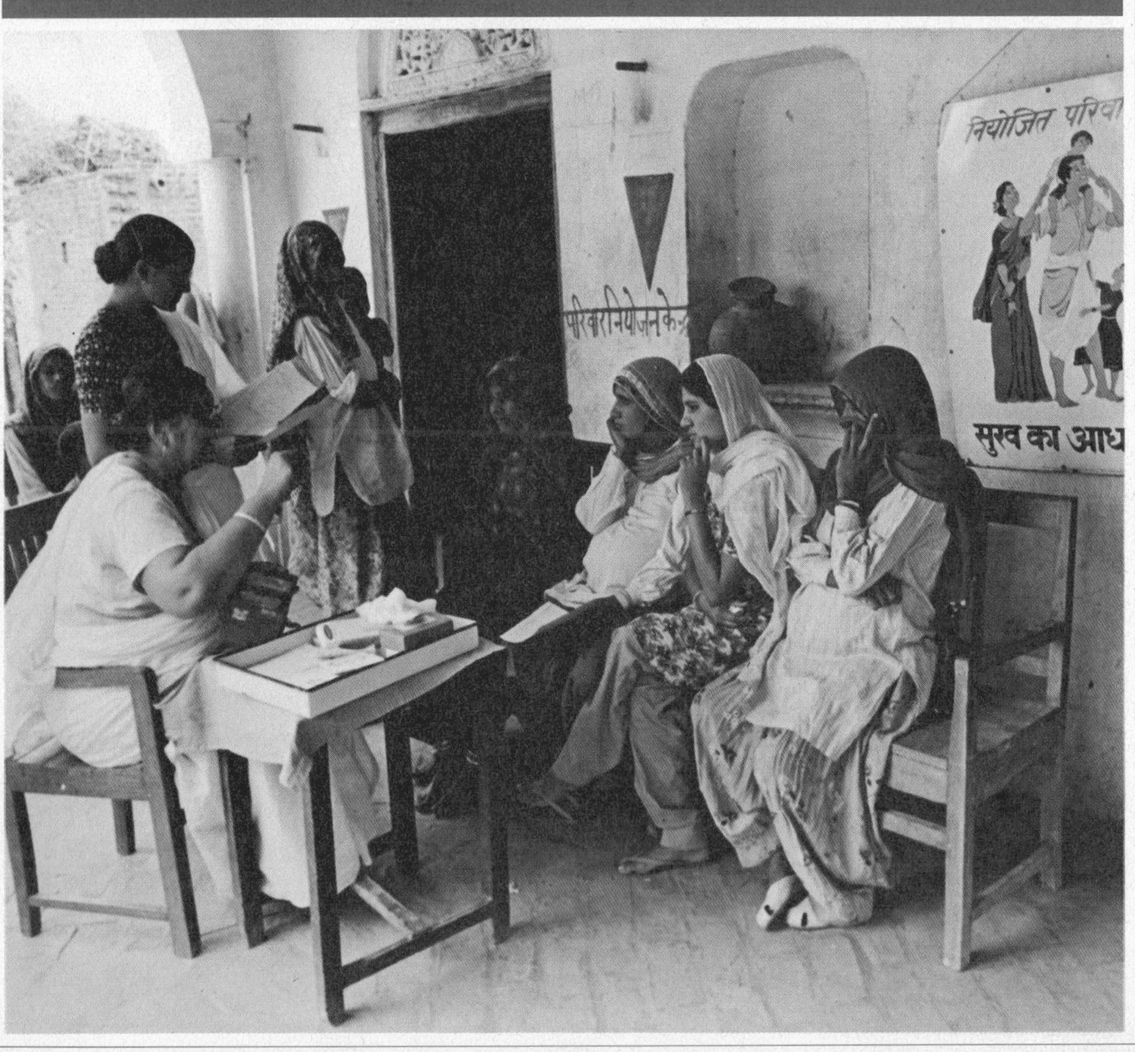

The term *developing country* is a euphemism for an extremely poor country that may or may not be making substantial efforts to raise its national income and, ultimately, its standard of living. In order to develop, such a country faces the difficult task of marshaling its scarce resources sufficiently to sustain a high rate of growth for several generations. Only such rapid and sustained growth will enable the developing country to escape the grinding poverty that has heretofore been its lot.

Placing a single label on a whole group of countries, each at a different point of development and each with a unique set of characteristics and problems, poses something of a dilemma. One such label used is the Third World, which refers to the position of these countries as a third economic and political force in the cold war between the free world and the Communist bloc dominated by the USSR. It is a negative description, since it spells out what the developing countries are not and sidesteps the problem of finding a common denominator. How should we compare, for example, Venezuela and China? What yardstick would allow us to evaluate the progress of two countries exhibiting such diverse growth patterns? The usual measure of per capita income is widely used and does give some basis for comparison. But it leaves the lingering suspicion that meaningful comparison and analysis are not quite so simple. After all, does one dollar in per capita income in China have the same effect and meaning as a dollar in Venezuela?

Furthermore, it can be argued that all countries are developing. Certainly, no nation has yet filled all the needs of all its people. Even the United States, with the highest per capita income of any nation, continues to have extensive, persistent pockets of both urban and rural poverty. In the developing nations, this situation is dire. Two out of three of the world's people live in countries where per capita income is less than $300 a year. One out of eight lives in a country in an intermediate group, with annual per capita income between $300 and $1500. Only one out of five lives in a developed nation, where annual income exceeds $1500 per capita. Table 18-1 lists the largest countries in these three income groups.

The gap between rich and poor nations is widening. The poorer countries as a group have experienced per capita income growth of slightly over 50 percent since 1950. Still, this represents a gain of only about $100 per capita. In 1972 alone, per capita income in the United States rose by nearly $500!

By definition, then, incomes are very low in developing nations. This means not only that living standards are low, but that personal saving is impossible for most families. In India, for example, where the per capita income is below $100, few

TABLE 18-1 Per Capita Incomes of Selected Developing and Developed Countries, 1960 and 1969 (In current U.S. dollars)

Country	1960	1969	Change 1960–69
Brazil	$ 196	$ 296	$ 100
India	70	88	18
Indonesia	76	98	22
Pakistan	78	132	54
All Developing (Noncommunist)	130	190	60
Japan	421	1410	989
West Germany	1505	2251	746
United Kingdom	1482	1826	344
United States	2559	4137	1578
All developed	1360	2480	1120

When it is said that there is a widening gap between the developing and developed nations, reference is usually being made to the per capita income. Brazil, one of the most rapidly developing nations, increased its per capita income by only $100 during the 1960s. The United Kingdom, which has experienced very sluggish growth, raised its per capita income by $344. The reason it will take a long time for developing nations to even begin to close this gap is that developed nations have much higher income bases. Brazil, which had a per capita income about two-fifteenths the size of the United Kingdom in 1960, would have had to grow seven and a half times as fast as the latter to raise its per capita income by the same amount.

SOURCE: United Nations, *Statistical Yearbook, 1960, 1970* (New York: United Nations, 1961, 1971).

Opening photo courtesy of United Nations

people earn enough money to live on, let alone to set aside any savings.

Per capita income is an index of a country's development, not the cause of that development. Development itself hinges on production, which is in turn dependent on capital accumulation. Generally, a developing country does not utilize the most advanced technology, as this requires capital accumulation well beyond its means. Thus, production is low; when this is divided among a rapidly growing population, as is the case in most developing nations, the resulting per capita income is extremely small.

THE PROBLEM OF DEVELOPMENT

Characteristics

The economies of most developing countries are dualistic. On the one hand there is a developed, export-oriented sector, while on the other hand 70 to 90 percent of the population is engaged in subsistence agriculture. Farm machinery is beyond the reach of these subsistence farmers, and the work is done almost entirely by human and animal power. There is high underemployment, with a substantial portion of the populace working far below its capacity. This is coupled with a shortage of skills, including managerial and administrative skills.

Exports consist of one or only a few items. These are usually raw materials and agricultural produce, whereas imports consist of more expensive, manufactured products. Rather than functioning as a national economy, the country's markets are fragmented by such factors as topography, language, and lack of transportation.

There is little hope for most people in developing areas to improve their lives, since a wealthy elite usually controls the processes of government there. This small group is anxious to preserve its privileges, is usually limited in economic competence, and is not motivated to alter the status quo.

The Vicious Circle

There is at work in the poorer countries of the world a phenomenon called "the vicious circle of poverty." Because productivity is low, incomes are low. Low income means low saving, which means low capital formation. And if there is little capital, productivity is low.

If we start with low productivity (which would be inevitable in a country with few plants, little equipment, and scarce trained labor), the demand for factors will be low. Since income is paid for the factors of production, incomes will necessarily be low.

Tangible output normally consists of two kinds of goods: consumption goods and capital goods. A poor society cannot afford to devote a very large proportion of its production to capital goods, since it is hard put to provide sustenance for the burgeoning population. Likewise, at the family level, only a small proportion of income can be saved, since most families earn scarcely enough to meet their barest needs.

Low saving leads to low capital formation, and industrial development depends on the use of accumulated capital (savings) to purchase the tools of production. Low capital formation leads to low productivity. Compare the productivity of the American farmer with that of the Indonesian farmer. The Indonesian is limited to perhaps a pair of oxen and a wooden plow, whereas the American is likely to work with the most modern implements.

Where does this circle of poverty begin? The answer is that a circle has no beginning: Any point can be taken as the starting point. Begin anywhere—at low income or at low capital formation—and trace the circle. The inevitable conclusion is that any of these factors can set the vicious circle of poverty in motion. Unsatisfactory as it is, there is but one answer: These nations are poor because they are poor. The more important question is how can a developing nation break out of the circle. We know that this is possible to do, because developed nations at one time faced the same problems.

Before discussing the obstacles to development and the solutions to the development dilemmas, we should note that not all production, income, and savings are entrapped within the vicious circle. As mentioned earlier, most developing nations have dualistic economies. The elite is able to save a substantial part of its income. However, this saving frequently takes the form of personal holdings of valuables or of foreign bank deposits. For example, it has been estimated that during U.S. involvement in the war in Vietnam, the inflow of American aid to that country was matched by an outflow of money deposited in Swiss banks. Therefore, the private savings of those inhabitants who are able to save (a function of unequal income distribution) is frequently of little benefit to a developing country. Aside from this, of course, a great deal of the profits generated by the local economy (which could represent potential savings) accrue only to foreign entrepreneurs, and are immediately withdrawn from the country.

OBSTACLES TO DEVELOPMENT

Geography and Culture

The degree of a nation's development has been commonly attributed to the culture of that nation. Nearly every developed country, so this line of reasoning goes, lies in the Northern Hemisphere (exceptions are New Zealand, Australia, and the Republic of South Africa); all of them, with the single exception of Japan, are of European cultural background. Therefore, the conclusion is that a temperate climate coupled with a strong infusion of European culture is the proper mix for the establishment of a developed country.

Matters of geography and climate are probably accidental, or at most of minor consequence in economic development. Matters of culture may complicate development, particularly when attempts are made to graft European patterns on other nations. Indeed, time and again those development measures that have ignored cultural attitudes have proved unworkable. There are two approaches to coping with cultural problems: (1) to work within the indigenous cultural framework, or (2) to try to effect cultural change (for example, to curb birthrates or encourage saving, both of which may be counter to traditional practice in a locality). The choice of method depends on individual situations, but the pivotal concept is that cultural factors cannot be ignored.

Natural Resources

A somewhat greater role in development can be given to the presence of abundant natural resources. However, the mere presence (or absence) of coal beds, iron ore, or oil deposits does not necessarily determine the extent of a country's development. Most developing nations possess some natural resources that are of potential value in world markets, but all too often remain untapped. A recent example of what happens when these resources are exploited is Libya, a country that formerly subsisted largely on exports of olive oil. Today, because of the discovery of vast quantities of oil under the Libyan Desert little more than a decade ago, that formerly poor nation is becoming a power in the Arab world. Libya's new position of economic strength is entirely due to wealth resulting from exports of crude oil and certain refined products, as well as of liquefied natural gas.

Where there is a dearth of varied resources, the deficiency can be partially offset by trade agreements. In the past, both England and Japan compensated for their lack of a wide range of natural resources through trade and conquest.

Population

In some countries such as Bangladesh, the pressure of population on the limited amount of available land is becoming so intense that millions of people are forced to live and work on marginal land. The 1971 tidal wave that swept in from the Bay of Bengal and killed hundreds of thousands was not unexpected. Every few years a tidal wave floods this area, but the pressure of population is so great that no land is left untilled. This area is again under cultivation.

Table 18-2 provides a capsule view of the rapid rates of population growth in the developing parts of the world. More alarming than the rates of population increase is the fact that these rates are actually accelerating. This is due not to a higher birthrate, but to a lower death rate. Until the 1930s, there

The post–World War II development of mainland China is virtually without parallel in modern economic history. This can be said regardless of statistics concerning GNP or per capita income. For more than two decades, China has provided over three-fourths of a billion people with food, clothing, shelter, and health care, and has educated most of them through at least six primary grades.

This should not be taken as evidence of an economic and social utopia on the Asian mainland. Indeed, such a conclusion would simply not agree with the facts. Rather, it should be viewed as a remarkable recovery for a nation formerly ravaged by hunger, disease, poverty, and illiteracy.

China is still poor. Her per capita income is estimated at about $145 U.S. equivalent. We must allow for distortions caused by spotty information and the fact that we are almost certainly dealing with an apples-and-oranges comparison aggravated by our use of Western economic yardsticks. Even so, we can say with assurance that the average inhabitant of China lives at a subsistence level. If this seems a depressing fact, a slight change of viewpoint assures us that that same inhabitant of China is protected from starvation, a situation which did not always prevail at the end of World War II.

It is difficult to equate China's progress with that of other developing nations. The figures that emerge cannot be directly compared with those from other developing countries and hence are subject to considerable estimating, weighting and fudging. Nevertheless, there have been significant gains in agricultural and industrial production. According to U.S. government projections, the GNP of the People's Republic of China rose from $99.5 billion in 1967 to $125 billion in 1971, an average of $5.1 billion per year. Taking this figure as anything more than a well-informed guess is not advisable, but it does generally indicate that China is making steady economic progress.

What Western economists view as progress is not necessarily the same as progress through Chinese eyes. Certainly the Maoist wishes to see his nation prosper, but his primary goal is social rather than economic. For him, a rise in GNP is incidental to the eradication of starvation. He must create a thriving economy to avoid the alternative of poverty and its attendant ills. But he is first and foremost concerned with the role of the individual human being in Chinese society.

The Chinese Communist following the precepts of Mao is much more likely to work toward the development of each person as a kind of universal man. The worker is not specialized in a single occupation. It is considered desirable that he be able to perform a variety of functions well. This is precisely why Chinese office workers are required to spend months at a time doing farm work. If this practice carries a penalty in slightly reduced productivity, it is of little consequence to the Chinese. Far greater importance attaches to the development of the human being as a versatile and happy worker, cheerfully contributing his labor to the common good. Only secondarily is the individual viewed as a producer of material goods.

The Westerner has difficulty reconciling this with the physical and intellectual regimentation that is so obviously an essential element of Chinese life. Clearly, the priorities of the two societies, and their concepts of what a free, whole person is, differ.

United Press International Photo

TABLE 18-2 Annual Population Growth Rates and Population Doubling Times of All Developing Countries, by Area, 1950–60 and 1960–70

	1950–60		1960–70	
Area	Annual growth rate	Years required to double	Annual growth rate	Years required to double
Africa	2.0	35	2.5	28
Latin America	2.3	30	2.9	24
Asia	2.1	33	2.3	30
All developing countries	2.2	32	2.5	28

In each major developing area—Africa, Latin America, and Asia—high birth rates accompanied by sharply declining death rates have caused a high and rising rate of population increase. In Latin America, the fastest growing of the developing areas, the population is doubling every 24 years—and the time required to double may actually be declining! Several Asian countries have recently adopted family planning programs, which may slow the rate of population growth in that region in future years. Such rapid rates of population growth eat away at gains in national income and thwart attempts at raising living standards.

SOURCE: United Nations, *Statistical Yearbook, 1961, 1966, 1971* (New York: United Nations, 1962, 1967, 1972).

was only very slow net population growth because the high fertility rates were matched by high death rates. Beginning in the thirties, widespread public health measures (malaria control, smallpox vaccine) were introduced, sometimes by the colonial powers, sometimes by independent governments, and later with aid from the World Health Organization. The results were dramatic. The high death rates in developing countries fell, not gradually, but almost immediately. Within a single generation those countries had the same death rates as the already developed nations. But since birthrates remained at the previous level, the result was a population explosion. Although death rates cannot fall much further, since they already approximate those of developed countries, there is little hope that fertility will decline appreciably within the next 20 years. This prediction is based on the experiences of the developed nations during the early stages of their development, when birthrates remained constant or rose slightly.

Rapid population growth hinders economic development, mainly through its effect on capital formation. When scarce resources must be diverted to food and clothing in ever increasing amounts, less is available for investment. Thus, the increased labor supply from population growth may not result in increased output. Another way of measuring this effect is to look at the growth rates of national income as measured by the United Nations' equivalent of GNP, real Gross Domestic Product, and real Gross Domestic Product per capita (Table 18-3). Real GDP for all developing nations rose by 150 percent between 1950 and 1970; real GDP per capita rose by only 51 percent. Had the population been stable, per capita GDP would certainly have grown faster and even total GDP might have grown faster because of more rapid capital formation.

What, then, should developing countries do to curb their fertility rates? Some economists and demographers believe that a fertility decline will accompany continued economic development. This has happened in every developed nation, although usually not until 50 to 70 years after industrialization began. If this same pattern were followed, we could not expect this decline to materialize in the

TABLE 18-3 Index of Real GDP and per Capita Real GDP for All Underdeveloped Countries, 1950–70 (1950 = 100)

Year	Real GDP	Real GDP per capita
1955	126	115
1960	157	123
1965	196	135
1970	250	151

Since 1950, real GDP per capita has increased by more than 50 percent in the developing world. Had it not been for the spectacular rise in population during this period, real GDP per capita would have been considerably closer to the more than 150 percent rise in real GDP.

SOURCE: United Nations, *Statistical Yearbook, 1961, 1966, 1971* (New York: United Nations, 1962, 1967, 1972).

developing world until about the year 2000. By then the populations of most of these nations would have doubled (see Table 18-2).

In an effort to hasten this anticipated fertility decline, many developing nations have commenced family-planning programs. As of 1973, several nations with these programs had realized appreciable fertility decline: Barbados, Hong Kong, Singapore, Malaysia, Taiwan, and South Korea. However, demographers caution that the programs ultimately succeed only if people are positively motivated to have smaller families; this motivation is not usually widespread until after some degree of economic growth has been attained. It is a vicious circle, because this economic growth may never come, due to the country's overpopulation. Family-planning programs are probably the best hope for breaking this vicious circle. Medical science achieved dramatic results in lowering death rates. But those efforts did not face one problem that is frequently encountered in efforts to lower fertility rates. This is the problem of values. Large families carry various religious, property, status, and other sociological meanings in some societies. Such entrenched values are slow to change. For the developing nations, then, management of population growth is a sensitive policy matter.

Of even greater importance for growth than quantity of people is *quality* of people. Although developing nations have disguised unemployment in the form of underemployed workers, there is a shortage of skilled and semiskilled labor at all levels. One way to meet this shortage is to alter the goals of the educational system so that primary and secondary schools concentrate on practical training for agriculture, business, industry, and construction rather than on preparation for university entrance exams. Likewise, the colleges could emphasize middle-level skills as opposed to high-level skills. This would broaden the base of available draftsmen and technicians, for example, rather than engineers and scientists. For a developing nation, investments in human capital are as important as investments in facilities. It is the need to assign priorities to the various educational sectors that strikes some people as bureaucratic and impersonal. However, as with the industrial sectors, it is seldom possible to pursue all goals simultaneously.

Capital and Technology: The Colonial Heritage

Much of development comes down to the problem of capital formation. As we have previously noted, the developing nations are poor, largely because they have not generated sufficient savings that could be converted into plants, equipment, and human capital. Most of the developing nations were colonies prior to World War II. Almost by definition their colonial status meant that the parent countries were tapping them for raw materials and using them as markets for manufactured products. The effect was to retard independent economic development in the colonies. In the decades since World War II, many of these colonies have achieved political independence. Economic independence, however, remains elusive for them. What typically remains is the same setup as before: continued economic control by the former colonists, or functional colonialism.

Modernized Enclaves During the colonial period many rich nations established enclaves of modernized economic sectors within poor countries for the purpose of importing certain raw materials to their home shores. This meant that reasonably sophisticated, export-oriented money economies existed side by side with simple rural agrarian sectors that operated at a subsistence level. These enclaves of modernization have existed for many decades for the sole purpose of siphoning off the natural resources of the developing nations for the economic benefit of the developed countries. But raw materials are not the only asset such enclaves drain from a country. From the surrounding area an enclave pulls in whatever talent is available. It also attracts savings, no matter how meager they may be.

The economic enclave does not exist in a vacuum; it is rather an outpost, a remote extension of an advanced foreign economy. Its purpose is to serve the needs of its developers rather than those of the host country. Typically, it is based on a single industry such as rubber, coffee, oil, or sugar. The enclave of modernization is not only a damaging influence from the standpoint of those things it takes away from a developing country, such as natural resources, human talent, and capital, but it also frequently causes misallocation of economic resources. An example of this is the railroads of east Africa, all of which run from east to west to facilitate shipments to Indian Ocean ports. This would not have been the case if construction capital had been locally controlled. We can assume that in that case the railway system would have catered to internal as well as export-oriented transportation needs.

Dualism Aside from the existence of economic enclaves, the developing nations have generated a form of dualism. Whereas enclaves are single-industry economic phenomena, dualistic sectors are much larger and encompass entire regions of a country. In operation, this dualism is similar in many respects to a feudal estate, even though legal sanctions are not generally as stringent as those of the classic feudal societies of medieval Europe. There are nevertheless several similarities between the two:

A few elite families own a large portion of the land.

A peasant class works this land in return for subsistence. Uneducated and unskilled, its members have little choice but to accept their lot because their opportunities elsewhere are almost nonexistent.

The population increase creates a surplus labor supply, further diminishing any hope of options for the peasants.

The peasant farmer keeps only what he can eat. The landowners appropriate the remainder of the crop. The amount collected from each peasant farmer is small, but the aggregate amount from the many farmers controlled by a single owner is large.

This agricultural surplus is sold for export by the landowners in return for cash.

To varying degrees, the income produced benefits the landowners, the limited middle class, the governmental structure, and the commercial urbanized sector.

Eventually, increased communication reveals to the peasant farmer that a better life is possible but that the current situation is widening the gap between the privileged and the deprived. Such knowledge, however rudimentary and unsophisticated, leads to a great deal of discontent and frequently to violent rebellion.

Poor Terms of Trade The developing nations seldom come out ahead in international trade. They are at a trading disadvantage because (a) the prices of the primary products they export are highly vulnerable to fluctuations in world market conditions, and thus these prices swing up and down broadly, and (b) at the same time, the manufactured products imported are expensive to begin with and their prices tend to rise.

SOLUTIONS TO DEVELOPMENT DILEMMAS

The many obstacles to development present a formidable set of problems for the poor nations. As we have mentioned repeatedly, the crux of the problem is capital formation. This is central to the theoretical work discussed in the following section. The two sources of capital, foreign aid and domestic savings, are discussed in the final two sections of the chapter.

Theoretical Approaches

The Stages of Economic Growth W. W. Rostow, who later became a leading architect of the Johnson administration's Vietnam policies, first gained worldwide prominence by outlining five stages of growth in the development process.[1] The first three stages are relevant to our discussion: (1) the traditional society, (2) the preconditions for take-off, and (3) the take-off. Other stages are (4) the drive to maturity and (5) the age of high mass-consumption.

In the traditional society, production is based on a limited knowledge and understanding of the physical world. Modern science either is unknown or is

1 W. W. Rostow, *The Stages of Economic Growth* (New York: Cambridge University Press, 1960).

not systematically applied. Hence, only the crudest technology exists. The central fact of production is that a ceiling exists on the level of attainable output per head.

The second stage, the preconditions for take-off, is that growth phase in which a country begins to throw off the limitations of the traditional society. The country begins to evolve new, alternative courses of economic action that lead to rapid economic progress. During this stage, there is increasing acceptance of the idea that economic growth is both possible and desirable. Individual entrepreneurial talent begins to appear, the mechanisms and institutions for mobilizing capital come into being, investment increases, and the scope of commerce widens.

And then there is the take-off itself. This is the point at which a society emerges from traditional and limited economic activity to modern orientations and practices in which growth is central. This third stage is normally accompanied by an ambience of nationalism and common cause, as opposed to the narrow and self-interested focus of the traditional society. The rate of saving and investment may rise from 5 percent to 10 percent. The technological and entrepreneurial skills necessary to create new industries become manifest. These new industries in turn (through their need for supportive services and supplies) give rise to still other industries.

Balanced Growth Rostow's theory provides a historical chart of the course of growth actually followed by most Western nations. Today the governments of most developing countries are more interested in plans that will bring immediate and widespread results. Two such plans are for balanced growth and unbalanced growth.

Ragnar Nurkse, a leading proponent of the balanced growth theory, poses this view in terms of consumer demand and industrial demand.[2] When an economy is composed of many industries and is geared to satisfying consumer demand (consumers in this case being other industries as well as individuals), then the various industries become complementary to each other and balanced growth occurs. This theory is really just a restatement of Say's Law (supply creates its own demand), which has little application to the mature money economy (as we saw in Chapter 8) and perhaps only limited application to a developing economy.

The balanced growth theory probably assumes too much with respect to developing nations. When an infant learns to walk, we do not expect him to mow the lawn and shovel snow—not for a few years anyway. The crawling stage is behind him, but any semblance of physical maturity is still some years in the future. Neither is it ordinarily practicable for newly developed countries to support a broad range of industries and provide the full complement of skill (entrepreneurial, production, managerial) to run them all.

Unbalanced Growth According to Albert Hirschman, economic growth "... is the end result of a series of uneven advances of one sector followed by the catching-up of other sectors. If the catching-up overreaches its goal, as it often does, then the stage is set for further advances elsewhere."[3] The process of development, then, is uneven, with forward and backward linkage between industries. For example, setting up an automobile industry will induce investment in a steel industry, a rubber industry, and a glass industry (backward linkage between industries). It will also provide employment for salesmen and auto loan agency workers (forward linkages).

For policy-makers the problem in the unbalanced growth approach is which economic sector to emphasize. It is not sufficient merely to identify the probable forward and backward linkages associated with a given sector. Rather, the planning should (a) first establish needs and priorities and (b) then determine specific measures that will zero in on these needs.

Social Revolution Rostow's theory of the stages of growth, as well as the theories of balanced and

2 Ragnar Nurkse, *Problems of Capital Formation in Underdeveloped Countries* (New York: Oxford University Press, 1962).

3 Albert Hirschman, *The Strategy of Economic Development* (New Haven: Yale University Press, 1958), p. 63.

unbalanced growth, presumes economic development through orderly processes. They are all in the same theoretical corner. At the other corner of growth theory is social revolution. Advocates of the revolutionary approach to achieving economic development feel that it is necessary to deliberately introduce disruptive elements into a society. Such elements can be social or technological, but their effect is always to deliberately upset the status quo. The major criticism of this approach is that it is open-ended and that it largely precludes planning.

Capital Formation through Foreign Aid

The developing nations have a very natural desire to rapidly attain the institutions and material benefits common to highly industrialized societies. They tend to yearn for a kind of instant balanced economy. As discussed in the preceding section, this is not a realistic aspiration. To amass capital stock, a nation must forgo a certain amount of immediate consumption: This is at best difficult where living is at the subsistence level. So these understandably impatient countries must frequently postpone copying the technology of the richer nations, unless there is some outside source of funds that will lessen the impact of industrialization on their own limited supplies of capital. This is where foreign aid comes in. The developing nations may turn to the governments or private industries of foreign nations or to international agencies for outside assistance. The problem with that approach, of course, is that the institution providing the aid has interests of its own that may conflict with those of the nation needing the aid.

Bilateral Aid Bilateral aid means that one country helps another directly. Several forms of bilateral aid are available to the developing nations, through either governments or private firms. The chief categories of foreign aid are money, materials, and technical knowledge and personnel. When a direct transfer of capital or machinery is made, the agreement between the two countries involved usually carries a stipulation that the materials will be used only for a stated project or that the money will be used to purchase goods only from the donor country. Quite obviously, the Soviet Union does not wish to lend money to a poor country that (if not restricted to a particular project) might use it frivolously or unwisely. Similarly, the United States would be loath to participate in a program where its money was used to purchase tractors from China. "Borrow from me, buy from me" is the usual deal. However logical for the donor country, this practice can lead to inefficiency, if the goods could be obtained at a lower cost elsewhere or if the funds for a project could contribute more to growth if used in another way.

Such problems are less obvious in technical assistance programs, which involve the sharing of knowledge and the temporary transfer of personnel capable, for instance, of breaking in an industrial plant. These programs originate either out of multilateral agreements set up among several nations on a cooperative basis, or as bilateral arrangements that exist entirely between the donor and recipient countries, or through private technical collaboration. The Point Four Program is a major example of a foreign aid program incorporating both financial and technical assistance. It was set up by the United States at the end of World War II to help raise the living standards of war-ravaged countries by lending aid in the areas of agriculture, public health, and education. Part of this work is now performed by the United Nations.

GOVERNMENTAL AID Other United States–sponsored assistance programs have included the Peace Corps, which deploys large numbers of mostly young people into many developing nations to bring their skills to the task of training local people; the Alliance for Progress, which is aimed at financing economic advancement for nations in Latin America that agree to adopt tax and land reform; and several banks whose programs go beyond the scope of the International Bank for Reconstruction and Development (the World Bank), which is described later in this chapter. The Agency for International Development (AID) is probably the most important organization established by the United States in the field of foreign aid. It administers funds intended to provide economic, technical, and defense assistance to free-world nations.

The United States is not alone in providing bilateral aid. The Soviet Union and other countries have since the early 1950s contributed a significant and growing percentage of foreign aid. Undoubtedly, both the United States and the Soviet Union dispense foreign aid to speed development and to obtain ideological allies throughout the Third World. Closely related is the desire to secure foreign military bases. Two additional motives are the promotion of domestic production of the donor nation (wheat, computers, vodka, caviar) and the assurance of access to raw materials (Arabian oil, southeast Asian rubber, Chilean copper).

To put foreign aid into proper perspective, one must understand not only the underlying motivations, but the scope of these programs. America's annual aid expenditures are currently running slightly in excess of $1 billion, which is about 1/10 of 1 percent of GNP. The USSR aid program, which peaked at $2.2 billion in 1969, is about one-half of one percent of that country's GNP. Given the enormous capital requirements of the developing nations, it is clear that the so-called competition between the two superpowers is not providing very substantial material results.

PRIVATE FOREIGN INVESTMENT Private foreign investment is another important source of capital for the developing nations. An average of $3 to $3.5 billion annually flows into Third World countries. Most of this money is devoted to manufacturing and to the extraction of petroleum and mineral resources. Some 75 percent of this money goes into foreign-owned plants and other facilities; this partially explains the frequent hostility in the host countries to foreign capital. The profits, which could provide a good source of saving, are usually drawn out of the country by the foreign owners.

WHO GETS BILATERAL AID? Some economists now advocate the "key countries" approach to aid-giving. They argue that the finite amounts of money and resources available for foreign aid would be better spent if they were spread less thinly. They advocate strengthening those nations which (1) exhibit the greatest economic potential for growth; (2) show a willingness to reform land and tax structures and to establish sound fiscal, monetary, and governmental policies; and (3) are strategic in terms of size, politics, or geographic location. Advocates of the key countries approach base their case not just on the humanitarian hope for progress but also on the political advantages. Because the Soviet Union concentrates most of its foreign aid on 10 or 12 nations, it is able to take credit for great economic advances in those countries; the United States scatters its limited largess over some 95 developing countries. If this other approach were implemented, say the advocates, the United States would be in a more competitive position to demonstrate to uncommitted nations that the free world can offer them the chance to develop through nontotalitarian techniques.

Adoption of the key countries approach would entail severe cutbacks of aid to some countries and substantial aid increases to others. There is a political gamble involved. U.S. influence could slip badly in those areas temporarily put on short rations. The key countries approach does, however, offer three distinct advantages for the United States. The United States would be in a position to significantly advance several key countries to the point where they would require much less assistance. The United States would subsequently be able to devote much more to the remaining countries—now reclassified as the *new* key countries. In the process, the United States would be able to develop demonstration models.

WHO IS REALLY HELPED BY BILATERAL FOREIGN AID? Regardless of who receives the aid, there are always problems involved in its acceptance. As discussed in the earlier section on modernized economic enclaves, foreign aid carries its own potential burden. What has happened in many cases is that an economy has developed that is actually complementary and subordinate to the interests of the donor country rather than to those of the country to which the aid was given. This has happened especially where there is a desire on the part of the donor nation to maintain a chain of strategically located and dependent friendly nations from which to drain capital and raw materials. Beyond possible misallocation of resources and the danger of either inflation or a growing imbalance of trade, the poorer country must also contend with the problems of debt servicing and repayment.

For all of these reasons, economic and technical assistance is inextricably bound up with international politics. Because the Third World needs development aid, it must deal with the richer nations on their own terms. This has led to repeated charges of neocolonialism against the donor nations. Regardless of benefits that may accrue to recipients, the critics charge that the chief concern of the richer countries is to set up favorable and even exploitative relationships. The alternative to this is some form of multilateral aid.

Multilateral Programs The United Nations was set up following World War II to provide an international forum for the peaceful settlement of disputes. Equally important, the United Nations was also to provide a wide range of services to the developing areas of the world, and agencies were established for this purpose. It quickly became apparent that these U.N. agencies alone could not handle the worldwide need for economic assistance. Another mechanism that developed at the same time was the International Bank for Reconstruction and Development, informally called the World Bank. This institution was designed to ease the transition to peace and postwar reconstruction and to aid the development of the poorer nations. Unfortunately, the flow of capital through the World Bank and its companion programs—the International Finance Corporation (IFC) and the International Development Association (IDA)—has been disappointingly small. Although the World Bank has certainly provided many countries with capital for important development projects, it has also been criticized for failing to provide sufficient capital to the poorer countries to stimulate private investment, for not making full use of its lending ability, for following too conservative a lending policy, and for not always putting its money where the greatest need exists.

Bilateral versus Multilateral Aid There is a clear consensus among development economists that multilateral aid (many countries funneling their assistance through an international agency) is better for the aid recipient than bilateral aid (one country aiding another country directly). Some advantages often cited are that multilateral aid (1) can be used to buy goods from the cheapest source, (2) has no strings attached, (3) encourages regional integration among developing countries, (4) encourages a more widespread sharing of the burden, and (5) is better suited for many large development projects that require experience and expertise that even the biggest bilateral aid agencies cannot offer.

A valid, although less convincing, case can also be made for bilateral aid. Probably the strongest argument is that citizens of the donor country are more willing to give bilateral than multilateral aid. This is largely because they believe (rightly or wrongly) that bilateral aid helps promote their country's foreign policy objectives. Historical ties and responsibilities felt toward former colonial territories encourage substantial aid (especially from France and England). In these cases, too, donors justifiably contend that they have a better understanding of local conditions than do multilateral organizations. There is an argument that bilateral aid permits a developing country to play off one donor against another. While this argument may be valid in isolated instances, it is probably highly overrated, especially in light of the small amounts of aid received by most countries.

It is unlikely that multilateral aid will soon replace bilateral aid. However, while the United States and the Soviet Union are not likely to be increasing their foreign aid programs, the multilateral programs have enlarged rapidly. Since 1960, when some $500 million was funneled through international agencies, this type of aid has been increasing rapidly; it will probably reach $2 billion before 1975. Perhaps there will be some shift from bilateral to multilateral aid, but as long as the Third World remains a cold war battleground, bilateral aid will continue as the dominant form.

The Role of Domestic Capital Formation

Although the developing nations are too poor to save very large portions of their production (if indeed they can save anything at all), most capital formation must come from domestic savings, since foreign aid covers only a fraction of their capital requirements. This type of savings can come from three main sources: (1) individual savings, measured as the difference between household income and expenditures; (2) corporate savings, which represent undistributed profits; and (3) governmental savings.

There is no criterion by which we can group the developing nations concerning the composition of their savings. There are wide variations, due to differences in economic organization and behavior. In general, however, household savings are far more important to the developing nations than to the highly industrialized nations. This is because the mature, richer nations have well-developed industrial and governmental sectors on which they can rely for their domestic savings needs.

Most of the developing nations have more than attained Rostow's figure of 10 percent as the saving rate at which the take-off occurs. Why, then, has there been no more development than that which we see in these countries? The answer lies in the *form* of savings and in the unequal distribution of income. Many developing countries do not possess adequate banking and financial structures to provide for either a tradition of individual monetary saving or—and this is important—a smooth transfer of funds from saving to investment. Therefore, many people who are financially able to save prefer tangible assets (such as livestock, real estate, or gold) to financial assets. Also, many of the rich prefer to deposit their holdings in foreign banks and foreign investments. Add to this the fact that there are tremendous disparities in income, ranging from subsistence on a grossly inadequate diet to absolute luxury, and it becomes clear that 10 percent as a saving level may be a misleading figure. It often simply is not matched by levels of private domestic investment.

Corporate savings in a developing nation will not be sufficient to produce a major source of potential investment capital, since about three-fourths of the labor force is engaged in subsistence farming and since the foreign ownership exports a portion of the already small profits. What is left, then, is governmental savings. We can characterize governmental savings in those Third World countries outside the Communist bloc as arising out of easily distinguished tax structures: (1) The ratio of tax revenues to GNP falls generally in the 10 to 20 percent range, compared with figures as high as 30 or 35 percent in the richer nations; (2) unlike the highly developed countries, most developing nations impose taxes that are indirect (on commodities) rather than direct (on income and wealth); and (3) for political and/or administrative reasons, the agricultural sector is directly taxed either lightly or not at all.

Government is nonetheless expected to do the job, for who else is there? All too often, however, the government squanders the meager resources on three standard prestige items that bring few direct economic returns: well-equipped armed forces (more to repress domestic opposition than to repel invasion), a national airline (which cannot handle more than 1 percent of the nation's freight and passengers), and a seat in the United Nations. (Since nonmembers can receive aid, the only economic advantage to U.N. membership is perhaps selling votes.)

Despite these unfortunate circumstances, fairly rapid growth *is* taking place in most developing nations. The progress in China and India is due largely to governmental efforts. Given the government's limited ability to provide investment funds, its prime development role is as a catalyst. Once sustained growth has taken place, the government's job will ease. Not only will the private sector be capable of carrying an increasing burden (as well as be induced to do so, according to Hirschman's analysis), but tax revenues will increase as income rises.

THE NEXT THIRTY YEARS

The next 30 years will be crucial for most developing nations. Although most of them have already attained Rostow's preconditions for the take-off, they must now sustain their growth for perhaps 30 years to be well into the take-off stage. During this period they must increase food production drastically, in order to feed their growing populations. But more important, they must increase their agricultural productivity. Only this will free a substantial number of workers to switch from agriculture to industry.

INDIA

The 547 million inhabitants of India (1971 census) comprise 14 percent of the world's population—and most of them are in trouble. Part of the problem is the population: Every year this number swells by 2.4 percent, or roughly 13 million people. Per capita income (based on an estimated GNP of $50 billion) is $91 U.S. equivalent. According to Dr. P. V. Sukhatme, director of the Statistics Division of the United Nations Food and Agriculture Organization, at least one in every four Indians lives in continuing hunger; one out of two suffers from malnutrition arising from the poor quality of the food that is available.

Tragically, this situation was not always India's lot. In the seventeenth century, she reached her zenith as a great manufacturing and agricultural country. What brought India to her knees was the cumulative effect of British colonial rule. In the early decades of the twentieth century, Britain annually appropriated over 10 percent of India's gross national income. Had this economic surplus been invested back into the country, India's current economic state would almost certainly not be so desperate.

Today India is struggling to escape from the debilitating effects of exploitation. She has growing unemployment (approximately 14 million in 1971). There is a severe inequality of wealth distribution and a dearth of entrepreneurial talent. The burden is on economic development and on reducing the birthrate through family planning. In short, India must extricate herself from the so-called population trap; this means her real GNP must always increase faster than her population.

Modern India has doubled industrial production in the last decade, and is making progress in education and public health. She is improving agricultural output in order to achieve higher levels of food production. Some analysts predict that she will become self-sufficient in food production by the mid-1970s.

How is this being done? One highly important effort is government-sponsored family-planning programs geared to the reduction of the birthrate from 41 per thousand per year to 22 per thousand by 1978. This thrust is vital to the economic advancement of India, but is impeded by widespread illiteracy and opposing cultural values.

Another important factor is foreign aid. India is the largest single recipient of U.S. development aid, which consists mainly of fertilizer, grain, the construction of fertilizer factories, and farm technology designed to increase yields per acre. This aid also includes development of power sources, construction of transportation facilities, and building industrial plants. Between 1947 and 1971 some $9.1 billion was given to India for such projects.

Perhaps the most important element in India's recovery has been the green revolution, which was much heralded in the late 1960s as a breakthrough in increasing grain production. This program involves (1) cultivation of the new miracle seeds, which offer a higher yield per acre; (2) heavy applications of fertilizer; (3) new approaches to irrigation such as tubewells, which are more efficient on a farm-to-farm basis for the distribution of large quantities of water than are huge dams, which tie up massive amounts of capital; and (4) improved farm practices.

Agriculture is the pivotal sector in India's development, and the evidence is that it is succeeding. The yield take-off year for wheat production was 1967; there was an abrupt increase from 11,393,000 metric tons to 16,568,000 metric tons. The growth of rice output has been slower, but the high-yield seeds are raising incomes and living standards for millions of farm families. In the state of Mysore, the technique of farming around the calendar has been introduced. Farmers there are now harvesting three crops of corn every 14 months.

If India can combine agricultural advances with a broadening industrial base and successful family-planning programs, she will be in a position to alleviate the poverty and economic chaos that have been her lot since the introduction of British colonialization in the eighteenth century. Independence has meant that she could chart her own course, but only gradually has she been able to steer away from the effects of her subservient past.

United Nations

The Green Revolution: A Source of Hope

Perhaps the single most hopeful development promising economic advancement and escape from the vicious circle of poverty is the so-called green revolution. The outcome of intensive research, this phenomenon concerns the new high-yield seeds of rice and wheat. Combined with new irrigation strategies and massive applications of fertilizer, the new "miracle" seeds promise to revolutionize agricultural production. Already many developing nations are using these seeds with extraordinary results. In two years (1967–69), Pakistan increased its wheat harvest nearly 60 percent. At the beginning of that period Pakistan had been the second largest recipient of U.S. food aid; now she is virtually self-sufficient in cereal. During the same period, Pakistan also became a net exporter of rice.

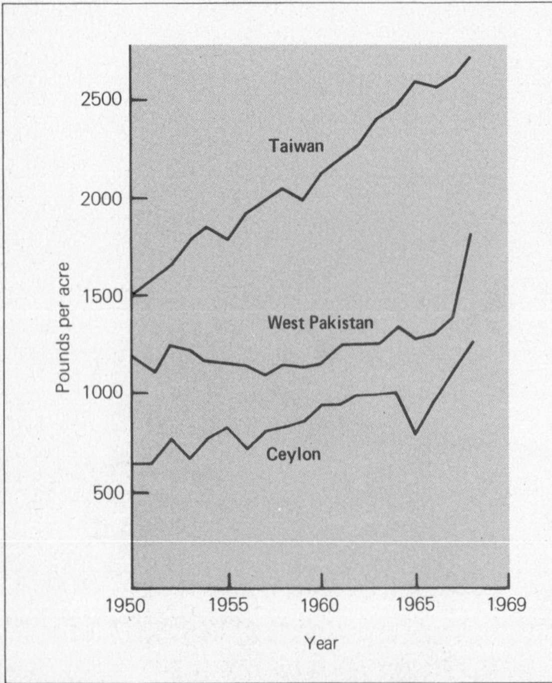

FIGURE 18-1 RICE YIELDS IN WEST PAKISTAN, CEYLON, AND TAIWAN, 1950–69 The remarkable increase in rice yields recently experienced in West Pakistan and Ceylon were foreshadowed by Taiwan's experience. One should note that only a small percentage of the farmers in these countries have begun to use the high-yield strains. That means that those who have been using them have pulled up the *average* yield by more than one-third in some years.

SOURCE: Lester Brown, *Seeds of Change*, P. 39. © 1970 by Praeger Publishers, Inc., New York. Excerpted and reprinted by permission.

Naturally, this is only a beginning, although a highly auspicious one. A nation no longer subject to widespread starvation (but unfortunately, we cannot yet count Pakistan among these) may in time develop its industrial sectors based on capital gained from agricultural exports. In the meantime, there will inevitably be problems between regions within the developing nations, between have and have-not nations, and even between the highly developed nations, as political lines are redrawn around formerly needy nations now facing the prospect of agricultural success. As one region attains relative self-sufficiency and perhaps even affluence, as one nation becomes less dependent upon another, and as the major powers experience shrinking influence over formerly subject countries, there will be periods when violence may temporarily win over the advocates of orderly change. We can, however, be sure of one thing: The green revolution promises profound changes worldwide in the structure of society.

Conflicts

Within Developing Nations Two areas of possible conflict during these next 30 years in many developing nations are (1) between the enclaves and the subsistence sectors and (2) between the rich and poor farmers. Generally, it is the elite from the foreign-oriented enclaves who control the government and who receive the lion's share of whatever development funds are available. In some cases, material disparities between regions are reinforced by ethnic differences—for example, East Pakistan (now Bangladesh) and West Pakistan, Biafra and Nigeria, or northern and southern Sudan.

Differences in wealth between the rich and poor farmers stand to be multiplied by the green revolution. Since only a few farmers can afford these new seeds, can take the risk of crop failure (which is far more likely), and are sufficiently skilled to cultivate the new varieties, only those farmers who are already fairly well off will benefit. As the disparity of incomes grows, so too will animosity between the poor majority and the rich minority of farmers.

Between Have and Have-not Nations Paralleling the widening gap between rich and poor farmers is that between rich and poor nations. Despite the fairly rapid growth of the poor nations, the gap in per capita income between rich and poor nations has been widening since World War II. The richest poor nation (with per capita income of $300) would have to grow five times as fast as the poorest rich nation (per capita income of $1500) just to stay even—a virtually impossible feat. At a more realistic rate, how long would it take for this richest poor nation to attain a per capita income of $1500? Provided the country could maintain an annual per capita income growth rate of 2.5 percent (the average for all developing countries during 1950–70), it would still take 65 years! And by then, of course, the currently developed nations would have per capita incomes well beyond the present range of $1500 to $5000.

The mathematics of growth is clear and it is depressing. What it adds up to is that poor countries are going to be around for a long time. A few of the developed countries (for example, Sweden) have effectively eliminated poverty within their own borders. In time, it may even be possible for the United States to erase her own poverty areas—most likely through transfer payments to the needy.

It is unlikely, however, that this same method of transfer payments in the form of massive foreign aid can entirely eliminate world poverty. There are several reasons for this pessimistic view: (1) More money is needed than is available, and there is the additional problem of sustaining aid on an indefinite basis; (2) most Americans feel less obligation to foreign nations, however needy they may be, than to their own poor; (3) when all is said and done, there is little real pressure for an all-out attack on world poverty.

The poor nations are acutely aware of the disparity between their own situations and that of the richer, highly developed nations. It is in this light that one should evaluate the nationalism, the jealousy, and the chauvinistic displays that make newspaper headlines. We can expect increasingly frequent showdowns with those poor nations that are nevertheless rich in certain valuable natural resources. For example, the United States may have little choice but to pay grossly high prices for oil. To some people this may seem to be extortion; others may view it as a Robin Hood type of behavior—robbing the rich to give to the poor. In any event, its effect will be to help redistribute the world's income.

The problems inherent in development are well known and well documented. The mathematics of development predicts no quick solutions. Perhaps no answer will be forthcoming, and we can expect political volatility on this planet for many years to come.

SUMMARY

1 Developing nations are those with extremely low per capita incomes, the dividing line being about $1000. Generally, such nations are characterized by high birth rates, dualistic economies, and government by an elite. To develop, these countries must break out of the vicious circle of poverty: Low income leads to low saving, which, in turn, means low capital formation and slow growth.

2 Among the possible obstacles to development are geography and culture, lack of natural resources, rapid population growth, low stock of capital, low rate of capital formation, dualism and enclaves, and poor terms of trade.

3 The theoretical answers to overcoming these obstacles to development are varied. Rostow's stages of development are really a description of how the institutions of the Western nations evolved sufficiently to permit development. Two

mutually contradictory theories have been advanced by Nurkse and Hirschman. The former, balanced growth, advocates the simultaneous growth of all related industries, since each will serve as supplier as well as consumer to each of the others. Hirschman notes that growth is generally unbalanced. One sector grows relatively quickly, inducing the others to catch up by providing a growing demand for their production. Some theorists argue that revolution is the precondition of growth.

4 In a practical sense, capital formation, from either foreign or domestic sources, is a key to breaking the circle of poverty. The developed nations can help by providing foreign aid in the form of capital or technical assistance. This aid may be bilateral (directly between developed and developing nations) or multilateral (involving an international agency such as the U.N. or the World Bank). Most economists favor the latter because multilateral funds can be used to buy goods from the cheapest source, there are no strings attached, it encourages regional integration among developing countries, it encourages a more widespread sharing of the aid burden, and it is better suited for many large development projects that require an experience and expertise that even the biggest bilateral aid agencies do not possess. Most capital formation must come from domestic sources since foreign aid covers only a fraction of capital requirements. There are three main domestic sources: individual savings, corporate savings, and government savings.

5 Perhaps the single most hopeful development promising economic advancement is the so-called green revolution. New varieties of wheat and rice have enabled farmers to double and triple their yields. However, since only a small percentage of farmers are able to afford these new seeds, can take the risk of crop failure, and are sufficiently skilled to cultivate these new varieties, only those already fairly well off will benefit at first.

SUGGESTED READINGS

Brown, Lester R. *Seeds of Change.* New York: Frederick A. Praeger, 1970.

Cochrane, Willard W. *The World Food Problem.* New York: Thomas Y. Crowell, 1969.

Gill, Richard T. *Economic Development: Past and Present.* 2nd ed. Englewood Cliffs, N.J.: Prentice-Hall, 1967.

Meier, Gerald M., ed. *Leading Issues in Economic Development: Studies in International Poverty.* 2nd ed. New York: Oxford University Press, 1970.

Shaffer, Harry G., and **Jan S. Prybyla**, eds. *From Underdevelopment to Affluence: Western, Soviet and Chinese Views.* New York: Appleton-Century-Crofts, 1968.

QUESTIONS

1 Review

a. the vicious circle in which developing nations find themselves,

b. geographical and cultural obstacles to development, the problem of population growth, and difficulties of capital formation,

c. the take-off into growth and balanced versus unbalanced growth,
d. the means by which developing nations can form additional capital,
e. the ways in which the green revolution might ultimately assist in the problem of capital creation.

2 Leaving aside the political objectives to be served by foreign aid, what would Thomas Malthus have to say about the long-term economic effects of foreign aid to a developing nation and why?

3 There are large numbers of students from developing nations in educational institutions in industrialized nations. How might their education be considered an investment by the developing nation? What difficulties, if any, might you anticipate for the developing nation in making use of this talent?

4 Assume that a developing country has a rather feudalistic type of organization in which the peasant farmer turns over half of his harvest to his feudal lord. How does this arrangement affect the incentives of the peasant to employ capital (such as improved seed) in increasing his productivity? (Note that he must foot the total bill for his capital.)

5 Assume that a developed country is having trouble with its balance of payments; more of its currency is leaving the country than is coming back through purchases of its products. How would foreign aid to a developing nation affect its payments problem? Assume that a condition of the aid is to buy from the donor country.

6 In developing countries, foreign-owned companies often run such enterprises as oil refineries and diamond mines. The companies are often criticized for sending profits back to the mother country. One solution has been to nationalize industries. What effects might be anticipated? Are there alternative ways to hold profits in the developing country?

7 In the summer of 1973, when the dollar was hitting new lows in popularity in Europe, Mexico placed ads in several financial newsmagazines requesting that Americans consider putting their dollars in Mexican savings and banking institutions. What might be the effect on Mexican chances for growth if Americans increased their deposits in Mexican institutions in the short run? In the long run?

8 One dramatically successful development with the assistance of foreign aid occurred among the war-ravaged countries of Europe immediately after World War II. The United States provided enormous quantities of aid through the Marshall Plan. Would you consider this example as providing great hope for the usefulness of foreign aid to developing countries? Why or why not?

9 Assume that there is a developing economy in which the elite are landowners. Anyone who wishes to rise in status will generally do so by trading or engaging in small-scale manufacturing, saving diligently, and then finally with great pride purchasing a fair-sized piece of land. What would be the prospects for development for this country? Why?

CHAPTER 19
U.S. GROWTH

In developing nations, over 90 percent of a family's income may go for necessities—a limited range of food, housing, clothing, and household supplies. That world seems remote from the United States, in which per capita income is now about $4500. Only two centuries ago, the United States was itself a developing nation, yet today it produces roughly one-third of the world's economic output. The United States is an outstanding example of a nation that not only has developed, but has sustained a relatively high growth rate once it became industrialized.

The record of U.S. growth is truly remarkable. It is particularly noteworthy since 1840, when industrialization began to gain momentum. Crude estimates reaching back to 1840 show U.S. population was then expanding at 2 percent per year, and the labor force at 2.2 percent per year. National product was growing even faster, at 3.6 percent per year. By 1960, per capita product (one measure of living standards) was over six times larger than in 1840.[1] In human terms, these statistics translate into more food in greater variety, better housing for most Americans, and more labor-saving devices for almost everyone. In short, Americans today have six times the goods and services that their forebears had in 1840.

What makes U.S. growth so remarkable is that the country has been able to sustain improving standards of living despite a rate of population growth well above that of other developed nations. To accomplish this feat, the U.S. aggregate product has had to grow at an even greater rate than population.

Whether the United States *can* and *should* continue its rapid pace of GNP growth is a subject of much current debate. Certainly, changes in GNP hardly tell the whole story of growth. Growth is sought because it improves material welfare, but not all welfare is captured in GNP statistics. The same things that make GNP grow can be the source of either comfort or discomfort for individuals. New technology can either spew more waste into the atmosphere or it can result in better, cheaper means of pollution control. New management techniques can result either in arbitrary bureaucracies or in better government services. More education can create an intellectual mandarinate or it can enhance the use of leisure time. A new definition of growth that includes these by-products of growth might provide a more agreeable goal.[2] Chapters 6 and 17 began constructing such a definition.

Perhaps the days of traditional growth are at an end in any event. Perhaps it was a unique set of circumstances that led to a century of unparalleled growth. As the high-pressure economy steams along, perhaps these circumstances can never really be duplicated. If this is true, then it may be unrealistic to expect growth to be as rapid as in the past. De-

1 Simon Kuznets, "The Pattern of U.S. Growth," in *The Goal of Economic Growth*, rev. ed., ed. Edmund S. Phelps (New York: W. W. Norton, 1969).

2 James Tobin and William Nordhaus, "Is Growth Obsolete?" in *Economic Research*, Fiftieth Anniversary, V (New York: National Bureau of Economic Research and Columbia University Press, 1972).

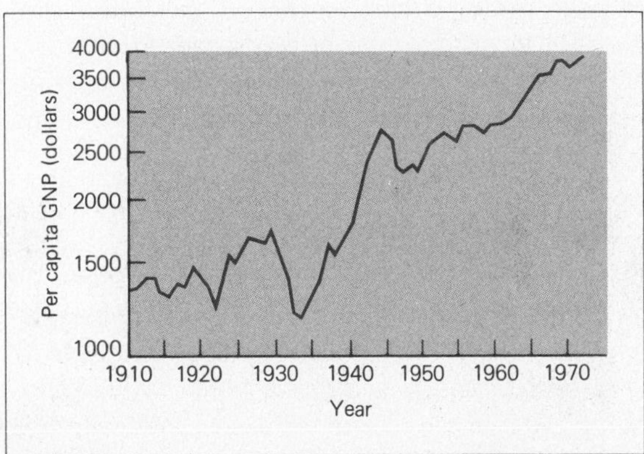

FIGURE 19-1 U.S. REAL PER CAPITA INCOME GROWTH, 1910–72 (In 1958 dollars) Perhaps the most widely used measure of economic growth is real per capita income. In the United States, real per capita income has grown substantially since 1910, but that growth has not been smooth. The Great Depression marked a particularly large setback. Since World War II, the United States has suffered six relatively mild recessions, each of which has been responsible for a brief downturn in real per capita income. This graph affords a good basis of comparison of living standards among various times over the last 60 years. Although there are shortcomings to this measure, the tripling of the real per capita income since 1910 is a reasonably good indication of the improvement in the material life of the average American.

SOURCE: U.S. Department of Commerce.

termining those factors that contributed to U.S. growth can help in the decisions about whether the United States should grow and, if so, how.

SOURCES OF GROWTH

The traditional ingredients of growth are already known from Chapter 17: sufficient factors of supply, flexible resource allocation, and adequate demand. But it is their relative proportions that explain how growth has occurred. Little can be said about the earliest stages of U.S. growth because accurate data are meager. Furthermore, the United States no longer has a large frontier, burgeoning immigration, or a predominantly rural population. Nor does it still have many of the institutional patterns that resulted from these other factors. Consequently, the sources of growth have shifted over the years.

One important trend since industrialization has been a constantly accelerating productivity. Productivity is measured by output per unit of input. Labor productivity, for example, can be expressed as GNP/man-hours employed = output per man-hour. We have already encountered the productivity of capital in the capital/output ratio.

John W. Kendrick has compared the productivity increases of all inputs between 1879 and 1919 with those between 1919 and 1957. He found enormous gains in the latter period.[3] When eliminating the government and service sectors (whose productivity is harder to measure and grows more slowly), Kendrick found that the rate of increase jumped from .8 percent in the earlier period to 2.4 percent annual growth in productivity.

Such increases in productivity are not the whole story. There are any number of reasons why output rises: more diligent workers, more machinery, better machinery, better industrial organization, larger markets. These reasons are systematically examined by Edward F. Denison, author of the most wide-ranging study of growth in the United States.[4] Denison looked at the trends behind U.S. growth from 1909 to 1957 to determine the relative contribution of all inputs as well as changes that might accelerate future growth. Table 19-1 summarizes Denison's weightings. Denison attributes a shade over two-thirds of the growth during the period between 1929 and 1957 to increases in the quantity and quality of inputs. The remaining one-third is ascribed to (1) increased productivity from new knowledge or better application of existing knowledge, and (2) economies of scale. To Denison, labor increases—in both quantity and quality—are still the most important factor, although somewhat less important than they were earlier in this century. Simple growth in capital stock (machinery, factories) was surpassed in importance by gains in productivity from advances in technology (new types of machinery, assembly lines, computers) during the 1929–57 period. Since Denison's data end at 1957, the weightings would be different today. Nevertheless, his work provides a convenient survey of the most important factors in U.S. growth.

3 J. W. Kendrick, *Productivity Trends in the United States* (Princeton, N.J.: National Bureau of Economic Research, 1961).

4 Edward F. Denison, *The Sources of Growth in the United States and the Alternatives Before Us* (New York: Committee for Economic Development, 1962).

TABLE 19-1 The Sources of American Economic Growth, 1909–57

Source	Percent of total growth 1909–29	1929–57
Increase in quantity of labor	39	27
Increase in quantity of capital	26	15
Improved education and training	13	27
Improved technology	12	20
Economies of scale and all other	10	11
Total	100	100

Between 1909 and 1929, U.S. economic growth was due mainly to increasing quantities of labor and capital. While these two factors remained important during the period 1929–57, still more important were improved education, training, and technology.

SOURCE: Edward Denison, *The Sources of Economic Growth in the United States and the Alternatives Before Us* (New York: Committee for Economic Development, 1962).

Natural Resources

Although the natural resources of the United States are set, their availability is not. Should a birdwatcher stumble across vast deposits of coal in the Florida Everglades, the nation's natural resources would seem to increase. Denison argues that technology (in this case the process of extracting coal from the swamp) makes resources available, and therefore technology, not the natural resources themselves, is the actual source of growth.

The real worry currently, of course, is that the availability of resources in the United States is declining—that we will run low on coal, oil, and other key materials provided by nature. Rising prices induced by shortages may discourage less efficient uses, encourage recovery of scarce resources, and stimulate the search for foreign sources and substitutes, thereby staving off depletion at least for a time. In this respect the future will be somewhat different from the recent past, when natural resources seemed virtually inexhaustible.

Human Resources

Changes in Quantity The importance for economic growth that Denison ascribes to the labor force may seem surprising, given the great efforts to eliminate dependence on labor by automation. Nevertheless, labor is the basic input for the growth process. In an underpopulated country, population increases are synonymous with economic growth, as more fields can be cleared or more herdsmen become available. Even in the United States, sheer increases in the quantity of labor accounted for about two-fifths of the aggregate growth between 1909 and 1929, and about one-fourth of the aggregate growth between 1929 and 1957.

Simon Kuznets has pointed out how much faster the population has grown in the United States than in most other developed nations, especially because of immigration.[5] Since 1900 the U.S. population has nearly tripled. When such population growth is translated into more people at work, then output should grow.

5 Kuznets, "The Pattern of U.S. Growth," p. 196.

However, some of this increase in the number of people working may be due to the shortened work-week. We know that the 1970 worker put in 11 fewer hours a week than did his grandfather in 1909. If individuals work fewer hours, it often takes more people to achieve the same output. To a certain extent, this decline in working hours offset some of the gains in economic growth, particularly between 1919 and 1957. But workers were probably better rested and healthier due to shorter working hours, and this in itself has contributed to increased output—and more importantly, to the quality of life of the worker.

Changes in Quality Although the labor force has remained a more or less constant percentage of U.S. population, the proportion of children and older people in the labor force has declined. Offsetting this decline has been an increase in the number of working women. In themselves, these changes in the composition of the labor force have had little effect on growth. What they do reflect is the changing quality of available labor, which has matched in importance the increase in the quantity of labor.

EDUCATION There are fewer children in the labor force today than at the turn of the century because young people now stay in school much longer than previously. In 1910 only half the population continued beyond the eighth grade; less than 15 percent finished high school. In 1970 over half the U.S. adult population had finished high school and over 20 percent had some education beyond high school. In addition, the school year has increased in length over the years. Thus, the average worker in 1960 had spent at least 2½ times as many days in school as his or her grandfather back in 1910.

This education prepares today's worker for different types of jobs than in the past. In today's economy, Horatio Alger's diligent grade school dropouts would probably be drawing unemployment compensation. The proportion of the work force employed as common laborers, for example, dropped from 25 percent in 1910 to about 9 percent in 1956.

WORKING WOMEN More important than the increased proportion of women in the labor force is the upgrading of the quality of their contribution. Because women now maintain a career longer than in the past, their greater experience adds to their effectiveness. And as the barriers to career advancement for women have begun to fall, women of talent are less likely to be permanently trapped behind a typewriter. Women constitute a large, untapped human resource, as do members of other groups barred by prejudice from achieving economic equality. Eliminating discrimination is a step toward economic growth as well as human advancement.

Capital Formation

The simple addition of more labor to fixed natural resources must eventually result in diminishing returns. But statistics show that per capita output has constantly increased. At the same time, the growth rate of real wages has approximately equalled increases in per capita output. Or put another way, over the years labor has earned about the same proportion of the total output. The quality of a labor force that can compile such a record has been continuously improving.

Such a spectacular increase in productivity cannot be attributed solely to enhanced use of natural resources or even to improvements in the quality of the labor component of growth. The efficiency with which workers can employ the materials at hand depends greatly on the facilities they have to work with. Their training would be largely useless if workers had no factories and offices, tools and powerful engines, or transport systems for producing and marketing finished goods. So a third essential feature of U.S. economic growth in the twentieth century is its swelling stock of capital goods.

The formation of capital in the United States has progressed faster than increases in either total population or the labor force. From 1909 to 1929, for example, gross capital stock rose 42.1 percent each decade; per worker it rose 24 percent each decade.[6] Given the relatively rapid rate of population growth, this is a remarkable score. For capital stock to grow, some of the investment must be used merely to replace worn-out capital goods, some simply to keep pace with growing numbers of workers, and finally some to expand the supply of capital goods available to each worker. This adds up to an enormous investment. From 1909 to 1918, for example, 22.1 percent of GNP was devoted to gross investment.[7]

When the amount of capital per worker increases, this is called **capital deepening.** Capital deepening is clearly one source of our increased output per man-hour. For example, think of how long it would take a worker to produce one sweater by hand. Then imagine the same worker equipped with a knitting machine; an entire sweater might be finished daily. Then envision our same worker at a console from which, by pulling levers and pushing buttons, he or she can whip up six dozen sweaters simultaneously!

There is some disagreement about the extent to which simply increasing the *amount* of capital through ever expanding investment will result in an improvement in the *quality* of capital—or, in more technical terms, whether capital embodies technical change. Denison separates capital and technology in his analysis.

Technology: Qualitative Capital

The importance of technology can be indirectly seen by comparing trends in GNP and other inputs. The growth of GNP cannot be entirely accounted for by the increases in capital stock and labor. The source of the residual increase is, for the most part, technology. Technology makes a qualitative difference in capital investment. Generally speaking, technological advance is the plus that yields more efficient use of resources and a more productive combination of workers and the tools they have to work with. Denison's figures confirm the importance of advances in production processes and management techniques. Although capital contributed 25 percent of the growth from 1909 to 1929, its impor-

6 Simon Kuznets, *Capital in the American Economy* (Princeton, N.J.: National Bureau of Economic Research, 1961).

7 Kuznets, *Capital in the American Economy*.

FUTURE SHOCK

If growth is to continue, technology is certain to play a role. Technology changes more than the means of production. It also affects people's lives by making their skills obsolete or by transforming their jobs. Because technology provides a steady stream of new products, it also changes the standard of living. As we have said, the rate of technological invention and innovation is speeding up and with it the impact on the economic system and individual human lives.

Future Shock by Alvin Toffler is an encyclopedia of speculation about human society in a world transformed by technology.* Ironically, the kinds of thinking that created advanced technology will no longer be of use in that society, and traditional notions of economizing will be obsolete. In a world continually in transformation, "gut" economy yields to "psyche" economy, in which the end products are not goods and services but human experience. When output is intangible rather than material, notions of efficiency (upon which technological thinking is based) become insubstantial.

Furthermore, because technology demands specialization, the members of society become interdependent. Yet the kind of specialized expertise called for by an advanced society concentrates decision making in the hands of an elite who are removed from the consequences of their decisions. The information they demand is based on criteria of efficiency rather than on the social situation as a whole. With rapid changes and inadequate information, the situation becomes highly unstable, unless technology is used to democratize decision making and give more people a say in the direction of the society.

If this seems a long way from economics and U.S. growth, perhaps we need only wait a half century. If economists can accept that growth changes standards of living, it is perhaps time they accepted that it likewise transforms styles of living.

* Alvin Toffler, *Future Shock* (New York: Random House, 1970), pp. 25–35, 234–237, 447–487 especially.

NASA

tance declined to 15 percent in the following period, while improvements in technology increased in importance.

The optimum meshing of human resources with technological advancement requires yet another element: scientific management. What was once simply business sense has become a science. The profession has acquired its own cadre of experts, and entire schools are devoted to its study. Systems analysis—a new way of thinking about social, military, and economic problems—has resulted in more efficient use of resources. Such problem-solving techniques rank in importance with tangible inventions as a technological advance.

Technological progress depends on managerial progress for its application; its very source is the research of both basic and applied scientists. Financing such work requires vast investments. Between 1940 and 1965 annual research and development expenditures in the United States increased twentyfold! Although part of this increase may be due to increased visibility of R&D expenditures, it nevertheless roughly indicates the technological explosion during this period.

The rate of diffusion of such new technologies in our society may also be accelerating. Between 1920 and 1944, the development and diffusion of technological advances took 18 to 20 years on the average; between 1890 and 1919, it took 30 or more years. For example, total development time for frozen foods was 83 years, for aluminum 37 years, for motor vehicle transport 27 years, for synthetic fibers nine years, for integrated circuits five years.[8] The difference in lag times may account for some part of economic growth, but this acceleration of the cycle of rise and decline of products has produced what Alvin Toffler and others call "future shock."

Economies of Scale

When we add up all those shares of growth accounted for by increases in the conventional growth sources (that is, human and natural resources, capital formation, and technology), there is still some growth left over. Under the category of "all other," we can assign some value to economies of scale, according to Denison. He believes that economies of scale "increased the contribution of all other sources to economic growth by 10 percent" between 1929 and 1957. This increase came primarily from the growth of national markets, which enabled specialization of both labor and capital.

8 Frank Lynn, "The Rate of Development and Diffusion of Technology," in *Automation and Economic Progress*, eds. Howard R. Bowen and Garth Mangum (Englewood Cliffs, N.J.: Prentice-Hall, 1966). A recent study of a limited number of technological developments indicates that this may be only partially true.

OBSTACLES TO GROWTH

Resource Allocation

When resources are held in inefficient uses, the nation is robbed of output. There are numerous causes of misallocated resources—tariffs, fair trade laws, monopoly power, featherbedding, racial prejudice. In each of these cases a special interest group seeks to protect its economic advantage by limiting the movement of resources. A still more technical example is that of taxation and its effects. Differential tax rates cause some industries to receive more investment capital than others. Since investment depends on net return, taxes are an added cost that raises the gross return needed to show a satisfactory profit. Investments are curtailed for those industries with higher taxes; to achieve the same net return, the gross return must be higher than for the same investment in tax-favored industries.

One important reason for fostering resource mobility is that it promotes the rapid technological change upon which growth depends. Capital and labor must be free to shift to their most productive uses, or a gap will open between the potential growth rate and the actual growth rate. Conversion of resources is not always easy. The problem, of course, is that such movements can cause dislocations when capital and people shift from region to region and from use to use.

Capital Immobility Ideally, capital is invested in its most productive use. But this ideal ignores the obvious problems of (1) getting the funds accumulated by savers into the hands of businesses ready to invest and (2) having businesses decide on the best uses for this capital. Growth particularly complicates matters, since it creates mammoth business organizations whose investment needs are only dimly known to savers. Accelerating changes in technology make it even more difficult to evaluate alternative uses of capital.

In the United States, an added problem is posed by the sheer size of capital needs. Not only must we find sufficient capital to keep the current stock of capital goods intact, but we must also somehow finance new industries. Saving must keep pace in order to finance added investment.

Labor Immobility Whereas capital cannot move or stay put of its own free will, labor can. But the efficient utilization of labor does not always coincide with the welfare or wants of the worker. Even though high productivity industries may offer high wages, the worker may prefer to stay where he grew up, or where his training is fully used, or where his working hours are to his liking. He may also be unaware of better opportunities. Labor mobility has probably been declining since 1929, and its further decline is likely. People cannot readily switch from a job as a machinist to one as an airline pilot. Moreover, most present pension systems are tied to jobs rather than workers, seniority rules encourage workers to stay put, other benefits are linked to length of service, and unemployment compensation ties people to a geographic location. Even though these practices were instituted to protect workers, reduced labor mobility is an unintended by-product, and this may impede growth.

Demand

No amount of efficient production from highly motivated and educated workers on the best of assembly lines contributes to economic growth without the consumption of the products that flow into the marketplace. Unless they are bought, all these goods and services count for nothing. Insufficient demand can prevent an economy from fully using its productive potential; excessive demand can cause rampant inflation.

Sufficient levels of demand may be promoted through stimulation of consumer purchases, business investment, and government spending. The choice between the three sectors is not an indifferent one for promoting growth. As James Tobin has observed, a gain in employment "will make no contribution if it is all consumed."[9]

The significance of Tobin's observation lies in the word *consumed.* To consume means to use up, to devote resources to things like food, clothing, television sets, and vacation campers—all items that produce no other benefits than sustenance or satisfaction. In the short run, increasing consumption may work. Investment, on the other hand, utilizes resources for goods that produce other goods. The government is unlike other sectors in that it can readily devote resources to consuming or investing or to promoting these same activities in the private sector. Regardless of where the decision is made—in the private or the public sector—the choice must be made whether to consume or invest. So the most fundamental priority set in choosing growth as a goal is the sacrifice of present consumption. Phrased another way, growth builds the future capacity of the economy at the expense of present consumption.

HOW TO KEEP GROWING

What Matters Most?

Among all the sources of growth, which ones promise the greatest lift to the economy—and at what costs? Should the United States stop shortening the workweek, or would it be better to cure alcoholism, thereby reducing absenteeism? Should we promote education or devote our greatest attention to encouraging investment?

Future growth need not be haphazard. We now have some knowledge of the sources that nourish economic growth. We know, for example, that growth is seldom if ever the result of any single factor. We also know that any single factor, by itself, has a limited potential for changing the future course of growth. In growth planning, the trick is to select a

9 James Tobin, "Growth through Taxation," in *Problems of the Modern Economy,* eds. Edmund S. Phelps et al. (New York: W. W. Norton, 1966).

balanced diet of those items that will contribute to a healthy economy. The menu from which to choose presents the planner or policy-maker with a wide range of policy alternatives, but not all are equally nutritious for sustained economic growth. The complexity of choice and the fact that any single policy alternative has limited impact are what make policy formation difficult.

As we have seen, the most important means of ensuring growth is by increasing employment. Lengthening the workweek is one way of employing resources more fully, but this can be done only at the expense of leisure time. A more practical goal is to reduce idle resources—those involuntarily not in use. Policies to reduce unemployment are covered in detail in Parts Two and Three of this book.

There are three other areas in which resources can be devoted to promoting growth: education, investment, and research. In a way, all three are forms of investment. Education builds up the quality of human resources by postponing present output and earning in order to obtain improvement in the individual's future productivity. Research advances knowledge and improves the quality of capital through technological progress. Investment builds up the stock of capital goods.

Education

Although in the short run, increasing the education level will reduce the labor force and thereby detract from growth, in the long run such an increase may improve labor productivity and add to economic growth. One obstacle to this solution in the past has been that the individual bears a double burden: the expense of a college education, while forgoing income during his years in college. More community colleges with little or no tuition is one answer to this problem. Another proposal would give tax credit for some part of college costs.

While the overall educational level has been rising, equality of education has remained a hollow promise for certain segments of American society. Both adequate educational standards and educational opportunities have been denied to many of our citizens on the basis of their socioeconomic class or their color. In human terms, selective upgrading of opportunities for these educationally deprived groups would wipe out the inequities. In economic terms, it would produce a dramatic effect on labor productivity and therefore on national growth potential.

The overall quality of education could be improved in three ways: better teaching better techniques, and better integration with job training. The last is probably the most promising area, although in a rapidly changing economy, specific skills soon become obsolete. This drawback might be overcome by continuing education at intervals throughout a person's working life.

Investment

Denison points out that it takes a whopping increase in investment to bring about even a small increase in the growth rate. However, compounding can make tiny increments significant over the years. So the promotion of investment is still essential to economic growth.

Investment can be stimulated in a number of ways. One approach is through fiscal policy using tax incentives. By reducing corporate taxes, by liberalizing depreciation allowances to increase cash flow, or by allowing tax credits for investments, the government can reduce the cost of investment and encourage businesses to venture their capital. One other way of encouraging investment is through monetary policy, using easy money to lower interest rates.

Without sufficient saving, investment cannot occur. Transferring money from consumption to investment can be done by fiscal policy. By raising taxes sufficiently, the government can create a budget surplus, hence savings of its own. If these savings are used to pay off part of the federal debt, the money finds its way into the capital market, where it becomes available for investment borrowing. Moreover, the influx of money lowers interest rates and makes investment more attractive.

A budget surplus and easy money seem to be a common prescription for economic growth among economists. However, lower interest rates may harm a nation's balance of payments, as savings dollars flow to countries offering a higher return; and easy money policies involve inflationary pressures. The higher personal taxes needed to trim inflation may be impossible to pass. So that what may be an intricate but sound economic policy is political dynamite.

Research and Development

Few people question the importance of research and development programs. But a great deal of controversy rages around sources of funding, control, and direction of R&D. This was not always the case. When the federal government started pouring money into R&D after World War II, the move received strong support from prominent scientists and other groups as a way of ensuring high, stable levels of support for R&D. Between 1953 and 1961, total R&D spending grew at 11.3 percent per year in constant dollars. Then between 1967 and 1972, R&D expenditures dropped 1 percent per year in constant dollars. The reason was a cutback in federal spending on R&D by more than 3 percent per year, in reaction to criticism of federal goals and overinvolvement in this area. Nonetheless, over half of R&D spending came from federal sources in 1972. Even this figure is deceptive, since industry and universities performed 80 percent of the projects.[10] This new pattern of federal funding for private execution may well become a permanent feature of R&D. There are even proposals to devote a constant percentage of GNP to research and development.

In the past, military and defense projects have been the primary recipients of R&D expenditures. Today this long-standing imbalance is being challenged by many individuals and groups who feel that U.S. R&D priorities are indeed out of order. They feel that the technological fallout from space and defense development is not sufficient and that it is too slow. They call for the planned, purposeful development of those means that will afford us cleaner air, better transportation, adequate housing for all, and other socially desirable amenities. It should be obvious that the real debate over R&D does not center on what goes on in the research laboratory; it lies at the very base of the whole issue of policymaking for national growth.

10 The data in this section are based on National Science Foundation estimates published in Henry H. Villard, *The Growth of the American Economy* (New York: Joint Council on Economic Education, 1972,) p. 35.

THE GROWTH DEBATE

Growth policies presume growth as a goal; they are concerned with whether or not a country can grow as fast as it wants to and the means to that end. Behind this presumption is the belief that growth is a means to (1) greater material abundance, (2) solving many social problems without necessitating sacrifices, and (3) proving the vitality of capitalism (or whatever the system is).

Critics of growth deny that it actually achieves these aims. Growth can be channeled into the arms race or superfluous technology rather than into solving domestic problems. The race to the moon, a result of growth and a stimulant to more growth, has been pointed out as an example of mistaken priorities. Growth, moreover, can be unbalanced, with the well-to-do reaping the bulk of the gains while the hard-core unemployed are left behind. While U.S. growth in the postwar era has been substantial, relative income shares have changed very little. Everyone may be better off in absolute terms, but the poor are still relatively just as poor as they were before. In the short run, income redistribution could do what growth has not been able to do: eliminate poverty and with it the social problems caused by malnutrition, poor health, and poor housing. This accomplishment would do more than any amount of growth to gain international prestige, critics contend. Such arguments do not attack growth as such, however. One might still choose to grow to supplement the benefits of income redistribution.

There are other arguments against growth that are more clearly dependent on its costs. As it is presently defined, growth sacrifices consumption for saving and present goods for future goods. According to critics, it also sacrifices public goods for private

JAPANESE GROWTH

In recent decades Japan has overtaken and passed the United States in the sustained growth rate sweepstakes. Since 1950, Japan has grown at over 10 percent per year in *real* terms. In 1970 her nominal growth rate was 17.3 percent; her real growth rate, 10.8 percent. Among capitalist nations, Japan's GNP is second only to that of the United States, and continued growth at this pace could put her ahead in the third millennium A.D.

Like that of the United States, Japan's growth can be traced to no single factor. Certainly abundant natural resources have not been the key; only 19 percent of Japan's land is under cultivation, and Japan is growing increasingly dependent upon foreign sources for raw materials and food. What have been important are:

"1 The closing of the technical gap by the import of new technology.

2 An exceptionally high rate of investment buttressed by a very high rate of saving, both institutional and personal [+30 percent of GNP and 20 percent of DI, respectively].

3 The direction of investment into uses which yield quick returns and the absence of wasteful investment in armaments.

4 The large reserve army of workers at the beginning of the period of growth and successful transference of huge numbers from low-productivity occupations [9 percent per annum growth in labor productivity].

5 The reconstruction of the *Zaibatsu* and the creation of other business groups capable of organizing development.

6 A monetary system and policy which were successful both in providing industries with the finance needed for expansion and also in cutting back credit quickly whenever the economy became 'overheated.'

7 A taxation system which kept clear of measures likely to curb industrial investment and damage personal incentives.

8 The effective use of official controls over foreign trade and payments."*

Of these, perhaps most important has been imported technology. By modernizing older industries and creating new ones based on techniques already tried and proven, the Japanese were able to sustain rapid rates of growth. According to Henry Rosovsky of Harvard, since 1958, 10 percent of all Japanese manufacturing has relied on imported

* G. C. Allen, "Japan's Economic Expansion: Achievement and Prospects," in *From Underdevelopment to Affluence: Western, Soviet, and Chinese Views*, eds. Harry G. Shaffer and Jan S. Prybyla (New York: Appleton-Century-Crofts, 1968), p. 289.

technology, and the figure is as high as 30 percent in some sectors. Rosovsky points to the burst of entrepreneurial talent as a strong reason for the success of this tactic. The Japanese have not been solely imitators; they have adjusted foreign processes to squeeze even more out of them than did the originators.†

Now that the technology gap is closing, rapid growth may be harder to come by for the Japanese economy. Despite growing labor productivity from a mobile, disciplined, and educated labor force, Japan ranks only fourteenth in per capita income, indicating the presence of backwater sectors of the booming economy. Many of these sectors have problems that are less amenable to technological solutions. Moreover, the labor surplus that fueled the growth is over, and wage increases have caught up with productivity, lessening the profits that provide investment incentives. A change in the world's foreign trade climate could hurt Japan seriously. Finally, because rapid growth has not widened the social services, nor curbed the pollution from the constantly expanding GNP, the Japanese are taking a closer look at growth policies. Whether the year 2000 marks the beginning of the century of Japan will depend on how Japan meets these problems.

† Henry Rosovsky, "Japan's Economic Future," *Challenge*, July/August 1973, pp. 6–17.

United Nations

goods, leisure for work, and environmental quality for material output.

Social Starvation

One consequence of growth has been the creation of what John Kenneth Galbraith terms "the affluent society"—one characterized by a profusion of consumer goods and a relative paucity of social goods. This imbalance is not due to any lack of demand for social goods. Indeed, as a nation's income rises, it evolves from a rural society to an urban society, and from one in which subsistence is barely possible to one that desires education, roads, and perhaps even armies. Known as Wagner's Law, this phenomenon of rising demand for social goods occurs as per capita incomes rise.

Satisfying these wants is no simple matter, however. In order to obtain public goods, an individual cannot pay directly as he does in the marketplace for his new gold nose ring or other baubles. He must pay taxes (which may even eliminate any baubles this year). And he receives nothing directly for his outlay (which he has no choice but to pay). The citizen may drive over roads paved by taxes. He may borrow books from libraries built and supported by taxes. He may listen to weather reports prepared by people paid by taxes. The separation of payment and goods received allows him to take the goods for granted while begrudging the tax levy. Moreover, some of his tax money goes for things he may neither want nor use: education, dams, or jet bombers, for example. And their benefits do not provide the same immediate satisfaction of cash traded for a chocolate bar. Nor are their costs measured by a price tag, so waste (or imagined waste) may creep in. Governments have a harder time justifying the goods and services they provide, particularly those like banding ducks or collecting folk music on tape. Since government does not normally advertise, it cannot compete for favor with private goods. For all these reasons, people are more willing to spend for private than public goods.

Strange as it may seem, the remedy for this situation is not necessarily cutbacks in private spending per se. Disarmament is one route to providing more social goods growth itself can help achieve the balance. Finally, it may mean levying higher taxes as a means of diverting private funds into government spending.

Those who argue against this imbalance may deny that it exists by pointing to rising public expenditures, particularly at the state and local levels. Moreover, even if a nation does need a better health care system or more colleges and scholarships, public spending is no guarantee that needs will be met. To get the needed goods may mean accepting lower priority items. Pork barreling is as wasteful as annual automobile model changes. Both substitute

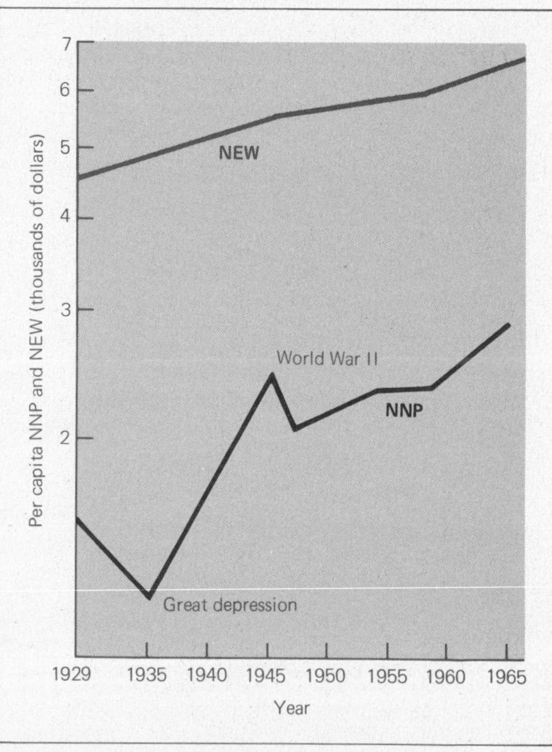

FIGURE 19-2 NET ECONOMIC WELFARE AND PER CAPITA GNP, 1929–65 GNP measures production, not consumption. Yet consumption is the goal of economic activity. A measure of this concept of economic welfare is NEW. Although it remains substantially above GNP. it is rising at a slower rate because an increasing proportion of U.S. GNP is actually a disamenity (such as pollution) or an instrumental expense (such as defense).

SOURCE: William Nordhaus and James Tobin, "Is Growth Obsolete?" *Economic Growth,* Fiftieth Anniversary, Colloquium V (New York: National Bureau of Economic Research and Columbia University Press, 1972), p. 58.

low-priority items for ones that could stimulate growth more. Finally, many of the needs are of a quasi-public nature. No one really knows which sector can deliver health care or college educations more efficiently. The costs of governmental control may be too high. By absorbing resources, government control may actually hinder growth.

Toward a New Definition of Growth

The remaining criticisms dealing with leisure and environmental degradation are partly a matter of definition. If growth is an increased standard of living as we have suggested in Chapter 17, then an increase in leisure time or an improvement in environmental quality is as much growth as is an increase in available goods and services.

This is an idea economists are just now beginning to develop. As we saw in Chapter 6, Tobin and Nordhaus have laid the groundwork by revising GNP in a number of ways, including adjustments to reflect the positive value of leisure time and the negative value of environmental problems. Tobin and Nordhaus provide a hint about the problem of social goods by classifying government expenditures as either consumption, investment, regrettables, or intermediate goods. Only the first two (which are primarily used to raise productivity or provide services to households) are counted. Excluded are defense and other costs of what the authors call "instrumental outlays."[11]

Except for the problem of assigning a dollar value to leisure time, this concept is relatively straightforward and has been discussed elsewhere in this book. The questions of environmental standards are more complex. Tobin and Nordhaus divide these into (1) disamenities associated with urban life and (2) depletion of environmental capital.[12] These problems are covered in the next two chapters. There we will examine in detail what the growth debate is all about. Like goods and services that show up in GNP, better urban land use and cleaner air are outputs of an economic system; resources may be devoted to realizing more urban amenities or better environmental quality. Here is yet another problem of economizing—this trade-off of GNP for other kinds of goods and services.

11 Tobin and Nordhaus, "Is Growth Obsolete?" pp. 26–28.
12 Tobin and Nordhaus, "Is Growth Obsolete?" pp. 49–51.

SUMMARY

1 American economic growth has been remarkable, especially since its population has been expanding rapidly throughout its history. Whether the United States *can* and *should* continue its rapid pace of GNP growth is a subject of much current debate. The same things that make GNP grow can be the source of either comfort (more goods and services) or discomfort (loss of leisure time and increased pollution).

2 One worry, currently, is that the availability of resources in the United States is declining—that we will run low on coal, oil, and other key materials provided by nature. Labor, however, remains the basic input for the growth process. The increase in the size of the labor force has been of paramount importance, but this is now matched in importance by the increase in the quality of workers, according to a leading student of U.S. growth, Edward Denison.

3 The simple addition of more labor to fixed natural resources must eventually result in diminishing returns. But statistics show that per capita output has constantly increased. Part of this can be accounted for by the growth in capital stock.

4 However, the growth of GNP cannot be entirely accounted for by the increases in capital stock and labor. The source of the residual increase is, for the most part,

technology, which includes advances not only in technical knowledge, but also in management.

5 In addition to sufficient factors of supply, growth is stimulated by flexible resource allocation and adequate demand. When resources are held in inefficient uses, the nation is robbed of output. There are numerous causes of misallocated resources: tariffs, fair trade laws, monopoly power, featherbedding, and racial prejudice. However efficiently our resources are allocated, growth cannot continue unless the goods and services produced are bought.

6 The most important means of ensuring growth is increasing employment, through full-employment policies. There are three other areas in which resources can be devoted to promoting growth: education, investment, and research.

7 The debate over growth pits the costs of increasing GNP against the benefits of increased material well-being. Proponents say that growth provides greater material abundance, a means to solve pressing social ills, and proof of economic viability. Opponents deny that growth achieves these aims and add that growth demands the sacrifice of consumption for saving, present goods for future ones, public goods for private ones, leisure for work, and environmental quality for material abundance.

8 If growth is defined as an increased standard of living rather than simply higher per capita GNP, then an increase in leisure or an improvement in environmental quality can be considered as much growth as an increase in available GNP. Economists are just now beginning to develop this new definition of economic growth.

SUGGESTED READINGS

Denison, Edward F. *Sources of Economic Growth in the United States and the Alternatives Before Us.* New York: Committee for Economic Development, 1962.

Nordhaus, William, and **James Tobin.** "Is Growth Obsolete?" *Economic Growth.* Fiftieth Anniversary, Colloquium V. New York: National Bureau of Economic Research and Columbia University Press, 1972.

North, Douglass C. *Growth and Welfare in the American Past: A New Economic History.* Englewood Cliffs, N.J.: Prentice-Hall, 1966.

Shapiro, Edward. *Macroeconomic Analysis.* 2nd ed. Chaps. 21 and 22. New York: Harcourt Brace Jovanovich, 1970.

U.S. Domestic Council Committee on National Growth. *Report on National Growth 1972.* Washington, D.C.: Government Printing Office, 1972.

Villard, Henry H. *The Growth of the American Economy.* New York: Joint Council on Economic Education, 1972.

QUESTIONS

1 Review

a. the sources of economic growth in the United States and their relative importance at various points in American history,

b. major obstacles to economic growth of the United States,

c. factors and policies in the United States that contribute to economic growth,
d. suggestions for redefining economic growth.

2 Assume that an economy is determined to be suffering from inflation due to excess demand. One proposal for reducing that demand is to limit the money supply and thereby raise interest rates. Could you argue that while this policy might be helpful in the short run, the excess demand is more likely to be met in the future if some other means were found to fight inflation? Why?

3 In the mid-1960s, several oil companies announced that they had located rich new sources of oil in Alaska. Could this discovery be considered to be an addition to America's natural resources? Why or why not?

4 In the late 1960s the courts decided that it is unlawful for states to stipulate that eligibility for welfare include strict residence requirements. How might this decision affect the mobility of labor and labor immobility as an obstacle to growth?

5 How did America's relatively open immigration policy in its early history contribute to economic growth? What effects may there have been from the more restrictive present policy? How might diminishing returns fit in your answer?

6 Do you think that there might be any difficulty in distinguishing between the contributions to economic growth from education and technology? Why or why not? Might there be a tendency to underestimate the contribution made by technology? Why or why not?

7 Assume that in a hypothetical economy, the saver and investor is basically the same person, a business owner-operator. Do you think that the allocation of capital under this type of organization would be more efficient and contribute a greater measure of economic growth than a system in which financial institutions serve as intermediaries between savers and investors? Why or why not?

8 In the summer of 1973, the Nixon administration imposed a price freeze. How would such a price freeze tend to affect long-term growth?

9 Some argue that the question of whether or not the American economy should continue to grow is simply a question of semantics. Do you agree or disagree? Why?

CHAPTER 20

URBAN PROBLEMS

Rapid and sustained growth has transformed the United States from a rural to an urban society. Not all sectors have benefitted from this shift, however. The inequities are underscored by the vast difference between the quality of life in the inner city and in the suburbs in almost every metropolitan area. Average annual family income figures only hint at the difference: In the inner city, the average falls below $7500; in the suburbs that ring the city, the figure ranges from $7500 to $15,000. Far greater disparities are evident in unemployment rates, crime rates, reading levels, housing, pollution levels, and most other measures of well-being.

Neither government nor private enterprise seems to be coping successfully with the problems of the cities. Outside government, there appears to be little incentive to take responsibility. Private enterprise prefers to ignore the problems of the cities. Political boundaries enable suburbanites to enjoy the benefits of the city without paying city taxes or concerning themselves with the plight of its poorer inhabitants. These boundaries, considered archaic by regional planners, prevent city and suburban governments from getting together to work on problems that affect them both. Even within city jurisdiction, governments are not meeting the problems. The problems of crime, poverty, and substandard housing and schooling continue to outgrow the budgets appropriated to deal with them and to raise questions about the uses to which public money is being put.

The bulk of this chapter deals with the most serious problems affecting urban areas—housing, transportation, and finance—and the extent to which each is a problem of inequity or of inefficiency. Their solutions cannot be seen in isolation, since each is competing for the limited resources of the area, and the solution to one problem may conflict with the solutions to others. The ultimate problem of the cities may be one of allocative efficiency, of setting priorities that are coherent and that offer the greatest hope of improving the urban society.

Opening photo by Elliott Erwitt, Magnum Photos

THE DEVELOPMENT OF METROPOLITAN AREAS

Since American cities are, at the most, no more than four centuries old, they have grown very rapidly, when compared with the rest of the cities of the world. A city was often initially settled because it lay at the mouth of a river or at the confluence of two rivers, or because it was otherwise strategically located with respect to defense, economic activity, or transportation. As economic and population growth took place, the cities often broadened their boundaries.

Since economic activity and population have spilled over the cities' boundaries into the neighboring suburbs, analysis of the economic problems of urban areas should not be confined to the central city itself. Therefore, we shall think of metropolitan areas as including the urban core and the outlying areas within the city, as well as the surrounding suburbs.

Definition of a Metropolitan Area

A metropolitan area is defined by the Bureau of the Census as a county or group of counties containing at least one city of 50,000 inhabitants. Two cities may count as one and contiguous counties are included if they are socially and economically integrated with the central city. Urban areas are defined by the Bureau of the Census as any settlements having a population of 2500 or more. When we are told that America is becoming increasingly urbanized but that the cities are losing population, we can resolve this seeming contradiction by noting that the big urban gainers are the suburbs.

The urban population has grown from 119 million people in 1960 to 139 million in 1970. Within the standard metropolitan statistical areas (SMSAs), however, the central cities have grown at less than 1 percent per year during that period, while the suburbs have grown at 2.4 percent per year. Most of the urban population increase, then, is due to the rapid rise in population in the suburbs, which may be compared with the rest of the United States in Table 20-1.

TABLE 20-1 Urban America

Residence and race	Population, 1970 total (in thousands)	Percent	Percent change, 1960–70	Average annual percentage change, 1960–70
Total	203,212	100.0	13.3	1.3
SMSAs	139,419	68.6	16.6	1.5
Central cities	63,797	31.4	6.4	0.6
Outside central cities	75,622	37.2	26.8	2.4
Nonmetropolitan areas	63,793	31.4	6.8	0.7
White	177,749	100.0	11.9	1.1
SMSAs	120,579	67.8	14.6	1.4
Central cities	49,430	27.8	−0.2	−0.1
Outside central cities	71,148	40.0	27.6	2.5
Nonmetropolitan areas	57,170	32.2	6.6	0.6
Black	22,580	100.0	20.2	1.9
SMSAs	16,771	74.3	32.0	2.8
Central cities	13,140	58.2	32.1	2.8
Outside central cities	3630	16.1	31.5	2.8
Nonmetropolitan areas	5810	25.7	−4.5	−0.5

Two of the most striking population changes since World War II have been the rapid growth of the suburbs and the migration of blacks from rural areas. Between 1960 and 1970, the suburban population in the United States grew by 26.8 percent; these suburbs contain well over half the urban population. In the central cities between 1960 and 1970, the black population rose by 32.1 percent. Blacks, who constitute 11 percent of the national population, constitute over 20 percent of the population of the central cities, but only 5 percent of the suburban population.

SOURCE: U.S. Department of Commerce, *Statistical Abstract of the United States*, 1972.

The Economic Basis of Cities

Traditionally, the economic activity of most American cities has centered around the port or railhead. Until the beginning of the twentieth century, this concentration was necessitated by the difficulty of transporting people and goods within the cities. Even manufacturing, which required relatively large amounts of space, was located near the hub. The presence of large numbers of people provided a sizable market for goods, and ready transportation gave access to the markets of other regions. Industrial concentration enabled greater specialization and encouraged further clustering. And the cities provided an **infrastructure,** or set of facilities such as power or a rail terminal, that no one company could ever afford.

The growth of the cities has been fueled by the flight from the land. Increasing agricultural productivity has freed large numbers of people to work in factories—factories located in urban areas.

The Suburbanization of America

The Flight Begins People began moving away from the cores of cities long before business could afford to move farther out. The advent of the trolley, first horse-drawn and then electrified, provided a cheap means of commuting. Businesses, however, were tied to the central cores of the cities by the railroads, then the cheapest mode of transportation for goods and raw materials.

Power was another important determinant of central-city location. In old mill towns, such as Lowell and Fall River, Massachusetts, textile factories were built alongside rivers so that the water wheels could be turned. The advent of steam power enabled these factories to move farther from the water.

Better modes of transportation and more diverse power sources permitted outward expansion from the central cities, a trend that was hastened by the rising cost of land in the old central business districts. Those districts ceased to be the central points of economic activity; now distribution of goods was taking place at several points simultaneously. Somewhat later, the internal combustion engine was to influence the distribution of people as well as the distribution of production facilities.

The Exodus Although automobiles were being mass produced during the 1920s, it was not until the late forties that the move to the suburbs began in earnest. Relatively low land prices, clean air, green space in which children could play, and perhaps the "snob appeal" of suburbia provided much of the impetus.

As the suburban exodus gathered momentum, an increasing number of businesses relocated in the suburbs. Corporate executives, who themselves had moved out of the city, opted for the relocation of their firms. Furthermore, a ready-made labor force was available in the towns that encircled most central cities. Once certain businesses made the move, there was less reason for others to stay. The downtown business district was no longer the only place to do business.

Suburban locations were cheaper, more spacious, and better suited to new production techniques requiring one-story buildings.[1] Another lure was the tax advantages offered by some towns. Probably the most significant factors in the move of manufacturers from central cities were the building of a nationwide highway network and the shift of freight carriage from railroads to trucks.

In most of the large metropolitan areas, the proportion of the population inhabiting the central cities has been falling since about 1900. Today, about 75 percent of those residing in metropolitan areas are outside the central cities. During most of the period since 1900, the central cities' share of manufacturing and wholesale and retail employment has been declining. Today, the relatively smaller manufacturing firms are generally located in the core while the larger ones are closer to the periphery. A firm that grows so large that it finds it more economical to take on added transportation and building costs than to continue coping with traffic congestion and lack of space will move toward the city's periphery or beyond, to a suburb. The process of suburbanization, then, has been going on for some time. But only after World War II was there a pronounced move beyond the boundaries of the central cities.

Influx of the Rural Poor Before the cities started losing their middle class, an influx of the rural poor had already begun. Blacks had begun to migrate from the South to northern cities in the hope of finding better jobs as well as escaping discrimination. While this migration has averaged 100,000 annually since 1940, the black population of the South has at the same time been increasing due to a high fertility rate. What this probably means, unless the South's changing attitudes bring a reversal, is a continuing enlargement of northern ghettos as well as a dispersion of children of migrants throughout urban society.

The Puerto Rican migration is similar to the black migration in that Puerto Ricans are primarily rural, relatively poorly educated, and unskilled. New York City alone has approximately one million people of Puerto Rican origin, most of them migrants or the children of migrants.

The migration of blacks and Puerto Ricans to the large northeastern cities during the 1950s was about equal in number to the immigration of Italians 40 years earlier. The middle class exodus has recently accelerated, taking with it most of these early immigrants and their by-now grown families. The influx and exodus have balanced out, halting the growth of most large cities and in a few cases producing

1 There has been a marked shift away from the "gravity-flow" approach to manufacturing, where production began on the top floor, proceeding down to the first floor shipping room. Today, industrial engineers consider the continuous flow (assembly line) approach more efficient. Since production is to take place on a single floor, considerably more space is required.

small declines. What is different from the cities' population redistributions of earlier years is that the middle class and many businesses have moved, not within the cities' boundaries, but outside to other political jurisdictions. Politically, the metropolitan area has become balkanized, with the poor trapped in the central cities. The economic implications of this pattern are examined in the following sections of this chapter.

HOUSING

A metropolitan area is often composed of a series of concentric circles. The core is the declining central business district surrounded by the ghetto. In the North, this ghetto is black and Puerto Rican, and in the Southwest and West, Mexican-American and black. As one leaves the city's core, the neighborhoods become progressively more desirable, especially beyond the city line.

Not all housing conditions have deteriorated in recent years. In fact, between 1948 and 1967, a population increase of 8 million in the central cities was matched by an almost equal number of new housing units. Since several people live in each housing unit, this represents a substantial improvement. As a result of this construction, the proportion of central city residents inhabiting seriously substandard units declined on a national basis, from 25 percent in 1950 to 7 percent in 1966.

But the distribution of these units was less than equitable. Central city conditions for nonwhites actually deteriorated during the 1950s. Over 30 percent of all housing occupied by nonwhites in most large cities could be classified as slums.

The Allocation of Housing

The Ghetto The term *ghetto* originated in medieval Italy, where it referred to those parts of the cities to which the Jews were confined. As the term is used in the United States today, it refers to the black (and to a lesser degree, Puerto Rican or Mexican-American) section of a central city. It is usually more centrally located and poorer than other poverty areas within the city. Unlike the earlier ghettos in this country, which contained diverse ethnic groups, the black ghettos are homogeneous entities. Aside from their poverty, all the residents have one thing in common—race.

Whatever the urban problem, it is usually more acute in the ghetto. Problems of transportation, crime, and poverty hit the ghetto areas the hardest. Health and education, despite recent efforts at improvement, lag well behind the standards in other parts of the city. Obviously, then, ghetto residents face more than a housing problem. But housing certainly is a major concern. Despite the fact that many of the dwellings are dated and rat-infested, the poor are forced to pay exorbitant rents.

Why don't they move out? An increasing number is doing just that. But there are three things holding many others back. Residents are often too well integrated into the ghetto community to want to make the move into an unfamiliar, presumably hostile world. Second, many are unable to afford to move. Finally, there is a very substantial degree of discrimination in housing in most large northern cities. As a popular saying goes, "Down South they don't mind how close you get as long as you don't get too big. Up North they don't mind how big you get as long as you don't get too close."

The Sources of the Housing Problem

Apart from the very real problems of discrimination that are reinforced by the political splintering of a metropolitan area, there are other, economic forces at work that retard the repair or replacement of substandard, low-income housing. In the United States, housing is furnished to the poor by the private market through the process of filtering. As described in Chapter 10, older housing is vacated by those moving into newer, better housing. This makes room for the poor, who are attracted by the relatively low rents on housing that has seen its better days. The low rents provide no incentives for landlords to make repairs, and even if there is a strict building code, landlords may find it cheaper to buy off a building inspector than to replace a balky heating system. The landlord may even abandon the building when taxes are higher than revenues from rents. Such disinvestments in housing are enormous; in 1965 they amounted to an estimated $25 million in the Bedford-Stuyvesant section of Brooklyn alone. But landlords are motivated by private costs and private benefits, not public ones.

A key problem in the housing market, then, is the presence of externalities. An externality is a social cost or benefit that is not construed by the individual as part of the private cost or benefit of the good or service he is producing or consuming. Externalities have led to the perpetuation of slums. For example, refuse-filled lots and dilapidated buildings present potential fire and health hazards to the community. To the owners of these properties, correcting the hazards represents a cost, not a benefit. Here, private decision making has led to inadequate protection for the community. This has led to government intervention. In theory, the government can take into account the costs and benefits external to the private market in ruling that an action needs to be taken by a landlord. In practice, this approach has had some undesirable consequences.

Urban Renewal One popular effort to eliminate slums is urban renewal. This consists of bulldozing slum buildings and putting up either private housing, business structures, or various public buildings, including housing. The local government, using the right of eminent domain, condemns all the property in a given area, clears that area of all structures, and helps relocate the former residents. Usually the federal government will lend about two-thirds of the necessary funds.

Area-wide development overcomes the problem of externalities that discourage landlords in slum areas from improving housing. Urban renewal projects can thus be justified on the ground of efficiency if the net social benefits that result are larger than would be derived from alternative programs designed to handle the housing problem.

To determine the wisdom of a particular investment, one must know *all* the costs and benefits. Like slumlords, urban renewal authorities may misallocate resources in particular areas by not taking into account externalities, but unlike slumlords, they may overallocate resources rather than underallocate them. Like the private landlord, the local government that carries out an urban renewal project may deal inefficiently with its resources from a community standpoint, because it has not considered all social costs. Unexpected costs that arise from the shifting of populations by urban renewal are reflected not only in the urban renewal area but throughout the city. These arise from changes in relative land values and the crowding of certain sections. Regardless of such costs, urban renewal is undertaken because the funding system makes it possible. Since the federal government usually provides about two-thirds of the funds, a project that would not have otherwise been carried out by a local government (because the private and social costs would have exceeded the private and social benefits) may be pushed through.

Many urban renewal projects fail the efficiency test, and even more of them would fail an equity test as well, since projects demolish substandard housing, leaving the dispossessed tenants unable to afford the better housing that replaces it. These tenants are merely being shunted from one slum to another, forcing up already high rents.

For example, urban renewal in Baltimore from 1951 to 1964 eliminated the equivalent of over one-fifth of the housing stock occupied by low-income blacks in 1950. By itself and considered on a metropolitan basis, the impact of each renewal project was small, but the total costs in decreased housing and increased rents were large and disproportionately borne by the low-income black population.

Since many urban renewal sites are developed into middle- and upper-income housing, the poor are, in effect, subsidizing the well-to-do. This may be partially compensated for, in the long run, by the additional taxes paid by these new residents. If the displaced slum dwellers were able to move into the homes and apartments vacated by the urban renewal tenants (which they generally are not), then the equity test would be passed. The most that the very

TALLY'S CORNER

The world of the ghetto is one apart from the rest of society. Isolated by discrimination, the ghetto forms an underdeveloped nation within America. A microcosm of this world is described in *Tally's Corner.**

The economic structure of the ghetto is different from that of society at large. Its resources are exported: Savings in ghetto banks are used for bank investments outside the ghetto; the infrastructure of the ghetto is depreciating so that there is disinvestment in the area; and profits from ghetto businesses flow to owners outside the ghetto. The income in the ghetto comes from sources different from the rest of society—from transfer payments, from illegal activity, or from low-paying jobs. This situation exists because ghetto residents are chronically unemployed or underemployed, forming a large pool of low-wage workers.†

Nicholas de Sciose, Rapho Guillumette

. . . the most important fact is that a man who is able and willing to work cannot earn enough money to support himself, his wife, and one or more children. A man's chances for working are good only if he is willing to work for less than he can live on, and sometimes not even then. On some jobs, the wage rate is deceptively higher than on others, but the higher the wage rate, the more difficult it is to get the job and the less the job security . . . some of the low-paying jobs are scaled down even lower in accordance with the self-fulfilling assumption that the man will steal part of his wages on the job.‡

Liebow emphasizes the effect of exclusion from economic success on the worker's self-esteem and on his whole living pattern. The street corner society Liebow describes is present-oriented because the future is hopeless. It is marked by transience of employment, family, friendship, and residence and by a set of values that provides a sanctuary from failure. Liebow concludes that the solution to the problems of the ghetto is not barred by cultural differences but by economic conditions and interests.

* Elliot Liebow, *Tally's Corner* (Boston: Little, Brown, 1967).
† Daniel R. Fusfeld, *The Basic Economics of the Urban Racial Crisis* (New York: Holt, Rinehart and Winston, 1973).
‡ Liebow, pp. 50–52.

poor can usually hope for is the public housing project, and even this less-than-ideal solution is available to relatively few families.

Public Housing Public housing is another alternative having serious defects with respect to both efficiency and equity. Like urban renewal, it is generally built by a local government authority and subsidized by federal funds. Since public housing must be built within the jurisdiction of the central city, it fails from an efficiency standpoint because it is built on relatively expensive land. Suburban land is cheaper, but suburban governments, with their relatively few low-income families, are averse to projects that would increase their number. This is unfortunate, not only because it prevents a better quality of life for lower-income central city residents, but because it excludes a labor supply for the increasing number of industrial jobs in the suburbs. Attempts by the U.S. Department of Housing and Urban Development to disperse low-income housing throughout the suburbs have met with considerable political resistance, however.

The total stock of public housing now provides aid to less than one-tenth of the eligible low-income families. To provide equivalent assistance to even half those eligible would cost $5 billion annually over a 10-year period.

Another argument against public housing is that it restricts the choices of its recipients. It is not left up to the people most affected to choose where to live, or, for that matter, to decide that available funds might be better spent on food or clothing. Poor housing is only part of the problem of being poor, and different families may have different priorities. For this reason, income grants have been suggested as a better alternative.

Housing Subsidies Most housing subsidies are given to middle-income and upper-income families through income-tax deductions of mortgage interest and through FHA or VA guaranteed loans. In 1973, President Nixon suspended mortgage subsidies to the poor, along with several other federal housing programs, because of scandals and misadministration.

Direct income subsidies have been proposed by a wide variety of observers, and prototypes were included in President Nixon's housing message. But they cannot work without an increase in the supply of housing. Without an increase in supply, such subsidies may simply drive up rents or house prices. In order to encourage new building, President Nixon has infused even more money into traditional mortgage markets, presumably relying on the filtering down principle to increase the supply of housing to the poor.

In sum, increasing the total supply of housing available to the urban poor is an essential need in our society. New technologies, such as prefabrication, offer an answer to the high cost of building. At present, archaic building codes and union opposition are blocking the widespread use of new building systems, but it is expected that these obstacles will be surmounted. When they are, the question is whether or not the increased supply of housing will be in the reach of people with low incomes. To ensure that it is, rent subsidies and subsidized mortgages can offer financial assistance. Sustained efforts to end discriminatory housing practices will ensure that the other measures do not perpetuate the housing plight of impoverished Americans.

EDUCATION

Like housing, education also involves externalities—positive ones if education is good and negative ones if it is poor. Because of the benefits to society of literacy—as well as the enormous expense involved—education has been virtually monopolized by the public sector. In the metropolitan areas, however, this sector is fragmented, resulting in the same kind of inequities of distribution as are found in housing. By any measure of performance—reading scores, dropout rates, pupil-staff ratios, or expenditures per pupil—inner city schools fall below suburban schools.

The financing of public education is in part responsible for such inequalities. By and large the funds for education come from property taxes. Tax rates are often higher in poorer areas, yet they raise fewer funds. A challenge to this funding practice met with no success in the Supreme Court.

Equalizing the tax base is only one means to the goal of equalizing educational opportunity. Eliminating inefficiencies in the present budgets raises the amount available to improve the quality of education. One means of providing incentives for efficiency is to make schools more directly responsible to "consumers" by the use of some form of voucher system. A voucher issued to each student could be used at any school—public or private. Competition for students would provide incentives for improving quality and for diversifying the options of each student. Without controls, however, such a system could maintain existing segregation by race and income, and relegate problem children to public schools. Another proposal is the use of some form of performance contracting. Performance contracting in essence turns public education over to private firms, which are compensated according to results. This provides incentives for efficiency and might lead to better education in the inner cities, since firms would be rewarded for significant improvements. Neither program would equalize per pupil expenditures but either would provide incentives to make the best use of available resources.

CRIME

The pattern of crime is similar to the pattern of housing and education. Poverty and population density are at the root of all three.

Crime is a particularly urban problem: More serious crimes per capita are being committed in cities than in the rest of the country. According to the Eisenhower Commission, about 45 percent of all major violent crimes[2] are committed in the 26 largest cities, which contain about 17 percent of the nation's population. A further breakdown of violent crime, by size of city, shows that crime rates increase rapidly with increases in population. Furthermore, the overall crime rate is rapidly increasing. There has been an apparent increase in the crime rate in cities of all sizes since 1960.

Crime also varies with age: people between the ages of 15 and 24 are more than three times as likely to commit crimes as the rest of the population over 10. Cities have had an increasing proportion of their populations in the 15- to 24-year-old age group, which partially explains the relatively high urban crime rates.

Violent crime is dwarfed, however, by the impact of organized crime on the ghetto, with its gambling rings, loan sharks, narcotics pushers, and receivers of stolen goods. Although these criminal industries provide some employment and income to ghetto residents, their net effect is to drain off the already meager resources of the area. It has been estimated that more money leaves Harlem through the numbers game than comes in in the form of welfare payments.

Crime of any kind imposes costs on society. Recent estimates of costs on a national scale suggest the dimensions of the problem. Figure 20-1 shows that these costs fall into two categories: costs imposed by crime itself and costs incurred in preventing it or in prosecuting those apprehended. To reduce the first category of costs—loss of property, lost wages, injuries due to crimes—society incurs the costs of prevention, apprehension, and prosecution. Most of the time, decisions concerning the amount to be spent on law enforcement are made intuitively, based on balancing the need for safety against all the other perceived needs of the city. In practice, the decisions to buy safety are often made either by those in least danger or by those employed in the safety field. The result is that increases in protection expenditures may have little effect on crime rates—a form of technological inefficiency.

One cost of combating crime not included in Figure 20-1 is that of welfare. Some crime bred by poverty may be eliminated by dealing directly with poverty rather than by adding burglar alarms or more policemen to the force. Evaluating expenditures on welfare as a way to prevent crime is another area in which the principles of allocative efficiency and technological efficiency may be applied.

TRANSPORTATION

If suburbanization exacts a price from the poor in the form of substandard housing, poor education,

2 See Joseph G. Metz, "The Economics of Crime," in *Economic Topic Series, 1970–71* (New York: Joint Council on Economic Education, 1971), pp. 2 and 4.

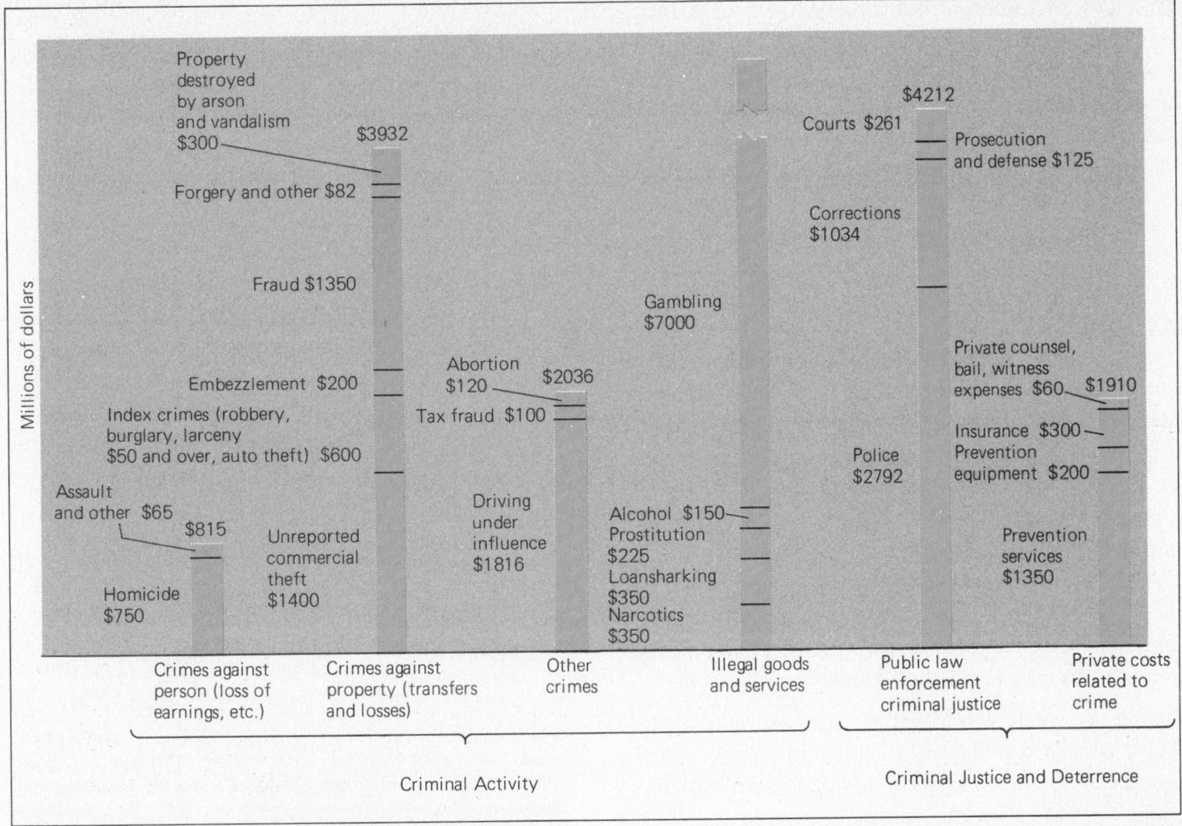

FIGURE 20-1 THE ECONOMIC IMPACT OF CRIME, 1967 Costs of crime fall into two categories: costs to crime victims and costs to deter crime. We must stress here that only the *economic*, and not the social or truly personal, impact of crime on the victims is shown here. These figures represent the dollar cost that falls on the public, private, and social spheres, but the psychological cost of being mugged, the trauma of returning home to find that someone has broken in, and the grief felt by those close to someone who has been killed are incalculable. The cost of police protection and security systems and that of actual loss to various forms of theft are fairly easily calculated. Losses to individuals in terms of lost earning power are determined with more difficulty. Of all criminal activity, gambling has by far the greatest economic impact.

SOURCE: *Crime and Its Impact.* The President's Commission on Law Enforcement and Administration of Justice, 1967, p. 44.

and closer proximity to crime, it exacts a price from the more affluent suburbanite in the form of commuting. In most cities commuting is done by car. Mass transit began losing passengers to cars following World War II, and although mass transit patronage stabilized during the 1960s, it is currently less than half its 1950 level.

Part of the explanation for the shift from public to private transportation lies in the dispersal of people and industries throughout the suburbs. Obviously, mass transit cannot succeed economically unless there is a concentration of passenger traffic along relatively few routes. In addition, urban automobile transportation has been subsidized heavily during the post–World War II period. The highway lobby, which has long had a lock on congressional transport policy, has seen to it that every cent of the highway trust fund (accumulated from federal gasoline taxes) has gone into highway construction, at least until recently. People use roads because they are there and seem to be free.

Consumers are being sent the wrong signals by the

structure of transportation charges. From an economic standpoint, the proper signals would tell each commuter the full opportunity costs (private plus social costs) of his decision. This failure becomes manifest during rush hours, when commuters, encouraged by the accessibility of highways, persist in using their cars to get to and from the urban core.

Congestion

The problem of traffic jams occurs in part because price signals do not reflect the full cost of the service. The auto commuter gets his roads free; he sees only the marginal cost of gasoline—and if he is conscious of his actual costs, the incremental depreciation on his car plus the time wasted in jams. The price of public transportation, however, may be set to reflect all operating costs, not simply marginal cost. But unless the commuter receives better signals from the price system or other incentives, he will continue to ply the roadways until he retires.

There are really two urban transportation problems: (1) a short-run problem in achieving technologically efficient use of existing transportation facilities, and (2) a long-run problem of allocating resources to build the most efficient transportation network.

Short-run Pricing Solutions Since in the short run, highway and mass transit systems are fixed, the only way of reducing congestion is either to stagger working hours or to make the car owner realize how he or she can benefit by not using roads during peak traffic hours. Differential tolls are one method. William Vickrey has described an ingenious system of installing sensors linked to computers that record individually identified autos as they pass key points and provide billing for the use of roadways at different hours.[3]

If drivers were charged enough, there would be a sizable reduction of peak-hour traffic. Shoppers would put off trips until later in the day, and some drivers would either join car pools or use public transportation. Variable prices on mass transit could also help the system spread its service throughout the day and could be an incentive to use a bus or train instead of a car. A tax on parking spaces during peak hours might also be used to discourage driving. Whatever the form of rationing, however, it would merely be a short-run solution utilizing present transportation facilities.

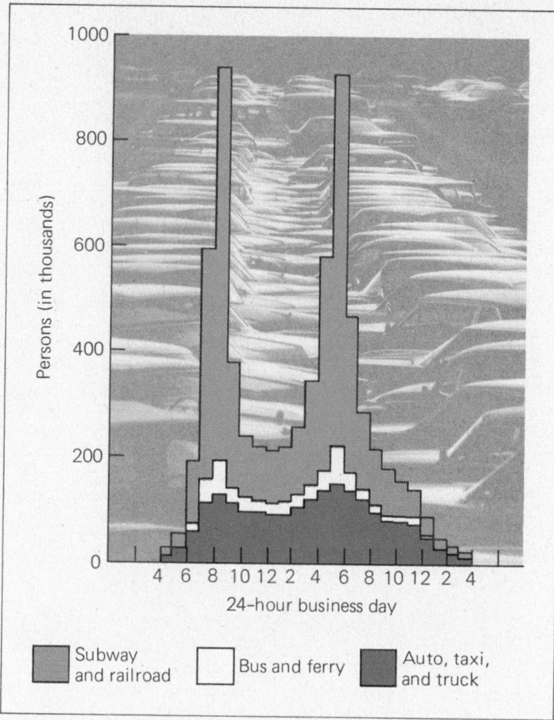

FIGURE 20-2 RUSH HOUR IN NEW YORK CITY (Typical Business Day, 1965) The real peak loading in New York City occurs not on highways but on mass transit. Transit capacity stands idle for all but a few hours a day. This is why mass transit operates at a deficit. Changing traffic patterns and charging more are alternative solutions. Eliminating the excess capacity is probably impossible without changing work patterns, and eliminating the deficit by charging high fares makes transit riders bear the entire cost of that means of transport which creates the least pollution while doing much to reduce traffic jams for auto users. Thus, because traffic patterns are so difficult to change, and because there is a limit to how high a fare can be charged, it may be that cities will have to rely on subsidies for their mass transit systems.
Photo by Tim Kantor, Rapho Guillumette.

SOURCE: William A. Caldwell, ed., *How to Save Urban America*. The Regional Planning Association. Fig. 4, p. 65.

3 William Vickrey, "Current Issues in Transportation," in *Contemporary Issues in Transportation*, 2nd ed., ed. Neil W. Chamberlain (Homewood, Ill.: Irwin, 1973), p. 242.

There is an equity consideration to be made: The imposition of price rationing of, say, so much money per mile of highway use would tend to price lower-income individuals off the road. But since higher-income people are by far the larger users of highways, they would be most directly affected.

Long-run Solutions The answer to congestion in the past has been "build more roads." But to build for peak capacity means that there will be substantial excess capacity during most of the day. On the other hand, limiting capacity and using variable tolls to spread the traffic load is viable as a long-term as well as a short-term strategy. This would enable society to take advantage of what Vickrey calls "economies of intensity," or declining average unit cost of service with increased density of use.[4]

The key long-term solution is providing better mass transportation. This alternative is safer and would move people at lower cost. Furthermore, it would not contribute as much to pollution. In New York City each car inflicts an estimated $400 of pollution-related damage each year, so for each car that stays home, the society will get a $400 hidden subsidy. Improved mass transit is blocked by the same obstacle that blocks the solution to most other urban problems, namely, lack of money.

URBAN FINANCE

A lagging perception of local finance has generated the view that the cities are on the edge of bankruptcy. Big-city mayors hold meetings and issue joint communiqués warning the public that the end is near. And no one will dispute that the costs of operating city government have been on an endless spiral. Crime, poverty, transportation, and other city problems, plus the rising cost of bureaucracy, have saddled city governments with phenomenal expenses in the past decade, with no end in sight.

To keep pace, taxes have been rising. After the federal and state governments have taken huge bites out of the taxpayer's budget, the cities must extract what they can. City governments receive the major part of their revenue from property taxes. They have therefore been compelled to raise property taxes repeatedly during recent years—a raise reflected in ever increasing rent hikes—and to introduce sales and income taxes or to raise them where they already existed.

These grim facts are common knowledge, but what is less known is that local governments in general—suburban as well as city—have been running large budget surpluses since 1968. The tax base in most central cities (essentially property values, retail sales, and personal incomes) has been growing substantially. More important, total federal aid to state and local governments has risen from $8.8 billion in 1963 to about $43.5 billion in 1973. Such surpluses may not continue, however, because of the changes in the revenue sources and the continued rise in expenditures.

The basic demographic problem of the central cities discussed earlier in the chapter—the influx of the poor and the exodus of businesses and the middle class—is clearly reflected in the fiscal problems of the cities. Rising expenditures can be traced to the rising proportion of poor people, since they require more government service per capita than the well-to-do. The departure of many corporations and well-off taxpayers has diminished the ability of city governments to pay for these services.

Large cities like New York have experienced particular difficulty in the areas of welfare and public employee compensation. The vast administrative apparatus, together with the huge caseload of 1.3 million recipients, constitutes a heavy drain on the city's fiscal resources. In themselves, welfare payments do not impose an unbearable strain on most central city budgets, but with ever increasing demands of public employees for higher wages, funding poses a problem of mounting gravity.

During the past 10 years, municipal employees in cities of over 50,000 have increased their salaries by about 75 percent. The most important reason is the advent of municipal workers' labor unions. A

4 Vickrey, p. 220.

TABLE 20-2 City Finances

Item	41 large cities and their school districts		
	Percentage increase, 1962–70	Percentage of 1962–70 increase	Percentage of 1970 budget
Direct general expenditure, total	112	100	100
Education	109	37	36
Highways	14	1	4
Public welfare	264	16	11
Health and hospitals	101	7	7
Police and fire protection	94	11	12
Sewerage and sanitation	56	3	5
Financial administration and general control	81	2	3
Interest on general debt	92	3	3
Other	135	20	18
General revenue, total	108	100	100
Intergovernmental	217	46	36
Property taxes	57	24	35
Other taxes	108	16	16
Current charges and miscellaneous revenues	90	12	13

Public welfare, health and hospitals, and education are the fastest growing urban expenditures. However, education remains, by far, the heaviest expenditure of the cities. On the revenue side, the fastest growing receipts are those from the state and federal governments, vying with property taxes as a main revenue source.

SOURCE: Excerpted from Charles Schultze et al., *Setting National Priorities: The 1973 Budget,* p. 301.

sharp rise in the number of public employee strikes, which began in 1966, was followed by an upsurge in the wages of municipal employees. A second reason for the jump in wages was the interest of politicians in the votes of municipal employees.

With the emergence of blacks and Spanish-Americans as a political force, local governments have expanded employment opportunities for these groups. Often this has meant hiring the "new minorities" in jobs that once were the prerogatives of the older ethnic groups—the Irish cop, the Italian sanitation man, and the Jewish teacher. Large wage increases in some cases may have been designed to placate these groups for their loss of hegemony over public service employment.[5]

5 Charles L. Schultze et al., *Setting National Priorities: The 1973 Budget* (Washington: Brookings Institution, 1972), p. 299.

Still another reason for the sharp rise in local government expenditures is an unprecedented increase in services. Community colleges, pollution control, family planning, day-care centers, drug rehabilitation, and consumer protection are among the programs that were started and rapidly expanded during the last decade in most cities. These new services were often spurred by federal programs such as Model Cities or compensatory education.

The central cities, whose extensive problems have made them outspend their suburban neighbors on a per capita basis, have been able to do so only because of massive infusions of state and federal aid over the last 15 years. This is shown in Table 20-3, which displays figures for the largest metropolitan areas. Of the 25 areas covered, only in Hous-

TABLE 20-3 City and Suburban Spending

Region and standard metropolitan statistical area	1970: Per capita total expenditure (dollars)		1970: Per capita state and federal aid (dollars)		Percentage increase in per capita expenditure, 1957–70	
	Central city	Outside central city	Central city	Outside central city	Central city	Outside central city
Northeast						
Boston	531	365	224	73	95	102
Newark	735	441	276	102	202	144
New York City	894	644	385	216	248	148
Philadelphia	495	325	134	88	200	136
Pittsburgh	450	309	111	95	139	141
Providence	392	265	111	71	145	168
Washington, D.C.	1006	425	358	118	321	224
Midwest						
Chicago	478	346	146	86	137	144
Cleveland	512	368	187	66	180	91
Columbus	398	290	75	77	140	86
Detroit	474	462	189	131	135	131
Kansas City	485	347	90	100	161	210
Minneapolis–St. Paul	540	520	177	228	192	177
St. Louis	463	292	99	83	211	135
South						
Atlanta	554	315	97	95	251	215
Dallas	352	279	54	70	91	158
Houston	305	307	61	73	97	64
Louisville	508	302	108	94	214	165
Miami	481	387	137	129	113	129
New Orleans	334	325	100	116	105	171
West						
Denver	502	306	149	94	135	108
Los Angeles–Long Beach	624	529	209	227	134	161
San Diego	484	472	194	202	153	150
San Francisco–Oakland	768	596	298	201	244	159
Seattle–Everett	524	471	137	162	201	232

In 24 out of 25 metropolitan areas shown here, expenditures in the central cities exceed those in the surrounding suburbs. However, on a per capita basis, state and federal aid is greater in only 16 of the central cities when compared with the suburbs. The disparity in expenditures will probably decline in the near future as suburban problems continue to grow. At present, in 12 of the 25 metropolitan areas shown here, central city government expenditures are growing faster than those of their suburbs.

SOURCE: Excerpted from Charles Schultze et al, *Setting National Priorities: The National Budget*, p. 294. Copyright © 1972 by The Brookings Institution, Washington, D.C.

ton do suburban per capita expenditures exceed those of the central city. In only 16 of these areas is federal and state aid per capita larger for the suburbs than for the central cities. Finally, in most cases, between 1957 and 1970, this aid has been increasing much more rapidly to the central cities than to the suburbs.

Regardless, the fiscal outlook of central cities is uncertain—in large measure because the extraordinary federal aid of the last decade may taper off considerably over the next few years. Revenue sharing which was justified as a panacea for the urban fiscal crisis, has temporarily led to cuts in specific (grants-in-aid) programs, resulting in declines in federal aid to most large cities. Moreover, the increase in the urban tax base is slowing as more businesses and middle-class families move to the suburbs. It will be increasingly difficult for cities to obtain sufficient revenue without raising their already-high tax rates, a move guaranteed to accelerate the exodus of the two prime groups of taxpayers.

Alternatives

Since the fiscal dilemma of the big cities is that public service expenditures threaten to outrun revenues, two courses of action suggest themselves: Cut expenditures or raise revenues. The first measure is largely self-defeating because, like raising taxes, it would contribute to the flight of business and the middle class. Possibly expenditures could be reduced by increasing municipal efficiency, but there has been little progress in this direction despite the grandiloquent claims of various city administrators.

Federal Takeover of Welfare Shifting the cost of the services to state and federal levels has been a popular proposal, particularly in the area of welfare. However, the takeover of all welfare payments by the federal government would provide little fiscal relief to the large cities: In 34 states, localities pay less than 5 percent of total welfare expenditures. Only New York City and San Francisco are heavily burdened by welfare payments, because of large caseloads and the unavailability of suburban financing.[6] The large northern cities might be helped indirectly, however, by increased welfare aid to the South. This might stem the migration of the southern poor to the northern cities, where welfare benefits are presently higher than in the South. Perhaps more significantly, it would encourage the return home from the cities of some of the rural poor.

Revenue Sharing This funding scheme returns a portion of federal taxes to the state and local levels for use as these governments see fit. The reasoning goes that the federal tax base is larger, and federal tax collection is fairer and more efficient. Revenue sharing would allow for equalizing revenues between richer and poorer areas, and it would eliminate the categorical grants that lead cities to develop programs because federal funds are available rather than because they meet the most pressing needs.

Revenue sharing is not universally hailed. It may be used to replace local revenues and lower taxes rather than to expand the services of the cities. Moreover, it "divorces the joyful privilege of spending public revenue from the burdensome responsibility of raising it."[7] This lessens the accountability of local government and may lead to allocative and technological inefficiency. Furthermore, since revenue sharing is based on political jurisdiction, it provides no incentive for the consolidation of some of the 81,000 local jurisdictions across America.

GENERAL SOLUTIONS TO URBAN PROBLEMS

The crises we have discussed in transportation, housing, crime, poverty, and education have been left to the central city governments to solve, but they are metropolitan in scope, affecting a wide area beyond the central city, and they must be solved through the efforts of the entire metropolitan area.

6 These two cities are coterminous with the counties they occupy: Since there are no suburban areas within these counties, there are no suburban tax contributions available at the local level.

7 Melville Ulmer, "The Limitations of Revenue Sharing," in *Current Issues of Economic Policy*, ed. Lloyd G. Reynolds et al. (Homewood, Ill.: Irwin, 1973), p. 433.

This not only raises a question of competing priorities, but it also focuses attention on the interdependency of problems that may appear unrelated.

A typical metropolitan problem (as opposed to one confined to the central city) is transportation, involving large numbers of commuters from the suburbs to the city, as well as a smaller number of reverse commuters. The location of businesses is also closely related to the metropolitan transportation problem. If the distribution of plants were planned along regional lines, not only could the transportation network be more efficiently utilized, but the labor supply could be more evenly distributed and people would not have to travel so far to get to work. Land could be put to better use and the urban sprawl that characterizes much of the suburbs could be minimized. But a solution would have to be found for the problem of housing for the workers employed by suburban plants.

Two inferences may be drawn here: (1) metropolitan governments should replace the hodgepodge of local jurisdictions, and (2) urban problems call for a certain degree of regional planning.

The major barrier to metropolitan government is the opposition of the suburbs. By and large, these communities do not want to pay higher taxes to cover the city's rising expenditures. They do not want children from the city's slums bused into their schools, nor do they want the city's poor moving into their neighborhoods. They do not heed the inefficiency (much of it in the form of social costs paid by someone else) and the inequities, which, of course, they themselves do not suffer, and hence they are resistant to any metropolitan alliance.

The existence of quasi-governmental bodies such as the Massachusetts Transit Authority and the New York Port Authority offers a hope of metropolitan cooperation in transportation as well as other areas. Suburban residents can accept regional bodies if they themselves can be helped by them. Perhaps regional agencies that are set up to meet specific needs, such as crime prevention, pollution control, business development, and possibly housing, offer the most feasible way of cutting across the jurisdictional lines of local government.

To provide incentives for the suburbs to get together with the cities, planners need to carefully weigh the benefits to all concerned. They need to plan for efficiency, not simply in doing the job well at the least possible cost, but in the selection of objectives. Every expenditure of public money should start with the questions: Who will be the beneficiaries, and is the undertaking worth its cost in terms of its potential for the greater good? As we have seen, shortsighted, piecemeal solutions lead to nothing but bigger and knottier problems in urban government.

SUMMARY

1 While the United States has experienced rapid economic growth, the inner cities have been left far behind with respect to income, unemployment rates, crime rates, reading levels, housing, pollution levels, and most other measures of well-being.

2 American cities have generally been located along transportation routes. The sizable market and available labor force, economies from specialization, and the presence of an infrastructure led to growth of cities.

3 Decentralization has been taking place for over a century in most American cities, leading to the balkanization of metropolitan areas. Since about the turn of the century, the cities' share of the metropolitan populations has been declining. Most of the immigrants to the cities have been blacks and Spanish-Americans from rural areas, while those leaving for the suburbs have been middle-class whites.

4 Metropolitan areas are plagued by a constellation of problems, one of the most serious being housing. A disproportionate percentage of slum housing is occupied by nonwhites, who are trapped in ghetto areas. Viable solutions to the problem have come from neither private industry nor government. Low rents in these areas provide no incentives for landlords to make repairs. Such repairs would be beneficial to the tenants and the community, but the landlord would pay the cost. Urban renewal projects may overallocate resources from a community standpoint, because funding is two-thirds federal. Usually these projects end by dispossessing the former residents, without providing them with alternative housing of an equivalent nature. Public housing is another alternative having serious defects with respect to both efficiency and equity. Housing subsidies that could give the poor leverage in the private market have been earmarked primarily for the middle class.

5 Crime is a nationwide problem, but the major violent crime rate is three times the national average in the 26 largest cities. Violent crime is dwarfed, however, by organized crime in the ghetto—gambling, loan sharking, narcotics, and the fencing of stolen goods. Solutions to crime need to measure the benefits from crime prevention programs against the costs. So far, traditional approaches to problems seem to have failed.

6 The problem of urban transportation is one of peak-loading. In the short run, differential tolls and other changes in pricing may encourage more even use of facilities. In the long run, better mass transportation may alleviate congestion.

7 Urban finance, while a serious problem, is somewhat exaggerated, since local governments have been running large budget surpluses since 1968. Federal aid, too, has increased fourfold between 1963 and 1973. One trend has been the spectacular rise in the wages of municipal employees (about 75 percent during the last decade).

8 The problem of fragmented jurisdictions stands as an obstacle to the solution of metropolitan difficulties.

SUGGESTED READINGS

Chamberlain, Neil W., ed. *Contemporary Economic Issues*. rev. ed. Homewood, Ill.: Irwin, 1973.

Downs, Anthony. *Urban Problems and Prospects*. Chicago: Markham, 1970.

Fusfeld, Daniel R. *The Basic Economics of the Urban Racial Crisis*. New York: Holt, Rinehart and Winston, 1973.

Schultze, Charles L.; **Edward R. Fried**; **Alice M. Rivlin**; and **Nancy H. Teeters**, with **Robert D. Reischauer**. "Fiscal Problems of Cities." *Setting National Priorities: The 1973 Budget*. Washington, D.C.: Brookings Institution, 1972.

Thompson, Wilbur A. *A Preface to Urban Economic Problems*. Baltimore: Johns Hopkins Press, 1968.

QUESTIONS

1 Review

a. general changes in the complexion of American urban areas especially since the 1940s,

b. problems in housing and types of government assistance programs,
c. problems in providing equitable education,
d. problems of crime control,
e. difficulties in providing transportation within metropolitan areas,
f. main sources of revenues to city governments,
g. some suggested solutions for city problems.

2 By the late summer of 1973, interest rates had risen to an all-time high, reflecting continued anti-inflation measures by the Nixon administration and the Federal Reserve Board. How would this development affect the problem of providing housing in urban areas? Might there be offsetting effects from other government programs? How?

3 The movement of new residents into an area produces external diseconomies felt by the previous residents. How? Does this effect encourage the exodus from the city or neighborhood? Which residents are most likely to leave?

4 Some local governments offer homestead exemptions on property taxes. New Orleans, for example, allows a new homeowner several years of residence tax-free. When the exemption period has elapsed, the resident must pay the property tax. How does such a system of taxation affect the incentives of individuals to move into and out of the city? Does the policy accurately reflect externalities?

5 Some experts in urban planning believe that there is no real economic or social reason for the megalopolis. From an economic standpoint, how might you support or refute such a belief? What role might improved communications play?

6 Proponents of mass transit have been eying the gasoline tax, traditionally used to build highways, as a source of funds for transit construction and operation subsidies. Should the revenues from this tax be reserved for highways? Give reasons for your response.

7 The higher density populations in urban ghettos may provide economies of scale for illegal activities. How?

8 Should the key countries approach described in Chapter 18 be applied to selected American cities? What obstacles might there be? What benefits?

9 Traffic jams might be solved if no one needed to leave home in order to work. Discuss some of the economic and social effects if computer terminals and visual phones were installed in every home. Would the problems of peak loading simply be shifted to another area?

CHAPTER 21
ECOLOGY
&
ECONOMICS

Although there is a vast difference between economics and ecology, both words have their origins in the Greek word *oikos*, meaning household. Thus, *ecology* could be broadly defined as a study of the household of nature, while *economics* could be thought of as dealing with the household of man. The human race, however, is a guest in the household of nature, a family member with certain obligations and responsibilities. The rules of the household are liberal and allow humanity to create its own household within that of nature, but it must not disrupt the basic functioning of its host's household. There is a very good reason for this. The economy, powerful and complex as it is, is still dependent upon the household of nature. And it will remain so as long as people remain creatures who need nourishing food to eat and clean air to breathe. Humanity lives on nature. Its economic system is based on channeling the resources of the environment into a system that yields products for its needs. Man, then, needs nature, but nature does not need man.

Ecology is the study of the relationships between living organisms and their environment. The interactions between these organisms and the environment are not haphazard, but on the contrary are highly organized. This organized interaction between organisms and their environment is called an **ecosystem.** Ecosystems are characterized by numerous cycles of relationships that operate in part through the food chain. At the beginning of the cycles are the nonliving elements: sunlight, soil, water. Through the process of photosynthesis and other reactions, these are converted by green plants into food substances usable by animals. These animals in turn are eaten by other animals. The food chain recycles its materials. The waste products of the animals, as well as the remains of dead animals and plants, are broken down into their chemical components by bacteria and fungi, allowing them to return to replenish the soil and air so that the cycle can continue.

Unlike human economic systems, which, as we have seen, are primarily concerned with the problem of reconciling scarce resources with infinite demand, nature's ecosystems, under natural conditions, have eliminated the problem of scarcity through unending cycles of materials. Scarcity is a less visible problem in nature than overabundance. Simple organisms at the bottom of the food chain, such as plankton, algae, and bacteria, multiply with incredible speed when not kept in check by consumers. Most animals and plants reproduce in such large numbers that most of their output can serve as food for other organisms or perish through other causes, and still serve to maintain the population level of the species. Also unlike human economic systems, ecosystems do not exist for the benefit of consumers. The jungle, for instance, is not a vast farm, organized for the express purpose of seeing that each lion has a succulent rump of okapi every day. Rather, the consumers in an ecosystem, insofar as they can be said to exist for a purpose, serve to maintain balance—to see that the overwhelming abundance of the system is kept under control, so that no single element grows to exert demands that the system as a whole cannot handle.

Opening photo by J. Paul Kirouac

THE PROBLEM

The modern industrial system interferes with the natural balance of the environment in a number of ways. Rather than recycling materials, the economic system survives by taking resources from nature, processing them, consuming the product, and discarding the waste. Petroleum is pumped out of the earth, refined into gasoline and other products, and used to fuel cars, whose exhaust introduces over 100 billion tons of noxious emissions into the air every year. Such a system of throughput

- depletes scarce resources,
- overloads the ecosystem with wastes,
- poisons the ecosystem with foreign materials it is unequipped to handle.

It also frees man from the population constraints that nature imposes on the rest of her creatures, since he can devise ways of eluding death by raising his own food supply, wearing protective garments, curing disease, and so on.

The obvious clash between ecology and economics finds its bleakest expression in what Robert Solow has called the "doomsday models,"[1] exemplified by the MIT-Club of Rome study *Limits to Growth*.[2] By projecting current trends in population, pollution, food supplies, and other nonrenewable resources, the computerized model predicts the collapse of the industrial economy within the next century from the depletion of resources, the ill effects of pollution, or the problem of overpopulation. Even if the rates of growth of these problems are varied to allow for corrective measures, the models are hardly cheerful oracles. Hence the cries for drastic solutions, the two most common being Zero Economic Growth and Zero Population Growth.

1 Robert M. Solow, "Is the End of the World At Hand?" *Challenge* (March/April, 1973): 39–50.
2 Dennis Meadows et al., *Limits to Growth* (New York: Universe Books, 1972).

ARE DRASTIC MEASURES NECESSARY?

Growth and No-Growth

Our economic system is based on growth. GNP is expected to go up each year (4 percent is considered a comfortable increase). One faction of environmental activists believes that this attachment to rising GNP is chiefly responsible for the rising level of pollution. A rising growth rate, they argue, means a growth in industrialization and consumption—and in the pollution they foster. Some time in the seventies, for

"Excuse me, sir. I am prepared to make you a rather attractive offer for your square."

example, production of solid refuse will reach one ton annually for every man, woman, and child in America, if present trends continue. Further, such critics charge that even a rise in per capita GNP is no indication of an increased standard of living. When allowances are made for increased prices, and when inconvenience, poor health, and ugliness due to pollution are given monetary values and balanced against growth, it becomes clear that economic growth is only a sort of fool's treadmill and that we had best get off before it is too late. Accordingly, these critics say that economic growth should be reduced, or eliminated entirely, and that we should concentrate instead on distributing more equitably the assets that our society already possesses.

Does the no-growth argument makes sense? Yes and no. Rising GNP does mean more industrialization, which, all other things being equal, does mean more pollution. But this does not necessarily mean that the answer to pollution is to stop growth, any more than the cure for heart disease is to stop the heart. The essential ingredients in Zero Economic Growth are stabilizing output, stopping technological growth, and maintaining zero capital accumulation. Advocates of no-growth policy forget that if the United States were to abandon increasing output in order to concentrate on distribution, the standard of living would probably decline and the resources available to deal with the problems of poverty and discrimination would be restricted. The poor will hardly be mollified if they are told that everyone is worse off. If the United States is to have any chance at all of feeding the hungry, and providing education, housing, and medical attention to all its citizens, the nation needs growth *as well as* greater equity in its distribution system.

Stabilization of outputs *without* any decline in the standard of living of the population would require a perfect knowledge of the quantity and quality of existing resources. It would also require advance knowledge on when substitutes would be available to replace finite resources and what disposal method would be least damaging to the environment. But if all this were known, why place any limits on output? Output at this point could be the result of the costless sort of growth outlined in Chapter 19.

Growth, in fact, could benefit ecological balance, particularly if technology were used to control pollution instead of simply increasing productivity. Although technological advances have harmed the environment in the past, not all technology is harmful. Many existing problems of resource shortages and existing residues will not be cured unless new means of using resources or curbing effluents are found. Recent technological advances have already made possible the removal of sulfur from coal before burning and the elimination of fluoride emissions from some aluminum smelting processes. Technology can solve environmental problems, and since technological advance requires capital accumulation, zero accumulation is not in the best interests of pollution abatement either.

All these arguments lead to the conclusion that the three components normally assumed to be essential ingredients in Zero Economic Growth—zero capital accumulation, no technological advance, and stable output—are not essential to an ecologically sound economy. Changes are needed, particularly in the ends to which technology is put, but ZEG is not the answer.

Overpollution and Overpopulation

Ecological reformers have seized upon population growth, as they have seized upon economic growth, as a possible explanation of the spread of pollution. Just as the reasoning in the case of economic growth was a simple equation—more growth, more pollution—the reasoning in the case of population is equally simple—more polluters, more pollution. As irrefutable as such a formulation may sound, it is open to question. The problem is that human beings do not produce equal quantities of waste products per individual. Obviously, an upper-income suburban family in the United States with three cars, a power lawn mower, a garbage disposal unit, a washer, a dryer, a dishwasher, plumbing, heating, and a magnificent annual intake of glass, metal, and paper-packaged goods is contributing far more toward

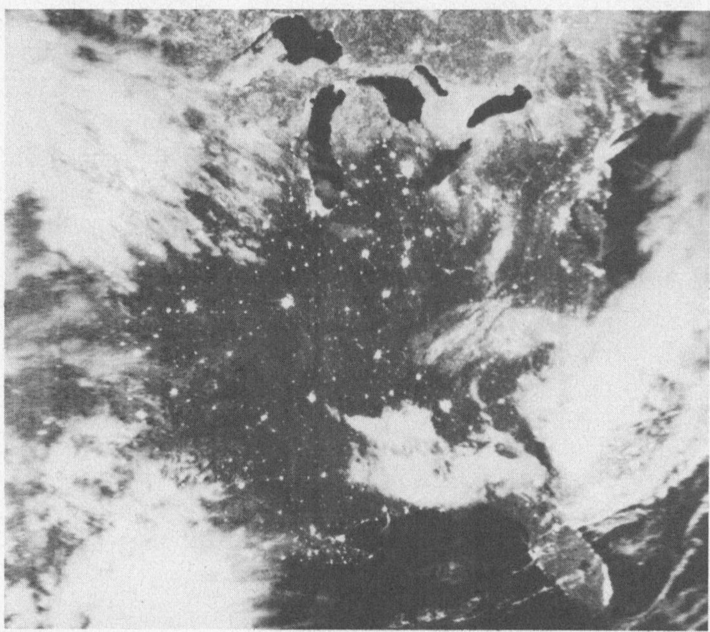

FIGURE 21-1 POPULATION This night satellite photograph of the United States shows graphically the nation's population density and indirectly the impact of man on the earth. The areas unobscured by clouds show the lights of the cities as they glow out into space. The east coast from Washington to Maine is a solid band of light, as are the Great Lakes area around Chicago and the Florida coast around Miami. The effects of such concentrations of people are far greater than simply the glow of lights. U.S. Air Force Photo

polluting the environment than a family of Indian Untouchables who live in a hut and subsist chiefly on rice. The truth is that pollution is not directly linked to population at all, but rather to affluence and life-style.

The example of the United States contradicts the advocates of zero population growth. The United States has in recent years already achieved the ZPG birth rate, although it will be some years before the population actually stops growing. The United States has, moreover, only about 6 percent of the world's population, but it produces more than one-third of all toxic substances released into the air and water and half of the world's industrial pollution. By contrast, the population density of India is almost 10 times that of the United States, and yet a child born in the United States is likely to be 60 times more of a burden on the environment than a child born in India. This difference is due to the fact that less industrialized economies have a low level of dependence on synthetic products and tend to return waste products to the earth. Primitive economies operate as closed systems in which materials are continually recycled. Advanced countries, like the United States, however, have throughput economies, which generate both an affluent society and a high level of pollution.

It becomes clear, then, that simple zero population growth cannot solve environmental problems any more than zero economic growth can.

SOLUTIONS: THE CARROT AND THE STICK

Solving the ecological problem entails a dual task: cleaning up the environment, and stopping or reducing the present sources of environmental degradation. Little can be done to accomplish the first task until some encouraging effects have been achieved in the second. There is little point in sweeping out a house while the fireplace is still pouring clouds of soot into the living room. Fortunately, however, the environment, unlike a living room, is partially self-cleaning.

The question remains: How can a nation most quickly and effectively stop environmental degradation? There are basically two approaches, which can be characterized as the stick and the carrot. In other words, a nation can stop pollution through prohibitions and punishments, or through incentives that make nonpollution more attractive than pollution. The two methods are roughly associated with ecologists and economists.

"... [T]he dedicated environmentalist [thinks] in terms of exponential rates of deterioration, thresholds, flash points, and of absolute limits to be dealt with by absolute bans."[3] The environmental strategy of ecologists, therefore, tends to focus on lobbying for strict limits on pollution levels or depletion rates and on shaming and scaring people into better practices. Some of their activity has already been effective in reducing pollution, and, in certain cases, where emergency action is required, the "stick" approach is obviously the most practical.

Economists, insofar as they see the problem at all, tend to see not just the outcome, but also the procedures for achieving the results. They look at the economic system and observe that for certain identifiable reasons it is more profitable to pollute or to deplete resources than not to. And since businesses are motivated to seek increased profits, expecting them to stop is unrealistic. The problem, then, is not in discovering how to enforce sanctions more effectively, but in using the market mechanism to remove the profit from unwanted activities.

The economist, therefore, looks to the price system to capitalize on its automaticity in digesting information and responding to it, its ability to integrate a vast range of decisions, its stimulus to natural resource conservation, and its lowering of demands on the government bureaucracy. More concretely, the price system can make it more expensive to deplete resources than to conserve them. As resources become scarcer, their prices rise. If the resource is not renewable, then the rate of its depletion is slowed as firms use less of it and search for better extraction methods or for substitutes. If the resource can be recycled, one of the substitutes is scrap or wastes of that resource. The reason that firms ignore scrap today is that it is cheaper to use virgin material. When the price of the virgin resource rises, scrap (or a more thorough extraction process) finally will become competitive in price. If the price of virgin material rose high enough, the resource might be supplied entirely from recycled scrap.

The problem for the economist is to get the price system to reflect the actual conditions. In the case of pollution, this is complicated by the presence of externalities. Pollution is profitable because not all of its costs are borne by the polluter. Traditionally, when a business figures total costs, it includes such

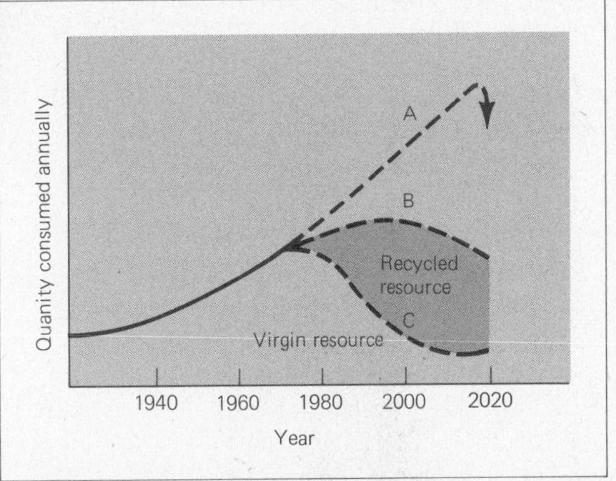

FIGURE 21-2 CONSERVATION AND THE PRICE SYSTEM The price system works to conserve resources. If prices of a resource such as iron would remain constant, then the world might exhaust its available supplies, as in A. However, as iron becomes scarce, its price is bid up and several things happen. Substitutes for it that were once ignored as being too expensive become more competitive. Extractive processes that used to cost too much become feasible, thereby expanding the supply. This reduces consumption of virgin material to path B. Further conservation is possible if higher prices make reclaiming used iron economically feasible. In this case, consumption may follow path C, with recycled iron meeting the rest of the demand.

3 Walter W. Heller, *Economic Growth and Environmental Quality: Collision or Co-Existence?* (Morristown, N.J.: General Learning, 1973). p. 3.

ENERGY CRISIS AND THE PRICE SYSTEM

Americans have always been used to cheap and plentiful sources of energy. The price of energy has not risen at the same pace as most other prices in the economy. For most people there was little question that the supply was never-ending. Today, however, most people know that there is not only a question of supply; there is a definite energy shortage. The immediate reaction has been to try to expand *supplies* of energy.

In his April 1973 energy message, President Nixon urged further exploration to develop domestic supplies of fuel at the same time that he relaxed restrictions on imports to meet the immediate needs. The urgency to expand supplies has weakened some of the environmentalists' successes. Most auto emission controls, for example, use more gasoline, and coal is presently dirtier to use but more abundant than oil or gas. The debate over which type of electrical generating plant to build—a hydroelectric plant or a cleaner nuclear plant—to try to meet the rapidly rising rates of consumption may no longer center on environmental questions, but rather on the issues of speed and price. How many of the environmental control measures will have to be sacrificed or temporarily postponed to meet the energy shortage is still in doubt.

The focus on supply has obscured the actual cause of the energy crisis—rising demand. Today's projections of huge increases in energy use in the coming years are based on past behavior—behavior influenced by the cheap prices and apparent abundance of energy resources. Rising prices limit demand, stretch existing supplies further, and encourage suppliers to increase output. Rising prices are induced by scarcity and by the current attempts of society to internalize the social costs of energy production. They may be further increased by changes in rate structures that traditionally give the lowest rates to high-volume users.

United Press International

Such price increases provide a strong incentive to cut back on energy consumption. Many of the big industrial users of electricity have cut energy costs by as much as 15 percent. Eliminating pilot lights on gas stoves would cut their gas consumption in half; and according to the Environmental Protection Agency, cutting the average weight of an American car from 3500 pounds to 2500 pounds would save 2.1 million barrels of crude oil a day—more than the proposed Alaska pipeline would deliver. Not all of the energy-saving changes can be made overnight; for instance, the current generation of heavy cars will be in use for another decade. In the long run, however, the price system may make current projections of energy needs excessive. Whether this will slow economic growth is hard to tell.

things as raw materials, labor, taxes, rent, and normal profits. But it does not include such things as the use of "free" commodities, such as water or air, for the disposal of harmful wastes. These things are not included in total costs because the business does not have to pay for them. But other people do. When businesses pollute the air and water with poisonous effluents, the cost of this disposal is borne by the public at large. For example, when steel mills dump wastes into lakes and rivers, the waters become polluted, leading to a reduction in the fish population. The fishing industry is hurt by this reduction and, as a result, must charge a higher price for its catches. Thus, the cost is passed along to all fish-eating people in society. But it does not end there. The fish-eaters are driven by higher prices to look for substitutes, such as meat. Increased demand then drives meat prices upward. So it goes until the cost incurred by the steel mill is absorbed by the economy as a whole. Because these costs are paid outside the business with which they originate, they are called externalities. The problem of the economist is to "internalize" these externalities. If externalities are included in the firms' total costs, the desire to reduce costs will result in a reduction in pollution.

Notice that the ultimate goal of the economist is quite different from that of the ecologist. The ecologist talks of eliminating pollution; the economist, of attaining acceptable levels of pollution. Given the limited resources of society, only so many can be devoted to any one objective. Allocative efficiency probably precludes a total clean-up. In theory, "the right solution, to an economist, would be the one that pushes depollution to, but not beyond, the point where costs—the foregone satisfactions of a greater supply of additional goods and services—just equal the benefits, which are the gained satisfactions of clear air, water, landscape, and reduced noise level."[4] Since finding that point is beyond the technique of the sciences and social sciences, setting the acceptable level is really a political decision. The economist then applies his tools of marginal analysis to measures of technological efficiency, the lowest cost method of achieving a certain level of environmental quality.

KNOW

POLLUTION ABATEMENT ALTERNATIVES

Methods of dealing with pollution can be grouped into three categories: (1) moral suasion, (2) limits or bans on harmful emissions, (3) use of the price system. Economic analysis can be used to weigh whether or not each method is likely to obtain the desired results, and at what cost.

Moral Suasion

One way to eliminate social costs is to persuade consumers and businesses to act against their own short-term interests in pursuit of the long-term goal of social welfare. On the one hand, consumers must be convinced to buy certain products not because they are cheaper than competing products, but because their manufacturers employ conservation-

FIGURE 21-3 PLEASE KEEP OFF THE GRASS This sign is an attempt at moral suasion. Other ways of preserving the grass might be fines for trespassing on it, licenses to sit on it, and bribes *not* to sit on it. After finishing this chapter, see if you can explain why moral suasion might be the appropriate college policy in this instance. United Press International Photo

4 Heller, p. 3.

oriented methods of production. On the other hand, corporations (or governments) must be convinced to use their profits (or tax revenues) to install antipollution devices and to alter their production methods to incorporate recycled materials.

This rhetorical approach is considered the most efficacious means of dealing with pollution only by those who, like Rousseau, believe that man is basically good and is corrupted only by evil practices. According to this line of thought, we have only to show corporation presidents or voters enough pictures of dead fish and they will stop their corporations or municipalities from pumping wastes into the rivers. Unfortunately, this method does not seem to be very effective. Even the potentially more effective attempts by public interest stockholder groups to pressure business firms to adopt nonpolluting methods of production have fallen on deaf ears. There is always an equally strong group of stockholders who are more concerned with earnings per share. Consumers and voters are as hard to persuade as corporation executives. Consumers who are guided by conscience to change their purchasing habits may pay higher prices and therefore can buy less than the person who selects the cheapest brand or product, regardless of its environmental effect. And voters who demand better sewage treatment will find their taxes raised to pay for this. No doubt the persuaders have had some effect, but of a type that can only be called "educational." They will not have succeeded in convincing many people to actually change their behavior, but they will have succeeded in convincing a substantial portion that they *ought to* change. This is important, since it paves the way for stronger measures. When regulations and special tax laws are put into effect, these educational methods may have succeeded in giving people the impression that they are being compelled to do something that they should have done on their own, rather than being forced to do something that they never wanted to do and see no reason for doing.

Limits and Bans

Another method of dealing with pollution is by passing laws, enforceable by the courts, which state exactly how much of a certain pollutant a factory may lawfully emit. If the company is convicted of overstepping this limit, it must pay a fine. Other laws may ban a polluting substance entirely, such as the recent ban on the use of DDT. Or a law may require an industry to install certain antipollution equipment in its products, as does the regulation imposed by the federal Environmental Protection Agency requiring the auto industry to meet emission control standards by 1975.

Such laws play a useful and very necessary role in the fight against pollution. In certain cases they are the only possible means of dealing with urgent environmental problems. Substances found to be injurious to human health, such as DDT, lead, and thalidomide, must be eliminated from consumer products completely. There can be no halfway measures. Similarly, when wildlife is threatened with extinction or when pollution reaches a critically destructive threshold, the most direct methods of pollution prevention are through legal action. Government must reserve the right to say "no" to certain practices. In certain situations, to do less would be to invite disaster.

In other situations, however, legal limits and bans have severe disadvantages. The legal requirements of due process specify a minimum of 58 weeks before the Environmental Protection Agency can even bring a polluter into court. Moreover, penalties handed down by environmental agencies are more a punishment for past actions than a solution to problems. They are deterrents rather than incentives, and the long history of the use of deterrents to prevent other types of crime should throw doubt on their effectiveness in the case of pollution. Moreover, direct regulations offer no incentive to companies to develop pollution-free production methods.

The most important objection to direct regulations, however, is that they are more expensive than they need be and their expense is ultimately reflected in costs to the consumer. Not only do the added costs of eliminating pollution from the production process increase the price of the item, but the consumer must pay again in the form of taxes to support the extensive bureaucratic machinery necessary to police and prosecute industry. Figure 21-4 shows the

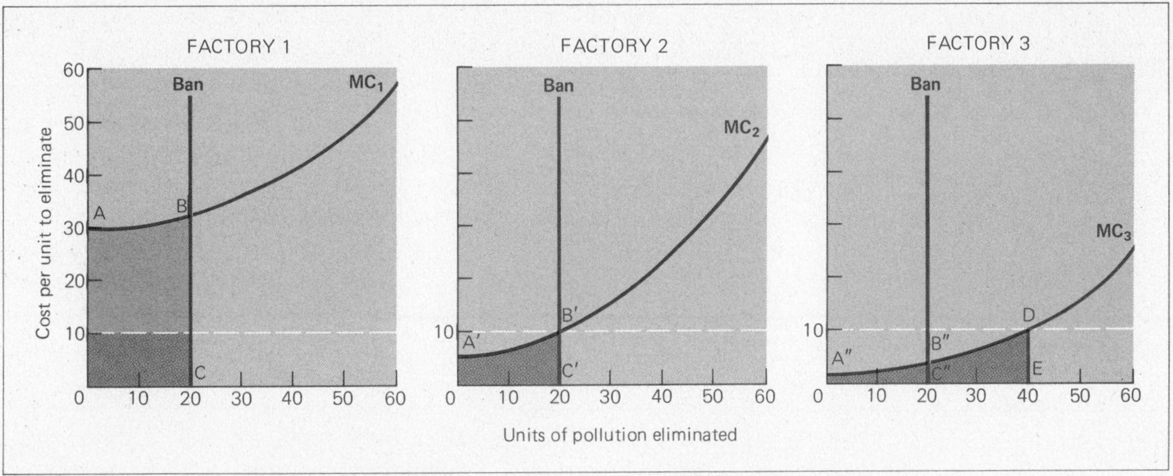

FIGURE 21-4 BANS VERSUS EFFLUENT CHARGES Suppose that a community wants to eliminate 60 units of pollution. It can impose a ban of 20 units on each of its three factories. This rough sort of justice does eliminate 60 units, but the costs to the factories differ markedly. The total cost is the sum of the areas 0ABC, 0A′B′C′, and 0A″B″C″. The community can use another alternative, an effluent charge set at $10 per unit of pollution. In this case, each factory would eliminate pollution up to the point at which the charge equalled the cost of controlling pollution. Thus, although factory 1 continues to pollute, factory 3 finds it economical to eliminate 40 units of pollution. In total, 60 units disappear. The total cost is zero to factory 1, the same to factory 2, and the area 0A″DE to factory 3. This method absorbs far fewer resources than the ban, so the cost to society is less if the town uses the effluent charge. (The effluent charge itself is not counted as a cost, since it is simply a transfer payment.)

costs when a town makes each of its factories cut back on 20 units of pollution. Each factory must eliminate 20 units regardless of its cost structure. The total cost is the total of areas 0ABC, 0A′B′C′, and 0A″B″C″. In the next section we can see how to achieve the same results at a lower cost.

Using the Price System

Right now the government offers to oil and other mining operations subsidies that encourage the use of these resources by reducing costs and prices. The government also uses subsidies in promoting environmental quality. But it could reverse the process by charging for the depletion of nonrenewable resources or for the deterioration of environmental quality. In this case the objective is to make the cost of an additional unit of deterioration greater than the cost of eliminating that unit. The externalities would be reflected in the price, and the higher price would reduce demand, thereby reinforcing the reduction in pollution. There are several ways of imposing such charges, effluent charges and licensing being the most prominent proposals.

Effluent Charges The most familiar effluent charge is the fine levied on polluters who exceed minimum standards.

With a true effluent charge, each corporation pays a tax on only the amount of pollutant that it emits into the water or air. The government sets a charge that it hopes will keep pollution within tolerable limits; and in theory it could set the rate high enough to reduce pollution altogether. This method, however, does not usually reduce pollution to zero, but it has the advantage of attacking the problem through the price system rather than from outside it. It is a most effective way of internalizing the externalities, of making it less profitable to pollute.

In Figure 21-4, we see that this method can achieve the same cutback in pollution at a cost lower than a government-imposed limit. Under direct regulation, all companies have to reduce pollution to a

ECONOMIC INCENTIVES FOR ZPG

Although zero population growth may not guarantee zero pollution growth, limiting the population may be a necessary first step in conserving natural resources and controlling pollution. But what method can bring about effective population control? Is it basically a cultural change that is needed or can economic incentives play a part in convincing people to limit the size of their families? The problem has bedeviled sociologists and economists for more than a century. It took on particular importance from the time of Malthus in the early 1800s. He predicted that based on the geometric progressions by which population was increasing, it would eventually outstrip the food supply. His solution to the problem was to have people postpone marriage until they could support a family.

One nation that has taken Malthus's advice quite literally is Ireland. Faced with a severe shortage of resources and jobs, economic constraints have had a dramatic limiting effect on the Irish population. Years of emigration have contributed to the declining Irish population, but those who remained in Ireland have been forced to postpone marriage until their parents died and left them the family farm. Only in this way would they have a home and the means to support a family.

Another less serious proposal for population control also came from Ireland. The Anglo-Irishman Jonathan Swift in his essay "A Modest Proposal" suggested selling unwanted babies as food to provide a source of income for an impoverished nation. Infanticide is practiced in some primitive societies to limit population, but it hardly seems an acceptable alternative to people outside these cultures.

In a plan suggested by Kenneth Boulding, one could sell children before they were born, rather than afterward, as in Swift's ghoulish scheme. Boulding's plan would utilize the market system to stabilize population. Under his plan each individual would be given slightly more than enough green stamps to entitle the person to have one child. Individuals who did not want children could sell their stamps to couples who wanted more than two children. In this way if everyone in a society wanted a large family, the price of the stamps would rise and tend to discourage births, but if everyone in a particular society wanted few children, the price of the stamps would go down, thus encouraging births. If there were many illegal children born in a society, the number of green stamps given to each individual would be reduced and sterilization might also be introduced as a penalty for anyone's having illegal children.

Other ways of "pricing" children may be more practicable. Many war-ravaged countries have sought to replenish their population by offering child subsidies and tax credits for each child. The U.S. tax exemption system has a similar effect. Might it not be a good idea to reverse the exemption system so that individuals are taxed for each child above a certain allotted limit?

It may seem harsh to talk, in economic terms, about the number of children a person has, but economic forces may be used to promote social goals. It is certainly preferable to offer economic incentives to regulate population than to have arbitrarily set limits or to see population outstrip the supply of food.

certain level, but this is more of a hardship for some than for others.

Under taxation, however, each company would be free to reduce pollution according to the principle of cost minimization. Those whose cost curves rose steeply as pollution was reduced could elect to pay a higher tax, while those that could reduce emissions cheaply would minimize their tax by polluting less. Because each company would be free to make its own adjustment, the total increase in costs for the industry would be less than under direct regulation.

With effluent charges administrative costs remain low. The regulatory agency simply installs a metering system to measure the amount of pollutant produced by a factory, and bills the company. This method imposes a tax on pollution and has the long-run effect of shifting industrial production away from high-pollution technology or products toward those that cause less damage. During the shift in industrial production, there are bound to be periods of dislocation, production cutbacks, and unemployment that cause hardships to the economy. Eventually, new jobs in pollution-control or low-pollution industries would replace those lost in the transition, and employment would rise.

Licensing With effluent charges, the government sets a price on pollution that it hopes will limit pollution to a certain level. Under licensing, the government would set that level of pollution and let the market set the price. According to this plan, society would estimate how much pollution constituted tolerable levels for a given time and place. Licenses or certificates would then be issued, entitling the bearer to pollute up to a certain amount. The total of these pollution allowances would add up to the tolerable level. These certificates would become negotiable items, going up and down in price in the same way as stocks and bonds on the open market, subject to the laws of supply and demand. For industries with high costs of curbing pollution, demand for pollution rights would be high, driving up the price of the certificates. The high price would stimulate corporations with high antipollution costs to invest in research to find ways of eliminating pollution from the production process. Those industries with costs lower than the price of the certificates would probably eliminate pollution since this approach would be cheaper.

Subsidizing Pollution Abatement Efforts The subsidy approach to pollution control is a form of effluent charge that shifts the burden away from those who actually do the polluting and back onto the public. Advocates of the subsidy approach call on the government to help pay the costs of a polluting firm's clean-up activities. They suggest that the government offer outright grants for the reduction of pollution levels, payments for installing control devices, exemptions from local property taxes on control equipment, and stepped-up depreciation allowances and tax credits for the purchase of pollution control equipment.

If improperly structured, subsidies do not encourage business to find new production methods or develop new control devices. They simply encourage companies to install the most expensive equipment regardless of whether it is the most effective. Payment for installation of equipment should be determined by how much a firm has lowered its discharge rate. But in many cases, there are no preinstallation measurements of emissions on which to base such a determination. Subsidies are also inefficient if they specify a certain way of accomplishing the task when there might be alternative methods that are more efficient and less costly. For example, most subsidies are paid to firms that install waste treatment equipment. In some cases, however, pollution might be reduced by making changes in the production process itself, but under the subsidy plan, firms would have no incentive to discover such a method. The failure of improperly designed subsidy plans is shown by its poor record during the years 1960 to 1973. During this period, federal subsidies to cities that built waste treatment plants amounted to $5½ billion. However, a study conducted by the General Accounting Office in 1972 has shown that serious misallocations have resulted from the program and that the rivers that the plan was supposed to save appear worse off than ever.[5] Despite their poor performance, subsidies should not be rejected entirely, for there is little difference in effect between properly designed subsidies and effluent charges, except in their effects upon income distribution.

ECOLOGY, ECONOMICS, AND EQUITY

Cleaning up the environment is only one of the goals to which society may devote its resources. The poor are particularly suspicious of programs that save wildlife rather than people. If pollution control raises prices, it affects the poor disproportionately. If local taxes are raised to pay for abatement programs, the regressive nature of these taxes decreases the disposable income of the poor proportionately more than that of the rich. If shifts in industrial methods and output create economic dislocations, the poor are more likely to suffer unemployment.

Economic growth in its fullest sense includes an increase in the living standard of all. Redistribution of income to cushion the regressive impact of environmental programs ensures that this larger goal is met. And substitution of careful analysis for sloganeering ensures that abatement programs operate economically so that more resources are available in meeting the other priorities of society.

5 Heller, p. 14.

SUMMARY

1 Ecology can be broadly defined as a study of the household of nature, while economics can be thought of as dealing with the household of man. Economics is really part of ecology. Ecological systems are characterized by cycling of materials and by balanced interactions, whereas industrialized economic systems are based on throughput.

2 The modern industrial system interferes with the natural balance of the environment by depleting scarce resources, overloading the ecosystem with wastes, poisoning the ecosystem with foreign materials it is unequipped to handle, and freeing man from the population constraints that nature imposes on the rest of her creatures.

3 Since an industrialized economic system is based on growth, there is more and more industrialization, consumption, and ecological damage. The most extreme solutions to the problems of growth include halting economic growth and/or population growth. To halt economic growth means to prevent an increase in output, technology, and capital accumulation. However, stopping output means lowering the standard of living and having fewer resources to solve pressing problems such as poverty. Technology—and capital accumulation which enhances its progress—can be either ecologically harmful or the means of cleaning up the environment. ZEG confuses growth with its preventable consequences. Population growth is not intrinsically a source of ecological damage; a high level of consumption is the real problem. Attacking population size again confuses growth with other consequences.

4 The ecologist and the economist view the problems somewhat differently. Hence, the ecologist is likely to depend on moral suasion or limits on pollution levels, while the economist is more likely to depend on proper pricing. The price system

can make it more expensive to deplete resources than to conserve them or to pollute than not to, largely by making externalities part of costs.

5 There are several alternative methods for adjusting the price system to discourage ecological damage. Effluent charges upon each unit of pollution make it cheaper to eliminate pollution up to the point at which the cost of control equals the effluent charge. Effluent charges in effect estimate the quantity of pollution to be eliminated in setting a price upon the quantity. Licenses, on the other hand, set the quantity of pollution allowed and let the price be set on the licenses by the market system. Properly designed subsidies are similar to effluent charges, except for their effects upon income distribution. Charges are paid by the polluter to the public, whereas subsidies are paid by the public to the polluter.

6 The equity of ecological programs involves not just charges versus subsidies, but the larger question of whether ecology is a luxury paid for by the poor in the form of higher prices, taxes, and unemployment.

SUGGESTED READINGS

Council on Environmental Quality. *Environmental Quality: Annual Report* (Washington, D.C.: Government Printing Office, annual). The environmental equivalent of the *Economic Report of the President.*

Dolan, Edwin G. *TANSTAAFL: The Economic Strategy for Environmental Crisis.* New York: Holt, Rinehart and Winston, 1969.

Freeman, A. Myrick, III. *The Economics of Pollution Control and Environmental Quality.* Morristown, N.J.: General Learning, 1971.

Hammond, Allen L. *"Energy Needs: Projected Demands and How To Reduce Them." Science* 178 (December 15, 1972):1186-1188.

Heller, Walter W. *Economic Growth and Environmental Quality: Collision or Co-Existence.* Morristown, N.J.: General Learning, 1973.

QUESTIONS

1 Review
   a. the unique relationship between the natural ecosystem and the industrial system,
   b. the controversy between those who propose economic growth and no growth as a solution to pollution and shortages,
   c. the merits of the suggestion that population growth be reduced to reduce the pressure on the environment,
   d. externalities and the basic methods of dealing with pollution.

2 The effect of ZPG would be to increase the median age of the population. What might be some of the consequences of that change?

3 Though an individual worker may be aware that an increase in wages for all workers will contribute to inflation, he is unlikely to refrain from asking for a raise for himself. After all, he reasons, his raise alone will not make much difference. Are there any parallels that may be drawn with the effectiveness of moral sua-

sion in the fight against pollution? In identifying those cases in which suasion might be effective?

4 Might there be greater dislocations and social cost arising from limits and bans as opposed to effluent charges? Why or why not?

5 Do government subsidies for developing and installing pollution control devices tend to correct "overproduction" in pollution-heavy industries? Why or why not? Is there any way of arranging subsidies without some misallocation of resources?

6 Which types of antipollution programs discussed would be most likely to encourage the effort to find substitute products, substitutes that may be produced without much pollution? Which program or programs are likely to discourage discovery and development of such substitutes?

7 There has been great criticism of the American automobile industry for failing to meet federal emission standards in the proposed 1974 models. Some foreign manufacturers did meet the standards. The American industry has been given an extension. What factors do you think contribute to the reluctance of big producers to meet standards on polluting merchandise? Would you expect any differences in behavior in an industry made up of a large number of small firms? Why or why not?

8 Should the poor be suspicious of conservation? Why or why not? Should GNP be discarded as an indicator? Are full employment and pollution control incompatible goals?

9 Can Figure 21-4 justify leaving some rivers polluted while cleaning up others, if each curve represents the costs of river restoration? Include problems of equity in your answer.

PART 5

PRODUCT MARKET

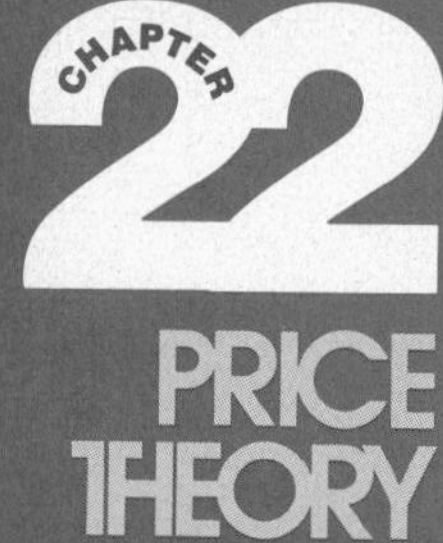

PRICE THEORY

The preceding chapters have dealt with such economic aggregates as national income and employment. The study of how government fiscal and monetary policies can be used to promote full employment, price stability, and economic growth has traditionally been called macroeconomics. In dealing with externalities in the later chapters of Part Four, we began to turn our attention to the individual producer—how he is affected by the national aggregates and how he in turn affects them. Since the behavior of firms, and of consumers, hinges primarily on the prices of products and the cost of resources, this area of study is called **price theory,** or **microeconomics,** because it deals with individual buyers and sellers.

Microeconomics is not merely a fancy name for marketing studies or business economics, although its tools may be applied in these areas. Microeconomic analysis may be applied to contemporary problems such as pollution, poverty, sexism, and strikes by public employees. Even noneconomic behavior, such as voting, has been studied with the tools of price theory. This chapter begins the study of microeconomics by viewing and extending the theory and application of price theory outlined in Part One.

REVIEWING THE MARKET SYSTEM

We already know that there are two markets, the product market and the resource market. The product market, which is covered in this part, is mainly concerned with the interaction of the buyers and sellers of goods and services through the medium of price. The goal of consumers is to maximize their satisfaction; the goal of producers is to maximize their profits. The resource market is shaped by the demand for the inputs used to produce goods and services. It determines both the allocation of resources and the distribution of income. The resource market is covered in Part Six.

In both markets, the motivating forces are the maximization of benefits and the minimization of costs. Decisions by both consumers and producers are assumed to be rationally made on the basis of marginal analysis. Consciously or unconsciously, consumers compare how much satisfaction they think they will derive from an additional unit of a product, with its price, and will stop buying it if the price outweighs the satisfaction. Similarly, producers will keep producing a product until the additional cost matches the additional revenue derived from its sale. If everything takes place according to the mechanism of a competitive market system, the result is full employment and the most efficient use of resources. At this point, any change cannot make anyone better off without making someone else worse off.

If this theory is correct, then the direct intervention of the government in setting price controls or the indirect intervention through taxation or subsidy (which also raise and lower price) is going to affect the amount of output and the efficient use of resources. In the first half of the chapter we examine the effects of direct controls. In the second, we see how the responsiveness of quantities to price changes affects the business firm and the consumer in a competitive market situation and under indirect controls.

PRICE CONTROLS

During Phase III½, when food prices were strictly controlled, chicken farmers responded by slaughtering thousands of baby chicks before they were ready for market. Simple economic theory could have predicted this; let us see how.

The Competitive Market

The basic laws of the market are those of supply and demand, which deal with the relationship between prices and quantities. In the real world, just about nothing is constant, but to see the laws of supply and demand clearly, we can imagine that quantity varies only with changes in price. The

Opening photo by J. Paul Kirouac

lower the price of chicken, the more chicken consumers will want; the higher the price of chicken, the more farmers will supply. (To simplify matters we will assume consumers buy directly from farmers.)

Columns 1 and 2 of Table 22-1 are a market demand schedule for chicken. It shows the inverse relationship between price and quantity demanded: The higher the price, the fewer chickens demanded. Columns 1 and 3 of Table 22-1 are the chicken farmer's supply schedule. It indicates that price and quantity supplied vary directly: As the price of chickens goes up, the number supplied by the farmer also increases.

Figure 22-1 plots these relationships in the form of demand and supply curves. Over the entire price range for chickens, there is only one point at which quantity supplied equals quantity demanded—the equilibrium price. At this point there is no reason for the price to change.

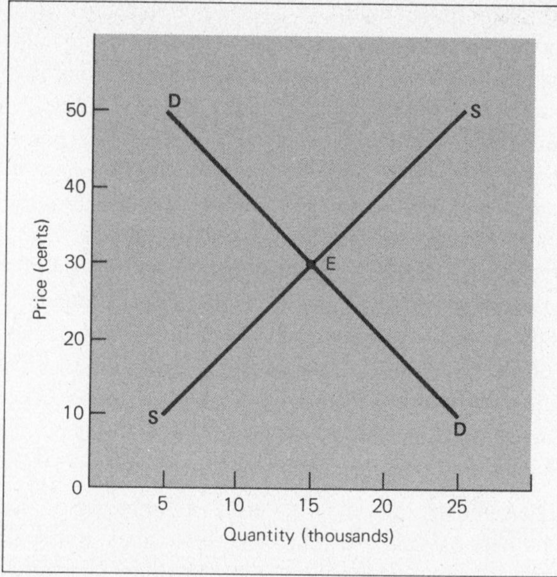

FIGURE 22-1 EQUILIBRIUM OF DEMAND AND SUPPLY At the equilibrium point, E, the quantity demanded and the quantity supplied are equal. This intersection establishes the equilibrium price. At a higher price, suppliers will furnish more chickens than consumers want; at a lower price consumers will want more than suppliers are willing to furnish.

When a change in price affects the quantity demanded, the relationship is shown on a single demand curve. But as we indicated, the strength of demand is determined by more factors than price. The most obvious is income. If people have more income, they will be able to afford more than chicken and they may buy something else. Another determinant is the prices of closely allied products (such as stuffing) or substitutes (such as beef). If the price of beef drops enough, consumers may want more of it and less chicken. Even the prices of totally unrelated products may affect the demand for chickens. Other factors such as changes in consumer taste or population growth may also affect demand. When any of these change, the curve itself shifts.

TABLE 22-1 Demand and Supply in a Competitive Market (Hypothetical)

Price per pound	Quantity demanded	Quantity supplied
50 cents	5000	25,000
40 cents	10,000	20,000
30 cents	15,000	15,000
20 cents	20,000	10,000
10 cents	25,000	5000

Consumers and suppliers respond to prices differently. As price drops, quantity demanded increases, but quantity supplied decreases; only when the two are equal is the market in equilibrium.

The supply curve shows the amount the farmer will supply at any given price. The curve shifts position only when other things change. For example, a new law subsidizing farming, a new technique that fattens chickens for market faster, or greater fertility in the chicken population will cause the curve itself to shift.

When there is a shift in the entire demand curve, as in Figure 22-2 (or in the entire supply curve), the result is a new equilibrium price. It is important to remember that most of the determinants of supply and demand change slowly over time, and that

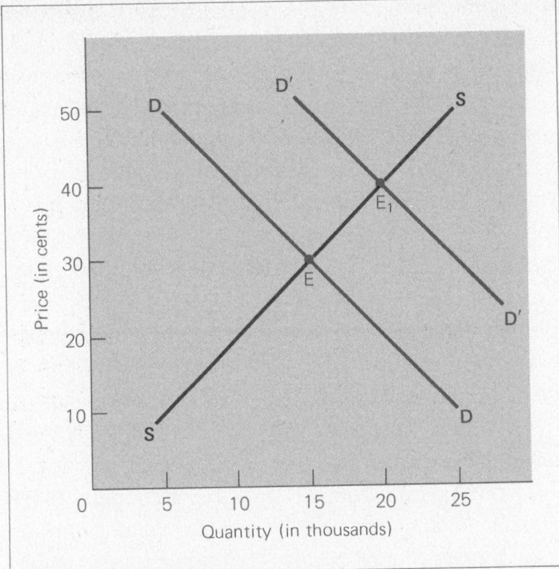

FIGURE 22-2 SHIFT IN DEMAND CURVE A shift in demand is shown here. A shift from DD to D′D′ represents an increase in demand, because D′D′ lies above and to the right of DD. A decrease in demand would be represented by a shift from D′D′ to DD. In either case, a new equilibrium price is set.

prices, far from finding their new equilibria instantly, usually lag behind those changes. Thus, we distinguish between **normal, or equilibrium, prices** and **market prices.** A market price is not necessarily in equilibrium. It is usually approaching a new equilibrium, but may actually never reach it because the market forces continue to change, determining new equilibria all the time. The prices consumers pay, therefore, are the prevailing market prices; the normal, or equilibrium, prices are usually a mere abstraction, signifying the direction in which market prices are moving. However, in situations in which prices remain stable for long periods of time, it can be assumed that the market price has caught up with the equilibrium price and that there is no difference between the two.

Wage and Price Ceilings

In theory, price is set primarily by changes in supply and demand. But government can set prices above or below the market price. Wage and price ceilings set the market prices of labor and products below the equilibrium prices. Such devices have been traditionally used to cope with persistent inflation or scarcities in times of national emergencies such as war. In wartime, when goods for the civilian population are in short supply, price ceilings prevent the prices from skyrocketing. During inflation, when the prices are already rising rapidly, price ceilings are used to put the lid on. The ceilings in Phases I through IV were

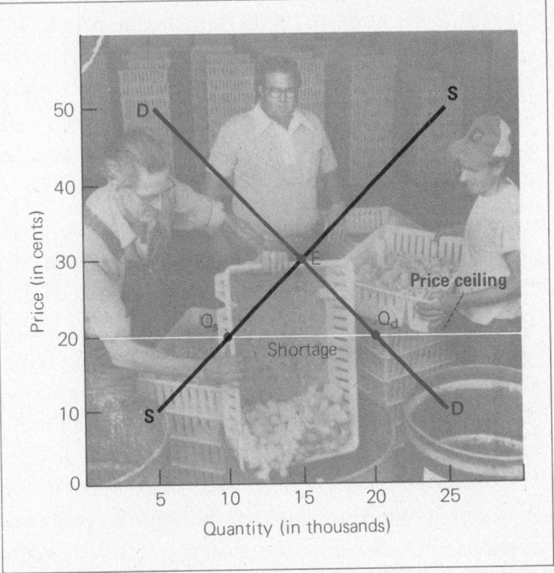

FIGURE 22-3 EFFECT OF PRICE CEILING The horizontal line depicted here as a "price ceiling" appears as if it were a floor. After all, isn't the horizontal line below the equilibrium price? Why, then, isn't that line a price floor? In a competitive market, if the market price is below the equilibrium price, it will be bid up until market price is set at equilibrium. Equilibrium price and market price are then identical. When the government sets a price ceiling, it makes charging over a certain price illegal—a price usually below the equilibrium level. The market price acts as a ceiling. Were it not for that ceiling the price would not have been 20 cents a pound, but 30 cents a pound. A ceiling, after all, prevents prices from going higher. There is, however, a shortage of some 10,000 units at the market price of 20 cents a pound. In other words, buyers would have liked to purchase 10,000 more units than they were able to at that price. Ceilings, then, cause shortages.

United Press International Photo—farmers suffocate chicks to fight price ceiling by reducing supply.

aimed at controlling the inflation that was hampering efforts at reducing unemployment and was harming the balance of payments. Once inflation is expected in an economy with marked concentration of power in many industries and in labor, halting the spiral of wages and prices is difficult. Controls are one way of breaking through the inflationary psychology. This is particularly crucial when relatively high unemployment levels accompany inflation, and attacks on inflation cannot be made at the cost of even higher unemployment.

When the government sets the price below the equilibrium level, shortages result. Because of low prices, chicken farmers cannot afford to supply all the chickens that people want. The wholesale destruction of baby chicks occurred because the cost of feeding the chicks to maturity was greater than the going price. Shortages ensued—at the ceiling price consumers demanded Q_d, while farmers supplied only Q_s.

Because the Nixon controls were not applied to all commodities, this created the danger of arbitrarily shifting resources to uncontrolled areas of the economy. The highest profit activities are most likely to attract capital, which is used to increase output. Since ceilings limit profits, capital and other resources may be attracted away from controlled goods, so that shortages become even more severe, and pressure on artificially set prices even greater. (Even in across-the-board ceilings such misallocation may occur since costs in one industry may change faster than in another.)

One hidden way of avoiding the impact of price controls is to lessen the quality of the goods while keeping output and price constant. In the early stages of Phase I, in 1971, George Meany graphically demonstrated this with a fable about his favorite soup that had just reduced the number of matzoh balls by one instead of raising prices. The problem with chickens is that such ploys are less possible. This phenomenon illustrates another problem in enforcing controls, since some industries can cut quality more easily than others, thereby affecting profits and resource allocation. Because the Nixon controls were limited in duration, the dangers of misallocation of resources and lowered quality were lessened. If the controls had not been lifted and severe shortages had ensued, the question would then have become, "Who gets Q_s?" Rationing is the usual method of ensuring equality of distribution. Everybody gets some, but usually much less than he wants. One other way of apportionment is by queuing. This imposes a nonmonetary price, since time is spent in place of money. Queuing may also cause a redistribution of income, since an unemployed person has plenty of time to wait in line to get steak whereas the opportunity cost of waiting in line may be astronomical to the business executive. Consequently, the rich business executive may subvert the ceiling by buying ration coupons or a place in line, bribing the butcher, or going through a black market. In a black market, a larger output may be available at higher prices. The higher prices represent a "crime tax" collected by those suppliers who take the risk of circumventing the law.

Simple microeconomic analysis predicts that wage-price ceilings lead to inevitable distortions in the economy. Such distortions become even more complex in the real world, where imperfect competition, political constraints, foreign trade problems, and the Phillips curve all complicate the choice between the problems of controls and the problems of no controls.

Wage and Price Floors

Wage and price floors mean that the government sets the floor price higher than the equilibrium. These price supports are generally used to help sectors of the economy in which incomes would otherwise fall too low. Farm prices have long been supported. If the price of chickens had a minimum floor, as in Figure 22-4, consumers would demand only Q_d, while suppliers would furnish Q_s, resulting in a surplus of $Q_s - Q_d$.

A price floor can be maintained only if the government actively supports it, and not simply decrees it. After all, if the surplus cannot be sold, producers will have wasted their resources and will suffer losses. But since consumers cannot be forced to buy a product at a high price, the government must

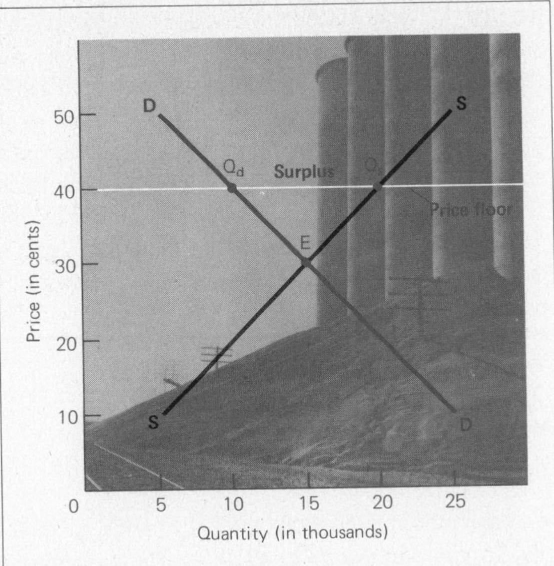

FIGURE 22-4 EFFECT OF PRICE FLOOR Much of the analysis in Figure 22-3 applies here as well. A price floor that keeps market price above equilibrium price creates surpluses. In this case, the price floor has been established at 40 cents and the surplus is 10,000 units. It is essential to understand that if the government did nothing the price would fall to 30 cents. Thus, by setting the price at 40 cents, the government has set a floor under prices (the price cannot go below this floor). The government administers a price floor by purchasing the entire surplus. This method has been used extensively by the Department of Agriculture to keep farm prices at certain levels (see Chapter 26). The greatest surpluses have been in wheat.

United Press International Photo

step in and buy up the surplus at the price it decreed. It can then either store it, distribute it to poor people or underdeveloped countries, or destroy it. The U.S. government has done all these things during the years it supported farm prices.

As a consequence of the artificially high prices, however, government has also priced a number of consumers out of the market, depriving them of what they would have been able to buy at equilibrium prices. In Figure 22-4, the government absorbs the surplus units at the floor price; at the equilibrium price all of these would have been demanded by consumers. In effect, the government is forcing one segment of consumers out of the market and making another segment pay more than it would normally have to. The sole reason is to help the producer of the good in question. He is the primary beneficiary of government-supported price floors.

The problem becomes more difficult when we examine wage floors, or minimum wage laws. Minimum wage legislation is supposed to guarantee people a living wage. But this is not necessarily so. If producers are forced to pay a higher wage rate, they will try to replace labor with other inputs, such as machinery. And instead of being paid more, workers may find themselves unemployed. Or the minimum wage may raise the prices of goods so that workers are no better off in terms of purchasing power. Thus, if the government intends to raise personal income, it may not necessarily succeed. The increases in unemployment may well outweigh the higher wage rates of some workers. Nonetheless, minimum wage laws cannot be rejected out of hand. In the United States, there are imperfections in the labor market that may unduly depress wages. In addition, higher wages may be offset by higher productivity if the employer is induced to use labor more efficiently or if the quality of the worker is improved due to the higher income. Here again, reliance on simple microeconomic analysis provides a useful but incomplete picture of the issues. The choices involve trade-offs between the distortions of controls and the problems that controls were supposed to correct.

ELASTICITY

The question of who is helped and who is harmed by government intervention varies from commodity to commodity, depending upon a characteristic called **elasticity.** Elasticity determines what effects a price change will have upon the firm and the consumer. Imagine yourself in a supermarket. The softly piped music stops, and there is an announcement that the price of chicken has just been reduced by 30 percent. Buyers scurry to snap up the fryers. Then there comes an announcement that paper diapers are down 50 percent. Few people seem to pay any attention.

You have witnessed two examples of the responsiveness of quantity demanded to changes in price. The price of chicken fryers went down 30 percent, but the quantity demanded probably increased by a much higher percentage; consequently, we say that demand for chicken is very **price-elastic.** The price of diapers was reduced 50 percent, without any appreciable increase in sales; therefore, we say that demand for paper diapers is **price-inelastic.**

Calculating Elasticity

Elasticity is a term indicating responsiveness. A rubber band responds to a pull, then springs back when it is released. It is elastic. In economics, elasticity expresses the response of a change in a dependent variable to a change in an independent variable. In measuring elasticity, we want to know if the initial change in the independent variable (in this case, price) causes a greater or lesser change in the dependent variable (in this case, quantity). We measure changes in percentages.

Demand for a product is termed *price-elastic* if a given percentage change in price results in a larger percentage change in quantity demanded. Demand is *price-inelastic* when a given percentage change in price results in a smaller percentage change in quantity demanded.

The same definitions go for the price elasticity of supply. The reason we specify *price* elasticity is that quantity may also respond to other factors, such as income.

The degree of elasticity is measured by the **coefficient of elasticity,** or E_d in the formula

$$E_d = \frac{\text{percentage change in quantity demanded}}{\text{percentage change in price}}$$

For a price-elastic product, the coefficient will be greater than 1; for a price-inelastic product, less than 1.

The Midpoints Formula The only question to be settled is how to calculate percentage change. Do we use the amounts before or after the change as a starting point? Using one or the other will yield different answers. If chickens were reduced from \$.90 a pound to \$.60 a pound, the reduction would be 33⅓ percent using the higher amount as the base, and 50 percent using the lower price as the base. The same problem occurs with the quantities demanded. Economists have conventionally used the midpoint between the two quantities to solve this problem. Thus, if we let

Q_1 = old quantity,
Q_2 = new quantity,
P_1 = old price,
P_2 = new price,

we can subtract $(Q_2 - Q_1)$ for the change in quantity. To arrive at the *percentage,* we must divide the change in quantity by the average of both quantities $\left(\frac{Q_2+Q_1}{2}\right)$. This division is expressed as

$$\frac{Q_2 - Q_1}{\frac{Q_2+Q_1}{2}} \quad \text{or} \quad \frac{\text{change in quantity}}{\text{average quantity}}$$

The same process holds true for the percentage change in price, and we get

$$\frac{P_2 - P_1}{\frac{P_2+P_1}{2}} \quad \text{or} \quad \frac{\text{change in price}}{\text{average price}}$$

The formula for the elasticity coefficient then looks like this (the 2s cancel out):

$$E_d = \frac{\frac{Q_2 - Q_1}{Q_2+Q_1}}{\frac{P_2 - P_1}{P_2+P_1}} \quad \text{or} \quad \frac{\frac{\text{change in Q}}{\text{average quantity}}}{\frac{\text{change in P}}{\text{average price}}}$$

Slope, Elasticity, and Midpoint The emphasis in all these calculations is on percentage change. Thus, we cannot simply assume that the gentle slope of the demand line in Figure 22-5A indicates elastic demand. The slope of a line merely indicates the absolute changes in price and quantity demanded. It is a function of the price and quantity scales we apply. A straight line has the same slope at every point. But if we work through the elasticities of the demand lines in Figures 22-5A and 22-5B, we discover that each has elastic and inelastic portions. In fact, they represent the same demand schedule. In Figure 22-6, Point M is exactly at the halfway point between the axes; therefore, it is called the midpoint. (This midpoint should not be confused with the midpoint between price changes or quantity in the midpoints formula.) If the demand curve is a straight line, the midpoint of that line always is the point of change between elastic and inelastic demand. Above the midpoint, demand is elastic; below, it is inelastic. At exactly the midpoint, demand has unitary elasticity, or a coefficient of 1. Obviously, then, different points on a single curve have differing degrees of elasticity and inelasticity.

Elasticity of Demand

Of paramount importance to a producer is the question of how elastic the demand for his product is. Most of his production and pricing decisions hinge on the answer. Elasticity to him means the saleability of a product, sales mean revenue, and revenues—up to a point—profit.

Total Revenue As a matter of fact, the only concrete way of measuring demand is by measuring the quantity demanded of a product, or, from the producer's point of view, the volume of sales. The producer gauges demand by the **total revenue** (PxQ) he realizes from sales. He gauges elasticity of demand by the changes in total revenue in response to price adjustments. He knows that if he lowers the price of his product and his total revenue increases, people are buying more and demand

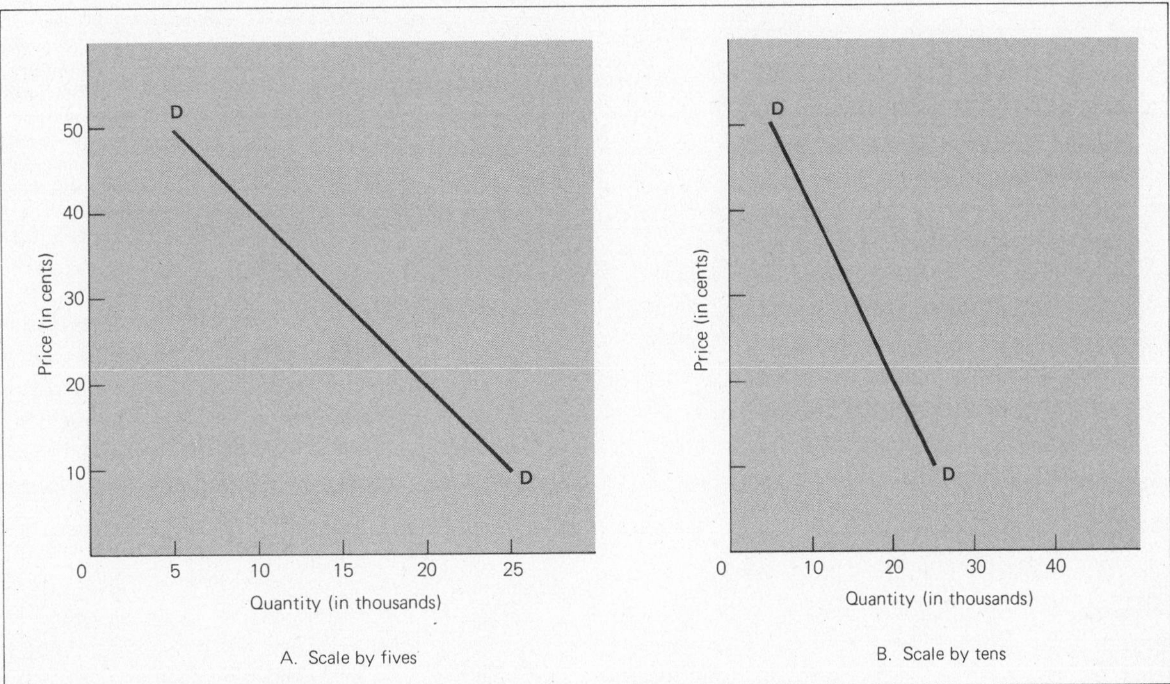

FIGURE 22-5 LOOKS ARE DECEPTIVE If we could rely on appearance, curve A looks more elastic than curve B. But the two plot identical data. They have the same elasticities and slopes. This apparent difference is explained by the wider quantity scale used in A. The scale chosen can make elasticity *appear* to be greater or less.

is elastic. It will be to his advantage to continue lowering the price as long as his total revenue goes up more than total cost. When the FCC ordered Ma Bell to lower long distance telephone rates, for example, the increased quantity demanded provided even higher total revenues than before, even though the price of a single phone call was lower than before. If, however, a producer lowers his product's price, and consumer reaction is so slight that his revenues actually shrink, he will conclude that demand is inelastic. Given these conditions, it will actually be to his advantage to raise his price, for he will find that though he may lose a few buyers, his total revenue will go up, costs will not increase, and profits will improve.

Figure 22-6 illustrates the connection between elasticity of demand and total revenue. The shaded rectangles delineate total revenue: price times quantity sold. The larger the area of a rectangle, the greater is total revenue. We see that in the elastic portion of the curve, total revenue increases as the price is lowered, while in the inelastic portion, total revenue increases as the price goes up.

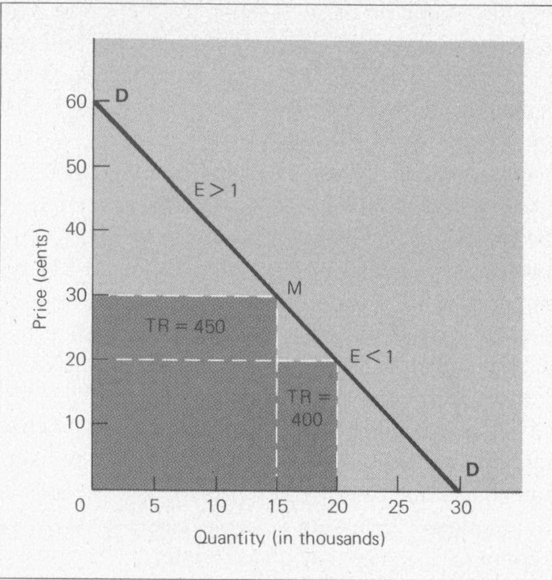

FIGURE 22-6 ELASTICITY AND TOTAL REVENUE Since total revenue is price times quantity, graphically it is the area of the quadrangle formed with P and Q. As a rule of thumb, when the demand curve is a straight line, total revenue is maximized at its midpoint. At the same point, elasticity will equal 1. For all demand curves, whether straight lines or curved, when elasticity equals 1, total revenue is maximized. Furthermore, for all demand curves, if elasticity is less than 1, total revenue can be increased by increasing price; and for all with elasticity greater than 1, total revenue can be increased by reducing price. Obviously, then, the business person out to maximize total revenue will keep increasing or reducing price until elasticity equals 1. Maximizing total revenue is not the ultimate objective, however; the ultimate objective of the firm is to maximize *profits*.

Marginal Revenue The change in total revenue when quantity sold increases by one unit is called **marginal revenue.** (If quantity decreases, we cannot speak of marginal revenue.) Marginal revenue is positive as long as total revenue increases; it is negative if total revenue decreases. As with total revenue, we can deduce the elasticity of demand from marginal revenue. For instance, if quantity increases as the price decreases but marginal revenue is negative, demand is inelastic.

The relationships between price, total revenue, marginal revenue, and elasticity are as follows:

There are three other possibilities concerning demand elasticity. **Perfect elasticity,** with an elasticity coefficient of infinity (∞), occurs only for individual firms under conditions of perfect competition. Such firms are too small to affect the market price, and therefore sell all they can produce at that price.

Demand	Coefficient of elasticity	Price change	Quantity change	Total revenue change	Marginal revenue
Elastic	Greater than 1	Decrease	Increase	Increase	Positive
Elastic	Greater than 1	Increase	Decrease	Decrease	
Inelastic	Less than 1	Decrease	Increase	Decrease	Negative
Inelastic	Less than 1	Increase	Decrease	Increase	

Graphically, perfectly elastic demand is depicted as a horizontal line, such as the one shown in Figure 22-7A: At the market price, any quantity can be sold by any one firm.

Perfect inelasticity (Figure 22-7B) assumes that, no matter how high the price of a product rises, the quantity demanded will remain the same. Salt is such a product. There is no readily available substitute for it. Even if the price rose sharply, the cost would still represent such a small portion of a family budget that the impact on demand would be negligible. Furthermore, salt is commonly regarded as a necessity, not a luxury, so that, once again, change in price is not likely to have a dramatic effect on quantity demanded.

Economists distinguish a third special case of elasticity—**unitary elasticity.** Over the segment of a demand curve for which elasticity is unitary, any change in price results in an equal percentage change in quantity demanded; the elasticity coefficient then is exactly 1. In this range, total revenue will stay the same and marginal revenue will be 0 (Figure 22-7C).

Determinants of Elasticity of Demand But what actually makes demand elastic or inelastic? Knowing *how* and *why* consumers tend to respond to changes in the prices of particular kinds of products can make or break a firm.

SUBSTITUTABILITY If there are many close substitutes for a product in the market, the demand for that product will be elastic. If the price of one product is raised and the prices of its substitutes remain unchanged, then consumers will simply start buying the substitutes. Where product differentiation has led to imperfect competition, the substitutability factor becomes less important in determining elasticity of demand. Through skillful advertising, a producer can point out the difference of his product compared with similar products and thus justify a difference in price.

Products for which there are no true substitutes will have a highly inelastic demand, when those products are necessities. If someone needs a certain drug to treat a fatal disease and if no other drug can prevent death, then that person will not care much about fluctuations in the price of the drug. Because there is no substitute for it, the quantity demanded will not change, no matter what the price may be. In the absence of substitutability, demand will be inelastic.

URGENCY This factor is similar to substitutability. It implies that at a given time there is no substitute for a product or service. If someone needs to get to the hospital for an emergency appendectomy, he will not put it off merely because medical care is more expensive this week than the week before. Because he needs to get to the hospital in a hurry, he will take a taxi instead of a bus, even though the bus would be cheaper. The choices are determined by the urgency of a situation, and demand for products and services urgently needed will tend to be inelastic.

If, on the other hand, someone is planning to go on a vacation or buy a second car, he can choose leisurely and carefully, because he really does not need either one at a given time. For luxury items in general, quantity demanded tends to be responsive to price changes. Lower the air fares to Europe, and a lot more people will decide that they want to take European vacations.

PROPORTION OF INCOME How much of a family's income is required to purchase a certain product may have a direct bearing on demand elasticity for that product. Though one might reasonably conclude that elasticity generally would be high for luxury items and for expensive goods such as automobiles, this judgment requires a little refinement. One could just as reasonably conclude, for example, that a family with an annual income of $60,000 would be less sensitive to an increase in the price of Cadillacs than a $12,500-a-year family would be to a rise in the price of Chevrolets. Thus, proportion of income assumes significance in the determination of relative demand elasticities.

TIME Changes in consumption patterns take time.

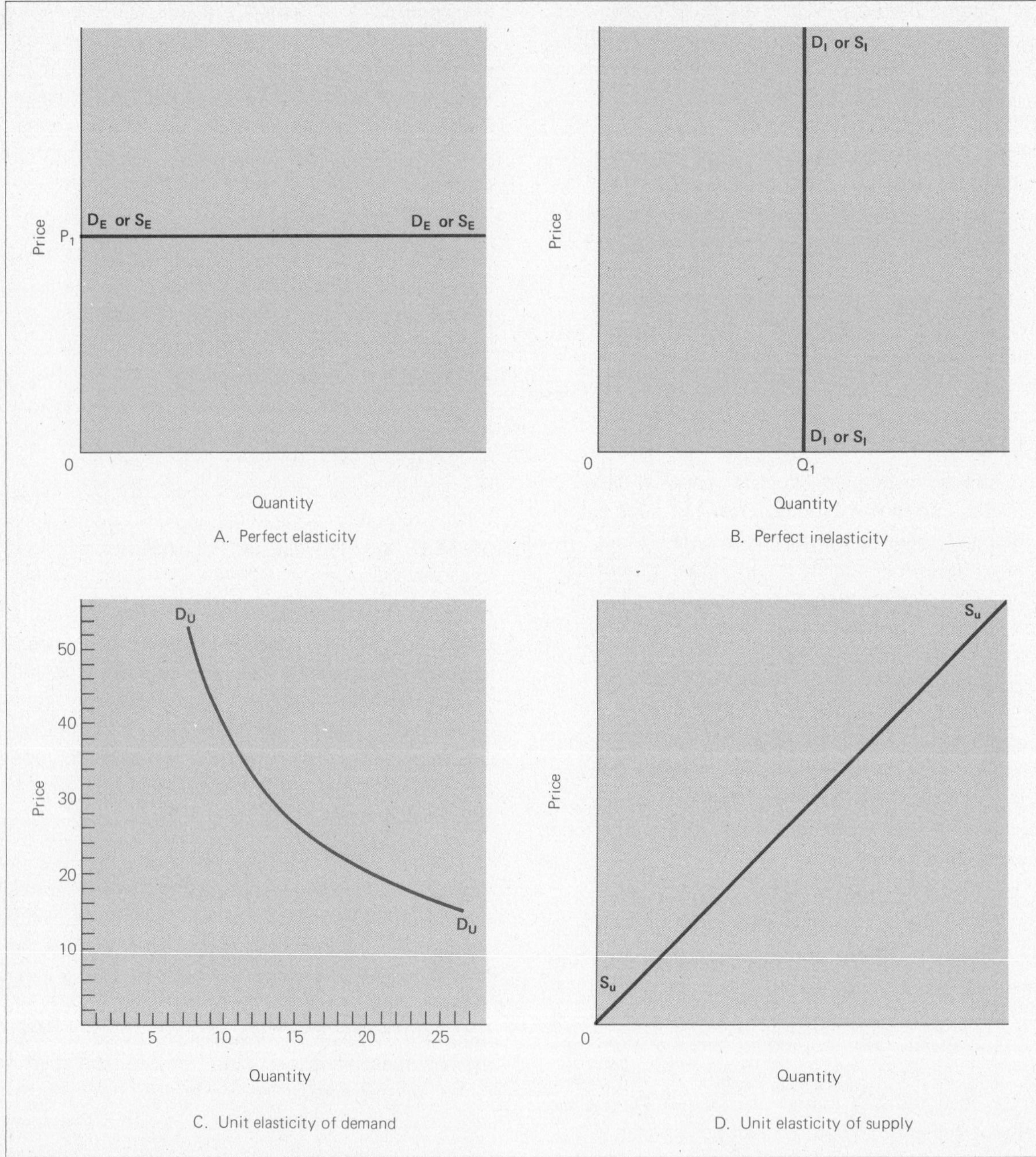

FIGURE 22-7 SPECIAL CASES OF ELASTICITY (A) Perfect elasticity: Curve D_ED_E or S_ES_E is a perfectly elastic demand (or supply) curve. The price, P_1, is set. People would be willing to buy or sell any quantity of the product at that price. (B) Perfect inelasticity: Curve D_ID_I or S_IS_I is a perfectly inelastic demand (or supply) curve. The quantity buyers are willing to purchase (or sellers sell), Q_1, is completely unresponsive to price. (C) Unit elasticity of demand: Figure 22-6 showed that total revenue is maximized when elasticity of demand is 1. By definition, when a curve is unit-elastic, elasticity is always equal to 1. Therefore, total revenue is maximized (and equal) at all points on a demand curve of unitary elasticity. It is left to the student to test this statement. (D) Unit elasticity of supply: Here is a sharp divergence from the demand counterpart shown in C. The unit-elastic supply curve is a straight line rising from the origin at a 45 degree angle.

In the short run, demand for many products tends to be inelastic because consumers, out of ignorance or habit, do not react to price changes altogether rationally. It will take a while before the rising price of a product relative to other goods will make people question their habitual use of it. If consumers are used to low gasoline prices, they may be slow to cut back on their use of autos when gas prices rise. Thus, demand for gasoline may be inelastic in the short run. But as consumers find less expensive substitutes (walking, bicycling or mass transit), demand will gradually become more elastic.

Elasticity of Supply

The concept of elasticity of supply is similar to elasticity of demand. It measures the percentage change in quantity supplied of a product in response to a given percentage change in price:

$$E_s = \frac{\text{percentage change in quantity supplied}}{\text{percentage change in price}}$$

The formula for calculating the supply elasticity coefficient is similar to that for calculating the demand elasticity coefficient:

$$E_s = \frac{\dfrac{Q_2 - Q_1}{Q_2 + Q_1}}{\dfrac{P_2 - P_1}{P_2 + P_1}}$$

The only difference is that Q_1 and Q_2 now stand for quantities supplied. As with the elasticity of demand, if the coefficient of elasticity is smaller than 1, supply is inelastic; if it is exactly 1, it is unitary; and if it is greater than 1, supply is elastic. On an inelastic curve, producers will be relatively unresponsive to changes in price; on an elastic curve, they will be relatively responsive to price changes.

Unlike demand elasticity, elasticity of supply can easily be deduced from the slope of a supply curve. The reason is that quantity—in most cases at least—changes directly with price, whereas on the demand curve the change is inverse. In Figure 22-7, the flat curve (A) represents the elastic supply; the steep one (B), inelastic supply; and the line going at a 45 degree angle between the axes (D), unitary elasticity.

Because price and quantity vary directly on the supply curve, the complex relationships between elasticity, marginal revenue, and total revenue that we worked out for the demand curve do not hold for the supply curve. Total revenue always increases as price goes up.

Furthermore, a perfectly inelastic supply curve is a very real possibility. It is most common with perishable goods brought to market by farmers and fishermen. A day's catch of fish must be sold at whatever price can be obtained on the market. If it is not sold, it will spoil. On the other hand, even if demand pushes up the price inordinately, supply for the day cannot be increased.

Still other products, mostly minerals and agricultural commodities, are sold in advance on the basis of a projected market price—all of which points up that the responsiveness of suppliers to ruling market prices is not the same as that of consumers. In some cases the incongruity of market price and quantities produced is so drastic that the producer may decide to destroy his product—as in the case of the chicken farmers. In such cases, the cost of bringing the product to market (transportation, storage) outweighs the revenue obtained from sales, and the producer simply cuts his losses by destroying goods.

Determinants of Elasticity of Supply The most important factor in determining the elasticity of supply is the length of time producers have to adjust to price changes. In the short run, producers have no time to raise or reduce their output. In the middle term, some adjustments can be made: Unused equipment can be activated, overtime shifts scheduled, or personnel laid off. Only in the long run, however, can producers adjust fully to price changes. They can build new plants, raise capital, hire and train labor—or, if the market contracts, phase out some operations.

Thus, in the short run, supply tends to be inelastic—that is, relatively unresponsive to price changes; in the middle run, it is somewhat more elastic; and in the long run, it is elastic.

ELASTICITY AND THE TAX BURDEN

Elasticity of supply or demand measures the responsiveness of changes in quantity to changes in price. But equilibrium price is set by both supply and demand, so that the relative elasticity or inelasticity of the two lines becomes crucial. Such a situation is illustrated by tax incidence—in effect, how an increase in price affects producers and consumers under differing conditions of elasticity.

How much of a tax on a good comes out of a consumer's pocket depends heavily on the elasticities of supply and demand. Whether a subsidy (negative tax) is more beneficial to the consumer or the producer also depends on these factors. An ignorance of elasticity can create unwanted side effects in taxation and subsidies—output will be affected and resources shifted.

Specific and Ad Valorem Taxes

Specific, or per unit, taxes add a flat amount to the price of every unit of a product sold. The amount of the tax never varies, even though the price of the product may. Figure 22-8A shows what happens when a 50 cent specific tax is imposed on a gallon of Dirtz, a phosphate detergent. Since the increase is the same for all price levels, the immediate effect is a shift of the supply curve up to S_TS_T, which will be parallel to SS. At the old equilibrium point, (E), 30,000 gallons of the product were sold at $1.00 per unit; at the new equilibrium, (E_T), 20,000 units are sold at a price of $1.20.

What happened? The government is collecting its 50 cent tax on every sale, but the price to the consumer has risen only 20 cents. That means that the producer is absorbing 30 cents of the tax and that his actual revenue on every sale is only 70 cents. At that price, which is lower than the old equilibrium price, he will be induced to supply only 20,000 gallons to the market, which is a 33⅓ percent reduction in his output.

In Figure 22-8A, we find that demand is elastic. Figure 22-8B illustrates the impact of a 50 cent specific tax when demand is inelastic. Here the equilibrium shifts from $1.00 and 30,000 units to $1.40 and 26,667 units. The consumers end up paying 40 cents of the tax, while the producers pay only 10 cents. The reduction in output is 3333 units, or 11 percent. So price has gone up more and quantity fallen less than when demand was elastic. Thus, the less elastic demand is, the more such a tax will cause a price increase. Figure 22-8C shows the demand curve of 22-8A with a less elastic supply curve. The tax causes less change in price and quantity than when supply was *more* elastic.

How does the effect of a specific tax in an elastic situation differ from one imposed in an inelastic situation? Clearly, the more inelastic demand is, the more prices will rise and the less quantity will fall as taxes are added. If demand is inelastic, then the tax is shifted forward onto the consumer in the form of higher prices. The consumer may grumble, but since he must have a certain amount of whatever commodity is taxed, he will pay the increase. The government makes use of this behavior by imposing cigarette and liquor taxes. Its revenues are high because the added tax does not cut demand, even though the burden of payment is on the smoker or drinker. If supply is inelastic, the tax is shifted backward onto the producer in the form of higher costs and lower profits.

Conversely, the more elastic demand is, the more quantity will fall, and the less price will rise. So as demand is relatively more elastic, there is less tax shifted to the consumer, since he will refuse to buy at higher prices. As supply is relatively more elastic, more tax is shifted to the consumer.

Similar effects occur when the government imposes an *ad valorem* tax, or sales tax. This is a percentage tax imposed on the sale of a product. It is widely used as a national tax in Europe and has been suggested as a way of raising more revenue in the United States. The one difference between the graphs for this tax and those for the specific tax is that since the absolute amounts of a percentage tax vary with price, the new supply curve, S_TS_T, will no longer be parallel to the old one, but will diverge as the price rises. Again, there is less decline in output when demand or supply is inelastic, and the brunt of the tax is felt by the more inelastic side of the market.

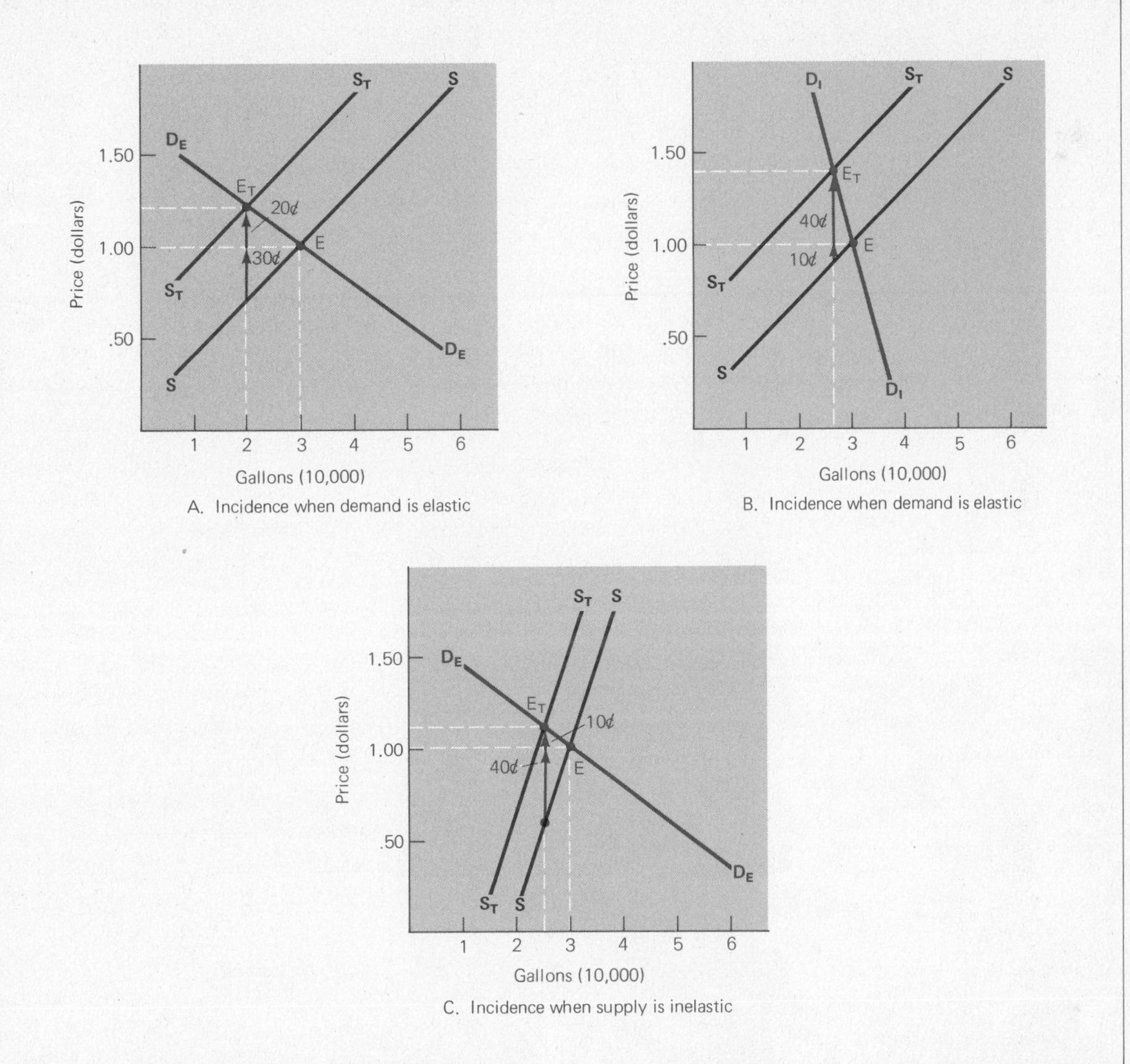

FIGURE 22-8 THE EFFECTS OF A SPECIFIC TAX (A) When demand is elastic: If a specific tax of 50 cents is added to the price of each unit sold, this creates a new supply curve, S_TS_T, a new equilibrium price, and a new level of output. With elastic demand, price increases somewhat and quantity demanded drops. The tax is split between the consumer and the producer with the producer paying the larger share. Confirm that demand is elastic using the total revenue test. (B) When demand is inelastic: The new supply schedule here sets a much higher price than before, but the quantity drops off only slightly. The consumer pays the bulk of the tax. (C) When supply is inelastic: The new supply schedule results in a reduction in output but a small rise in price. The producer pays the bulk on the tax.

WHO PAYS CORPORATE TAXES?

The discussion of tax incidence shows the multiple potential effects of taxes in the marketplace. When the tax falls on a corporation, the effect is similar. Corporations, after all, are not individuals but legal entities, which pay salaries to their employees and dividends to their stockholders. Those individuals subsequently are taxed on their income. But a corporation pays taxes on its profits before it can even pay out dividends. Such federal levies have varied from 42 percent to 52.8 percent since 1950 and currently stand at 48 percent.

Since corporate profits come from sales to consumers, the consumers are the ones who pay corporate taxes and, consequently, dividends to stockholders. Furthermore, since the consumers pay taxes on their incomes, they actually pay three types of taxes: income, corporate, and the levy on stockholders' dividend income.

But the stockholders can argue that corporate profits are actually funds accrued to them for the risk of holding stock in a company. So they are doubly taxed—once on corporate income, and again on the residual paid out in dividends. If they decide to sell stock that has increased in value, they then pay a capital gains tax.

Who, then, does pay corporate taxes? In general, corporations tend to be more solicitous of stockholders than consumers. They will therefore try to pass on taxes to consumers by raising product prices, rather than reduce dividends to shareholders. But this is not always feasible. Like other cases of tax incidence, if demand for a corporation's product is price-elastic, it is better for the corporation to absorb the greater part of tax costs rather than pass them on and lose sales. If the product is price-inelastic, then the bulk of tax costs can be passed on to consumers, without risk of substantial effect on sales. Thus, shareholders absorb the greater proportion of additional taxes if the demand is price elastic and consumers bear the major incidence if the demand is price inelastic.

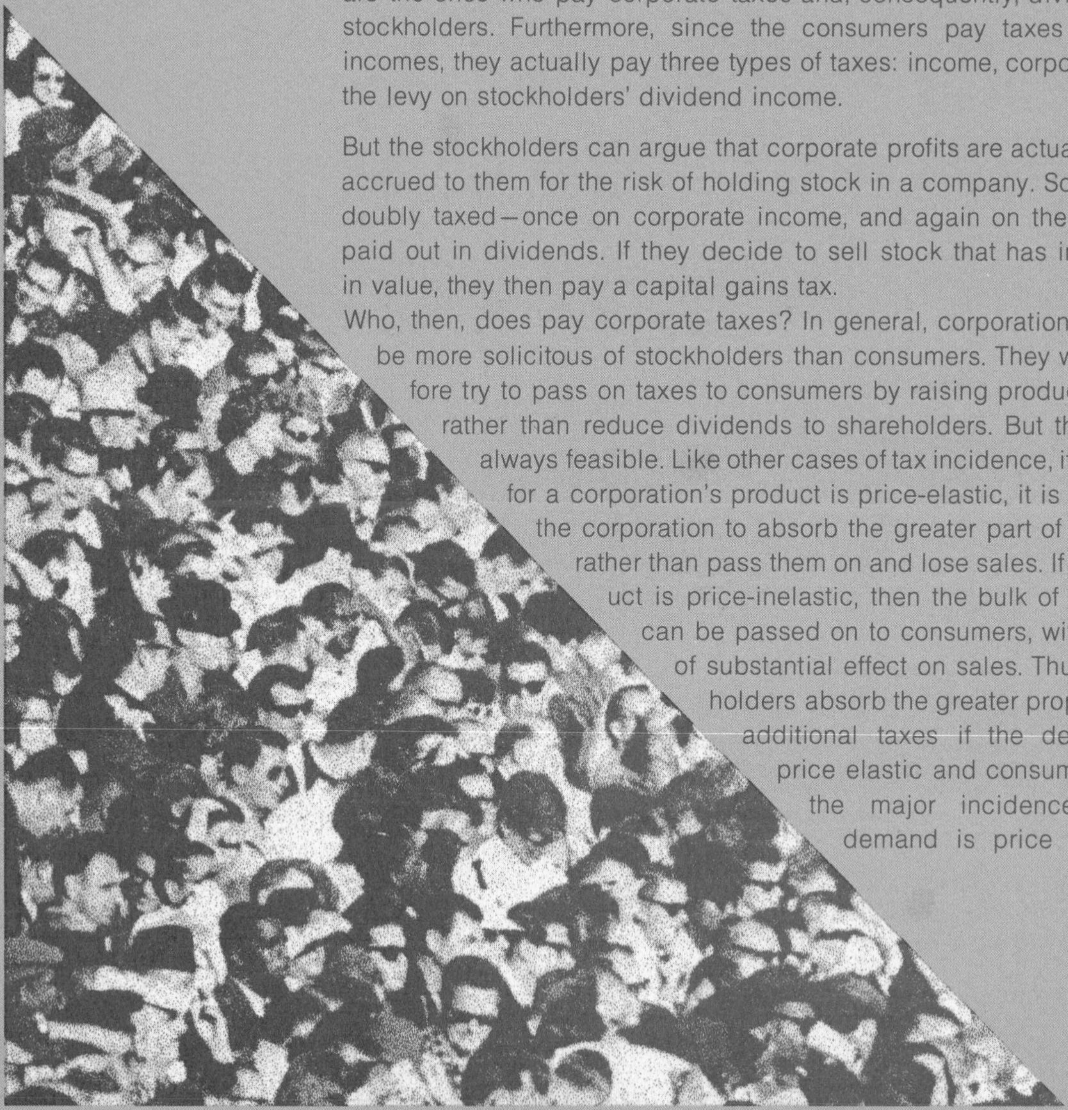

Other Effects This is but one lesson of the relationship between elasticity, tax incidence, and the economy. The policies of taxation on specific products can affect the level of employment and income, the level of revenues raised, the distribution of income, and the allocation of resources. When the objective is to raise substantial revenue without raising prices, taxes should be imposed on commodities characterized by inelastic supply. Although the major tax burden will fall on the producer, the cutback in output will be less than with a more elastic product, and employment levels will be relatively unaffected.

For goods with inelastic demand, taxation rates may take into account the kind of good—high for luxury items in order to generate adequate revenue yield from a small segment of the population, and low on commonly used items with comparatively low unit prices.

In most cases, the incidence of taxation on consumers and producers will be shared in line with relative elasticities of demand and supply: The more inelastic the demand, the higher the proportion of taxes that will be borne by consumers. Thus, tax policy can indirectly redistribute income. And finally, tax policy also affects resource allocation. In the example of Dirtz, the phosphate detergent, we saw that the tax increase caused not only a hike in price, but a cutback in output. By judicious taxation on goods with elastic demand, the government could discourage not only pollution but the consumption of empty calories in snack foods—results that direct legislation might fail to accomplish. The distributive and allocative effects of the effluent charges discussed in Chapter 21 depend upon the elasticities involved.

Subsidies

A subsidy is a kind of tax in reverse. A tax raises costs and can be used to discourage production; a subsidy lowers costs and can be used to encourage production. For whatever reason, the government decides to keep the price of a product or service lower than it would ordinarily be without setting the price directly. In the United States, subsidies have gone to farmers, railroads, shipping firms, and other industries.

By reversing the direction of movements in the previous figure, we can depict what happens when a 50 cent specific subsidy (or an *ad valorem* subsidy) is paid to producers. In all cases, the supply curves shift to the right and result in new equilibria. There is a decrease in prices and an increase in output levels. But the magnitude of these changes varies depending upon whether demand and supply are elastic or inelastic.

Subsidies to products with inelastic supply cause relatively smaller price reductions and smaller increases in output than subsidies to products with elastic supply. Subsidies to products with elastic supply cause greater price reduction and a greater increase in output. If government seeks to stimulate production to bring about economic expansion in general, subsidizing products with elastic demand would be more effective.

Although a subsidy always appears to be helping producers at the taxpayer's expense, the benefits of imposing a subsidy are actually shared by the producer and the consumers. To the extent that product prices are lowered, the consumers benefit, while the balance of the subsidy is added profit for the producer.

SUMMARY

1 The basic laws of the market are those of supply and demand, which deal with the relation between prices and quantities. The inverse relationship between price and quantity demanded is shown on a demand curve. The direct relationship between price and quantity supplied is shown on a supply curve. The intersection of the demand and supply curves determines the equilibrium price. The prevalent

market price—the price at any given time—may differ from the equilibrium price. Shifts in the determinants of demand (or supply) will shift the curve and set a new equilibrium price.

2 Prices are usually set by market forces, but the government can affect prices directly or indirectly. It can directly set prices above or below the equilibrium price. Wage and price ceilings set the market prices of labor and products below the equilibrium prices, thereby creating shortages. Price floors raise prices above their equilibrium levels, thereby producing surpluses.

3 Government can affect prices indirectly by imposing taxes or by providing subsidies. Either method affects the costs of the supplier and shifts the supply curve, creating a higher or lower equilibrium price. The full effects cannot be understood, however, without the concept of elasticity.

4 Elasticity indicates responsiveness. Price elasticity of demand or supply measures the relative change in quantity demanded or supplied resulting from a change in price. The coefficient of elasticity,

$$E = \text{percentage change in Q/percentage change in P},$$

expresses this mathematically. If E is greater than 1, the demand or supply is elastic; if less than 1, the demand or supply is inelastic.

5 Total revenue is the product of price times quantity, and it is affected by elasticity of demand. If a firm lowers the price of its product and if its total revenue increases, demand is elastic. In this case it might be to the firm's advantage to lower its price still further (depending on its cost structure). If a firm raises the price of its product and if its total revenue increases, then demand is inelastic.

6 Demand tends to be elastic over time; it also tends to be elastic if there are many close substitutes for a product, or if the product or service is not needed urgently, or if it requires a large proportion of a family's income. The most important factor in determining the elasticity of supply is the length of time that producers have to adjust to price changes: The longer the period of adjustment, the more elastic the supply schedule.

7 Specific, or per unit, taxes add a flat amount to the cost of every item of a product sold—the amount of the tax never varies. These taxes result in an upward shift of the supply curve. An *ad valorem* tax, or sales tax, is a percentage tax imposed on the sale of a product. The new supply curve will no longer be parallel to the old one, but will diverge as the price rises. If a tax is imposed, there is less decline in output when demand or supply is inelastic. A subsidy is a kind of tax in reverse. A tax raises costs and can be used to discourage production; a subsidy lowers costs and can be used to encourage production. Policies for raising revenues, promoting full employment, and curbing output selectively need to take elasticity into account.

SUGGESTED READINGS

Dorfman, Robert. *Prices and Markets.* Englewood Cliffs, N.J.: Prentice-Hall, 1967.

Leftwich, Richard H. *The Price System and Resource Allocation.* 4th ed. Chaps. 1–3. Hinsdale, Ill.: Dryden Press, 1970.

Mansfield, Edwin. *Microeconomics: Theory and Applications.* Chap. 1. New York: W. W. Norton, 1970.

Miller, Roger L. *Economics Today.* Chap. 20. San Francisco: Canfield, 1973.

QUESTIONS

1 Review
   a. equilibrium and market prices,
   b. methods of calculating elasticities of demand and supply,
   c. the relationship between elasticity of demand, total revenue, and marginal revenue to the firm,
   d. the determinants of elasticity of demand,
   e. the elasticity of demand and supply and the incidence of specific and *ad valorem* taxes,
   f. the distribution of benefits between consumers and producers in the case of subsidies.

2 Assume that you work in a bookstore and that the manager of the store decides to place an art book on sale, reducing the price from $15 to $10 per copy. As a result of the reduction, his sales increase from 60 to 100 copies. What must be the elasticity of demand for this particular book? If the manager is facing a cost of $9 per copy, is the sale a good idea? Why or why not?

3 For each of the following products, indicate if the demand for the product would be relatively elastic or inelastic, and give your reasons.
   a. camper trailers,
   b. electricity,
   c. peanut butter,
   d. bread,
   e. surfboards,
   f. medicine for heart conditions,
   g. Picasso drawings,
   h. paperback novels.

4 What is wrong with the following statement? "The demand for automobiles must be less elastic than the demand for stereos because a $50 reduction in the price of cars does not affect the number sold nearly as much as does a $50 reduction in the price of a stereo."

5 Suppose that you have a friend who roams the countryside and seashore to collect rocks and shells. She mounts the rocks and shells on polished wood blocks with brass or copper fittings and distributes them to gift and specialty shops. Would the supply of these products tend to be elastic or inelastic? Why? Would the elasticity of supply in this case be typical of that of other products?

6 In the summer of 1973, prices for beef remained frozen while the ceiling on other products was lifted. Shortages of beef began to develop. Although there was no real change in price during this period, the behavior of the consumer was similar, in some respects, to what one might expect if the price of beef actually rose. What would you have predicted for the demand for beef substitutes? Complementary products? What are those products?

7 Most states, as well as the federal government, tax gasoline by a specific tax per gallon—the revenues to be used largely for roads. One argument in favor of such taxes is that the users of the roads are the ones who are being taxed. Is this correct? Why or why not?

8 Do you agree that there may be temptation on the part of the state and local governments to tax necessities, and hence the poor more than the rich? Why or why not?

9 Until recently the federal government of the United States has supported the prices of many agricultural products by buying up surpluses. Who do you think most benefits from these subsidies? Give your reasoning.

Opening photo by J. Paul Kirouac

CHAPTER 23
CONSUMER DEMAND

In the preceding chapter, we started to explain the shape of the demand curve through a consideration of elasticity. But the basic property of the demand curve, its slope downward to the right, remains unexplained. Why in fact does the standard demand curve always have this shape? A demand curve does not just float down from heaven, but is controlled by the determinants listed earlier in the book: income, prices of other goods, and individual preferences. However abstract, it represents a part of reality.

Business firms know this and spend a great deal of effort on marketing studies to learn about the characteristics of consumer demand for their product. The braver, or more foolhardy, may use direct experimentation—cutting prices in one locality to see how total revenue responds, and raising it in another, varying the advertising budget or approach. These experiments lack vigorous controls, and can backfire and lose sales. Statistical analysis of actual behavior is sometimes used—how much did we advertise, how much did we sell? Direct interviews are another approach, although few people will be able to answer how much soap or cottage cheese they would buy at different prices. Indirect questions or simulated market situations are used by researchers, academic and otherwise, to get inside the head of the consumer. These approaches are strictly empirical. An economist gets at consumer demand a bit differently, through the use of a model. By making certain assumptions about how people behave and by following them through to their logical consequences, the economist attempts to explain consumer demand.

A FIRST LOOK AT THE DEMAND CURVE

The assumptions on which this economic model of consumer demand is based are relatively few and simple: that the consumer is rational and tries to get maximum satisfaction for his or her limited amount of money; that he or she is able to make free choices; and that other things like income, tastes, or the prices of other goods are constant. Such assumptions are hardly realistic, and many of the attacks on microeconomic theory challenge them, but for the moment, let us see what they reveal.

Taken together, our assumptions give us a picture of a consumer who, with a limited income, must continually make choices between alternative sources of satisfaction. He is not able to buy everything, so for whatever he does buy, he must forgo buying something else of comparable price. This limitation makes it especially important that the consumer choose his purchases wisely. He must ask himself in each case if the proposed purchase is worth its price, not only abstractly, but to him, in his present situation.

Substitution and Income Effects

Effective demand depends on the willingness and ability of the consumer to purchase certain quantities of items at certain prices. Note that desire alone is not enough to create demand. A tribe of Amazonian Indians may develop the desire to own high-performance sports cars. Their subsistence way of life, however, could not possibly supply them with the purchasing power needed to acquire an automobile. Thus, while there is desire, there is no ability to fulfill it, and we would say that the demand among these Indians for sports cars is, for all purposes, nil.

The universal relationship between price and quantity may be explained by the substitution and income effects. As the price of a product declines, a buyer is *willing* and *able* to buy more.

A shopper who is faced with skyrocketing meat prices is less inclined to buy as much meat as before. If the price goes high enough, he may become a vegetarian, substituting bean protein for beef protein. The decline in beef consumption, reflected in the downward-sloping demand curve for beef, is partially a result of the **substitution effect.** This also works when the price of the product declines. As beef becomes cheaper, the shopper is tempted to substitute it for the soybeans on which he had previously been subsisting.

When faced with a price increase, the consumer in effect has had his income cut. What bought two steaks six months ago now buys one steak. Fewer goods can be obtained with the same amount of money. This is known as the **income effect.** It refers only to the effect of a change in price on the consumer's purchasing power. It does not refer to the effect of a change in income; that is shown by a shift in the demand curve.

Together the income and substitution effects define why the demand curve slopes downward from the left. At higher prices, consumers are less willing and less able to buy large quantities of a commodity than they are at lower prices.

Snob Goods and Giffen Goods But there are a few goods whose behavior does not follow the customary pattern. If the price of a sweater in a chic boutique is raised, more people may buy it believing that it is of higher quality or a rarer design. These are **snob goods.**

If the price of chicken necks and wings is raised, paradoxically, poor people may have to buy more of them. The price increase means that for a poor family to buy meat, it has had to forgo the dab of hamburger it could once afford and stick to chicken. These are **inferior**, or **Giffen, goods.**

An easier way of understanding these exceptions is to hold price constant and vary income. This can be done using an Engel curve, with income on the x-axis and quantity on the y-axis. As incomes rise, people buy disproportionately more of a snob good. At higher incomes, people buy disproportionately less of an inferior good. Helicopter taxis are a snob good; long-distance bus travel is an inferior good.

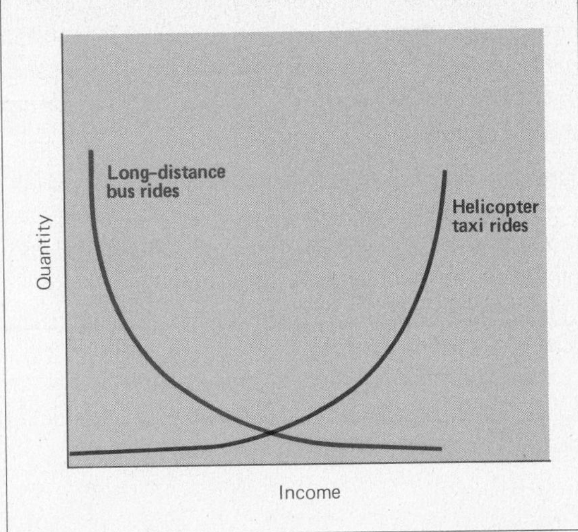

FIGURE 23-1 ENGEL CURVE OF A SNOB GOOD AND OF A GIFFEN GOOD An Engel curve plots the quantities purchased at different income levels, holding prices constant. Fewer quantities of the inferior good—long-distance bus rides—are used as incomes rise, since better substitutes are readily available for those who can afford them. The snob good (helicopter taxi rides) is consumed in greater and greater amounts as income rises.

Marginal Utility

There is a second way of examining the relationship between price and quantity demanded—through marginal utility. It is probably true that our wants, in general, are insatiable. No matter how much we have, there is always something more we desire. It is the very rich who buy the most, despite the fact that they have already accumulated more than anyone else. However, for a single item, during a limited period of time, there is a satiation point, a point at which the consumer declines to purchase more units of the item, even if he can afford them. This is the point at which an item's subjective value to the consumer falls below the value of other goods that he would have to forgo in order to purchase it. The term *utility* is not to be confused with *usefulness.* Utility does not necessarily mean practical applicability. A signed drawing by George Grosz or a bottle of *Trockenbierenauslesen* may have no usefulness, but each may have a great deal of utility to people who appreciate it. Utility is a subjective concept, and though it may differ widely between different individuals for the same product, general trends can often be observed.

The subjectivity involved in the concept of utility is the chief impediment to its use in quantified studies. However, for the sake of demonstration, we shall assume that it is possible to measure a *util,* or the amount of satisfaction gained through the purchase of successive units of a product.

The amount of satisfaction gained through the purchase of the last unit of a product is known as marginal utility.

With each successive unit consumed, the marginal

utility decreases. For example, the second cup of coffee consumed at a lunch counter will have less utility than the first, and the third less than the second. This principle is known as the **law of diminishing marginal utility**.

The law of diminishing marginal utility helps explain the shape of the demand curve. A consumer expects the money he spends on an item to correspond with his desire for it, which is to say, its utility. If the item's utility decreases, the consumer will no longer buy it at the same price. He will buy it only if the price goes down in proportion to his diminishing desire for it. Thus, on the demand curve, the greater the quantity sold, the lower must be the price.

CONSUMER DECISIONS

We have developed a tool for determining how much of something the consumer will buy. Now we are left with the question: How does the consumer choose *what* he is going to buy? For this purpose we need some method of comparing the marginal utility of different items, to discover what mix of goods will give the consumer the greatest satisfaction.

Utility Maximization

When we try to compare the marginal utility of different items, we run into the problem of trying to add apples and asparagus. Different things may offer the same amount of satisfaction, but for one item a consumer may have to spend $5 while for the other he may pay $1. We need a common denominator to allow us to reduce different scales of satisfaction to the same unit of measurement. We derive this formula by dividing marginal utility by price, giving the utility per dollar expended, or

MU/P.

The aim of the consumer is to achieve maximum satisfaction, or utility, with every purchase. Since his means are limited, he must do this by carefully balancing his expenditures, until the last dollar spent on any purchase yields the same marginal utility as the last dollar spent on every other purchase. At this point, the consumer will have no incentive to buy more of one product than another. He will be in a state of equilibrium, which can be expressed by the formula:

$$\frac{MU_1}{P_1} = \frac{MU_2}{P_2} = \frac{MU_3}{P_3} = \frac{MU_n}{P_n}$$

An example may make this clearer. Suppose that a rock music enthusiast with $10 in his pocket passes the window of a record store and sees that there is a sale on the albums of two of his favorite groups, Dark Victory and the Parameters. Dark Victory is selling for $1, the Parameters for $2. He has many things to consider. Dark Victory is interesting, but seems to lack vitality and has been repeating itself in recent recordings. The Parameters, in their first album, introduced a whole new kind of music—a synthesis of bluegrass and Gregorian chant—but the group seems to have lost something with the demise of its electric oudist, Joachim Peabody. The enthusiast mentally totes up his desires for the albums, as shown in Table 23-1, and buys one Parameters album, giving up $2 and obtaining 48 utils for an MU/P score of 24. He now has $8 left and can obtain equal satisfaction from a purchase of Dark Victory or Parameters, so he buys both. Now he has spent $5. So he can buy either three more Dark Victory albums and one Parameters album or two Parameters albums and one Dark Victory album. Will he opt for quantity? Not if he is utility maximizing. At four Parameters and two Dark Victories he has exhausted his budget and maximized utility.

Now suppose that he had $15. Then he would buy two more Dark Victory albums because they furnished greater satisfaction rather than buying a fifth Parameters album. Having money left, he will finally buy one more of each to reach equal satisfaction and the limit of his budget.

This idea can be applied to hours as well as dollars. There are only 24 hours in a day; some can be spent at leisure, others in working. The decision to work or not to work balances the satisfaction per hour worked against the satisfaction per hour at sleep or

TABLE 23-1 UTILITY MAXIMIZING (Hypothetical)

	Dark Victory ($1)			Parameters ($2)		
	Total expended$_v$	MU_v/P_v	Choice	Choice	MU_p/P_p	Total expended$_p$
1	$1	20	2	1	24	$ 2
2	2	16	4	2	20	4
3	3	14	5	3	18	6
4	4	12	6	4	16	8
5	5	10	7	7	10	10
6	6	8			4	12

At each step, the buyer chooses the album that yields the greatest satisfaction per dollar spent. His spending ends as his budget is exhausted and the purchases yield equal satisfaction. To see if you understand the MU/P principle, recalculate this table reversing the prices.

play. If price is now in hours, we have the same utility maximizing formula:

$$\frac{MU_L}{P_L} = \frac{MU_w}{P_w}$$

Indifference Curve Analysis

The problem with the concept of marginal utility is that a util is something that does not exist. There is really no such thing as a unit of satisfaction. Satisfaction cannot be quantified. You may feel that you get more satisfaction from early Mick Jagger than you do from late Wayne Newton, but it would be extremely difficult to say exactly how much. An alternative approach that avoids this difficulty is indifference curve analysis.

Suppose that a consumer, Mr. Mudd, is interested in buying two commodities, earth and water. The table below shows nine combinations of earth and water that would yield equal satisfaction to Mr. Mudd. Therefore, he is *indifferent* to which of the combinations he gets.

Focusing on the two commodities separately, we see that getting more water compensates for giving up some earth. The terms on which Mr. Mudd will substitute water for earth are known as the **marginal rate of substitution.**

Earth (pounds)	Water (quarts)	Marginal rate of substitution
41	1	
33	2	8/1
26	3	7/1
20	4	6/1
15	5	5/1
11	6	4/1
8	7	3/1
6	8	2/1
5	9	1/1

These quantities of earth and water may be plotted on a graph. The resultant curve, called an **indifference curve,** moves down and to the right, showing that as he gives up water, he must get more and more earth to maintain his level of satisfaction. The curve also becomes flatter as it descends, which shows that as Mr. Mudd acquires more and more units of water, his desire for water diminishes and he is willing to give up fewer and fewer units of earth to acquire additional units of water. In economic terms, we would say that Mr. Mudd is exhibiting a **decreasing marginal rate of substitution.**

Anywhere along the indifference curve Mr. Mudd would be equally satisfied. But if we put him anywhere along an indifference curve to the right of this one, he would be more satisfied. If we put him anywhere along an indifference curve to the left of this one, he would be less satisfied. We are assuming, of course, that the more units of earth and water Mr. Mudd possesses, the more satisfied he will be. Such a series of curves showing the range of consumer preferences is called an **indifference map**.

But in order to discover which combination of earth and water Mr. Mudd will actually buy, we must know more. We must know how much earth and water cost and we must know how much money Mr. Mudd has to spend. Let us say that water costs $1 per quart and earth costs 50 cents per pound. Mr. Mudd has $20. The following table shows the different combinations of earth and water that Mr. Mudd could buy with his $20.

Earth	Water
40	0
36	2
32	4
28	6
24	8
20	10
16	12
12	14
8	16
4	18
0	20

Note that this table merely shows the various possibilities open to Mr. Mudd with the amount of money he has. Unlike the indifference curve, it says nothing about which combinations of earth and water Mr. Mudd would prefer. Because it does not contain this element of preference, the curve does not flatten out as does the indifference curve when the combinations are plotted on a graph. Instead, the combinations plot a straight line, slanting down and to the right. This is called the **budget constraint line.**

We can superimpose the budget constraint line over the indifference map. This allows us to compare Mr. Mudd's preferences with his spending capability. There are many points at which the budget line intersects the indifference curves, but there is only one point at which it is tangent to an indifference curve. At this point Mr. Mudd will be getting the most satisfying combination of earth and water his budget will allow.

Geometrically, at the point of tangency the slope of the indifference curve is exactly equal to the slope of the budget line. Since the slope of the indifference curve is the marginal rate of substitution (MRS), and the MRS indicates the ratio of marginal utilities, this slope may be expressed as MU_1/MU_2. Since the slope of the budget line is the ratio of the prices, this slope may be expresed as P_1/P_2. Since these values are equal at the point of tangency, at this point $MU_1/MU_2 = P_1/P_2$, or in its more familiar form, $MU_1/P_1 = MU_2/P_2$. The indifference curve is simply another way of expressing the same insight about consumer behavior. From the indifference curve we can derive a demand curve, as shown in Figure 23-3.

VALUE THEORY

What we have been considering here is *marginal utility,* but in choosing the greater satisfaction at each stage, the end result is greater total utility. Total utility is the sum of all satisfaction from the goods consumed.

In the difference between total value and marginal utility rest two important insights about the basis upon which people buy things and the value they attribute to them: the paradox of value and consumer surplus.

The Paradox of Value

The concept of utility allows us to explain why it is that diamonds are very expensive while water is cheap. From the point of view of total utility, the prices should be the other way around. Water is essential to life and therefore very valuable. Diamonds are mere decorations: It is much easier to live without them than it is to live without water; therefore they should be cheap. In a sense, this reasoning actually holds up in reality. A consumer may be willing

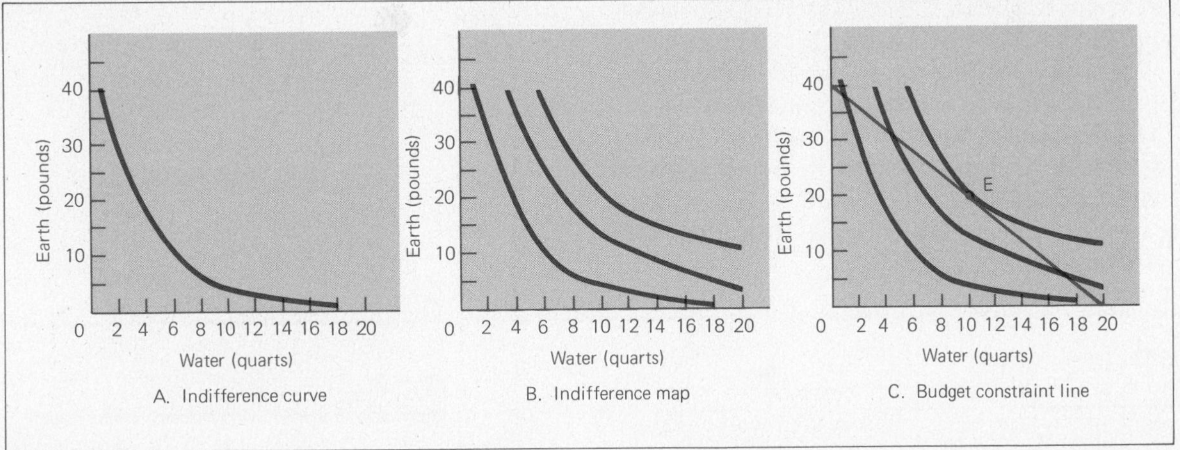

FIGURE 23-2 CONSUMER CHOICE (A) Indifference curve: This curve plots those combinations of goods that furnish the consumer with equal satisfaction. (B) Indifference map: The set of indifference curves that represents an individual's preferences is called an indifference map. The higher the curve, the higher the level of satisfaction. (C) Budget constraint line: The budget constraint line shows the combination of goods that the consumer's budget allows him to buy. Where this line is tangent to the indifference curve, the consumer will receive the most satisfaction from his limited budget. For Mr. Mudd this combination is 20 pounds of earth and 10 quarts of water.

to pay several thousand dollars for a diamond, but if he were dying of thirst, he would be willing to pay even more for a glass of water. This is because water, being one of the essentials of life, has a very great *total utility*. However, price is not determined by the total utility of an item, but by the *marginal utility* of

FIGURE 23-3 DERIVING A DEMAND CURVE To derive Mr. Mudd's demand curve for water from the indifference map shown here, we must assume that his budget and the price of earth remain constant. With a budget of $20 and a price of $2 per pound, we know that Mr. Mudd can buy no more than 40 pounds of earth. We now vary the price of water. As the price of water increases from $1 to $2 to $5, Mr. Mudd will be able to purchase fewer and fewer quarts of water with his $20 budget. This gives a series of budget lines originating from the same point on the earth axis and terminating at different points on the water axis. It is unlikely, however, that Mr. Mudd will devote his entire budget to either one of the two commodities. All that remains is to see what quantity of water Mr. Mudd will actually buy as the price rises. This is shown by the points of tangency on the indifference map. With water at $2 a quart ($P_2$), Mr. Mudd will buy 6 quarts of water; raise it to $5 a quart ($P_3$) and he will cut his purchase to 3 quarts. We can make up Mr. Mudd's demand schedule for water by reading the price-quantity combinations off the indifference map and then plotting a demand curve from the schedule.

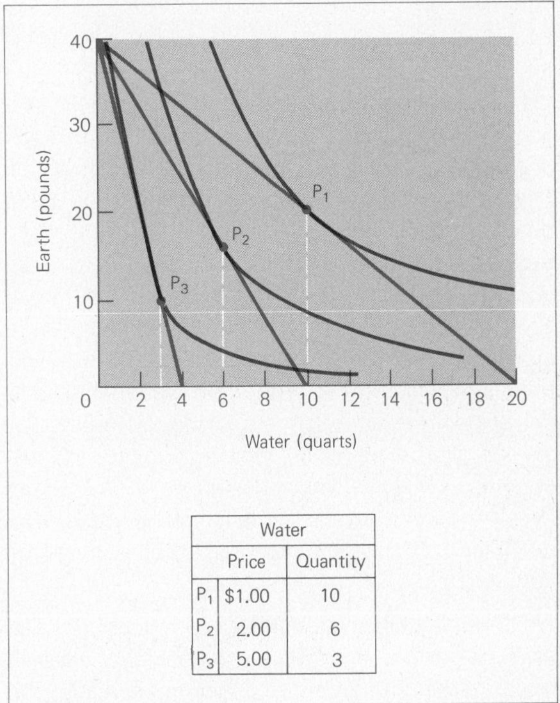

	Water	
	Price	Quantity
P_1	$1.00	10
P_2	2.00	6
P_3	5.00	3

the last unit purchased. Since water is so abundant and since most people are not dying of thirst, the marginal utility of water is very low. The last unit purchased yields only a small amount of satisfaction. Diamonds, on the other hand, while they may have a smaller total utility than water, have much greater marginal utility. They are extremely scarce, so their marginal utility remains quite high. Thus, the price remains high.

Consumer Surplus

If the price of an item is determined by the marginal utility of the last unit purchased, then the consumer is getting a bonus. The price of an item is constant, whether it is paid for the first unit or the last unit. But as we have seen, the first unit purchased has greater utility than the last unit. The consumer would have been willing to pay a higher price for it. If we add the prices the consumer would have been willing to pay based on the marginal utility of each unit purchased, this amount would be greater than the actual amount paid. The difference between the two is **consumer surplus.**

Let us say that a consumer, Mr. Botticelli, goes to his local aquarium supply store to buy seashells. Figure 23-4 shows the marginal value of successive seashells to Mr. Botticelli. He finally decides to buy four shells, because the marginal value he places on the fifth shell is 50 cents, while the store price is 75 cents. The four shells he buys at 75 cents each amount to a total expenditure of $3, but if we add the total value to him of his purchases, we find it comes to $4.50. Mr. Botticelli therefore has $1.50 worth of consumer surplus. When reading Figure 23-4, it is important to remember to read down, not up, the vertical scale. The highest figure at the top represents the marginal utility to Mr. Botticelli of the first unit purchased. Marginal value then drops with each successive purchase, until it falls below price. The magnitude of consumer surplus is represented by the triangular area in Figure 23-4.

What does consumer surplus represent? It is a measure of the benefits of technology, capital, skilled labor, and an ordered market economy. The more abundant goods become, the lower their price and the greater the consumer surplus. A person in the wilderness who has to make his or her own clothes and gather his or her own food pays a higher price for them than a person in a society where specialization affords a wide variety of goods and services.

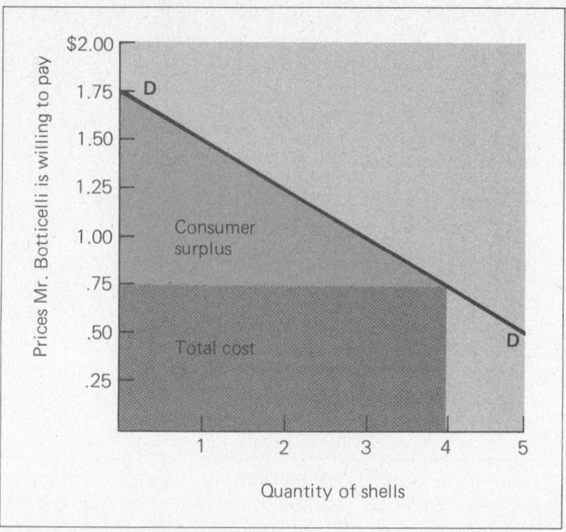

FIGURE 23-4 MR. BOTTICELLI'S CONSUMER SURPLUS If DD depicts Mr. Botticelli's demand schedule and the selling price of shells is 75 cents, Mr. Botticelli will buy four seashells. Since he pays only 75 cents for each shell but would have been willing to pay higher prices for the first three, Mr. Botticelli is getting a bonus. This bonus, or difference between what he would have been willing to pay and what he did pay, is measured by the triangular area and is known as consumer surplus. The cost of his purchase is measured by the rectangular area.

Market Demand and Allocative Efficiency

In studying economics, we are less interested in the problems of one man struggling for survival in the wilderness than in problems peculiar to a large and complex society. In order to understand some of these problems, we must be familiar not only with the demand curve of the individual, but also with the market demand curve.

In order to ascertain market demand, we must add the quantities of goods purchased at each price by each individual consumer. The plotting of points based on these totals will then give us a demand curve for a good, representing the entire market. (See Chapter 3, Figure 3-5 for the graph of this process.) This market demand curve is made up of all the individual consumer decisions to maximize utility.

If the market is competitive and every individual is maximizing his or her own utility, this means that the greatest amount of satisfaction, or general welfare, is also achieved. It means that resources are being devoted to that combination of goods that best satisfies the society. Utility maximizing is the force behind allocative efficiency.

SOCIETY AND DEMAND

In theory, then, utility maximization works to the advantage of society. But this theory depends on a number of assumptions, not the least of which is that shoppers look for the most satisfaction for the least cost and that they know what they are buying. These assumptions may be overly optimistic, however.

High-pressure salesmanship coupled with downright fraud are well-documented tactics of many furniture dealers in the ghettos. Luring in the customer with ads for low-priced goods, the dealer then says that the advertised goods have been sold and shows higher-priced items. Once the customer signs the easy credit terms, the dealer sells the note to a bank or other agency that can collect whether or not the dealer delivers the promised goods.

In theory, such dealers will go out of business because people will refuse to patronize them again. The buyer can choose *not* to buy. In practice, the buyer may only be able to afford to shop in such places or he may believe that such practices are the norm.

Downright fraud coupled with shoddy quality is only part of the problem, however. The array of goods available in the economy does not always work to the advantage of the consumer. For example, a group of housewives armed with a 14-item shopping list and instructed to buy the lowest price for each item failed to do so on about half the items. Moreover, they spent nearly 20 minutes longer than average in shopping.[1] In this case, the problem involved no wrongdoing on the part of individual businesses, but the result was still not maximizing utility.

For consumers to get what they want, they need both information and power. Prices in terms that allow for comparison and information on the quality and safety of products are a first step. To get these, consumers may need more than the power of the individual purse. The consumer movement offers a collective voice to balance the power of large and influential business firms. To this, the consumer movement wishes to add the power of government enforcement.

Product safety is one of the chief areas in which government regulation is applied. Home and recreation products, for example, are involved in about 20 million injuries per year, 17 million of which require medical attention. These findings have led to the signing into law of the Consumer Product Safety Act, which protects the consumer against product safety risks, as well as providing a program of product analysis and information.

Making products safer and consumers better informed confers benefits, but it also incurs costs. Naive consumer advocates often forget this in their rush to keep consumers out of harm's way. Higher prices and a growing bureaucracy are two major consequences. As presently structured, federal consumer protection is fragmented among as many as 50 agencies, often working at cross purposes and easily subverted by firms. The Food and Drug Administration (FDA), for example, conducted a 13-year law suit over the peanut content of products calling themselves peanut butter, a monumental waste of federal resources.

Cost-benefit analysis is one way of evaluating regulatory schemes. But this analysis is made more difficult because many consumer problems are confined to the poor and the vulnerable, so that the costs fall on only one class. Studies have found that the poor pay more not just proportionately but also absolutely for food, credit, and other goods.[2] Efforts to regulate such differential effects have been far

1 E. B. Weiss, "Marketers Fiddle While Consumers Burn," *Harvard Business Review*, July–August 1968, p. 48.
2 David Caplowitz, *The Poor Pay More* (New York: Free Press, 1963).

ABOLISH THE FDA?

If any regulatory agency seems necessary to protect the public, the Food and Drug Administration does. Consumers and even doctors can hardly know all the dangers a specific drug may pose, nor can they test its worth. A National Academy of Sciences report for the FDA found that of the 4300 drugs put on the market in the 24 years before 1962, only two out of every five could be proved effective and of the 16,000 therapeutic claims made for them, there was evidence to support only one in five.* In 1962, tighter restrictions were put on the drug industry.

Although nobody wants to die of a drug-related reaction or spend money on drugs that do not work, nobody wants to die of a disease that could be treated by a drug. The problem of drug regulation is one of balancing the costs of allowing the sale of harmful or ineffective drugs against the costs of impeding the introduction of beneficial drugs. It is upon this that Milton Friedman builds his argument to abolish the FDA. In a widely noted column in *Newsweek*† based on an unpublished paper by a UCLA economist, Friedman blasts the 1962 amendments to the Food, Drug and Cosmetic Act as imposing more than $250 million of costs annually above the benefits from protection offered, or in Friedman's more graphic language, "It is as if a 5 to 10 percent tax were levied on drug sales and the money so raised were spent on invisible monuments to the late Senator Kefauver." A two-year delay in introducing a drug effective against heart disease, for example, would overshadow by 10 to 100 times the costs of even a thalidomide disaster, according to the paper upon which Friedman bases his claims. The FDA retorted that the decline in new drugs was not confined to the United States and that there was a trend that began half a decade before the stricter laws were passed. Only a small percentage of new drugs consists of genuine innovations, and this percentage has remained stable over two decades.

This battle is like many others over consumer protection. It pits two desirable but to some extent mutually exclusive priorities against each other and provides no simple formula for picking one or the other.

* Nicholas Wade, "Drug Regulation: FDA Replies to Charges by Economists and Industry," *Science*, 179 (1973):775.
† "Frustrating Drug Advancement," *Newsweek*, January 8, 1973, p. 49.

less vigorous than those aimed at collective problems.[3] But perhaps new approaches such as financial education, consumer class actions, extended legal services programs, or precinct ombudsmen may be better investments than the large-scale regulatory agencies of the past.

3 Mark Nadel, *The Politics of Consumer Protection* (Indianapolis: Bobbs-Merrill, 1971), p. 223.

SUMMARY

1 To determine why the demand curve slopes downward and to the right, economic theory starts from several assumptions: that the consumer is rational and tries to get maximum satisfaction for his limited money; that he is able to make free choices; and that other things such as income, tastes, or the prices of other goods are constant. Whatever he does buy, he must forgo buying something else of comparable price. The shape of the demand curve can be explained in several ways: the income and substitution effects, marginal utility, and indifference curve analysis.

2 Effective demand depends on the willingness and ability of the consumer to purchase certain quantities of items at certain prices. As the price of a product declines, a buyer is willing and able to buy more. A shopper confronted by rising prices will look for substitutes (substitution effect) and buy less of the higher-priced product. Since a price increase means that fewer goods can be purchased with the same amount of money, the consumer's income has been cut (income effect). Together, the income and substitution effects define why the demand curve slopes downward from the left. Exceptions are snob goods and Giffen goods, the consumption of which rises with price.

3 Alternatively, demand can be explained by the declining additional satisfaction a good yields as more units are purchased. The amount of satisfaction from a product gained through the last unit purchased is known as its marginal utility.

4 Marginal utility provides a common denominator to reduce different scales of satisfaction to the same scale of measurement. The consumer tries to attain maximum satisfaction with his limited means. He can do this by balancing his expenditures in such a manner that the last dollar spent on any purchase yields him the same marginal utility as the last dollar spent on every other purchase. His equilibrium may be expressed:

$$\frac{MU_1}{P_1} = \frac{MU_2}{P_2} = \frac{MU_3}{P_3} = \frac{MU_n}{P_n}$$

5 An indifference curve shows those combinations of two goods that afford a consumer equal satisfaction. An indifference map contains curves for different levels of satisfaction. The budget constraint line shows the combination of goods the consumer is *able* to buy. The combination that affords the consumer the most satisfaction within his budget may be found from the point at which the budget line is tangent to an indifference curve.

6 From the point of view of total utility, it is impossible to explain why diamonds cost so much and water so little: Water is essential to life, while diamonds are mere decorations. This problem is known as the paradox of value and can be

resolved, since price is not determined by the total utility of an item, but by the marginal utility of the last unit purchased. Because water is so abundant and most people are not dying of thirst, the marginal utility of water is very low, and so is its price.

7 If the price of an item is determined by the marginal utility of the last unit purchased, then the consumer is getting a bonus. If we add all the prices a consumer would have paid for successive units of a product based on the marginal utilities, this amount will be greater than the total price of all the units purchased. This difference is known as consumer surplus. The more abundant goods become, the lower their prices and the greater the consumer surplus.

8 A market demand curve for a commodity can be drawn by adding the quantities of goods purchased at each price by each consumer. If the market is competitive and every individual is maximizing his own utility, the greatest total amount of satisfaction is also achieved. This means that resources are being devoted to that combination of goods that best satisfies the society.

9 Are shoppers really looking for the most for the least and do they know what they are buying? What about high-pressure salesmanship and fraud? For consumers to get what they want, they need both information and power. In addition to collective action, the consumer movement may need the power of government enforcement.

SUGGESTED READINGS

Galbraith, John Kenneth. *The Affluent Society.* Rev. ed. New York: New American Library, 1970.

Haveman, Robert H., and **Kenyon A. Knopf.** *The Market System.* Chap. 3. New York: John Wiley & Sons, 1966.

Mansfield, Edwin. *Microeconomics: Theory and Applications.* Chaps. 2–4. New York: W. W. Norton, 1970.

Spencer, Milton H. *Contemporary Economics.* Chap. 21. New York: Worth, 1971.

Veblen, Thorstein. *The Theory of the Leisure Class.* Reprint. New York: New American Library, 1954.

QUESTIONS

1 Review
   a. substitution and income effects resulting from changes in price,
   b. snob and inferior goods,
   c. the law of diminishing marginal utility,
   d. consumer choice using utility maximization,
   e. consumer choice using an indifference map,
   f. consumer surplus and the paradox of value.

2 One of the assumptions for the model of consumer behavior covered in this chapter is that the consumer tries to buy the most for the least. In order to put this principle into practice the consumer must spend time and energy to obtain information. Is it possible to argue that the consumer is still behaving rationally even if he or she buys something at a higher price than charged elsewhere? How? On what types of items is the consumer most likely to search out the highest quality for the lowest price? Why?

3 Which of the following might be inferior goods and why?
   a. beans
   b. perfume
   c. wine
   d. lobster
   e. rice

4 Some economists have suggested that the behavior of demand for snob goods does not actually defy the law of demand. Instead, the consumer reevaluates the utility he expects from the good and behaves accordingly. How might you show this change on a consumer's indifference map?

5 Assume that a consumer is about to stock up on groceries and must decide between eggs at $1 per dozen and cheese at $2 per pound. The consumer has $8 to spend. Draw a budget constraint line to match these conditions. Now assume that the cheese goes on sale for $1 per pound. Draw in the new budget constraint line. Is the consumer likely to increase his purchases of cheese only or of both eggs and cheese? What would the indifference curve look like in either case?

6 Use concepts of indifference, diminishing marginal rates of substitution, and opportunity costs to discuss whether public policy should be aimed at zero or some low level of pollution.

7 Use the concept of marginal utility and price to explain why most families have only one washer while they may have two televisions.

8 The paradox of value can be explained by the law of diminishing marginal utility. Use this law also to explain why many consumers are now willing to pay in one way or another for clean air and quieter surroundings.

9 Would you say that the average householder's consumer surplus is greater for water than for garbage disposal? Why or why not?

10 Look now at the hypothetical indifference map. Assume that this consumer is deciding between bread and fishing rods. Several budget constraint lines are drawn in and represent possible combinations of purchases with the same budget but with different prices per loaf of bread. According to this map, is the consumer's demand for bread likely to be elastic or inelastic? Why? How about the demand for fishing rods? What, in effect, does a drop in the price of bread do for this consumer?

CHAPTER 24
COSTS

In the previous chapter, we examined consumer demand, describing how the individual consumer makes buying decisions. The layman, reading about demand theory, may be surprised to find his behavior described in terms of marginal utility, indifference theory, and the substitution effect, but as soon as he understands these ideas, it becomes clear that they are fairly accurate descriptions of what the consumer actually does. The laws of supply are a different matter. Unless one happens to be a business executive, chances are that he or she rarely thinks about the principles that govern the flow of goods into markets. We know that somebody, somehow, does supply the canned pineapple or cigarette papers that appear on the shelves of stores. But it rarely occurs to us to wonder how the manufacturer decided to produce these goods at all, much less how much of them and by which processes. The subject of supply is a rather complex one. Suppliers must take quite a number of factors into account when making production decisions.

Economic theory assumes that a firm's primary consideration is the maximization of profits. In ordinary usage, profit is what is left over after total costs are subtracted from total revenue. Revenue is the barometer of consumer demand. But revenue is not directly under the control of the firm. To a greater extent, the costs of production are under its control. And costs are of paramount importance when a business makes decisions about supply—the quantity of a product it is willing to supply to the market at a given market price.

SOME PRELIMINARIES

Assumptions

Most businesses operate quite prosperously without explicitly using the economists' model of the world. If businesses use models at all, they are probably based on linear programming, in which decisions involving hundreds and sometimes thousands of choices among processes (and the extent to which they are used) are readily resolved through mathematical manipulations. The availability of a certain grade of motor oil or the shipment patterns of an auto plant may depend on the solutions reached by linear programming. Even if firms do not use marginal analysis in their decision making, however, their behavior can be described as if they did.

As with the theory of consumer demand, the theory of the firm is based on a model that is in many ways idealized. First, we shall assume that firms produce a single product. This is in the interest of simplicity. Everything that we shall say could be applied to firms that produce more than one product, but it would make our analysis unnecessarily difficult. Other assumptions that simplify reality, but which we make for the sake of convenience, are that (1) factor prices are fixed, (2) factor supply is infinitely elastic, and (3) factors are available in small increments—say, one dollar's worth of a linotype machine at a time. We also assume that we can vary one input, while holding the others constant. This may not always be possible in actuality, but it enables us to project hypothetical situations under controlled conditions.

Finally, as in the case of the consumer, we assume that the entrepreneur is rational. But while rationality for the consumer means maximizing satisfaction, rationality for the entrepreneur means maximizing profits. As we have seen, profit maximization requires minimizing costs by being technologically efficient. Any other motives, however exalted, are not rational in the strict sense of the word.

What Is Cost?

We all know that cost does not always entail money. Cost means a sacrifice of something in order to obtain something else. The "something" that is sacrificed can be many things besides money. It can be goods, personal security, leisure time, prestige, or pleasure. Generally, then, costs can be divided into two categories: explicit (or monetary) costs and implicit (or opportunity) costs.

Explicit costs are those that involve money. For the business firm, they include wages paid to employees,

Opening photo from United Nations

payment for production equipment, raw materials, and utilities such as gas, oil, and electricity. Money spent on insurance, rent, advertising, and taxes also comes under the category of explicit costs. Explicit costs are also known as accounting costs, for they can be precisely measured and entered into the firm's books.

The other category of costs is **implicit costs.** Implicit costs can also be viewed as the opportunity costs of being in business (or the value of a resource in an alternative use). A knowledge of implicit costs can mean big money to a firm. Del Monte, for example, calculated the cost of having sufficient inventory to ensure 100 percent availability of its products, its traditional practice. By reducing availability to 98 percent, Del Monte saved more than enough money to finance the purchase of a Guatemalan banana operation, presumably a venture with a higher rate of return than an inventory of canned goods.

When we speak of *total cost* throughout this analysis, we are referring always to both explicit costs and implicit costs. Therefore, it follows that when total revenue exactly equals total costs, a firm is earning a **normal profit.** This is because implicit costs include the return a firm could have earned if it had employed its resources in some alternative use. If total revenue is sufficient to cover both explicit and implicit costs, the firm must be earning a normal return on its resources—that is, a normal profit. Any revenue that the firm earns above this level is known as **excess profit,** or **economic profit.** Excess profit, then, occurs when total revenue exceeds total cost.

THE PRODUCTION FUNCTION

Fixed and Variable Inputs

In order to estimate the total cost of producing a certain quantity of goods, it is first necessary to understand the relationship between input and output. Output refers to the goods produced by a firm; input, to the resources required to produce them. Thus, to calculate the total cost of a given level of output, a business must know precisely what inputs it must employ and in what quantities to employ them. This relation between input and output is known as the **production function.**

In the short run, a firm's ability to increase or decrease certain inputs is limited. If General Motors wants to step up production of Chevrolets, it can order more steel and engine components, hire more workers, and put on a third or fourth shift in all of its plants. But at some point the existing plants will reach full capacity. No matter how ingenious corporate executives may be, in the short run there is a limit to how many Chevrolets can roll off G.M. assembly lines each day. This is because in the short run certain factors of production—the size of the factory, the amount of capital equipment—are fixed. This short-run limitation applies to most types of businesses; capital equipment and physical plant are typically **fixed inputs.**

Other factors of production, however, can be altered in the short run. Such factors are called **variable inputs.** In the short run, a shoe manufacturer can increase or decrease its orders for leather, and hire or lay off workers; without much delay, these inputs can be varied in whatever way the manufacturer thinks will be most profitable. For many industries, then, labor and land resources are variable in the short run.

To the economist, the distinction between fixed and variable inputs is really a matter of time.

Variable inputs are those resources that can be increased or decreased in the short run; fixed inputs are those resources that cannot be altered in the short run. In the long run, however, all inputs, including fixed inputs, can be increased or decreased.

The Short Run and the Long Run

We have defined fixed and variable inputs in terms of the short run and the long run. But what exactly do we mean by the "short run" and the "long run"? In economics, these terms do not designate specific periods of time. Rather, the short run is simply that period of time in which some of the firm's inputs are fixed. In the short run, the firm can decide only how much to produce given its existing capacity. It can hire more workers or order more raw materials, but because the size of its plant facilities cannot be altered, output possibilities are limited.

The long run is that period of time in which a firm can change all of its inputs, including the size of its plant. In the long run, a firm can expand its capacity to any size that will be profitable; conversely, it can contract its capacity by closing down a factory or deciding not to replace worn-out equipment. Of course, the time it takes to alter plant capacity varies from industry to industry. It could take General Motors several years to design and construct a new factory, while the corner drugstore might be able to build a new wing in a matter of a few months. In the long run, however, both firms can adjust in any way they choose to changing market conditions.

Total Product Curve

How many workers should an employer hire? How much fertilizer should a farmer order? How much leather should a shoe manufacturer purchase? Businesses are well aware that correct answers to such questions are vital. Too little of any one of these factors will mean, of course, lessened output, but too much could produce a drop in output as well. The reason is explained by the law of diminishing returns.

As explained in Chapter 17, the law of diminishing returns was first perceived in the realm of agriculture in the late eighteenth and early nineteenth centuries, but it holds equally true for any business. It states that, when added to a fixed factor of production, successive increases in a variable input will, beyond a certain point, result in smaller and smaller quantities of additional output. The total product curve is a way of demonstrating the operation of the law of diminishing returns.

Figure 24-1 is the total product curve for the Old Dobbin Glue Company. It is based on the information contained in Table 24-1. Column 1, showing units of variable input, forms the horizontal axis of the curve, while column 2, total product, forms the vertical axis. Since the total product curve can only show change in one variable input at a time, we shall designate the particular input shown in column 1 as labor.

At zero input, output is also zero. Nothing can be produced without any workers. As the number of workers increases, output also increases, but slowly. This initial slowness of response reflects the fact that there are still too few workers to operate the company's equipment effectively. But as labor is increased still more, output begins to climb more quickly and by larger and larger additional units. This part of the curve is known as the range of increasing marginal returns. Increasing marginal returns ends at point A, the point of inflection. It is here that additional units of input begin to yield pro-

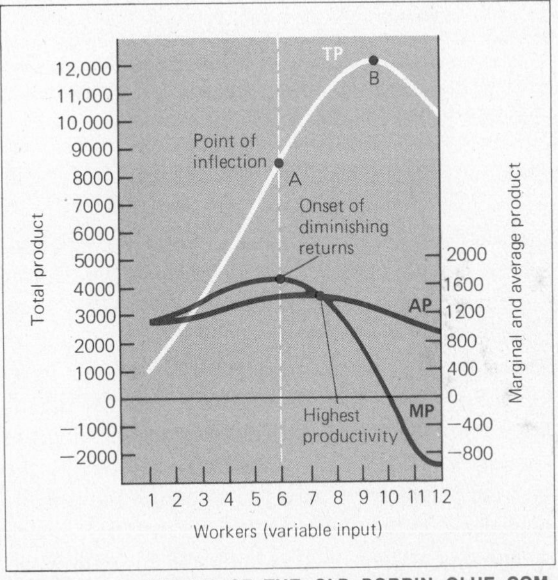

FIGURE 24-1 OUTPUT OF THE OLD DOBBIN GLUE COMPANY **The total product curve is plotted on the left axis and the marginal and average product curves on the right axis. Each shows diminishing returns in a different way. When the marginal product curve peaks and then begins to decline, diminishing returns have set in. On the total product curve this occurs at the point of inflection, after which TP begins to increase at a decreasing rate, reaching a peak at 10 workers. After that point, there will be negative returns, indicated by the negative values for the marginal product curve after 10 workers and the decline in total output. The effect on productivity appears on the average product curve. As long as marginal product is greater than average product, the latter will continue to increase. After seven workers, however, average product will begin to decline, as marginal product falls below average product.**

TABLE 24-1 The Production Function of the Old Dobbin Glue Company

(1) Variable input (labor)	(2) Total product	(3) Marginal product	(4) Average product
1	1000	1000	1000
2	2200	1200	1100
3	3600	1400	1200
4	5200	1600	1300
5	6900	1700	1380
6	8600	1700	1433
7	10,100	1500	1443
8	11,300	1200	1413
9	12,000	700	1333
10	12,000	0	1200
11	11,200	−800	1018
12	10,200	−1000	850

The relationship between input and the output or product of a firm is known as its production function. Total product is the sum of the output of all workers; marginal product is change in total product/change in input; average product is total product/total input. The relationship between these three concepts is shown in Figure 24-1.

gressively smaller additional units of output. Total returns are still climbing, but by smaller amounts with each successive unit of input. The part of the curve between the point of inflection and the peak is known as the range of diminishing marginal returns. Thus, from the origin to point B, total returns are constantly increasing, but the rate of increase first rises, then diminishes. Finally, at point B, the highest point of the curve, total output reaches its peak. Beyond this point workers begin to get in each other's way and total output begins to fall. Remember that it is not that the workers themselves are becoming less efficient; we are assuming that each worker is exactly as efficient as every other. But after point B, there are simply too many workers. The part of the curve after point B is called the **range of negative marginal returns.**

Marginal Product Curve

The management of the Old Dobbin Glue Company may also want to know exactly how much output is gained with each additional unit of variable input—in this case, labor. This information is represented by the marginal product curve. To calculate marginal product, we divide the change in total product by the change in variable input:

$$\text{MP} = \frac{\text{change in total product}}{\text{change in variable input}}$$

Thus, what the marginal product curve actually represents is the slope of the total product curve. This becomes obvious when we remember that the slope of a curve between any two points on that curve is equal to the change along the vertical axis divided by the change along the horizontal axis.

Looking at the MP curve, we see that it first rises steadily, showing that each successive unit of variable input is yielding greater and greater additional output. The curve reaches a peak, and then begins to decline, as additional units of input yield diminishing amounts of extra output. Finally, the curve descends below zero, showing that additional units of input now cause total output to decline. Thus, the shape of the marginal product curve, like the total product curve, is governed by the law of diminishing returns.

Plotting the marginal product curve and the total product curve on the same graph, we see that the MP curve reaches its peak prior to the TP curve. This is because MP shows output for each additional unit of input, while TP shows output for all units of input. The highest point on the MP curve represents the largest incremental gain in output; after this, marginal output starts to decline, and so does the curve. However, total output is still rising, but by diminishing marginal units. Thus, the highest point on the MP curve falls at the point of inflection on the TP curve. Total output does not begin to fall until additional units of input begin to yield negative returns. This means that the highest point on the TP curve corresponds to the point at which the MP curve falls to zero.

Average Product Curve

The total product curve tells us how much of a product a given number of workers will produce; the marginal product curve tells us the extra output resulting from additional units of input. These do not reveal at what point output per worker, or productivity, is maximized. To determine this ratio, called average product, we must divide total product by total variable input:

$$AP = \frac{\text{total product}}{\text{total variable input}}$$

For example, with one worker producing 1000 bottles of glue, average product will be 1000/1, or 1000. With two workers producing 2200 bottles of glue, the average product will be 2200/2, or 1100; each worker is producing 1100 bottles of glue. With three workers producing 3600 bottles, the average product is 1200, and so on.

Plotted on a graph, the average product curve rises to a peak and then falls. The highest point on the curve represents the greatest amount of output per unit of input. When we compare the average product curve with the total product curve, we see that AP reaches its peak while TP is still rising. If the AP curve is still rising production will normally be increased, for workers are not utilizing the fixed factors of production at maximum efficiency.

If we plot the average product curve on the same graph with the marginal product curve, we notice that the MP curve intersects the AP curve at its highest point. Any marginal product curve and average product curve drawn from the same set of data will have this relationship. When the MP curve is above the AP curve, each additional worker is producing more extra output than the average output of all workers up to that point. Thus, the marginal product of the additional worker will force AP to rise. When, on the other hand, the MP curve is below the AP curve, each additional worker is producing less extra output than the average output of all workers up to that point. In this case, the marginal product of the additional worker will force the average product down. It is easy to see how this relationship operates in a concrete situation. Suppose that your instructor administers a short exam every Friday and your average grade (AP) on these exams is B. If on your next exam (MP) you receive a grade of A, your average will go up. If you get a D, your average will go down.

At the point where MP and AP intersect, AP reaches its peak. After that point, AP begins to decline, but more slowly than MP, since it is derived from marginal units of output averaged in with all previous units of output.

Returns to Scale: A Long-Run Concept

The law of diminishing returns affects firms only in the short run. Its effects depend upon there being some fixed factor of production, but in the long run, all inputs can be altered. What, then, happens to the relationship between input and output when all factors of production are increased simultaneously? If a firm is made twice as large, does its output automatically become twice as great? Not necessarily. Actually, three situations are possible.

First, increases in inputs may result in proportionately greater increases in output. This is known as **increasing returns to scale.** Such a relation between input and output in the long run may be due to several factors. As a firm increases in size, it may be able to use certain equipment and operations—such as open hearth furnaces or the assembly line—that are not available to the small firm. And greater numbers of customers may provide larger firms with a more stable market. Increasing returns to scale are realized by all business firms at very low levels of output, but at higher levels of output they are most significant in mass production industries, such as steel, auto manufacturing, and public utilities.

A second possible situation is that of **decreasing returns to scale,** in which increases in inputs result in proportionately smaller increases in output. Decreasing returns to scale are usually blamed on the limitations of management. As firms become larger, the strain placed on communications systems becomes greater and greater; as a result, it becomes increasingly difficult for management to ascertain exactly what is happening throughout the firm and to issue orders to workers and see that they are carried out. In effect, this situation could also be viewed as an example of the law of diminishing returns. The fixed factor of production is the coordinating abilities of management. When the firm reaches a certain size, additional resources will result in declining marginal product because managerial skills cannot increase, even in the long run.

Decreasing returns to scale theoretically affect any firm beyond a certain size, although the vastness of certain present-day firms seems to belie this assumption. Actually, what has happened is that communications systems, information storage and retrieval systems, and surveillance systems have increased tremendously in efficiency due to recent technological breakthroughs. The computer alone has revolutionized many industries. Thus technology has, for many industries, delayed the effects of decreasing returns to scale. However, in certain types of businesses, such as restaurants, theaters, research groups, and engineering companies, decreasing returns to scale are encountered much sooner. In such firms, costs rise quickly when the business grows beyond a certain size.

The third possibility is **constant returns to scale,** in which increases in inputs produce proportionately constant increases in output. Empirical evidence indicates that constant returns are relatively common in many manufacturing industries.

TABLE 24-2 Cost Schedules of the Old Dobbin Glue Company

(1) Output (in thousands)	(2) Total fixed cost	(3) Total variable cost	(4) Total cost	(5) Marginal cost
1	$2000	$ 1000	$ 3000	$1000
2	2000	1800	3800	800
3	2000	2600	4600	800
4	2000	3300	5300	700
5	2000	3900	5900	600
6	2000	4500	6500	600
7	2000	5200	7200	700
8	2000	6000	8000	800
9	2000	7000	9000	1000
10	2000	8500	10,500	1500
11	2000	10,500	12,500	2000
12	2000	13,000	15,000	2500

As output rises, costs rise too. However, total fixed cost, by definition, remains the same throughout the entire range of output. Therefore, the rise in total cost is due to the rise in variable cost.

SHORT-RUN COST CURVES

So far, we have been looking at the production function, or the relationship between input and output. At this point, it is necessary to recognize that everything that comes under the heading of inputs has a price tag. One additional worker costs a certain amount per hour; one bottling machine costs so many thousands of dollars. Just as there are fixed inputs and variable inputs, so are there corresponding fixed and variable costs. In the short run, fixed costs remain the same while variable costs may be altered to increase or decrease the level of output.

To examine the relation between cost and output, we can draw up a table that shows both change in costs and change in output. Table 24-2 contains this information for the Old Dobbin Glue Company. Column 1 shows the quantity of output, each unit representing 1000 bottles of glue. Each of the other columns lists a different type of cost. In the following analysis, we shall illustrate the relationship between output and each of these types of costs by means of graphs.

Total Cost Curves

Since a firm's total inputs are composed of both its fixed and its variable factors of production, it follows that total costs must be the sum of fixed costs and variable costs at any given level of output. The formula for total costs is:

$$TC = TFC + TVC.$$

Variable costs are the costs of all variable factors of production—number of workers, quantity of raw materials, and so on. To plot a total variable cost curve, we simply need to know the quantities of all variable inputs needed to produce different levels of output and how much those inputs will cost. Essentially, then, a total variable cost curve is another way of looking at the information contained in a total product curve. The difference is that we are now attaching a price tag to units of input.

We can see this close relationship between the total variable cost curve and the total product curve by looking at Figure 24-2. (This variable cost curve is based on the information contained in the third column of Table 24-2.) The variable cost curve shows the same data as the product curve; the only differences are that the axes of the graphs have been reversed and that variable inputs, which now have price tags on them, are expressed in terms of cost rather than number of units. As in the case of the product curve, the shape of the cost curve reflects the effect of the law of diminishing returns. At zero output, there are no variable costs. As inputs are added, costs rise but at a decreasing rate. This portion of the curve corresponds to the area of increasing marginal returns on the total product curve. Eventually, the curve hits a point of inflection and begins to rise at an increasing rate. Again, this upper portion of the TVC curve corresponds to the area of diminishing marginal returns on the TP curve.

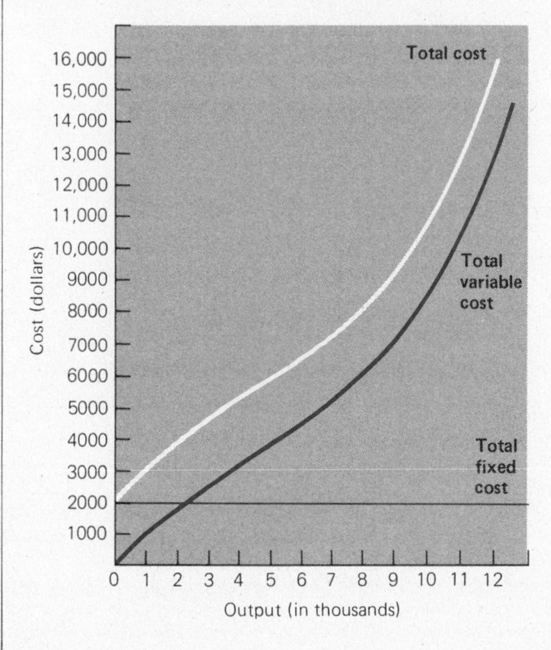

FIGURE 24-2 FIXED COST, VARIABLE COST, AND TOTAL COST OF THE OLD DOBBIN GLUE COMPANY **No matter what the level of output, costs such as rent on the factory and the salary for the night watchman must be paid. Total fixed cost is represented here as a horizontal line throughout the entire range of output. Although both variable and total costs keep rising from zero units of output, there is a $2000 differential between these two curves at each level of output. That differential is due to fixed cost.**

As we have said, variable costs are only one component of total costs. The other component is fixed costs. Therefore, in order to determine total costs, we must add fixed costs to variable costs. As we can see from column 2 of Table 24-2, total fixed costs remain the same regardless of the level of output. Because fixed costs remain constant in the short run, they are represented in Figure 24-2 by a straight, horizontal line. Adding fixed costs to variable costs, then, is simply a matter of adding the same amount at each level of output. When total costs are plotted, we see a curve that follows the variable cost curve, at an equal vertical distance above it. This equal distance is the amount of total fixed costs.

Like the total product curve, the total cost curve can tell us only one aspect of the input/output relationship. To fill out the cost picture, we shall also have to consider the average cost curve and the marginal cost curve.

Average Cost Curves

From one point of view, average cost curves are more useful than total cost curves. The units of output that a firm produces do not all cost the firm the same amount. Yet all must be sold for the same price. Therefore, it is important to know the average cost per unit of output.

In calculating average costs, we must take into account, as we did in calculating total costs, both fixed and variable costs. **Average fixed cost,** unlike total fixed cost, does not form a straight, horizontal line when plotted on a graph. This is because average fixed cost is derived from dividing total fixed cost by the number of units produced:

$$AFC = \frac{TFC}{TP}.$$

TABLE 24-3 Average Cost Schedules of the Old Dobbin Glue Company

Output (in thousands)	AFC	AVC	ATC
1	$2000	$1000	$3000
2	1000	900	1900
3	667	867	1534
4	500	825	1325
5	400	780	1180
6	333	750	1083
7	286	745	1031
8	250	750	1000
9	222	778	1000
10	200	850	1050
11	182	955	1137
12	167	1083	1250

Average fixed cost, TFC/TP, unlike total fixed costs, constantly declines in magnitude. Both average variable costs, TVC/TP, and average total cost, TC/TP, decline at first, then rise showing the impact of diminishing returns. These are shown graphically in Figure 24-3.

In other words, a constant figure (total fixed cost) is divided by a constantly increasing figure (units of output). The result is a number that is continuously diminishing. On a graph, average fixed costs form a downward-sloping curve. All average fixed cost curves have a similar downward-sloping shape.

Average variable cost is derived by dividing total variable costs by the total number of units produced.

$$AVC = \frac{TVC}{TP}.$$

When plotted on a graph, average variable costs produce a curve similar to that shown in Figure 24-3. At first the curve slopes downward, indicating the increasing marginal returns that result from initial increases in variable inputs. But eventually total variable costs begin to rise, due to the law of diminishing returns. All average variable cost curves resemble the one shown in Figure 24-3.

In order to calculate **average total cost,** we simply add average fixed cost and average variable cost for each level of production. Or we can find average total cost by dividing total cost at each level of output by the number of units produced. This is the way in which the formula is generally written:

$$ATC = \frac{TC}{TP}.$$

When average total cost is plotted, the result is a curve that reflects the influence of both its components: average fixed cost and average variable cost. The ATC curve falls rather sharply at first, as does the steadily declining AFC curve and the AVC curve. Even

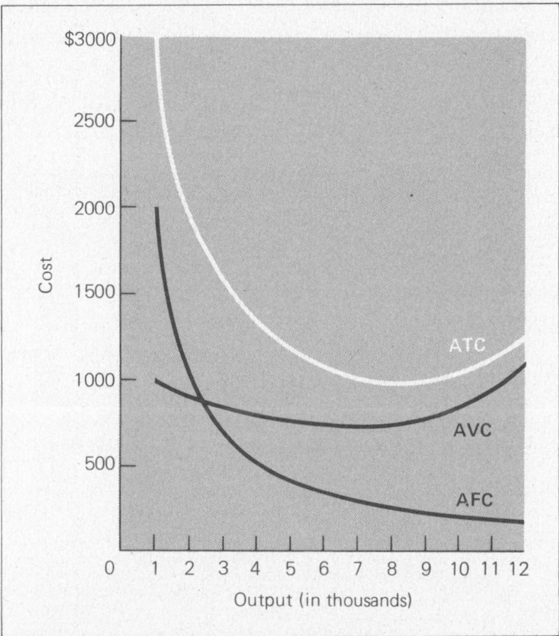

FIGURE 24-3 AVERAGE FIXED COST, AVERAGE VARIABLE COST, AND AVERAGE TOTAL COST CURVES OF THE OLD DOBBIN GLUE COMPANY **Several observations may be made here which hold for all average fixed, variable, and total cost curves. Average fixed cost approaches the output axis asymptotically (approaches without ever quite touching). Since fixed cost is being divided by larger and larger outputs, eventually average fixed cost becomes negligible. Average total cost remains higher than average variable cost over the entire range of output since it is the sum of AVC and AFC. However, the two grow increasingly close as output increases, because AFC becomes a smaller and smaller part of the total. Because AFC helps keep down the average total costs, the lowest point on the ATC curve occurs after the AVC curve reaches its minimum. Both ATC and AVC show the effects of diminishing returns in their characteristic U shape.**

after AVC begins to rise because of the effects of diminishing returns, the ATC curve falls, under the influence of the declining average fixed costs. But the ATC curve does not continue to fall indefinitely; it is eventually affected by the rising AVC curve which, in turn, is influenced by the law of diminishing returns. Thus, the ATC takes on a U shape which is characteristic of all ATC curves.

Marginal Cost Curves

The marginal cost curve is also very helpful because it shows the cost of producing additional units of a good. For this reason, the MC curve shows whether the firm is likely to produce more, to continue at the same level, or to decrease output. The data on which the MC curve is based are contained in the total cost curve. If we look at Table 24-2 for the Old Dobbin Glue Company, we can see how the figures for the MC curve are derived. The first unit of output costs \$3000 to produce. But when output is increased to two units, the cost is \$3800. The cost of producing the second, or marginal, unit is therefore \$800. Marginal cost is the cost of producing one additional unit; we can calculate it by dividing the change in total cost by the change in output:

$$MC = \frac{\text{change in TC}}{\text{change in output}}.$$

Actually, the marginal cost curve represents the slope of the total cost curve for the same reason that the marginal product curve represents the slope of the total product curve.

When plotted on a graph, the marginal cost curve forms a characteristic U shape. It drops sharply at first, due to initial increasing marginal returns. Then the law of diminishing returns begins forcing the curve upward. The low point on the MC curve corresponds with the point of inflection on the total cost curve, the point at which total costs begin to increase at an increasing rate.

If the MC curve is plotted on a graph along with the average total cost curve and the average variable cost curve, as in Figure 24-4, an interesting relationship becomes apparent. The MC curve intersects

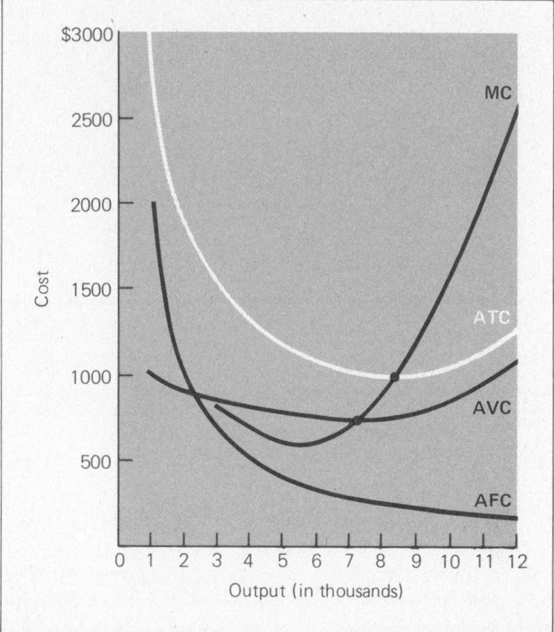

FIGURE 24-4 AVERAGE FIXED COST, AVERAGE VARIABLE COST, AVERAGE TOTAL COST, AND MARGINAL COST CURVES OF THE OLD DOBBIN GLUE COMPANY The marginal cost curve is U-shaped, like those of average total cost and average variable cost. Note that the marginal cost curve intersects the average variable cost curve and the average total cost curve at the minimum point. When marginal cost is below either average variable cost or average total cost, the latter is declining. However, when marginal cost lies above average variable cost or average total cost (and is rising), the latter will be rising.

The explanation of these relationships becomes clear when we define marginal cost. Marginal cost is the additional cost of producing one more unit of output. In Table 24-2, we have taken each 1000 units of output as one unit. To determine the marginal cost of producing the sixth unit of output, for example, we take the difference in total cost. To produce five units, total cost is \$5900; to produce the sixth, total cost is \$6500. Therefore, the marginal cost of producing the extra unit of output is \$600. Similarly, to produce a seventh unit of output, the marginal cost is also \$700 (\$6500 total cost to \$7200 total cost).

Now we are ready to explore why average variable cost and average total cost rise and fall with marginal cost. At output five, average variable cost is \$780 and average total cost is \$1180. If it costs an additional \$600 to produce another unit, this will pull down average variable cost, because \$600 additional cost for the sixth unit is lower than the average cost for the first five units. Average variable cost for six units = \$3900 + 600/6 = \$750. Similarly, average total cost = \$5900 + 600/6 = \$1083.

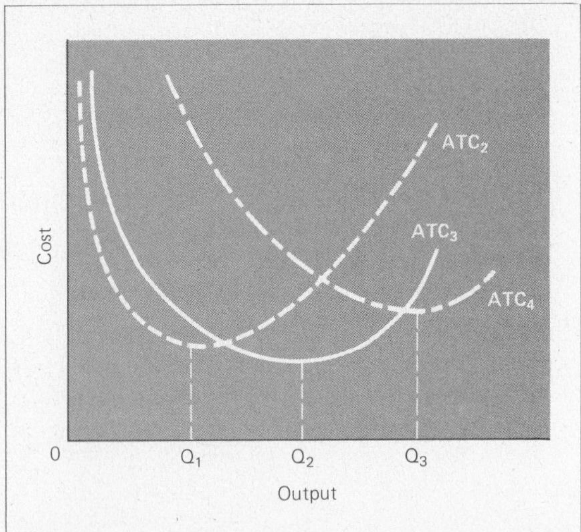

FIGURE 24-5 SHORT-RUN AVERAGE TOTAL COST CURVES We have shown here three short-run average total cost curves, ATC_2, ATC_3, and ATC_4, with corresponding optimal outputs of Q_1, Q_2, and Q_3. The lowest possible average total cost occurs on ATC_3, at output Q_2, which happens to be the size and output of the Old Dobbin Glue Company. If that company wished to produce output Q_1 or Q_3, it would have to do so, in the short run, with plant ATC_3. In the long run, however, it would be possible to build or buy a new plant.

the other two curves at their lowest points. This will always happen, with curves plotted from any one set of data. What does this relationship mean? It indicates that if the marginal cost exceeds the average cost, the average cost will rise. Conversely, if the marginal cost is less than the average cost, the average cost will decline.

COSTS IN THE LONG RUN

The cost curves we have considered so far are short-run curves. In the short run, a firm's plant and equipment remain fixed, and only its variable inputs can be altered. In the long run, however, plant size can be changed as well. In order to maximize profits in the long run, a firm can select the plant size that will produce the quantity of goods it wishes to supply to the market at the lowest possible per unit cost. This point of long-run minimum costs can be located by referring to a long-run cost curve, which indicates the lowest possible input cost for different levels of output, using different sized plants.

Figure 24-5 shows the short-run ATC curves for a number of different sized plants that are being considered for construction by the Old Dobbin Glue Company. The plant in which the firm is now located is represented by ATC_3. If the Old Dobbin Glue Company wanted to reduce its level of production by building a smaller plant that would allow it to produce, at optimum cost, output Q_1, it would do best to build the plant represented by ATC_2. If, however, it wished to expand its production in the long run to Q_3, the plant represented by ATC_4 would be the best choice.

It is interesting to note that the lowest possible average total cost occurs on ATC_3 at output Q_2, which also happens to be the Old Dobbin Glue Company's present position. The firm will find that if it wishes to produce less than Q_2, the optimum level for its present plant, it will be cheaper for the firm to underutilize a plant by producing less output than the lowest cost capacity rather than overutilize a smaller plant. Conversely, if the firm wants to increase production, it will be cheaper to overutilize a plant by

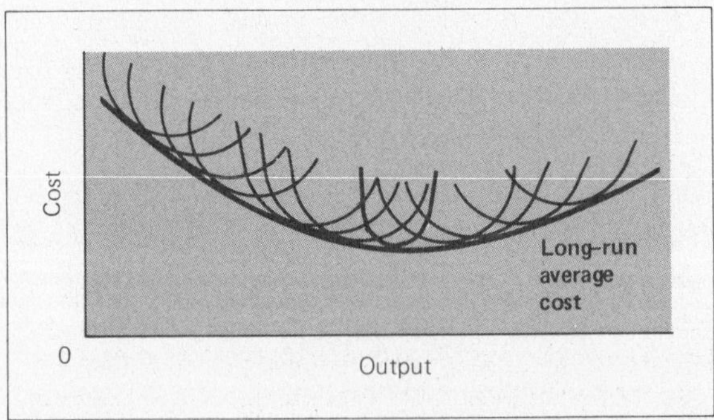

FIGURE 24-6 THE LONG-RUN AVERAGE COST CURVE If we drew every possible short-run average cost curve and drew a curve that would be tangent to each of these short-run average cost curves, we would have a long-run average cost curve, or envelope curve. Note that the LRAC curve would be tangent to the minimum point of only the lowest short-run average cost curve. The LRAC curve indicates the minimum cost per unit of producing at each level of output over the long run.

producing more output than the lowest cost capacity, rather than underutilize a larger plant.

The long-run average total cost curve demonstrates this principle. It is formed by projecting an infinite number of short-run average cost curves and drawing a line that is tangent to all of them. Note that the resulting curve does not connect the lowest points on all the short-run cost curves; therefore, it does not indicate the minimum unit costs for each individual plant size. What the long-run average total cost curve does show is the minimum cost per unit of producing each level of output over the long run. Figure 24-6 shows that at levels of output less than Q_2, the points of tangency fall to the left of the point of minimum cost, showing that the plant is being underutilized. Conversely, at levels of output greater than Q_2, the points of tangency fall to the right of the point of minimum cost, showing that the plant is being overutilized.

Economies and Diseconomies of Scale

What gives the long-run average total cost curve its characteristic U shape? This time the answer is not the law of diminishing returns. Rather, it is the principle of economies and diseconomies of scale, which is simply another way of looking at increasing and decreasing returns to scale.

Economies of Scale Whenever long-run average total costs diminish as output increases, the firm is encountering economies of scale. Economies of scale may be the result of several factors, most of which we have already outlined when discussing increasing returns to scale. As the firm becomes larger, there is more possibility for specialization. When both human and machine labor are concentrated on more specialized tasks, greater efficiency results. A larger firm is also able to utilize equipment that is not available to the small firm. For example, a small dairy would not be able to utilize an automatic milking machine, and so must do the job by hand. And a large firm can buy variable inputs at reduced unit costs, because it is buying in bigger quantities. Because of their size, large firms can also utilize by-products more effectively. For example, if the Old Dobbin Glue Company had the necessary capital, it could expand into the dog food business. Finally, economies of scale may encourage the growth of and, in turn, benefit from, auxiliary facilities. Examples include a number of individual farms benefiting from a collective irrigation project, or large companies reaping the benefits of their scholarship programs in the form of trained personnel.

Diseconomies of Scale When a firm continues to expand, eventually it will probably reach a point at which long-run average costs begin to rise. While previous expansion brought diminishing costs, now increasing size serves to raise costs. Circumstances that bring on long-run increases in average cost are two: the limitations of management in coordinating the production process (which have already been discussed) and competition for resources. Competition for resources becomes a factor leading to diseconomies of scale, because as a firm grows larger it becomes a more important force in the resource market. As it bids competitively for labor and raw materials, it has a bigger impact on driving up the prices of these inputs. Consequently, its costs tend to rise.

Long-Run Average Cost Curves and the Structure of Industry

Why does one rarely find steel mills in sixth floor lofts, or luncheonettes covering several square blocks? We are now in a position to answer this question. The solution lies in the long-run average cost curve and the variations in shape that it can take.

One type of long-run average cost curve is that shown in Figure 24-7A. It indicates that economies of scale are substantial, while diseconomies of scale do not begin to occur until very high levels of output. Consumer demand and the technology of the industry may be such that there is room in the market for only a small number of large producers, but this depends on the size of the market since a very large output need not be a great percentage of the output if the total is high enough.

SCHOOL DECENTRALIZATION

To lower the costs of education, the trend has been to enlarge or consolidate school districts. The reasoning, of course, is that as school districts increase in size, the average cost per pupil declines. Opponents of city decentralization plans also use this argument to buttress their case. Economic analysis partially contradicts this assumption: Growth in the size of a school district does not necessarily result in economies of scale.

The reasons are several. First, if a school district is expanded, this does not necessarily mean that the schools within that district are similarly consolidated or enlarged. Very large schools, it appears, are quite inefficient, except in very densely populated areas, for operating costs rise rapidly when children must be transported long distances. Consequently, schools within a district remain fairly constant in size, regardless of the extent to which the district itself expands.

The long-run ATC curve for a typical school, then, remains essentially the same, whatever the district size. Moreover, observation suggests that most schools are already operating at minimum per student costs. This is because the short-run ATC curve for a typical school tends to be very flat at the bottom. Most schools are quite flexible in the number of students they can accommodate, and when the area of increasing costs is finally reached, there are usually few obstacles to building another school.

Thus, expansion of school districts has little effect on the size of individual schools or on their short-run ATC curves. Expansion of a district merely means that more schools of similar size and with similar cost functions will be integrated under a single administration.

Observation also seems to indicate that some of the cost reductions enjoyed by other large-scale horizontally integrated industries do not apply to education. School districts, no matter how large, do not purchase inputs in large enough quantities to enjoy reductions in factor prices. The only resource purchased in truly large quantities—labor—is unionized; therefore, the costs of labor are unaffected by increases in scale. Moreover, as school districts enlarge, some suspect that diseconomies due to political patronage and administrative top-heaviness are introduced.

The conclusion, then, is that for public education, the long-run ATC curve, like the short-run curve, tends to be horizontal over a very wide range.*

*Analysis based on "Appendix—Economies of Scale," *Analysis of the Rising Costs of Public Education*, Study Paper No. 4, Materials Prepared in Connection with the Study of Employment, Growth, and Price Levels, for consideration by the Joint Economic Committee, Congress of the United States, November 10, 1959 (Washington, D.C.: GPO, 1959), pp. 41–43.

The focus on plant size ignores other aspects of education, however. For special education—both for the advanced and the retarded—a larger school district may be necessary. Few districts would devote their limited resources to developing a Bronx High School of Science or High School of the Arts. Decentralized school districts may also perpetuate economic and racial segregation.

The financing of schools may also be inequitable if the districts are atomistic. Schools are financed through property taxes, and valuations differ markedly from area to area. In California, for example, the range of per pupil valuations is $103 to $952,156. If the revenue is raised locally, or if "each tub stands on its own bottom," then the wealthier districts may tax at a lower rate yet raise more per pupil than the poorer ones. Revenue may be raised by a unit different from the one that controls educational policy, but this issue cannot be ignored in deciding about school decentralization.

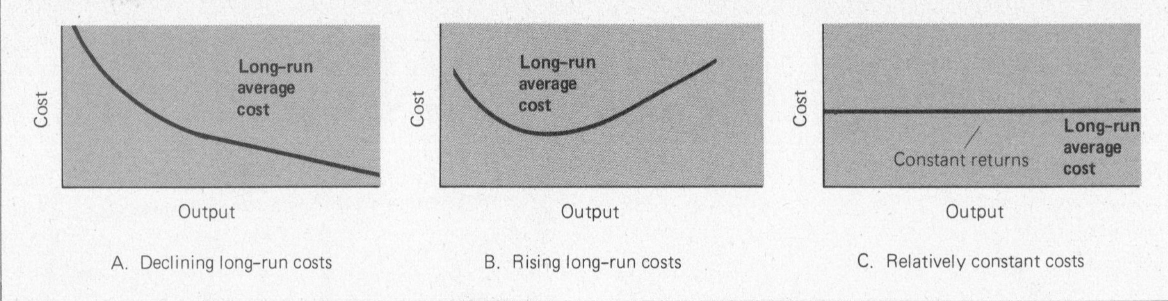

FIGURE 24-7 VARYING COST STRUCTURES Long-run average cost curves translate into optimum plant size. Some industries have enormous plants, whereas others, such as in retailing, have very small plants. The difference is explained by the difference in the onset of diseconomies of scale and can be seen in the different shapes of the LRAC. Those industries with large plants do not encounter diseconomies of scale until very high levels of output; long-run costs decline over a wide range of output, as in A. Those with relatively small plant sizes begin to experience diseconomies of scale, or rising long-run costs very early, as in B. Most industries have similar costs, or constant returns to scale over a range of output, as in C.

Figure 24-7B shows the opposite situation. In this case, diseconomies of scale begin to appear at a relatively early point. Since lowest costs in this industry occur at a rather low level of output, the market favors a large number of small producers. Such a situation is typical of the retail trades and some farming.

In Figure 24-7C, we see a situation in which large firms and small firms exist side by side, both incurring similar costs for dissimilar levels of output. Actually many industries are characterized by a range of constant returns, but the point of minimum efficient size varies widely. In the auto industry, output must be quite large. In other industries, this point occurs much earlier.

THE QUESTIONS OF PROFIT MAXIMIZATION

All these descriptions of costs assume that the rational entrepreneur maintains technological efficiency, or produces at the lowest possible costs. In theory, the entrepreneur is out after profits and watches every paper clip in the supply room if he can cut costs by doing so. The behavior of real business firms, however, often suggests that something besides profit is being maximized, and empirical studies provide some support for this.[1]

It does seem reasonable that a single owner of a business would want to maximize profits. But most firms are no longer owned by single entrepreneurs. In large corporations, the firm owners and the firm managers are not even the same people. The owners are the stockholders, whereas the managers are a large, dispersed group of specialists, each with a different area of responsibility. Moreover, profit is only an expectation when most business decisions are made, so that firms operate under a high degree of uncertainty rather than with perfect knowledge. Given such conditions, the assumption that maximization of profits is a firm's only possible goal cannot go unchallenged.

One suggestion is that the typical firm does not maximize profits but rather "satisfices"[2]—that is, it aims at some figure that is agreed upon as satisfactory. The goal that is agreed upon depends on business conditions and on the firm's past performance.

One theory suggests that rather than maximize profits, most firms attempt to maximize sales revenues. This theory goes hand in hand with the first theory of satisfactory profits. It is assumed that firms maximize total sales while keeping an eye on profits. As long as profits remain above a certain satisfactory minimum level, all is well. If profits sink be-

1 Gerald R. Nordquist, "The Breakup of the Maximization Principle," *The Quarterly Review of Economics and Business* 5, no. 3 (Fall 1965):33–46, summarizes the debate.

2 Herbert Simon, *Models of Man* (New York: John Wiley, 1957).

low this level, the firm will shift its attention from sales goals to watching profits. The same reasoning applies to other substitute indicators such as stock value or stable accounting ratios.

Beyond the goal of attaining a "satisfactory" return, by whatever measure, lies the politics of the firm. In many large firms with several product lines, the managers wrestle for power or for higher compensation, and it is these goals that form part of their strategy rather than simple profit maximization. If the company can produce enough profit to keep the stockholders happy, then management's future is secure.

Efficiency and Equity

Whether firms maximize profit is of more than theoretical interest. A firm may add to its costs not only by having an oversized sales force or an elaborate executive dining room, but also by spending for community day-care centers or for air pollution control equipment more advanced than that of their competitors.

For example, safety in coal mining is better in companies owned by steel corporations than in other commercial coal mining operations because the steel companies use the coal themselves and place less cost pressure on their mining subsidiaries than the competitive pressures of the market place on the commercial coal operations. The coal division of U.S. Steel had 2.72 injuries per million man-hours and 0.28 fatalities per million man-hours, compared with 18.68 injuries and 1.52 deaths in Consolidation Coal's operation. "Safety is a cost we're willing to bear. It can be said that if more money has been spent on safety, profit has been less," according to one coal mining executive in the steel industry.[3] Behind the question of profit maximization, then, lies the issue of corporate responsibility.

To those who value technological and allocative efficiency, the prime social responsibility of the firm is to meet market demand for its goods at the lowest possible cost. Any other use of funds is a usurpation of power, which arbitrarily redistributes income from the stockholders to other groups, and becomes a form of private taxation that raises prices of goods. In the words of the *Wall Street Journal,* "The objective of the profit maximizing ethic ... is to promote efficient use of resources, so that there will be a bigger pie to split among profits, wages, and lower prices, to the total benefit of the entire community."[4]

To some extent the equity argument boils down to a larger definition of costs. The accounting costs of a firm are only part of its total costs to society. The social costs of mine deaths, air pollution, or discriminatory hiring practices are not usually paid by the firm. Voluntary assumption of these costs places the burden on those who created the problems and the consumers who buy their products. Used in this sense corporate responsibility is not simply an ethical term, but an economic one as well.

3 "Safety Underground," *Wall Street Journal,* January 18, 1973, p. 1.

4 "Some Thinking To Do," *Wall Street Journal,* December 18, 1972, p. 14.

FIGURE 24-8 CORPORATE RESPONSIBILITY AND SOCIAL COSTS **The conflict between profit maximization and corporate responsibility is dramatized by this West Virginia mine disaster in which 22 miners were killed. The issue could just as well revolve around the problem of strip mining, the pollution caused by the mines, black lung disease, or any other instance where private costs differ from total social costs.**

United Press International Photo

SUMMARY

1 The goal of the business firm in economic theory is to maximize profits. To do so, the company must minimize costs.

2 Costs may be explicit (actual outlays) or implicit (the opportunity cost of resources in one use rather than another). Normal profit is a part of a firm's costs. Thus, the firm enjoys a profit when the total revenues exactly equal costs. If total revenues are larger than costs, the difference is excess or economic profit.

3 Costs depend on factor prices, the amount of factors (or inputs) used, and the output (or product) yielded. The relationship between input and output is known as the production function.

4 In the short run, a firm's ability to increase or decrease certain inputs is limited, so that there are some fixed and some variable inputs. At some point, the existing plants will reach full capacity. In the long run, however, all costs become variable, and output is not limited by the capacity of a given plant.

5 The law of diminishing returns states that when added to a fixed factor of production, successive increases in a variable input will, beyond a certain point, result in smaller and smaller quantities of additional output. The additional output yielded by the use of an additional unit of variable input is known as the marginal product. The marginal product curve depicts the law of diminishing returns directly; the total product and average product curves also show the effects of diminishing returns. The relationship is shown in the figure below.

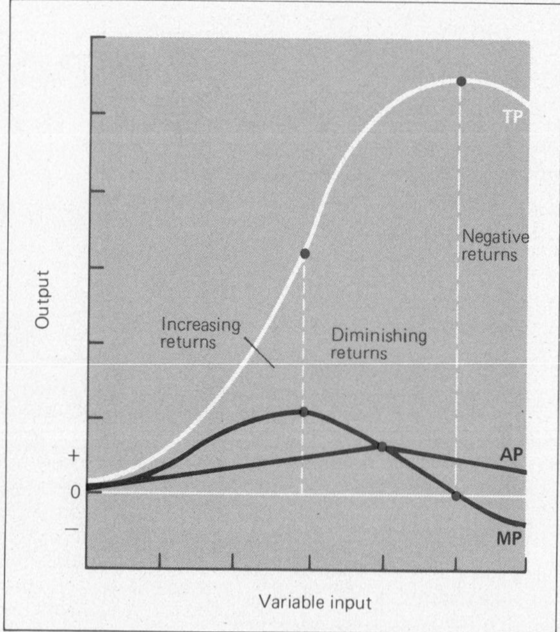

6 In the long run, increases in inputs may result in proportionately greater increases in output (increasing returns to scale), or in proportionately smaller increases

in output (decreasing returns to scale), or in constant increases in output (constant returns to scale).

7 Fixed, variable, and total costs at various levels of output can be represented graphically. Fixed costs are represented by a horizontal line, since they remain the same at all levels of output. Variable and total costs usually increase at a decreasing rate, and then at an increasing rate as diminishing returns set in.

8 Average fixed cost, unlike total fixed cost, does not form a straight, horizontal line, because average fixed cost is derived by dividing total fixed cost by output (that is, the denominator increases steadily). Average variable cost is derived by dividing total variable cost by output. An average variable cost curve is generally U-shaped, as is an average total cost curve. Average total cost is calculated by dividing total cost by total output.

9 Marginal cost, the additional cost of producing one more unit of output, is calculated by dividing change in total cost by change in output. It is also generally U-shaped, dropping at first due to increasing marginal returns, but rising at the onset of diminishing returns. The marginal cost curve intersects the average variable cost curve and average cost curve at their minimum points. The relationships are shown below.

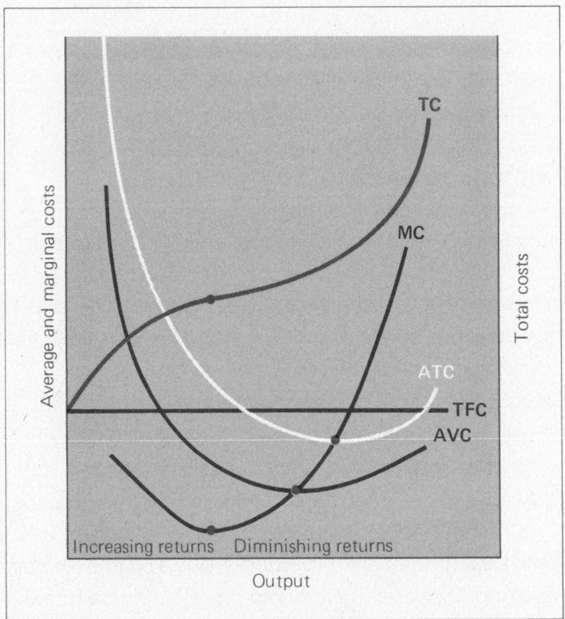

10 In the long run, a firm can select the plant size that will produce the quantity of goods it wishes to supply to the market at the lowest possible cost per unit. This point is located on the long-run average cost curve, which is a line drawn tangent to every possible short-run average cost curve. It shows the minimum cost per unit of producing each level of output over the long run.

11 Whenever average total costs are diminishing in the long run, the firm is encountering economies of scale. Specialization and the utilization of sophisticated and expensive equipment are two contributing factors. Increasing size may raise cost: Management may have difficulty coordinating the production process and resource prices might be bid up. The firm is then encountering diseconomies of scale.

12 The assumption of profit maximization is open to question on empirical grounds and on the grounds of equity.

SUGGESTED READINGS

Dorfman, Robert. *Prices and Markets.* Englewood Cliffs, N.J.: Prentice-Hall, 1967.

Haveman, Robert H., and **Kenyon A. Knopf.** *The Market System.* Chap. 4. New York: John Wiley & Sons, 1966.

Leftwich, Richard H. *The Price System and Resource Allocation.* 4th ed. Chaps. 7 and 8. Hinsdale, Ill.: Dryden Press, 1970.

Watson, Donald S., ed. *Price Theory in Action.* 2nd ed. Boston: Houghton Mifflin, 1969.

QUESTIONS

1 Review
   a. opportunity and direct costs of business,
   b. the shapes of total, average, and marginal product curves,
   c. the economist's definitions of short and long run,
   d. diminishing returns and returns to scale,
   e. the shapes of total, average, and marginal cost curves,
   f. long-run cost curves and economies of scale.

2 What would the average and marginal cost curves look like for an industry facing constant returns to scale?

3 In 1973 the price of feed for livestock more than doubled that of 1972. How would you show the effect of this increase on the marginal cost curve for, say, chicken or beef?

4 In some parts of the country a beefalo, a cross between a beef animal and a buffalo, is being raised for meat. The animal puts on weight faster with less high-cost feed. How would the marginal cost curve for beefalo differ from that of beef?

5 Assume that you are a manager of a small plant producing bottles. In a meeting with the board of directors of the company you suggest that the plant would be more efficient if expanded. One of the board members points out, however, that you are not completely utilizing the capacity that you already have and asks how you could justify a request for expansion. How would you answer?

6 For a number of years the United States government paid farmers a fee for acreage that they withheld from production. Although the soil bank program was designed to be a subsidy to farmers, could one argue that the program actually increased the cost of production? How?

7 Is it true that marginal cost curves reflect variable cost exclusively? Why or why not?

8 Suppose that a labor union settles for a new contract in which the company pays the premiums for medical insurance. Would this added cost to the company be a fixed or variable cost? Why? What would be the effect on the average and marginal cost curves?

9 California levies a tax on inventories held by businesses. The wineries must pay such a tax on all of the wines that they hold through the aging process. How does such a tax affect the cost curves for wineries?

10 Assume that you are managing a plant that produces a product that you can sell for $5 each. Your plant is unionized and so you must pay a total of $10 per hour in wages and benefits for each of your workers. The first worker that you hire is able to produce 10 units, the second brings total production to 15 units, the third to 20, the fourth to 23, the fifth to 25, the sixth to 26, and the seventh to 27. How many workers should you hire and why?

11 Why does the average variable cost curve reach its minimum point before the average total cost curve? Why does the marginal cost curve intersect the average variable cost curve and the average cost curve at their minimum points?

12 Explain how the total cost curve reflects the total product curve, using these graphs.

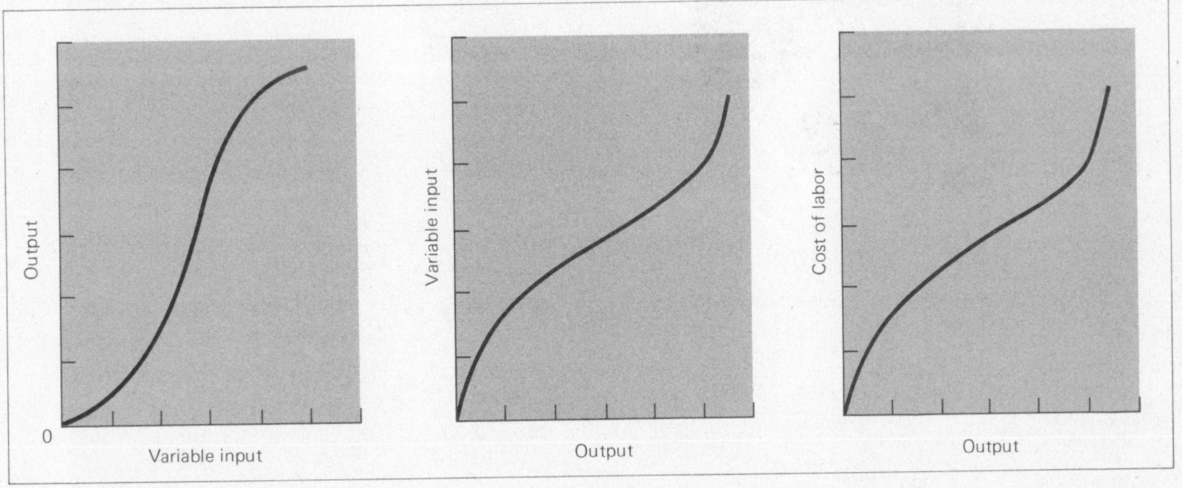

CHAPTER 25 PERFECT COMPETITION

When economists speak of perfect competition, they imply no value judgment. They do not mean "perfect" in the sense of "the best." A condition of perfect competition, as the economist means it, would be impossible in the real world and, probably, undesirable.

What, then, is meant by perfect competition? The economist's system of perfect competition is an abstract model based on, but not realistically descriptive of, the way some markets actually function in any economy. As a picture of reality, then, the model of perfect competition is limited by both selectivity and simplification. But it is not as a picture of reality that the model is prized. It is rather as an analytical tool that allows us to study the economy as an intelligible entity. The economy, after all, is not as accessible, as easily observed, as the objects of study in some other sciences. The economy is all-encompassing. We are part of it, and because of this, our experience of it is limited. In order to see the whole, we must step back. And the only way in which we can step back is in imagination. We build a model of what we observe, a model that we can carry in our heads or reproduce in the form of graphs and tables.

The model of perfect competition began with Adam Smith's *Wealth of Nations* (1776). Smith looked carefully at the bustling capitalist system that was growing in strength and size in England, France, Germany, and the Netherlands, and tried to discover the laws that made the system self-sustaining. He isolated, as the mechanism that coordinated the consumer's desire to buy cheap with the merchant's desire to sell dear, the principle of supply and demand. As Smith saw it, consumers and suppliers were balanced on either side of a pivot: price. Although the pivot was slightly movable, allowing the beam to tip in one direction or the other, the fluctuations were self-correcting: on the average, consumer and supplier were in perfect equilibrium. Smith, in a flight of anthropomorphism, identified the instigator of this ideal condition as "the invisible hand."

Smith's model has since been the subject of much criticism—some of it constructive, some destructive. Some economists, such as Marx, attempted to undermine the model. Others, like Marshall and Keynes, tried to refine it. Both have contributed to the model's development. Since Smith, much has been added, much has been changed, and much has been qualified. Marshall, Jevons, and other late nineteenth-century figures added the concept of marginalism, thus providing a workable solution to the problems of value and cost. John Maynard Keynes contributed a cogent analysis of the causes of imbalance. But, even with all these additions, the basic concept remains intact.

A model is, as we have said, an analytical tool. Insofar as it is a tool, it is judged on how well it performs—how effectively and economically it integrates and explains available data. Although it is a tool and not an exact picture of reality, it must still be judged by how well it corresponds to reality. To take an example from another science, Ptolemy's geocentric model of the universe was accepted for many years because it explained, after a fashion, the observed facts. But when the telescope provided new facts that could not be accounted for in Ptolemy's system, astronomers were forced to accept the Copernican heliocentric universe as the better model. The annals of economic thought are full of thinkers who sought to effect a Copernican revolution in economics. Some of them have succeeded. Marx and Keynes have certainly altered the way we view the economy. And surely there will be many more alterations in the future. There is nothing sacred about the model of perfect competition. It is, after all, simply a tool.

PROPERTIES OF THE MODEL

Homogeneous Product

Firms in a perfectly competitive market produce goods that are indistinguishable from one another and, hence, interchangeable. Within a particular market, the good sold does not vary in quality and has no distinguishing features that would cause a consumer to prefer the product of one firm over the product of another. The steel market and the wheat

Opening photo from Culver Pictures

market approximate this condition. Yet even here there may be differences in quality as well as type, grade, and suitability for certain uses.

Resource Mobility

Under perfect competition, firms are free to enter or leave an industry, to change the size or scale of their operations, or to shift their resources into some other activity.

Although such mobility is variable in the real world, there are some industries that come close enough to the model to assist us in analyzing how perfect competition functions. Agriculture has many of the characteristics of a perfectly competitive industry. Small farms are therefore often used as hypothetical examples of perfect competition in action. It is possible for a small farm to start operation or to change from one product to another (for example, from spinach to carrots) within a single season. But such a shift is by no means as effortless or instantaneous as it would be under conditions of perfect competition.

Perfect Knowledge and Equal Access

Under perfect competition firms would not enjoy patents, copyrights, or trademarks. No trade secrets would exist. Every discovery could be immediately exploited by rival firms, because they would learn of it at once and could use the totally flexible resources to begin employing it immediately. Consumers, too, would be fully informed about the prices of all goods and would have equal access to all sellers so that they could obtain the most satisfaction from their budget at the lowest cost. This world would be a frictionless one, where information, goods, and resources move without encountering all the obstacles of the real world. Consumers would not be too busy to shop for the best buy; entrepreneurs would not be hindered from adopting a process because of ignorance, legal barriers, or limitations of resources and productive processes.

Price Takers versus Price Makers

A market that is perfectly competitive contains a large number of small firms, all selling an identical product and each with perfect knowledge of the market. Although these firms compete with one another, they do so only in a certain way and according to certain rules. The firms can compete through the market only. They do not launch advertising campaigns to polish their image and blacken that of their competitors. They do not spy on one another in order to gain inside information. They do not entice one another's staff with offers of higher wages. They do not buy out one another. They *could* do these things, but it would be futile, since buyers and competitors would have immediate knowledge of these ploys and since any firm would have such a small share of the market that it could sell its entire output without resorting to these tactics.

The relation of the real business world to the world of perfect competition is roughly that of a street brawl to a karate match. In the real business world, we are constantly aware of behavior that supposedly would have no effect under conditions of perfect competition. Advertising can be effective in establishing a product image that stimulates sales, and there can be considerable competition based on product style and quality. Furthermore, perfect knowledge is rarely present among all participants in a competitive industry, and few of them are really able to adjust their factory processes and resources instantaneously in order to switch from products that bring low profits to those that offer better returns.

The consequences of perfect competition are even more important than the general characteristics of the model. Because there are so many firms, none of them can have any effect on the price of the items they sell. In reality, some firms do have enough market power to change product prices. But these firms are monopolies or near-monopolies. They do not fit into the perfect competition framework. Because of their small size, firms under perfect competition cannot affect prices through any action of their own. If a firm did raise its price, its customers would simply cease to patronize it and would buy the same product from the firms that were still charging the lower price. Therefore, firms under perfect competition are known as **price takers.**

A firm that is a price taker has no reason to lower

price, because it can sell all it wants at the existing price.

This means that for the individual firm in a perfectly competitive market, demand is perfectly elastic. In other words, the individual firm can always sell 100 percent of what it produces at the current market price. Therefore, the demand curve faced by an individual firm is represented graphically as a straight, horizontal line at the market price, as shown in Figure 25-1.

WHAT HAPPENS UNDER PERFECT COMPETITION?

In order to analyze how output decisions are made in a perfectly competitive market, it will be useful to have an example. Farming, as we have mentioned, comes closest to resembling a perfectly competitive industry. Farmers are, generally speaking, price takers rather than price makers. No one farmer, no matter how large his operation, has the power to affect market prices to any significant degree. Although farmers can affect prices by lobbying, even here they are effective only as a group, not as individuals. The products that farmers supply are nearly homogeneous. And the demand for these products from the viewpoint of the individual producer is almost perfectly elastic; it is possible, in most cases, for a farmer to sell as much of a product as he could conceivably grow.

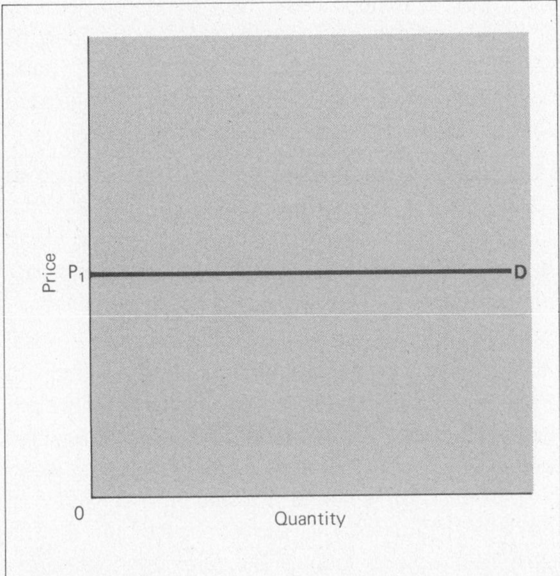

FIGURE 25-1 DEMAND CURVE OF A PERFECT COMPETITOR
The demand curve faced by a perfect competitor is invariably a horizontal line fixed at the current market price. This price is subject to change as demand changes, but the perfectly competitive firm is so small that it cannot influence price and can sell all of its output at the market price.

We must remember, however, that perfect competition is an abstraction. No actual market can meet all these requirements. We must keep this in mind while selecting our hypothetical example. Since cucumbers, cows, chickens, and the like are too much a part of the real world for our purposes, we shall rule them out. Our abstract farmer must grow an abstract product. Let it be triangles.

How many bushels of triangles will he produce? Our farmer (call him Farmer Euclid) will produce as many triangles as is necessary to keep his profits at a maximum. If he is unfortunate enough to earn no profits, he will strive to do what is virtually the same thing: keep his losses at a minimum. Farmer Euclid, like anyone else in business, strives to "buy cheap and sell dear." We have already explored the factors involved in his buying cheap in Chapter 24. Because Farmer Euclid wishes to maximize his profits, which equal revenues minus costs, he is equally interested in the other side of the equation, the part having to do with price or revenue. But under perfect competition Farmer Euclid has no control over price. He must sell his triangles at the going price or else leave the market.

As we have seen, the demand curve for such a firm (or farm) is a horizontal line at the market price. In other words, a firm can count on selling as much of its product as it can produce, at the market price. The demand curve of the entire market, however, will have the traditional downward-sloping shape. The market demand curve represents the sum of all the individual demand curves of all consumers in the market. The point at which the market demand

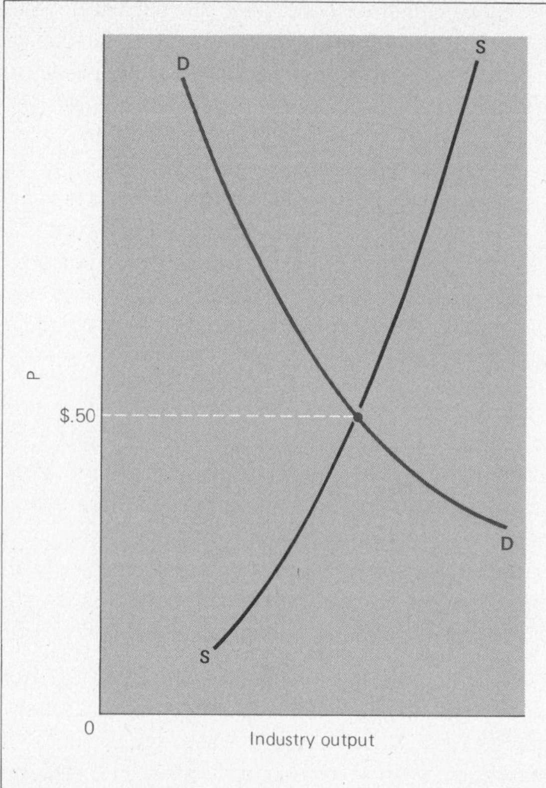

FIGURE 25-2 MARKET DEMAND AND SUPPLY FOR TRIANGLES **We have seen that the demand curve faced by the perfect competitor is a perfectly horizontal line. On the other hand, the demand curve faced by all suppliers, taken together, is an unmistakably downward-sloping curve, shown here. How can we reconcile the horizontal demand curve faced by the individual seller with the downward-sloping demand curve faced by all suppliers, taken together? Since each supplier is so small that he can sell all he wants at the going price, shown here as 50 cents, as far as each is concerned, his demand curve *is* horizontal. However, for the market to sell more triangles, the price must be lowered, hence the downward-sloping market demand curve.**

curve and market supply curve intersect will determine the price. In our example, we will make that price 50 cents per bushel of triangles.

Maximizing Short-Run Profits

The price that the firm charges is set by the market. The quantity that it produces is under its control. Since the firm can sell any amount at the going price, how does it select the quantity it will supply? The answer is: the quantity that earns the greatest profits—or incurs the smallest losses. If the firm's revenues are greater than its costs, then the quantity will be set at the point at which there is the greatest difference between revenues and costs; here profits will be maximized. If the firm's costs are greater than its revenues, the firm may continue operating for a while. Then the quantity will be set at the point at which there is the smallest difference between costs and revenues; here losses will be minimized.

Total Costs and Total Revenue One way in which this point may be determined is by comparing total costs and total revenues at different levels of output. Total cost is determined by adding the firm's total fixed costs and total variable costs. Total revenue is determined by multiplying the price of a single unit by the number of units sold ($TR = P \times Q$). The level of output at which there is the greatest difference between total cost and total revenue is the one at which total profit is greatest—assuming, of course, that revenues exceed costs. Note that this is excess, or pure, profit, since normal profit is included as part of total cost. It is very important to keep in mind the concept of excess profit in order to understand long-run equilibrium under perfect competition.

Table 25-1 shows the quantitative steps leading to computation of total excess profit. Note that at either end of the supply curve (at both a very high and a very low rate of production), profit, paradoxically, becomes negative. That is, the firm is losing money.

Column 7 in the table shows net revenue or total profit. These figures are arrived at by multiplying price per unit (column 5) by the number of units manufactured in one day (column 1) to get total revenue (column 6). From total revenue we then subtract total cost (column 4), which is the sum of total fixed cost (column 2) plus total variable cost (column 3). The remainder equals total profit. Greatest total profit occurs when production is 700 bushels of triangles. At this point excess profit equals $85.

In order to show this same information in graph form, we must plot two overlapping curves, one based

TABLE 25-1 Costs, Revenue, and Profit for Farmer Euclid

(1) Output (bushels)	(2) Fixed cost	(3) Variable cost	(4) Total cost	(5) Price per unit	(6) Total revenue	(7) Total profit
100	$100	$25	$125	$.50	$50	$–75
200	100	45	145	.50	100	–45
300	100	60	160	.50	150	–10
400	100	70	170	.50	200	30
500	100	90	190	.50	250	60
600	100	120	220	.50	300	80
700	100	165	265	.50	350	85
800	100	230	330	.50	400	70
900	100	315	415	.50	450	35
1000	100	425	525	.50	500	–25

As output rises, fixed cost remains the same, variable cost rises, and total cost increases at varying rates. Total revenue is derived by multiplying price per unit by output. Since price per unit is the same for all outputs, total revenue rises proportionately with output. By subtracting total cost from total revenue, we obtain total profit, which varies considerably over the range of output.

on the figures in column 4 of the table (total cost) and the other based on the figures in column 6 (total revenue). The shaded areas between the curves depict the information in the last column of the table, total profit. Note that one of the curves, the TC curve, slopes upward and to the right, reaching a point of inflection; the other curve, the TR curve, is a straight, ascending line. The difference in shape occurs because the TC curve, like the TC curves we encountered in Chapter 24, is influenced by the law of diminishing returns, while the TR curve is not. The slope of the TR curve, remember, is equal to the change in total revenue over the change in quantity. Since, in perfect competition, price remains constant for every level of output, and price is one of the factors of total revenue, it follows then that the change in TR will be determined only by the other factor, change in quantity. Obviously, if Farmer Euclid is to maintain a profit, the TR curve must at some point be above the TC curve. The two places at which the cost and revenue curves intersect are the **break-even points.** At those levels, Farmer Euclid will simply be matching income and expenses (including a normal profit); he will realize excess profit only at production levels between the two points, where TR exceeds TC. At the level of output where the distance between TR and TC is greatest, total profit is maximized.

Marginal Cost and Marginal Revenue In Chapter 24, we introduced marginal, total, and average cost curves. Here, too, in the study of output decisions, we can employ marginal concepts. By comparing marginal cost and marginal revenue, we are able to determine, just as we did using total cost and total revenue, the point of greatest total profit. Let us see how this is done.

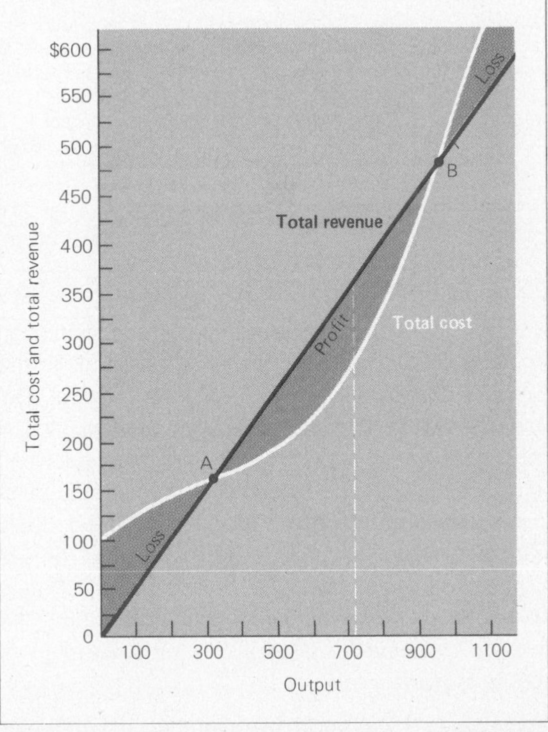

FIGURE 25-3 TOTAL COST AND TOTAL REVENUE OF FARMER EUCLID **Total cost is the familiar curve from Chapter 24, showing the effects of diminishing returns and increasing costs. Total revenue is the straight line passing through points A and B. Points A and B are break-even points, since total cost and total revenue are equal. The outputs between these two points are profitable, since total revenue exceeds total cost. At an output of 700 bushels of triangles, total revenue exceeds total cost by the greatest possible amount; this is the quantity selected if Farmer Euclid is profit maximizing.**

TABLE 25-2 Marginal Cost, Average Variable Cost, Average Total Cost, and Marginal Revenue

Output (hundreds of bushels)	(1) Marginal cost	(2) Average variable cost	(3) Average total cost	(4) Marginal revenue
1	$ .25	$.25	$1.25	$.50
2	.20	.225	.725	.50
3	.15	.20	.533	.50
4	.10	.175	.425	.50
5	.20	.18	.38	.50
6	.30	.20	.367	.50
7	.45	.236	.379	.50
8	.65	.288	.413	.50
9	.85	.35	.461	.50
10	1.10	.425	.525	.50

Marginal cost represents the additional cost of producing one more unit of output and is calculated by dividing change in total costs by change in output. Each unit of output represents 100 bushels of triangles in this table. Average variable cost is total variable cost divided by output. Similarly, average total cost is total cost divided by output. Marginal revenue is change in total revenue divided by change in output. These figures are used to draw the curves in Figure 25-4.

You will recall that marginal cost is the amount it costs a firm to produce one additional unit of the product. Marginal revenue is a new concept. But familiarity with marginal concepts tells us that it must be the amount of money the firm receives when it sells an additional unit. But price, under perfect competition, is constant. Marginal revenue, then, cannot change. Therefore, it is represented on the graph as a line parallel to the horizontal axis at the level of market price. Under perfect competition the marginal revenue curve represents the demand curve for the individual firm.

In Figure 25-4 the two curves marginal cost and marginal revenue are plotted along with the familiar duo average total cost and average variable cost.

Marginal revenue is represented by a straight, horizontal line at the level of 50 cents, the market price for a bushel of triangles. Average total cost is U-shaped and intersects the MR curve at two points, A and B. Points A and B represent, respectively, the smallest and greatest number of bushels of triangles that Farmer Euclid may produce and still make a profit. If he produces to the left of point A, there will be too few units sold to cover costs. If he

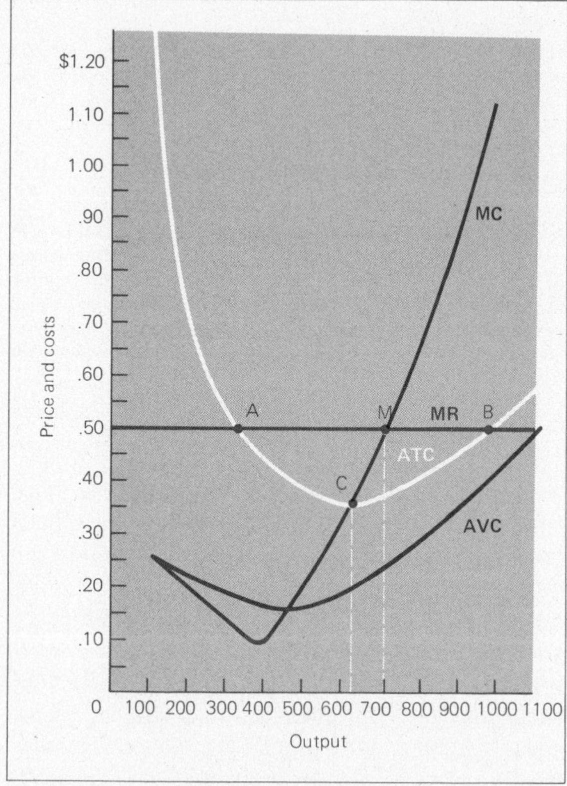

FIGURE 25-4 PROFIT MAXIMIZING These curves are drawn from the figures provided in Table 25-2. Points A and B are the break-even points, since average total cost is equal to marginal revenue (price). If average cost is equal to price, Farmer Euclid is neither making excess profits nor losing money. However, to go beyond point B or to fall short of A would entail losing money, since average cost would exceed price. Notice that all outputs between A and B are profitable, since price exceeds average cost. The most profitable output is *not* that of lowest average cost—that is, the cost that yields the highest profit per unit of output. It is more profitable to produce at point M than at point C. At point M, marginal cost and marginal revenue are equal, and profit is at a maximum. This is the output Farmer Euclid will select. Below that, producing one more unit of output will add more to revenue than to costs, and Euclid will keep expanding production to add to profits. Once the additional cost equals the additional revenue, there is no reason to expand output, since beyond that costs will be increasing faster than revenue.

produces to the right of point B, the farm's productive capabilities will be stretched to such an extent that inefficiency will push costs above revenue. Points A and B are the break-even points.

Farmer Euclid knows that if he produces somewhere between points A and B on the MR curve, he will be making some profit. But Farmer Euclid, remember, is eternally fated to strive after profit maximization. He must know at exactly what point his farm will be making the highest profit. How is he to find that point?

Farmer Euclid might reason that the point of highest profit must be the point of lowest average total cost, point C. He might, but he would soon realize his mistake. Farmer Euclid has periods when he is quite obtuse, but they are compensated for by times when he is correspondingly acute. During one of these moments he would undoubtedly discover that point C merely represents greatest *average* or per unit profit. Farmer Euclid wants to maximize *total* profits. Therefore, if by producing past the point of greatest average profit, he can increase the farm's total profit, Farmer Euclid will opt for that increase.

Now let us look at the marginal cost curve, which shows the cost of producing each additional unit. The MC curve intersects the MR curve at point M. Point M is still within the break-even area defined by points A and B, so we know that Farmer Euclid is still making a profit. We also know that if he produced one more unit of triangles, his total profit would diminish. This is because the cost of producing an additional unit past point M would be greater than the revenue received for that unit. Also, if Farmer Euclid produced one less unit of triangles, his total profit would decline, because the reduction in revenue would overbalance the reduction in cost. The point of greatest profit maximization, then, must be M, the point at which MR = MC.

The Firm's Short-Run Supply Curve With a market price of 50 cents per bushel of triangles, the point of greatest total profits lies, as we have seen, at point M. What would happen if the market price of triangles fell to 25 cents per bushel? We can determine this simply by drawing another horizontal line at the 25 cent level. The point at which this new marginal revenue curve (MR_3) intersects the marginal cost curve would represent the amount of triangles Farmer Euclid would be willing to supply at that market price. In fact, each point along the MC curve represents the units of triangles that Farmer Euclid would supply at a particular price. The MC curve, then, is the supply curve of the farm. It records the different amounts of his product that Farmer Euclid

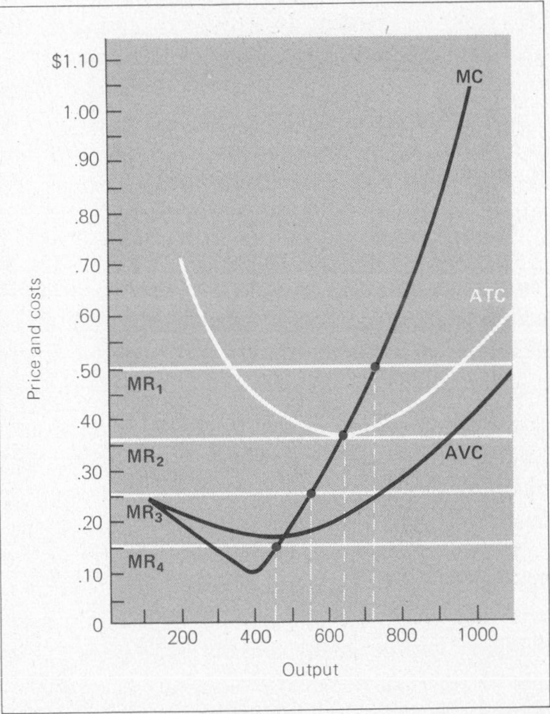

FIGURE 25-5 PRICE CHANGES AND OUTPUT OF FARMER EUCLID Since under perfect competition P = MR and the quantity a firm chooses to produce is determined by the intersection of the MR and MC curves, the MC curve shows the quantities supplied at any given price level and is therefore the supply curve for a perfectly competitive firm, above the shutdown point. The relationship between the MC = MR point and the ATC and AVC curves shows whether the firm will make a profit, incur a loss, or close down altogether. MR_1 will yield excess profits, since price exceeds average total cost. At MR_2, Farmer Euclid will break even, since P = MC = MR = ATC. At MR_3, he will lose money, but keep operating in the short run, since he is more than covering his variable costs. He will shut down operations if price falls below the lowest point on the AVC curve, such as at MR_4.

would be willing to supply at each and every price. But there are prices at which Farmer Euclid would rather shut down than offer any triangles for sale. Therefore, the MC curve above this shutdown point is the supply curve.

In a sense, profit maximization is merely the other side of the coin of loss minimization; faced with either a profit or a loss situation, an entrepreneur under perfect competition (or, indeed, in the real world) will react in a similar way. Let us see how. Suppose that the market price of triangles drops from 50 cents to 25 cents. With marginal revenue at 25 cents, the average total cost of producing the units is larger than the per unit price at which they can be sold (25 cents). This means that the business is losing money. "Drat!" mumbles Farmer Euclid and, to cool his anger, recites *pi* under his breath to 16 places. "This means I'll have to shut down the farm."

But Farmer Euclid is wrong, as he soon realizes. He hurries down to the lower forty to announce to his employees that he would like production cut down to a level at which the farm's MC curve intersects the new MR curve.

The reason behind Farmer Euclid's decision is this: This triangle farm, like any other business, has two different kinds of cost—fixed costs and variable costs. The ATC curve shows the average variable costs plus the average fixed costs. Fixed costs are those costs that would have to be paid no matter what the level of production. These include such things as rent, insurance, and the like. Farmer Euclid has perceived that while he is losing money selling triangles at 25 cents, he is not losing quite as much money as he would if he shut down. As shown in Figure 25-5, the MR curve at 25 cents is below the ATC curve, but above the AVC curve at some points. This means that at these points, while revenue is not covering total costs, it is more than covering variable costs. As long as total revenue is greater than total variable cost, it is more profitable, or rather less unprofitable, to keep the business running than to shut it down. For example, suppose that fixed costs for Farmer Euclid's triangle farm amount to $100, while variable costs are $150, giving us total cost of $250. Now suppose that the market price of triangles sinks to 25 cents (at this price, P = MR = MC at 800 bushels); at this level of output, average total costs are not being covered, and obviously the farm is operating at a $50 loss. However, if it shut down entirely, it would still incur fixed costs of more than this loss. Since revenue would then be zero, this would mean losing more by closing down. Therefore, Farmer Euclid keeps his losses down by producing fewer units of triangles. Only if the marginal revenue curve lies below the AVC curve at all levels of production will Farmer Euclid shut down the farm, for he will lose more by continuing to produce at any level than he will by simply paying fixed costs from his own pocket. Over this range of prices, his output will be zero. Therefore, only the region of the MC curve above its intersection with the AVC curve is the firm's supply curve.

Short-Run Equilibrium

Let us review the various levels of output at which a business may either maximize its profits or minimize its losses under perfect competition. Figure 25-5 shows various short-run situations. At a price of 50 cents, MR_1 is above the lowest point on the ATC curve. As in any position, the firm adjusts production so that MC = MR. Because at this point the firm receives more in revenue than it incurs in costs, we say that it is making an excess profit. Next, market price drops to a point exactly equal to the lowest average cost of production, shown as MR_2. Again output is adjusted so that MC = MR. Here P = MC = MR = ATC. At this point the firm is making a normal profit. If the market price drops to a point below the ATC curve but above the AVC curve, as shown by MR_3, the firm suffers a loss, but that loss can be minimized by producing at the level where MC = MR. If the market price descends lower than the lowest point on the AVC curve, however, the firm will have no choice but to shut down, since it will no longer be possible to minimize losses by continuing to produce. Each of these positions is known as an equilibrium position, since in each case the firm is either maximizing its profits or minimizing its losses. They are short-run equilibrium positions because the firm has no chance to change the fixed costs of production by altering its plant size.

In the short run, demand may change, but the supply schedule of an individual firm remains the same. In Figure 25-6A we see the result of this situation. Because of a government report praising the nutritive value of triangles, the market demand for them has increased. This is shown by the movement of the demand curve to the right, and the increase in the equilibrium price. The only response that an individual triangle grower can make to this situation is to increase variable inputs such as labor and raw materials. Fixed inputs remain unchangeable. The producer merely moves production to a higher level on the already existing marginal cost or supply curve, as in Figure 25-6B.

Figure 25-6B shows the profits enjoyed by Farmer Euclid's triangle farm during the triangle boom just mentioned. The equilibrium level, as always, falls at the point at which MC = MR. Notice that this point occurs far above the point of average total cost for this level of output. This means that at this level of production, Farmer Euclid will receive excess profits. Since all triangle farmers under perfect competition

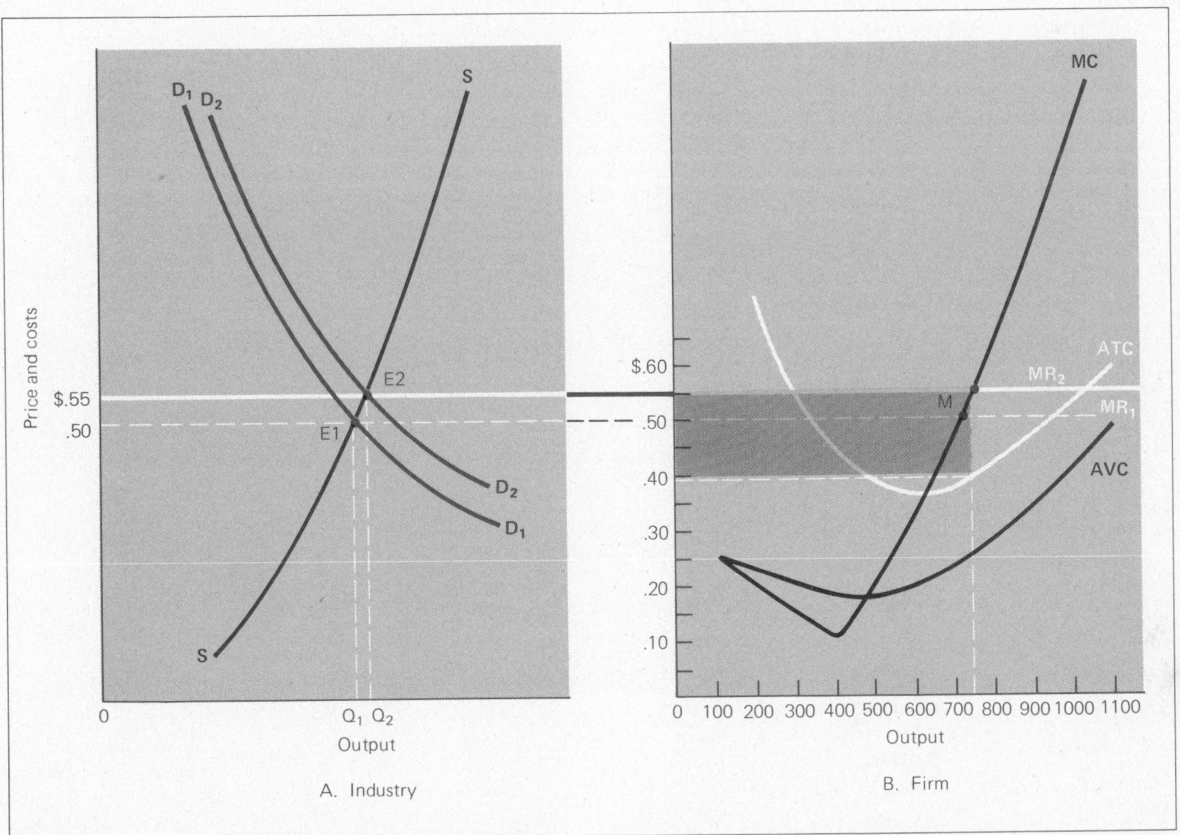

FIGURE 25-6 SHORT-RUN CHANGES WHEN DEMAND SHIFTS **When the market demand curve shifts up, this raises the equilibrium price for all firms, as shown in A. The individual firm, as in B, now receives a higher price, which furnishes greater excess profits, represented by the shaded rectangular area. Note that the excess profits are measured from the level of average total costs for that output rather than from the lowest point on the ATC curve. These excess profits are a short-run condition, since ultimately the industry will expand supply to bring prices down.**

must sell their product at the same price and because all of them face similar market conditions, they will enjoy excess profits simultaneously.

Long-Run Equilibrium

The farmers will not enjoy these excess profits for long, however. In the long run, the excess profits created by increased demand will disappear. The increased demand for triangles will induce some growers of hexagons, squares, and dodecahedrons to enter the triangle market. These additions to the triangle industry will result in a new market supply curve, to the right of the previous one, as in Figure 25-7A. This new curve establishes a new short-run equilibrium level.

The new supply curve gives a new equilibrium price, one lower than the previous value (in Figure 25-6). Price has fallen from 55 cents, while quantity has risen from Q_1 to Q_2. None of the farmers in the triangle market has any choice about whether to sell his product at the new price level. If Farmer Euclid is stubborn and attempts to sell at the older, higher level, his triangles will simply be passed over by consumers.

Figure 25-7B shows the profits that Farmer Euclid now enjoys in the expanded market. Expansion con-

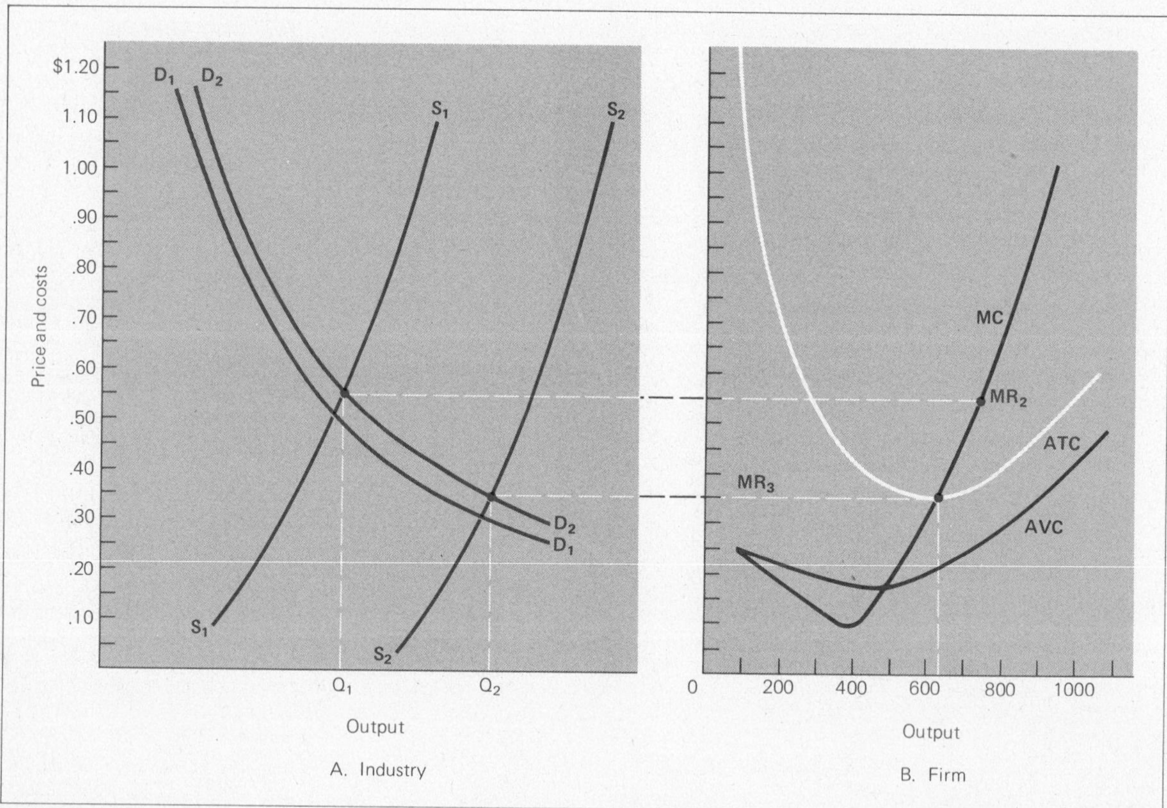

FIGURE 25-7 LONG-RUN EQUILIBRIUM UNDER PERFECT COMPETITION YIELDS NORMAL PROFIT An upward shift in the industry demand curve, from D_1D_1 to D_2D_2, in the short run raises the price to 55 cents. However, in the long run the high profits in the triangle industry attract an increasing number of farms, raising industry supply until it settles at S_2S_2. At that output, each farm makes no excess profits because price just covers average total cost. There is no incentive for new farms to enter the industry, since other industries earn the same normal profits.

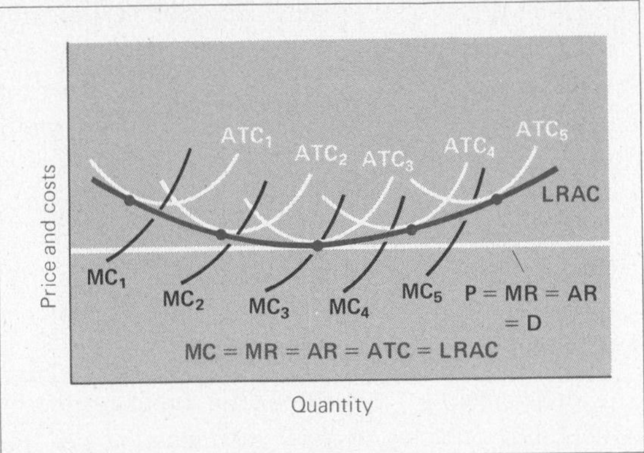

FIGURE 25-8 LONG-RUN EQUILIBRIUM FOR A FIRM UNDER PERFECT COMPETITION **Firms will strive to reach a plant size that will give them minimum average costs equivalent to those of ATC_3. Any other scale of operations will have a higher minimum cost and will incur losses earlier than the optimum size firm, forcing them to leave the industry.**

tinues as long as any excess profits exist. Farms keep entering the triangle industry until the long-run equilibrium is reached. Long-run equilibrium occurs when the price of triangles is exactly equal to the minimum average total cost of all triangle farms in the industry (P = MR = MC = ATC). At this point there are no longer any excess profits, and, hence, there is no incentive for industry expansion. Under perfect competition this new equilibrium will exist until there is a new shift in demand or supply.

When an entire industry is in a state of long-run equilibrium, only a shift in the market demand curve or a change in the costs of production can cause a change in price or in output of any firm. Thus, we can see that under perfect competition, the phenomena of both excess profits and loss exist only in the short run. When there are excess profits within a market, new firms will enter the industry until price drops to a point at which all excess profits are squeezed out. When price falls to the lowest point on the ATC curve, the market is at long-run equilibrium and will tend to stay there unless there is some change, either in demand or in the costs of production. If firms are suffering losses, some firms will drop out of the market entirely. This contraction of the market will cause a rise in price. The supply curve will shift to the left until, again, price is equal to the lowest point on the ATC curve. In this way, too, long-run equilibrium is established.

This pressure means that in the long run, only firms with optimum size plants will survive. Larger or smaller plants can survive only when excess profits are being made, since their costs are higher than costs of the optimum size firm. The long-run equilibrium price permits only normal profits, so that plants that are not of optimum size will be squeezed out in time. The remaining firms will be operating at a level of output where MC = MR = AR = ATC = LRAC, as shown in Figure 25-9. MC = MR means that the firm is in short-run equilibrium and is maximizing profits, since any increase in output will increase costs more than revenues and any decrease in output will decrease revenues more than costs. Because price equals marginal cost (P = MC), resources are devoted to producing the quantity consumers want and the firm is allocatively efficient. Since price is also average revenue, ATC = AR means that price exactly covers unit costs, so that although there are no excess profits to attract new firms, normal profits provide incentive for firms to remain in the industry. MC = ATC indicates

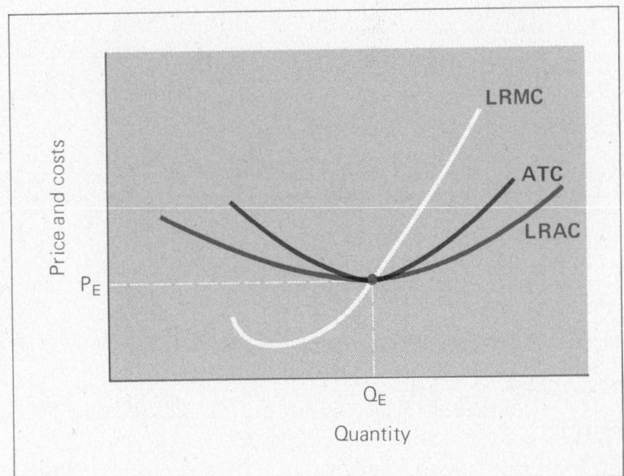

FIGURE 25-9 LONG-RUN INDUSTRY EQUILIBRIUM UNDER PERFECT COMPETITION **In the long run the industry will be operating at a normal profit. Long-run marginal costs will equal both minimum average total costs and minimum long-run average costs, so that the firm is technologically efficient in its use of its plant and in its choice of plant size.**

that the firm is operating at the lowest point on the ATC curve and is technologically efficient in the short run. MC = ATC = LRAC indicates that the firm is using the optimal plant size and is therefore technologically efficient in the long run.

The Long-Run Industry Supply Curve The long-run tendency of price to settle at a level that provides normal profits does not mean that the long-run price is forever constant. This would be the case if resource prices remained unchanged as the industry expanded. This process is shown in Figure 25-10A. Demand increased from D_1 to D_2, temporarily raising prices and creating excess profits as the equilibrium rested at E_2. But other firms saw the excess profits and entered the industry, shifting supply from S_1 to S_2. Because resource prices remain constant, the equilibrium price returns to the original level, even though the industry is much larger than before. This is known as a **constant-cost industry.**

But increased competition for resources often does raise their prices. Once the industry starts expanding, more firms are bidding for the same resources, and the price of the resources goes up. This raises the costs of production, shifting the ATC curve upward. This partially offsets the competitive effects of having more firms in the industry, so that while price declines from E_2, it does not return to its original level because excess profits disappear earlier than before. The long-run supply curve, then, slopes upward in an **increasing-cost industry.**

The long-run supply curve does not directly show the effects of economies or diseconomies of scale. This appears on the long-run average cost curve. The long-run supply curve shows the shifting of the industry LRAC as more firms enter and costs change.

IS PERFECT COMPETITION "PERFECT"?

The model of perfect competition, as we have been emphasizing, is a picture neither of how things actually are nor of how they ought to be. Neverthe-

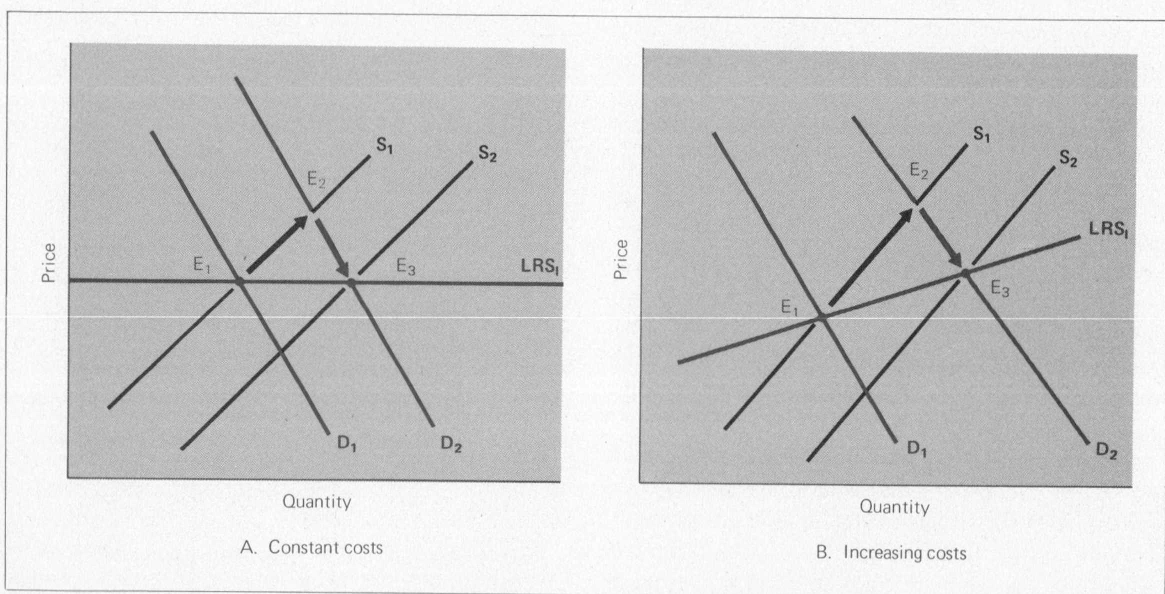

FIGURE 25-10 LONG-RUN INDUSTRY SUPPLY CURVE The long-run industry supply curve shows the effects of resource prices as the industry expands. A constant-cost industry, as in A, has a perfectly elastic long-run supply curve. An increasing-cost industry, as in B, has a long-run supply curve that slopes upward.

less, the model, as it has evolved through the work of economists from Adam Smith to the general equilibrium theorists of today, has had a considerable influence, not only on economic theory, but on political ideology as well. The line between a purely analytical tool and a pattern of perfection is, unfortunately in this case, disturbingly indistinct. Often the model of perfect competition, despite all disclaimers, has been used as an ideal, or at least a source of justification for certain practices of the capitalist economy. Theorists like Milton Friedman see capitalism as at least a pale reflection of the efficiencies of perfect competition and bridle at attempts to impose regulations.

Positive Aspects

Technological Efficiency Perfect competition does encourage technological efficiency. Since, in the long run the price of a good must be equal to the minimum average cost of production, all firms in an industry must strive to produce that good as efficiently, and therefore as cheaply, as possible. Otherwise they will lose profits. The search for efficiency will involve careful planning to choose the optimum plant size for the level of production that the firm expects to achieve in the long run. The resources from less profitable plants may be readily shifted away into more productive uses, making for greater output and a better chance for full employment of all resources.

In a competitive market firms will avoid expenditures such as costly advertising campaigns. All resources will be devoted strictly to production. This is favorable to consumers, since it offers them a better chance to buy goods at the lowest possible price.

Allocative Efficiency This search for the most profitable enterprise means that consumers will be able to obtain the goods they want, since firms will shift resources out of unprofitable industries into more profitable ones, where demand is higher. Examination of the marginal cost concept can give a clearer picture of allocative efficiency. If, for example, the price that society is willing to pay for a certain product is greater than the marginal cost of producing another unit of that product, society is in fact saying that more resources should be applied to the output of that product rather than to making another product that uses similar resources.

Consequently, as we have seen, there is a tendency in such cases for producers to maximize consumer satisfaction and their profit by planning output at levels where price equals marginal cost. Where marginal cost exceeds price, it is clear that resources are being overallocated to that product. Society will not pay the price and is, in effect, voting for a shift of productive resources to another product. Thus, in the 1960s, a greater emphasis by consumers on convenience in clothes care shifted demand in yarns and basic fabrics toward synthetic fibers and drip-dry materials, which gradually rose in price relative to comparable natural fiber items. (Of course, since this is the real world, the range of actual final product prices of wearing apparel items was also influenced by factors that would not exist under perfect competition, such as product differentiation in style, color, workmanship, and the effects of advertising in stimulating preference for certain labels and designer names.)

Political Consequences Under perfect competition there would be no ITT lobbyists cozying up to the Justice Department because there would be no ITT. All firms would be too small, not only to fix market price but to "fix" anything. Economic power would be dispersed, rather than concentrated as it is today in firms whose budgets are often larger than those of most states and all but a few nations. And the power over lives exercised by giant firms that shuffle people about in time to bureaucratic rhythms would be reduced.

Negative Aspects

According to the defenders of perfect competition, the consumer is king. His willingness or unwillingness to pay the price for a good has a direct effect in regulating how much of that good will be produced and how much will be charged for it. But does the

O BRAVE NEW WORLD!

A truly competitive world would bring many changes. A supermarket stocking the output of perfectly competitive firms would look very different from today's wonderamas, for example. There would be little reason to increase costs by packaging goods in supergraphic cartons with cuddly babies or tempting dishes on them, since the same product would be identical, no matter who the producer was.

Nor would there be that profusion of unproducts—the zillions of breakfast cereals or the "new" version of the old detergent. The fake additives—and the dangerous ones—would impose unnecessary costs, and a fully informed buying public would ignore them. The consumer would no longer need the FTC, the FDA, or even Ralph Nader.

Wherever perfect information came from, it would probably not be from TV, radio, magazines, and newspapers as we know them today. These now survive on revenues from advertising. Under perfect competition these revenues would dry up because advertising would represent unnecessary expense for the firm. So the entertaining commercials that enliven the great wasteland would jingle in some historical archive instead of between segments of the Johnny Carson show.

Genuine innovation might disappear as well, along with the colorful cartons, the unproducts, and the advertising campaign. Because the excess profits gained from an invention would soon disappear as other firms immediately took advantage of the innovation, firms would have little incentive to innovate. Moreover, since firms could sell their entire output at the existing market price, there would be little incentive to develop a new product or a cost-cutting method of production. So fewer new products and processes would appear than under the present system. This is a major drawback indeed to perfect competition.

1984

consumer really have the power that is attributed to him?

Many of the areas in which competition fails to ensure consumer sovereignty have already been treated at length in earlier chapters, so we need only list them briefly.

1 – Externalities. Allocative efficiency, as represented by the P = MC principle, is effective only if MC includes all costs, social as well as private. As Chapter 21 showed, the minute a firm flushes unprocessed wastes into a river, the gap between the two costs opens. As we saw at the conclusion of Chapter 24, competitive pressures may make firms less socially responsible because they will not survive if they assume costs that could be externalized.

2 – Social starvation. Perfect competition seems very efficient at providing private goods, but less so in providing public goods, such as adequate fire protection or equal educational opportunities. The relationship between the public and private sectors is treated at greater length in sections of Chapters 3 and 29.

3 – Poverty. Unequal income distribution based on unequal control of productive resources means that some people have very few of their wants met. This consequence of the connection between private property and income distribution is the core of the radical critique of capitalism to be covered in Chapter 36.

For the individual business firm perfect competition may be even less palatable. What seems orderly and balanced in the perfect competition model may, when translated into reality, become rather terrible. After all, when we speak of firms having free exit from the market, what we actually mean is that they have permission to go bankrupt. This instability is just the problem encountered in agriculture. The next chapter takes up this problem in greater detail.

SUMMARY

1 A market that is perfectly competitive contains a large number of small firms producing identical products. Each has perfect knowledge of the market, resources move freely, and because there are so many firms, none of them can have any effect on the price of the items they sell. Because an individual firm can sell as much as it wishes at the market price, its demand curve is perfectly elastic – a straight, horizontal line at the market price.

2 The market demand curve is downward-sloping, since consumers will buy more only if the price is lowered. The point at which the market demand curve and the market supply curve intersect will determine the price.

3 Since the firm cannot set price, it can maximize profits only by selecting the proper level of output. The level of profit maximization is that quantity at which total revenue exceeds total cost by the greatest amount. Total cost is determined by adding the firm's total fixed costs and total variable costs. Total revenue is determined by multiplying the price of a single unit by the number of units sold. Another way of finding the level of greatest total profit is by choosing the level of production at which marginal cost and marginal revenue are equal. Below that level, MC $<$ MR, so the firm can add to profits by increasing output. Above that level, MC $>$ MR, so the firm is adding more costs than revenues.

4 The MR curve is the demand curve for the individual firm. The MC curve above its intersection with the AVC curve is the supply curve for the individual firm.

5 In the short run the firm will continue operations as long as it can cover at least its average variable costs. It is possible, then, for the firm to operate in the short run, even though it is doing so at a loss. The short-run equilibrium will show the firm maximizing profits (including zero economic profits) or minimizing losses.

6 In the long run there will be only normal profits (P = MR = ATC). If there were excess profits in the short run, the entry of new firms would bring down the price, squeezing out profits. If firms were sustaining losses, some would leave the industry (in the long run), thus reducing industry supply and raising market price so that those firms remaining make normal profits. All firms would operate plants that afford them optimal capacity (LRMC = LRAC).

7 Depending on the cost of resources used the industry might be one of constant or increasing long-run costs. A constant-cost industry will supply a varying range of output at approximately the same price, because its resource costs neither rise nor fall over this range. Increasing-cost industries charge increasing prices as output rises, to reflect the increasing resource costs as output expands.

8 Perfect competition ensures technological efficiency because firms will operate at the lowest point on both the short-run and long-run average cost curve (P = MR = MC = ATC = LRAC). It ensures allocative efficiency because price reflects the value that consumers place on the product (P = AR = MR = MC). It also prevents concentrations of power. This can be accomplished only if there are no public goods and no externalities. Perfect competition, moreover, does not ensure equitable income distribution or stability for the individual firm.

SUGGESTED READINGS

Dooley, Peter C. *Elementary Price Theory.* Chap. 4. New York: Appleton-Century-Crofts, 1967.

Dorfman, Robert. *Prices and Markets.* Englewood Cliffs, N.J.: Prentice-Hall, 1967.

Friedman, Milton. *Capitalism and Freedom.* Chicago: University of Chicago Press, 1962.

Haveman, Robert H., and **Kenyon A. Knopf.** *The Market System.* Chap. 5. New York: John Wiley & Sons, 1966.

Stigler, George. *The Theory of Price.* 3rd ed. New York: Macmillan, 1966.

QUESTIONS

1 Review
   a. assumptions for the perfect competition model,
   b. conditions for maximizing short-run profits or minimizing short-run losses,
   c. the supply curve for the individual firm,
   d. long-run equilibrium for the industry and the long-run industry supply curve,
   e. advantages and problems associated with perfect competition.

2 During the price freeze in the summer of 1973, the prices of processed meat

were frozen. Unbutchered meat, however, was exempt from the freeze and prices began to rise. As a result, many meat packers shut down their operations. Describe the conditions that must have prevailed in these companies.

3 Why would such industries as automobiles, chlorine bleach, frozen foods, and steel not fit into the model of perfect competition?

4 Since agriculture is relatively close to the model of perfect competition, how could you argue that allocative and technical efficiency in food production would be high? How would you evaluate the market's capability of handling the use of pesticides by individual producers?

5 The U.S. government's antitrust policy, while aimed at protecting the public from excesses and inefficiencies associated with monopolies, does not aim at producing conditions of perfect competition. Why might this be the case?

6 **Annual Costs of Production of Confidential Recording Company, Inc.**

Output	Total cost	Average total cost
1000	$2000	$2.00
2000	3800	1.90
3000	5400	1.80
4000	7000	1.75
5000	9000	1.80
6000	11,400	1.90
7000	14,700	2.10
8000	18,800	2.35

Assume that in the long run all the firms in this competitive industry have a cost structure identical to that of the Confidential Recording Company.

a. What will be the long-run equilibrium price in the industry?
b. What will be the long-run average cost?
c. What will be each firm's annual output?
d. Suppose that the total market demand for confidential recordings is unit elastic and that $35 million is spent annually on this product, whatever the price. How many firms will there be in this perfectly competitive industry?

7 The largest number of business failures in the United States is among small proprietorships. From what you know about the conditions of perfect competition, why might this be so?

8 On a Saturday afternoon you may elect to go to the flea market and you may find that the same item is offered for sale by several owners at widely varying prices. Why might this occur? Would the flea market fit into the model of perfect competition in this case? Why or why not?

9 Those people who have control of a fair amount of capital may wish to weather a short-term loss. In fact, such an entrepreneur may expect to recover those losses some time in the future. How could he support such an expectation?

10 Assume that an economy is characterized by perfect competition in all industries. In one of the industries, costs begin to rise while the price for the final

product remains constant. What conclusions can you draw about consumer preferences in this economy?

11 The following graph depicts the average cost and marginal cost curves of the perfect competitor, in the long run. Draw in his demand and marginal revenue curves and determine his output and price.

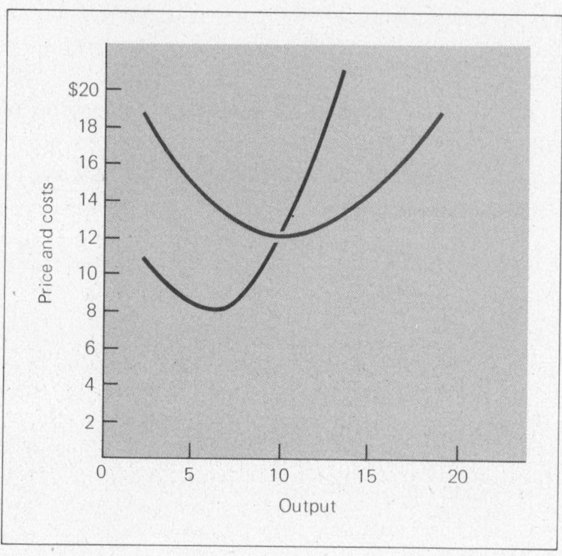

AGRICULTURE

Agriculture is an example of perfect competition, and an example of why the "perfect" in perfect competition is only a technical term, not a description of what life is like under those circumstances. Like the imaginary Farmer Euclid, a real farmer sells a uniform product in a market so large that his bit of wheat or hogs or whatever can never affect market price. But the rigors of this world have been so far from perfect, in a qualitative sense, that vast amounts of government aid—direct and indirect—have been poured into this industry, and accounted for one-fifth of all farm income by the late 1960s.

The irony of the American farm problem is that it results in part from overabundance. Growing capital stock and technological innovations, from tractors to high-yield strains of wheat, have kept agricultural output growing at about 2 percent annually for the last 40 years. A century ago, each farmworker produced enough food to feed himself and four people. Today that same worker puts food on the tables of about 50 people.

This success has been slow to show up in farm incomes. Since the turn of the century per capita farm income has been about half that of urban incomes. This figure underestimates the value of the homegrown produce and the intangible satisfactions of farm life, but even so, farming has been a depressed industry for many years. This disparity of incomes has been narrowing since the late sixties, but this may or may not be a permanent trend.

The gradual rise in per capita farm income is partially a result of the decline in farm population. One-third of the U.S. population lived on farms before World War I. Today less than 5 percent are still on the old homestead. A more rapid movement from the land occurred in the fifties and sixties (contributing to many of the urban problems encountered in Chapter 20).

As the farm population shrank, so too did the number of farms. During the 1950s the number of farms fell by about 4 percent a year; during the late sixties the decrease had slowed to 1.6 percent. And as the number of farms has declined, their average size has nearly doubled—from 213 acres in 1950 to almost 400 acres in 1972. The farms that were disappearing were the smaller, more marginal ones whose operations could not withstand the rapid increases in costs sustained since 1950. Figure 26-1 shows how the prices farmers pay have outstripped the prices their products can command. Although such a condition has driven over 3,500,000 off the land since World War II, even today there are over 500,000 farms that bring in a net income of less than $2500 a year. In the first section of the chapter we examine the economics behind the traditional farm problem of persistent poverty side by side with increasing abundance.

The future may hold new problems. The sharpest pangs from shifting agricultural labor to other sectors may be over, as evidenced by the closing gap between urban and rural incomes in the late sixties and the slowing rate of decline in the number of farms. What may lie ahead are problems of shortages, not surpluses. The concern is threefold. First, the gains in output are based on technological innovation, such as the widespread use of fertilizers. The law of diminishing returns makes applications of fertilizer or any other input useful only up to a point. When that point is reached, further gains in productivity from that source are impossible, and only other innovations can keep output rising. Second, more pessimistic ecologists believe that even the initial gains may be temporary, since practices such as one-crop farming and the heavy use of fertilizers and insecticides, which may provide fast increases in output in the short run, may in the long run upset the balance of nature and affect the generative powers of the earth. Third, the number of mouths to be fed is increasing, both at home and abroad. In the second section of the chapter we consider the possibility of this new type of farm—or rather food—problem.

THE TRADITIONAL FARM PROBLEM

Unstable and low incomes are the crux of the farm problem. In the short run, the conditions facing today's farmer make his income unstable. In the long run, these conditions also limit his income. Over

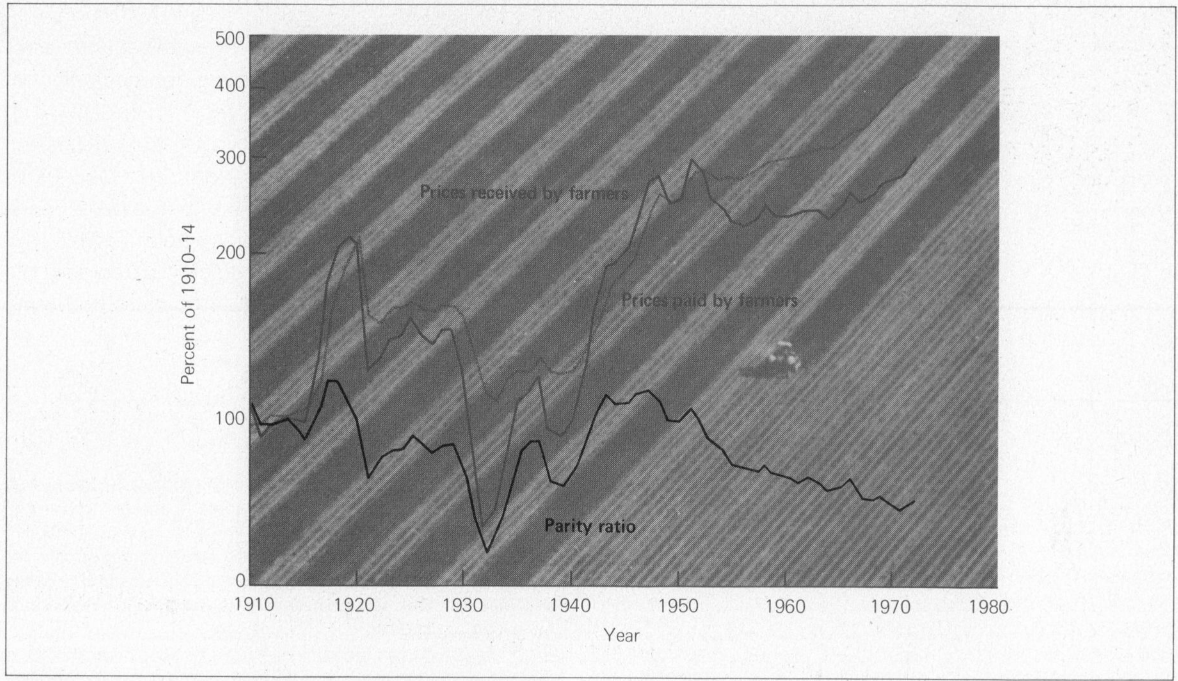

FIGURE 26-1 THE COST SQUEEZE The prices that farmers receive for their goods have not risen as rapidly as the prices they have to pay for other goods. Moreover, price declines of farm goods have been greater during depressions than declines of other prices. These problems have made agriculture a depressed industry for at least half a century.

Photo by Georg Gerster, Rapho Guillumette

SOURCE: U.S. Department of Agriculture.

half of all farms in 1971 brought in less than $5000, and many farmers were forced to supplement their earnings with nonfarm jobs.

The Short Run

Total farm income has fluctuated more widely than nonfarm income, despite the fact that total farm output has been more stable than industrial output. A primary reason for this curious predicament is the variability of farm prices.

Price Elasticity The greater fluctuations in income can be explained by the price inelasticity of supply and demand for agricultural products. Although a farmer may switch from crop to crop as prices change, this switch takes time. Fixed costs are such a large percentage of the farmer's total costs that the farmer is likely to harvest and sell his crops over a wide range of prices. Agricultural supply, then, is relatively price-inelastic.

Consumers, too, respond relatively little to price changes. Regardless of how low the price of corn drops, any one consumer can stomach just so many ears of corn. Similarly, regardless of how high food prices rise, there is a certain minimum level that everyone is going to buy. What this means is that a small change in quantity supplied (or demanded) means a large change in price, and in farm revenues. The Russian wheat deal of 1972 increased demand, and prices went up appreciably.

Dynamic Elements The short-run inelasticity of supply does not mean that farmers never cut back output in response to price. Certain products such as hogs and cattle exhibit regular cycles, geared

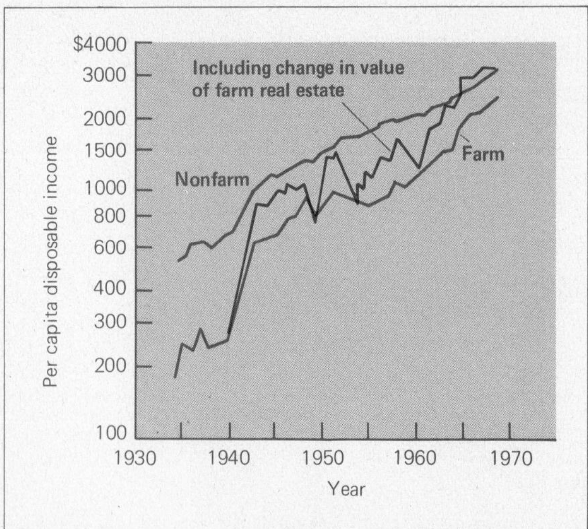

FIGURE 26-2 LOW FARM INCOMES Per capita farm disposable income has been lower and more unstable than nonfarm income. Farm incomes have been rising faster, but the gap has not been closed.

SOURCE: U.S. Department of Agriculture

to feed grain prices as well as market prices for the animals. The reasons for this behavior can be explained only if we examine the dynamic elements of market adjustment through the **cobweb theorem.**

Up to now, the explanation of equilibrium presumed that immediate adjustments to market conditions were always possible. However, the price level upon which a hog farmer made his output decisions may no longer apply when it is time for him to take his pigs to market. Referring to Figure 26-4A, suppose that output fell to Q_1, raising price to P_1. To take advantage of this price, farmers would grow enough hogs to supply Q_2, but at that output the price will fall to P_2. Quantity chases price, forming a pattern that resembles a cobweb, hence the name of this theorem. Depending upon the elasticities of the curves, the differences in price over time could diminish, grow increasingly larger, or continue to oscillate in a regular pattern. Of course, farmers may eventually catch on to the pattern, but the potential for instability is inherent in the structure of the agricultural industry.

The Long Run

Ever since the 1920s America has had a farm problem. The early years of this century, particularly from 1910 to 1914, were the golden years for the American farmer. Then, rising prices for agricultural goods enabled farmers to pay off their debts on expensive equipment they had purchased in previous years. World War I continued this prosperous era by adding large foreign demand to domestic demand. But the depression came early to agriculture and hung on longer there.

FIGURE 26-3 INELASTIC SUPPLY AND DEMAND: INCREASE IN SUPPLY A bumper crop can actually bring a decline in farm income. An increase in supply (from SS to S_1S_1) leads to a large decline in price, because both demand and supply are inelastic. These lower prices cause a decline in total revenue and income. This situation describes most of the markets in American agriculture.

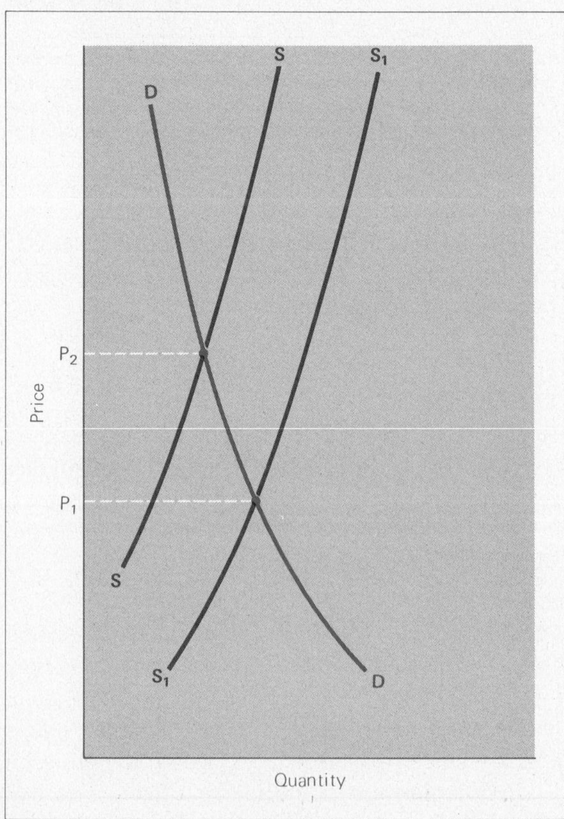

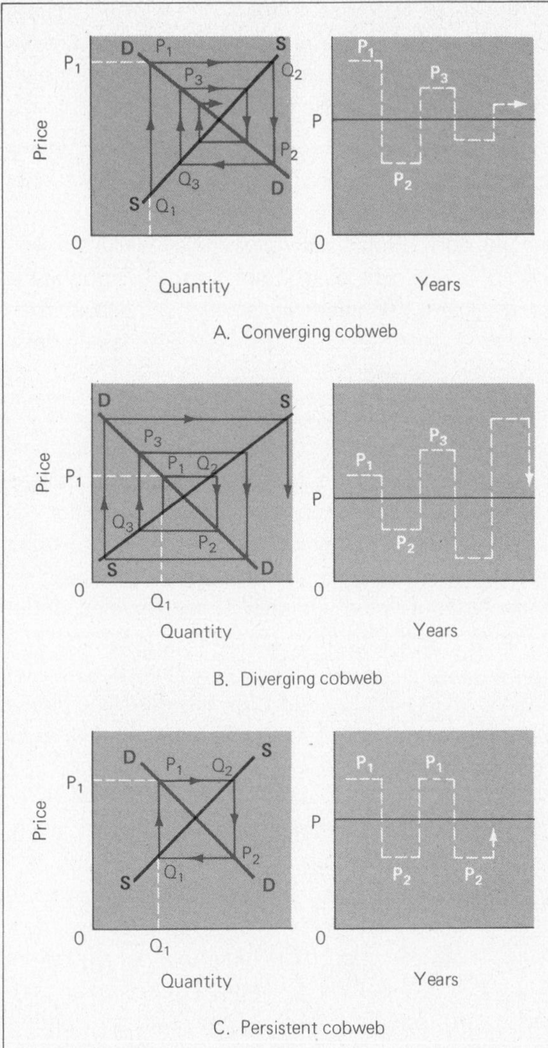

FIGURE 26-4 COBWEB THEOREM The mad chase of supply and demand may take different patterns, depending on the elasticities of supply and demand. If demand is more elastic than supply (as in A), then the changes in price will progressively diminish, though it may take many seasons before equilibrium is reached again. Graphically, this process can be charted like a *converging* cobweb spun around the supply and demand curves.

In B, supply is more elastic than demand, and the result is a *diverging* cobweb, with the swings between supply and demand growing ever more distant.

When the elasticity of supply equals that of demand (as in C), the oscillations, once started, will continue in the same pattern until some outside factor shifts them to a different box. We call this a *persistent* cobweb.

The problem has been that supply has grown faster than demand. For the last half century, productivity has grown at 2 percent annually but demand has increased at only 1.3 percent. The rise in demand has been due primarily to increases in domestic population rather than to increases in exports or to greater consumption at home. Unlike many products, for which demand increases as incomes rise, agricultural products are relatively insensitive to increases in income. Demand, then, is income-inelastic as well as price-inelastic.

The increases in supply have been due to rapid technological changes. Vast sums have been invested in agricultural research (mainly by the government), yielding techniques that increase farm output. The market structure is highly conducive to the adoption of this new technology; because the typical farmer cannot influence the price of his product, he is always on the lookout for ways of cutting costs. If only a few farmers took advantage of a certain new technique, they would not affect total output appreciably, price would not be driven down, and reduced costs would result in higher profits. However, since many farmers are using new techniques, prices fall with rising output, squeezing out any increased profits that would have gone to an individual innovator.

The result has been surpluses, low farm income, and excess capacity. In theory, these should be temporary conditions. If food is being overproduced, surpluses will be eliminated by falling prices. Similarly, food shortages will cause prices to rise, stimulating more production. This solution might work well for the consumer, but it creates another problem for the farmer—that of maintaining adequate levels of income by eliminating excess capacity.

In a perfectly competitive market, you will recall, price equals average cost. This means that price just covers all the costs of an operation, including the normal profit that rewards the entrepreneur for using resources for this purpose rather than for another enterprise. As prices fall, the less efficient producers will be squeezed out of the industry and resources will be shifted to other sectors whose profits are more attractive. This has happened to some extent in agriculture, but there still remains a substantial group of marginal farmers. The industry is moving toward an equilibrium, but the problem is compounded by a continually changing equilibrium level as productivity continues to rise.

The Situation Today

Agribusiness Because there are economies of scale in agriculture, larger farms will be more profitable. However, the capital required for a good-sized farm is prohibitive for the average farmer. According to a recent *Fortune* article,[1] the ideal one-man soybean operation in Indiana requires an investment of $610,000 in land and machinery. A wheat farm in Kansas and a cotton farm in Mississippi require investments of $255,000 and $335,000, respectively. The rapidly escalating costs of farming, especially the increasing amounts of machinery necessary to take advantage of economies of scale, have made for more and more concentration. The alliance of the large commercial farms, the feed grain dealers, and the giant marketing corporations such as Ralston-Purina, General Mills, and Cargill, Inc., has formed the agribusiness complex. These farms today constitute a small but powerful segment of the industry.

Viable Family Farms The nature of farming has been changing steadily for the last century and a half, but that change has accelerated drastically since World War II. The farmer depends on nonfarm suppliers for seed, fertilizer, pesticides, power, and equipment. Often he buys not only materials, but the machinery and manpower to apply them. Instead of spreading fertilizer himself, he hires the local farm supply cooperative to apply liquid fertilizer with machinery he could not himself afford to own.

The trend to larger, more heavily capitalized farms would probably be speeded even more were financial capital more readily available. (As it is, farm debt has increased to 5½ times the 1950 level.) But lending policies ration funds, and particularly hard hit are small businesses like farms with fluctuating annual income and limited equity. Consequently, many farmers who would expand or improve the efficiency of their operations cannot do so.

Although this may mean the elimination of the smaller family operation, it does not mean that giant corporate farms are the only viable form of commercial farm. Farms that involve half a million dollars in investment may seem large in agriculture, but they are still relatively small businesses when compared with other industries. The family farm cannot be counted out.

The elimination of inefficient farms may reprieve the consumer, who is hard-pressed by rising food prices. But if these farms are replaced by agribusinesses that demand returns on their capital equal to that of investments in other sectors, pressures on price may continue. The low profit margins accepted by family farms in return for other benefits such as independence hardly figure in corporate accounting. The trends in farm organization are, therefore, of interest to all of society, since they may affect the prices the general public pays at the supermarket or at the clothing store.

The Rural Poor Although the small farm is a dying institution, the transition to large-scale farming is a slow and often painful process. Many farmers remain on land that gives them only a subsistence living. There are about 17 million rural poor, of whom about 700,000 belong to migrant farmworker families. Low-production farms, poor land, and undercapitalization are the direct causes of most rural poverty. The migrant farmworkers are a special case, since they do not operate or rent their own farms, but follow the harvest. That most are Mexican-Americans and blacks has added the stigma of discrimination.

The rural poor remain so because they have little alternative. They usually live far from urban centers, where new nonfarm jobs are located. Furthermore, even if they heard about these jobs and could apply, they could not attain them because they tend to be poorly educated and untrained in the necessary technical skills.

1 Juan Cameron, "A Golden Chance to Get Uncle Sam Off the Farm," *Fortune*, July 1973.

Even with the relative immobility of farm labor there has been continuous flow of surplus rural labor from two sources: a relatively high rate of natural population increase (excess of births over deaths) and the displacement of farmworkers by new technological advances. The industrial sector cannot accommodate all of the labor surplus.

Since very little capital is required to become a low-production, low-income farmer, setting up a farm may seem preferable to migrating to the city. These farms are doomed from the start, however, because of inadequate resources—poor land, equipment, and livestock. Such farmers are underemployed because they produce only a small fraction of what they could if they were working on an adequate-sized, adequately capitalized farm.

Government Response

The government has tried to deal with the economic dislocations in the agricultural industry in several ways—by acting directly upon prices, by creating its own artificial demand, and by limiting supply. Direct federal outlays on farm subsidies have consumed over $5 billion annually. This infusion of aid has profoundly affected the structure of the industry.

Parity A mainstay of American farm policy has been to return agriculture to the prosperity of those happy years between 1910 and 1914. This policy is known as parity and is designed to maintain a constant relationship between farm prices and farm costs (or prices paid by farmers). This relationship is called the parity ratio, and anything below 100 means that, in a sense, farmers are worse off than in the base period, 1910–14. Figure 26-1 shows this ratio. Looked at another way, parity tries to keep farm and nonfarm prices in line so that a farm can count on a bushel of corn bringing in enough income to buy a given amount of goods and services.

Parity protects not only farm income but farm wealth as well. The higher the prices goods from the land bring, the greater the value of the land itself. Recall Ricardo's theory of rents. As prices rise, less productive land may be brought into use and rent on more productive land rises. Much of the investment of the farmer is tied up in his land, so that declining prices hurt his land values as well as his income. "Most of the subsidy programs are vested not in the farmer but in his land."[2]

The problems with parity stem from one encountered earlier in a more abstract form in Chapter 22. Parity is a price floor, and price floors create surpluses if they are higher than the equilibrium price. This, in turn, affects resource allocation and income dis-

2 "Who Benefits from Farm Subsidies?" *Brookings Bulletin* 8, no. 1:5.

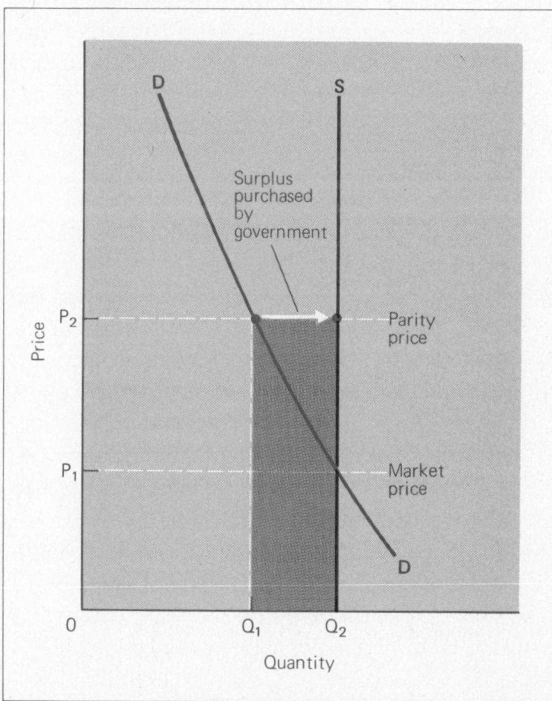

FIGURE 26-5 PRICE SUPPORTS The effect of price supports at parity or otherwise is generally to drive the price of the supported commodity upward. This happens when the price level desired by government lies above what would have otherwise been the market price. The usual manner of supporting the price is for the government to buy up exactly that amount of the commodity (surplus) that would otherwise have gone unsold in the market. In this hypothetical illustration, the government has raised the market price from P_1 to P_2 by purchasing the difference between Q_1 and Q_2. At the market price consumers would have bought Q_2, so the effect on the public is to reduce the amount it buys and to raise the prices it pays.

tribution. Consumers want less because they must pay more. One estimate put the costs of higher agricultural prices at $4.5 billion in 1969, a rather hefty hidden tax.

Suppliers, on the other hand, are encouraged to increase output and thus use resources that might otherwise be devoted to different commodities. The whole concept of parity ignores the larger economic picture. To say that a bushel of wheat should buy today what a bushel bought in another era is actually not keeping the farmer equal to his urban neighbors but redistributing income in a disguised form. Farm productivity has been growing faster than productivity in other sectors. An hour of farm labor produces many more bushels of wheat (or whatever) than before. The change is signaled by lower price. Parity keeps prices artificially high to support farm income, thereby interfering with the true economic parity between agricultural goods and other goods. And it calls forth more output than the equilibrium price would.

In its original form, parity had a particularly bad effect on resource allocation because only goods whose surpluses could be stored came under the programs. Thus, prices were high for wheat where demand was not growing rapidly, but they were low for other commodities like fruits and dairy products whose demand was actually growing faster than the supported commodities. This trapped resources in uses that were allocatively inefficient. Congress finally liberalized the parity formula to correct somewhat for this problem by figuring in price performance of the previous 10 years as well as price of the base year. Expanding the cost index and changing the weighting of the formula can also adjust for changes in the economic picture. But full parity will always create higher prices, resource misallocation, and surpluses, as long as agricultural productivity continues to grow more rapidly than productivity in the rest of the economy.

Purchasing Surpluses The price support program has been thinly disguised as a loan program for agricultural surpluses. As early as the Hoover administration, a Federal Farm Board was established with a $500 million fund to make loans to farm cooperatives that wanted to purchase and store surpluses until prices rose. During the Depression the government replaced the cooperatives through the Commodity Credit Corporation. In effect, the government lends farmers money on their excess output through what is called a nonrecourse loan. If the farmer can sell the output at a higher price, he does so and repays the loan. Otherwise, the government "forecloses" on the surplus and the farmer keeps the loan. The government will never ask for its money back because the terms of a nonrecourse loan bar this.

The government then has a surplus of farm commodities to deal with. During the 1950s and 1960s these surpluses filled granaries, warehouses, anchored ships, converted movie theaters, airplane hangars, and other storage areas. The cost of storage was enormous, sometimes running a million dollars a day.

Not all these surpluses were left to sit and rot, however. Although there has been spoilage and deliberate destruction of surpluses, the government has also sold and given away surpluses at home and abroad. In 1954, for example, Congress passed PL480, providing for the sale of agricultural commodities to developing countries for their own currencies rather than for dollars. Between 1954 and 1962, some $9 billion worth of surpluses moved abroad, but domestic storage bins still bulged. Foreign dumping, in which American surpluses were sold abroad at cut rates to compete with the produce of other agricultural nations, has been another way of reducing U.S. surpluses. The United States might have given away or dumped still more but was afraid of disrupting world markets as well as discouraging agricultural progress in the developing nations.

By 1973, the granaries were empty. Expanded foreign sales, particularly the Russian wheat deal, had eliminated U.S. surpluses, and Secretary of Agriculture Earl Butz was talking of bringing idled acreage back into production.

Production Cutbacks The idled acreage that Butz spoke of was taken out of production by federal

TABLE 26-1 Vanishing Surpluses (Bushels at start of harvest)

	1963	1969	1973 (est.)
Wheat	1.1 billion	163 million	30 million
Corn	810 million	295 million	0
Grain, sorghums	351 million	111 million	0

Except for a small carry-over held by grain dealers and farmers, the government is the holder of our grain surplus. As shown here, this surplus has disappeared during the last decade, largely because of rising foreign demand.

SOURCE: U.S. Department of Agriculture.

measures. Limits on production help curb the surpluses that price supports cause. Acreage allotments, marketing quotas, and the Soil Bank program were aimed at the supply side of the problem, unlike the parity/surplus loan program, which worked on demand and actually encouraged expanded output. To control this adverse side effect, farmers have to agree to limit acreage if they receive surplus loan aid. The government also pays direct subsidies by renting acres from farmers who earmark them for the Soil Bank. By early 1973, a total of 60 million acres had been removed from production by federal measures, but some 40 million were released for spring planting that year.

A catch to acreage restriction is that it limits land use, not output. Output may actually increase as the remaining acres are farmed more intensively. Between 1953 and 1960, the number of acres of wheat under cultivation was reduced by 30 percent, yet wheat production jumped 17 percent. In addition to the failure of acreage restriction to achieve its purpose, this program seems technologically inefficient because farmers use less land and more land substitutes than are actually required to minimize costs.

Acreage restriction is allocatively inefficient as well. Like price supports, production controls create higher prices for consumers. When farm surpluses disappear, as they did in 1972, the restrictions on output put the squeeze on rising food prices even more. All in all, production controls are an expensive way of tackling the problems of low and unstable farm incomes.

Income Supports A cheaper way to raise farm income is to make direct payments that close the income gap. If the market price is set by free-market forces at the equilibrium level, the consuming public is spared the expense of higher prices. The only expense is the direct payments the government makes to farmers between the market price and the parity level or some other target level of prices, as shown in Figure 26-6. Although these direct payments may involve larger government outlays, the total cost may be smaller because the hidden tax of higher output and restricted output has been eliminated. This program has the added advantage of

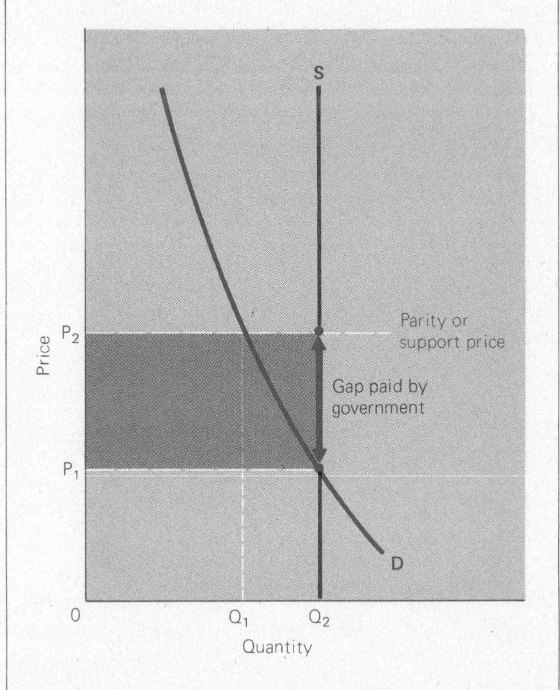

FIGURE 26-6 DIRECT INCOME SUPPORTS Under this plan, the government allows the price to settle at the level that will clear the market. Consumers get Q_2 rather than Q_1, as under price supports, and they pay only P_1. To support farm income, the government pays the difference between P_1 and P_2. The tax bill is higher under this program, but the total bill is lower, since consumers do not have to pay higher prices.

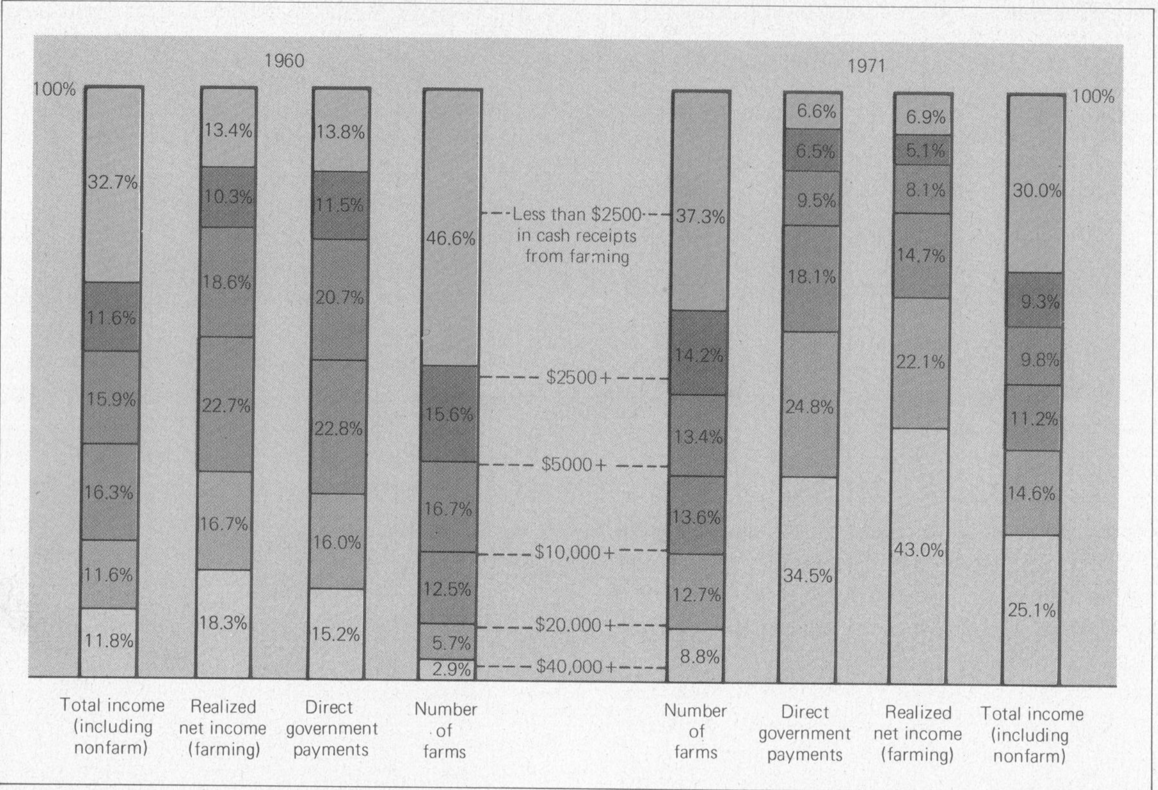

FIGURE 26-7 WHO RECEIVES GOVERNMENT AID? Since direct government aid to agriculture depends upon output, the larger farms receive more aid than the more marginal farms. The low-income farms depend upon nonfarm income to supplement their farm earnings. In the middle are the viable family farms. These farms receive crop-based supports but may need help with capital investment in order to stay competitive. Government aid, therefore, is in a form that does not help those most hurt by low and unstable incomes.

SOURCE: U.S. Department of Agriculture.

eliminating surpluses, since the market price falls to the level that will clear the market of all output.

Despite its economic logic, this program has had a stormier political career than its more expensive alternatives. It was a feature of the ill-fated Agricultural Adjustment Act of 1933, struck down as unconstitutional by the Supreme Court. In 1949 it was revived by Agriculture Secretary Charles F. Brannan, but met thundering opposition from the farm lobby and Congress. Its apparent expense makes it difficult to enact because taxpayers look only at the higher tax bill, not at the promise of lower prices, and the farm lobby prefers to keep its subsidies hidden. In recent years only cotton has been completely supported by direct income subsidies, while feed grain growers have received about half their subsidies in this manner. The expense of these programs has led to a search for more efficient and equitable farm programs.

Equity and Efficiency in Agriculture The U.S. farm program as it is presently structured represents a massive redistribution of income from the general public to the farmer. Despite extensive cutbacks in aid to agriculture under the Nixon administration, the fiscal 1974 budget still contained over $5 billion earmarked for agriculture. This represents only

THE 1973 FARM BILL

In August 1973, President Nixon signed into law a new four-year farm bill—the Agriculture and Consumer Protection Act of 1973—which is applicable to crop years 1974 to 1977. There have been claims that the bill is a giant step toward returning agriculture to the free market. It was anticipated that, in 1974, direct payments to farmers, which previously had been $5 billion annually, would be less than $1 billion and that acreage restriction on most major crops would be removed for the first time in many years.

Actually, the primary reason for these dramatic changes was not the new legislation but the tremendous increase in the demand for agricultural goods. The farm bill still provides for payments by the federal government if farm prices are too low as well as acreage restrictions if surpluses threaten to develop. But because the demand for farm products has risen so significantly, such measures may not have to be imposed to the extent they have been in the past.

Among the major provisions of the 1973 act is the establishment of "target prices" for cotton, wheat, corn, and some other feed grains for 1974 and 1975. If prices fall below the target prices, the government will pay the difference. For 1974, market prices were expected to be substantially higher than target prices, thus the apparent return to the free market. For 1976 and 1977, target prices will be adjusted to reflect increases in production costs (increases in factor costs adjusted for increases in per acre productivity).

The Secretary of Agriculture can impose acreage restrictions as a condition for receiving price subsidies. For the 1974 crop, it was neither necessary nor desirable to use this power for cotton, wheat, corn, or other feed grains. On all crops covered by target prices, except cotton, the Secretary can impose whatever acreage limitations he deems necessary. However, the bill states that this cannot be less than 11 million acres for cotton—a result of southern dominance of the House and Senate Agriculture Committees.

The 1973 farm bill also places a $20,000 a year limit on the total payments any one person can receive under the cotton, wheat, and feed grain programs. This should help reduce the percentage of benefits going to large farms.

Whether the bill means a reduced role for the federal government depends primarily upon supply and demand. If a worldwide food shortage develops and persists, prices will remain high. But if the United States and other countries are successful in substantially increasing their agricultural production, prices will fall, the government will begin making direct payments, surpluses will develop, and acreage restrictions will be reinstated.

part of the bill, however. Farm prices have been inflated as much as 15 percent by farm subsidies, at a cost of $4.5 billion to the consumer.[3] Nearly $10 billion a year has gone to agriculture in order to stabilize and raise income, and one-fifth of farm incomes in 1972 came from government supports.

The recipients of these subsidies are not the poorest farmers. All the main farm subsidies are closely linked to output, so the larger the output the greater the subsidy. In the United States about one-fifth of all farms accounts for three-fourths of the sales of farm products. This factor is reflected in the distribution of farm subsidies. In 1971 farms with cash receipts over $40,000 constituted only 8.8 percent of the number of farms but received 34.5 percent of direct government payments. Two-thirds of these payments went to farms with over $20,000 in cash receipts. The direct income program has proved such a windfall to large farms that Congress has limited to $20,000 the amount that any one person can receive.

At the other end of the scale are farms with cash receipts of under $2500. These constituted 37.3 percent of U.S. farmers in 1971, yet they received a scant 6.6 percent of the government outlays. Inequities seem to have worsened, since in 1960 these impoverished farms received twice the proportion of government aid as in 1971.

Of course, this inequity, by withholding aid from the less efficient farms, does help squeeze the excess rural population off the farm. Correcting the inequity by providing more aid to these marginal farms may actually retard chances for the solution of the farm problem unless this aid helps farmers cut costs and increase productivity to make their farms more viable. A better approach might be to focus aid on programs that would open a place in the more productive sectors of society for the black sharecropper, the Appalachian dirt farmer, and the rest of the marginal farmers. Right now some of these people, of necessity, supplement their incomes by working at extra jobs outside agriculture, and could be absorbed into the nonfarm work force. The separate problem of migrant labor is dealt with in a later chapter.

Can Farm Programs Be Eliminated? Even if average farm income were raised by easing the transition of marginal farmers out of agriculture, the return to a free-market condition could not be immediate. When one-fifth of all income in a sector issues from the government, the structure of that industry accommodates itself to that fact. The cost structure of many of the larger farms is based on this income, and discontinuing it abruptly would drive many potentially viable farms into bankruptcy. And removing price supports could pare $30 million to $50 million from the value of U.S. farmland—a drastic shift. Apart from the fact that such economic conditions give farmers a big incentive to fight for the continuation of government support, an immediate return to the free market is inadvisable because the disruptions caused by an abrupt halt of the programs would probably harm all of society.

Abolishing farm programs altogether may never be desirable, even if incomes can be raised. There would still be the problem of instability. Perhaps some form of income floor similar to unemployment compensation could buoy farm incomes during lean years from mandatory contributions made during the fat years. This would still not attack the sources of instability, however.

Because output decisions are based on past prices and future expectations, instability is inherent to agriculture. The hog cycle is an example of the swings that plague certain commodities. More stable prices could help farmers in their planning. This is the idea behind **forward prices.** The government (or even large processors) would announce well in advance its predictions of market conditions and would set a price expected to clear the market. Farmers could then sow crops or breed livestock based on this price. The price would not involve parity or any guarantee of fair return, but it would help in planning output.

Conclusion Reform of farm programs seems more possible today than ever before. Redistricting of

3 Charles L. Schultze, *The Distribution of Farm Subsidies: Who Gets the Benefits?* (Washington, D.C., Brookings Institution, 1971).

Congress and the urbanization of the United States has reduced the political power of the farm bloc. Rising food prices have made consumers impatient and receptive to alternatives that might give them some relief. The exposés of the Russian wheat deal and the continuing inequities that give large agricultural combines millions of dollars in subsidies have created a new political climate. And a new economic climate has also arisen as the agricultural problem appears to have shifted from one of excess supply to one of excess demand. The important thing now is to adopt structures that provide a transition to programs with a sounder economic footing.

FEAST OR FAMINE?

Traditional farm policy has been centered around the problems in dealing with surpluses. In the later part of this century agriculture may enter a new phase marked by conflicts between the short-run need to expand output rapidly through the use of advanced technology and long-run need to preserve the environment.

The need for more and more food and fiber is real and growing. Malnutrition is a constant presence for one-third of humanity, and population is growing most rapidly among that very segment, doubling every 25 years in some areas.

The Increasing Costs of Increasing Productivity

To expand output means to use more arable land or to improve productivity. In either case, costs are involved. According to the authors of *The Limits to Growth,* bringing arable land in unsettled areas under cultivation costs about $1150 per hectare (2½ acres)—beyond the means of many developing nations. The green revolution brings hope of improved productivity through better strains of plants, increased use of fertilizer, disease and pest control, increased irrigation, and tillage and harvesting equipment. But this also imposes costs.

> Each doubling of yield from the land will be more expensive than the last one. We might call this phenomenon the law of increasing costs. The best and most sobering example of that law comes from an assessment of the cost of past agricultural gains. To achieve a 34 percent increase in world food production from 1951 to 1966, agriculturalists increased yearly expenditures on tractors by 63 percent, annual investment in nitrate fertilizers by 146 percent, and annual use of pesticides by 300 percent. The next 34 percent increase will require even greater inputs of capital and resources.[4]

Even wealthy nations may not be able to afford the real costs of increased productivity, for ecological as well as financial consequences are already beginning to appear. Because land has been made more and more expensive by price supports, the United States has turned to developing land substitutes that make each acre more productive. The greater the productivity, the lower the per unit cost—to the farmer. To society, however, the cost may be much higher because these land substitutes, such as DDT or fertilizer, leave residuals that adversely affect other parts of the ecosystem.

Barry Commoner provides an example of how externalities occur because of residuals. Fertilizer has appreciably improved corn yields in Illinois in the course of two decades, from 50 to over 90 bushels per acre. But as the law of diminishing returns predicts, successively larger quantities of fertilizer have produced successively smaller gains in yields.

> Local farmers find that if they receive only about an 80 bushel per acre return from their corn crop, they just about meet expenses. To operate at a profit, yield per acre must be increased above that point, and under present conditions this can only be achieved by using fertilizer nitrogen at levels that are utilized very inefficiently by the crop.
>
> Farmers are not concerned by this inefficiency because the cost of fertilizer is very low. But, of course, the inefficient uptake of the last few pounds of nitrogen per acre means that a good deal of it must go somewhere else. The fate of this "lost" nitrogen was suggested by Illinois State Water Survey data which showed that between 1950 and 1965, when fertilizer nitrogen use increased fivefold, there was a significant increase in the nitrate levels of a number of the rivers that drain Illinois farmlands.[5]

4 Dennis Meadows et al., *The Limits to Growth* (New York: Universe Books, 1972), p. 53.

5 Barry Commoner, "Illinois Earth," in *The Closing Circle: Nature, Man, and Technology* (New York: Bantam Books, 1971), p. 82.

To say that food prices rose steeply during the first half of 1973 would drastically understate what took place. Before Nixon's mid-June price freeze went into effect, food prices had risen at an annual rate of 21.5 percent since the first of the year. Was this a precursor of shortages to come or a result of temporary conditions?

Rising food prices have traditionally been blamed on the middleman, who gets two-thirds of the average food dollar. This cow, for example, was an attempt by cattle growers to publicize their plight despite rising meat prices. However, between March 1972 and 1973 the total amount paid for food by the average consumer rose by $102, and the farmer received $86 of the increase.

On the supply side, there were several contributing factors. The fall and winter of 1972 were unusually wet, preventing full soybean and corn harvests. Snow and rain turned hog and cattle feed lots into quagmires, causing very slow weight gains and a very high rate of animal deaths. In addition, a shift in the Humboldt Current off the coast of Peru caused a sharp decline in the anchovy catch, a major source of animal fodder. This drove up feed grain prices even higher. Meanwhile, the government was still paying farmers to keep over 60 million acres idle, and the freeze on food prices during Phase III½ caused a cutback in supplies going to market.

Foreign demand was swelled by poor harvests in the USSR as well as in Argentina and Australia, both major grain exporters. The harvest failure in the USSR prompted the wheat deal that shipped one-quarter of the U.S. harvest to the Soviet Union. The price of wheat shot up from $1.49 in early July 1972, when the deal was disclosed, to $2.26 by mid-September 1972.

Most farmers were unable to profit from this increase because they had already sold their wheat to the large wheat dealers. The question was: Had the large dealers such as Continental Grain, Ralston-Purina, and Cargill received advance word of the huge Russian purchase? This suspicion was not allayed when several Department of Agriculture officials who had participated in the trade negotiations soon left the department to work for the firms that had profited.

Adding to the controversy was the low price the USSR had paid for the wheat—$1.65. This had been made possible through an export subsidy paid by the Department of Agriculture. (This subsidy had been paid since 1949 to keep U.S. agricultural exports competitive in the world market.) Apparently the U.S. might have driven a harder bargain with the Russians in view of their disastrous harvest.

United Press International

In a report to Congress in July 1973, the General Accounting Office noted that the export subsidies paid were excessive, and G.A.O. blamed the deal for much of the increase in U.S. food prices. By May 1973, wheat had reached \$3.00 a bushel and by August it had topped \$4.00, causing price rises not only in flour-based products, but also in beef, pork, poultry, eggs, and dairy products due to higher feed grain costs.

Nitrate itself is not poisonous but can be converted into nitrite by intestinal bacteria. Nitrites can reduce the oxygen-carrying capacity of the blood and may cause death in infants. Here is a cost that shows up long after and at a distance from the place where the benefits were reaped. This situation results from "the overvaluation of land and the undervaluation of the social costs of residuals from agricultural processes."[6] Making the price system reflect the full costs of production through measures such as those outlined in Chapter 21 can reduce the ecological damage. This may be unacceptable, however, if it retards efforts to meet the needs for increasing output more and more rapidly. Future farm policy will have to shift its single focus from raising farm incomes to include the interests of society at large.

6 Vernon W. Ruttan, "Technology and the Environment," *American Journal of Agricultural Economics*, 53:712.

SUMMARY

1 The traditional farm problem has been one of unstable and low incomes, resulting in a declining farm population.

2 Total farm income has been more unstable than total output because of price variations. Both demand and supply are relatively unresponsive to price changes; a small change in either one results in a large change in price. In addition, certain products such as hogs and cattle exhibit regular cycles. This is caused by the lags in response of output to price conditions and can be depicted by the cobweb theorem.

3 Over the long run, farm incomes have been consistently lower than nonfarm incomes. Rapid technological change has increased farm productivity at a rate faster than productivity in most other sectors. However, demand for agricultural products is relatively income-inelastic and has increased primarily because of population growth. Because supply has grown faster than demand, the industry has been plagued with surpluses, excess capacity, and low incomes.

4 In theory, these conditions should be temporary. Falling prices will eliminate surplus, but will cut farm revenues. Less efficient operators will not receive normal profits, and resources will be shifted to other sectors.

5 Government programs have retarded this shift. Parity programs, designed to keep farm and nonfarm prices equivalent to years when farming was a prosperous industry, provide supports to certain commodities. Because the formula ignores the relatively more rapid growth of farm productivity, it does not maintain true parity but is a disguised form of income redistribution to agriculture. It raises prices that consumers pay and encourages suppliers to produce surpluses. To cope with the surpluses created by price supports, the government buys excess output and encourages farmers not to produce. One other method of raising incomes has been direct income supports, which let the market determine the price and pay the farmer the difference between price and parity.

6 The results of farm aid have been large government outlays, higher prices for consumers, and the retention of resources in inefficient uses. Moreover, because these programs are linked to output, they have been of little benefit to the truly poor farmer. Agribusiness and viable family farms produce the greater proportion of output and receive most of the government aid. One-fifth of farm income now comes from the government, and land values are $30 to $50 billion higher than

if no price supports were given. An immediate return to free-market conditions would be disastrous and would still leave the problem of income instability.

7 In the future, scarcity rather than overabundance may be the problem. The need for increasing amounts of food and fiber will impose increasing monetary and social costs.

SUGGESTED READINGS

Bickel, Blaine W. "Revolutions in American Agriculture." *Federal Reserve Board of Kansas City, Monthly Review* (June 1972):3–9.

Cochrane, W. *City Man's Guide to the Farm Problem.* New York: McGraw-Hill, 1966.

Ruttan, Vernon W., Waldo D. Arley, and James P. Houck, eds. *Agricultural Policy in an Affluent Society.* New York: W. W. Norton, 1969.

Schultze, Charles L. *The Distribution of Farm Subsidies: Who Gets the Benefits?* Washington, D.C.: Brookings Institution, 1971.

Weiss, Leonard W. "Pure Competition and Agriculture." In *Case Studies in American Industry.* 2nd ed. New York: John Wiley & Sons, 1971.

QUESTIONS

1 Review
   a. the short-run problem of income instability caused by price inelasticities and lags in adjustment,
   b. the long-run problem of low incomes caused by income inelasticity and technological change,
   c. the effects of output restrictions, income supports, parity and surplus-loans upon the level of output, resource allocation, and incomes,
   d. the distribution of government aid and its effects on equity and efficiency,
   e. prospects for scarcity from increasing outlay and social costs.

2 The perfect competition model assumes that entrepreneurs will readily switch from manufacturing one product to manufacturing another if price changes warrant. Evaluate this assumption as it applies to farming in the United States and indicate how surpluses and low incomes may be perpetuated even in the relatively long run.

3 In the early summer of 1973, President Nixon imposed an export embargo on certain types of agricultural products. Why do you suppose the export restrictions were imposed? What might be some of the dangers in prolonging such restrictions?

4 Although larger farms are emerging on the American scene, some types of operations tend to remain on a relatively small scale. The dairy industry is one such example: Herds rarely number over 1000, a number capable of supplying only a small fraction of the market of an urban area. How would you describe the conditions in these areas by using long-run cost curves?

5 Dairy cows are frequently sold as meat animals when their milk production drops off or when they can no longer be used profitably as milk producers. The price

of meat rose rapidly along with the price of feed in early 1973. What would tend to happen in the dairy industry in the short run? In the long run?

6 Draw hypothetical demand and supply curves for agricultural products and discuss the effects on the curves of each of the following:
   a. parity price floors
   b. acreage quotas
   c. loan-purchase agreements with the government

7 In the face of rising food prices many consumers began to band together in cooperatives to take advantage of lower prices available by purchasing in bulk. According to arrangements of many of these cooperatives, members donate their time and skill in performing the functions normally performed by the supermarket. Could it be argued that the cooperatives' members are not actually getting more for less? Under what conditions?

8 In arid areas of California, Israel, and Hawaii, water sources have been used successfully to convert desert lands into high-producing food lands. What are the prospects for projects of this type in, say, the American Southwest if food prices continue to rise? How high would prices have to rise?

9 What are the consequences of free international trade when, for example, the Japanese are willing to pay $7 and up per pound for American beef?

Opening photo by J. Paul Kirouac

CHAPTER 27 MONOPOLY

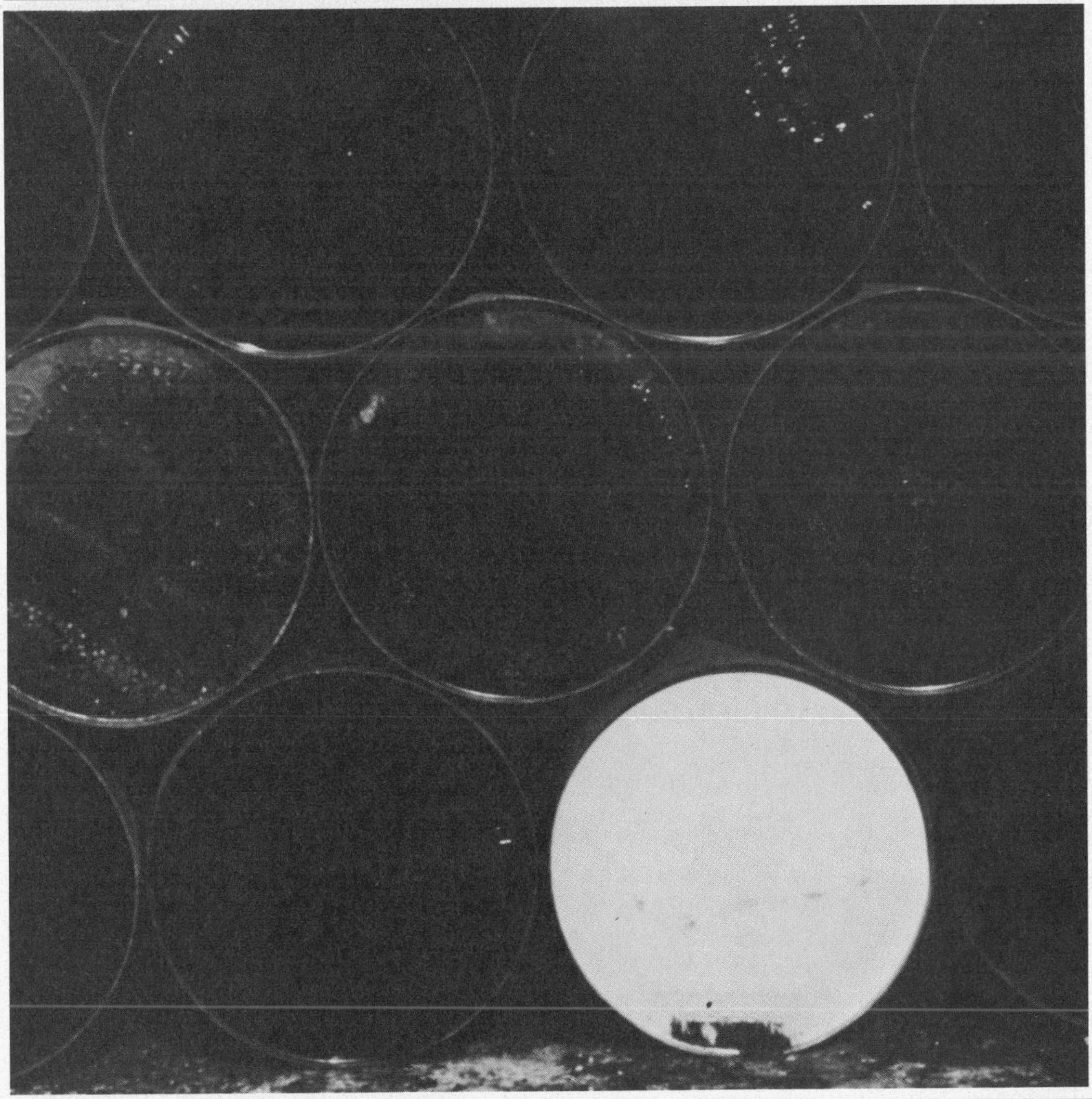

We now return to the world of the abstract. "Pure" monopoly does not exist in the real world any more than perfect competition does. Monopoly is at the other end of the spectrum from perfect competition, with various kinds of real firms falling between. Like the model of perfect competition, the model of pure monopoly is not meant to be a faithful portrait of reality or to be a form of perfection toward which firms in the real world should be striving. Rather, the model of monopoly is an analytical tool that helps us understand certain aspects of the real world.

DEFINITION OF MONOPOLY

In popular usage, the word *monopoly* has negative connotations. We tend to think of competition as healthy and good and of monopoly as pernicious and evil. The competitor is someone who acts in the public interest; he is somehow more sportsmanlike than the monopolist, who acts only out of greed.

Such an interpretation is entirely incorrect. The competitor is no better, socially or morally, than the monopolist. Both are motivated solely by the desire to maximize profit. Neither is, on the abstract level at least, community-minded or sportsmanlike. To pass judgment upon the respective characters of the competitor and the monopolist is to mistake effect for cause. With respect to society, whatever differences exist between monopoly and competition usually are the result of the nature of the systems themselves and not of the personality or morality of the individuals behind them.

What exactly is a monopoly? When one firm is the only producer of a commodity for which there are no close substitutes, it is a monopoly. Utilities such as electric companies may approach being monopolies. For instance, an electric company may have a monopoly of power used for lighting (the number of people who use kerosene lamps or candles being negligible). This monopoly, however, may not extend to all uses of power; for heating, many consumers may choose to substitute gas and oil.

The main characteristic of monopoly, then, is the domination of the market by one firm. Under conditions of perfect competition, there are a large number of firms selling the same product; no one firm can affect market price, and all can sell as much as they want at the market price. These firms are *price takers*. For the individual firm, the demand curve is a horizontal line at the market price; only the market demand curve is downward-sloping. But in a monopoly the firm and the market are one. The demand curve is downward-sloping, so that by restricting output the firm can charge a higher price. It is a *price maker.* Although both price takers and price makers aim to maximize profit, their behavior is rather different.

What Creates a Monopoly?

Although pure monopolies are probably as rare in the real world as is perfect competition, there are many firms that control a substantial portion of certain markets—enough so that they are able to drastically affect prices through their own rate of production. These firms are generally classed as monopolies, as are those firms that have exclusive rights to a particular market but which must obey certain restrictions imposed by government. All monopolies arise because of one essential condition: For one reason or another, potential competitors are prevented from entering the market.

Economies of Scale In some industries efficient, low-cost production is possible only when firms are small; in other industries it is possible only when firms are relatively large. The idea of the restaurant or pet shop industry being dominated by one establishment is preposterous. Equally implausible is the idea of a tiny automobile firm effectively challenging "the big three." Why this difference in industries?

The technology employed in some industries is such that the individual firm's average total cost declines or is constant over a long-range expansion of output. That is, diseconomies of scale are not encountered until firm size is very great. This means that costs can be minimized only when the individual firm controls a certain portion of the industry.

In addition to the automobile industry, this situation

prevails in the aluminum and steel industries and in heavy industry in general. Although these firms tend to be very large—not only in relation to the market, but absolutely—this is not always the case. In some cases, monopolies may occur when the size of the individual firm is large relative to the industry, but not absolutely. Most of the cast-iron cookware in the United States, for example, is manufactured by two firms, both located in Sydney, Ohio.

NATURAL MONOPOLIES Utilities, such as electric and gas companies, bus and railway firms, water companies, and communication services, are often characterized by high set-up costs and economies of scale. It would be extremely inefficient, for example, if a dozen different companies were operating public telephone lines in a single area. Each company would have to publish its own telephone directory, and people wishing to find a number would have to search through 12 books instead of one. Moreover, unless some cooperative arrangement were made, owners of telephones from firm A could be reached only on other phones from firm A. This would mean that anyone wishing a full range of communication would have to invest in 12 different phones and, at the end of each month, pay 12 different bills. For these reasons alone, such industries not only lend themselves to, but positively demand, a monopoly structure. This is why they are called **natural monopolies.** To ensure order the government grants exclusive franchises to one firm in each of these industries. In return, the government acquires special rights in the management of the firm, such as the right to limit its level of profits. Such regulations ensure that these monopolies will not charge overly high prices.

Control of an Essential Factor of Production

Sometimes a firm will monopolize an industry simply because it has exclusive rights to the raw material from which the product is made. For example, the Aluminum Company of America (Alcoa) for many years owned the only known, significant deposit of bauxite (raw material from which aluminum is made) on the North American continent. It is only since World War II that other companies have discovered bauxite deposits of their own. These discoveries (combined with antitrust litigation) enabled other firms to challenge the exclusive monopoly of Alcoa. Other examples of this type of monopoly are nickel and diamonds.

These firms operate on a national or international scale, but most monopolies are probably small, local enterprises. The only doctor in a small town has a corner on the skills of medicine, and therefore runs a kind of monopoly. The important concept is the **supply space,** rather than the size of the firm. A firm may be quite small, even in its industry, yet have no competitors in its supply space.

ARTIFICIAL MONOPOLIES Sometimes the control of an essential factor is a temporary circumstance, granted by government. For example, according to American patent laws, a firm may acquire exclusive rights over an original invention for 17 years. The government grants patents in order to encourage innovation and the improvement of products. Under perfect competition, you will remember, all firms in an industry were assumed to immediately assimilate any improvements that were developed by individual firms. This tended to destroy the incentive for innovation. Patent laws create temporary monopolies to reward innovation and thus avoid the stagnation inherent in competition.

The technological improvements protected by patent laws may prove to be self-perpetuating, leading to the general development of the industry, with the benefits eventually reaching the consumer. However, the danger of an artificial monopoly is the same as the danger of a natural one—that the firm will restrict output and raise prices in the absence of competition.

Copyrights are a kind of patent granted to protect and reward artistic innovations (literature, songs) rather than technical ones. They, too, create a sort of monopoly, but with one difference. The monopoly that a publishing company holds by virtue of having bought the copyright to a best-selling book cannot be exploited to the same degree as can the monopoly created by a patent on a new and successful invention. This is because in the realm of art necessity is not the mother of invention. You do not *need* to read the current best-seller in quite the same way you need electric light. A best-seller may be popular, but it has many close substitutes, in all the other popular books on the market. A publisher that decided to charge twice the usual price for a popular novel would very soon find it slipping from the charts.

HOW THE MONOPOLIST MAKES DECISIONS ON PRICE AND OUTPUT

As we mentioned earlier, a monopolist is no different from a competitor in that the prime motivating force behind his activity is the desire to maximize profit. Competitors and monopolists are, in fact, identical agents operating within different market systems. How, then, do the systems differ?

Monopoly and Demand

The demand curve for a monopoly is the same as the industry demand curve under perfect competition. Given the fact that the monopolist faces a downward-sloping demand curve, it follows that his decisions on price and output generally must be governed by considerations different from those of the competitor. A competitive firm is able to sell as much as it can produce at the current market price. A monopolist, however, can sell more of a product only if he lowers prices.

As in Chapter 25 on perfect competition, it will be helpful if we have a hypothetical example of the type of firm we are discussing. Farmer Euclid's triangle farm will not do here; since points and lines, the raw materials of triangles, are infinite, there could be no effective barriers to entry. We need a firm whose product is totally unique. Let our example therefore be the Acme Phoenix Hatchery. In the early days of its existence, this monopoly encountered the difficulty of being too pure; only one phoenix could be born in the world every 500 years. However, through diligent cross-breeding (which took considerable time) the species was improved to the point where

TABLE 27-1 Cost and Revenue Schedule for Acme Phoenix Hatchery

(1) Output	(2) Price and average revenue	(3) Total revenue	(4) Total cost	(5) Average total cost	(6) Marginal cost	(7) Marginal revenue	(8) Profit
0	–	–	$ 5	–	–	–	$– 5
1	$12	$12	9	$ 9	$ 4	$12	3
2	11	22	12	6	3	10	10
3	10	30	17	5.67	5	8	13
4	9	36	22	5.50	5	6	14
5	8	40	30	6	8	4	10
6	7	42	41	6.83	11	2	1
7	6	42	56	8	15	0	–14
8	5	40	76	9.50	20	–2	–36
9	4	36	104	11.56	28	–4	–68

The cost and revenue schedules for Acme show the profit levels at various outputs. As in perfect competition, the monopolist will produce at MC = MR. At this point profits are maximized. Note that in this case MR exceeds MC at unit 4 and MR is less than MC at unit 5. Therefore, the firm has no incentive to produce the fifth unit and profits are maximized at 4 units.

enough birds could be hatched to turn a profit. This involved the use of electronic funeral pyres and other equipment, which make Acme, at least as long as its patents hold out, a perfect monopoly.

Setting the Level of Output

The behavior of the monopolist in selecting the level of output is identical to that of the perfect competitor. The managers of the Acme Phoenix Hatchery, like Farmer Euclid, look at total cost and total revenue and at marginal cost and marginal revenue to choose a level of output that affords them the greatest profits. Because of the difference in market structures, however, the shape of these curves will be different.

Total Cost/Total Revenue The cost and revenue figures for Acme are shown in Table 27-1. Note that the price declines as output increases. To see its profit picture, the firm will look first at column 8.

As we can see, Acme would certainly not want to hatch as many as 7 phoenixes since at this level, profit would become negative; the firm would be losing money. Four units is the level at which the difference between total cost and total revenue is greatest with positive profit. This is the point at which Acme's total profits are greatest, although it may not necessarily be the point at which per unit profits reach their highest level. But like the competitor, the monopolist's primary goal is to maximize total profits. So, 4 units would be the level at which Acme would produce.

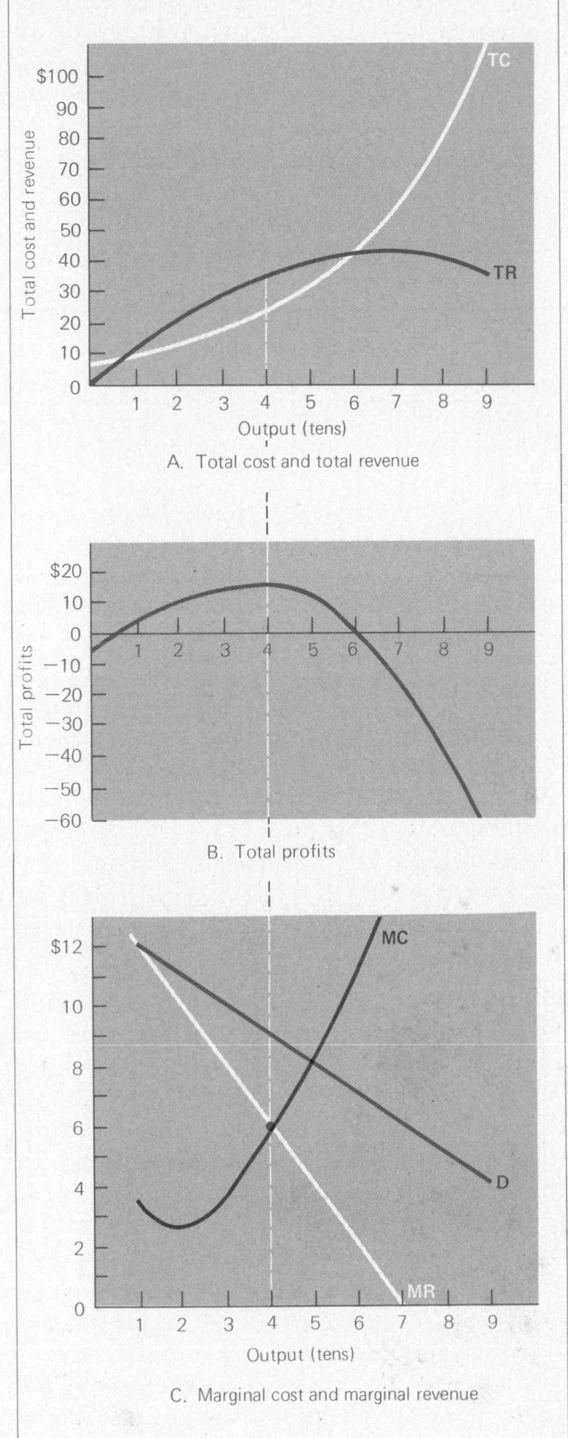

FIGURE 27-1 PROFITS AT THE ACME PHOENIX HATCHERY (A) Total cost and total revenue: Like perfect competitors, monopolists receive the greatest profits at the point where the total revenue curve lies farthest above the total cost curve. The total revenue curve appears different from that of perfect competition because price declines as output increases. (B) Profits: The difference between total cost and total revenue indicates the total profit above the normal profit included as part of total cost. Profit may be positive or negative. The peak of this curve shows the level of profit maximization. (C) Marginal cost and marginal revenue: The marginal revenue curve lies below the demand curve. Output is nonetheless set where MC = MR. This coincides with the level of greatest profits in A and B.

As with the firm under perfect competition, the relationship between total cost and total revenue can be shown by means of a graph as well as a table. We have merely to plot the information from columns 3 and 4 in the table, as shown in Figure 27-1. The total revenue curve rises to a high point and then descends, because the increase in output is accompanied by a decrease in price. The total cost curve slopes upward at an increasing rate as diminishing returns set in. The greatest positive distance between the two curves occurs when the level of output is at 4 units. At this output the slope of the total cost curve is equal to the slope of the total revenue curve. To change the level of output in either direction would result in a decline in profits.

Marginal Cost/Marginal Revenue Under perfect competition a firm reaches its point of greatest total profits when marginal cost equals marginal revenue. And if the firm cannot make a profit, losses are minimized if MC = MR. In this case, what is true for the competitive firm is true for the monopolist. The monopolist, like the perfect competitor, will produce additional units of his product as long as such activity adds more to revenue than to cost. When MR = MC, any increase in production will mean that marginal costs will start exceeding marginal revenues, so that profits will begin to decline. Similarly, when MC = MR, any cutback in output will also mean that profits will begin to drop since the decrease in revenue will be greater than the decrease in cost.

The marginal revenue curve for a firm in a perfectly competitive industry is a horizontal line at the level of the price. In fact, under perfect competition, the marginal revenue curve, the price line (or average revenue curve), and the demand curve are identical. The marginal revenue line merely reflects the fact that under perfect competition, the firm receives an identical increment for each unit sold. The monopolist, however, receives less for each unit sold. In fact, he must steadily lower his price if he wishes to sell more. Therefore, unlike the competitive firm, the monopolist faces a downward-sloping marginal revenue curve (see Figure 27-1C). As you can see from column 7 of the cost and revenue schedule for the Acme Phoenix Hatchery, at a certain point marginal revenue becomes negative. This point occurs when production increases from 7 to 8 units.

When we plot the numbers in column 7 on a graph (Figure 27-1C) to produce a marginal revenue curve, we notice a significant relationship between the MR curve and the demand curve. Throughout the entire schedule of production, marginal revenue is below the demand curve, or price.

Thus, a major difference between the perfectly competitive firm and the monopolist is that for the monopolist, price is always greater than marginal revenue.

Setting the Price

Under conditions of perfect competition, the intersection of MC and MR curves determines both price and quantity directly. Under monopoly conditions, the intersection of the MC and MR curves determines only quantity directly. Under perfect competition the MC curve—or, more specifically, that portion of the MC curve that lies above the average variable cost curve—is the firm's supply curve. In a monop-

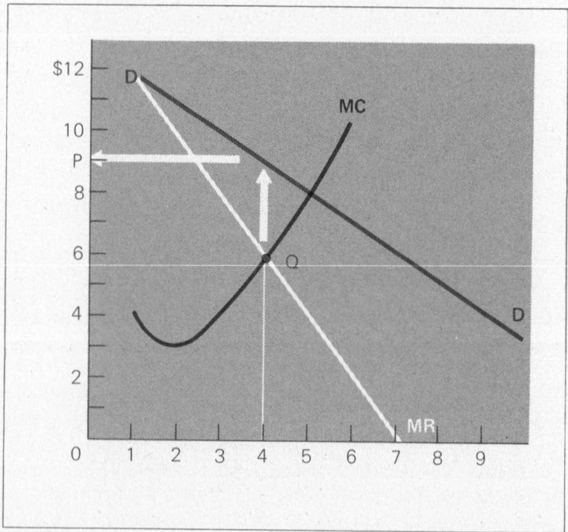

FIGURE 27-2 SETTING PRICE AND OUTPUT In the previous figure we saw that the level of output was established at MR = MC. Price is found by reading off the demand curve at the chosen output level. Under monopoly, then, price equals neither marginal revenue nor marginal cost.

olistic firm this is not true. The MC curve is not, as it is under perfect competition, made up of points indicating the price levels at which the firm would be willing to produce at each level of output. For the monopolist the demand curve indicates the highest price he can charge for a given level of output. Therefore, the monopolist does not have a supply curve in the same sense that the perfect competitor has one.

The monopolist sets output at the level MC = MR, but sets price on the demand curve. We can find the price by drawing a vertical line through the point at which MC = MR. The intersection of this vertical line and the demand curve will determine price.

This results in the second major difference between the perfectly competitive firm and the monopolist: Price will always be greater than marginal cost for the monopolist.

Equilibrium Levels

This does not mean that the monopolistic firm is always making enormous profits. Although the price it can charge is higher than that charged by a perfectly competitive firm, it cannot set any price it wishes. It is constrained by the prices set by the demand (or AR) curve.

Whether this price enables the firm to earn excess profits or normal profits, or whether it makes the firm incur a loss, depends on the position of the average revenue and average total cost curves. The quantity is set by MC = MR; if price is greater than ATC at this quantity, then the Acme Phoenix Hatchery will receive excess profits, as in Figure 27-3A.

If a decrease in demand or an increase in costs were to force the firm into the position shown in Figure 27-3B, it would still be operating at a point where MC = MR, but it would no longer be earning an excess profit. Price would just equal ATC, and Acme would be earning only a normal profit. Unlike normal profit for a perfectly competitive firm, however, normal profit for a monopolist does not necessarily occur at the lowest point on the ATC curve, so that the firm has higher per unit costs than it would under competitive conditions.

In Figure 27-3C we see the firm operating at a loss, since price is less than ATC. Acme is still managing to cover the average variable costs (frankincense, myrrh, and so on); therefore, it can still minimize its losses by continuing to produce at a point where MC = MR. However, it is not covering its average total costs. The firm cannot continue in this position any more than a competitive firm can. No firm can operate at a loss in the long run. The monopolistic firm must either find some way of increasing demand for its product, lower its costs, or else shut down.

In Figure 27-3D we have relaxed the conditions to allow the threat of competition. The monopolist then may choose to produce not where MC = MR, but rather where AR = ATC. The firm is making normal profits, although on all units above Q it is incurring a loss. The monopolist is forgoing excess profits. Why would any firm break all the rules of profit maximization? The reason is simple: to prevent competitors from entering the market. Excess profits attract other firms; by lowering its profit margin, the monopolistic firm keeps a low profile and discourages other firms from trying to enter the industry. It may also be trying to avoid an antitrust suit by increasing output and making only normal profits.

The long-run equilibrium of a monopolistic firm can be predicted by theory only if we exclude any threat of potential competition. Certainly it will shut down if it is continuously losing money, but under other conditions it can opt either to maximize profits by producing at the MC = MR level of output, to minimize competition by producing at or near the AR = ATC level, or to pursue some other corporate goals such as $1 billion annual sales. Excess profits can be sustained indefinitely by a monopolistic firm, unlike a perfectly competitive industry. And the firm need not operate at the lowest average cost.

CONSEQUENCES OF MONOPOLY

In a monopoly the consumers are getting less output and a higher price than they would if the industry were perfectly competitive. And a monopoly can sustain higher costs of production indefinitely. Con-

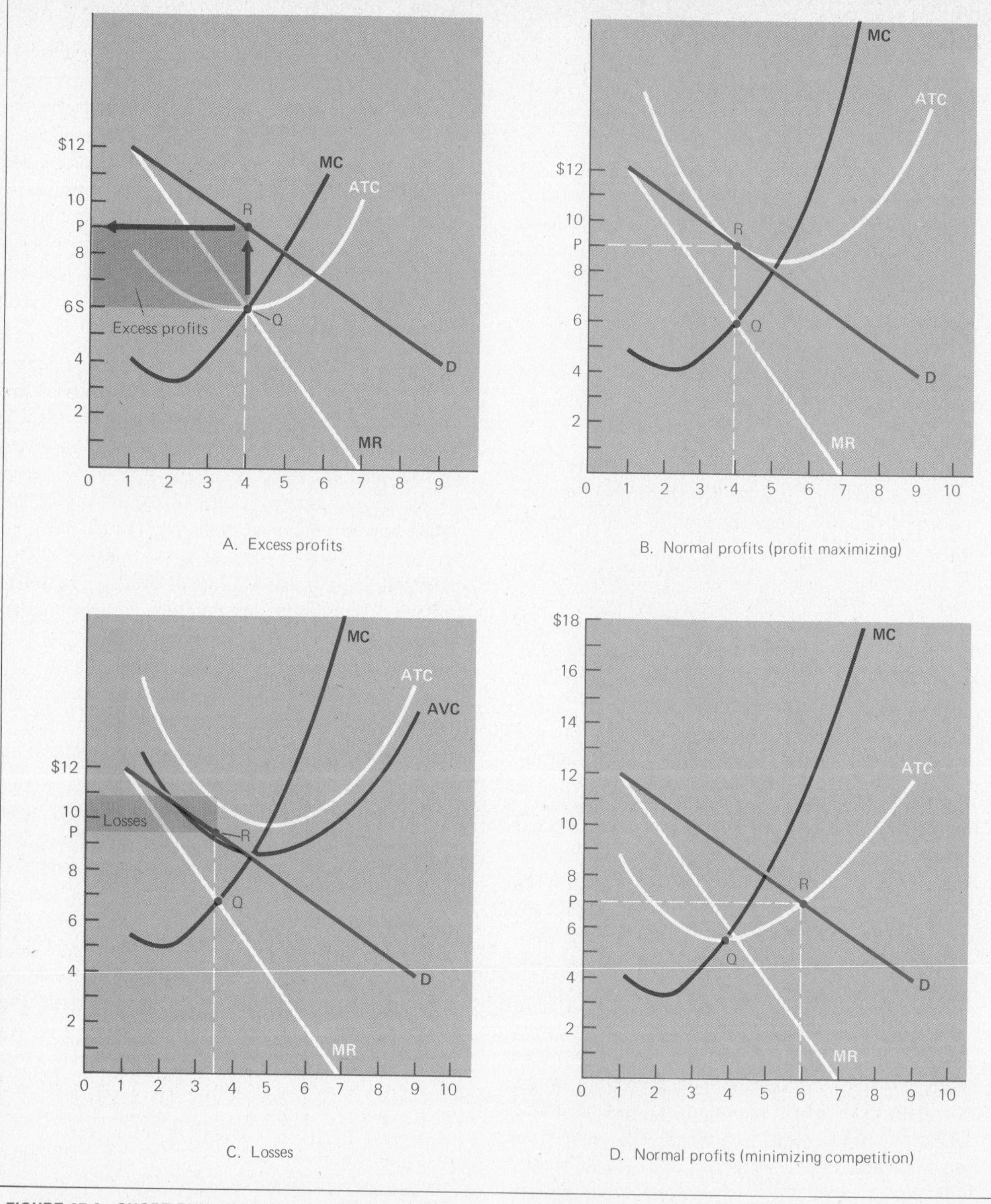

FIGURE 27-3 SHORT-RUN EQUILIBRIUM POSITIONS OF THE ACME PHOENIX HATCHERY MONOPOLY (A) Excess profits: Although MC = MR at minimum average cost, the firm is enjoying excess profits. (B) Normal profits under profit maximization: An increase in costs would force the firm into the position shown here. MC would still equal MR, but profits would be zero, since ATC equals price. (C) Losses: Any further increase in costs would cause losses for Acme. Since average variable costs are covered, the firm will continue operations in the short run. However, as was the case under perfect competition, the firm will go out of business in the long run unless it at least breaks even. In the short run, then, the monopolist will minimize losses by operating at that output at which MC = MR. (D) Normal profits under competition threat: Although this firm is losing money on its marginal units above MC = MR, it is still making normal profits. By forgoing excess profits, the company may be trying to keep from attracting competitors or the attention of antitrust prosecutors.

sequently, a monopoly may be both allocatively and technologically inefficient.

Allocative Inefficiency

The profit-maximizing monopolist always sells at a price greater than marginal cost, which automatically results in allocative inefficiency.

A simple example will illustrate how a monopoly will cause inefficient resource allocation. This example involves an economy with two industries—leather doublets and belts. The belt industry is a monopoly and the doublet industry is perfectly competitive. Both industries are in equilibrium and both are operating at a level of output at which marginal costs equal $5. In the doublet industry, price equals marginal cost and is therefore $5. In the belt industry, price is greater than marginal cost and is $10. In this situation resources are not allocated efficiently between belts and doublets. There are too many resources devoted to doublet production and too few to belt production. An additional belt could be produced by shifting $5 worth of resources from doublet to belt production. Consumers would lose one doublet that they value at $5, but they would be better off because they would gain a belt that they value at $10. In other words, the marginal social value of a belt is $10. Since both require the same amount of resources, doublet production should be decreased and belt production increased.

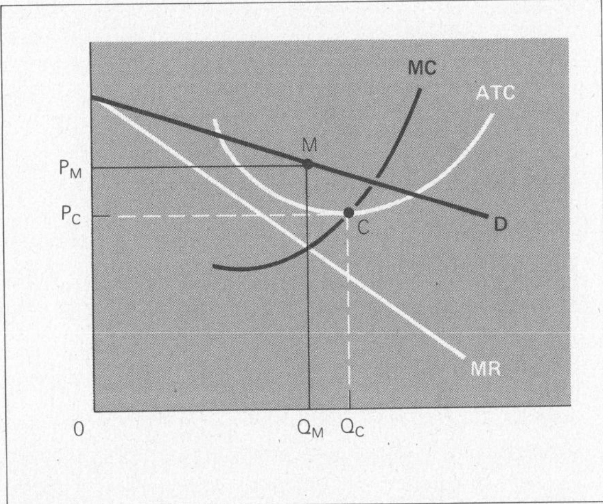

FIGURE 27-4 MONOPOLY VERSUS PERFECT COMPETITION Compared here are the price, output, and cost structure of a monopoly and of a perfectly competitive industry. Output under monopoly is different from the level consumers want or the level costs dictate. Because P is greater than MC, society would benefit if production were increased. If the monopolist produces at a cost above the lowest point on the ATC curve as in this figure, resources are being wasted. Under perfect competition, P = MC = MR = ATC, and the firm produces a level of output that is technologically and allocatively efficient.

As a general rule, if price is greater than marginal cost (and there are no externalities), this means that marginal social value is greater than marginal social cost, and production of that good should be increased. As this happens, the price will fall and marginal cost will rise until P = MC, or efficient resource allocation is achieved. If the price is less than the marginal cost, the reverse should occur.

In our example, if the belt industry were suddenly to become competitive, belt production would increase because price is greater than marginal cost, and firms would be earning excess profits. The price of belts would fall as resources shifted from doublets, until the price of a belt equalled its marginal cost. Allocative efficiency would then ensue.

Price Discrimination The monopolist not only may charge *one* higher price, but also may charge different prices to different groups of consumers. A single price may work if buyers have the same elasticity of demand, but if readily identifiable submarkets have less elastic demand, the monopolist may charge higher prices in those submarkets without losing sales. The U.S. government, for example, sells grain surpluses abroad at prices lower than the domestic price. It can do so only because the foreign buyers cannot turn around and export the grain to the United States at a price that undercuts our domestic price.

Price discrimination, or charging different prices for the same product or service, may occur when the market is segmented into groups with differing elasticity of demand and each segment can be sealed to prevent those who obtain the product at a lower price from reselling it to those who obtain it at a higher price.

What the monopolist is doing is increasing his revenues at the expense of consumer surplus.

TAPPING THE DEMAND CURVE This skimming of consumer surplus is most readily seen when the monopolist gives discounts not warranted by cost differentials. He could sell the same quantity by charging the "discount" price to everyone, since this is the price level indicated by MC = MR. If he charges differential prices, he can take in even more revenue without losing customers, as Figure 27-5 shows. The single-price revenue is the area of the rectangle $0Q_3R_3P_3$. With different prices, the monopolist can tap the demand curve and collect revenues equal to the area of all the rectangles.

This behavior is no more or less rapacious than that of the perfect competitor. The perfect competitor is prevented by the structure of the market from charging different prices, since those to whom he charged higher prices could take their business elsewhere.

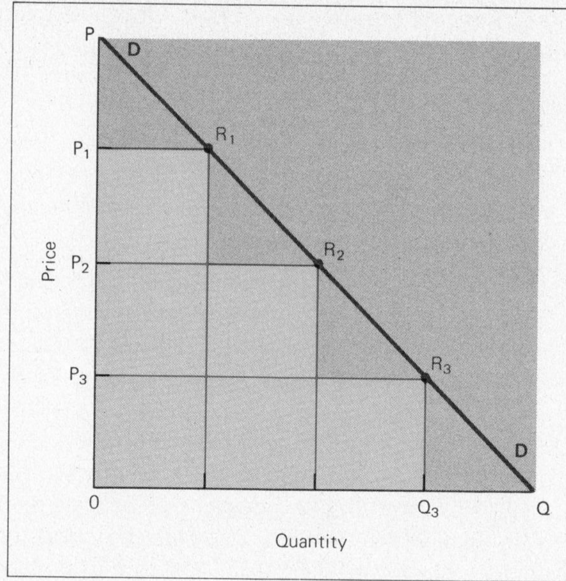

FIGURE 27-5 TAPPING THE DEMAND CURVE Because MC = MR at output level $0Q_3$, the monopolist will maximize profits at this output. He will charge price P_3 for all units, receiving a total of the area $0Q_3R_3P_3$. However, the monopolist can increase revenues if he can charge different prices for this output. The monopolist will still produce at the level $0Q_3$ but will set higher prices for some consumers. His total revenue equals the area of all the rectangles. If he charged a price that changed for every unit purchased, his revenue would be the area 0QP and he would have converted all consumer surplus into his own revenues.

DUMPING The case of U.S. grain sales abroad is somewhat more complex. At home demand is relatively inelastic, so a higher price can be charged. Abroad quantity demanded is much more sensitive to price, so the price must be lower. To set the level of output, we need to know where MC = MR (see Figure 27-6C). If MC is the same in each market, equating MC with the MR curves of the domestic and foreign markets (Figures 27-6A and 27-6B) indicates the profit-maximizing levels of output. The prices are found on the respective demand curves. The domestic price is much higher than the foreign price.

Businesses as well as government engage in foreign and domestic dumping. Even firms that are not complete monopolies can take advantage of dumping. As any penny-wise business school student soon learns, whiskey manufacturers sell the same liquor under prestige labels at a higher price and under lesser known brand names at a lower price. One empty bottle of the high-priced brand and a funnel can convert Old Snort into Luxury Liquor. Most buyers do not know this, however, and the whiskey manufacturers can reap higher revenues with the same output.

The effect on allocative efficiency of these practices may be to increase output, since the price structure shifts the MR curve to coincide with the demand curve. Marginal cost will then intersect at a higher level of output. Price will equal marginal cost at the last unit of output, but the monopolist will be charging higher prices for earlier units and so the consumer's surplus will disappear. The firm may or may not be operating with technological efficiency, depending on the location of the ATC curve. It could be operating at the lowest point on the ATC curve, but

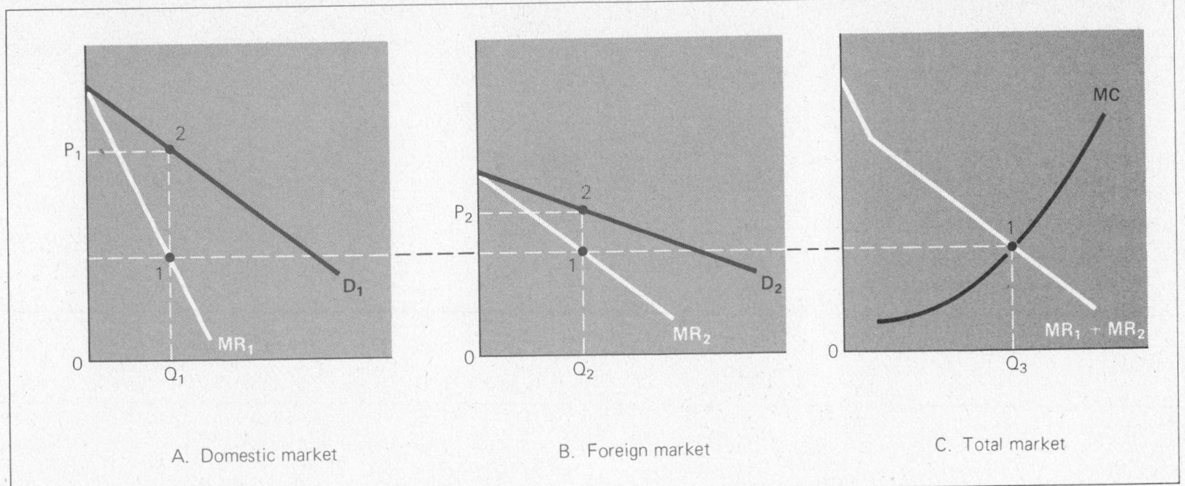

FIGURE 27-6 DUMPING The marginal revenue of the domestic market (A) and the foreign market (B) form the kinked curve of the total market (C). Since MC is the same for each market, output is set at the level of MR = MC found at (1). Price is then set on the demand curve for each market (2) and will be relatively high at home but low abroad. Would it be price discrimination if MC, as well as MR, were different in each market?

this is not inevitable, as it is under conditions of perfect competition.

Technological Efficiency

Whether monopoly will be technologically efficient cannot be answered by theory alone. It is possible that MR = MC = minimum ATC, as in Figure 27-7. However, this need not be the case. If MC = MR at some other level of output such as Q_N or Q_L, then the firm will be operating at higher than minimum cost, even though it is on its ATC curve.

The firm may not even be on this curve. It could produce at Q_M and be incurring costs of K Such a situation may occur for a number of reasons.

Although the excess profit of a monopoly may not attract competitors, it may spur labor to increase its wage demands. The monopolist does not have quite the same incentive to refuse these demands, and its costs may be higher than they would be under perfect competition. Add to this the resources the monopoly may devote to averting the threat of competi-

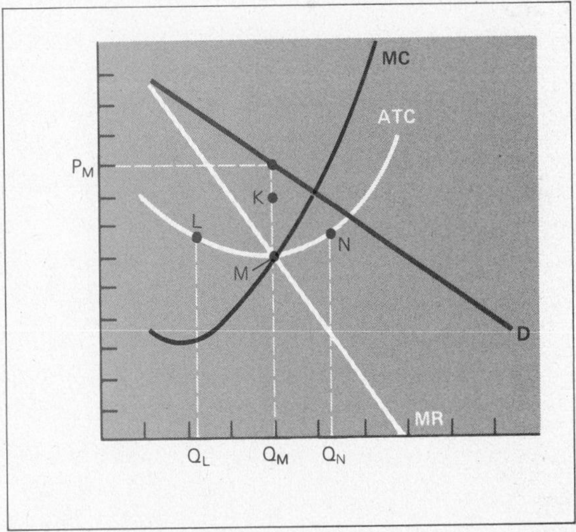

FIGURE 27-7 TECHNOLOGICAL INEFFICIENCY The cost and revenue curves for this firm mean that it will operate at minimum average cost, which ensures technological efficiency. However, were MC = MR to set output at Q_L or Q_N, the firm might still continue to operate even though costs are above minimum. In fact, the firm may produce Q_M yet have costs of K, which is not even on the ATC curve.

THE BALL-POINT PEN MONOPOLY

Today people are accustomed to walking into a drugstore and picking up a ball-point pen or two for under a dollar. But these pens once sold for $12.50 because they were produced by a monopoly.

The ball-point pen was first patented by Milton Reynolds in 1945. After being granted a patent, which, theoretically at least, should have barred the entry of other firms from the market for the next 17 years, Mr. Reynolds formed the Reynolds Pen Company and began producing the new writing implement.

The cost of producing each pen was estimated to be about 80 cents, but since Mr. Reynolds did not initially have to worry about competitors, he was able to charge a price that brought him a considerable excess profit. The first Reynolds pens were sold by Gimbels department store for $12.50 each. On the first day they were offered for sale, 10,000 were sold. Encouraged by the popularity of the new pen, Reynolds expanded production. Within a few months, he was producing 30,000 pens a day. His profits at this time were as much as $500,000 per month, or almost 20 times his original investment of $26,000.

Despite his patent, Reynolds did not have the market to himself for very long. Other firms either found ways to circumvent the restrictions or, irresistibly attracted by the high profits to be made, simply defied Reynolds' claim, thereby risking litigation. Macy's department store, for example, soon began importing a rival pen from South America, while Sheaffer and Eversharp came out with models of their own, which they sold at even higher prices. A little over a year after Reynolds had introduced his pen, he was confronted with about 100 rival companies. Competition had succeeded in forcing down price to the point where some pens were selling for $2.98. Continued competition forced price down even more. By the late forties and early fifties, the 39-cent and 25-cent ball-point pen had become commonplace.

The story of the ball-point pen illustrates several interesting points about monopoly in the real world. First, where demand for a product is high, a monopolistic firm can charge prices drastically above cost and, consequently, make a tremendous profit. Second, the artificial barrier to entry created by patent laws may not be adequate to keep rival firms out of an industry when profits are sufficiently attractive. Third, the competitive situation that results when rival firms enter the market soon drives down prices to a point where they reflect the true costs of production. And finally, despite the failure of the patent laws and despite the destruction of the original monopoly by rival firms, the establishment of a monopoly on even a short-run basis may be so profitable as to be a strong incentive for innovation.

Buy this Reynolds International pen tomorrow, October 29, 1945—don't fill it again until October 29, 1947! Here is the fantastic, atomic era, miraculous fountain pen that you've read about, wondered about, waited for! Imagine a pen like this! You can go to the remotest ice floe in the Aleutians where ink has never been heard of. You can stay there for two whole years—and this veritable camel of a pen won't ask for a drink. That alone would be enough to make you storm Gimbels door, flood Gimbels with phone calls, deluge Gimbels with letters and wires. But this Buck Rogers baby has more tricks up its sleeve. It writes in the stratosphere at 20,000 foot altitude or higher without leaking. It will write on cloth—under water. And you get the handsome desk stand—so you need only one for office and pocket.

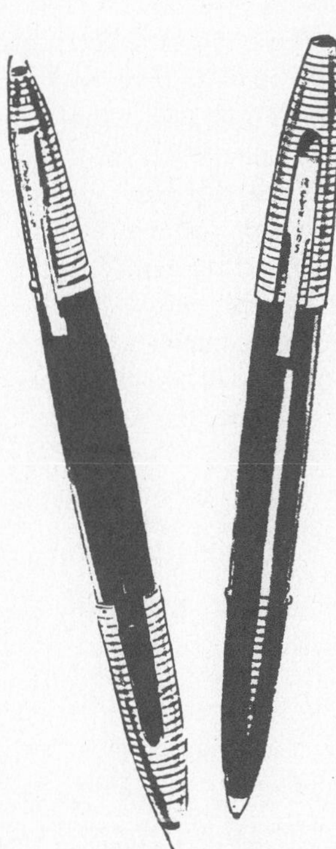

Guarantee

If the Reynolds International Pen fails to write during 2 years after the day of purchase, return it to Gimbels and we will immediately give you a NEW PEN!

SPECIAL OVERSEAS PACKAGE — We will mail first class to anyone in the armed services a special package containing the Reynolds pen. The U. S. Postal authorities assure us that if the pen is mailed promptly it will reach anyone in the armed services before Christmas. No request is needed. Gimbels will pay the postage.

phone PEnn 6-5100 or mail coupon

Gimbels, 33rd & B'way, New York 1, N. Y.

Send me ____ Reynolds pens at 12.50 each.

Name ________________

Address ________________

charge ☐ check ☐ money order ☐ c.o.d ☐

shipping charge 14c beyond Gimbels delivery area

tion either from antitrust actions or from would-be entrants to the market, and the costs rise even higher.

These costs may offer some social benefits. As we saw in Chapter 24, increased costs may be spent on better working conditions. Monopoly may also provide greater stability than the tumultuous world of perfect competition, where changes in price switch resources (and firms) in and out of industries.

Monopoly and Innovation One extra cost is that of research and development (R&D). Competitive firms, we have seen, have little incentive to innovate. There is some debate about whether or not this is true of monopolies. In the absence of competition, firms need not select the lowest cost level of output, nor need they employ available technology to the fullest extent. Since monopolistic firms are not immediately threatened by competition, they have no reason—other than making even greater profits—to develop new methods to reduce their costs of production. Moreover, when new methods do come to light, monopolistic firms have been known to suppress them if these methods undermine their secure hold on the market. On the other hand, R&D is a way of keeping one step ahead of possible competitors and has been used with great effectiveness by firms like IBM, which are on the frontier of an industry. And because there is less incentive to operate at the lowest cost, a monopoly may be more willing to maintain advanced research facilities than a firm in a competitive industry. The prospect of a new monopoly in an allied area was enough to encourage a small Rochester, New York, specialty paper company to invest millions in a process called xerography.

Is Monopoly Equitable?

We have already established that monopolies, by nature, produce less and charge more than competitive industries. This difference in production and price creates what amounts to a "private tax" on consumers. The extent of this tax will be covered in Chapter 29. By paying this tax when they purchase the goods produced by monopolistic firms, consumers make possible the substantial excess profits that are often enjoyed by the owners of monopolistic firms, namely the stockholders. Owners of stock in our society, and especially owners of large quantities of stock, tend to be people in the upper-income brackets. This means that the structure of monopoly tends not only to misallocate resources, but also to distribute income unevenly, concentrating it in the hands of the well-to-do. Whether or not this situation is inequitable is a value judgment, not susceptible to economic analysis. Some people would say that it is simply in the nature of things that there should be rich and poor, and because a particular economic model accentuates the dichotomy is no reason to discard it. Others might say that the solution is to convert the private tax into a public tax by levies on monopoly profits. Others insist that the regressive effects of monopolies, combined with their obvious inefficiencies, require that they be broken up into competitive units or be treated as public utilities. In Chapter 29, we shall take a closer look at the public policy issues involved in monopoly and other forms of imperfect competition.

SUMMARY

1 Pure monopoly, which is at the other end of the spectrum from perfect competition, does not exist in the real world any more than does perfect competition. A monopoly is the only producer of a commodity for which there are no close substitutes; it faces the downward-sloping industry demand curve rather than the perfectly elastic demand curve of a competitive firm.

2 All monopolies arise because of one essential condition: For one reason or an-

other, potential competitors are prevented from entering the market. Economies of scale may produce natural monopolies (usually public utilities); control of an essential factor of production may be gained independently or by a government license that creates an artificial monopoly.

3 Although both the monopolist and the perfect competitor seek to maximize profits by producing that output at which marginal cost and marginal revenue are equal, the monopolist will inevitably charge a higher price and produce less than would the industry if it were perfectly competitive. This is because the demand curve (which is also the price line and AR curve) is above the MR curve. The monopoly firm sets output at MR = MC but sets price on the demand curve. Furthermore, the firm need not operate at the lowest point on the average cost curve.

4 Although the monopolist charges a higher price than that charged by the perfect competitor, he may or may not earn a greater than normal profit. If he operates at that point where the demand curve intersects (or is tangent to) the average cost curve, profits will be normal (zero). This is, however, only one of an infinite number of possibilities, all of which mean greater than zero economic profit. (If economic losses were to be sustained in the long run, the monopolist would leave the industry, as would the perfect competitor.)

5 From society's viewpoint, the monopolist is allocatively inefficient, since people would like to have more of the product. Because marginal cost is lower than price, society is signaling to have resources shifted to this industry. By charging a higher price than would obtain under perfect competition and by producing a lower output, the monopolist fails to hire enough factors of production to reach the level of production that is allocatively efficient. Price discrimination, through either tapping the demand curve or dumping, can increase output, but only at the cost of reducing or eliminating consumer surplus.

6 The monopolist may also be technologically inefficient because there is no guarantee that MC = MR at a level of output that also allows the firm to operate at minimum average cost. Furthermore, the cost curves may be higher than under perfect competition, since the monopolist has fewer incentives to minimize costs. These extra costs may include research and development that lead to innovations, but there is some debate on this point.

7 Monopoly constitutes a hidden tax on the consumer in the form of higher prices and restricted output. This redistributes income from the public to the shareholders of the monopoly, who are usually in higher income brackets.

SUGGESTED READINGS

Haveman, Robert H., and **Kenyon A. Knopf.** *The Market System.* 2nd ed. Chap. 6. New York: John Wiley & Sons, 1970.

Leftwich, Richard H. *The Price System and Resource Allocation.* 4th ed. Chap. 10. Hinsdale, Ill.: The Dryden Press, 1970.

Mansfield, Edwin, ed. *Monopoly Power and Economic Performance.* rev. ed. New York: W. W. Norton, 1968.

Stonier, Alfred W., and **Douglas C. Hague**. *A Textbook of Economic Theory*. 2nd ed. Chap. 8. New York: John Wiley & Sons, 1961.

Weiss, Leonard W. *Case Studies in American Industry*. 2nd ed. Chap. 3. New York: John Wiley & Sons, 1971.

QUESTIONS

1 Review
   a. factors that contribute to the creation of monopolies,
   b. price and output decisions of the monopolist,
   c. distortions created by monopoly,
   d. discrimination in pricing,
   e. incentives for innovation and increased technological efficiency by monopolies.

2 Is the monopolist's self-denial of excess profits a contradiction of the assumption of long-run profit maximization? Why or why not?

3 The existence of monopoly places a kind of tax on the consumer, reducing supply and increasing price. Would a subsidy for each unit produced beyond the monopoly level correct the situation? Why or why not?

4 Fill in columns 3, 4, 6, and 7.

(1) Price	(2) Output	(3) Total revenue	(4) Marginal revenue	(5) Total cost	(6) Average total cost	(7) Marginal cost
$10	1			$ 8		
9	2			12		
8	3			15		
7	4			19		
6	5			23		
5	6			28		
4	7			35		
3	8			45		

   a. Draw a graph showing this monopolist's demand, marginal revenue, marginal cost, and average total cost curves.
   b. Indicate on the graph the most profitable output and the price charged at that output.

5 What are the relative price and output distortions from monopoly in the case of extremely inelastic demand? Extremely elastic demand?

6 Assume that a local doctor has an official high price schedule for those patients who are willing and able to pay. For those he believes unable to pay, he scales down his charges or waives payment completely on some of the services he provides. Draw a demand curve for his services and identify the doctor's revenue and the consumer surplus, if any.

7 Patents are one way in which a firm can establish a monopoly position at least for a while. How does the existence of patent protection affect a potential com-

petitor's incentives to develop substitutes over which it may have exclusive control?

8 Which of the following might be a natural monopoly and why?
   a. urban mass transit
   b. grain storage facilities
   c. space exploration
   d. hospitals offering special equipment for organ transplants

9 Might there be a greater tendency for small, local monopolies to take excess profits than for large, regional monopolies? Why or why not?

10 Some monopolies are denied excess profits by regulatory agencies. How might this policy tend to affect the firm's willingness to innovate?

CHAPTER 28
IMPERFECT COMPETITION

In the previous two chapters we explored the models of perfect competition and monopoly. It was explained that neither of these models is an accurate picture of reality, but that both are useful as analytical tools that allow us to see more clearly how the economy (more particularly, the price system) operates. The worlds portrayed by these models are admittedly abstract, ideal (but not in the prescriptive sense), and, above all, imaginary. Perfect competition and monopoly were said to stand at opposite poles of a continuum, each describing an extreme situation, while reality stood somewhere in the middle. Now we are going to explore that middle. It is the world of imperfect competition. And within that world we shall be looking at two distinct market structures: oligopoly and monopolistic competition.

OLIGOPOLY

The literal definition of oligopoly is "a few sellers," but to the economist the word means something more specific.

An oligopoly is an industry in which the number of firms is small enough so that changes in the price and output of one firm will affect the price and output of the others.

In the abstract worlds of perfect competition and monopoly, firms were independent of one another. Competitive firms were able to sell as much as they could produce without affecting market price, while monopolies could not affect other firms because there were no other firms to affect. In the real world of oligopoly, however, firms are interdependent.

When we think about the products we use in daily life, we realize that a great many markets follow the oligopolistic pattern. Industries such as automobiles, typewriters, breakfast cereals, canned soups, cigarettes, laundry detergents, and light bulbs are dominated by a handful of big firms. And behind these are manufacturers of products such as steel or aluminum that go into the machinery that makes the goods on the shelves and in the showrooms. Concentrated market power is a feature of the American marketplace as well as of the theory of the business firm.

Opening photo by Cornell Capa, Magnum

Price and Output in Oligopoly

Since pricing and output decisions on the part of one firm can have a direct effect on the industry as a whole, there will be a natural tendency on the part of all firms to avoid "rocking the boat." Oligopolistic firms cannot afford to compete with one another in a no-holds-barred fashion. The emphasis, rather, is on outguessing the other fellow's strategy and then suitably adjusting one's own behavior. Sometimes, as we shall see, more than guessing is involved. In any case, the interdependence of oligopolistic firms gives rise to a special type of competition in which price plays a minimal role. Most oligopolistic firms tend to avoid price competition. Competition between oligopolistic firms is conducted largely on a nonprice basis, consisting of such things as product changes, advertising, customer service, and other "public relations" practices.

The "Kinked" Demand Curve The demand curve for a competitive industry, you will remember, was a horizontal line at the current market price, demonstrating that demand under perfect competition is perfectly elastic. The demand curve for a monopolistic firm, being identical to the demand curve for the entire industry, is downward-sloping. The demand curve for an oligopolistic firm cannot be so easily described without knowing more about the structure of the industry and the behavior of competing firms.

One model that helps explain oligopoly behavior is the kinked demand curve. This demand curve for an oligopolistic firm has a shape that is essentially different from either of the other two market structures. It is kinked or bent at the current market price. This kinked demand curve helps explain why oligopolistic firms avoid competing with one another on the basis of price.

Figure 28-1 represents the market situation of a typical oligopolistic firm. The Golden Dragon Cig-

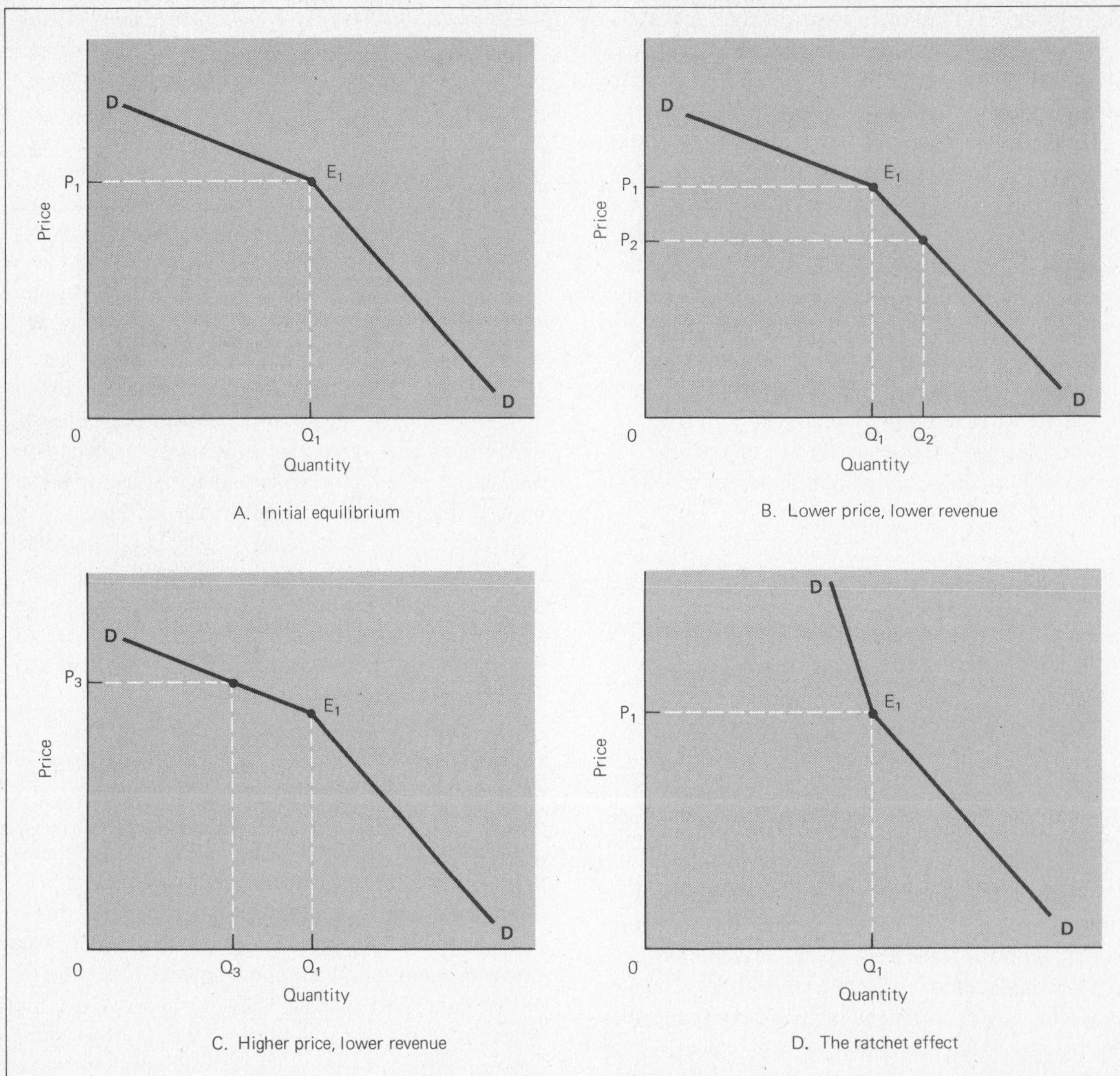

FIGURE 28-1 KINKED DEMAND CURVE In graphs A, B, and C, demand is relatively elastic for outputs less than Q_1 and relatively inelastic for outputs greater than Q_1 because of the behavior of the oligopolist's competitors. Graph A represents the initial situation (equilibrium point E_1, when price is P_1 and quantity, Q_1). Graph B shows that if the oligopolist lowered his price from P_1 to P_2, he would gain little competitive advantage because his competitors would also cut prices to P_2. Lowering price would not appreciably increase the amount sold. In C, a price increase from P_1 to P_3 brings about a sharp decline in quantity demanded because the competitors will keep prices at P_1. The demand curve in D differs from the previous three demand curves in that it is relatively inelastic for outputs less than Q_1. When all the firms in an oligopolized industry are operating at capacity, any reduction in price would not be matched by competitors because each is already producing at capacity. It would pay no one to cut price—why should anyone cut price when he is producing and selling all he can at P_1? Were one of the oligopolists to raise price above P_1, however, the others would immediately match this increase, because they would not stand to lose too many sales. Since everyone is following the leader, the consumer would have no choice but to pay the increase.

PERILS OF THE PRICE WAR

In 1972 A&P, one of the leading firms in the oligopolistic food chain industry, began a new pricing policy, which was presented to the public as WEO (Where Economy Originates). The policy, described by one A&P spokesman as a "tonnage recovery program," had some features common to oligopolistic competition, in that it involved nonprice competition. Old stores were closed and new, larger, more attractive stores were opened. At the same time a huge advertising and promotion campaign was launched. A&P's WEO program contained another feature, however, not usually part of the repertoire of oligopolistic firms' competitive apparatus. A&P proposed to attract new customers by underselling its rivals. It was prepared, in other words, to start a price war.

How has A&P fared with its unconventional behavior? So far, not too well. A&P instituted the WEO program to bolster its falling profits. In 1970, A&P's profits were $50 million. In 1971 they were down to $14.6 million. The WEO program was expected to reverse this trend, and while it is true that the new policies have brought an $800 million sales increase, the firm's expansion program, selling costs, and other factors resulted in a loss of $51.3 million for the 1972 fiscal year.

In part this failure may be attributed to the oligopolistic system's lack of tolerance for price competition. A&P could not hold the slight edge which its lowered prices gave it over the rival firms. When the WEO program went into effect, competing supermarkets had no choice but to cut their prices to similar levels. So thorough was the industry-wide leveling of prices that a later study by an independent firm showed that A&P's prices on all but a few items were the same as or even higher than other chain food stores.

Moreover, in starting the price war and forcing other firms to diminish their profits, A&P has lost much of the goodwill of the industry. Spokesmen for rival firms speak bitterly of A&P's tactics and predict failure for its efforts.

The picture may not be thoroughly bleak, however. Others affirm that A&P's attempt to get and keep a new type of consumer may prove successful. The firm may pull through its present distress with increased profits. In this case, the example of A&P's WEO will have to be recorded as an exception to, rather than proof of, the rule that oligopolies cannot tolerate competition on the basis of price.

arette Company is earning a comfortable profit, but it would like to earn even more. The president of Golden Dragon calls a board meeting to discuss possible ways of achieving this aim. One board member suggests that the company might simply raise its prices and count on the loyalty of Dragon's satisfied customers to keep sales at or near their present level. This suggestion is dismissed, however, when another board member points out that customers are never that loyal—that when one firm in an oligopolistic industry raises its price, a great portion of its customers is sure to switch its allegiance to the competition. In other words, in this situation, demand would prove *highly elastic*. If one firm raised its price and the other firms did not, the firm charging the higher price would experience an immediate and severe decline in sales.

At this point another board member says: "Well, if that's the case, why don't we *lower* our price? The other firms' customers will leave them and come to us and our sales will increase." But this suggestion does not fare any better than the first one. Another board member points out that if one firm in an oligopolistic industry cuts its price in order to attract customers away from the others, then the others are almost certain to cut their prices to precisely the same level in order to prevent the success of such a plan. Thus demand would become *highly inelastic*. With prices cut all around, each firm would still have the same share of the market, but proportionately smaller revenues. The plan would have backfired.

Thus, the kinked demand curve: As price increases, above point E, the curve flattens, approaching the horizontal. A small increase in price brings a large change in quantity demanded and a drop in total revenue. As price decreases, below point E, however, the curve descends more sharply, approaching the vertical. A large decrease in price will increase quantity demanded very little, and again revenues will drop. Given this situation, Golden Dragon will probably decide to give up its plan to increase profits and be satisfied with the present state of things.

The kinked demand curve is common to many oligopolies, but the kink is more extreme in oligopolies that deal in homogeneous products. The reason for this is simple: With nothing to distinguish the product of one firm from that of another, customers will more readily switch their patronage, and sellers will react to these changes more swiftly.

RATCHET EFFECT If the firm and the industry in general are operating at capacity, expectations—and behavior—are somewhat different. Firms still have no incentive to lower prices because even if they did they could sell no more output because their plants are at capacity. A firm might increase its prices, however, since demand is great enough and supply so limited that buyers might not be able to switch to another supplier. The other firms would raise their prices, too, in order to profit from higher revenues.

This creates a climate for creeping inflation. When the economy is slack, price will not fall, since firms fear that they will trigger a price war. When the economy is booming, however, the industry will raise prices. Knowing this, labor unions may ask for large wage increases during booms, and firms are more likely to assent since this provides a justification for a price hike.

Marginal Cost/Marginal Revenue What relevance does the kinked demand curve have to the determination of price and output of oligopolistic firms? The answer to this question becomes clear when we examine the marginal revenue curve of the Golden Dragon Company. As you can see, there is a large break in the MR curve. Now the maximum total profit position of an oligopolistic firm, as in any other firm, is MC = MR. Because of the break in the MR curve, marginal cost may fluctuate between points F and E without changing price. This situation contributes to the relatively high degree of price stability enjoyed by the firm.

Price Uncertainty However, this stability, at least from the point of view of the firm, is quite arbitrary. The kinked demand curve provides no particular reason why price should stabilize at the point it does. Once it does stabilize, it becomes difficult to dislodge, as we have seen. But unless the firm can know the behavior of its competitors in advance or can insulate itself from them, it will be subject to a great deal of uncertainty in setting its price.

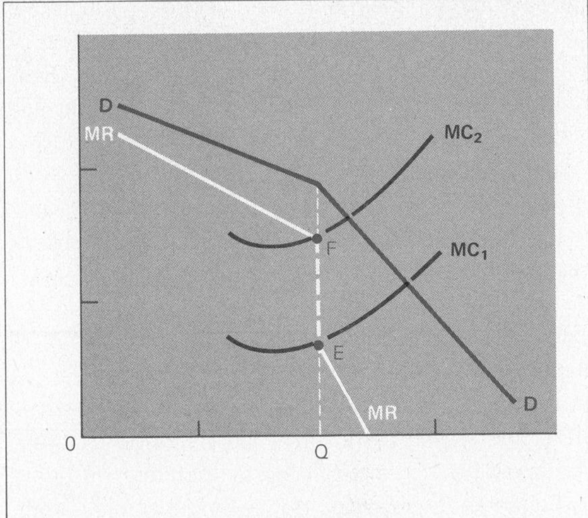

FIGURE 28-2 MR CURVE AND PRICE RIGIDITY When there is a kink in the demand curve, there will always be a discontinuity in the marginal revenue curve. This discontinuity is represented by the vertical broken line at quantity Q. Since the quantity sold (and the price) is determined by the point at which the MC and MR curves intersect, any MC curve between MC_2 and MC_1 will intersect the MR curve at quantity Q. Quantity and price will remain unchanged, then, over a range of costs. Thus, the oligopoly market situation is often one of price rigidity, since the seller is reluctant to change price, and only large changes in cost can induce him to alter the price.

The kinked demand curve depends upon knowing that the competition will respond in certain ways to price changes; other responses make other models necessary. All we can say for sure is that price and output will fall somewhere between the perfect competition combination and the monopoly combination. Chances are that price will be higher than that of perfect competition, so that resources will be misallocated. But oligopoly is characterized by price uncertainty, and firms will be anxious to find means to reduce this uncertainty.

Minimizing Uncertainty

Collusion Collusion is a broad term, encompassing many different types of price-setting behavior common to oligopolistic firms. **Overt collusion**, its most extreme form, involves the formation of a **cartel**, or central decision-making association entrusted with managing the price-setting policies of all firms in the industry. The trust of late nineteenth century America was a form of cartel. Since all firms are able to act as one, an oligopolistic industry under the control of a cartel is virtually identical with a monopoly in terms of price and output determination. The price can be at a level that allows joint profit maximization for all the firms. This is easier if the firms have similar cost structures, but it can work even if the firms have different costs. Price is frequently set high enough to allow inefficient firms to survive. For society the results are as if these firms actually formed a monopoly. Cartels of this type are against the law in the United States, although they do exist in other countries and on an international basis. But while formal cartel arrangements can be prevented fairly effectively by law, informal arrangements between heads of oligopolistic firms, often taking place on the golf course or at cocktail parties, cannot. It is these informal cartels that are most common in the United States. Despite their clandestine nature, they are nonetheless illegal, and can be dealt with by law when discovered.

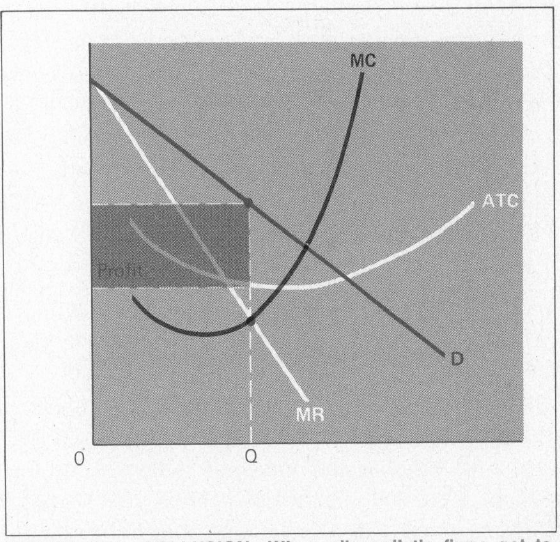

FIGURE 28-3 COLLUSION When oligopolistic firms get together and set a price, through collusion, the result is as if they were a monopoly. With similar cost curves, the MC = MR point will be similar, and collusion will enable joint profit maximization.

Price Leadership Even where no cartel exists, formal or informal, certain rules of the game, or **tacit collusion**, may evolve. Firms can signal each other by announcing that they are considering a new price schedule. When one breaks ranks the others follow suit. After a while one firm may always make the first move. This is known as **price leadership.** The price leader sets its price at a level that meets its corporate goals and that it believes will not outrage the rest of the industry. The other firms in the industry then match that price. The profit-maximizing position of the leader will probably not be the profit-maximizing position for the other firms, but in most cases, the price arrived at by the leader will yield at least normal profits for all concerned and often allows continued operation of inefficient firms. Price leadership is not illegal, and this fact, combined with the advantage it provides of effectively avoiding damaging price wars, has made it a method of price determination throughout most oligopolistic industries in the United States.

Barriers to Entry Oligopolies have every reason to keep out newcomers to the industry that might upset fixed arrangements. Take an industry in which several firms are enjoying excess profits. If a firm attracted by those profits finds it possible to enter the industry, the market shares and profits of the original firms will decline. In addition, the more firms there are in an industry, the more difficult it will be for them to "get together" and for any form of collusion to take place. Thus, in order to protect collusive arrangements and their advantages, oligopolistic firms find it beneficial to maintain barriers to entry. These barriers are a result of oligopoly and help to maintain it.

For example, one firm, which holds the patent rights to a machine whose use is crucial to the manufacture of a product, leases the machine to the existing firms and refuses it to new firms. Existing firms may also bar access to essential raw materials. Artificial barriers may also take the form of government franchises or licenses granted to a limited number of firms with the ostensible purpose of protecting the public by maintaining high standards within the industry. Such franchises are common in the public transportation industries, including taxi services, municipal and interstate bus lines, and air transportation. If all else fails, established firms may frighten away entering firms. This involves intimations that they will lower prices drastically if the new firm enters the industry. Entering firms will be apt to take such threats seriously since, having no established share of the market, they will be far less able to absorb losses incurred in a price war.

Mergers The problem with all these methods of avoiding competition is that a firm can never be absolutely sure that its rivals will always hold the price line. When there are a large number of firms, one aspiring upstart can try to increase its share of the market by lowering prices. In the ensuing competition, prices will fall below the level at which joint profit maximization is enjoyed. Maintaining price also depends upon relatively close cost and demand structures for all firms. The profit-maximizing level for one firm may actually call for a price above or below the established one. This firm may try to set clandestine prices in order to withstand a recession or get ahead of its competitors. If its customers turn around and demand the same discount from other firms, the secret is out and a price war may ensue.

One of the most effective ways of averting a price war is for two or more of the firms in the oligopolistic industry to merge. With one element of uncertainty thus eliminated, the remaining firms can maintain or raise existing profit levels.

Nonprice Competition

Because of the uncertainties about the elasticity of demand, oligopolistic firms tend to avoid competition on the basis of price. Prices can be changed very rapidly; a gas war, for example, may reduce the price of gasoline by 50 percent in a single week. However, this does not mean that the firms avoid competition altogether. Competing firms take longer to change a product or to introduce a sales gimmick, so oligopolists prefer to gain market advantages on this basis.

Perfectly competitive firms that wanted to indulge in

nonprice competition would probably find it hard to raise the necessary capital, since in the long run they receive only normal profits. Oligopolies, on the other hand, may earn excess profits in the long run. From this larger financial base they can mount annual model changes or devise ingratiating ad campaigns. If they are selling primary products like steel instead of consumer goods like autos, they can use lavish expense accounts to woo customers, promise better service, guarantee supplies, or make the steel to the customers' specifications.

Nonprice competition takes the form of product differentiation, which fosters the notion that one brand is different from the rest, either through physical changes or through advertising.

Physical Product Differentiation Physical product differentiation often, though not always, forms the basis of advertising campaigns. Many oligopolistic firms spend large amounts of money on "research and development" in the hope that improvements made on the product will make it more attractive to the public. Rival firms, of course, do not sit idly by and allow such claims to be made unopposed. They conduct research efforts of their own as well as match innovations made by one firm with their own imitations or variations. Such intense rivalry over product differentiation is most obvious in the automobile industry, where such things as power steering, power brakes, electronic ignition, and the rotary engine are introduced as totally unique innovations one year, only to become standard equipment, or at least easily available options the next. Some of these innovations actually do increase the safety or performance of autos and, as such, are in the interests of the consumer. Others are merely added for the purpose of producing a new model for the coming season and serve only to raise the price that the consumer must pay. Estimates for the decade 1950–60 place the total cost of annual model changes at $5 billion per year, with an added $7.1 billion in extra gas consumption of the heavier, faster autos.

The principle of product differentiation may also be applied to the products of a single firm. A firm may offer product models of different price and quality, not to compete with one another, but to appeal to different segments of the buying public. Again, the automobile industry best exemplifies this process. A single firm will produce an entire range of cars from a small economy car to appeal to those who doubted whether they were able to afford a car at all, all the way up to the luxury model for the person accustomed to treating himself to the best. By dealing with a broad range of economic groups, the firm tries to secure a larger share of the total market and, as a result, to increase its total revenue.

Advertising Sometimes advertising creates or suggests physical differentiation where it does not actually exist. Some products, such as aspirin, are essentially the same, no matter who manufactures them. Some firms, however, will not allow the public to accept this fact and spend great amounts of money on advertising campaigns to convince the public that their product is somehow different and superior. The public, meanwhile, accustomed to thinking that the products of rival firms must necessarily be arrangeable in terms of "good, better, best," accepts the advertiser's imaginary claims and gratefully pays a higher price for what it has been convinced is a better quality product.

The aim of advertising is both to shift to the right the demand curve faced by the individual seller and to make it less elastic. The shift of the demand curve to the right will absorb the effects of such changes that would normally touch off a price war. The decrease in elasticity allows the seller to sell a larger quantity of his product while maintaining or perhaps increasing price.

The purpose of an advertising campaign is not simply to attract a greater buying public for a product, but to attract consumers away from the competition. Sometimes these valiant efforts have been crowned with conspicuous success. For instance, the Marlboro man boosted sales of that brand when the advertising first appeared. But this success demonstrates only one function of advertising. Advertising campaigns for rival products may settle down into a virtual cold war, without winners or losers. Such a situation is customary in the ciga-

POSITIONING, OR HOW DIFFERENTIATED CAN YOU GET?

We see them on our TV screen: the rugged men who have just returned from an afternoon of throwing the hammer, or putting the shot, or tossing around the old anvil. They want a beer to satisfy the massive thirst they have built up. Wisely, they choose Schaefer, "the one beer to have when you're having more than one." Presumably, under less demanding conditions they would have chosen differently. They would have picked, say, Miller's, which as the song says, is appropriate only "when you've got the time."

Of course, nobody really believes that Schaefer's is inherently suited to quantity guzzling or Miller's to leisurely sipping—any more than anybody really believes that Nyquil, the "night time cold remedy," is any more effective in the dark than the daytime remedies (what if you live in the land of the midnight sun?), or that Correctol, "a woman's gentle laxative," has anything in it that especially suits it to feminine intestines. But advertising is not based on having consumers make rational choices. It is based on conditioning. And apparently enough people can be conditioned to believe these artful fabrications to make them worthwhile.

These advertising techniques are known as positioning. Positioning is really a new approach to an old activity common to imperfect competition: product differentiation. Product differentiation can be based on actual innovations, or it may be totally a matter of image, created by advertising, promotion, and packaging. Positioning by and large, is of the latter type. The difference is that it relies on specialization for its appeal. The Schaefer Company, for example, discovered through market research that a large portion of beer drinkers drank in quantity and that their major complaint was fading flavor as the bottles were emptied. Schaefer quickly adjusted its advertising to appeal to this newly identified minority. Similarly, Nyquil discovered that, since cold symptoms were most troublesome during the night, an appeal to "night sufferers" would pay off.

Laughable as these examples are, it is nonetheless true that ad campaigns such as these cost a great deal of money and that these selling costs must ultimately be paid by the consumer. Because of positioning, we must pay higher prices for our beer, our cold medicine, our laxatives—and not only for those products promoted by means of positioning, but for all products in the industry. Positioning then shows us quite clearly one of the liabilities of imperfect competition: higher prices through high selling costs.

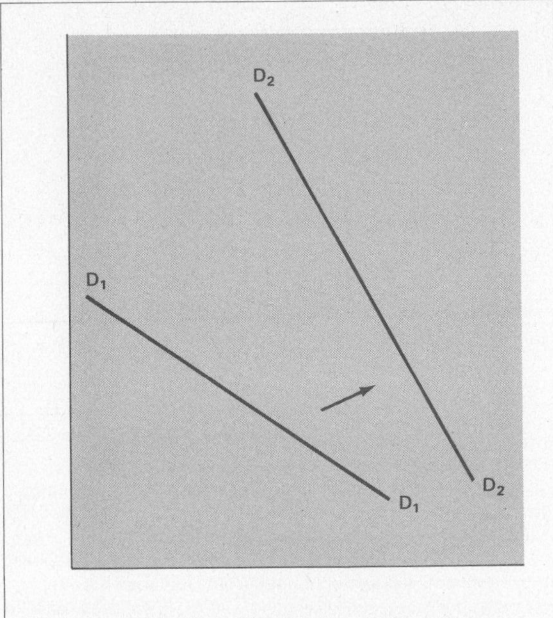

FIGURE 28-4 PRODUCT DIFFERENTIATION AND ADVERTISING MAKE DEMAND CURVE LESS ELASTIC When the demand curve is less elastic, a price change will have less effect on quantity demanded. By differentiating its product (in this case, autos) in the minds of consumers, either through physical features such as tail fins or through ad campaigns emphasizing the unique, sexy quality of the product, the oligopolist may shift the demand curve from D_1D_1 to D_2D_2.

rette industry, where each firm feels that it must continue to advertise merely to keep its name before the public and to retain its share of the market. Banning cigarette ads on TV and radio was not an unmitigated disaster for tobacco companies, since it enabled them to lower costs.

Oligopoly and Efficiency

When successful, product differentiation and advertising can distort resource allocation because firms create or modify consumer demand rather than respond to it. As the case of the cigarette industry shows, however, competition by means of advertising may be like competition by means of price. When one firm cuts prices, everyone cuts prices, revenues fall, and the industry is worse off than before. When one firm advertises more, everyone increases the advertising budget, costs go up, but market shares remain exactly as before.

Price competition imposes fewer costs than competition by means of product differentiation or advertising. Even if prices are not increased to reflect these extra costs, resources are absorbed that might be used more productively in other sectors. Over $20 billion is spent on advertising annually, in the United States alone, forming a "blandishments tax" of $100 per person.

The price rigidities in oligopolistic industries mean that during recessions output will fall instead of prices. This intensifies instability, and further adds to technological inefficiency, since plants are built with low break-even points to withstand recessionary periods, creating large amounts of excess capacity.

Oligopoly, then, is subject to all the criticisms of monopoly—restricted output, higher prices, and average cost above minimum—plus a few of its own caused by the added costs of nonprice competition.

On the positive side, oligopoly may produce innovation for much the same reason as monopoly or may be more efficient than perfect competition if it produces sizable economies of scale.

MONOPOLISTIC COMPETITION

At first glance the phrase *monopolistic competition* seems to be a contradiction in terms. If an industry is monopolistic—composed of just one firm—who can there be to compete with? But we encounter this contradiction only because we are still thinking in terms of the imaginary worlds of perfect competition and monopoly. When we think in terms of the real world of imperfect competition, the phrase becomes understandable.

Monopolistic competition refers to a situation in which there are many small firms—so many and so small that the price and output decisions of one can have no effect on the price and output decisions of the others. In this respect the situation resembles perfect competition. While firms in a perfectly competitive industry produce a homogeneous product, firms under monopolistic competition produce products with a degree of individuality. The products are differentiated.

The degree of differentiation may be great or small; it may be virtually nonexistent except as an advertising ploy. But whatever the degree, the differentiation of products within the industry results in each firm having a "partial monopoly" on the product it sells. Examples of industries characterized by monopolistic competition are the clothing industry, the shoe industry, the furniture and household goods industries, as well as certain services, such as those provided by doctors, dentists, and optometrists. Products and services in these industries may serve as substitutes for one another. If you cannot afford a particular brand of shoes, you may consider selecting another brand. The more sharply various brands within an industry are differentiated, the more resistance there will be to substitution and the more disparity there will be in price.

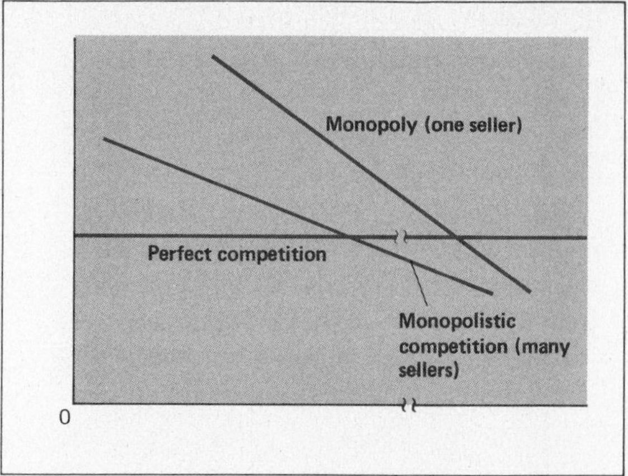

FIGURE 28-5 DEMAND CURVE UNDER MONOPOLISTIC COMPETITION Theoretically, we could have an identical demand curve for the monopolist and the monopolistic competitor, since both are downward-sloping. Were you asked to identify a single demand curve, say, the right-hand one in this graph, you would be hard put to identify it as that of the monopolist or the monopolistic competitor. If the industry were a monopoly, however, and many other firms entered to create monopolistic competition, the demand curve for the original firm would shift sharply to the left and become more elastic. Were there many firms selling an identical product rather than differentiated ones, the curve would become perfectly elastic.

Price and Output under Monopolistic Competition

Demand Because products under monopolistic competition are differentiated to the extent that consumers develop loyalties to one brand or another, a firm may be able to raise its price somewhat without a significant loss of customers. The loyalty of customers to certain brands also means that a firm will gain only a small number of new customers by lowering its prices. Other firms are not threatened by such small shifts in consumer preference and so do not retaliate with price cuts of their own. Thus the price wars that threaten oligopoly are less feared by those in monopolistic competition.

Although price cuts attract relatively few customers under monopolistic competition and price increases lose relatively few, the extent to which firms can affect their demand curves *is* of some significance. Firms under monopolistic competition face a demand curve that is not perfectly elastic. Instead it slopes downward, showing that a rise in price will decrease sales, while a drop in price will increase them. This sloping demand curve must always be considered against the background of product differentiation. For example, a person who drinks an expensive imported beer at $3 per six pack rather than a domestic brand for $1.50 per six pack will probably stick to his brand even if the price goes up a few cents or if the price of the domestic brand goes down by a similar amount. If, however, the imported beer went up to $4, he might consider abandoning it. Similarly, if the domestic beer lowered its price to $1, he might think of laying in a supply, perhaps for undiscriminating guests.

Price and Output As might be surmised from the above discussion, there is no single industry price for a product under monopolistic competition. Instead there is a range of prices. Each firm must decide individually, based on the unique cost and demand requirements it faces, how much of its product it should produce, and how much it should charge for the product in order to maximize profits.

Certain firms facing favorable cost and demand conditions may find themselves in a position to earn excess profits. However, since entry under monopolistic competition is relatively easy, the existence of excess profits will attract new firms. Under perfect competition the entry of new firms causes the market price to fall because of the shift in the industry supply curve. Under monopolistic competition the outcome is not so simple. There is no market price, so the effect of entry must be more general. What actually happens is that the entry of new firms increases the elasticity of demand and shifts the demand curve to the left, indicating that each firm now has a smaller share of the market.

In Figure 28-6 we see a firm under monopolistic competition that is earning excess profits. Note that the firm, according to the universal rules, sets output at the point where MC = MR.

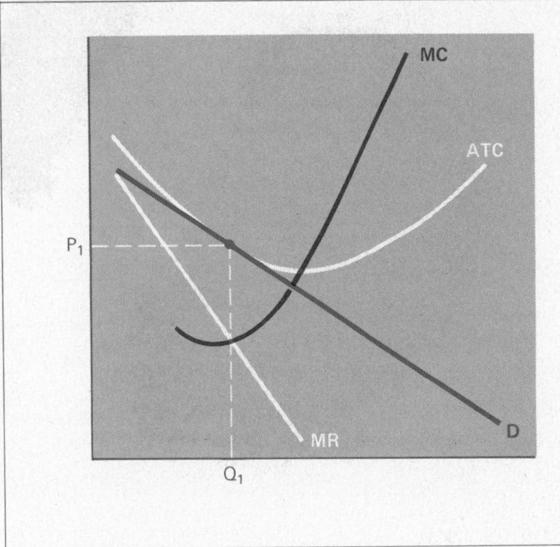

FIGURE 28-7 LONG-RUN EQUILIBRIUM FOR MONOPOLISTIC COMPETITION **Like perfect competition, monopolistic competition cannot sustain excess profits in the long run. Price will equal average cost and normal profits will be earned. But unlike perfect competition, monopolistic competition will operate above minimum average cost, so there will be excess capacity.**

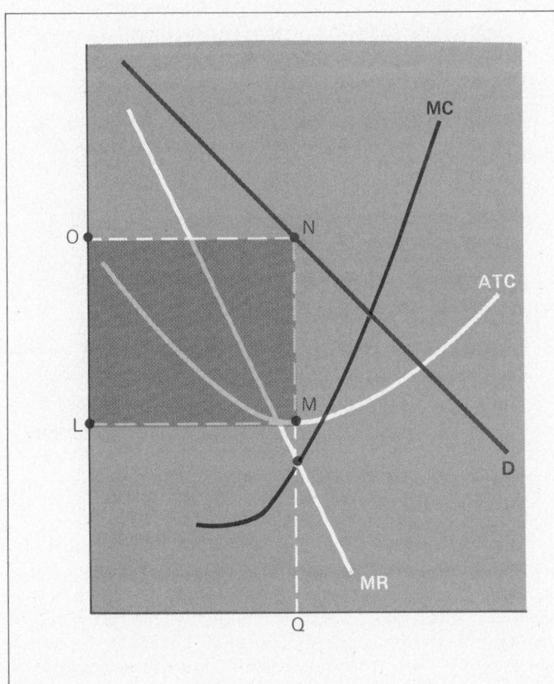

FIGURE 28-6 SHORT-RUN EQUILIBRIUM FOR MONOPOLISTIC COMPETITION **In the short run, the monopolistic competitor may earn profits, shown here by box LMNO. However, since there is ease of market entry under monopolistic competition, enough additional firms will be drawn into the market so that there will be no excess profits in the long run.**

Long-Run Equilibrium This situation does not last. Attracted by excess profits, more firms enter the industry. The demand curve shifts and becomes more elastic and the sales of each firm drop. The firm is left with excess capacity, but normal profits are being made. Here is where the industry will reach equilibrium.

Efficiency

The long-run equilibrium level of monopolistic competition no more guarantees efficiency than did monopoly or oligopoly. Price still exceeds marginal cost, indicating that this industry should keep increasing production.

Nor is the industry able to minimize costs. Because the firm's demand curve slopes downward, it cannot

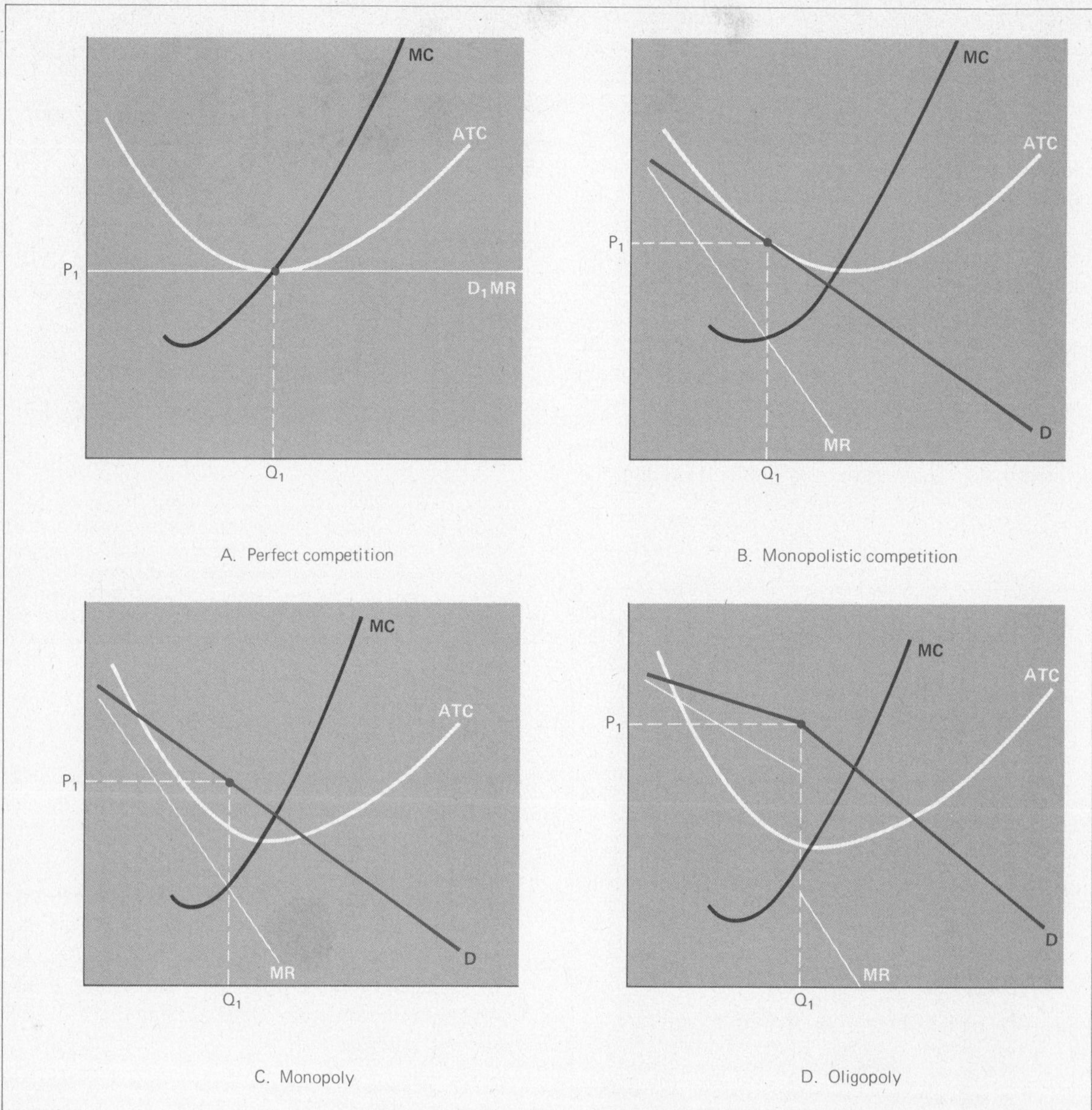

FIGURE 28-8 COMPARING MARKET STRUCTURES These four graphs give us a chance to make certain comparisons among the long-run equilibriums of (A) the perfect competitor, (B) the monopolistic competitor, (C) the monopolist, and (D) the oligopolist. Note first that the average total cost curve and the marginal cost curve for each of these competitors are identical. This is to emphasize that their differences lie in their demand curves and derivative marginal revenue curves, as well as in the relationships among all the curves. Price, output, and profits in each of these market structures are described in the text.

be tangent to the average total cost curve at its lowest point. Instead it will be tangent to the left of the lowest point. This indicates that the firm, even when it is earning only normal profits, cannot produce at minimum costs, or looked at another way, the firm always has excess capacity.

Firms under monopolistic competition then are guilty of misallocating resources and of setting prices "unnaturally" high. In this they resemble monopolies. However, the characteristic sins of monopolistic competition may be even greater than those of monopoly. This is because under monopolistic competition a major cause of wasted resources and higher prices is the high selling costs incurred as a result of the necessity for product differentiation. And there is no limit to these costs. They vary according to the way the management of the individual firm views the market situation. Moreover, high selling costs may infect an entire industry, so that there is no way the consumer can escape from them.

Finally, because entry is relatively easy, many industries under monopolistic competition end up glutted by too many small firms selling too many differentiated products. When this happens we say that the industry is "sick." The result of such a situation is that nobody earns much of a profit, and prices consequently are high. Although marginal firms are forced out of business by such a situation, ease of entry makes it possible for new firms to take their place. Thus a "sick" industry can be perpetuated almost indefinitely. A common example of this is the cluster of gas stations seen on roadways; sometimes there is one station on each corner of an intersection. Should one fail under one brand name, a new owner may appear to operate it under another name.

MARKET STRUCTURE AND MARKET PERFORMANCE

Over the past four chapters the market structures of perfect competition, monopolistic competition, monopoly, and oligopoly have been described. Figure 28-8 summarizes these in graph form. What these graphs show is:

1. All market structures except perfect competition have a gap between price and marginal cost that leads to restricted output, higher prices, and therefore allocative inefficiency. Under oligopoly and monopoly, price discrimination may allow increases in output at the cost of eliminating consumer surplus.
2. All market structures except perfect competition need not produce at a level at which average costs are minimum. Such technological inefficiency is particularly true of monopolistic competition, in which considerable excess capacity is the rule.

The case is not that simple, however. The structures of the cost curves may reflect pressures within the market to incur extra costs or to find ways of reducing costs. Oligopoly and monopolistic competition rely on advertising and product differentiation, which raise the average cost curve. Output may increase, moving the firm down the higher AC curve to a point lower than before, but there is no guarantee that this will happen. The oligopolist may try to find lower cost methods of producing his goods, since he (like the monopolist) has excess profits to finance the search. (But these excess profits also allow the monopolist or oligopolist to forgo profit maximization in favor of reducing competition, thereby intensifying technological inefficiency.) Perfect competition may not induce innovation, since the benefits are quickly shared by other competitors, so that its cost curves may actually be higher than other market structures. If all the cost structures are the same (as in Figure 28-8), then perfect competition will always have the lowest cost. But since these structures vary, there is no way to predict which structure actually offers the lowest cost.

What these curves do not show is the interaction of market structure with the society at large. The next chapter takes up this topic in some detail.

SUMMARY

1 Imperfect competition embraces oligopoly and monopolistic competition.

2 Oligopoly consists of an industry in which there are a few firms whose actions are interdependent. For example, if one firm lowers price, the others might—resulting in lower revenues for all. But if one firm raises price, the rest might grab his customers by holding to the lower price. This situation may be shown using the kinked demand curve and the break in the MR curve that holds output and price stable over a range of costs.

3 In order to minimize price uncertainty firms may engage in overt or tacit collusion, price leadership, manipulating barriers to entry, or merging with competitors. This enables joint profit maximization, the economic effects of which are nearly identical to those that would occur if the industry were a monopoly.

4 To escape the problems of price competition entirely, oligopolists use nonprice competition. Product differentiation and advertising set the output of one firm apart from that of its competitors, but impose added costs.

5 Monopolistic competition also involves the use of product differentiation and advertising. In this market system there are many firms, each trying to distinguish its product in some fashion. The effect of this on the firm's demand curve is to make it less elastic and move it to the right.

6 Unlike the oligopolist, the monopolistic competitor cannot maintain excess profits indefinitely; in the long run the demand curve will shift until it is tangent to the AC curve, and the firm earns normal profits. The monopolistic competitor is plagued by overcapacity and is neither technologically nor allocatively efficient.

7 Market structure shapes market performance. If the cost structures of each industry are identical, then perfect competition will allocate resources so that profits are maximized for the firm but do not exceed the normal level, resources are allocated so that the price people are willing to pay equals the marginal cost of producing the last unit, and the firm is using the optimum size plant and is producing at minimum cost with that plant. However, cost structures may differ, complicating the evaluation of the relationship between market structures and market performance.

SUGGESTED READINGS

Adams, Walter, ed. *The Structure of American Industry*. 4th ed. New York: Macmillan, 1971.

Caves, Richard. *American Industry: Structure, Conduct, and Performance*. 3rd ed. Englewood Cliffs, N.J.: Prentice-Hall, 1972.

Leftwich, Richard H. *The Price System and Resource Allocation*. 4th ed. Chap. 12. Hinsdale, Ill.: Dryden Press, 1970.

McDonald, John. *Strategy in Poker, Business, and War*. New York: W. W. Norton, 1950.

Weiss, Leonard W. *Case Studies in American Industry*. rev. ed. Chap. 5. New York: John Wiley & Sons, 1971.

QUESTIONS

1 Review

a. the major models of imperfect competition: oligopoly and monopolistic competition,

b. the kinked demand curve for the oligopolist and the tendency to try to minimize uncertainty,
c. the ways in which oligopolists tend to restrict entry and attempt to differentiate products,
d. price and output under conditions of monopolistic competition,
e. inefficiencies inherent in oligopolistic and monopolistically competitive markets.

2 Indicate the model that would most likely describe each of the following industries and give your reasons.
a. nonprescription drugs
b. air travel
c. hair-care products
d. soybean meal
e. dog food
f. apartments

3 In the early 1970s there was a rapid increase in the popularity of American Indian jewelry. Because of the increase there have been entries of many more Indian jewelry producing firms, many of which do not employ Indians. A large number of Navajos and Zuñis, among others, have been bringing suits to try to establish that these firms cannot market their wares as "Indian" unless they are actually made by Indians. According to the models discussed in this chapter, how would you describe this move on the part of the Indians? What is the effect on the demand curve for their wares? Their profits?

4 Under what circumstances would you say that the drive-in fast-food service is a sick industry? How does easy access to franchises contribute to the problem?

5 On occasion, presidents have been able to roll back or prevent a price increase by an oligopolist by persuasion. Why might a president have such success in the case of the oligopolist and not in the case of local farmers' markets?

6 In 1973, the Nixon administration placed a price freeze on almost all consumer goods. However, some raw materials such as unprocessed food were exempt from the freeze. In some cases, this policy allowed increases in costs to the firm while the price of the final product was fixed. One of the models of imperfect competition would predict little if any price change on the part of the firm even though the costs of production varied. Which model? Why?

7 In the case of monopolistic competition the purpose of advertising is product differentiation. How would each of the following affect the demand curve for a given firm's product?
a. The assertion that a particular brand of aspirin is suited especially for arthritic pain
b. A ruling by the Federal Trade Commission that no claim can be made in advertising unless the company can substantiate that claim upon demand
c. A law that provides that all beauty aids must have a list of ingredients on the package

8 Which of these graphs represents the long-run equilibrium situation of the monopolistic competitor and which represents the short-run equilibrium situation? Why?

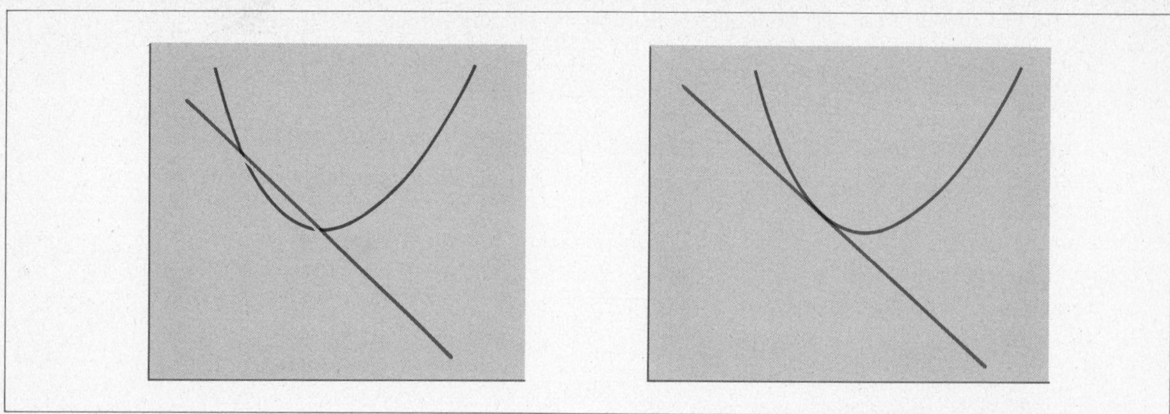

9 Explain the economics behind this cartoon using the graphs of long-run equilibrium for monopoly and oligopoly.

Culver Pictures

CHAPTER
29
BUSINESS &
GOVERNMENT

A major theme of this book has been to investigate the advantages and disadvantages of alternative methods of organizing or controlling economic activity. The emphasis has been on analyzing the market system as a means of achieving society's economic goals, with some analysis of government control as a complement or an alternative to the market. This analysis has shown that a market system without governmental restraints or assistance will fall far short of attaining society's economic goals. Government action is needed in order to maintain full employment, price stability, a satisfactory rate of growth; to provide public goods and services such as national defense and police protection; to alleviate the problems caused by externalities such as air and water pollution and so forth.

Government activity is more than a supplement to market control of economic activity; it is necessary to the very existence of a market system. A government is necessary to establish and protect property rights, to enforce contracts, to establish a monetary system, and to collect taxes to pay for these services. Even the strongest advocates of *laissez faire* must admit the necessity of governmental actions and institutions that establish the legal framework and political stability within which a market system can operate.

On the other hand, few if any economic activities in a mixed economy such as ours are strictly in the realm of government control. Government agencies buy from and sell to private business; they compete with businesses for labor and other factors of production; their very existence depends upon their ability to tax businesses and individuals. Accordingly, the oft heard question, "Should government or business be involved in this activity?" is not quite appropriate. In our economy, government *and* business are almost always involved.

The questions that should be considered by all those concerned with economic policy are, "What mix of government and business will make the economy work best?" and "What forms of governmental and what forms of market control will make the economic system most likely to fulfill society's goals?"

Opening photo by J. Paul Kirouac

Previous chapters have shown that the term *market* actually embodies a number of different ways of organizing economic activity—from competition through monopoly. We have seen that in many cases competition is to be preferred, but that there are situations in which because of economies of scale or faster technological change, some degree of oligopoly or monopoly may enhance the operation of the system.

The term *governmental control* also embodies a variety of forms of control. One aspect of this is determining the appropriate level of government—federal, regional, state, county, and municipal. But of even more importance is the issue of *how* the governmental agency attempts to achieve its goals. For example, different governmental actions designed to improve the provision of medical care can have significantly different consequences, as shown in Chapter 2. In Parts Two and Three, alternative ways of attempting to achieve full employment and price stability were examined. Chapter 21 revealed that alternative pollution control policies can have significantly different costs.

Contemporary economic analysis has articulated the conditions under which markets fail to be efficient. Governmental control can fail also. Poorly designed or poorly administered programs may fail to improve the general welfare. All of this suggests that a study of the relationship between business and government should focus on the probable consequences of alternative forms of governmental and market control of economic activity. This requires a careful look at the relevant dimensions of the economic problem to be considered (which vary considerably among different problems) and a careful look at the elements of the government policy and the market structure that are involved.

ECONOMIC CONCENTRATION

Playing with Economic Blocs

A glance at the financial section of any newspaper shows that there are many enormous firms in the United States. General Motors, for example, has

TABLE 29-1 The 30 Largest Industrial Corporations in the United States, 1972

Rank '72	Rank '71	Company	Sales (in thousands)	Assets (in thousands)	Rank	Net Income (in thousands)	Rank
1	1	General Motors (Detroit)	30,435,231	18,273,382	2	2,162,807	1
2	2	Exxon (New York)	20,309,753	21,558,257	1	1,531,770	2
3	3	Ford Motor (Dearborn, Mich.)	20,194,400	11,634,000	4	870,000	5
4	4	General Electric (New York)	10,239,500	7,401,800	10	530,000	9
5	7	Chrysler (Detroit)	9,759,129	5,497,331	13	220,455	19
6	5	International Business Machines (Armonk, N.Y.)	9,532,593	10,792,402	5	1,279,268	3
7	6	Mobil Oil (New York)	9,166,332	9,216,713	7	574,199	6
8	8	Texaco (New York)	8,692,991	12,032,174	3	889,040	4
9	9	ITT (New York)	8,556,826	8,617,897	8	483,303	10
10	10	Western Electric (New York)	6,551,183	4,309,899	17	282,941	13
11	11	Gulf Oil (Pittsburgh)	6,243,000	9,324,000	6	197,000	24
12	12	Standard Oil of California (San Francisco)	5,829,487	8,084,193	9	547,070	7
13	13	U. S. Steel (New York)	5,401,773	6,570,009	11	156,988	33
14	14	Westinghouse Electric (Pittsburgh)	5,086,621	3,843,291	19	198,667	23
15	15	Standard Oil (Ind.) (Chicago)	4,503,372	6,186,242	12	374,740	12
16	17	E. I. du Pont de Nemours (Wilmington, Del.)	4,365,900	4,283,700	18	414,500	11
17	16	Shell Oil (Houston)	4,075,898	5,171,600	14	260,480	15
18	19	Goodyear Tire & Rubber (Akron, Ohio)	4,071,523	3,476,668	23	193,159	26
19	18	RCA (New York)	3,838,180	3,137,312	27	158,104	32
20	21	Procter & Gamble (Cincinnati)	3,514,438	2,360,458	38	276,310	14
21	20	LTV (Dallas)	3,514,181	1,784,924	57	8,838	385
22	26	International Harvester (Chicago)	3,493,274	2,574,344	31	86,554	60
23	28	Eastman Kodak (Rochester, N.Y.)	3,477,764	3,757,454	20	546,250	8
24	23	Continental Oil (Stamford, Conn.)	3,414,984	3,249,705	26	170,181	30
25	22	Atlantic Richfield (Los Angeles)	3,320,793	4,629,013	16	195,561	25
26	32	Tenneco (Houston)	3,275,411	4,838,123	15	203,017	22
27	25	Union Carbide (New York)	3,261,322	3,718,342	21	205,241	21
28	27	Swift (Chicago)	3,240,931	935,848	127	37,003	172
29	30	Kraftco (Glenview, Ill.)	3,196,789	1,245,193	96	88,335	56
30	29	Bethlehem Steel (Bethlehem, Pa.)	3,113,602	3,645,375	22	134,584	38

Shown here are the sales, assets, and net income of the top 30 industrial corporations, each with sales of over $3 billion. Oil and autos dominate the list. The oil industry, in particular, has six representatives among the top 15 industrial corporations in sales, and nine in the top 25. Not only do General Motors, Ford, and Chrysler constitute the auto industry's Big Three, but all are among the top five in the sales listing. ITT, LTV, and Tenneco represent a relatively new phenomenon—the conglomerate. Such enormous economic power wielded by these industrial giants cannot help but be translated into political power over state and national policies.

SOURCE: *Fortune*, May 1973, p. 222.

sales greater than the GNP of most nations. But sheer size is not the same thing as economic concentration.

The exact definition of economic concentration varies depending on the indicators used. Thus, economists can say the trend toward concentration in the United States is increasing and decreasing at the same time. It all depends on which indicator they are looking at.

One measure of concentration is the number of firms

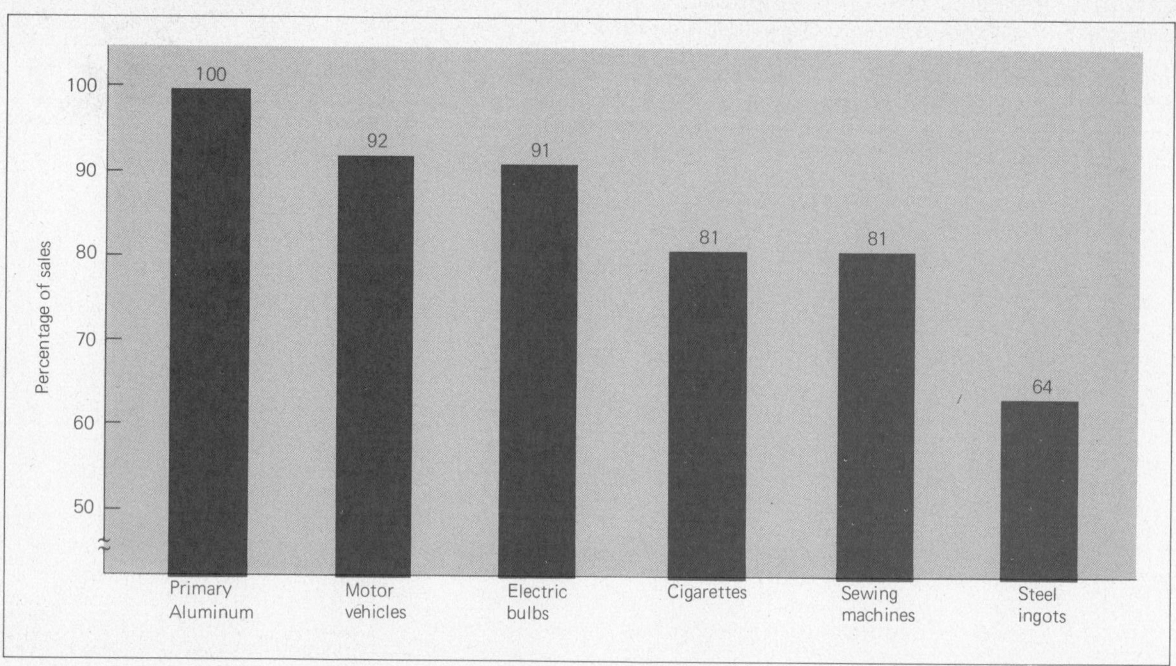

FIGURE 29-1 ECONOMIC CONCENTRATION (PERCENTAGE OF INDUSTRY OUTPUT OF FOUR LARGEST FIRMS, 1967) Industry concentration ratings are a measure of oligopoly in an industry. In the cases shown here, the top four firms produce all, or nearly all, of the output in a given industry. However, the market share of the individual firms may vary considerably. For example, in cigarettes, R. J. Reynolds is the dominant firm, producing a little less than one-half the industry's output, while U.S. Steel and Bethlehem Steel dominate that industry, although they produce less than one-half the output, since the other firms are relatively small.

SOURCE: U.S. Bureau of the Census, *Census of Manufacturers*, 1967. Special Report Series: Concentration Ratios in Manufacturing, M67(S)-2.1, Table 5.

in the industry and their relative size. Industry concentration ratios quantify this. Concentration ratios are computed by the Department of Commerce for various industries in the United States. They indicate the percentage of total sales of the four largest firms in each industry. For example, in 1972, total sales of cigarettes were $4.1 billion, with the four largest firms accountable for about $3.3 billion. The concentration ratio was 81, or 81 percent of the sales accounted for by the top four firms. Such a high ratio shows that the cigarette industry is an oligopoly and implies that it is not highly competitive. Contrast this with the wood furniture industry, with a concentration ratio of 11, suggesting that the wood furniture industry is more competitive than the cigarette industry.

By this measure a substantial portion of U.S. manufacturing industries are still reasonably competitive. In 1970, for example, 116 manufacturing industries had concentration ratios above 50, 166 were between 25 and 50, and 140 had ratios below 25. About three-quarters of all U.S. industries then had less than one-half their output sold by the top four firms. Furthermore, comparisons of these figures with those of previous years indicate that concentration may have even decreased during the 1960s.

A number of observers, however, maintain that competition is decreasing rather than increasing. As evidence, they point to a different measure of concentration, aggregate concentration. This indicator measures the relative size of the largest firms regardless of their industry designation. In 1947 the 100 largest manufacturing firms accounted for 39.3 percent of the assets of all manufacturing firms and the largest 200 for 47.2 percent; in 1968 these figures were 48 and 61, respectively. Thus aggregate concentration appears to have increased substantially even though industry concentration has shown a slight decline.

The significance of these two measures has been widely disputed. Many economists say that industry concentration ratios tell us more about competition than do aggregate ratios. In recent years, however, there has been a growing concern that the increase in aggregate concentration is adversely affecting the performance of the economy. To many observers, these indicators have been viewed as evidence of an alarming increase in economic and political power in the hands of a relatively few people, a decrease in competition, and a deterioration in the performance of the market system.

Alarm is heightened by the concentration of power in the financial community. In 1970 the largest 100 commercial banks had 47 percent of all deposits in the U.S. (a drop, however, from 57 percent in 1940) and the largest 20 life insurance companies (with total assets of approximately $200 billion) held 75 percent of all life insurance policies. Add to this the corporate interest groups controlled by such families as the Rockefellers, the Mellons, and the Du Ponts, which have a major financial interest in or control a wide range of enterprises. Such control can be maintained through interlocking directorates. While it is illegal for an individual to be on the board of directors of competing companies, it is not uncommon for one person to be on a number of noncompeting boards—holding seats, for example, on the boards of a large bank, an insurance company, a public utility, a large retail chain, and perhaps several large manufacturing companies that are not in direct competition, such as General Electric and Gulf Oil. Obviously, such arrangements make possible the concentration of a vast amount of economic power.

Bigger Is Better?

Critics of bigness charge that freedom from competition has given the consumer inferior merchandise. They point out that, by maintaining excessive profits, bigness has contributed significantly to inflation and, by maintaining excess capacity, to unemployment. They have condemned large corporations as a source of foreign imperialism and political corruption and have decried discriminatory hiring practices. They have identified large corporations as major culprits in pollution, that have steadfastly resisted public pressures—as witnessed by the resistance of auto makers to antipollution devices and the oil industry's pursuit of an Alaska pipeline. The problem is in testing these charges empirically, calculating their economic impact, and determining whether they stem from concentration rather than some other source.

The dimensions and effects of such concentration have been subject to considerable investigation in recent years, with a number of studies supporting allegations that wasteful advertising, higher prices, and misallocation of resources are direct results of bigness. Ralph Nader, for example, cited such studies in 1973 to charge that $4 billion a year was being wasted on advertising by the food industry. This expenditure, he declared, not only inflated the cost of food products to the consumer but furthered monopoly power by keeping out competitors who lacked the means for large-scale advertising.[1]

In a comprehensive study, F. M. Scherer estimated that in recent years actual GNP was 6.2 percent below potential GNP because of the concentration of market power.[2] Table 29-2 summarizes the causes of this failure to reach potential. Although Scherer recognized that each of the individual estimates was subject to a wide margin of error, he was confident that the total estimate was not unreasonable. If he is correct, concentration of market power has not been an overwhelming burden on the system, but in recent years it has cost about $70 billion a year, which is twice the annual cost of the Vietnam War at its height.

Concentration of market power also has some impact upon income distribution, since monopoly

1 *New York Times*, July 18, 1973, p. 16.
2 F. M. Scherer, *Industrial Market Structure and Economic Performance* (Chicago: Rand McNally, 1970), pp. 408–411.

TABLE 29-2 Economic Cost of Concentration

Percentage of GNP lost	Cause
0.9	Resource misallocation in unregulated sectors
0.6	Pricing distortions in regulated sectors
2.0	Inefficiencies due to deficient cost control by firms insulated from competition
0.6	Deficient cost control by defense and space contractors
1.0	Wasteful promotional efforts
0.3	Undercapacity or overcapacity
0.2	Distorted location decisions
0.6	Excess capacity due to collusive profits
6.2	Total cost of market power

When the Vietnam War was drawing to a close, everyone spoke of the "peace dividend" from decreased war spending. The "concentration dividend" from eliminating the ill effects of monopoly and oligopoly would be twice as large, according to one estimate. The greatest burdens are technological inefficiency of deficient cost controls and promotional spending. These alone equal the "peace dividend."

SOURCE: Frederic M. Scherer, *Industrial Market Structure and Economic Performance*, © 1970 by Rand McNally and Company, Chicago, p. 408. Reprinted by permission of Rand McNally College Publishing Company.

profits are in effect a redistribution of the income of consumers to the stockholders of giant corporations. Scherer estimated an annual redistribution on the order of 3 percent of GNP.

Technology and Concentration Whatever the consequences, concentration may be inevitable and perhaps even necessary. This argument depends upon the link between concentration, size, and technology. First, largeness may permit greater technological efficiency. Second, concentration may generate more rapid technological change and therefore more rapid economic growth. To those who hold this view, bigger may well be better.

TECHNOLOGICAL EFFICIENCY Common sense and experience tell us that economies of scale are possible in the production of many items. Is there any systematic relationship, then, between size and technological efficiency?

Somewhat surprisingly, studies reveal that in almost every highly concentrated industry in the United States the average cost of production for the largest firms is approximately the same as for many of the smaller firms. Figure 29-2 shows a typical long-run average cost curve estimated in these studies. A firm that has become big enough to produce at just 5 percent of the output of the industry has reached its minimum efficient size (MES); any further increase in size will not reduce costs since there are constant returns to scale beyond MES. In most industries a firm can achieve its MES with less than 5 percent of the industry output. Thus, if the concentration ratio of the four largest firms in an industry is 20, those firms can be producing with technological efficiency. This implies that although perfect competition is not feasible, the current level of concentration in many industries is not necessary. In fact, reduction of market power might enhance technological efficiency, as indicated by Table 29-2, which shows a 2.0 percent GNP loss due to deficient cost control by firms with inadequate competitive pressures.

TECHNOLOGICAL INNOVATION A most eloquent proponent of the idea that concentration promotes tech-

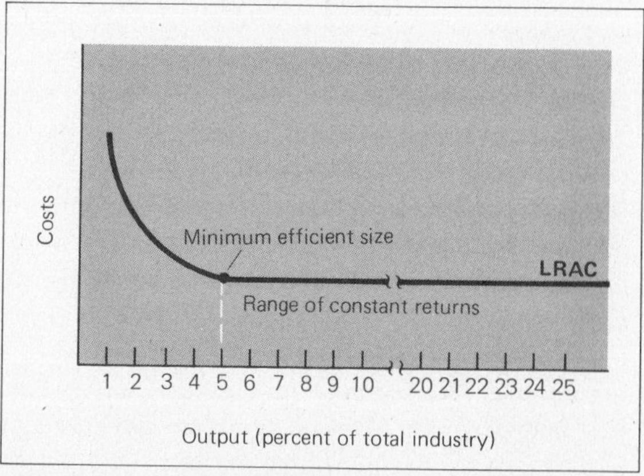

FIGURE 29-2 MINIMUM EFFICIENT SIZE The argument that technological efficiency depends upon the size of the firm is based on increasing economies of scale as size increases. However, the long-run average cost curves for many industries show constant returns to scale over a wide range of output. Once the minimum efficient size is reached, increases in size will not lower costs. If the MES occurs at 5 percent of industry output, 20 firms can operate as cheaply as four or five much larger firms.

nological innovation is Joseph Schumpeter.[3] He stresses that oligopolies have the financial resources to innovate, since excess profits free them from dependence on capital markets. And these firms have the incentive to innovate. Innovation in cutting costs is simply another means of nonprice competition. In the event of a price war, having lower costs than those of rivals helps the efficient firm weather the storm. And market power ensures that the innovator profits from his investment, unlike under more competitive conditions.

However, like the relationship between firm size and efficiency, the relation between concentration and technological change cannot be taken for granted. Schumpeter's argument seems reasonable, but there are other factors at work. Bureaucratic organization tends to stifle inventiveness and creativity, and the absence of competitive pressures may breed lethargy: Because these firms have market power, they may also deliberately withhold new ideas, processes, and products in order to protect their existing products and investment. A surprising number of major inventions have been developed by independent workers or by small research organizations. Included in this list are the helicopter, air conditioning, the automatic transmission, power steering, the cotton picker, insulin, cellophane, quick freezing, and the catalytic cracking of petroleum. Research laboratories of large firms have been responsible for some major inventions, but the list is much smaller. Moreover, in many cases innovations developed by large firms have been the result of defense projects financed by the federal government. By contrast, oligopolistic industries that do not ordinarily attract defense contracts, such as producers of food products and agricultural machinery, usually spend only small amounts on research. In sum, research indicates that medium-size firms and industries that have a moderate amount of concentration tend to be more innovative than the very largest corporations.[4]

The New Industrial State One renowned economist who disagrees with such an evaluation of the role of technology and technological change is John Kenneth Galbraith.[5] He believes that modern technology is making the small competitive firm a relic of the past. This has resulted in more than the ill effects of oligopoly and monopoly that are predicted by conventional economic theory. In *The New Industrial State,* Galbraith details the inevitably dangerous union between business and government, which he believes modern technology has created.

Galbraith argues that in recent years the nature of technology has changed dramatically. It now requires highly specialized capital equipment, highly specialized labor, huge amounts of financial capital, and long time lags between the commitment of funds to a project and the receipts of any revenue from the project. Accordingly, firms can no longer afford the uncertainties associated with a competitive market or with the normal interaction of supply and demand. They must be able to plan, and planning requires, among other things, stable prices—of both inputs and the products sold.

This means that corporations will work hard to ensure that the demand for their products will be there when they finally reach the markets. This forces heavy advertising. It also implies a close relationship with the federal government. The easiest way to handle the need for planning is through a government contract. This guarantees not only that the product will sell, but that any unexpected costs will be no problem, since such contracts usually allow for some form of cost-plus compensation.

If the product cannot be sold to the government, the corporation still relies upon the federal government to ensure an adequate level of aggregate demand. Despite corporate pronouncements about fiscal responsibility, American corporations are among the strongest proponents of government spending, according to Galbraith.

This is especially true when considered in conjunction with the corporate drive for growth. Given the growing separation between ownership and management, Galbraith believes that profits have become

3 Joseph Schumpeter, *Capitalism, Socialism, and Democracy,* 3rd ed. (New York: Harper & Row, 1950).

4 John Jewkes, David Sawers, and Richard Stillerman, *The Sources of Invention* (New York: St. Martin's Press, 1958).

5 John Kenneth Galbraith, *The New Industrial State,* 2nd rev. ed. (Boston: Houghton Mifflin, 1971).

secondary to the growth of the corporations as a management objective, because increased size provides the bureaucrats (or "technostructure" as Galbraith calls them) with autonomy and security. The easiest way to achieve corporate growth, he says, is through a close relationship with the federal technostructure, which is also committed to the goal of growth.

The result of all this is an economy that is avidly pursuing the goal of economic growth, but growth in the wrong direction! Instead of consumer sovereignty, there is the "revised sequence." Producers decide what to make and then create the demand for these products. The government ensures that there is sufficient aggregate demand and itself undertakes projects, such as sophisticated weaponry and spacecraft, that mean growth for the existing large corporations.

The academic community and the labor movement are largely agreeable to all this because their own personal needs appear to be well met by such a system. But the poor are left out, as are many social services and projects that would truly improve our quality of life. Thus, Galbraith sees the New Industrial State as both inefficient and inequitable.

Workable Competition Most American economists would not go this far. Concentration of economic power need not eliminate competition. Drawing on J. M. Clark, some argue that competition in the United States, while far from perfect, is at least workable.[6]

Shifts in demand may make market power temporary. Many firms that enjoyed enormous power at one time have lost it or have ceased to exist because the goods or services they produced no longer play an important part in our culture. For example, the Central Leather Company, seventh largest corporation in America in 1909, was forced out of the market when plastics and other materials began to replace leather. Similarly, the growing popularity of alternate forms of transportation forced the Pullman Company and the American Locomotive Company into drastic decline, while the rise of synthetic fabrics sheared away much of American Woolen's former glory.

Furthermore, concentration in an industry need not preclude competition. Imports often challenge domestic goods. And the threat of potential competition always exists, even for the most entrenched company, not only from firms in its industry but from other sectors as well. Since ultimately all goods are substitutes for one another, competition for the consumer's dollar still exists *between* industries, even when there is considerable concentration *within* industries. Workable competition may not be sufficient to counteract the ill effects of concentration entirely, however.

6 J. M. Clark, *Competition as a Dynamic Process* (Washington, D.C.: Brookings Institution, 1961).

GOVERNMENT REGULATION

The problems created by market power have led to intervention by government. This has taken two forms: antitrust enforcement to protect competition and regulation in areas where no competition is possible. In this way the government does not operate businesses but merely sets the ground rules for the economy.

Antitrust Enforcement

The grandaddy of antitrust laws is the Sherman Act of 1890. The legislation bearing the name of Senator John Sherman of Ohio has little resemblance to the bill he introduced. Unfortunately, there are few records of the congressional debate in shaping passage of the act, so we have little record of the thinking behind its final form. But the Sherman Act probably reflects a compromise between those who wanted no antitrust bill but realized that the political situation required one, and those who wanted a strong bill but realized that a compromise was required if there was to be any bill at all.

The basic elements of the Sherman Act are contained in the first two sections. Section 1 outlaws "every contract, combination in the form of trust or otherwise, or conspiracy, in restraint of trade...." Section 2 makes it illegal to "monopolize, or attempt to monopolize .. any part of the trade or commerce among the several states. . ." If these provisions are enforced and interpreted very strictly, they would appear to be quite powerful tools in maintaining a competitive economy. However, the rather general wording of the act has allowed for much evasion, and the act has not always been vigorously enforced. Judicial interpretation has further reduced its effectiveness. The Sherman Act was scarcely enforced during the administrations of Harrison, Cleveland, and McKinley. Only 18 cases were initiated under these three presidents. It appeared that the opponents of antitrust had succeeded. The political pressure for an antitrust bill had been eased, but the law did not mean anything—a situation that is not unique to the Sherman Act. However, during the administration of Theodore Roosevelt the climate changed, and 44 cases were brought.

The Rule of Reason and the Meaning of Monopoly

In the next decade two problems of interpretation emerged—problems that still dominate debate over antitrust policy. The first involves the question of whether the law should be interpreted "literally" or "reasonably." In 1911, in its Standard Oil opinion, the Supreme Court opted for the second interpretation.[7] But the question of what constituted "reasonable" enforcement remained. If "reasonable" is too loosely defined, the law becomes meaningless. For example, firms have tried to defend price-fixing agreements on the grounds that the prices they agreed upon were "reasonable"—that is, they were not exorbitant and did not lead to monopoly profits. The Supreme Court has stated unequivocally that price fixing is always an unreasonable restraint of trade and is thus illegal. But what constitutes price fixing? Overt agreements may be clearly defined as such, but what about price leadership—the ability of one firm to set prices for an entire industry? Price leadership has not generally been adjudged to be price fixing, but there is a notable exception. In 1946, the three major tobacco companies were found guilty of restraint of trade, despite lack of evidence that they had overtly conspired to fix prices. In this case the results of price leadership in an oligopoly were indistinguishable from the profit maximizing behavior of monopoly. What is apparent in this is that normal oligopoly behavior and price leadership may circumvent the law, but if firms become too proficient at coordinating their pricing policies they may find that they have violated the Sherman Act.

Another continuing controversy over the Sherman Act and the rule of reason involves the interpretation of the word *monopolize* in Section 2. Does it mean being a monopoly, acting like a monopoly, becoming a monopoly, trying to become a monopoly, or simply having a large share of the market? Basically the question boils down to whether the mere possession of market power is illegal, or whether this power must be misused before the law has been violated. Later in this chapter several cases are discussed to show the evolution of judicial opinion on this issue.

Later Laws

By the time the Sherman Act reached its twentieth birthday, there was wide concern that it was much too easy to circumvent. It had not been able to stop a tremendous number of mergers and a substantial increase in the concentration of economic power between 1890 and 1910. The law was put to use in actions against the worst abusers of monopoly power—for instance, to break up monopolies such as Standard Oil and American Tobacco—but only after damage had already been done. It did little to prevent monopoly from developing. As a result, two new antitrust laws were enacted in 1914—the Clayton Act and the Federal Trade Commission (FTC) Act.

THE CLAYTON ACT

The Clayton Act was much more specific than the Sherman Act in its prohibitions. It focused on practices that "lessened competition" and was designed to prevent or forestall the development of monopoly rather than correct the abuses of monopoly power.

Four sections of the Clayton Act proscribe specific types of business activity. Section 2 outlaws price discrimination when the effect is a substantial reduction in competition; Section 3 prohibits tying contracts and exclusive dealing arrangements that lessen competition; Section 7 attempts to prevent

7 *U.S. v. Standard Oil Company of New Jersey*, 221 U.S. 1 (1911).

mergers that may reduce competition or create a monopoly; and Section 8 makes interlocking directorates among competing firms illegal. Each of these prohibitions was aimed at practices that flourished under the Sherman Act and contributed to the growth of economic concentration after its passage. But the trouble with specific prohibitions is that determined people can find other methods of accomplishing the same end.

Nowhere is this better illustrated than by Section 7 of the Clayton Act, which made it illegal for a firm to acquire the stock of a competing firm if the effect "may be to substantially lessen competition." Any merger achieved by some means other than stock acquisition—as by buying up a firm's physical assets—was beyond the reach of the Clayton Act. The sponsors of the Act undoubtedly wanted to prevent all mergers that lessened competition, but in being so specific they left so wide a loophole that almost no mergers were prevented until the loophole was finally closed in 1950.

Mergers had been a major factor in the increase in concentration and the reduction of competition under the Sherman Act, and they continued to play the same role under the Clayton Act. Again those who saw capitalism as relentlessly monopolistic had reason to argue that public pressure for reform had brought about no real reforms. In fact, it could be argued that antitrust laws, at least until 1950, actually contributed to economic concentration. Since the Sherman Act stopped price fixing and other cartel arrangements, the only way for some firms to avoid the rigors of competition was to merge—which they did. Although the extent of such activity is debatable, in some instances the effect of antitrust laws was to substitute mergers for collusion.

FTC ACT The other antitrust law passed in 1914, the FTC Act, has two main features. The first of these is Section 5, which prohibits "unfair methods of competition," a catchall designed to stop anticompetitive practices not specifically mentioned in the Clayton Act and not as flagrantly monopolistic as required for successful prosecution under the Sherman Act.

Presumably one of the intentions of the authors of the FTC Act was to restrict practices unfair to consumers or the general public. In an early test case, the Supreme Court indicated otherwise. A firm was charged with violating Section 5 because it had engaged in deceptive advertising. It was exonerated, not with the consumer's welfare in mind, but on the grounds that deceptive advertising was not an unfair method of competition because competitors all had an equal opportunity to use this kind of advertising. As a result of this interpretation, the Wheeler-Lea Act was passed in 1926, prohibiting "unfair and deceptive acts or practices."

Another major feature of the FTC Act was the establishment of the Federal Trade Commission as an alternative to the Justice Department to enforce antitrust laws. The FTC is an independent, quasi-judicial agency, composed of five members appointed by the President. The term of appointment is seven years, and no more than three commissioners may belong to the same political party. It enforces the FTC Act and shares responsibility with the Justice Department for enforcing the Clayton Act; enforcement of the Sherman Act remains with the Justice Department.

The rationale for creating the FTC was twofold. As an independent, regulatory agency, it would be free to act without political interference and without compromising antitrust goals with other goals of the executive branch, a problem sometimes faced by the Justice Department. Second, it was foreseen that the FTC members would have more expertise in antitrust law than most judges who presided over cases brought by the Justice Department. A stronger, more consistent application of the law was therefore predicted. As events have shown, the FTC's performance has fallen short of expectations.

ROBINSON-PATMAN ACT Section 2 of the Clayton Act permitted the charging of different prices to different buyers if the differences were based on the seller's cost differences in the respective transactions. In 1936, Section 2 was amended by the Robinson-Patman Act in a move aimed at the growing power of the chain stores, in particular A&P, whose ability to obtain lower prices from suppliers put it in a position to drive smaller retailers out of business. The Robinson-Patman Act makes it more difficult for firms to engage in price discrimination on the grounds of differences in cost. It even prohibits certain types of savings from being passed on to consumers. Many economists feel that it has stifled price competition and fostered the survival of inefficient retailers.

CELLER-KEFAUVER ACT The last major addition to the antitrust laws was the Celler-Kefauver Act, enacted in 1950. This act amends Section 7 of the Clayton Act by closing the loophole that limited prosecution to mergers by stock acquisition. It also extends the coverage of the law in another way. The original law applied to mergers of companies selling similar products, or **horizontal mergers.** The amended law also applies to mergers of buyers and sellers, or **vertical mergers,** and mergers of firms with unrelated products, or **conglomerate mergers.** This does not make all mergers illegal; rather it prohibits those in which the effect "may be substantially to lessen competition or tend to create a monopoly." Since a horizontal merger is much more likely to reduce competition and be subjected to antitrust prosecution under this act, an increasing number of mergers in the United States have been either vertical or conglomerate. In fact, between 1964 and 1969, nearly 80 percent of all acquisitions of firms with assets of more than $10 million were conglomerate mergers. This led to increased pressure on the Justice Department and the FTC to challenge conglomerate mergers.

Conglomerates

Although antitrust authorities have been quite vigorous in challenging horizontal and vertical mergers, they have shown less zeal with respect to conglomerate mergers. As a result, much of the merger activity in the United States since 1960 has been in conglomerates. Conglomerates are large firms that have absorbed other firms in a wide variety of noncompeting areas. Textron, a typical conglomerate, has divisions in electronic equipment, textiles, aircraft, machine tools, pharmaceuticals, golf carts, and several other diverse manufacturing operations.

The basic reason for this neglect of conglomerates by the Justice Department and the FTC has been uncertainty over the effects of such mergers on competition. There is still substantial disagreement as to whether a merger between firms in unrelated industries will affect competition in either industry.

During most of the 1960s the Justice Department hesitated to move against conglomerate mergers because its antitrust lawyers believed that such mergers did not lessen competition in the traditional economic sense. Many of them felt somewhat uneasy about the concentration of power represented by conglomerates, but they did not see Section 7 of the Clayton Act as the appropriate remedy, abiding by the traditional narrow economic definition of competition.

The FTC was the pathbreaker in challenging conglomerate mergers. In 1967 the Supreme Court upheld the FTC's ruling that Procter & Gamble's acquisition of Clorox was illegal, primarily on the grounds that the merger would lessen potential competition because both Procter & Gamble and Clorox were already the dominant firms in their respective industries.[8]

After President Nixon took office in 1969, the Justice Department finally instituted what appeared to be significant action against conglomerate mergers by challenging the Ling-Temco-Vought acquisition of Jones and Laughlin Steel Company and three ITT acquisitions. Three explanations have been offered for this belated attack. The first is that economic theory had finally caught up with conglomeration. As conglomerate firms became increasingly conspicuous in the U.S. economy, economists began to give more thought to their impact. When a firm takes over a company that manufactures a particular kind of product instead of producing that product itself, there is a loss of potential competition. The conglomerate hurts competition by its use of reciprocity, when its suppliers are forced to buy from its subsidiaries. Also, by further promoting the fortunes of

8 *FTC* v. *Procter & Gamble Company*, 386 U.S. 568, 573-4 (1967).

Most antitrust cases are familiar only to scholars in that field, but the ITT case of 1972 made headlines with allegations of financial assistance for the Republican convention, the flight and subsequent reappearance of ITT lobbyist Dita Beard in a Denver hospital, and E. Howard Hunt's visit disguised in a red wig. Despite the circus atmosphere, the ITT case provides some insight into the maneuvering involved in a large antitrust case.

The case began several years before when Richard McLaren assumed his duties as head of the Justice Department's Antitrust Division. One of his top priorities was stopping the increasing number of conglomerate mergers. Among the cases he initiated were three against ITT, one of the largest, fastest growing, and most merger-hungry conglomerates in the United States. The challenge involved ITT's proposed acquisition of Canteen Corporation, Grinnell Corporation, and Hartford Fire Insurance Company. McLaren believed that if the three cases were to appear simultaneously before the Supreme Court, the government would prevail. Winning these cases would accomplish two goals for the Justice Department. First, it would stop the growth of ITT. Secondly and most important, it would establish the precedent that Section 7 of the Clayton Act was clearly applicable to conglomerate mergers, providing a new weapon against economic concentration.

However, two years later, the Justice Department agreed to permit the mergers. Why? To many observers the answer was obvious. It was simply a matter of politics. However, although ITT kept the three companies in question, in order to do so it had to make some concessions. ITT agreed to divest itself of a string of companies with assets of more than $1 billion, and it consented not to make any major acquisitions for 10 years. Even with this relatively favorable settlement, the price of ITT stock dropped sharply when the settlement was announced.

Defenders of the Justice Department's action also point out that it had lost all three cases in the lower courts and therefore was not assured of winning them before the Supreme Court. In discontinuing the litigation, it did accomplish the first goal, namely stopping the growth of ITT. The second goal, establishing anticonglomerate precedents, was not as important in 1971 as in 1969, because the conglomerate movement had already lost much of its appeal to the firms involved and to Wall Street.

Critics of the settlement point out that it was basically quite satisfactory to ITT. The conglomerate was allowed to keep the firms it wanted most and to spin off those it wanted least. They also felt that ITT's warnings about the adverse effects on balance of payments and on the stock market were convincing arguments that its economic power should be reduced, that no single company should be able to hold an economy hostage. They believe that the government forfeited a golden opportunity to establish strong precedents against such mergers, since the Supreme Court in recent years has consistently ruled against bigness.

United Press International

a leading corporation it has enveloped, the conglomerate discourages the entry of smaller competitors.

The second explanation for the belated activity against conglomerates is that the public became increasingly concerned over their growth, demanding that some action be taken. Congress was holding hearings on the problem and was beginning to consider passing new antitrust laws aimed at conglomerates. A third explanation is that many blue-chip corporations were beginning to feel threatened by conglomerates and were able to use their political influence to persuade the Justice Department to take action against them.

The Justice Department has set forth specific criteria for its challenges of conglomerate mergers. The attack on conglomerates rests on Section 7 of the Clayton Act but relies on an interpretation that is broader than the economist's traditional concept of competition. The final say is up to the Supreme Court. It is conceivable that the justices will eventually hold that a firm is too big, regardless of any demonstrable effect upon the traditional variables of price and quantity.

Antitrust: Structure versus Behavior

In the controversy over antitrust policy a major issue has been the question of the extent to which such policy should center on market structure or on market behavior. Differences of opinion on this issue reflect disagreements over the underlying economic relationship between the market's structure and its performance. On one side of the issue are the structuralists, those who see a close link between market structure and market performance. They believe that highly concentrated industries generally exhibit monopolistic behavior and, as a consequence, poor economic performance. To this group the best antitrust policy is one that focuses on market structure: breaking up existing large firms and preventing new ones from developing.

The behavioralists believe that such an approach is too simple and potentially harmful because the relationship between market structure and performance is not very predictable. They argue that some highly concentrated industries may be quite competitive and may demonstrate better performance than some industries with low concentration. Accordingly, they believe that antitrust policy should concentrate on behavior, preventing anticompetitive practices such as price fixing, rather than indiscriminately attacking big business in general.

The evolution of judicial interpretation of Section 2 of the Sherman Act phrases the conflict in this form: Does, or should, the word *monopolize* refer to market structure alone or is behavior also involved? In the U.S. Steel case of 1920, the Supreme Court ruled that monopolistic behavior is required for a firm to be guilty of monopolizing.[9] Based on the rule of reason the Court concluded that U.S. Steel was a "good" monopoly, that although it possessed market power, it did not abuse this power and therefore was not monopolizing. Thereafter, many companies with large market shares were acquitted on these same grounds.

This interpretation established a precedent that was eventually modified by the Alcoa decision.[10] The final decision in this case was made by the Second Circuit Court of Appeals, since a majority of the Supreme Court disqualified themselves on the grounds of previous involvement in the case. Written by Judge Learned Hand, the opinion is probably the most famous and oft quoted of all antitrust rulings. Judge Hand determined that because Alcoa had 90 percent of the aluminum ingot market in the United States, it was a monopoly. And because such a share of the market could not be maintained accidentally, Alcoa was also guilty of monopolizing.

Thus, Judge Hand equated monopoly with monopolizing—an apparent victory for the structuralists, who saw in this a precedent enabling the Justice Department to use the Sherman Act to attack and break up many highly concentrated oligopolies. Subsequent cases dashed these hopes. The Supreme Court upheld a charge of monopolizing against the United Shoe Machinery Corporation, which had 85 percent of the market, but refused to order dissolu-

9 *U.S. v. U.S. Steel Corporation*, 251 U.S. 417 (1920).
10 *U.S. v. Aluminum Company of America*, 148 F 2nd 416 (1945).

tion.[11] In other cases involving smaller but nevertheless substantial market shares, the court has required evidence of monopolistic behavior as a violation of the Sherman Act.

These interpretations of the Sherman Act have probably prevented American corporations from developing into true monopolies but have not prevented the development and prosperity of highly concentrated oligopolies. Because the law continues to evolve, structuralists have not lost hope. In 1969, the government brought suit against IBM for monopolizing and attempting to monopolize the digital computer market. A decision against IBM could make this one of the most significant of all antitrust cases and have a profound impact upon the structure of American industry.

Since 1950 the use of Section 7 of the Clayton Act has also raised the hopes of structuralists, especially with respect to horizontal mergers. The Celler-Kefauver Act, which put teeth in Section 7, activated the Justice Department and the FTC, and the Supreme Court responded extremely favorably to their antimerger efforts. The case that firmly established the power of the new Section 7 involved a proposed merger between Brown Shoe, primarily a shoe manufacturer, and Kinney Shoe, primarily a shoe retailer.[12] Both shoe manufacturing and retailing were quite unconcentrated and the firms involved in the merger had small market shares. Brown accounted for 4 percent and Kinney for 0.5 percent of the shoes produced in the United States. Kinney also accounted for 2 percent of the retail shoe stores. While the Court recognized that the industry was unconcentrated and that the merger would not significantly change the situation, it ruled that both the horizontal and vertical aspects of the merger continued a trend of increased concentration in shoe manufacturing and retailing that should be stopped before it was too late. Thus, the doctrine of **incipiency** was articulated: Anticompetitive trends need to be stopped before concentration has developed.

When reminded of the difference between its interpretations of Section 7 of the Clayton Act and the Sherman Act, the Supreme Court has answered that it simply interpreted the law: A merger of two firms each with 5 percent of a market may *lessen competition* but a firm with 50 percent of the market is not necessarily monopolizing. If the two laws are inconsistent, it is up to Congress not the Court to remedy the situation.

The precedent established in the Brown-Kinney case has prevailed and has been strengthened during the relatively brief period the Celler-Kefauver Act has been in effect. The Justice Department has indicated that it will probably challenge any horizontal merger in which the acquiring firm has as much as 5 percent of the market and the acquired firm has 5 percent. For vertical mergers, the percentages are 10 and 6, respectively. If a trend toward increased concentration has been observed or if the markets are already highly concentrated, the percentages are even lower. Exceptions may be made in the case of failing firms, but as a general rule these percentages prevail.

These antitrust developments have met with opposition from the behavioralists, who protest that mergers that show little probability of reducing competition are being prohibited. They claim the antitrust authorities' obsession with market shares is preventing mergers that would improve economic performance by permitting greater economies of scale.

This raises an interesting question: Should mergers that lessen competition but reduce costs because of economies of scale be permitted? The law does not mention this possibility and perhaps it should.

Critics of current antimerger policy claim that its emphasis is upon protecting competitors rather than competition, asserting that the authorities have the one-sided view that mergers, by lowering costs, can only lessen competition. The issue hinges on the definition of competition. The legal form, as interpreted by the Supreme Court, has included social and political as well as economic factors. The Court has, in effect, defined competition as being characterized by a large number of firms in the marketplace, with

11 *U.S.* v. *United Shoe Machinery Co.*, 110 F Supp 295 (D Mass 1953).
12 *Brown Shoe Company* v. *U.S.*, 370 U.S. 294 (1962).

each firm holding a small market share. By contrast, competition in conventional economic theory is primarily concerned with the equalizing of price, marginal cost, and minimum average total cost. The use of resources with allocative and technological efficiency rather than market share is important to the economist.

Anti-Antitrust

It is an irony of government that when one of its branches is attempting to achieve a goal, another may be pursuing policies to frustrate achievement of that goal. Antitrust is no exception. Although the federal government, through the FTC and the Antitrust Division of the Justice Department, attempts to promote competition, price supports and other assistance for farmers, military and other government procurement policies, subsidies to large firms such as Lockheed, and many other such practices have reduced the free competition sought by antitrust laws. In many instances the policies were aimed at other goals and reduced competition inadvertently.

But the government may also choose to grant temporary monopolies or charter public utilities. In these cases its intention is to gain the benefits of monopoly and to reduce the ill effects of this concentration by establishing limits and ground rules.

Patents The firm that receives a patent receives a legal monopoly on the patented product or process for a period of 17 years. The rationale for curbing competition in this way is that patents reward and encourage invention, whose benefits to the economy offset the competitive loss during the temporary monopoly. The courts generally interpret patent laws in such a way as to encourage competition while maintaining a nominal protection of original inventions. This is done by extending the protective influence of the patent, not to the product itself, but to the production process. If a competitor can produce a product similar or even identical to a patented product, he is welcome to do so, so long as he does not employ an identical production process. n this way innovation is still rewarded, but the public is given some protection from patent-protected monopolies earning enormous excess profits at the consumer's expense.

The effects of the patent system have not always confirmed this rationale. Frequently, by patenting minor improvements in a product, a firm is able to maintain a patent monopoly well beyond 17 years. Also, by cross-licensing patents among selected competitors and excluding all others, oligopolists often are able to increase and extend their market power. As a result, in some industries patents have made a significant contribution to the strengthening of monopoly power.

Among the suggested reforms of the patent system are establishing a shorter period for the patents or for improvements of existing patents, and mandatory cross-licensing of patents for a reasonable fee.

Public Utility Regulation Public utilities comprise a large sector of the American economy in which competition is not considered appropriate, although the means of production are privately owned. For these businesses, direct regulation by a regulatory commission of prices, output, and other activities takes the place of regulation by competition. Public utilities are natural monopolies; their economies of scale are so great that costs are minimized when the service is produced by only one firm—as is usually the case for the production of electric power, telephone service, railroads, and other essential public services. Accordingly, public policy has been to grant the firm a monopoly, so it can realize the economies of scale, but to regulate it to prevent it from charging monopoly prices.

Public utility regulation is common only in the United States; in most other market economies the transportation, power, and communications industries have been nationalized. In the United States public utilities are regulated by public utility commissions. Each state has such a commission, and there are several independent federal regulatory commissions, such as the ICC, FPC, and FCC. The commissions have two basic tasks: to determine the cost of providing the service, including a fair return on investment, and to set prices that will ensure that revenues cover costs.

Public utility regulation began in the late nine-

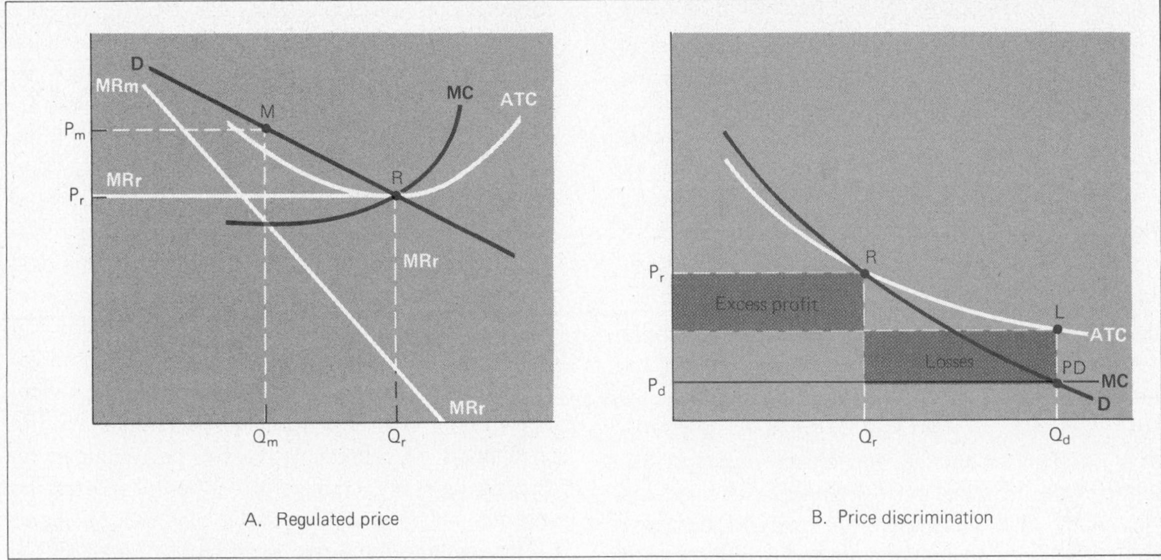

FIGURE 29-3 PUBLIC UTILITY PRICING An unregulated utility may charge a monopoly price such as P_m in part A, thereby restricting output. If the regulatory commission sets price to equal MC in order to assure allocative efficiency, then the utility will increase its output to Q_r. This happens to coincide with the point at which P = AC, which means that the utility is breaking even. This need not happen, as shown in B. These curves are more typical of a utility with declining average costs over a wide range of output. Here regulators must choose. Either the utility breaks even because the regulators set price to equal average cost (P_r) but the result is allocatively inefficient, or the utility is allocatively efficient because the price is equal to marginal cost but it incurs losses. One solution is to charge some customers P_r and others P_d, so that the excess profits on the output sold at P_r just offset the losses on the output sold at P_d. Then, the utility will break even, yet also be allocatively efficient.

teenth century when the Supreme Court ruled that the government could regulate the price a firm charged only if it was "affected with the public interest."[13] After 60 years of struggling over the substantive issue of which industries met this standard, the Supreme Court finally broadened the powers, so that for the past 40 years government has had the power to regulate any business enterprise as long as due process is observed. In the main, regulatory commissions have construed due process to mean ensuring the stockholders a fair return on their investment in the regulated firm, a practice that neglects other vital economic goals.

COSTS Determining costs is a very technical, complex task. The regulated firm tries to claim all the costs it can because it can then set prices to cover them. The commission must determine if the claimed costs were actually incurred and, if so, which were legitimate or consistent with good management. Given its limited resources and expertise, the commission may easily fail to recognize costs that are padded or the consequences of inefficient management. There is little clear incentive for the regulated firm to economize. This is especially true in regard to the cost of capital. Determining how much capital the firm requires and what the proper rate of return on investment should be is the most difficult aspect of rate regulation. When a firm is regulated it may have less pressure to be technologically efficient than if it were faced with even a moderate amount of competition.

PRICES Once the commission has determined which costs to allow, it must approve a schedule of prices. The regulation of price attempts to reduce the effects of monopoly power by lowering prices and increasing output. Figure 29-3A shows how this may be accomplished. The unregulated monopolist would

13 *Munn* v. *Illinois*, 94 U.S. 113 (1876).

charge P_m and produce Q_m, but by setting the price at P_r, the utility commission causes the firm to enlarge its output to Q_r. With this regulated price of P_r, the firm's marginal revenue curve is the discontinuous line, and MC = MR at Q_r. The regulation has enabled the consumers to benefit from the technological efficiency of the natural monopoly and has achieved allocative efficiency by setting the price so that it is equal to marginal cost at the firm's profit-maximizing output.

However, the achievement of P = MC is not so simple in many cases, because the cost curves do not resemble those in Figure 29-3A. For most public utilities, fixed cost is high and marginal cost is relatively low. This situation is illustrated in Figure 29-3B, which shows hypothetical demand and cost curves for a utility. If all consumers are charged the same price, the price must equal average total cost. If Q_d is produced, average total cost will fall to L, but consumers will pay only P_d. Price will equal marginal cost at this level of output, so the firm will be allocatively efficient, but it will be operating at a loss, because price will not equal average cost. In order to get Q_d, substantial government subsidies could make up the losses.

Another way out of this dilemma is to employ price discrimination. The demand curve represents a variety of individual demand curves. Some consumers are willing to pay more for their electricity or telephone service than others. Through judicious price discrimination, Q_d can be produced. Part of it will be sold for P_r and the other part for P_d. Thus average price will equal average cost, revenues will cover cost, price will equal marginal cost for the last unit produced, and everyone will pay a lower price than if a uniform price were charged. With more price discrimination, everyone might enjoy a lower price than P_r. Price discrimination results in a more efficient use of plant and equipment, but some consumers—those paying the higher price—may feel cheated. There is room for considerable discretion by the commission in determining the exact form the price discrimination will take, and the results may not be consistent with one's notion of equity.

PROBLEMS OF PUBLIC UTILITY REGULATION Public utility commissions function under less than ideal conditions. They are confronted with extremely complex issues and limited resources and must frequently rely upon the regulated companies themselves for information. They are subjected to a variety of pressures from one group or another that feels entitled to low rates. They are usually understaffed and underpaid—especially the state regulatory commissions—so that even the best intentioned, hardest working commissions often fall short of perfection. In addition to such handicaps, the commissions are often crippled by apathy. Appointments to the commissions are frequently made to pay off political debts rather than on the basis of expertise. It is not uncommon for representatives of the regulated industries to sit on commissions, which often explains why commissions have tended to be more concerned for the welfare of the regulated industry than for the welfare of the general public.

Regulation frequently has been used as a device for guaranteeing profits to the regulated firms and shielding them from competition and public pressure. Firms may often make a show of opposing regulation, but essentially they appreciate its value in protecting them from competitive pressure. A few years after the ICC was established, the U.S. Attorney General wrote to a railroad president, "The commission ... is, or can be made, of great use to the railroads. It satisfies the popular clamor for a government supervision of the railroads, at the same time that the supervision is almost entirely nominal. Further, the older such a commission gets to be, the more inclined it will be found to take the business and railroad view of things ..."[14]

The history of the ICC substantiates this charge. The ICC was established in 1887 to regulate railroads, because they appeared to be a natural monopoly service essential to the livelihood of many individuals, yet in many areas rates were exorbitant. The railroads were not entirely opposed to regulation because in areas where railroads were in direct competition with each other, services were duplicated and prices had fallen to unprofitable levels.

14 Reported in Grant McConnell, *Private Power and American Democracy* (New York: Alfred A. Knopf, 1966), excerpted in David Mermelstein, ed., *Economics: Mainstream Readings and Radical Critiques*, 1st ed. (New York: Random House, 1970), p. 197.

The ICC therefore gained the authority to set minimum as well as maximum rates.

In 1935, trucks and busses were placed under ICC regulation in an action that has met with strong criticism. Trucks and busses are not a natural monopoly. Capital costs are relatively small, fixed costs are relatively low, and economies of scale are not exceptional. The reason given for the new regulation was "a coordinated national transportation policy," but the indications are that it emerged because of pressures from truck companies that wanted protection from competition. Since then the CAB has been established to regulate airlines, and inland water carriers and oil pipelines have been placed under the jurisdiction of the ICC.

This has hardly resulted in a coordinated control of national transportation policy or a system that protects the consumer or the railroads. The rules governing the various forms of transportation vary significantly; for example, for agricultural commodities the ICC sets a minimum rate for railroads but not for trucks, which enables trucks to underbid railroads. Railroads are no longer a natural monopoly because of the intense competition from other modes of transportation. The elaborate system of price discrimination (there are 75,000 different rates) that worked when railroads were monopolies does not work in the face of competition. The competition takes away the high-profit business and leaves the railroads with the marginal operations. Moreover, regulation takes place at a high cost to society; conservative estimates place waste of resources due to transportation regulation at $4 billion annually. For these reasons, many people favor a relaxation of regulation, one that will permit competition in freight transportation. The most vocal opponent has been the trucking industry. This is not an isolated example of the power of a single industry to determine government policy.

GOVERNMENT CONTROL

Regulation of public utilities, with all its shortcomings, represents a means by which government attempts to serve the people by controlling industry—as it does when it issues licenses and patents, or institutes wage-price regulation and pollution control. Another form of economic service pertains to the fulfillment of such essential needs as fire and police protection, highway construction and maintenance, education, and national defense—in short, the provision of public goods. Because these public goods are usually free and available to all, resource allocation by price does not apply in the public sector in quite the same ways it does in the market, complicating matters of comparing allocative and technological efficiency within the two sectors.

Even for the market system these questions are often impossible to answer quantitatively. When it actually comes down to evaluating a specific industry, it is rarely possible to determine whether the industry is operating efficiently, but if the industry is reasonably competitive and there is no significant evidence of externalities, it may be assumed to be reasonably efficient. The same generalized approach can be used in evaluating government performance.

Economizing on Government

In the U.S. economy the market is the preferred method of economic organization, unless government intervention or ownership can improve the situation markedly. Where indications are that either can achieve the same economic goals, we generally prefer the market system. Milton Friedman has "codified" this preference into a set of eight guidelines for "cutting government back to size":[15]

1 Concentrate on general rules for individual behavior rather than specific intervention.
2 Refrain from activities unless clearly needed.
3 Finance specific activities without administering them.
4 Finance beneficiaries, not producers.
5 Permit competition for all activities it administers in order to have a yardstick.
6 Buy resources, not commandeer them.
7 Charge the user for services it produces.

15 Milton Friedman, "Cutting Government Back to Size—Eight Guidelines," in *The Political Economy of Federal Policy*, eds. Robert Haveman and Robert Hamrin (New York: Harper & Row, 1973), pp. 23–25.

8 Only as a last resort, finance, administer, and deliver free of charge.

Under these guidelines Friedman can advocate making education in effect a private industry by means of the voucher system or abolishing welfare in favor of the negative income tax. These guidelines are an attempt to make each government dollar count as much as possible, just as the assumption of competitiveness is believed to ensure efficiency in the private sector.

Even with such rules of thumb, however, it is extremely difficult to evaluate most government programs. The unemployment rate can tell us how successful fiscal policy has been, but how do we evaluate the Head Start program? Which statistics tell us if OEO is a wise use of money? How do we evaluate alternative policies of pollution control, especially when billions of dollars must be spent before we know whether a program has done any good? One method is balancing costs against benefits.

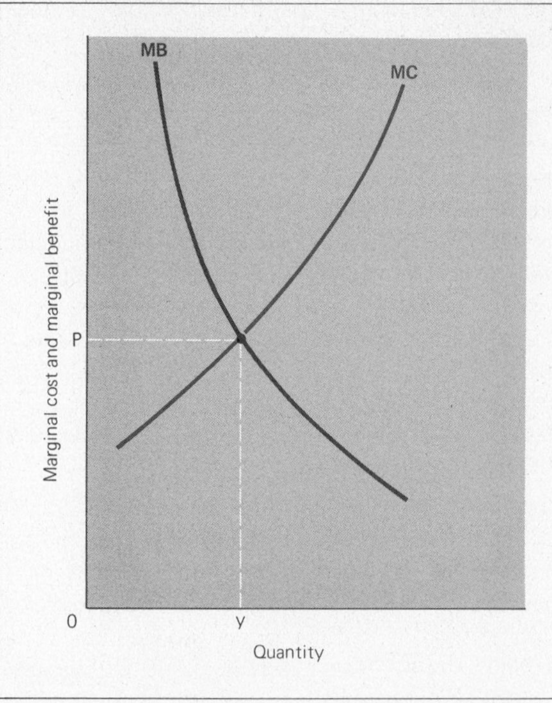

FIGURE 29-4 THE MARGINAL COST AND MARGINAL BENEFIT OF A GOVERNMENT SERVICE **All government programs have costs and all presumably provide benefits. If these benefits could be measured, they would signal the demand for an additional unit of the service. The costs of a particular government program are treated in the same way as the costs of a business. Marginal cost is the cost of producing an additional unit of the service. When MC = MB, the government is producing the optimal output, from the viewpoint of society. If more than OY is produced, the additional costs exceed the social benefits: if less than OY is produced, production should be increased, since it would yield benefits greater than the added costs.**

Costs and Benefits

An efficient government program not only reaches its goals at the least possible cost, but is also allocatively efficient; its costs are not too high for the expected benefits. Figure 29-4 provides a simple illustration of this. MB represents the marginal benefit of some government service, and MC the marginal cost of the technologically efficient way of providing this service. Thus, if OY is produced, marginal cost and marginal benefit are equal, and efficiency is achieved. If more than OY is produced, the additional costs exceed the benefits; if less than OY is produced, more should be provided, since the benefits exceed the costs.

How simple this seems! But how do we measure MB, for example? This is really the market demand curve for this particular good. Instead of summing the curves horizontally to see how much different consumers would buy at a given price as with market demand, the curve in this case is summed vertically because at any price, everyone (in theory) can consume the same amount. Even this is oversimplified, since not everyone benefits equally from a school lunch program or a ship construction subsidy. The analysis has to be concerned with the distributive effects, for even if MC = MB for all programs, we would be offended if the effect were to take from the poor and give to the rich.

Built into this analysis is the presumption that public investments should provide a "return" comparable to that of private industry. Benefits, therefore, are discounted to ensure that the "yield" will be equalized between sectors. If capital earns 10 percent for corporations, then economists discount benefits by 10 percent. Failure to do this will overallocate resources to the public sector. Conversely, if public projects that yield more than average returns cannot be funded because of budget limits, then resources may be underallocated to the public sector.

Even with these modifications the whole analysis is a fiction, since finding the public demand curve is really a political process. It is folly to pretend, as economists sometimes do, that such cost benefit analysis can be the government's ultimate yardstick for economic control.

Too Much and Too Little Economic analysis *can* be extremely useful in determining the full cost of a program. Knowing the full cost provides incentive for the rational use of resources. What can happen when such incentives are nonexistent is illustrated by a notable example of military inefficiency. For years commanders of military bases were not charged in their budgets for the use of military personnel. As a consequence, they tended to overuse military personnel and to underuse civilian personnel, equipment, and other factors of production. The result was that the real cost of running the base was higher than it should have been. As another example, the Defense Department does not pay for atomic warheads for its nuclear weapons; instead it requires the AEC to provide them. Defense planners, therefore, have little incentive to minimize the stockpiling of nuclear weapons. If the Defense Department had to pay for them, the mix of nuclear and nonnuclear forces might better reflect the real costs of defense.

In graph form this situation means the cost curve is too low. MC_a represents the actual marginal cost of defense or national security, whereas MC_p represents the perceived costs; items such as atomic warheads and merchant marine subsidies are not included in the defense budget. Given this situation, society is likely to choose OX units of defense as appropriate, but it would choose only OY units if it knew the real cost of defense.

This can also be illustrated by the production possibilities curve in Figure 29-5B. If society knew the real cost of defense, the political process would determine that point Y was the optimal choice between defense and all other goods, but since it does not know the true opportunity cost of defense it chooses point X.

In general, then, if the cost of a service provided by the government is underestimated, there is a tendency to overproduction. This is especially true when groups of people receive substantial benefits from a government program but do not pay their share of the cost or are not conscious that they pay a share indirectly. They will be much more enthusiastic about public spending for the service than those for whom the reverse is true. For example, currently an "airport crisis" is in the making in this country. Existing and planned airports are not sufficient to handle the expected increase in air traffic over the next decade. Airlines and those who rely heavily on them are anxious to see new facilities constructed with the use of public funds. But a more efficient and equitable solution might be to raise airline fares. This would place the financial burden on those who cause the congestion by using the airlines. It would also motivate some passengers to seek other means of transportation.

Another example of what may be seen as either overproduction or inequitable distribution of benefits relative to costs is federal water resource policy. Many waterways maintained by the federal government benefit people who pay a small fraction of their cost of operations. The barges that use them pay nothing for this service. The large, politically influential farming industries that benefit from federal irrigation projects pay very little for them. If the farm groups had to pay a larger percentage of cost, there might be less political pressure for projects once it was shown that they did not meet the test of allocative efficiency.

To many, the underprovision of services is a much more serious problem than the overprovision just discussed. Underprovision results from the overestimation of costs. Reversing MC_a and MC_p in Figure 29-5A illustrates this. Certainly one of the reasons we are reluctant to impose meaningful pollution controls is that the estimated costs seem too high.

It is also true that overestimation of costs often goes hand in hand with the choice of technologically inefficient means to solve a problem. We underallocate to pollution control because the method used to curb effluents is far more costly than need be.

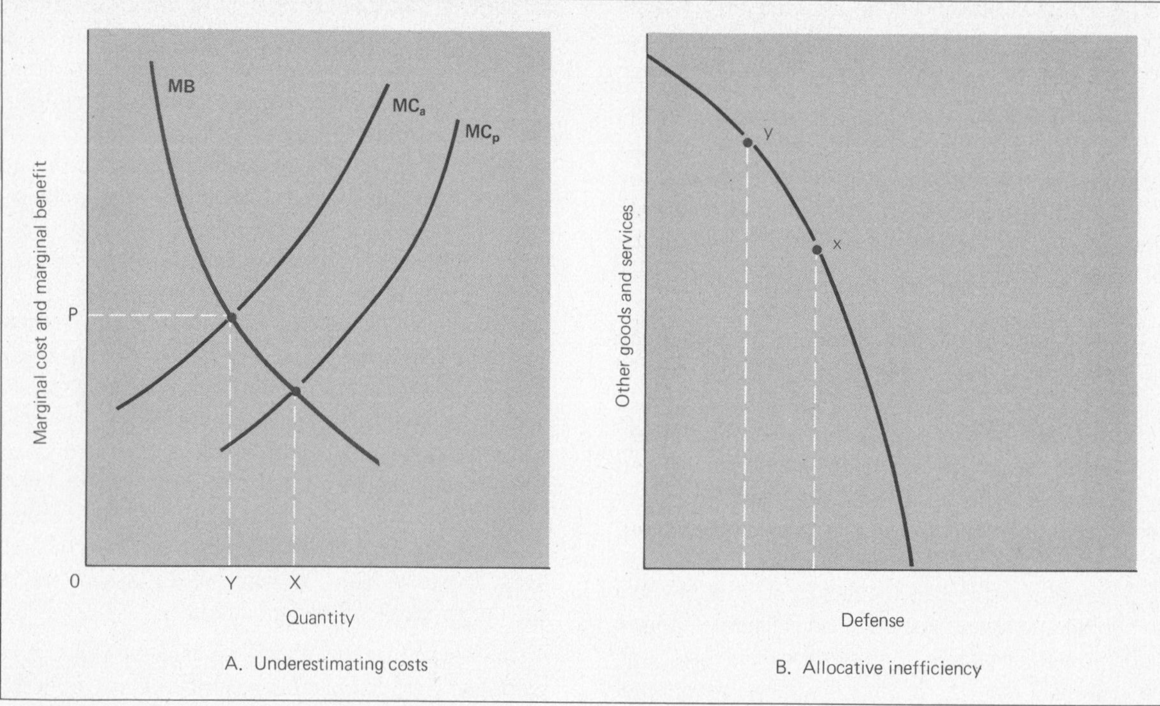

FIGURE 29-5 ACTUAL AND PERCEIVED COSTS When perceived costs are less than the full social cost (as in A), society will overinvest in that good or service. On the production possibilities curve (B), society will be at point X; were the true costs known, it would devote fewer resources to that good or service and produce at point Y. Now explain underinvestment using the same kind of analysis.

Economics and Power As mentioned earlier, there is really no way to determine precisely whether a program provided by the government is technologically efficient or provides the proper amount of a particular service. But these are questions to which at least approximate answers are possible. If public policy is to be efficient and equitable, economic analysis can be very useful in determining what can and cannot be answered, and within these limits which programs offer the greatest chances of success. But a major impediment to the realization of well conceived programs in the public interest has been the self-interest of powerful groups inside and outside the government. A glaring example is in the relationship between the military and the giant private contractors. This provides a case study of regulation and control under politically charged conditions.

GOVERNMENT AND THE MILITARY-INDUSTRIAL COMPLEX

The term *military-industrial complex* entered the American vocabulary when President Eisenhower warned of its dangers in a speech at the very close of his second term in 1961. Eisenhower described an alliance between an immense military establishment and a large arms industry with an influence "felt throughout the nation." Such an alliance includes military personnel, especially high-ranking officers, some of whom upon retirement find employment with defense contractors; the corporations whose profits depend upon defense spending; unions whose members are employed in defense production; and politicians whose reelection depends on the defense contracts they bring to their districts. It also penetrates the educational establishment. (M.I.T., for example, was getting one-half its budget from weapons funding during the late 1960s.) What this all boils down to is that a large number of groups have a significant economic interest in maintaining high military spending.

The U.S. economy did not always depend so heavily on the military. For a variety of reasons, U.S. political leaders since World War II have been much more willing to spend money for defense than other purposes. Because of the cold war mentality that pervaded this nation for many years, it was considered almost treasonous and certainly political suicide not to give the defense establishment what it requested to protect us from foreign dangers, especially communism. Politicians otherwise unable to support deficit spending as a means of maintaining full employment could vote for defense outlays as a means of supplying jobs. Few economists say that a capitalistic economy actually requires high defense spending to maintain full employment, but to many legislators during the 1950s and 1960s, it seemed the only feasible way.

The impact of the military-industrial complex on our economy is immeasurable. The defense budget stands at around $90 billion per year, somewhat under 10 percent of total GNP. As the employer of almost 8 million Americans, including over 60 percent of all scientists, engineers, and technicians in the United States, it has an enormous power base. Property owned by the Defense Department constitutes about 10 percent of total U.S. assets. As overseer of this vast enterprise, the Department of Defense is proud of its sophisticated weaponry and its military readiness.

From the viewpoint of efficiency, it has less to be proud of. The waste and cost overruns in the military and defense industries have been well documented by now. The cost overruns on the C5A planes, for example, have ballooned above $2 billion. Politicians have tended to concentrate on these cost overruns in their criticism of the Defense Department because they are easily detected, they make headlines, and they are readily expressed in terms people understand—dollars. They are also relatively noncontroversial; no one likes gross waste. But there are more serious issues to be reckoned with.

By its contracts with major corporations, the military has favored concentration at the expense of competition. By its absorption of public resources, it has raised important questions about allocative efficiency. By its impact on the political system, the complex has had significant effect on the direction of national policy in both foreign and domestic affairs. These effects are far more significant than exposure of the scandal that it costs the United States $20 billion to obtain a weapons system that could have been bought for $18 billion.

The concentration of contract awards is quite marked. In 1969, over two-thirds of major defense contracts went to 100 companies. Four firms received 86 percent of the contracts for airplane engines; one firm monopolizes production of attack aircraft carriers. Small businesses received only 20 percent of all defense contracts in 1969, as opposed to 57 percent a decade earlier.

The effect on allocative efficiency is also pronounced. One of the opportunity costs of a powerful military-industrial complex is the sacrifice of production of other needed items, both public and private. We might not willingly pay these opportunity costs if we knew the real costs and benefits of defense spending.

Another cost of the military-industrial complex is in its tendency to make us provocative and imperialistic in foreign policy. This generates similar behavior by other countries, which is then used as a justification for further increases in our own defense spending. The facts that the nation is not at war and that arms limitations agreements have been signed do little to reduce defense spending. Despite the initial SALT agreement between the United States and the USSR and the "peace with honor" proclaimed in Indochina, U.S. military expenditures have continued to rise.

The impact of the military-industrial complex upon the goal of equity is not easy to assess. To the extent that military expenditures absorb funds that would otherwise be used for social welfare programs, achievement of equity is hindered. However, if the military is a disguised public works program to promote full employment, then it helps redistribute income to those who might otherwise be unemployed. This rationale probably explains the low pay scales that prevailed in the military until recently. Ostensibly, these made it seem as though those in uniform had sacrificed income to be soldiers; this was true only if they were not going to be unemployed in civilian life.

To the extent that defense contracts yield higher than average profits, military expenditures redistribute income from those who pay for them to those who profit from them. This probably does occur despite the disclaimers of defense contractors, since profits on military commodities have traditionally been higher than on those in the civilian economy.

There is also the question of whether the political system is truly responsive to our wishes, when it offers us defense instead of health care and housing. To many people the military-industrial complex typifies what is wrong with our economic system, but they see little hope of eliminating it without massive political and social reform. To some observers the defense establishment is the inevitable consequence of government efforts to stabilize and direct our economy. Consequently, the efforts to rationalize and to bring efficiency to government that were examined in the preceding section are doomed to failure. The economic and political power of the military-industrial complex will see to that.

One need not be as cynical and pessimistic as these critics to recognize that there is a military-industrial complex and to believe that its distortions endanger American society. In using pressure upon government for policies that serve its interests, this complex is little different from other sectors in which a governmental service is allied with private industry. We might as easily make reference to a medical-care–industrial complex or an agricultural-industrial complex. Eliminating the ills of such alliances, like the improvement of any misconceived government program, is no overnight project. Given a favorable political climate, most economists are optimistic that rational application of basic economic principles can help us reach our goals more efficiently with a better distribution of gains.

SUMMARY

1 A market system without government restraints or assistance will fall far short of attaining society's economic goals. Government action may be necessary to maintain full employment, price stability, and a satisfactory rate of growth, as well as to provide public goods.

2 The effects of economic concentration have reduced GNP by about 6 percent and redistributed about 3 percent of GNP regressively, according to one estimate. Concentration has been defended as necessary to technological efficiency and innovation, but evidence indicates the necessary degree of concentration is low. Other defenders assert that its dangers are controlled by "workable competition."

3 Antitrust regulation is the government weapon against economic concentration. The Sherman, Clayton, FTC, Robinson-Patman, and Celler-Kefauver Acts, as interpreted by the Supreme Court, constitute the government's arsenal against monopoly.

4 A key issue in antitrust policy is that of behavior versus structure. The structuralists see a close link between structure and market performance; they believe that highly concentrated industries generally exhibit monopolistic behavior and, as a consequence, poor economic performance. The behaviorists argue that some highly concentrated industries may be quite competitive and may demonstrate better performance than some industries with low concentration. Accordingly, they prescribe examining behavior and preventing anticompetitive practices such as price fixing, rather than indiscriminately attacking big business in general.

5 The effect of antitrust laws may be to protect competitors rather than to protect competition.

6 While seemingly anti-antitrust, patents and utility regulation place bounds on anticompetitive situations. In theory, public utility regulation places a lid on monopoly pricing, yet allows a fair return to the utility. In practice, the regulatory agency may be a captive of industry interests.

7 Government-run enterprise is an alternative to the market. In the United States the market is usually preferred.

8 Measuring the efficiency of either market or government is difficult. Comparisons of costs and benefits can show whether the society is underproducing or overproducing a public good, if benefits and costs are carefully identified. If MB = MC, the project is presumed to be allocatively efficient.

9 The basis for governmental decisions is often political rather than economic. The military-industrial complex is an example of the effects of political power on efficiency and equity. Its technological inefficiency has been loudly decried, but it may have more serious effects on the society by promoting concentration, diverting resources from other social necessities, and increasing international tensions. In its pressure upon government, the military-industrial complex is little different from other sectors; rational application of economic analysis can help curb the excesses.

SUGGESTED READINGS

Bain, Joe S. *Industrial Organization.* 2nd ed. New York: John Wiley & Sons, 1968.

Caves, Richard. *American Industry: Structure, Conduct, Performance.* 3rd ed. Englewood Cliffs, N.J.: Prentice-Hall, 1972.

Galbraith, John Kenneth. *The New Industrial State.* 2nd rev. ed. Boston: Houghton Mifflin, 1971.

Haveman, Robert H., and **Robert D. Hamrin,** eds. *The Political Economy of Federal Policy.* New York: Harper & Row, 1973.

Kaysen, Carl, and **Donald F. Turner.** *Antitrust Policy.* Cambridge: Harvard University Press, 1959.

Scherer, F. M. *Industrial Market Structure and Economic Performance.* Chicago: Rand McNally, 1970.

Shepherd, William G. *Market Power and Economic Welfare: An Introduction.* New York: Random House, 1970.

QUESTIONS

1 Review
   a. measures of business concentration,
   b. factors contributing to a high concentration of economic power,
   c. possible loss in GNP from high concentration,
   d. the provisions of the Sherman Act and the difficulties in its enforcement,
   e. major provisions of the Clayton, FTC, Robinson-Patman, and Celler-Kefauver Acts,
   f. the belated attacks against conglomerates,
   g. areas in which monopoly control is tolerated,
   h. problems in evaluating efficiency in government intervention.

2 Milk and ready-mix cement are products for which the effective markets may be somewhat localized. Why? What conclusions, if any, could you draw from a low industry concentration ratio?

3 In 1973, the government brought suit against seven major oil companies for conspiring to restrict the supply of gasoline. To prevent such occurrences in the future, government sought to divest the companies of either their retail operations or their refining and wholesale operations. Would you say that this move is a victory for the structuralists? Why or why not?

4 Somewhere between horizontal mergers and conglomerates is the case of mergers between substitute products. In one such case, the Continental Can Company, the country's largest producer of can containers, wished to merge with a large producer of glass containers. The court argued that the two firms together would account for 22 percent of an industry of can and glass container producers. In commenting on this case, Phillip Areeda claims that the court gerrymandered an industry that does not really exist as such.* Why would he advance this argument? What are the implications for other proposed mergers, say, between a producer of lumber and a producer of plastic?

5 Public utility industries, along with other regulated industries, must justify their requests for rate increases before government authorities. Could it be argued that these companies do not have much incentive to reduce costs? Why or why not?

6 If the American public were to decide that child care services should be offered to allow young mothers to enter the labor force, which policy would Friedman tend to prefer and why?

a. a subsidy for private child care centers,
b. a direct payment to the mother for each child,
c. government-operated, free centers located in key areas,
d. loans to working mothers to be paid back when the children no longer need care.

7 There is a certain momentum in government spending for existing programs, and switching programs frequently becomes quite costly for the government. What are the implications for allocative efficiency?

8 Milton Friedman believes that if we give the consumer a chance to either pay or not pay for a service or good, he is giving us a measure of his priorities. How might this be an improvement over writing to your congressman? Is this possible for all types of goods?

9 The move to a "volunteer" army will tend to dramatize the true cost of maintaining a large peacetime armed force. Why?

10 Until the news exposés of the late 1960s, few people knew that the American government was in the business of producing deadly stocks for germ warfare. As a result of the public outcry, the government began to destroy its inventories and convert its facilities to other uses. How did the secrecy of the government's program contribute to overproduction in this area? How does secrecy in general tend to complicate the efficiency problem?

*Phillip Areeda, "Structure-Performance Assumptions in Recent Merger Cases," in *Public Policy Toward Mergers*, eds. J. Fred Weston and Sam Peltzman (Pacific Palisades, Calif.: Goodyear Publishing Co., 1969), p. 40.

PART 6

FACTOR MARKET

CHAPTER 30

FACTOR DEMAND

In *Animal Farm* a band of barnyard animals sets out to create an egalitarian community.[1] After the farm has degenerated into a dictatorship of the pigs over the other animals, the final article of the constitution, "all animals are equal," is altered to conclude with the words, "but some animals are more equal than others."

Some people are more equal than others, too. Why, for example, might an engineering professor with a doctorate earn $18,000 while an engineer in industry with a master's degree earns $40,000? The answer to the question of differences in income lies not in the familiar world of Part Five, where cars, breakfast cereals, football tickets, and dry cleaning were bought and sold in the product market, but in the union hiring hall, the brokerage house, and the corporate office, where factors of production are exchanged for income.

Individuals receive income as payment for providing factors of production. These factors are their own labor or entrepreneurial talent, land they may own, or capital they may have accumulated or inherited. Each of these factors is essential to the production process, and their availability ultimately determines the level of national output.

The value the individual places on his own resources matters little if there is no demand. Someone may have invested thousands of dollars in education to become an expert in Byzantine art, and still be unemployed. Another person may have few skills, but have no trouble finding employment as a janitor because nobody else wants to do the work. Someone may own a thousand acres of desert land and be unable to rent it to anybody. But if that person owned only one acre in Manhattan, he or she would earn a fortune. What matters is how much the resources are needed by firms and entrepreneurs in the production of their goods and services. These firms will employ the available factors of production in the proportion that results in the desired level of output at the least cost. They will not hesitate to substitute one factor for another to lower their cost still more. Demand for inputs will determine the price of these factors and, therefore, the income of those who provide them. Thus, differences in factor income depend on the variations in factor prices. It does not matter how large the quantity of a factor a person can provide; if there is no demand for it, that person will be poor. The factor market operates similarly to the product market. Indeed, the factor market is the reverse side of the product market. In Part Five we looked at the cost of production as something constant in the supply of finished products. Now we must examine how the cost of production is determined and how inputs are used. There is a supply of an input and a demand for it. The interaction of supply and demand determines factor prices and, consequently, incomes. This chapter concentrates on the demand side of the factor market, while the next chapter treats the determinants of supply.

The underlying concern is how the criteria of efficiency and equity are satisfied in the factor market. Are all resources allocated optimally? Are they employed efficiently? And what is the resultant distribution of income? Is it equitable? This chapter begins explaining the economics needed for the answer. A full consideration of income distribution, however, will take up all of Part Six, concluding with an alternative view of the economics of income distribution.

1 George Orwell, *Animal Farm* (New York: New American Library, 1971).

Opening photo courtesy French Embassy Press & Information Division

CHOOSING FACTORS UNDER PERFECT COMPETITION

When faced with any competition at all, a firm must seek to minimize its production costs—if it wants to stay in business and make a profit to boot. The pressure on the perfect competitor is especially great, since only those in the industry who have the optimum-size operation and produce at the least possible cost will survive.

How does a firm decide on its optimum resource mix? Resources are limited, and therefore any given firm will find itself in competition for them with other firms. If land is not used for farming, it can be rented to industrial enterprises or used for housing. If labor is not employed in the production of one good, it can be employed elsewhere. The capital accumulated in banks can be used for investment in any productive enterprise. Thus, while resources are limited, they are also versatile and can be shifted among alternate uses in the long run. As in the product market, demand will work to allocate resources where they are most needed.

To develop the theory of factor demand, let us return for a while to the triangle farm of perfect competition. When Farmer Euclid studies his catalogue to order angles and points or when he contemplates the number of field hands needed for next season, he considers several interrelated variables:

- the price of the factor
- the prices of other factors
- the output of each factor
- the market price of the final product.

A change in any one of these can spark a shift in what Euclid will use.

Demand for a Single Factor

The decision-making process for choosing factors is similar to that of choosing output. Recall that each unit of output is viewed in terms of its contribution to a firm's total revenues and total cost. Under perfect competition, a firm will produce up to the point at which the marginal cost (MC) of producing an additional unit is equal to the incremental revenue (MR) it produces. And MR is equal to market price of a final product under perfect competition. Instead of seeing how much an additional unit of *output* adds to costs and revenues, Farmer Euclid goes one step back and sees how much an additional unit of a *factor* adds to output and thus to revenue. He then compares this with the price he has to pay to add that increment of the factor. If Farmer Euclid is deciding how many field hands to hire, it will pay Euclid, or any other perfect competitor, to employ them up to the point at which the price of the factor (in this case, the wage rate) equals what the output from the factor will bring on the market.

Factor Price In the ideal world of perfect competition, Farmer Euclid can hire as many workers—or buy as much of any other factor—at the going rate as he needs. The marginal cost for every unit of input is the same—the factor price.

$$MC_F = P_F$$

Thus, the MC curve, or supply curve, for Farmer Euclid is perfectly elastic. In Figure 30-1 this appears as a horizontal line at the market price.

Marginal Productivity The contribution to output by each worker is known as his **marginal physical product.** How much a worker produces is only the first step in calculating his worth to the enterprise, however. What Euclid really wants to know is how much that worker adds to revenues, or **the value of the marginal product.**

The value of the marginal product (VMP) is the increase in revenue due to using one additional unit of the factor when the market is perfectly competi-

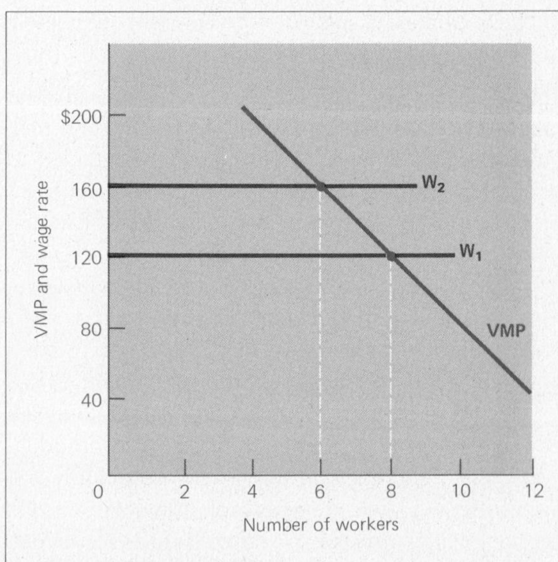

FIGURE 30-1 THE VMP CURVE Using the data given in Table 30-1, we have plotted the VMP curve. This curve is the demand curve for labor. We can determine the number of workers the perfect competitor would hire by looking at the going wage rate. If that rate were $120, eight workers would be hired. If the rate were $160, then only six workers would be hired.

TABLE 30-1 Demand for a Factor under Perfect Competition

(1) Wage rate	(2) Number of workers	(3) Marginal physical product	(4) Product price	(5) Value of marginal product
$120	4	100	$2	$200
120	5	90	2	180
120	6	80	2	160
120	7	70	2	140
120	8	60	2	120
120	9	50	2	100
120	10	40	2	80
120	11	30	2	60

Since the price of the goods remains the same no matter how many units are sold (or how many workers are hired), the value of the marginal product varies with the marginal physical product of each additional worker. We have assumed here that diminishing returns sets in immediately, so the VMP declines steadily throughout the range considered. The number of workers is selected not by the size of VMP but by its size in relation to the wage rate. When VMP is equal to the wage rate, the firm's costs and revenues are in balance, so there is no incentive to change the number of workers.

tive. It is equal to the marginal physical product (MPP) times the price of the good purchased.

$$VMP_F = MPP_F \times P_G$$

For example, if Farmer Euclid hires a field worker, Isosceles, who produces an additional 100 bushels of triangles that Euclid can market at $2.00 each, then the VMP of this field worker is $200. Table 30-1 continues the example, and from it we can determine how many of Isosceles' relatives Farmer Euclid will hire. As long as the VMP in column 5 exceeds the wage rate in column 1, the firm's total revenue will increase more than its total cost, and the firm will increase the quantity of the input—in this case, labor. With the addition of the eighth unit, the VMP falls to $120, which is also the wage rate for that unit. At this point, the firm will stop adding inputs.

If the wage rate changes, say to $160 because Isosceles' relatives join a union, then the number of workers Farmer Euclid will hire also changes. In Figure 30-1 we see that Euclid will hire only six workers. From this figure we also see that the VMP curve shows how many workers will be sought at different prices. Since a demand curve, by definition, shows the quantity demanded at different price levels, the VMP curve is also the factor demand curve. As the price of the factor declines, the amount of the factor demanded increases. Looked at another way, the more workers on hand, the less the last one contributes to Farmer Euclid's revenues and the lower the worker's wage rate will have to be to induce Farmer Euclid to hire him.

DIMINISHING MARGINAL PRODUCT The reason for the declining contribution to revenue of additional workers lies in what by now should be a familiar concept—the law of diminishing returns. As more workers are added to inputs that are fixed, the marginal physical product declines. The marginal physical product on Euclid's triangle farm does not drop as he brings on more workers because he is forced to hire the clumsier and more slothful members of the Isosceles clan; all of Isosceles' relatives are equally diligent and resourceful. The decline occurs simply because of the limitations of the fixed inputs. Although under perfect competition the price of a product remains constant, the VMP of a factor will decline because the MPP declines as additional units of the factor are employed.

But simply because a factor has a diminishing MPP does not mean that additional units will not be employed. Up to what point will a firm increase the quantity of one factor in relation to others?

As long as the VMP is greater than the cost of the additional unit of the factor (P_F), a firm will increase its profit by employing that unit. But if the price of a factor unit is higher than its resultant VMP, it would be unprofitable to employ that additional unit. The proper input level is obviously where the VMP of a factor equals the price of that factor.

$$VMP_F = P_F$$

Demand for Several Factors

Farmer Euclid is not just interested in hiring farm hands; he wants to produce the greatest number of triangles at the lowest total cost, labor being only a part of that total. All factors may vary, not just the single factor, labor. Farmer Euclid could sow the pasture land on the south forty or he could try fertilizing the remaining acreage more heavily; he could hire more hands or invest in a new, mechanized straight edge. Farmer Euclid has to look at the whole operation, first for its productivity and then for its cost. Euclid does not look at cost alone or output alone. He might be able to hire 15 farm hands for the price of the new straight edge, but he may pick the machine anyway because it can produce more triangles and, therefore, more revenue. Or he may be able to get the same number of bushels of triangles (and the same revenue) with several different combinations of land, labor, and capital; he is not indifferent about the choice, but picks the combination that incurs the lowest cost. By weighing MPP against cost, he finds the optimum resource mix.

The optimum resource mix occurs when the MPP of the last dollar spent to purchase a resource equals the MPP of the last dollar spent to purchase every other resource.

$$\frac{MPP_{F1}}{P_{F1}} = \frac{MPP_{F2}}{P_{F2}} = \frac{MPP_{FN}}{P_{FN}}$$

This principle is familiar from the discussion of the product market, where the consumer wanted to maximize the satisfaction gained from his limited budget. If these ratios are not equal, then more is gained from one input (say, labor) than another (say, land) and it will pay to shift purchases to labor. The shift, of course, changes the MPP of both; the MPP of labor falls because of diminishing marginal productivity as workers are added, while that of land rises. Eventually, the ratios of MPP to factor price will be equal. (This presumes, of course, that factors can be easily shifted and are ready substitutes for one another.)

Elasticity of Factor Demand

The Individual Firm The effect of a change in factor price upon the amount of that factor the firm will use depends in part upon the ability of firms to substitute one factor for another. If one factor can easily be used in place of other factors, then its **substitutability** is high. If so, it also will be price elastic, for only a small decrease in its price will encourage a firm to use it instead of other factors. But if it cannot easily be used in place of other factors, demand for it will be less responsive to price changes, or price inelastic.

Technology determines **the rate at which MPP declines.** If MPP declines rapidly, a small change in factor price would not induce a firm to use more, whereas if MPP declines slightly, a small change in factor price may justify using more or less of that factor.

Time is important in these adjustments. In the long run, demand is much more elastic because firms can change their setup to take advantage of relative changes in factor prices. For example, if the price of leather goes up, a firm may hire more skilled doublet makers to ensure that not a scrap is wasted, thereby substituting labor for leather. Changing the composition and size of the work force or the production methods is easier in the long run, so that elasticity is usually greater over time.

If the **supply of other inputs** is relatively elastic, then the demand for a particular input will also be elastic. A high elasticity of supply from other factors will heighten their competition with the one variable factor. Since producers can obtain much larger quantities of other factors by raising their prices only slightly, their demand for the one variable factor will be very sensitive to changes in its price. Demand elasticity for one factor, therefore, is tied to the supply elasticities of all other factors.

The **cost of a factor relative to the total cost** of all inputs affects its price elasticity. If a factor accounts for only a very small part of the total cost of the product, a change in its price will not affect total cost by much. Demand for it will be inelastic. If a factor accounts for only 1 percent of production cost and its price goes up 100 percent, it will merely have caused a rise in total cost of 1 percent, which can be absorbed easily by the firm.

Finally, if the demand for the final product is elastic,

then the demand for the factor will be elastic as well. If factor price goes up, raising costs, the firm may respond by charging a higher price for its product. If demand for the final product is elastic, however, the price increase will lose customers. Output—and factor demand—will decline. Therefore, what happens in the product market affects what happens in the factor market.

Derived Demand: A Digression Because factor demand depends upon consumer demand, it is a derived demand. Consumers have desires and seek satisfaction from the goods they purchase. In contrast factors are not bought or rented because they give any intrinsic satisfaction to producers, but because they are used to make products that can be sold at a profit. This profit potential depends on the strength of consumer demand. A change in product price, therefore, will cause a change in factor demand. The effect is different from the changes in factor price, since that resulted in movements *along* the VMP curve. A change in product price changes the VMP and shifts the curve.

Today, for example, the service industries are growing rapidly, as consumer demand shifts away from products people already own to services required for the upkeep of the products. Because people are needed to perform most services, firms in this field are labor intensive, and the demand for labor is greater than if the society were simply manufacturing goods in automated plants. As demand for services increases, their price increases, raising the VMP of each worker. The firm will, therefore, hire more workers at a given wage rate and its VMP curve for labor will shift to the right. Should the demand for services slacken, the firm would hire fewer workers at a given wage rate and the VMP curve would shift to the left.

Market Demand Because factor demand is a derived demand, finding the market demand for a factor is somewhat more complicated than finding the market demand curve for products. Recall that in the product market the market demand curve is simply the sum of the individual demand curves.

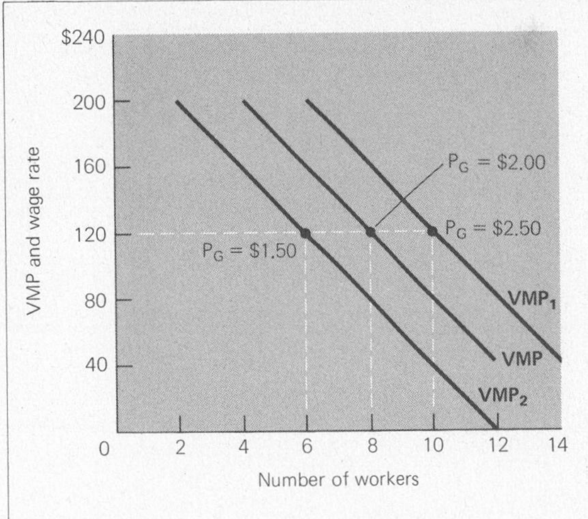

FIGURE 30-2 THE DERIVED DEMAND FOR LABOR **Since demand for the final product determines how much labor will be hired, the demand for labor is a derived demand. Whenever the price of the final product shifts, so too does the VMP schedule. Let us begin with the VMP curve of the previous figure, when price was $2.00. Were price of the final product to rise to $2.50, the VMP of each worker would increase and the VMP curve would shift upward to VMP_1; at the going wage, 10 workers would be hired instead of the eight hired when the product sold for $2.00. A decline in product price to $1.50 would result in a downward shift in VMP to VMP_2, with only six workers hired.**

Such an approach for factor markets would overestimate the amount of the factor in use because the factor demand curve reflects not only increase in output, but the repercussions this increase might have in the product market.

Suppose that the wage rate of triangle hands fell, perhaps because of a large wave of immigration. As the price of labor falls, more workers are hired and output increases. But this increase in total output changes the equilibrium in the product market. Although production of a single firm cannot affect the market price of its product, a higher output by the entire industry can. A greater amount supplied on the product market depresses the price of the product. This in turn lowers the VMP of inputs and reduces demand for them. The firm's VMP curve shifts downward. Thus, the increases in quantity demanded are not as great as we assumed initially.

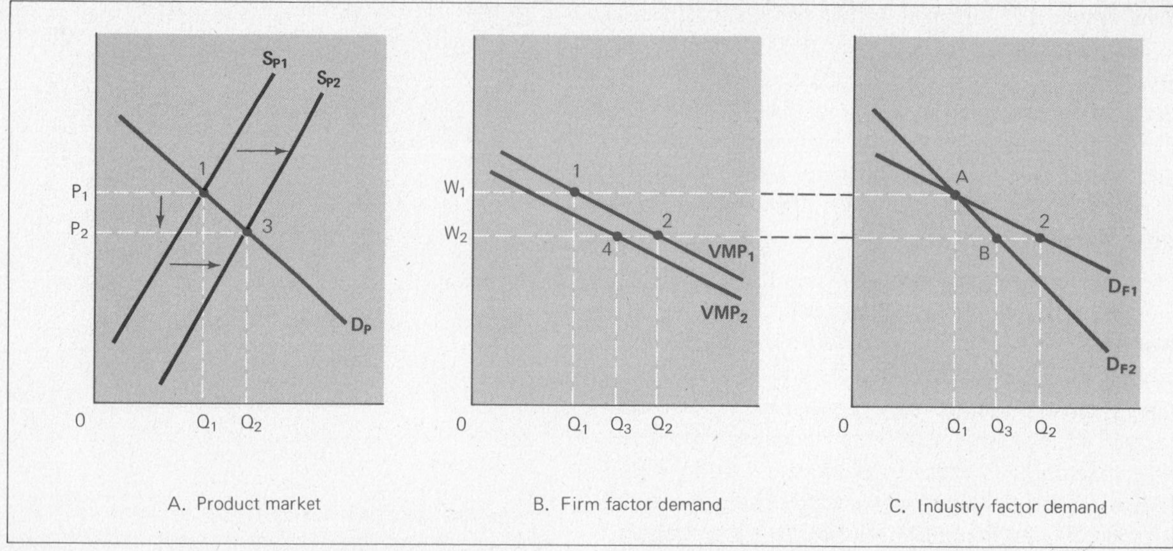

FIGURE 30-3 THE MARKET DEMAND CURVE Lowering the wage rate sets off a chain reaction that makes the market demand for labor less elastic than the demand of the individual firm. When the wage rate is W_1, the product market is in equilibrium at point 1; the firm finds its factor demand from point 1, and the market is at A. When the wage rate drops to W_2, each firm hires more workers, represented by point 2. Because total output then rises, the entire output cannot be sold at P_1 in the product market. The shift in the product supply curve from S_{P1} to S_{P2} causes equilibrium to fall to point 3 and product price to fall to P_2. Because product price determines VMP the VMP curve then shifts downward to VMP_2 and the number of workers is determined at point 4. Point B indicates the final equilibrium in the factor market, and the curve connecting A and B shows the more inelastic market demand resulting from these events.

Figure 30-3 shows how the market demand curve is derived under these circumstances. On the original VMP curve for the individual firm, when labor receives \$150, the firm will hire Q workers. If all firms are identical to this, we can multiply by the number of firms in the industry and obtain point A in the right-hand graph, which charts market demand. When the price of labor drops to \$100, the repercussions we described above will shift the individual firms' VMP curve down, and rather than demanding quantity Q_2 of the factor at the lower price, the individual firm will demand quantity Q_3. Multiplied by the number of firms in the industry, this will give point B in the market demand graph. If we now draw a line through AB, we see that the market demand curve has a much steeper slope than the individual VMP curves and is, therefore, not a simple multiple of individual firms' demands. Rather, it reflects the downward shift of the individual curves as a result of price changes, both for factors and products.

The result would be reversed if a factor's price rose. Firms would employ less labor and supply fewer products to the market. Consumers would react to the shortage by bidding up the price of the product. A higher price means a greater VMP for the individual producer. His VMP curve would shift upward, mitigating the effect on quantity demanded as a result of its higher price.

Market demand, then, is less sensitive to price changes than demand of the individual firm, and is less elastic.

Equity and Efficiency in Perfect Competition

So far we have concentrated on the firm. Factors are employed according to their marginal productivity, which is the measure of their contribution to the output and revenues of the firm. If $\frac{MPP_{F1}}{P_{F1}} = \frac{MPP_{FN}}{P_{FN}}$, the firm is using the least-cost combination of factors and making the greatest profits. Technological efficiency is assured if the firm uses the least-cost combination of factors.

Allocative efficiency is also achieved because the firm chooses that level of input at which the price of the factor equals its VMP and selects inputs whose VMP is highest. Assume that two firms in perfect competition are producing the same good. If one firm utilizes a factor of production in a process yielding a VMP that is less than the VMP that can be obtained by another firm using a more efficient productive process, the latter firm will bid the productive factor away from the firm with the less efficient productive process. By the same token, if two firms producing different goods require the same factor input, that input will be available only to the firm that achieves the higher VMP on its output. This results in allocative efficiency for society at large. And, presumably, it results in a sort of economic justice in which a laborer who is paid less than his VMP will not remain in that industry but will shift to where wages better reflect his or her economic contribution.

The equity of this arrangement is ambiguous, since payment according to marginal productivity means that incomes are unequal. After all, the factors supplied to firms are owned by individuals who are compensated for them. When a firm pays for a factor on the basis of its marginal productivity, then that is the income of the individual who supplies the factor. Inequality arises partly because not all individuals own factors with the same marginal productivities; through no fault of their own, these individuals earn less than others. A maid is paid $2 an hour and a fashion model $50 an hour, but both supply what is, in one sense, the same factor: labor per unit of time. Landlords in the city collect higher rent for their property than landlords in rural areas, yet they both own land. And many owners of land and capital have a higher income than working people, yet they do not ever have to lift a finger. Although differing marginal productivity accounts for part of the differences in income, inequality also arises because of imperfect competition in the product or factor markets.

FACTOR DEMAND UNDER IMPERFECT COMPETITION

Monopoly

Even if the firm participates in a perfectly competitive factor market, income distribution is affected if the firm is monopolistic. With perfect competition in the product market, the market price of a final product is the same for all sellers. The individual firm cannot affect it. It can sell as many units of a product as it can produce at that price. In this situation, the consumer demand curve for a firm is a horizontal line. But the monopolist faces a downward-sloping demand curve. Such a firm can only sell more of a product at steadily declining prices for every unit of output. In this situation, a factor's VMP no longer equals the marginal revenue a firm will realize from its employment, for a declining final product price affects the revenues from that factor and also reduces the revenues of all factor units already used to make products that must now be sold at the lower prices.

A firm's demand curve for a factor in a monopoly situation, therefore, will no longer be that factor's VMP curve. It will no longer be a factor's MPP multiplied by a stable price. Rather, demand for a factor will reflect the MPP multiplied by the marginal revenue (MR) it produces, which is declining. Now we no longer speak of a factor's VMP, but of its MRP, or marginal revenue product.

$$MRP_F = MPP_F \times MR_G$$

Table 30-2 relates the variables based on monopoly in the product market. Note that we still assume perfect competition to exist in the factor market and that the input price and marginal factor cost therefore do not change.

MRP is simply the change in total revenue due to using an additional unit of a factor. The firm will hire additional input units until the MRP of a unit equals its price.

$$MRP_F = P_F$$

In Table 30-2 that point is reached with the addition of the sixth unit of input. Under monopoly, therefore, the MRP curve will be a firm's demand curve for a factor (Figure 30-4). It declines more steeply than

TABLE 30-2 Demand for a Factor under Imperfect Competition

(1) Wage rate	(2) No. of workers	(3) TP	(4) MPP	(5) PP	(6) TR	(7) MRP
$120	4	100	100	$2.00	$200	$200
120	5	190	90	1.88	357	157
120	6	270	80	1.77	477	120
120	7	340	70	1.66	564	87
120	8	400	60	1.55	620	56
120	9	450	50	1.44	658	38
120	10	490	40	1.33	652	−6
120	11	520	30	1.22	634	−18

Columns 1, 2, and 4 here are identical to the first three columns of the preceding table. Since this buyer of labor is an imperfect competitor he faces a downward-sloping demand curve. He must charge a lower price to sell additional units of output, so there is a declining product price in column 5. Column 6 is derived by multiplying total product (column 3) by product price (column 5); some rounding has been done. Marginal revenue product, column 7, is derived from column 6, total revenue; it is the difference between total revenue at one level of input (and product price) and total revenue for the next level of input with its lower product price.

the VMP curve because it not only reflects the diminishing MPP of a factor but also the declining market price for the product.

Because factor demand is basically derived from product demand, imperfections in the product market affect the remuneration of inputs. A factor's VMP is society's measure of its contribution to output. But since a firm will pay all factor units at the rate of the MRP of the last unit added, all units will be paid less than they contribute. The suppliers of inputs, of course, feel exploited since they receive less than their full contribution. This need involve no vicious intent on the part of the monopolist, however. Firms act to profit maximize in response to certain market conditions. The real cause of the inequity is the imperfection of the market.

To society this means that resources are underallocated to the monopolistic industry. Consider, for example, a situation in which both a competitive firm and a monopolistic firm use purple dye. The price per pound is $5, and the competitive firm produces until $P_F = VMP_F$, whereas the monopolistic firm produces only until $P_F = MRP_F$. The monopolist's VMP at this point is $10. This means that without market imperfections, purple dye with a VMP of $5 could be shifted to a use that yielded a VMP of $10. Society would get $10 worth of product and give up only $5, clearly a wise use of resources. From the point of view of allocative efficiency, then, the monopolist is underutilizing this factor.

Monopsony

Consider, too, the effect of **monopsony**, where the firm may be the only buyer of a particular resource, although it may be a perfect competitor in the product market. In the labor market, monopsony is frequently encountered in small towns, where one

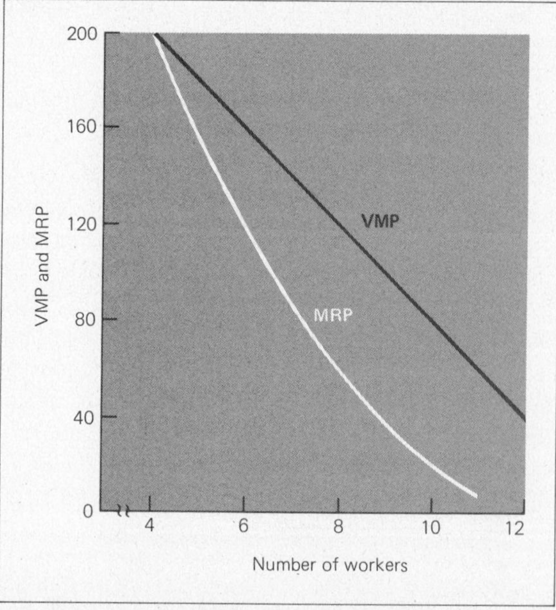

FIGURE 30-4 THE MARGINAL REVENUE PRODUCT CURVE OF THE IMPERFECT COMPETITOR **The MRP of the imperfect competitor is much more inelastic than that of the perfect competitor (both of whose labor has the same marginal physical product schedule), because both the MPP *and* the product price decline as the imperfect competitor sells additional units of output. At a salary of $120, the imperfect competitor will hire six rather than eight workers (the amount hired by the perfect competitor at the same wage rate).**

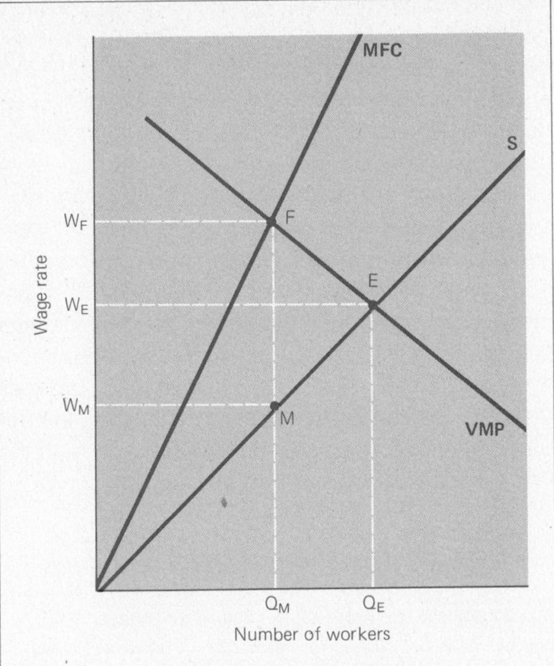

FIGURE 30-5 THE WAGES OF MONOPSONY If a monopsonist sells his product in a perfectly competitive market, its demand curve is its VMP curve. However, because the monopsonist's firm is the entire market for labor, it faces the upward-sloping market supply curve; it cannot hire additional workers at the going rate, but must increase wages in order to entice more workers. In deciding how many workers to hire, therefore, it is not guided by the intersection of supply and VMP at point E but by the intersection of the marginal factor cost curve with the VMP curve. Here cost and revenue are in balance at F. The monopsonist need not set the wage rate at W_F. The wage rate is read off the supply curve, not the MFC curve, because a wage of W_M will call forth the requisite number of workers. Because factor price is below VMP the workers are being paid less than their contribution to revenues, or, in technical terms, they are being *exploited*. Society is receiving less than it wants, as well.

company employs most of the labor force. Thus, people have a choice of working for that company at whatever wage it pays or not working at all. The firm, on the other hand, is not a resource price taker, able to hire any number of workers at a going market price, as would be the case under competition. Its supply curve is identical to the market supply curve, so it pays higher wages to attract more workers, up to a point at which the marginal factor cost equals the VMP of the unit employed (point F in Figure 30-5). If the employer paid the employee a wage equal to his or her VMP, then all employees should be paid W_F. But the monopsonistic firm need not do that. It need only look at its supply curve

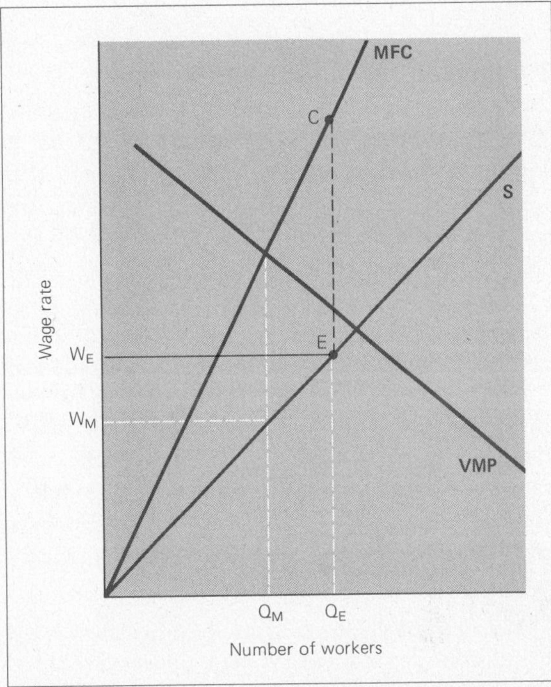

FIGURE 30-6 A MINIMUM WAGE UNDER MONOPSONY As we saw in Figure 30-5, the monopsonist would hire fewer workers at a lower wage rate than if he were competing for labor. To offset these effects, government may set a minimum wage at W_E. If a minimum wage were set at W_E, the monopsonist would have to pay his workers at least that. That wage would mean that the new supply curve of labor is W_EES and the MFC curve is identical to the supply curve 0 to E. Beyond point E, the original MFC curve is applicable, so there is a discontinuous portion (the dotted vertical line EC) at the kink in the supply curve. (This is similar to the oligopolist's marginal revenue curve, which is discontinuous at the output where the market price is set.) Since the monopsonist will hire that number of workers at which MFC and VMP are equal, he will hire Q_E workers. A minimum wage of W_E applied to a monopsonistic situation raises wages, employment, and presumably output. Under other circumstances, the minimum wage raises wages but cuts back employment. The debate over raising the minimum wage, then, depends in part on how monopsonistic the labor market is believed to be.

to find the wage rate that will call forth the necessary number of workers. Wages of W_M will be all the monopsonist needs to pay. In a competitive factor market, the quantity of workers employed and the corresponding wage rate would be at the equilibrium level, E. Many would call this exploitation, since workers are receiving less than their VMP. Workers accept it because there is no alternative employment.

EVALUATING MARGINAL PRODUCTIVITY

There are two questions to be answered concerning marginal productivity: *Does* it account for actual income distribution and *should* it account for income distribution? The first is an empirical question, and there are some problems in calculating the exact MRP or VMP of a given input. In a highly industrialized society, production processes have become so complex that it is especially difficult to assess the contributions of individual factors. Stockholders of a corporation have provided the capital for venture, but employees do all the work. What is their relative contribution to the output of that firm? Furthermore, how can one really measure the marginal product of a janitor, a secretary, or an executive all employed by the same company, which perhaps produces soap?

Institutional obstacles prevent the free flow of factors to the uses that ensure the highest contribution to output and revenues. Individuals, even if they own the same factors, do not always have the same opportunity to offer them. Factors may be immobile, as is land and even labor at times. Union seniority may tie down a worker, or tariff barriers may hold resources in an industry and may limit their use. And discrimination may mean that labor is underused or underpaid.

Despite these problems, income provides a rough reflection of the marginal productivity of most factors. Gains in compensation of labor, for example, have kept pace fairly steadily with rises in productivity—at least in the private sector. The use of factors by the public sector is a separate problem, considered in the final section of the chapter.

The link between productivity and income is good or bad depending on one's values. There is a tension between efficiency and equity in this issue. If factors are compensated according to their marginal productivity, technological efficiency should follow. Because of the differences in marginal productivity of the breadwinners, however, a family of seven may have less to live on than a family of three. If the market is imperfectly competitive, the worker will receive compensation lower than his or her VMP, redistributing income from the worker to the owners of the firm and making the distribution of resources allocatively inefficient. The normative issues depend, therefore, on the value placed on efficiency, the degree of imperfect competition in the society, and the value placed on relatively equal living standards.

GOVERNMENT DEMAND FOR FACTORS

When the government decides to provide certain public goods and services, it becomes in effect an entrepreneur, a single firm in business to meet common needs. While the government can hardly be called a profit-maximizing institution, it does have an obligation to supply its services at minimal cost. In that sense, it has to act like a firm searching for the least-cost combination of inputs. Its operation is complicated, however, by the fact that the services it provides generally have a rather inelastic demand. As a nation, Americans demand a certain level of national defense, health care, law enforcement, and so on. Locally, they expect adequate educational facilities, fire protection, and sanitation services. As long as government taxes and bond issues are not too onerous, little public account is taken of individual programs.

A change in prevailing sentiments may suddenly turn demand quite elastic, however. For example, the once sacrosanct defense budget has come under sharper scrutiny in the wake of public disenchantment with the Vietnam War. When citizen control over the purse strings is direct, as it is for local school taxes or bond issues, spending may be abruptly curtailed. The problem is that the expression of

STOPPING CRIME

The issue of crime in the streets has elected officials and unmade police commissioners since the first consolidated urban police force was organized in 1844 in New York. During the 1960s this issue swelled the budgets of crime control agencies by 145 percent (including inflation), creating larger police forces with special—and often controversial—street crime programs such as those in Detroit and equipping police with tanks, labs, dogs, and so on.

The output of these factors is supposed to be crime prevention. Justifying these expenditures involves finding first of all the marginal productivity of added expenditures on law enforcement. During the 1960s the FBI crime rate went up just as fast as the outlays for law enforcement. The more spent on crime, the more crime there was. Seemingly, the marginal productivity of law enforcement was low, or perhaps even negative.

Matters are hardly that simple, of course. Problems of measurement of crime and crime control, more reported crimes, changes in police budgeting, and so on complicate the conclusion. But more sophisticated studies found that just because one city outspent another on crime control, its crime rate might not be lower. The conclusion is not that wholesale budget cuts are in order or that increased budgets might have no effect, but simply that "observed marginal differences in law enforcement efforts have little apparent effects on crime rates."*

In a study by Thomas Pogue, crime rates correlated closely with poverty and race, suggesting that attacks on income inequality and racial discrimination might control crime more effectively than stepped-up street patrols. If the marginal productivity of welfare, day-care centers, and school integration is positive, then more dollars should be spent there and less on police. This principle of shifting resources to activities that offer a higher VMP applies to efficiency in the provision of all government services, not simply police versus welfare.

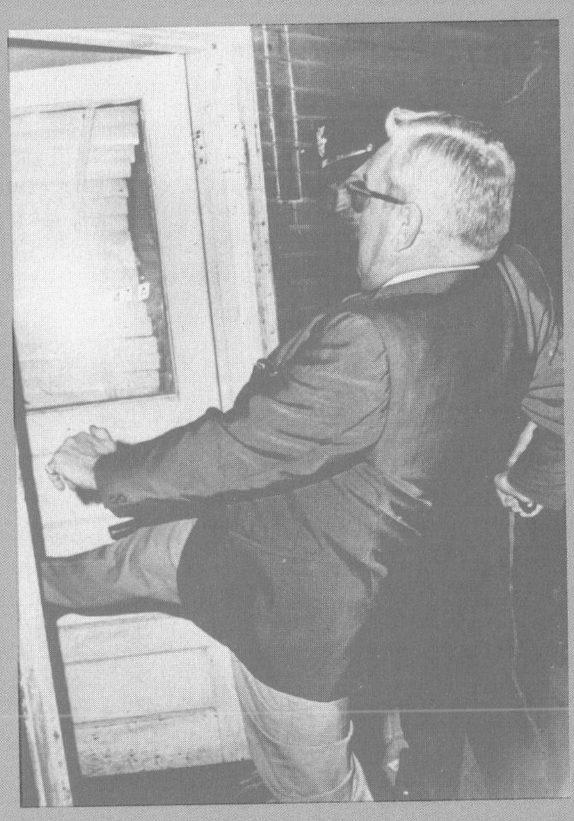

United Press International

* Thomas F. Pogue, *An Econometric Analysis of Inter-City Differences in Crime Rates* (Iowa City: Bureau of Business and Economic Research, University of Iowa, 1973).

consumer demand is usually indirect, making the demand for factors more complicated.

Moreover, it is sometimes hard to distinguish between inputs and outputs of programs. Are the Tomcats of Chapter 1 an output or simply a factor in the production of the government service called defense? If they are a factor, then the government can measure the Tomcat capability against submarines or missiles to determine the least-cost combination of factors for a given level of defense.

Since there are sporadic or indirect pressures from the product market, no profit-making incentives, and some question about what output actually is, what keeps government from ignoring the least-cost combination of factors? Competition between programs for the limited funds available is a major source of pressure. This is oftentimes political, not economic competition, but it serves to make those who appropriate or administer funds examine their use of resources. Within the executive branch, the Office of Management and Budget trims or expands programs. Congressional scrutiny, while haphazard, is also a feature of this process and can be a pressure for economizing. The General Accounting Office, the committee system, and legislative powers can control spending. Other incentives employing market features were discussed in Chapter 29.

The search for the least-cost combination of factors is only one aspect of efficient factor allocation. "A program may be well run and highly efficient . . . but still waste national resources if it pursues the wrong objectives."[2] We have already examined many examples of this problem—in health care, urban transportation, pollution control, and defense. It will recur when we take up solutions to the problems of income distribution.

2 Charles L. Schultze, "Perverse Incentives and the Inefficiency of Government," in *The Political Economy of Federal Policy*, eds. Robert Haveman and Robert Hamrin (New York: Harper & Row, 1973), p. 15.

SUMMARY

1 Firms demand inputs for the production of consumer goods in order to make profits. The factor market, therefore, directly determines the allocation of resources. It determines the distribution of income, since individuals own factors and receive their income from supplying these factors.

2 A firm will keep adding a factor until its addition to cost equals its contribution to revenue. Under perfect competition, the marginal factor cost equals the factor price at all levels of factor use. The contribution to revenue is the addition to output (MPP) times the price this output can be sold for (P_G). This is known as the value of the marginal product (VMP). Because the MPP declines as additional units of one factor are added to fixed factors, the VMP also declines. The VMP curve is the demand curve of the firm.

3 The firm seeks the least-cost combination of factors by adding and subtracting units until the marginal output for the last dollar expended is the same for all factors.

$$\frac{MPP_{F1}}{P_{F1}} = \frac{MPP_{FN}}{P_{FN}}$$

4 The responsiveness of the firm to changes in factor price (or the elasticity of the VMP curve) is determined by substitutability, the technology of the firm (which determines the rate at which MPP declines), time, the cost of a factor relative to the total cost, and the price elasticity of the final product.

5 Since factor demand is a derived demand, a change in the price of the final product will change the amount of a factor a firm will hire at a given factor price and will thus shift the VMP curve. An increase in P_G will shift the VMP to the right; a decrease in P_G will shift it to the left.

6 A change in factor price will have less effect on total quantity demanded than expected, because this change affects the product price, which then changes the demand for the factor and modifies the amount of the factor in use. The market demand curve is, therefore, less elastic than demand curves of individual firms.

7 For the firm, employing factors according to their marginal productivity ensures the least-cost combination and the greatest profit. Although income distribution will be unequal, technological and allocative efficiency are achieved. Efficiency is guaranteed only if the product and factor markets are perfectly competitive.

8 If a firm is monopolistic, it can sell more output only by lowering price. This is shown by its marginal revenue product, which declines because of both declining MPP and declining product price. Hence a firm's MRP, or demand curve, is less elastic and lower than the VMP would be if the firm were perfectly competitive. The firm will hire workers only until MRP equals factor price. This leads to lower wages and curtailed output, and means that the monopolist is allocatively inefficient.

9 If the firm is monopsonistic, it can employ more of a factor only by raising factor price, since it is the only firm in the factor market. Its MFC curve is, therefore, above its supply curve. The firm employs a factor up to the point at which marginal factor cost equals VMP, but it determines the wage level from the supply curve. The factor is paid less than its contribution to the firm's revenues, since P_F is less than VMP This constitutes exploitation of labor and creates allocative inefficiency, since the use of resources has been curtailed.

10 The demand for factors may occur in a nonmarket setting. The government employs factors, but lacks the simple decision-making system and the incentives that ensure the use of factors with technological and allocative efficiency. Devising such incentives constitutes an important contemporary economic problem.

SUGGESTED READINGS

Douglas, Paul H. *The Theory of Wages*. New York: Augustus M. Kelley, 1934.

Haveman, Robert H., and **Robert D. Hamrin**, eds. *The Political Economy of Federal Policy*. New York: Harper & Row, 1973.

Haveman, Robert H., and **Kenyon A. Knopf**. *The Market System*. New York: John Wiley & Sons, 1966.

Hunt, E. K., and **Howard J. Sherman**. *Economics: An Introduction to Traditional and Radical Views*. Chap. 15. New York: Harper & Row, 1972.

Leftwich, Richard H. *The Price System and Resource Allocation*. 4th ed. Chaps. 13 and 14. Hinsdale, Ill.: Dryden Press, 1970.

Mansfield, Edwin. *Microeconomics: Theory and Application*. Chaps. 12 and 13. New York: W. W. Norton, 1970.

QUESTIONS

1 Review
   a. basic explanations for unequal income distribution,
   b. how a perfect competitor chooses the amount of a given factor he will use and the factor mix that he will use,

c. the factors that affect the elasticity of demand for individual inputs,
d. why the industry demand for a factor of production is generally less elastic than that of an individual firm,
e. the MRP curve for a monopolist and the quantity of an input that the monopolist would choose to employ,
f. the shape of the monopsonist's demand curve for a factor of production,
g. the distortions in allocative efficiency resulting from imperfect competition,
h. characteristics of government demand for factors of production.

2 Assume that you are managing a glass jar plant and that you must inform the personnel office as to the personnel needs for the plant for the next few months. You call in all your foremen and from their estimates draw a MPP curve for labor in the plant. What further steps would you need to take to decide upon the number of workers you need? Now suppose that there is some transportation difficulty that leaves you with a virtual monopoly in glass jars in your new supply space. What would happen to the VMP curve and why? What might happen to the number of workers you decide to hire?

3 Suppose that in anticipation of increased food prices, people wish to store their home-grown produce in glass jars. Since the produce is generally maturing over a period of two or three months throughout the country, there is a sudden and very rapid increase in the demand for jars. You are a perfect competitor but you nevertheless may wish to make some adjustments in your plant. Why? What is likely to happen in the long run?

4 There have been frequent increases in the federal minimum wage over the years. Assume that the minimum wage is raised again and, since your glass jar plant ships across state lines, you are subject to the new law. How might the new law affect your hiring decisions? Under what conditions might you lay off some of your existing work force? Is it possible that an increase in the minimum wage might not affect your hiring practices?

5 Because of a large increase in the demand for low-phosphate detergents, detergent producers have begun to use potash, a phosphate substitute. Potash is an important ingredient in the production of glass, however, and because of price controls the price of potash is fixed. What effect would you predict in these industries? If there were no controls, what might happen to (a) the price of potash, (b) the amount used in glass production, and (c) the quantity of potash produced?

6 Your plant is the largest employer in town and exercises a practical monopsony over certain labor skills. From your point of view, what does the labor supply curve look like? How does its shape affect the marginal factor cost curve for labor? Why might a labor leader charge that management is either underhiring or paying too little?

7 Assume now that your glass jar plant has become unionized. The union wants a 50 cent per hour increase but agrees to supply all the labor that your plant could possibly use for the union wage. Now what does the labor supply curve look like? The marginal cost curve? Does the wage equal the value of the marginal product?

8 The cost of gasoline to independent retailers went up in the summer of 1973,

but the retailers were unable to pass on the increase due to Phase IV controls. Retailers complained bitterly about the inability to pass on the increase to the consumer. Why would these retailers want to pass on the increase to the consumer? What might be the elasticity of demand for gas? How about the substitutability of gas as a factor of production for the gasoline retailer?

9 Indicate whether factor demand is likely to be elastic or inelastic for each of the following:
   a. wheat flour to cereal producers
   b. costumes for theaters
   c. wood products for mobile home producers
   d. wool for clothing manufacturers

10 Assume that a monopoly is regulated so that the price for its final product is fixed. Is there any possibility that the MRP would equal the VMP? Why or why not?

Chapter 31 Factor Supply

It is impossible to say whether supply or demand determines the market price for a factor and, therefore, the distribution of income and the allocation of resources. In the previous chapter, supply was taken for granted; workers, land, capital, and entrepreneurs appeared to accept recompense at the market rate. But in reality, supply varies, too. Waves of immigration provide an abundant labor supply, floods temporarily take land out of production, and so on. These fluctuations affect the abundance of a factor and the price it can command.

FACTOR SUPPLY CURVE

As might be expected, the factor supply curve shows the relation between the amount of factor supplied and the price of the factor. In the case of labor, for example, the supply curve shows the relation between the quantity of labor supplied and the wage rate. The elasticity of supply is the percentage change in the quantity supplied divided by the percentage change in the price of the factor. Since it takes time to adjust to a price change, the elasticity of supply will be greater in the long run than it is in the short run. It takes time for labor to be hired and trained or retrained, land to be cleared and made productive, and capital to be made available. No matter how much the prices of these factors shoot up, additional quantities may not be immediately available. The response of suppliers will be felt only gradually.

For instance, consider the case of arable land. An individual farmer can purchase at the market rate as many acres of arable land as he desires since, assuming perfect competition, the supply of a factor is infinitely elastic to an individual firm. But if too many farmers want to purchase the same arable land, there will be a sharp rise in its price, for the amount of arable land is fixed in the short run. In the long run, however, with a large increase in the price, some poor or marginal land may be transformed (by drainage, clearing, or irrigation) into arable land, thereby increasing total supply.

Opening Photo by J. Paul Kirouac

For purposes of analysis, we generally consider the supply of land to be completely inelastic—represented graphically by a straight vertical line—and it is true that a given acre cannot be reproduced. But, depending on the demand for land (which we explore in a later section of this chapter) it is possible to retrieve land for almost any use. In Chapter 20 on urban problems we have seen the supply of land contract for low-income housing and expand for high-rise luxury apartment buildings as a result of urban renewal.

It can be argued, on the other hand, that factor supply in its totality, even in the long run, must always be inelastic. There is only so much land and a fixed amount of natural resources within the boundaries of a nation.

Economists, however, have come to distinguish between absolute limitations and the relative amounts of a factor that are in use. Capital accumulation is the result of that portion of our funds that is not spent on consumption. We could increase the stock of capital by consuming less and saving more, up to the point at which we simply have no more money to save. Similarly, the supply of labor is limited ultimately by the size of the population, but ordinarily the labor force is only a fraction of the total population. In the long run, the labor supply could be increased by inducing more women to enter the labor force, by persuading workers to retire at a later age, or even by altering child labor laws.

SUPPLY OF LABOR

Labor is the factor that most of us supply to the economy. In the United States, about three-fourths of the national income consists of payments made to blue- and white-collar workers, professional people and self-employed business persons—in short, payments for personal services of one sort or another. Although we shall refer to the income received by labor as wages, these may actually take the form of salaries, bonuses, commissions, and the profits realized by the owners of small, independent businesses.

Supply Curve of Labor

A pencil vendor will sell you as many pencils as you want, but a worker will not necessarily sell you as many hours of his labor as you want. Every hour devoted to work is an hour that could have been devoted to leisure. It is also true that every hour devoted to leisure is an hour that could have been devoted to earning more money at work. So an obvious question at once comes to mind: How does a worker decide how to divide his waking hours between work and leisure?

To answer this question, consider the choice a carpenter might have to make after working eight hours: He can go home and drink a beer, or he can work an extra hour and earn an additional $5. The carpenter has to decide whether an hour with a beer is worth more to him than an extra $5. His decision will depend on how tired he is, how much he needs the money, and other considerations such as how much he enjoys the company of his wife. Since he has already worked eight hours, thereby earning $40, he may opt for the beer. After only four hours of work, he would be more likely to continue working. In economic terms, he will work until he reaches the point at which the marginal utility of his hourly wage is equal to the marginal utility of an extra hour of leisure.

We have assumed so far that the carpenter's wage is fixed at $5 per hour. Let us now consider what happens if his wage is raised to $7 per hour.

The carpenter now has to sacrifice $7 for an hour's leisure. That is to say, the price of leisure has risen to $7 per hour, since every hour of leisure costs precisely the amount of money that could be made working during that hour. Leisure can be looked upon as just another good a person desires. So when the price of leisure rises in relation to the prices of other goods, the carpenter's consumption of the relatively expensive good will decline and he will buy more of the other goods. The carpenter will tend to work more and take less leisure. Economists call this the **substitution effect**.

If the carpenter's income keeps rising, he will gradually become susceptible to another phenomenon called the **income effect**, which will tend to increase the number of hours he devotes to leisure. The more money he has, the more he will be able to afford all goods, including leisure. Few people want to work constantly, earning more and more money without having an opportunity to spend it. The carpenter wants to reap the benefits of having more money, and that includes a weekend excursion to

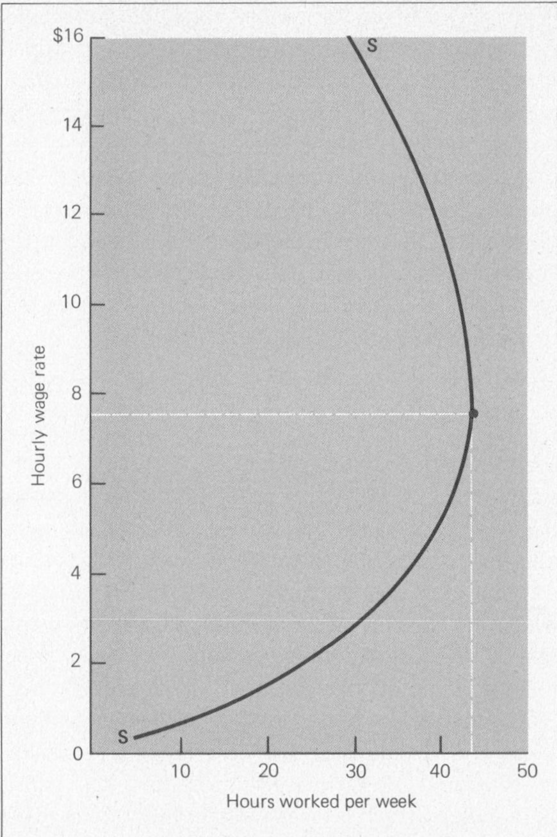

FIGURE 31-1 THE BACKWARD LABOR SUPPLY CURVE (Hypothetical) As the hourly wage rate is increased, the quantity of labor supplied by a worker increases, but at a decreasing rate. Beyond the wage rate of $7.50, the amount of labor offered by a worker begins to decline. At very low wages, then, a worker is not willing to sacrifice very many hours of leisure for employment, but as the wage rate increases, so does the worker's willingness to work. At some point, however, a worker will forgo additional wages in favor of leisure time, and this is the point at which the labor supply curve bends backward.

the beach or a vacation in Florida. The more money he earns, the more easily he can afford such pleasures without having to sacrifice any of the other goods that satisfy him.

The carpenter's understandable desire to lie underneath the Florida sun is reflected in the peculiar shape of the supply curve of an individual worker. While the supply curves of factors generally slope upward and to the right, the labor supply curve for the individual may bend backward beyond a certain point (Figure 31-1). The substitution effect will cause the amount of labor supplied to increase when wages rise from relatively low levels. Once they have reached a certain point, however, the income effect will predominate, and any further increase in the wage rate may actually cause a reduction in the quantity of labor supplied.

Since not all workers' supply curves bend backward at the same time, we usually proceed on the assumption that the market supply curve for labor will be positively sloped throughout. At any wage rate, the majority of workers will work more if wages increase.

Why Wage Rates Differ

Labor, then, is supplied by individuals who seek to obtain income with which to buy the goods and services they need. As a factor, however, labor is far from homogeneous. Clearly, human mental capabilities vary; and there are variations in training and education that affect the skills possessed by different individuals and therefore contribute to wage differentials in the labor market.

Qualitative Differences in Skills In the complex workings of a modern economy, there is a need for both brain surgeons and auto mechanics. But brain surgeons earn as much as $100,000 per year, while auto mechanics earn much less. Why are brain surgeons paid so much money? Their work is socially useful, of course; but the work of auto mechanics is also useful.

Brain surgeons are highly paid because the supply of brain surgeons is highly inelastic. In other words, a large increase in the fees paid to brain surgeons will result in but a small increase in the availability of their services. Why is this so? First of all, brain surgery requires a great deal of training. Only a limited number of people have the time and money to study four years in college, four years in medical school, and several more years in internship and residency—regardless of the level of the fees paid to brain surgeons. Second, surgical aptitude is relatively scarce. In other words, a relatively small portion of the American population has the innate talent and intelligence necessary to learn brain surgery—regardless of the level of the fees.

However, the supply of brain surgeons is not totally inelastic. In the short run, some surgeons may work a few more hours per week as fees rise. (But because of the income effect, at a higher level of pay some may work less!) And in the long run, an increase in fees may induce not only more medical students to study brain surgery but also more foreign brain surgeons to immigrate to the United States.

Wage Differentials among Labor of Similar Quality Yet there are also income differences among persons who perform the same type of labor. How do we explain this? Basically, it is the result of short-term shifts in demand. Bricklayers may have the same degree of skill as carpenters, but if housing demand switches from brick buildings to wooden structures, then carpenters will earn more money because the greater demand for them will drive up their incomes. Only in the long run will horizontal mobility result in bricklayers being retrained for carpentry work. The degree of this horizontal mobility is another cause of income differences between similar types of labor. The less mobility, the greater will be the wage differentials.

The supply of labor for similar occupations may be influenced by considerations other than monetary ones. The classic example is the high school graduate capable of working either in a bank or on an automobile assembly line. The latter would give him roughly twice the income, yet he may decide to become a bank clerk, because he prefers the clean, air-conditioned environment of a bank to the noise and monotony of the assembly line. He sacrifices a higher income for what he considers better working conditions.

Similar considerations can affect the wages paid in occupations with high prestige. For years, teachers—particularly college professors—have received incomes far below those in other fields that require similar qualifications, training and experience. Presumably public esteem of the teaching profession made up for the income deficiencies.

Immobilities Sometimes workers at identical jobs are paid different wages due to geographic, institutional, or social immobilities that block the free flow of labor to the highest bidder.

Geographical immobility is caused by people's attachment to their milieu. Workers, after all, are human beings, not machines. They may resist leaving their families, friends, and home town, even though they could make more money in another area. The psychic stress of resettlement outweighs the lure of a higher income. Or workers may simply be

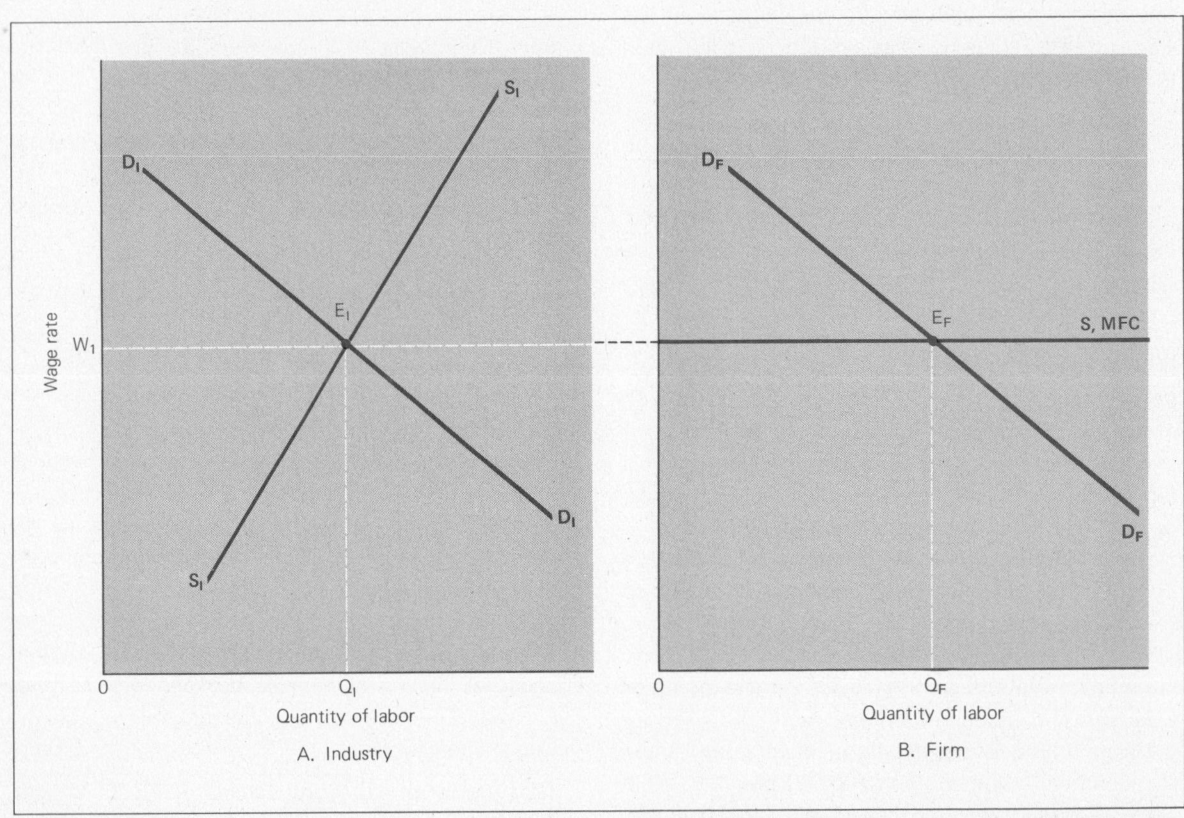

FIGURE 31-2 INDUSTRY AND FIRM SUPPLY AND DEMAND CURVES FOR LABOR The labor supply curve faced by the entire industry slopes upward to the right, because it takes higher wages to attract more workers to an industry. The point of intersection of the labor supply curve and the demand curve determines the wage rate for the entire industry.

The quantity of labor hired by the competitive firm is determined by the intersection of its labor supply curve and its VMP curve. Since the firm can obtain all the labor it needs at the market wage rate, the labor supply curve faced by the firm (which is also its MFC curve) is a horizontal line. D_F, the firm demand (or VMP) curve, slopes downward and to the right, since the marginal physical product of additional workers eventually declines. This parallels the relation between individual demand and market demand in the product market: The perfect competitor could sell all he wanted at the market price; here he can buy all the labor he wants at the market wage.

ignorant of pay and working conditions in other regions.

Institutional immobility often results from the restrictive membership practices of trade unions. Closed shops may operate to reduce the normal supply of labor to assure a higher income for union members. Thus, nonunion construction workers may earn only a fraction of the income earned by unionized construction workers, even though they do the same work. Schools and universities usually require formal academic credentials or published research from those they hire, notwithstanding an applicant's knowledge or ability to teach. Again the result is that people with essentially the same skills receive different incomes.

Social immobility also contributes to market imperfection. Despite legislation to the contrary, women and members of ethnic minorities continue to receive lower-than-average payments for their labor.

Analysis of Wage Determination

With perfect competition in the labor market, there will be many buyers and sellers of labor. Figures 31-2A and B contrast the slopes of the labor supply curves faced by an industry and a single firm. In the left-hand graph, D_I is the sum of the value of the marginal product (VMP) curves of all the firms in the industry. Like most demand curves, it slopes downward. S_I slopes upward and to the right because when an industry seeks a greater quantity of labor, it has to increase the wages it pays to lure workers from other markets, occupations, and localities. This is the only way that the amount of labor supplied to any market can be increased under conditions of perfect competition and full employment.

In Figure 31-2B, a firm's demand for labor is represented by its VMP curve, which again is downward sloping. But it is faced with a perfectly elastic supply curve, since at the going market price of labor, it can hire as many units as it wants. Since at a steady wage rate the supply curve is also the marginal factor cost curve, the firm will employ labor in such quantity that MFC equals VMP. It has no control over the wage rate it pays; but it can adjust the quantity it hires according to its VMP. To maximize profits it will hire that quantity at which the market wage equals the VMP

Imperfect Competition

In Chapter 30, we saw that the effects of monopoly in the product market and monopsony in the demand for factors were to lower the wage rate and reduce the quantity demanded. Society is deprived of output, and workers are exploited, in the technical sense.

Monopoly of Supply Monopoly in the labor market can also have detrimental effects on resource allocation. In this case, however, the beneficiaries are on the supply side of the market. They are usually represented by one powerful union that deals with a

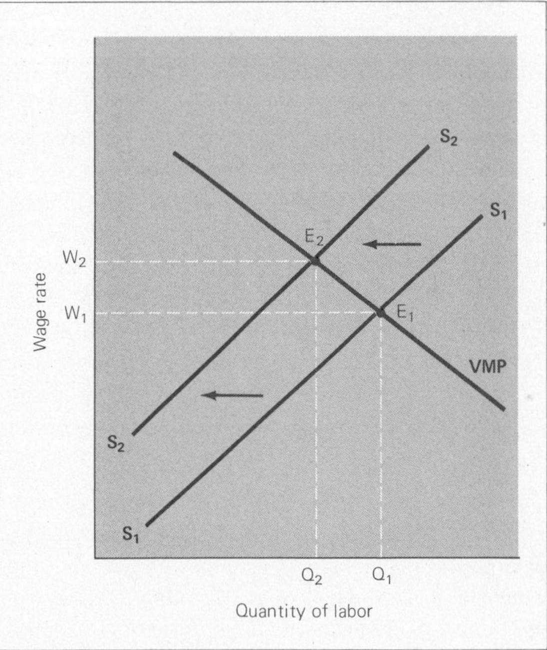

FIGURE 31-3 UNIONIZATION OF A COMPETITIVE INDUSTRY The unionization of a competitive industry (many firms now buying labor from a single union) may result in higher wages and a smaller quantity of labor purchased. The supply of labor may be restricted by initiation fees, restrictive membership rules, and long apprenticeships, as well as by restrictive work rules. This lowers the supply of labor from S_1S_1 to S_2S_2. Wages rise from W_1 to W_2, while the quantity of labor hired declines from Q_1 to Q_2.

large number of small firms. Like any monopolist, the union can restrict supply (labor in this case) to command a higher price (wages in this case). It can do so through restrictive membership rules, high initiation fees, and long apprenticeships. This will cause the supply curve of labor for an industry to shift to the left. Given the industry's factor demand, the wage rates will increase as the supply of labor is reduced. Other effects of unions are discussed in Chapter 33.

Bilateral Monopoly If a factor market consists of one seller of the factor (a monopolist) and one buyer of that factor (a monopsonist), what will happen? This situation, called bilateral monopoly, is approximated in many labor markets in the United States where a large union bargains with one or a few large corporations. Automobile manufacturing and steel are examples of American industries in which bilateral monopoly can be said to exist.

Figure 31-4 illustrates these market conditions. Curve S is the labor supply curve; curve MFC represents the marginal factor cost to the monopsonist; and MRP is the demand curve for labor. The employer will seek to maximize profits by hiring Q_1 employees at a wage rate of W_1. The union will seek the highest possible wage rate, which for Q_1 employees would be W_2. Our theory cannot predict the precise outcome of the bargaining between labor and management, but we would expect the wage rate to settle somewhere between W_1 and W_2. The greater the bargaining power of labor, the closer the wage rate will be to W_2; the greater the bargaining power of management, the closer it will be to W_1.

If the wage rate is W_1, clearly only Q_1 will be employed. In this case, line W_1abMFC becomes the MFC curve, and MFC = MRP at Q_1. However, if the wage rate is between W_1 and W_2, more than Q_1 will be employed. For example, if the agreed upon wage rate is W_3, the MFC curve becomes line W_3cdMFC and MRP = MFC at Q_2. In this case, the countervailing power of the union has offset the power of management and the result is a wage rate and a level of employment equal to those under competitive conditions. Thus, when monopoly exists on both the demand and supply sides of the labor market, the result may well be wage and employment levels closer to the competitive model than if monopoly prevailed on one side of the market only.

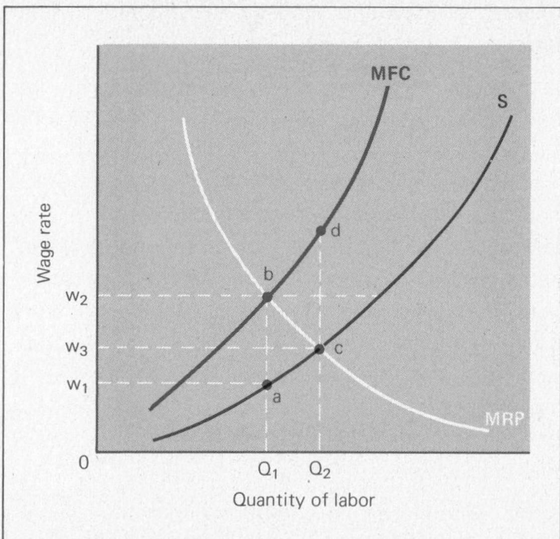

FIGURE 31-4 BILATERAL MONOPOLY IN THE LABOR MARKET Bilateral monopoly in a factor market exists when there is one seller of the factor of production (a monopolist) and one buyer of that factor (a monopsonist). In labor markets, such a situation is approximated when a powerful union bargains with one or a few large corporations. The employer will seek to hire Q_1 workers at a wage rate of W_1; the union will seek the higher wage rate W_2. Bargaining between the union and management will result in a wage rate somewhere between W_1 and W_2, in which case more than Q_1 workers will be employed. If the wage rate is settled at W_3, wages and employment will equal those that would prevail under competitive conditions.

Wages and Productivity

We could expect the mechanics of wage determination under various competitive conditions to be reflected in the relation between wages and productivity. A look at wage rates in general indicates that they are closely tied to the productivity of labor. Figure 31-5 shows that as productivity in the United States has increased, so have wage rates. It is important, however, to distinguish between money wages and real wages. Money wages are simply the amount of money the supplier of labor is paid for his services, while real wages determine the purchasing power of his income, or the amount of goods and services he can purchase with his wages.

Real wage rates, therefore, are a more accurate reflection of the productivity of labor. If, for instance, money wages rise faster than productivity, as they have since the mid-1960s, this difference will probably result in an increase in consumer prices.

Gains in productivity are due partly to the improved health, education, and training of the work force, and partly to the growth in quantity and quality of other factors of production, notably capital. With technological advance, output per worker will increase, and so will his income. We shall take a closer look at productivity, labor unions, and other aspects of labor economics in Chapter 33.

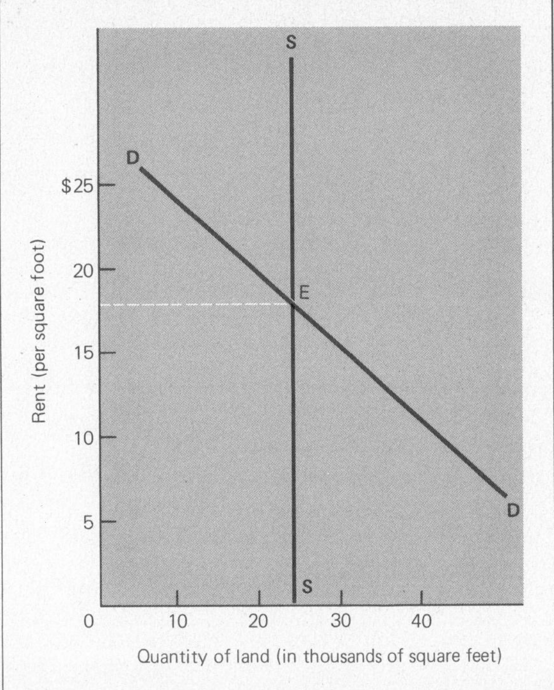

FIGURE 31-6 DEMAND FOR AND SUPPLY OF LAND AT A GIVEN LOCATION The supply of land, SS, is perfectly inelastic. Its price, the rent charged, is determined by the intersection of the demand curve and the supply curve. In this graph, the rent is $18 per square foot and the quantity of land purchased is fixed at 24,000 square feet.

SUPPLY OF LAND

Let us start by assuming that land is nonreproducible. The economy has a certain quantity of land, and that's that. It is true that within certain limits existing land can be transformed by clearing drainage, and irrigation, so in the long run, depending on the level of demand, it is possible to increase the supply of a given type of land. However, traditional economic analysis tells us that such effects result in only a small increase in the total amount of land supplied, especially in the short run, and that therefore we may assume that land and other natural resources are in virtually fixed and inelastic supply.

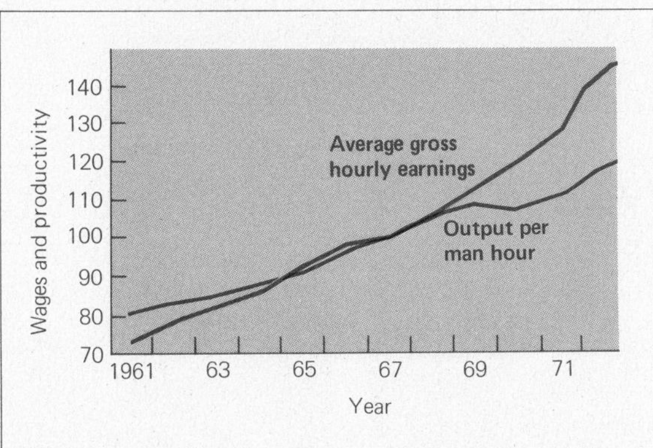

FIGURE 31-5 PRODUCTIVITY AND WAGE RATES (1967 = 100) Between 1961 and 1972, both productivity and wage rates rose substantially. Since 1967, however, wage rates have risen more than twice as fast as output per man-hour. When money wages rise faster than productivity, this difference will tend to result in an increase in consumer prices, which has indeed occurred during these years.

SOURCE: *Economic Report of the President*, January 1973.

Whenever the supply of a good or a factor is perfectly inelastic, its price will be determined by the demand for it. In Figure 31-6, the inelastic supply of land is represented by the vertical line SS. The equilibrium price (E) depends on the position of the demand curve alone. The greater demand is,

MONOPSONY IN PROFESSIONAL SPORTS

The owners of America's professional baseball clubs exercise rigid control over the services of their employees, the players. A reserve, or option, clause is written into the contract of each athlete. It requires that each player must negotiate only with the club that holds his contract. If another club wants to acquire a particular player, it cannot negotiate with the athlete directly, but must instead buy his contract from the club that presently owns it. Moreover, baseball clubs, like teams in many other sports, do not compete with one another in trying to attract new talent. Instead, they rely on a draft system in which the lowest ranking team in each league is given first choice of all graduating high-school players. A club cannot negotiate with an athlete who has been drafted by another club.

The reserve clause and the draft system severely reduce a player's ability to maximize his income, since athletes are not free to bargain with whatever club they choose. The ballplayer must either play for the club that drafts him or owns his contract, at the salary the club offers, or not play at all. That this immobility diminishes the bargaining power of athletes is demonstrated by the case of Ken Harrelson. A few years ago, Harrelson found himself in the unusual position of having been released unconditionally by his team while still capable of playing major league baseball. Eventually, he negotiated a salary of $75,000 a year, substantially above the salary he had been receiving previously.

The labor market for professional ballplayers illustrates the monopsonistic model developed in Chapter 30, for major league clubs have essentially joined together to form a cartel. The graph below shows that

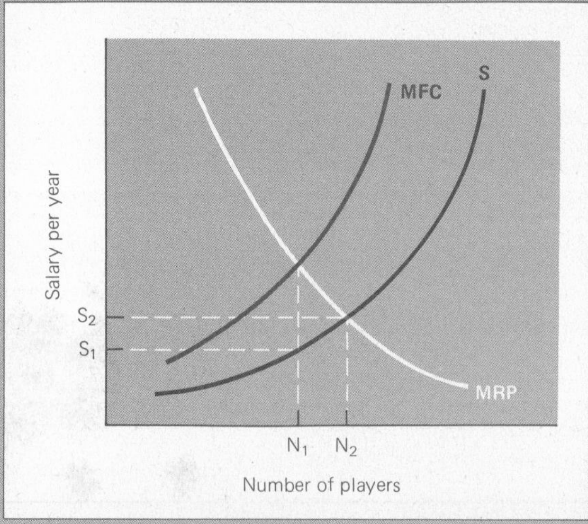

United Press International

club owners will choose to hire N_1 players, since this is the number at which MFC = MRP. The salary level needed to attract this number of players is S_1. Clearly, both salaries and the number of players hired will be lower under these conditions than they would be in a competitive situation, where salaries and employment would be at S_2 and N_2 respectively. Of course, if the players were organized to the extent that workers are organized in many industrial unions, a situation of bilateral monopoly could develop which might raise salaries substantially.

Efforts have been made to challenge in the courts the monopoly power of major league baseball clubs. In 1970, baseball player Curt Flood argued that the reserve clause constitutes a restraint of trade, which is outlawed under the Sherman Act. But the Supreme Court upheld its 1922 ruling that baseball is outside the scope of federal antitrust laws.

While the courts have been upholding the reserve clause in baseball, Congress has been approving the merger of rival leagues in other sports—which also serves to diminish the bargaining power of athletes. When the American Football League was formed in 1960 and started to compete with the National Football League for talent, player salaries shot up dramatically. The same effect resulted from the formation of the American Basketball Association in 1967. Congress subsequently legislated approval for a merger between the AFL and the NFL, and a merger has also been sought by the American Basketball Association. Such mergers, of course, negate the benefits for athletes springing from the competition of rival leagues. In fact, the motivation behind the merger of the ABA and the NBA "is solely one of cost reduction—lowering the salaries of players," according to a study by the Brookings Institution.

the higher the price of land will be. If demand shifts, the price will change accordingly, but the quantity of land supplied remains constant.

Economic rent is the price paid for the use of land (or any other resource whose supply is completely inelastic). Economic rent constitutes a pure surplus to the landlord, since he would be willing to supply the land even without it. An alternate definition of economic rent is the excess over the opportunity cost of the land or other factor of production—the amount just higher than the factor could command at its next most profitable use. For example, economic rent equals the cost to Farmer Euclid of keeping his farmland in the production of triangles rather than selling it to the Happy Homes Development Corporation or using it to pasture unicorns.

The economic rent paid for land is completely determined by the demand for land, which is largely determined by the price of the product grown on the land and the productivity of the land. If the price of the product were to fall because people began to desire other goods, there would be a decrease in the demand for the land and less economic rent would be paid for it.

The payment to any input in temporarily fixed supply, such as a firm's plant, is called **quasi-rent.** It is possible to expand a firm's plant or adapt the plant to another productive purpose, but only in the long run.

Allocative Function of Rent

In explaining the concept of rent we assumed explicitly that the supply of land is fixed, and implicitly that it has, if only in the short run, one specific use. In reality, land can be used for any number of purposes. Once land use is split among several productive areas, the supply of land to any single productive purpose is no longer limited. Different users will bid for the land, and owners can provide more land to the user who bids highest. Land, then, can be switched from one use to another according to the profitability of the different uses, which in turn depends upon the productivity of land. A high productivity allows a land user to pay a relatively high rent. Much, of course, depends on the quality and location of the land. A strip of desert may have a low productivity if one wants to raise corn, but if the land overlies oil deposits, it will be of high productivity to the petroleum industry. The mountains of Montana may be of very little use to anybody, but if they contain copper reserves, their productivity will be high to the copper industry, and that industry will pay high rent for the land.

Now suppose that oil is discovered in Oklahoma and Texas. Which location will command higher rent payments? Probably Texas, because it is closer to the seashore, and this means that the oil can be transported more easily to other parts of the country. Location is an important determinant of the value of land, as any real estate agent will tell you. Rent in populated areas is higher than in areas of sparse population. Land close to the centers of transportation and communication will command a higher return than land in isolated areas.

While the rent mechanism may assure a fair degree of efficiency, it may not always take into account social costs and benefits involved in land use. The supply of oil and minerals may be abundant at any given time, and their exploration may be profitable and beneficial to one generation. But what about future generations? Sooner or later these deposits will be exhausted, and society will then be deprived of their use. The rent mechanism does not serve to ration now-abundant natural resources over time, although, as the resources become scarcer through depletion, price will ration the remainder. Nor does it reflect certain social costs of exploitation. Strip mining may be the most efficient way to exploit some minerals, allowing firms to pay the highest rent for the land they mine, but it destroys the natural beauty of land from which society as a whole derives enjoyment. It is clear that the phenomenon of externalities is not limited to the question of land use and rent, but rather the problem is inherent in the pricing mechanism as a whole. In the last few years laws have been passed to ensure that the allocation of natural resources reflects the costs incurred by the public through pollution, but some of the more economically efficient tactics are still to be employed, as Chapter 21 indicates.

Land Distribution and Income Distribution

What is the justification for the private ownership of land? After all, the land was there before the people. Nobody owned it initially. So why should some people have to pay for its use, while others collect rent?

These interesting questions were posed by, among others, Henry George, a famous nineteenth century economist and social reformer. George recommended that only rent income be taxed, and taxed heavily, for three reasons: Land is distributed unequally, and the owners of land should not gain from its possession at the expense of the public; rent is a pure surplus and is not tied to any service landlords must render or to the supply of land; and taxing rent income will not affect the supply of land. Let us consider each of these three arguments.

It is obvious that land is distributed unequally in the United States. However, it does not necessarily follow that owners of land should not gain from its possession. After all, many things are unequally distributed in this country: ownership of stocks and bonds; physical beauty; athletic ability. If we deny people the right to own land, then should we not deny Vida Blue the right to own his pitching arm?

George's second argument—that rent is a pure surplus—is valid, since the owners of land do not have to work or offer any other service to collect rent for their property. Unlike expenditures for other resources, rent payments do not affect the supply of land. Whether rents rise or fall, a given acre of land will have the same productivity. Whatever rent a landlord receives, therefore, is like a bonus to him—a pure surplus.

The theory behind George's third argument, that taxing rent income will not affect the supply of land, seems quite valid, since landlords will not be able to pass on the effect of such a tax to the users of land. Demand for land, as we have seen, is determined by the demand for products this land helps produce. If landlords raised rents to offset fully the tax imposed, the new rents might price some of the users out of the market. If a firm faced by a substantial rent increase could not, in turn, pass this on to the consumer, it might well be forced out of business. Then the land would not be rented at all. Faced with the prospect of receiving no rent, landlords will choose to absorb the full impact of the tax. Figure 31-7 illustrates the situation. Note that no distortion of pro-

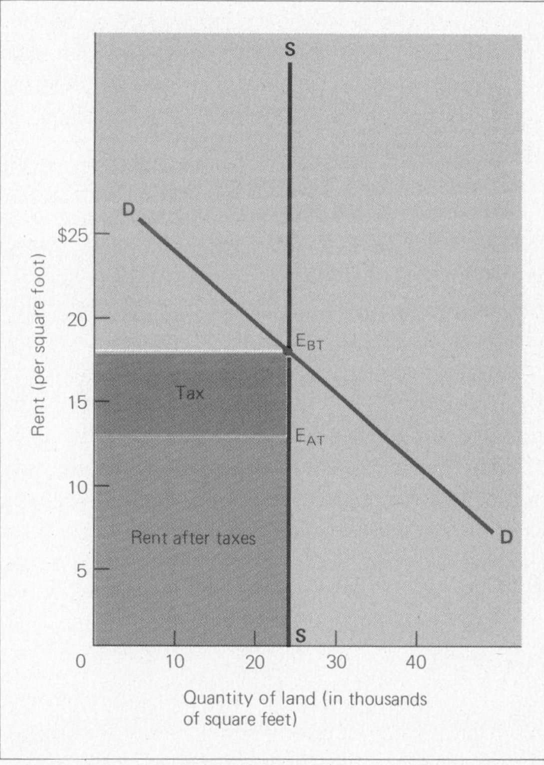

FIGURE 31-7 THE ABSORPTION OF A TAX ON RENT BY LANDLORDS Given the demand and supply curves, DD and SS, a tax of $5 per square foot of land must be absorbed entirely by the landlords, since the tax will not change either the supply of land or the quantity demanded. The total amount of the tax is shown by the upper area, while that part of the rent retained by the landlords after paying the land tax is the lower rectangle. Only the landlord's income is affected by the tax; the supply of land remains the same, tax or no tax.

duction incentives or efficiency takes place. The supply of land will remain the same—reflecting its fixed nature and price inelasticity—and the demand for land will also remain constant as long as conditions in the product market are unchanged. The rent equilibrium to land users will still be at E_{BT}, but the rent retained by landowners will be at E_{AT}, the difference reflecting the amount of the tax imposed. The tax, of course, is imposed by government, and thus its effect is that part of rent income in the economy reverts to the public. Henry George felt that by judicious use of these funds, poverty could be eliminated. This position attracted a considerable following In 1886, George ran for mayor of New York City on a single-tax platform, and was defeated only through a coalition effort by his opponents. Although his single-tax concept has not been revived since, the questions he raised are serious and important, as well as interesting.

SUPPLY OF CAPITAL

We distinguish between financial capital and physical capital. Physical capital is the resource that is actually involved in the production of goods, along with labor and land. It consists of the plant and equipment that firms require for efficient production of their goods. But such equipment is usually very expensive—too expensive to be bought with the funds a firm might have available at any one time. The purchase of physical capital frequently requires financial capital—money accumulated in the economy, which is loaned to the business enterprises that need it.

While financial capital does not by itself contribute to the production of goods and services, it does enable individuals and firms to acquire the physical capital they desire. It is for this use that borrowers are willing to pay interest.

Who supplies financial capital and why? An important source of capital is the savings of individuals. Of course, to contribute to financial capital, these savings must be deposited in banks as time deposits or invested in securities—corporate and government bonds. In either case, the savings supplied will draw interest at a rate which is established by conditions in the money market.

Past and present savings of business firms are the other source of financial capital. These savings may take the form of undistributed profits or depreciation allowances on already existing physical capital. Such funds are most often used internally by the firms that have accumulated them, but since they are sizable, they must be listed here as a significant source of financial capital supply. (After all, if a firm can draw on internal funds, this will affect its demand for other financial capital.)

Allocation of Capital

Physical capital can never constitute the sole factor input. Even if we could conceive of a production process that is totally automated and requires no labor, physical capital would still be used in conjunction with land.

As with the other factors of production, the marginal product of capital diminishes when its quantity is increased relative to that of the other factors. Firms will use additional capital up to the point at which its price equals the marginal revenue product (MRP) (which is also the value of its marginal product VMP if the industry is perfectly competitive).

Since physical capital is acquired through financial capital, its price is actually the interest paid for borrowing the financial capital. As long as the expected return on the physical capital—its marginal revenue product—equals or exceeds the interest charged on the borrowed financial capital, entrepreneurs will continue to demand it. As we learned in Chapter 14, such a relationship between interest rate and the quantity of capital demanded is shown by the MEI curve. The determinants of the interest rate were also treated at some length in that chapter, so we need not repeat that analysis of the supply of and the demands for money. In that analysis, only one interest rate was shown, but this was an oversimplification, as we shall see.

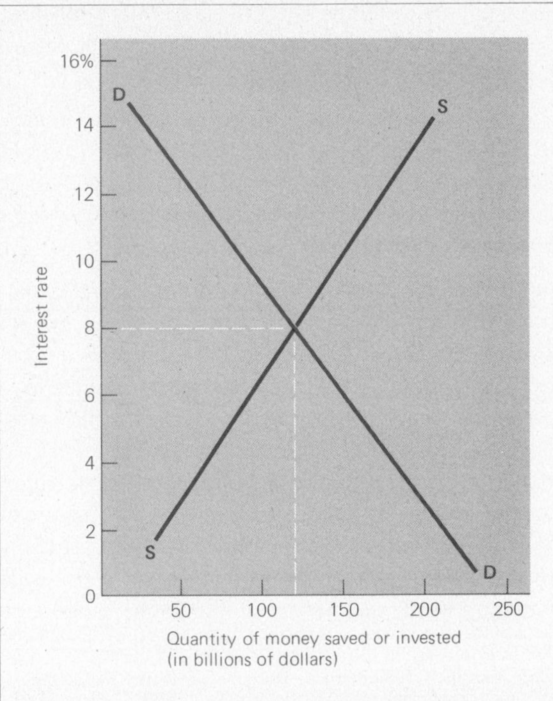

FIGURE 31-8 DETERMINATION OF THE INTEREST RATE The interest rate is determined by the intersection of the demand for and the supply of loanable funds. The market rate is the sum of the individual curves. The individual firm will employ capital up to the point at which the market interest rate shown here equals the marginal revenue product of capital.

Interest Rates

Interest is not only the price firms pay to borrow money but also the payment offered to attract the funds they subsequently lend out. It follows that there are at least two distinct interest rates. In fact, there are many different interest rates in effect at any given time. These rates depend on the amount of money borrowed, the length of time of the loan, the risk of the investment, and the reliability of the borrower.

In 1973, time deposits at banks earned interest at a rate between 5 percent and 10 percent depending on the amount of money on deposit and the length of time it would be left at the bank. The 10 percent rate applied to savings certificates of $100,000, for 10 years. By depositing his or her savings, of course, the individual is in effect lending money to the bank—which then loans it to others. If an individual buys bonds, issued by corporations or governments, he is lending money to these institutions as well. They may offer him higher rates than commercial banks—6 to 10 percent, or even higher.

Traditionally, the lowest lending rate of banks, the major lending institutions in the economy, is the prime rate. In recent years, it has ranged from 5 to 10 percent. Low-risk borrowers such as large corporations pay the prime rate; all other borrowers pay a higher rate. For example, depending on state law, households borrowing money from banks may pay up to 18 percent. If an individual has a poor credit rating he may not be able to borrow from banks at all, and may have to get a loan from a finance company, whose interest rates range up to 36 percent.

The risk of lending money is usually greater in the long run than the short run. Long-term lenders suffer greater inconvenience and forgo other lending opportunities that might return them more money. Thus, long-term loans normally have a higher interest rate than short-term loans.

All loans involve certain administrative costs, and those costs will be reflected in the interest rate. They will be proportionally higher for loans of small amounts than loans of large amounts. Sizable loans will therefore command lower interest rates than small loans.

Interest rates are not determined solely by market forces. The supply and demand of capital are so crucial to the stability and growth of the entire economy that the government has increasingly intervened to regulate them. Through the Federal Reserve System, the government maintains a fairly tight control on the money market, enabling it to counteract destabilizing forces. States also regulate interest rates to prevent **usury**, or charging interest rates higher than a "reasonable" level set by law. Sometimes the interest of the Fed and the prohibition of usury conflict.

The severe inflation that continued throughout 1973 led to a rather ironic change in the prevailing structure of interest rates in the United States. The Fed was putting the brakes on the economy, and the result was an increase in interest rates not covered by usury laws. Because commercial loans are not covered by state usury laws, the prime lending rate continued to creep up—to the point that it actually exceeded, for example, the strictly controlled long-term interest rate for home mortgages by 1½ to 2 percent. Before we start rejoicing that finally Mr. and Mrs. Average American received some advantage over the industrial giants, it must be pointed out that there is a great difference between the interest rate charged and the amount of money available at that rate. Although in theory savings and loan associations were founded for the express purpose of making mortgage loans, the regulations have gradually been changing to allow them to make some commercial loans, and it would be rather naive to assume that the neighborhood S&L would continue to make mortgage loans at a long-term interest rate that is lower than could be obtained if it loaned the funds, instead, to business borrowers for a shorter time period. Thus, money for mortgages became quite scarce and access to funds was still greater for those borrowing at the prime rate.

Equity of Interest Rates The interest-rate structure has favored large corporations and wealthy individuals. Since wealthy borrowers are more established in the marketplace and are able to offer more collateral, they are able to borrow capital at lower rates than small firms and poor individuals. In other words, the wealthy have found it less expensive to increase their wealth than the poor have found it to make ends meet.

ENTREPRENEURSHIP

It is obvious that labor, land, and capital do not spontaneously come together to participate in the production process. These resources must be organized by an entrepreneur toward producing a marketable good or service. Some economists therefore consider entrepreneurship a separate factor of production, comparable to land or labor.

But we must stress again that what we have in mind is pure, or economic, profit. It is economic profit that remains after all explicit and implicit costs, including a normal profit, have been subtracted from total revenues.

In addition to earning a positive return on the capital he owns or borrows, the entrepreneur will expect some returns on his labor, or some minimum profit from his venture, that would be comparable to a salary he could earn by working for somebody else. Perhaps we could understand the entrepreneurship concept better in concrete terms. Product designer James Acme, a long-time employee of American Automatic Ovens, Inc., decides to leave the security of his weekly pay check to embark on a phoenix-hatching venture. A normal profit will be just enough for him to keep his venture going. Anything less than that would constitute a loss. But if after accounting for explicit and implicit costs and normal profits, there is still some income left, then this residual constitutes pure or economic profit, which is what James Acme, and indeed every entrepreneur, strives for.

Risk and Uncertainty

The entrepreneur must face risk and uncertainty in committing his resources and ability to a venture. Risk implies a predictable chance of loss; the whole insurance industry is based on the predictable rates of death, accidents, and other disasters. So long as a business knows that so many accounts will never be paid or that its machinery can be expected to be out of service for repairs a certain percentage of the time, it can build such probabilities into its costs either through insurance or through a separate accounting item. What cannot be built in is protection against uncertainty. Uncertainty implies the impossibility of knowing or predicting the outcome of a venture. The firm knows a machine will be out so many hours for repairs, but it does not know that the machine will quit in the midst of a rush order from a new customer who has been promised priority service. With uncertainty comes the possibility of loss—the waste of time, energy, and resources on an objective that was not attained. But while there is a possibility of loss, there is also a possibility of profit beyond the normal gain an entrepreneur would realize if he devoted himself to an activity that did not involve uncertainty. It is the prospect of this pure profit—also called economic or excess profit—that outweighs the possibility of loss and motivates the entrepreneur. Since uncertainty is at the heart of this analysis, this concept is generally called the **uncertainty theory of profit.**

Innovation

One of the happy sorts of uncertainties is the possibility for innovation, for finding a better product, a more effective form of management, a cheaper way of producing goods than the competition uses. Profits, according to Joseph Schumpeter, are the reward for such innovations, since successful changes lower costs or open new markets, both of which are a source of excess profits. Such rewards do not inevitably go to the person who first discovers them—the inventor—but rather to the entrepreneur who applies them successfully to the marketplace—the innovator. Excess profits may spread through the economy as other innovators provide ancillary services or serve as suppliers for the original innovating firm.

Profits are a result of disequilibrium, and they disappear as equilibrium is reestablished. Other firms, attracted by the excess profits, enter the picture to expand supply, lower price, and eventually erase excess profits—until the next novelty appears. Thus, the source of business enterprise is also the source of business cycles, according to Schumpeter.

Monopoly

One way to perpetuate excess profits from innovation is to establish monopoly power. By preventing entry of competitors, the monopolist can protect itself against the threat of competition and continue to enjoy excess profits. Unfortunately for society, as we have seen in earlier chapters, monopoly profits come at the expense of reduced output and employment.

What to do about the concentrations of market power is the subject of heated debate. On one side are those who feel that free-market forces should be given freer rein to eliminate such allocative inefficiency as it occurs. On the other side are those such as Galbraith who feel that a modern economy depends upon such concentration and that allocative efficiency can be restored only by diverting excess profits to social uses. Both groups see that institutional rigidities prevent the free flow of resources within the economy, but to the first group they are aberrations, whereas to the other they are inevitable. The first group emphasizes profits as an incentive; the other, profits as a product of inefficient distribution of resources.

Marx on Profit

Those with a passing acquaintance with the current radical critique and its blasts at the domestic and foreign empires of such giants as ITT or Dow Chemical would be likely to imagine that monopoly profits are central to Marx's analysis of capitalism. Marx's attack, however, begins in the theoretical world of perfect competition. To Marx, labor is the source of value and all returns are derived from it. Profits are a result of private property, since those who own the means of production can set the number of hours worked above the amount paid to labor to sustain it. The difference between the value of the output and the wage bill is *surplus value,* or profit derived from labor but retained by the capitalist, who need never soil his hands.

The labor theory of value is a weak link in the causal chain, but even today radicals who reject it point to a surplus not accounted for by the marginal productivity of all inputs. The entrepreneur keeps this surplus, but his claim to it is not supported by his marginal productivity nor by equity. From a theoretical point of view, therefore, marginal productivity cannot account fully for income distribution, say the radicals.

CONCLUSION

In this chapter we have dealt with the forces that underlie factor supply in the economy. Since the price of a factor represents income to its owner, we have also discussed the effect of factor supply on income distribution. The theory of marginal productivity is the cornerstone of employment patterns and income distribution in a market economy. Labor, land, and capital inputs are employed and reimbursed according to the marginal product they generate. While labor is the most significant single factor of production in the United States, accounting for three-fourths of national income, the owners of land and capital command by far a higher per capita income than do working people.

We shall learn more about the problems of relying exclusively on marginal productivity in the policy chapters of this section, but it should be clear already that behind the demand and supply curves we have been manipulating in this chapter are the social and even psychological factors that affect factor demand and supply. A worker's productivity is the result of intelligence, education, mobility, and a host of other things. For example, if the education system is failing minorities, then the marginal productivity, wages, and income of this group are affected.

Supply may be affected as well. As we have seen, unions can limit the labor supply. Both farm price supports and oil depletion allowances affect the supply of land—and the income derived from it. The lower capital gains tax and depreciation allowances favor returns to capital, in effect increasing its supply. In fact, just about any practice or institution—pollution laws, birth control, building codes, and so on—can affect the factor market. A figure such as 31-8 hides such issues in bland simplicity. After a brief survey of how all the curves in product and factor markets interrelate, we can begin to explore the determinants of income distribution more thoroughly.

SUMMARY

1 The supply of factors shows the same basic relation between the price and quantity supplied as supply in the product market.

2 Under perfect competition, factor supply to the individual firm is infinitely elastic, but to the economy as a whole, at least in the short run, it is quite inelastic. In the long run, the elasticity of factor supply becomes greater.

3 The quantity of labor supplied by an individual increases as wages rise, up to a certain level. Above this it may decrease again. This reflects the demand for leisure time, which increases at higher income levels. The firm faces a horizontal factor supply curve at the wage rate determined by the intersection of the market supply and demand curves. The price of labor is closely tied to its productivity, but it is also affected by market imperfections, such as monopoly, monopsony, or bilateral monopoly.

4 Total land supply is inelastic, at least in the short run. Rents reflect the demand for land as derived from the demand for products for which the use of land is necessary. The rent mechanism allocates land to the most productive uses. Quasi-rent refers to income from factors whose supply is temporarily inelastic.

5 Unequal land distribution is a cause of inequalities in income distribution. The single tax imposed on rent is a method of redistributing income from land. It will not affect supply of land and will be absorbed completely by the landlord.

6 Financial capital consists of the savings of individuals and firms. It is used to

purchase physical capital, which is used in the production process. The price of capital is the interest rate paid by borrowers of financial capital to its lenders. There are many interest rates in the money market, reflecting the risk, amount, and length of time of a loan. Interest rates are also affected by market imperfections and by government regulation.

7 Entrepreneurship can be regarded as a separate factor necessary for the production of goods.

8 Inequalities in income and wealth distribution result from the ownership of the various factors. These inequalities are a product of social factors as well as marginal productivity.

SUGGESTED READINGS

Chamberlain, Neil W., and **Donald E. Cullen.** *The Labor Sector.* 2nd ed. Chaps. 17 and 18. New York: McGraw-Hill, 1971.

George, Henry. *Science of Political Economy.* New York: Robert Schalkenbach Foundation, 1962.

Haveman, Robert H., and **Kenyon A. Knopf.** *The Market System.* New York: John Wiley & Sons, 1966.

McConnell, Campbell R. *Economics: Principles, Problems and Policies.* 5th ed. Chaps. 32 and 33. New York: McGraw-Hill, 1972.

Smith, Adam. *Wealth of Nations.* New York: Random House, Modern Library, 1937.

Stonier, Alfred W., and **Douglas C. Hague.** *A Textbook of Economic Theory.* 3rd ed. Chaps. 13 through 15. New York: Longmans, Green, 1964.

QUESTIONS

1 Review
   a. elasticity of supply of factors of production in the short run and long run,
   b. the point at which an individual will cease to supply additional labor,
   c. the individual and market supply curves for labor,
   d. factors that contribute to wage differentials,
   e. the supply of land and economic rent,
   f. the relationship between the MRP of capital and the interest rate,
   g. the supply of entrepreneurship and the potential for economic or pure profit.

2 In recent negotiations in the automobile industry, workers were asking for the right to refuse to take overtime without suffering retribution. How would you describe the point that has been reached in the collective preference of union workers in this industry?

3 The cost of capital to a given firm can be shown as a horizontal line at the market interest rate. Draw a hypothetical MRP curve for capital equipment for the firm and show how changes in the price of the final product and the interest rate would affect the firm's demand for capital. What must happen elsewhere in the economy for that capital to be supplied?

4 Would you say that it is likely for wages to ever become absolutely equal for the same job across the country? Why or why not?

5 Recall that the labor supply tends to swell as jobs become more plentiful and wages increase. Would this be evidence for or against a backward-bending supply curve for labor? Why?

6 Most employment is arranged so that the worker puts in approximately 40 hours per week. The worker does not really have the option of working 25, 26, or 39 hours. The wage earner must decide whether to take the full 40-hour job or perhaps no job at all. Would the person represented by the supply curves below be willing to take a 40-hour job if he could not work less? Why or why not?

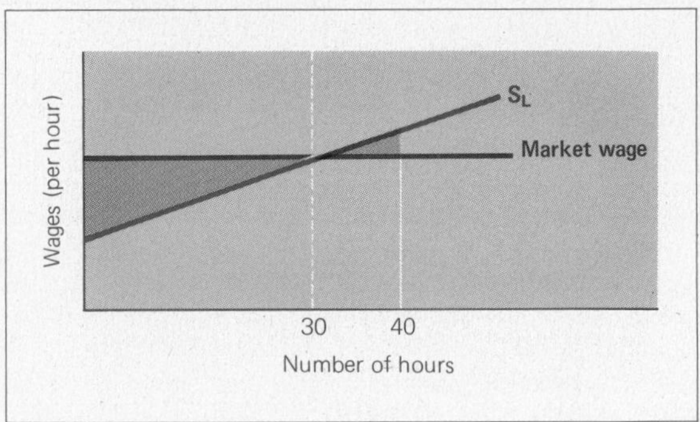

7 Is there any possibility that the social custom of requiring workers to work full time in some industries provides the employers with any advantage in the labor market? Explain.

8 Would the salary of David Brinkley or Eric Sevareid be partly economic rent? Why or why not?

9 Would you predict that there would be no quantity of entrepreneurship available if economic profit were zero throughout the economy? Why or why not? How then might you draw the supply curve of entrepreneurship if plotted against economic profit? Do you think that the supply of entrepreneurship would be elastic or inelastic? In the short run or long run? Why?

10 Petroleum is a natural resource that is generally included in the factor category land. Does the price we pay for gasoline or natural gas contain some economic rent? Why or why not?

Opening photo by J. Paul Kirouac

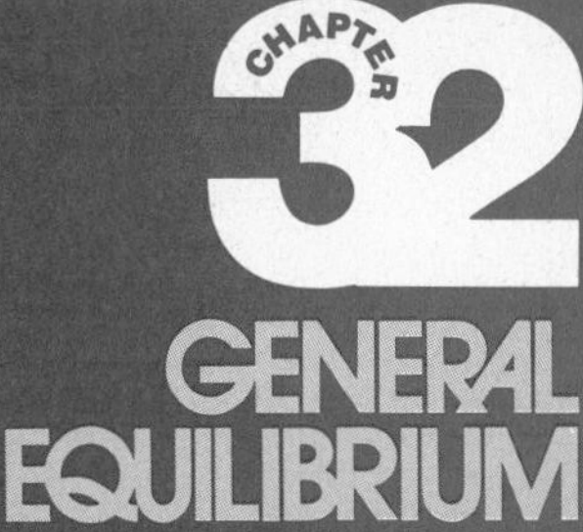

GENERAL EQUILIBRIUM

The economy is like an intricate set of finely meshed gears: as one turns faster or slower, so do many others. We have ignored this interconnection by holding a number of factors constant and varying only a few in either the product or the factor market.

When analyzing the demand curve for a certain product, for example, we assumed that the prices of all other goods remained constant. This assumption is simply a convenient device for examining and explaining the operation of individual markets.

The study of equilibrium prices and output in specific markets, holding all other effects constant, is called partial equilibrium analysis.

In the real world, however, changes in one market inevitably spill over into other markets. A change in the price of steel will be felt in the markets for automobiles, refrigerators, canned okra, computers, auto workers, okra pickers, and others. The changes in each of these markets will in turn affect supply or demand in many other markets, which in turn will affect even more markets. In theory, every economic event can affect the equilibrium in all other markets in the economy, although a change in the price of jade rings, for example, will probably have a negligible effect upon the market for cotton pickers.

Partial equilibrium analysis is convenient and even necessary in examining the behavior of individual markets. To attempt to handle all the variables involved whenever some economic change occurs would be too complex and would unduly limit effective use of economic analysis. Nevertheless, always limiting the variables hampers the full exploration of economic effects.

General equilibrium analysis describes and explains the interactions among markets as well as the interaction of supply and demand within markets.

AN EXAMPLE OF INTERCONNECTIONS

An example of the problem of general equilibrium can be seen in the effects of the sale of American wheat to the Soviet Union in 1972. The political and legal aspects of the deal are still the subject of much debate, but the basic economics of the sale are apparent. In the summer of 1972, the USSR agreed to purchase at least $250 million of wheat each year for three years from the United States at the then current world price for wheat of $1.65 a bushel. The USSR, whose own wheat crop was lower than the U.S. negotiators had realized, purchased $1 billion worth the first year. This substantially reduced the amount of wheat available for other purchasers, and as a result the world price of wheat climbed to $3.00 in early 1973. However, most American farmers did not benefit from the higher price, because they had sold or contracted to sell their wheat before the price increase. The dealers who had purchased the wheat were the major beneficiaries of this windfall.

Getting the wheat to market created a shortage of railroad cars with which to ship agricultural products. The shipment of wheat to the USSR put tremendous pressure upon the national and international transportation systems, diverting many trains and ships from their normal usage. Thus, a strange situation developed—a relative shortage of agricultural products, but also a shortage of railroad cars in which to ship them, because U.S. wheat was being shipped much farther than usual. This created more frustration for the American farmer. Prices were high, but frequently the farmer could not sell his crops. Dealers would not accept them because their warehouses were full and transportation was not available.

As grain prices rose with increased demand, the prices of substitutes also rose. Events in other sectors exacerbated this situation. Because 1972 was an election year, the administration followed the traditional practice of ensuring farm votes by keeping agricultural prices up. This required limiting planting in 1972 so that the "market" price of agricultural products would be high. The weather cooperated, or over-cooperated, by raining or snowing too little or too much, depending on the location or season, and kept crops below anticipated levels. For example, early snows left many soybeans rotting in the fields and the price of soybeans began to escalate.

Complicating this situation was the anchovy shortage. Anchovies and soybeans may appear to be unlikely substitutes, but both are important sources of protein and livestock feed and are, in fact, almost interchangeable for some uses. The anchovy catch in early 1973 was well below previous levels, putting even greater pressure on the price of soybeans, sending their price to an unheard-of level. A number of factors had combined to greatly increase the price of wheat, soybeans, and other grains: the Russian wheat deal, quotas, price supports, bad weather, anchovy shortage, the railcar shortage. Which of these was most important is impossible to determine and this is perhaps a meaningless question. Any one of these factors alone would have had some effect, but without the others it might not have been serious.

Since they did all occur within a fairly brief period, the effects were serious. For most Americans, inflation was the most significant consequence. Before the imposition of Phase III½, increased food prices were in no small measure caused by the events discussed above. For example, much of the rapid increase in meat prices may be attributed to the high cost of feed grains.

It seems clear that the wheat deal contributed to instability in the American economy, even though it was only one of several causes of instability. This instability caused by the wheat deal may have been simply a short-run consequence of an otherwise beneficial development. Although it did not work out quite as well as anticipated, the wheat deal was an important step in opening up trade between the two countries—a development that will benefit the citizens of both countries.

We may all benefit in the long run, but the question of who benefitted in the short run has raised much controversy. In the presidential campaign of 1972, Senator McGovern charged that the American farmer had been cheated and that a few businesses had profited greatly from the administration's handling of the wheat deal. The Russians had agreed to purchase the wheat at the world price of $1.65 a bushel. Their purchases raised the world price of wheat, and the U.S. government paid the difference between the contract price and the market price to those who sold wheat to the Russians. However, most of the wheat was sold by a few large grain companies that had already purchased the wheat at lower prices before the deal was announced. As a result, they received the bulk of the $300-million subsidy paid by the federal government. Senator McGovern charged that the administration informed the grain companies of the sale ahead of time so that they could buy the wheat and make the profit that otherwise would have gone to the farmers. Whether this is true is still under investigation. By July 1973, some irregularities had been uncovered and hearings had started before a Senate investigating committee.

In any event, whether due to corruption, mismanagement, or simply the impersonal interaction of market forces, it appears to date that the Russians benefitted, a few grain companies benefitted, some farmers benefitted while others were hurt, and the American consumer and taxpayer paid the price.

On balance, what were the effects of the sale of wheat? On the positive side, it helped our balance of payments and was perhaps a step toward free trade, which may ultimately add to the income of American farmers. On the negative side, its short-run effects were inflationary and in the opinion of many its effects on domestic income distribution were inequitable. Because the factors were interrelated and so complex, however, supporting evidence can be found for almost any conclusion about causality or equity, a common characteristic of economic problems.

THE THEORY OF GENERAL EQUILIBRIUM

The father of the modern theory of general equilibrium is Leon Walras, whose work was discussed in Chapter 5. Walras, through the use of mathematics, showed that in a competitive economy the interaction of self-seeking consumers and producers will result not only in equilibrium in individual markets (partial equilibrium), but in a general equilibrium in all markets in the system. This equilibrium is defined by two conditions: (1) Each person's consumption of goods and services is in perfect balance, so that it is impossible to increase utility any further, and (2) the quantity of goods and services supplied in the economy as a whole is exactly equal to the quantity demanded. This is simply another way of saying that the economy is operating efficiently.

General equilibrium analysis does not attempt to incorporate all possible variables into its model of the economy. As with any economic model, it is limited to those variables that are believed to be most significant. It is like partial analysis in this respect. It differs, not in the types of variables involved, but only in that it incorporates the interaction of these variables among all markets in the economy.

A simple two-product, two-factor model permits illustration of the general equilibrium principle without resorting to the mathematics that a full-fledged model would require. Figure 32-1 shows the results of partial equilibrium analysis for two products (cars and TV sets) and two factors of production (labor and capital). Let us assume that car production is relatively capital intensive and that TV production relatively labor intensive. All four markets are perfectly competitive and in long-run equilibrium. Therefore, each consumer is maximizing his utility with respect to his consumption of cars and TV sets. The firms producing cars and TV sets are minimizing costs and maximizing profits. The value of the marginal product of labor in producing cars is equal to the VMP of labor in producing TV sets. And the VMP of capital for TV manufacturers is equal to the VMP of capital for car manufacturers. The economy is in equilibrium and there is no incentive for change; no one can be made better off without making someone worse off; the economy is both technologically and allocatively efficient.

At equilibrium, everyone is working as much as he or she wants. In other words, everyone is working up to the point at which the marginal utility of an hour's leisure is just equal to the marginal utility of the goods that can be purchased with an hour's wages. After existing in this tranquil world for a while, let us assume that something happens to people's preferences for work and leisure. Some people now place a higher value on leisure than they did previously. The initial effect of this is a decrease in the supply of labor, or a leftward movement of the labor supply curve, which in turn causes an increase in the wage rate and a decrease in the quantity of labor hired. Since capital is now relatively less expensive than labor, the demand for it may increase somewhat. The increase in capital will partially offset the reduction in labor, but the net effect will be a decrease in the supply of autos and TV sets with the usual consequences for price and quantity. All these effects are shown in Figure 32-2. Since the TV manufacturing process is relatively labor intensive, the supply of TV sets will be affected more than the supply of automobiles.

However, this is not the whole story. Because of the decrease in the amount of hours worked, incomes will fall, which will result in a decrease in the demand for both TV sets and cars, and both demand curves will move to the left. Ultimately, a new equilibrium will be reached at a higher price, reflecting the change in preferences of society.

Efficiency and Equity

People are working less and consuming less, but enjoying more leisure. Because of the differences in the technologies of TV and car production, TV production and consumption have fallen relative to those of cars. Prices are equal to marginal cost, factor prices are equal to VMP, and total costs are minimized while consumer utilities are maximized. Again the economy is technologically and allocatively efficient.

Problems of equity do not appear serious in this situation, because the changes have been a result of changes in preferences. But not everyone's preferences changed, only those of some. As a result, those whose preferences remained the same are paying higher prices because some people have decided to work less. In the abstract example, there is no basis for making any judgment about the equity of this situation, but it is clear that decisions by some people affect the welfare of others. And it is hard for those with constant preferences to see how

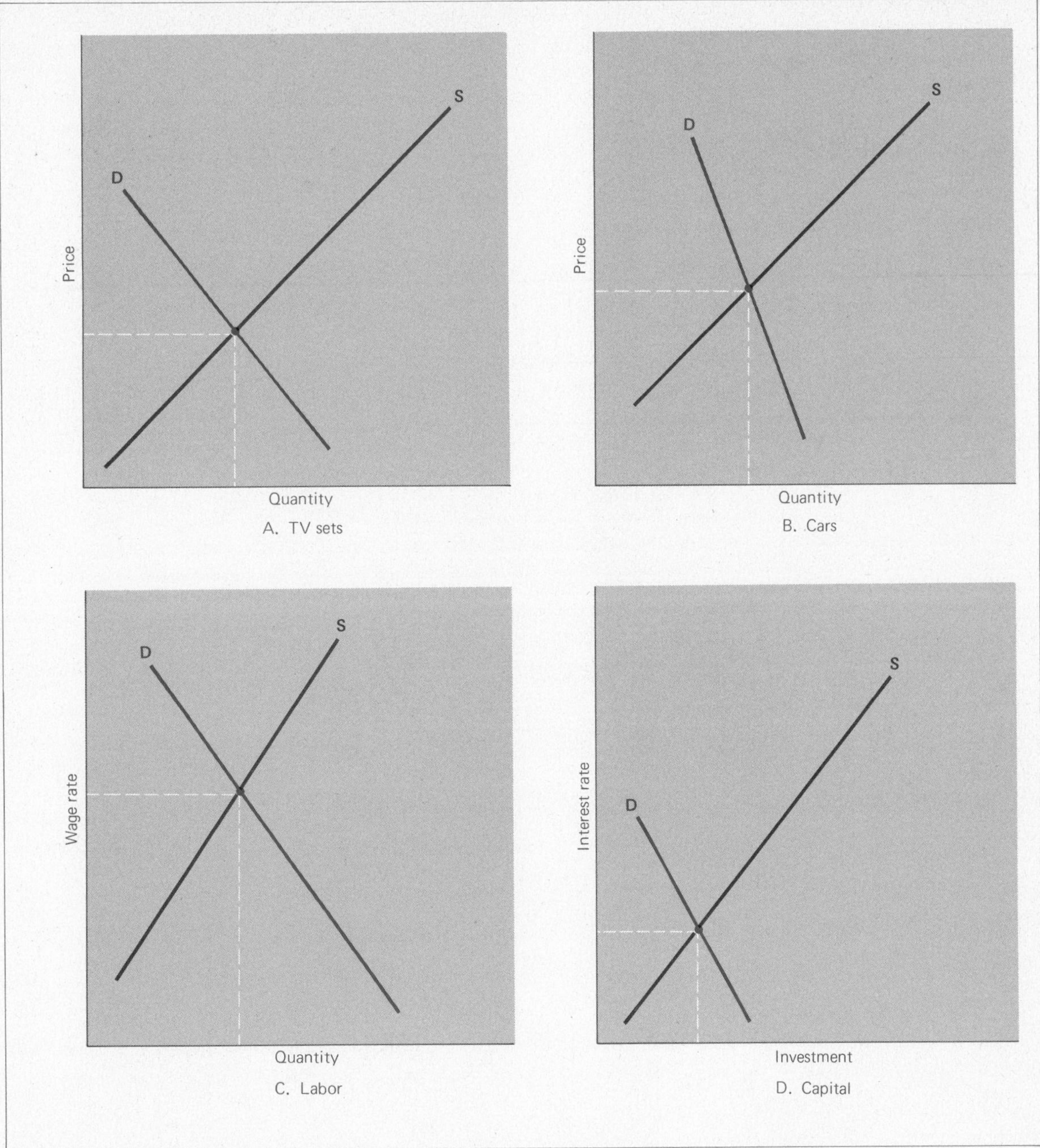

FIGURE 32-1 AN ECONOMY IN EQUILIBRIUM Both the product markets (A and B) and the factor markets (C and D) in this hypothetical economy are in equilibrium. Consumers are receiving the same amount of utility on the last dollar spent, whereas firms are receiving equal VMP for the last dollar of factor used. The economy is technologically and allocatively efficient.

GENERAL EQUILIBRIUM AND UNEMPLOYMENT

One of the more persistent criticisms of a market economy is that there is always some unemployment. Even under ideal conditions this occurs, and theory easily reveals why. Since the normal state of affairs is disequilibrium, the best we can expect is to be moving toward an ever changing equilibrium, and thus have some unemployment, which we call frictional. Our definition of full employment recognizes 3 or 4 percent unemployment, or about 3 million people unemployed, as inevitable.

But how about when we are in equilibrium? When a market is in equilibrium, by definition there is no unemployment, but some people are reluctant to define away the problem of people without work so easily. Consider the situation represented by the figure below. At a wage rate of W_1, the amount of labor supplied and demanded is Q_1. The labor market is in equilibrium. There is no unemployment. However, if the wage rate were higher, say at W_2, the labor supplied would be Q_3 and labor demanded would be Q_2—clearly a disequilibrium. Lowering the wage rate to W_1 restores equilibrium. Equilibrium is restored in part because the amount of labor demanded increases as the wage rate falls, but also because fewer people are now seeking work. Thus, unemployment has been eliminated by making wages so low that some people no longer want to work. Is that really full employment? Is that really an equitable solution to the problem of unemployment? This question underlies much

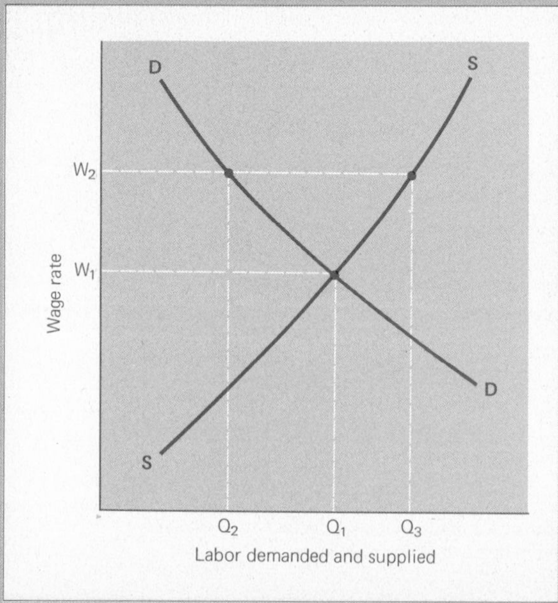

of the controversy about macroeconomic policy and about what interference with market-determined wage rates is appropriate.

As we have seen, classical economists believed that full employment is the natural state of affairs in a market economy. In large measure this is due to their definition of the term *full employment*. If more people are willing to work than are demanded at the existing wage rate (W_2), they will accept lower wages (W_1) in order to get work. Refusal to accept lower wages is evidence that they do not really want work, and thus there is no unemployment.

Regardless of whether lowering wages is the efficient way of handling decreases in demand, decreases in money wage rates are relatively rare events in the United States because of minimum wage laws, union contracts, and other institutional factors. Thus, one of the classical remedies for unemployment is apparently not available in this country. However, one way in which real wages may be reduced is through inflation severe enough that prices increase more rapidly than money wages. This is a fairly common way of restoring full employment in the U.S. and it is a relatively painless way of doing so. A little inflation can be achieved more easily than wage decreases and tends to be more evenly spread among the members of the economy than unemployment. The way we attempt to restore equilibrium may be as important as whether we are there or not.

Low-equilibrium wage rates for some individuals are undoubtedly among the most disturbing aspects or costs of equilibrium. One suggested remedy for low incomes is a minimum wage rate. The appeal of such a proposal is obvious: if the wage rate is lower than is consistent with our social goals, then pass a law that prohibits such a low wage. The problem, of course, is that the number of people hired by a profit-seeking firm cannot be legislated. This is also illustrated in the figure. If the equilibrium wage rate (W_1) is considered to be too low and if a minimum wage (W_2) is established, employment will fall from Q_1 to Q_2. To some people, this is a fatal flaw in a minimum wage law. By raising the costs of labor, the minimum wage law induces the firm to shift its combination of resources away from labor and (especially in markets greatly affected by labor costs) to underproduce goods, causing unemployment. If there is good unemployment insurance (or if there is widespread monopsony), then maybe the increased minimum wage does more good than harm. On the other hand, there are other ways of ensuring a decent income. If the federal government established a good negative income tax, there might be no need for a minimum wage law.

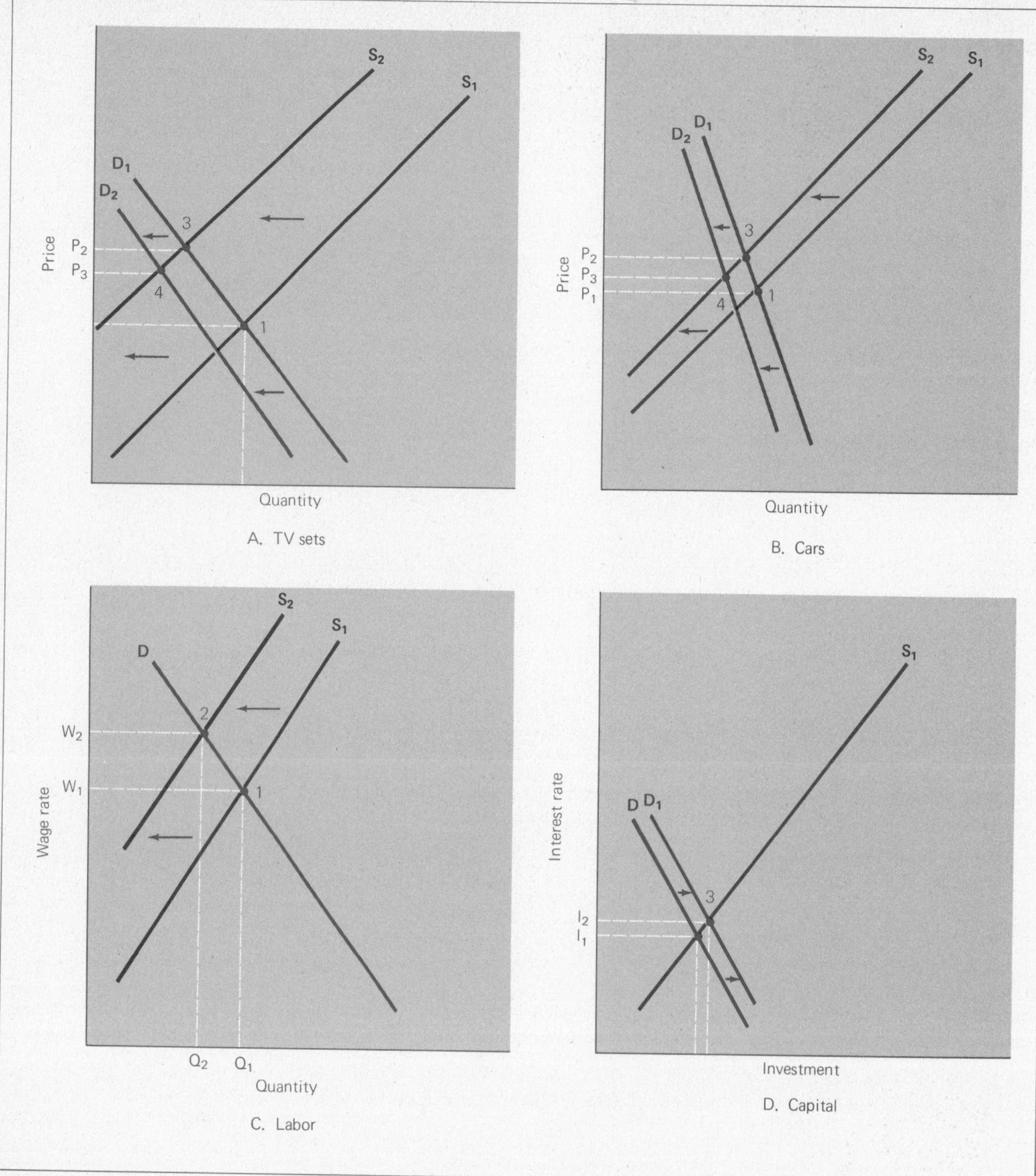

FIGURE 32-2 THE EFFECTS OF MORE LEISURE When people want more leisure, the supply of labor decreases, affecting the supply of TV sets and cars. Although wages are higher, incomes are lower because of reduced production. Therefore, the demand for goods decreases. Equilibrium is reestablished with more leisure and fewer, higher-priced goods.

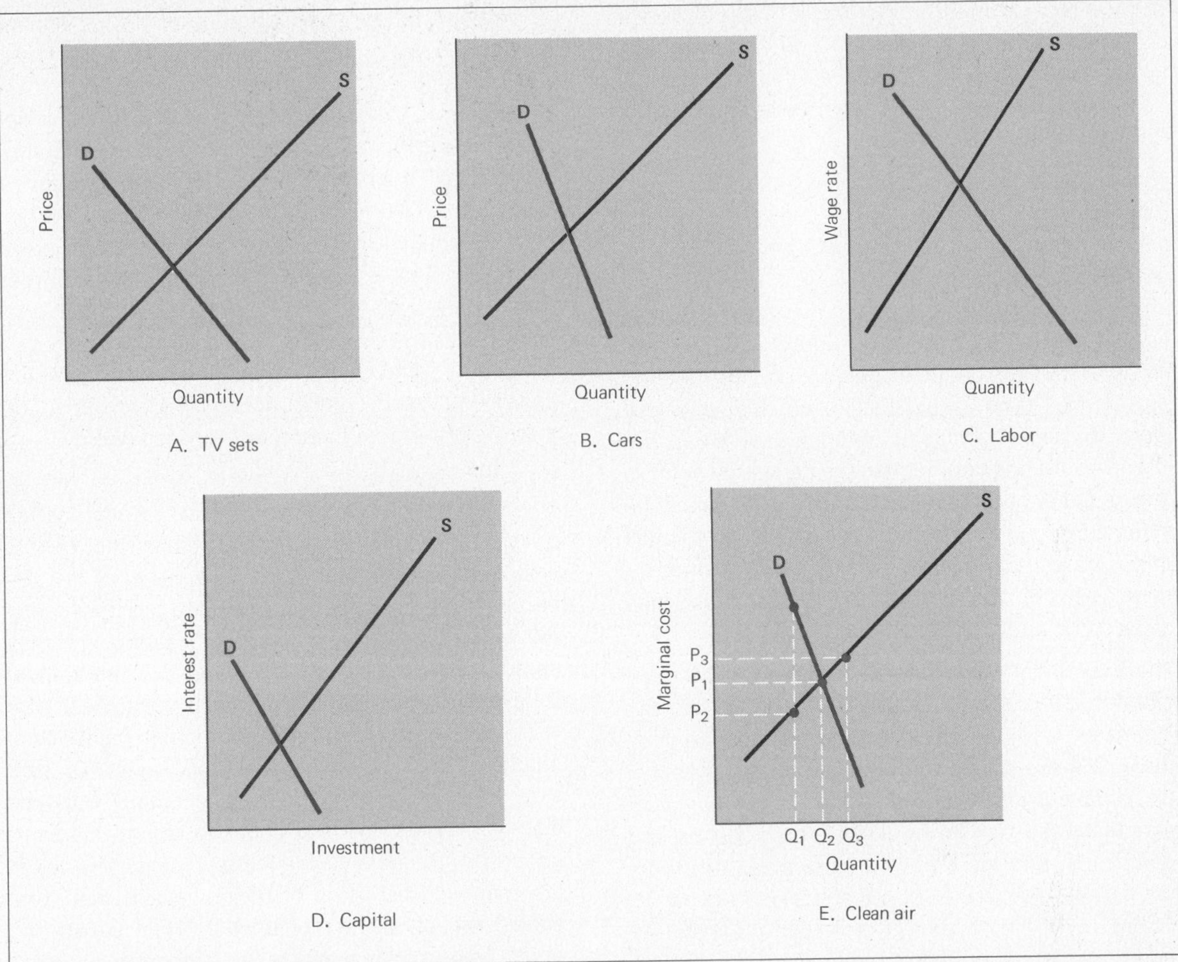

FIGURE 32-3 MARKET FOR CLEAN AIR The original equilibrium in A–D ignores the social costs of air pollution. In E, we see that this market is out of equilibrium when clean air is at Q_1. Resources are underallocated to this sector. The equilibrium level of clean air is at Q_2. If Q_3 is obtained, then society is paying more for its clean air than it wants to and resources are being overallocated to this sector.

the second equilibrium is as "good" as the first. But from the perspective of the general equilibrium theory, the second is as "good" as the first because both equilibria are efficient.

Problems with the model are not confined to equity. It is unrealistic to assume that consumers always act rationally when surrounded by goods designed to appeal to subconscious urges, that imperfect competition is absent, or that there are no externalities. With these elements present, the analysis changes. It can even help show how to offset the deleterious effects of these imperfections.

Internalizing Externalities

What about the attempts by government to internalize externalities? Can their effects be shown through general equilibrium analysis? Let us consider a simple illustration of this by returning to the TV-car example. Let Figure 32-1 represent equilibrium again, but now there is an externality that prevents this equilibrium from being an efficient one. The manufacture of cars causes air pollution, but this is an external cost that is ignored by the auto makers and is not reflected in the price of cars.

This situation is shown in Figure 32-3, which duplicates Figure 32-1 except that a fifth set of supply and demand curves (E) has been added. The new graph shows the supply and demand curves for clean air. Remember that the supply curve is the marginal cost of stopping pollution. In Figure 32-3 the market for clean air is not in equilibrium. Q_1 is being provided at price P_1, but people are willing to pay more to obtain additional amounts of clean air. However, the market mechanism cannot respond to this demand, because clean air is not and cannot be supplied through the market. As long as production and consumption decisions in the auto market ignore the externality of dirty air that car production causes, the equilibrium will not be efficient.

The answer to this problem, conceptually, is quite simple, as we saw in Chapter 21. A tax or effluent charge for each car produced can be imposed upon the auto makers. This will raise the marginal cost of car production and thus shift the supply curve for cars to the left. Now fewer cars will be produced and purchased, and there will be more clean air. If the tax or effluent charge is set at the correct, or efficient, level, the amount of clean air available will be Q_2. If it is set too low, the quantity will be somewhere between Q_1 and Q_2. If it is set too high, the quantity of clean air available will be greater than Q_2, such as Q_3. It is too high, because at this point people would willingly sacrifice some clean air for more cars. On the other hand, when less than Q_2 is available, consumers are willing to sacrifice some cars in order to get cleaner air.

The imposition of the effluent charge affects not only the car market and the environment but also the factor markets and the distribution of income. As a result of the drop in auto production, some labor and capital previously used in car production will be unemployed. This in turn will lead to a decrease in the price of labor and capital. This is shown in Figure 32-4C and D by the leftward shifts of the demand curves for labor and capital and the movement along their supply curves. As a result of the lower prices for the factors of production, the marginal cost of cars and TV sets will fall. This will partially offset the effects of the effluent charge. In the new equilibrium, more TV sets and fewer cars will be produced than before the imposition of the effluent charge. Now that market prices better reflect the true costs of production, the pattern of resource allocation between cars and TV sets has changed. Since consumer tastes are better satisfied and the new equilibrium is efficient (if exactly the right effluent charge is used), most economists would argue that it is preferable to the original equilibrium.

However, the move from the inefficient to the efficient equilibrium is neither a costless one nor one devoid of equity problems. Consider the people who initially lose their jobs as a result of the decrease in auto production. How long are they unemployed before finding a new job? What about a poor person who does not mind dirty air, but needs a car to take his sick child to the doctor every week? He will have a hard time believing that the effluent charge is making the system work better. Or consider the stockholder in the car company who was counting on his dividend check to pay for his son's education. Because of the reduced sales, dividends are omitted. The point, of course, is not that there should be no effluent charge, but that social and moral values, in addition to economic analysis, must be used in making public policy.

To complicate matters further, economic analysis suggests that we may not even want to make each particular market as efficient as possible in order to come as close as possible to general efficiency. The principle underlying this assertion is known as the theory of the second best.

Theory of the Second Best

A general equilibrium in which all markets are competitive and in which there are no externalities and no public goods means that the economy is both technologically and allocatively efficient. An inevitable consequence of such a situation and a neces-

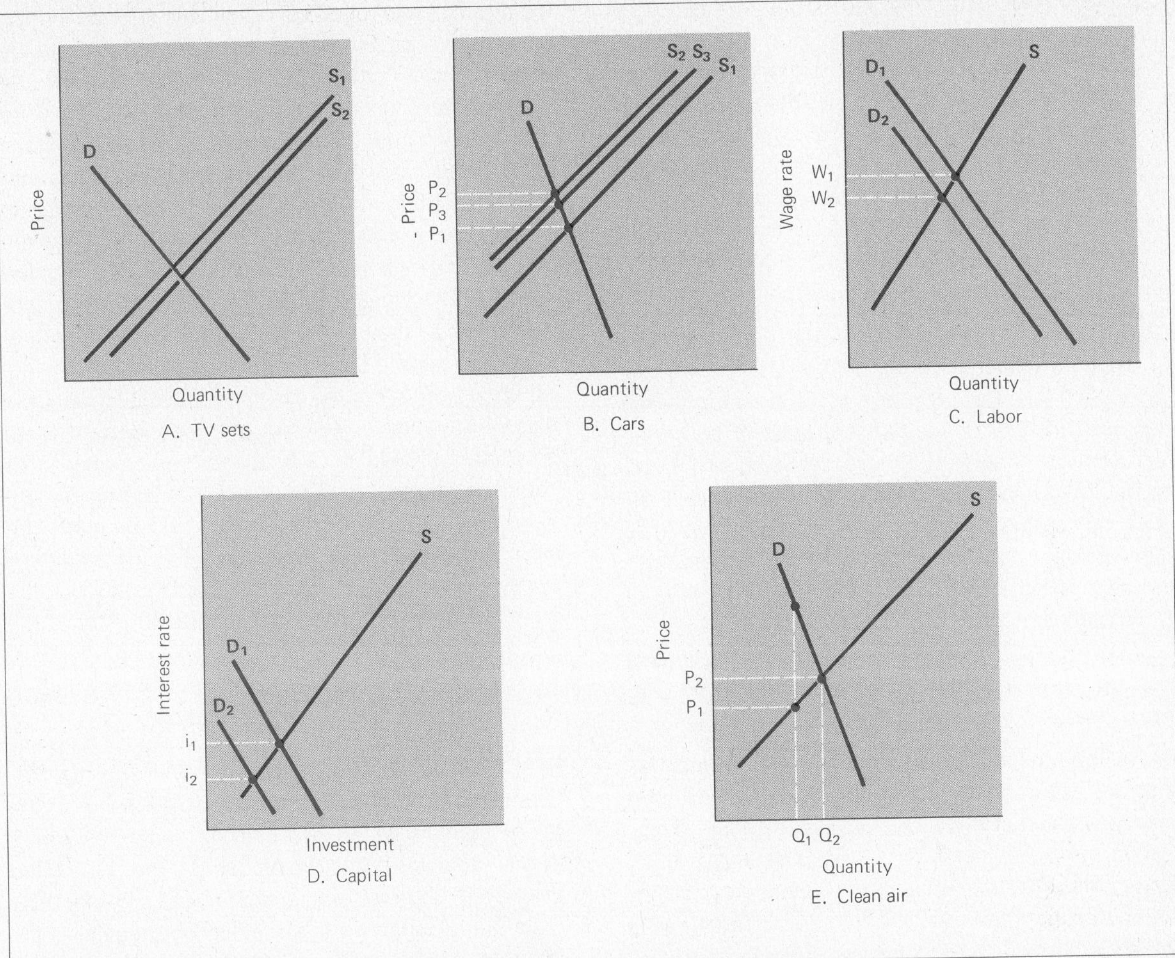

FIGURE 32-4 THE EFFECTS OF AN EFFLUENT CHARGE When society imposes an effluent charge, it may obtain more clean air. This also raises the cost of automobiles and reduces their production, reducing the demand for labor and capital. As the factor prices drop, costs of production are reduced, partially offsetting the effects of the effluent charge. The result is cleaner air, more TV sets, and fewer, more expensive cars. The economy is now technologically and allocatively efficient, but there have been costs of adjustment and effects on income distribution.

sary condition for allocative efficiency is that the price of a good equals its marginal cost. Now suppose that some part of the economy is imperfectly competitive or that there are externalities that cannot be internalized. And suppose that this condition is inevitable. Thus we must accept a world in which at least one market is not perfectly competitive or in which there are unmanageable externalities and attempt to design a public policy to do the best possible with this imperfect world. Is the proper prescription to have perfect competition wherever possible and P=MC wherever possible? The theory of the second best says no. If imperfect competition and P > MC is inevitable in one market, there may be a set of prices in other markets that will make people better off than if P=MC in all other markets.

For example, imagine an economy with three industries. Each produces one-third of GNP Industry

C is perfectly competitive, industry M is a privately owned monopoly, and industry G is government-owned and operated. The marginal cost of producing one unit of C, M, or G is $1.00 The price of C is $1.00 and the price of M is $2.00. What should be the price of G? If both C and M were competitive and pricing at marginal cost, G should also price at marginal cost. This would be the best solution. But since the monopoly in industry M cannot be eliminated, we must look for the second best solution.

Assume that the production of one additional unit of G draws resources equally from C and M. Thus, production of one more unit of G means one-half unit less of C and one-half unit less of M, or the loss of production that is valued at $0.50 and $1.00, respectively, since their prices are $1.00 and $2.00. Thus, the marginal social value of the resources used to produce one unit of G is $1.50. Accordingly, the second best solution is to set the price of G at $1.50 rather than at its marginal cost of $1.00. To set the price below $1.50 would result in overproduction of G, because it is undervaluing the resources drawn from the monopoly.

Since the United States does have many markets that are not perfectly competitive, we cannot automatically say that P = MC is always the best policy.

Urban Mass Transit One of the factors contributing to the transportation problem in many urban areas is the misuse of the pricing system. Prices charged to commuters do not reflect the marginal cost of providing the service for the users of the highways or of mass transit systems. The marginal cost of driving a car or riding a subway is higher during rush hour than it is the rest of the day. At this time subways must use their least efficient equipment, extra lanes on highways must be constructed for rush hour commuters, and the external costs (increased traffic jams, waiting time, and so on) greatly increase social cost during this period.

The differences in costs in mass transit for different times of the day are relatively easy to determine. For example, in New York City, if the cost of operating the subway at peak usage is 10 times that of normal operation, economic efficiency seems to dictate that the price of riding the subway during these hours be increased. However, this would be so only if other modes of transportation followed the same system. If only subway rush hour fares were raised, some people would drive rather than take mass transit. However, this would be even less efficient than the current system, because the marginal social cost of driving a car during rush hour is even greater than the marginal social cost of using the subway. Therefore, it would be better to leave subway rates as they are unless a way could be found to charge people the marginal social cost of driving, which would, of course, be the best solution. But the current situation is still not the second best. Rush hour fares should not be raised, but off-hour fares could be lowered, thus bringing relative prices more in line with relative costs, which would be more efficient. This would necessitate a subsidy to the subway system to make up the lost revenues, but it would be a subsidy whose benefits would exceed its costs.

INPUT-OUTPUT ANALYSIS

One method of analyzing the interrelationship of different markets in an economy is known as input-output analysis. This technique is the brainchild of Wassily Leontief, winner of a Nobel prize in 1973. Input-output analysis is a method of quantifying the interrelationship between various markets.

One reason for the close relationship between events in one market and those in other markets is that every output is also an input. For example, the output of a steel company becomes an input for the truck industry, whose output in turn becomes an input for the transportation of wheat, which then becomes input, and so on. In order to fully comprehend this problem of general equilibrium, it is necessary to know more than that changes in the steel industry cause changes in the bread industry. We must also be able to measure or predict the extent of such changes. The input-output model attempts to do just that. Table 32-1 is an input-output table for a simplified economy with only three industries. In the right-hand column, it shows the value of the total output

TABLE 32-1 Input-Output (in millions of dollars)

	Primary metals	Pollution control equipment	Automobiles	Final consumption	Total output
Primary metals	200	100	600	100	1000
Pollution control equipment	100	50	150	200	500
Automobiles	500	50	250	700	1500
Labor	200	300	500	(1000)	
Total value of inputs	1000	500	1500		(3000)

of each of the three industries. Each horizontal row shows the distribution of this output, indicating how much of the total output is an input to each industry. The column labeled *final consumption* shows how much is consumed by households directly rather than being used as an input. In a more realistic table, there would be a number of final consumption columns—for governments, exports, households—but in this simple model, we limit ourselves to households as the source of all final demand. The vertical rows show how much (in dollars) of the different inputs is required by each industry to produce its total output. For example, Table 32-1 reveals that in order to produce $1000 worth of primary metals, the required inputs are $200 of primary metals, $100 of pollution control equipment, $500 of cars, and $200 of labor. This totals $1000, exactly the value of the total output of primary metals. Reading the table horizontally, we see the following distribution of the industry's output: $200 to the primary metals industry itself, $100 to the pollution control equipment industry, $600 to the auto industry, and $100 to final consumption demand.

The information about the inputs required enables us to calculate the value of each input needed to produce an additional dollar's worth of any output. This is done by dividing the requirement for each input by the total inputs required for that product. These results, called input coefficients, are shown in Table 32-2.

With the coefficients shown in this table, it is possible to determine the consequences of a change in demand in one industry on all three industries. Suppose that the final consumption demand for autos increases by 20 percent. As a result, not only will an additional $140 million worth of cars be needed to supply final demand, but another $24 million (.17 × $140 million) of autos will be needed as input by the auto industry. And $56 million worth of primary metals (.40 × $140 million), $14 million of pollution control equipment (.10 × $140 million), and $46 million worth of labor (.33 × $140 million) will be required. The sum of the value of the additional inputs, of course, must and does equal the value of the additional output—$140 million.

TABLE 32-2 Input Coefficients

	Primary metals	Pollution control equipment	Automobiles
Primary metals	.20	.20	.40
Pollution control equipment	.10	.10	.10
Automobiles	.50	.10	.17
Labor	.20	.60	.33
Total value of inputs	1.00	1.00	1.00

TABLE 32-3 Input Coefficients after a New E.P.A.

	Primary metals	Pollution control equipment	Automobiles
Primary metals	.19	.19	.38
Pollution control equipment	.15	.15	.15
Automobiles	.47	.09	.16
Labor	.19	.57	31

The increase in demand for autos has set into motion a series of changes throughout the economy. If we have accurately determined the input-output coefficients, then the coefficients enable us to predict accurately the total effect of the change in one industry. In the real world, of course, there are many more markets, and the problem of determining the coefficients is a complex one. Nevertheless, with the help of computers, such estimates are constantly being made and refined and are used for planning purposes by both business and government.

One of the problems with an input-output table is that the numbers are continually changing and it must be constantly updated if it is to be useful. For example, in our simple model, consider what would happen if a new Environmental Protection Act were passed that set stiffer emission limits for all manufacturing processes. This would raise the coefficients for the input of pollution control equipment and necessarily lower the coefficients for the other inputs, since they must total 1.00. Perhaps after such a law was passed, the coefficients would be those shown in Table 32-3. Can you analyze the effects of such legislation on profits and employment in all three industries? What assumptions about full employment and resource mobility are involved in your analysis?

SUMMARY

1 The study of equilibrium prices and output in specific markets is called partial equilibrium analysis. But an economy never has such isolated markets. What happens in one may affect many others. General equilibrium analysis describes and explains the interactions among markets as well as the interaction of supply and demand within markets.

2 General equilibrium theory shows how the society may achieve efficiency if the analysis assumes that all markets are perfect, the consumer is rational and sovereign, and there are no externalities. The economy will eventually reach a point at which: $P_g = MC$ for all goods, and utilities are maximized; $P_f = VMP$, and total costs are minimized for all firms. The economy is technologically and allocatively efficient. However, it does not guarantee adequate income for all.

3 If there are externalities, internalizing them will have repercussions throughout the economy; in theory, everyone will be better off, but the costs of adjustment are borne more by some groups than others.

4 When there are inherent imperfections, society may have to settle for less than optimum conditions in more markets than simply the imperfect one, according to the theory of the second best.

5 Because goods may be simultaneously an input and an output, the connections between seemingly disparate markets may be quite close. Input-output analysis quantifies the interrelationships between the various markets. Input coefficients

reveal the proportion of an input needed in a given process and allow the calculation of the value of input required to produce an additional dollar's worth of output.

SUGGESTED READINGS

Bowen, Howard R. *Toward Social Economy*. Chaps. 15 and 16. New York: Holt, Rinehart and Winston, 1948.

Carter, Anne. *Structural Change in the American Economy*. Cambridge, Mass.: Harvard University Press, 1970.

Gill, Richard T. *Economics*. Chap. 22. Pacific Palisades, Calif.: Goodyear, 1973.

Köhler, Heinz. *Welfare and Planning*. New York: John Wiley & Sons, 1966.

Leftwich, Richard H. *The Price System and Resource Allocation*. 4th ed. Chap. 17. Hinsdale, Ill.: Dryden Press, 1970.

Leontief, Wassily W. "The Structure of the U.S. Economy." *Scientific American* 212 (April 1965): 25–32.

Stigler, George J. *The Theory of Price*. Rev. ed. Chap. 16. New York: Macmillan, 1952.

QUESTIONS

1 Review
   a. the conditions for general equilibrium as defined by Walras,
   b. how changes in preferences may be reflected throughout an economy producing two goods with two factors,
   c. how the imposition of an effluent charge on one industry may be reflected throughout the economy,
   d. the theory of the second best when there is imperfect competition,
   e. input-output tables and how they may be used to predict effects of changes in one industry throughout the economy.

2 Suppose that an economy produces beef and furniture and that the economy produces these goods with land and labor. Assume also that the beef industry is land-intensive while the furniture industry is relatively labor-intensive. If the economy is in general equilibrium as described by Walras, how would you characterize that position with respect to the production of goods and the allocation of resources?

3 Now assume that consumers in the economy described above change their preferences in favor of furniture. Trace the effects throughout the economy. What if people decide that they do not wish to supply any additional labor for the furniture industry?

4 Suppose that the American government adopts a policy of imposing effluent charges on the power-producing industries. Assuming that the power industries are capital-intensive, what changes would you predict throughout the economy?

5 A hypothetical economy produces automobiles and wheat. Due to innovative entrepreneurship, a new wine industry is introduced into this economy. What changes would you predict and under what conditions? In the purchases of consumers? In the distribution of factors and factor income?

6 From an equity standpoint what problems would result from a change in consumer preference in favor of additional clean air? What is the basis for these equity problems?

7 As a result of the devaluation of the dollar in 1973, there was an increase in foreign demand for American products. Would this change tend to disrupt general equilibrium if the economy were in equilibrium? Why? Would you expect a shift in production from some products to others? Why or why not?

8 Consider the input-output table below representing a hypothetical economy. Assume that in this economy there is a change in consumer preference so that consumers now wish to use some of the commercial fertilizer for their home gardens. Assume that consumers want $1.6 million (about 10 percent of present production) from the fertilizer industry. How might the change be felt in other industries? What if the economy is below capacity? At full employment?

Input-Output ($ millions)

	Wheat	Fertilizer	Food Processing	Final Consumption	Total Output
Wheat	50	10	190	150	400
Fertilizer	150	5	2	0	157
Food processing	100	120	20	150	390
Labor	100	22	178	(300)	
Total value of inputs	400	157	390		(947)

9 Assume that the economy represented by the input-output table above experiences a bad crop year in wheat. Production falls by 25 percent. What would be the effect on other industries? Assume that the demand for wheat is extremely inelastic. What might happen in the final consumption column? Why?

10 Following the failure of the wheat crop, the economy was lucky enough to be able to adopt a new resistant high-yield strain of wheat, which resulted in a 25 percent increase in output from the original level. What would this change do? Would the existing input-output table be accurate? Why or why not?

11 Assume that an economy produces electronic equipment and machinery. Both industries require about the same proportions of inputs, but the machinery industry is perfectly competitive while the electronic equipment industry is a monopoly. The government in this economy decides that there simply must be a mass transit system and that, therefore, it must call for a redirection of resources away from electronic equipment and machinery for the production and operation of mass transit. According to the second best solution, which industry would give up the larger amount of inputs and why?

Opening photo by Michael Tzovaras

CHAPTER
33
LABOR

Chapters 30 and 31 explained how the prices of the factors of production—including labor—are determined under perfect competition. In the everyday world, however, most labor markets are very different from the idealized model of perfect competition: Workers lack mobility and full knowledge of the job market, employers discriminate, one or a few employers may control the demand side of the market, and labor unions (to which some 20 million or approximately one-fourth of all American workers now belong) may dominate the supply side. In this chapter we shall investigate the role of unions in the labor market. What are the goals of unions, and how do these goals relate to those of the workers whom the unions represent? What tools does organized labor have to accomplish its objectives, and how successful has it been?

THE GOALS OF LABOR UNIONS

In the stereotype of the American labor union, the union's one overriding objective is to secure higher wages. This, however, is not really the case. Unlike the business firm, whose first and foremost objective is profit maximization, the labor union has no single primary goal. The typical union seeks various goals: increased wages and fringe benefits, improved working conditions, expanded membership, and freedom from arbitrary demands imposed by management. And often trade-offs are involved in choosing among these many aims.

Clearly, wages are an essential part of any union's bargaining demands. But increasingly, union negotiations involve requests for fringe benefits as well as wages: The 1973 UAW contract, for example, provided for annual wage increases of only 3 percent, but 5 to 6 percent increases in fringe benefits. Pensions, health and welfare provisions, and paid holidays are the basic fringe benefits. Recently, the form of the pension fund has attracted special attention. Today, some plans provide not only a pension for the retired worker, but also survivor benefits payable to a spouse if the worker dies before retirement, and portability or vesting provisions so that the worker can take some of his pension rights with him if he switches to another job or another industry. Another popular innovation is expanded health benefits, which in some cases now cover dental care, eye care, and allowances for prescription drugs. There has also been increased emphasis on longer vacations (5 to 6 weeks for long-time employees) and more holidays. Many steelworkers, for example, are entitled to a paid day off on their birthdays.

For many unions, the level of union membership is also an important goal. For example, industrial unions, such as the auto workers, consider all the workers in a given industry potential union members—the unskilled men and women at the bottom jobs on the assembly line, the semiskilled workers, and even many of the craftsmen. Such a union is under great pressure to increase its membership. If it fails to do so and leaves a large supply of nonunion labor available to employers, it is in a relatively poor bargaining position when the time comes to renegotiate its contract, for it does not have the ultimate weapon of threatening to deprive the employer of his entire working force. This is one of the reasons why recognition of the union as the sole bargaining agent, the union shop (in which nonunion members may be hired but must join the union as a condition of employment), and the check-off (a system through which the employer acts as a collection agent for the union by withholding union dues from paychecks) are often given primary importance in labor negotiations. A farsighted union frequently trades off current wage or fringe benefits for procedures that will ensure its growth.

A third objective of labor unions is industrial justice. Sumner Slichter has defined industrial justice as "a method of introducing civil rights into industry. . . . of requiring that management be conducted by rule rather than by arbitrary decision."[1] Thus, industrial justice reflects the desire of workers to replace the "uncontrolled discretion of management" with a system of established rules and policies.

The way in which an industrial justice issue is translated into policy and practice varies from union to union. It may be incorporated into hiring and train-

1 Sumner Slichter, *Union Policies and Industrial Management* (Washington, D.C.: Brookings Institution, 1941), p. 1.

ing procedures, promotion policies, grievance procedures, or the rights of shop committees. Moreover, the desires of different unions are not always the same on a given issue. Some unions, for example, insist on seniority rules to govern reduction of the work force, whereas others request that the available work be shared among all members. But whatever the details, the important point is that workers now feel that "the days are coming to an end when the boss's word, no matter how unreasonable, is law."[2] Instead, they favor the development of a system of industrial justice in which specific rules and policies provide the framework for what management can and cannot do with its work force.

United Auto Workers' negotiations in 1973 offer an example of how the issue of industrial justice has assumed increasing importance as a goal of American labor unions. The year 1973 was a boom one for the automakers, and many workers had been putting in 10-hour days, 7 days a week for extended periods. Such overtime had always been compulsory in the automobile plants; it was considered a matter over which management could exercise its own discretion, leaving the worker, or his union, with no voice. Despite the excellent overtime pay, the practice was extremely unpopular with workers, who felt that it was an unfair intrusion by the company on their personal lives. As a result, compulsory overtime became a prime issue in the 1973 negotiations. Although strong inflationary pressures at the time might normally have encouraged the unions to give primary importance to wage hikes, the UAW was willing to settle for a relatively minor wage package in exchange for a set of rules limiting compulsory overtime.

HOW DO UNIONS ATTEMPT TO RAISE WAGES?

Restricting the Supply of Labor

Wage increases are, of course, an important goal for every worker, and labor unions have channeled much effort into negotiating higher pay scales for their members. One approach the union can use in attempting to raise wages is to restrict the supply of labor. In the past, this has been accomplished through such methods as child and woman labor laws, strict immigration quotas, and maximum workweek legislation. The recent emphasis on early retirement can also be interpreted as an effort to restrict the size of the work force. The automobile workers, for example, have supported the concept of "30 and out," a plan under which a worker, regardless of age, can retire on a pension after 30 years in the plant. Craft unions, organizing such groups as plumbers, carpet layers, and elevator installers, whose work involves a particular skill, have been especially successful in raising wages through this approach. Typical craft unions require long apprenticeship periods, charge high initiation fees to prospective members, and, in general, limit the number of members they will admit into their unions. As shown in Figure 33-1, such policies can be graphic-

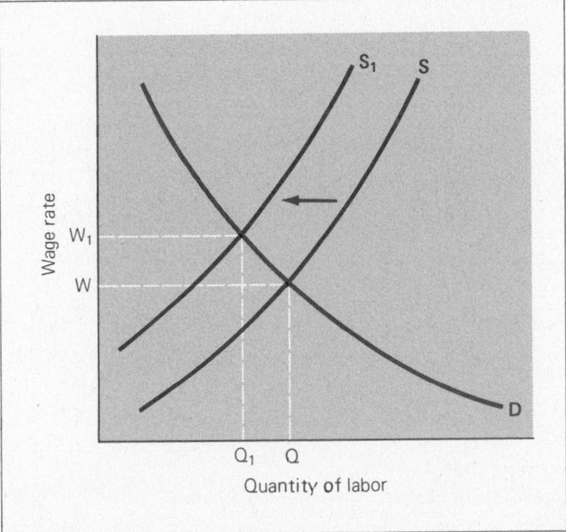

FIGURE 33-1 RAISING WAGES BY RESTRICTING THE LABOR SUPPLY **A craft union will generally offer membership only to those deemed qualified. Since not everyone who would otherwise seek employment in that line of work is admitted to the union, the supply of labor is restricted. The advent of a craft union will shift the labor supply curve to the left (from S to S_1). This decrease in the labor supply forces the wage rate up from W to the restricted rate W_1, while the level of employment declines from Q to Q_1. Such an outcome may also be the result of restrictions other than those imposed by a craft union—strict immigration quotas or discriminatory practices that keep blacks and women out of the labor market, for example.**

2 Slichter, *Union Policies and Industrial Management*, p. 1.

ally illustrated as a shift in the labor supply curve to the left, so that it intersects the demand curve at a higher wage level.

Imposing a Higher Wage Rate

Higher wages can also be achieved when a union is able to control nearly all available workers in an industry. The UAW, for example, has succeeded in imposing higher wages on the automobile industry because the industry no longer has access to a supply of workers outside the UAW. As a result, the labor supply curve does not have a typical upward-sloping shape; instead, over most of its range, the supply curve is a horizontal line at the negotiated wage rate, as shown in Figure 33-2.

Figures 33-1 and 33-2 illustrate two important methods used by craft unions and industrial unions, respectively, to increase wage rates. A craft union generally attempts to raise wages through policies that restrict the supply of labor; an industrial union, through policies that increase its strength and size, is able to impose wage rates on the industry. In both cases, a side effect of the higher wages is a reduction in the number of workers employed. Thus, despite the higher wages achieved, such efforts may have negative consequences for the union, for if a significant number of union members are laid off, union solidarity may be eroded.

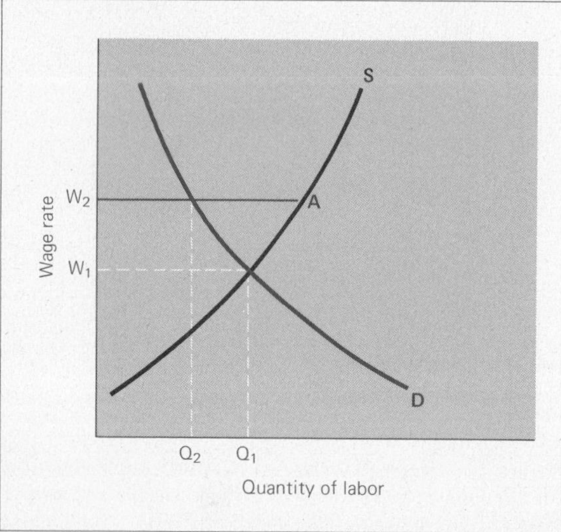

FIGURE 33-2 RAISING WAGES BY IMPOSING HIGHER PAY SCALES **An industrial labor union seeks to represent all workers in a particular industry, regardless of craft. If it succeeds in controlling virtually all the available labor supply, it is in a good position to impose higher wages on employers. If the imposed wage rate is W_2, the labor supply curve for that industry will become W_2AS, a straight horizontal line over most of its range. In this case, the number of workers hired would drop from the competitive level Q_1 to Q_2.**

What determines the extent of the decline in employment that will accompany a given wage increase? The determining factor is the elasticity of demand for labor in that particular industry, which in turn is dependent upon the elasticity of demand for the final product, the relative importance of wages in total costs, and the availability of other resources that could be substituted for the now more expensive labor. If, for all these reasons, demand is highly inelastic—as in the case of waiters at a resort hotel during a short summer season—the resulting unemployment may be minuscule. If, however, the demand is very elastic, the long-term effect on employment may be disastrous—as the textile workers in many New England communities have discovered.

In theory, then, the threat of such a decline in employment should act as a restraining force on unions during bargaining sessions. In practice, however, the declines in employment opportunities resulting from wage increases are usually very gradual. It takes time for employers to shift their resources to other enterprises, to replace high-priced workers with machines, or to move to a low-wage area. Moreover, there are some unions that have taken the position that higher wage rates for those employed are worth the cost of reduced employment in the long run. In the 25 years from 1945 to 1970, employment in the coal mining industry dropped from 400,000 to 146,000, but the coal miners, formerly one of the lower-paid groups in the United States, were earning weekly wages 40 percent higher than the average of all manufacturing industries. The United Mine Workers apparently felt that this was a satisfactory trade-off.

There are, however, ways that labor unions can attempt to artificially maintain the number of workers employed in an industry at the going union wage, even when technological change has made many jobs obsolete. Featherbedding—rules imposed by unions on the number of workers hired, job assignments, output quotas, and the kinds of equipment used—is one such tactic. The railroad unions, for example, have fought for "full crew" laws, which require that the number and types of workers needed to operate a steam engine be maintained on diesel trains. And the American Federation of Musicians, a very strong craft union, requires that a certain number of musicians be hired for any public performance, regardless of whether it is live, taped, or recorded. Thus, a TV producer would have to hire the minimum number of union musicians for a show, even though recorded music was actually being played.

Affecting the Demand for Labor

Another way that unions can increase wages is by affecting the demand for labor. (See Figure 33-3.)

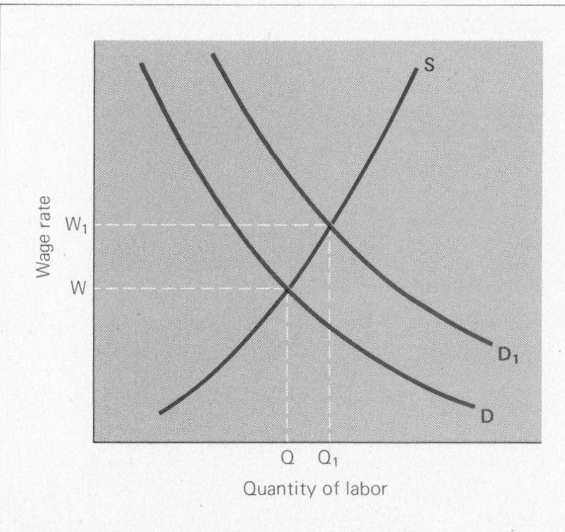

FIGURE 33-3 RAISING WAGES BY INCREASING THE DEMAND FOR LABOR OR FOR THE FINAL PRODUCT Labor unions can raise wages by shifting the labor demand curve to the right. This could be accomplished either by raising the productivity of workers or by increasing the demand for the final goods that workers produce. If the demand curve is shifted from D to D_1, wages will increase from W to W_1 and the number of workers hired will also rise, from Q to Q_1.

Raising productivity is one method unions can use to shift the demand curve for labor to the right. The International Ladies Garment Workers Union, for example, has been very active in working with management to increase productivity.

The demand for labor can also be increased if the demand for the goods that workers produce can be increased. This is because the demand for labor is a derived demand. Since advertising can help increase the demand for a product, labor unions sometimes launch their own ad campaigns. The plasterers' union, for example, has sponsored full-page ads in local newspapers featuring the slogan "Get Plastered" in an attempt to extol the virtues of plaster walls over wallboard. Lobbying for tariffs or import quotas is another method of accomplishing the same objective. Organized labor has been a prime supporter of the Burke-Hartke Bill, a measure that would severely limit the quantities of foreign goods that could be imported by the United States. Generally, however, unions have engaged in such lobbying efforts primarily as a way of maintaining a potentially declining demand, rather than as a device to increase overall demand.

HOW SUCCESSFUL ARE UNIONS IN RAISING WAGES?

Do unions actually raise wages? Our theoretical models would certainly indicate that one main thrust of union activity is to engage in policies that will raise wage scales. Moreover, the statistics reveal that the unionized segment of the labor force receives average wages approximately 10 to 15 percent higher than the nonunionized segment. Nevertheless, a closer look at the picture raises doubts about the direct responsibility of the unions for these wage gains and also some provocative questions about their source.

Have Union Wages Come Out of Excess Profits?

One way of explaining the higher wages earned by union workers is that the unions have managed to carve out for their members some of the excess profits that would otherwise be earned by the large corporations. Actual statistics, however, do not appear to confirm this thesis. It is true that the employee compensation share of U.S. national income did increase from approximately 55 to 65 percent during the first three decades of this century. But from the 1930s on, the period in which unions grew most significantly, the employee compensation share of NI has remained relatively constant at around 65 percent, suggesting that wage gains by labor unions have come from another source.

Have Union Wages Come at the Expense of Nonunion Workers?

Several studies suggest that the wage increases of unionized workers may have been achieved at the expense of nonunion workers. The very lowest-paid workers in our economy have always been the nonunionized ones—domestic workers and clerks in small retail shops, for example. It is possible that their low wages are directly related to the higher pay received by union workers. As we saw in Figures 33-1 and 33-2, one side effect of higher union wages may be a cutback in the number of workers employed in the unionized industry. The workers who have been laid off are consequently added to the ranks of those competing for jobs in the nonunionized labor market, and the result is lower wages for all workers in those nonunion jobs. This situation is illustrated graphically in Figure 33-4. Graph A shows the decline in employment from Q to Q_1 that occurs when an industrial union raises the wage level from W to W_1. Those workers who are unemployed because of the shift from Q to Q_1 join the job-seekers in the nonunionized labor market, graph B, shifting the supply curve to the right, from S to S_1, and reducing the wage rates from W to W_1.

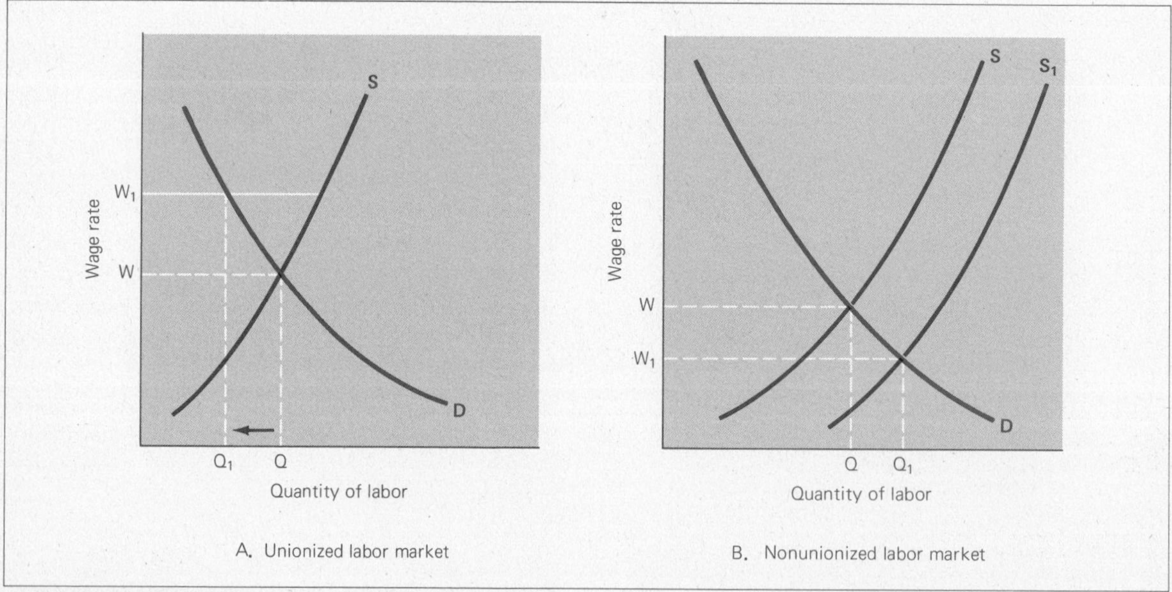

FIGURE 33-4 UNION AND NONUNION WAGES The higher wages paid to union workers may be at the expense of nonunionized labor. A by-product of higher union wages may be a drop in the number of workers hired. This is shown in graph A as a decline in employment from Q to Q_1 at the higher union wage W_1. Those workers who are laid off may be forced to seek employment in the nonunionized segment of the labor market, shown in graph B. Here the supply of labor curve shifts to the right (from S to S_1) as the result of the influx of new workers seeking jobs, and the wage rate drops from W to W_1.

Union Wages and the Nature of Unionized Industries

It is also possible to explain the gap between union and nonunion wages by the fact that unions have had their greatest success in organizing workers in highly profitable and growing industries, frequently ones with market power. In such industries, the productivity of labor tends to be high, so workers would typically earn higher-than-average wages. For example, the automobile industry was a relatively high-paying industry, even before unionization. It can, therefore, be claimed that the high wages in unionized industries do not necessarily reflect the effectiveness of the union, but rather the ability of the industry, because of market factors, to pay high wages.

The Diminishing Gap between Union and Nonunion Wages

In recent years, the wage gap between union and nonunion workers has appeared to be diminishing. This can be attributed in part to recent union activity in those enterprises that were formerly both nonunionized and very low paying—hospitals, laundries, and restaurants, for example. In addition, many union leaders claim that pay for nonunionized workers is affected by the gains achieved by the unions. When unions are successful in establishing higher wages for their members, they may force nonunion employers to meet or to approach these standards, particularly in a tight labor market. Certain large, nationwide employers routinely follow a policy of paying comparable wages in their union and nonunion plants. Thus, a wage increase earned by a union in one operation will be matched throughout the company.

Clearly, economists differ in their evaluations of the overall effect of unions on wage rates. The consensus appears to be that unions have had modest success in increasing overall wages above the level to which they might have risen without unions. Wage gains, however, are largely confined to union members in industries where productivity has been growing rapidly. And the gains in union wages have been, at least to some extent, at the expense of nonunion workers. These conclusions raise important questions about the effectiveness of unions as vehicles through which wages can be raised and about the equity considerations involved.

COLLECTIVE BARGAINING

Once a union is organized, its task is to represent the interests of its members in every facet of employment—wages, fringe benefits, working conditions, job security, and retirement. Elected union officers negotiate with management to settle issues on which the two sides disagree. This process of collective bargaining is the main tool labor unions use to attempt to achieve their goals. The aim of collective bargaining is to negotiate a contract between union and management that covers the rights and duties of each over a given period, usually a two- or three-year span, and to provide a means of enforcing the provisions of the contract. In order to avoid conflicts, the two parties may sometimes leave parts of the settlement vague, hoping that any problems that arise can be worked out at a later date. But differing interpretations are still there to be resolved in the everyday give-and-take of labor-management relations.

Contrary to the impression one may get from newspaper pictures of haggard executives and union chiefs emerging with a contract after a 36-hour negotiating session, collective bargaining does not occur in a marathon session once every several years. Rather, it occurs day-in and day-out at all levels in the firm. Nor is any given contract the final word on an issue. An agreement hammered out in one contract may be discarded in the next. For example, the number of workers covered under cost-of-living clauses (which provide that wages will rise by a certain amount in proportion to the officially determined cost of living) totaled 4 million in 1960. Several years later, however, cost-of-living clauses had been dropped from many union contracts because the economy was enjoying a period of relative price stability. In 1963, the number of workers affected by such clauses had decreased to only 1.85 million. And yet by 1971, when the economy was again experiencing substantial inflation, cost-of-living clauses were back, with 4.7 million workers covered.

Collective bargaining, then, never provides a final answer, but occurs in the context of a changing industrial environment. It is not self-enforcing, but involves a continuous process of negotiation, and it covers more than simply wage determination.

The Issues

Watching labor negotiations is like watching a sport. It helps if you know what to look for and it helps to know the rules. One of the curious features of this sport, however, is that the same ideas can be used to justify diametrically opposed positions. The arguments used for and against wage and benefit increases provide an example.

Wages and Benefits Extremely important bargaining points in almost every labor-management dispute are the salaries and benefits that the workers will receive. On what basis is the size of the compensation package determined? First, a union will tend to demand that workers receive a package comparable to those packages paid by other firms in the industry, provided, of course, that the other firms' compensation is higher than what the workers are already getting. If workers are receiving higher compensation than that paid by other firms, management uses this argument to justify its restraint on wages and benefits. Second, the success of the firm in the preceding fiscal year will be brought up as justification for higher compensation, simply on the principle that the firm is in a position to afford it. If the firm lost money, however, management can plead poverty. Third, inflation is often used as a strong bargaining argument in favor of higher wages and benefits. This method has become more popular in recent years as a result of increased public awareness of the cost-of-living and consumer price indices. Unions often demand cost-of-living clauses, but management may reply that giving in to these demands will rob workers of purchasing power because of the inflation such a settlement would bring. Fourth, paradoxically, recession may also be used as an argument in favor of higher wages, the point being that if workers are paid more, they will spend more, and thus help to revive the failing economy. Finally, the productivity of the firm may be claimed as the basis of a raise. This argument is similar in principle to the one based on cost-of-living increases, in that it is agreed that wages will be raised in proportion to improvements in the firm's output per worker.

Contracts, in addition to spelling out the size of the compensation package, vary in terms of the form that such a package will take. Will it be allocated primarily as current wages or will it show up largely as benefits? Will the fringe benefits be items, such as improved pensions, of greatest concern to older workers, or will they take the form of longer vacations for new employees or employer subsidies for further education? How much of a sacrifice in hourly wages should the union accept to receive dental care? Another paid holiday? The right to retire a year earlier?

Working Conditions In the area of working conditions, the issues often become much more specific, involving such things as the rate of the assembly line, the working environment, and what happens when layoffs or hiring becomes necessary. Most of these issues were once *management prerogatives,* a term denoting inviolable powers. Over the years, however, management has found itself bargaining over more and more of its "prerogatives." The latest issue being raised is management's traditional power to make overtime compulsory. Workers once eager for the extra income are now more eager for leisure time, or at least fewer hours on the assembly line.

The Process

If we were to design a playing field for the sport of collective bargaining, it might resemble the shaded area in Figure 33-5. Outside this area, either group will refuse to play. Labor masses at the upper end, management at the lower end, and the game begins, with each side trying to capture as much area as it can. The problem is that each side needs the

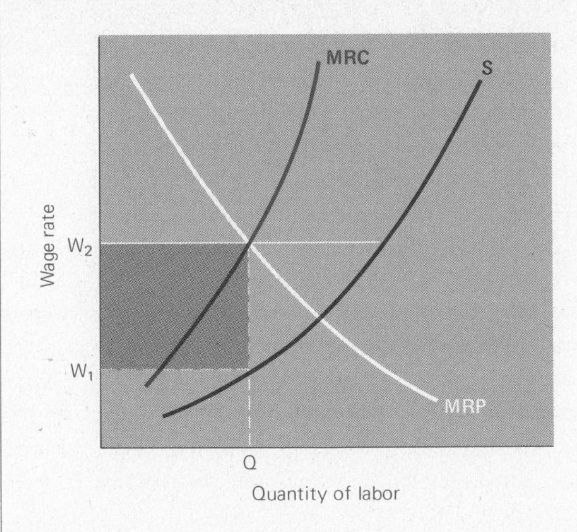

FIGURE 33-5 THE LABOR UNION VS. THE MONOPSONISTIC EMPLOYER **The bilateral monopoly model discussed in Chapter 30 indicates what labor and management are arguing about in wage negotiations. The employer (in this case a monopsonistic or oligopsonistic employer) wants to set the wage rate at W_1, whereas the union wishes to establish the higher wage rate W_2. If the wage was set at W_1 instead of W_2, the workers would forfeit the shaded area in lost income. If, on the other hand, the wage was set at W_2, the employer would pay the shaded area in higher costs. The shaded area, then, represents the income and the costs that the two sides are bargaining over. Undoubtedly, the final wage rate will be established somewhere between W_1 and W_2, depending upon the relative strength of labor and management.**

other, so concessions are made on both sides, until a mutually acceptable standoff is reached.

Grievances Even though a contract is signed, disagreements over terms or new issues may arise. Although some collective bargaining agreements are many pages long, they cannot possibly include provisions for every eventuality. Most contracts between labor and management, therefore, contain a clause outlining the steps to be taken by both sides in the event that an issue arises about which there is disagreement. For example, if a worker is discriminated against by the firm, he may file a grievance with the shop steward, who will try to resolve it with the foreman. If the foreman and the steward cannot settle the grievance, it may then be taken up by the local union leadership and the plant manager; and, if it is still unresolvable at this level, it may go even one step higher—to the national union and management of the firm. Usually, the contract calls for compulsory arbitration to settle grievances if other channels do not work. Typically, outside parties are called in to resolve the issue. Such grievance procedures are essential to a workable contract; without them, labor could enforce the contract only by a wildcat strike.

Strikes An agreement between labor and management is possible only if both parties are willing to be tugged into the standoff zone. If one or the other stands fast on a position unacceptable to the other, a strike ensues. Most strikes are brief, lasting less than a week, and the total loss to the economy is relatively small, as shown in Table 33-1. In most years, time lost due to strikes never amounts to even one-third of 1 percent of total man-hours worked. Such a loss is the cost society has chosen to incur in order to have collective bargaining.

As far as the parties immediately involved in a strike are concerned, the purpose of the strike is to shift the bargaining to areas of potential agreement. This is done by the aggressive method of forcing the other side to consider terms that it had previously rejected. And it is not always labor that displays such aggression. On the surface, the union is always the one to cause a strike; after all, it announces the walkout. In reality, however, management can easily provoke a strike by adopting a patently unreasonable bargaining position.

As the strike draws on, it becomes a test of the resourcefulness and the resources of union and management. The union tries to support its members from its strike fund and to keep morale up. The company must continue to pay fixed costs, such as rent and interest, while forgoing operating revenue. Usually, the financially weaker side will start making concessions first. It will scale down its terms for settlement when it realizes that a continued strike will cost it more than it could hope to gain from its original demands.

TABLE 33-1 Work Stoppages and Time Lost, 1945–72

Year	Number of stoppages	Number of workers involved (in millions)	Man-days idle: Number (in millions)	Man-days idle: Percentage of total
1945	4750	3.5	38.0	.31%
1946	4985	4.6	116.0	1.04
1947	3693	2.2	34.6	.30
1948	3419	2.0	34.1	.28
1949	3606	3.0	50.5	.44
1950	4843	2.4	38.8	.33
1951	4737	2.2	22.9	.18
1952	5117	3.5	59.1	.48
1953	5091	2.4	28.3	.22
1954	3468	1.5	22.6	.18
1955	4320	2.7	28.2	.22
1956	3825	1.9	33.1	.24
1957	3673	1.4	16.5	.12
1958	3694	2.1	23.9	.18
1959	3708	1.9	69.0	.50
1960	3333	1.3	19.1	.14
1961	3367	1.5	16.3	.11
1962	3614	1.2	18.6	.13
1963	3362	.9	16.1	.11
1964	3665	1.7	22.9	.15
1965	3963	1.6	23.3	.15
1966	4405	2.0	25.4	.15
1967	4595	2.9	42.1	.25
1968	5045	2.6	49.0	.28
1969	5700	2.5	42.9	.24
1970	5700	3.3	66.4	.37
1971	5100	3.3	47.6	.26
1972	5100	1.7	26.0	.14

In only one year since World War II did work stoppages cause the loss of more than 0.5 percent of total working time. That was in 1946, when labor unions, restive after four years of patriotic restraint, demanded huge wage increases. One of the consequences of these strikes was the election of a Republican Congress and the passage of the Taft-Hartley Act, limiting labor's power somewhat. Those who would prohibit unions from striking often cite the work stoppages as too high a price to pay for the freedom to strike. These figures seem to belie such assertions. Furthermore, the very threat of a strike probably encourages employers to bargain in good faith. However, whether the power of the labor unions, derived largely from the ultimate threat of a strike, has led to much of the inflation we have suffered in recent years remains an open question.

SOURCE: U.S. Department of Labor, "Current Labor Statistics," *Monthly Labor Review*, July 1973, p. 109.

Mediation and Arbitration When negotiations between labor and management become deadlocked, so much so that the distance between the disputants on certain areas obscures the possibilities for agreement, rather than having the situation culminate in a strike, the two sides will sometimes agree to try settling their differences through the intervention of a third party. There are two basic forms of third-party involvement: mediation and arbitration. In mediation, the third party is given no particular authority over the disputants, save for what he commands by virtue of his experience and prestige. He merely acts as a go-between. His function is to present the arguments of both sides in their best possible light and to draw attention to potential avenues of concordance. Both labor and management have the prerogative of ignoring the mediator's counsel, of achieving agreement on their own, or of going on with a strike.

Arbitration, on the other hand, involves intervention by a third party in whom both parties have agreed to invest final authority to decide the issues in question. This form of decision making is known also as "binding arbitration." Labor and management usually agree to try arbitration when neither side wants to force the issues through a strike or when both sides want to terminate a walkout. In a few cases, arbitration of disputes in key industries has been made compulsory by state legislatures. By and large, however, the emphasis in the United States has been on mediation rather than on arbitration. The federal government, in fact, has set up mediation services, as have several state governments.

But because strikes in a major industry, such as automobiles, or in an essential service, such as air traffic control, can be so crippling to the entire economy, some have suggested that strikes be prohibited and a form of compulsory arbitration be required. One such proposal was offered by President Nixon, early in his administration, as a solution to a threatened rail strike. The President proposed that when labor and management reached an impasse, both sides would have one last opportunity to make an offer. Then an arbitrator would be called in to choose either one or the other offer. Knowing this, both sides would be encouraged to make their final offers as reasonable as possible, and the prospects for a fair and mutually satisfactory settlement would be enhanced.

Another provocative proposal offers an added monetary incentive to settle rather than to strike. When an impasse in bargaining occurs, labor and management would be given one final 90-day period in which to negotiate. During this period, operations would continue, but all wages and profit would be put into a trust fund. If, during the 90-day period, an agreement were reached, the monies would be distributed to the workers and the corporation. If no agreement were reached, the entire sum would be forfeited.

EVOLUTION OF THE AMERICAN LABOR MOVEMENT

The American system of labor relations has evolved over several centuries. Collective bargaining is in part a creation of the courts, the legislature, and administrative agencies. For much of America's history, unions were not even recognized as legal organizations, and certainly their full power did not surface until the New Deal.

In the United States, the labor movement started with the formation of craft unions after the American Revolution. These were local unions that organized workers in particular trades, such as bakers, carpenters, printers, and teamsters. For a long time, unions were strenuously opposed by employers, who viewed them as conspiracies in restraint of trade. On several occasions, unions were even punished by the courts as illegal organizations. In 1842, however, a Massachusetts court held that a trade union was a lawful organization with the right to represent workers and bargain with employers. But employers continued litigation. Courts turned antitrust laws against unions and employed injunctions to prevent the use of boycotts, strikes, and picketing, by which unions could enforce their demands. Employers, meanwhile, discharged union organizers and sympathizers, often blacklisting them to ruin their chances for employment elsewhere. Yellow dog contracts forced employees to agree not to join a union. And employers offered strictly company-controlled unions as substitutes for meaningful bargaining units.

Despite the hostile climate, unionism spread to almost every craft and to most cities. Several local unions joined to form national federations and succeeded in negotiating trade agreements with employers. The first such federation was the National Typographic Union, organized in 1852.

Craft unions are referred to as horizontal unions because they are comprised of workers in several localities or in several industries, all of whom have a particular skill. The National Typographic Union, for example, had members in several areas of the country, employed by newspapers, book publishers, and other types of firms. In contrast, the industrial unions of today are referred to as vertical unions because they include all workers in a particular industry, regardless of their different skills. An example of a vertical union is the United Auto Workers.

The Knights of Labor, founded in Philadelphia in 1869, was the first major vertical union. It attempted to unify workers nationally without regard to their skills. After winning several strikes against the railroads, its power and influence grew, until, by 1886, its claim to membership exceeded 700,000. But along with the Knights of Labor's popularity came its downfall. Several craft union leaders became dissatisfied with its all-inclusive philosophy. In 1886, the American Federation of Labor was formed, and, under its president, Samuel Gompers (who served it almost continuously until 1924), the AFL became the dominant force in the American labor movement.

The philosophy of the AFL was based chiefly on three principles: federalism, voluntarism, and business unionism. Federalism guaranteed the autonomy of the various national craft unions that joined. Each union was allowed to control its own trade without interference from the federation. The principle of voluntarism was an attempt to protect the parties involved in the bargaining process from government intervention. Unions were to refrain from direct political affiliation (for example, from forming a labor or socialist party), while government, in turn, was not to intervene in bargaining or in matters of labor organization. Business unionism focused on concrete gains: an eight-hour day, child labor laws, higher pay, elimination of sweatshops. Gompers had no use for class warfare or utopian social reform.

From the 1880s onward, the Knights of Labor declined in importance, finally disbanding in 1917. In the meantime, AFL membership rose to unprecedented proportions, reaching 1 million at the turn of the century. This growth was achieved despite tremendous public hostility against unions. Often state and federal governments supported business interests in disputes with labor, and often police and the military were called in to break strikes. Still, unions managed to win a shorter workweek and higher wages.

The labor movement, however, was not free from internal dissent. Some leaders in the AFL felt that the union overrepresented skilled workers while ignoring the needs of the unskilled and the semiskilled. This argument, which was essentially a revival of the old dispute over the efficacy of horizontal and vertical unions, resulted in the expulsion of several industrial unions from the AFL in 1938. Under the presidency of John L. Lewis of the United Mine Workers, these unions formed the Committee (now Congress) of Industrial Organizations (CIO), which became very successful in organizing workers in mass production industries such as steel and automobiles.

Both the AFL and the CIO continued to grow after World War II. Many people hoped that the two giant unions would someday be reconciled and their power thereby increased. Finally, in 1955, this hope was realized. The two federations merged to form the AFL-CIO, which, under the leadership of George Meany, has survived until today. In 1968, the United Auto Workers withdrew from the AFL-CIO and, together with the Teamsters, formed the Alliance for Labor Action. The current memberships of the UAW and the Teamsters, as well as of some of the major unions belonging to the AFL-CIO, are shown in Figure 33-6.

Trade Union Legislation

For more than a hundred years, organized labor in the United States had almost no support from the law-making branch of government. Decisions involving labor-management disputes were settled by the courts, and, without legislative guidance, the courts invariably ruled in favor of the employers. Even the landmark Massachusetts decision of 1842, which declared unions to be legal organizations, was only of limited usefulness, since the unions' only significant weapon, the strike, was still regarded by the courts as an unlawful conspiracy in restraint of trade. The Clayton Act of 1914 finally recognized the ideas that labor is not merely another commodity and that unions per se are not a violation of antitrust laws.

The 1930s saw the full legitimization of organized labor. Many people felt that unions, by encouraging workers to demand higher wages, might increase spending and help alleviate the depression. The first act of Congress to express this new feeling was the **Norris–La Guardia Act** of 1932. Basically, the Norris–La Guardia Act helped organized labor in two ways. First, before the act was passed, it had been relatively easy for an employer to obtain an injunction against a union and thereby legally prevent a threatened strike. The Norris–La Guardia Act made it more difficult for employers to obtain such injunctions. Second, the act made yellow dog contracts unenforceable.

The **Wagner Act**, or **National Labor Relations Act**, of 1935 was the second and more powerful piece of pro-union legislation passed during the Great Depression. Specifically, the act forbade certain "unfair labor practices," among them interference by employers with the workers' right to organize unions, establishment by employers of "company unions," discrimination by employers on the basis of a worker's union membership or lack thereof, discrimina-

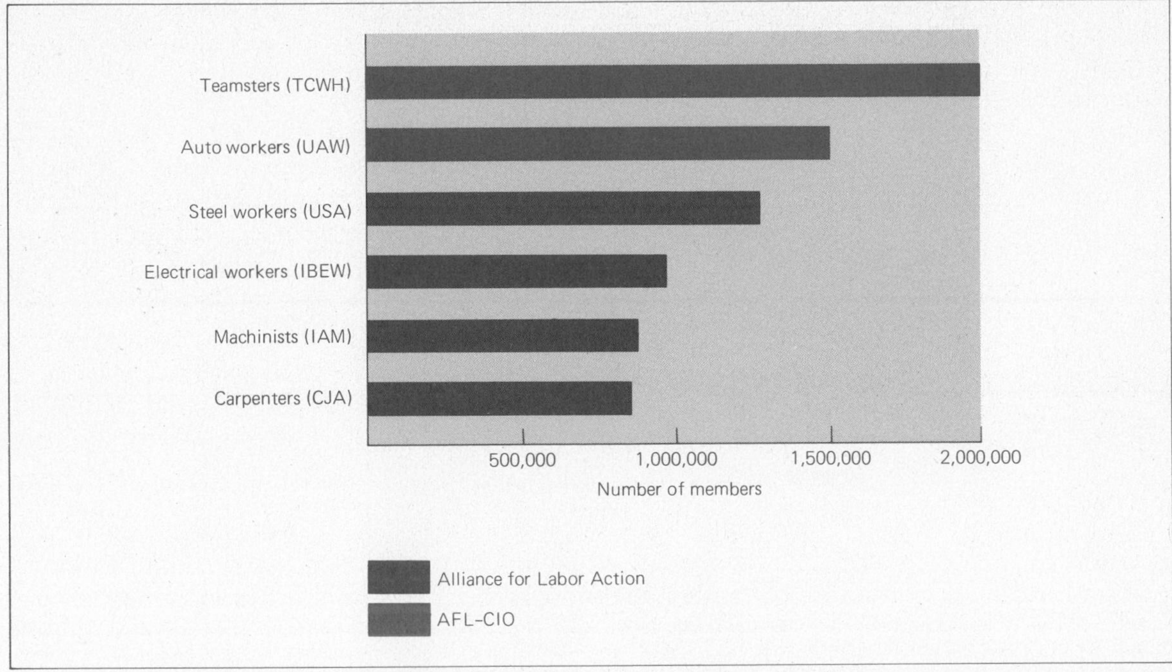

FIGURE 33-6 MEMBERSHIP OF SIX MAJOR UNIONS, 1972 These six labor unions are among the most powerful in the United States. The Teamsters could bring the entire nation to a standstill, since most goods are shipped by truck. The auto industry, directly and indirectly, provides jobs for one out of six workers in the United States.

tion by employers against workers who give evidence or register charges under the act, and the refusal of employers to bargain in good faith with the representatives of a duly established union. This act amounted to a Magna Carta for labor and recognized the necessity for unions to equalize bargaining power. The act also provided for the establishment of a National Labor Relations Board to investigate unfair labor practices and to ensure fairness in union practices. Under the protection of the Wagner Act, organized labor made enormous gains, increasing total union membership from 4 million in 1935 to 15 million in 1947.

The **Taft-Hartley Act** of 1947 reduced and qualified some of the power given to labor by the earlier Wagner Act. In part it was the result of an anti-union backlash. Many people felt that the unions had initiated too many strikes during the years after World War II and that, in addition to endangering the nation's security, they were responsible for the rapid inflation that followed the war. Consequently, the Taft-Hartley Act was designed to impose certain limitations on organized labor. The provisions of the act were many and complex, falling into four general categories. The first category outlawed specific union practices. These included jurisdictional strikes, secondary boycotts, and certain kinds of sympathy strikes; exorbitant dues or initiation fees; featherbedding; and the refusal of union leaders to bargain in good faith with management.

The second category of provisions affected the internal affairs of unions. Unions were required to make financial records accessible to both members and the National Labor Relations Board. Contributions by unions to political campaigns were prohibited, and, as originally stated in the act, union leaders were forced to swear that they were not Communists.

One group that has remained exempt from the jurisdiction of the National Labor Relations Board is agricultural laborers. This exemption has kept food prices down, but at what cost?

Child labor is a common practice in harvesting crops and a financial necessity for migrant labor families. One survey placed the weekly wages of a migrant breadwinner at $32, supplemented by $48 earned by his wife and children. Such poverty condemns the children of agricultural workers to a life of migrant labor—if they survive. In one Texas camp, 96 percent of the children had not tasted milk in the last six months. A California survey revealed that two-thirds of the children under three had never received smallpox vaccinations or immunization against diphtheria, whooping cough, or tetanus. The average life expectancy of a migrant farm worker is over 20 years less than that of the average American.

Since World War II, the government has actually promoted migrant labor by allowing braceros, or foreign labor, to be imported for the harvest season and trucked back to Mexico when the crops were in. Not until 1964 were the most notorious of these programs eliminated. Migrant labor in some areas is still heavily foreign because of laws permitting permanent resident alien status.

Organizing agricultural laborers is difficult, not only because they lack the protection of the NLRB, but also because their frequent moves make it impossible to sustain suits. Many farm workers are aliens, some illegally in this country. Economic vulnerability and physical danger make union organizing a hazardous occupation at best.

The most successful organizer of migrant farm workers has been Cesar Chavez. Although Chavez began organizing in 1952, it was the grape boycott in the mid-1960s that drew national attention to his efforts. The United Farm Workers became a member of the AFL-CIO in 1966, and until recently it was competing against Teamster locals for the right to represent agricultural laborers. Many of the Teamster locals were willing to sign "sweetheart," or pro-management, contracts in return for recognition, a tactic publicly repudiated by the Teamsters International. Eventually, however, an agreement was reached whereby representation of workers would be divided between the UFW and the Teamsters, depending upon whether the crops involved were to be sold as canned goods or as fresh produce.

If the UFW were covered by the NLRB, it would find its most effective weapons—jurisdictional strikes and the boycott—curtailed because it would also come under the Taft-Hartley Act, which prohibits certain types of boycotts and all jurisdictional strikes. But if the UFW is able to increase its membership significantly, it may be strong enough to forgo earlier tactics and to make use of the provisions of the National Labor Relations Act.

United Press International

The third category of provisions detailed specific arrangements that were forbidden in collective bargaining agreements. The closed shop (an arrangement whereby only union members could be hired) was outlawed. And state legislatures were given the right to outlaw the union shop (an arrangement whereby all nonunion workers hired are required to join the union within a specified period) if they wished. At present about 19 states have right-to-work laws, which forbid compulsory union membership. In addition, the Taft-Hartley Act specified that unions could no longer demand that dues be deducted from paychecks unless the individual worker gave his signed approval. Management was to work in conjunction with unions in the administration of pensions and welfare. And, finally, unions and management were required to give each other warning of their intention to change or to terminate an existing contract no less than 60 days before that contract expired.

The fourth category of provisions of the act outlined a way in which the President could issue an injunction against any major strike if it endangered the national interest. The injunction lasts 80 days and is known as a "cooling-off period." If labor and management have still not reached an agreement at the end of this period, the strike may go on, unless the President sees fit to exercise his final prerogative: placing the entire industry under government control, an action that is of doubtful constitutionality.

In 1959, the **Landrum-Griffin Act** was passed. Its official name was the Labor-Management Reporting and Disclosure Act, and essentially it was an extension of the Taft-Hartley Act in that it placed further regulations on unions. The Landrum-Griffin Act required unions to hold regular elections of officers by secret ballot. It also required union officers who handle funds to be bonded, and it made the theft of such funds a federal offense. Moreover, the act stipulated that Communists and ex-convicts could not, except under special circumstances, hold union offices.

The history of union legislation, then, is roughly divided into three periods. After a long period in which the legislature punished the labor movement by ignoring it, Congress actively encouraged labor during the New Deal by passing the Norris–La Guardia Act and the Wagner Act. Then during the 1940s and 1950s, Congress tried to contain burgeoning union power and union abuses with the restrictive Taft-Hartley Act and Landrum-Griffin Act. It is clear in looking at this pattern that the government has tried to fill a regulatory function in attempting to establish a balance of power between management and labor.

THE LABOR MOVEMENT TODAY

The merger of the AFL and the CIO in 1955 seemed to herald a new era of solidarity in the labor movement in the United States. But, compared with the rapid expansion of membership in the 1930s and 1940s, organizing activity actually seems to have leveled off following the merger. This trend is shown clearly in Figure 33-7, which charts the growth of union membership in this century against the growth of the labor force. As a percentage of total civilian employment, union membership has remained fairly stable during the past 20 years. The main reason advanced for this stagnation has been the shift in the composition of the labor force from blue-collar workers, who are typically unionized, to white-collar workers, who are not. The unions themselves are concerned about this trend. As one AFL-CIO report states:

> A recent Labor Department study shows 48 million job openings occurring in the national workforce from 1968 to 1980. Thirty million are replacements, while 18 million are new jobs. White collar dominated 2½ to 1 over blue collar in these new openings. Half of the white collar openings, 14 million, will be new jobs, while only 4 million of the new jobs will be blue collar. Eleven million of these "job openings" will occur in clerical jobs.
>
> Total employment in clerical jobs is expected to reach 17.3 million in 1980, with professional, technical and kindred jobs reaching 15.5 million for a total between these two low-union-level groupings at nearly 33 million. It is estimated that 85 percent of blue collar workers are unionized, with about 15 percent of white collar workers in unions.
>
> The impact of these radical shifts in the complexion of the workforce on union organization has, according to one analyst, cost the union movement nearly 2½ million members from 1947 to 1966 simply by growth occurring where

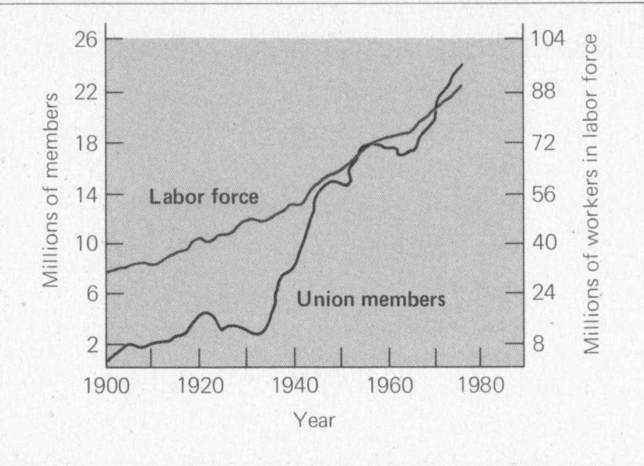

FIGURE 33-7 U.S. LABOR FORCE AND UNION MEMBERSHIP, 1900–73 In 1900, there were only about a million union members in the United States, and in 1933 there were only a little more than two million. But under the administration of Franklin Roosevelt, union membership soared to more than 14 million. Since World War II, however, union growth has been much less steady and much slower. Public resistance, as well as the fact that unions had already skimmed the most receptive recruits from the labor force, has accounted for much of this slackening. Since 1945, white-collar workers, who traditionally have avoided union membership, have comprised an increasing percentage of the labor force. But white-collar resistance to unionization may be changing. Much of the union membership gains in the 1960s and '70s has come from this group, especially from among municipal employees.

SOURCE: U.S. Department of Labor.

unionism was sparse and contraction occurring where it was widespread. Stated another way, union jobs disappeared while non-union jobs increased.[3]

Moreover, union membership is concentrated by geographical area. Ten states contain 70 percent of all union members; the entire southeast has fewer union members than New York State alone, partially because of the prevalence of right-to-work laws in the South.

Public Unions

One sector in which unionism is on the rise is government. Strikes by letter carriers, policemen, sanitation workers, and teachers have given public unions high visibility.

During one three-month period, not so long ago, a casual check showed social workers' strikes in Chicago, Sacramento, and White Plains; slowdowns of firefighters in Buffalo and of policemen in Detroit; strikes among university maintenance employees at Ohio State, Indiana, and the University of Kansas Medical Center; a three-day "heal-in" by the interns and residents of the Boston City Hospital; "informational" picketing, with a strike threat, by the Philadelphia School Nurses' Association; teachers' strikes in a dozen communities, ranging from West Mifflin, Pennsylvania, and Gibraltar, Ohio, to South Bend, Indiana, and Baltimore, Maryland.[4]

The real growth of public unions started during the 1960s. Before then, limitations on the right to organize were strict, and strikes were banned outright. In January 1962, Executive Order 10988 liberalized federal policies toward the recognition of unions and the right of collective bargaining, but maintained the prohibition against strikes. It is over the right to strike that much conflict has occurred.

Why is the right to strike considered so necessary among public employees? First, strike bans "warp the vital process of collective bargaining," according to Jerry Wurf, President of the American Federation of State, County, and Municipal Employees. Second, the public sector is indistinguishable from the private sector in many instances; therefore, why should a clerk in the Social Security Administration be denied the same rights as a clerk working for John Hancock?

Objections to these arguments range from the gut reaction, "Who's going to collect the garbage if the sanitation men are out on the picket lines?" to legalistic arguments over the sovereignty of the government. All rely on distinctions between public and private functions. The public sector is both stronger and weaker than the private sector. Its strength lies in the doctrine of inviolable powers—that the legislature has the ultimate authority to determine conditions of employment. Its weakness lies in the fact that it *does* provide essential services and that the costs of a strike are imposed upon a hapless public—or as Calvin Coolidge more bluntly put the idea during the Boston police strike of 1919, "There is no right to strike against public safety by anybody, any-

3 AFL-CIO, *Proceedings and Executive Council Reports,* 9th Constitutional Convention, 1971, p. 55.

4 Everett M. Kassalow, "Trade Unionism Goes Public," *Public Interest,* Winter 1969, p. 118.

THE JOB BLAHS

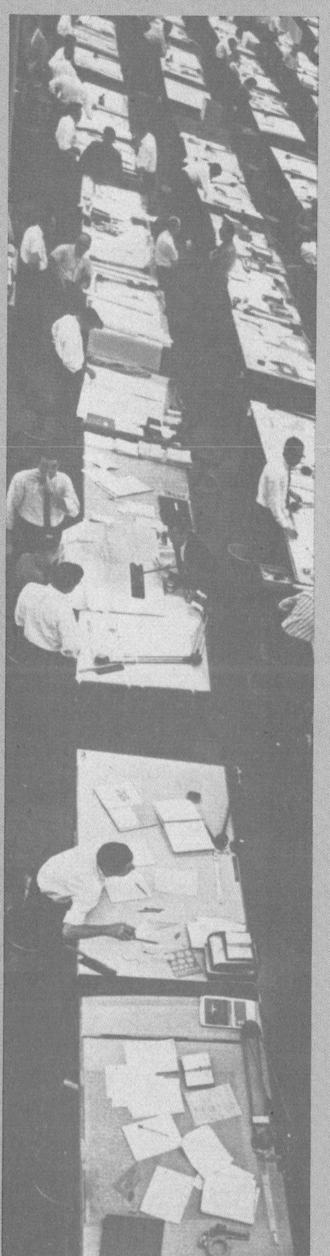

Although Americans seem to have a commitment to work, work does not always bring satisfaction. People work for reasons other than money—to fill time, to give life a purpose, to confirm self-worth. Prolonged unemployment is hard on people; it shows up in anxieties, generalized hostilities, and even physical symptoms such as loss of sexual drive. Most Americans prefer working. In one survey, 80 percent of those who replied said that even if they inherited enough to retire, they would continue to work, a fact confirmed by studies showing that people with increased incomes do not work less. In effect, the individual labor supply curve is not backward-bending, but rather has a vertical region.

Paradoxically, the expectations created by such a strong belief in work may lead to job dissatisfaction. This is at its highest among people who work in a hierarchical structure with little autonomy, little chance for advancement, and heavy personal financial responsibilities. The symbol of this is the assembly line, but only 2 percent of the work force is employed there; some studies, in fact, indicate dissatisfaction is higher among white-collar workers. Such conclusions are still not accepted by all; an HEW study, *Work in America,* which concluded that there was alienation among the American labor force, was promptly denounced by many.*

The job blahs are in part a consequence of the reduction of work into simple, easily mastered tasks. Such specialization increased productivity when it was first introduced, but when carried to an extreme, boredom and decreasing productivity may set in. One group of management consultants discovered that the office workers they studied were producing at about 55 percent of their potential. Allowing greater autonomy can bring payoffs in better work: At Travelers Insurance, one experiment in consolidating and varying tasks produced a 26 percent increase in productivity and a 24 percent decrease in absenteeism.

One economic incentive to increase job commitment is a profit-sharing plan. But unions look askance at profit sharing because they feel it makes workers part of management and limits increases in pay to a measure manipulated by management and not always reflecting increased productivity. However, if profit-sharing plans could be tied closely to worker productivity, as suggested by *Work in America,* they would allow workers to share directly in the fruits of their labors.

* Harold Shepherd et al., *Work in America: Report of a Special Task Force to the Secretary of Health, Education, and Welfare* (Cambridge, Mass.: MIT, 1973).

Elliott Erwitt, Magnum Photos

where at any time." Because the government has no profit motive to keep costs down, unions have greater leverage to exact demands from a government fearful of public outcry over the loss of potential services. Furthermore, there is a fine line between collective bargaining and political influence. It may be one thing for teachers to strike over pay and another thing for them to strike over per pupil allotments. As voters, the public employees have a further weapon against a stubborn government official. For these reasons, governments have maintained laws against strikes by public employees, with penalties for those who defy the ban.

Obviously, prohibitions do not always work. Today, the search is on for flexible, effective means to avert strikes and to overcome the difficulties of collective bargaining in the public sector. Many states and cities have had no guidelines to govern behavior toward unions, and many officials have little familiarity with the array of tools that could bring out areas of agreement and conciliation between the sides. The way in which this challenge is met may change the way in which collective bargaining is viewed. ". . . the right to resort to economic warfare has greatest prominence among those who regard collective bargaining as a marketing procedure, involving the sale of labor services. In this view the right not to contract is supreme. By contrast, if one looks upon collective bargaining as a system of group government or joint management pertaining to the employment relationship, the strike and the lockout cease to be essential. It is still possible for each party to influence the other by other methods."[5]

5 George H. Hildebrand, "The Public Sector," in *Frontiers of Collective Bargaining*, ed. John H. Dunlop and Neil W. Chamberlain (New York: Harper & Row, 1967), p. 151.

SUMMARY

1 Increased wages and fringe benefits are certainly important goals of labor unions but they are not the only goals. Labor unions seek various objectives, and often trade-offs are involved in choosing among them. For many unions, the level of union membership is a very important objective. And today, the issue of industrial justice is assuming great significance.

2 Unions can attempt to raise wages in one of several ways. Attempting to restrict the supply of labor is one approach. It is an especially common tactic among craft unions, whose members possess a particular skill. Higher wages can be imposed when a union is able to control nearly all available workers in an industry. Large industrial unions often possess this kind of market power. Finally, unions can attempt to increase wages by affecting the demand for labor, either by raising productivity or by increasing the demand for the goods the workers produce.

3 The unionized segment of the labor force receives wages some 10 to 15 percent higher than the nonunionized segment, although this gap has been declining in recent years. Data indicate that, contrary to popular belief, the wage gains achieved by unions have not come out of corporate profits. Several studies have suggested that the higher wages enjoyed by union members may be at the expense of nonunionized workers. It is also possible to explain the gap between union and nonunion wages by the fact that typically unions have organized workers in highly profitable and growing industries, where wage scales were high even before unionization.

4 Collective bargaining is a continuous process of determining wages, benefits, working conditions, and other policies. Negotiation of a contract involves a process of bluff and acumen to find areas of agreement without sacrificing one's own

interests. Even after the contract is signed, disagreements may occur; these are dealt with through grievance procedures. A strike is a means of changing the bargaining relationship to force an agreement; its costs are part of having a system of collective bargaining. Deadlocks may be resolved through the use of a neutral negotiator, either with the power to force a settlement (arbitration) or without it (mediation).

5 The system of collective bargaining has been shaped by governmental controls. Until 1842, courts did not recognize unions as legal, viewing them instead as illegal groups in restraint of trade. The Clayton Act of 1914 exempted unions from the antitrust laws, but it was not until the New Deal that unions received active federal protection. The Wagner Act of 1935, the Magna Carta of labor, forbade unfair labor practices and established the National Labor Relations Board. Following World War II, government intervened to curb certain union practices, primarily through the Taft-Hartley Act.

6 Today the traditional sources of union membership are no longer growing. The public sector has become an area for organizing, raising the issue of whether the unique responsibilities of the government permit the ultimate weapon of collective bargaining, the strike.

SUGGESTED READINGS

Bloom, Gordon F., and **Herbert R. Northrup.** *Economics of Labor Relations.* 6th ed. Homewood, Ill: Richard D. Irwin, 1969.

Bowen, William G., ed. *Labor and the National Economy.* New York: W. W. Norton, 1965.

McConnell, Campbell R. *Perspectives on Wage Determination.* New York: McGraw-Hill, 1970.

Marx, Herbert L., Jr., ed. *Collective Bargaining for Public Employees.* New York: H. W. Wilson, 1969.

Reynolds, Lloyd G. *Labor Economics and Labor Relations.* 5th ed. Englewood Cliffs, N.J.: Prentice-Hall, 1970.

QUESTIONS

1 Review
   a. types of union objectives,
   b. ways in which unions seek to increase wages,
   c. the success of unions in improving the employment conditions of members,
   d. the process of collective bargaining,
   e. major legislation affecting unions,
   f. efforts to unionize workers in the public sector.

2 As the expiration date for an existing labor contract approaches, the union generally seeks to maintain or improve the solidarity of its membership. In this attempt, the union may be seeking to affect the elasticity of supply of labor. In what way? Why?

3 Edward Chamberlin has argued that "monopoly wages, like monopoly prices,

are paid in the end by the public . . ."* Under what circumstances could you argue that the increased costs would be passed on to the consumer? What are the implications for the danger of cost-push inflation?

4 How would you describe the prospects for success of a union of migrant farmworkers in raising wages and improving working conditions? Consider the ability of the union to attract membership, the elasticity of demand for agricultural products, ability to restrict other sources of cheap labor, and so forth.

5 Suppose that a commentator argues that featherbedding is not such a bad practice because the price eventually paid by the consumer would be paid in other ways. Is he right? Why or why not? What about the short run versus the long run?

6 A union organizer points out that unionization is quite difficult in those industries composed of large numbers of small establishments. What factors might contribute to this difficulty? How might unions try to overcome these problems? Do you see any evidence that they are trying to penetrate these industries?

7 There is considerable reluctance on the part of many public employees such as teachers and welfare workers to resort to a strike. Why do you think this is the case? Would you expect less reluctance on the part of workers who do not deal directly with customers?

8 Though unions frequently try to protect workers from layoffs due to innovation, could you argue that unions themselves may have contributed to technological unemployment? How?

9 Assume that a union has been successful in increasing productivity and shifting the marginal product curve to the right. Is it likely that the workers would reap the entire benefit of the increase? Why or why not? What factors would determine the way in which those gains are distributed between wages and profits?

10 Though unions in the steel and automobile industries may actually be bargaining with oligopolies, they may feel as though they are dealing with a monopoly. Why?

* Edward H. Chamberlin, "Can Union Power Be Curbed?" in *Readings in Economics*, 6th ed., ed. Paul A. Samuelson (New York: McGraw-Hill, 1970), p. 250.

CHAPTER
34
POVERTY

Affluence rather than poverty is the exception in most societies. Since the beginning of recorded history, most societies have been structured as aristocracies—a handful of very wealthy people at the top surrounded by literally starving masses. In El Salvador, for example, the distribution of income is still such that 10 percent of the population receives 45 to 50 percent of the income; the remaining 90 percent make do with about 50 percent of the income. Even in a country like India that has more equal income distribution (95 percent of the nation gets 80 percent of the income), per capita income is so low that malnutrition is a constant presence and many people have no permanent shelter.

"That is India," we say—we, the well-fed, middle-class, who contribute to CARE and feel comfortable that the United States has a foreign aid program to alleviate some of the hard-core poverty existing in much of the nonindustrialized world. But it came as a rude shock to many Americans during the 1960s to discover that despite the affluence of the United States there is poverty here as well as in India and Latin America—a poverty that is particularly heartbreaking and senseless in a nation that prides itself on its record of economic growth. In this chapter we look for an explanation for poverty in the United States, why it exists, and what we have done and can do to try to eliminate it.

We know something of the economic theory underlying the distribution of income—why physicians receive higher pay than janitors. We have also seen, however, that marginal productivity does not always determine income distribution in a just fashion. There is ample evidence today that the actual structure of wages and salaries for certain groups departs substantially from the theoretical model of marginal productivity. Customary social restrictions—such as those against women and the elderly—and overt discrimination further aggravate the disparities of income distribution. In the United States, as Table 4-2 in Chapter 4 indicates, the most glaring disparities continue to exist between the incomes of whites and nonwhites. Despite the recent civil rights laws and court decisions affirming the political and social equality of these groups, the facts remain that the percentage of nonwhite households afflicted by poverty is three times that of white households, that the unemployment rate of nonwhites is almost twice that of whites, and that the level of education of nonwhites lags far behind that of whites.

Opening photo by Charles Gatewood, Magnum

Until the last decade, economic theorists as well as policy-makers in the United States were loath to consider poverty as a separate problem. They assumed that maintaining a high level of economic growth, thereby eliminating unemployment, would wipe out poverty as well. Unfortunately, this approach has proven to be overly simplistic. The poor are sometimes the victims rather than the beneficiaries of economic progress.

DISTRIBUTION OF WEALTH AND INCOME

Historically, the income of the poorest 20 percent of the U.S. population has averaged only 4 to 5 percent of total national income (Table 34-1). This discrepancy can be partially explained by the unequal distribution of wealth in the country. Indeed, differences in personal abilities (theoretically, the marginal productivity of labor) do not account for differences in income so much as the differences in property (land and capital) owned by various individuals. It is quite clear that unequal ownership of wealth is a prime source of unequal income distribution. It is startling to learn that 96 percent of all corporate stock in the United States is owned by only 20 percent of all families and that 1 percent owns 61 percent of this stock. Fully half the wealth in the United States, not counting residences, is controlled by 5 percent of the population.

How has such tremendous wealth been accumulated by so relatively few? Often, it has been through plain luck. Two hundred, one hundred, or ten years ago, someone discovered some natural resource or invested in some likely enterprise, assuring the wealth of his descendants ever since. Sometimes ingenuity or perseverance played a role, sometimes

TABLE 34-1 Income Distribution (percentage, by household)

Quintile	1929	1935–1936	1944	1955	1967	1972
Lowest	12.5	4.1	4.9	4.8	4.5	4.2
Second		9.2	10.9	12.2	10.5	10.5
Third	13.8	14.1	16.2	17.7	17.6	16.8
Fourth	19.3	20.9	22.2	23.7	24.7	24.6
Highest	54.4	51.7	45.8	41.6	42.7	43.9
Total	100.0	100.0	100.0	100.0	100.0	100.0
Top 5 percent	30.0	26.5	20.7	16.8	15.3	16.1

Has there been a trend toward income equality? Between 1929 and 1972, the lowest two-fifths of the families increased their share of total personal income from 12.5 percent to 14.7 percent. This is not a very impressive gain, and there has even been a decline in their share from 17.0 percent in 1955. Furthermore, since a 40 percent share would indicate income equality, the 14.7 percent share of these two groups is quite low. The lowest fifth has been losing ground steadily since 1944 because its income has been increasing at a slower rate than the income of the other groups. The share of the top 5 percent has declined considerably since 1929, as has that of the highest fifth, although the latter has increased its share of total personal income since 1955.

SOURCE: U.S. Bureau of the Census, *Current Population Reports*, Series P-60, No. 89.

crookedness. In any case, individual wealth today is, for the most part, inherited rather than earned. This serves as one explanation for the pattern of income distribution in the United States since the turn of the century. While the absolute amounts of income received by the rich, the not-so-rich, and the poor have risen, their proportion has remained virtually unchanged.

Some respected economists support the status quo of unequal income distribution on grounds that such inequality is necessary to assure a sufficient rate of capital formation. People with high incomes have a high propensity to save, and these savings are essential to capital formation. Since a high ratio of capital to labor is also a means to increased productivity and higher income for workers, an unequal distribution of income ultimately benefits even people with relatively low incomes. There is, however, conflicting evidence as to whether unequal income distribution is indeed necessary for an adequate rate of capital formation. In Norway, for example, great strides have been made toward a more equal distribution of income, and yet a very high rate of capital formation has been maintained since World War II. This does not mean that private savings have necessarily remained high; public capital formation plays a larger role in the Norwegian economy, for instance.

The unequal distribution of wealth may account for differences in income but need not account for poverty. We can distinguish between inequality and poverty. After all, most people who are not wealthy are still not poor. Even if there is a highly unequal distribution of income (even greater than that in the United States), the people at the poorest end of the scale may not be in want. Why, under these circumstances, should it matter that a tiny percentage is "fabulously" wealthy? The answer is, of course, that in the United States today the people at the bottom of the ladder *are* poor and *are* in need of basic necessities. It is the contention of many, particularly the radical economists (see Chapter 35), that the elimination of poverty will necessitate the elimination of all forms of inherited wealth because wealth forms a power base to perpetuate inequality.

Another argument sometimes advanced in favor of income redistribution is that to persons with low incomes money has a higher marginal utility than to people with high incomes. Therefore, if society takes a dollar away from the rich and gives it to the poor, the utility to the poor will have increased by a

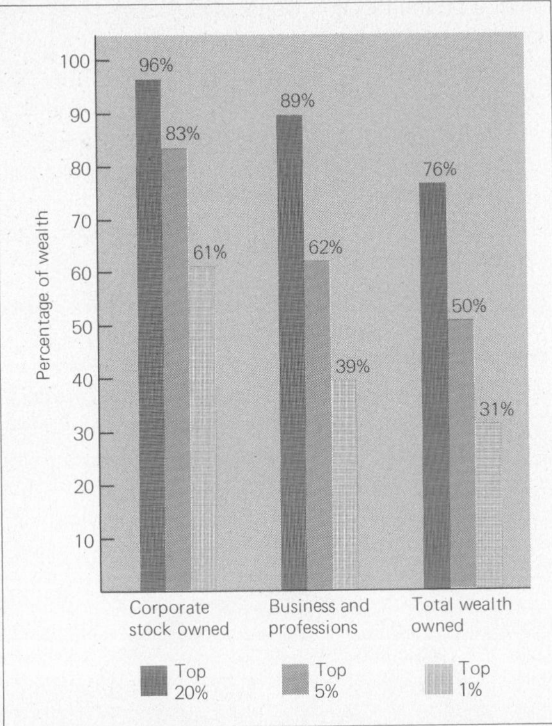

FIGURE 34-1 TOTAL WEALTH OWNED BY WEALTH GROUPS, 1962 An alternate way of looking at the distribution of resources is to examine holdings of wealth. Inequality of wealth is much more pronounced than inequality of incomes alone. Here we have omitted homes owned, which constitutes the third component of total wealth owned and would broaden the distribution appreciably. That the top 1 percent of the population owns such a huge share of certain resources is dramatic proof of the vast differences in economic well-being in the United States.

SOURCE: Based on data from Frank Ackerman *et al.*, "Income Distribution in the United States," *Review of Radical Political Economics*, Summer 1971, pp. 22–25.

greater amount than the utility to the rich will have decreased. There will have been a net increase in utility to society as a whole. The problem with this argument is that utility is a purely subjective concept. We cannot really know that the person who earns $10,000 does not get as much satisfaction from spending his last dollar as the man who earns $2000. Perhaps his greater income has enabled him to cultivate more expensive tastes and habits, and his personal loss in utility will be just as great as the gain of the poor.

On the other hand, it can be argued that even the wealthy have—or should have—*some* interest in a redistribution of income. Humanitarian reasons aside, simple self-interest would dictate this. Wide income disparities naturally produce envy and may cause serious social unrest. The control of such unrest puts an additional burden on society as a whole (in the form of increased taxes, which are, at least in theory, borne more by the rich than by the middle class); if the social unrest grows to such proportions that it cannot be suppressed, it leads to violent acts against the property of the rich and perhaps even revolution.

DIMENSIONS OF POVERTY

Poverty in present-day America is not what it is in India or even what it was here during the Great Depression. Some experts have suggested that all poverty is necessarily relative—that a person who is poor here might be considered rich in India and that a person who earned a comfortable $3000 in 1920 would live in poverty on that income today. Taking such relativity into account, some economists have suggested that any household receiving less than half the median income in the economy at any given time should be considered poor.

Government authorities in the United States, however, have used absolute standards to define poverty. Thus, when the Census Bureau estimates that 13 percent of all Americans live in poverty, it refers to a poverty cutoff line at $4275 per year for a nonfarm family of four and somewhat less for a four-member farm family. This standard has risen by some $1000 over the past decade to allow for inflation, but it has not risen as much as the overall standard of living (determined by the increase in per capita income).

These figures were determined by estimating minimum subsistence needs, including a minimum food plan established by the Department of Agriculture. This level of income should provide a family with indoor plumbing, a double bed for every two family members, enough utensils to allow the entire family to eat at one time, and other minimum essentials.

However, most of us will be quick to note the obvious omissions. For example, the government experts have neglected to include dental care and have allowed for very little medical care in general. Little provision has been made for fresh fruit, vegetables, and meat in the high-carbohydrate diet established for those at the threshold level. There is no allowance whatever for entertainment, and very little for clothing, even for school-age children. Including even minimal costs for these items would raise the official poverty line and, of course, the number recognized as living in poverty. In 1969, for example, the Department of Labor estimated a "moderate but adequate" income for a family of four to be $9100, which was just a little less than the median income then.

If we accept the $4275 cutoff, we can perhaps better grasp the magnitude of the poverty problem in the United States today. If income is distributed so unevenly that more than 25 million people (equal to the combined population of New York and New Jersey) are considered poor, then maybe it is time to take steps to restructure the pattern of distribution. Some economists argue that there is no reason that poverty must continue in the United States, that if priorities were shifted poverty could be eradicated in a relatively short time. But the mere fact that this has not been done tends to support the argument that economic forces are much stronger than any government policy and that whatever distribution of income exists is basically unalterable.

This argument is supported by research into public attitudes toward poverty. There is little sympathy for people at the low end of the income scale. Rather than viewing them as victims of circumstances beyond their control, they are considered lazy, immoral, and even criminal. People who are neither poor nor rich will tend to moralize downward, not upward, on the social scale. They are quick to condemn the apparent promiscuity of welfare mothers while condoning and even envying the well-publicized escapades of the rich. They will demand punishment of welfare chiselers, but be unmoved by the manipulations of price fixers. The man unable to hold a job is considered "worse" than the landlord unwilling to fix a heating system. Studies have shown that welfare chiseling amounts to a mere fraction of the total money lost by the government through income tax evasion by the rich, yet "welfare Cadillacs" are of far greater public concern. It is not that the public is unaware of the transgressions of the rich, but these deeds are judged differently. A stigma is attached to economic failure whereas success is viewed with respect.

Who Are the Poor?

More than half the people classified as poor receive no income from work at all. These are the old, the disabled, the children—who clearly have not the

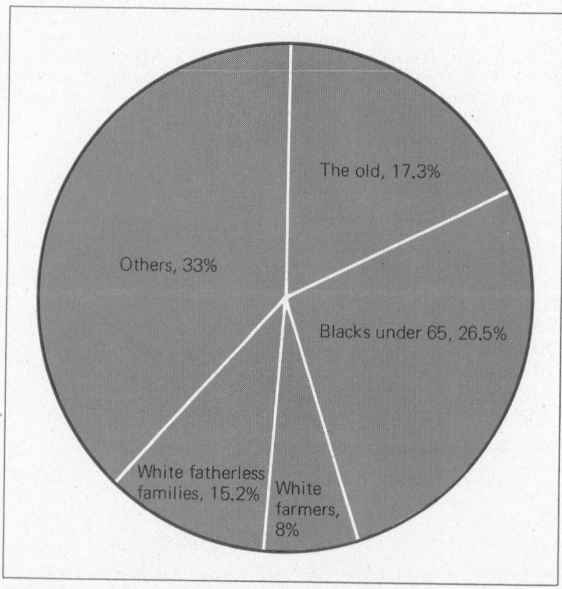

FIGURE 34-2 POVERTY GROUPS IN THE UNITED STATES, 1972 In 1972, the poverty level for a nonfarm family of four was $4275. There were 5,075,000 families (representing over 25 million people) whose incomes fell below this level. Some 29 percent of all black families and only 7.1 percent of all white families have incomes below the poverty level. Thus, those who are black and/or old constitute nearly one-half of the poor. In addition, families headed by women and rural families tend to have high incidences of poverty. About one-third of the poor do not fall into these categories. Many live in depressed areas, some have low intelligence, and most are poorly educated.

SOURCE: U.S. Bureau of the Census, *Current Population Reports*, Series P-60, No. 88, June 1973.

physical ability to work—and the mothers of dependent children for whom working outside the home may create more financial problems than it solves.

The majority of the remaining poor do not participate fully in the economy due to lack of training and education, racial and sex discrimination, geographical immobilities, and similar reasons. Seven million are members of families whose head is underemployed or works irregularly, and 5 million are members of families whose head does work full time and is simply not paid enough to raise the family above the poverty level. There is also a high incidence of poverty among farm families.

Farm Families The plight of many farmers, caught in the transition from an agricultural to an industrial society, continues today. Despite massive migration from the farms since 1945, over 50 percent of the farms had receipts of less than $5000 in 1973. Moving off the farm, however, may not be the answer, since as we saw in Chapter 20, migration to the city may simply move the families into the ranks of the urban poor.

Inner-City Families Studies of urban dwellers have shown that the more affluent people are, the farther removed from the city's center they live. For whatever reason, the poor cluster around the central commercial district and get a chance to move to surrounding areas only when the middle class moves still farther out. Chapter 20 on urban problems has shown that overcrowding and lack of income result in the decay of the central cities, which in recent years has become a national problem. Government programs to reshape the urban environment have had limited success. Generally they have not benefited the poor as much as other segments of society. Razing slum housing and erecting middle-income dwellings in which the poor cannot afford to live has concentrated poverty still further. Public housing projects in middle-income areas have run into stiff opposition from residents there. A more promising approach has been to give rent subsidies to low-income families, who then can afford to move to better neighborhoods or improve their living quarters. But because of the influx of poor people from other areas, living conditions in the inner cities on the whole seem to be getting worse.

FIGURE 34-3 POVERTY OF THE AGED One of the saddest reflections on our society is the neglect of the elderly. They constitute a major poverty group, which will increase considerably over the next few decades as a growing percentage of the U.S. population reaches 65. The median income for those over 65 is under $2000. Over 85 percent of those over 65 receive social security payments, which average less than $1500 annually; less than a third of the aged receive retirement pensions, most of which provide considerably less than social security. Contrary to popular opinion, the inadequate savings of the elderly poor are due to low lifetime incomes rather than to profligacy when money was being earned.

U.S.D.A. Photo

The Young, the Aged, and the Ill Mostly because they cannot work and have no independent income, the young, the aged, and the ill have always been more susceptible to poverty. Discrimination by employers against old people, pressures from unions for an earlier retirement age, and restrictions by the social security program on the income recipients may earn limit the income-producing activities of the elderly. Today, just over 17 percent of all poor people are aged 65 and over. Primarily because they are dependents, the young also suffer. On the average, poor families have more children than well-to-do families. No wonder, then, that about 40 percent of the poor are children under 18 years of age. Finally, the incidence of disease is higher among the poor. Ignorance and unsanitary conditions breed illness, and lack of money often rules out adequate treatment and sufficient time for recuperation. A grave illness in a poor family has much more disastrous consequences than in a family that is well off.

The Physically and Mentally Disabled Persons with handicaps number about 5 million in the United States, including about 400,000 in mental hospitals. Of the physically disabled, only about one-third will eventually be rehabilitated and join the labor force. Many of the rest live on disability and other types of insurance.

Families Headed by Women This is one of the largest groups among the poor. The strains of living in destitution cause poor families to break up at a higher rate than other families do. Desertion is far more common than divorce, usually leaving the mother to provide for the children. Over one-half of the black families and one-quarter of the white poor families are headed by women.

Nonwhites These figures reinforce what most other statistics also show: that for many nonwhites, poverty is a way of life. Nonwhites make up over one-eighth of the total population but one-third of the poor population. More than half of all nonwhite children today are growing up in poverty. We shall take a closer look at this group in the next chapter, which examines discrimination.

Persons without Market Power The poor usually are not union members. They usually are not in a position to be licensed as barbers, beauticians, or taxi drivers. Institutional barriers prevent them from obtaining a degree of market power that might help them escape poverty. Thus, even the 32 percent of all poor who work full time do so on the fringes of the economy. They are easily replaced and do not have institutions protecting their interests.

WHAT'S BEING DONE ABOUT POVERTY

A society that does nothing about the poverty in its midst can be sure that a private form of income redistribution will develop. It is called the Robin Hood Principle or, more baldly, theft. Since the thief is assumed to have fewer economic resources than his victims, mugging, burglary, and so on serve to redistribute income. If the victim is insured, the loss is shared by those who have made premium payments to the insurance company, and theft insurance becomes a kind of voluntary taxation designed to distribute the burden of reallocating wealth to an economically deprived segment of our society. In the United States, the losses from burglary, robbery, larceny, and auto theft amounted to $600 million in 1967 alone.

Of course, there are negative economic aspects to this approach, let alone the social and political implications. If a thief is apprehended, there will be no redistribution of income and there will actually be increased costs to society (court costs, imprisonment, and so on). Few societies have been willing to rely on this system alone. Usually the government intervenes. Using taxation, the government may take proportionately more from the rich. It may then redistribute income or goods and services to the poor.

Taxation as a Form of Income Redistribution

What constitutes an ideal system of taxation? In the United States, the federal income tax is based on the principle that government expenses should be divided among the people based on their ability to pay. Moreover, the tax system that was established in the 1930s was intended to effect a certain degree of income redistribution. On the surface we have a progressive income tax system, with marginal rates ranging up to 70 percent (before 1954 it was over 90 percent) on earned income. However, many people at the high end of the income scale do not depend on work for their income, and income from property is taxed more favorably than are wages and salaries. In addition, numerous legal loopholes allow various politically powerful interest groups to whittle down their tax burdens still further. These loopholes are usually not relevant to the average taxpayer, and taking advantage of them requires expensive legal services—something that only the wealthy can afford.

According to the Brookings Institution, the federal tax structure has actually become more regressive in the last decade. Their study cites figures showing that the payroll tax has virtually doubled as a source of total tax revenue between 1960 and 1970 (increasing from 16 percent to 30 percent), while corporate income-tax revenue has declined from 23 percent to 14 percent during the same period. The study goes on to state that, particularly since 1970, changes in the federal tax structure have "dramatically increased the burden on those with very low wages." Taxes on the poor are heavy, and the tax system as a whole does little to alter the very unequal distribution of pre-tax income.

That income redistribution through taxation is indeed negligible can be seen from Table 34-2. In low-income brackets federal taxes cause only a small percentage increase in disposable income, while in high-income brackets federal taxes decrease disposable income only slightly. In fact, the disparity of income distribution has not been reduced much since 1929, as Table 34-1 showed.

State and Local Taxes Because most state and local taxes are taxes on consumption and property, their effect is regressive. A flat percentage tax on sales, for instance, affects the poor as well as the rich, but hurts the poor more because it takes a larger share of their income. While the poor pay less in income tax, it has been estimated that sales, excise, and property taxes amount to an average 27 percent of incomes under $2000 annually and to 28 percent of incomes in the $2000–$3000 bracket. This is a sizable burden and counteracts whatever income redistribution has been achieved through other forms of taxation.

Government Antipoverty Programs

The tax system provides little relief to the poor, but specific government programs have been established to eliminate poverty from American life. We know from photographs of bread lines during the Depression and of turn-of-the-century immigrants that there has always been poverty in the United States. However, it was not until the civil rights movement focused on black poverty, TV and newsmagazine documentaries vividly depicted destitution in Appalachia and political campaigners spoke of millions of Americans going to bed hungry every night

TABLE 34-2 The Effect of Federal Taxation (percentage distribution)

Income quintile	Total income before taxes and transfers	Total income after income and payroll taxes	Cash transfers received	Total income after taxes and transfers
Lowest	1.7	1.8	40.2	6.3
Second	6.6	7.0	26.8	9.1
Third	14.5	14.8	13.1	14.6
Fourth	24.1	24.4	10.3	22.8
Highest	53.1	51.9	9.6	47.1
Total	100.0	100.0	100.0	100.0
Total dollar amount, in billions	$772.1	$620.4	$ 80.1	$700.5

Without transfer payments, the federal tax system does little to redistribute income. The payroll tax, which constituted 30 percent of the fiscal 1974 revenues compared with only 16 percent in 1960, has made the system more regressive.

NOTE: Data in Tables 34-1 and 34-2 are not directly comparable.

SOURCE: Edward Fried et al., *Setting National Priorities: The 1974 Budget*, © 1973 by the Brookings Institution, Washington, D.C., p. 50. Details may not add up to totals because of rounding.

that poverty became, in the early 1960s, a subject of national concern.

Previously, various amounts of money had been spent by the government to ease the plight of the poor, but no attempts had been made to attack the root causes of poverty. Finally, in 1964, Congress passed the Economic Opportunity Act and the "war on poverty" began. The Act established the Office of Economic Opportunity to administer such programs as the Job Corps, VISTA, loans to small businesses through the SBA, and various community action programs. These called for "maximum feasible participation" by the poor themselves in the planning and administration, but a major problem was that this participation never materialized and was never effectively sought by the government planners. In addition, much emphasis was placed on manpower and development programs, but given the overwhelming percentage of elderly and children within the poverty group, this approach seems rather beside the point. From the very beginning, too, the war on poverty was handicapped by a severe shortage of money.

In effect, many of the government programs did not address themselves to the causes of poverty, and there appeared to be little concern with either the efficiency or the equity of distributing available funds.

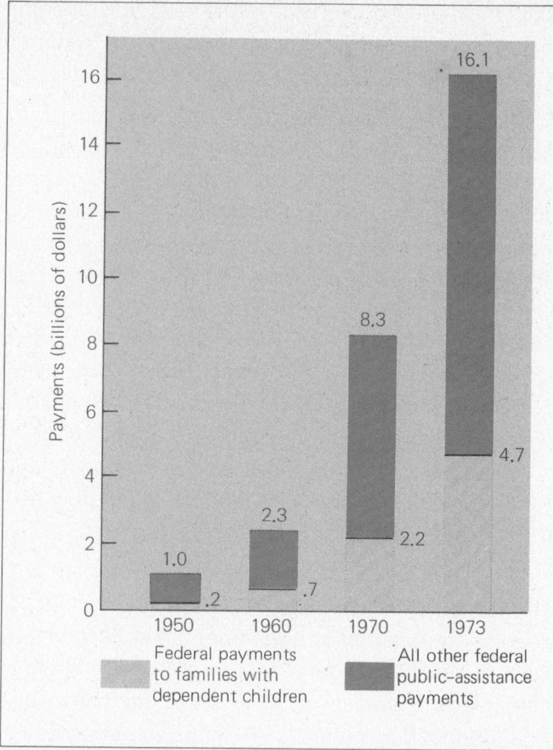

FIGURE 34-4 FEDERAL PUBLIC ASSISTANCE PAYMENTS, INCLUDING PAYMENTS TO FAMILIES WITH DEPENDENT CHILDREN (Billions of dollars) Public assistance payments have increased drastically over the past 13 years. During this time there has been a continuing migration of largely black, rural poor to the northern cities after they have been displaced by farm mechanization. The inauguration of Medicaid in the early 1960s and the 1969–70 recession further added to the relief rolls.

SOURCE: Charles Schultze et al., *Setting National Priorities: The 1973 Budget*, © 1972 by the Brookings Institution, Washington, D.C., p. 176.

Transfer Payments *Transfer payments* is a collective term for funds that are transferred to people who meet certain criteria. For instance, social insurance programs provide unemployment, disability, and old-age benefits. Well over half of the federal cash transfers are made under these programs. By their very nature, however, such transfer payments are primarily available to those with some record of participation in the labor force and to many people who are not poor.

The federal government has joined with the states to fund **categorical assistance programs** aimed at the nonemployable, who are even more likely to be classified as poor. These programs include old-age assistance for persons who do not qualify for Social Security, aid to dependent children, and aid to the blind. In 1970, about 8 million people were assisted by these programs, but, typically, the benefits received were too small to lift these people above the poverty line.

If a person is destitute and cannot qualify for social insurance or for categorical relief programs, he or she may become eligible for general public assistance. General assistance is financed and administered entirely by state governments, and, as a result, the benefits vary widely. However, if a person is poor but works, his relief payment is often reduced by the amount he has earned. This constitutes a 100 percent tax on income and is obviously a strong disincentive to work at all. It also entails a loss to society, which forgoes the additional product that could be produced if more poor people could be encouraged to work.

How far do transfer payments go toward lifting low-income people above the poverty line? Benjamin Okner of Brookings has estimated that in 1966 the pretransfer poverty gap stood at $22 billion and 15.2 million families had incomes below the poverty line.[1] Although $18 billion was transferred to the poor that year, the poverty gap after transfers stood at $9.9 billion and 10 million families still remained in poverty. The reason is that for the 5.2 million families removed from poverty, the poverty gap was overfilled by nearly $6 billion. Red tape and ignorance as well as lack of funds prevent the neediest from receiving help. In 1966, 4.2 million poor families received no transfer payments at all.

Subsidies in Kind As an alternative measure, it has been suggested that low-income families be subsidized in kind rather than through cash payments. Government could provide goods and services to the poor free or below cost. To a certain extent, this already happens. The federal Medicare program and some states' Medicaid programs reimburse hospitals and doctors for health care administered to the poor. Public housing projects accommodate low-income families at rentals below full cost. The food stamp program, ineffective as it is, is also a subsidy in kind, as is the lunch program for poor school children.

These programs have been criticized as depriving poor consumers of their freedom of choice, thereby reducing the utility of the money spent, and being wasteful. But we must remember that consumption by one family has effects on other people. The amounts spent on medical care and education affect not only the welfare of one household, but to a degree the welfare of the entire neighborhood and even of future generations. Many would argue that it is in the public interest to channel consumption into such socially desirable areas. Subsidy in kind accomplishes this.

Another argument for such subsidies is that some markets do not operate efficiently in meeting consumer demand, especially when the consumers are poor and powerless. In housing for example, inner-city residents might well express their demand for better tenements. But even if they have the necessary incomes to back up such a demand, it is unlikely that any slum-clearing project will get under way. Financing, relocation, transportation facilities, and the like must be planned and coordinated. In these areas, then, government has a valid role to play. The problems of administering these programs have been enormous, however. This constitutes the greatest criticism of the subsidy-in-kind approach.

The Welfare Mess

The problem of welfare has surely been tackled but scarcely solved. The costs of poverty—human and economic—are recognized; poverty constitutes a large drag on GNP and may waste human lives. But the cures for poverty have proved neither efficient nor equitable.

As we have seen, neither federal nor state and local taxes redistribute income to any great extent. State and local taxes are the most regressive, but as the payroll tax grows more important, the federal tax grows less progressive.

Transfer payments do constitute an important source of income to those in the deepest poverty. But these payments vary from state to state, so that a poor person in Mississippi receives AFDC benefits of $14.41 a week while a sister in Boston receives $95.01 a week. In addition, many poor families are headed by wage earners whose income is insufficient to raise the household above the poverty line. Many of these families receive no benefits whatsoever. On the other hand, as Table 34-2 indicates, cash transfers go to all levels of society; even the richest fifth receives 9.6 percent of all transfers. By far the largest programs are Social Security, other retirement programs, and public as-

1 Benjamin Okner, "Transfer Payments: Their Distribution and Role in Reducing Poverty," in *Redistributing to the Rich and the Poor: The Grants Economics of Income Distribution*, eds. Kenneth E. Boulding and Martin Pfaff (Belmont, Calif.: Wadsworth, 1972), pp. 62–77.

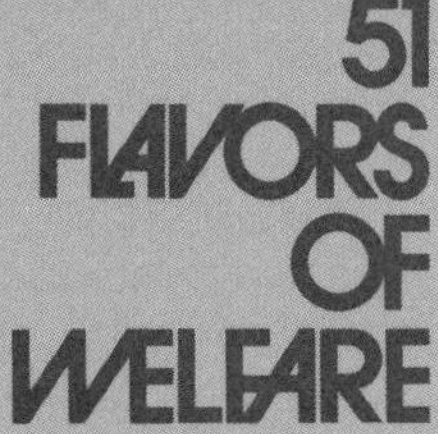

51 FLAVORS OF WELFARE

Administration of the various public assistance programs has become a nightmare. In 1972, welfare recipients alone numbered about 15 million nationwide; of these, almost 11 million were members of families with dependent children. California and New York showed a dramatic lead over all other states in the number of indigent as well as in the amount of payments made to them. No wonder, then, that in these two states efforts began in the early 1970s to tighten the dispensation of welfare funds, particularly to reduce welfare fraud. But these efforts have not really struck at the heart of the administrative problems—the varying standards and the maze of programs.

Whereas an efficient system could be expected to give equal treatment to people in similar economic circumstances regardless of their place of residence or other demographic criteria and to keep administrative costs within reasonable limits, the existing system is a labyrinth of overlapping and often conflicting programs. A recent study indicates that more than one-fourth of households receiving some kind of public assistance were enrolled in two or more programs. In the early 1970s, there were 51 separate programs with varying eligibility standards, and new ones were being added. No wonder, then, that the mechanics of welfare administration have become so monstrous that paperwork alone threatens to smother the system. Processing a welfare applicant in Atlanta, for instance, requires 27 forms; workers dispensing food stamps in Detroit must cope with 40 different forms. Recipients cannot keep up with the multitude of constantly changing regulations, and neither can caseworkers. It is obvious that the confusion and work load reduce the quality of welfare administration. Working conditions lead to a high staff turnover and inadequate training and supervision, which further impair the effectiveness of the programs.

Thus, added to the uncertainty of the approach to the poverty problem are the structural weaknesses of the present system. They cannot be remedied easily because in most cases they are laid down by law. One must indeed ask if the perpetuation of this system does not guarantee job security to the army of middle-class bureaucrats who administer it more than it guarantees economic security to the poor.

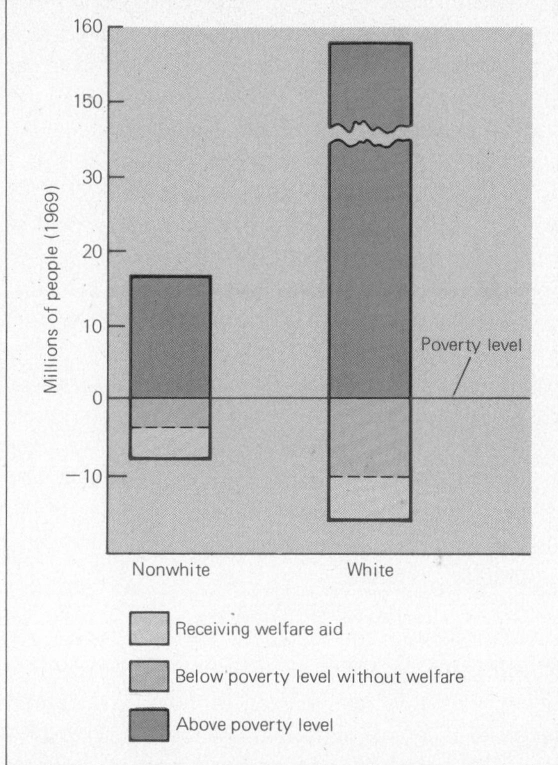

FIGURE 34-5 POVERTY DOES NOT MEAN WELFARE Poverty and welfare do not go hand in hand. About half of the poor in 1969 received no public assistance. Over a third were members of families whose breadwinner worked more than 35 hours a week, 50 to 52 weeks a year, yet could not earn enough to raise the family above the poverty line.

SOURCE: Lester C. Thurow, *The Economics of Poverty and Racial Discrimination* (New York: Joint Council on Economic Education, 1972), p. 6. Reprinted by permission.

sistance to the blind and disabled, which in the 1974 budget amounted to $76.9 billion, compared with $9.6 billion for unemployment and AFDC. These constitute a large and growing part of the federal budget, yet millions remain below the poverty line.

The categorical approach with its proliferation of forms, eligibility standards, and regulations, creates a bewildering array of programs that deters people from knowing what they may receive. In addition, the waste of resources is enormous. The subsidies-in-kind suffer from the fact that they often go to the supplier rather than to the recipient, resulting in a severe rationing in which some people receive public housing or medical care, while others in equal need do not.

Perhaps the most controversial aspect of the current system is the extent to which it reduces the incentive to work. Objections to current practices often come from those who do not recognize that many of the poor do work and that many others do not work because of legitimate disabilities or barriers. But the problem is a crucial one, since any program that pauperizes some members of society makes no sense. There is an inherent tension in providing for an equitable standard of living for all without eliminating work incentives.

ECONOMIC ALTERNATIVES

Economic Growth

If the current methods of attacking the poverty problem are inadequate, what hope is there that poverty will ever be eliminated? Several alternative solutions are possible. The one alternative that most economists point to even today smacks of classical doctrine: General, sustained economic growth will reach even the poor and will raise their incomes without causing undue social and political antagonism. If aggregate demand can be raised to levels at which unemployment and underemployment cease to exist, then at least the working poor—and those willing to work—will be helped.

Since any direct subsidy of poor people always seems to create social and political conflict, some experts have argued that government should simply confine itself to injecting funds into the economy generally—that through the multiplier effect the poor will benefit almost as much as from direct subsidies. Social discord would be avoided. Thus, the argument that in the 1960s the Vietnam War siphoned off funds that otherwise would have been spent on antipoverty programs is rejected with the contention that Congress would not have allocated such funds to combat poverty anyway. In the meantime, however, the economic boom generated by the war expenditures tightened the labor market and substantially eased poverty.

Recent studies indeed indicate that high aggregate demand is especially beneficial to minority groups among which the incidence of poverty is most common. As more and more people are employed, employers will eventually dip into the pool of low-skilled, relatively unproductive workers. Once this happens, the income gains of this group will be especially dramatic. This idea has been strongly supported by data on the economic fluctuations between 1954 and 1966. For a 1 percent gain in white employment in times of economic boom, employment of nonwhites rose 3.3 percent. During recessions, however, these relative gains of nonwhites were erased. Thus, if high demand and employment conditions cannot be sustained, neither will the economically disadvantaged realize permanent gains.

Backwash Thesis While most experts agree that economic growth has a salubrious effect on those at the poorest end of the economic scale, some point out that certain subgroups among the poor are so isolated from society that their condition will not improve as a result of general economic growth. They suggest that special programs are needed to reach this "backwash" element and that such programs will probably have to be devised by social psychologists rather than by economists or politicians.

One need not accept the backwash thesis to realize that full employment will not solve the problem of low-wage employment or unemployment. After all, the reason that many persons who are employed full time are still classified as poor is that their wages are below the poverty level. Consequently, some form of income supplement or wage subsidy is essential if they and their families are to rise above this level.

Radical Perspective

Certain radical critics have argued that wages are not at all the key to eliminating poverty. They cite statistics showing that the higher a person's income, the less it is derived from work—that income from capital underlies most prosperity. They advocate a redistribution of income-producing capital or at least a redistribution of the income derived from capital. A 1966 study showed that nearly all income of under $10,000 annually comes from labor, only half of it in the $20,000 to $50,000 range, one-third in the $50,000 to $100,000 range, and only 15 percent of income in excess of $100,000. If a transfer of income to bring all families to the moderate but adequate living standard of $9100 were to be achieved, it would involve the redistribution of about $119 billion, or roughly 20 percent of total personal income. Since this is also about the proportion of income derived from capital, the equalizing effect of a redistribution of income-producing capital is established. Under the current political system in the United States, however, such a solution cannot be regarded as realistic.

Negative Income Tax

Economists of various ideological hues have agreed for some time that by far the cheapest and most effective substitute for the current welfare mess is some form of negative income tax. Its principle is that the income of all people should be brought to some minimum level and that incentives to increase this income through work should be maintained. The income guarantee need not be at the poverty line; in fact, few proposals advocate the guarantee be set that high. This minimum income is really little different from welfare without the second feature: the marginal tax rate. The traditional welfare program deducts any earnings from the welfare allotment, so that working does not raise the recipient's income. The marginal tax rate is 100 percent; the incentive to work is near zero. But suppose that in addition to the guaranteed income, people earning below a certain level were allowed to keep part of their earnings. The marginal tax rate might be 50 percent and the guarantee $1500. If the recipient earned an additional $1500, he or she could keep $750 of the earnings plus the $1500 guarantee. Disposable income would be $2250. If the recipient earned $3000, the tax would take $1500, exactly offsetting the $1500 allotment and resulting in no taxes, either positive or negative. Above $3000, the traditional form of taxation would begin. Suppose that the program were more generous—a $4000 guarantee and a marginal tax rate of one-third. Then people earning up to $12,000 would be getting some portion of the income guarantee.

The economic advantages of a negative income tax are many. It would be simpler and less costly to administer than the present welfare programs. The program would help the working poor as well as the nonemployable. Depending upon the specific formula, it could provide strong work incentives by allowing the people to retain a substantial percentage of earnings. There would be only a simple income test for eligibility. Fathers would no longer need to abandon their families and there would be no demeaning investigations into morals or lifestyles.

One problem of such a program, however, is that it would not bridge the poverty gap completely—unless the break-even income level is set high enough so that the income floor falls above the poverty line. In addition, to provide suitable work incentives, the rate at which income is supplemented would have to be relatively high. There is a conflict between the two objectives since if the minimum income guarantee is high enough to take care of those who cannot work and the rate at which benefits are reduced is low enough to provide incentives for those who can, the costs will be enormous. The costs of a program with a $4800 minimum and a 50 percent tax rate have been estimated at $27.1 billion, over twice the existing costs of unemployment compensation and AFDC and probably well beyond what Congress could reasonably be expected to pass.[2]

Of course, lowering the minimum guarantee and keeping the 50 percent tax rate would reduce the cost while preserving work incentives. But this would penalize those who cannot work at all. Maintaining the income floor at the poverty cutoff line and increasing the marginal tax rate would solve this dilemma—at the cost of reducing work incentives.

The choice appears clear enough. We cannot keep costs within politically acceptable limits while providing both a decent income to those who cannot work and strong work incentive for those who can, without making the arbitrary distinctions characterizing the present system. Any program of reform will probably have to sacrifice one or more of these objectives.

Family Assistance Plan One compromise between the conflicting objectives is the Nixon plan to revamp the government's approach to poverty, embodied in the Family Assistance Plan. FAP was first submitted to Congress in 1969 and again in 1971, but was left to die in both sessions.

As originally proposed, the plan outlined a "workfare" program with some features of a negative income tax. It would set national standards for welfare disbursements, giving an annual allowance of $1600 to a family of four without any other income. However, this amount could be supplemented through state-run welfare programs. The Nixon plan also would expand the food stamp program and tie it directly to family assistance. Payments beyond the basic $1600 allowance would be structured to maintain incentives to work. The first $720 earned would be left untaxed; after that, benefits would be reduced by 50 cents for each additional dollar earned.

A major feature of the Nixon proposal is its emphasis upon work. All applicants for family assistance, except mothers with preschool children, would have to register with state employment agencies for training or suitable employment, and day care would be provided for mothers with dependent children. Initial cost of the entire program was estimated at $4 billion annually.

The bill passed the House of Representatives twice, but died in the Senate. Liberal critics argued that the proposed level of assistance was much too low and would leave recipients below the poverty line. Conservatives contended that it smacked too much of guaranteed income plans. Nixon himself repudiated this charge by emphasizing its strong work provisions. While it did not go so far as guaranteeing a

2 Edward R. Fried et al., *Setting National Priorities: The 1974 Budget* (Washington, D.C.: Brookings Institution, 1973), p. 83.

job to every American, it called for expanded manpower training programs which would assist at least those of working age. It also proposed that the government assume the cost of relocation for securing employment and of commuting to distant jobs—an undertaking in which the United States has traditionally lagged behind some European countries, notably Great Britain and Sweden.

Outlook

Over the long run, eliminating poverty in the United States will require a combination of sustained economic growth, specific government programs, and a certain amount of income redistribution. If the tool of income redistribution is a negative income tax with a meaningful income floor, there is some real hope of achieving both equity and efficiency. By eliminating the administrative costs of the existing programs, the negative income tax would result in more efficient resource use. An ancillary benefit of a successful negative income tax plan would be a probable reduction of theft and robbery and consequent lower costs in police protection.

Progress may come slowly. Most social legislation in the United States has begun small and gradually expanded. There is no reason to expect that the negative tax, once enacted, will be any different. The initial bill may meet only partially the goals of decent income for those who cannot work, incentives to work for those who can, equitable standards of eligibility, and moderate cost. Costs and work incentives will probably be emphasized most at first, as matters of efficiency usually are.

It is also possible that progress toward income equality may come at some expense to efficiency. Economists point to the burdens created by government interference in the marketplace. If taxes become too steeply progressive, it is said that willingness to work hard or to make risky investments may be profoundly affected. Other programs such as freezing prices and profits or setting minimum wages alter production and employment patterns. Such adjustments necessarily entail some inefficiency in the operation of the economy. Drastic attempts to redistribute income, therefore, may have some undesirable economic effects.

It is clear that many causes of poverty lie outside the realm of economics. The hard core and seemingly hopeless poverty that has evolved in the United States is as much an outgrowth of social discrimination and alienation as of purely economic factors. Therefore, the establishment of a realistic negative income tax containing strong work incentive provisions while extending social service programs would be a giant step in the right direction, but may not be the entire answer, because poverty may be caused not just by lack of income but by conscious exclusion from economic power.

SUMMARY

1 Income distribution in the United States is hardly equal. The poorest fifth receives only 4 to 5 percent of the national income. The distribution of wealth partially accounts for this inequality and for poverty. Some economists support inequality on the grounds that it is necessary for a sufficient level of capital formation. Others argue for redistribution based on the varying utility of money at different income levels. Radicals see wealth as the basis for economic and political power. All would probably agree that sufficiently unequal income distribution will result in social unrest.

2 Poverty may be defined either absolutely or relatively. In the United States, the poverty level is defined by the amount of money required to ensure a minimum level of subsistence rather than by the more relative standard of those below a certain percentage of the median income. Socially, poverty is defined rather un-

sympathetically; the poor bear a stigma and their activities are judged more harshly than similar behavior by the rich.

3 The popular impression of the shiftless poor is not supported by the data. More than half are old, disabled, or under 18. The families of the working poor constitute a large group; farm families particularly are likely to be poor, as are those headed by women, especially nonwhite women.

4 Although theft is one form of income redistribution, society prefers to leave income transfers to the government through taxation, transfer payments, and subsidies in kind.

5 The federal tax system is progressive if the effects of payroll taxes, notably Social Security, are ignored. These payroll taxes constitute a growing percentage of federal revenues, however, so that the federal system is growing less progressive. State and local taxes are regressive in their effects. In total, therefore, the tax system is not the primary instrument of income redistribution.

6 Antipoverty programs proliferated during the 1960s, but their effects were not entirely efficient or equitable. Transfer payments include social insurance programs, categorical assistance programs, and general public assistance. Social insurance goes to many who are not poor, categorical assistance includes only specific groups, and general public assistance is administered by the states, with varying eligibility requirements and levels of benefits. A majority of the poor, particularly the working poor, receive no public assistance at all. Subsidies in kind provide medical care, food, and so on, at the cost of rather large inefficiencies.

7 The problem of welfare has been tackled but not solved. In addition to the drawbacks of the individual approaches, there is the general problem of balancing the need for a decent standard of living against the necessary incentives to work.

8 Economic growth is one answer to the welfare mess, since it opens jobs for rich and poor alike. Minorities are more widely employed during times of prosperity and high demand. However, there are those in the "backwash" for whom special training and counseling may be necessary. The radicals see wholesale income redistribution as being necessary.

9 The negative income tax is the most likely approach to be taken to reform welfare. This program combines an income guarantee with provisions for retaining earnings as an incentive to work. Ideally, the negative tax would offer a decent income to those who cannot work and a strong incentive to those who can work—at a reasonable cost and without arbitrary distinctions in eligibility. These goals conflict, however; any program of reform will probably stress work incentives and moderate cost at the expense of broad coverage and generous benefits. Nixon's Family Assistance Plan is such a reform, with certain extra features.

SUGGESTED READINGS

Bowman, Mary Jean. "Poverty in an Affluent Society." In *Contemporary Economic Issues*. Edited by Neil Chamberlain. Rev. ed. Homewood, Ill.: Richard D. Irwin, 1973.

Ferman, Louis A., Joyce L. Kornbluh, and **Alan Haber,** eds. *Poverty in America*. Rev. ed. Ann Arbor: The University of Michigan Press, 1968.

Fried, Edward R., Alice M. Rivlin, Charles L. Schultze, and **Nancy H. Teeters.** *Setting National Priorities: The 1974 Budget.* Chaps. 3 through 5. Washington, D. C.: Brookings Institution, 1973.

Harrington, Michael. *The Other America.* Baltimore: Penguin Books, 1962.

Hunt, E. K., and **Howard Sherman.** *Economics: An Introduction to Traditional and Radical Views.* Chap. 19. New York: Harper & Row, 1972.

Kershaw, Joseph A. *Government against Poverty.* Chicago: Markham, 1970.

Will, Robert E., and **Harold G. Vatter,** eds. *Poverty in Affluence.* 2nd ed. New York: Harcourt Brace Jovanovich, 1970.

QUESTIONS

1 Review
   a. the distribution of wealth in the United States and its effect on income distribution,
   b. the extent of poverty in the United States,
   c. characteristics of the poor,
   d. the effectiveness of taxation in redistributing income,
   e. major government programs designed to assist the poor,
   f. economic growth as a possible way of reducing poverty,
   g. radical arguments and proposals for eliminating poverty,
   h. negative taxation.

2 Conservative economist Milton Friedman has argued in favor of the adoption of a negative tax. Friedman has also suggested, however, through his permanent income hypothesis, that people do not necessarily make their spending and saving decisions on the basis of current (one year's) income. Do you see any difficulties or inequities arising because the negative tax program is based on income in a single tax year?

3 In 1972 a new federal provision took effect which placed a tax ceiling of 50 percent on earned income—that is, income in the form of wages and salaries—leaving a 70 per cent ceiling on unearned income (such as income from investments). How might this provision tend to affect income distribution? Is there any possibility it might have no effect? Under what circumstances?

4 Consider the suggestion that private firms be given subsidies in the form of reduced taxes for each member of the poor that they train and employ. What effect would you predict for the overall problem of poverty and why? Might there be any advantages over direct government training?

5 The congressman from your district is holding an informal hearing among his constituents on a proposed increase in the minimum wage. He states that he is particularly interested in hearing opinions since his district contains a poverty pocket. As a disinterested observer, what would you tell this congressman as to the possible effects of the bill, especially in his district?

6 How might the use of an income definition of poverty tend to distort the picture of well-being in individual cases? (Note that not all property is income-earning property.) Might there be a tendency for young households to be classified as poor when they should not be? Why or why not?

7 Some liberals argue that while economic growth may not automatically eliminate

poverty, it may nevertheless produce a greater willingness on the part of society to tackle the problem with more resources. Why would they be unable to rely entirely on economic growth? Use the concept of marginal utility to explain why society might be more willing to tackle the problem.

8 Use the marginal cost and return concepts to describe the optimum investment by the government in manpower training

9 Assume that a single woman head of household with several dependents is encouraged to work through a government program that provides free training, free child care, and very little reduction in her welfare check. Is it possible to describe in marginal cost and benefit terms how much this mother should work and under what circumstances she should not? Recall that she will have to incur private costs for processed foods, clothing, transportation, and so forth in addition to the costs incurred by the government for training and child care.

10 Some critics of welfare programs argue that the benefits rarely get to the very disadvantaged because these people are frequently unaware of the programs and the regulations for qualifying. What advantages might there be to a negative tax in this particular case?

CHAPTER 35

DISCRIMINATION

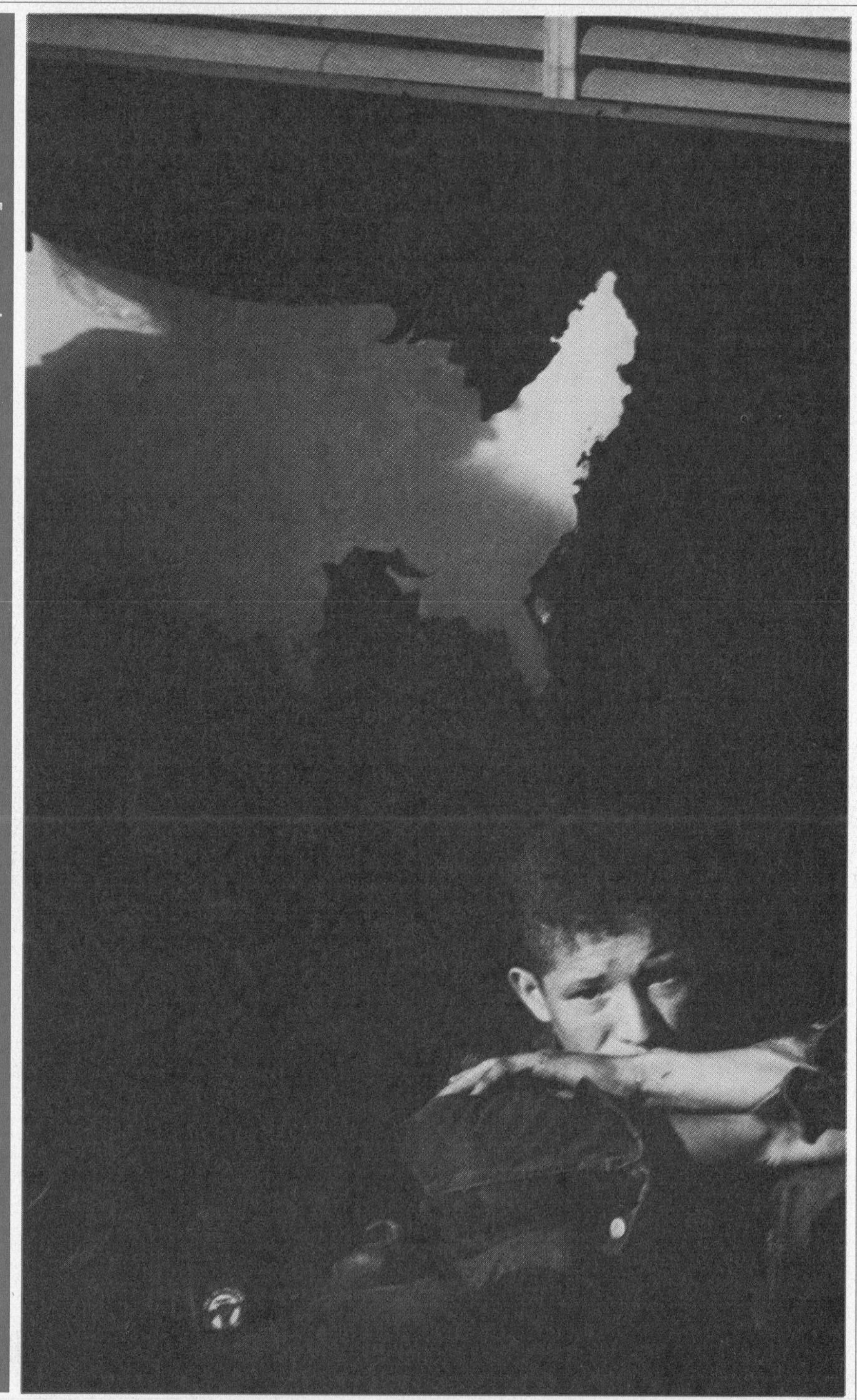

The position of blacks and women in the American economy is clearly inferior to that of white males. Black unemployment rates seldom run less than 100 percent higher than white rates, and the median family income of blacks is less than two-thirds the income of whites. Women's unemployment rates run about 60 percent higher than men's, and the average woman employed full time earns about 60 percent of the average man's salary. Both blacks and women are underrepresented in high-paying professions: Only about 1 percent of American lawyers are black and only 3 percent are women.

How are such inequalities to be explained? Racists and sexists see them as the inevitable result of the natural inferiority of blacks and women. Most observers, however, feel that these inequalities are largely the consequence of economic and social discrimination.

ECONOMIC DISCRIMINATION

There are two obvious kinds of economic discrimination—in hiring and in paying **Job discrimination** occurs when people are denied employment because of characteristics that are irrelevant to their productivity—such as race or sex. **Wage discrimination** occurs when people are paid lower-than-normal wages because of these irrelevant characteristics. Although race, sex, and religion are the most common areas of discrimination in our society, people may also be discriminated against because of other characteristics. For example, the University of Pittsburgh discovered that its business school graduates over six feet tall were offered beginning salaries 4 percent higher than shorter graduates, despite the better scholastic performance of the shorter people.

Discrimination is not always easy to identify. Sometimes a black or female applicant simply does not have the qualifications necessary for a particular job, as a consequence of prior social or economic discrimination. The black is a high school dropout; the woman can work only part time because of family obligations. Is the employer discriminating against them or is his decision based on an estimate of lower marginal productivity from these workers?

Thus, job and wage discrimination, whether or not the employer is racist or sexist, may result from previous discrimination in the acquisition of **human capital.** From an economic point of view, education or job training is an investment in people, or human capital, just as buying a new machine is an investment in capital goods. Both sorts of investments add to productivity. Many of the wage differentials between whites and nonwhites stem from a lack of investment in human capital; according to one estimate, the lack of education for urban nonwhite males reduces their income 23 to 27 percent below that of whites.

Opportunities for education or training that are not available to members of a group at a given time often have lasting consequences. A woman denied a place on the executive training squad will probably not qualify for future top management positions. A black refused a spot in an apprentice program may never become a union member, with union job security, union wages, and the middle-class housing and education for his children that union status would bring. So, even if all economic discrimination ended today, its effects could continue for years or generations.

Explaining Discrimination

To understand economic discrimination, it is necessary to understand the theory of **occupational crowding.**[1] This theory proposes that most jobs open to blacks and women are in certain low-status occupations and that blacks and women are "crowded" into these occupations. It follows that the wages in crowded occupations tend to be low, because there will be an artificially increased supply of labor available to them. At the same time, the supply of labor in other occupations is artificially limited, thereby leading to higher wage rates in those oc-

Opening photo by Geoffrey Gove from Rapho Guillumette

1 Barbara R. Bergmann, "The Effect on White Incomes of Discrimination in Employment," *Journal of Political Economy*, March/April 1971, pp. 294–313.

TABLE 35-1 Inequality of Blacks, 1972

	Whites	Blacks
Income		
Median income	$11,549	$ 7,106
Percent of households under $10,000	33.7	59.2
Percent of households in poverty	11.7	41.5
Education		
Percent of age group 25–29 who are high school graduates	81.5	64.0
Percent of age group 25–29 who are college graduates	19.9	8.3
Employment		
Professional and technical	14.6	9.5
Unemployment rate	5.0	10.0
Life expectancy at birth	72.1	65.5

It is evident that blacks are at a disadvantage not only economically, but with regard to education and health as well. If you are black, you are about four times more likely to be poor and twice as likely to be unemployed than if you are white. Whites go to school longer and live longer.

SOURCES: Bureau of the Census; National Center for Health Statistics; Bureau of Labor Statistics.

cupations. Crowding, however, does not explain why blacks or women receive lower pay when they perform the same jobs as white males.

The Black Experience in the United States Again and again the effect of crowding has worked against black Americans. During the slave era, blacks were routinely engaged in the least attractive jobs in the community. Since the marginal cost of keeping a slave was less than the cost of hiring a free man, slave labor was generally concentrated in those fields where marginal productivity was low, and there was no cost pressure on owners to give their slaves the opportunity for developing skills. After the Civil War, both social pressures and the absence of skills crowded blacks into only a few occupations. The sharecropping system, which provided a livelihood for most blacks in the South between 1860 and 1930, was a direct result of the lack of alternatives open to them. Finally, when the mechanization of agriculture in the South forced blacks to move to northern cities, the crowding principle applied again. Lacking education, skills, and a familiarity with urban ways of work, and discriminated against by northern employers, blacks were restricted to a very few areas of employment, generally unskilled work. In printing and publishing in 1967, blacks had only 1.3 percent of the professional and technical jobs and only 1.6 percent of the craft jobs, though their shares based on educational experience would have been 4.7 and 9.6 percent respectively. On the other hand, twice as many laborers and three times as many service workers were black as would have been expected.

Unfortunately for these new migrants, unskilled jobs were drying up in the cities; for example, the total U.S. work force grew by 32 percent from 1950 to 1970, but the number of laborer jobs increased by only 5 percent. Meanwhile, professional and technical jobs, which were less available to blacks, increased by 14 percent during this period and clerical jobs by 80 percent. The results have been low wages and unemployment for blacks.

Women The occupational crowding of women is even more prevalent than crowding by race. Blacks and whites work side by side on the assembly line at General Motors, but there are only a handful of women in the design department and no men in the secretarial pool. Very few men work in occupations where women have wide representation; instead, there is an ingrained feeling throughout the economy that certain jobs are "fit" for women and certain others for men.

Anthropologists and sociologists point out that as societies become more industrialized, there is little reason to allocate work according to sex. The particular sexual distribution of labor we know is culturally determined. Thorstein Veblen explained this development in terms of his theory of **conspicuous consumption.** A man wealthy enough to have a wife or a daughter or a mistress who had to do very little (or nothing) of economic value had surely achieved more status than one whose female dependents were engaged in useful employment. More radical economists see sex discrimination as part of the general exploitative pattern of capitalism. The low wages that result from crowding large numbers of women into a few occupations mean larger profits for the capitalist. More importantly, sex discrimination divides men from women and weakens the class struggle.

Whatever its origins, sex discrimination has intensified as more women have entered the labor force. Between 1910 and 1940, female participation in the labor force was fairly constant, with about 25 percent of working-age women employed. In contrast, between 1950 and 1970, the number of women working increased by 70 percent, as opposed to a 15 percent increase in male workers. And today, 44 percent of all women of working age are members of the labor force. Women are hardly better off by some measures, however. In all, the gap between men's and women's wages has widened slightly. In 1947 the median money income of all women was 58 percent of men's income; in 1970, it had dropped to 54 percent. (Not all of this differential is accounted for by job discrimination, however. There are also significant wage differentials between men and women performing the same jobs. In 1970, a government survey reported that women payroll clerks were paid 27 percent less than men, female tabulating machine operators earned 11 percent less than their male co-workers, and female janitors earned 15 percent less than men.)

Even well-educated women are not exempt from

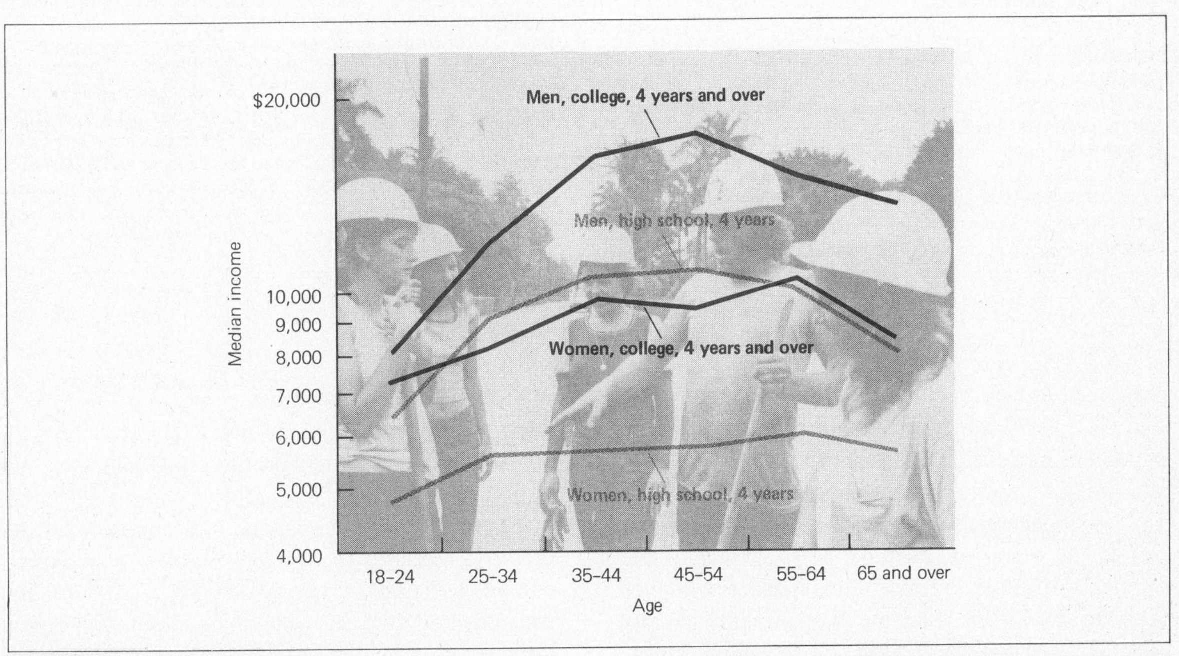

FIGURE 35-1 ECONOMIC DIFFERENCES BETWEEN THE SEXES (Full-time workers, 1971) It pays more to be a man with a high school diploma than a woman with a college or graduate degree. If differences in hours worked and the earnings of part-time workers were included, the gap would open even wider. Those women who remain single manage to have appreciably higher earnings than other working women, but they are still earning 15 to 20 percent short of what males in the same age bracket are earning. We cannot conclude that all the differentials are a direct result of intentional discrimination; life styles make women hold jobs more erratically and choose jobs that are more "feminine." But being a woman is clearly an expensive proposition. *New York Times* Photo

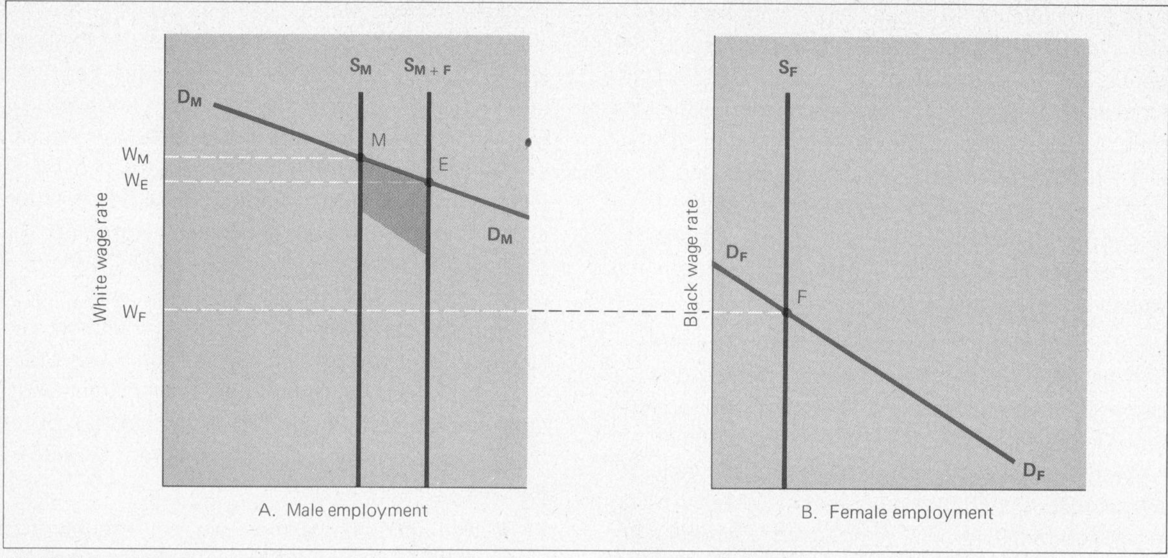

FIGURE 35-2 EFFECT OF DISCRIMINATION ON WAGES AND TOTAL ECONOMIC PRODUCT Assume that there are an equal number of males and females in the labor force, but that the male half of the labor force has exclusive employment rights in three of the economy's four industries. The demand curve for males is D_M and that for females is D_W. Men are paid at wage rate W_M and women, W_F. Were discrimination ended, both men and women would be employed in each industry, with wage rate W_E paid to all workers. The shaded area measures the gain in GNP that would result from the elimination of the discrimination. These two graphs also demonstrate the crowding theory of wages and, indirectly, the effect of discrimination on GNP. Although there are numerous federal, state, and municipal fair employment laws on the books, in many occupations there are two separate labor markets for blacks and whites. Because blacks are not permitted to work at the higher paying jobs, in the more prosperous industries, they are forced to accept low pay in the crowded occupations.

Until discrimination ends, the United States is placing people in jobs for which there are others who might be better suited, and hence more productive. A former vice president once remarked that he would not like to be operated upon by a surgeon who had gotten into medical school on a racial quota that is, because he was black); for several hundred years, nowever, the United States has been filling many jobs with 100 percent white quotas, at the expense not only of blacks, but of GNP and ultimately at the expense of most whites as well.

crowding. Recent studies reveal that 48 percent of women workers with 1 to 3 years of college and 14 percent of those with four years of college are clerical workers, and a survey of starting salaries for 1971 accounting graduates of Northwestern University found that men average $845 a month and women, $793. Juanita Kreps, professor of Economics at Duke University (and the only woman director of the 32-member New York Stock Exchange Board), has suggested that, realistically speaking, many women have "erred in the direction of overinvesting in their education" and that in today's working world, women are typically overeducated for the jobs they are able to find.

Who Benefits? Who Pays?

Crowding theory suggests that costs and benefits are different for different groups. Figures 35-2 shows the consequences of excluding women from three-quarters of the occupations. All the women (or blacks, or Puerto Ricans, or homosexuals) are excluded from three-quarters of the occupations and are crowded into the remaining quarter. This difference in demand is shown by the curve D_FD_F. The result is that more jobs are open to men and at higher wages, whereas fewer jobs are open to women and at lower wages. According to the *Economic Report of the President* for 1973, such differentials may amount to as much as 20 percent of the difference between men's and women's salaries.[2] Women suffer less from wage discrimination than from role differentiation that pigeonholes women in low-paying jobs.

At first glance, then, it seems as though those discriminated against are bearing the costs of discrimination. But society is paying higher costs for the male-dominated industries, costs not entirely offset by the lower ones in female-dominated industries. Moreover, society is forgoing GNP. If equality reigned, output would be at E, and wages would be equal for all. Some of this would come at the expense of males but part would come because women were more productively employed. The gain in GNP appears as the shaded area.

This model primarily describes job discrimination. Wage discrimination is another matter. Many industries are open to women or minorities, if they are willing to accept lower wages than men. In effect, there are two demand curves, one for white men and one for the objects of discrimination. Gary Becker explains that this is a result of nonmonetary costs the employer feels he incurs by hiring blacks or women or whatever.[3] The "taste for discrimination" lowers the demand curve, as in Figure 35-2, so that the employer will hire 19 men at $2.00, but only 11 women at that same wage. To induce the employer to hire 19 women, the wage rate would have to drop to $1.25.

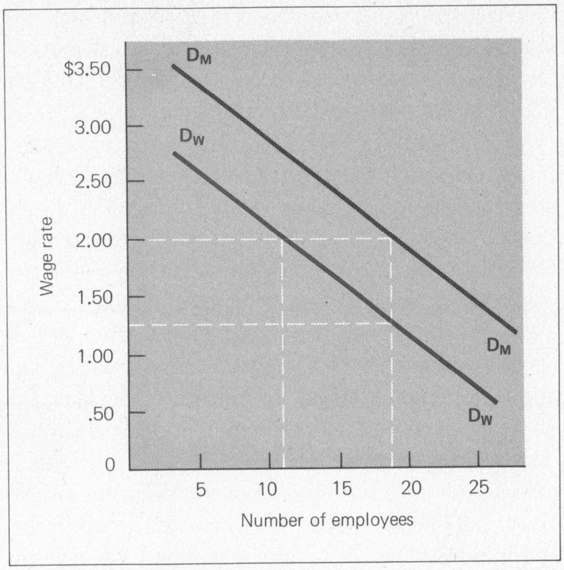

FIGURE 35-3 DISCRIMINATION AGAINST WOMEN: UNEQUAL PAY FOR EQUAL WORK **The sexist employer is willing to hire women for certain jobs under either of two conditions—that no males are available or that women are willing to work for lower wages. This employer has two separate demand schedules for labor, D_M and D_W, one for men and the other for women. This is reflected in the pay they receive.**

The Employer

These models hint that it is the employer who discriminates. Radical economists support this thesis. Blacks, for instance, are

> an available source of labor when needed by the economy and at the same time a group set apart that can be confined to certain types of work (low-paying, hard, and unpleasant jobs). They have been given the worst jobs the society has to offer. When labor is scarce they are given the lower rungs of better jobs; when economic conditions decline, whites move in to take even the jobs previously set aside as "Negro work." The blacks act as a buffer pool, keeping labor costs from rising. In this way the entire white society benefits by receiving goods and services more cheaply and white unemployment is cushioned.[4]

Excluding workers does impose costs on the discriminating employer, however. The racist or sexist can indulge his taste for discrimination only if he (or she) is willing to pay the higher wages resulting from the restricted labor supply. In theory, at least, this should act as a check on the employer. Milton Friedman argues that employers with prejudicial attitudes will be driven out of business in a competitive economy. "A businessman or an entrepreneur who expresses preferences in his business activities that are not related to productive efficiency is at a disadvantage compared to other individuals who do not. Such an individual is in effect imposing higher costs on himself than are other individuals who do not have such preferences. Hence, in a free market,

2 "The Economic Role of Women," *Economic Report of the President*, Chapter 4 (Washington, D.C.: Government Printing Office, 1973), pp. 89–111.

3 Gary S. Becker, *The Economics of Discrimination*, 2nd ed. (Chicago: University of Chicago Press, 1971).

4 William K. Tabb, *The Political Economy of the Black Ghetto* (New York: W. W. Norton, 1971), p. 26.

they will tend to drive him out."[5] Economic discrimination will persist only in monopolistic situations, for only monopolistic employers are able to bear higher costs, according to Friedman.

The Consumer In the case of a monopoly, or highly inelastic product demand, the costs of discrimination can be passed on to the consuming public. This price may be exacted because the employer wants to discriminate due to his own personal prejudices. But it is also possible that the employer is simply responding to a consumer demand for discrimination. For example, if consumers prefer male airplane pilots, an airline might find its business dropping off if its jets were piloted by women. Thus, rather than being driven out of business by higher costs, the discriminating firm may thrive while the integrationist or liberationist is shunned. A study by Victor R. Fuchs found evidence that indirectly confirmed this hypothesis.[6]

ELIMINATING DISCRIMINATION

Because the analysis of the causes and consequences of discrimination differ, the prescriptions for its cure differ as well. A wide range of solutions has been proposed—from compensatory education to hiring quotas. In examining the solutions, try to determine the assumptions about causes and costs upon which they are based.

The Melting Pot

The traditional American answer to racial or ethnic discrimination has been to assume that it is temporary. Earlier in America's history, the Irish, Scandinavians, Germans, and Jews were crowded into less attractive employment, but eventually they were absorbed into the mainstream of American life, with ready access to economic opportunities. This argument, however, does not explain the current plight of the American Indian (who, after all, preceded all others to America) or the black Americans or Mexican-Americans, who have been here for generations, to say nothing of the vast numbers of American women whose mothers and grandmothers came to the United States at the same time as their fathers and grandfathers. In this light, it is no longer possible to fall back on the melting pot solution to economic discrimination, with all of its comforting, do-nothing implications; instead, a better understanding of the problem is needed in order to reach out for solutions.

5 Milton Friedman, *Capitalism and Freedom* (Chicago: University of Chicago Press, 1962), p. 109.

6 Victor R. Fuchs, "Difference in Hourly Earnings Between Men and Women," *Monthly Labor Review*, May 1971, pp. 9–15.

The Public Sector

Antidiscrimination Legislation A common prescription for discrimination is to pass laws against it. The 14th Amendment prohibits some forms of racial discrimination, and, if passed, the Equal Rights Amendment would expand this prohibition and extend it to sex discrimination as well. The real progress in enforcement came in the 1960s for blacks and, to a lesser extent, for women. Title VII of the Civil Rights Act of 1964 made it illegal for employers or unions with more than 25 employees or members and engaged in interstate commerce to discriminate on the basis of race or sex. It also created the Equal Employment Opportunity Commission, which in 1972 was given additional authority to sue for compliance, and which since that date has instigated suits against violators as prominent as General Motors.

The Equal Pay Act of 1963 required employers to pay men and women the same amount for the same work. Title VII of the Civil Rights Act prohibits discrimination in hiring, discharging, and compensation on grounds of sex as well as race. A 1971 Executive Order requires that contractors employing more than 50 workers and holding federal contracts of $50,000 or over formulate written affirmative action plans to ensure equal opportunities for women. Under such legislation, certain dramatic antidiscrimination moves have been taken. In 1973, AT&T was forced to make payments of $38 million to 13,000 women who suffered wage discrimination, and the company has promised to end any sexual stereotypes associated with its jobs.

Full Employment As Chapters 7 and 34 have shown, full employment helps minorities more than other groups. Fiscal and monetary policy are indirect tools against the economic suffering of minorities. Unfortunately, full employment has recently been secondary to the other goal of fiscal and monetary policy, that of controlling inflation. Government stabilization efforts to control inflation have been particularly burdensome to blacks. Moreover, since black ownership of fixed-value assets (bank accounts, bonds, insurance policies) tends to be substantially lower than that of whites, the value of such anti-inflationary policies is perhaps somewhat less important to them. In other words, it can be argued that blacks have paid most of the unemployment price of government efforts to combat inflation, while whites have received most of the benefits.

There are more direct means of promoting full employment than fiscal and monetary policy. Public service employment and government as an employer of last resort have been proposed as means of offering training and a start on a career to the unemployed—minorities and otherwise. Economist Barbara Bergmann suggested this solution in testimony before a congressional committee:

> Public service employment is a necessary tool for breaking down patterns which have led to high turnover and high unemployment for youth, blacks, and women, simply because it is too much to expect the private economy to solve this problem all by itself. The public service already plays a role in giving blacks and women a better deal than does the private labor market. Its role must be expanded and whatever patterns of discrimination that remain within the governmental service must be broken up.[7]

The Private Sector

Unions Although certain segments of the trade union movement have received considerable publicity in the media as discriminators against blacks, recent studies reveal that on balance, "there is apparently less discrimination against black workers in the average unionized labor market than in the average nonunion labor market."[8] This statement should not be taken to mean that no union discriminates; obviously, the low percentage of nonwhite union members in many of the construction unions, for example, is evidence that many blacks still find it impossible to achieve union membership. Nevertheless, in several important industries, the proportion of black workers who are union members is virtually identical to the proportion of white workers who are members. And even more important, the average wage of blacks as compared with whites is frequently higher in unionized job markets than in nonunionized markets.

The industrial unions in particular have been open to black membership. Where industrial unions predominate, about the same proportion of black workers as white workers has joined the appropriate union. Although there is still a gap between black wages and white wages among these union members, the gap is significantly smaller for union members than for nonunion workers.

The record is less impressive for craft unions. Here, the percentage of unionized blacks is only about half that of whites, and wage differentials between black workers and white workers are about the same on union jobs as in nonunion work. It would appear that blacks are less likely to be granted membership in craft unions and that the unions themselves have had little impact on reducing pay differentials.

In summary, it appears that the role labor unions have played in fighting economic discrimination has been too often understated. The record of the industrial unions has been outstanding, and the potential of the craft unions, although as yet untapped, is enormous.

Black Capitalism Presumably black employers do not practice economic discrimination against blacks. A possible solution to the problem of discrimination, therefore, is black capitalism, which has as its objective increased black control of business, particularly those businesses that serve the black community.

7 U.S. Congress, Joint Economic Committee, 92nd Cong., 2nd sess., "Reducing Unemployment to 2 Percent." *Hearings*, October 17, 18, and 26, 1972 (Washington, D.C.: Government Printing Office, 1972), p. 49.

8 Orley Ashenfelter, "Racial Discrimination and Trade Unionism," *Journal of Political Economy* 80, no. 3 (May/June 1972):462.

MA BELL AND THE EEOC

In 1969, there were only eight male telephone operators in the entire United States. By the end of 1973, their ranks had grown to several thousand and there may well be tens of thousands within a few years. All of this is one result of the agreement in 1973 between the American Telephone and Telegraph Company, the U.S. Department of Labor, and the Equal Employment Opportunity Commission (EEOC). The decision appears to signify a turning point in the legal attack on discrimination. It broadens the definition of what constitutes job and wage discrimination to include considerably more than the original equal-pay-for-equal-work concept. In addition, the $38 million settlement imposed on the telephone company in the form of back pay and wage increases is expected to spur other companies to comply voluntarily.

AT&T is the largest nongovernment employer in the world, with approximately one million workers, of whom 60 percent are women. The company had been described by EEOC as "the largest oppressor of women workers in the United States." Women were almost entirely restricted to unskilled jobs, primarily as secretaries, operators, and service representatives. For example, in 1971, 99.8 percent of all telephone operators were women, while 98.9 percent of the highly skilled craft operators were men. The jobs held by women not only paid less but also had smaller advancement potential, and, as a result, less than 2½ percent of all managers above the first level were women.

In presenting its case, the government focused its attack not on the issue of equal pay for equal work, but on the Bell System as an example of institutionalized discrimination. In the words of EEOC lawyer David Copus, "We wanted to present the whole sociology and psychology of sexual stereotypes as it was inculcated into the Bell System," in other words, to expose the entire structure of AT&T's employment policy as it was designed to channel women into some jobs and men into others. The government's objective was to force the company to build procedures into its employment practices that would permit minorities and women to receive promotions previously denied.

The government believes that the settlement to which AT&T agreed should go a long way toward accomplishing this objective. First, it provides specific guidelines and timetables for the employment of women and minority workers. The goal for women is 19 percent of the outside craft jobs and 40 percent of the inside ones. (In 1971, women held only 1.1 percent of all craft jobs.) Moreover, in a dramatic attempt to eliminate stereotyped job placements, the settlement also included specific job goals for men—10 percent of all new operators and 25 percent of all new clerical workers must be males. But although some success has been achieved in filling traditionally female jobs with men, the reverse is not the case: many traditionally male jobs remained staffed primarily with men.

A key aspect of the case is the substantial costs incurred by AT&T. The $38 million in back pay and wage increases is vastly more than the settlement in any previous job discrimination ruling. Moreover, in many earlier cases, employers found guilty of discrimination were able to make peace with the EEOC by promising to hire more women; now, however, employers can be held responsible for past action, and this could cost them a lot of money. As one lawyer in the field put it, "Making discrimination expensive is what will end it faster." It is hoped that the threat of enormous back pay settlements similar to those imposed on the telephone company will motivate other employers to take a new look at their current employment practices, and produce immediate results rather than taking their chances as part of the 60,000–70,000 case backlog of complaints now in the files of the EEOC.

Most recent activities by the EEOC suggest that it will continue this approach of concentrating on large, widely known employers. In September 1973, the EEOC notified GM, Ford, General Electric, and Sears Roebuck that charges of job discrimination had been filed against them and that court action was possible if a satisfactory out-of-court arrangement could not be reached.

The proponents of black capitalism see the black ghetto as a form of underdeveloped country or colony, in which outsiders (whites) own the resources (stores, apartment houses) and exploit the indigenous population. Moreover, they claim that just as in many colonial areas, the scarcity of capital makes it impossible for the local people to compete.

To correct this situation, both massive infusions of capital and a higher level of entrepreneurial skill would be required. Unfortunately, just as in many underdeveloped nations, neither has been available in sufficient quantities. Some government help and some private assistance have been given to emerging black businesses in the form of loans, but the substantial long-term lending or equity capital needed to provide a solid basis for larger size enterprises has not been forthcoming. In addition, the "brain drain" so characteristic of many new Asian and African nations is also a problem for the ghetto: The brightest children seldom return after college.

Furthermore, some questions have been raised as to whether black capitalism is a viable approach to the elimination of economic discrimination against blacks. Black economist Andrew Brimmer, of the Federal Reserve Board, suggests that the road to black economic equality must be through "full participation in an integrated national economy." He believes that black capitalism, with its emphasis on black ownership of small businesses, may be running against the mainstream of American life. Small business has become increasingly risky in our economy and has a high failure rate; it is in the professions and in salaried jobs with big businesses that most of the opportunities now lie.

Are the Solutions Working?

Some observers have attempted to dismiss the problems examined in this chapter on the grounds that they are gradually disappearing. Unfortunately for many blacks and women, the statistical evidence does not support this optimistic viewpoint.

Blacks In 1973, Ben J. Wattenberg and Richard M. Scammon announced that blacks were marching "across the invisible line into the lower-middle and middle classes" and, in fact, "a slender majority, but a majority nevertheless" could be said to have reached the middle class where they "have enough to eat . . . adequate if not necessarily expensive clothes to wear . . and housing that is safe and sanitary."[9] The authors quoted Census Department figures showing that the median income of black families nearly doubled during the 1960s, while the median income of white families grew by only 69 percent; that nearly half the members of minority groups now earn $7000 a year, as compared with barely 10 percent in 1951. Confirming the Wattenberg-Scammon thesis, there is definite evidence that blacks are now moving into many of the better paying job categories. For example, 60 percent of all nonwhite workers were employed in skilled or semiskilled jobs in 1970 as compared with only 42 percent in 1960.

Unfortunately, however, the most recent figures cast doubt on whether the improvement in the black economic condition reported by Wattenberg and Scammon is the whole story. Unquestionably, black income has increased, both absolutely and relatively, from the levels of 20 or 10 years ago. But by some measures it does not appear that any progress has been made since the mid-sixties. In 1967, the median income of blacks was 59 percent of whites; it grew to 61 percent in 1969 and 1970, but has declined in both 1971 and 1972. The Census Department study also showed that the number of low-income black households headed by women in 1972 stood at 1 million, up 300,000 from 1968. The unemployment statistics are equally disappointing. In 1972, the black unemployment rate again exceeded twice the white rate after falling to less than 2:1 between 1968 and 1971. And the black teenage unemployment rate—26.3 percent in 1967—soared to 33.5 percent in 1972.

Even if one accepts the premise that black family income appears to be approaching white family income, these economic gains may be the result of more black wives working. A recent Census Depart-

9 Ben J. Wattenberg and Richard M. Scammon, "Black Progress and Liberal Rhetoric," *Commentary*, April 1973, pp. 35–44.

with about half of them working full time, while in the white families, only 54 percent of the wives worked, and only one-third worked full time. In other words, to a considerable extent, black income parity appears to be based on the two-worker family; the white family, on the other hand, manages to achieve the same income level with only one wage earner.

Women In the case of economic discrimination against women, progress has been even slower, and there is some evidence of backward movement. For example, the percentage of female college presidents, professors, and instructors was significantly higher in 1920 and 1930 than it is today, and the percentage of women dentists in 1970 was only just returning to the 1910 and 1920 levels.

Looking ahead to the 1980s, a mixed picture with pessimistic overtones appears. Female participation in the job market will undoubtedly increase; one estimate is that the number of women in the work force will grow from about 33 million in 1973 to 37 million in 1980, and will constitute 37 percent of the labor force, up nearly 5 percent from 1960. At the same time, however, there is a possibility that employment of women in better paying, higher status jobs may actually decline. Most of the better jobs available to women have traditionally been in a few of the professions. Teaching, library work, nursing, home economics, and social service have provided two-thirds of all women's professional employment. Over one-third of all women professionals are teachers. These fields (especially teaching) appear unlikely to generate enough new jobs for the college-educated women who will be seeking work within the next few years. The more limited growth in "women's" work is not the only factor that will determine how women will fare in the next decade, however. Should the entire economy slow its growth, either because of a conscious choice by society to preserve the environment or because of stagnation, then career opportunities will be restricted. Higher ment survey showed that the incomes of young black families in the North are very close to those of comparable young white families. However, in the families surveyed, 63 percent of the black wives worked, rates of participation by women could increase competition for jobs; and failure to eliminate barriers could intensify crowding. The key, really, is the rate of economic growth, since a healthy economy creates a greater demand for labor that can offset the ill effects of other developments.

A Myth

One myth that makes people fear the end of sexism and racism depicts gains by one group only at the expense of other groups. Higher salaries for women or blacks mean lower salaries for white males, goes the tale. If "they" gain jobs, it can only mean that "we" lose them! Like most myths, this one has some truth to it. One study found that while integration would have only minor effects on the overall wage rates for whites, the costs would be primarily borne by white males with less than an elementary school education and white females with less than a high school education. Spread over time, however, and with proper compensatory programs, the effects might be slight indeed. In fact, rather than falling, it is more likely that wages for white males simply would not rise as rapidly for a while.

The reason that gains are not entirely exacted by one group from another is shown in Figure 35-2. At first there are two markets—one with low wages, the other with high wages. In the low-wage market, the employers can use labor in inefficient ways because it is cheap; therefore, productivity may be low. When both markets are combined in a nondiscriminatory way, wages are equalized. Blacks receive appreciably higher wages, but whites receive only slightly reduced checks in their pay envelopes. The black gain comes less at the expense of whites than from increased black productivity. Instead of pushing a broom, a plow, or a drug, the black can work up to his or her educational level. The individual benefits, and society receives added GNP as well (shown by the shaded area).

As labor shifts among industries, relative wage rates change. Some occupations lose in "popularity," and, as wages increase, employers have an incentive to increase the productivity of the remaining workers.

The scenario depends, to some extent, on the shape of the demand curve; whites may lose more or less in wages if the shape changes. But society will always gain some increase in GNP from the elimination of sexism and racism—a strong economic argument for their elimination.

SUMMARY

1 The discrepancies between white male income and employment rates and those of minorities and women cannot be explained entirely by differing marginal productivity. Such inequalities are the result of discrimination.

2 Job discrimination occurs when people are denied employment because of characteristics that are irrelevant to their productivity. Wage discrimination occurs when people are paid lower-than-normal wages because of irrelevant characteristics. Discrimination also is met in obtaining access to opportunities that enhance human capital, and may have continuing effects on the economic potential of a person.

3 One explanation for their lower incomes and higher unemployment rates is that minorities and women are denied access to many types of jobs, crowding them into certain industries and thereby depressing wages. Occupational crowding of blacks began with slavery and continues today, as blacks are overrepresented in such jobs as laborer. Such industries are not growing as fast as the rest of the economy, making unemployment even more severe. The occupational crowding of women is even more prevalent than crowding by race.

4 Crowding can be represented by two demand curves, one for white males and one for those discriminated against. More jobs will be open to white men, at higher wages than others. The effects are broader than this, however. Society is paying higher costs for the white male-dominated industry, costs not entirely offset by the lower ones in female- or minority-dominated industries. Moreover, society is forgoing GNP. This occurs whether it is the employer or the customer who discriminates.

5 The melting pot solution has not provided the answer to discrimination. Government acts directly to eliminate discrimination with legislation prohibiting it and indirectly to eliminate its effects with full-employment policies. On balance, unionized industry has discriminated less than the rest of industry, although the record of craft unions is less impressive. Black capitalism offers a chance for self-determination, but may not be viable since it begins with small business, a risky sector of the economy.

6 Whether such solutions have worked depends on whether one sees the glass as half full or half empty. In absolute terms, blacks and women are enjoying higher income than ever before. However, the gap between their incomes and those of white males is growing slightly wider. In many black families that enjoy an income close to that of whites, both the husband and wife work, whereas white families achieve the same level with only one wage earner.

7 Hostility to integration and women's liberation is based to some extent on the myth that gains by one group come at the expense of another group. Because of the increase in productivity from the elimination of discrimination, GNP increases, and

white male wages are affected only slightly, while the others receive much higher income. There will be some dislocation, especially among people without high school education and in industries that have benefitted from the depressed wages of discrimination.

SUGGESTED READINGS

Becker, Gary S. *Economics of Discrimination.* Chicago: University of Chicago Press, 1957.

Beer, Samuel H., and **Richard E. Barringer**, eds. *The State and the Poor.* Cambridge, Mass.: Winthrop, 1970.

Economic Report of the President. Chap. 4. Washington, D. C.: Government Printing Office, 1973.

Fusfeld, Daniel R. *The Basic Economics of the Urban Racial Crisis.* New York: Holt, Rinehart and Winston, 1973.

Kain, John F., ed. *Race and Poverty: The Economics of Discrimination.* Englewood Cliffs, N.J.: Prentice-Hall, 1969.

Myrdal, Gunnar. *Challenge to Affluence.* New York: Random House, Pantheon Books, 1963.

Schultz, Theodore W. "Investment in Human Capital." *American Economic Review* 51 (March 1961):1–16.

Tabb, William K. *The Political Economy of the Black Ghetto.* New York: W. W. Norton, 1971.

QUESTIONS

1 Review
   a. the similarities and differences between job and wage discrimination,
   b. the concept of occupational crowding and how it tends to keep wages low for minorities,
   c. various solutions suggested such as the melting pot solution, legislation, and full employment,
   d. the effect of unions on discrimination,
   e. black capitalism,
   f. the myth concerning those who gain and those who lose from nondiscrimination.

2 In what way can it be said that a woman overinvests in human capital? (Use a marginal cost and return approach.) From an employment standpoint? From her own standpoint?

3 Can you make a case that the investment in human capital by the black worker may be underinvestment from the economy's point of view but not necessarily from the point of view of the individual? Why does this happen?

4 For black capitalism to be very effective there would need to be a higher marginal propensity to save among blacks than among whites. Why? Is there a likelihood of such an occurrence?

5 Legislation against discrimination was one of the most fervent hopes of the civil rights movement in the early 1960s and resulted in rather strong legislation in the form of the 1964 Civil Rights Act. However, some 10 years later serious problems remain. Do you believe lack of economic power to be the crux of the matter? Why or why not?

6 Milton Friedman argues that the employer who discriminates may be incurring a higher cost. Can you give a counter argument stemming from some consumer preferences? Why can the higher cost be maintained only in the case of monopoly?

7 "Full employment alone may not solve the problem of discrimination in jobs and wages, but it may be an important part of a setting that is conducive to the elimination of discrimination." Do you agree or disagree? Might you have to wait for a recession for the proof? Why?

8 Does the socialization of minorities tend to contribute to occupational crowding and low wages? How? Give an example for the case of women.

9 The employment position of the black American has been affected by institutional and structural changes in the economy. Since World War II, over 90 percent of the growth in employment has been in white-collar jobs. How would this shift affect black employment in your opinion? Why?

10 Examine below the two labor demand curves of a given employer, the first for white males and the second for all others. Assume that there is now a change so that the employer's demand curves are combined. He will no longer show a preference for white males in hiring or pay. Draw a new curve and show what wage needs to be paid for his original force of 250 workers. Look back at the original demand curves and discuss the question of who gained and who lost. Is there any reason to believe that the demand curve for "All others" might shift? Why? In what direction? How would the shift affect the solution?

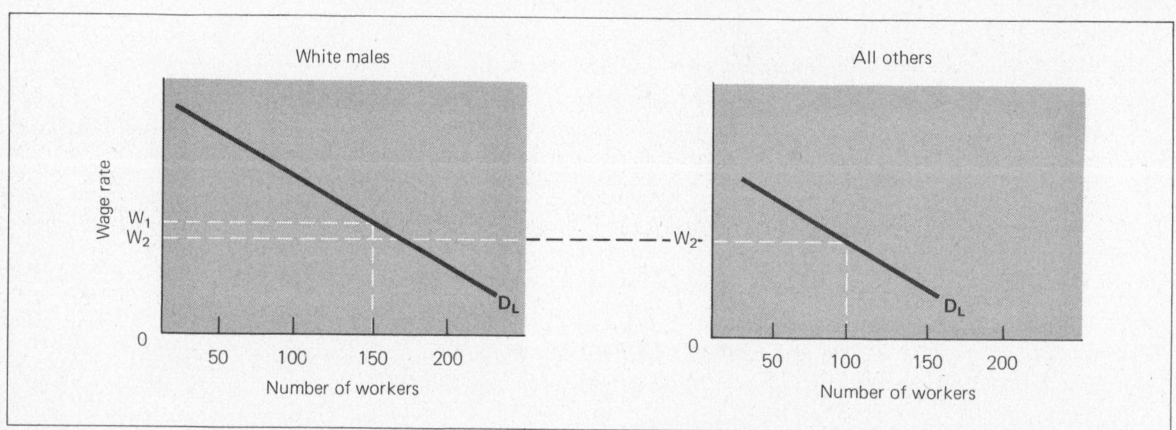

Opening photo by J. Paul Kirouac

CHAPTER 36
RADICAL CRITIQUE

The 1960s were traumatic years for America. It was a decade that started with high hopes for a better way of life at home and abroad, but which ended with shattered illusions on both counts. For many young idealists, the election of John F. Kennedy was to be the catalyst for young men and women with new ideas to create a better world. Social scientists and other academicians were finally to have a chance to put their theories to work in creating a better society for all mankind.

Somewhere along the way, however, something went wrong Foreign policy was still dominated by a cold war mentality, which intensified the arms race and led to the war in Indochina. This was the product of men who eagerly left the most prestigious universities in the country to come to Washington to help make the world safe for democracy. They were in the words of David Halberstam, "the best and the brightest." Yet what they created was, to many Americans, an unmitigated disaster.

At home, the results were not much better. John Kennedy had promised to "get this country moving again." The dramatic application of Keynesian economics did result in a rapid growth of GNP. But had the quality of life improved? The problems of pollution, poverty, inflation, discrimination, substandard housing, crime, drugs, and alienation did not disappear. In many cases, they seemed to worsen during this period of unparalleled affluence.

A growing number of people began to raise some serious questions about their economic and political system. They reasoned that if this was the best the system could do, there must be a better system. Capitalism itself was at fault. Only some form of socialism would bring the social and economic justice that a good society requires.

People also began to wonder about the techniques that created the policies of the sixties. If the best that the best and the brightest could come up with was a half-hearted war on poverty and a lot of quibbling over whether 4 or 4½ percent was the optimal unemployment rate, there must be something wrong with the way in which these learned men and women were looking at the world. Conventional economics, they argued, simply was not capable of dealing with, or finding solutions to, the economic problems of contemporary America.

In recent years, the radicals, or the New Left, have voiced these criticisms and have seen their number grow. The radical critique rejects the foundation of the U.S. economy as unredeemable and rejects the usual tools of economic analysis as totally inadequate. According to the New Left, conventional economics is at best naive about the real power relations in society and at worst a tool of those who hold power. Because of this, the traditional solutions for the problems of the economy merely modify the present mix of government and free enterprise rather than attacking the underlying causes.

In an effort to find another way of organizing the economic system and another system of economic analysis, the radicals found their way to Karl Marx who, more than a century ago, conceived of a new philosophic, economic, and historical analysis. Marx is the spiritual father of the radical critique and the author of the idea that capitalism itself—and not some technical malfunction within it—is the cause of the miseries of modern civilization.

Although most economists reject the radical message as polemics with little constructive content, many believe they should be listened to. At the very least they have raised important questions that conventional economics does not or cannot handle very well. And they have made the orthodox economists a little less smug about the power of their scientific analysis. Radicals, of course, are not satisfied with such a patronizing pat on the head. They demand a fuller hearing.

PROBLEMS OF CAPITALISM

Writing in *The Yale Review* in 1933, John Maynard Keynes said that capitalism "is not intelligent, it is not beautiful, it is not just, it is not virtuous—and it doesn't deliver the goods." He then set about showing, in his *General Theory*, how to make capitalism work again, after the debacle of the Great Depression.

Radicals agree with Keynes's analysis of and conclusion about capitalism. What they disagree with is the effort he subsequently invested to reform the system, for the New Left has little interest in schemes to reform capitalism and make it work. Even the so-called radical policies of presidential candidate George McGovern—a more progressive tax system, more antitrust, more welfare, more aid to education, and so forth—were actually marginal changes to the existing system. The radicals reject this approach. Most believe that the socioeconomic system built upon capitalism is rotten at its roots. It is their position that the theory of capitalism overemphasizes the greedy and competitive aspects of humans and the capitalistic system fosters these tendencies. At the same time, both theory and practice give inadequate weight to cooperation toward the common good and to a concern for shared values. The New Left also maintains that the economic and social problems that face modern societies are not aberrations or technical deficiencies, but rather the inevitable products of 300 years of capitalism—a system that began with the intrinsically exploitative and inequitable enclosure laws of seventeenth century England and that today remains firmly grounded in the twin propositions of exploitation and inequality.

Radicals have written extensively about the abuses of the capitalist economic system and about the orthodox economic theory underlying this system. In this chapter, four of the many areas of the system that radicals have criticized—income distribution (actually maldistribution), alienation, racism and sexism, and imperialism—are examined, as are the economic theories underlying the radical critique.[1]

Income Distribution

In many ways, it is over the theory of income distribution that radical thought is in most fundamental disagreement with orthodox economics. As pointed out in Chapters 30 and 31, the traditional concept of the distribution of income rests upon marginal productivity theory: Supply and demand mechanisms of the market determine which goods and services can be produced at a profit; this in turn determines which factors of production are needed; income then flows to the owners of those factors. If everyone in the system works so as to maximize utility and self-interest, the resources of the economy will be allocated in the most efficient manner possible and the most wants will be satisfied. People who contribute to the satisfaction of those wants receive income. People who do not contribute to the satisfaction of those wants do not receive income.

Orthodox economists accept this circular flow of factors and products on one side and income on the other as inherent in and necessary to the market system. It is the contribution that these factors of production make to satisfying wants, rather than who the owners or controllers of these factors are, that determines their relative importance to the system. Since these various factors differ in productivity and since they are unequally distributed among owners, the amount of income they earn is different. Orthodox economists accept this unequal distribution of income, too, as inherent in the system. Some people think that this also confers a degree of justice or equity upon the system. People are paid in accordance with their contributions to production. Exploitation is not possible and everyone gets what he contributes and, thus, deserves.

Radicals often claim that this theory is used by conventional economists as a justification for existing patterns of income distribution. Such a charge is somewhat exaggerated. Most modern economists realize that efficiency does not imply equity and they do not advocate an income distribution based solely upon marginal productivity.

To correct at least some of this maldistribution of income and to guarantee that enough of the population will have sufficient income to generate a level of demand able to make the market system work, many orthodox economists recommend policies such as a minimum guaranteed annual income for all people, regardless of their productivity, and tax reform to redistribute some of the income and wealth of society. They argue that this would main-

1 For an in-depth analysis of these problems and others, see Assar Lindbeck, *The Political Economy of the New Left: An Outsider's View* (New York: Harper & Row, 1971) and "Symposium: Economics of the New Left," *Quarterly Journal of Economics* 86 (1972):632–683.

tain the efficiency of the market system while also resulting in an equitable income distribution.

The radical charge does contain some truth. The work of many economists is concerned solely with the question of efficiency. By directing their teaching and research in this area and by proclaiming the efficiency of marginal productivity as a basis for income distribution, they neglect or obscure the issue of equity. Thus, they confer unintended legitimacy upon an inequitable situation.

The radical economists reject the orthodox analysis of the system, the system itself, and the redistribution ideas of the orthodox economists for other reasons as well. In the view of the New Left, income distribution is based on power relations in society, not on market relations. The greater the political and economic power of a group (or class in Marxist terms), the greater its income. The group without such power receives the least income. The New Left further accuses the orthodox economists of being unable, or unwilling, to see that this superior-subordinate power relationship pervades society but particularly economic affairs.

What accounts for the differences between the orthodox and radical views of the world? One explanation put forth by the radicals is that in the eighteenth century, when the orthodox approach to economics was originally developed, power was so diffused that it was possible for each person, acting as both consumer and producer, to be sovereign. However, since that time, enormous changes in the economy have brought about a situation in which capitalists (and their minions) have become increasingly powerful, and the workers increasingly powerless. Radicals believe that if the orthodox economists were able to accept the idea that the economy is a dynamic social institution rather than a static one with unchanging relationships, they would be able to see how power relations have replaced market relations in determining how income is distributed. To the degree that orthodox economists maintain that the fundamental economic relationships between men are those of the market system, they will continue to misperceive the reality of the modern economic situation.

Since the current method of distributing income rests on a market system with entrenched vested interests, radicals in their total rejection of this system maintain that no reforms within it—be they changed tax structure, increased welfare, or whatever—can adequately provide for truly equitable

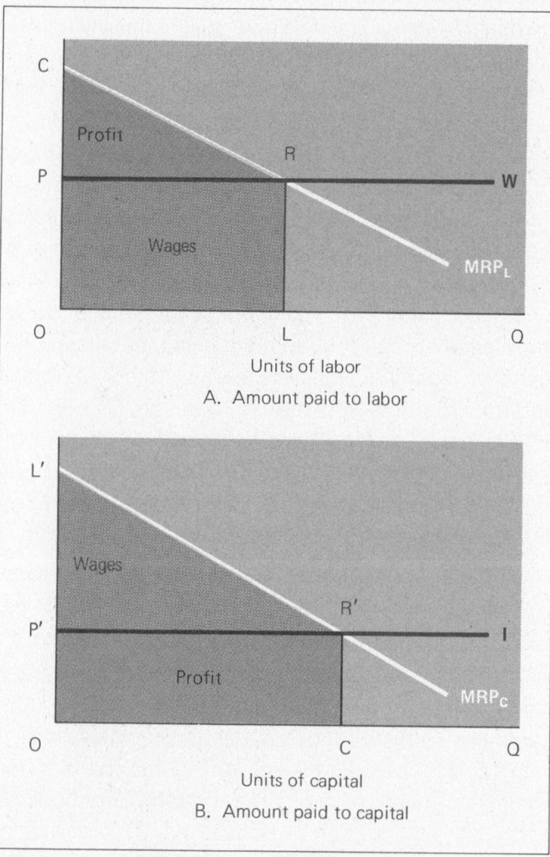

FIGURE 36-1 WHOSE SURPLUS? Marginal productivity theory presumes that returns to a factor are equal to the value of its contribution to production and that the total value of the marginal product for all factors equals the value of the total product. If there is a discrepancy—if the area of the rectangle (wages) in graph A is not equal to the area of the triangle (wages) in graph B—then one factor is creating a surplus whose distribution is based on something other than marginal productivity. Because the two areas are equal only under conditions of perfect competition in a constant-cost industry, analysis based on marginal productivity provides only partial insight, and economists must look elsewhere for a full theory of income distribution. The radicals find their answers in power relationships based on class interests.

income distribution. None of these suggestions will work because they will not alter the basic power structure in the society. Only through abolishing private ownership of the means of production and divorcing the distribution of income from ownership and productivity of the factors of production can a truly equitable means for distributing income be achieved.

The radicals see yet another flaw in the theory of marginal productivity. Marx argued that the value of a product was based upon the value of the human labor used to produce the product. The wages in a market system were less than the true contribution of labor. The difference, or the profit paid to capital, was surplus value. Marx believed that capitalists would try to expand this surplus value by continued exploitation of labor. Economic theory, on the other hand, says that capital will be paid the value of its marginal product as will all other factors of production. The sum of the value of the marginal products for all factors is the total revenue. There is no exploitation, and there is no surplus value to fight over.

It can be mathematically shown that paying each factor the value of its marginal product will use up the entire revenue from the product. But this will occur only if all markets are competitive and all industries have constant costs. Neither condition exists in any economy. So radicals argue that there is surplus value, or some part of the total product, to be fought over. Determining who gets what depends upon the relative power of the competing groups. Thus, income distribution is determined by power relations, not marginal productivity, and conventional theory does not deal with the problem at all.

Alienation

According to the New Left, alienation is likely to result when individuals lack political and economic power and when their behavior cannot determine the outcomes that they want, particularly in areas such as work satisfaction and income. Following Marx, the radicals describe alienation in the following way. Under the market system, workers sell their labor for wages and, in effect, are separated from their own minds and bodies. They give up control of their lives for the period of time that they are working. What they produce is independent of them and its use is no concern of theirs. The activity of work, which is itself external to and independent of the individual workers, offers them little personal satisfaction or fulfillment. Laborers follow the directions of others. The result of all this is a compartmentalization of the individual worker—he is separated from other workers and from a sense of community.

Workers are employed in producing commodities for exchange rather than for their own use. Under the market system, commodities exist only for their exchange value; that is, how many other commodities or, in advanced economies, how much money they can be exchanged for. The workers who make these commodities are only concerned with receiving money for their labors. The commodities have no intrinsic use value to them, whereas the money can be exchanged for other commodities, made by other workers.

To a worker the forces of the market system appear to be far beyond individual control. Securing and retaining a job in order to earn money means adjusting to the forces of the economy, doing whatever kind of work the system at that time requires, rather than adjusting the economy to a worker's own needs as an individual and a member of a family.

However, according to the New Left, this attitude of the workers toward the inevitability of conforming is not a realistic one. If they were able to see their situation in true perspective, the workers could assume control over the forces of the economy, end private ownership as the means of production, and, in so doing, end their alienation. But as long as the workers perceive these acts as beyond their capability and believe that because they sell their labor for a wage, they are exercising free will, alienation will continue as an inevitable outcome of the market system. Workers are, in fact, the exploited captives of the capitalists, but while the exchange of commodities, particularly through the use of money, still

FIGURE 36-2 STUDENT ALIENATION The dehumanization of the universities was a New Left rallying point during the 1960s. Universities were attacked as tools of the military and supporters of the economic and political status quo. At Sir George Williams University in Montreal, as at many other schools, the computer became the symbol of university-student relations. Here the streets are lined with computer cards and printout sheets in the aftermath of a building seizure. Student uprisings over similar issues occurred not only in North America but also in Europe and around the globe. United Press International Photo

obscures the reality of the relationship between the capitalists and the workers, the workers will not assume control over the forces of the economy.

Racism and Sexism

The New Left believes that discrimination by race and sex is essential to the capitalist system and will continue as long as capitalism exists. Racism and sexism benefit the ruling class, the capitalists, by dividing the work force against itself.

White male workers see their interests as being separate from the interests of nonwhite male workers and female workers; minority workers see their interests as being separate from those of white workers; and female workers see their interests as being separate from those of male workers. Thus, the workers are unable to join and assert their common interests.

In addition, the New Left sees racism and sexism as providing the capitalists with a pool of workers who have been socialized to accept, without protest, a clear and undisguised subordinate role. Minority and female workers provide a mobile, marginal work force that is available to the capitalists when and where they need it. These workers can be laid off and otherwise discarded by the capitalists whenever it suits their needs. Female and minority workers accept low-paying jobs and, in the past, have received lower pay than white male workers for the same jobs. In many marginal enterprises, it is this discrimination alone that makes for a profit that allows the business to continue.

Female and minority workers also serve the interest of the capitalists by providing scapegoats upon which white male workers can vent their frustrations and anger. Capitalists endeavor to make white male workers consciously think of themselves as free and unexploited. But in reality, according to the New Left, the subordination of white male workers to the capitalists and their managerial stand-ins engenders in these workers feelings of inferiority and envy. Were these feelings directed toward the capitalists, their authentic target, the capitalist system itself would be endangered. Thus, by separating certain groups as scapegoats, the capitalists are able to diffuse this hostility and protect themselves. The capitalists, in effect, provide a means whereby white male workers can also feel superior—at least over minority and female workers.

The radicals believe that racism and sexism can be eliminated only by changing the mode of production and then developing a society in which feelings of superiority and inferiority and the need to dominate or to be dominated are not part of the acculturation process. Their position is that as long as capitalism exists, racism and sexism will exist too, because they are necessary to the continued operation of the market system.

Imperialism

There is an ever widening gap in income between the rich and poor countries of the world, which radicals feel the orthodox economists are unable to explain or suggest remedies for. However, the New Left sees nothing mysterious about this widening and views it as the inevitable consequence of capitalism.

In explaining the existence of this gap, the New Left looks to the origins of capitalism, pointing out that much of the accumulation of wealth that enabled the market system to take root came from exploitation of the human and natural resources of what is today known as the Third World. Since that time, the trade, investment, and, more recently, aid policies of the more industrially developed countries toward the less-developed ones have been devised with the aim of keeping the less-developed countries less developed, while at the same time using the raw materials of these poor nations to sustain domestic growth. According to the radicals, this keeps the nations of the Third World in a state of dependence and prevents them from developing their own technology and productive base.

Given these conditions, the radicals maintain, a gap between the rich and poor countries is the only possible outcome. And the one way to change the situation is to build a new international economic order, one that is not based on this kind of exploitation of the poor by the rich.

REFORMING THE MARKET SYSTEM

The attitude of the radicals is that these four, and other, problems of capitalism cannot be solved by reform. The organization of the market system itself, rather than any difficulties in making it operate properly or any aberrations within it, accounts for these problems. The market itself creates and nurtures the many evils that face us today, and merely reforming the system will not do away with the inherent problems.

To the orthodox economists who attribute many of today's problems to capitalism's departure from the "pure" market system, the radicals answer that capitalism is an evolving system, completely different in its form today from what it was at its inception, and that to compare capitalism as it exists today with some pure model and draw inferences from that comparison is illogical. To the radicals, the model of pure capitalism has no relationship to the present economy.

To the orthodox economists who admit that there are indeed problems today in the workings of the free-market system but who maintain that these problems could be corrected by proper governmental

POWER AND THE MARKET SYSTEM

"Neoclassical or neo-Keynesian economics . . . has a decisive flaw. It offers no useful handle for grasping the economic problems that now beset the modern society. . . . Rather in eliding power—in making economics a nonpolitical subject—neoclassical theory, by the same process, destroys its relation with the real world."* In his presidential address to the American Economic Association in December 1972, John Kenneth Galbraith thus assaulted the irrelevance of conventional economics.

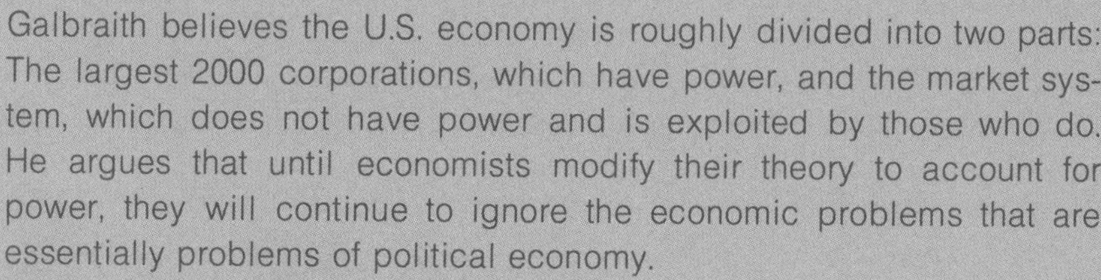

Galbraith believes the U.S. economy is roughly divided into two parts: The largest 2000 corporations, which have power, and the market system, which does not have power and is exploited by those who do. He argues that until economists modify their theory to account for power, they will continue to ignore the economic problems that are essentially problems of political economy.

According to Galbraith, even those problems that are recognized by conventional economics are completely misunderstood because power and the resulting political context are not considered. For example, Galbraith claims that the problem with monopoly and oligopoly is not that they underproduce as price theory predicts, but that they overproduce: we have a surfeit of cars, electric appliances, cosmetics, and so on because the large corporations have power over resources, consumers, and the government.

Galbraith also argues that economic theory is misleading as far as monetary policy is concerned. Traditional monetary policy is an acceptable means of stopping inflation because it leads to a lower level of investment by corporations. However, in the real world, large corporations are relatively immune to tight money because they have an assured supply of funds from retained earnings or "morally affiliated banks."

The solution, in Galbraith's opinion, is not to destroy the power of the large corporations, for this is impossible. The answer, rather, is to extend power to those who do not have it, through a new socialism—one that would provide the protection and power of the planning system to the existing market system.†

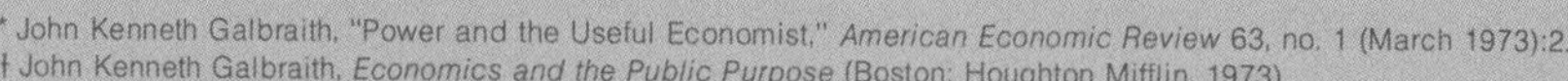

* John Kenneth Galbraith, "Power and the Useful Economist," *American Economic Review* 63, no. 1 (March 1973):2.
† John Kenneth Galbraith, *Economics and the Public Purpose* (Boston: Houghton Mifflin, 1973).

Bruce Davidson, Magnum

action, the radicals point out that the governments of the modern capitalist states are under the control of the capitalists. The tremendous impact on and involvement by modern governments in economic affairs in recent history have occurred under the sponsorship of the capitalists themselves. Therefore, the radicals maintain, it is foolish at best and self-deceptive at worst to expect such client governments to undertake any serious reform. True reform would endanger the continued existence of capitalism. Since the problems stem from the structure of capitalism itself, any reform that could solve these problems would have to replace that structure. The New Left thus believes that any governmental attempts at economic reform are cosmetic rather than substantive.

Along this same line of thinking, the radicals reject the position of many orthodox economists who see the increased governmental activity in the economy as a sign of coming socialism. They maintain that, if anything, this increased governmental influence, under the guidance of the capitalists, represents the possible onset of statism or fascism. And even as the radicals reject the market system as a dehumanizing and impersonal force with control over all of people's activities, they have an even deeper and more abiding hatred for the kind of control implicit in any kind of fascism.

REFORMING ECONOMICS

The current economic system, according to the radicals, is beyond hope of redemption. There is no meaningful alternative except to replace it. Similarly, they maintain that orthodox economic thinking is hopelessly unrealistic. It neither describes the economic situation as it exists today nor has the tools to develop solutions to the problems that beset modern society. To the New Left, orthodox economics is increasingly irrelevant and impotent. Only by first building a new economic model—one that accurately reflects the power relations in society—and then using that conception to build a new economic structure can these problems be meaningfully attacked and a better way of life emerge.

The New Left grants that in its original formulation the orthodox conception of the economy may have been valid. Individuals may very well have acted on their own, seeking their own self-interest apart from that of any group. Since that time, however, economic life has undergone enormous changes, yet the orthodox conception has remained the same, only becoming more technical. In modern society, individuals, acting as individuals, rarely make any decisions that have direct effect on the economy. The really important economic decisions are now made by organizations: trade associations, corporations, labor unions, and government bureaucracies. There is an interaction between economic decisions and political and social situations that has a profound effect in all areas. Yet the model of the free-market system does not in any way take into account these kinds of restraints and modifications on economic decision making.

Orthodox economics has also developed a complex analytic methodology, which the radicals feel suffers from gross misdirection because the kinds of problems it can solve are not the problems that people in modern society face. The radicals maintain that regardless of how high-powered this methodology is, it is a sterile and useless instrument because it cannot speak to real problems like poverty, alienation, discrimination, and imperialism. Of paramount importance to the radicals in the development of their new economics is the search for ways to relate the theory and the methodology of their new model to solving pressing problems. The New Left is more interested in improving the quality of life than in developing abstract propositions and theorems, and, to this end, it is as much an activist movement as an intellectual position.

REFORMING THE ECONOMY: PROS AND CONS

What exactly are the characteristics of the new economy that the radicals seek? Primarily, their recommendation is that the present wage-labor market system be superseded by a new relationship of men to the means of production, in which the people control the system, rather than vice versa.

The radicals suggest that people should organize

FIGURE 36-3 THE COMMUNE MOVEMENT Not all protest has been violent. The commune movement has been a small but conscious effort to create new foundations for society. Marxist analysis is only one strain of this movement; ecological sensitivity to the dangers of mass consumption, new psychological theories, and oriental philosophies have also contributed to visions of a new, commune-based society. Photo by Dominique Darr, Sygma

themselves into new social units of moderate size, called "communes" by some New Left writers, which would act in a political as well as in an economic context. These communes are envisioned to be self-governing, self-managing entities in which each individual would take his turn doing the administrative work, where the distinction between the directors and the directed would disappear, and where major decisions affecting the group would be arrived at by a kind of consensus.

Orthodox economists deride many of these suggestions as naive. They point out that the radicals have ignored the fundamental problem of how to provide for the incentives that cause people to work and the coordination that ensures that their work will be beneficial to the group. In any society, regardless of who owns the means of production, if specialization exists at all, these tasks must be accomplished. In addition, unless the communes are small enough to enable each person to communicate directly with every other person, the collection, organization, and dissemination of information within the group, let alone among the various communes, will not take place. In many ways, it is the allocation of information that forms the basis for class distinction.

Orthodox economists also point out that many of the problems that exist in capitalist societies, problems that the radicals properly denounce, also exist today in socialist societies such as the Soviet Union and its eastern European satellites. These societies also have their share of poverty, violence, alienation, and unequal distribution of power. Radicals counter this argument by saying that as far as they are concerned, the Soviet Union and its satellites in eastern Europe are class societies that are fast becoming indistinguishable from their capitalist counterparts. Radicals now point to China, where, they say, there is some evidence to support the proposition that a totally new kind of society, classless and cooperative in nature, can be built.

CONCLUSION

The New Left has developed from a concern with the economic problems that are readily apparent in the United States and other capitalistic countries. They see these problems as a result of capitalism.

Traditional economists see most of these problems as manifestations of the universal problem of scarcity and problems that have not yet been solved by any socialist or communist systems. Defenders of capitalism tend to argue that problems found in socialist systems are inherent in the system but that problems found in capitalist systems can be corrected by more, less, or different forms of government intervention. Radicals, of course, see existing problems in socialist systems as being temporary ones that can be solved by better planning and more or less centralization. Each group complains that the other is unfairly comparing the actual with the ideal. There appears to be little hope of resolving these basic differences by empirical or analytical means.

Traditional economists argue that their system of

thought does permit comparison of the two systems and analysis of the real economic problems. But much of the radical critique is aimed precisely at this framework, or paradigm, for examining economic systems and problems. A paradigm has been compared with a flashlight, which illuminates part of the problem but leaves the rest in the dark. The New Left believes that the traditional paradigm illuminates the wrong part of the problem and leaves the crucial issues in the dark. For example, marginal analysis and supply and demand curves reveal little about racism or the power of large corporations over legislation. Conventional economists answer that they can shed some light on these problems but that some aspects of them are beyond the realm of economics or any other social science. Radicals answer that the light they do shed is harmful because it diverts attention from the real problem and therefore confers legitimacy on basically corrupt institutions. Traditionalists then reply that the radicals' argument is basically noise and that they have not been able to substitute anything better than, or even as good as, conventional economics.

Radicals say that conventional economists are not concerned about the quality of life. Traditionalists say that concern with unemployment, wages, inflation, pollution, and poverty is nothing but concern for the quality of life and admit that other problems such as alienation and the origin of consumer tastes are beyond the realm of formal economics. Radicals reply that this proves their point.

Many orthodox economists feel that the biggest weakness in the radical critique is its simultaneous rejection of the market system and of bureaucracy in general. Although the radicals have indicated the need for a new kind of social and economic organization, they have not suggested any way that the present American economy, imperfect as it is, but also as huge and complex as it is, could be reorganized into commune-type units without enormous resistance, dislocation, and loss of productivity. It is more likely that the market will be replaced with a vast bureaucracy, which means more control, more power, and more alienation than any market system. The radicals reply that this proves the bankruptcy of the traditional paradigm. In their ideal system, what bureaucracy and control there is will be based upon cooperation and solidarity, and thus the results will be different from bureaucracies under capitalism. Most traditional economists remain skeptical.

SUMMARY

1 The radical critique of capitalism and orthodox economics rejects the foundation of the U.S. economy as unredeemable and the usual tools of economic analysis as totally inadequate. This approach is in accordance with Marxian analysis, which pinpoints capitalism itself, and not some technical malfunction within it, as the cause of the miseries of modern civilization.

2 Radicals believe that capitalism overemphasizes the greedy and competitive aspects of humans, while neglecting cooperation toward the common good and concern for shared values. Capitalism is intrinsically exploitative and inequitable, resulting in income maldistribution, alienation, racism, sexism, and imperialism.

3 To correct at least some of the maldistribution of income, many orthodox economists recommend policies such as tax reform and a minimum guaranteed annual income for all people regardless of their productivity. To radical economists, such ideas are naive because income distribution is based on power relations, not market relations. Surplus value created in the marketplace is taken by capitalists, and only the abolition of private property offers true hope of redressing the imbalances of power and income.

4 According to the New Left, alienation is likely to result when individuals lack political and economic power and when individuals' behavior cannot determine the outcomes that they want, particularly in areas such as work satisfaction and income. The Marxian description of the brutality of the mid-nineteenth-century English factory system has been adapted by the radical economists to describe the current discontent among American blue-collar workers, especially those who work on assembly lines, simply turning screws or tightening bolts eight hours a day.

5 Racism and sexism are seen as benefitting the ruling class by dividing the work force against itself. In addition, the New Left sees racism and sexism as providing the capitalists with a pool of workers who have been socialized to accept, without protest, a clear and undisguised subordinate role. Further, they provide scapegoats upon which white male workers can vent their frustrations and anger.

6 According to the radical economists, much of the accumulation of wealth that enabled the market system to take root came from exploitation of the human and natural resources of the Third World. Even though much of that area is now politically independent, the trade, investment, and aid policies of the more industrially developed countries toward the less-developed ones have been devised to keep the less-developed countries mere suppliers of raw materials, at low prices.

7 The main recommendation of the New Left is that the present market system be superseded by a new relationship of men to the means of production, in which the people control the system, rather than vice versa. They recommend the formation of self-managing communes in which each individual would take a turn doing the administrative work, where the distinction between the directors and the directed would disappear, and where major decisions affecting the group would be arrived at by a kind of consensus.

8 Orthodox economists question how incentives will be provided and whether the communes would not be subject to the same liabilities that plague us now.

SUGGESTED READINGS

Edwards, Richard C., Michael Reich, and **Thomas E. Weisskopf.** *The Capitalist System: A Radical Analysis of America.* Englewood Cliffs, N.J.: Prentice-Hall, 1972.

Heilbroner, Robert L., and **Arthur M. Ford.** *Is Economics Relevant? A Reader in Political Economics.* Pacific Palisades, Calif.: Goodyear, 1971.

Hunt, E. K., and **Howard J. Sherman.** *Economics: An Introduction to Traditional and Radical Views.* New York: Harper & Row, 1972.

Lindbeck, Assar. *The Political Economy of the New Left: An Outsider's View.* New York: Harper & Row, 1971.

Mermelstein, David, ed. *Economics: Mainstream Readings and Radical Critiques.* 1st and 2nd eds. New York: Random House, 1970, 1973.

QUESTIONS

1 Review

a. the basic criticisms of the radical economists concerning the use of the traditional economic model of the world,

b. distribution of surplus value,
c. characteristic alienation of the worker under capitalism,
d. the functions of racism, sexism, and imperialism for the capitalist according to the radical economists,
e. the radicals' view of the possible effectiveness of government in initiating and enforcing reform,
f. alternatives suggested by the radicals.

2 During the 1972 Presidential campaign, George McGovern was called a radical because he advocated a more progressive tax system, stronger antitrust policies, higher transfer payments to the poor, and a large cut in defense expenditures. Did the radicals accept this approach? Why or why not?

3 The radicals have cited many abuses of the capitalist system. Which abuses do they consider most blatant and what solution do they propose to eliminate them?

4 The radical economists might be considered revolutionaries, the more liberal among the orthodox economists, reformers. Explain why this is so.

5 The radicals would like to change the present mode of production into one in which the people control the means of production. Major decisions would be arrived at by consensus and there would be no distinction between directors and workers. Why do the orthodox economists call these plans naive? Do you agree or disagree?

6 According to the radical economists, the capitalist divides the labor force by fostering racism and sexism. To what extent do you think this charge true? Is this division mitigated by the formation of unions?

7 Charles Wilson, who was drafted from General Motors by President Eisenhower to serve as Secretary of Defense, told a panel of Senators at his confirmation hearing that what was good for General Motors was good for the country. This did little to allay the fears of those who were alarmed at the dominance of such corporations in our economic system. How does this concentration of economic power square with the orthodox model?

8 Small companies have a high mortality rate, frequently because they are inadequately financed. When a large company finds itself in financial difficulty, it is often able to obtain a government subsidy in the form of a loan guarantee: witness the cases of the Pennsylvania Railroad as it neared the shutdown point and of Lockheed Aircraft when it announced it would probably go bankrupt. How does this experience differ from what the traditional model would predict? What role does efficiency play with respect to the survival of small and large companies?

9 One of the arguments against the assertion that American policy toward the Third World is imperialistic is that the foreign component of our national income is small. Yet the radical economists point to many examples of what they consider to be American imperialism: the role of ITT in Chile (during the early 1970s), the intervention of the United Fruit Company in Guatemala (it supported a revolution there in 1954), as well as the involvement of American corporations in the countless coups and revolutions in Asia, Africa, and Latin America. How would the orthodox economists explain such events?

PART 7

INTERNATIONAL ECONOMICS

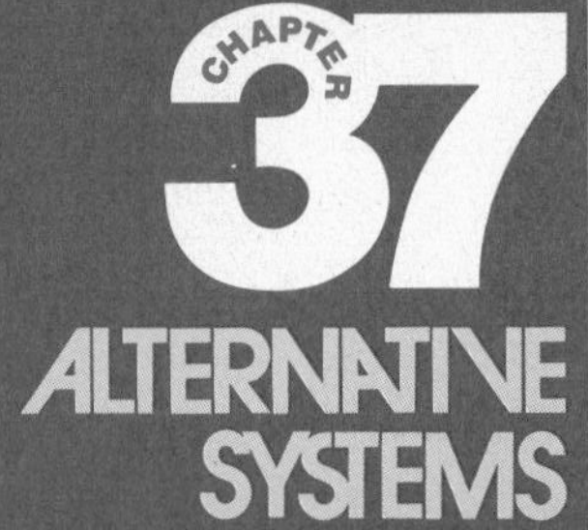
CHAPTER
37
ALTERNATIVE
SYSTEMS

Throughout this book, we have been primarily concerned with the operation of a capitalist market economy. But a market economy is only one of the systems man has devised to answer the basic economic questions of what to produce, how to produce it, and for whom. Much of the world's population, in fact, lives under economic systems far different from the one with which Americans are familiar.

This chapter examines and contrasts alternative economic systems. What are the economic arrangements under which many people of the world now live? How are decisions about production, allocation of resources, and job assignments made in each of these systems? What are the goals of each economy and what incentives are used to achieve these goals? And finally, how are the results of the productive process distributed within the economy?

In addition to seeking answers to these questions, we shall also attempt to evaluate the performance of each economy, using the criteria of efficiency, equity, stability, and growth. Does one system offer a higher level of allocative and technological efficiency? How equitable is the distribution of income in each? Which systems have the best records in maintaining full employment and price stability? And finally, what is the overall rate of growth that each economy has achieved? It is important to recognize, however, that the answers to these questions will not necessarily provide us with definitive judgments about the superiority of any one system. In the last analysis, any such judgments must depend on the relative importance assigned to each criterion. Moreover, many believe that the choice among economic systems is not a strictly economic issue; philosophical and ideological considerations are of equal or even greater importance.

CLASSIFYING ECONOMIC SYSTEMS

There are many different ways a society can organize the production and distribution of the goods and services it needs. In simple primitive economies, the family produces almost all the goods and services it requires. By contrast, in complex modern economies, the production process is highly specialized; households purchase most of the products they need with the money they earn by selling their labor or other resources. In this chapter, we shall confine our analysis to complex industrialized economies, which are generally classified in terms of two variables: the mechanism that coordinates the production process and the ownership of the means of production.

The market system is one mechanism for coordinating economic production. In a market economy, the questions of what will be produced and how incomes will be distributed are answered by individual decisions about what to buy and what to produce. Consumers choose among various products and between current and future consumption; workers choose among various jobs and between work and leisure; producers choose among possible product lines and between alternative production methods. All these millions of individual decisions are coordinated in the marketplace by the forces of supply and demand. Production in a command economy, in contrast, is coordinated by central economic planning. Decisions about what will be produced are made by a relatively small group of top-level managers. And, typically, there is also top-level planning regarding the allocation of raw materials, the assignment and utilization of labor, and the distribution of the goods and services.

A second variable often used to classify economic systems is ownership of productive assets. Under pure capitalism, the means of production are privately owned; under pure socialism,[1] they are owned by society as a whole or by groups of workers.

Opening photo from United Press International

1 It may be useful at this point to distinguish between socialism and communism. In the theory of Karl Marx, socialism is merely a transitional stage between capitalism and communism, a stage in which productive assets are owned by the state and the state is directed by the workers. Communism is the final stage in historical development. When it is achieved, the state will no longer be necessary, since all men will be internally motivated to produce those goods required by society. Although this is the distinction between socialism and communism offered by Marx, in everyday usage the two terms have rather different meanings. To some people socialism refers to any economic system that to some extent substitutes public for private ownership of the means of production, whereas communism refers to an economic system in which both public ownership and centralized planning predominate. Others tend to connect socialism and communism with political organization, assuming that a communist system is generally more totalitarian.

Although we have distinguished between market and command economies and between public and private ownership, in the real world none of these characteristics is found in its pure form. Instead, the various economies of the world might be said to form a spectrum, each including some mix of the market and command mechanisms and of private and public ownership.[2]

The Mix of Market and Command Mechanisms

Although the United States is generally classified as a market economy, many production and consumption decisions are made by planners. Government purchases of goods and services account for more than one-fifth of our GNP, and many of these spending decisions are determined by relatively small groups in the Office of Management and Budget, in congressional subcommittees, and in the federal and state bureaucracies. When implementing its economic policies, government also imposes centralized planning on the private sector. For example, macroeconomic planning is used to establish stabilization goals, and a handful of experts on the Federal Reserve Board, the Council of Economic Advisers, and congressional committees have the responsibility for timing and controlling the monetary and fiscal measures that will achieve these goals. Microeconomic planning is perhaps even more prevalent. Zoning regulations, acreage allotments for farmers, antidiscrimination laws, and specific provisions of the tax code are planned controls that affect many industries, firms, workers, and consumers. Finally, it can be argued that the output of many industries in the United States is not determined by market forces; instead, giant firms have the power to manipulate the market in order to dispose of planned levels of production.

Similarly, there are many elements of the market system in every command system. In the USSR, for example, higher wage levels are assigned to jobs in locations such as cold and distant Siberia and in industries such as machine goods, leaving market forces to attract sufficient workers to these regions and occupations. There are also market elements in the retail sector of the Russian economy. Although decisions about the overall level and composition of consumer goods are made by planners, people can choose in the marketplace among the goods that are available. Moreover, there is recent evidence that Soviet planners are becoming somewhat more responsive to consumer preferences, indicating that the market does, to some extent, augment central planning as a determinant of production goals.

No economy, then, is a pure market or a pure command system. Soviet planners realize that in a complex modern economy, total planning would be so ponderous as to prove unworkable, while even the most conservative American capitalist recognizes that the "anarchy of the market" could be a real threat to our institutions, in the complete absence of planning. Other nations, however, have gone even further than the United States and the USSR in seeking some form of compromise between the market and the command economies. Among the capitalist nations of the West, Sweden, the Netherlands, and France have developed extensive planning mechanisms, with responsibility being shared among government, employers, unions, and the public. Among socialist nations, on the other hand, Yugoslavia has been outstanding in the development of a viable market sector within the framework of a planned economy.

The Mix of Private and Public Ownership

A similar mix of systems can be seen when we compare economies in terms of private versus public ownership. Although the United States is theoretically a bastion of private ownership, its economy includes many public or quasi-public operations. Its mail, water, and garbage disposal services have traditionally been supplied by publicly owned enterprises, as have most of our intercity passenger rail services since the advent of Amtrak.

2 Although public ownership is frequently combined with a command system, and private ownership with a market system, this is not necessarily the case. Nazi Germany is an example of a command economy that operated within a framework of private ownership, while Yugoslavia is a case of public ownership combined with widespread use of the market mechanism.

Similarly, private ownership exists within nations generally classified as having public ownership. In the USSR, members of the agricultural cooperatives are also permitted to work on small, privately owned plots (one-half to two acres in size) and to sell the produce from these plots in the free market; in addition, professionals (doctors, dentists) are permitted to engage in private practice, and craftsmen (shoemakers, tailors) may operate their own businesses.

EVALUATING ALTERNATIVE ECONOMIC SYSTEMS

In evaluating the alternative economic systems that now exist, we are confronted by a choice of criteria. Shall we confine ourselves to economic measures of success, or shall we broaden our standards to include philosophical and ideological issues as well? Here we shall briefly review some of the major criteria—both economic and noneconomic—that are used in comparing and evaluating alternative economic systems.

Efficiency

Throughout this book, we have defined technological efficiency as a condition in which resources are used to their utmost capacity, such that no change can be made in the use of inputs to increase the output of one product without decreasing the output of another. There appears to be considerable evidence that market economies are often more technologically efficient than command economies. Some people suggest that this is the result of factors intrinsic in a command system: cumbersome bureaucracies, the stifling of individual initiative, a lack of flexibility.

If we define allocative efficiency as the ability to produce that combination of goods and services that people prefer, it seems that the market system is superior to the command system in this regard as well. In a command society, the allocation of resources is determined by a small group of planners who make judgments about what they think is best for society; in a market economy, in contrast, allocation is governed by consumers themselves.

There is some question, however, about whether allocative efficiency is an appropriate criterion for evaluating performance in command economies. Is satisfaction of consumer preferences necessarily a primary goal in all economic systems? To those who have adopted a command economy, it is only of secondary importance. Allocative efficiency, therefore, may not be a fair yardstick by which to compare market and command systems.

And, even in a market economy, allocative efficiency is not necessarily an unqualified blessing. Many observers have suggested that consumer demand does not always lead to the production of those goods and services that society needs most. John Kenneth Galbraith, for example, has written of the cravings of American consumers for color TVs, electric toothbrushes, and snowmobiles at the expense of quality education, clean air, and good public transportation.

Equity

In a market economy, output is distributed according to income. Income, in turn, depends on the quantity and quality of labor an individual has to offer in the marketplace, as well as on the contribution to production made by whatever other resources (land or capital) he owns. Capitalism, then, appears to include certain built-in inequalities: Some people simply possess more resources than others or resources that are in greater demand, for reasons that have nothing to do with their own efforts. It has been suggested by some that these inequalities should be eliminated—that goods and services should instead be allocated on more humanitarian grounds. To a certain extent, this point of view is accepted today in even the most extreme market economies. No society advocates that children, the blind, the old—or even the able-bodied but unemployed—should starve because they cannot produce. Nevertheless, in the United States and other capitalist economies, there are still huge differences in income between those who own the means of production and those who work them, between the highest-level managers and

THE SWEDISH EXPERIENCE

In Sweden, economic planning and capitalism are combined in an attempt to provide high degrees of efficiency and equity. The Swedish economy employs the market mechanism to encourage both technological and allocative efficiency. With the exception of a few public utilities and some cooperative retail outlets and manufacturing plants, private enterprise prevails, and the traditional market institutions determine what is produced, what resources are used, how goods are priced, and what workers are paid. Central planning, however, is superimposed on this market system, largely to control cyclical fluctuations. The planning elements include a novel investment reserve system by which Swedish businesses are encouraged, through tax incentives, to set aside part of their annual profits as investment reserves. When economic activity declines, the government "activates" these reserves, which are then used for investment purposes. Swedish planners believe that this investment reserve system has proven helpful in avoiding the wide fluctuations of investment spending that characterize many market systems, and which result in recurring bouts of unemployment and inflation. The unemployment rate in Sweden, for example, has generally remained between 1½ and 3 percent.

The Swedish system is deliberately designed to guarantee a minimum standard of living for all its citizens—a minimum that is very high indeed even by U.S. standards. Benefits include maternity grants of about $500, free meals at school for students, hospitalization at $2 a day, unemployment insurance of up to $150 a week, and retirement pay equal to two-thirds of average income earned. These programs are financed by the highest income tax schedule in the world: 58 percent of each dollar earned above $6000 goes to the government, and the rate climbs to 70 percent after income hits $12,000. Thus, the combination of widespread low-cost benefits and a high income tax rate have created an economy in which there can be few extremes of poverty or wealth, in which everyone is assured a comfortable minimum, but almost no one has the after-tax income to provide very much more.

At the present time, the key question in Sweden is whether the Swedes have sacrificed efficiency and growth for equity. Those who are disenchanted with the system tell of the "flu epidemic" that hits Sweden every November, when workers realize that their annual income has reached a tax bracket where further earnings will go mostly to taxes. Instead of working, they call in sick, and collect tax-free sick benefits for the rest of the year. Similarly, there are reports of workers who choose jobs primarily on the basis of how easy it is to conceal income earned from the tax collector. For example, a choice source of income for many Swedish

SIS (Swedish Information Service)

SIS

women is "black" (tax-free) money earned by privately caring for neighborhood children. Similarly, the increasing movement of Swedish funds to Swiss bank accounts suggests that considerable efforts are being made to conceal "black" money earned. Thus, critics claim that the high Swedish tax rates, which are essential if the system is to achieve its high standard of equity, divert resources from their most efficient uses.

On the other hand, the Swedish economic statistics are unquestionably impressive. From 1965 to 1970, the nation's domestic growth rate was 3.9 percent, somewhat better than the 3.3 percent experienced by the United States. In mid-1973, the Swedish per capita income was approximately 80 percent of the U.S. figure. Swedes own proportionately more cars and telephones than any of their European neighbors and more TV sets than Americans. More than 500,000 families (or about 1 in 4) spend vacations in their own summer cottages or on privately owned boats.

To many observers, the Swedish experience represents a curious paradox. Why is there discontent in a society that has apparently met and conquered so many of the economic challenges that are still besetting the rest of the world? But to the Swedish people, the welfare state they have created is far from a utopia. In the words of one Stockholm University sociologist, "A welfare society is not a society of happy pigs. Sweden is in a healthy state of dissatisfaction."

the lowest-level workers. Of course, differences in income also exist in socialist nations, but these differences are much smaller than those in capitalist countries. The extremes of poverty found in some rural areas and urban ghettos of America have been virtually eliminated in the USSR and China.

Stability

Stability is a goal that all economic systems seek. A stable economy is one in which fluctuations in the level of employment are eliminated, or at least minimized, and in which prices remain essentially constant, with no significant inflation or deflation. Wide swings in economic activity are characteristic of market economies, and in the last several decades, capitalist countries have directed much effort toward developing tools that will stabilize both employment and prices. Command economies, on the other hand, because of their ability to equate saving and investment, have managed to avoid the economic ups and downs of the business cycle. In terms of stability, then, the command system seems to outperform the market system.

Growth

Another criterion for evaluating the performance of alternative economic systems is the overall rate of growth. Growth remains an objective, even for highly developed economies, since growth allows a society to have more of the many goods and services its people desire. Comparisons of capitalist market economies and socialist command economies in regard to economic growth reveal that success is mixed. During certain periods in their histories, several command systems, notably those of the USSR and China, have achieved impressive rates of economic growth. Other command economies, however, have been far less successful. Similarly, market economies vary in the rates of growth they have achieved, Japan and West Germany having the most outstanding records in recent decades. It appears, then, that a high rate of growth is perhaps related less to the general economic system a nation has adopted and more to the current conditions and the stage of economic development of that country.

Ideological Factors

When we attempt to evaluate economic systems in terms of philosophical and ideological values, we are entering ambiguous territory. Most Americans defend the market system on the grounds that competition not only spurs economic abundance, but also provides a climate in which individual liberties and values can best flourish. The Maoist Chinese, on the other hand, claim that the equalitarianism, self-reliance, and cooperative spirit of a command system produce not only superior economic performance, but also a higher level of personal development and well-being.

It is especially important to avoid the error of associating any particular economic system with political freedom. Although the Soviet Union and China, the two largest communist countries, do not enjoy such democratic institutions as free elections and a free press, there are other communist nations, such as Yugoslavia, that appear to offer some of the political institutions we consider important. And although many Western capitalist countries are classified as democracies, there are capitalist societies, such as Spain and Greece, that can be described as dictatorships.

In the remainder of this chapter, we shall analyze the workings of several alternative economic systems and use the criteria outlined above to evaluate their performances. The Soviet Union, being the oldest socialist command economy in the world, provides a good introduction to how such a system operates. Then, the economies of China and Cuba offer interesting examples of how differences in ideology, resources, and history can produce socialist command systems quite removed from the basic Soviet model. And, finally, the case of Yugoslavia illustrates one way in which public ownership can be combined with the market mechanism to create a rather unique economic arrangement.

THE SOVIET UNION

Planning outweighs all other economic concerns in the Soviet Union. Should the planning system be centralized? Decentralized? To what extent and at what point should lower-level administrators or managers participate in the planning process? How much of a role should be assigned to market factors? To consumer preferences? Clearly, it is an immense task to regulate all the economic activity between people and institutions in a country as large as the Soviet Union, and the problem of exactly how this planning should be organized is a constant and difficult one.

Setting Economic Goals

In the Soviet Union, long-term goals have usually been outlined in five-year or seven-year plans. These plans specify major objectives, such as the overall rate of growth, and set target percentage increases for each segment of the economy. For example, the Five Year Plan for 1966 to 1970 called for an increase of 47 to 50 percent in total industrial output, 15 to 17 percent in coal production, 25 percent in agricultural output, and 121 to 145 percent in motor vehicle production. The process of translating these long-term plans into action, however, is primarily embodied in the nation's short-term, or annual, plans, which lie at the heart of the Soviet economic system.

Primary responsibility for the Annual Plan rests with GOSPLAN, the state planning commission. Planning begins with the assignment of production goals for the coming year to the leading industries. These goals are submitted to the appropriate ministries, which in turn break them down by industrial subdivision. Moving through various levels of administrators, the original goals are finally assigned as individual quotas to particular plants or farms. The individual producing units provide some feedback to the official planning agencies; each estimates its own productive capacity for the coming year, and comments about the feasibility of the assigned quotas. The final plan, which must eventually be approved by the top-level Council of Ministers of the USSR, is a product of compromises between the original quotas of GOSPLAN and the central ministries, and the views of the particular producing units. Since most Russian plant managers are rated (and in some cases paid) according to their success in achieving or surpassing their quotas, they have a vested interest in receiving quotas that are as low as possible. Consequently, there is continuous interplay between the local plants and the central planners at the administrative levels, who wish to set higher quotas.

The Coordination Problem

One fundamental problem facing any command economy is that of coordination. It is one thing to mandate a 15 percent increase in steel production; it is quite another to ensure adequate supplies of iron ore, coal, and labor so that this increase will be accomplished. Suppose, for example, that the iron mining industry fails to achieve its quota, either because of a lack of machinery or because transportation is not available. As a result, its output will be inadequate to supply the needs of the steel industry, and the steel industry will not reach its assigned production level. And the repercussions of a shortage of iron ore do not stop with the steel industry. If the steel quota is not met, the machinery quota will not be met, and if the machinery quota is not met, all industries that rely on the use of machinery will be similarly affected.

There are more than 200,000 industrial enterprises in the Soviet Union. The central planners must ensure that resources are allocated to each enterprise in the correct amounts and at the right time to keep production moving. This involves, quite literally, billions of planning decisions, all interrelated. It is an enormous undertaking, and Soviet economists and mathematicians have pioneered the use of sophisticated mathematical techniques and computers in their attempts to handle the planning function in a complex modern economy.

Input-output analysis, which was discussed in Chapter 32, is the basic tool of Soviet planners. It indicates the interrelationships between industries by listing the amount of output of each industry that is eventually used as an input in other industries. In this way, planners can easily recognize the changes in output in, say, steel that will be required to achieve a given increase in the machinery industry, or any other industry that uses steel as an input. This input-output approach helps the planners avoid bottlenecks that can occur throughout the economy if production quotas in any one area are not met because of miscalculations.

Another planning technique used in the Soviet Union is the establishment of priorities. Certain segments of the economy, such as heavy industry, are given special status as "leading links," while others, such as consumer goods or agriculture, are assigned lower priority. When shortages develop because goals are not achieved, resources are channeled to the leading links. For example, if steel production should be inadequate to meet all the input requirements of Soviet industry, the available steel would be used for dam construction and heavy electrical equipment, while allotments to automobile and tractor factories would be cut back.

Finally, the Soviet planners often depend on reserves as a way of avoiding the bottlenecks of poor planning. If sizable inventories of grinding wheels or rubber hoses or ball bearings can be maintained, industries requiring these inputs will not have to close up shop should current production be inadequate.

Although such techniques enhance the workability of the central planning process, they do not guarantee a high degree of efficiency. Furthermore, an inevitable problem with such an ambitious planning system is the bureaucracy it requires. Numerous control agencies must be established to supervise the creation and implementation of plans, and the time spent formulating and frequently reevaluating quotas slows the production process. Thus, even when a command economy works, the enormous administrative overhead involved in central planning detracts greatly from its efficiency.

Soviet Economic Institutions

The Individual Firm In Soviet industry, the individual firm or "enterprise" is responsible for carrying out its assigned production goals using a predetermined allotment of resources. A typical plant manager, for example, will be told not only what his production quota is, but also how many people he can employ, the established wage rates for each job category, and the quantities of raw materials he may use for each unit of output. Managerial discretion is generally restricted to attempts to increase production within the limits of resource allocations.

The types of resources allocated to individual firms depend upon the nature of the industry and the priority assigned to it. Because capital goods have always been relatively scarce in the USSR, highly capital-intensive plants have been restricted to priority sectors. But whenever possible within these sectors, Soviet designers and managers of individual plants have turned to capital-intensive production methods. In part, this reflects the technical or engineering background of most managers. But it also reflects the Marxian view that interest should not be considered a cost of production, a view that, in the past, has led Soviet planners to provide capital equipment with no interest cost. As a result, capital-intensive plants often appeared to be cheaper to operate than those using larger quantities of labor.

The Labor Market The labor market in the USSR combines both planned and free-market mechanisms. Nominally, wage rates are established by the government. But workers usually have the right to choose their own jobs and to change them as they wish. In fact, because of the shortages of trained labor in most fields, there is a good deal of job turnover. Moreover, market forces operate to some extent within the fixed wage scales. First, the central planning authorities deliberately set pay rates higher for jobs in priority enterprises. Second, individual plants have a certain degree of flexibility in determining job classifications, so that it is possible to attract workers to a particular job by assigning a higher rating to that job. Finally, fringe benefits, desirable housing in particular, are often tied to jobs and can be used as incentives to attract or hold employees.

Pricing Practices Most retail trade in the USSR takes place through state-owned or cooperative stores, where prices are fixed by planners. The only exception is the kolkhoz market, where peasants may sell the produce from the small private plots they are permitted to cultivate and where prices are set by supply and demand. Kolkhoz sales accounted for about 4 percent of all USSR retail sales in 1964.

Outside the kolkhoz markets, pricing procedures in the USSR are very different from those in a market economy. In the United States, prices reflect production costs and market conditions. In the USSR, the prices assigned to goods are not necessarily related either to costs or to market demand, but rather reflect policy decisions. Food and housing are generally priced significantly below cost, while those goods that planners consider luxuries are priced considerably above cost through the use of an excise or turnover tax. A turnover tax ensures that market demand and supply remain in equilibrium. Assume, for example, that the cost of producing a washing machine is 2000 rubles. At any price near this, however, the quantity of washing machines demanded will exceed the low-priority quota the central planning agency has set. In order to avoid shortages, the government will impose a turnover tax of 100 percent or more on washing machines. The turnover tax, then, ensures equilibrium in the product market and also provides the government with a very effective stabilization device. One of the reasons the USSR has been so successful in avoiding inflation is its use of the turnover tax to eliminate excess buying power. Moreover, the turnover tax is the largest source of revenue for the Soviet government.

The Agricultural Sector The agricultural sector of the USSR is divided primarily into two types of farms: the state farms, which are state-owned and hire labor for wages, and the collective farms, whose members pool their land, machines, and labor, and who share in the profits. In addition, each peasant family is allotted a small individual plot of land, which it can cultivate privately, selling the produce at market prices in the kolkhoz markets.

Both the state and the collective farms are huge, even by U.S. standards. A state farm resembles an industrial firm in its organization. Its manager is appointed by the state; it is assigned production quotas and allocated the labor, seed, fertilizer, tractors, and other resources that it must use to achieve these quotas. Profits belong to the state. Since Khrushchev's regime, the use of the state farm has been significantly increased. But at one time the state farms were the means through which the "virgin lands" in the east were brought under cultivation in an attempt to solve the persistent Russian food shortage.

Most of the older Soviet farms are operated as collectives, although the collectives have had a generally unsatisfactory record in Soviet history. They were originally introduced by Stalin in 1929 to replace the inefficient small family farm as a way of increasing agricultural production. Collectivization was strongly opposed by the peasants, both because of personal preferences and because the prices the state paid for agricultural goods produced by collectives were set deliberately low in order to keep down food costs for urban workers. The immediate effects of this forced collectivization included a considerable decline in agricultural output, widespread famine, and the death of millions of Soviet peasants. It also resulted in the wholesale slaughter of livestock by farm families who would otherwise have starved, a slaughter that disrupted meat, dairy, and poultry production in the USSR for years to come. Finally, forced collectivization created a climate of distrust for the central government, which has been compounded over the years because of government pricing policies that continue to favor the urban worker at the expense of the farmer.

Recently, attempts have been made to raise the prices paid to the collectives, and some success has been achieved in raising agricultural productivity. Nevertheless, the private plots of land, which occupy only 3 percent of the total cultivated land in the USSR, produce about one-third of the total value of farm output. This is partly because these plots are primarily devoted to higher-value goods such as meat and dairy products, but the statistics do raise some fundamental questions about the applicability of a command system to agriculture.

The Soviet Economy: An Evaluation

Accomplishments The most outstanding accomplishment of the Soviet command economy has been its rate of growth. And what makes this accomplishment even more impressive is the fact that a high growth rate has been achieved without the cyclical unemployment and persistent inflation that have characterized the market economies of other industrialized nations. It also appears that the USSR has achieved a higher degree of equity in the distribution of its goods and services than many market economies.

GROWTH With the exception of the war years, the Soviet growth rate has indeed been impressive. From 1950 to 1965, for example, real GNP increased at a rate of 6.2 percent, a dramatically better record than the 3½ percent rate achieved by the United States over the same period. Since 1965, however, there has apparently been some slowdown in Soviet growth: During the late sixties, the Russian growth rate probably did not exceed 5 percent, and current figures may be even lower. Furthermore, although the Soviet Union has consistently outperformed the United States in terms of growth during the post–World War II period, the market economies of capitalist West Germany and Japan have reported higher growth rates than the USSR since the mid-sixties, as has the market economy of socialist Yugoslavia.

The high Soviet growth rates can be attributed, at least in part, to deliberate policy decisions. As compared with the United States, the Soviet Union has chosen to devote relatively more of its GNP to investment than to private consumption. In addition, much of this investment spending has been concentrated in the heavy industry sector, where it has the most effect on future growth. Soviet investment is much more likely to be channeled into dams or factories, for example, than into freeways or shopping centers.

STABILIZATION One important advantage of a command economy is its ability to equate saving and investment so that the economy is always in balance, thus avoiding the cyclical unemployment and inflation that characterize business cycles in capitalist nations. Soviet economists, unlike their American counterparts, do not have to worry about the possibility of unemployment[3] resulting from a gap between saving and investment: Investment levels are planned so that such a gap is impossible. Nor is price inflation a major problem, at least in the sense that we have experienced it in recent years. The excesses in demand that would, in a market economy, be reflected in higher prices throughout the economy, are carefully channeled into a few sectors in the Soviet Union. Food, housing, and other necessities are rigorously price-controlled, and the high turnover taxes on luxuries absorb excess buying power.

But, despite the use of the turnover tax, there are many examples of **repressed inflation** in the Soviet economy. This is characterized by shortages of many commodities and by long lines of consumers waiting to buy the scarce goods. Technically, however, there is no inflation in such cases, since the prices of the scarce goods remain stable.

EQUITY How equitable is the distribution of income under the Soviet system? Comparing Soviet and U.S. pay scales is not always revealing because of the differences in fringe benefits, income tax policies, and prices in the two economies. For example, salary figures might show that the manager of a medium-sized Russian factory is paid five to six times as much as a low-level worker in his plant. But these figures may actually understate the manager's relative income, because he may also receive a car, desirable housing, and elaborate free vacations—all of which may not be available at any price to the ordinary worker. Moreover, in comparing the range of salaries in the United States to that in the Soviet Union, we should note that federal income taxes on earned income run as high as 50 percent in the U.S., whereas in the USSR those in the top bracket pay only 13 percent. Thus, there is evidence that wage differences in an individual firm may actually be greater in the Soviet system than they appear.

Many experts believe that there are also significant inequalities in the distribution of income between urban and rural sectors of the Soviet economy. Russian policy, from its inception, has been based on the premise that rapid industrialization was essential to protect the nation from its potential enemies. To spur industrialization, prices paid to

3 We refer here only to cyclical unemployment. Structural and frictional unemployment exist in the USSR just as they do in most capitalist nations.

farmers were deliberately set at low levels, both to encourage migration from the countryside to the urban factories and to provide a cheap source of food for the urban masses. Although some increases in farm prices have been introduced in recent years, it still appears that the average rural dweller in the United States is relatively better off than his counterpart in the USSR.

Nevertheless, there is considerable evidence that income is more equally distributed in the USSR than it is in many Western capitalist nations, including the United States. The absence of private property such as real estate or stocks means that there is no unearned income from rents or dividends to distort earned income distribution patterns. Nor, under the Soviet system, are there any individuals who receive the very high incomes earned by a few corporate executives, private entrepreneurs, or superstars in the capitalist market economies. Finally, there are many items, such as education, housing, medical care, or even vacations, that can be a major expense for lower- and middle-income Americans, but which are free or very cheap in the USSR. Such free or subsidized goods and services can reduce the significance of reported differences in take-home pay. Thus, pay differentials exist in the USSR, but these differentials are probably less than those in the United States. Extremes of poverty and wealth are not generally found in the Soviet Union. Moreover, in terms of real income, the distribution is perhaps even more equal because of the impressive list of goods and services that are supplied on a free or subsidized basis by the Soviet government.

Failures Many of the shortcomings of the Soviet system can be grouped under the collective heading of failures of efficiency, both technological and allocative. There is evidence to suggest that despite the country's excellent growth record, Soviet planners do not always specify the particular resource mix that maximizes production. Nor does the system appear to provide the Soviet consumer with the variety, quality, or quantity of goods he would otherwise prefer.

TECHNOLOGICAL INEFFICIENCY Many experts feel that the industrial sector of the Soviet economy has been relatively unsuccessful in achieving the largest output at the lowest cost. The heavy emphasis on centralized planning leaves the individual plant manager with little room for innovation: His allotment of labor, capital, and raw materials is assigned, and he has almost no discretion to vary it. In particular, the fact that relative scarcities of resources are not reflected in prices hinders both the planners and the plant managers in adjusting the resource mix to achieve a high level of technological efficiency. For example, if cottonseed oil is especially plentiful and therefore cheap in the United States, margarine manufacturers will switch at once from alternate inputs such as soybean oil. But such a switch would be more difficult and cumbersome in the Soviet Union because of the many levels of administrators who would have to approve the projected substitution and because of the absence of price changes as a signaling device.

Another source of technological inefficiency in industry has been the heavy emphasis on capital-intensive production methods as a result of early Soviet accounting practices, which did not charge an enterprise interest on capital equipment. Even today, interest charges are probably too low in light of the severe shortage of capital in the USSR. As a result, it is possible that many enterprises are operating inefficiently in terms of true costs and that a different resource mix, involving less capital, might be preferable.

It is in the agricultural sector that Soviet technological inefficiency has perhaps been most apparent. Although agriculture employs more than 30 percent of the Soviet labor force, as opposed to approximately 5 percent of the U.S. labor force, the industry has periodically been unable to supply enough foodstuffs for the nation. Part of the failure can be attributed to a lack of rich land, a short growing season, and unpredictable weather. The problem, however, has doubtless been compounded by planning errors, resulting in inadequate supplies of fertilizer and capital equipment, and a farm-pricing system that does not provide suitable incentives.

ARE THE SOCIALIST AND CAPITALIST SYSTEMS CONVERGING?

One of the intriguing questions now facing economists is whether we are in the midst of a convergence or rapprochement between the socialist command economies and the capitalist market economies. Of course, in the real world there are no pure socialist or capitalist, command or market, systems: every economy includes some mix of these various elements. But in recent years it appears that private ownership and the market mechanism have become increasingly important in the socialist nations, while, at the same time, the capitalist nations have adopted more planning and more public ownership. Many economists have suggested that these are signs that a convergence of the two systems is taking place.

A number of changes now occurring in the socialist nations seems to confirm this thesis. In the Soviet Union, the Eastern satellites, and Yugoslavia, there now appears to be less concern with equalizing income. These nations are also placing new emphasis on using market criteria to determine production goals, with the result that more consumer goods are being produced. And decentralized planning, often based on market factors, has replaced centralized planning in many areas.

Similar changes are taking place in the market economies of the West. The public sector has become increasingly important: in Western Europe, public utilities, coal and steel works, and banks and insurance companies are often state-owned; in the United States, intercity rail services have recently become publicly operated under Amtrak. Higher income and inheritance taxes, more public education, and more free medical care have resulted in a more equitable distribution of income. Centralized government planning has superseded the market mechanism in many segments of the economy: the United States, for example, has had over 40 years of government-administered production allotments for agriculture and several years of nationwide wage-price controls.

Granted there are still many significant differences between socialist command and capitalist market economies. The public sector in socialist countries is still much larger than in capitalist nations, there is more control of prices, centralized planning is more prevalent, and the distribution of real income is more equal. Nevertheless, some maintain that these remaining differences will probably become less distinct in the years to come.

Most Soviet economists, however, reject the convergence theory, arguing that it merely provides evidence of "the bankruptcy of the traditional forms of attacking socialism." Because socialism has been so successful, say the Soviets, capitalists can no longer dismiss it as a failure; instead, they attack it more subtly by insisting that socialism is merely one step in an evolution toward capitalism. In the view of one Soviet economist the differences between capitalism and socialism are so basic as to minimize any superficial similarities. In capitalist nations the profits "land in the pockets of capitalists, the safes of monopolies . . ."; in socialist nations, they are "used in full, to the last kopek, for the good of society." Under capitalism, prices are fixed "through destructive competition"; under socialism they are determined "according to plan." Under capitalism, the goals of the national economy are determined by the "selfish interest of capitalists"; under socialism, "by the interests of the people [as] represented by . . . the Party and the State."*

*L. L. Leontiev, "Myth about 'Rapprochement' of the Two Systems," *Reprints from the Soviet Press* 4, 3 (February 9, 1967).

Marc Riboud, Magnum

ALLOCATIVE INEFFICIENCY Allocative efficiency occurs when an economy produces the combination of goods and services that most satisfies society; no change can be made in the allocation of resources without making someone worse off. In the United States, the market mechanisms help to ensure that consumer preferences will be met. In the Soviet Union, however, the product mix is determined by a small group of planners in accordance with their view of the relative importance of alternative satisfactions. In other words, the Soviet system, like that of any other command economy, reflects the planners' preferences rather than the consumers' preferences. Soviet planners have consistently favored capital goods over consumer goods. Moreover, within the consumer goods sector, the Soviet citizen does not necessarily find the items he prefers, partly because the overall shortage of consumer goods means that there are rarely oversupply pressures forcing producers to please their customers.

As a result, it appears that the Soviet Union is significantly behind Western capitalist nations in satisfying consumer preferences. Housing is scarce and crowded, clothing is shoddy, per capita consumption of meat is much lower than U.S. levels. The full extent of the Soviet lag in consumer goods, as seen through Western eyes, is exemplified by the automobile industry. In 1973, there were 90 million private cars in the United States, or almost one car for every two people. In the Soviet Union, there were only 2 million cars in all, or about 1 for every 125 people. Part of this difference is due simply to lower per capita GNP in the Soviet Union as compared with the United States, but it also reflects a lower priority to consumer preferences in the USSR.

Recent Changes in the Soviet Economy

As the Soviet economy has grown, becoming wealthier and more complex, there has been an increasing awareness of technological and allocative inefficiencies. Pressures for reform have been exerted. In particular, pressures for change have arisen in the consumer area, and Soviet economists have attempted to devise a more effective method of satisfying consumer preferences. **Libermanism,** named for Yevsei Liberman of Kharkov University, is the label given to the institutions and practices recently introduced into the Soviet economy in an attempt to achieve these reforms.

Under these innovations, the Soviet economy has tried to some extent to "plan from below." Individual enterprises are now permitted to accept "orders" for consumer goods from the state retail stores, which can specify the types of merchandise and the quality standards they believe consumers desire. This is a major innovation, since it is no longer the planners alone, but also the retailers, who decide what is to be available for consumption. In this way, it is hoped that the new system will lead to a closer match between what the consumer wants and what he gets.

Other market-style innovations include drastic changes in the incentives under which the individual Soviet enterprise operates. The objective of the plant manager is no longer merely to meet or exceed his production quota in physical terms. Instead, an elaborate "profit" indicator has been developed, and managers and workers are rewarded, to some extent, in terms of their profits. This profit indicator is related to costs as well as to the quality of the finished product, which is reflected in revenue. Thus, under the new incentive system, the plant manager is motivated both to improve the technological efficiency of his operation by cutting costs and to produce better quality goods. Moreover, since the reforms also allow increased independence for the individual enterprise manager (for example, the right to set his own wage rates), he has been provided with the freedom, as well as the incentive, for improving production techniques and quality.

These economic reforms, which now affect perhaps as many as half of all Soviet enterprises, have met with a mixed reception. Old-line socialists mistrust the introduction of market institutions into the framework of their centralized planning system. They wonder if an economy can function with a half-market, half-command mechanism. In addition, they question whether the increasing use of the profit motive will have ideological implications throughout the system: Can the rigorous control that has characterized Soviet political life since Lenin's time be maintained in the face of a decentralized economic system? Undoubtedly, the answers to such questions will emerge in the years to come.

THE PEOPLE'S REPUBLIC OF CHINA

The Ideological Base: Maoism

The ideological differences between the USSR and China partly explain many of the unique institutions and practices that characterize the People's Republic of China. The Chinese interpret quite literally much of Marxian doctrine: They view private property and the profit motive as innately evil, believing that these institutions are inevitably accompanied by social injustices and dehumanization. Using these Marxian tenets as a base, Mao Tse-tung, Chairman of the Chinese Communist Party, has developed a distinctive ideology, called Maoism. According to Maoist thought, the function of the state is to promote not only economic development and material well-being, but also spiritual well-being. The Maoist man is a well-rounded, self-reliant human being, not a helpless cog in a machine. He is an unselfish person, who cooperates rather than competes.

Such a concept of man must inevitably have an effect on economic organization. It also makes comparisons of China's economy with those of other nations almost impossible, for the Chinese goals are very often social rather than material. Certainly the Maoist wishes his nation to prosper, but he would consider an increase in GNP incidental to the development of a versatile and cooperative work force that willingly contributes its labor to the common good.

The Historical Background

When the Chinese Communists came to power in 1949, they found a nation devastated by years of war with Japan. The technological base was small, there were few capital goods, and there was runaway inflation and vast unemployment. The first Five Year Plan (1952–1957) was directed at alleviating these problems. In an attempt to industrialize, it placed primary emphasis on heavy industry. Far-reaching changes were also introduced in the agricultural sector, with collectivized farms replacing the traditional large landowner system.

The first Five Year Plan achieved remarkable success in industrializing the nation. Output increased spectacularly, vast numbers of new plants were built, and production of such basic commodities as coal and steel quadrupled. In 1958, a new plan, the Great Leap Forward, was introduced. The objectives were an even higher rate of growth and continued emphasis on heavy industry and capital goods. But because of poor planning, unrealistic goals, lack of coordination, and neglect of agriculture, the Great Leap Forward ended in disaster, and, since its failure, the entire direction of the Chinese economy has changed.

Since 1961, the Chinese strategy has been to give highest priority to the agricultural sector, with the industrial sector taking a secondary role and being evaluated largely in terms of its effect on agriculture. New investment in heavy industry, for example, is more likely to be channeled into a fertilizer plant than into a cement or plastics plant. Furthermore, the nonagricultural heavy industries are often forced to take a back seat, even to consumer goods. Even consumer goods take precedence over heavy equipment when those goods are intended for farm consumption.

China's Economic Institutions

The People's Communes China is a command economy. But, beginning with the period of the Great Leap Forward, Chinese leaders have had an ideological commitment to decentralization. The vehicles for this decentralization have been the People's Communes, geographical and administrative subdivisions of government, varying in size from fewer than 5000 to more than 40,000 people. The People's Communes also serve as the basic producing units. Each commune is assigned a production task, but it is encouraged to use its own initiative to improve production methods and work assignments, to develop local sources of raw materials, and so forth.

The Labor Market The economy of China is characterized by full employment. This has been accomplished by channeling most of the labor force—perhaps 75 percent—into agriculture, which is still extremely labor-intensive. Even within the industrial sector, much of the emphasis is on labor-intensive light industry, rather than on capital-intensive heavy equipment.

Perhaps nowhere does the command economy affect the daily life of the Chinese citizen more clearly than in his job. Occupations, specific jobs, and places of residence are assigned by the state: The individual has little choice as to what he will do or where he will do it. For example, under most circumstances, a young rural resident who has just completed school cannot leave for the city if he so desires. He automatically becomes a member of the commune in which he has grown up, and he must continue to live and work there. Reinforcing this practice is the requirement that factories and urban employers may not recruit in the countryside unless they have specific permission from the planning authorities to do so.

Pricing Practices Prices in China are set by the state and remain very stable. In fact, prices have actually declined in parts of the industrial sector in recent years. This is in keeping with a government policy to reflect productivity increases in real income by decreasing prices rather than by raising money wages.

Overall, inflationary pressures have not been a major problem for the Chinese planners, partly because of the relatively high proportion of GNP devoted to consumer goods and partly because most of the population lives in rural communes, which are relatively self-sufficient. In addition, the government is committed to a balanced budget. The state does no borrowing and has no internal or external debt. As a result, the inflationary pressures that can arise from a budgetary deficit or an excessive expansion of the money supply, and which are characteristic of many developing nations as well as some highly industrialized ones, are absent in China.

The Agricultural Sector The agricultural sector of the Chinese economy is organized through the commune system, with an individual production team comprising 100 to 150 members. Each team cultivates the land assigned to it by the commune. The team is responsible for allocating tasks among its members and for organizing the way work will be carried out. The commune keeps what it needs for its own consumption, selling the rest to the state retail outlets. Part of the proceeds of these sales (15 to 20 percent) is kept by the commune for local public services, state taxes, and so forth; the remainder is returned to the individual teams, where the members of the team decide among themselves how it should be distributed.

In addition to the communally worked land, each peasant in the commune is permitted to cultivate a small plot for his personal use. Unlike the Russian kolkhoz system, however, the peasants are required to keep the output from these plots for their own use; they may not sell it in the open market.

The Chinese Economy: An Evaluation

In evaluating the performance of the Chinese economy, we are confronted by two major difficulties. The available statistical data are limited, often out of date, and based on accounting concepts that are very different from our own. The Chinese, for example, consider services an unproductive activity and do not include them in their GNP figures. In addition, the Maoist emphasis on nonmaterial, nonquantitative measures of economic success makes it virtually impossible to apply Western economic yardsticks to the economy of China.

Achievements: Growth, Stability, and Equity For the 15-year period 1950 to 1965, estimates are that the Chinese growth rate approximated 4 percent annually. Most of this growth took place during the early years of the first Five Year Plan; there were significant declines in many sectors during the

Great Leap Forward. It would appear, however, that the growth rate has accelerated since then and may be close to 6 percent at the present time.

Economic stability is a significant achievement in the People's Republic of China. The unemployment and underemployment that plagued pre-Communist China have been eliminated, a notable accomplishment. We may, however, question the methods used—strict control over freedom of movement and use of labor-intensive agricultural production techniques. Inflation, too, is not a problem; the record of the Chinese government in maintaining stable prices is truly outstanding.

Equity is a third area of economic achievement in China. By Western standards, China is still a very poor country, with an average per capita GNP of perhaps only $145. Nevertheless, it has made remarkable economic advances over the past 20 years. China now feeds, clothes, and houses more than 800 million people. It also provides health and educational services to its citizens. Although many of China's people still live at the subsistence level, no one starves. It is possible that during the last decade, China has experienced less malnutrition due to maldistribution of food than has the United States.

Income differences still exist within the People's Republic of China. Industrial wages are substantially higher than peasant income, and there are wage differentials among workers in the same enterprise. But the available data suggest that these differentials are much smaller than those in either the USSR or the United States. In one department store, for example, wages were reported as ranging between 36 and 80 yuan a month; and, in a Shanghai hospital, the average wage for all staff members was 67 yuan a month, and only 85 for doctors. Maoists say their objective is to further reduce these differentials, because they believe that monetary incentives are not necessary to achieve a high level of output.

Failures of Efficiency To Western eyes, the Chinese command economy is not an efficient one. We need cite only a few examples to illustrate this. Capital investment is not channeled primarily into heavy industry, where it would have the most significant and immediate effect on economic growth. Specialization, a key factor in any system attempting to increase output, is often ignored in China. For example, office workers or college students are sent periodically to the countryside to do farm work for a few months. Most important, the agricultural sector has been supported at the expense of the industrial sector, despite the fact that productivity in agriculture is very low—perhaps only one-seventh that of average productivity in industry.

On the other hand, perhaps we should view these "failures" as the Maoist might. Although the official policy has produced a society that is still 80 percent rural, it has also managed to avoid the social problems that routinely accompany the rapid growth of urban areas. "There are no beggars on the streets, no idlers on the streets . . . litter goes into litter cans with a regularity that would astound and delight Mayor Lindsay of New York. Streets, parks and public lavatories are clean. . . . In all these public places, your person and property are secure day and night."[4]

A similar case could be made for the Chinese emphasis on labor-intensive craft industries and for their distaste for extreme specialization. Certainly the problem of alienation among American workers seems to buttress the Maoist point of view. Moreover, the final accounting is not yet complete: We do not know at this point whether the Maoist version of the versatile and cooperative worker who willingly contributes his labor to the common good will prove, in the long run, to be more efficient than his bored and frustrated Western counterpart.

CUBA

Cuba provides an example of a socialist command economy whose institutions have been determined to a large extent by the historical and geopolitical circumstances peculiar to it. When Fidel Castro

4 J. Tobin, "The Economy of China: A Tourist's View," *Challenge*, March-April, 1973, p. 26.

came to power in 1958, Cuba was one of the more economically advanced nations of Latin America, with a comparatively high per capita GNP. But the average figure masked an economy in which the unemployment rate stood at 16 percent, with perhaps another 10 percent underemployed, and in which there were very wide inequalities in income distribution, much illiteracy, and extreme economic dependence on one crop—sugar. Equally important was the great distaste among the underprivileged, the intellectuals, and, in particular, the leaders of the revolution for the humiliating client relationship they claimed characterized U.S.–Cuban dealings.

Cuba's Economic Goals

As a result, the initial objectives of the Cuban revolution were to eliminate both social injustices and one-crop economic dependence. During the first years of the revolution, major attempts were made to deemphasize sugar through massive investments in heavy equipment as well as in cattle, tobacco, and nickel production. At the same time, considerable efforts were devoted to improving the living conditions of the rural and urban poor. In 1961, for example, about one-half of all investment was channeled into social services in education, housing, and public health.

By 1963, however, it became apparent that the original plan was overly ambitious, given the relatively small size of the nation, its lack of minerals and energy sources, its climate, and the low industrial base with which it started. Production, therefore, shifted back to sugar, which now absorbs a significant part of the nation's investment spending, although crop yields do not seem to have reached the official goals. Attempts at diversification continue. Nickel production, for example, has more than doubled since 1959.

The Cuban economy differs from the Soviet model not only in its primary emphasis on agriculture as opposed to industry, but also in its relatively small allocation of resources to investment as opposed to consumption. Investment spending in Cuba has averaged 18 to 20 percent of GNP, rather than the 25 to 30 percent achieved in the USSR. This is probably due to Cuba's proximity to the United States, which makes Cuba reluctant to depress consumption to levels that might provoke internal dissension and encourage U.S. military intervention. Another factor has been the large amount of assistance supplied to Cuba by the Soviet Union, both in the form of direct aid, estimated at close to half a billion dollars a year, and in the form of purchases of Cuban sugar and nickel at prices higher than those prevailing in the world market.

The Cuban Economy: An Evaluation

It is in the structure and quality of Cuban social institutions that the most important achievements of the revolution are found. The regime reports that 100 percent of the school-age children are now in school, that since 1959 the number of teachers has increased from 20,000 to 109,000, and that illiteracy has dropped to below 4 percent. Polio, malaria, and diphtheria have disappeared. Income distribution is unquestionably more equitable: The wealthier middle and upper classes have had their property confiscated and their incomes reduced, or they have left for the United States, while the poorer Cubans have benefitted from the elimination of unemployment, the vast expansion of public services, and policies that keep the cost of certain necessities, such as rent, at very low levels.

On the other hand, the Cuban experience has certainly not been an unmixed success. In 1973, basic consumer goods—food, clothing, and gasoline—were still rationed, with the Cuban citizen entitled to only three-quarters of a pound of meat per week. Indications are that the productivity of the Cuban worker, which actually declined during the early years of the revolution, has not increased significantly since then. These facts raise questions about the effectiveness of the Cuban planning system, the moral (or collective) incentives it has chosen to use, and its attempts to totally abolish markets and private property. The government planning agency, JUCEPLAN, has had only limited success in diversifying the pre-Castro one-crop economy, and it has merely replaced the United States with the USSR and Eastern Europe as the economy's most important customer. Overall, Cuba's growth rate does not appear impressive, although it is difficult to allocate responsibility for this failure between the nation's basic lack of resources and the particular economic system it has adopted.

Despite the drawbacks, however, the psychological impact of Castroism, especially in Latin America, should not be underestimated. It is true that the revolution has produced only a limited economic impact; nevertheless, its record in achieving a more equitable distribution of those goods and services the economy does produce and, in particular, its success in breaking Cuba's dependence on the United States, the nation's colonial patron, are admired by many developing nations.

YUGOSLAVIA

The Yugoslavian economic system, usually described as **market socialism,** involves some elements of a publicly owned economy superimposed on what resembles a market system at the lower levels. Its development is closely related to the political break with the Soviet bloc that occurred in 1950. The primary differences between the Yugoslavian economy and the Soviet model are in the degree of autonomy given the individual enterprise and in the widespread acceptance of market forces as the coordinating mechanism for much of the economy.

Yugoslavian Economic Institutions

Under the Yugoslavian system, the role of the central government is limited to a few basic areas. It determines the overall allocation of GNP between investment and consumption. (The specific allocation of investment funds among individual enterprises, however, is left to market forces: The state simply sets an interest rate at which it estimates the total demand for investment funds will be equal to the total it has decided to supply, and, given this rate, the individual enterprises decide whether or not to borrow.) The state also makes several other fundamental planning decisions, deliberately diverting some investment spending to those areas of the country or to those ethnic groups that are relatively depressed. In addition, the state provides and enforces guidelines within which the individual enterprise may compete. For example, Yugoslavia has an antitrust system and minimum wage laws. Finally, the government siphons off some of the profits of each enterprise in the form of taxes.

In the industrial sector of the economy, all enterprises are state-owned. However, they are run by the employees, who elect Workers' Councils and appoint the chief executive or director of the enterprise who serves for a term of four years. Working with the director, the Workers' Council sets its own input mix, production methods, capital requirements, marketing procedures, and pricing practices. Wages are determined by collective bargaining. Profits after taxes and after allocations made by the Council for Reinvestment are paid out in bonuses to the director and the workers. In contrast to the industrial sector of the economy, the agricultural sector has remained primarily in private hands.

The Yugoslavian Economy: An Evaluation Proponents of the Yugoslavian market socialist system emphasize that it is more efficient than command socialism. Because the economy is decentralized, there has been no need to develop an extensive planning bureaucracy. The use of the market system as a coordinating mechanism has apparently been very effective in providing both a method and an incentive for increasing production. The 8 percent annual growth rate reported by Yugoslavia since 1949 provides impressive evidence of the system's technological efficiency, while the wide variety of consumer goods and absence of shortages indicate that the economy is satisfying the economic wants of its consumers to a degree uncommon in other socialist countries.

But there are also drawbacks to the system. Managers of enterprises often complain that the Workers' Councils emphasize short-run objectives, that they are most concerned with current wages and bonuses, and that they are not inclined to invest in expansion or research. Another difficulty has been the tendency of a few individual enterprises to become extremely successful and to dominate their markets. Monopolies in certain industries charge unduly high prices and engage in practices that limit entry into the industry by potential competitors and restrict production.

As a result, the economy has experienced many of the stabilization problems that confront nonsocialist market economies. There is unemployment in Yugoslavia, and every year thousands of its citizens are forced to seek jobs in other European countries. In addition, the economy has been plagued periodically with serious inflation. For example, in 1965, prices were increasing at such a fast rate that the central government was forced to intervene with a general price freeze.

Because Yugoslavia's economy is socialist, many of the inequities that characterize income distribution in a capitalist market economy are absent. Since all industrial firms are publicly owned, there is no unearned income from dividends, interest, profits, or rent. Nevertheless, major differences in income do exist. Workers in enterprises that are very profitable, either because of high productivity or because they have carved out a monopoly position, often earn considerably more than the peasants in depressed rural areas and than less fortunate members of the urban labor force.

Overall, Yugoslavia is generally admired as a successful adaptation of the original Soviet socialist economy. It has provided the model for many of the reforms that have occurred in other Eastern European socialist nations in recent years—in East Germany, Czechoslovakia, and Poland. Moreover, many economists see in the Yugoslavian experience a possible convergence of the market-oriented and the command-oriented systems.

SUMMARY

1 Economic systems are generally classified in terms of two variables: the mechanism that coordinates the production process and the ownership of the means of production. The market system is one mechanism for coordinating economic production; the command system, characterized by central economic planning, is another. Ownership of productive assets can take the form of private ownership, as in a capitalist society, or public ownership, as in a socialist society.

2 Although we have distinguished between market and command economies and between public and private ownership, in the real world none of these characteristics is found in its pure form. Instead, the various economies of the world might be said to form a spectrum, each including some mix of the market and command mechanisms and private and public ownership.

3 Some of the criteria that can be used to evaluate the performance of alternative economic systems are efficiency, equity, stability, and growth. In general, market systems appear to outperform command systems in terms of both technological and allocative efficiency. Command systems, on the other hand, have typically achieved more equitable distributions of income than market systems. And command systems have also managed to avoid the cyclical swings in employment and prices that characterize market economies, although in command systems inflation is usually replaced with shortages of various commodities. In regard to the criterion of growth, the record of alternative economic systems is mixed.

4 In the last analysis, however, any judgment about the superiority of any one system must depend upon the relative importance assigned to each of the various

criteria employed. Moreover, many believe that the choice among economic systems is not a strictly economic issue; philosophical and ideological considerations are of equal or even greater importance.

5 Outweighing all other economic concerns in the Soviet Union is the question of planning. The state planning commission (GOSPLAN) has primary responsibility for the Annual Plan, which begins with the assignment of production goals for the leading industries. Individual quotas are assigned to particular plants by intermediate ministries. After some feedback from the individual plants, each of which estimates its own capacity, the final plan is approved. One fundamental problem facing any command economy is that of coordination. The central planners must ensure that resources are allocated to each enterprise in the correct amounts and at the right time to keep production moving.

6 In Soviet industry, the individual firm or "enterprise" is responsible for carrying out its assigned production goals using a predetermined allotment of resources. Managerial discretion is generally restricted to attempts to increase production within the limits of resource allocations. The labor market in the USSR combines both planned and free-market mechanisms. Nominally, wage rates are established by the government, but workers usually have the right to choose their own jobs and to change them. Most retail trade in the USSR takes place through state-owned or cooperative stores, where prices are fixed by planners. The only exceptions are the free kolkhoz markets, where peasants may sell the produce from the small private plots they cultivate. The agricultural sector of the USSR is divided primarily between the state farms, which are state-owned and hire labor for wages, and the collective farms, whose members pool their land, machines, and labor, and share in the profits.

7 Since 1961, the Chinese have reversed their initial emphasis on heavy industry and instead have given highest priority to the agricultural sector. The Chinese also have an ideological commitment to decentralization, a commitment that is primarily carried out by administrative subdivisions called the People's Communes. Work assignments are quite strictly controlled in China, most of the labor force being channeled into agriculture. Prices are set by the state and remain very stable.

8 During the first years of the Cuban revolution, major attempts were made to break the traditional dependence on one crop—sugar. At the same time, considerable efforts were devoted to improving the living conditions of the poor. In general, Cuba appears to have solved many of the problems of equity but still faces the problem of economic growth.

9 The Yugoslavian economic system, usually described as market socialism, involves some elements of a publicly owned command economy superimposed on what resembles a market system at the lower levels. The primary areas of divergence from the Soviet model are in the degree of autonomy given the individual enterprise and in the widespread acceptance of market forces as the coordinating mechanism for much of the economy.

SUGGESTED READINGS

Bornstein, Morris, and **Daniel R. Fusfeld,** eds. *The Soviet Economy*. 3rd ed. Homewood, Ill.: Richard D. Irwin, 1970.

Feiwel, George R., ed. *New Currents in Soviet-Type Economies.* Scranton, Pa.: International Textbook Company, 1968.

Galenson, Walter, and **Nai-Ruenn Chen**. *The Chinese Economy Under Communism.* Chicago: Aldine, 1969.

Jacoby, N., and **J. E. Howell**. *European Economics: East and West.* New York: World Publishing Company, 1967.

Loucks, William N., and **William G. Whitney**. *Comparative Economic Systems.* 8th ed. New York: Harper & Row, 1969.

Shaffer, Harry G., and **Jan S. Prybyla**, eds. *From Underdevelopment to Affluence: Western, Soviet and Chinese Views.* New York: Appleton-Century-Crofts, 1968.

Sherman, Howard. *The Soviet Economy.* Boston: Little, Brown, 1969.

QUESTIONS

1 Review
   a. ways in which economic systems are generally classified,
   b. elements of command systems and public ownership in the American economy,
   c. elements of a market system and private ownership in the Soviet economy,
   d. the relative performances of command and market economies in the areas of efficiency, equity, stability, and growth,
   e. basic features of and problems faced by the Soviet, Chinese, Yugoslavian, and Cuban economies.

2 Critics of big business in the United States sometimes argue that executives may not make use of a highly productive innovation as quickly as they might because they wish to show long-term steady growth in output and profits. Is there any similar interest on the part of the Soviet manager? Why or why not?

3 There has been some difficulty in the Soviet Union because of the ways in which quotas are specified. For example, the quota for a factory producing nails may be stated in terms of a certain number of tons of nails or in terms of a certain number of nails. What difficulty might you predict in each case? What are the incentives for the manager to produce nails in a variety of sizes?

4 The Yugoslavian method of promoting long-term growth of the economy is in many ways similar to that used in the United States. In what ways?

5 Between 1928 and 1937 the rate of investment in the USSR grew from 12.5 to 26 percent of GNP. In addition the USSR also made a very large investment in education, the first nation to plan its education systematically to promote economic growth.* Given the history of the USSR and its special problems, why would it be essential for the Soviets to invest substantially in education?

6 Because of the peasant resistance to collectivization under Stalin, Soviet leadership could not trust the management of collectives to the then existing farmers. What would be the implication for the choice of managers and their effectiveness in raising the efficiency of the collective?

7 While Japan and the USSR have both had remarkable records of economic

*Angus Maddison, *Economic Growth in Japan and the USSR* (New York: W.W. Norton, 1969), p. 100.

growth, some experts point out that Japan did not have the constraint of a large military budget as did the USSR. Why would the military be a constraint?

8 One pair of writers on Cuban economic policies has argued that "It is apparent ... that Che's [Guevara] real concern was not maximizing efficiency but rather to devise a system of economic organization that would favor rather than inhibit the development of socialist consciousness and behavior."† In his beliefs, was Che Guevara closer to the Soviet leaders or the Maoists? Why?

9 Apparently the Soviet Union like the United States is plagued with difficulties of pollution. What advantages would the Soviet Union have in dealing with such problems? Why do you suppose that the problems are arising?

10 It is fairer to judge the effectiveness of an economic system in terms of achieving those goals the nation concerned deems important. Contrast briefly the criteria we generally use to evaluate the performance of Western economies and the criteria considered important among socialist economists and philosophers. What role seems to be played by the belief that there is a political and military threat from foreign powers?

†Leo Huberman and Paul Sweezy, "Socialism in Cuba," in *Economics: Mainstream Readings and Radical Critiques*, ed. David Mermelstein (New York: Random House, 1970), p. 471.

CHAPTER 38

INTERNATIONAL TRADE

To most of the countries of the world, international trade is vital to economic well-being. As Table 38-1 indicates, many major nations export between 10 percent and 20 percent of their GNP's. In the United States, however, exports total less than 5 percent of GNP, and the net balance of exports minus imports is generally only a few billion dollars. But because the American economy so far outranks in size those of most other countries, our relatively small foreign trade commitment is huge in money value. The approximately 4 percent of U.S. GNP exported in 1972 was worth nearly $50 billion, by far the largest volume of exports for any nation, and it contributed about 13 percent to total world trade. Consequently, our international trade has an enormous impact on the smaller nations with whom we do business. For example, exports and imports between the United States and the United Kingdom were nearly equal in 1971—both approximately $2.4 billion. That $2.4 billion, however, represented only ¼ of 1 percent of American GNP, but almost 2½ percent (or 10 times as much) of British GNP.

In addition, trade relationships have an impact on our domestic economy. Trade is clearly of concern to those directly involved in importing or exporting: to the farmers who grow wheat for export to the USSR; to the merchants who buy cocoa from Ghana or TV sets from Japan; to the American consumers who enjoy Brazilian coffee, Hong Kong shirts, and Swiss watches. Foreign trade is also of concern to those who make domestic stabilization policy. Because foreign purchases can influence the level of total spending in our economy, foreign trade has an impact on the level of national economic activity. And finally, foreign trade is of concern to those affected by the current American balance of payments problem. In recent years, chronic balance of payments deficits have created burdensome economic and political problems for the United States both at home and abroad, and attempts to solve these problems have at times seriously compromised our stabilization objectives. In this context, the need to understand the mechanics of foreign trade, its benefits and its limitations, takes on increased importance.

This chapter investigates the reasons for international trade. What are its objectives? What advantages or disadvantages does it offer a nation? In the next chapter, we examine the mechanics of foreign trade, including foreign currencies, exchange rates, and balance of payments statements. Finally, in Chapter 40, we review some of the international economic problems currently facing the United States and its expanding list of trading partners, and analyze some of the possible solutions to these problems.

What yardsticks do economists use to evaluate foreign trade policies? Essentially, the criteria are much the same as those employed in analyzing domestic economic measures: International trade is judged in terms of its efficiency and equity as well as its effect on economic stability and growth.

Foreign trade is efficient when it results in a greater amount of goods and services available in each of the trading nations. One very popular argument for expanding trade between the United States and

TABLE 38-1 Volume of Exports for Major Trading Nations, 1970 (in billions of U.S. dollars)

Country	Exports	GNP	Exports as a % of GNP
United States	$43.2	$970	4.5%
Japan	19.3	201	9.6
West Germany	34.2	186.4	18.3
France	18.1	147.5	12.3
United Kingdom	19.4	121	16.0
Italy	13.2	93.2	14.2
Canada	16.7	85	19.6

As a percentage of GNP, the volume of exports from the United States is clearly much smaller than that of any other major trading nation. For example, for West Germany and Canada, exports as a percentage of GNP are nearly four times the comparative figure for the United States. In absolute terms, however, the volume of U.S. exports far exceeds that of any other nation, a fact that makes the United States an important force in international trade.

SOURCES: *International Financial Statistics*, International Monetary Fund, September 1973; and *U.N. Statistical Yearbook, 1971.*

Opening photo by J. Paul Kirouac

the USSR is that of efficiency. It is claimed that the net effects will be both more natural gas for American households and more meat for Russian consumers.

Equity is another yardstick for evaluating foreign trade, for international trade policies can affect the distribution of income. It was argued, for example, that the oil import quotas of the 1960s benefitted the high-income stockholders of American oil companies at the expense of the low-income fuel oil and gasoline consumers forced to pay higher prices.

A third criterion for judging international trade policy is stability. How does foreign trade affect the level of domestic employment and prices? Is some degree of instability a reasonable price to pay for the economic expansion obtained through exploiting foreign markets?

Finally, international trade can be evaluated in terms of its impact on economic growth. Government officials must therefore consider trade policy when planning an overall rate of growth. Can India, for example, increase its GNP faster by exporting rice and importing steel, or by building up a domestic steel industry?

To find the answers to questions such as these, we shall use many of the same micro and macro tools developed in our study of the domestic economy. Our analysis is complicated, however, by circumstances peculiar to foreign trade: Each nation uses a different currency; the free flows of labor, capital, and finished goods between markets are often impeded and are subject to restrictions, limitations, and special costs; and finally, unlike the domestic market, where profit considerations are usually the major determinant of production decisions, political and military factors frequently have a major impact on foreign trade policies.

THE REASONS FOR INTERNATIONAL TRADE

Why do nations trade? Why should it be advantageous for the United States, with a gross national product approximately five times that of its closest free world competitor and with large supplies of raw materials, capital, and educated manpower, to trade with the rest of the world? One obvious reason for foreign trade applies to those goods that a nation cannot produce at home because it lacks the appropriate natural or technological resources. The early European fur traders in North America swapped muskets for fur pelts. Both they and the Indians with whom they traded found the deals satisfactory because neither could produce by themselves the goods they sought.

But even when it is possible to produce a good domestically, foreign trade may be advantageous. The Scottish economist Adam Smith provided an explanation for this some 200 years ago in *The Wealth of Nations:*

> It is the maxim of every prudent master of a family, never to attempt to make at home what it will cost him more to make than to buy. The tailor does not attempt to make his own shoes, but buys them of the shoemaker. The shoemaker does not attempt to make his own clothes but employs a tailor. The farmer attempts to make neither the one nor the other, but employs those different artificers. All of them find it for their interest to employ their whole industry in a way in which they have some advantage over their neighbors, and to purchase with a part of its produce, or what is the same thing, with the price of a part of it, whatever else they have occasion for.

Smith applied his advice—never produce what it costs you more to make yourself than to buy from someone else—not only to individuals, but also to nations. According to him, when one nation produces less of a good than another nation at the same cost, it should import that good rather the producing it at home. Using hot houses, hand fertilization, and elaborate moisture controls, Great Britain could probably produce its own tea, but the costs in terms of labor and other resources would be perhaps 20 times the cost of tea grown in Ceylon. Ceylon, then, is said to have an **absolute advantage** over Great Britain when it comes to tea production, and Smith argued that the English would be well advised to obtain their tea from Ceylon rather than produce it domestically.

Comparative Advantage: Opportunity Cost as the Basis for Trade

The theory of absolute advantage, however, does not adequately explain the basis for international trade.

If it did, a nation with an absolute advantage in the production of all the goods that its potential trading partner produced would have no incentive to trade. But this is not the case, as the nineteenth century economist David Ricardo proved with his theory of **comparative advantage.** According to Ricardo, foreign trade is mutually beneficial, even when one nation is *absolutely* more efficient in the production of every good, as long as there are differences in the *relative* costs of producing the various goods in the two potential trading nations. Thus, the theory of comparative advantage is closely tied to the concept of opportunity costs. An example will help to clarify how this principle works. Assume that Dr. Tarsus can clean her office twice as fast as the janitor to whom she pays $5 an hour. But Dr. Tarsus can also earn $30 an hour as a chiropodist. Therefore, despite the fact she has an absolute advantage in janitorial services, it is not worth her while to save $5 an hour in cleaning expenses at the cost of $30 an hour as a physician. She is better off using her labor to treat patients' feet, even though she is also the most efficient janitor in town.

The same principle applies to nations. Assume that the United States can produce either 30 units of wool or 30 units of steel with a given amount of resources and that Australia can produce either 20 units of wool or 10 units of steel with the same resource input. (See Table 38-2.) It is clear that the United States has an absolute advantage in both wool and steel production, since it can produce both more steel and more wool than Australia with an equal quantity of inputs. Nevertheless, it will be worthwhile for the United States to specialize in producing steel and to use its surplus steel to trade with Australia for wool. This is because the United States can produce 1 unit of steel for each unit of wool it forgoes, whereas the Australians can produce only ½ unit of steel for each unit of wool they give up. Thus, if Americans produce their wool at home by cutting back on steel production, their opportunity cost is 1 unit of steel for each unit of wool. The opportunity cost in Australia, on the other hand, is only ½ unit of steel for each unit of wool. Because the cost of wool, in terms of steel, is relatively less in Australia than in the United States, the Australians are said to have a comparative advantage in wool production. It will therefore pay the Americans to specialize in steel production and procure their wool from Australia, where a unit of wool can be obtained for ½ unit of steel, rather than to make it at home, where the opportunity cost of a unit of wool is 1 unit of steel.

TABLE 38-2 Production Possibilities

Country	Units of wool	Units of steel
United States	30	30
Australia	20	10

Conversely, the United States has a comparative advantage in steel as far as the Australians are concerned. The opportunity cost of 1 unit of steel in Australia is 2 units of wool; that is, Australians must forgo 2 units of wool in order to obtain 1 unit of steel. In the United States, however, the opportunity cost of a unit of steel is only 1 unit of wool. Because steel, in terms of wool, is relatively cheaper in the United States, the Australians would do well to put their resources into wool production, trading some of the surplus for American steel. It would not make economic sense for Australia to produce steel instead of wool.

To summarize, we can say that one nation has a comparative advantage over another in terms of a given product when its opportunity cost for producing that product is less than that of its neighbor. Comparative advantage, then, is based on differences in relative, rather than absolute, costs. Although the United States had an *absolute* advantage over Australia in terms of both steel and wool, it was advantageous for Americans to buy their wool in Australia, because Australia had a *comparative* advantage in wool, as compared with steel. Moreover, trade between two nations each of which specializes in producing the goods in which it has a comparative advantage will prove mutually beneficial. Using some simple arithmetic, we shall demonstrate this point concretely, showing that the United States and Australia will end up with larger quantities of both steel and wool if each specializes in producing the item in which it enjoys a comparative advantage.

Demonstrating the Benefits of Specialization and Trade

The advantages of specialization and trade according to comparative advantage can be demonstrated through the construction of production possibilities curves. Previously, we saw that the United States can produce either 30 units of wool or 30 units of steel with a given quantity of resources. It can, of course, also produce various combinations of these goods—15 units of steel and 15 of wool, 10 of steel and 20 of wool, and so on. Several of these alternatives are shown in Table 38-3. This information can then be plotted to form the production possibilities curve shown in Figure 38-1. The curve shows that for each unit of wool the United States chooses to produce, it must give up one unit of steel. (To simplify, we have assumed that the opportunity cost remains constant.) Table 38-4 is the production possibilities schedule for Australia. This economy can produce 20 units of wool at capacity, and it must forgo 2 units of wool for each unit of steel it desires to manufacture. Thus, its production possibilities schedule includes such combinations as 20 units of wool and zero units of steel, 18 units of wool and 1 unit of steel, 16 units of wool and 2 units of steel, and so on. The production possibilities curve plotted from this information is shown in Figure 38-2.

What happens if the United States and Australia decide to be self-sufficient, meeting their steel and wool needs from domestic production exclusively? Each must select one combination from its production possibilities schedule. Let us assume that the United States decides that its optimum product mix is 18 units of steel and 12 units of wool (point A on Figure 38-1), and Australia chooses 8 units of steel and 4 units of wool (point A on Figure 38-2). Under these circumstances, the total output available for consumption in each nation would be as follows:

TABLE 38-3 Production Possibilities Schedule for the United States

Units of steel	Units of wool
30	0
24	6
18	12
12	18
6	24
0	30

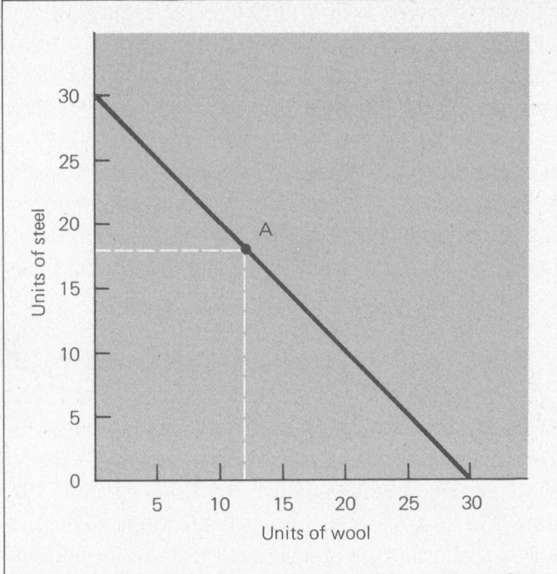

FIGURE 38-1 PRODUCTION POSSIBILITIES CURVE FOR THE UNITED STATES **Without international trade, the United States has the capability to produce and consume only those combinations of steel and wool located along its production possibilities curve. If Americans decide to consume 18 units of steel and 12 units of wool, output would be designated by point A.**

Output and Consumption Before Specialization and Trade

	Steel	Wool
United States	18	12
Australia	8	4
Total	26	16

Suppose, however, that both nations decide to specialize, each limiting its production to that

TABLE 38-4 Production Possibilities Schedule for Australia

Units of steel	Units of wool
10	0
8	4
6	8
4	12
2	16
0	20

good in which it has a comparative advantage. The United States would devote its full resources to steel and Australia to wool. Total output after specialization would be as follows:

Output After Specialization

	Steel	Wool
United States	30	0
Australia	0	20
Total	30	20
Change in output	+4	+4

We see at once that total output is larger under specialization than it was when each nation attempted to produce its own steel and its own wool.

Earlier, we said that specialization and trade increased the quantity of goods available in both trading nations. In this case, the Australians trade their surplus wool for American steel, and the United States exports its surplus steel and imports Australian wool. But what will be the terms of this trade? That is, how will the additional 4 units of wool and 4 units of steel resulting from specialization be divided between the United States and Australia?

It is clear that specialization will prove advantageous to Australia only if it can obtain a unit of steel from the United States at an opportunity cost that is less than the 2 units of wool it would have to forgo to produce the steel at home. Similarly, the United States must work out an arrangement for purchasing Australian wool that is somewhat more attractive than the 1 unit of steel it must forgo to produce a unit of wool domestically. In other words, Australians will be ahead if they pay less than 2 units of wool for 1 unit of steel; Americans will benefit if they get more than 1 unit of wool for each unit of steel. Both the Americans and the Australians, then, will find the trading arrangement satisfactory if the terms of trade fall somewhere between

1 steel = 1 wool
and
1 steel = 2 wool

In the real world, the exact terms of trade will depend on such factors as possible substitutes for each of the two goods, and other available sources of supply. If the terms of trade settle closer to 1 steel = 2 wool, they will favor the United States because Americans will be required to give up only slightly more than 1 unit of steel for every 2 units of wool; if, however, they settle closer to 1 steel = 1 wool, they will favor Australia because Americans will be re-

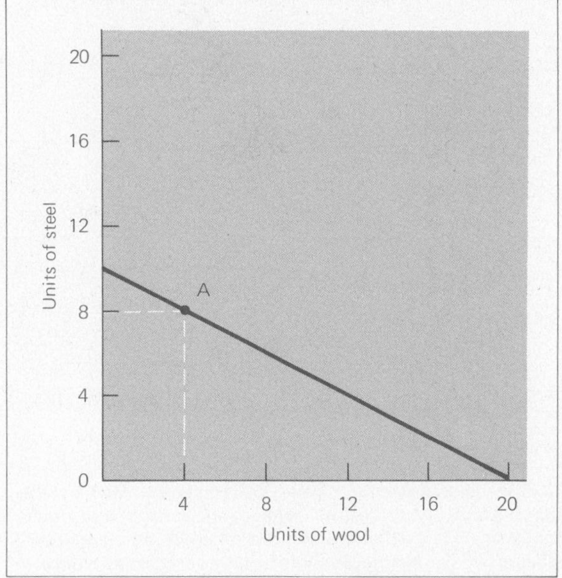

FIGURE 38-2 PRODUCTION POSSIBILITIES CURVE FOR AUSTRALIA In the absence of trade, consumption of steel and wool in Australia is also limited by domestic production capabilities. At point A, Australians have chosen to produce and consume 8 units of steel and 4 units of wool.

quired to deliver 1 unit of steel for approximately 1 unit of wool.

Suppose that the terms of trade settle halfway between the two extremes, so that the United States and Australia trade 1 unit of steel for 1½ units of wool. In Figure 38-3, these terms of trade are reflected in the orange lines, which represent each nation's new **consumption possibilities curve**. With specialization and trade, consumption in the United States and Australia is no longer limited by domestic production possibilities frontiers. Instead, both countries can now consume beyond their own production frontiers, choosing any product mix allowed by the terms of trade line. This is because specialization enables a more efficient use of resources and, therefore, an increase in total world output.

Let us say that consumers in the United States want to keep 20 of the nation's 30 units of steel for domestic use, leaving the remaining 10 units to be exported to Australia in exchange for 15 units of wool. Australians, on the other hand, choose to keep 5 of their 20 units of wool for domestic consumption, receiving 10 units of steel in return for the 15 units of wool exported to the United States. This information can be summarized as follows:

Consumption After Specialization and Trade

	Steel	Wool
United States	20	15
Australia	10	5

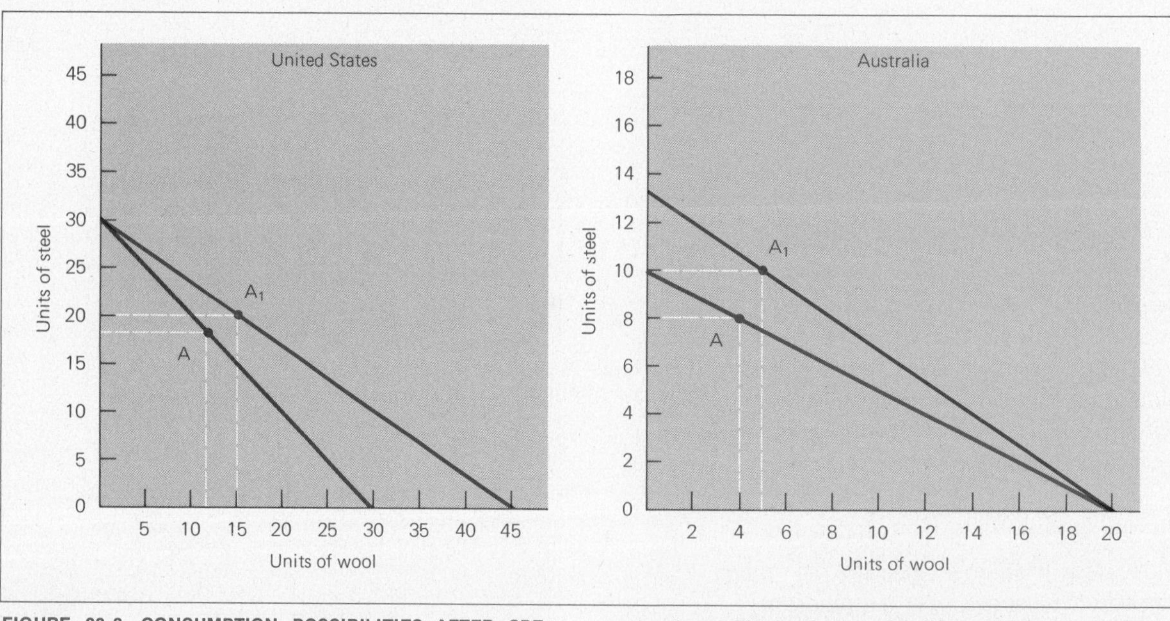

FIGURE 38-3 CONSUMPTION POSSIBILITIES AFTER SPECIALIZATION AND TRADE With specialization and trade, consumption in the United States and Australia is no longer constrained by the two nations' production possibilities frontiers; both countries can enjoy a higher standard of living. Before specialization and trade, the United States consumed at point A on its domestic production possibilities curve. By specializing in steel production (producing 30 units of steel), the United States could trade 10 units of steel to Australia in return for 15 units of wool. This has improved the United States' consumption position to point A_1, which provides 20 units of steel and 15 of wool. Note that point A_1 represents an improvement in the consumption level of both steel and wool for the United States. Applying the same analysis, we see that Australia similarly stands to gain by specializing in wool production. Twenty units of wool are produced, 15 of which are exported to the United States in exchange for 10 units of steel. At point A_1, Australia consumes both more steel and more wool than at point A.

Compare these figures with the quantities of each good consumed before specialization and trade. Not only has the total output of both wool and steel increased—from 26 to 30 units of steel and from 16 to 20 units of wool—but, in addition, each nation has shared in the higher output. There are now larger supplies of both wool and steel in Australia and the United States, and consequently a higher standard of living in each nation. As shown in Figure 38-3, specialization and trade permit each nation to consume at A_1, a point beyond its original production possibilities frontier.

This example illustrates a fundamental principle of international economics. When one nation has a comparative advantage over another nation in the production of a certain good, it should specialize in producing that good, rather than diverting its resources to the production of other goods. It should then use its surplus output for trading purposes, obtaining other goods it requires from nations enjoying a comparative advantage in producing those goods. As a result of such specialization and trade, both nations will benefit, because each will have more goods to consume.

Sources of Comparative Advantage

Comparative advantage is the justification for most international trade, but what are the sources of comparative advantage? What conditions enable one nation to produce a certain good relatively more cheaply than another nation? The simplest answer ties comparative advantage to differences in the quantity and quality of resources in a given nation. Kuwait has extensive petroleum deposits; the United States is favored by huge plains well suited to growing grain; Canada has the combination of bauxite and water power needed to produce aluminum. Differences in resource endowment also apply to labor. Hong Kong enjoys a large semiskilled work force ideally suited for the assembly of transistor radios; the United States has a labor pool consisting of a relatively large number of highly trained engineers and scientists who can specialize in designing new products or production processes. And there are differences among nations in the availability of capital. The United States and Western Europe have large pools of capital and will therefore have a comparative advantage in producing capital-intensive goods such as automobiles and heavy machinery. Many of the underdeveloped nations in Asia and Africa, on the other hand, are capital-poor and, as a result, are frequently unable to compete in world markets in the production of capital-intensive goods.

This factor-endowment approach to explaining the sources of comparative advantage has been explored in some detail by two Swedish economists, Eli Heckscher and Bertil Ohlin. Heckscher and Ohlin emphasize both the differences in capital, labor, and land endowments among nations and the differences in capital, labor, and land requirements for various products. They suggest that, given free trade, each nation will specialize in those goods requiring the resources in which it is especially rich, obtaining other goods through trade. Australia, for example, a land-abundant country, will produce wheat and wool; it will obtain its capital-intensive steel and airplanes from the United States and Western Europe and its labor-intensive TV sets and sewing machines from Japan. The United States, in contrast, is both land-abundant and capital-abundant, but labor is relatively scarce. As a result, the United States has historically concentrated its production efforts in capital-intensive goods—electric machinery, automobiles—and land-intensive goods—wheat, soybeans, cotton. American needs for labor-intensive merchandise, on the other hand, are met through imports from the Far East, South America, and Africa. In brief, factor endowments—labor, capital, and land—vary from one nation to another, and the trading patterns that develop are based on the exploitation of these differences.

The Equalization of Factor Prices: A By-Product of Trade

Heckscher and Ohlin, however, do not stop here. They also point out a frequent side effect of the growth of trade based on factor-endowment differences. Without trade, the prices of factors of production will vary widely in different nations, depending on their relative scarcity. Under free trade conditions, however, factor prices tend to equalize among the trading nations.

We can understand the mechanisms through which this equalization occurs by examining the prices of labor and capital before and after trade in two hypothetical countries: Alpha, which has considerable capital but a small labor force, and Beta, with a large labor supply but not much capital. Assume first that the two countries attempt to produce domestically both labor-intensive and capital-intensive goods. Since Alpha has abundant capital, the price of capital (interest rates) will be low, but wages will be high, reflecting the small labor supply. Conversely, Beta, with a large work force but little capital, will experience low wages and high interest rates. Once Alpha and Beta begin to trade, however, factor prices will change. The demand for labor will drop in Alpha because its producers will stop making labor-intensive goods, preferring instead to import them. As a result, wages will fall from their previous high levels. At the same time, interest rates will rise because of the increasing demand for capital to meet the needs of the export market for capital-intensive goods.

The reverse, of course, will occur in Beta. Both the demand for labor and wage rates will climb, since Beta is now increasing its production of the labor-intensive goods in which it has a comparative advantage. Simultaneously, interest rates will fall in response to the decline in demand for capital that occurs as Beta switches some of its production efforts from capital-intensive to labor-intensive goods.

This tendency for world trade to reduce differences in factor prices provides an additional argument for free trade. Without trade, high interest rates or low wages resulting from particular national resource allocations might continue indefinitely. Consequently, essential investments might never be made in an underdeveloped nation because of high capital costs, and the unfortunate workers living in an economy highly endowed with labor might be trapped forever in a pattern of low wages. With trade, however, there are long-run forces at work that tend to equalize resource prices. Trade, in other words, substitutes for the actual movement of the factors of production themselves, movements that are often restricted because of resource immobility and political conditions. In so doing, trade acts to reduce the differences in the costs of resources in different economies.

The Benefits of Trade: Some Qualifications

Although the theoretical benefits of specialization and trade according to comparative advantage are clear, it is important to recognize that the discussion so far is simply a model. Like all models, the model of comparative advantage is based upon certain assumptions that may not hold true in the real world.

First, the theory of comparative advantage assumes that before trade each nation is producing along its production possibilities frontier—that is, that there is no domestic unemployment. Furthermore, it is taken for granted that the introduction of trade does not cause the level of employment to fall. This may not actually be the case. As a nation shifts its production from one industry to another, unemployment problems may result, particularly if the shift is from labor-intensive industries to capital- or land-intensive ones. It is possible that the reduction in national income due to unemployment may be great enough to offset the rise in the standard of living due to trade.

Of course, domestic stabilization policy can do much to counteract any declines in the level of employment, and manpower training programs can help speed the switch from disadvantaged to advantaged industries. The important point to remember is that, regardless of short-run dislocations, the advantages of specialization and trade will tend to be realized in the long-run.

A second assumption of the model of comparative advantage is that the relative prices of goods in each nation reflect the relative scarcities of resources. But if prices do not reflect real costs, it is possible that trade will not result in a better use of resources. For example, a government wishing to increase steel exports may subsidize steel production. Given such a policy, a country with a comparative disadvantage in steel production may become a net exporter of steel. However, despite the misallocation resulting from this policy, other nations should not be deterred from trade, for they will still be able to increase their own production possibilities by engaging in trade. If one nation wishes to subsidize other nations by keeping the price of steel below costs, the other nations should not hesitate to take advantage of this misguided, or unrealized, generosity. This is true as long as they can maintain full employment or adequate unemployment compensation.

Inefficiencies due to trade may also arise when externalities are present. If the external costs (such as pollution) of steel production differ substantially between two countries (due to, say, different atmospheric conditions), then steel prices in the two countries will not reflect real costs, and trade may flow in the wrong direction.

A lack of competition may also cause distortions in relative prices. For example, if there is a steel monopoly in a country that has a comparative advantage in steel production, the price of steel may not reflect that advantage.

However, it is still true that other nations will continue to benefit from international trade in spite of these distortions in price-scarcity relationships. If they attempt to compensate for the distortions by keeping out low-cost imports, or polluting their own air, or creating their own monopolies, they will find themselves worse off than if they took advantage of the principle of comparative advantage.

A final assumption of the theory of comparative advantage is that there are no barriers to the free movement of goods among nations. But as we shall see in the following section, this is seldom the case.

BARRIERS TO FREE TRADE

In theory, free trade leads to the most efficient allocation of world resources and provides higher standards of living for all participants. Nevertheless, free trade has been the exception rather than the rule throughout much of modern history. Indeed, even in the United States, which has led the way in reducing trade restrictions during the post–World War II period, there is now considerable public pressure for reimposing trade barriers, and some steps have already been taken in this direction.

Protectionist Devices

Tariffs Tariffs are simply taxes on imported goods. They are levied for two basic reasons: to raise revenue and to protect domestic industries. Revenue tariffs are generally modest, for if they were too large, they would discourage imports entirely, thus defeating their objective. During the 1790s, such tariffs accounted for around 95 percent of total federal government receipts. Today, however, their contribution to total revenue is minuscule, and as a practical matter, tariffs now have almost no significance as a revenue source. Protective tariffs also serve as sources of revenue, but their primary purpose is to "protect" domestic producers by increasing the prices of competing goods from abroad. In the United States, such goods as foreign automobiles, shoes, and steel are currently subject to protective tariffs, and many other industries are hard at work trying to obtain similar protection.

In general, tariff rates in the United States are set by Congress. The record of American tariff policy, shown in Figure 38-4, illustrates the broad swings that have occurred over the years. The highest tariffs occurred in 1828 and about 100 years later, in 1930. The Tariff of Abominations (1828) was an attempt by Northern manufacturers to protect the domestic markets that had developed when English imports were cut off during the Napoleonic Wars. The Hawley-Smoot Tariff (1930) had similar objectives. American agriculture had expanded rapidly during World War I, as had various other industries, such as chemicals. When normal trade channels reopened after the war, these industries faced sharp foreign competition. When the unemployment resulting from this competition was compounded by the domestic depression that began in late 1929, Congress tried to safeguard American jobs by imposing protective tariffs. Unfortunately, other nations did the same, and world trade declined to about half its pre-depression level.

Many experts now feel that the wave of protectionism that characterized the pre–World War II period was a major contributor to the length and severity of the Great Depression, both in the United States and abroad. As a result, following the end of World War II, there was considerable interest in eliminating tariff barriers as a way of ensuring world prosperity. The 1947 General Agreement on Tariffs and Trade (GATT), to which the United States and most of the other leading trading nations of the world eventually became signatories, was an important first step. Its most significant aspect was the "most favored nation" clause, which provided that a tariff reduction arranged between any two members of GATT must be extended to all other members. As Figure 38-4 indicates, average U.S. tariff rates dropped sharply during the early postwar period, primarily as a result of the implementation of this "most favored nation" clause. Further tariff reductions occurred during the 1960s, after the Kennedy administration persuaded Congress to pass the Trade Expansion Act of 1962 permitting the President to cut all tariffs by as much as 50 percent if other nations would respond with similar reductions and if such tariff cuts would not injure domestic industry by idling labor or machinery.

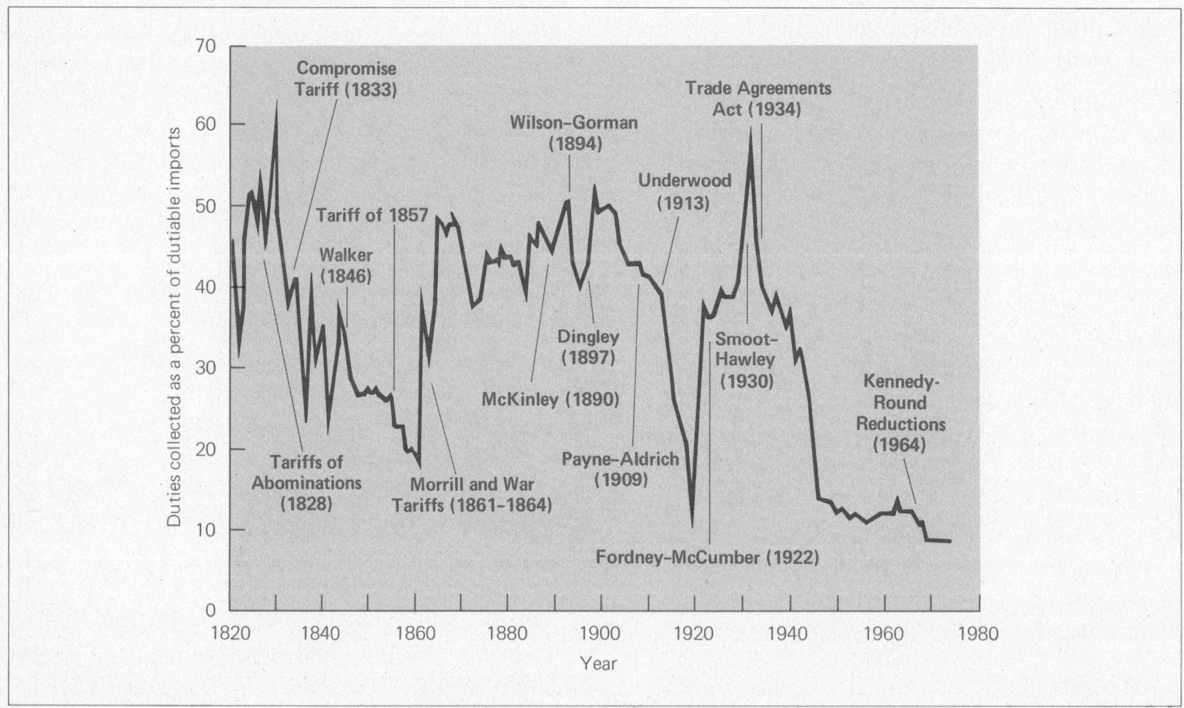

FIGURE 38-4 AVERAGE U.S. TARIFF RATES, 1820–1973 Average tariff rates in the United States have fluctuated widely over the past 150 years. In recent decades, tariffs have been reduced from their peak in 1930. But other restrictive measures, such as import quotas, some of which are applied on a voluntary basis by such exporters as Japan, have been on the increase. (These measures are not reflected in this graph.) President Nixon has had a mixed record on trade restrictions, pushing for reductions in tariffs for most goods, while opting for increased protection for textiles and import quotas on oil (costing American consumers about $6 billion annually).

SOURCES: U.S. Department of Commerce, *Historical Statistics of the U.S.* and *Statistical Abstract of the U.S.*, 1972.

THE MULTINATIONAL CORPORATIONS

Traditionally, the primary participants in foreign trade have been firms located in a single nation. An American lumber company, for example, will export some of its product to Japan, while a Japanese electronics firm will export computers to the United States. Since 1950, however, the international economic system has been revolutionized by the growth of multinational corporations (MNCs), giant firms with subsidiaries producing goods around the globe.

By 1973, the volume of sales for MNCs totaled nearly $500 billion a year, and it was growing at an annual rate of about 10 percent. Most of this output comes from investments made abroad by American companies, which presently account for about 60 percent of all direct foreign investments. The recorded value of American MNC foreign investments passed $100 billion in 1973, up eightfold from the 1950 total of $11.8 billion, and growing at a faster rate than corporate investment here in the United States. General Electric increased the number of its overseas plants from 21 to 82 between 1959 and 1969, and other corporations like Raytheon, ITT, Westinghouse, and IBM now have as many as 160 affiliates abroad. In all, it has been estimated that foreign operations currently account for between 20 and 25 percent of total U.S. corporate profits.

United Nations

In some ways, the multinational corporation represents the logical next step in the evolution of a large domestic corporation. As a company grows, it develops new products for home markets, and eventually attempts to increase sales and profits by exporting these products abroad. If the product is successful, however, the threat of foreign competition will appear, and the domestic producer (especially if it is an American corporation producing goods with high-cost American labor) will feel forced to build plants abroad in order to forestall serious foreign competition. Ultimately, if the cost differential between its foreign plants and its domestic plants is big enough, the corporation may reduce or eliminate domestic production, supplying domestic markets from foreign plants.

This pattern is clearly seen in the U.S. auto industry. At first, foreign markets were supplied with cars produced domestically by the U.S. firms. Today, however, most foreign sales by GM, Ford, and Chrysler are cars made in their foreign plants—Ford, for example, produces the English Ford for the British market, and GM supplies the Continent with the German-made Opel. Moreover, a significant part of the U.S. domestic auto market is supplied either with automobiles made abroad by foreign affiliates of U.S. companies and imported into the United States, or with ostensibly U.S.-produced cars, which, however, contain a substantial number of foreign components. (The transmission and engine for the Ford Pinto, for example, are produced in Ford's German plants, and its steering gear and carburetor are made in England.)

Although initially it was the large U.S. corporations that provided the stimulus for the growth of MNCs, corporations from other nations are now expanding in a similar manner. Direct investment abroad by Japanese firms grew at a 30 percent annual rate during the late 1960s and early 1970s. Here in the United States, the Michelin Tire Co. of France provides tires for its U.S. dealers from a 1200-worker plant it owns in Greenville, South Carolina; Kikkoman Shoyu, Ltd. of Japan turns out soy and teriyaki sauce for the U.S. market in a plant near Walworth, Wisconsin; Sony assembles color TV sets in San Diego; and both the Swedish Volvo and the West German Volkswagen have announced that they are considering building plants in the United States.

Advocates of the MNC claim that it provides an efficient means of integrating national economies. Moreover, the MNC has become the vehicle through which technological know-how and production and marketing skills are spread rapidly from more advanced to less advanced nations. Multinational firms not only build new plants in foreign nations, they also train local people to work in these plants and, in some cases, to manage them. In this way, they provide the foreign economy with an indigenous supply of technology and trained personnel which can eventually be used to spur the development of locally owned and operated businesses. Finally, the MNC works to equalize the cost of factors of production around the world. For example, American firms build plants in Spain and Ireland and Taiwan because of the availability of low-cost labor, but the ultimate consequence is usually an increase in the demand for labor in these countries and therefore higher wages. It is true that this could also be accomplished by the traditional single-nation producer exporting his goods abroad. But very often trade barriers such as tariffs or quotas create obstacles to free trade. The multinational corporation provides a way of bypassing the barriers that would otherwise impede the free flow of goods among markets.

Critics, however, attack the MNCs on several grounds. Some fear that the MNCs, because of their enormous assets and market shares, will destroy world competition. Although most nations have domestic antitrust laws, there is no supranational authority to protect the consumer from price-fixing or other anticompetitive actions by the MNCs. The tremendous power of the MNCs also poses the risk that they may threaten the sovereignty of the nations in which they do business. ITT, for example, admitted it had played a very active role in the Chilean elections of 1972 in an attempt, although unsuccessful, to defeat former President Allende.

Organized labor in the United States has criticized the MNCs because of their effect on domestic employment. George Meany, president of the AFL-CIO, claimed that foreign operations of U.S.-based MNCs led to the loss of 500,000 jobs in the 1960s. He warned that the United States was "in danger of becoming nothing more than a nation of hamburger stands" if the exodus of U.S. production to overseas plants continued. The MNCs, on the other hand, claim that on balance they create jobs in the United States. IBM, for example, has stated that "one out of every eight jobs in its U.S. plants depends on shipments abroad that it would not be sending if it did not also produce abroad." Other firms have quoted similar statistics on the importance of foreign operations to research, development, and adminstrative employment in the United States.

At this point, the future of the MNC is somewhat unclear. In the United States, the Burke-Hartke Bill (Foreign Trade and Investment Act) introduced in Congress in 1972 would seriously restrict the operations of many American MNCs by increasing their taxes, curbing capital flows, limiting the transfer of patents and technology to foreign affiliates, and otherwise curtailing the ability of these corporations to produce certain goods abroad for eventual import into the United States. While passage of the bill in its original form is questionable, it appears possible that Congress may at least remove some of the present advantages enjoyed by MNCs. Current tax laws permit them to defer payment of U.S. taxes on foreign earnings until these earnings are actually transferred to this country, rather than paying taxes on profits as earned. Moreover, in 1973 the Senate Foreign Relations Committee began an investigation of the Overseas Private Investment Corporation (OPIC), a government agency that insures investments by MNCs in developing nations. Operating behind OPIC guarantees, many MNCs have in effect been able to enjoy all the benefits of foreign operations, with the U.S. taxpayer assuming most of the risks. On an international level, the UN took a first step toward regulation of the MNCs in 1973, when it appointed a committee to investigate their role in national political matters and to establish a code of behavior and international machinery to control the relations between individual countries and the MNCs.

By the 1970s, however, a reaction against these lower tariffs took hold, spurred by the unfavorable U.S. balance of payments position, the 1970–71 domestic recession, and a growing feeling that foreign nations were reaping the benefits of our lower tariffs while using other trade barriers to keep U.S. goods out of their domestic markets. Responding to these criticisms, President Nixon, in 1971, imposed a 10 percent surcharge (or additional tariff) on all imports.

Quotas A quota sets a maximum on the quantity of a good that may be imported during a given period of time. In its initial form, the extremely protectionist Foreign Trade and Investment Act (Burke-Hartke Bill), introduced in Congress in 1972, proposed that most imports be limited to the average annual amount imported during the years 1965 to 1969. In recent years, similar mandatory quotas have been imposed by Congress on such commodities as oil. And in the case of certain textile products, producers from major exporting nations (Japan, Hong Kong, Korea, and Taiwan) have agreed to voluntary quotas in the hope of escaping more stringent mandatory restrictions.

The current trend as far as trade barriers is concerned appears to be moving away from the use of tariffs. In the United States, for example, the Burke-Hartke Bill proposed to cut imports primarily through import quotas, taxes on foreign earnings, and restrictions on capital movements. Other nations often restrict trade by imposing time-consuming and expensive customs procedures or by refusing to permit local citizens to purchase foreign currencies to pay for certain imports. But the most significant barrier to free trade today is probably the import quota.

Who Benefits from Protection?

Although free trade benefits nations as a whole, certain industries may suffer when trade policies are liberalized, and those involved with such industries will understandably favor the adoption of protective measures. Workers in disadvantaged industries, for example, benefit from protection. Without tariffs or import quotas, disadvantaged industries would be unable to compete in world markets and would consequently suffer contractions. Workers in these industries would lose both jobs and income until their skills could be adapted for use in other areas of the economy.

Producers, too, benefit from protection. Because protective measures increase the prices charged for imported goods, domestic producers are able to remain competitive with foreign-based firms. In some cases it is likely that American producers could not compete at all if imports were permitted in unlimited amounts. For example, many U.S. textile mills were forced to close down once the American consumer discovered that shirts made in Hong Kong undersold comparable American-made merchandise by several dollars. In other cases, domestic firms can manage to survive the onslaught of imports, but their profits will be substantially reduced unless tariff or quota protection can be arranged. Without the import quotas imposed on oil during the 1960s, domestic producers would have been forced to meet the lower foreign prices in the open market and to suffer a loss in revenue and profits.

In every case, of course, it is ultimately the consumer who pays the extra costs. In a recent year, for example, tariffs added $.65 to the $4.35 price of a typical imported woman's umbrella, $4.15 to an average $25 man's cashmere sweater, and $2.40 to a $17 pair of woman's shoes. Quotas also add to the cost of living by eliminating low-cost imports from certain American markets, leaving consumers with no alternative but to buy the higher-priced domestic products. But perhaps most important from a long-term point of view is the fact that protection removes many of the incentives that might otherwise force American industry to seek out more efficient methods of production. An industry protected by a tariff or quota is under no pressure to produce a better or lower-cost product in order to maintain its markets against foreign competition.

Infant Industries One of the oldest arguments in favor of protection comes from those who feel that new domestic industries must be shielded temporarily from foreign competition. The case for protecting America's "infant industries" was first presented in the eighteenth century by Alexander Hamilton, in his report on manufactures. Hamilton claimed that because a new industry may lack trained workmen, established suppliers of raw materials, and the necessary technological know-how, it should be protected from low-cost imports until it achieves the level of efficiency of its foreign competitors. Recent versions of the infant industry argument stress that unless such an industry is granted protection, its volume of sales may never reach the level where it can enjoy economies of scale. In theory, then, the protection of infant industries is seen as temporary. Once the new industry reaches efficient levels of production, it will be able to compete in terms of price with foreign competitors, and tariffs or quotas can be removed.

It is difficult to make a strong case for the infant industry argument in mature economies like those of the United States, Western European nations, or Japan. In developing nations, it may have more validity, although even there it is often difficult to determine which industries are truly infant industries with the potential to compete in world markets and which will never reach the required levels of efficiency. In addition, the record shows that protection originally afforded as a temporary measure frequently persists even after an industry has reached maturity and has become an efficient producer. The result is permanently higher prices for the consumer and frequently higher profit margins for the fortunate industry. Finally, many point out that even in those cases where an infant industry legitimately deserves some help, there are cheaper ways than tariffs or quotas to accomplish this end, including direct cash subsidies, government manpower training programs, and tax abatement.

National Security The national security argument in favor of protection holds that certain industries are essential to the nation's defense and must therefore be protected despite the fact that cheaper sources of supply are available in peacetime. This was, for example, the prime argument for the quotas imposed on oil imports during the 1960s. The domestic oil producers claimed that the higher prices resulting from such quotas would encourage exploration for new oil deposits in the United States, and the nation would need new domestic sources of supply if it was to remain self-sufficient during wartime. The same argument has been used to defend tariffs on imported steel.

The national security argument for protection is particularly susceptible to overuse. In the last analysis, almost any industry, from shoes to copper to watches, contributes in one way or another to the nation's capacity to wage war. Indeed, it is difficult to argue that the watchmaker's skills were not used to make bomb sights in 1942 or that boots were not essential to winning World War II.

Two points, however, should be kept in mind in evaluating the merits of requests for tariffs or quotas on national security grounds. The first is that, once again, there are less expensive and more equitable methods of protecting those industries judged vital to our national defense. Direct government subsidies to the domestic watchmaking industry, for example, would be cheaper, and would also allocate the cost of preserving these essential wartime skills among all Americans rather than only among those who buy watches. Second, tariffs based on national security needs should be evaluated in the context of present-day military technology. Just how meaningful are steel, oil, bomb sights, and 3 million pairs of combat boots in a world where most of the potential combatants have atomic weapons?

Protection Against Cheap Foreign Labor The cheap foreign labor argument in favor of protection holds that since wages in the United States are substantially higher than in other nations, tariffs and similar barriers are necessary to keep out goods produced by low-paid foreign workers. Otherwise, low-cost imports will outsell American-made goods, and the result will be widespread domestic unemployment or lower wages and living standards for American workers.

Although this argument has great appeal, especially to the industries and workers threatened by imports produced in low-wage nations, in many cases it is

THE COST OF TRADE BARRIERS TO CONSUMERS

In dollars and cents, what do the trade barriers imposed by the United States against foreign imports cost the American consumer? A survey of current practices revealed not only that the actual dollar costs are substantial, but that it is also the less affluent U.S. citizen who is paying most of the bill. In addition, the same survey indicated that the widely accepted view of tariffs as the primary barrier to free trade is no longer true; instead, quotas and "voluntary" export restraint agreements do more to raise domestic prices than traditional tariffs on imports.

Estimates are that the total cost of tariff and nontariff trade barriers is a minimum of $10 billion a year, with some suggesting that it may actually exceed $15 billion. Of this, $2 billion represents direct markups on imported goods because of tariffs: the tariff on automobiles, for example, is 7.2 percent, or an average of $140 per car. A more serious problem, however, are the quotas presently imposed on textiles, sugar, steel, and other goods. These raise the prices paid by American consumers in a more subtle way. First, they tend to remove the least costly imports from the market, because a foreign producer, faced with quantity controls on what he can ship to the United States, will usually eliminate his lower-priced items rather than his higher-priced, more profitable ones. This leaves the U.S. consumer with no choice but to buy a more costly alternative. For example, inexpensive shirts from Japan, Taiwan, and Korea are no longer available in most U.S. stores. Second, quotas increase prices because they enable American manufacturers (especially those in monopolistic industries) to raise prices and/or cut quality on domestically produced merchandise, which they would not do if competitive foreign goods were permitted free entry into the United States.

Data suggest that oil quotas alone have cost us $5–6 billion annually. Foreign oil has usually sold for about a dollar a barrel less than domestically produced oil, but quotas kept much of this cheap foreign oil out of the United States, and Americans were forced to buy the more expensive domestic product. In much the same way, dairy quotas prevent us from drinking milk produced in New Zealand, where production costs are one-third lower than they are in the United States. It is estimated that these quotas add about $500 million annually to our food bill.

Another example of the costs of trade restrictions can be seen in the case of textile fabrics. It would appear that we pay an additional $1.3 billion a year for apparel because of import quotas. And since most of the excluded merchandise consists of the lowest-priced items, it is the poorest Americans who are most directly affected by these textile quotas. Meat quotas, which cost us about $350 million a year, have similar consequences: They keep out of the U.S. market meats from

Australia, Ireland, Mexico, and Central America, which might be sold as low-priced hamburgers and frankfurters here.

Although the impact of the "voluntary" steel restraints instituted in1969 is not quite so obvious, it is possible that they have had an even more significant effect as far as the entire economy is concerned. Steel or steel products are the raw materials for an infinite number of finished goods; thus, any increase in the price of steel is bound to have economy-wide repercussions. Faced with heavy foreign competition, steel companies kept their prices reasonably stable during the early and mid-1960s. However, between 1969, when the quota system was first introduced, and 1972, steel companies increased their prices five times as much as they had in the preceding eight-year period, despite the fact that the industry was experiencing declining demand and had unused capacity of 25 to 50 percent. It appears, then, that once blessed with quota protection, the steel companies felt free to raise prices; and because of the central role of steel in our economy, these increases unquestionably contributed to the accelerating rate of inflation experienced since 1969.

Some Industries Enjoying Quotas or Voluntary Export Restraints in 1973

- animal feeds containing milk or milk derivatives
- brooms of broom corn
- cattle
- cotton—raw, waste, etc.
- crude petroleum & petroleum products
- dairy products
- fish & fish products (fresh, frozen or filleted)
- meat & meat products
- peanuts
- potatoes, white or Irish
- sugar & sugar-containing products or mixtures incl. candy & confectionery
- textiles & apparel of cotton, man-made fibers & wool
- stainless steel flatware
- steel
- wheat & wheat flour

United Nations

simply irrelevant. The cheap foreign labor argument ignores the fact that labor is not the only factor of production. A low-wage area may not be able to compete efficiently in those commodities that require substantial amounts of land, capital, or highly trained, specialized labor. Korea may have a large supply of low-cost labor, but it poses no threat to American computer design companies or to our huge capital-intensive airplane factories.

Moreover, protection may not be appropriate even for labor-intensive products which can be produced more cheaply using lower-paid foreign workers. According to the principle of comparative advantage, it will be advantageous in the long run to purchase labor-intensive goods from nations that can produce them at relatively lower cost. It is true that the Americans employed in making radios or shoes may be severely hurt by such a policy in the short run. In the long-run, however, the nation should realize significant benefits from free trade. Moreover, it is cheaper for a society to compensate, retrain, and relocate workers, than it is to subsidize indefinitely a comparatively disadvantaged industry.

The Foreign Trade Multiplier A special version of the cheap foreign labor argument is often heard during periods of economic depression. Based on the formula $Y = C + I + G + X$ (where X represents net exports), this argument holds that because an increase in any one of the components of national income will stimulate the economy and raise the level of employment, an attempt should be made to increase X. In the short run, the simplest way to increase X often appears to be reducing imports by imposing tariffs and quotas. The weaknesses of such an approach, however, have been illustrated time and time again. Since one nation's imports are another nation's exports, any attempts to increase domestic employment in country A through reducing imports from country B will have a negative effect on country B's net exports and employment. If country B did nothing, such a "beggar my neighbor" policy on the part of country A would prove successful. In reality, however, country B would soon reciprocate with its own tariffs and quotas, and A's exports to B would decline. For example, the Hawley-Smoot Tariff, imposed by Congress in 1930, was reasonably successful in keeping some European chemicals and agricultural products out of the United States, but the retaliatory tariffs levied by foreign nations led to a steady decline in American net exports: from $1.1 billion in 1929 to $0.5 billion in 1931 to $0.1 billion in 1935.

Thus, tariffs and quotas usually fail as devices for stimulating net exports and domestic employment. It is true that initially some domestic industries will expand, but very soon employment in the traditional export industries declines in response to the imposition of retaliatory measures by foreign nations. In other words, the final result is rarely an expansion of overall economic activity. Instead, the previous pattern of exports and imports is replaced by a less efficient use of resources, as workers shift from the former export industries in which the nation had a comparative advantage into protected high-cost industries.

The Case Against Protection

The case against protection is, in the last analysis, merely a restatement of the benefits of specialization and trade based on comparative advantage. To special interest groups, tariffs and quotas will often be advantageous. For the country as a whole, however, they lead to an inefficient utilization of resources. Because free trade permits each nation to specialize in the goods it can produce most cheaply, the result is more and cheaper goods for all. Protection, on the other hand, diverts resources into goods that could be produced more efficiently elsewhere.

Logically speaking, a country should avoid fostering or protecting domestic industries that cannot compete with foreign competitors. It makes more sense to let such firms go out of business and to shift the labor and capital into industries enjoying a comparative advantage. Of course, it is difficult to convince those industries currently threatened by imports of the wisdom of this approach. New England shoe manufacturers and South Carolina textile mill owners are perfectly correct in thinking that high tariffs and low quotas will help solve their problems, at least in the short run. Consequently, they are probably not going to be very receptive to suggestions that they abandon the shoe or shirt business and start turning out electric generators or supersonic airplanes. But in terms of the larger national interest, such a switch would be beneficial, at least in the long run. For this reason, we would be wise to explore alternative means of compensating those groups threatened by imports. Tariffs and quotas are permanent, expensive taxes on consumers. Retraining employees, providing loans for relocation or new equipment, and offering temporary subsidies may prove to be less expensive ways of easing the dislocations in domestic industries caused by foreign competition.

SUMMARY

1 The United States is less affected by international trade than most other nations, for our volume of trade is small relative to the size of our GNP. Nevertheless, the United States is the world's largest importer and exporter, accounting for approximately 13 percent of total world trade.

2 According to the principle of absolute advantage, formulated by Adam Smith, when one nation produces less of a good than another nation produces at the same cost, the first nation should import that good from the second nation rather than produce it domestically. In this case, the second nation is said to have an absolute advantage over the first nation in producing that particular good.

3 The theory of absolute advantage does not adequately explain the reasons for international trade. Actually, foreign trade is mutually beneficial, even when one nation is absolutely more efficient in the production of every good, as long as there are differences in the relative costs of producing the various goods in the two potential trading nations. This is the principle of comparative advantage. It is the basis for international trade.

4 For example, suppose that the United States can produce either 30 units of wool or 30 units of steel with a given quantity of resources, whereas Australia can produce either 20 units of wool or 10 units of steel with the same resource input. In terms of opportunity cost, the United States can produce 1 unit of steel for each unit of wool it forgoes, whereas the Australians can produce only ½ unit of steel for each unit of wool they give up. It will therefore pay the Americans to specialize in steel production and procure their wool from Australia, while the Australians specialize in wool production and import their steel from the United States. With specialization and trade, the two nations will be able to consume both more steel and more wool, and domestic standards of living will rise.

5 The simplest explanation of comparative advantage ties it to the differences in the quantity and quality of resources in a given nation. Accordingly, nations should specialize in producing those goods that require the resources with which they are richly endowed. An interesting by-product that often accompanies the growth of trade based on factor-endowment differences is the equalization of factor prices among the trading nations. Essentially, trade serves as a substitute for international mobility of factors of production.

6 The primary barriers to free trade are tariffs and import quotas. Tariffs are taxes on imports, often so high that relatively cheap imports are kept out completely. Import quotas prohibit the importation of more than limited quantities of par-

ticular commodities. These barriers to free trade raise the prices a nation's consumers must pay, since they are subsidizing the relatively inefficient domestic producers.

7 There are few valid arguments in support of trade barriers. A few commonly advanced are: (a) Protection of infant industries. This argument is seldom applicable to industries in mature economies, and in developing nations it is often difficult to determine which industries have the long-run potential to compete in world markets. (b) Protection of industries vital to national defense. In the last analysis, however, almost any industry contributes to national defense, making it difficult to decide where to draw the line. (c) Protection against cheap foreign labor. Economists counter this argument by pointing out that the United States should specialize not in labor-intensive goods, but in those commodities for which we enjoy a comparative advantage. (d) Stimulation of domestic employment. This argument is weak, since other nations may retaliate by imposing tariffs of their own, thus contributing to a decline in employment in traditional export industries. In the long run, output will be higher if resources are allocated to more efficient uses.

8 Although free trade may cause dislocations in the disadvantaged industries that suffer a contraction, in the long run the economy as a whole will benefit from specialization and trade according to comparative advantage. Tariffs and quotas are permanent and expensive taxes on consumers, and there are less expensive ways of easing the dislocations in domestic industries caused by foreign competition.

SUGGESTED READINGS

Balassa, Bela. *Trade Liberalization Among Industrial Countries: Objectives and Alternatives.* New York: McGraw-Hill, 1967.

Haberler, Gottfried. *A Survey of International Trade Theory.* Princeton: International Finance Section, Princeton Univ., 1961.

Kenen, Peter B. *International Economics.* 2nd ed. Chaps. 1, 2, and 4. Englewood Cliffs, N.J.: Prentice-Hall, 1967.

Kindleberger, Charles P. *International Economics.* 4th ed. Chaps. 1-4. Homewood, Ill.: Richard D. Irwin, 1968.

Miller, Roger LeRoy, and **Raburn M. Williams.** *The New Economics of Richard Nixon: Freezes, Floats & Fiscal Policy.* Chap. 10. San Francisco: Canfield Press, 1972.

Ross, Irwin. "Labor's Big Push for Protectionism." *Fortune,* March 1973, pp. 92 ff.

Snider, Delbert A. *Introduction to International Economics.* 5th ed. Chaps. 1-9. Homewood, Ill.: Richard D. Irwin, 1971.

QUESTIONS

1 Review

a. the importance of international trade to the United States,

b. absolute and comparative advantage as the basis for trade,

c. forms of trade restrictions,

d. arguments in favor of protectionism,

e. changing attitudes toward protection through the 1960s and early 1970s,

f. the tendency for factor prices to equalize under conditions of free trade.

2 Assume that the United States must give up one barrel of oil for one bushel of wheat. The USSR must give up one barrel of oil for one-half bushel of wheat. If the United States were to specialize in oil, it could produce 10 million barrels. If it specialized in wheat it could produce 10 million bushels. The USSR could produce 10 million barrels of oil or five million bushels of wheat. How should the two countries specialize and what effect would specialization have on the world production of oil and wheat? Where would the terms of trade fall?

3 Although the production possibilities curves of the United States and the USSR in the example above were assumed to be straight lines, most production-possibilities curves are not shown as straight lines. Why? What is the implication for specialization? In the case above, would the United States be likely to produce only wheat?

4 Protectionists sometimes argue that some industries need to be protected for defense reasons. Could you argue that specialization does not necessarily mean that industries would totally disappear?

5 Is a country's comparative advantage likely to remain in the long run? Why or why not?

6 A large supply of oil has been discovered beneath the floor of the North Atlantic. Since the North Atlantic is not "owned" by any particular nation, which nations are most likely to exploit these resources? Are factors somewhat mobile in this case? Are there any equity problems or distribution problems? For example, should the companies be required to pay rent to the rest of the world for the oil taken?

7 Suppose that trade has been established between two countries, one labor rich, the other capital and land rich. Is it possible that trade might accentuate an inequitable distribution of income in the capital and land rich country? Why?

8 Assume that there is a monopoly in an export industry in an underdeveloped country. What are the effects of monopoly prices on the flow of trade? Why?

CHAPTER 39 EXCHANGE

According to the principle of comparative advantage, international trade can prove beneficial to consumers, workers, and businesses in all the countries involved. Yet, although total world output can be increased through trade, artificial barriers to trade such as tariffs and quotas are the rule rather than the exception. The reasons are many and complex. In this chapter we consider some of the mechanics peculiar to international business dealings that make such dealings more difficult and often more risky than transactions occurring within a country. Since we have concluded that expanded international trade is desirable, our emphasis will be on evaluating alternative international trade arrangements in order to determine which system is most conducive to a high level of trade.

The most important difference between foreign and domestic trade is that different currencies are used in different nations. There are over a hundred sovereign nations in the world; almost every one uses its own currency domestically and must become involved with foreign currencies every time it buys or sells abroad. For example, an American Volkswagen dealer in Philadelphia sells his cars for dollars. But the German factory from which he buys the cars needs German marks to pay its workers, steel suppliers, and electric bills. So the German manufacturer will require eventual payment in marks rather than dollars. Fortunately, over the years, we have developed extensive international monetary institutions that facilitate such payments and permit citizens of different countries to buy and sell each other's products. Here we will examine these institutions, exploring the process through which the dollars of the American car dealer are transformed into the marks required by his German car supplier.

But first, it is useful to consider the factors that contribute to a workable international monetary arrangement. Various types of international monetary system have existed in the past, and one of the major international problems facing us at present is the shape that system will take in the future.

Opening photo by James Andanson, Sygma

What, then, are the criteria for evaluating an international monetary system?

First, such a system must be efficient. It must provide institutions and procedures that permit businesses or governments to exchange currencies easily, quickly, and safely, so that trade will not be discouraged. For example, a mail order house may find that English sweaters are a better value at current prices than comparable American merchandise, and may consider ordering these sweaters for inclusion in its catalog. However, if it is too complicated or burdensome or risky to obtain the necessary English pounds, the buyer may decide to purchase domestic goods instead. In other words, unless an efficient international monetary system exists, the benefits of comparative advantage may well be lost to consumers, even if tariff or quota barriers are removed.

Second, the system must be fair. If an international monetary system has built-in inequities, there will be pressures to circumvent or subvert the system. One of the key issues surrounding the current efforts to reform the international monetary system is how to equitably distribute the costs and benefits of any new arrangement. Unless the mechanisms for international monetary adjustment are fair, they will not be acceptable to all the trading nations involved, and, thus, no matter how technically efficient, such mechanisms will not work for long.

Finally, the system must balance the need for international stability with the need for domestic stability. A good international monetary system must leave room for a nation to pursue its domestic stabilization goals; it cannot require that a country assume the burden of widespread unemployment or spiraling inflation as the price of an efficient, risk-free international monetary arrangement. Both the traditional gold standard and the post–World War II Bretton Woods arrangement (which we examine later in this chapter) involved such requirements to some extent. In 1931–32, for example, the Federal Reserve Board, in an attempt to preserve the gold supply on which international monetary arrangements were based, raised domestic interest rates drastically. Many feel that this move was an important factor in extending and deepening the depression then underway. Today, most observers agree that any international monetary system necessitating such a move is unacceptable. Indeed, confronted with a similar problem 40 years later (1970–71), the Nixon administration decided to abandon the Bretton Woods agreement rather than subvert domestic stabilization objectives.

A good international monetary system, then, must facilitate trade. It must provide those engaged in foreign commerce with easy access to the foreign currencies they require. Ideally, it should be no more difficult or risky for an American supermarket to order and pay for Australian lamb than for beef shipped in from Kansas City. In addition, the system must be fair to all the trading nations involved. If the costs and benefits of international monetary adjustments are not equitably distributed, the arrangement may not long survive. And finally, the system must not interfere with domestic stabilization needs, for an international monetary system that does is not likely to survive for long.

THE MECHANICS OF INTERNATIONAL PAYMENTS

Foreign Exchange

How can an American auto dealer pay for Volkswagens purchased from a German manufacturer? Conceivably, he could use a barter system. If he wants to buy a Volkswagen carrying a 6000 mark price tag in Munich, he could try to negotiate a direct swap of perhaps 600 bushels of wheat for the car. Or he might search for an American farmer currently in the process of selling wheat to Germany and offer to exchange his dollars for the marks the farmer will get from his German customer. Both of these methods, of course, are extremely complicated and time consuming. In real life, an American importer who needs foreign currency (or foreign exchange, as such currencies are called in international dealings) will simply go to a bank or foreign exchange dealer who will trade his American dollars for foreign money. The ratio or price at which this exchange is made is called the **foreign exchange rate.** In mid-1973, for example, the foreign exchange rate for German marks was about 2½ marks to the dollar, or approximately 40 cents per mark. This means that our hypothetical Volkswagen importer could obtain the 6000 deutsche marks he requires for $2400 (2½ × $2400 = DM 6000).

Obviously, the foreign exchange rate is a key element in determining whether or not the transaction will take place. An American importer may be eager to buy a Volkswagen at an exchange rate of 1 DM = 40 cents, or a cost of $2400. But what would happen if the foreign exchange rate changed to 2 DM to the dollar (1 DM = 50 cents)? The importer would then have to spend $3000 to obtain the necessary 6000 marks (2 × $3000 = DM 6000), and the purchase might appear much less attractive.

Foreign exchange rates, then, are an essential factor in determining the levels of international trade. They can, in fact, be substituted for quotas and tariffs as devices to encourage or discourage exports and imports. In the case of cars, for example, a change in the foreign exchange rate from 4 marks to the dollar to 2½ marks to the dollar may discourage imports and protect the U.S. automobile industry as effectively as an increase in the tariff on imported cars.[1] Because exchange rates play such a central role in international trade, it is important to understand the alternative methods through which they may be established and the advantages and disadvantages associated with each method.

Floating Exchange Rates

Under a system of floating exchange rates, the price of a foreign currency will be determined like the price of any other commodity—that is, by supply and demand. However, supply and demand in foreign currency markets are unique in that they are based upon the supply of and demand for other goods and services. Under normal circumstances, nobody wants marks or dollars for their own sake; they are desirable only because they can be used to purchase

1 Such a change in the exchange rate for marks actually occurred between 1969 and 1973 and was largely responsible for the decline in Volkswagen sales in the United States.

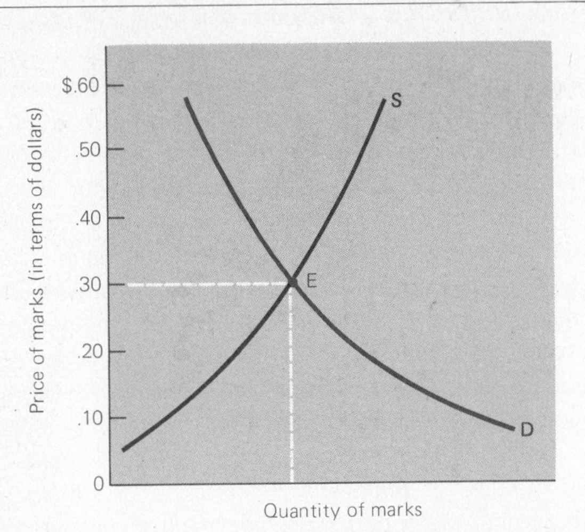

FIGURE 39-1 THE SUPPLY AND DEMAND FOR MARKS The setting of floating exchange rates (in this case, the price of marks in terms of dollars) is just one more example of supply and demand analysis. Given a demand for and a supply of marks, an equilibrium rate is determined. Here, the intersection of the demand curve, D, and the supply curve, S, occurs at equilibrium point E, at which the mark is valued at 30 American cents.

German or American merchandise.[2] Consider, for example, a market in which there are only two participants: the United States and Germany. The foreign exchange demand for marks would be based on the American demand for German goods. Similarly, the supply of marks entering the foreign exchange market would be based on the German demand for American products. The price of marks will settle where the supply and demand curves intersect.

Figure 39-1 shows this supply and demand relationship graphically. Curve D is the demand curve for German marks, which is derived from the American demand for German products. It slopes downward as typical demand curves do. This means that if the mark is selling at a higher dollar price, German goods will cost more in the United States, and the quantity of German goods demanded will drop. For example, at 25 cents a mark, a 400-mark camera would cost an American buyer \$100; at 40 cents a mark it would cost him \$160. Thus, as the price of marks in terms of dollars rises, the quantity of marks demanded declines. Curve S is the supply curve for marks, which is derived from the German demand for American goods. Like a typical supply curve, it slopes upward, indicating that a higher price for the mark means that each mark will buy more American goods, thus encouraging Germans to buy American products and to supply a larger quantity of marks to the foreign exchange market. For example, at 1 mark = 25 cents, a German family of four touring the United States can dine on McDonald's 25 cent hamburgers for 4 marks. If the exchange rate changes to 1 mark = 33⅓ cents, however, the family can buy those same four hamburgers for only 3 marks. Under such circumstances, the number of German tourists in the United States should increase, as should the number of marks these tourists offer in the foreign exchange market. Note that the supply and demand curves for marks intersect at point E, where the demand equals the supply. Thirty cents per mark is therefore the equilibrium foreign exchange rate.

Of course, changes in the exchange rate will occur if there are shifts in either the demand curve (the American demand for German goods) or the supply curve (the German demand for American goods). Assume, for example, that because of gasoline shortages, the U.S. demand for low-fuel-consuming German automobiles increases at every price level and that there is no corresponding change in the German demand for U.S. goods. Graphically, this would mean that the demand curve for marks has shifted to the right (from D to D_1), while the supply curve remains unchanged. Figure 39-2 shows the effect this shift has on the exchange rate. The rate rises to a new equilibrium level (E_1). At this higher exchange rate, American goods that were formerly too expensive for German consumers will now appear attractively priced, and the quantity of American products demanded by Germans will expand enough to supply the additional marks needed to meet the increased American demand for German cars.

2 This description of the demand for marks is considerably oversimplified. It ignores the nonmerchandise demand for foreign currencies, including both long- and short-term capital accounts. These are explained in the section on balance of payments.

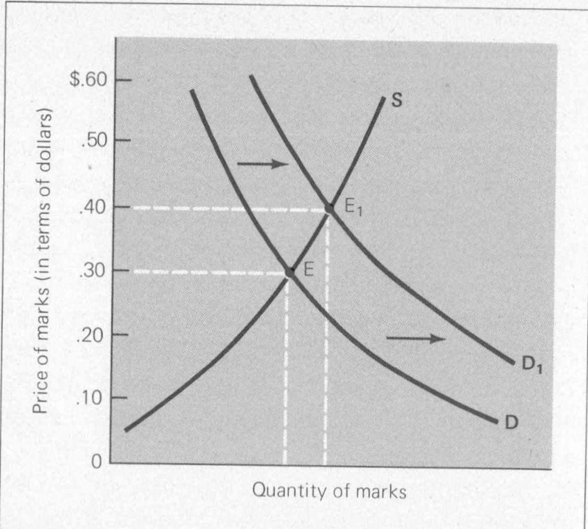

FIGURE 39-2 A SHIFT IN THE DEMAND CURVE FOR MARKS The shift in the demand curve for marks from D to D_1 represents an increase in the desirability of marks relative to dollars. The cause of the shift may be an increase in the demand for German goods. The result is a rise in the price of marks, from 30 to 40 American cents.

Similarly, a shift in the supply curve for marks (which is derived from the German demand for U.S. goods) would also have an effect on the foreign exchange rate. For example, a long-term switch by German housewives from domestic pork products to imported American steaks would increase the supply of marks seeking dollars in the foreign exchange market; that is, it would shift the supply curve to the right. Assuming no change in the U.S. demand for German goods, such a shift would lead to a new, lower equilibrium price level for marks, as shown in Figure 39-3. At this lower exchange rate, German goods would become increasingly attractive to American buyers, and the quantity of German marks demanded by U.S. buyers would increase to a level equal to the higher supply of marks now offered in the foreign exchange market.

Under a system of floating exchange rates, then, the price of a foreign currency is established in the marketplace, varying with supply and demand conditions. The major advantage of such a system is that it provides a means through which imbalances between exports and imports will be adjusted automatically by changes in the exchange rate, rather than through lengthy, expensive, and frequently disruptive domestic measures. For example, the United States suffered a persistent foreign exchange imbalance during the late 1960s and early 1970s, with the value of the foreign currencies U.S. citizens demanded exceeding the value of the dollars foreigners demanded by several billion dollars annually. Under a system of flexible exchange rates, such an imbalance would have been corrected automatically: The prices of the foreign currencies would have increased (resulting in a decline in the quantity of higher-priced foreign goods demanded in the United States), and the price of the dollar would have dropped (resulting in an increase in the quantity of America's relatively cheaper goods demanded in other nations). Instead, the United States struggled for many years under a fixed exchange rate system and was forced to use a wide range of measures, including controls, higher tariffs, and even a measure of internal deflation, in an attempt to discourage Americans from buying foreign goods

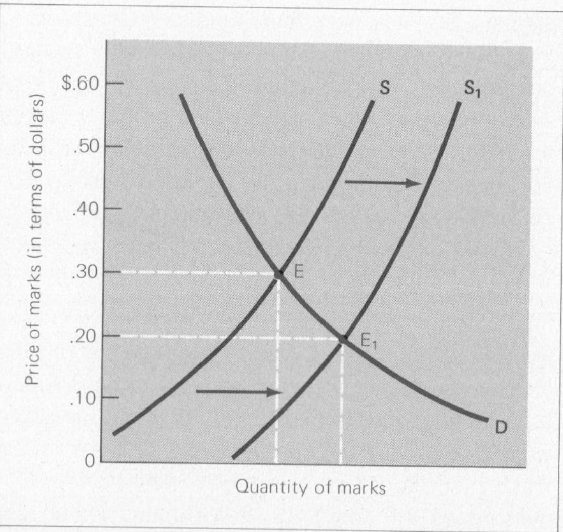

FIGURE 39-3 A SHIFT IN THE SUPPLY CURVE FOR MARKS An increase in the supply of marks, from S to S_1, will drive down their price from 30 to 20 American cents. Such an increase may be due to a higher level of demand in Germany for American products.

and to encourage foreigners to acquire U.S. merchandise and services.

But floating exchange rates have certain very important drawbacks. Primarily, they tend to complicate business arrangements. Consider the case of an American department store contemplating placing a March order for French gloves to be sold at $5.50 at Christmas time. The quoted price is 20 francs a pair; at the current exchange rate of 5 francs to the dollar, the store's cost is $4 a pair. However, the order will not be delivered and paid for until September. Under floating exchange rates, the price of francs could change substantially during the next six months. If the exchange rate should drop to 4 francs to the dollar, the store's cost would be $5 a pair and its profit negligible. As a result, the firm might prefer to stick with domestic merchandise for which the dollar costs are fixed.

There is a definite possibility, then, that floating exchange rates will discourage foreign trade, because they add a currency risk to the normal risks of business enterprise. On these grounds, many consider a floating exchange rate system undesirable. And often, even those who favor flexible rates on principle prefer some limit on the range within which foreign exchange rates can fluctuate.

Advocates of flexible exchange rates, however, contend that there are ways of circumventing currency risks. These methods involve the purchase of currency "futures" contracts. An importer agreeing in March to buy 10,000 francs worth of gloves for delivery and payment in September could simultaneously purchase a futures contract for 10,000 francs. The seller of such a contract would guarantee delivery of 10,000 francs in September at a stated price, regardless of the actual market price of francs in September. The importer would probably pay a small premium for the contract, but it would guarantee him the necessary francs at a stated price and protect him from any changes in foreign exchange rates. Such contracts have proven to be an effective and relatively cheap way of eliminating the excessive risks involved in floating currency systems.

A second drawback to floating exchange rates is the destabilizing impact they may have on domestic economic activity. As exchange rates fluctuate, a nation's volume of exports and imports will change as well. For example, if the dollar were to appreciate (rise in value relative to other currencies), U.S. goods would be less favorably priced in world markets, and U.S. exports would consequently decline. At the same time, the goods of other nations would become more competitive in the United States, and the level of American imports would increase. The overall effect, then, would be a drop in net exports and a corresponding drop in the domestic levels of income and employment. Conversely, a depreciation of the dollar (a decline in value relative to other currencies) would encourage foreigners to purchase American goods, and U.S. exports would therefore increase. It would also make foreign products less attractively priced in the United States, so that America's volume of imports would drop. As a result, U.S. net exports would increase, and if the economy were already operating at the full employment level, inflationary pressures would arise. These effects, of course, would be most severe in nations that rely heavily on foreign trade.

Fixed Exchange Rates

Under a fixed exchange rate system, maintaining stable exchange rates is the most important objective. When a trade imbalance[3] occurs, it is corrected by domestic adjustments of one sort or another, but the price of the currency does not change. For example, with fixed exchange rates, an American buyer ordering French gloves in March at an exchange rate of 5 francs to the dollar can be confident that the rate will be the same when payment is due six months later. This absence of currency risk is believed to create a climate of confidence in which foreign trade will flourish; it is generally given as the primary rationale for a fixed exchange rate system.

The major disadvantage of fixed exchange rates involves the adjustment process through which trade imbalances are handled. With flexible rates, such

3 Again, we are using the concept of trade imbalances as a convenient substitute for the broader total payments imbalances, which include capital accounts.

adjustments are automatic: The price of the currency itself changes. With fixed rates, however, imbalances between the foreign transaction demand and supply of a nation's currency require more complicated adjustments and generally involve government participation. For example, assume that an excess of francs is available for sale in foreign exchange markets because the quantity of dollars demanded by Frenchmen to buy U.S. merchandise exceeds the quantity of dollars supplied by Americans seeking to purchase French goods. Under a flexible rate system, normal competitive forces would lower the price of the franc. Under a typical fixed exchange rate system, however, the Bank of France would intervene, acquiring the surplus francs at the fixed rate. Because of these purchases, the exchange rate for the franc in terms of the dollar will remain constant regardless of changes in the supply and demand curves for francs and the changes in the demand for French and American goods these curves reflect.

Of course, in order for such a system to operate, the central banks responsible for stabilization must have some assets to work with. If the French central bank is to continue to provide $1 for each 5 francs, it must have dollars on hand to exchange for these francs or some other assets that it can speedily exchange for dollars. Such assets are called **international reserves.** In the past, gold has been the classic international reserve, but dollars and pounds (known as "key currencies") have also served this purpose, and other alternatives ("paper gold") are now being introduced.

Although the various forms of international reserves are significant in distinguishing one fixed exchange rate system from another, these differences are not important to a general understanding of how a fixed rate system operates. What is important is a recognition of the consequences of a prolonged and severe drain on a nation's international reserves, whatever they may be. For example, if an imbalance between francs and dollars persists, the French central bank may eventually run out of dollars, or of pounds or gold which it might exchange for dollars. Faced with such prospects, nations with persistent reserve drains have only one alternative under a pure fixed rate system: They must attack the underlying causes of the imbalance between imports and exports. It is likely that the imbalance will be related to domestic price levels. French goods, for instance, may be so expensive that no one will buy them in world markets. The classic way of correcting such a situation is through domestic deflation: raising interest rates, imposing higher taxes, cutting government spending, and generally accepting a lower national income and a higher unemployment rate in an attempt to reduce the inflation that has priced domestic goods out of world markets. If these measures work, exports will increase, the trade imbalance will be eliminated, and the reserve drain ended. But for obvious reasons, such measures often prove to be highly unpopular at home.

Of course, a nation with a fixed rate system does have another alternative when faced with a reserve drain resulting from an imbalance between the demand for and supply of its currency: It can decide to change its exchange rate. Such a move will not only remove the immediate need for central bank intervention in the foreign exchange markets; it will also correct the basic cause of the imbalance. The French government, for example, might decide to change the official exchange rate for the franc from 5 francs to $1 (20 cents per franc) to a price nearer that which would prevail in the free market under competitive conditions—say, 8 francs to the dollar (12½¢ per franc). At this new exchange rate, American customers who were formerly paying $2 for a bottle of 10 franc sauterne would find that it now costs only $1.25. Other French products would be similarly reduced in price in the American market, and hopefully U.S. imports from France (and therefore the U.S. demand for francs) would increase enough to eliminate the need for intervention by the French central bank in the foreign currency market.[4]

However, changes in the official exchange rate are not without costs. During the late nineteenth and early twentieth centuries, when the gold standard was at its peak, devaluation meant a loss in interna-

4 A reduction in the official exchange rate is called *de*valuation; an increase is known as a *re*valuation.

tional prestige, for such changes were regarded as a sign of weakness characteristic of a third-rate power. Moreover, any nation that indulges in exchange rate changes may find them backfiring: Speculators, anticipating further changes, may engage in speculative currency transactions that significantly accentuate the reserve drains caused by ordinary trade imbalances, and other nations may decide to change their exchange rates too, thus negating the effects of the first nation's move.

The Gold Standard From the early nineteenth century until the post–World War I period, most of the major industrialized nations of the world and their trading partners operated, at least nominally, under a fixed exchange system called the gold standard. Under this system, each nation defined its currency in terms of gold. For example, in 1900, the dollar was equal to 1/20 of an ounce of gold, the pound to 5/20 of an ounce. In addition, each nation agreed to convert its paper money into gold on demand, and there were no restrictions on the shipment of gold from one country to another. Thus, an American ordering an English sweater priced at 1 pound was assured that he would have to pay $5 in U.S. currency. If he could not buy 1 pound for $5 in the foreign exchange market, he could always exchange his $5 for 5/20 of an ounce of gold at his U.S. bank and use this gold to buy 1 pound at the Bank of England. Of course, only very rarely would a normal business transaction require direct exchanges of gold for currency. But the fact that such an option was available assured businesses that the foreign exchange rate for the pound would remain at 1 pound = $5.

What would happen during a given period if Englishmen bought $15 million (3 million pounds) worth of goods and services from the United States, but Americans purchased only 2 million pounds ($10 million) worth of merchandise from Britain? Because foreign exchange dealers could supply only $10 million in U.S. currency to British buyers, the remaining $5 million would have to be obtained by the shipment of gold from Great Britain to America. Englishmen would in effect be required to bring 1 million pounds to the Bank of England, obtain gold for it, and send this gold to the United States in exchange for the additional $5 million they needed. In other words, the payments imbalance would be solved by a decline in British gold reserves and an increase in U.S. gold holdings.

Such a procedure raises the question of what would happen if there was a prolonged trade imbalance in Great Britain. Would the gold drain continue until the Bank of England lost all its reserves and the system collapsed? Writing in 1752, the British philosopher David Hume explained why this was unlikely. His explanation is based on the premise that under a gold standard all monies, both those used in foreign exchange and those used at home, are convertible into gold. Therefore, the supply of money depends on the amount of gold a nation has. Combining this fact with the classical economists' claim that the price level depends on the quantity of money, we can see that changes in the gold supply within a nation will affect prices. Consequently, if there is a gold outflow from England to the United States because of a trade imbalance, prices in England will decline and prices in the United States will rise. English goods will become more attractive to American buyers, American goods less attractive to English buyers. In other words, the trade imbalance that caused the original gold drain will reverse itself, and Britain will regain its lost gold reserves.

According to Hume's analysis, then, the gold standard would provide an automatic adjustment process through which trade imbalances between countries would self-correct. Moreover, this correction process would theoretically be painless. Although a nation suffering a gold outflow would undergo deflation, such deflation, as the classical economists saw it, would mean lower prices throughout the economy. Wages might be cut, but prices would fall proportionately, and everyone would maintain his original buying power.

Despite this idealized description of the gold standard, it became increasingly clear over the years that the system had several important drawbacks. The first involves the rigidities that develop as economies become more complex. We now know that a decline in the supply of money does *not* affect all segments of the economy equally. Prices in monopolistic industries and wages in highly unionized trades may refuse to fall. As a result, deflation resulting from a gold outflow will be especially burdensome to certain groups, particularly small businesses and nonunionized labor. In addition, it is possible that the gold outflow may not provide the automatic adjustment for trade imbalances that classical economists expected, because the prices of exports may well be among those that do not decline.

A second drawback of the gold standard concerns the shortages of gold that developed in certain nations, beginning after World War I. Many of the major trading nations found their gold reserves depleted because of the huge expenditures they had made in the course of the war, the disruption of normal export markets during and after the war, and, in the case of Germany, the reparations it was forced to pay to the victors. As a result, these nations simply did not have the gold reserves required to handle even temporary trade imbalances, and many nations imposed tariffs, quotas, and other trade restrictions in an attempt to cut imports and thus preserve whatever gold they did have. Germany, for example, negotiated most of its foreign trade on a barter basis, and, at one time, South America was flooded with German chemicals obtained in exchange for Argentine beef, Brazilian coffee, and so on. All these measures, which were instituted at least in part in response to the dwindling supplies of gold reserves, led to a collapse of world trade. By the mid-1930s annual world trade had dropped to half its earlier level.

The shortage of gold was even worse after World War II. By 1949, two-thirds of the world's gold reserves had moved to the United States, and other trading nations lacked adequate supplies of gold to serve as a reserve asset. Nor was the problem merely one of maldistribution of total world gold supplies. Rather, there was a worldwide shortage of gold. The volume of world trade had the potential to expand very rapidly, but the world gold supply did not. Increases in the total supply of gold were limited to the relatively small outputs of a handful of mines in South Africa, Australia, and North America, plus an uncertain quantity from the USSR. And because the nonreserve demands for gold (for dentistry, jewelry, hoarding, and so forth) were increasing at a rapid rate, only very small amounts were available each year as additional monetary reserves. Consequently, there was pressure for the development of a new monetary system that would either replace or augment gold as the international monetary reserve.

Gold Exchange Standards The gold exchange standards that have evolved since World War I are similar in some respects to the old gold standard: They attempt to provide fixed exchange rates through the use of reserve assets, and their primary mechanisms for adjusting payment imbalances are transfers of reserve assets and internal measures. However, the gold exchange standards differ from the gold standard in that "key currencies" (at first the pound, and later the dollar) serve along with gold as reserve assets. Over the years, these key currencies, rather than gold, have assumed an increasing role in the settlement of international payments imbalances.

THE BRETTON WOODS SYSTEM The Bretton Woods system, established at an international monetary conference in Bretton Woods, New Hampshire, in 1944, represented the culmination of efforts to develop a workable gold exchange standard. It lasted, despite severe strains in its later years, until 1971. Under the Bretton Woods system, the value of the U.S. dollar was set at 1/35 of an ounce of gold, and the United States promised that all U.S. dollars in the hands of central banks would be redeemed in gold upon demand. Every other nation then defined its currency in terms of the dollar and/or gold. The pound, for example, was originally given a fixed value of $4.00 or of 4.0 × 1/35 of an ounce of gold.

Under the Bretton Woods agreement, trading in currencies was left to the market as long as the demand for and supply of the currencies was such that the free market price stabilized around the established par values. When trade or capital movement imbalances moved the price of a currency more than 1 percent above or below its stated par value, government action was mandated. Assume, for example, that the par value for the franc is 20 cents (5 francs = $1). If the French demand for U.S. goods were to soar, an excess of francs and a shortage of dollars in the currency market would result. Under normal circumstances, this would mean that the price of the franc would fall. Under the Bretton Woods system, however, the French government, through its central bank, was required to enter the market, supplying $1 for every 5 francs, regardless of demand or supply conditions.

Thus, the stabilization process under the Bretton Woods gold exchange system required reserve assets, just as it did under the gold system. The difference was that nations kept their reserves not only in gold, but also in dollars. They were willing to do this because of the U.S. guarantee to exchange dollars for gold on demand. In this way, the Bretton Woods arrangement solved one of the major problems of the gold exchange system: It permitted the expansion of world monetary reserves at a much quicker rate than a system restricted only to gold. But the key factor in guaranteeing the workability of the system was the acceptability of the dollar. If anything were to happen that would shake world confidence in the ability or desire of the United States to continue exchanging dollars for gold, the system might very well collapse.

In many ways, the adjustment process under the Bretton Woods system was similar to that under a pure gold system. Nations with a persistent trade or capital flow imbalance would find their reserves depleted, and they would be under pressure to deflate internally in order to correct the imbalance. The system, however, provided two means of assisting nations with severe reserve drains. First, a new world monetary body, the International Monetary Fund, was created. Among its other functions, the IMF was assigned the role of aiding nations whose reserves were temporarily inadequate to meet currency imbalances. Each nation contributed certain reserve assets (gold, dollars, or its own currency) to a central pool, and each nation was then assigned a prescribed quota of these reserves (called its gold tranche), on which it could draw automatically in times of need. The second means of assistance involved devaluation. Under the Bretton Woods system, devaluation was an acceptable alternative in cases of persistent payment imbalances. Any nation could unilaterally change the par value of its currency by as much as 10 percent, and even larger changes were permissible if approved by the IMF.

SDRs AND PAPER GOLD By the late 1960s, it had become evident that there were problems developing in connection with the reserve assets on which the Bretton Woods system was based. While most nations were satisfied to keep their increased reserves in dollars, some took advantage of the Bretton Woods convertibility clause, exchanging dollars for gold. As a result, U.S. gold reserves declined: from $20 billion in 1959 to $10 billion in 1971. At the same time, foreign dollar holdings increased, and nations began to wonder if the United States could maintain its convertibility guarantee forever. In the light of these doubts, the dollar began to look somewhat less attractive as a reserve asset, and the search for an alternative began.

In March 1968, at a meeting of the leading nations of the world in Stockholm, plans for a new world reserve asset were announced. Special Drawing Rights (SDRs) were to be created by the IMF and credited to each nation's account in proportion to its original IMF contribution of gold or currencies. These SDRs (also called "paper gold") could be used to help a nation with a balance of payments problem. For example, if France needed additional marks to support the franc, but had already used up its gold, dollars, and gold tranche reserves, it could turn to its allotment of SDRs. By 1972, $9.5 billion worth of SDRs had been created. Although this was less than 10 percent of total world monetary reserves, many authorities believe that SDRs will play an increasing role in any world monetary system based on international reserves.

THE BALANCE OF PAYMENTS

Until now we have described the imbalances between the demand for and supply of a currency in

TABLE 39-1 U.S. Balance of Payments, 1972 (in billions of dollars)

	(a) Credits	(b) Debits	(c) Net	(d) Major balances
I. CURRENT ACCOUNT				
A. Private goods and services				
1. Merchandise trade				
a. Merchandise exports	+48.8			
b. Merchandise imports		−55.7		
Balance on merchandise trade			−6.8	
2. Investment income[1]				
a. U.S. investment abroad	+13.8			
b. Foreign investment in the U.S.		−5.9		
Balance on investment income			+7.9	
3. Other services, net (travel, transportation, etc.)			−1.8	
B. Government current account				
1. Military transactions, net			−3.5	
2. Remittances, pensions, and other transfers, net			−1.6	
3. Government grants[2]			−2.2	
BALANCE ON CURRENT ACCOUNT				−8.0
II. CAPITAL ACCOUNT				
A. Long-term				
1. Direct private investment				
a. U.S. direct investment abroad		−3.3		
b. Foreign direct investment in the U.S.	+ .3			
Balance on direct private investment			−3.0	
2. Other long-term capital flows, net[3]			+1.8	
BALANCE ON CURRENT ACCOUNT AND LONG-TERM CAPITAL ACCOUNT (BASIC BALANCE)				−9.2
B. Short-term				
1. Nonliquid short-term private capital flows, net			−1.6	
2. Allocation of SDRs to the U.S. by IMF	+ .7			
3. Errors and omissions, net			−3.8	
NET LIQUIDITY BALANCE				−14.0
4. Transactions in U.S. liquid short-term assets, net			−1.1	
5. Transactions in U.S. liquid liabilities to other than foreign official agencies, net			+4.8	
OFFICIAL RESERVE TRANSACTIONS BALANCE				−10.3
III. RESERVE ASSETS MOVEMENTS				
Financed by changes in:				
1. U.S. government and U.S. bank liabilities to foreign official agencies			+10.3	
2. U.S. NET TOTAL			*	
				0.0

1 Includes direct investment fees and royalties.
2 Excludes military grants of goods and services.
3 Excludes official reserve transactions and includes transactions in some short-term U.S. government assets.
* Less than $0.05 billion.

Note: Details will not necessarily add to totals because of rounding.

terms of merchandise exports and imports. Other transactions, however, also create demands for and supplies of currencies. For example, American purchases of Swiss watches result in a demand for Swiss francs, but so do American purchases of Swiss ski lift rides or hotel rooms. And demand for foreign currencies also occurs when an American multinational corporation decides to build a factory in France or Taiwan. Similarly, supplies of foreign currencies result from any transaction requiring a foreigner to obtain U.S. dollars. These can include expenditures by Japanese tourists in the United States, purchases of U.S. stocks by German investors, and payment of interest or dividends to U.S. corporations by their foreign subsidiaries.

A balance of payments statement is a summary of all the international financial dealings in which a nation engages over a stated period of time, typically a year. The U.S. balance of payments statement shown in Table 39-1 lists in column (a) the value of various types of transactions resulting in an inflow of money from other nations to the United States; these are called credit (+) transactions. It lists in column (b) all transactions creating an outflow of money from the United States to other nations; these are called debit (−) transactions. In column (c), credits and debits for each item are totaled to arrive at a net credit or debit figure. Finally, section III of the table indicates how the United States dealt with any gap between total net credits and net debits; in other words, this part of the balance sheet shows the movements of reserve assets and/or borrowings that the United States was forced to employ.

The United States has experienced a deteriorating balance of payments position since the late 1950s. There are several reasons for this: military expenditures abroad (particularly for the war in Vietnam), foreign aid, and, most recently, a reversal of America's traditional trade surplus. Her trade deficits have been due to relatively high prices in the United States compared to those in Japan, Canada, and Western Europe. But this problem appears to have been corrected by recent policy measures, and the United States should be having trade surpluses over the next few years.

SOURCE: U.S. Department of Commerce.

Balance of Payments Statement: The Individual Accounts

Current Account

Section I of Table 39-1 is called the current account. The largest item in this section of the balance of payments statement is private merchandise transactions—that is, imports and exports. In earlier times, this item was even more important than it is today. When exports exceeded imports, a nation was said to have a favorable **balance of trade,** or a trade surplus; when imports exceeded exports, as they do in the 1972 U.S. statement, a nation was said to have an unfavorable balance of trade, or a trade deficit. The balance of trade should not be confused with the other, broader payments balances discussed below. These distinctions are particularly important today, when the nonmerchandise accounts have assumed increasing importance.

Other private goods and services entries, in addition to the "visible" merchandise category, are those often referred to as the "invisible" items. These include tourist travel, shipping expenditures, insurance payments, and other services that Americans buy from foreigners or that they buy from Americans. Also included are private remittances; for example, monies sent by Americans to their families still living in Europe or Hong Kong. A final invisible item is investment income, a large net credit entry representing interest and dividend payments made to U.S. investors who own or have lent money to foreign businesses. Investment income received by American multinational corporations is a large component of this category.

In all, the balance on the private goods and services portion of the current account amounted to a $0.7 billion deficit in 1972. When this is combined with the net debits due to government transactions—foreign aid, government remittances, pensions and other transfers, military transactions—the resulting **balance on current account** comes to −$8 billion, a sizable deficit.

Capital Account

LONG-TERM CAPITAL MOVEMENTS The long-term capital account represents both private and government loans and investments abroad. The private long-term capital account for 1972 showed a substantial deficit, because U.S. investors (primarily the multinational corporations) were lending and investing considerably more in foreign markets than foreigners were investing in the United States.

If we combine the net balance from the current account with the balance resulting from these long-term capital transactions, we arrive at the "basic" U.S. balance of payment position. Since the **basic balance** includes only those transactions arising from the normal course of business and government operations, many authorities consider it the most useful measure of a nation's balance of payments position.

SHORT-TERM CAPITAL MOVEMENTS The balance of payments statement differentiates between long-term capital movements, which are closely related to longer-term business or government operations, and short-term capital movements, which occur primarily to take advantage of transitory conditions. For example, if interest rates are temporarily higher in Germany than in New York, investors may switch dollars into marks to benefit from this short-term situation. The most important short-term capital movements in recent years, however, have been speculative. In 1972, speculators became convinced that the exchange rate between the U.S. dollar and the yen (then about $1 = 320 yen) was unrealistic because at this rate Japan was exporting considerably more merchandise to the United States than the United States was selling there. They suspected that shortly, in an attempt to reduce Japanese exports to the United States, the yen would be revalued upward, so that American importers would receive perhaps only 280 yen to the dollar. Anticipating this, speculators sold dollars and bought yen at the current rate, figuring that if they were right, they could later replace each dollar for only 280 yen, making a nice profit on the trade.[5] Such speculation has the effect of increasing the demand for yen, just as U.S. purchases of Japanese goods do; therefore, it is recorded as a debit on the balance of payments statement. In some versions of the statement, these speculative movements of capital are lumped together with other short-term movements. In the official version, however, they are usually included under the heading "errors and omissions." This is because many speculative movements of capital are not recorded, partly because in some countries speculation is illegal and partly because of general inadequacies in recording procedures.

If we combine the basic balance with the balance on short-term capital transactions, we arrive at another balance of payments figure: the **liquidity balance.** When the liquidity balance is adjusted by the amount of liquid private capital flows (a complex procedure involving transfer of short-term assets and liabilities mainly among U.S. and foreign commercial banks), a final total, the **official reserve transactions balance,** results.

Reserve Asset Account How did the United States manage to finance its huge 1972 payments deficit? Where did Americans find the $10.3 billion by which the U.S. demand for foreign currencies exceeded foreigners' demand for U.S. dollars? There are only a few alternatives open to a country with such a problem, and the United States used them all. She sent some of her reserve assets—gold, foreign currencies—abroad. But her major solution involved a form of borrowing. She persuaded foreign governments (largely central banks) to increase their holdings of dollars by almost the entire amount of her deficit, and in that way she avoided the unpleasant necessity of having to provide them with the foreign currencies, gold, or SDRs they might otherwise have received in exchange for these dollars.

THE U.S. BALANCE OF PAYMENTS PROBLEM

U.S. Balance of Payments Trends Since World War II

The monetary problems that caused the breakdown of the Bretton Woods system in 1971 have their roots in the balance of payments problems confronting the United States in the late 1960s and early 1970s. Here we shall trace the development of these problems. What caused the United States to move

5 They were right. The yen was revalued in late 1972, and speculators reaped enormous profits.

from a balance of payments surplus of $4 billion in 1947 to a deficit of over $29.8 billion in 1971?

The end of World War II found the productive capacity of Europe and Japan largely destroyed. Consequently, the United States supplied these nations with huge amounts of both merchandise and capital. The typical American balance of payments statement during the fifties and early sixties showed the accumulation of an enormous balance of trade surplus, which was offset almost entirely by private and government capital movements abroad. In a typical year (between 1950 and 1967) the net result of these transactions was a small overall balance of payments deficit ($2 to $4 billion), which was handled by a gradual decline in the U.S. gold supply and a very sharp increase in foreign holdings of U.S. dollars.

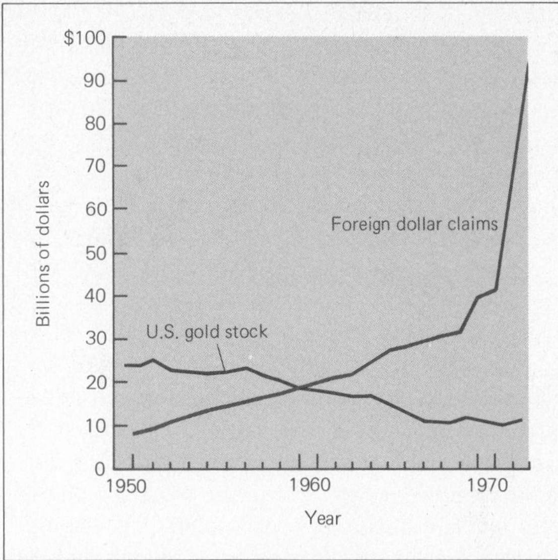

FIGURE 39-5 OFFICIAL GOLD STOCK AND FOREIGN DOLLAR CLAIMS, 1950–72 Since the United States began incurring balance of payments deficits in the late 1950s, her reserve position has deteriorated steadily. As the stock of gold held by the United States declined, the volume of foreign dollar claims mounted rapidly. Clearly the United States government does not hold enough gold reserves to cover these dollar claims.

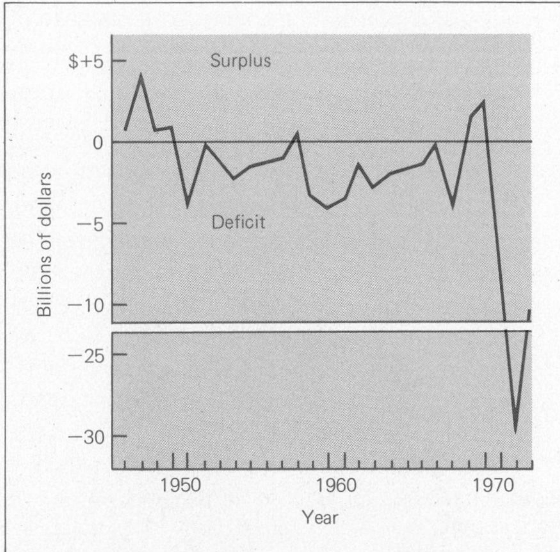

FIGURE 39-4 U.S. BALANCE OF PAYMENTS, 1946–72 During the 1950s and 1960s the United States experienced balance of payments deficits almost every year. Typically, these deficits averaged about $3 billion annually, and caused concern because they were eroding the gold and foreign currency reserves of the United States. Then, in 1970, the U.S. payments deficit began to soar, culminating in the $29.8 billion deficit of 1971, which set off a series of international monetary crises. America's loss of trade surplus and the growing net outflow of short-term and long-term capital contributed to this huge deficit. Although these trends have been reversed, by 1972 the United States had only started to eliminate its enormous balance of payments deficit.

SOURCE: U.S. Department of Commerce.

In the late 1960s, however, it became obvious that the forces underlying these fairly modest deficits were accelerating. As shown in Figure 39-4, the U.S. payments deficit took a quantum leap—from a $2.2 billion average in 1960–64 to $9.8 billion in 1970 to $29.8 billion in 1971. This was accompanied by a further decline in U.S. gold holdings and a tremendous increase in foreign short-term dollar claims. (See Figure 39-5.)

One important reason behind the growing payments deficit involved the U.S. merchandise account. Every year from 1900 to 1970 this account had produced a surplus. Typically, this surplus, along with credits resulting from income from U.S. investments abroad, was almost enough to offset the deficits resulting from certain account items, such as tourist spending and remittances, and from long-term government and private capital flows. By the late 1960s, however, it had become obvious that the United States was losing its traditional primacy in world export markets. European nations and Japan had recovered from the devastation of the war, their productivity was growing more quickly than that of the United States, and in some cases they could undersell American competitors because their domestic inflation rates were lower than that of the United States. In addition, the development of the European Economic Community (the Common Market) provided its member nations with the advantages of size and the removal of tariff barriers. The result was both the loss of some of the U.S.'s traditional foreign markets and the introduction of new, very efficient competitors into some U.S. domestic markets. Another factor detrimentally affecting the U.S. trade balance was the imposition of trade barriers against U.S. goods by nations such as Japan. Finally, the high level of both private and government investment abroad continued. American direct private investment abroad increased from an annual level of $1.8 billion during the early 1960s to $4.8 billion by 1971, largely reflecting the increased power and size of the American multinational corporations; and to this was added accelerated spending on Vietnam, which continued throughout the late 1960s.

The 1971 Monetary Crisis and Its Aftermath

By mid-1971 it was becoming increasingly clear that the U.S. dollar was in trouble. The nation had just reported its first trade deficit in this century. This in itself suggested that our basic balance of payments account would show a severe deficit, but the problem was compounded by speculative transactions that dumped billions of dollars for sale in world markets. Indeed, by the year's end, that provocative account—Errors and Omissions—would show an astounding deficit of $11.1 billion.

A country with a growing payments deficit and declining reserve assets has only a few alternatives. It can attempt internal deflation, but, in 1971, with the unemployment rate already at 6 percent and a presidential election coming up, the Nixon administration could not take this path. Other alternatives involve cutting the price of the currency, either through a single devaluation or through adopting floating exchange rates. Gradually, the major foreign holders of dollars began to accept the inevitability of one of these solutions. As a result, foreign banks became increasingly reluctant to continue the stabilization procedures that were daily expanding their dollar holdings, and speculators and multinational corporations became very eager to unload dollars (which they felt would soon be worth less) and to acquire other currencies instead. Thus, the international monetary system was confronted with two interrelated problems. On the one hand, there was a tremendous desire to sell dollars; on the other hand, the traditional buyers of these dollars—the foreign central banks—were no longer willing to purchase. The eventual outcome was a collapse of the institutions and procedures underlying the Bretton Woods system.

The Collapse of the Bretton Woods System Although the Bretton Woods monetary arrangements officially came to an end on August 15, 1971, there were two key events that preceded its demise. The first occurred in March 1968, when a two-tier gold system was introduced. Under the Bretton Woods system, the world market price of gold had been set at $35 an ounce. Not only did official reserve transfers take place at this price, but, in addition, many central banks sold gold at $35 to private individuals. The Bank of France, for example, for many years had redeemed francs for gold for any private citizen; in the United States such sales were also made, although they were restricted to people with a legitimate trade interest (jewelers, dentists, and so on). The net effect of these private transactions was to reduce the gold reserve assets of the nations involved, especially when the speculative demand for gold began to increase in the late 1960s.

The two-tier market was an attempt by IMF member nations to limit such gold drains. It provided for an **official tier**, within which existing gold reserves would be used only for settlements of international trade imbalances. Movements of gold within the of-

THE MNCs AND INTERNATIONAL MONETARY CRISES

The role of the giant multinational corporations in precipitating international monetary crises is currently a topic of great controversy. A recent study by the U.S. Tariff Commission charged that "much of the funds which flow internationally during a crisis doubtlessly is of multinational corporation origin." In fact, the multinationals are fast becoming the primary culprits at whose door responsibility for recurring international financial instabilities and breakdowns is laid.

This is due to the MNCs' huge holdings of very mobile money. When a particular currency shows weakness (as did the dollar most recently), the multinational corporations act to protect their assets by dumping their holdings of the weak currency in exchange for a stronger one (frequently the mark). As a result, the weakness of the dumped currency is aggravated. This tendency to abandon the weak for the strong had precipitated monetary crises long before the advent of the MNCs, but the volume of short-term capital flows has been greatly enhanced by these huge corporations.

United Press International

In the view of some observers, few nations can withstand the financial power of the multinationals. Their $268 billion in short-term liquid assets as of the end of 1971 (according to the Tariff Commission study) dwarfed the less than $68 billion in reserves held by the major central banks. Thus, even a proportionately small shift in the liquid assets of the multinationals may be sufficient to plunge the international system into a crisis. In the winter of 1972–73, for example, less than $10 billion in multinational financial maneuvering was enough to prompt the events leading to the second devaluation of the dollar, in February.

The actions of the MNCs may be viewed as logical defensive actions taken to avoid substantial losses (if, say, dollars are devalued and/or other currencies are revalued). While bigness is certainly no crime, the very possession of huge currency holdings makes such defensive actions both necessary and inevitable. Unless international monetary authorities are able to avert the effects of those short-term flows or curb them in some way, the monetary crises of the future might be still more acute.

There is, of course, the temptation for those MNCs so inclined to speculate in currencies, since they are in a most favorable position to do so. But even if no speculation took place—and there is considerable evidence to the contrary—many argue that the world's monetary system is captive to the whim as well as the self-interest of the MNCs' international money managers.

ficial tier would continue to take place at the official price of $35 an ounce. The United States, for example, would continue to redeem dollars held by central banks at the rate of one ounce of gold for each $35. But it would no longer sell gold to private citizens, and it would no longer guarantee to buy gold at $35 from any private seller. Instead, all such nongovernment transactions in gold would take place in the **free-market tier,** where the price would fluctuate in accordance with supply and demand.

The objectives of this two-tier market were, first, to conserve the existing gold reserve assets by stopping gold drains to private sources; and second, to discourage speculation in gold by eliminating in the free-market tier the $35 guaranteed price. But the two-tier market provided only a brief respite. After all, the primary reason behind the enormous gold losses suffered by the United States during the post–World War II years had not been private demand, but the payments deficit—and this deficit was still growing. Moreover, it is possible that although the two-tier system was designed to preserve the Bretton Woods system by protecting reserve assets, psychologically it may actually have hastened the decline. Once the United States had suspended the convertibility of the dollar into gold for a given group (the private, noncentral bank holders of dollars), the suspension of all convertibility became an implicit possibility. Under such conditions, the dollar became an even less attractive long-term holding.[6]

During the next two years, the flight from the dollar took many forms. The price of gold in the free-market tier rose steadily, as did the supplies of dollars accumulating in the hands of foreign central banks. In May 1971, traders in the foreign currency market were seeking to exchange an enormous number of dollars for German marks. For a while, the West German central bank adhered to its Bretton Woods commitment and continued to trade dollars for marks at the official exchange rate of 1 mark = 27.3 cents. Finally, however, the central bank withdrew from the foreign exchange market and permitted the mark to float in the open market. It finally settled at approximately 31 cents. This action by the West German government marked the first time since the end of World War II that a major trading nation had discarded the concept of fixed exchange rates maintained by central bank intervention.

6 In November 1973 the two-tier market for gold was abandoned since central banks were no longer willing to buy or sell gold at the official price. Thus the free-market price for gold prevailed in all transactions.

President Nixon's New Economic Policy On August 15, 1971, President Nixon issued his New Economic Policy, the price-wage freeze and projected wage-price controls being the most important domestic innovations. Simultaneously he announced a very significant international move: The United States would completely abandon its Bretton Woods convertibility guarantee. Three years earlier, with the introduction of the two-tier system, the United States had stopped gold transactions with all buyers and sellers except central banks. It now announced that it would not redeem paper dollars for gold even from these sources. Confronted with this development, foreign governments felt free to dispense with their Bretton Woods commitments, too. One central bank after another announced that, since dollars were no longer convertible into gold, it was no longer obliged to buy dollars to support the official exchange rates of its currency. Instead, currencies were left free to be traded in the open market and find their own levels. This floating exchange rate system continued for the next four months, with almost every major currency rising in price relative to the dollar. President Nixon hoped that eventually these higher prices for foreign monies would correct the U.S. payments imbalance, but, for the time being, the payments deficit continued, compounded by the huge supply of dollars already in foreign hands because of earlier imbalances.

The Smithsonian Agreement Although four months of floating exchange rates did not cause international trade chaos, as feared by some, there was still considerable pressure for the development of a new monetary system involving some form of fixed rates. In December 1971, representatives of the Group of Ten (the 10 largest trading nations) met at the Smithsonian Institution, and produced the Smithsonian agreement. Under this agreement the dollar was officially devalued by about 8 percent (to $38 an ounce), and many other currencies were appreciated relative to the dollar: the yen by 17 percent, the mark by 14 percent, and most other European currencies by somewhat under 10 percent. Overall, the dollar was depreciated by an average of approximately 12 percent.[7] Central bank stabilization efforts were still mandated as under Bretton Woods, but such efforts were not required unless the open-market price of a currency rose or fell more than 2¼ percent above or below the official price. (Under the Bretton Woods system, stabilization efforts were required after a deviation of only 1 percent.) It was hoped that these new higher prices for foreign currencies would correct the U.S. payments imbalance and that the new exchange rates were realistic enough that the central banks would not be forced to intervene.

For a while, the new arrangements seemed to work. In mid-1972, however, the British pound was subjected to a wave of selling. The Bank of England used billions of its reserves in an attempt to maintain the Smithsonian agreement price ($2.60 less 2½ percent), but, finally, in June 1972, it abandoned further stabilization efforts, withdrew from the foreign exchange market, and permitted the pound to float.

The pound was the first casualty of the new Smithsonian arrangement; it was not, unfortunately, the last. In early 1973, world currency speculators attacked the dollar. Again, West Germany bore the brunt of the attack. In one six-week period, the West German central bank, in accordance with the Smithsonian agreement, was forced to acquire more than $8 billion worth of U.S. currency from sellers anticipating a further decline in the relative value of the dollar. Then, in February, President Nixon announced a 10 percent devaluation of the dollar (from $38 to $42.22 an ounce). But the European countries had had enough. In mid-March, prodded by the Germans, six of the leading nations of Europe (West Germany, France, Belgium, the Netherlands, Luxemburg, and Switzerland) announced that they would replace the Smithsonian agreement. Under the new system, these nations would confine stabilization efforts to maintaining the current fixed price relationship only between their own currencies, allowing their currencies to float against all others. This "joint float" would ensure a fixed exchange rate for the mark in terms of the franc or the guilder, but would permit the price of the mark in terms of the dollar to vary in accordance with supply and demand.

During the next few months, world monetary conditions remained confused, with some nations operating under the rules of joint float and others, such as Great Britain and Italy, apparently permitting their currencies to float freely against all others. Fluctuations occurred in the prices of all monies, but the general trend was toward a depreciation of the dollar. (See Table 39-2.) This was somewhat upsetting to many Americans, who remembered that a few years ago a dollar would buy 4 marks rather than 2½, or 360 yen rather than 270. Overall, however, it was clear that these realignments in exchange rates were having a very posititve effect on the U.S. bal-

TABLE 39-2 The Rising Prices of Foreign Currencies

	Dates			
Type of currency	12/31/70	12/31/71	12/31/72	9/18/73
West German mark	$0.2741	$0.3060	$0.3123	$0.4147
Japanese yen	0.0028	0.0032	0.0033	0.0037
British pound	2.3938	2.5522	2.3481	2.4175
French franc	0.1812	0.1914	0.2280	0.2353

With the exception of the British pound, the value of each of the currencies shown here has steadily risen relative to the dollar. This is particularly important to importers, consumers of imported goods, and tourists. Although the tourist going to England is least affected by the recent currency devaluations, a tourist vacationing in Germany would find things about 50 percent more expensive than they were three years ago.

SOURCE: U.S. Congress, Joint Economic Committee, and *New York Times*, September 19, 1973, p. 70. Reprinted by permission.

7 It is important to understand the distinction between a depreciation and a devaluation. A decline in the value of a currency under a system of floating exchange rates is called a depreciation. But when the value of a currency in terms of gold and other currencies is reduced through direct government action under a fixed exchange rate system, it is called a devaluation. Similarly, a rise in the value of a currency under floating exchange rates is an appreciation, while an increase in the value of a currency in terms of gold and other currencies through government action under a fixed rate system is a revaluation.

ance of payments position. For example, in August 1973, the Ritz, a traditional haunt of Americans in Paris, was reported two-thirds empty, while the number of foreign tourists in the United States climbed 22 percent over the previous year. In particular, the U.S. trade position improved significantly. After showing deficits for a year and a half, the balance of trade account was in surplus by the middle of 1973. It is true that this development also reflected factors other than the new exchange rates: The inflation rate abroad was accelerating and a world shortage of foodstuffs, a major U.S. export, occurred. Nevertheless, the primary cause of the 1971 monetary crisis, the U.S. payments deficit, seemed to be correcting itself.

It is interesting to note that during this period of flexible exchange rates, world trade continued at a high level, with exporters, importers, and even tourists adjusting in one way or another to the new, uncertain world of floating currencies. Yet many experts expressed fears about the long-term effects of the current system, especially on the multinational corporations. "If we do not begin to rebuild an efficient international payments mechanism," wrote Donald Platten, Chairman of the Chemical Bank of New York, "we can be certain that expansion of world trade and investment will begin to grind to a halt." Reflecting this fear, a world monetary conference was convened in Nairobi in September 1973, from which it was hoped a new and more permanent world monetary system would emerge. Once again, however, no decision was reached, largely because several nations insisted upon the inclusion of world trade in the discussions. Agreement on other issues, such as dollar convertibility and balance of payments adjustments, was postponed. The conference ended after setting a July 31, 1974 target date, by which time agreement was to be reached on a new world monetary system.

SUMMARY

1 Since over 100 different currencies are used in international trade, it has been difficult to provide satisfactory international monetary arrangements to expedite the worldwide flow of goods and services. There are several criteria for evaluating an effective international monetary system. First, it must be efficient; second, it must be fair; and third, it must not promote domestic instability.

2 International trade revolves around exchange rates. How many yen or pounds or marks one gets for a dollar affects whether or not a transaction will take place.

3 Under a system of floating exchange rates, the price of a foreign currency will be determined by supply and demand. The major drawback to floating exchange rates is that they add a currency risk to the normal risks of business enterprise. This problem, however, might be overcome through the purchase of currency futures contracts.

4 Under a system of fixed exchange rates, the stability of the exchange rate is the most important objective. When an imbalance occurs, it is corrected by domestic adjustments of one sort or another, but the price of the currency does not change. However, when a severe drain on any major currency occurs, the par value of that currency may have to be adjusted.

5 Until the 1920s, most major trading nations were on the gold standard, a system that provided for automatic adjustments of any currency drains, but at the price of domestic instability. If a country had a long-term adverse balance of payments, it would be forced to ship gold to other countries. Since gold was the basis of a country's currency, an outflow of gold would mean domestic deflation. Such defla-

tion, however, would encourage foreign purchases of a nation's products, and thus the balance of payments deficit would eventually reverse itself.

6 After the Bretton Woods agreement of 1944, most of the major trading nations of the world adopted a gold exchange standard. The system was similar to the old gold standard in that it attempted to provide fixed exchange rates and the primary mechanisms for adjusting payments imbalances were transfers of reserve assets and internal measures. However, the gold exchange standard differed from the gold standard in that "key currencies" (the dollar and the pound) served along with gold as reserve assets.

7 A balance of payments statement reflects more than trade alone. Investments, tourism, and foreign aid, as well as other international transactions, are included in a nation's balance of payments statement. The U.S. balance of payments difficulties have stemmed from several sources. American goods have recently become overpriced in the world market (this trend was reversed in 1973), the United States has invested heavily abroad, and the U.S. government has spent more than $100 billion in foreign aid since the end of World War II. The Vietnam War further contributed to the U.S. payments deficits.

8 At the beginning of 1974, the monetary system of the world was in disarray. Nothing was decided at the September 1973 conference in Nairobi and the issues of dollar convertibility and balance of payments adjustments remained unresolved.

SUGGESTED READINGS

Ellsworth, Paul T. *The International Economy*. 4th ed. Chaps. 18–24. New York: Macmillan, 1969.
Ingram, James C. *International Economic Problems*. 2nd ed. New York: John Wiley & Sons, 1970.
Kenen, Peter B. *International Economics*. 2nd ed. Englewood Cliffs, N.J.: Prentice-Hall, 1967.
Letiche, John M. *Balance of Payments and Economic Growth*. New York: Augustus M. Kelley, 1967.

QUESTIONS

1 Review
   a. the effects of foreign exchange rates on the volume of trade between two or more countries,
   b. floating exchange rates, advantages and disadvantages,
   c. advantages and disadvantages of fixed exchange rates,
   d. the gold standard,
   e. gold exchange standards,
   f. major categories of the balance of payments statement,
   g. international monetary arrangements and major events since World War II.

2 Assume that the world consists of the United States and Japan. Draw hypothetical demand and supply curves for dollars in terms of yen. Show the effect on those curves and the resulting change in the exchange rate given each of the following events:
   a. Japanese consumers develop a taste for American fruits such as apples and pears.

b. To protect the American meat producers against the high cost of feed, the United States government imposes an export embargo on soybeans.
c. Japan decides to subsidize shipping costs for any Japanese companies wishing to sell in American markets.
d. Americans decide to purchase more Japanese automobiles and television sets.

3 Draw hypothetical demand and supply curves for yen in terms of dollars, and show the shifts that would occur for each of the circumstances described above.

4 Would the elasticity of demand for the goods produced by another country affect the elasticity of demand for that country's currency? Why or why not? Would you expect Japan's demand for dollars to be elastic or inelastic if Japan's imports from the United States are largely foods? What about substitutes?

5 One argument against floating exchange rates is that the wealthy are able to speculate in currencies. However, speculation in the case of floating exchange rates is stabilizing while speculation in the case of fixed rates is destabilizing. Why?

6 In a world on the gold exchange standard, in which gold is basically international money, why would the gold supply need to expand along with the expansion of international trade?

7 How would each of the following show up in the balance of payments statement?
a. Macy's department store imports a shipment of figurines from Germany.
b. Macy's purchases a building in London and opens a new store.
c. A college transfers some of its endowment funds from an American to a Mexican savings institution.
d. Although illegal for him to do so, a South Vietnamese citizen, in 1966, obtains dollars on the black market in exchange for domestic currency.

8 By 1973 the West German mark was one of the strongest currencies in the world. Suppose that West Germany agrees to peg the mark at a specific value in terms of gold and always to redeem the mark for gold. You hold a large number of marks inherited upon the death of your great grandfather and held in a West German bank. If West Germany begins to suffer an imbalance in its international payments, would you be inclined to trade your marks for dollars? Why or why not?

9 According to David Hume's reasoning, a gold standard would automatically correct imbalances in international payments. Why?

10 On the gold standard, the expansion of the gold supply would depend to some extent on the elasticity of the supply of gold, assuming that the price of gold could change. Do you believe that the supply of gold would be elastic or inelastic? Why? Would it be advisable to have the basic components of the international money supply elastic or inelastic or neither? Why?

11 The two-tier gold system adopted by the United States to prevent erosion of its supply for international payments may very well have preserved existing gold supplies, but how would the system affect the supply of new gold for international payments? Where would most of the new gold produced tend to be channeled?

Opening photo from United Press International

CHAPTER 40 CURRENT PROBLEMS

The ideal aim of international trade policy is to expand world trade so that the benefits of comparative advantage may be fully exploited and a higher standard of living provided for all nations. Within the past few years, however, we have been confronted with a breakdown of the international monetary system under which trade has flourished since the end of World War II. Coincidentally, there have been signs indicating a resurgence of the kind of protectionist policies that devastated world trade during the 1930s. In this chapter, we shall examine these problems and analyze some of the solutions that have been offered.

BACKGROUND OF THE CURRENT CRISIS

Monetary Problems

The breakdown of the Bretton Woods monetary system was closely related to the persistent U.S. balance of payments deficit, which eroded American reserves and foreign confidence in the dollar. The cause of these deficits can be traced to several sources. On the domestic front, the U.S. payments deficit was closely tied to the rapid inflation of the late 1960s. American goods were being priced out of world markets, and the decline in the American trade surplus (and eventually the American trade deficit) was the inevitable outcome of this domestic inflation. (See Figure 40-1.) Government spending abroad, both on the Vietnam War and on foreign aid, contributed to the problem, as did the growing level of foreign investment by American firms. Investments by the multinational corporations have represented major debit items in our long-term capital accounts, and the speculative currency flows that these firms often initiate were an important factor behind the 1970–71 flight from the dollar that was the immediate cause of the Bretton Woods collapse.

But the U.S. balance of payments problem and the failure of Bretton Woods cannot be attributed to U.S. activities alone. In large part they were an almost

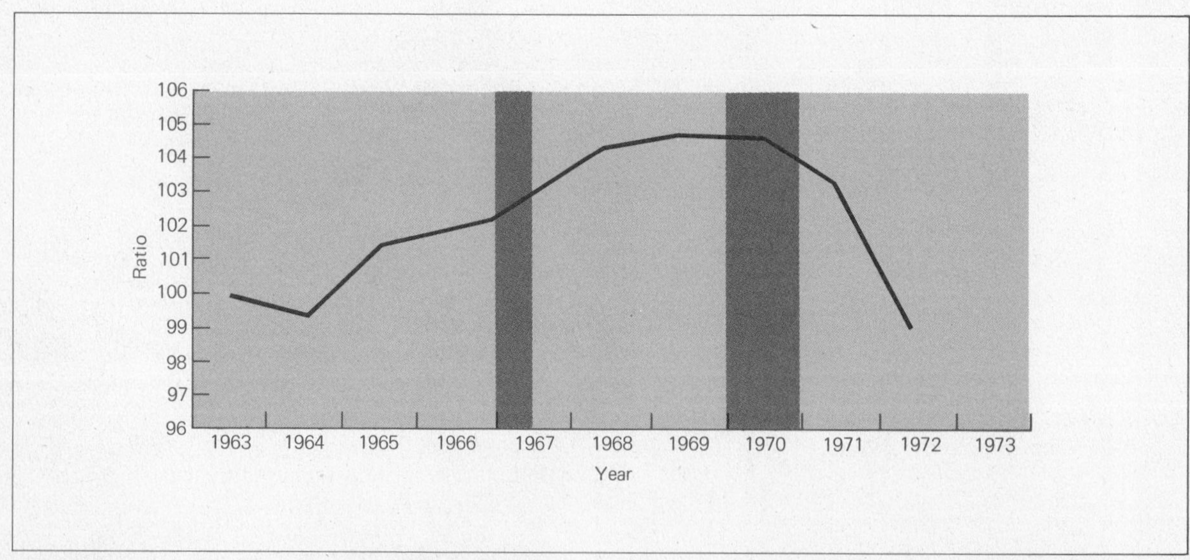

FIGURE 40-1 U.S. EXPORT PRICES RELATIVE TO FOREIGN EXPORT PRICES American export prices relative to foreign export prices rose during the decade of the sixties, but have been on the decline since mid-1970. The relatively high rates of inflation in Western Europe and Japan compared to our own rate of inflation, as well as the devaluations in the U.S. dollar, have helped make American exports more competitive. (*Note:* Index is ratio of U.S. export average values to weighted index of several major trading partners' export averages.)

SOURCE: International Monetary Fund, Organization for Economic Co-operation and Development.

inevitable consequence of the resurgence of Europe and Japan in the years following World War II. The Bretton Woods agreement was based on the supremacy of the American economy and, consequently, of the American dollar. Over the years, however, other nations found ways of competing successfully with the United States. For example, the United States began the postwar period with the advantage of size, but, by 1970, the major Western European nations had joined forces in the European Economic Community (EEC or Common Market), establishing a highly competitive economic entity. Japan, too, successfully strengthened its competitive position. In the 1950s, Japan had ranked substantially behind the United States in almost every measure of economic activity. But by achieving a much faster rate of growth than the United States, it has managed to narrow the gap. (See Table 40-1.) Other nations have also managed to increase their economic power relative to the United States by employing tariffs, quotas, currency regulations, and other barriers to trade.

TABLE 40-1 The ECC and Japan: Formidable Economic Competitors for the United States.

	EEC	Japan	United States
1971 GNP *(billions of dollars)*	$706.7	$225.0	$1068.8
1971 population *(millions)*	253.5	104.7	207.0
1971 per capita GNP	$2790	$2150	$5160
1970 crude steel production *(millions of metric tons)*	138.0	93.3	119.6
1970 electrical energy production *(billions of kilowatt hours)*	842.1	359.5	1638.0
1972 exports *(billions of dollars)*	$154.9	$ 28.6	$ 49.8
1972 imports *(billions of dollars)*	$154.5	$ 23.5	$ 59.0

The United States is no longer the unchallenged economic leader it was up to a decade ago. We have already been surpassed by the Common Market in steel production, imports, and exports. Japan, the fastest growing industrial country, might soon attain our level of steel production, and there is even speculation that her per capita income will be higher than our own by the 1980s.

SOURCES: Federal Reserve Bank of Chicago, March 1973, p. 11; *International Financial Statistics*, International Monetary Fund, Washington, D.C., August 1973, pp. 36–37.

During the late 1960s and early 1970s, many monetary authorities (especially those in other countries) blamed forces within the United States for undermining the international monetary system. As a result, the solutions they offered—internal deflation in the United States, reduced American commitments abroad, devaluation of the dollar—involved only the United States. Today, however, there is a growing recognition that the U.S. balance of payments problem was not a purely domestic matter, but represented a world monetary disequilibrium, for which the nations with balance of payments surpluses (for instance, Germany and Japan) must also bear responsibility. This new approach stood at the heart of the U.S. position on monetary reform in mid-1973. If it prevails, the new international monetary system replacing Bretton Woods will encompass an adjustment process that involves both nations with payments deficits and those with payments surpluses.

Trade Problems

Although currency revaluations and the weakness of the dollar make headlines, international trade practices (such as foreign lending, tariffs, and export and import quotas) play an equally important role in determining the volume of trade. Since the earliest post–World War II years, regulation of such trade practices has been closely tied to the development of the international monetary system. And today, many believe that once again we must deal with trade and monetary matters together. They argue that because these problems overlap, progress in one area can be offset by failures in the other. For example, even a strong and effective world monetary system may not necessarily lead to a greater volume of world trade, unless it is also accompanied by liberalization of trade restrictions, investment funds for underdeveloped nations, and some means of ensuring free international flows of scarce commodities.

International Lending Agencies During the years following World War II, various attempts were made to create institutions through which the less developed nations of the world could participate in world trade. The United States has traditionally played a major role in fostering and financing these efforts. The International Bank for Reconstruction and Development (also known as the World Bank) was established at the Bretton Woods Conference in 1944, the same meeting at which the details of the postwar international monetary system were worked out. The Bank provides a vehicle for dispensing loans for less developed nations. Funds for loans come from the Bank's capital, which has been subscribed by the member nations, and from monies that the Bank raises by selling its own bonds. World Bank bonds have been sold to investors in the United States, Switzerland, and Japan among other nations; they are considered safe investments because they are backed by the capital investment of the World Bank members. The Bank has also established a system through which it will insure private loans to underdeveloped nations for a small fee. In addition to the World Bank, U.S. participation in international lending institutions is channeled through the Inter-American Development Bank and the Asian Development Bank.

In some ways, these lending operations have proven very successful in providing substantial sums for new industries in underdeveloped countries—sums that these nations would not have been able to borrow from private banking sources. Recent signs, however, indicate that the United States, the major source of funds, may be losing interest in supporting such international lending operations. In mid-1973, the United States was more than a year behind schedule in the most recent round of contributions to the International Development Association, a World Bank subsidiary that provides easy-term loans to the poorest of nations. Furthermore, Congress had not approved a $100 million pledge to a similar division of the Asian Bank, and it had voted to cut in half the pledged amount for the Inter-American Bank. These actions reflected the general apathy and even hostility in Congress toward all foreign aid measures. The Nixon administration claims that the reluctance of Congress is upsetting not only its long-term political relations with the uncommitted nations of the Third World, which are the prime candidates for such loans, but, more immediately, its efforts to work out a new world monetary system. On the other hand, it is possible that the adminstration has not yet made a whole-hearted attempt to press for congressional approval of these funds in order that U.S. negotiators at world trade and monetary conferences will be able to use the promise of future U.S. contributions as a lever in eliciting support from the underdeveloped nations for the kind of monetary and trade systems the United States wants.

GATT A second major world trade problem concerns the liberalization of trade barriers. In 1947, a General Agreement on Tariffs and Trade (GATT) was signed by 23 leading nations, including the United States. Since that time, many other nations have joined. The objectives of GATT were the elimination of tariffs and other barriers to trade among member nations. Significant progress was made in reducing tariffs and import quotas, especially through the six rounds of tariff reductions that took place between 1947 and 1964.

Since the last set of GATT talks (the so-called Kennedy Round in 1964), however, important changes have occurred in the U.S. position. The United States spearheaded the previous rounds of tariff cuts, but many Americans are no longer sympathetic to such objectives. In Chapter 38, we discussed the Burke-Hartke Bill, which was designed to use tariffs, quotas, and other methods to protect U.S. industry from foreign competition. Although in mid-1973 it appeared doubtful that the Burke-Hartke Bill would pass, at least in its most extreme form, the bill nevertheless represented a point of view that would make it more difficult for President Nixon to obtain the further tariff cutting powers from Congress that he had requested. New GATT trade negotiations were scheduled for 1973–74, with the first session to be held in Tokyo. In 1973 the position the United States would take at these meetings was still unclear. Pressures from protectionists might limit the opportunity for U.S. participation in further trade liberalization, especially if the economy should take a downturn or if U.S. negotiators are unable to obtain trade concessions from other nations. On the other hand, long-term U.S. policy since the end of World War II has always favored the liberalization of trade, and President Nixon has been outspoken in his support of such objectives.

Although in 1973 observers were uncertain about the details of any new trade program that would come out of the 1974 GATT meetings, they were reasonably sure that this round of negotiations would cover much more than simply tariffs. The United States has become aware that the nontariff measures used by other governments to control trade are becoming increasingly important; such matters as foreign export subsidies and incentives, safety standards, customs procedures, and government procurement policies may influence the level of U.S. exports even more than tariff rates. For example, the currency restrictions and import quotas imposed by Japan, a nation with a huge surplus in its U.S. trade account, will probably come up for discussion. Similarly, the United States has been very displeased by the common agricultural policy of the European Economic Community, which discriminates against U.S. agricultural exports.

It is also likely that trade negotiations will attempt to provide rules through which resources in short supply will be allocated among the nations of the world. Americans have recently been affected by such resource shortages. As importers, Americans have been worried about the cutback in oil supplies and the higher prices imposed by the Organization of Petroleum Exporting Countries. As exporters, Americans have contributed to world instability by an embargo on shipments of U.S. soybeans abroad. Unless some system can be implemented that will prevent similar disruptions of normal supplies in the future, there will be tremendous pressures on governments to develop domestic sources of supply, despite the fact that these commodities can be produced more cheaply elsewhere. The net effect could be a decline in the overall volume of world trade.

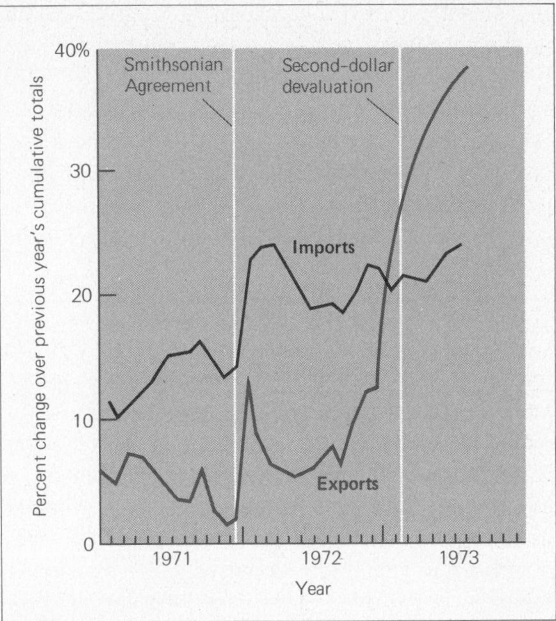

FIGURE 40-2 THE TURNAROUND IN U.S. TRADE: PERCENTAGE CHANGE IN EXPORTS AND IMPORTS By mid-1973, the balance of trade position—which suffered deficits in 1971 and 1972—seemed to be reversing. The extent of this turnaround can be seen clearly by comparing cumulative monthly import and export figures for each year with the same figures for the previous year. Exports have grown at a rapid pace since the fall of 1972. By mid-1973, exports had gained nearly 38 percent over the previous half-year total. The increased world demand for U.S. goods can be attributed to several factors, among them the adjustments in the price of the dollar that occurred between 1971 and 1973. (*Note:* Monthly trade statistics have been totaled separately for each year and compared with the corresponding figures for the previous year to arrive at percentage changes.)

SOURCE: Bureau of the Census; seasonally adjusted data.

The Changing Picture: 1973

In mid-1973, faced with preparations for tariff negotiations and a conference on international monetary reform, the United States was in a much stronger position than it had been in years. America's trade balance for July 1973 showed a $106 million seasonally adjusted surplus; for 1973 as a whole, estimates were that the trade account might wind up in equilibrium, a significant improvement over the $6.8 billion deficit of 1972. (See Figure 40-2.) This improvement reflected several factors. First, U.S. goods appeared more attractively priced in world markets, both because of the devaluation of the U.S. dollar and because of the accelerating inflation rate abroad. Second, the United States was benefitting from several bad growing seasons in the USSR and other parts of the world, which had created a world shortage of grain, rising prices, and an increased world demand for U.S. foodstuffs.

This projected improvement in the U.S. balance of payments position did not, however, stop with the trade accounts. There were indications that America's capital account deficit for 1973 would also be more modest. Foreign multinational corporations have found attractive investment opportunities in the United States, where their revalued currencies can now buy 20 to 50 percent more dollars than they could a few years ago. Conversely, the substantial increase in the price of the mark, the yen, and the Swiss franc has caused some American firms to take a second look at new investments abroad. Furthermore, there are indications that the speculative flows of short-term capital out of the United States have lessened, both because of the tremendous appreciation in the prices of other currencies and because the absence of government supports under the new floating exchange rate system has made such speculation more risky. Finally, a booming economy in the United States prompted the Federal Reserve Board to raise domestic interest rates to very high levels. Although the primary objective of this move was to cool the domestic economy, a by-product has been the movement of some foreign monies to the United States to take advantage of these high short-term interest rates.

By 1973, then, the United States was no longer operating from a position of weakness. Although U.S. reserves were seriously depleted by years of payments deficits, and although a huge quantity of dollars (100 billion) was accumulated by foreigners, there are many reasons for thinking that the dollar, after two years of attrition, was by 1973 an undervalued currency. Believing this to be true, American officials saw an important impetus for foreign governments to move for the speedy creation of a new monetary system that would enable them to handle any runs against their currencies that might develop. And the United States also believed it had acquired additional bargaining power in its efforts to ensure that the new system meets American objectives.

RESHAPING THE INTERNATIONAL MONETARY SYSTEM

In 1973 leading trading nations of the world were confronted with the opportunity to design a new exchange rate system. The form that system would take was still open to question. Would they return to a fixed system based on fully convertible reserves like the old gold system? Would they opt for floating rates such as those prevailing for some countries at various times since 1971? Or would the new system involve a combination of both flexible and fixed exchange rates? In choosing among these alternatives, monetary experts would unquestionably be influenced not only by the lessons of Bretton Woods and the immediate problems confronting international trade, but also by the unexpected ability of world trade to flourish under the quasi-flexible rate system that has existed since 1971.

The Monetary System since 1971: Temporary Alternatives

A brief review of the U.S. experience since 1971 illustrates the wide range of exchange rate systems under which world trade has recently operated. During the period immediately following the Smithsonian Agreement of December 1971, the world exchange rate system was theoretically a fixed one. The Agreement established a parity price for the dollar in terms of every other currency and a range —2¼ percent on either side of the parity price—within which open market fluctuations were permitted. The responsibility for maintaining these parities was left primarily to foreign central banks, which were obliged to intervene in exchange markets and to buy or sell dollars any time the value of their currencies in the open market deviated from the Smithsonian limits. The main U.S. contribution to the new system was a 10 percent devaluation of the dollar.

By February 1973, however, the behavior of the dollar in foreign exchange markets suggested that, at least in the short run, the 10 percent devaluation had not been adequate. Because of the U.S. devaluation and foreign revaluations, the dollar in terms of many of the leading foreign currencies depreciated 15 to 32 percent from December 1971 to February of 1973. Nevertheless, in the foreign exchange markets, there was still an excess of dollars for sale, and foreign central banks were consequently forced continually to intervene and buy dollars. On February 12, 1973, the United States devalued by another 10 percent, with the intent that this new devaluation and the new exchange rates resulting from it would accomplish what the first devaluation had obviously failed to do—that is, provide a set of exchange rates that could be maintained without central bank intervention.

Following this second devaluation, generally stable conditions prevailed until early May 1973. Then the Watergate crisis and the accelerating inflation in the United States led to a new run on the dollar, involving such enormous sums that very shortly the major European governments abandoned all stabilization efforts for the dollar. The dollar was left to float, and the result was devastating: In one brief two-week period, the dollar depreciated by another 10 percent.

At this point, the U.S. government decided that it could not permit any further declines in the price of the dollar without grave, long-term political and economic consequences. Foreign governments were also dismayed because every precipitate drop in the price of the dollar represented an equally rapid increase in the price of their own currencies. This meant that they might eventually be priced out of export markets if their currencies continued to appreciate. It was clear, however, that foreign central banks, loaded as they were with U.S. currency, would no longer accept full responsibility for stabilizing the dollar. Instead, the Federal Reserve Board, with currencies borrowed from other governments, entered the market, using marks, francs, guilders, and so on, to buy dollars. This was a historic development, because it represented the first time that the United States had publicly and on a large scale accepted the fact that it, rather than foreign central banks, would play a central role in maintaining the price of the dollar.

By late summer, it appeared that the U.S. "dirty float" adventure was paying off: The Fed's intervention in the floating exchange rate market had worked. The dollar rebounded somewhat from its July lows, and it stayed above these lows for the next few months. Very probably, however, this recovery in the price of the dollar was also related to the improved U.S. balance of payments statistics, which were being released at about this time. Nevertheless, the performance of the dollar following the Fed intervention and the Fed's announcement that it might intervene again illustrated the role that occasional "dirty floats" can play within a flexible exchange rate system.

Monetary experts interpret differently the recent U.S. experience. Neither fixed exchange rates, nor floating exchange rates, nor the dirty float has been completely satisfactory. In August 1973, the Subcommittee on International Economics of the Joint Economic Committee of Congress issued its evaluation of the entire period. The Committee was very positive in its feeling that free floating rates had proved to be the most successful alternative. Members spoke out firmly against any premature unilateral return by the United States to fixed rates, recommending that such a step wait until the IMF worked out permanent monetary reform on a worldwide basis. The Committee further objected to occasional "dirty floats" within a free-floating system, claiming that such interventions by governments in currency markets are rarely effective as permanent solutions to problems. In other words, the Committee appeared to suggest that the successful intervention by the Fed in June 1973 would have failed had not the U.S. balance of payments position been improving.

On the other hand, it seems clear that most business executives and government officials, both in the United States and abroad, want some form of fixed rates as a permanent solution to world monetary problems. Firms are more comfortable conducting international business when they know what the exchange rate will be three months or six months or a year hence. This is particularly true for the multinationals, which are constantly engaged in making commitments that will involve shifts of funds from one country to another. For this reason, the consensus seems to favor fixed rates as part of any permanent new world monetary order. Nevertheless, until the IMF nations approve such a new order, it does not appear likely that any nation, including the United States, will unilaterally return to a system involving massive and continuous central bank intervention as a way of ensuring fixed rates. For one, the costs are too great. And as both the Germans (who tried such intervention to keep the mark from rising) and the English (who tried it to keep the pound from declining) know from experience, the chances of permanent success are small if the parity price is an unrealistic one. It appears, then, that fixed rates are the objective of any new, permanent international monetary system, but, in the interim, most governments do not seem to have much choice but to adopt some form of floating exchange rates.

The International Monetary System: Permanent Structural Reform

Objectives

Regardless of the specific details of any new, permanent world monetary system, most experts agree that there are certain basic structural problems that it must solve. Among them are the adjustment problem, the reserve problem, and the dollar overhang and convertibility problems.

THE ADJUSTMENT PROBLEM If a new monetary system is to endure, it must provide a method for adjustment whenever payment imbalances occur. It appears unlikely at this time that nations will ever again settle for an adjustment process that relies primarily on internal inflation or deflation. Instead, it would seem that the new adjustment process will involve adjustments in exchange rates. Such a system, however, must also be able to discourage sudden and enormous flows of short-term money when an adjustment is anticipated.

The United States has taken a strong stand on one aspect of the adjustment process. It holds that no country has the right to maintain a "disequilibrium" exchange rate—that is, one that causes it to gain or lose vast amounts of reserves. Accordingly, any new IMF plan must place equal responsibility for corrective action on those nations with payments surpluses as well as those with payments deficits. A nation with a persistent surplus must move to increase its exchange rate just as a nation with a deficit must move to devalue its currency.

THE RESERVE PROBLEM Even if an effective adjustment process that will prevent the accumulation of huge payments surpluses and deficits is established, under a fixed rate system there will be times when transfers of reserves between nations are required. With the world gold supply growing at only a 2 percent annual rate, it is probable that the role of gold as the primary international reserve will continue to diminish. Some gold may be added to international reserves, but it is likely that Special Drawing Rights (SDRs) will grow in relative importance. As far as key currencies are concerned, there appears to be some feeling that the dollar could be joined in this role by other strong currencies such as the yen and the mark. Under such a system, the monetary reserves of most nations might consist of a mix of gold, SDRs, and key currencies.

THE DOLLAR OVERHANG AND CONVERTIBILITY PROBLEMS One objective of any new monetary system must be some arrangement for dealing with the $100 billion overhang of U.S. dollars now in the hands of central banks around the world as a result of U.S. payments deficits of past years. Until a way is found to neutralize this overhang, any new monetary system will be in jeopardy. In particular, the overhang precludes the acceptance by the United States of any meaningful form of convertibility, because it has the potential to wipe out U.S. reserves overnight.

C. Fred Bergsten, a senior fellow at the Brookings Institution, has suggested that we try to persuade Europe and Japan to cancel, at least temporarily, the American debt embodied in the overhang, perhaps by exchanging these dollars for a new issue of SDRs. These SDRs could then be used as reserves to settle international imbalances in much the same way as dollar reserves. But by eliminating the dollar overhang, the exchange would permit the United States to return to convertibility. Bergsten mentions the post–World War I Hoover Moratorium on European debt to the United States and the post–World War II Marshall Plan as two comparable circumstances under which the United States behaved with similar generosity toward an impoverished Europe. At this time, however, we cannot determine the specific measures that will eventually be taken to deal with the dollar overhang problem.

Possible Solutions

RETURN TO THE GOLD STANDARD One of the interesting by-products of the flight from the dollar that occurred in 1972–73 was the soaring price of gold, shown in Figure 40-3. Speculators, convinced that the dollar was going to decline in price in world currency mar-

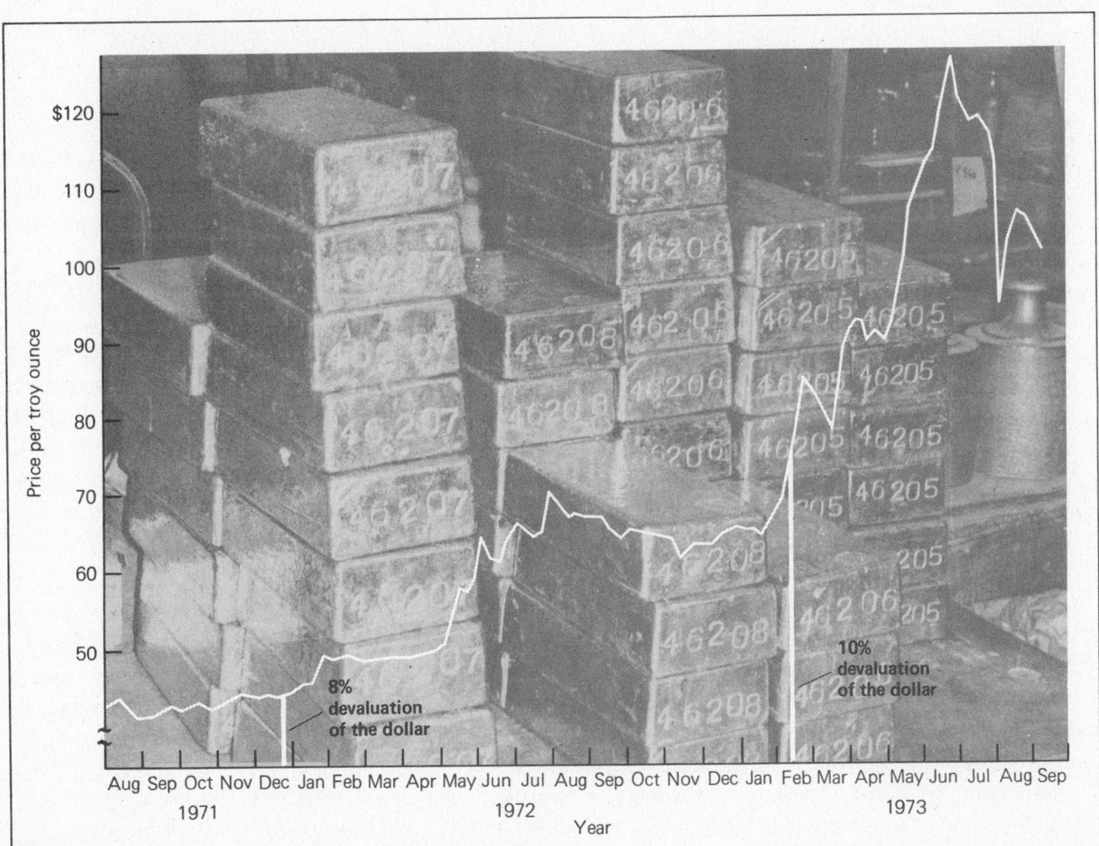

FIGURE 40-3 GOLD PRICES, LONDON OPEN MARKET, 1971–73 The price of gold tripled between 1971 and 1973, largely due to a rapid deterioration in foreign confidence in the dollar. When Nixon called a halt to dollar convertibility in August 1971 and subsequently devalued the dollar in December of that year, he was only acting out what had already been anticipated by gold speculators. The speculators were betting against the dollar, saying in effect that the dollar was not really worth its stated value of 1/35th of an ounce of gold. Because of balance of payments deficits in 1971 and again in 1972, speculators began to bet even more heavily against the dollar, further driving up the price of gold. This rise was given additional impetus by the second devaluation, in February 1973, hitting a peak of $127.00 in late June 1973. But then the price of gold declined considerably as the U.S. balance of payments position improved. Photo: A.F.P. from Pictorial

SOURCE: U.S. Department of Commerce.

kets, sold their dollars not only to buy marks and francs and yen but also to buy gold. The price of gold reached levels well over $100 an ounce. As a result, the reserve assets of every nation with substantial holdings of gold have been automatically increased in value. For example, in August 1971, the United States owned about 300 million ounces of gold worth about $10 billion at $35 an ounce. But at the free-market price of $100 an ounce, the August 1973 price, these reserve assets were worth $30 billion. Other nations have enjoyed a similar increase in the value of their reserve assets. Theoretically, then, it would be somewhat easier for nations to return to a form of gold standard, at least as far as the adequacy of present reserves is concerned, and simply revalue their gold at the current market price. However, any return to the gold system also implies the necessity for internal deflation or inflation every time substantial gold inflows or outflows occur. It is doubtful that there would be much enthusiasm for this approach among most nations today. Support does come, however, from South Africa and the USSR, major gold producers, which would like to see the market price remain high. It also comes from speculators who have bought gold and who fear an abrupt price decline unless gold is given a prime position as a reserve asset in any new world monetary order.

FLEXIBLE EXCHANGE RATES The prospect of the 140 IMF member nations approving a flexible exchange rate system does not appear likely. It is true that such a system might offer many advantages. It would solve the adjustment problem by leaving the adjustment process to the forces of supply and demand in foreign exchange markets. It would solve the reserve problem and the dollar overhang problem because neither reserves nor convertibility is essential in a system in which exchange rates are left to the marketplace. Nevertheless, there is widespread opposition to flexible rates. Industrial nations object because their multinational corporations feel that they cannot operate without some form of monetary stability. The underdeveloped nations object because of the extreme dependence of their economies on exports and imports. In brief, most authorities believe that a floating exchange rate system will never receive official IMF approval. Of course, it is possible that such a system will emerge de facto, should the IMF be unable to devise a satisfactory fixed rate system of its own.

THE WIDER BAND Various alternatives have been proposed that offer a combination of the stability of fixed rates and the smooth adjustment process provided by flexible rates. One such alternative is the "wider band." The original Bretton Woods Agreement provided for a 1 percent range or band around parity within which currencies could fluctuate in free-market trading without requiring central bank intervention. Thus, as far as stabilization activities were concerned, parity was not an exact price, such as 1 pound = $2.60, but a range, such as 1 pound = from $2.574 to $2.626. The Smithsonian Agreement widened the band to 2¼ percent on either side of parity, or 4½ percent in all. Current suggestions involve a further widening of the band, perhaps to as much as 10 percent.

Such a wider band allows for increased flexibility within the framework of a fixed exchange rate system. It permits a currency to vary by as much as 10 percent in free-market trading before central bank stabilization activities are mandated. As such, it provides more protection for central bank reserve assets when temporary payments imbalances occur. At the same time, it pleases businesses by reducing their currency risk from the unlimited amount inherent in a free-floating system.

Critics of the wider band system emphasize that it is no panacea. It can work only if the underlying parity rate is reasonably realistic—that is, within striking distance of the price that would prevail in the free foreign exchange market. Otherwise, it will be only a question of time until the free-market price will reach the outer limit of the band. At this point, central bank intervention will be required and the old familiar problems of reserve asset loss or accumulation of unwanted foreign currencies will recur. In other words, the widened band may make a fixed exchange rate system more palatable for central banks by keeping them out of the currency markets under normal conditions; it will not, however, save them if a currency is fundamentally mispriced.

THE CRAWLING PEG (OR GLIDING PARITY) In recent years, we have observed many examples of unrealistic parity rates imposing tremendous stabilization burdens on central banks. Attempts to maintain parities that were too high resulted in enormous reserve drains for Britain in 1972 and 1973; attempts to maintain parities that were too low led to the vast accumulations of U.S. dollars that are now in the hands of the German central banks. Under Bretton Woods, the only way of correcting such a parity error was through formal devaluation or revaluation. The very possibility of such changes in parity, however, was in itself a destabilizing factor, because speculators would rush to buy any currency that appeared likely to increase its parity or to sell any currency for which devaluation looked imminent. The crawling peg proposal appears to offer an effective way of changing parities without attracting these speculative flows.

Under a crawling peg (or gliding parity) system, a nation with a chronic payments imbalance would be permitted to change the parity price of its currency by a stated small amount at periodic intervals. For example, a country might have the right to change its parity by 1 percent every six months. In this way, a nation with a persistent deficit could devalue by 2 percent within one year and by another 2 percent in each subsequent year, until the new exchange rate resulted in a payments balance. Because each adjustment is small, the speculative flows that accompanied revaluation under Bretton Woods would be avoided, but the required changes in parity would be accomplished. Most monetary experts believe that a combination of wider bands with a crawling peg may characterize the upcoming IMF monetary reform proposals.

RESERVES AND CONVERTIBILITY IN ANY NEW FIXED RATE SYSTEM How will the IMF handle the problem of reserves in any new monetary system? This problem is of course closely tied to the adjustment process and the various alternatives discussed above. If the IMF designs a system with an effective adjustment process through which changes in exchange rates occur smoothly and promptly in response to payments imbalances, then the reserve problem will to a certain extent solve itself. Huge movements of reserves (and therefore huge supplies of reserve assets) are required only when huge payment imbalances occur. It is assumed that under any new IMF monetary system, the nations of the world will be given the tools and the mandate to correct such imbalances early. Nevertheless, world monetary reserves must be expanded, if only to meet the growing volume of world trade. It now appears as if new issues of SDRs will probably be authorized as the source of most new world reserve assets. It is also likely that IMF rules will be changed to make SDRs, which now operate under various limitations, fully equal to gold and dollar reserve assets. For example, at the present time there are limitations on the percentage of a nation's total IMF allocation that can be held in the form of SDRs; no such "holding limits" exist for gold or dollars.

Of all the international monetary problems, that of convertibility will probably be the most difficult for the IMF member nations to solve. It is complicated by the existence of the dollar overhang, by uncertainties about the nature and quantity of world reserves, and by doubts about the effectiveness of any new adjustment process. At the heart of the problem is the U.S. position. As of mid-1973, it did not appear that the United States had either the reserve assets or the prospects of acquiring them that would permit an early return to convertibility. However, America's improving balance of payments position and the possibility of new SDR allocations do offer some reason for optimism.

In 1973 and 1974 the nations of the world have the opportunity to determine the direction in which international monetary and trade matters will move through the remainder of the 1970s. The seventh round of GATT trade talks is scheduled for 1973–74, and the IMF member nations will also be meeting to work out a new monetary order. It is clear that new and intense forms of international cooperation will be needed for world trade to continue expanding. The threat of a revival of the protectionist spirit is a real one and could easily be aggravated by the inability of the nations to come to some agreement on monetary reform. For this reason, most economists believe that it is essential that some workable international monetary system emerge from the upcoming IMF meetings, and they urge member nations to be realistic in evaluating the alternatives.

Distributing the Costs and Benefits of International Monetary Reform

No monetary system, of course, is perfect; each has built-in costs that cannot be avoided. For example, if a system with wider bands is selected, then the currency risk for businesses is increased. On the other hand, if the bands are narrowed, then the danger of too much central bank intervention increases. Similarly, an excessively permissive gliding peg arrangement encourages speculation, whereas an overly restrictive one may lead to payments imbalances. The task of the IMF members, then, is to determine which costs are least painful to most of the nations involved in international trade.

The problem of international monetary reform, however, is complicated by the fact that each of the IMF member nations would prefer a system that meets its own particular needs, but whose costs would be borne by other countries. As a result, the problem is not so much one of finding a viable solution (actually there are several different international monetary proposals that would work) but rather of resolving the power struggle among the various trading nations over how the costs and benefits of a new international monetary system should be distributed.

One key issue is the adjustment process. The United States favors an automatic adjustment process as part of any fixed exchange rate system. It has advocated a plan based on "objective indicators," such as changes in the level of a nation's reserves. When the indicator reached a predetermined mark, the nation would be required to change its foreign exchange rate. This system would provide important benefits to the United States; it would, for example, ensure that the accelerating American balance-of-payments deficits of the 1960s and early 1970s would not be repeated. The costs of the system, however, would be paid primarily by the Europeans and the Japanese, who would probably be forced to revalue their currencies should the American plan be adopted. These nations are very reluctant to have vital decisions about the timing and extent of changes in their exchange rates removed from their direct control. Exchange rates are a crucial issue in West Germany, Japan, and France, where large percentages of GNP are devoted to exports. The jobs and incomes of the citizens of these nations are very closely tied to exchange rates, and their leaders view with alarm any system that would require automatic revaluation regardless of the domestic political or economic situation. Imagine, for example, the plight of the Japanese government, confronted with a slowdown in the domestic growth rate and an upcoming election, but forced to announce a revaluation of the yen because its foreign exchange reserves had reached a certain level.

On the other hand, it would appear that the plans offered by some of the European nations are equally objectionable from the American point of view. The Europeans have proposed systems under which the benefits would accrue mostly to themselves, while the United States would be required to pay the costs. The primary objective of the European nations is to restore and maintain the convertibility of the dollar, so as to provide a framework for a return to some form of fixed exchange rates. The plans they offer, however, place the major part of the burden for maintaining convertibility on the United States. These plans emphasize the responsibility of the United States, as a deficit balance-of-payments nation, to take whatever measures are necessary (including higher domestic unemployment and interest rates, reduced imports, and fewer military activities abroad) to eliminate its deficits and thus protect its reserves and guarantee convertibility.

How will this power struggle eventually be resolved? It is probable that some compromise will emerge. The United States, for example, may be willing to accept some form of a return to dollar convertibility, but only if other nations agree to share the burden, so as to ease the American problem of controlling balance-of-payments deficits. For example, the United States may insist that the Japanese remove their tariffs and quotas on computers, feed grains, and rice. For the Japanese, the cost of doing so would be a reduction in the growth rate of their computer industry and the risks of greater dependence on American agriculture, but perhaps Japan will be willing to accept this cost in return for the benefits of dollar convertibility. Or, as another compromise, it is possible that the European nations may agree to some version of an automatic adjustment process in exchange for signs that the United States is willing to move toward a return to convertibility.

Clearly the current negotiations toward international monetary reform involve a power struggle among nations, each pressing for a system that will distribute the costs and benefits of trade in its own favor. In this struggle the United States seems to be in a much stronger position than it has been in years. The improvement in the U.S. balance of payments, the somewhat stronger performance of the dollar in foreign exchange markets since mid-1973, and the relatively lower inflation rate in the United States as compared with other nations have reduced America's feeling of urgency for international monetary reform. It now appears that the United States can afford to stay with floating exchange rates, at least in the short run. If European nations and Japan are to enjoy the benefits of fixed rates and a return to dollar convertibility, which they so strongly desire, they may have to bear greater costs than they have previously been willing to accept.

SUMMARY

1 To fully exploit the benefits of comparative advantage, world trade must be expanded. However, such efforts have been confounded by a breakdown in the international monetary system as well as by a resurgence of protectionist sentiment both in the United States and abroad.

2 The international monetary breakdown was closely related to the persistent U.S. balance of payments deficit, which eroded U.S. reserves as well as foreign confidence in the dollar. The rapid inflation of the 1960s, the Vietnam War, and the growing level of foreign investment by U.S. firms contributed to the American payments deficit.

3 Even a strong and effective world monetary system may not necessarily lead to a greater volume of world trade, unless it is also accompanied by liberalization of trade restrictions, investment funds for underdeveloped nations, and some means of ensuring free international flows of scarce commodities. The U.S. Congress has been increasingly reluctant to approve funds for international agencies that make loans to developing nations, which will use these funds to import needed capital equipment. Furthermore, the United States, which spearheaded the previous rounds of tariff cuts under GATT, has become less sympathetic to future reductions in trade restrictions.

4 By 1973 it appeared that the U.S. balance of payments position was improving, not only in the trade account, but also in the capital account. The United States, then, was no longer operating from a position of weakness, although $100 billion worth of U.S. currency had been accumulated by foreign central banks. In fact, the dollar may have become an undervalued currency, a condition that would create an important impetus for foreign governments to move for the speedy creation of a new monetary system that would enable them to handle any runs against their currencies that might develop.

5 By 1973 the trading nations of the world were faced with the need to design a

new exchange rate system, but it was uncertain if they would return to a fixed system based on fully convertible reserves like the old gold system or adopt a floating exchange rate system, which has essentially prevailed for some countries since 1971. Most business executives and government officials, both in the United States and abroad, wanted some form of fixed rates as a permanent solution. Nevertheless, until the IMF nations approved such a new order, it did not appear likely that any nation, including the United States, would unilaterally return to a system involving massive and continual central bank intervention as a way of ensuring fixed rates.

6 If a new monetary system is to endure, it must provide a method for adjustment whenever payments imbalances occur. Such adjustments, rather than relying on internal inflation or deflation, will involve changes in exchange rates. But the system must also discourage sudden and enormous flows of short-term money when an adjustment is anticipated. The United States has insisted that equal responsibility for corrective action must be placed on those nations with payments surpluses as well as those with payments deficits.

7 Another problem that a new, permanent world monetary system must solve is that of supplying adequate reserves, for under any system some reserve transfers are inevitable. With the growing inadequacy of the gold supply, it is likely that Special Drawing Rights (SDRs) will play an increasingly important role as reserve assets in any new international monetary order.

8 A third problem is the $100 billion of U.S. currency in foreign hands—the dollar overhang. Any forthcoming solution will have to take into account the problems and special interests of all IMF members.

9 Various alternatives to fixed and flexible exchange rate systems have been proposed. They offer both the stability of fixed rates and the smooth adjustment process of flexible rates. One such alternative is the wider band which increases the range around parity within which currency prices can fluctuate without requiring central bank intervention. Another alternative is the crawling peg, or gliding parity, under which a nation would be permitted to change the parity price of its currency by a stated amount at periodic intervals.

10 Any international monetary system has built-in costs and benefits. The task facing the IMF member nations is to construct a system that distributes the costs and benefits in a way that is acceptable to all participants.

SUGGESTED READINGS

Birnbaum, Eugene A. "A Cure for Monetary Discord," *Fortune*, May 1973, pp. 210ff.

Economic Report of the President, 1971. Chap. 5. Washington, D.C.

Einzig, Paul. *The Euro-Dollar System*. 4th ed. New York: St. Martin's Press, 1970.

Miller, Roger LeRoy, and **Raburn M. Williams.** *The New Economics of Richard Nixon: Freezes, Floats & Fiscal Policy*. Chap. 10. San Francisco: Canfield Press, 1972.

Snider, Delbert A. *Introduction to International Economics*. 5th ed. Chaps. 13–21 and 25. Homewood, Ill.: Richard D. Irwin, 1971.

Vernon, Raymond, ed. *The Technology Factor in International Trade*. New York: National Bureau of Economic Research, 1970.

QUESTIONS

1 Review
  a. factors leading to the current international monetary crisis,
  b. American trade problems and the change in attitude toward liberalized trade,
  c. objectives to be reached by any new monetary system,
  d. the problem of the dollar overhang,
  e. possibilities for new monetary systems; advantages and disadvantages of each.

2 In the case of a domestic economy, the relationship between the money supply, velocity, prices, and output was stated as an identity, $MV = PQ$. Is there any analogy that you can draw with world trade? Explain.

3 How would the rapid inflation experienced by the United States from the mid 1960s to the early 1970s affect American trade and the position of the American dollar?

4 Some critics of the gliding peg arrangement point out that corrections in exchange rates are made only after the fact and that there is a danger that they may never catch up. How would you evaluate this criticism?

5 Any system of fixed exchange rates will encourage a certain amount of speculation that is destabilizing. Why doesn't there seem to be much worry concerning speculation in the case of flexible exchange rates?

6 In the spring of 1973 the United States took the unusual action of placing export embargoes on certain food crops, creating serious disruption of food supplies for some other countries such as Japan. Though the embargo was later lifted, how is the American action likely to affect the future flow of trade between these countries? Their tendency to hold reserves? The tendency to rely heavily on one exporter?

7 American-owned airlines and shipping companies predicted a dramatic rise in business after the devaluation of the dollar. Why?

8 Inflationary pressures were increasing in Europe by 1973. How would these pressures affect short-term monetary flows? How might they complicate European interests concerning a new monetary arrangement?

9 If Adam Smith was right that the wealth of a nation consists of goods and services, is there any defense for a nation with a strong currency and large reserves trying to maintain these reserves? Why or why not?

Glossary

absolute advantage: Nation or enterprise is said to have an absolute advantage in the production of a good or service when it is able to produce the good or service at a lower cost than that at which it can be produced elsewhere.

acceleration principle: Principle that any changes in total output may result in much greater percentage changes in investment in new plant and equipment.

ad valorem tax: Percentage tax on the value of the product sold such as a sales tax.

aggregate concentration: Indicator of economic concentration that measures the relative size in assets of the largest firms regardless of their industrial designation.

aggregate demand: Total goods and services that all members of the economy are willing and able to buy at various levels of national income; includes consumption, investment, government expenditures, and net exports.

aggregate supply: Total number of goods and services suppliers are willing and able to sell at various levels of national income; Keynes assumed that producers would be willing to supply all the goods consumers would be willing to purchase, so supply would equal demand at all income levels up to the full-employment level of income.

agribusiness: Alliance of large commercial farms, grain dealers, and marketing corporations.

alienation: According to the radical economists, alienation occurs under the market system when workers sell their labor for wages and are, in effect, separated from their own minds and bodies; they give up control of themselves during the work period. Whatever they produce is independent of them and is therefore of no concern to them. The worker finds little satisfaction and is separated from other workers and lacks a sense of community.

Alliance for Labor Action: Affiliation of the United Auto Workers and the Teamsters formed in 1968.

allocative efficiency: Degree to which the economy produces the combination of goods and services that most satisfies society. Allocative efficiency is achieved when no change in resource allocation can be made without making someone worse off or when $\frac{MU_1}{P_1} = \frac{MU_N}{P_N}$ and $P = MC$ for all goods and services.

American Federation of Labor (AFL): Federation of labor unions formed in 1886 under the leadership of Samuel Gompers and committed to the principles of federalism, voluntarism, and business unionism. Since 1955, it has been allied with the Congress of Industrial Organizations (CIO).

annually balanced budget: Government budget in which revenues and expenditures are equal during the course of the fiscal year.

arbitration: Intervention in the collective bargaining procedure by a third party whom both parties have agreed to invest with final authority to decide the issues in question.

automatic stabilizers: "Built-in" fiscal stabilizers that work automatically as countercyclical forces. These include transfer payments and progressive taxes.

average fixed cost: Total fixed costs at any level of output divided by the total quantity of output.

average product: Total product divided by the quantity of a variable input used to produce that product.

average product curve: Curve plotting the ratio of total product to the amount of a variable input needed to produce that product.

average propensity to consume: Percentage of total income consumed:

$$\frac{\text{Consumption}}{\text{Disposable income}}$$

average propensity to save: Proportion of total income saved:

$$\frac{\text{Saving}}{\text{Disposable income}}$$

average total cost: Total cost at any level of output divided by the total quantity of output.

average variable cost: Total variable costs at any level of output divided by the total quantity of output.

balance-of-payments statement: Summary table of all the international financial dealings in which a nation engages, generally during the period of one year. Individual accounts include the current account, the capital account, and the reserve assets account.

balance sheet: Device for showing the assets of a business along with the claims against these assets at a specific time.

balanced budget multiplier: Effect of an increase in government expenditures and a simultaneous and equal increase in taxes that is to raise national income by the exact amount of the budget increase; or the effect of a decrease in expenditures and an equal decrease in taxes that is to reduce national income by the exact amount of the budget decrease.

balanced growth: Simultaneous development of all sectors of an economy.

barter: Exchange without the use of money; trade of goods.

behavioralists: In antitrust policy, those people who believe that highly concentrated industries may nevertheless be quite competitive and exhibit a good economic performance.

bilateral monopoly: Situation in which a monopoly sells to a monopsony, such as when a monopoly labor union is organized into a monopsonistic industry.

bimetallic monetary standard: Monetary standard under which the unit of currency is defined according to the fixed weight of two metals (usually gold and silver).

black capitalism: Approach to economic improvement for blacks that emphasizes increased black control of business, especially business that serves the black community.

break-even point: Level of production at which a firm is just covering its costs. Also the point at which the value of the marginal product for a given factor of production is equal to the price of that factor.

Bretton Woods agreement: International monetary arrangement in which the price of the dollar was set at 1/35 of an ounce of gold and the United States promised to redeem for gold all dollars in the hands of foreign central banks; adjustments were made through transfers of reserves. It collapsed in January 1971, when the United States declared that it would no longer maintain convertibility to gold.

budget constraint line: Line showing the greatest number and combinations of two goods that can be purchased with a fixed amount of money.

business cycles: Recurrent but irregular fluctuations of economic activity that occur over a period of years. Cycles are characterized by changes in output, employment, and prices.

business fixed investment: Part of the investment component of GNP that includes expenditures for buildings constructed for business purposes plus the equipment and machinery needed to produce goods.

business investment: Creation of new plant and equipment or repair of old, and changes in inventories. It may be intended or unintended through inventory accumulation.

businesses: Firms that produce goods and services with resources for a profit.

capital: In economics, man-made resources such as plant and equipment, which are used to produce other goods and services.

capital account: Portion of the balance-of-payments statement showing the volume and movements in both long- and short-term investment by foreigners in the United States and by Americans abroad, as well as the investments of multinational companies.

capital consumption allowances: Component of GNP consisting of expenditures to replace worn-out equipment used in the production process.

capital deepening: Condition in which the amount of capital per worker increases.

capital mobility: Capability to use capital in the production of alternative goods and services.

capital stock (or goods): Plant and equipment for producing goods.

cartel: Organization of firms entrusting price-setting decisions to a centralized association. It acts basically as a monopoly in price and output decisions, and is illegal in the United States.

Celler-Kefauver Act (1950): Amended Section 7 of the Clayton Act by closing the loophole that limited its application to mergers by stock acquisition. It also extended coverage to vertical and conglomerate mergers.

ceteris paribus: Latin phrase meaning "other things being equal." It is used to denote the change of only one variable or one set of variables at a time.

circular flow: Process consisting of both the real flow of resources and commodities and the money flow of expenditures and income between businesses and households.

Clark, John Bates (1847–1938): First American economist to receive international attention, by extending marginal analysis to costs and supply. He suggested the theory of marginal productivity—that the income earned by each factor of production is the value of added goods and services it can produce.

Clayton Act (1914): Antitrust act prohibiting specific practices such as price discrimination, exclusive dealing arrangements, mergers, and interlocking directorates when the effect is to substantially reduce competition.

cobweb theorem: One way of explaining why price may be unstable in those cases in which suppliers must rely on significant periods of time to adjust production levels.

collective bargaining: Process by which a union acts as an agent for all members in bargaining with the employer for conditions of employment. The objective is to negotiate a contract between union and management covering rights and duties of each for a given period, usually two or three years.

collusion: Agreement by two or more firms on noncompetitive behavior. Collusion on prices is illegal in the United States.

command system: Economic system characterized by a centralized government authority over economic goals planning.

comparative advantage: A nation is said to have a comparative advantage in the production of a good or service when the opportunity cost of producing the good is lower than the opportunity cost of producing the same good or service in the other trading nations. The theory, advanced by David Ricardo, was considered to be the basis of trade between nations and it functions as a substitute for the mobility of resources.

compensation: Component of national income consisting of wages, salaries, and fringe benefits paid to the labor force in the production process.

complementary good: Good that is typically purchased to be used with another, such as automobiles and gasoline.

composition/division fallacies: False assumptions that what is true of the parts must be true of the whole, or what is true of the whole must be true for the parts.

Comprehensive Health Manpower Training Act of 1971: Legislation designed to increase the number of physicians by providing aid to medical schools and by providing scholarships and loans to students in health care professions.

concealed unemployment: That portion of the population which would be willing and able to work if jobs were available, but have become discouraged and have dropped out of the labor force. This kind of unemployment is believed to increase as the unemployment rate increases.

conglomerate: Large firm that has absorbed other firms in a wide variety of noncompeting areas. It accounts for much of the merger activity in the United States since 1960.

Congress of Industrial Organizations (CIO): Affiliation of unions formed in 1938 by industry-wide, or vertical, unions. It became very successful in organizing workers in mass production industries. In 1955 it merged with the AFL.

constant dollar GNP: Value of gross national product expressed in prices prevailing in some base year.

constant returns to scale: Increases in all inputs produce proportionately constant increases in output.

consumer durables: Those goods purchased by consumers that have a long life, such as washing machines and lawnmowers. They are easily postponable purchases. The quantity demanded varies widely with the business cycle.

consumer surplus: Difference between the total utility derived from a purchase and the price consumers are willing to pay, which represents marginal utility.

consumption schedule: Table showing the relationship between disposable income and consumption, the amount a family spends at various levels of income.

contraction: Movement of the economy to a lower level of national income and employment.

Corn Laws: Nineteenth century English laws designed to prevent imports of cheap grain.

corporate profits: Earnings of an incorporated business. Earnings before distribution of dividends to shareholders.

corporate taxes: Portion of corporate earnings paid to the government in the form of taxes.

corporation: Business organization with stockholders, limited liability, and unlimited life.

cost: The sacrifice of something (monetary or nonmonetary) in order to obtain something else (the use of a resource or a finished good).

cost-benefit analysis: Tool for judging the desirability of a given course of action by comparing the cost with the benefits expected. It is used frequently in areas outside the market price system as, for example, with government programs.

Cost of Living Council: Cabinet-level body created by the Nixon administration to administer price controls.

cost-of-living (or escalator) clause: Feature of a union contract specifying that wages will rise by a certain amount in proportion to the officially determined cost of living.

cost-push inflation: Rising prices occurring when producers, for one reason or another, are required to pay higher prices for the factors of production. The higher costs are not offset by increases in productivity and are passed on to the consumer.

countervailing power: John Kenneth Galbraith's term for competition between power blocs, such as large corporations and large unions.

crawling peg system (gliding parity): System in which exchange rates are fixed, but a nation with chronic payments imbalances would be permitted to change the parity price of its currency by a stated small amount at periodic intervals.

creeping inflation: Slow but steady increase in the price level over a long period of time.

current account: Portion of the balance-of-payments statement showing the volume of exports and imports.

current dollar GNP: Value of gross national product expressed in prices prevailing in the year of measurement.

cyclical unemployment: Unemployment that occurs when the economy operates below full employment.

cyclically balanced budget: Government budget that balances over the course of the business cycle and that surpluses during peak periods, canceling deficits incurred during recessions.

decreasing returns to scale: Increases in all inputs result in proportionately smaller increases in output.

deflation: Decreases in the general price level.

deflationary gap: Gap between an insufficient aggregate demand and the aggregate dollar level required to maintain full employment in the economy.

demand deposit: Money placed in checking accounts at commercial banks, which may be withdrawn on demand. It is considered to be part of the money supply.

demand-pull inflation: Increases in prices due to a demand for larger quantities of goods and services than the economy is providing—"too much money chasing too few goods."

demand schedule: How much of a good individuals are willing and able to buy at various prices during a given period of time.

deposit expansion multiplier: Reciprocal of the reserve ratio. It measures the extent to which money may be created or destroyed by the banking system through the use of excess reserves.

depreciation (capital consumption): Wearing out of productive resources during the production process; the expenditures made to replace worn-out equipment used in the production process.

depression: Period of severe economic downturn characterized by low levels of consumption, investment, and employment. Public confidence is also at a low ebb.

derived demand: Term frequently used to describe factor demand since factor demand is dependent upon consumer demand for final products.

devaluation: Reduction in the official exchange rate, reducing the price of domestic currency to the foreigner and increasing the price of foreign currency. It has the effect of raising the prices of imports and reducing the prices a foreigner pays for the country's exports.

discount rate: Interest rate charged by the Federal Reserve for loans to member banks.

discretionary tools: Deliberate actions available to the government that will alter national income and employment. These include changes in taxes, expenditures, and interest rates.

diseconomies of scale: Increasing long-run average costs as an enterprise increases in size, caused by (1) diminishing returns to management or (2) rising input costs.

disposable income: A measure of dollars actually available to households for consumption or saving. It is equivalent to personal income minus personal taxes, plus transfer payments.

doctrine of incipiency: Articulated in the Kinney and Brown shoe merger case, in which the court ruled that it is better to stop concentration before it occurs than after.

dollar overhang: The $100 billion still in the hands of central banks around the world as a result of United States payments deficits.

double counting: Statistical error of counting more than once the same item in arriving at a total, such as GNP. It is avoided by counting only final goods or by using the value-added method, which counts only the value added at each step of the production process.

dualism: In developing countries, sharply contrasting characteristics stemming from a developed, export-oriented sector and an undeveloped, agricultural sector employing 70 to 90 percent of the population and feudalistic social organization.

dumping: The practice of selling a good or service in a given market for a lower price than elsewhere.

easy money: Easy availability of credit; expansionary monetary policy associated with increases in the money supply and reduced interest rates. It is used to stimulate the economy to the full-employment level.

ecology: The study of the household of nature.

economic concentration: Relative size of large firms. An index of the power of such firms frequently measured by an industry concentration ratio, by the percentage of total industry sales of the four largest firms in the industry, or by aggregate concentration, the relative size of firms regardless of industrial designation.

economic growth: Outward expansion of the production possibilities frontier; traditionally measured by changes in GNP or per capita GNP.

economics: Process of exchange and allocation; the effect of individual and collective decisions on that process; satisfaction-seeking as a basis for these decisions; and the necessity of choice that results from the inevitability of scarcity.

economies of scale: Decreasing long-run average costs as an enterprise increases in size caused by (1) specialization of resources, (2) more efficient utilization of equipment, (3) reduced unit costs of inputs due to quantity buying, (4) utilization of by-products, or (5) growth of auxiliary facilities.

economizing: Allocating the limited material resources of a society for the efficient production of inevitably scarce goods and services to satisfy best the needs and wants of society.

ecosystem: Organized interaction between living organisms and their environment.

effluent charges: Fines or taxes levied on polluters for the amount of pollutant emitted into the air or water.

elastic demand: Demand is price elastic if a given percentage change in price results in a larger percentage change in the quantity demanded. A drop in price will result in an increase in total revenues.

elastic supply: Supply is price elastic if a given percentage change in price results in a larger percentage change in the quantity supplied.

elasticity of demand: Responsiveness of the quantity demanded to a change in price. It is defined as

$$\frac{\text{Percent change in quantity demanded}}{\text{Percent change in price}}$$

and calculated as

$$\frac{\frac{Q_2-Q_1}{Q_2+Q_1}}{\frac{P_2-P_1}{P_2+P_1}}$$

elasticity of supply: Percentage change in the quantity supplied resulting from a given percentage change in price. It is defined as

$$\frac{\text{Percent change in quantity supplied}}{\text{Percent change in price}}$$

and calculated as

$$\frac{\frac{Q_2-Q_1}{Q_2+Q_1}}{\frac{P_2-P_1}{P_2+P_1}}$$

Employment Act of 1946: Set forth as a responsibility of government the goals of high employment and price stability. It created the three-man Council of Economic Advisers and the Joint Economic Committee of Congress to advise the President.

entrepreneurship: Factor of production performing the functions of organizing, directing, and managing the other factors or production. Income from entrepreneurship is known as profit.

equation of exchange: Relationship between the money supply (M), the velocity of circulation (V), the price level (P), and the output of goods and services (Q), expressed by the identity $MV = PQ$.

equilibrium income: That level of national income for which the quantity of goods supplied equals the quantity of goods consumers have demanded.

equilibrium price: That price for which the quantity consumers are willing and able to buy equals the quantity suppliers are willing and able to sell. The intersection of the demand and supply curves for a given product. Also, "normal" price.

equity: Idea of justice based on the values and judgments of society; usually excluded from scientific or positive economic analysis.

expansion: Movement of the economy from a point below full employment closer to the full-employment level. It involves increases in income and employment. Expansion may produce rising prices if it occurs near the full-employment level.

explicit costs: Monetary costs of buying and processing resources.

external diseconomies: Costs incurred by someone other than the producer or individual consumer.

external economies: Benefits incurred by someone other than the producer or individual consumer.

externalities: Costs or benefits incurred by someone other than the producer or buyer.

factors of production: Resources used to produce goods and services. Land, labor, capital, and entrepreneurship.

false-cause fallacy: False assumption that because two events occur together, one must be the cause of the other.

Family Assistance Plan (FAP): Proposal submitted by President Nixon to the Congress in 1969 and 1971. It would provide a minimum income to those without income and would tie in the food stamp program. It requires recipients to register with the state employment agencies and it provides day care for mothers with dependent children.

featherbedding: Rules imposed by unions specifying the number of workers hired, job assignments, output quotas, and the kinds of equipment used beyond actual requirements and for the purpose of expanding employment.

Federal Deposit Insurance Corporation: Government agency responsible for guaranteeing deposits in banks.

Federal Reserve System (Fed): Independent central banking authority in the United States. It consists of 13 district banks and a centralized decision-making body, the Board of Governors. The Fed provides currency upon demand by member banks, check-clearing services, and it regulates the money supply.

Federal Trade Commission: Independent regulatory agency established by the Federal Trade Commission Act of 1914. It is an alternative to the Justice Department in the enforcement of antitrust laws.

Federal Trade Commission Act (1914): Antitrust act prohibiting "unfair methods of competition" and establishing the Federal Trade Commission as an alternative to the Justice Department to enforce antitrust laws.

fiat money: Money designated as legal tender by decree of the government.

fiscal drag: Tendency for the progressive tax system to generate rapidly growing tax revenues as national income grows and the tendency of that tax to generate surpluses that prevent the economy from reaching new levels of full employment as the economy grows.

fiscal policy: From the Latin *fiscus* meaning state or royal treasury. It encompasses the entire realm of public finance or governmental policies relating to expenditures and raising funds by taxation and borrowing.

fixed costs: Costs that remain constant in the short run (in the long run there are no fixed costs, since all costs are variable in the long run).

fixed exchange rates: System in which exchange rates between trading countries are pegged at a certain rate.

The rates are maintained through reserve flows, actions by central banks, and domestic inflation or deflation.

fixed input: Those factors of production (essentially plant and equipment) that are available in a given quantity in the short run.

floating exchange rates: Price of any foreign currency is determined the same way prices of other commodities are, by supply of and demand for the currencies, which are based in turn on the supply of and demand for goods and services produced by the trading countries.

foreign exchange rate: Ratio or price at which two currencies are exchanged; for example, the exchange rate between the American dollar and Mexican pesos may be 1 dollar = 150 pesos.

fractional reserve banking: Banking in which some proportion of total deposits is held in reserve. The system as a whole has the capability of expanding and contracting the money supply, thereby affecting national income and employment.

frictional unemployment: That percentage of the labor force which expects to begin work shortly but is presently unemployed because of job changing. It is estimated to consist of 1½ to 2 percent of the labor force.

functional finance: Approach to government budgeting that ignores the question of equating revenues and expenditures but concentrates on reaching the goals of full employment and price stability.

game theory: Theory applied to economics by John Von Neumann (1903–1957) and Oskar Morgenstern (b. 1902). It attempts to use mathematical methods to determine what each firm in a market will do when faced with a certain number of competitors.

General Agreement on Tariffs and Trade (GATT): Agreement reached between major trading nations in 1947. It generally tended to encourage liberalization of trade. The agreement included the "most favored nation" clause, which specified that any reduction in tariffs between two members of GATT must be extended to all other members.

general equilibrium: Defined by Leon Walras as an economy meeting two conditions: (1) each person's consumption of goods and services is in perfect balance so that it is impossible to increase utility, and (2) the quantity of goods and services supplied in the economy as a whole is exactly equal to the quantity demanded.

George, Henry (1839–1897): Economist and social reformer who recommended that only rent income be taxed since rent is a pure surplus not tied to services given by landlords or the supply of land.

ghetto: The black (to some extent the Puerto Rican or Mexican-American) section of a central city. It is characterized by poverty, high crime rates, and poor housing.

Giffen good: Good for which a price increase results in a greater quantity sold. The income effect of a price increase is great enough that consumers can no longer afford as many higher-priced substitutes; also known as "inferior goods."

gliding parity (crawling peg system): System in which exchange rates are fixed but nations with chronic payments imbalances are permitted to change the parity price of their currency by a stated small amount at periodic intervals.

GNP gap: Difference between the actual GNP and that which could have been achieved assuming a 4 percent unemployment level and a normal rate of GNP growth.

gold bullion standard: Monetary standard in which a unit of currency is defined in terms of a fixed weight of gold in the form of bars or ingots that do not circulate.

gold exchange standard: System similar to the gold standard but which also allows the use of key currencies such as the dollar as additional reserves. The Bretton Woods agreement established a gold exchange system that lasted from 1944 to 1971.

gold standard: Currencies are defined in terms of a given weight of gold; exchange rates remain fixed; adjustments are made through shipments of gold reserves. David Hume believed the system to be self-regulating, since shipments of gold would affect the supply of money and the relative prices of goods between the trading countries.

GOSPLAN: State planning commission in the Soviet Union. It is primarily responsible for developing the Annual Plan and quotas for the following year.

gray area: In a city, areas in the central city that are largely white-occupied; have aging neighborhoods of four- and six-story apartment houses, frame walkups, and two-family row houses; and low rents.

Great Depression: Historical period of worldwide economic decline lasting from the stock market crash of 1929 until World War II. The greatest economic catastrophe in American history, causing heavy unemployment and drastic declines in output and prices.

Great Leap Forward: Program established in China in 1958 calling for a very high rate of economic growth with an emphasis on heavy industry and capital goods. It failed due to poor planning and neglect of the agricultural sector.

green revolution: Outcome of intensive research in agriculture, which has produced new, resistant, high-yield seed and new cultivation strategies.

Gresham's Law: Tendency for coins of one metal in a bimetallic monetary system to leave circulation if their market value rises above their mint value. "Cheap money drives out good."

gross investment: Value of total spending on productive assets, including that needed to replace worn-out assets.

gross national income: Sum of all income components in the economy, including compensation, rent, interest, proprietors' profits, and corporate profits, plus the nonincome components. Capital consumption allowance and indirect business taxes.

gross national product (GNP): Dollar value of all final goods and services produced in an economy in a year. It may be measured in terms of either income or output.

Harrod-Domar growth model: Theory of economic growth that emphasizes the instability caused by too much or too little investment.

Health Maintenance Organization (HMO): Comprehensive group medical practice that charges a flat annual fee to cover all or most medical expenses the consumer incurs for the year. It is based on the principle of risk sharing.

horizontal union: Labor union comprised of workers in different localities or industries, all of whom have a particular skill. Examples include the Amalgamated Meat Cutters and the United Brotherhood of Carpenters and Joiners.

households: Individuals, couples, or groups of people who are both consumers and controllers of the factors of production.

hyperinflation: Sometimes called "runaway" inflation, hyperinflation occurs when a flood of money is added to circulation or when there is a general loss of confidence in the official medium of exchange.

imperfect competition: Market in which buyers or sellers have some measure of control over the price of the product. It includes monopoly, oligopoly, and monopolistic competition.

implicit costs: Opportunity costs of production that are not recorded in financial records.

income distribution: Either where households get their money (functional distribution) or who gets how much (personal distribution).

income effect: Increase in the price of a good reduces the overall purchasing power of the buyer's income and the consumer cannot afford to buy as many goods and services as before. Also, a fall in the price of a good will raise the purchasing power of the consumer's income. This effect helps to explain the slope of the demand curve downward and to the right.

income statement (profit-and-loss statement): Financial statement denoting a firm's flow of receipts and expenditures over a given period, usually the fiscal year.

incomes policy: Any method, voluntary or compulsory, that attempts to control inflation by direct limitations on price or wage increases.

inconvertible paper standard: Monetary standard in which currency is not convertible into gold or other precious metals. However, a unit of currency may or may not be expressed in terms of a fixed weight of gold.

increasing opportunity costs: Tendency for the opportunity cost of a given product to rise as the economy produces ever higher quantities of that product.

increasing returns to scale: When increases in all inputs result in proportionately greater increases in output.

indifference curve: Curve denoting the combinations of two possible purchases; each combination that would yield equal satisfaction.

indifference map: Series of indifference curves showing a range of consumer preferences for combinations of two possible goods or services. Each indifference curve shows an increased level of satisfaction from left to right across the map.

indirect business taxes: Nonincome component of GNP consisting of sales and excise taxes, property taxes, and license fees.

industry concentration ratio: Percentage of total industry sales of the four largest firms in the industry.

inelastic demand: Demand is price inelastic if a given percentage change in price results in a smaller percentage change in the quantity demanded. A drop in price will result in a drop in total revenues.

inelastic supply: Supply is price inelastic if a given percentage change in price results in a smaller percentage change in the quantity supplied.

infant industries: New domestic industries that may not be expected to compete successfully with efficient foreign competitors for some short period of time and must therefore be protected temporarily by tariffs or quotas.

inferior goods: Good for which a price increase results in a greater quantity sold. The income effect of a price increase is great enough that consumers can no longer afford as many higher-priced substitutes. Also known as "Giffen goods."

inflation: Generally rising level of prices.

inflationary gap: Gap between aggregate demand which is above the level required to maintain full employment and the aggregate dollar level required to maintain full employment.

infrastructure: Set of facilities or services that is essential to the operation of the economy, including highways, railroads, communication systems, and power companies.

input: Resources required to produce goods or services.

input coefficient: In an input-output table, the coefficient enabling one to determine the value of an input needed to produce an additional dollar of output in a given industry.

input-output analysis: Analysis of the interrelationships of industries and sectors of an economy by determining the destinations of the output of all industries and the mix of inputs used to produce that output. The analysis was introduced by Wassily Leontieff. It attempts to show the effect on all industries of a change in production in one industry or sector.

interest: The price for borrowing money. Also, the component of national income consisting of payments by business to lenders for the use of borrowed funds.

International Bank for Reconstruction and Development (World Bank): Established at Bretton Woods in 1944 to serve as a vehicle for making loans to less-developed nations. Loans are made from the bank's capital, created by the subscriptions of members and by the sale of bonds.

Interstate Commerce Commission (ICC): Established in 1887 to regulate railroads, which appeared to have a natural monopoly. Now it extends to cover other forms of transport between the states.

inventory: Goods produced but not yet sold.

inventory accumulation: Part of the investment component of GNP consisting of changes in the value of finished goods, goods in process, and raw materials produced but not sold during a period of time.

investment: In economics, the use of resources to form new capital such as machinery or plant. The component of GNP that consists of spending by private business firms and individuals on output that increases or replaces real productive assets.

investment demand schedule: Shows the amount of investment that would take place at various rates of interest.

Iron Law of Wages (Malthus's): While population grows at a geometric rate (1, 2, 4, 8, 16, etc.), output at best increases only arithmetically (1, 2, 3, 4, 5, etc.), inevitably forcing the standard of living of the working class to the subsistence level.

Iron Law of Wages and Profits (Ricardo's): An economy inevitably must reach an equilibrium in which there is no population growth, a subsistence level of consumption, a stationary supply of capital, and therefore economic stagnation. This state is reached through a series of steps in which profits encourage capitalists to expand, which leads to increased competition for labor and subsequent increases in wages, which fosters population growth requiring an increase in the food supply. The demand for more food brings relatively unproductive land under production, which drives up rent on the more productive acreage. Higher rents increase the cost of food, driving up wages further and shrinking profits so that capital accumulation is arrested.

IS curve: Graphic representation of equilibrium in the product market. It indicates all levels of income and interest rates at which savings and investment are equal.

"jawboning": Effort by the President or other governmental officials to affect the economy, especially wages and prices, through persuasion.

job discrimination: Condition in which people are denied employment because of characteristics irrelevant to their productivity.

Keynes, John Maynard (1883–1946): Published *The General Theory of Employment, Interest and Money* in 1936, in which he argued that supply will not necessarily create its own demand and may result in a glut on the market. The resulting unemployment cannot be reduced through easy money since businesses do not want to expand nor do banks want to lend. The only remedy is for the government to get money directly into the hands of those who will spend it.

"kinked" demand curve: Model of a demand curve for an oligopolist, in which the oligopolist assumes that if he lowers his price, all competitors will follow suit, and if he raises his price, none will raise theirs. There is inelastic demand below the existing price and elastic demand above the existing price.

Kolkhoz market: Market in which Soviet peasants are permitted to sell the produce from the small private plots they may cultivate. It accounts for a high proportion of agricultural produce sold in the Soviet Union.

labor: Factor of production from the expenditure of human energy. Income to labor is a wage.

labor force: Consists of all those who hold jobs and all those actively seeking employment.

labor mobility: Capacity of labor to relocate in new geographical areas or in new occupations.

laissez faire: Literally translated means "leave alone." The principle that government intervention in the economy should be minimized and the economy left to regulate itself.

land: In economics, refers to all natural resources. Income from land is known as rent.

Landrum-Griffin Act (1959) (also the Labor Management Reporting and Disclosure Act): Required unions to hold regular elections by secret ballot, to bond officials who handled funds, and to forbid Communists and ex-convicts from holding office except under special circumstances.

law of demand: Quantity of a good demanded varies inversely with the price of that good.

law of diminishing marginal utility: Principle that with each successive unit of a good obtained, the marginal utility, or additional satisfaction derived, decreases.

law of diminishing returns: Continued addition of one factor of production while others remain fixed will eventually produce smaller and smaller additions to total output. If carried far enough, total output may actually decline.

law of supply: Quantity supplied of a given product varies directly with the price obtained for the product.

Libermanism: Label given to the institutions and practices introduced into the Soviet economic system to promote greater responsiveness to the preferences of consumers.

liquidity: Property of an asset that enables it to be easily exchanged for something else of value.

liquidity preference curve: Curve showing the relationship between the demand for money, or liquidity, and the interest rate.

liquidity trap: When the interest rate is already so low that increases in the money supply will not reduce it further. The flat portion of the liquidity preference curve.

LM curve: Representation of equilibrium in the money

markets. It indicates the various combinations of income and interest rates for which the demand for money (L) will equal the supply (M).

the long run: That period of time in which a firm can increase or decrease all of its inputs (that is, when all inputs are variable).

long-run average cost curves: Curves enveloping all possible short-run average total cost curves over a range of output representing different plant sizes.

Lorenz curve: Graphic description of a society's income distribution comparing population percentages with the percentages of total income received.

M_1: Component of the money supply consisting of coins, currency, and demand deposits.

M_2: Component of the money supply consisting of M_1 plus savings accounts held in commercial banks, mutual savings banks, savings and loan associations, or credit unions.

M_3: Component of the money supply, loosely defined as M_1 plus M_2 plus United States government bonds owned by individuals or businesses, and cash values of insurance policies.

Malthus, Thomas Robert (1766–1834): Most famous for his essay on population, in which he maintained that population would grow at a geometric rate while food supplies would grow at only an arithmetic rate. The general population would be doomed to subsistence standards of living and suffer periodic setbacks through famines, war, and disease.

Maoism: Ideology developed by Chairman of the Chinese Communist Party Mao Tse-tung. The function of the state is to promote not only economic development and material well-being but also spiritual well-being.

margin requirement: Percentage of the price of a stock purchase that must be paid as a down payment.

marginal cost: Additional cost incurred by producing one additional unit of output.

marginal efficiency of investment curve (also investment demand curve): Shows the expected rate of return for every level of investment.

marginal physical product (MPP): Change in total output resulting from the use of an additional unit of a given input.

marginal product: Addition to total product due to an increase in one unit of a variable input.

marginal product curve: Curve defining the amount of additional output obtained when one additional unit of variable input is used.

marginal propensity to consume: Percentage of any additional income used for consumption:

$$\frac{\text{Change in consumption}}{\text{Change in disposable income}}$$

marginal propensity to save: Percentage of any increase in income that will be saved:

$$\frac{\text{Change in saving}}{\text{Change in disposable income}}$$

marginal rate of substitution: On an indifference curve, the ratio of the amount of one good that the consumer is willing to give up to the amount of the other good he must receive in order to remain equally satisfied.

marginal revenue product (MRP): Term used in the case of imperfect competition or monopoly to designate the increase in revenue due to the use of an additional unit of a given factor of production: $MRP = MR \times MPP$.

marginal utility: Utility or satisfaction to be gained from the last unit obtained. It is generally believed to fall as the number of units obtained increases.

market: Interaction of supply and demand, the buying and selling of goods and services by individuals and businesses in an attempt to satisfy their own economic wants.

market price: Prevailing price for a given product; it may or may not reach equilibrium.

market socialism: Term used frequently to describe an economic system in which the means of production are publicly owned but market forces provide the coordinating mechanism; an example is Yugoslavia.

markets: Mechanisms through which prices are set and goods and services exchanged through the interaction of supply and demand.

mark-up pricing: Practice common in retailing in which the firm decides to charge a price a certain percentage above cost.

Marshall, Alfred (1842–1924): One of the most outstanding of the nineteenth-century marginalists, Marshall advanced the theory of marginal utility along with other price theorists. He introduced the tool of partial equilibrium analysis.

Marx, Karl (1816–1883): With Friedrich Engels published the *Communist Manifesto* in 1848, advancing the theory that capitalism itself contained the factors that would result in its inevitable downfall—a downfall to be brought about by class-consciousness and a unified proletariat in revolt against the bourgeoisie, the owners of capital.

maximizing utility: Basic motive of consumers according to price theorists, accomplished through balancing purchases until the last dollar spent on any purchase yields the same amount of utility as the last dollar spent on every other purchase:

$$\frac{MU_1}{P_1} = \frac{MU_2}{P_2} = \frac{MU_n}{P_n}$$

mediation: Intervention of a third party acting as a go-between in the collective bargaining procedure; the mediator has no particular authority over the disputants save for that which he commands by virtue of his reputation.

mercantilism: One of the first attempts at organized thinking about the behavior of firms and markets. It included the beliefs that government should intervene to arbitrate competing interests and maintain order and that gold stocks possessed by a nation determined its well-being (a belief now held to be incorrect).

merger: Legal and economic joining of two or more firms.

metropolitan area: Economically and socially integrated area of high population density. Defined by the Bureau of the Census as counties or groups of counties containing at least one city of 50,000 inhabitants, it may include more than one city or county if they are economically and socially integrated.

microeconomics: Study of the behavior of individual units within the economy. Consumers and producers and the markets in which these individuals perform.

military-industrial complex (MIC): Described first by Eisenhower in a speech close to the end of his second term; an alliance between an immense military establishment and a large arms industry.

model: Simplified version of reality, expressing the theoretician's understanding of how reality works.

monetarists: Those theoreticians believing that monetary tools are more effective in stabilizing employment and income at full employment and avoid many of the dangers of fiscal tools.

monetary standard: Laws of a nation that define the value of its currency and the regulations to which that currency may be subject.

monetization: Creation of money by the bank's accepting for a loan the borrower's promise of repayment.

money: Anything accepted as a medium of exchange that can function as a means of payment, a unit of value, a standard of deferred payments, and a store of value.

money flows: Payments for economic resources and goods and services (which move in the opposite direction of real flows).

money markets: Markets in which the demand for and the supply of money establishes the price of money (the interest rate).

money supply: Total quantity of coins, currency, and demand deposits existing in the economy. It sometimes also includes time deposits and other near money.

monopolistic competition: Condition in which many firms produce similar products but with some individuality, resulting in each firm having a "partial monopoly." Each firm has some control over price and output levels.

monopoly: Model in which the market is dominated by a single firm; a price maker.

"most favored nation" clause: Feature of the 1947 General Agreement on Tariffs and Trade. It specifies that any reduction in tariffs between two members of GATT must be extended to all other members.

multiplier: Number of times a change in aggregate spending is magnified in a change in national income:

$$\frac{1}{1-MPC} \text{ or } \frac{1}{MPS}$$

multiplier effect: Any change in aggregate demand has not one effect but a whole series of effects on total spending. National income eventually rises by some multiple of the original change in aggregate demand.

national consumption schedule: Table showing the amounts that all consumers in the economy would spend at various levels of income.

national income: Sum of all income components in the economy, including compensation, rent, interest, proprietors' profits, and corporate profits.

natural monopolies: Domination of a market by one firm resulting from enormous efficiencies, eliminating duplication. Examples include public utilities.

near money: Assets that are not accepted as such in exchange for goods but may be converted easily and quickly into money.

negative income tax: System by which a household whose income fell below a specified level would receive an automatic subsidy and would keep a declining percent of that subsidy as income rises. The idea is supported by many economists of varied political persuasions.

net exports: Component of GNP that consists of expenditures by foreigners on goods and services produced in the United States (exports), minus expenditures by the government and residents of the United States on goods and services produced abroad (imports).

net investment: Value of total spending on productive assets less an allowance for depreciation.

net national product (NNP): Dollar value of a nation's total output of goods and services less the depreciation of its capital goods.

"new economics": Policy that avocates aggressive use of fiscal policy to maintain full employment, based on the belief that private savings and investment decisions will not necessarily yield full employment.

nondurable goods: Those goods that are purchased and replaced frequently, such as clothing and food. They are characterized by relatively inelastic demand and little change in demand over the course of the business cycle.

normal price: That price at which the quantity consumers are willing and able to buy equals the quantity suppliers are willing and able to sell. The intersection of the demand and supply curves for a given product. Also, "equilibrium" price.

normal profit: Normal rate of return on investment. A rate equal to that in other industries. Or a return that just covers the opportunity cost of the investment.

normative economics: Study of economics that favors a value-oriented, humanistic approach.

Norris–La Guardia Act (1932): Assisted organized labor by making injunctions against strikes more difficult to obtain and by making yellow dog contracts unenforceable.

occupational crowding: Term describing a situation in which a segment of the population is denied entrance into high-paying occupations and so "crowd" into low-status occupations, thereby depressing wages in these occupations.

Office of Management and Budget: Created from a reorganization of the old Bureau of the Budget in 1970. It handles all requests for appropriations, allowing close Presidential control over the size of the budget.

oligopoly: Industry in which the number of firms is small enough so that changes in price and output of one firm will affect the price and output of the others. Competition between firms is based largely on a nonprice basis.

open market operations: Buying and selling of government bonds on authority from the Federal Reserve, directed by the Open Market Committee and carried out by the District Bank of New York.

opportunity cost: Amount of one good or service that must be sacrificed in order to obtain another or additional units of another.

optimum plant size: That size plant associated with the lowest average cost curve; the technologically efficient size of operation.

optimum resource mix: That mix for which the marginal physical product of the last dollar spent to purchase a resource equals the marginal physical product of the last dollar spent on each of the other resources.

output: Goods and/or services produced by a firm or any other economic enterprise.

overinvestment theory of the business cycle: Theory that swings in investment are primary factors in business cycles. Investment swings are largely a result of changes in profits and profitability, which are in turn affected by changes in production costs and selling prices. The theory emphasizes the intrinsic nature of business cycles.

paper gold (also Special Drawing Rights, SDR's): Created by the International Monetary Fund and credited to the account of each nation in proportion to that nation's original contribution of gold or currencies. The rights are to be used as additional monetary reserves.

paradigm: Simplified model or view of the world and framework for analyzing its problems.

paradox of value: Why does a good that is essential to life such as water, have little or no value while goods such as rubies—only decorations—command high prices?

parity ratio: In farm policy, the ratio between farm prices and farm costs (1910–1914 = 100).

partial equilibrium analysis: Technique of analysis by which the interaction of supply and demand in one market is examined while conditions in other markets are assumed to remain unchanged.

partnership: Business firm owned by two or more people, with each partner liable for the firm's debts.

patent: Legal monopoly over a product or process granted by the government for a period of 17 years.

people's commune: Political, social, and economic unit in the People's Republic of China. The basic production unit is managed by a group of the commune's members.

perfect competition: Economic model in which firms produce homogeneous products, are free to enter and leave the industry, have perfect knowledge, and are unable to affect the market price through their own actions; price takers.

perfect elasticity: Horizontal demand or supply curve. The seller can sell any quantity he wishes at the given price or the buyer can buy any quantity he wishes at the given price.

perfectly elastic demand: Horizontal demand curve. The firm can sell as much as it wishes at the market price.

performance contracting: In effect, turns public education over to private firms, which are compensated according to results.

permanent income hypothesis: Theory developed by Milton Friedman, in which a family makes saving and consumption decisions on the estimated size of expected annual lifetime earnings (permanent income) rather than on current income.

personal consumption expenditure: Component of GNP that consists of spending by households on consumer durable goods, consumer soft goods, and consumer services.

personal income: Measure of the dollars actually received by households. It is equivalent to national income minus profits retained by corporations, corporate taxes, individuals' social security contributions, plus transfer payments.

personal taxes: Excise and income taxes paid to the government out of individuals' incomes.

physiocrats: Economic philosophers who emerged after mercantilism. They believed that there was a natural order that governed man and that one could achieve harmony by discovering and obeying those natural rules. The philosophy was most completely expressed in *Tableau Economique* by Francois Quesnay (1694–1774).

positive economics: Study of economics as a science; matters of value are treated as separate issues.

price ceiling: Maximum legal limit imposed on the price of a good. That price normally falls below the equilibrium price.

price discrimination: Charging of different prices for the same product or service. This may occur when the market is segmented into groups with differing elasticities of demand and each segment can be sealed to prevent those who obtain the product at a lower price from reselling it to those who obtain it at a higher price.

price floor: Minimum legal limit imposed on the price of a good, a price that normally falls above the equilibrium price. It can be maintained only through supports.

price leader: One firm in an oligopolistic industry that signals a new pricing system for all by breaking ranks and announcing a price increase or decrease. All others follow with similar price changes.

product differentiation: The attempt to make a product seem different from its rivals. The objective is to move the demand curve for the product to the right and to make the demand curve more inelastic. This is frequently accomplished through advertising and packaging.

production possibilities frontier: A curve showing the combinations of goods that may be produced by an economy operating at peak technological efficiency and full capacity.

productivity: Output per unit of input. In the case of labor, for example, productivity is

$$\frac{\text{GNP}}{\text{Man-hours employed}}$$

profit maximization: Process by which the firm seeks to make the highest possible profits (setting marginal cost equal to marginal revenue).

propensity to consume schedule: Table showing the relationship between disposable income and consumption, the amount a family spends at various levels of income.

proprietors' income: Profits earned by unincorporated businesses, usually the smaller owner-operated enterprises. It also includes the earnings of professional practices of doctors, lawyers, accountants, and the like.

prosperity: Period of high output and employment, high public confidence, and high levels of consumption and investment. It may also result in price increases.

protectionist devices: Any policies designed to protect domestic industries from competition from imports, usually by direct restrictions on quantity to be imported or by tariffs.

public debt (or national debt): Debt owed by the government. In the United States it is owed primarily to private American citizens and institutions, being held by those parties in the form of government bonds.

purchasing power: Measurement of the value of money in terms of the amount of goods and services it can buy.

quantity theory of money: See "equation of exchange."

quasi-rent: Payment to any factor of production in temporarily fixed supply.

"ratchet" effect: Tendency for oligopolists to raise prices when operating at full capacity but not to lower prices when operating below capacity for fear of touching off a price war.

real flows: Exchange of goods and services among households and businesses.

recession: Period of economic downturn—milder than a depression—in which output and employment drop, with declines appearing in consumption—especially for durable goods—and in investment.

recovery: Period following a recession or depression in which consumption spending increases, is followed by a rise in investment spending and then an increase in output and employment.

Regulation Q: Authority of the Federal Reserve to set ceilings on the amount of interest that member banks may pay on time deposits.

Regulation X: Authority vested in the Federal Reserve designed to limit the flow of money into housing construction.

relative income theory: Developed by James Duesenberry, in which the amount a family spends is based not merely on its income, but on how its income compares with that of other households.

rent: Income to the factor of production land. Return to a factor with an inelastic supply. Also the component of national income consisting of payments for the use of land, and facilities or equipment used in the production of goods and services.

reserve assets account: Portion of the balance of payments statement showing how a nation handled its deficit or surplus; that is, changes in reserves.

reserve ratio, or reserve requirement: Percentage of deposits member banks are obliged to keep in reserve with the Federal Reserve or to hold as vault cash. Its reciprocal is the deposit expansion multiplier.

residential construction investment: Part of the investment component of GNP that includes expenditures for the construction of one-family and multi-family homes.

resource mobility: Degree of flexibility of factor of production in shifting from one use to another.

retained earnings: Portion of corporate profits not distributed to shareholders or paid out in taxes.

revaluation: Increase in the official exchange rate increasing the price of the domestic currency to the foreigner and decreasing the price of foreign currency. It has the effect of reducing the price of imports and increasing the price the foreigner pays for the country's exports.

revenue sharing: Funding scheme to return a portion of federal taxes to state and local governments for use as these governments may choose.

Ricardo, David (1772–1823): Predicted a somewhat gloomy future in which workers and manufacturers would be commanding low incomes and the landlords (controlling the production of food) would be receiving an ever increasing share of the income pie through rents.

Robinson-Patman Act (1936): Amended Section 2 of the Clayton Act to make it more difficult for firms to engage in price discrimination on the grounds of differences in costs.

rule of reason: Supreme Court opinion in the Standard Oil case of 1911 that antitrust laws should be applied "reasonably."

saving schedule: Table showing the amount a family saves at various levels of income.

Say, Jean-Baptiste (1767–1832): Contended that the amount of money paid out for the production of goods and services will be used to buy back the total output from that production—the principle known as Say's Law. The economic system will automatically reach full employment.

Say's Law: Principle that the amount of money paid out for the production of goods and services will be used to buy back the total output from that production. In essence, supply will always create its own demand.

Sherman Act of 1890: Antitrust act outlawing "every contract, combination in the form of trust or otherwise, or conspiracy, in the restraint of trade, " and monopolizing or the attempt to monopolize.

the short run: That period of time in which some of the firm's inputs are fixed.

shortages: Quantities still demanded by consumers but which suppliers will not supply. Shortages result from a price that is lower than the equilibrium price. They bring about competition among consumers for the quantity available and they pressure an increase in the price.

slope of the demand curve: Absolute change in price associated with a given absolute change in quantity demanded. It is not to be confused with elasticity of demand.

Smith, Adam (1723–1790): Well-known scholar and author of *The Wealth of Nations*. He advanced the theory that goverment intervention in the economy should be minimized because the economy will automatically regulate itself to the benefit of all. This ability, Smith termed the "invisible hand." Smith disagreed with the mercantilist view of wealth, maintaining that wealth consisted of goods, not money. Smith also believed in economic growth largely through increases in productivity from division of labor and capital accumulation. He was the founder of "classical economics."

Smithsonian Agreement: Agreement among the 10 largest trading nations in 1971 to devalue the dollar and revalue many other currencies. It was abandoned in 1973.

snob good: When the price rises, there is a greater quantity sold. This occurs in the case of some products such as perfume, cosmetics, and jewelry.

sole proprietorship: Business firm owned by a single individual. The most numerous type of firm.

Special Drawing Rights (SDR's) (also paper gold): Created by the International Monetary Fund and credited to the account of each nation in proportion to that nation's original contribution of gold or currencies; the rights are used as additional monetary reserves.

specific tax: Fixed tax on every unit sold.

speculative demand for money: Amount of money demanded to be held in the form of cash and demand deposits awaiting more favorable conditions in the securities market. It varies inversely with the interest rate.

stability: Absence of fluctuations in output and employment levels.

stagflation: Relatively new phenomenon in the United States that combines an uncomfortably high unemployment rate with an uncomfortably high rate of inflation.

structural inflation: General increases in prices, sometimes initiated when, for one reason or another, prices rise in certain basic industries.

structural unemployment: Percentage of unemployment occurring because of a mismatch between the jobs that are available and the skills of those looking for work. It is estimated to consist of 1½ to 2 percent of the labor force.

structuralists: In antitrust policy, those economists who believe that industrial concentration necessarily results in monopolistic behavior and poor economic performance.

subsidy: Negative tax paid by the government to lower costs, to encourage production, or to raise a person's income.

substitutability: Degree to which one product, service, or factor can be used in place of another.

substitution effect: As the price of a good rises, the buyer has a tendency to turn to other goods as substitutes. Or if the price falls, the buyer is more likely to buy the product as a substitute for other higher-priced products. This effect helps to explain the slope of the demand curve downward and to the right.

supply curve: Shows the quantity the supplier is willing and able to sell at each price. Under perfect competition the short-run supply curve is the firm's marginal cost curve.

supply schedule: How much of a good suppliers are willing and able to supply at various possible prices during a given period.

surplus: Excess quantity in the hands of supplier. It results from a price that is higher than the equilibrium prices, and it constitutes pressure to lower the price.

tacit collusion: Informal price-setting arrangements between heads of oligopolistic firms.

Taft-Hartley Act (1947): Imposed limitations on the power of unions in six general areas: (1) specific practices such as certain types of strikes and featherbedding, (2) internal organization and accounting, (3) specific arrangements in collective bargaining, (4) the use of a presidential injunction against a strike requiring an 80-day cooling off period, (5) outlawing the closed shop, substituting the union shop, and (6) permitting states to pass right-to-work laws (prohibiting the union shop).

tax incidence: Degree to which the consumer or producer bears the burden of tax payment.

technological efficiency: Degree to which all resources are being used to their utmost capacities. An economy is operating at 100 percent technological efficiency when no change can be made in the use of resources that would lead to an increase in the output of one product without necessitating a decrease in the output of another product.

theory of the second best: In an economy in which it is

inevitable that the price of at least one good does not equal its marginal cost, the optimal price for another good may not be its marginal cost. When one condition for optimal resource allocation is violated, the second-best solution may not be to achieve normally optimal conditions in other markets.

third world: Label used for the very poor countries, relating to the position of these countries as a third economic and political force in the cold war.

tight money: Difficulty in obtaining credit. Contractionary monetary policy associated with decreases in the money supply and rising interest rates. It is used to combat inflation or the threat of inflation.

time deposits: Deposits in savings and loans and in the form of certificates of deposit or passbook accounts that require advance notice of withdrawal; not checking accounts.

total costs: All costs of production. The sum of total fixed costs and total variable costs. The sum of implicit and explicit costs.

total product curve: Curve showing the amount of output that the firm can produce with a given plant by changing the quantity of a variable input such as labor.

transactions demand for money: Money demanded to be held on hand in the form of cash and demand deposits to pay day-to-day expenses. It varies directly with income.

transfer payments (public): Payments made by the government but not in exchange for goods or services. They include such payments as welfare and social security.

two-tier market: Attempt to preserve the supply of gold for international dealings under the Bretton Woods arrangement. It provided an official tier within which gold transfers would take place at the official rates and a free-market tier in which all nongovernmental transactions would take place.

unbalanced growth: Development of one sector or a few sectors of the economy at a more rapid pace than others.

uncertainty theory of profit: Theory that entrepreneurs face the risk of possible loss, but also the potential for more than normal gain. It is the potential for pure profit that provides incentive for the entrepreneur to make his services available.

underconsumption theory of the business cycle: Changes in consumption spending patterns provide the primary impetus for fluctuations in economic activity. This theory emphasizes the intrinsic nature of business cycles.

unemployment: Existence of idle capacity. It is most frequently associated with the inability of all those who are willing and able to work to find jobs.

unemployment rate: Percentage of the labor force (those working plus those actively seeking employment) who do not have jobs.

union shop: Nonunion members may be hired by management but the new worker must join the union within 30 days after being hired, as a condition of continued employment.

unitary elasticity: Percentage change in price results in an equal percentage change in the quantity demanded. Elasticity equals one.

utility: Subjective value or satisfaction to be obtained from a given course of action or a given product.

utopian socialists: Nineteenth-century group that advocated harmonious, group-oriented economic systems. It included such figures as industrialist Robert Owen.

value of the marginal product (VMP): Increase in revenue due to using one additional unit of a factor, when the market is perfectly competitive. It is equal to the marginal physical product times the price of the good.

variable costs: Costs that vary directly with the firm's output. (In the long run all costs are variable.)

variable input: Those resources that can be increased or decreased in the short run (such as raw materials, electricity, and so forth).

velocity: Number of times the money stock changes hands during any given period.

vertical union: Labor union comprised of workers in a given industry regardless of their different skills. Examples include the United Mine Workers and the United Auto Workers.

vicious circle of poverty: In underdeveloped nations income is low, so saving and capital formation are low. Therefore, productivity is low resulting in continued low income.

wage ceiling: Maximum legal limit imposed on wages. A wage that normally falls below the equilibrium wage.

wage discrimination: Condition in which people are paid lower-than-normal wages because of characteristics irrelevant to their productivity.

Wagner Act (also the National Labor Relations Act of 1935): Legislation guaranteeing labor's right to organize; forbidding company unions, discrimination on the basis of a worker's union membership or his giving evidence under the act; forbidding employers to refuse to bargain in good faith with a duly established union; and establishing the National Labor Relations Board.

Walras, Leon (1834–1910): First important economist to extensively use mathematical techniques in his work. He described a state of general equilibrium in which no person could increase his utility by changing his purchases, and the economy supplies exactly the combination of goods and services that best satisfies society's demands.

World Bank (International Bank for Reconstruction and Development): Established at Bretton Woods in 1944 to serve as a vehicle for making loans to less developed nations. Loans are made from the bank's capital, created by the subscriptions of members and by the sale of bonds.

yellow dog contract: Contract in which an employee promises not to join a union. It was outlawed by the Norris–La Guardia Act of 1932.

Index

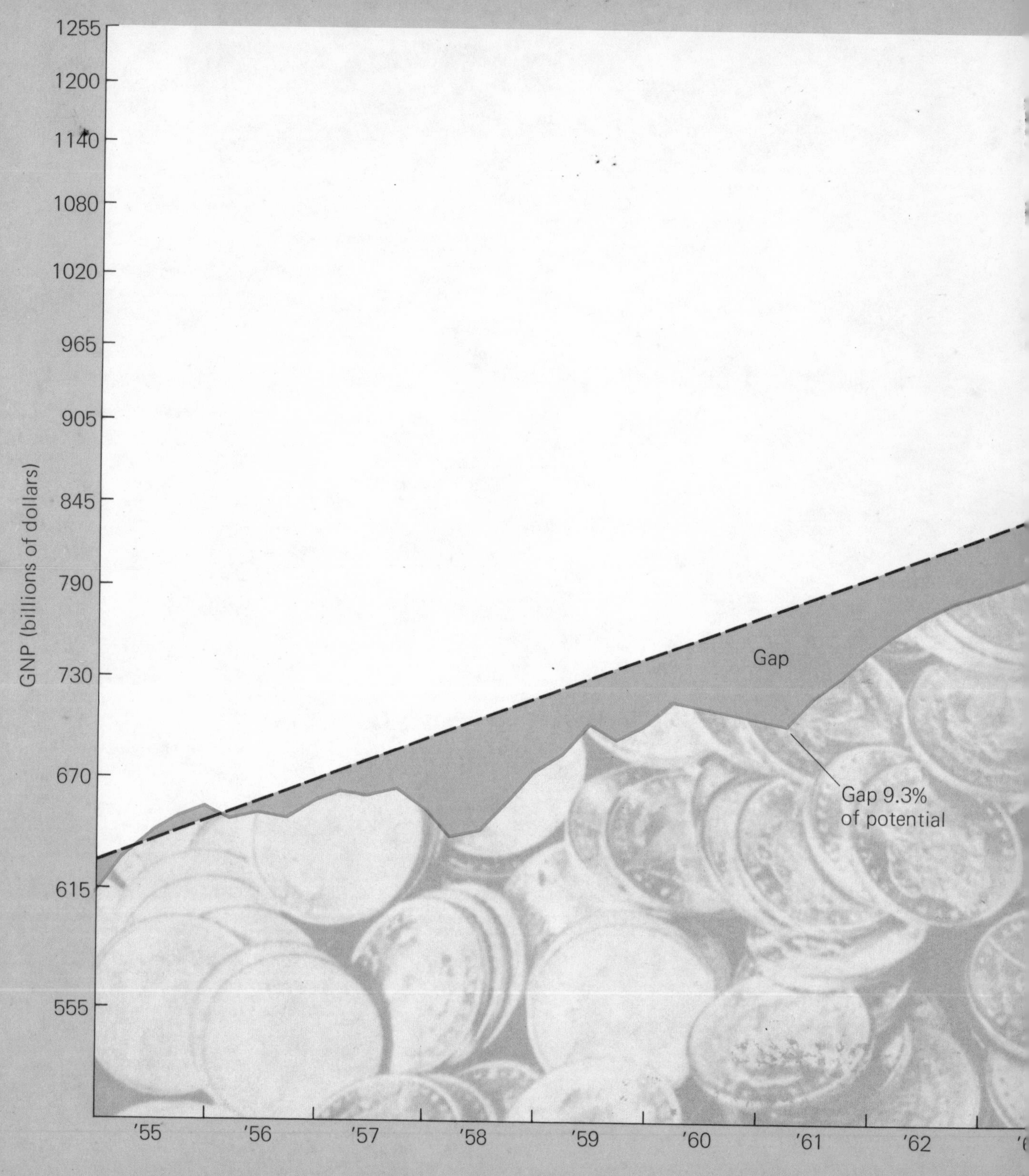
1255
1200
1140
1080
1020
965
905
845
790
730
670
615
555
GNP (billions of dollars)
Gap
Gap 9.3%
of potential
'55
'56
'57
'58
'59
'60
'61
'62